1001 SONGS
YOU MUST HEAR BEFORE YOU DIE

1001 SONGS
YOU MUST HEAR BEFORE YOU DIE

GENERAL EDITOR ROBERT DIMERY

PREFACE BY TONY VISCONTI

UNIVERSE

A Quint**essence** Book

First published in the United States of America in 2010 by
UNIVERSE PUBLISHING
A Division of Rizzoli International Publications, Inc.
300 Park Avenue South
New York, NY 10010
www.rizzoliusa.com

2010 2011 2012 2013 / 10 9 8 7 6 5 4 3 2 1

ISBN: 978-0-7893-2089-6

Library of Congress Control Number: 2010923719

QSS.1SON

This book was designed and produced by
Quint**essence**
226 City Road
London EC1V 2TT
www.1001beforeyoudie.com

Project Editor	Philip Contos
Associate Editor	Bruno MacDonald
Editors	Irene Lyford, Fiona Plowman, Frank Ritter
Editorial Assistant	Simon Ward
Designer	Jon Wainwright
Design Assistant	Tom Howey
Production Manager	Anna Pauletti
Editorial Director	Jane Laing
Publisher	Tristan de Lancey

Color reproduction by Pica Digital Pte Ltd., Singapore.
Printed in China by Toppan Leefung Printing Ltd.

CONTENTS

PREFACE

By Tony Visconti, Record Producer and Musician

In the beginning there was the single, a stand-alone recording of a song. The phonograph, invented by Thomas Alva Edison in 1877, had a cylinder, slightly larger and thicker than the cardboard core of a toilet roll, that stored about two minutes of music or recitation—that was the limit of the medium. Made of wax compounds, cylinders lasted for just a few dozen plays, until they were worn smooth. As for the sound, it was tinny and awful, degenerating more with every playing. Cylinders made of plastic, a superior medium, later became the standard and lasted longer, although the music still sounded as if it was recorded in a chip-frying factory. Undismayed, the public was hooked on buying singles.

Edison was smiling all the way to the bank when an upstart inventor, Emile Berliner, introduced a new form of recording and playback medium: the flat platter. Revolving at seventy-eight revolutions per minute, the disc came in basic black, just like Mr. Ford's Model T. Berliner could argue that his platter produced a superior sound (it did), and also that it offered an additional two minutes of music on its reverse side. Despite the obvious merits of Berliner's invention, Edison foolishly defended his cylinder format to the point of bankrupting his company as he tried to maintain its status as the only recorder in town. Berliner not only defeated Edison (as did Nikola Tesla, the inventor of alternating current), he also invented, inadvertently, the musical B-side—but more about that later.

My father, Anthony, was an avid collector of singles. As a boy I would watch his 78s spin at a dizzying speed and try to freeze the label with a blink of my eye. Music poured out of our record player—short jazzy tunes by the Glenn Miller Orchestra, the Dorsey Brothers (Tommy and Jimmy), close-harmony singing by The Pied Pipers (lead singer Frank Sinatra), even Egyptian singles sung in Arabic from Arab immigrant shops on Atlantic Avenue in Brooklyn. I would observe Dad's ritual of sliding a precious black shellac-based disc out of its sleeve and carefully placing it on the turntable, see the delicate descent of the tone arm into the lead-in grooves, and breathlessly anticipate the moment when the loud scratchy surface noise suddenly became music—this was an experience I would relive countless times in my life, despite having been told not to even think of touching my dad's records or his record player.

I had to learn the hard way to respect this delicate recording medium. At the age of four I was suddenly inspired to hold the brittle 10-inch shellac discs parallel to the floor, release them, and delight in seeing them smash into many small pieces. I had decimated a serious part of his collection in the space of five minutes when my not very well padded posterior became the recipient of several hard whacks, accompanied by a flood of tears, not just from me but from him, too.

On a brighter note my father loved comical music records. In the 1940s he gleefully played me the surreal parodies of contemporary pop songs by bandleader Spike Jones and his City Slickers. My favorite was the comic song "All I Want for Christmas Is My Two Front Teeth," in which the tooth-whistling singer (trumpeter George Rock) made me laugh by the way he sang the word "Christmas," enunciating both S's with a canary-like trill. But when I heard Jones's "Cocktails for Two," I instinctively knew that the band could not play their instruments and produce those garish sound effects at the same time (I was already a young and enlightened ukulele player). Something fishy was going on in the studio and I wanted to know what it was and how to do it. Suffice to say, I've spent countless hours in recording studios since then, trying to perfect the arcane art of doing something fishy!

The first record I bought for myself was Fats Domino's "Blueberry Hill." By this time I was responsible enough to operate Dad's phonograph, and I played the shiny black 78-rpm single until I had memorized every nuance, from the eight solo piano notes of the intro to the snare-drum flourish that brings the last dying chord to an abrupt halt. I played the second side even more, because I never heard that song on the radio. The B-side was "Honey Chile," sung with such a thick New Orleans accent (for me at the time) that I couldn't decipher the first line of the song, although I memorized it phonetically. This single was my property, my cultural property! It was a wonderful start to my small collection of 78-rpm singles, which grew to include "Tutti Frutti" by Little Richard and "Flying Saucer" by Buchanan and Goodman (I was still enjoying comical music). I would play these three records (and the B-sides) incessantly after school, and often my dad would come home from work and bellow: "Shut that damn record off!" My father's music was my music, but my music was not my father's music—clearly!

Shortly after I started the addictive hobby of record collecting, I became a victim of the now all-too-familiar format wars. Almost unbreakable vinyl was the new medium, with a durable surface that could stand the wear and tear of the tone arm to a far greater extent than its predecessor. Vinyl singles were smaller and more compact than shellac, and many of them fitted into a highly portable box with a little plastic handle that I still own. I was an only child, and my 45s were my constant companions. I bought singles by my singing guitar heroes: Elvis Presley, Chuck Berry, Buddy Holly, Buddy Knox, and Mickey (Baker) & Sylvia (Vanderpool), whose "Love Is Strange" (B-side "No Good Lover") was the epitome of guitar tone. Working on my guitar, I gleaned everything I could from Mickey "Guitar" Baker's style by playing that 45 over and over again. In 1957 I met my hero outside the stage door of the Brooklyn Paramount. Mickey and Sylvia were on the bill, playing up to six shows a day. Mickey, who was rushing out after the morning show, probably to get a cup of coffee and a jellyroll donut, kindly stopped and signed my album sleeve. He even gave me a guitar pick, which I kept in my wallet for several years until I used it at a gig and broke it.

My earliest 45s were "That'll Be the Day" (1957) by Buddy Holly & The Crickets; "You Can't Catch Me" (1956) by Chuck Berry—although I fell more in love with the captivating B-side, "Havana Moon"; "All Shook Up" (1957) by Elvis Presley; "Let the Good Times Roll" (1956) by Shirley and Lee; "To Know Him Is to Love Him" (1958) by The Teddy Bears (Phil Spector's debut as a group member and a producer); "A Rose and a Baby Ruth" (1956) by George Hamilton IV (and I memorized every word of the B-side, the verbose rockabilly song "If You Don't Know"); and an extremely obscure pre-psychedelic version of "Muleskinner Blues" that was renamed "Good Morning Captain" (1956) by Joe D. Gibson. But eventually it was the singles of the British Invasion of the 1960s—The Beatles, The Rolling Stones, The Zombies, and one single in particular by The Who, "Happy Jack"—that collectively extracted me from New York City and transplanted me to London Town, where I learned how to make singles for T. Rex, for starters.

That extremely fertile period of early progressive rock 'n' roll makes up about 50 percent of my musical DNA. The singles, the smell of vinyl, the colorful labels with their cryptic messages (the writers' surnames in parenthesis, the serial numbers, the legal warnings) are part of me; they are what made me who I am and what I do. Sure, at about this time the record companies made larger 12-inch vinyl discs that ran at 33 rpm, but they were for grown-up Doris Day fans and were way too expensive for kids. I hardly ever bought albums because even then there didn't seem to be any value in re-buying the same singles and B-sides just to get the few quickly recorded songs that filled the remaining space, the "fillers." When I bought a single from an artist I loved, I got maximum bang-for-buck value, such as "Oh Boy" by The Crickets with the amazing "Not Fade Away" on the B-side. The record biz called a single a "unit"; to me, it was a unit of sheer pleasure.

Eventually the album, with its longer-duration "album cuts," was embraced by pop artists who wanted to express more depth and nuance without being subjected to the commercial pressure that record labels exerted when it came to singles. In the United States during the Seventies, the single was forced to take a back seat when FM radio stations boldly played entire LP sides. The popularity and prestige of the rock concept album was peaking, and radio singles served merely as adverts for albums (even though a hit single didn't always ensure a hit album). But I continued to buy singles because some were "orphans" that did not appear on parent albums; others had enigmatic B-sides, such as the irrelevant "Tandoori Chicken," the flip side of Ronnie Spector's "Try Some, Buy Some."

However, the vinyl LP, followed by the album-length CD and then the Internet download, changed the way people buy their music. In *1001 Songs You Must Hear Before You Die*, you will find many of the songs that I collected as singles, alongside many that were released as album tracks and which people can now download in single form. Now, more than ever, people can decide for themselves which songs they want most, and which they think deserve to be hits.

Yet singles, and particularly 45s, not only played a profound revolutionary role in music and culture, they also changed a draconian business model. Until the end of the Sixties, all standard recording contracts stated that the company was entitled to withhold up to 10 percent of the artist's royalties for "breakage," even though from the mid Fifties very durable 45s and 33s were the only form of music delivery. When Andrew Loog Oldham, manager of The Rolling Stones, was renegotiating a contract for his clients with Decca Records, he insisted that the 10 percent breakage clause be removed. When the label executive asserted that the obsolete clause (from 78-rpm days) was "standard," Oldham took a 45 (disc, not revolver) from his coat pocket, slammed it on the executive's desk with great force, and challenged him to "break that!" The clause does not exist anymore.

Finally, why are most 45s black, even today? The chemicals that make up vinyl are essentially clear but in the manufacturing process the discs easily became discolored with impurities. The alternative to maintaining a clean factory is to add coal dust to the formula, turning the vinyl black. I know, many people have a record in red, blue, green, yellow, or even transparent clear vinyl, but these are really expensive to manufacture, and, I assume, were made in a pristine, germ-free, dust-free factory high in the Swiss Alps by a James Bond villain.

On a more serious note, you really must buy, beg, steal, or borrow the 1001 songs recommended in this book. I don't know if I'll ever accomplish that, but as the title suggests, I will die trying.

Tony Visconti, Greenwich Village, NYC

INTRODUCTION
By Robert Dimery, General Editor

It's hard to believe that five years have passed since *1001 Albums You Must Hear Before You Die* first hit the shelves. Putting together that selection of premier LPs of rock and pop proved a real challenge, prompting heated debates among the creative team behind it—and among readers, of course. If anything, this time the challenge was even harder: choosing 1001 essential tracks from popular music's rich and impossibly varied heritage. For starters, musical preferences can be hopelessly subjective and are prone to regular revision. You'll probably come to the end of this book and decide you'd have opted for a very different choice of 1001 songs. And you're not alone: over time, I'd probably do the same.

So, where to start? Well, from the outset, by way of sharpening our focus a little more, we restricted ourselves to songs that have lyrics. So, no instrumentals are included—which means Jimi Hendrix's "The Star-Spangled Banner" will have to wait for another book. Even so, the choosing proved a Herculean task, with wish lists being constantly revised, left-field song selections giving way to more familiar fare (and vice versa), and, naturally, more of those heated debates.

Unsurprisingly, although my name is emblazoned on the front of *1001 Songs You Must Hear Before You Die*, this has been a highly collaborative effort, with input from all the writers, the editors, and the publishing houses that issue this book worldwide. The latter, in particular, have been instrumental in broadening the scope of *1001 Songs* to include key tracks from a host of different countries and cultures. It's a big world out there, but it's getting smaller all the time, with Western musicians borrowing freely from non-Western artists and styles—and influencing their own music in turn.

We hope you'll find a grab bag of unexpected musical pleasures in these pages alongside the better-known hits. The book kicks off with "O sole mio" and ends with tracks released in the few months before our publishing deadline. In between, you'll be able to trace the growth of jazz and the blues, and the evolution of R&B and western swing into rock 'n' roll. You'll sample the infinite riches of the Great American Songbook and witness soul music bloom into exhilarating statements of black consciousness and pride in the Sixties and Seventies. You'll encounter highlights of French chanson, Portuguese fado, Spanish flamenco, Caribbean calypso, and Latin American bossa nova. And along the way you'll uncover fascinating stories about extraordinary songs and their equally extraordinary performers. How Fela Kuti's incendiary Afrobeat brought the wrath of the Nigerian military down on his head. How the morbid reflections of a Métro conductor gave Serge Gainsbourg a hit. And how R.E.M.'s Michael Stipe didn't always know what his own lyrics meant.

Indeed, among the beauties of a book such as this is the fascinating trivia it throws up. Often, the most remarkable revelations have concerned not so much the household names who became famous for singing these songs, but those working in the shadows. This seems an appropriate moment to honor one of them, so step forward Hal Blaine, a genuine legend in the world of popular music. As a session drummer, and a member of the famous Wrecking Crew studio band, Blaine has played on more hits than any of his peers during the rock era. And while we're handing out plaudits, The Funk Brothers are due their share. As Motown's in-house band from the end of the Fifties to the start of the Seventies, they backed a firmament of stars, including Marvin Gaye, The Supremes, Stevie Wonder, The Temptations, and Martha & The Vandellas—all of whom you'll find in these pages.

I'd like to finish this introduction with a few words about our presentation of the 1001 entries in this book. The dates that we provide for each entry are for the first appearance of the version of the song under discussion. This isn't always the same as the date of its first release as a single, of course, as sometimes tracks appear on albums before getting a life of their own as a single.

Alongside the details you'd expect to find for each song, we've often added some extra information at the end of each entry. The ◄ symbol indicates a song that may be seen as influential on the song in question; the ► symbol suggests a song that this song may, in turn, have influenced. In some instances, the influence is widely acknowledged—often by the songwriters themselves—and commonly accepted. In others, however, the degree of "influence" is sometimes fairly subjective. We are certainly not suggesting that the artists intended the songs to sound similar. Look on this feature of the book, rather, as playful speculation that suggests a shared musical heritage between two tracks—then seek out the songs themselves and see if you think we're near the mark or hopelessly wide of it. Finally, toward the end of the book you'll find a long list of songs that are also worthy of your attention—and which, in an alternative *1001 Songs*, might well have been covered in more detail. All told, that brings the total number of songs listed in this book to the 10,001 mark!

We have endeavored to keep up-to-date with changing writing credits—for example, where names have been retrospectively added to songs featuring samples—so they may not match those on the original releases. Where possible, credits have been cross-checked against the ASCAP and BMI databases, but we welcome corrections for future reprints of this book.

But, in the words of Spinal Tap's Marty DiBergi: enough of my yakkin'. These songs have changed the world. Find out why. Then listen to them.

Index
of Songs

- Bessie Smith has a major hit in 1925 with "St. Louis Blues"

- Musical films supply song standards, such as 1939's "Over the Rainbow"

- Bing Crosby releases the top-selling movie song "White Christmas" in 1942

- Columbia Records introduces the 33-rpm LP in New York in 1948

- Hank Williams raises the profile of country music with a series of hits

PRE 1950s

O sole mio
Enrico Caruso (1916)

Writer | Giovanni Capurro, Eduardo di Capua
Producer | Uncredited
Label | Victor Talking Machine
Album | N/A

Just as Charley Patton and Robert Johnson made their Mississippi Delta universal, Enrico Caruso has lent Naples a status that the richer and more celebrated Italian cities of Rome and Florence can never hope to match. The tenor singer had a beautiful voice and became one of the world's first superstar entertainers.

Caruso is the great icon of *canzone napoletana* (Neapolitan song), and "O sole mio" remains the city's anthem—an epic ballad that effortlessly blends popular song and opera. The masters of *canzone napoletana* can be regarded as forefathers to the Sinatra/Martin axis; indeed, Caruso was the original role model for all male ballad singers. His version of "O sole mio" builds and broods with great Neapolitan character. Despite Caruso being one of opera's greatest tenors, it is this anthem of his home city that most listeners know him by.

"O sole mio" translates as "my sun," and the song begins by celebrating a sunny day, before moving on to unfold as a great love song. It was popular before Caruso recorded it (the song was written in 1898), but Caruso's recording popularized the song internationally. His rendition of it at New York's Metropolitan Opera was so well received that audiences demanded he sing it ever after. Both in concert and on vinyl, Caruso helped make "O sole mio" a standard—and effectively turned it into an alternative Italian national anthem. **GC**

St. Louis Blues
Bessie Smith (1925)

Writer | W. C. Handy
Producer | Uncredited
Label | Columbia
Album | N/A

"St. Louis Blues" was, and remains, a phenomenon—a fully composed (rather than traditional hand-me-down) blues song that became a massive hit. W. C. Handy wrote it in 1913, at a time when there were no charts to register a song's popularity. Yet some measure of its success comes from the income it generated through sheet-music sales. For more than forty years, the song brought in an annual sum of around $25,000, making Handy a multimillionaire by today's reckoning.

The song has been recorded by many blues and jazz musicians, but no finer version exists than the one by Bessie Smith. Accompanied by just Fred Longshaw on harmonium and a magisterial Louis Armstrong on cornet, Smith mournfully relates the tale of how her love has run away with a chic St. Louis woman. Handy said he was inspired to write the song after meeting a woman in St. Louis bemoaning the absence of her husband. "Ma man's got a heart like a rock cast in da sea," she remarked—a line Handy wrote into the song.

Handy's skill is evident in the way in which he alters the traditional twelve-bar blues structure by introducing a sixteen-bar bridge in the habanera rhythm—an irregularly accented beat known as the "Spanish Tinge"—after the second verse. It adds contrast to the simple blues refrain and transforms the song into one of the most heartfelt laments of the century. **SA**

Empress of the blues: Bessie Smith in a 1923 studio publicity shot. ➜

Allons à Lafayette
Joe & Cléoma Falcon (1928)

Writer | Traditional
Producer | Uncredited
Label | Columbia
Album | N/A

On April 27, 1928, Joe Falcon and his wife, Cléoma Breaux, were recorded in New Orleans performing the clever two-step Cajun dance number "Allons à Lafayette" (Let's go to Lafayette). This was the first ever recording of Cajun music, and its success surprised the young American music industry by proving a demand for Louisiana swamp music.

The Cajuns are a French-speaking people descended from French settlers deported from the area around present-day Nova Scotia by the British in the mid-eighteenth century and refugees from Haiti who fled the slave revolt of 1791. Their distinct language and culture (and residence in the Louisiana bayous) kept them largely apart from mainstream America, yet their dynamic music—a mix of traditional seventeenth-century fiddle tunes and influences from the German and African settlers they were forced by location to mingle with—went on to create a uniquely American hybrid. Cajun music has influenced both country music and rock 'n' roll, and given birth to a black French music called zydeco.

Joe and Cléoma shaped their sound playing local dances. Joe played the accordion, while Cléoma played striking percussive guitar. Both took turns at singing. This recording, with its suggestive lyric and swinging groove, made them very famous among their fellow Cajuns. Heard eighty years on, Joe and Cléoma still swing. **GC**

Lágrimas negras
Trio Matamoros (1928)

Writer | Miguel Matamoros
Producer | Uncredited
Label | RCA Victor
Album | N/A

One of the most influential groups in the development of Cuban son, Trio Matamoros were founded in Santiago de Cuba in 1925 by guitarist and singer Miguel Matamoros. Matamoros also wrote their songs, which combined sophisticated but accessible lyrics with simple, unforgettable melodies. One of his most famous and enduring compositions is "Lágrimas negras" ("Black Tears").

Matamoros was inspired to write the lovesick meditation on rejection when he overheard a woman crying near the residence where he was staying while visiting Santo Domingo, the capital of the Dominican Republic. He first composed it as a tango, but the version he recorded is considered to be the first example of a new genre, a fusion of *son* and *bolero*, called, understandably, *bolero-son*.

Covers of the song include a feverish, jazzy instrumental by pianist Angel Rodrígues and versions by Cubans Compay Segundo and Omara Portuondo. In 2003, a radical revision of "Lágrimas negras" became the title track of an inspired collaborative album between veteran Cuban pianist Bebo Valdés and the rising Gypsy singer Diego El Cigala. Acknowledging the influence of Andalusian Gypsy music on that of Cuba, El Cigala improvises new lyrics in his vital, sobbing wail of a voice, and there is a lovely alto sax solo by Paquito D'Rivera. The album was a huge hit in both Spain and Latin America and won a Latin Grammy. **JLu**

Pokarekare | Ana Hato (with Deane Waretini) (1929)

Writer | Traditional, arranged Paraire Tomoana
Producer | Uncredited
Label | Parlophone
Album | N/A

Commonly known as "Pokarekare Ana," this is a Maori love song of disputed origins that has become New Zealand's unofficial national anthem. It has also been extensively exploited for political, sporting, and commercial purposes.

The first recorded version was by Ana Hato, who appeared in concert parties performing traditional Maori *waiata* (songs) for tourists at the "thermal village" of Whakarewarewa in the Rotorua area of central North Island. She made an acoustic recording of "Pokarekare" with choral backing there in 1927. Two years later, in Sydney, she made this more widely heard "electric" version, which finds Hato's keening vocal accompanied by violin, cello, and piano, with harmony vocals by her cousin and frequent collaborator Deane Waretini.

Although it is most commonly associated with Rotorua, "Pokarekare" is thought to have originated in Northland (northernmost New Zealand), according to the songwriter Paraire Tomoana, who published his take on the song in 1921. He had heard it sung by Maori troops stationed in Auckland on their way to combat in World War I. The tune is believed to have come originally from Dalmatian, or even Irish, folklore.

Popular renditions recorded by other New Zealanders include those by Inia Te Wiata, The Howard Morrison Quartet, Dame Kiri Te Kanawa, Prince Tui Teka, and Hayley Westenra. **JLu**

St. James Infirmary Blues | Louis Armstrong & His Hot Five (1929)

Writer | Uncredited
Producer | Don Redman
Label | Okeh
Album | N/A

Those who only know Louis Armstrong as the singer of hits such as "Hello, Dolly!" and "What a Wonderful World" are often unaware that in the 1920s he was the most innovative figure in jazz. Armstrong was a musical revolutionary, a trumpeter who stepped out from the ensemble playing of the band to become the first great improvising soloist in jazz history.

He was also a singer, with a fine, deep voice that is heard to great effect on this classic song. It is based on an English folk song that tells of a sailor who spends his money on prostitutes and dies of venereal disease in St. James's Hospital, London. By the time Armstrong recorded the song, in 1928, the action had shifted to America, and related the tale of a man going to the hospital to find his girlfriend dead. As a traditional song, its author is long forgotten, although it is sometimes credited to Joe Primrose, a pseudonym for Irving Mills.

The Hot Five who perform here were, in fact, a sextet of piano, trombone, two clarinets and saxophones, banjo, and drums. They start with a funereal instrumental introduction, before the melody kicks in at mid-tempo. Earl Hines then lays down a light-fingered, honky-tonk piano solo before Armstrong, in all his majesty, sings the two verses of the song. A trombone solo follows until Armstrong plays out with a strong trumpet. Not a note is wasted. **SA**

El manisero | Don Azpiazú & His Havana Casino Orchestra (1929)

Writer | Moisés Simón (later "Simons")
Producer | Uncredited
Label | RCA Victor
Album | N/A

"Ma-ní!" is the cry that opens the song that kicked off the worldwide "rumba craze" in the early 1930s. During the previous decade, street vendors in Havana advertised their peanuts that way, with a jingle-like *pregón*. When songwriter Moisés Simón fused this idea with *son*—an umbrella term for Cuba's folkloric styles—he created "El manisero." His authorship has been disputed, but the song made him rich; sheet-music sales (then very important) topped a million copies, as did those of the 78.

Cuban starlet Rita Montaner recorded the first version, in 1928, but the one that took the world by storm was by Don Azpiazú & His Havana Casino Orchestra, with vocals by Antonio Machín. They cut it in May 1930, just after arriving in New York. There it became the biggest-selling song of 1931, and was also a hit in Japan and Europe.

Perhaps its most lasting influence was in West and Central Africa. Azpiazú's imported 78s, then labeled as a "rumba fox-trot," went down so well there that it is thought this is how the *rumba congolaise* got its name. For the rest of the century, "El manisero" was required repertoire for any large African "orchestre" in that enormous region.

"El manisero" has been recorded more than 160 times, with notable versions by Louis Armstrong (1931) and Stan Kenton (1947): a testament to the influence of Latin music on American jazz. **JLu**

Minnie the Moocher | Cab Calloway & His Orchestra (1931)

Writer | Cab Calloway, Irving Mills
Producer | Uncredited
Label | Brunswick
Album | N/A

The "Hi-de-hoh Man," as Cab Calloway was known, was one of the most successful big-band leaders of the 1930s, famous for his flamboyant performances. He was particularly renowned for his scat singing—that is, his use of nonsensical, ad-libbed words—for example, the "Hi de hi de hi de hi" refrain from "Minnie the Moocher" that gave him his nickname and first brought him fame.

"I forgot the lyric to another song that I was doing and I put in skee-tee-tuh-bee and the hi-de-hos and it became very effective," Calloway recalled in later years, speaking of his most famous song. "And then I sat down and wrote 'Minnie the Moocher.'" Musically and lyrically, the song was based on Frankie "Half-Pint" Jaxon's "Willie the Weeper" from 1927, which was performed by Bette Davis in the movie *The Cabin in the Cotton* (1932). It tells the tale of Minnie the Moocher, a good-time girl who was rough and tough but had "a heart as big as a whale." The song abounds in drug slang: Smokie, the man Minnie messed around with, was "cokey," or did cocaine, while in Chinatown, he "showed her how to kick the gong around," or smoke opium.

The song was an immediate and huge success, selling in excess of a million copies. The septuagenarian Calloway revived the song to charming effect in *The Blues Brothers* (1980), and it's still great fun today. **SA**

Cab Calloway, arguably the most flamboyant front man of the Big Band Era. ➜

Need a Little Sugar in My Bowl
Bessie Smith (1931)

Writer | Clarence Williams, J. T. Brymn, Dally Small
Producer | Frank Walker
Label | Columbia
Album | N/A

At first blush, one might think that Bessie Smith was singing a song in the vein of Ray Henderson's perky composition "You're the Cream in My Coffee" from 1928, a straightforward you-complete-me metaphor structured around popular condiments. Yet as the chorus's second line ("Need a little hot dog between my rolls") makes manifest, it is in fact an example of the under-the-counter sub-genre known as dirty blues. The likes of Sippie Wallace's "I'm a Mighty Tight Woman" (1929) were not adorned with patronizing "parental advisory" stickers, presuming that the listener was underage: they were performed by adults, for adults.

Smith's languorous performance on "Need a Little Sugar" makes it clear that this is a sensual woman with genuine needs and desires. Backed by only the polite tearoom piano of Clarence Williams (her first accompanist in 1923, playing here on one of her very last recordings for Columbia), Smith holds forth with a stentorian delivery based on that of her mentor, Ma Rainey—a voluptuous bellow designed to play up to the primitive microphones of the period. In the hands of the Empress of the Blues, the innuendo becomes a metaphor of touching tenderness.

It's worth remembering that the dirty blues also gave us the euphemism "rock and roll"—a phrase that resurfaced, to world-changing effect, as the name for the illegitimate child of the blues. **SP**

Brother, Can You Spare a Dime?
Bing Crosby (1932)

Writer | Jay Gorney, E.Y. "Yip" Harburg
Producer | Uncredited
Label | Brunswick
Album | N/A

Socialist by birth and nature, New York lyricist Yip Harburg was deeply affected by the mass unemployment and endless breadlines that became all too familiar in the United States after the Wall Street Crash in 1929. "Brother, Can You Spare a Dime?" crystallizes the despair of those dark days in the story of an Everyman who had helped build the nation's railroads and skyscrapers and fought its wars, but was now reduced to panhandling on the streets. There is anger and bemusement in the lyrics, the tone moving from the general to the personal: "Brother" becomes "Buddy," as the narrator tries, and fails, to awaken the memories and sympathies of his audience. "Say, don't you remember?" he pleads finally, with heartbreaking pathos, "I'm your pal!"

Written for the musical *Americana*, it stunned audiences, overshadowing the rest of the show. ("Plaintive and thundering," applauded the *New York Times*.) Al Jolson and Rudy Vallee both covered the number, but it's Bing Crosby's version that has lasted. Crosby was intensely moved by the song and delivered a mellifluous vocal, lilting and understated but becoming progressively more urgent, more vibrant, in those poignant end lines.

Seven years later, Yip Harburg captured the zeitgeist once more with "Over the Rainbow," a wistful recasting of the American Dream—battered but still standing. **RD**

Bing Crosby displays his eyebrow-raising guitar skills in a 1935 publicity still. ➡

Mal hombre
Lydia Mendoza (1934)

Writer | Traditional, arranged by Lydia Mendoza
Producer | Eli Oberstein
Label | Blue Bird
Album | N/A

Lydia Mendoza is one of the great pioneers of American music and a legend of Mexican music. Born in Houston, Texas, in 1916 to a Mexican family who had fled the chaos of the Revolution, she and her siblings were never sent to school. Instead, they performed with their mother on the streets and in the fields, busking to survive.

From an early age, Lydia showed herself to be a remarkable singer and player of the twelve-string guitar (she also played mandolin), and by 1934 she was celebrated in San Antonio, Texas, as a street singer and radio performer. This success led to the independent label Blue Bird recording her and issuing "Mal Hombre" (Bad Man) as her first 78. Lydia had learned the lyric of "Mal Hombre" from a bubble-gum wrapper (a novelty marketing promotion of the time) and set it to music. It is the tale of a ruthless womanizer, which Lydia sung stridently, providing her own sturdy accompaniment on twelve-string.

The song immediately struck a chord with listeners. It was her first—and greatest—hit, taking off right across the U.S. Southwest, making Lydia a star, and kicking off a Mexican-American recording boom in the process. Buoyed by her success, Lydia got on the road and crisscrossed the United States—and later Mexico, Colombia, and Cuba—her bell-like voice and resonant guitar-playing marking her out as a true original. **GC**

Hula Girl
Sol Hoopii (1934)

Writer | Sunny Cunha
Producer | Uncredited
Label | Brunswick
Album | N/A

Hawaiian music proved to be the first "world music" craze after it was introduced to the U.S. public at the San Francisco–Panama–Pacific Expo, in 1915. At the Expo, the grass-skirted dancers and Ki ho'alu ("slack-key") guitarists set off a craze in the United States for all things Hawaiian. While much of this was down to novelty kitsch, the lyrical Hawaiian guitar sound proved hugely influential. Mexican and Portuguese immigrants had brought guitars and ukuleles to Hawaii, and the indigenous Polynesian populace had retuned them, creating the slack-key guitar style. This involved playing the guitar in open tuning on your lap while sliding a steel instrument across the strings, and was developed in Hawaii in the late nineteenth century. Slack-key's resonant sound, especially its ability to suggest a droning, weeping effect, would prove a strong influence on blues (as slide guitar) and, especially, country music (as lap-steel guitar).

Sol Hoopii was the greatest slack-key guitarist of the 1920s and '30s. He brought in jazz influences and was technically brilliant in his use of chords, harmony, and phrasing. The tuning he developed led to the emergence of the pedal-steel guitar that would become omnipresent in country music. The bubbling "Hula Girl" finds Hoopii's genius at its finest: joyful, jazzy rhythms topped off by the fabulous excursions of his melodic, expansive solos. **GC**

Can the Circle Be Unbroken (By and By) | The Carter Family (1935)

Writer | A. R. Habershon, C. H. Gabriel, A. P. Carter
Producer | Ralph Peer
Label | Okeh
Album | N/A

In the 1920s and '30s, Alvin Pleasant "A. P." Delaney Carter; his wife, Sara; and her cousin Maybelle laid the foundations of country music and bluegrass one brick at a time, and each tune is as vital as the next to the integrity of the structure that stands today.

When the Carters recorded "Can the Circle Be Unbroken (By and By)" in 1935, they were already recognized trailblazers in the infant music industry. This farming family from the Appalachian Mountains had scored a few hits in the late 1920s, but had also succumbed to the afflictions of the Great Depression. Their haunting tales of want, loss, and faith provided the accompaniment to millions of shattered lives, not least their own.

A. P. was the restless innovator, rambling across countless miles of dusty plains and pastures to find and "work up" the folk songs of the day. Sara and Maybelle were the talent, devising rhythmic and melodic guitar stylings—the "Carter scratch"—that would be imitated for all time.

The Depression also saw the collapse of A. P. and Sara's marriage. Adapted from a hymn by Ada R. Habershon and Charles H. Gabriel, "Can the Circle Be Unbroken" finds a mournful son at his mother's funeral, imploring the undertaker to "please drive slow." But A. P.'s vocal tells another story—one of abandonment and fear that fuses love and loss. "Lord," he cries, "I hate to see her go." **MO**

Cross Road Blues

Robert Johnson (1936)

Writer | Robert Johnson
Producer | Don Law
Label | Vocalion
Album | N/A

This Mississippi bluesman's acoustic-guitar-driven song has taken on mythical status since first recorded in 1936. "Cross Road Blues" has the choppy, rhythmic guitar sound and plaintive vocal that inspired today's rock heavyweights to build a career during the 1960s and '70s. But it is the allegedly autobiographical nature of Robert Johnson's lyrics, set at the crossroads of highways 49 and 61 in the town of Clarksdale, that gives the song its notoriety. Here—or in nearby Rosedale, according to some—Johnson allegedly sold his soul to the devil in exchange for mastery of the blues.

Brian Jones (The Rolling Stones), Peter Green (Fleetwood Mac), John Mayall (The Bluesbreakers), and Jimmy Page (The Yardbirds and Led Zeppelin) were all in thrall to Johnson's sound, but it was Eric Clapton who did most to popularize the song. Clapton's electrified version—"Crossroads"—was a staple of his band Cream's live performances and featured on the trio's U.S. No. 1 album *Wheels of Fire*. Central to the story of the blues, the song—and Johnson's so-called pact with the devil—also inspired the movie *Crossroads* (1986).

Johnson's personal "Crossroads" story ends unhappily. Two years after the song was recorded, and as his career looked to be taking off, the legend began to take root. Poisoned by the jealous husband of a girl he had added to his list of affairs, his life ended at the age of twenty-seven. **DR**

Hellhound on My Trail
Robert Johnson (1937)

Writer | Robert Johnson
Producer | Don Law
Label | Vocalion
Album | N/A

So little is known about Robert Johnson that trying to untangle the myths from the facts becomes a fool's errand. How did he go from the pedestrian guitarist routinely laughed at by Son House and Willie Brown to the finest bluesman they had ever heard—in less than two years? How did he die? Where is he buried? This, of course, is just the way the devil would want it. Johnson may or may not have sold his soul at the Mississippi intersection of highways 61 and 49, but in life he was a man on the run and in death he's a reminder that the blues can be a supernatural force.

We do know that Johnson cut "Hellhound on My Trail" in Dallas, Texas, on June 20, 1937, during his second and final recording session. The vision of Satan's hounds emerging to drag sinners to hell was prevalent in Southern churches, and to listen to Johnson's eerie, piercing tenor and the turbulent striking of his strings, it seems clear that he wasn't evoking them for mere rhetorical effect. As he recounts in the song, Johnson lived the life of a nomad, traveling up and down the Delta to perform his innovative style of bottleneck guitar. "I got to keep moving, I got to keep moving / Blues falling down like hail, blues falling down like hail / And the day keeps remindin' me, there's a hellhound on my trail." According to witnesses, Johnson became violently ill on August 13, 1938; the Delta-blues king died three days later. **MO**

Strange Fruit
Billie Holiday (1939)

Writer | Abel Meeropol (credited as Lewis Allan)
Producer | Uncredited
Label | Commodore
Album | N/A

"Strange Fruit" began life not as a song but as a photograph. When high-school teacher Abel Meeropol saw an image of two black men hanging from a tree, ringed by a crowd of white onlookers, he was moved to pen a poem protesting against the lynching of African-Americans by white vigilantes. "Southern trees bear a strange fruit," wrote Meeropol, nodding to the scale of the problem in the Deep South but seemingly unaware that the photograph had been taken in the northern town of Marion, Indiana.

Meeropol's poem came to the attention of Billie Holiday, who added the song to her repertoire. Her first attempt at recording it fell foul of executives at Columbia Records, for whom the subject proved a little too hot to handle. But rival label Commodore stepped in where Columbia feared to tread. And, despite the best efforts of some radio stations, which refused to play it, and concert promoters, who stopped the singer from performing it, Holiday had an unlikely hit on her hands.

Meeropol's poem and Holiday's recording are deeply affecting, their message amplified by the simplicity of its transmission: a twelve-line extended metaphor filtered through an unvarnished vocal and a stark accompaniment. The song's influence has been profound, but it's still not heard often on the radio. "Strange Fruit" remains a deeply discomfiting listen. **WF-J**

Billie Holiday performs in 1947, the year she was first arrested for possession of narcotics.

Over the Rainbow
Judy Garland (1939)

Writer | Harold Arlen, E. Y. "Yip" Harburg
Producer | Uncredited
Label | MGM
Album | N/A

It's hard to imagine the movie without it now, but "Over the Rainbow" almost got dropped from *The Wizard of Oz*. After a preview screening, executives at MGM demanded that the song be removed on the grounds that it slowed down the action. Only the forceful intervention of Arthur Freed, a former songwriter then carving a new path for himself as a movie producer, kept the ballad in the picture. It later won the Oscar for Best Original Song.

The tune had come to Harold Arlen while he was driving along Sunset Boulevard in Los Angeles on his way to the movies. Lyricist Yip Harburg didn't immediately take to it. But when Arlen, acting on the advice of Ira Gershwin, sped it up a little and thinned out its ostentatious harmonies, Harburg was convinced, and went on to write a lyric with a dramatic arc that beautifully mirrored the rise and fall of the melody.

The song has since been recorded by singers as notable as Tony Bennett and Aretha Franklin; Arlen himself even had a crack at it, albeit with a voice as flat as Kansas. But it'll always belong to Garland, whose own off-screen existence came to embody the song's mix of wide-eyed optimism and desperate melancholy. As Harburg put it, "Her whole life, almost like a Dostoevsky novel, seemed to fit this beautiful little child's song that had color and gaiety and beauty and hope . . . and yet she was so hopeless." **WF-J**

The Gallis Pole
Lead Belly (1939)

Writer | Huddie Ledbetter, Alan Lomax
Producer | John Lomax, Alan Lomax
Label | Library of Congress
Album | N/A

Huddie Ledbetter's violent, mythic life has fascinated listeners ever since folklorists John and Alan Lomax first discovered him as a prisoner of Louisiana's notorious Angola Penitentiary in 1934. By then, Lead Belly had already supposedly sung his way out of prison once, but his violent temper found him locked up again. When the Lomaxes came through looking for singers supposedly "uncontaminated" by the modern world, they were hugely impressed by this big black man who played twelve-string guitar and knew literally hundreds of songs (including "The Gallis Pole," an old English ballad he had seemingly learned off hillbilly musicians and adapted). In the 1939 recording, Lead Belly builds up a busy rhythm on his guitar, over which he tells the tale of a condemned man desperately asking his loved ones if they have brought gold, silver, and other bribes to keep him from hanging.

Lead Belly became friends with, and an influence on, such American folk pioneers as Woody Guthrie, Josh White, Pete Seeger, Sonny Terry, and Brownie McGhee. Ironically, it was a young white audience who adopted his music—he sounded too "old fashioned" to win over much of black America. While alive, Lead Belly was never rich or famous, but his songs became hits for Lonnie Donegan and The Beach Boys, and entered the repertoire of many others. **GC**

Judy Garland sings "Over the Rainbow," the song always associated with her, on CBS radio in 1940.

Mbube | Solomon Linda
& The Evening Birds (1939)

Writer | Solomon Linda
Producer | Griffiths Motsieloa
Label | Singer
Album | *Mbube* (1939)

Java Jive
The Ink Spots (1940)

Writer | Milton Drake, Ben Oakland
Producer | Uncredited
Label | Decca
Album | N/A

"First the Zulu man made magic. Then white man made money. This is the secret history of . . . one amazing melody." Thus begins Rian Malan's *Rolling Stone* article "In the Jungle" (2000). The melody: South African musician Solomon Linda's "Mbube."

"Mbube"'s history is clouded by cultural exploitation. The story starts in Eric Gallo's Johannesburg studio, where migrant Zulu musician Linda and his group, The Evening Birds, were paid ten shillings for their original song. With its ecstatic a cappella vocals and haunting melody, "Mbube" ("Lion") was an instant hit, selling 10,000 copies in the Forties. A decade after its release, the record found its way to American folk musician Pete Seeger, who was enchanted by its Zulu refrain, which he misheard and turned into the pop hit "Wimoweh." In 1961, George David Weiss, Hugo Peretti, and Luigi Creatore added smoother arrangements and exotic lyrics, copyrighting what became "The Lion Sleeps Tonight."

Despite being "lionized" in South Africa, where he is regarded as the founder of Zulu choral (or Mbube) music, Linda died a pauper in 1962, he and his estate having received almost none of the royalties the song generated (including an estimated $15 million alone from its use in Disney's *The Lion King*). It was only in 2006, under threat of legal action, that publishers Alibene Music agreed to a financial settlement with Linda's heirs. **MK**

Long ago, before sex 'n' drugs ruled rock 'n' roll, The Ink Spots found time to sing in praise of the more innocent stimulation offered by the coffee jug.

The quartet first formed in Cincinnati, Ohio, in 1934. With their trademark ostinato guitar intros, and vocal harmonies as warm as a mug of steaming java, they rapidly became a crossover success with black and white radio listeners across America, even touring in the United Kingdom later the same year. They were to prove immensely influential on a host of famous R&B close-harmony outfits, perhaps most famously The Platters.

The original lineup of Orville "Hoppy" Jones, Ivory "Deek" Watson, Jerry Daniels (replaced by tenor Bill Kenny), and Charlie Fuqua underwent many changes, and there was considerable animosity between ex-members. None of that turbulence can be heard in the group's sweetly melodious recordings, however, which showcased what *Melody Maker* described as "beautifully balanced and exquisitely phrased vocalisms." "Java Jive," a caffeine fad song written in 1940 and recorded by The Ink Spots in July of that year, is fittingly a little peppier than the band's hypnotic lonesome-heart ballads. Its smart wordplay is couched in smooth harmonies and topped off with a playful vocal from Watson—who ironically had once performed in The Percolating Puppies; their "instruments" included coffee pots. **JD**

Gloomy Sunday
Billie Holiday (1941)

Writer | Rezs Seress, László Jávor, Sam Lewis
Producer | Uncredited
Label | Okeh
Album | N/A

Pop music thrives on myths, and one of the most enduring surrounds the song penned in 1933 as "Szomorú Vasárnap" by Hungarian composer Rezs Seress. To his captivatingly plaintive melody—influenced by *Magyar nota*, a Hungarian hybrid of Gypsy music and coffeehouse repertory—Seress paired lyrics by László Jávor portraying a heartbroken soul on the point of no return.

Translated for Western ears, "Gloomy Sunday" was first recorded in 1936 by Hal Kemp & His Orchestra. It has attracted covers from the likes of Paul Robeson, Serge Gainsbourg, Elvis Costello, and Björk, though its definitive reading came from Billie Holiday. To mournful, muted accompaniment from Teddy Wilson & His Orchestra, Holiday's sweetly sad delivery—almost coquettish at times—draws out the seductive pull and tug of the melody, and the defeat in the lyrics. Ending it all sounds beguilingly appealing.

The words, written by Sam Lewis, added the chilling line "Would they be angry if I thought of joining you?" implying suicide—something left vague in the original. Many radio stations, including the BBC, banned it outright. Bizarrely, over the years the song became associated with a string of genuine suicides.

Rezs Seress remained bemused by his song's unsettling reputation, right up to his death in 1968. He committed suicide. **RD**

Guantanamera
Joseíto Fernández (1941)

Writer | Joseíto Fernández
Producer | Uncredited
Label | RCA Victor
Album | N/A

Guantánamo is notorious for reasons other than music nowadays, but back in the Thirties, it became synonymous in Cuba with the most widely recognized Cuban song of all time. Almost everyone knows the tune and words of the chorus, which are also those of the original title. This may refer to a "woman from Guantánamo" or perhaps to the style itself, the *guajira*, a type of Cuban country music.

José Fernández Diaz (the stage name came later) composed the song in 1928, basing the words on a poem by celebrated Cuban nationalist José Martí. Actually from Havana, not Guantánamo, Fernández's own group debuted on the radio station CMCQ in 1935, using "Guajira Guantanamera" as their theme tune and improvising *décimas* (ten-line poems) to the melody. This was in the style of the *punto guajiro*, developed during the early eighteenth century by Cuban peasant farmers of Spanish descent.

It wasn't until 1941 that Fernández recorded the song as "Mi biografia" (My Biography). From 1943, he sang it on another station, using it as a template for a news and gossip slot. By the time the show was axed, fourteen years later, the tune was ingrained in Cuba's collective psyche. Yet it was only when U.S. folk icon Pete Seeger recorded it in 1962, during the Cuban Missile Crisis, that the rest of the world caught on. **JLu**

God Bless the Child
Billie Holiday (1941)

Writer | Billie Holiday, Arthur Herzog Jr.
Producer | Uncredited
Label | Okeh
Album | N/A

Renowned as an interpreter of other people's songs, Billie Holiday rarely wrote her own material. "God Bless the Child" was a rare exception. In her autobiography, *Lady Sings the Blues*, Holiday recalls one of the many fierce arguments she had with her mother, Sadie—this one concerning money. In the course of the row, she uttered the old proverb, "God bless the child that's got his own"—words that she later used as the starting point for a song.

"God Bless the Child" was recorded on May 9, 1941, in New York. Holiday's band was pianist Eddie Heywood's Orchestra, which featured a smooth three-man saxophone lineup and the renowned Roy Eldridge on trumpet, who delivers a succinct solo. Piano, guitar, bass, and drums make up the rhythm section.

Holiday opens the song with her own interpretation of a biblical observation (possibly Matthew 25: 29): "Them that's got shall get / Them that's not shall lose." Money brings friends, but poverty sees them leave again. But the child that stands on his own two feet is immune to fortune's whims and is truly blessed. As a statement of self-reliance, sung in Holiday's knowing but vulnerable voice against a restrained accompaniment, it is disarmingly effective. "Billie Holiday," noted Joni Mitchell in 1998, "makes you hear the content and the intent of every word that she sings, even at the expense of her pitch or tone." **SA**

Stormy Weather
Lena Horne (1943)

Writer | Harold Arlen, Ted Koehler
Producer | Uncredited
Label | Unknown
Album | N/A

Stormy Weather the movie is a musical loosely based on the life of its main star, the dancer Bill "Bojangles" Robinson. Robinson plays Bill Williamson, a dancer returning home from the war in 1918 and trying to launch his performing career. His invented love interest is a singer named Selina Rogers, played by Lena Horne. The short movie— only seventy-eight minutes long—was released to great acclaim in July 1943. It was notable for showcasing many of the top African-American performers of the time, including Cab Calloway and his band, and pianist Fats Waller, who died a few months after its release.

"Stormy Weather," the song that lent its title to the movie, is a decade older, written in 1933 by Harold Arlen, with lyrics by Ted Koehler. It was first sung by Ethel Waters at the Cotton Club in Harlem. Lena Horne recorded it in 1941 for RCA Victor, but in 1943 re-recorded it for the film soundtrack.

"Stormy Weather" is a song of disappointment and regret, the singer pining for her absent man. The bad weather acts as a metaphor for her feelings: "Don't know why there's no sun up in the sky / Stormy weather / Since my man and I ain't together / Keeps rainin' all the time." Unsurprisingly, the song has been much loved by torch singers and drag queens ever since. Noteworthy cover versions have been recorded by Judy Garland and Billie Holiday, among many others. **SA**

Rum and Coca-Cola
Lord Invader (1943)

Writer | Rupert W. Grant, Lionel Belasco
Producer | Uncredited
Label | Decca
Album | N/A

During World War II, around 20,000 U.S. GIs were stationed in Trinidad, ostensibly to deter any invasion. Unhappy with the situation, a local musician using the stage name of Lord Invader commented on this "American social invasion" in a calypso titled "Rum and Coca-Cola." The song is a ribald exposé of the informal prostitution that took place ("Both mother and daughter / Workin' for the Yankee dollar"). "Rum and Coca-Cola" was both the servicemen's preferred tipple and a metaphor for the "mixing" of the two cultures. Lord Invader had based the melody on a tune called "L'année passée," copyrighted by Lionel Belasco, another Trinidadian calypsonian. His song, in turn, was based on a folk tune from nearby Martinique.

The track was a huge hit in Trinidad in 1943. In 1945, a very similar-sounding song by The Andrews Sisters—with the same title, general subject, and even some of the same lyrics—became the biggest-selling song in the United States. It was credited to the writer Morey Amsterdam and two business associates. The Andrews Sisters' version makes light of the issues raised by Lord Invader and is sung in hammy faux-Trinidadian accents. In an ensuing court case, it was found that Amsterdam, who had visited the island when Lord Invader's hit was current, had indeed infringed copyright, and Lord Invader won an undisclosed sum in compensation. **JLu**

This Land Is Your Land
Woody Guthrie (1944)

Writer | Woody Guthrie
Producer | Moe Asch
Label | Folkways
Album | N/A

First recorded in 1944, Woody Guthrie's most influential song was actually written some four years previously as a response to Irving Berlin's "God Bless America," which Guthrie felt was trite. "This Land Is Your Land" has since become regarded as an alternative "Star-Spangled Banner."

Guthrie matched his original lyrics to large parts of the melody of The Carter Family's "Little Darlin', Pal of Mine," a technique he often used to increase the appeal of his songs. Given the economic climate of the 1940s, the song was most popularly sold in a hand-printed booklet with nine other songs and a selection of illustrations for twenty-five cents. This made the song hugely popular among those struggling with financial hardship and the effects of World War II.

The rousing nature of the lyrics has led to the song being championed as a folk protest song across the world. As is often the case with folk songs, the lyrics have been adapted to reflect different times, and geographical references have changed to reflect the local environment. Popular versions include those sung in India, Canada, and the Republic of Ireland.

In January 2009, Bruce Springsteen and—longtime friend of Woody Guthrie—Pete Seeger performed the song together at the inauguration of U.S. President Barack Obama at Washington D.C.'s Lincoln Memorial. **CR**

Lili Marleen
Marlene Dietrich (1945)

Writer | Hans Leip, Norbert Schultze, Mack David
Producer | Uncredited
Label | Decca
Album | N/A

The song "Lili Marleen" was first recorded in 1938, but its lyrics were written much earlier, in 1915, when Hans Leip, a young German soldier, attempted to express the nostalgia he felt while enduring that era's political upheavals. His poem was originally entitled "Das Mädchen unter der Laterne" ("The Girl Under the Lantern"); her name, Lili, was that of his girlfriend, and also that of a nurse he knew during World War I.

When Leip's work appeared in a collection of poems in 1937, composer Norbert Schultze set about turning it into a song. It was recorded by popular German singer Lale Andersen in 1939, but initially made very little impact. However, all that changed when German Forces Radio started broadcasting it to the Afrika Korps in 1941. The song's wistful romanticism struck a chord with both Germans and Allied soldiers (who were listening in), and English versions of the ballad were hurriedly recorded. Remarkably, both sides ended up broadcasting the song in both languages.

This unexpected cultural rapprochement was perfectly epitomized by the song's most famous singer, the German Hollywood actress and staunch anti-Nazi Marlene Dietrich. She became synonymous with the song, performing it for U.S. infantrymen "for three long years in North Africa, Italy, Alaska, Greenland, Iceland, and in England," as she later recalled. **DaH**

(Get Your Kicks on) Route 66
The Nat King Cole Trio (1946)

Writer | Bobby Troup
Producer | Uncredited
Label | Capitol
Album | N/A

While driving from Pennsylvania west across the United States to Los Angeles, the composer Bobby Troup came up with the idea of a song about the road he was then driving on, Route 66. He soon had the melody and title, although the lyrics proved trickier. Eventually, he settled on an itinerary of the towns along the road, from St. Louis and Joplin, in Missouri, to Flagstaff, in Arizona. He then backtracked east slightly so that we "don't forget Winona," before heading west again to San Bernardino in California and journey's end.

Troup wrote the song for Nat King Cole, whose trio had a big pop and R&B hit with it. "Route 66" celebrates the freedom of the road and, in the direction the road takes, the "manifest destiny" of the American people to settle their continent from coast to coast. Construction of Route 66 began in 1925 and the road was fully operational by 1932, initially running for 2,448 miles (3,939 km) from Chicago across the country to Los Angeles. It linked the rural south with the industrial cities of the north, but also the sunshine towns of California.

Cole's version of the song is lightly swinging, piano-led jazz, topped off with a characteristically stylish vocal, though others—notably Chuck Berry and The Rolling Stones—turned it into an R&B classic. As for the road itself, Route 66 has been replaced by interstate highways and other major roads and is now largely disused. **SA**

Al gurugu
La Niña de los Peines (1946)

Writer | Uncredited
Producer | Uncredited
Label | La Voz de su Amo (HMV)
Album | N/A

La vie en rose
Edith Piaf (1946)

Writer | Edith Piaf, Louiguy
Producer | Uncredited
Label | EMI
Album | N/A

Born in 1890 to a poor Gypsy family in Seville, the capital of Andalusia, Pastora Maria Pavón Cruz developed into the first major flamenco star of the twentieth century. Today she is widely regarded as the greatest female flamenco singer ever. Nicknamed "La Niña de los Peines" (the girl with the combs) early on, she began singing as a child to help support her family. Her voice's power and harsh timbre attracted attention beyond the Gypsy community, however, and soon the likes of the poet Federico García Lorca and the guitarist Andrés Segovia were championing her artistry.

At a young age, La Niña began touring Spain, and her first recordings were made in 1910. Fittingly, she married the great flamenco singer Pepe Pinto; fleeing the Spanish Civil War for Argentina, they returned in the 1940s to Spain, where she continued her career. "Al gurugu" is regarded by flamenco connoisseurs as one of the defining recordings of flamenco's golden dawn.

The song's title is a nonsense term comparable, say, to "doo-doo-doo." It works primarily as a vocal effect, around which La Niña improvised lyrics such as "My husband's left me all alone / He's gone to war in France." Backed by flamenco guitar and *palmas* (hand claps), "Al gurugu" displays La Niña at the height of her powers and stands as an intense performance of *cante jondo* (deep song). Here lives flamenco's raw Gypsy soul. **GC**

Loosely translated as "a life through rose-colored glass," Edith Piaf's iconic ballad embodies the cabaret singer's traumatic life and timeless work. It was given a Grammy Hall of Fame Award in 1998.

Colleagues and peers initially critiqued Piaf's signature song, written in 1945, as a bad choice, yet it became an instant hit with live audiences. Songwriting duties were shared, with Edith penning the lyrics and Louis Gugliemi (a Catalan musician writing under the nom de plume "Louiguy") composing the melody.

The song's unashamed romanticism, coupled with its sultry orchestral score, made it an international hit; Disney lyricist and songwriter Mack David soon translated an English version of the lyrics. The song has since become almost an alternative "La Marseillaise," representing new generations of French citizens.

This classic number continues to influence popular culture, featuring in Hollywood movies as diverse as Steven Spielberg's *Saving Private Ryan* (1998), Oliver Stone's *Natural Born Killers* (1994), and Pixar's *WALL-E* (2008). It provided the title for the Oscar-winning Piaf biopic *La vie en rose* in 2007. Ian Fleming named the thirteenth chapter of *Casino Royale* after "La vie en rose," in addition to referencing it in both *You Only Live Twice* and *Diamonds Are Forever*. In 1977, another diva—Grace Jones—reinvented it for a new generation. **KL**

Edith Piaf in concert in 1946; audiences were transfixed by the raw emotion of her performances. ➜

La mer
Charles Trenet (1946)

Writer | Charles Trenet, Albert Lasry
Producer | Uncredited
Label | EMI
Album | N/A

Charles Trenet was among the most respected and loved French artists of his generation. Yet despite crafting more than a thousand evocative chansons during his six-decade career, the singer-songwriter is most famous outside of his native country for one track—the symphonic classic "La mer."

A larger-than-life character, Trenet was initially known as "the Singing Madman," thanks to his exuberant stage presence and eccentric persona. Combined with his carefree and quirky vocal style, this proved a winning combination, but it wasn't until after World War II that Trenet really capitalized on his growing popularity, showcasing a clutch of new tunes that included "La mer."

Released in 1946, it's a poetic ode to the ocean, capturing its hypnotic qualities in almost surreal terms. Although the song became an international hit, little was known about its origins until an elderly Trenet revealed in 2001 that he'd written the lyrics of "La mer" as a poem when he was sixteen. He also divulged that the music was composed and scribbled onto railway toilet paper during a short train journey in 1943.

In the late 1950s, American songwriter Jack Lawrence transformed "La mer." He rewrote the lyrics and turned it into a romantic song of yearning, retitled "Beyond the Sea." This English-language version became a megahit for American heartthrob Bobby Darin. **BC**

White Christmas
Bing Crosby (1947)

Writer | Irving Berlin
Producer | Uncredited
Label | Decca
Album | *Merry Christmas* (1947)

Irving Berlin was never much of a musician. He lacked Jerome Kern's gift for harmony, George Gershwin's adventurousness, and Cole Porter's wit. He was a famously terrible pianist and never learned to write musical notation. Yet from this apparently unsophisticated hand came a catalog whose success remains unmatched by any songwriter before or since: more than eight hundred published songs, among them such unavoidables as "God Bless America," "There's No Business Like Show Business," and this, the Christmas song to end all Christmas songs.

First sketched out by Berlin in early 1940, "White Christmas" appeared in 1942, sung by Bing Crosby in the movie *Holiday Inn*. Although Crosby's recording was released at the height of summer, its timing couldn't have been better: with U.S. involvement in World War II escalating, the song's sentimentality struck a chord with listeners parted from loved ones. (It helped that Crosby's version omitted Berlin's original verse, which sets the singer's location in Beverly Hills.) The song was No. 1 by October and omnipresent by 1943.

Five years after the original hit, Crosby was asked to re-record "White Christmas" because of the degradation of the original master plate; it's this version that's most familiar today. It's since been covered by everyone from Louis Armstrong to Twisted Sister. **WF-J**

Good Rockin' Tonight
Roy Brown (1947)

Writer | Roy Brown
Producer | Jules Braun
Label | DeLuxe
Album | N/A

Roy Brown remains among the greatest "lost heroes" of rock and soul. With "Good Rockin' Tonight," he gave postwar America an anthem for the turbulent new music taking shape. The Louisiana-born Brown had grown up singing gospel. Initially a Bing Crosby imitator, he quickly reshaped his sound after witnessing Houston audiences throw money at blues singers.

A hugely popular live entertainer, Brown's athletic stage presence and musical versatility established him as the most popular black singer in New Orleans. He wrote "Good Rockin' Tonight" in 1946 and performed the song for boogie-woogie pianist Cecil Gant. So taken was Gant with the song, he rang Jules Braun of New Jersey's DeLuxe Records and got Brown to sing "Good Rockin' Tonight" to him over the phone. Braun promptly told Gant to give Brown a hundred dollars, get him a room at the Dew Drop, and keep an eye on him. Arriving in New Orleans two days later, Braun set up a recording session, and released "Good Rockin' Tonight" in May 1947.

Backed by a pumping band, Brown sang "Good Rockin' Tonight" as a call to arms, and the record captures the raw power and excitement of jump blues. An immediate hit in New Orleans, the song reached the national charts in 1948, though it went to No. 1 on the R&B listings when covered by leading blues shouter Wynonie Harris. **GC**

Nature Boy
The Nat King Cole Trio (1948)

Writer | Eden Ahbez
Producer | Uncredited
(arranged by Frank DeVol)
Label | Capitol
Album | N/A

The story goes that a few days after composer Eden Ahbez first presented Nat King Cole's manager with "Nature Boy" in 1947, Cole performed it live at the Bocage nightclub in Los Angeles. At the end of the set, before Cole had even reached the dressing room, Irving Berlin offered to buy it. This tale of a "strange enchanted boy . . . who wandered very far" was to be the making of Cole.

Pianist Nat King Cole had come to prominence in the late 1930s as the leader of a jazz trio. As a singer, with a beautifully smooth style and clear diction, Cole had a series of hits in the 1940s that appealed to a white audience. This was a difficult trick to pull off, as American music was then divided by race, and crossing over from black-jazz to white-pop acceptability was rare. Cole did it in style with "Nature Boy," which became a U.S. No. 1.

The melody echoes the Yiddish tune "Schwieg mein Hertz," as well as part of a Dvořák piano quintet. The original version, however, which Cole recorded on August 22, 1947, was transformed by the lush orchestrations of Frank DeVol, the in-house arranger of Capitol Records, whose use of strings and flute to suggest the strange enchantments of the nature boy made the song a massive hit, despite the simultaneous appearance of several cover versions. Cole himself only sings on the song, the piano solo taken by someone else. Cole the popular vocalist had arrived. **SA**

Saturday Night Fish Fry | Louis Jordan & His Tympany Five (1949)

Writer | Louis Jordan, Ellis Walsh
Producer | Uncredited
Label | Decca
Album | N/A

Few figures in black-music history have enjoyed greater success and wielded more influence than Louis Jordan. The singer and saxophonist got his start in New York during the 1930s with Chick Webb's big band, the same group with which Ella Fitzgerald found fame. But Jordan truly hit his stride with his own Tympany Five, helping to define the R&B sound while racking up an unmatched chart run during the Forties and early Fifties with a string of joyous, swinging singles.

Telling the tale of a police raid on a New Orleans house party, "Saturday Night Fish Fry" is in many ways a Jordan archetype: there's a little boogie-woogie piano, a bookending horn riff, an in-the-pocket rhythm section, and a comic narrative. By this point, the group (now a nine-piece) were swinging more fiercely than ever, with James "Ham" Jackson's cranked-up electric-guitar licks offering a direct link to rock 'n' roll.

Spending twelve weeks atop the U.S. R&B charts, "Saturday Night Fish Fry" was one of Jordan's last hits. By 1951, his ten-year chart residency had begun a decline that was only expedited by rock 'n' roll, the music he'd helped invent. It took four decades for audiences to rediscover his catalog, when *Five Guys Named Moe*, Clarke Peters's feel-good musical built around Jordan's songs, transferred from the London fringe to lengthy runs in the West End and on Broadway. **WF-J**

I'm So Lonesome I Could Cry | Hank Williams (1949)

Writer | Hank Williams
Producer | Uncredited
Label | MGM
Album | N/A

Country music has long toed the line separating craft and confession, artistry and authenticity. Yet it was Hank Williams who really tied together these opposite extremes. Williams was a skilled tunesmith and a gifted vocalist. More than any country performer before him, he carved his own life into his songs, whether wryly lamenting his lack of beer ("My Bucket's Got a Hole in It," making light of his debilitating alcoholism) or eerily anticipating his own demise ("I'll Never Get Out of This World Alive," released weeks before his death). Apparently written about his turbulent marriage, "I'm So Lonesome I Could Cry" is an archetypal blend of autobiography and imagination.

"I'm So Lonesome I Could Cry" is unusual among Williams's repertoire in that it was conceived not as a song but a poem. The singer had been booked to tape a series of spoken-word recitations in early 1950, and "I'm So Lonesome I Could Cry" had apparently been written with these sessions in mind. Williams had a change of heart, though, and instead set the words to a plangent, simple tune in three-quarter time.

Buried on the B-side of "My Bucket's Got a Hole in It," the song wasn't a hit in its day. However, it's since become a touchstone for Williams's ill-starred life, which ended, strung out on morphine and alcohol, in the back seat of a car on New Year's Day, 1953. He was twenty-nine years old. **WF-J**

Hank Williams's unadorned vocal delivery and poignant lyrics make him a giant of country music. ➔

- DJ Alan Freed begins to play black R&B for white listeners in 1951

- Black harmony groups initiate the American fad of doo wop in 1954

- Bill Haley & His Comets release "Rock Around the Clock" in 1955

- Elvis Presley electrifies America on *The Ed Sullivan Show* in 1956

- Berry Gordy Jr. founds the Motown label, dubbed "Hitsville USA," in 1959

1950s

Autumn Leaves
Jo Stafford (1950)

Writers | Joseph Kosma, Jacques Prévert, Johnny Mercer
Producer | Uncredited
Label | Capitol
Album | N/A

First finding fame as a member of close-harmony group The Pied Pipers, Jo Stafford became a favorite of U.S. troops during World War II, which led to her picking up the affectionate nickname "G.I. Jo." Dozens of hits followed, from melancholy ballads ("Some Enchanted Evening," "A Sunday Kind of Love") to lively duets with Frankie Laine ("Hambone," Hank Williams's "Hey, Good Lookin'"); all are distinguished by Stafford's rich, elegant, and beautifully understated deep soprano.

Although "Autumn Leaves" is now an American jazz standard, it's a French tune, written in 1946 and originally titled "Les feuilles mortes" (The Dead Leaves). The song crossed the Atlantic courtesy of songwriter Johnny Mercer, who wrote a new English lyric to Joseph Kosma's melody in the late Forties. Featuring an orchestra directed by Hal Mooney, Stafford's typically stately recording may have been the first to include Mercer's words.

Her success continued for around another decade, during which time she had her second No. 1 single in the U.K. ("You Belong to Me") and won an unlikely Grammy for Best Comedy Album. A thousand servicemen's hearts were broken when Stafford hung up her mic in 1966 while still in her forties, apparently dissatisfied with the quality of her voice. She retired, she said, "for the same reason that Lana Turner doesn't pose in a bathing suit any more." **WF-J**

Summertime
Sarah Vaughan (1950)

Writers | George Gershwin, DuBose Heyward
Producer | Joe Lippman
Label | Columbia
Album | N/A

Porgy and Bess has long attracted controversy for its representation of African-American life. Written in 1935 by a white Jewish musician, George Gershwin, and based on the 1924 novel *Porgy* by a white southerner, DuBose Heyward, who then wrote the libretto, the folk opera has been accused of sustaining white stereotypes of southern black life. No such criticism attaches to its individual songs, however, least of all to "Summertime," which became a popular jazz standard.

Gershwin based the song on black spirituals. It has a mainly pentatonic melody—that is, one that uses notes from a five-note scale rather than the more conventional heptatonic (seven-note) scale—a form common to many spirituals and gospel songs. The main theme uses only six notes and in its simplicity sounds like a traditional folk song, not a modern composition.

In Sarah Vaughan's hands, the song is transformed into something quite dramatic. After two sets of repeating and descending string and bass-drum riffs that echo throughout the song, Vaughan enters with a sense of purpose. Horn statements and lush string arrangements support her full, rich contralto voice. In her "Summertime," the "living is easy," but anxious and possibly threatening, too. Of all the many versions that exist of this standard, few are as arresting, or as original, as that of Sarah Vaughan. **SA**

Sarah Vaughan in concert in 1956, during a hectic schedule of jazz performances. ➔

Goodnight, Irene
The Weavers (1950)

Writer | Traditional; Huddie Ledbetter, John A. Lomax
Producer | Uncredited
Label | Decca
Album | N/A

Mambo No. 5
Pérez Prado (1950)

Writer | Pérez Prado
Producer | Uncredited
Label | RCA Victor
Album | N/A

Legend has it that "Goodnight, Irene" was spectacular enough to get the man that first popularized the tune out of prison in 1934. Huddie "Lead Belly" Ledbetter received a pardon from the crime of attempted murder due in large part to how much Louisiana's governor enjoyed the bluesman's recording of "Irene."

The exact origin of "Irene" is unknown. It's often credited to Lead Belly, but he learned the tune from his uncle, and its origins may stretch back to the 1880s and Gussie Lord Davis's "Irene, Good Night." Whoever was the first to spin this lovesick tale, listeners can thank musicologists John and Alan Lomax for recording Lead Belly's version—for the composition went on to become one of the greatest American folk standards of the twentieth century. The version that truly secured that lofty ranking, however, wasn't Lead Belly's, but the one by The Weavers.

Pete Seeger's folk quartet, which learned the tune straight from Lead Belly, omitted some of the composition's more controversial verses, including the suicidal "And if Irene turns her back on me, I'm gonna take morphine and die." Yet, these "prettied up" lyrics meant that millions would get to enjoy "Irene." The song went to No. 1 in the United States, stayed on the charts for nearly half a year and prompted countless others, spanning from Frank Sinatra to Raffi, to record their own versions. **JiH**

Pérez Prado, a brilliant bandleader, pianist, arranger, composer, and performer, left his native Cuba in 1947 after feeling stifled by his publisher, who was finding his innovative music "too weird." After living briefly in Puerto Rico and touring, he settled in Mexico, where his nascent "mambo" style was an instant hit, largely due to its appearance in many Mexican movies. He may not have invented the form, but it was Prado who really launched the worldwide mambo craze of the Fifties with this song, released as a 78 rpm.

"Mambo No. 5," one of several numbered Prado mambos, is a typically jerky, strutting example, bludgeoning the ears with high, squealing trumpets, punchy saxes, and hyperactive percussion. Suspenseful silences punctuate the track, most ending in one of Prado's trademark grunts, which soon became synonymous with the style itself. (Rather than emoting meaninglessly, he was saying "¡Dilo!"—"Say it!" or "Give out!")

In 1999, a previously unknown German artist of Ugandan and Sicilian descent called Lou Bega overhauled the original, retitling it as "Mambo No. 5 (A Little Bit Of . . .)." The result was no more intellectual, but it too was a massive worldwide hit. Bega's souped-up version sampled Prado's original (grunts included) and added a lyric consisting of a long wish list of sexual conquests. It has been covered and ruthlessly parodied ever since. **JLu**

Rocket 88 | Jackie Brenston & His Delta Cats (1951)

Writer | Jackie Brenston
Producer | Sam Phillips, Ike Turner
Label | Chess
Album | N/A

Often cited as the first rock 'n' roll record, "Rocket 88" features the pounding piano of one Izear Luster Turner Jr. several years before he met future wife Anna Mae Bullock and they found fame as Ike and Tina Turner. In March 1951, Turner and his band The Kings of Rhythm traveled north by road from Clarksdale, Mississippi, to cut a session at Sam Phillips's Memphis Recording Service (later Sun Studio) at 706 Union Avenue in Memphis, Tennessee. The band's vocalist/saxophonist and Turner's cousin, Jackie Brenston, sang lead on "Rocket 88," an ode to the pleasures of the Oldsmobile 88, first produced in 1949 and famed for its "Rocket V8" engine. Phillips leased the master to Chicago's Chess record label, who released it with the artist renamed as Jackie Brenston & His Delta Cats—to the chagrin of Turner, who watched the record soar to the top spot on the *Billboard* R&B chart. Brenston was also credited with sole authorship, which Turner disputed.

The recording features a distorted, fuzz guitar sound that Phillips said was the result of guitarist Willie Kizart's amp falling from the roof of the band's car on the way to the studio, thereby puncturing the speaker cone; Phillips tried to fix it by stuffing the rip with paper. Little Richard's "Good Golly, Miss Molly" (1958) reused Ike Turner's "Rocket 88" piano riff—which itself had been lifted from "Cadillac Boogie" (1947) by Jimmy Liggins. **JoH**

Cry | Johnnie Ray & The Four Lads (1951)

Writer | Churchill Kohlman
Producer | Uncredited
Label | Okeh
Album | N/A

In the early Fifties, Johnnie Ray was a new kind of singing sensation. His style owed everything to crooners such as Bing Crosby, but it was the drama and personality he added to his recordings that singled him out as a truly original performer.

"Cry" was the perfect embodiment of Ray's characteristic vocal delivery. The recording's gulping, tuneless, sob story sounds almost as though the singer is about to break down in tears—a feat he achieved in many of his concert appearances. A tormented childhood and an accident at age ten that left him requiring a hearing aid all added to Ray's frail appeal. "So let your hair down and go right on and cry" says the lyric, and fans took his advice and did just that. Ray's concerts were emotional experiences that would arguably be equaled in their intensity only by Sixties Beatlemania and the teenybopper era in the Seventies. Ray himself admitted that he sang "flat as a table"—which mattered not at all, as he was drowned out by hysterical screaming girls who frequently ripped the clothes from his back.

Churchill Kohlman's song, first made popular by Ruth Casey, had long since lost its original substance when Johnnie Ray made it his own and topped the *Billboard* Hot 100. The song lent itself to country covers more in keeping with its original creation and was recorded by artists such as Tammy Wynette and Crystal Gayle. **DR**

How High the Moon
Les Paul and Mary Ford (1951)

Writer | Morgan Lewis, Nancy Hamilton
Producer | Uncredited (Les Paul)
Label | Capitol
Album | N/A

Dissatisfied in the 1930s with his semi-acoustic guitar—too weedy by itself, too prone to feedback when amplified—Les Paul decided the solution was a fully amplified, solid-bodied instrument. So he built one himself from a length of lumber, adding two cut-away sides of an acoustic guitar for decorative effect, as audiences found its appearance freakish. Nicknamed "the Log," it was the first-ever electric guitar, the direct precursor to the later Gibson model named in Paul's honor.

His guitar-building success helped inspire the indomitable guitarist to resolve another irritation: the need to record live. Fidgeting with acetate discs in his garage in 1947, Paul cut an otherworldly version of the Rodgers and Hart song "Lover (When You're Near Me)," on which he overdubbed eight guitar parts. But the fun really started shortly afterward, when sometime recording partner Bing Crosby helped fund Paul's experiments in tape-recording technology, which made it far easier for Paul to layer tracks on top of each other.

One of the earliest songs cut by Paul on his souped-up Ampex tape recorder, "How High the Moon" still sounds dazzling nearly sixty years later, Paul's dozen fizzing tracks finding an opposites-attract marriage with Ford's graceful layered vocals. A *Billboard* No. 1 for nine straight weeks, it's perhaps the apogee of Paul's experiments in what he called "sound-on-sound recording." **WF-J**

London Is the Place for Me
Lord Kitchener (1951)

Writer | Aldwyn Roberts
Producer | Denis Preston
Label | Melodisc
Album | N/A

Lord Kitchener was born Aldwyn Roberts in Trinidad, the son of a blacksmith, in 1923. He grew up hearing the Spanish songs of the dance halls and the early calypso performed around the island. Along with Mighty Sparrow, Kitchener would popularize calypso across the globe.

By the late Forties, Kitch had already become a leading light of Trinidad's burgeoning calypso scene, and had traveled to the United States and United Kingdom to perform. He emigrated to the the latter country aboard the MV *Empire Windrush* in 1948 (newsreel of the time captures him, disembarking, and actually singing this song) and swiftly became a talismanic figure for Caribbean immigrants in London. Arriving in a strange land, they initially relied on themselves for community and entertainment alike, with calypso providing a commentary on everything from politics to sexual innuendo.

"London is the Place For Me" caught the optimistic feel of the time and offered some colorful island relief against the gray tones of the British capital. The opening and closing piano phrase from the song mimics the "Westminster Quarters" from the chimes of Big Ben, and establishes an iconic image of the city. The song proved popular not only with immigrants in the U.K., but also in the West African countries of the Commonwealth, and was a hit back in the Caribbean, too. **CR**

Married duo Les Paul and Mary Ford play along in a tongue-in-cheek 1955 publicity shot.

They Can't Take That Away From Me | Fred Astaire (1952)

Writer | George Gershwin, Ira Gershwin
Producer | Norman Granz
Label | Clef
Album | *The Astaire Story* (1952)

Music by George Gershwin, lyrics by brother Ira, "They Can't Take That Away From Me" first surfaced in the Fred Astaire and Ginger Rogers movie *Shall We Dance* (1937). Then accompanied by Johnny Green & His Orchestra, Astaire's first attempt was nominated for Best Original Song at the Oscars, only to lose out to Harry Owen's "Sweet Leilani" from *Waikiki Wedding*.

Astaire crooned the number to Rogers yet again in *The Barkleys of Broadway* (1949), but arguably nailed the song's easy charm later on, when he finally recorded his debut long player in 1952. *The Astaire Story*, a four-volume career retrospective that made its way into the Grammy Hall of Fame in 1999, featured pianist Oscar Peterson, famous for his Trio but here fronting a sextet. The producer was impresario Norman Granz, who had given Peterson his big break at Carnegie Hall a few years earlier, and together they improvised a jazzy, delicate, amiable version given spring by Astaire's sensitive and guileless performance. Not bad for the chap who "Can't act. Can't sing," according to that sniffy, possibly apocryphal, screen test report.

"They Can't Take That Away From Me" has, of course, enjoyed a rich afterlife. Covered by Sarah Vaughan in 1957, Ella Fitzgerald in 1959, and Frank Sinatra in 1962, to name just a handful, it stands tall as a fixture of the putative Great American Songbook, a signifier of a more romantic age. **MH**

Dust My Broom
Elmore James (1952)

Writer | Elmore James
Producer | Lillian McMurry
Label | Trumpet
Album | N/A

"Dust My Broom" has one of the most complex histories of any blues song, not least because it involves the enigmatic Robert Johnson. In November 1936, Johnson recorded his own composition called "(I Believe I'll) Dust My Broom." Both the title and the tune, however, were already around by that date in other songs. Elmore James has sometimes been credited as its composer, although he was only eighteen at the time Johnson recorded it and the two probably did not meet until 1937. What probably happened is that Johnson then taught James the song.

What is known is that in August 1951 the producer Lillian McMurry got Elmore James into a recording studio. She was unaware of Johnson's earlier composition and in good faith filed for copyright under James's name. His version of the song had the title "Dust My Broom" and slightly altered words, but most importantly was played not with the acoustic guitar used by Johnson but with an electric slide or bottleneck guitar.

Supported by harmonica, bass, and drums, James turns the song into a hardwired, amplified banshee wail. What the song actually means is debatable, "dust my broom" referring either to cleaning or being perhaps a sexual term. The song was a surprise hit when it was released in 1952, and its opening electrifying riff is one of the best-known sounds in modern blues. **SA**

Foi Deus
Amália Rodrigues (1952)

Writer | Alberto Janes
Recording Engineer | Hugo Ribeiro
Label | Valentim de Carvalho
Album | N/A

Fado (literally, "fate" or "destiny") is a distinctive Portuguese folk music, often melancholic in mood. Now acknowledged as the greatest *fadista* (fado singer) ever, Amália Rodrigues was already a huge star in Portugal when unknown songwriter Alberto Janes knocked on her door, touting his composition "Foi Deus" ("It was God"). Its lyrics seem to have been tailored specially for her: "It was God . . . who opened my eyes and let me embrace fado . . . it was God who gave me this voice." She recorded her most famous version two years later at Abbey Road Studios in London.

At just twenty-two, Amália had already fully realized her trademark swooping vocal technique, which married the precision and control of an operatic diva with the emotional honesty of a folk singer. This arrangement features the conventional trio of fado—acoustic bass, "Spanish" guitar, and the chiming twelve-string *guitarra Portuguesa*. At the time this song was considered almost heretical by some purists for its departure from tradition, which dictated that "proper" fados be sung to one of only two hundred or so traditional melodies.

"Foi Deus" is so associated with Amália that few others have dared to record it. That said, in 1992 Lisbon-based Angolan singer Waldemar Bastos cut a brilliant version. His stripped-down reading uses just guitar and voice, but he invests the song with plenty of his own private pathos. **JLu**

Le gorille
Georges Brassens (1952)

Writer | Georges Brassens
Producer | Jacques Canetti
Label | Polydor
Album | *La mauvaise réputation* (1952)

In 1952, nonconformist troubadour Georges Brassens found notoriety with one of the first songs he wrote, "Le gorille." The song had its origins in a German work camp he'd been sent to during World War II, where he had written songs in an attempt to keep his fellow workers amused. Once he'd escaped and reached Paris, Brassens fine-tuned one of the songs for publishing. The only line that remained, however, was "Beware of the gorilla!"—originally a reference to camp guards, although in the released song the (well-endowed) gorilla is a priapic figure, used by Brassens to attack authority figures in general, as well as the concept of capital punishment in particular. The climax sees the gorilla mistaking a judge (who has just sentenced a man to death by the guillotine) for an old woman, and sodomizing him.

The song caused a storm of controversy and was banned from French radio until 1955. Brassens was unfazed by the reception to the song, claiming that he had toned it down by deleting a final verse with an even stronger anti-authoritarian message. "Le gorille" made him briefly infamous, but Brassens found himself garlanded with awards and praise for his other work, and now his output is studied in many French schools.

Some still appreciate his rebellious track of 1952: controversial rapper Joey Starr paid homage in "Gare au jaguarr" in 2006. **DC**

Singin' in the Rain
Gene Kelly (1952)

Writer | Nacio Herb Brown, Arthur Freed
Producer | "Musical direction" credited to L. Hayton
Label | MGM
Album | *Singin' in the Rain OST* (1952)

"Though it's old," sings a teenage Judy Garland, introducing it in the 1940 movie *Little Nellie Kelly*, "it's a lovely song." And old it was, at least in relation to what was then a young Hollywood. "Singin' in the Rain" had featured in several film musicals since making its debut in *The Hollywood Revue of 1929*, but never quite caught on. It would probably still be languishing in obscurity were it not for the persistence of one of its co-writers.

Arthur Freed spent the first part of his Hollywood career as a jobbing lyricist, churning out songs on the MGM assembly line. Promotion in the late 1930s led him into movie production, but he never quite let go of his music. And so it was that in the early 1950s, flush with success from the likes of *Easter Parade* and *On the Town*, he decided to build a film around songs he'd written in the Twenties and Thirties with composer Nacio Herb Brown. The result was *Singin' in the Rain*.

It's near-impossible to hear the title number without also seeing it. Gene Kelly was never a great singer, but he could always sell a song, especially when he relied on his feet to do the selling. Heard without the visuals, it's a gentle little swinger but not much more; paired with the dance routine, though, it's irresistible. Since referenced by everyone from Stanley Kubrick to British comedians Morecambe and Wise (in a 1976 sketch), it's still musical shorthand for joy. **WF-J**

Just Walkin' in the Rain
The Prisonaires (1953)

Writer | Johnny Bragg, Robert Riley
Producer | Sam Phillips
Label | Sun
Album | N/A

In June 1953, five criminals—variously convicted of murder, sexual assault, and theft—ambled into Sam Phillips's now-legendary Sun recording studio in Memphis, Tennessee. But these jailbirds weren't going to rob the joint. Known as The Prisonaires, they were out on day release from Nashville's Tennessee State Penitentiary, and about to lay down one of the decade's most melancholic and beautiful ballads.

Composed by group founder and lead singer Johnny Bragg (who was serving ninety-nine years for rape, a charge he always denied) and burglar Robert Riley, the mournful "Just Walkin' in the Rain" perfectly captures the frustrations and regrets of an isolated life spent behind bars. Bragg sings of a man trying to forget his true love, his lead vocal line floating over the group's delicate doo-wop harmonies and a simple strummed guitar.

When the recording session ended, The Prisonaires headed back to jail. (Their guards had been waiting in the café next door.) But they were no longer just common criminals. Soon after its release, the song became a hit with local radio stations, and eventually made the U.S. R&B Top Ten. Three years later, the crooning "nabob of sob" Johnnie Ray covered the track, topping the British charts and reaching No. 2 in the United States. However, Ray's overblown interpretation did not possess the soul and intimacy of the original. **TB**

Please Love Me
B. B. King (1953)

Writer | Jules Taub (Joe Bihari), B. B. King
Producer | Jules Bihari
Label | RPM
Album | N/A

Riley B. King—the "B. B." moniker is an abbreviation of "Beale Street Blues Boy," after the famous street in Memphis, Tennessee—had his first R&B No. 1 in 1951. Two years later he hit the top spot again with "Please Love Me." King wrote the song himself, but, as was common for artists at the time, he was forced to share credits, and thus income from royalties, with management or record owners. In this case, the writing was co-credited to Jules "Taub," the pseudonym for Jules Bihari, one of the owners of RPM Records.

The song kicks immediately into action, the electrifying guitar intro closely related to Elmore James's classic "Dust My Broom." Over four verses set to a horns-led swinging beat, cymbals hissing, and with a voice straining with yearning, King stresses his love for his unnamed woman, pledging to satisfy her every whim. By the end of the song, he is even promising to buy "a Cadillac car just to drive me where ever you are." One brief coda from King's blistering guitar and the song is done.

This is a raucous slice of R&B more usually associated with T-Bone Walker (an early and key influence on B. B.) or Howlin' Wolf than with B. B. King. His guitar is heard only at the start and finish, for the beautifully structured and poised solos that were to distinguish such epics as "The Thrill is Gone" were still a few years in the future. But it is still a mighty fine song. **SA**

Crying in the Chapel
The Orioles (1953)

Writer | Artie Glenn
Producer | Uncredited
Label | It's a Natural (Jubilee)
Album | N/A

Eight years before a baseball team came to town and swiped its name, Baltimore's Orioles formed in 1946 and started drawing up the doo-wop rulebook. The vocal troupe, named after Maryland's state bird, soon became an R&B sensation, scoring several big singles by decade's end. The well began to dry up in the early Fifties, but not before these birds recorded the top doo-wop ditty "Crying in the Chapel."

The supple gospel composition, versatile enough to thrive in country, R&B, and pop readings, was the perfect vehicle for the high-flying vocals of The Orioles. The four singers meshed on this song as well as any combo in doo-wop history, with George Nelson (baritone) and Johnny Reed (bass) digging a tomb for all earthly burdens, and tenors Alexander Sharp and Sonny Til soaring off with the promise of a heavenly existence. It was an ode to "the Lord"—and yet, there was a bit of the devil in there as well.

"Crying in the Chapel" was a hit in many hands—including those of Elvis and Aretha—yet none would handle it better than Baltimore's finest. The Orioles' version went to No. 1 on the U.S. R&B charts, where it remained for five weeks, becoming the band's biggest—and last—hit. Two decades later, this signature rendition was introduced to new generations of listeners on the *American Graffiti* soundtrack. **JiH**

Riot in Cell Block No. 9
The Robins (1954)

Writer | Jerry Leiber, Mike Stoller
Producer | Jerry Leiber, Mike Stoller
Label | Spark
Album | N/A

Leiber and Stoller's comic "playlets" for The Coasters remain some of the most enduring mementos of the rock 'n' roll era. No less impressive is this influential single for their forerunners, The Robins.

Wailing sirens and the rat-tat-tat of Tommy guns open up a tale of a prison riot, based on a swaggering Muddy Waters–style riff. The lyrics are delivered in a wonderful couldn't-give-a-damn drawl by Richard Berry, the composer of "Louie Louie." The latter was truly insurrectionary—the FBI actually had *those* lyrics scrutinized—but Leiber always denied any deeper meaning to "Riot in Cell Block No. 9," claiming its origins (especially the sound-effects-heavy intro) came from radio show *Gang Busters*. That may be, but there's an edge to the track that suggests something more.

For a start, there's nothing in the lyrics that openly acknowledges the song as a joke. And the payoff at the end—"In the forty-seventh hour, the tear gas got our men / We're all back in our cells, but every now and then . . ."—suggestively hints that the action isn't over quite yet.

Elvis's "Jailhouse Rock," also penned by Leiber and Stoller, is a more lighthearted take on the same theme, but Sly Stone's classic 1971 album, *There's a Riot Goin' On*, is perhaps a truer descendant, picking up on the dark stuff in The Robins' original and using it to tell the tale of a country still twitchy about race, still in Vietnam, and still riven by riot. **RD**

Love for Sale
Billie Holiday (1954)

Writer | Cole Porter
Producer | Norman Granz
Label | Verve
Album | *Billie Holiday* (1954)

Cole Porter wrote "Love for Sale" for the musical *The New Yorkers*, which debuted on Broadway in December 1930. A prostitute's song, it offers a direct and arrestingly unromantic view of love ("Love that's fresh and still unspoiled / Love that's only slightly soiled")—though perhaps a broken heart lies beneath all that cold cynicism.

Initially performed by white actress Kathryn Crawford, Porter quickly transferred the song to black singer Elisabeth Welch. This change did little to diminish the song's controversy, because the Hays Code had been introduced that year to censor immoral content and "Love for Sale" was briefly banned from the radio.

Given the song's status, it is interesting that Billie Holiday recorded it only once. Although taped in April 1952 as part of a session with her six-piece orchestra, she performed it with just pianist Oscar Peterson as her accompanist. Once recorded, though, it would not appear until the eight-track *Billie Holiday* 10-inch album in 1954.

For Holiday, the subject of this song was undoubtedly raw. As a young woman in New York, she had once worked in a brothel and was imprisoned briefly for soliciting sometime around 1930, the same year the song made its Broadway debut. Certainly, she sings it with a regretful knowingness, but then that was her trademark. Either way, her version is a heartfelt classic. **SA**

The Wind | Nolan Strong
& The Diablos (1954)

Writer | Nolan Strong, Bob Edwards
Producer | Jack Brown, Devora Brown
Label | Fortune
Album | N/A

Doo-wop combo Nolan Strong & The Diablos got together at high school, naming themselves after a book Strong was studying for class, *El niño diablo*. In 1954, the group auditioned for Fortune founders Jack and Devora Brown, who promptly signed them. Fortune was a family-run label that recorded in a back room of a shop in Detroit.

The group's second single, "The Wind," is as captivating today as it was when it was first cut. Over creeping double-bass plucks, the group swell into harmony, crooning, "Wind, blow, wind." Then Strong begins to sing and it's a true goosebump moment, his pure, sweet falsetto swooning across the track. "The Wind" is a lullaby to lost love and comes complete with a spoken-word section—delivered with that hand-on-heart seriousness exclusive to teenagers.

"The Wind" became a big seller in the Midwest, but never nationally. Local boy Smokey Robinson was a big fan; another was Berry Gordy, who tried to sign the group to Motown for $5,000. Fortune countered with $15,000. Moving into the Sixties, Strong was still bound to a contract with Fortune that he'd signed in his teens. Frustratingly, Fortune refused to license the group's recordings out to bigger labels with better distribution. One can only imagine how painful it must have been for Strong to witness Motown's massive success while his own talent remained under lock and key. **SH**

My Funny Valentine
Chet Baker (1954)

Writer | Richard Rodgers, Lorenz Hart
Producer | Richard Bock
Label | Pacific Jazz
Album | *Chet Baker Sings* (1956)

When Chet Baker died in 1988 after falling from a hotel window in Amsterdam, his good looks and velvet voice had been wrecked by forty years of drug abuse. Despite that ending, Baker is perhaps best remembered as the handsome, fragile soul delicately crooning "My Funny Valentine."

Baker first encountered the ballad—originally written for the Broadway musical *Babes in Arms*—while playing trumpet with the Gerry Mulligan Quartet in 1952. "The song fascinated Baker," writes his biographer James Gavin in *Deep in a Dream*. "It captured all he aspired to as a musician, with its sophisticated probing of a beautiful theme and its gracefully linked phrases."

After recording an instrumental version with Mulligan, Baker returned to the song in 1954, this time singing with a sparse drum, piano, and bass backing. His elegantly restrained, hushed delivery summed up the "cool" style of West Coast jazz. While it didn't earn him the respect of critics—one described his singing as a "time-consuming habit" that distracted from his trumpet playing—it turned him into a teen icon.

More significantly, the perfect balance of toughness and vulnerability, introspection, and romance in Baker's vocals set the template for almost every flawed pop and rock hero to come. Today, Pete Doherty and Amy Winehouse are walking a path he paved fifty years ago. **TB**

West Coast wunderkind Chet Baker in 1956. ➡

Shake, Rattle and Roll | Big Joe Turner & His Blues Kings (1954)

Writer | Charles E. Calhoun
Producer | Ahmet Ertegun, Jerry Wexler
Label | Atlantic
Album | N/A

Big Joe Turner's remarkable career stretched from the 1930s to the 1980s. He initially came to New York from Kansas City as a blues shouter during the boogie-woogie craze. A disastrous appearance at Harlem's Apollo Theater fronting the Count Basie band saw Turner heckled viciously. Atlantic Records boss Ahmet Ertegun convinced Joe to sign with his label, though, and start cutting R&B.

Between 1951 and 1956, Turner had fourteen Top Ten R&B hits. The most memorable was "Shake, Rattle and Roll," which topped the R&B charts and went to No. 2 on the pop listings. Written by Kansas City jazz veteran Jesse Stone (under the pseudonym Charles E. Calhoun), "Shake, Rattle and Roll" possesses a hard-driving rhythm that allows Turner's vocal to celebrate his lover with joyous lust. The song was covered by Bill Haley and Elvis Presley (albeit in a bowdlerized manner that removed the innuendo—"Way you wear those dresses, the sun comes shinin' through / I can't believe my eyes, all that mess belongs to you").

Turner was forty-three when "Shake, Rattle and Roll" gave him the biggest hit of his career and he became an unexpected beneficiary of the rock 'n' roll phenomenon, with Cleveland DJ Alan Freed championing him alongside much younger singers. The hits faded after 1958, but Turner kept recording and performing right up until his death, aged seventy-four. **GC**

(We're Gonna) Rock Around the Clock | Bill Haley & His Comets (1954)

Writer | Max Freedman, Jimmy deKnight (aka James E. Myers)
Producer | Milt Gabler
Label | Decca
Album | N/A

A clean-cut, slightly chubby twenty-nine-year-old with a slicked-down spit curl was an unlikely face to launch a thousand rock 'n' roll songs—but Bill Haley belting out "Rock Around the Clock" to a musically undernourished (but demanding) white teenage audience did just that. Its jump-band beat, with dramatic rimshots, thumping double bass, and Danny Cedrone's twanging, gymnastic guitar breaks (albeit copied lick for lick from his solo on 1952's "Rock the Joint"), marked a radical sonic shift in America's segregated airwaves.

The band played hundreds of high-school dances, which helped them tailor their stage presence and performances to mimic teenage aspirations and slang. So the yodeling, polka-dance, and western-swing style went out, and in came the harder-edged boogie-woogie beat. Goodbye hillbilly, hello rockabilly.

The first hints of their new sound came with a cover of R&B hit "Rocket 88," in 1951, followed by 1953's "Crazy Man Crazy" (the first rock 'n' roll record to make the U.S. *Billboard* Top 100). "Rock Around the Clock" followed, but didn't chart as well: it took Hollywood to rescue the song behind the opening credits for a movie about teenage delinquents, *Blackboard Jungle* (1955). The film caused outrage in crew-cut America, but the teenagers loved it and the re-released single made No. 1 on July 9, 1955. **JJH**

Bill Haley & His Comets monkey around during a rehearsal for their first British performance. ➔

I Get Along Without You Very Well | Chet Baker (1954)

Writer | Hoagy Carmichael
Producer | Dick Bock
Label | Pacific Jazz
Album | *Chet Baker Sings* (1956)

Trumpeter Chet Baker was the James Dean of modern jazz. His striking looks made him the epitome of cool. As a trumpeter, if truth be told, his range was limited, but he was a supreme balladeer, his delicate, gossamer-light lines displaying a brittle beauty. "Walking on eggshells" is the apt description often applied to his fine solos.

Baker had first made his mark in 1952 on America's West Coast, where he partnered baritone saxophonist Gerry Mulligan in a piano-less quartet, an unusual lineup that matched his light and airy notes with the gruff harrumphing of a baritone sax underscored by bass and drums to surprisingly balletic effect. The idea that Baker might then sing on some tracks came from his record label boss, Dick Bock. "I encouraged him to sing and it turned out he had an exceptional talent for it," Bock recalled later.

Baker's emotionally restrained singing is musical in the proper sense. His bel canto–tenor vocals are achieved with perfect breath-control and relaxation, his notes completely in tune, his phrases perfectly measured throughout. On Hoagy Carmichael's well-loved song—as on the rest of its parent album—he is accompanied by just piano, bass, and drums, although on this occasion he plays no trumpet. It is a poignant performance, its seemingly effortless simplicity hiding considerable technique. **SA**

In the Wee Small Hours of the Morning | Frank Sinatra (1955)

Writer | David Mann and Bob Hilliard
Producer | Voyle Gilmore
Label | Capitol
Album | *In the Wee Small Hours* (1955)

The concept album is now a much-derided musical offering, usually judged to be the product of an overblown artistic imagination supported by crass commercial packaging. But the idea of an album containing music that is unified by theme or mood and specifically programmed from start to finish has an honorable precedent with Frank Sinatra, one of the first singers to realize the artistic potential of the format.

Sinatra had already experimented with collections of linked songs (*Songs for Young Lovers* and *Swing Easy*), but fully realized the concept album with *In the Wee Small Hours*. Opening with the title track, the sixteen songs—all ballads specifically recorded for the album and lovingly arranged for a small ensemble and string section by Nelson Riddle—describe a mood of nocturnal loneliness and remorse brought on by lost love.

The love in question was actress Ava Gardner, married to Sinatra since 1951 and with whom he enjoyed a turbulent relationship until they eventually divorced in 1957. The title track sets the scene, Sinatra ruminating on the woman he has lost and regretting the mistakes he has made. "In the Wee Small Hours of the Morning" was specifically written for this album, the rest of the songs being popular standards—by the likes of Cole Porter and Rodgers and Hart—that develop this narrative of loss. **SA**

Contact sheets record Frank Sinatra fully in command of a recording studio in 1955. ➜

Tutti Frutti
Little Richard (1955)

Writer | Richard Penniman, Dorothy LaBostrie
Producer | Robert "Bumps" Blackwell
Label | Speciality
Album | *Here's Little Richard* (1957)

With its wild opening, "Tutti Frutti" had been a popular part of Little Richard's stage act for some time. However, the singer had never expected the song to get released on record because of the highly sexual nature of the lyrics. Yet on September 14, 1955, at J&M studios in New Orleans, one of pop's defining recordings was conceived as Little Richard filled in time at the end of the session by bashing out "Tutti Frutti." Producer "Bumps" Blackwell was impressed by the song's energy and excitement and hired songwriter Dorothy LaBostrie to work on some less inflammatory lyrics.

With LaBostrie's "clean-up" job done, Little Richard's recording still found difficulty in getting sufficient radio airplay to win a chart battle against Pat Boone's clean-cut version. However, it was Richard's flamboyant "Tutti Frutti" that had the most lasting effect, transfixing teenagers as far away as Liverpool—where The Beatles became big fans—and beyond.

Mixing gospel, jump blues, and boogie-woogie piano, Richard still had one killer element that made him a key figure in pop history: his personality. His pompadour hairstyle, makeup, and frantic movement shocked and amazed conservative mid-Fifties America. "Tutti Frutti" was his breakthrough, the beginning of a career that exploded across the world a year later with his appearance in the movie *The Girl Can't Help It*. **DR**

Only You (and You Alone)
The Platters (1955)

Writer | Buck Ram
Producer | Buck Ram
Label | Mercury
Album | *The Platters* (1955)

A few songs are de facto anthems for musical genres—think Bob Marley & The Wailers' "One Love" for reggae, or Fela Kuti's "O.D.O.O." for Afropop. Doo-wop's pièce de résistance is arguably The Platters' "Only You (and You Alone)."

The song was the first hit for the Los Angeles quintet, charting stateside at No. 5. (Its follow-up, "The Great Pretender," went to No. 1.) "Only You" was also one of the earliest major "crossover" hits by a black act, at a time when "race" records rarely reached white audiences or the pop charts. So the group's induction into the Rock & Roll Hall of Fame in 1990—the first doo-wop group to be so honored—is wholly appropriate.

An initial session, for Federal Records, stalled; however, a second stab, for Mercury, proved rather more successful, and the song took off, despite competition from another version by The Hilltoppers. A performance of "Only You" in the movie *Rock Around the Clock* (1956) further cemented its legendary status.

Even heard with contemporary ears, "Only You" retains its appeal. Lead vocalist Tony Williams's singing is at once confident and vulnerable, breaking into a controlled quivering as he hits his higher register. The very nature of the song is also illustrative of a transitional period in music: Williams's vocal delivery is part swing-era crooner, part declarative rocker. **YK**

Cry Me a River
Julie London (1955)

Writer | Arthur Hamilton
Producer | Bobby Troup
Label | Liberty
Album | *Julie Is Her Name*
(1955)

When Arthur Hamilton wrote "Cry Me a River," it was his intention that Ella Fitzgerald would perform it in the 1955 movie *Pete Kelly's Blues*, but the song was dropped.

In the end, the honor fell to former jungle-movie actress Julie London—known as much for her sultry sleeve photographs as for her languorous voice—and its big-screen debut was in the Jayne Mansfield vehicle *The Girl Can't Help It* (1956). The jazzy number was a remnant of the past in a picture that otherwise celebrated the emergent beat of rock 'n' roll, but that didn't prevent its selling millions and becoming one of the most covered standards of all time.

Hamilton's jazzy blues composition reignited the smoldering torch song, but with a couple of new twists. Unusually for the genre, the singer is defiant, turning the tables when a man who rejected her—evidently a cad, given that his pretext was that love is "too plebeian"—comes crawling back. Its sparse arrangement, too, was unprecedented: where the torch singers of the past would have been backed up by piano and orchestra, here the vocalist is supported only by Ray Leatherwood's upright bass and arranger Barney Kessel's stark electric guitar. The pioneering sound inspired, among others, Brazilian guitarist João Gilberto to develop his minimalist take on samba, the bossa nova. **SP**

Sixteen Tons
Tennessee Ernie Ford (1955)

Writer | Merle Travis
Producer | Lee Gillette
Label | Capitol
Album | N/A

"Burl Ives has sung all the folk songs," sighed western-swing star Merle Travis in 1946, when Capitol asked him to record an album to cash in on the Woody Guthrie–inspired craze for American roots music. So Travis turned his thoughts to the work songs and chain-gang rounds of the Depression, and set some of the sayings of his father, a Kentucky miner, to music. The result was a gritty exploration of the U.S. miner's lot, where back-breaking toil was rewarded not with cash but "scrip"—promissory tokens that could be spent only at a company-owned store. In McCarthyite America, such sympathy for the working man was deemed downright subversive, and some radio stations even went so far as to ban Travis.

Nine years later, Tennessee Ernie Ford, a Pasadena-based DJ, revisited the tune. While Travis's recording had been an acoustic strum, Ford's reading luxuriated in a smooth jazz arrangement by bandleader Jack Fascinato, centered on clarinet, slap bass, and a muted trumpet *obbligato*. The infectious finger-clicking was supplied by Ford purely as a means to count in the band, but producer Lee Gillette recognized its rhythmic appeal and kept it in the mix.

Ford's warm baritone made the song—initially intended simply as a B-side—a huge international hit; it spent eight weeks atop the *Billboard* chart and sold a million copies inside a month. **SP**

I'm a Man
Bo Diddley (1955)

Writer | Ellas McDaniel
Producer | Leonard Chess, Phil Chess
Label | Checker
Album | *Bo Diddley* (1958)

Despite boasting the nickname "The Originator" and influencing everyone from Buddy Holly and The Rolling Stones to U2 and The Jesus & Mary Chain, Bo Diddley made for a pretty unlikely rock pioneer. Born Ellas Otha Bates in Mississippi in 1928, he was a chunky, myopic man who happily sported tartan-checked jackets and bow ties along with a rectangular guitar covered with rabbit fur. Yet his memory lives on through the ubiquity of his "Bo Diddley Beat."

Starting out playing music on Chicago street corners, in late 1954 Diddley recorded demo versions of two songs: "Uncle John" (the racy lyrics of which were later bowdlerized when it was retitled "Bo Diddley") and another, inspired by a Muddy Waters number from a few years before, called "I'm a Man." Built on the same guitar pattern as Waters's song, "I'm a Man" saw Diddley boasting of his sexual prowess over a lascivious blues ramble. Re-recorded at the legendary Chess studios, "I'm a Man" appeared on the B-side to Bo's debut single, a No. 1 hit on the R&B charts when it was released in March 1955. This was the version discovered by British beat bands when Bo toured Europe in 1963—the cover that appeared on The Yardbirds' American compilation album *Having a Rave Up* becoming the template for several thousand white, suburban garage-rock bands when it was released in 1965. **PL**

Blue Monday
Fats Domino (1956)

Writer | Fats Domino, Dave Bartholomew
Producer | Dave Bartholomew
Label | Imperial
Album | *This Is Fats Domino* (1957)

Rarely given enough credit for his pioneering role in the story of popular music, Antoine "Fats" Domino influenced legends from Elvis Presley and John Lennon to Otis Redding and Bob Marley. Today, the New Orleans pianist is perhaps most widely known through The Beatles' homage "Lady Madonna." In the Fifties, however, "Blue Monday" was his fifth No.1 on *Billboard*'s R&B listing. More significantly, it was his sixth smash on the pop chart: Fats's laconic, country-and-western-flavored style made him a multimillion-selling favorite with both black and white audiences.

The titular inspiration for New Order's 1983 classic, "Blue Monday" is—wrote Dave Marsh in *The Heart of Rock & Soul*—"the foundation of a rock and roll tradition of songs about hatred of the working week and lust for lost weekends." The teenage Fats had, in fact, toiled in a factory by day—playing in clubs by night—hence his charmingly grumpy lyric, "How I hate blue Monday / Got to work like a slave all day." These complaints are complemented by hammering drums and furry sax. An eight-bar break by his long-standing saxophonist Herb Hardesty was acclaimed by critic Hank Davis as "a gem of almost frightening economy."

Reportedly Fats's favorite of his own recordings, this super song remains rib-ticklingly relevant more than five decades later. **BM**

Burundanga
Celia Cruz (1956)

Writer | Oscar Muñoz Bouffartique
Producer | Uncredited
Label | Seeco
Album | N/A

She was born Úrsula Hilaria Celia de la Caridad Cruz Alfonso in Havana, Cuba, but is better known as Celia Cruz or the Queen of Salsa. However, Cruz was having hits with gentler Afro-Cuban numbers such as "Burundanga" long before the term "salsa" was cooked up.

Even to Spanish-speakers, the lyrics of this pan-American smash are rather impenetrable. They refer to Abakuá, a male-only secret society that traces its roots to southeastern Nigeria and western Cameroon, before its members were stolen away to Cuba by slave traders. It's not so much the content but the way that Cruz rolls the words off her tongue that really matters, though.

"Burundanga" was written by a maestro with whom Cruz had studied music, and was Fidel Castro's favorite musical accompaniment to clean his gun to while plotting the Cuban revolution in his mountain hideaway in 1959. Ironically, Cruz and her backing band, Sonora Matancera, left Cuba as exiles in July 1960.

Little did Cruz know she would spend more than half her life in New York City when she traveled there in 1957; she made the trip to accept a gold disc for the song. The success of "Burundanga" also led to her first tour of Colombia, where—in a sign of the times—the word now refers to scopolamine, a hypnotic substance used by robbers and rapists to drug their victims. **JLu**

Let's Do It (Let's Fall in Love)
Ella Fitzgerald (1956)

Writer | Cole Porter
Producer | Norman Granz
Label | Verve
Album | *Ella Fitzgerald Sings the Cole Porter Songbook* (1956)

Two days after she recorded the sublime "Ev'ry Time We Say Goodbye," Ella Fitzgerald continued work on the *Cole Porter Songbook* album by recording a droll and witty song about love.

Although on the face of it "Let's Do It (Let's Fall in Love)" is about love, in fact the whole song is one long euphemism for sex. Of all the great singers there have ever been, Ella Fitzgerald is not one you would immediately associate with the subject. Ella was a stately lady in build and demeanor. Sophisticated, yes; sexy, no. To hear her, of all people, singing about sex thus gives her version of this famous song a considerable frisson.

The song itself was written by Cole Porter in 1928 and featured in *Paris*, his first Broadway success. Its lyrics consist of a long list (a conceit that became a Porter staple) of suggestive pairings and preposterous double entendres. The song starts with the simple statement that "Birds do it, bees do it"—referencing a time-honored euphemism for sex. Verbal puns abound, the suggestion that "Lithuanians and Letts do it" immediately and alliteratively leading into "Let's do it." "Oysters down in Oyster Bay do it" works wonderfully as a line—oysters live in oyster beds, and we all know what beds are for.

Without a word out of place, this much-covered song is three and a half minutes of perfectly poised innuendo. **SA**

I've Got You Under My Skin
Frank Sinatra (1956)

Writer | Cole Porter
Producer | Voyle Gilmour
Label | Capitol
Album | *Songs For Swingin' Lovers!*
(1956)

Twenty years before Frank Sinatra made "I've Got You Under My Skin" his own, American singer and actress Virginia Bruce sang it in the musical *Born to Dance* (1936). Sinatra began singing the Cole Porter–penned song in the 1940s, but it was 1956 before a scintillating, swinging big-band arrangement by Nelson Riddle provided the singer with what many fans argue was his best recording. Its musical centerpiece—the slow-build crescendo, exploding into Milt Bernhardt's joyous slide-trombone solo—was inspired partly by Ravel's *Boléro*, although Bernhardt's contribution to Stan Kenton's "23 Degrees North 82 Degrees West" was an influence, too.

Opening Side Two of his No. 2-charting album *Songs For Swingin' Lovers!*, the track showed all the exuberance of a performer at the top of his game. The album went one better in the United Kingdom, topping the very first U.K. album chart, in July 1956, and—weirdly—even entering the singles chart a month earlier. However, "I've Got You Under My Skin" didn't get any additional exposure as a proper single release until much later.

Sinatra had an enduring passion for "I've Got You Under My Skin" that saw it feature in concert set lists right up to his final public performances, in 1994. And, paying credit where credit was due, the legendary singer often referred to it as "Nelson Riddle's shining hour." **DR**

Ev'ry Time We Say Goodbye
Ella Fitzgerald (1956)

Writer | Cole Porter
Producer | Norman Granz
Label | Verve
Album | *Ella Fitzgerald Sings the Cole Porter Songbook* (1956)

By the mid-Fifties, Ella Fitzgerald was a singer out of time. The commercial success she had enjoyed with Chick Webb's band during the swing era was now over. She was rescued by the advent of the LP era and a commercially and artistically astute record producer, Norman Granz. He signed her up to his new Verve record label and proposed she record a series of albums, each one dedicated to a great American songwriter.

The first, the *Cole Porter Songbook*, spread over two LPs, appeared in 1956 and was an immediate success. Among its many highlights was a song originally written by Porter in 1944 for the musical *Seven Lively Arts*. "Ev'ry Time We Say Goodbye" is a love song made all the more effective by its simple lyrics—just ten lines in all—and far-from-complex melody. The start of six of the lines—including the words of the title—is sung on a hypnotically repeating single note. As the melody reaches its sweeping climax, Porter underlines the melancholy theme of the song by echoing the concluding words with a key change from a happy major key to a sadder, more bluesy, minor key—a device used by Handel and other Baroque composers among others—the music mirroring the words.

Buoyed by the success of the Cole Porter album, Ella went on to make memorable recordings of the songbooks of Rodgers and Hart, Duke Ellington, Irving Berlin, and George and Ira Gershwin. **SA**

Be-Bop-A-Lula | Gene Vincent & His Blue Caps (1956)

Writer | Tex Davis, Gene Vincent
Producer | Ken Nelson
Label | Capitol
Album | N/A

Gene Vincent is rockabilly's dark prince, his startling Fifties recordings and short, troubled life lending him iconic status. "Be-Bop-A-Lula," his first record and biggest hit, remains an anthem, a song that continues to sound both sexy and eerie.

Vincent Eugene Craddock grew up listening to country, bluegrass, gospel, and blues at his parents' store in Norfolk, Virginia. During a stint in the U.S. Navy, he badly injured his left leg in a motorcycle accident. Focusing on singing, Vincent was spotted by local DJ Tex Davis, who, aware that Capitol Records in L.A. wanted some of the action being generated by Elvis, cut a demo on Vincent.

Gene Vincent & His Blue Caps were dispatched to Nashville. Producer Ken Nelson had no idea how to record rock 'n' roll, and session musicians were hired in case the Blue Caps proved incompetent. Instead, Vincent's band, led by guitarist Cliff Gallup, delivered a bravura performance, the rhythm section pulling out a slinky groove while Vincent whispers in a fine Presley imitation about his baby and how he "don't mean maybe." Gallup's spiraling guitar solos and the whoops of bassist "Jumpin'" Jack Neal helped create a rockabilly template that everyone from The Beatles to The Clash has attempted to emulate.

After "Be-Bop-A-Lula" scaled the world's charts, Vincent's career went steadily downhill. He died from alcoholism, aged thirty-six, in 1971. **GC**

Heartbreak Hotel
Elvis Presley (1956)

Writer | Mae Boren Axton, Tommy Durden, E. Presley
Producer | Steve Sholes
Label | RCA
Album | N/A

"I walk a lonely street." That line, taken from a suicide note and quoted in a local newspaper report, inspired writers Mae Boren Axton and Tommy Durden to pen Elvis's breakthrough hit—although initially it seemed anything but.

Demo vocalist Glenn Reeves thought the title daft and disliked the song so much that he wanted his name kept off it. Elvis's erstwhile mentor Sam Phillips denounced it as a "morbid mess"; RCA's A&R man, Steve Sholes, fretted that he'd signed the wrong Sun artist, and wondered whether he should have opted for Carl Perkins instead; his superiors told him to re-record it.

True, attempts to mimic the clean "slapback" reverb characteristic of Phillips's Sun recordings had been flawed at best. (RCA's engineers wound up recording in a hallway, for its echo, resulting in a far murkier sound.) But this lumbering, bluesy lament—quite unlike anything else in mid-Fifties pop—proved mesmerizing, from Floyd Cramer's ghostly barroom piano, to Scotty Moore's jagged solo, momentarily breaking up the somnolent mood. Elvis's trademark swooping, slurred vocal made it, of course. "His phrasing, his use of echo, it's all so beautiful," Paul McCartney reflected admiringly nearly fifty years later. "As if he's singing it from the depths of hell." Teenagers everywhere could relate to *that*, and they bought up this tale of alienation and rejection in droves. **RD**

Elvis holds a framed gold record of "Heartbreak Hotel" in the studio in 1956. ➡

Blueberry Hill
Fats Domino (1956)

Writer | Vincent Rose, Al Lewis, Larry Stock
Producer | Dave Bartholomew
Label | Imperial
Album | *This Is Fats* (1956)

By 1956, Fats Domino had already scored more than a dozen Top Ten R&B singles. The song "Blueberry Hill" had an equally impressive track record: published in 1940, the tune had been recorded by such notable entertainers as Glenn Miller and Louis Armstrong (in 1949—the recording that inspired Domino to cut the song). Domino's version of the song was forlorn yet not tearful, and the instruments revealed more heart than the words. His piano work was concise and gripping, while his voice remained steady as he told the story of love found, then lost, beginning with the famous line, "I found my thrill . . . "

"Blueberry Hill" was the natural choice to open *This Is Fats*, but it almost didn't make the cut. On the day the song was recorded, at Hollywood's Master Recorders, the sheet music was lost and Domino kept forgetting the lyrics. He never made it through a complete take, and the final product was spliced together by engineer Bunny Robyn from aborted efforts.

No one noticed, and "Blueberry Hill" reached No. 2 on the pop charts (it spent eleven weeks at No. 1 on the R&B listings). The song's success would quickly inspire other rockers, including Elvis Presley and Little Richard, to release their own renditions—and, reportedly, inspired the bass line to The Doors' 1967 breakthrough hit, "Light My Fire." **JiH**

Hound Dog
Elvis Presley (1956)

Writer | Jerry Leiber, Mike Stoller
Producer | Steve Sholes
Label | RCA
Album | N/A

In 1956, Mike Stoller returned from a European trip to be met by songwriting partner Jerry Leiber in New York harbor. Leiber cheerfully informed him that their song "Hound Dog" was a massive hit—not for Big Mama Thornton, who'd first recorded it in 1953, but for "some white kid named Elvis Presley."

Thornton's original is slow, sassy, and bluesy. Stoller initially found Presley's version "kind of stiff and a bit too fast—a little nervous"; to Leiber, it was "a lot of noise." In other words, grade-A rock 'n' roll. (In truth, Elvis's version was modeled on a spoof take on the song, with altered lyrics, by Freddie Bell & The Bellboys, whose act he'd caught in Las Vegas.) Elvis spits out his vocal, J. D. Fontana provides machine-gun drum fills between verses, and Scotty Moore delivers two scintillating guitar solos.

Performing the song on *The Milton Berle Show*, Elvis had tacked on his trademark half-speed ending, accompanied by a selection of bumps and grinds that had aroused a storm of protest. By way of publicly atoning for his "sins," the night before he recorded the song he had been hauled out wearing a tux on *The Steve Allen Show* and forced to sing the song to an unmoved basset hound. Irked, he put everything into his studio session the next day, running through some thirty takes and unleashing a raucous, sneering performance that crackled with energy. Result: a genre-defining, seven-million-selling, iconic U.S. chart-topper. **RD**

Fats Domino in the studio in 1956.

Honey Hush
The Johnny Burnette Trio (1956)

Writer | Big Joe Turner
Producer | Owen Bradley
Label | Coral
Album | N/A

When Johnny Burnette's guitarist, Paul Burlison, inadvertently knocked over his Fender Deluxe amp, he discovered that his clean, twangy guitar sound had mutated into a distorted growl. As a trained electrician, Burlison diagnosed that the effect was caused by a dislodged vacuum tube and that he could re-create it on demand. By fortuitous accident, he had invented fuzz guitar.

This vicious, electrifying new sound was unleashed on the trio's third single, which coupled Tiny Bradshaw's "Train Kept A-Rollin'" with a composition by avuncular man-mountain Big Joe Turner from 1953. As recorded by Turner, "Honey Hush" sounds almost like a dry run for his hit "Shake, Rattle and Roll" the following year—an uptempo twelve-bar blues over which the singer improvised light-hearted lyrics about keeping his woman in line (with a baseball bat, if necessary). The Burnette version injects the song with the primitive vigor of rockabilly—Johnny, howling and jabbering like a deranged hick, transforms Turner's good-natured jibes into something wild and menacing. Double-bass player Dorsey Burnette and session guitarist Grady Martin rattle along in the background, but it is Burlison's springy lead that holds the ear. One of the first instances of purposeful distortion committed to vinyl, it reverberates as if plucked on a rubber band. Guitar heroes of the future listened and took note. **SP**

I Walk the Line
Johnny Cash (1956)

Writer | Johnny Cash
Producer | Sam Phillips
Label | Sun
Album | N/A

"I find it very, very easy to be true," intoned Johnny Cash over half a century ago. Recorded by Sun Studio owner Sam Phillips at the dawn of Cash's career, "I Walk the Line" sounds simultaneously naive and profound. The same clanky instrumentation appeared on the early hits of Cash's fellow Sun signing Elvis Presley, and the simple guitar line cannot help but sound outmoded today, but the lyrics give the song an air of wisdom that has prevailed over the decades.

When Cash sings, "I keep a close watch on this heart of mine," it is his vulnerability that you hear, but without his having to spell it out clearly. The music is not predictable, either; each verse is preceded by a few seconds of humming, a mesmeric device that Cash explained helped him to find the right key (the original 1956 recording featured a key change before every verse) but which lends the song a contemplative air.

"I Walk the Line" was re-recorded for the album of the same name eight years after its release as a single, with a rearrangement and a cleaner production. The song also provided the title for a 1970 film and the better-known 2005 Cash biopic. He wrote bigger, more expostulatory songs across his long career, but few that spoke as clearly to people about the human condition as this one. "I Walk the Line" speaks with utter clarity to anyone prepared to listen. **JMc**

Johnny Cash smokes moodily for the camera in a 1957 studio portrait. ➔

Knoxville Girl
The Louvin Brothers (1956)

Writer | Traditional, arr. by Ira and Charles Louvin
Producer | Ken Nelson
Label | Capitol
Album | *Tragic Songs of Life* (1956)

Although the writing credit beneath "Knoxville Girl" reads "Traditional," the origins of the song are believed to lie some four thousand miles away from Knoxville, Tennessee, with either "The Bloody Miller," a 1680s song about a murder near the English town of Shrewsbury, or "The Berkshire Tragedy," another ancient English ballad. The song went through innumerable variations—"The Oxford Girl" and "The Wexford Girl" among them—before winding up in Tennessee and becoming the classic American murder ballad.

Having learned the song from their mother, Alabama-born brothers Ira and Charles Loudermilk took it with them when they started out as performers in the Forties. They soon dropped it in favor of gospel music, but "Knoxville Girl" returned to their repertoire when the pair returned to secular song in the mid-Fifties—their sponsor on radio staple *Grand Ole Opry*, Prince Albert tobacco, preferred non-gospel tunes. And, as Charlie pointed out: "Work a gospel show, make 500 dollars; work a country show, make 2,500."

Owing more than a little to a Thirties reading of the song by another pair of singing brothers, The Blue Sky Boys, the Louvins' plangent recording appeared in 1956. Charlie re-recorded the song just before his eightieth birthday, but Ira was not around to hear it: his tempestuous life ended in 1965, courtesy of a drunk driver in Missouri. **WF-J**

Ella
José Alfredo Jiménez (1956)

Writer | José Alfredo Jiménez
Producer | Uncredited
Label | RCA
Album | N/A

To Mexican-music lovers, José Alfredo Jiménez is comparable to, say, Hank Williams and Jacques Brel combined—a huge talent who went on to dominate and reshape the Mexican songbook.

Legend has it that in 1956 Jiménez was working as a waiter in a restaurant when the popular singer Miguel Aceves Mejía arrived to eat, and Jiménez pleaded that Mejía listen to his songs. They duly met a few days later, but when asked if Jiménez played guitar, the answer was no. Was this song a waltz or a *huapango*? Mejía was told, "I don't know," and he did not know what key it was in, either. He was about to give up on this wannabe when Jiménez began singing—and Mejía swiftly came to realize the waiter had already written dozens of great songs. One of these was "Ella" (Her), a frank tale of love thwarted by a girl's parents, who had rejected her suitor because he was a lowly waiter.

Jiménez was a singer in the ranchera style, the popular Mexican song form comparable to country or blues in that it lyrically details the hard times and misfortunes of the singer. He had written songs since childhood and possessed a great ear for melody, a gift for lyrics, and a voice that, while rough, dramatically sold his songs. "Ella" was one of the first songs Jiménez got to record, and it proved a huge hit, his soaring, impassioned vocal set against chirpy mariachi brass and swathes of bittersweet strings. **GC**

Take My Hand, Precious Lord
Mahalia Jackson (1956)

Writer | Thomas A. Dorsey
Producer | Mitch Miller
Label | Columbia
Album | *Bless This House* (1956)

Thomas A. Dorsey started out as a blues pianist with Ma Rainey, co-writing with Tampa Red "It's Tight Like That," a dirty blues that scored a huge hit in 1928. He subsequently branched out into the genre that would make his name—gospel.

Dorsey wrote "Take My Hand, Precious Lord" in 1932, heartbroken and disconsolate after his wife died in childbirth (the baby died soon afterward); the melody was borrowed from George N. Allen's 1844 hymn "Maitland." Immediately recognized as a gospel classic, the song established Dorsey as Chicago's preeminent gospel songwriter.

In 1929, the songwriter came across a teenaged Mahalia Jackson, not long in town from New Orleans and already capable of "wrecking" churches. Dorsey coached Jackson and the two toured together, she singing his songs and he selling the new gospel tunes as sheet music. When Jackson recorded ". . . Precious Lord" for Columbia in March 1956, the label arranged for the recording session to be as thorough as a jazz or pop session. The power and grace of the resulting recording made the singer a household name.

Dr. Martin Luther King Jr. named Mahalia's recording of the track as his favorite song. Her performance of the song at King's 1968 funeral gained her (and the song) headlines around the world. Four years later, Aretha Franklin would sing ". . . Precious Lord" at Jackson's own funeral. **GC**

Folsom Prison Blues
Johnny Cash (1956)

Writer | Johnny Cash, Gordon Jenkins (uncredited)
Producer | Sam Phillips
Label | Sun
Album | *With His Hot and Blue Guitar* (1957)

Although released in 1956, it was not until a re-release coinciding with 1968's *At Folsom Prison* live album that Johnny Cash's "Folsom Prison Blues" reached the U.S. *Billboard* No. 1 slot. Cash was moved to write the song after seeing the 1951 documentary *Inside the Walls of Folsom Prison* while serving with the U.S. Air Force in West Germany. He borrowed from the Gordon Jenkins song "Crescent City Blues," which led to a successful lawsuit from Jenkins following the 1968 album release.

Cash identified closely with the imprisoned and downtrodden, and combined two of the most popular elements of folk music—prison and train songs—in the song. For the memorable lines "I shot a man in Reno / Just to watch him die," Cash recounted, "I sat with my pen in my hand, trying to think up the worst reason a person could have for killing another person, and that's what came to mind. It did come to mind quite easily, though."

Cash would become a firm favorite with the incarcerated, though on the live version the whooping reception of the song's grimmest lines is said to have been added post-recording—the prisoners were too wary of guards' reprisals to react to any references to prison or criminal acts.

"Folsom Prison Blues" became a staple of Cash's live performances and the epitome of his man-in-black/rebel image, which saw him influence future music from rockabilly to punk. **CR**

I Put a Spell on You
Screamin' Jay Hawkins (1956)

Writer | Jalacy Hawkins
Producer | Arnold Maxon
Label | Okeh
Album | *At Home With Screamin' Jay Hawkins* (1958)

"I Put a Spell on You" is a truly extraordinary recording, branded "cannibalistic" and banned from radio programming when released on Columbia Records' R&B subsidiary Okeh in 1956. The band, including sax player Sam "The Man" Taylor, play a relatively subdued, bluesy waltz backing while former pugilist Hawkins screams, hollers, howls, and groans through the lyrics.

The track was never a major hit but eventually shifted a million copies—despite the record company's removal of Hawkins's grunts and moans from the ending of the song in later pressings. Hawkins liked to say that he had intended the song as a ballad and that his maniacal delivery was the result of a party in the studio at which he got so drunk he couldn't remember the recording. As a result, he allegedly had to learn the song's delivery from the record to perform it live. Encouraged by New York DJ Alan Freed, Hawkins developed an act to go with his oddball repertoire that involved arriving on stage in a coffin, wearing a cape, and carrying a skull called Henry on a stick.

"I Put a Spell on You" was used in the Jim Jarmusch film *Stranger Than Paradise* in 1984, and Hawkins himself acted as a desk clerk in Jarmusch's *Mystery Train* (1989). The influence of Hawkins's shock-horror rock 'n' roll has been wide ranging, with disciples including Alice Cooper, Arthur Brown, and Screaming Lord Sutch. **JoH**

Just a Gigolo / I Ain't Got Nobody | Louis Prima (1956)

Writer | L. Casucci, J. Brammer, I. Caesar, S. Williams, R. Graham
Producer | Voyle Gilmore
Label | Capitol
Album | *The Wildest!* (1957)

Down the years, countless musicians have attempted to disprove F. Scott Fitzgerald's thesis that "There are no second acts in American lives." Few, though, have sounded as if they had quite as much fun doing so as Louis Prima. Born to Italian parents in New Orleans in 1910, Prima found success during the Thirties as a bandleader in New York, but changing fashions eventually took him away from the spotlight. In 1954, Prima and his band, led by young New Orleans saxophonist Sam Butera and augmented by Prima's wife, Keely Smith, were booked to appear in the lounge of the Sahara casino in Las Vegas. Within months, the singer had revived his career, pretty much inventing the idea of Vegas lounge entertainment.

This glorious, live-in-the-studio medley was pretty much how they sounded back then: raucous, joyful, and irrepressible. Allied to a band that was clearly having a ball, Prima's listen-to-this vocals turn the track into a kind of Italian-American fusion of Louis Armstrong and Louis Jordan. Apparently joined together by Butera, the two songs are unrelated, but Prima's stamp is such that they are now regularly covered as a pair.

By the time The Beatles touched down in New York in 1964, Prima was once again struggling for relevance. He just about survived the rock 'n' roll era, before his show-stealing turn as King Louie in *The Jungle Book* gave him one last hurrah. **WF-J**

Screamin' Jay Hawkins and Henry the skull: a lesson in comparative dentistry.

Rock Island Line | Lonnie Donegan Skiffle Group (1956)

Writer | Uncredited
Producer | Hugh Mendl
Label | London
Album | N/A

"Rock Island Line" did more than any other record to popularize Britain's short-lived skiffle craze in the mid-Fifties. Glasgow-born Lonnie Donegan was dubbed "The King of Skiffle" after this version of an old Arkansas prison song—ostensibly about the Rock Island railroad that stretched from Chicago to Mississippi—hit No. 8 in the charts on both sides of the Atlantic. (Country-blues performer Lead Belly was the first to record the song, in 1930.) Lonnie Donegan's souped-up version, delivered at breakneck speed, was just what the new breed of British teenager had been waiting for. The song was also one of the first pop records to be promoted via television.

Don Cornell, in 1956, and Johnny Cash, in 1970, also covered the song with minor U.S. chart success—Cash had covered the song in 1957, too—but it was the energy evident in Lonnie Donegan's nasal delivery that captured the imagination of impressionable youngsters, such as the sixteen-year-old John Lennon, who set about copying Donegan's style of guitar playing and singing. Unlike the B-side, "John Henry," which has become a roots-music classic thanks to twenty-first-century covers by the likes of Bruce Springsteen, "Rock Island Line" has attracted comparatively few big-name artists of late, though there were cover versions in the Eighties by Mano Negra and Little Richard & Fishbone. **DR**

Whole Lot of Shakin' Going On
Jerry Lee Lewis (1957)

Writer | Sunny David (Roy Hall), Dave Williams
Producer | Jack Clement
Label | Sun
Album | N/A

Determined to audition at Sun Studio, Jerry Lee Lewis funded a trip to Memphis in late 1956 by selling eggs. Sam Phillips was away, but producer Jack Clement allowed the youngster to make an audition tape. Invited back, Lewis cut what would be his first Sun single, "Crazy Arms" / "End of the Road." At his second session, with Clement again producing, he cut "Whole Lot of Shakin' Going On," one of the most earth-shattering records in pop history.

The song was not new. A version produced by Quincy Jones and recorded by R&B singer and pianist Big Maybelle in March 1955 had failed, as had a recording the following September by Roy Hall, the song's co-author. But it had become a feature of Lewis's live set, and a rapturously received performance at a small Arkansas club in early 1957 persuaded Jerry Lee to try it at Sun.

Released to early indifference, the record owed its eventual success to television. Those raw, piano-pounding rhythms were one thing on the radio, but after millions saw the dramatic way Jerry Lee performed the song for his TV debut on *The Steve Allen Show*, the record began its rise up the *Billboard* chart in the summer of 1957, eventually selling more than six million copies. Jerry Lee Lewis had achieved his first hit (U.S. No. 3; U.K. No. 8). Every rock 'n' roller from Cliff Richard to Little Richard has attempted it, but it is Jerry Lee's seismic reading that has endured. **DR**

Mean, moody, multiple exposures of The Killer—Jerry Lee Lewis. ➡

That'll Be the Day
Buddy Holly & The Crickets (1957)

Writer | Jerry Allison, Buddy Holly, Norman Petty
Producer | Norman Petty
Label | Brunswick
Album | N/A

Buddy Holly's No. 1 hit "That'll Be the Day"—the title was inspired by a drawled John Wayne catchphrase in the film *The Searchers*—helped to establish one of rock 'n' roll's true legends. But that song was a far cry from his 1956 version, which was slower, higher-pitched and . . . well, just not rock 'n' roll. Perhaps Decca could be forgiven for not liking and not releasing it.

But dropping him from their roster was not a smart move (neither was rejecting The Beatles' demos, but that is another story), and a footloose Holly took his demo to producer Norman Petty. Petty's track record included Buddy Knox's "Party Doll" (a U.S. No. 1 in 1957). With a reshuffled band now called The Crickets—featuring Jerry Allison (drums), Joe B. Maudlin (bass), and Niki Sullivan (guitar)—Holly re-recorded a peppier version in a more comfortable vocal range so that Petty could pitch it to Knox's label, Roulette.

Roulette passed on it, as did Columbia, RCA, and Atlantic. But when Bob Thiele, A&R director at Brunswick (ironically, a subsidiary of Decca), heard the demo, liked it, and signed Holly, everything changed. Decca still owned "That'll Be the Day" by Buddy Holly, so Thiele released the re-recorded song under the group name The Crickets. With a two-guitar, drum, and bass lineup, and lead vocals replete with Holly's trademark hiccups, here was the modern-era rock band in the making. **JJH**

Little Darlin'
The Diamonds (1957)

Writer | Maurice Williams
Producer | Nat Goodman
Label | Mercury
Album | N/A

Doo-wop purists sneer at The Diamonds, a preppy Canadian quartet who carved out a career covering material by black vocal groups for a mainstream audience. But with "Little Darlin'"—laid down in a single take as the studio clock approached 4 a.m.—The Diamonds turned what could have been a lackluster carbon copy into a bona fide (U.S. No. 2) hit. The original version, cut by songwriter Maurice Williams with his group The Gladiolas, was an innovative melding of R&B with elements of rumba and calypso, but had been let down by its murky production (it had, after all, been recorded in the back room of a Tennessee record mart).

The Diamonds retained the song's original arrangement but brought to it a spirit of assured showmanship, from the opening flurry of castanets to the falsetto la-la-las from tenor Ted Kowalski. There are no drums—the drummer had already left. Lead vocalist Dave Somerville reshaped Williams's subdued delivery into something verging on parody, exaggerating the end of each line ("My dear-*ah*, I was wrong-*ah*").

In the middle eight, suave bassman Bill Reed stepped forward to deliver a spoken-word bridge in the mellifluous, dramatic fashion popularized by The Ink Spots' Hoppy Jones. This later inspired a performance by Bobby Pickett in the sepulchral tones of horror star Boris Karloff. That on-stage gooning led to the 1962 hit "Monster Mash." **SP**

Great Balls of Fire
Jerry Lee Lewis (1957)

Writer | Jack Hammer,
Otis Blackwell
Producer | Sam Phillips
Label | Sun
Album | N/A

This keyboard-pounding rock 'n' roll classic was Jerry Lee Lewis's biggest U.S. chart hit. Peaking at No. 2 in the *Billboard* Hot 100, it was pipped at the top spot by Danny & The Juniors' "At the Hop" but had no such problems in the United Kingdom, where it spent two weeks at No. 1 in 1958.

The song's two creators did not share the workload equally. Jack Hammer simply came up with the song title, while the songwriting was all down to Otis Blackwell, who penned a catalog of rock 'n' roll greats including "All Shook Up," "Don't Be Cruel," and "Return to Sender" for Elvis Presley.

Lewis, nicknamed "The Killer" for his aggressive, wild-eyed performances and sometimes shocking behavior, nevertheless had a certain sensitivity—certainly when it came to the opening line of his most famous song. The original line kicking off "Great Balls of Fire" was "Great God almighty. . . ." Doubtless mindful of his God-fearing upbringing, Lewis changed the line to "Goodness gracious, great balls of fire"—and one of the most memorable introductions in rock was born.

Among a select few who have covered the song are Dolly Parton, on her 1979 album of the same name, and Tiny Tim, whose very different version provided the B-side to his 1968 smash hit "Tip-Toe Through the Tulips with Me." The 1989 biopic *Great Balls of Fire!* starring Dennis Quaid as Lewis helped to reignite Jerry Lee's dormant career. **DR**

When I Fall in Love
Nat King Cole (1957)

Writer | Edward Heyman,
Victor Young
Producer | Lee Gillette
Label | Capitol
Album | *Love Is the Thing* (1957)

Nat King Cole first found fame in the late Thirties, leading a piano trio. By the Fifties, though, he had reached the mainstream as a singer, enjoying a string of pop hits that offered little evidence of the jazzer he had once been. On occasion, the sacrifice was great; some of his later recordings are just too sugary for comfort. But the LP *Love Is the Thing*, released in 1957, is lush, honeyed perfection. It was Cole's first album with Gordon Jenkins, who had arranged for crooners such as Dick Haymes and, later, Frank Sinatra. Unlike contemporaries such as Nelson Riddle, Jenkins never really swung, preferring ambrosial strings to driving horns. It took a good ballad singer to elevate Jenkins's sometimes schmaltzy scores. And in the late Fifties, Cole was as good as they came.

The pair are at their best on "When I Fall in Love," a song first heard in a 1952 Robert Mitchum flop called *One Minute to Zero* before being led into the charts by Doris Day. Cole was modest about his vocal abilities, but his phrasing here is immaculate, tracing a smooth arc over thick strings and, gliding in almost unnoticed, a gentle rhythm section. Jenkins, too, is on fine form; even that twinkling harp, a favorite trick, is put to good use. A U.K. hit on its first release, the recording returned to the British charts in 1987, six years before the song was brutalized by Céline Dion and Clive Griffin for *Sleepless in Seattle*. **WF-J**

You Send Me
Sam Cooke (1957)

Writer | Charles "L. C." Cooke (Sam Cooke)
Producer | Bumps Blackwell
Label | Keen
Album | N/A

The course of true love never did run smooth, and so it was with one of the great pop love songs of all time. Indeed, the soft caress of "You Send Me" belies its contentious birth. In 1957, Sam Cooke was singing gospel with the vocal group The Soul Stirrers on the Specialty label. Wishing to avoid alienating gospel fans, Cooke recorded and released a secular song, "Lovable," under the pseudonym of "Dale Cook." Few were fooled. The single led to Cooke's split from The Soul Stirrers and the beginning of his career as a solo artist.

Staying with Specialty, Cooke redoubled his efforts at a crossover, working with producer Bumps Blackwell on new material, including his own pop songs. But when label owner Art Rupe heard the distinctly Caucasian background singers on "You Send Me," he reportedly protested that Cooke and Blackwell had gone too far. The problem was effectively solved when Blackwell bought both Cooke's contract and the new masters from Rupe. "You Send Me" was then released on Bob Keane's new Keen label, with writing credits originally going to Charles "L. C." Cooke, Sam's brother, for legal reasons. On the B-side was an unusual take on Gershwin's "Summertime."

The single quickly shot up the charts, reaching No. 1 on both the pop and R&B charts and going on to sell over two million copies. Sam Cooke, the inventor of soul, had arrived. **TS**

It's Only Make Believe
Conway Twitty (1958)

Writer | Conway Twitty, Jack Nance
Producer | Jim Vienneau
Label | MGM
Album | *Conway Twitty Sings* (1958)

Harold Jenkins had once aspired to become a professional baseball player—until he heard the music of a hillbilly cat from Memphis. His thoughts turning to showbiz, Jenkins realized that he would need a *nom de guerre* as ludicrous and memorable as Elvis Presley, and he found one in a coupling of the city of Conway, Arkansas, with Twitty, Texas.

On his breakthrough single, Twitty affects Presley's delirious slur to perfection, while the barbershop ba-ba-ba-bums buoying up the melody are provided by none other than Elvis's own backing vocalists, The Jordanaires. Yet while its 1958 release date certainly capitalized on the King's national-service sabbatical, "It's Only Make Believe" goes beyond slavish pastiche to anticipate the songs of marital mistrust that characterize Presley's later, Vegas years. The song, a portrait of a one-sided love affair, is in similar territory to The Platters' 1956 hit "My Prayer," but whereas that was wistful and optimistic, this is abject and baseless. The pitch escalates with each successive line as Twitty itemizes his hopes and dreams, only to dismiss them with the howled refrain of the title.

The transatlantic No. 1 spawned dozens of covers, but it also contained the seeds of the heartfelt melodramas that Roy Orbison made his stock-in-trade in the early Sixties. Not a bad legacy for a song that was penned in just seven minutes during a concert intermission. **SP**

Sam Cooke relaxes in the unaccustomed mode of Delta bluesman for a 1960 portrait.

Johnny B. Goode
Chuck Berry (1958)

Writer | Chuck Berry
Producer | Little "Bongo" Kraus
Label | Chess
Album | *Chuck Berry Is on Top* (1959)

In 1977, NASA launched a gold-plated record into the vast silence of outer space. It included a ninety-minute collection of songs representing cultures around the world. Germany chose Bach and Beethoven. Britain picked a stately song, "The Fairie Round." The United States opted for Chuck Berry and the timeless "Johnny B. Goode."

The American selection offers remarkable testimony to how much a country can change its attitudes over fewer than twenty years. In 1958, when Berry wrote and recorded "Johnny B. Goode," the people who would eventually make the song their interstellar calling card were uneasy, to say the least, about what it represented. Elvis Presley's hips were cause for concern, sure, but here was a black man who wrote all his own songs, played the guitar better than anyone else on the radio, and had the gall to sing about turning this already alarming rock 'n' roll thing into big business.

Starting with a hair-raising riff (one that would eventually keep Keith Richards in fake teeth) that he had lifted straight off a Louis Jordan record, Berry told the story of a "country boy" who had little in the way of prospects but was destined to become rich and famous, thanks to his effortless guitar picking. By 1958, Berry had already pioneered much of rock 'n' roll's instrumentation and rhythm. With "Johnny B. Goode," he was to introduce its next vital feature: ego. **MO**

Move It!
Cliff Richard & The Drifters (1958)

Writer | Ian Samwell
Producer | Norrie Paramor
Label | Columbia
Album | N/A

In 1958, Britain woke up to its very own pouting, lip-curling version of Elvis: "Move It!" had arrived and was shaking up the soporific music scene.

Cliff Richard & The Drifters (later, via a series of lineup changes, The Shadows) got their big break at a Saturday-morning talent show at the Gaumont cinema, Shepherd's Bush, in London. Theatrical agent George Ganyou paid for the group to tape a demo for pitching to record companies. EMI producer Norrie Paramor was sufficiently impressed by recordings of rock 'n' roll classics "Breathless" and "Lawdy Miss Clawdy" to go ahead with an audition. The result was an acetate featuring American Bobby Helm's ballad "Schoolboy Crush" on the A-side. On the flip side was a rocking number written by London guitarist and one-time Drifter Ian Samwell. Samwell's guitar-booming track "Move It!" was a sensation when innovative TV producer and broadcaster Jack Good showcased Richard on his TV show *Oh Boy!* The exposure shot "Move It!" (now the A-side) up the U.K. singles chart to No. 2.

The echo-laden guitar intro proved a compelling way to start the record, but it was the smouldering sex appeal of the vocals that sold the song—and kick-started Richard's six-decade pop career. For the British, who might never see Elvis, "Move It!" was the closest thing to the real deal before the beat boom displaced rock 'n' roll. **DR**

Chuck Berry poses playfully with his Gibson semi-acoustic in the late 1950s.

La Bamba
Ritchie Valens (1958)

Writer | Traditional, arranged by Ritchie Valens and Bob Keane
Producer | Bob Keane
Label | Def-Fi
Album | *Ritchie Valens* (1959)

Los Angeles record man Bob Keane first encountered sixteen-year-old Richard Valenzuela playing an L.A. cinema. Recognizing Valenzuela's raw talent, Keane signed him to his Del-Fi label, shortening his polysyllabic moniker to Ritchie Valens. Keane helped Valens develop his material and paired him with fine session musicians such as drummer Earl Palmer and guitarist René Hall.

Valens hailed from a Mexican-American household and had grown up listening to mariachi, flamenco, and blues. When Keane heard him messing about with "La Bamba"—a popular Mexican wedding song by Vera Cruz—he suggested Valens transform it into a rocker. Valens was initially reluctant, not being a fluent Spanish speaker and also apprehensive that Mexicans might dislike a rocked-up take on this well-known tune. Keane prevailed, and together they created a blazing masterpiece of Mexican-American rock 'n' roll. It leaps out of the speakers, a musical hotrod, with Valens's wild guitar inviting listeners to a blasting Chicano party. The circling three-chord trick was an influence on many rock 'n' roll staples, notably The Isley Brothers' "Twist and Shout."

"La Bamba" was released as the B-side of Valens's second hit single, the swooning ballad "Donna." But then DJs started playing its flip side as well, and by January 1959 "La Bamba" too was rising up the U.S. charts, eventually hitting No. 22. **GC**

Yakety Yak
The Coasters (1958)

Writer | Jerry Leiber, Mike Stoller
Producer | Jerry Leiber, Mike Stoller
Label | Atco
Album | N/A

The Coasters were on a roll in the late Fifties. The Los Angeles vocal troupe scored fourteen R&B hits during their career, six of which were also pop Top Ten hits. But it was "Yakety Yak" that secured the band's legacy as a primary architect of rock 'n' roll.

Coming under the wing of the legendary songwriting team of Jerry Leiber and Mike Stoller in 1955, The Coasters found immediate success by spinning what their mentors called "playlets"—short, comedic story-songs. In the case of "Yakety Yak," the playlet addressed the everyday dance between parent and teen around the household chores. "Take out the papers and the trash," the parent orders. The kicker is that the kid simply translates the instructions as "yakety yak." The Coasters' doo-wop–inspired four-part vocal attack, confidently led by Carl Gardner, is nicely augmented here by Adolph Jacobs's rollicking guitar and King Curtis's squawking tenor saxophone (aka his "yakety sax")—a quirky and defining feature of many classic Coasters tracks.

The group followed with a trio of 1959 smash recordings—"Charlie Brown," "Along Came Jones," and "Poison Ivy"—before their brand of music fell out of fashion. "Yakety Yak," however, would not be silenced—it was passed down through generations, thanks to its inclusion in Fifties-music compilations, various soundtracks, and, perhaps most significantly, children's cartoons. **JiH**

At the Hop
Danny & The Juniors (1958)

Writer | Arthur Singer, John Medora, David White
Producer | Arthur Singer
Label | ABC-Paramount
Album | N/A

With its four opening "bahs" over a rollicking Jerry Lee Lewis–style piano, "At the Hop" hits you in the solar plexus and never gives you time to draw breath thereafter. This is consummate high-school dance music fifty years before *High School Musical*.

Baritone Joe Terranova calls the first "bah" (and "oh baby"), followed by lead vocalist Danny Rapp, then second tenor Frank Maffei, and finally first tenor Dave White. The four barber-shop-with-beat singers started as The Juvenairs in a Philadelphia high school. After playing school gigs, private parties, and occasional clubs, they were discovered by local record producer Arthur "Artie" Singer, of Singular Records. He gave them vocal lessons and persuaded them to change their name.

The group actually sang "At the Bop" on a demo given to Dick Clark, presenter of *American Bandstand* (think Corny Collins Show in *Hairspray*). He suggested to co-writers Dave White and John Medora that they rewrite the single using the slang term for high-school dances, "Hop," rather than that for last year's model dance craze, "Bop." The recut song hit No. 1 on *Billboard* on January 6, 1958, and stayed there for five weeks.

Today most people know "At the Hop" from Sha Na Na's frantic stage performance at Woodstock. Throughout the Seventies, that band, and a version of The Juniors, played the revival circuit, and "At the Hop" was a hit again in 1976. **JJH**

Stagger Lee
Lloyd Price (1958)

Writer | Traditional
Producer | Uncredited
Label | ABC-Paramount
Album | N/A

"Stagger Lee" relates the tale of Lee Shelton, a black American cab driver and pimp who, on Christmas Eve 1895, shot his friend William "Billy" Lyons in a bar in St. Louis, Missouri. The two had been drinking and started to argue about politics. Lyons snatched Lee's hat off his head and refused to give it back. In response, Lee shot Lyons, retrieved his hat, and calmly walked out of the bar. Lyons later died of his wounds; Shelton was tried and convicted of the crime and sent to prison.

The power of the song lies not in the fairly unremarkable crime but in the archetypal figure of Stagger Lee, a tough black man who is cool, amoral, and defies white authority and laws. The song itself originally appeared in black communities along the lower Mississippi River in the early years of the twentieth century and was first published by the folklorist John Lomax in 1910. Mississippi John Hurt recorded a definitive reading in 1928, and many other versions of the song exist.

Price turned the song into an R&B shouter, buoyed along by a big brass section, vocal responses, and a honking tenor-saxophone solo. He had first performed it while on military service in Korea and Japan in 1953–56, getting his fellow soldiers to act out a play he had written while he sang it. Out of the military, he revisited the song, achieving great success when it reached No. 1 on the *Billboard* Hot 100 chart in January 1959. **SA**

Summertime Blues
Eddie Cochran (1958)

Writer | Eddie Cochran, Jerry Capehart
Producer | Uncredited
Label | Liberty
Album | N/A

The definitive images of rock 'n' roll rebellion are a kid with a car, a kid with a quiff and a kid with a guitar. Eddie Cochran, who died at the cruelly young age of twenty-one, is intimately connected with all three. He had only two years as a musician, leaving his all-time classics, "Summertime Blues" and "C'mon Everybody," for the new generation of teenagers to cherish into their middle years and beyond. Along the way, those songs inspired a whole raft of rockers, from The Who to Marc Bolan.

Although Elvis Presley took rock 'n' roll into the U.S. charts a couple of years before Cochran, his image was more about sex than rebellion; Eddie added a twist of teenage anger to the mix, venting his displeasure at the voting age for U.S. citizens and thus giving a voice to a generation of disgruntled youth. "Summertime Blues" was not exactly Rage Against the Machine, but at the time, when teens were just beginning to find their own identity, this song was cultural dynamite.

The importance of the track has inevitably increased over the decades, with commentators on Cochran's work apparently unable to avoid using the "die young, leave a good-looking corpse" cliché when writing about him. His death in a car crash in England's West Country, caused by a tire blowout, deprived the world of more of his astute, raw expression. Who knows? He might have gone on to be another Bob Dylan. **JMc**

Dans mon île
Henri Salvador (1958)

Writer | Maurice Pon, Henri Salvador
Producer | Uncredited
Label | Barclay
Album | *Dans mon île* (1958)

"Quem não sentiu o swing de Henri Salvador?" asked Caetano Veloso. Who has not felt the swing of Henri Salvador? Very, very few—even if the name of the great chansonnier, who died in 2008, aged ninety, is unfamiliar. Salvador had been Django Reinhardt's second guitarist, playing with his American jazz heroes after hours in Paris, and had gone west with bandleader Ray Ventura shortly after the start of World War II.

Developing a style referred to as "chanson douce," Salvador sang softly and high, though with a rich timbre, accompanied by percussion and an acoustic guitar. Sophisticated harmonically and with Caribbean inflections, his approach brought him appearances on both *The Ed Sullivan Show* and Italian television. In 1958, the popular "Dans mon île" was added to the soundtrack of a long-forgotten Italian film that somehow found its way to a Brazilian cinema. One viewer who got far more than he bargained for was the composer Antônio Carlos Jobim, who had been looking for inspiration to give him an advantage over João Gilberto in their race to develop bossa nova. Here it was, fully formed and waiting. The rest is history.

Fittingly, Salvador's final album, *Révérence*, recorded in 2006, was a Brazilian album and featured both a new version of "Dans mon île" and duets with Veloso and Gilberto Gil, who at the time was the Brazilian Minister of Culture. **DH**

Lonesome Town | Ricky Nelson (1958)

Writer | Baker Knight
Producer | Jimmie Haskell
Label | Imperial
Album | *Ricky Sings Again*
(1959)

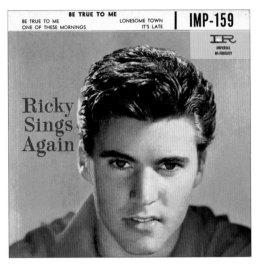

"He told us, 'When I get to recording, I want you guys to do some oohin' and aahin' behind me.'"

Gordon Stoker, The Jordanaires, 2000

◄ **Influenced by:** I'm So Lonesome I Could Cry • Hank Williams (1949)
► **Influence on:** Wicked Game • Chris Isaak (1989)
● **Covered by:** The Ventures (1961) • Shakin' Stevens and the Sunsets (1975) • The Cramps (1979) • Paul McCartney (1999) • Richard Hawley (2008)

By 1958, rock 'n' roll had told us of so many lovers nursing broken hearts that there was no hope of a mere hotel being large enough to accommodate them—they needed an entire city to themselves. But while Baker Knight's lyric for "Lonesome Town" is clearly indebted to the imagery of Elvis Presley's first RCA single, it is no simple retread of "Heartbreak Hotel." The town where "the streets are filled with regret" is a reference to that most unwelcoming of cities, Hollywood, home to the so-called boulevard of broken dreams.

Knight's minor-key ballad, inspired by the stark simplicity of Hank Williams's work, was written with The Everly Brothers in mind. But, perhaps appropriately, it was instead given to a singer with a distinctly showbiz background. Teenage idol Ricky Nelson had been a child star in the long-running sitcom *The Adventures of Ozzie and Harriet* (a precursor to such MTV fodder as *The Osbournes*, with the Nelson family starring as themselves). Ricky's recording career began as an attempt to impress a girl: after a date had gushed to him about how much she loved Elvis, he proclaimed that he too was a singer.

"Lonesome Town" was a game-changer for Nelson; his early LPs had been full of smoothed-down rock 'n' roll—not quite Pat Boone material, but far from the authentic voice of teenage rebellion. But with this mournful lament came a new maturity. In a move that anticipates his Sixties folkie phase as "Rick" Nelson, he performs without backing musicians, instead picking forlornly at an acoustic guitar. The only accompaniment comes from The Jordanaires, their moody harmonizing evoking the lost souls of the eponymous town. The wannabe Elvis had found his own voice. **SP**

Fever | Peggy Lee (1958)

Writer | Otis Blackwell (credited as John Davenport), Eddie Cooley
Producer | Dave Cavanaugh
Label | Capitol
Album | N/A

*"The rock 'n' roll stuff …
appeals [to young people]
because it stresses simple, basic
rhythm. … It's the rhythm."*
Peggy Lee, 1958

◀ **Influenced by: Calypso Blues** • Nat King Cole (1950)
▶ **Influence on: Bad Day** • Carmel (1983)
● **Covered by:** Frankie Avalon (1959) • Elvis Presley (1960)
Ben E. King (1962) • Conway Twitty (1963) • Suzi Quatro
(1975) • Boney M. (1976) • The Cramps (1980) • Joe
Cocker (1989) • Madonna (1992) • Beyoncé (2003)

"Fever" arrived on Peggy Lee's desk courtesy of Max Bennett, her bass player at the time. A 1956 hit for R&B singer Little Willie John, the song was first heard by Bennett at a minor club gig, and the bassist suspected it would suit Lee to a tee. The singer agreed; after stripping back the arrangement, working in a couple of key changes, and adding some verses of her own—but not copyrighting them: "It didn't occur to me," she mused regretfully, thirty years later—Lee had a considerable hit on her hands.

There is not much to choose between John's original and Lee's whitewashed reinvention. John's cracked vocal is dirtier and more desperate, and the band behind him is bigger. Lee's reading, though, is more mysterious and sultry, backed by nothing more than Shelly Manne's drums (beaten with his bare hands), Howard Roberts's finger-clicks, and, on bass, not Bennett but Joe Mondragon. Having suggested the song to Lee, presumably with one eye on playing its dominant bass line, Bennett then missed the session because he had gone on tour with Ella Fitzgerald.

Peggy Lee's cover outperformed Little Willie John's original, reaching the Top Ten on both sides of the Atlantic in 1958. It went on to become her signature song, a favorite of audiences in a performing life that ran for a further four decades. But perhaps the most interesting post-"Fever" career arc belongs to the then unfortunately absent but influential Bennett, a jobbing jazzer who later reinvented himself as an electric bassist. More than a decade later, he was to appear on on such disparate rock classics as Frank Zappa's *Hot Rats* and *Chunga's Revenge*, and Joni Mitchell's *The Hissing of Summer Lawns*. **WF-J**

One for My Baby (and One More for the Road) | Frank Sinatra (1958)

Writer | Harold Arlen, Johnny Mercer
Producer | Voyle Gilmore
Label | Capitol
Album | *Frank Sinatra Sings for Only the Lonely* (1958)

Conceived in the wake of the singer's split with Ava Gardner, three years before its release, *In the Wee Small Hours* was Sinatra's first successful concept album, sixteen ballads of lovelorn despair built around empathetic Nelson Riddle arrangements. After its release, which cemented the singer's transition from teen idol to adult artist, Sinatra continued to follow the themed-album path, following upbeat, swinging collections with melancholy affairs. *Only the Lonely* is in the latter category; "One for My Baby" is its keynote address.

With lyrics by Johnny Mercer, himself no stranger to alcohol-soaked misery, "One for My Baby" first appeared in the 1943 movie *The Sky's the Limit*, unconvincingly delivered by a too-smooth Fred Astaire. Sinatra later tackled it twice, but neither rendition had taken wing. So for *Only the Lonely*, he took the tempo down, asked Riddle to keep out of the way, and brought pianist Bill Miller into the spotlight.

Unlike Astaire, Sinatra does not oversell the drunken overtones. His "One for My Baby" is more memorable for how he inhabits the rest of the lyric: the near-whispered delivery of the first verse, the flat desperation as he urges the bartender to "make the music easy and sad," the way he backs away from the mic at the end. In his biography of the singer, Will Friedwald described it as "the finest piece of musical acting Sinatra ever turned in." **WF-J**

Le poinçonneur des Lilas | Serge Gainsbourg (1958)

Writer | Serge Gainsbourg
Producer | Denis Bourgeois
Label | Philips
Album | *Du chant à la une!...* (1958)

Porte des Lilas, proudly serving commuters since 1921, is one of the better-known Métro stations in Paris. Credit much of that to filmmakers—a 1958 Oscar-nominated movie bore the same name, and the station is featured in Meryl Streep's 2009 film *Julie & Julia*—and also to Serge Gainsbourg.

The famed provocateur-vocalist gave the station somewhat undesirable exposure with the hit French song "Le poinçonneur des Lilas" (The Conductor of Lilas). It told of a ticket-puncher who found his job so deadly dull that he daydreamed of quitting—not just the gig but life itself. "I make holes, little holes. . . . There'll come a crazed moment, when I'll take a gun / Make myself a little hole, a little hole. . . . They'll put me in a huge hole." Gainsbourg was not the first to have these kinds of morbid thoughts, but he was likely the first to turn them into a pop song. The piano-based tune chugged along on a rhythm like a speedy train. Sung with old-fashioned chanson gusto, it resonated with those stuck in dead-end jobs.

The song was offered up as track one on Gainsbourg's 1958 debut LP, which meant that listeners quickly discovered how this singer differed from most popular artists of the day. Gainsbourg continued to travel a controversial road throughout his career, which took in orgasmic sighs on 1969's "Je t'aime...moi non plus" and an eyebrow-raising duet with his daughter on 1985's "Lemon Incest." **JiH**

A reflective Serge Gainsbourg at the Théâtre de l'Etoile, Paris, in 1959. ➜

Nel blu dipinto di blu
Domenico Modugno (1958)

Writer | D. Modugno, F. Migliacci
Producer | Uncredited
Label | Fonit
Album | *La strada dei successi di Domenico Modugno* (1958)

It is hardly surprising that a song that translates as "In the Blue Painted Blue" came to be known simply as "Volare" (to fly), after its chorus hook. Although far from being a one-hit wonder in his native Italy, Domenico Modugno never matched the success of this breakthrough smash, which spent five weeks at the top of the U.S. charts in 1958 and earned him two Grammys and three gold discs. All through a lengthy musical career, and even when he became a politician, he was referred to by the nickname of "Mr. Volare."

According to co-writer Franco Migliacci, the idea for the words of "Nel blu dipinto di blu" came to him one day as he was gazing absentmindedly at the back of a packet of cigarettes. Somehow the visuals inspired a lyric about a man who dreams that he has swept up into the sky after painting his face and hands blue. Modugno helped to finish the words and added the tune. Wedded to a brassy big-band arrangement, the song was soon a hit.

After winning at the Sanremo Music Festival in 1958, the song became Italy's entry in that year's Eurovision Song Contest. Although it reached only third place at the time, it was voted the second most popular song in Eurovision history in the contest's fiftieth-anniversary celebrations, pipped by ABBA's "Waterloo." Cliff Richard, David Bowie, and the Gipsy Kings are among the many artists that have covered it, in various languages. **JLu**

All I Have to Do Is Dream
The Everly Brothers (1958)

Writer | Felice Bryant, Boudleaux Bryant
Producer | Archie Bleyer
Label | Cadence
Album | N/A

Brothers Don and Phil Everly began their chart career with two rock 'n' roll smash hits when debut "Bye Bye Love" and "Wake Up Little Susie" made No. 2 and No. 1 respectively on the *Billboard* Hot 100. But it was the slower, sleepy "All I Have to Do Is Dream" that best promoted the duo's unique selling point. Their sublime, apparently effortless, high harmonies were given the perfect vehicle by songwriters Boudleaux and Felice Bryant, who completed the song in just fifteen minutes.

"All I Have to Do Is Dream" was recorded in March 1958 and released a month later. The distinctive sound was managed by Cadence record label owner and producer Archie Bleyer. An even greater influence on the recording was Chet Atkins, who contributed the shimmering tremolo guitar effect that sets the tone from the opening second. "Chet Atkins was the reason we came to Nashville," admitted Phil Everly.

The song became the brothers' first of two transatlantic chart-toppers and continued to provide hits for a succession of artists. "One of the most important songs we ever recorded," reckoned Phil. Sixties genres such as surf pop and country rock would take their lead from the duo's singing style—Californian teenager David Crosby and Manchester youngster Graham Nash later co-formed Crosby, Stills & Nash, adapting the close harmonies on similarly seminal recordings. **DR**

Domenico Modugno's 1958 hit—inspired by blue, not by the blues.

To Know Him Is to Love Him
The Teddy Bears (1958)

Writer | Phil Spector
Producer | Phil Spector
Label | Dore
Album | N/A

No long slog to hit the top of the charts for Phil Spector: he struck gold with his first hit. Spector's ability to write, produce, and assemble a group was evident from the start, when three former Fairfax High School students from Los Angeles called themselves The Teddy Bears and recorded the plaintive "To Know Him Is to Love Him."

Inspired to write the song by the inscription on his father's gravestone, the teenage Spector picked his girlfriend's best friend, Annette Kleinbard (who later changed her name to Carol Connors and became a successful songwriter), to sing the song with Marshall Leib, the third Teddy Bear, and himself. After rehearsals, Spector arranged a session at which The Teddy Bears, plus debutant drummer Sandy Nelson, cut "To Know Him Is to Love Him" at Hollywood's Gold Star Studios in twenty minutes flat. Newly created label Dore relegated the track to a B-side, but a DJ in Fargo, North Dakota, had other ideas and began a trend by flipping the disc. A ten-week buildup of sales resulted in the single topping the *Billboard* Hot 100 in December 1958 for three weeks.

The song proved to be extremely adaptable. A favorite in early Beatles set lists, it charted again for Peter & Gordon and Bobby Vinton. It even managed to top the country chart in 1987, when beautifully hijacked by the legendary trio Dolly Parton, Linda Ronstadt, and Emmylou Harris. **DR**

Brand New Cadillac
Vince Taylor & His Playboys (1959)

Writer | Vince Taylor
Producer | Norrie Paramor
Label | Parlophone
Album | N/A

After many years in the United States, British-born Brian Holden returned to find his homeland's answer to rock 'n' roll was former jazzmen playing Bill Haley–inspired swing on the BBC Light Programme. Adopting the name Vince Taylor, he set about introducing Britain to the raucous, primitive beat of rockabilly. Taylor's early 45s were covers—Ray Smith's "Right Behind You Baby" and Johnny Ace's "Pledging My Love"—but on the latter's flipside was this self-penned number.

From its opening bars, driven by Joe Moretti's circling guitar, it was clear that this was something quite different. In a land of Ford Consuls and Morris Oxfords, the idea of an inamorata driving a tail-finned automobile was exotic and new. In direct contrast to the mannered style of his British contemporaries, Taylor's wild vocals could almost have been cut at Sun Studios. He even calls out, "Hangin' on Scotty, here we go!" before the second solo, as if addressing Elvis Presley's guitarist Scotty Moore rather than the Scottish-born Moretti.

Although subsequently revered by everyone from Van Morrison to Joe Strummer, the leather-clad rocker burned out rapidly. Increasingly addled by drink and drugs, he memorably informed a 1964 audience: "My name is Mateus. I'm the new Jesus, the son of God." Little wonder, then, that he became the model for David Bowie's tale of rock 'n' roll self-immolation on 1972's *Ziggy Stardust*. **SP**

What'd I Say (Parts 1 & 2)
Ray Charles (1959)

Writer | Ray Charles
Producer | Ahmet Ertegun,
Jerry Wexler
Label | Atlantic
Album | *What'd I Say* (1959)

The story behind "What'd I Say" reads like a classic piece of Hollywood let's-do-the-show-right-here hokum. According to legend, Ray Charles and his well-drilled band found themselves with a quarter-hour to fill at the end of a long supper-club date. Having exhausted the group's repertoire, Charles started vamping a keyboard riff, improvising lyrics over the top as the other musicians joined in. Cue audience pandemonium and a phone call to Jerry Wexler, with the singer suggesting to his producer that he might have a little something here.

Even in its subsequent studio recording, boiled down by engineer Tom Dowd into six and a half minutes and then split over two sides of a seven-inch single, "What'd I Say" sounds, gloriously, as if the group are playing by ear. From this point on, Charles ended every concert with this tune.

In terms of musical structure, "What'd I Say" is not much more than a handful of rhyming couplets hitched to a by-the-book twelve-bar blues. But records are not made on paper. The jumpy keyboard work, Milt Turner's propulsive, Latin-inflected drumming, and, most famously, Charles's own lascivious, gospel-inspired call-and-response vocal interplay with The Raelettes, all combine to elevate "What'd I Say" into something remarkably potent and thrilling. The single's success prove that sometimes it is not what you play but how you play it that counts. **WF-J**

I Only Have Eyes for You
The Flamingos (1959)

Writer | Harry Warren, Al Dubin
Producer | Uncredited
Label | End
Album | *Flamingo Serenade* (1959)

First heard as a part-sung, part-spoken duet by Dick Powell and Ruby Keeler in the 1934 movie *Dames*, "I Only Have Eyes for You" entered the standards repertoire quickly. As such, it was an easy target for the doo-wop scene, which enjoyed a love affair with Tin Pan Alley during the Fifties. The slight surprise is that the task of recording it fell to The Flamingos, a Chicago-based group who had issued more than a dozen largely unsuccessful singles between 1953 and 1958.

The arrival among The Flamingos of arranger Terry Johnson and producer George Goldner brought about a shift of focus. The group (a sextet) charted for the first time in early 1959 with "Lovers Never Say Goodbye," before Goldner encouraged them to turn toward Tin Pan Alley for inspiration. The success was immediate: grounded by a stately rhythm section, led by Nate Nelson's plaintive, elegant vocal and colored by an echo-soaked backing-vocal arrangement that blends the ethereal and the pungent, "I Only Have Eyes for You" became the group's biggest hit, and remains one of the most striking singles of the Fifties.

The group never matched the song's success. The recording, meanwhile, was assured of immortality when it was granted starring roles in George Lucas's 1973 movie *American Graffiti* and, twenty-five years later, an episode of *Buffy the Vampire Slayer*. **WF-J**

Ne me quitte pas | Jacques Brel (1959)

Writer | Jacques Brel
Producer | Uncredited
Label | Philips
Album | *La valse à mille temps* (1959)

"In those days [the mid- to late Sixties], hearing [Brel] sing was like a hurricane blowing through the room."

Scott Walker, 2008

◀ **Influenced by: Les feuilles mortes** • Yves Montand (1946)
▶ **Influence on: Once Was** • Marc & The Mambas (1983)
● **Covered by:** Nina Simone (1965) • Sandy Shaw (1967)
Scott Walker (recorded as **"If You Go Away"**) (1969)
Daniel Guichard (1972) • Serge Lama (1979)

Although he is forever destined to feature in that old saloon-bar challenge of coming up with the names of five famous Belgians, Jacques Brel had an uneasy relationship with the country in which he was raised. Brel left Brussels for Paris as a twenty-something in the mid-Fifties, and ever after regarded his country with a quixotic mix of affection and contempt. His fellow Belgians came to view him in something like the same way.

In disregard of his origins, Brel's music has come to represent a certain streak of Frenchness: impassioned, poetic, theatrical, and serious. Written for his onetime lover Suzanne Gabriello, who promoted Brel through her role as an MC at the Paris Olympia, and delivered with little more than a piano for accompaniment, "Ne me quitte pas" has come to symbolize Brel's milieu, despite the fact that its pleading melancholy is far from typical of a catalog of songs that are often shot through more with humor and social comment than romantic desperation.

Brel became more widely known after his songs were translated into English, first by hack poet Rod McKuen and later, for a hit off-Broadway musical devoted to Brel, by Eric Blau and Brill Building stalwart Mort Shuman. Literary precison is not always what is needed when it comes to the translation of songs, and it was McKuen's typically clumsy rewriting of "Ne me quitte pas," retitled "If You Go Away," that found favor with everyone from Frank Sinatra to Ray Charles. However, none of the versions matched the success of McKuen's even more hamfisted translation of another Brel song, "Le Moribond." Retitled "Seasons in the Sun," this gained the U.K. No. 1 slot for both Terry Jacks and, much later, Westlife. **WF-J**

Shout (Parts 1 & 2) | The Isley Brothers (1959)

Writer | O'Kelly Isley, Ronald Isley, Rudolph Isley
Producer | Hugo Peretti, Luigi Creatore
Label | RCA
Album | *Shout!* (1959)

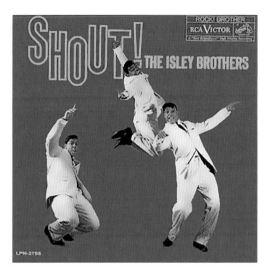

"It just grew out of . . . the sort of thing we'd do in church."

Ronald Isley, 1975

◀ **Influenced by: Lonely Teardrops** • Jackie Wilson (1958)

▶ **Influence on: White Lines (Don't Don't Do It)** Grandmaster Melle Mel (1983)

● **Covered by:** Lulu & The Luvvers (1964) • Joan Jett (1980) • Grandmaster Melle Mel (1983)

While riffing on call-and-response vocals in a live cover of Jackie Wilson's doo-wop weepy "Lonely Teardrops," The Isley Brothers threw in a winning line—"You know you make me want to shout"—and the Washington, D.C., crowd answered in kind. Swiftly picking up on the reaction, an RCA chief in the audience snapped the brothers up and suggested they might like to construct a song around this gambit. O'Kelly, Ronald, and Rudolph Isley had roots in gospel singing; now they were using their skills in secular style.

That is the legend. "Shout," the song they fashioned, became a standard and—eventually—a huge seller, in spite of modest chart performances. Produced by Brill Building duo Hugo & Luigi (Hugo Peretti and Luigi Creatore), the single was spread over both sides of the 45, the body of the song in Part 1, the full audience-participation workout ("A little bit louder now . . .") in Part 2. As a whole, "Shout (Parts 1 & 2)" is a thrilling party record, built around an invigorating call-and-response interplay that defied anyone not to get involved.

The inspiration that led to the song was fleeting, however, and the brothers would not find their flow until the Sixties were bedded in, although there would be further acts to their career, with perhaps even more life than in "Shout." Covers of the song have been plentiful, most famously Scot poppet Lulu's jolly, parping 1964 version. Lulu's take does not bother itself with the extended breakdown of Part 2, but that section was tackled with gusto in the memorable frat-party scene from 1978 movie *National Lampoon's Animal House*. Such was the strength of fictional band Otis Day & The Knights' performance, they were persuaded to record it for real. **MH**

Mack the Knife
Bobby Darin (1959)

Writer | Kurt Weill, Bertolt Brecht, Marc Blitzstein
Producer | Ahmet Ertegun
Label | Atco
Album | *That's All* (1959)

Slick and finger-clicking good, "Mack the Knife" was an extraordinary U.S. and U.K. chart-topper at a time when most pop hits sang of heartache, hunks of love, and loneliness. Here were lyrics describing death and robbery in a song written in 1928 for the Brecht–Weill ballad "Die Moritat von Mackie Messer"—the character of Messer being based on ne'er-do-well Macheath from John Gay's *The Beggar's Opera*—which served as the theme for their *Threepenny Opera*. Mark Blitzstein supplied English lyrics in 1954.

Bobby Darin was inspired to cover the song after hearing Louis Armstrong's 1956 version. He was unsure at first about releasing it as a single, but it stayed nine weeks atop the *Billboard* Hot 100 and Darin's jazzed-up rendition became *the* definitive version, according to Frank Sinatra.

Sinatra was a good judge. Darin's biggest hit gained him Grammy awards for Best New Artist of 1959 and Best Vocal Performance. Although he would never better "Mack the Knife," his Top Ten hits stretched to the mid-Sixties, after which, along with many other singing stars', his popularity waned in the post-Beatles singer-songwriter boom. But this show tune has never really gone out of fashion, covered by off-duty Who vocalist Roger Daltrey on the 1989 *Mack the Knife* movie soundtrack and by Kevin Spacey, who played Darin in the 2004 biopic *Beyond the Sea*. **DR**

It Ain't Necessarily So | Diahann
Carroll & The André Previn Trio (1959)

Writer | George and Ira Gershwin, DuBose Heyward
Producer | Jack Lewis
Label | United Artists
Album | *Porgy and Bess* (1959)

George Gershwin's "folk opera" *Porgy and Bess* opened on Broadway in 1935 to a mixed critical reception. Some were doubtful that it should even be called opera, while others were unsure of Gershwin's portrayal of African-Americans.

It took a long time for the opera to receive the attention it deserved, but two of its songs, "Summertime" and "It Ain't Necessarily So," soon became standards, recorded by the likes of Ella Fitzgerald, Billie Holiday, and Bing Crosby.

Porgy and Bess became an MGM film in 1959, featuring a cast including Sidney Poitier, Dorothy Dandridge, Sammy Davis Jr. and Diahann Carroll. As Carroll told the *Daily Telegraph* in the United Kingdom, "We were the only blacks on the Paramount lot." Despite the starry cast, many of the principals—including Carroll—had their voices dubbed by opera singers, including on the subsequent soundtrack album. Sammy Davis Jr. whose character, Sportin' Life, sings "It Ain't Necessarily So," had his own voice on the film—though he was dropped from the soundtrack release due to contractual obligations.

The film's score won an Oscar for André Previn, but he soon revisited it with his trio and Carroll in a sparser, jazzier style, with Carroll adding a subtle intensity to the song's mockery of biblical teaching. Carroll was herself later to win a Tony award and be nominated for an Oscar. **DC**

- Motown takes U.S. R&B and soul to a wider international audience

- The Beatles conquer America and trigger the "British invasion" in 1964

- Bob Dylan plays loud and electric at the Newport Folk Festival in 1965

- The Love Generation convenes at the Woodstock Festival in 1969

- Violence at Altamont in 1969 signals the end of the hippie dream

1960s

Wondrous Place
Billy Fury (1960)

Writer | Jeff Lewis, Bill Giant
Producer | Jack Good
Label | Decca
Album | *Billy Fury* (1960)

Pop idol Billy Fury, real name Ronald Wycherley, was a gifted recording artist, songwriter, and rock 'n' roller, also known for his stylish stage and TV work.

"Wondrous Place" proved to be the ideal vehicle for the man in the silver lamé suit. Penned by two of Elvis's songwriters, and originally cut in the United States by Jim "Handyman" Jones, this was British pop's own "Heartbreak Hotel," complete with echo-chamber delivery. TV pop svengali Jack Good was, like Fury, convinced that the strange otherworldly nature of the song was a perfect choice. "We both agreed that we wanted a steamy bayou thing: shades of Elvis Presley's 'Crawfish.' It was a wonderful stage number and Billy was terrific on stage," recalled Good.

With dramatic, eerie vocal pauses and minimal instrumental backing, the song proved a showstopper in concert. Fury liked it so much that he recorded it five times during his career. Although it is now classed alongside Cliff Richard's "Move It!" and Marty Wilde's "Endless Sleep" as a British rock 'n' roll classic, "Wondrous Place" made only No. 25 in the U.K. singles chart.

The song echoes down the decades. A turn-of-the-century TV commercial for the Toyota Yaris featured the Billy Fury recording, and indie darlings The Last Shadow Puppets recorded a truly wondrous version as a track to accompany their 2008 debut single. **DR**

Save the Last Dance for Me
The Drifters (1960)

Writer | Doc Pomus, Mort Shuman
Producer | Jerry Leiber, Mike Stoller
Label | Atlantic
Album | N/A

Post-Elvis and pre-Beatles, much of the best pop originated in New York's Brill Building. Pomus and Shuman were among its finest songwriters, notching up hits including "A Teenager in Love," "Sweets for My Sweet," "(Marie's the Name) His Latest Flame," and "Can't Get Used to Losing You."

But none was more affecting than this U.S. No. 1 for The Drifters. "Save the Last Dance for Me" features a Brazilian *baion* beat (Shuman was a self-confessed "mambonik") and is swathed in strings—innovative for the time, though The Drifters had employed both before, in 1959. The narrative—boy reminds girl who she will be leaving with after the dance—may seem well worn, but a careful listen reveals notes of genuine anxiety ("If he asks . . . can he take you home, you *must* tell him no") among the everyday.

A childhood bout of polio had left Doc Pomus unable to walk without crutches. At his wedding, in 1957, he warmly encouraged his new wife to enjoy herself on the dance floor, but the experience was bittersweet: he knew he could never partner her. A few years later, Pomus came across an old wedding invitation; those mixed emotions rose up again and he penned the song. At the recording session, Atlantic Records' Ahmet Ertegun told singer Ben E. King the origin of the words. Moved almost to tears, King turned in a beautiful vocal—and Atlantic's biggest hit single up to that point. **RD**

Chaje shukarije
Esma Redžepova (1960)

Writer | Esma Redžepova, Stevo Teodosievski
Producer | Stevo Teodosievski
Label | RTB
Album | N/A

Rightly hailed as the "Queen of the Gypsies," Esma Redžepova has brought Balkan Gypsy music to international audiences for more than fifty years. She was born in 1943 to a Roma family in Skopje, Macedonia, and sang and danced from childhood. Discovered by Macedonian bandleader Stevo Teodosievski after she won a talent quest in 1956, Esma left school to become a professional singer.

Singing in Macedonian, Serbian, and her native tongue, Romany, Esma became a favorite of President Tito, Yugoslavia's visionary (if autocratic) ruler. He sent Esma & Ensemble Teodosievski abroad as representatives of socialist Yugoslavia, and their dynamic blend of Oriental ballads and Balkan dance tunes won over huge audiences.

"Chaje shukarije" ("Beautiful Girl" in Romany) was one of Esma's first hits. The song tells of a young man in love with a beautiful girl who rejects him. Sung over a pulsing accordion, clarinet, and hand drum, "Chaje shukarije" rips along with a bright chorus that ensures audiences shout for it whenever Esma performs. The song has gone on to become a Balkan standard, performed by Gypsy brass bands, pop singers, jazz bands, and more. In 2007, it was used over the opening credits to Sacha Baron Cohen's comedy *Borat!* Esma is a living legend in the Balkans and has twice been nominated for the Nobel Peace Prize because of her work with refugees from the Yugoslav wars. **GC**

Oh Carolina
Folkes Brothers (1960)

Writer | John Folkes
Producer | Prince Buster
Label | Buster Wild Bells
Album | N/A

Of course, the Jamaican music industry already existed before "Oh Carolina" was released, yet to many it is this track that marks the beginning of Jamaica's musical maturity. Here is the first recording with a Rastafarian flavor, the first Prince Buster production, and the first example of how timeless Jamaican pop could be.

The Folkes Brothers—John, Mico, and Junior—had met Prince Buster at Duke Reid's liquor store, where they had gone to audition. The music they sang was *mento* (a shuffling 1950s-era Jamaican sound) in style, yet Buster recognized something distinctive about their songs. He had already made a name for himself running outdoor sound systems, and was now looking to set himself up as a producer and label owner. Buster was impressed by the brothers and invited them to record. Joined by Owen Gray on piano and Count Ossie, a Rasta elder who played the Nyahbhingi drum (which added a palpable African flavor), "Oh Carolina" came together in the studio as the brothers sang their hearts out.

The song was an immediate hit in Jamaica and established Prince Buster in the music business. The Folkes Brothers quickly faded from view, although John Folkes reappeared to fight (and beat) Prince Buster in court over who wrote "Oh Carolina" (and thus received publishing royalties) when Shaggy scored internationally with it. **GC**

The Click Song (Qongqothwane)
Miriam Makeba (1960)

Writer | The Manhattan Brothers, Miriam Makeba
Producer | Bob Bollard
Label | RCA Victor
Album | *Miriam Makeba* (1960)

She was a singer, actress, and political activist. She performed for presidents and had audiences with the pope. She was the first African woman to win a Grammy Award and was known as "Mama Afrika," the "Empress of African Song." But it is for a lullaby about a black dung beetle knocking its abdomen on the ground as a mating call that Miriam Makeba remains perhaps best known outside her native continent. Her interpretation of the traditional Xhosa folk song, "Qongqothwane" opened Western ears to African music.

American audiences were enchanted by the onomatopoeic range of vocalized clicks in Makeba's native Xhosa vernacular. *Time* magazine compared this distinctive sound, made with a percussive flick of the tongue off the palate, to "the popping of champagne corks," and hailed Makeba as "the most exciting new singing talent to appear in many years." From the first rhapsodic reviews in *Billboard* magazine in 1960, Makeba was tagged by journalists as the "click-click girl."

While "The Click Song" would become her signature tune in live performance over the next five decades, Makeba herself had a love/hate relationship with it. As a vocal proponent of black consciousness, she was all too aware of its novelty value as an "exotic" signifier. It was only after the end of apartheid that she recorded a new studio version on her final album, *Reflections* (2004). **MK**

Will You Love Me Tomorrow
The Shirelles (1960)

Writer | Gerry Goffin, Carole King
Producer | Luther Dixon
Label | Scepter
Album | *Tonight's the Night* (1961)

The Shirelles' 1961 *Billboard* No.1 is significant because it ushered in the era of the girl group, which would dominate pop music until The Beatles stormed America, and—in the wake of The Drifters' No. 2 "There Goes My Baby"—cemented the relationship between soul and riffs played on strings. Yet its most important achievement is the way it pushed the envelope regarding sexual explicitness, cannily bridging the divide between Eisenhower's America (when it was recorded) and Kennedy's Camelot (when it charted).

Nice girls didn't put out when Gerry Goffin added words to a tune his young wife, Carole King, had left on a tape recorder while she went to play mah-jongg, and Shirelles singer Shirley Owens was none too happy with the story she had to tell. Yet from here it would be a short, slippery slope to *Hair*, *Oh! Calcutta!* and free love. This is the *Lady Chatterley's Lover* of pop.

Although brilliantly sung and possessing a tremendous melody, the song is made by the unmistakable jeopardy in the lyrics. A teenage girl is considering surrendering her virginity and wants a commitment from her boyfriend that he will still be there should there be consequences (this is a song dating from the pre-Pill, pre-abortion era). The fact that you know Owens has already made up her mind makes her apparent uncertainty all the more powerful. **DH**

Love Hurts
The Everly Brothers (1960)

Writer | Boudleaux Bryant
Producer | Uncredited
Label | Warner Bros.
Album | *A Date with the Everly Brothers* (1960)

The Everly Brothers chose to highlight their family ties from the start: one of the duo's earliest albums, a spartan collection of traditional tunes, was called *Songs Our Daddy Taught Us*. In truth, though, the emphasis was unnecessary. The effortless way that Don and Phil Everly's voices blended, usually in sweet, keening thirds, gave the game away, eventually proving to be an influence on acts such as The Beatles and Simon & Garfunkel.

The brothers released their first single in 1956, when Don was nineteen and Phil a mere seventeen. Success came after the pair connected with Boudleaux and Felice Bryant, a husband-and-wife songwriting team who had moved to Nashville in the late Forties and seen their songs picked up by acts such as Little Jimmy Dickens and Carl Smith. "Bye Bye Love," the Everlys' first hit, came from the couple's pen, as did subsequent chart-toppers "Wake Up Little Susie" (by both Bryants) and "All I Have to Do Is Dream" (by Boudleaux alone). "Love Hurts," another Boudleaux composition, is simple, stately, and beautiful.

The Everlys had twenty-six U.S. Top Forty hits and thirty U.K. chart entries. Surprisingly, "Love Hurts" was not among them; it appeared only as an album track. However, it has become one of their best-known songs, thanks to covers by Joan Jett, Roy Orbison, and, perhaps most memorably, Gram Parsons and Emmylou Harris. **WF-J**

September Song
Ella Fitzgerald (1960)

Writer | Kurt Weill, Maxwell Anderson
Producer | Norman Granz
Label | Verve
Album | *Ella Fitzgerald Sings* (1960)

In April 1960, Ella Fitzgerald took a break from the arduous recording schedule of her *Great American Songbook* series. In the company of just a pianist, Paul Smith, she recorded thirteen songs for the soundtrack to *Let No Man Write My Epitaph*. The film is based on the 1958 novel by Willard Motley and is set in the poverty and crime of Chicago's South Side. Ella plays a junkie piano player, appearing alongside Shelley Winters and Burl Ives, among others. The film has long since disappeared, but the music can still be heard on CD under the title *The Intimate Ella*.

One of the songs included on the soundtrack was by the prominent German composer Kurt Weill, a Jewish refugee from the Nazis who had settled in the United States in 1935. Once in America, he moved away from his politically engaged music with Bertolt Brecht and immersed himself in the American musical and popular song. Among his first efforts was *Knickerbocker Holiday*, a 1938 Broadway musical with lyrics by Maxwell Anderson, which featured "September Song."

It is a delightful, slow-paced love song about a lover spending a "few precious days" with her beloved. Ella not so much sings the song as caresses it, toning down her full-bodied voice into a gentle croon. Pianist Paul Smith is her perfect foil, gently supporting her every word. An intimate moment in a perfectly subdued set. **SA**

Ella Fitzgerald's supreme musicality and three-octave range earned her the highest accolades. ➜

Shakin' All Over | Johnny Kidd & The Pirates (1960)

Writer | Fred Heath
Producer | Walter J. Ridley
Label | HMV
Album | N/A

"I was paid my fee of seven pounds ten shillings cash, as I had demanded, plus a quid for the overdub."

Joe Moretti, 2006

◀ **Influenced by: Whole Lotta Shakin' Goin' On**
Jerry Lee Lewis (1957)

▶ **Influence on: Back in Black** · AC/DC (1980)

● **Covered by:** The Swinging Blue Jeans (1964)
The Guess Who (1965) · Suzi Quatro (1973) · Alvin
Stardust (1979) · Cliff Richard (1981) · Mud (1982)

From Lonnie Donegan's incongruous talk of a "railroad" line outside New Orleans to Cliff Richard's Home Counties Presley impersonation, Britain's first, faltering steps toward rock 'n' roll had been made in borrowed suede shoes. It was only with the fourth seven-inch by London combo Johnny Kidd & The Pirates that British rock found its feet and learned to innovate rather than imitate. And yet, like Cliff's 1958 breakthrough, "Move It!" "Shakin' All Over" (a U.K. No. 1) was originally to be the flip of a much tamer single—in this case, hoary old trad-jazz number "Yes Sir, That's My Baby."

This B-side, hastily written in a Soho coffee bar the day beforehand, was churned out in a single take. In a discernibly English accent, the eye-patch-wearing Johnny Kidd (né Fred Heath) recites a litany of tremorous afflictions, based around a remark that he and his lothario friends would habitually exchange upon seeing a pretty girl: "She gives me quivers down the membranes."

The Pirates press-ganged Scottish session player Joe Moretti into service to provide the spooky, minor-key guitar hook; he created the overdubbed "shimmer" effect that precedes the chorus by sliding a cigarette lighter down the fretboard, receiving an extra one-pound session fee for this contribution.

The spectral feel is compounded by Alan Caddy's insectoid finger-picking, which floats around in the upper register like a pizzicato echo of Brian Gregg's bass line. And in Moretti's landmark solo—introduced by a skittering drum break from Clem Cattini (purportedly added to pad out the record)—can be heard the embryonic guitar sound of George Harrison and Keith Richards. At last, the British were coming. **SP**

An act of piracy? Johnny Kidd steals rock 'n' roll from the States. ➡

Non, je ne regrette rien

Edith Piaf (1960)

Writer | Charles Dumont, Michel Vaucaire
Producer | Uncredited
Label | EMI
Album | N/A

Written four years before its recording, "Non, je ne regrette rien" swiftly became Edith Piaf's signature song. The French songstress initially dedicated her recording to the French foreign legion, which at the time was engaged in the Algerian War. The First Regiment Foreign Paratroopers soon adopted the song when the civilian leadership of Algeria's resistance was broken. "Non, je ne regrette rien" has since become an integral part of the French foreign legion heritage.

Piaf's commitment to the interpretation of a song, the way she *inhabits* it, has influenced generations of singers since—and not only the obvious ones. "Edith Piaf is my particular idol," a Ziggy-era David Bowie declared in 1973. (He later cited epic *Ziggy Stardust* closer "Rock 'n' Roll Suicide" as Fifties rock flavored with Piaf-esque chanson.) "I've never seen her live, only seen her perform on film, and what I saw was the greatest amount of energy given out with the least amount of movement." Two years later, an admiring Emmylou Harris confessed, "I don't understand a word she's saying, but she just breaks my heart."

In 2000, Lou Reed paid heartfelt tribute to Piaf's ability to interpret the sentiments of song with the skill of an actor: "The *whole* thing is that you've got to *believe* the singer. You *believe* Edith Piaf." The passion and gusto of Piaf's delivery on "Non, je ne regrette rien" are ample confirmation of that. **KL**

Spanish Harlem

Ben E. King (1961)

Writer | Jerry Leiber, Phil Spector
Producer | Jerry Leiber, Mike Stoller
Label | Atco
Album | N/A

Soul singer Ben Nelson was born in North Carolina in 1938 and, aged nine, moved to Harlem, New York. He joined the Five Crowns doo-wop combo in 1958, but when the manager of The Drifters sacked the entire group later that year, he replaced them with The Five Crowns. Nelson sang on ten of The Drifters' songs, co-writing the hit "There Goes My Baby" in 1959, but left in 1960 when he failed to get a pay raise and a decent share of royalties.

Nelson then remarketed himself as Ben E. King and embarked on a successful solo career. His first hit was a song based on the area in which he grew up. Strictly speaking, Leiber's lyrics aren't quite up to his usual standard—it's not possible to "pick that rose *and* watch her as she grows in my garden"—but such carping is churlish given the charm of the piece and the sparkling arrangement. The song packs a lot into under three minutes. The opening marimba triplets, delightfully syncopated melody, swathes of echo, and warm vocal accompaniment (from vocal trio The Gospelaires, featuring Dionne Warwick) all combine to produce a real sense of Latinate longing.

"Spanish Harlem" was a success but not a massive hit, peaking at No. 15 in *Billboard*'s R&B chart and No. 10 in its pop chart. Subsequently, however, it has become a popular standard, with Aretha Franklin producing perhaps the most transcendent of the numerous cover versions. **SA**

Mad About the Boy
Dinah Washington (1961)

Writer | Noël Coward
Producer | Uncredited
Label | Mercury
Album | N/A

The arc of Dinah Washington's career may not have been smooth, but it was gentler than the bumpy ride she endured away from the stage. Born Ruth Jones in 1924, she joined Lionel Hampton's band in her teens as a raw blues belter, but gradually left her roots in favor of ballads and torch songs. At the close of the Fifties, she found mainstream fame through slick recordings such as "What a Diff'rence a Day Makes" and some flimsy duets with Brook Benton. Jazz diehards, who had previously called her one of their own, were appalled. Washington didn't seem to care. And it is from this controversial but commercially lucrative period that her 1961 reading of "Mad About the Boy" emerged.

Written by Noël Coward for his 1932 revue *Words and Music*, "Mad About the Boy" had first been recorded by Washington back in 1952, in a comparatively low-key and jazzy arrangement. Nine years later, though, rough edges and jazz inflections were largely absent from her second attempt. Quincy Jones's arrangement is handsome, even stately, and Billy Byers's trombone intro and coda linger in the memory. But the recording would be nothing without Washington, her faintly caustic vocal providing necessary counterbalance to an otherwise sweet setting.

Washington died just two years after recording "Mad About the Boy," accidentally overdosing on sleeping pills. She was thirty-nine. **WF-J**

Lazy River
Bobby Darin (1961)

Writer | H. Carmichael, S. Arodin
Producer | Ahmet Ertegun, Nesuhi Ertegun, Jerry Wexler
Label | Atco
Album | N/A

Bobby Darin was at the peak of his career at the beginning of the Sixties, having had a string of hits starting with the self-penned "Splish Splash" and "Dream Lover," followed by his big-band takes on the jazz standard "Mack the Knife" and "Beyond the Sea" (an Anglicized take on Charles Trenet's "La mer"). He was a hugely popular live act, regularly headlining at Las Vegas clubs and drawing sellout crowds at the Copacabana club in New York.

Darin's record label, Atco, was keen for him to make a shift in his style, hoping to cash in on the continuing rise of rock 'n' roll. In the end, though, Darin took the advice of his friend and publicist, Harriet "Hesh" Wasser, to carry on doing what he did best: jazz-pop numbers in a swing style.

The choice of "Lazy River" in 1961 seemed a surprising one. Written by Hoagy Carmichael in 1932 and performed by him in the laid-back manner the title suggests, it appeared unlikely material for Darin's full-on performing style. Previous covers had retained the feel of the Carmichael original, though in 1956 a version by Roberta Sherwood injected some pace and New Orleans jazz into the standard midway through. But with a powerful, fully orchestrated arrangement by Richard Wess, Darin transformed it into an upbeat number that truly swung, reaching the U.S. Top Twenty and confirming his status as one of the great swing singers. **MW**

Back Door Man
Howlin' Wolf (1961)

Writer | Willie Dixon
Producer | Willie Dixon
Label | Chess
Album | *Howlin' Wolf*, aka "The Rockin' Chair Album" (1962)

Willie Dixon was behind much of the best blues music made in post-World War II Chicago. Muddy Waters, Little Walter, and Howlin' Wolf received more attention, but they all did so with help from Dixon, who wrote, produced, and/or played on many of those bluesmen's top cuts.

None of those titans benefited more from their association with Dixon than Wolf. Having scored a hit with his 1954 recording of Dixon's "Evil," Wolf spent the first half of the Sixties focused almost exclusively on the Dixon songbook. The result was one of the most impressive runs in blues history, producing such classic cuts as "Spoonful," "The Red Rooster" (aka "Little Red Rooster"), and "Back Door Man." The latter was a perfect fit for Wolf—a midnight ramble of a song with boastful lyrics that were both scary and sexual. Wolf inhabited the song's character in a way that should have made all the husbands on his block nervous. He was utterly believable in the role of Casanova/predator, growling out such menacing lines as "When everybody's tryin' to sleep / I'm somewhere making my midnight creep." Musical accompaniment was a slow grind, turned out in after-hours style by Wolf's regular studio band.

The song was released as the B-side to "Wang Dang Doodle." Later collected on various albums, it became a blues standard. Its best-known cover is on The Doors' 1967 eponymous debut. **JiH**

The Red Rooster
Howlin' Wolf (1961)

Writer | Willie Dixon
Producer | Willie Dixon
Label | Chess
Album | *Howlin' Wolf*, aka "The Rockin' Chair Album" (1962)

"The Red Rooster"—it acquired the diminutive "Little" in later cover versions—is credited to composer and bass player Willie Dixon. Yet Wolf recalled hearing it sung years before by blues guitarist Charley Patton, and the Dixon song does indeed show great similarities to a Patton song from 1929. Other blues singers then took up the evocative imagery of a lost rooster, notably Memphis Minnie, who recorded "If You See My Rooster (Please Run Him Home)" in 1936.

Wolf's version features the composer on bass along with guitar, piano, and drums, but it is Wolf's lead slide guitar that steals the show. At a funereally slow pace, Wolf tells the tale of owning "a little red rooster, too lazy to crow for day." But once the rooster is on the prowl, "dogs begin to bark, and the hound begin to howl," and the narrator pleads for someone to drag the rooster home. The metaphor of the erring husband is clear, made all the more obvious in the cover version by The Rolling Stones, in which the singer clearly identifies himself as being said (red) rooster.

Issued as a single in 1961, the track featured on Wolf's eponymous second album, released in 1962. Soul singer Sam Cooke hit the R&B and pop charts with the song in 1963, and it was the mixture of Cooke's more soulful treatment and the purer blues approach of Wolf that made The Rolling Stones' 1964 cover version so successful. **SA**

Johnny Remember Me
John Leyton (1961)

Writer | Geoff Goddard
Producer | Joe Meek
Label | Top Rank International
Album | N/A

So-called "death discs" enjoyed a brief vogue in the pre-Beatles era, as tales of teenage melodrama escalated into doomed *Romeo and Juliet* affairs. Perhaps the finest example of the genre was recorded in the unlikely setting of an apartment on London's Holloway Road. Wires trailed between the various rooms, with the TV actor John Leyton singing in the sitting room, the backing vocalists in the bathroom, the string section camped out on the stairs, and Joe Meek at his mixing desk in the kitchen, heavily compressing the output to create his signature coruscating, trebly sound. The result was a bottled hurricane, with Billy Kuy strumming his guitar in a relentless flamenco while drummer Bobby Graham and bassist Chas Hodges (latterly of "rockney" duo Chas & Dave) laid down a galloping beat straight out of Vaughn Monroe's country hit "Riders in the Sky" (1949).

Songwriter Geoff Goddard avoided specifying that "the girl I loved and lost a year ago" was actually dead, although Lissa Gray's ethereal vocals left little room for ambiguity. But the connections with the spirit world ran deeper than a few eerie sound effects: Goddard informed journal *Psychic News* in September 1961 that the song had been dictated to him in a dream by the ghost of Buddy Holly; and in a follow-up séance, the bespectacled hitmaker popped up again to tell Goddard that it was a surefire No. 1. And so it proved. **SP**

I Fall to Pieces
Patsy Cline (1961)

Writer | Hank Cochran, Harlan Howard
Producer | Owen Bradley
Label | Decca
Album | *Patsy Cline Showcase* (1961)

She wasn't the first female singer to crack the country world; Patsy Montana and Kitty Wells, among others, both got there before her. Yet Patsy Cline pretty much wrote the book on country-music ballad singing, and the lessons she set out in it have since been read, absorbed, and put into practice by everyone from George Jones to Trisha Yearwood. While Montana brought a homespun sound to her records, and Wells sang with a twang that matched any delivered by her guitarists, Cline's fluid style combined country's yen for a good story with a pop singer's sense of drama.

She was helped by Owen Bradley, the head of Decca's Nashville operation when Cline signed to the label, in 1960. Cline had enjoyed her first hit in 1957 with "Walkin' After Midnight," but none of her subsequent singles had followed it into the charts. A change in labels brought a change in fortunes. The duo's first collaboration, "I Fall to Pieces" hit No. 1 on the country charts, also crossing over to reach No. 12 in the *Billboard* Hot 100.

When Cline followed "I Fall to Pieces" with "Crazy," one of the first hits written by Willie Nelson, her fame was assured. However, the singer's promising career ended abruptly in 1963 at the age of thirty, when the plane on which she was traveling with singers Cowboy Copas and Hawkshaw Hawkins crashed. The pilot was Randy Hughes, Cline's manager. **WF-J**

Stand by Me
Ben E. King (1961)

Writer | Ben E. King, "Elmo Glick" (Jerry Leiber and Mike Stoller)
Producer | Jerry Leiber, Mike Stoller
Label | Atco
Album | *Don't Play That Song!* (1962)

To write a song that becomes a contemporary standard is an exceptional achievement; with "Stand by Me," Ben E. King did exactly that. King had been The Drifters' lead singer on a series of magnificent late-Fifties hits written by Doc Pomus and Mort Shuman—"I Count the Tears," "This Magic Moment," "Save the Last Dance for Me"—and was groomed for solo stardom by Atlantic.

In 1961, King released "Stand by Me," a song he had shaped in the studio from an old gospel number. Leiber and Stoller, aware of how well Latin rhythms had suited The Drifters, added a pulsing Afro-Cuban groove alongside zigzagging cello and soft quartet harmonies. King's smooth tenor vocal, pleading yet strong, vulnerable yet authoritative, builds and builds (as does the initially sparse instrumentation) until "Stand by Me" almost explodes with tension and desire.

Beautifully performed and produced, the song topped the R&B charts, hitting No. 4 in the pop listings. Twenty-five years later, Stephen King's novella *The Body* was adapted by Hollywood as *Stand by Me*, and Ben E. King's song provided the film's theme; immediately, "Stand by Me" reentered the U.S. pop Top Ten. A Levi's jeans ad helped to push it to the U.K. No. 1 in 1987. The song possesses timeless appeal, conveying both fear and reassurance. "Stand by Me" is an ode to human unity. **GC**

Blue Moon
The Marcels (1961)

Writer | Richard Rodgers, Lorenz Hart
Producer | Stu Phillips
Label | Colpix
Album | *Blue Moon* (1961)

The overwhelming glut of vocal groups milling around the American pop margins in the late Fifties meant that it often took a stroke of luck for the best ones to get heard. The Marcels, though, got their break the old-fashioned way. In 1960, the Pittsburgh quintet (named, incidentally, after a hairstyle) sent some demos to Colpix Records, a subsidiary of Columbia Pictures. Label founder Stu Phillips liked what he heard and invited the group—comprising three black and two white singers—to New York for a session.

What actually happened in the studio remains a matter for debate. Some reports suggest the group wanted to cover The Collegians' single "Zoom Zoom Zoom" of 1958; Phillips disliked the song but liked the bomp-baba-bomp bass riff, and got the singers to marry it to the much-loved Rodgers and Hart standard "Blue Moon." Other accounts reckon that the bass line came not from the group but from Phillips himself. At any rate, The Marcels cut two takes of "Blue Moon" as the session drew to a close. The second, which bore more than a passing resemblance to "Zoom Zoom Zoom," got the thumbs-up.

The tape found its way via a Colpix promo man to renowned New York DJ Murray the K, who pretty much wore it out; within weeks, this daffy, dynamic piece of doo-wop fluff had topped the *Billboard* Hot 100. **WF-J**

Crazy
Patsy Cline (1961)

Writer | Willie Nelson
Producer | Owen Bradley
Label | Decca
Album | *Patsy Cline Showcase* (1961)

"Crazy" is one of pop's most common song titles, with more than twenty transatlantic chart hits to its name. Most enduring of these is Patsy Cline's country ballad, which she recorded in one take supported by Elvis Presley's vocal troupe.

When Texas-born musician Willie Nelson decamped to Nashville in the early Sixties, he began a double life as a performer and songwriter, forging himself a reputation as a respected country-music icon along the way. Nelson provided Cline with her most successful recording when he penned a country classic that was perfect for the sad, soulful, deep vocal pitch of the country star. Cline's gritty determination to get to grips with the song she at first hated was compounded by her lingering injuries, sustained in a near-fatal car accident two months before the recording sessions. The song wowed country fans, who gave her three standing ovations as she sang it—on crutches—at the Grand Ole Opry.

Cline's distinctive vocal is not the only reason the song is so well remembered. Less than two years after her recording of "Crazy," she was involved in yet another accident, when she was a passenger aboard a small aircraft flying en route to Nashville which crashed in rural Tennessee. This time, she failed to survive. The haunting, plaintive "Crazy" has become her signature song down the decades. **DR**

Tous les garçons et les filles
Françoise Hardy (1962)

Writer | F. Hardy, Roger Samyn
Producer | Chuck Blackwell
Label | Vogue
Album | *Tous les garçons et les filles* (1962)

Françoise Hardy was born to a single mother in Paris in 1944. Having received a guitar for her sixteenth birthday, she began playing both French and U.S. folk and pop songs. In 1961, she answered a newspaper advertisement looking for young singers. With her striking features, breathy voice, and introspective songs, she swiftly won a record deal. Her first 45, in June 1962, found the A-side, "Oh oh chéri," paired with Hardy's own "Tous les garçons et les filles," with a simple waltz rhythm placed beneath her casual yet intense vocal.

"Oh oh chéri" was not a success, and, when given the opportunity to perform on French TV in 1962, Hardy sang "Tous les garçons et les filles" instead. It promptly became a huge French hit, eventually selling more than 700,000 copies. The song finds the narrator musing on all the happy couples she sees around her while she herself remains alone, having never experienced love. Hardy later recorded the song in English as "Find Me a Boy."

Françoise Hardy went on to become one of France's most popular—and critically acclaimed—singer-songwriters. Her original songs displayed both emotional subtlety and a sonic resonance that makes them compelling even if the listener doesn't speak French. Both Bob Dylan and Blur have championed Hardy (the latter recording with her in 1994), while "Tous les garçons et les filles" remains a classic of Sixties French pop. **GC**

Françoise Hardy sports that iconic Sixties fashion accessory: the peaked cap. ➲

You've Really Got a Hold on Me
The Miracles (1962)

Writer | "Smokey" Robinson
Producer | "Smokey" Robinson
Label | Tamla
Album | *The Fabulous Miracles* (1963)

Signing to the fledgling Tamla label in 1959, The Miracles were integral to establishing the early Motown sound, scoring the label's first million-seller with 1960's "Shop Around." The intense ballad "You've Really Got a Hold on Me" was written by The Miracles' leader, William "Smokey" Robinson, in a New York hotel room after hearing Sam Cooke's "Bring It on Home to Me."

Robinson wanted to pen something similar, aping the tight vocal harmony from Cooke and fellow soul singer Lou Rawls. Stylistically, the song also exhibits the influence of doo-wop vocal acts such as The Moonglows. Its arrangement is simple, with Smokey's falsetto combining with a tenor vocal from bandmate Bobby Rogers and infectious guitar lines provided by Marv Tarplin and Funk Brother sessioneer Eddie Willis. The song's enduring appeal comes from Robinson's ingenious lyric, concerning a man madly in love with a woman who treats him badly, the song's opening line—"I don't like you but I love you"—neatly grabbing listeners at once and placing them in the confused mind-set of the lovelorn loser.

The Beatles covered the song on their U.K. chart-topping second album, *With The Beatles*, John Lennon singing lead and George Harrison providing the harmony. The Zombies and The Small Faces also recorded versions, as did Motown's The Supremes and The Temptations. **JoH**

Boom Boom
John Lee Hooker (1962)

Writer | John Lee Hooker
Producer | Uncredited
Label | Vee-Jay
Album | *Burnin'* (1962)

Perhaps better known from the cover version recorded by British R&B group The Animals in 1964, "Boom Boom" was originally recorded in Chicago in late 1961. Electric guitarist John Lee Hooker is supported on the track by a sextet packed with future Motown luminaries. Bassist James Jamerson was to go on to become renowned at Motown as the "father of modern bass guitar" with the label's in-house studio band, The Funk Brothers, alongside drummer Benny Benjamin. Two saxophonists, a pianist, and a second guitarist make up the sextet.

Hooker starts by picking out the song's signature riff, repeated by a light-touch piano with bass and drums, before launching into the vocals. Each suggestive vocal phrase is echoed by an instrumental response that slowly but surely builds up momentum before Hooker lets rip. The band then lays down a thundering beat behind his lead guitar that drives all before it until the vocals return. This time, Hooker growls out the words, his gruff, suggestive voice making it more than clear that, having taken his woman home and put her in his house, after she's walked that walk and talked that talk, it is: "Boom Boom Boom Boom."

Indeed. Hooker was virtually illiterate, yet his words here speak about sex with concise eloquence. This is two minutes, thirty-one seconds of raw, stomping R&B porn. Bliss. **SA**

He's a Rebel
The Crystals (1962)

Writer | Gene Pitney
Producer | Phil Spector
Label | Philles
Album | *He's a Rebel* (1963)

Turned down by its intended performers, The Shirelles, because of the controversial subject matter (for the time), "He's a Rebel" came to the attention of Phil Spector, who thought it would be ideal for The Crystals. That band, led by Barbara Alston, was then touring the East Coast of the United States, though, and could not make it to Spector's Los Angeles studio in time to record the song and release it before a rival version came out. As a result, Spector drafted in Darlene Love and her band, The Blossoms, to the recording—but used The Crystals' name for the release.

Although "He's a Rebel" does not feature strings, it is widely viewed as an early and definitive example of Spector's "wall of sound" production style. Spector took a track, accomplished as it was written, and developed it into an anthem—and, in this case, a U.S. No. 1. The song also marked a change in direction for girl groups, featuring the new allure of the "bad boy," which developed further with The Shangri-Las' "Leader of the Pack." The Crystals had previously courted controversy with their release of the Goffin/King single "He Hit Me (and It Felt Like a Kiss)."

The same lineup of Love and The Blossoms recorded the follow-up single, "He's Sure the Boy I Love," which reached No. 11 in the *Billboard* chart, though subsequent releases were by the "original" version of The Crystals. **CR**

Do You Love Me
The Contours (1962)

Writer | Berry Gordy Jr.
Producer | Berry Gordy Jr.
Label | Gordy
Album | *Do You Love Me (Now That I Can Dance)* (1962)

It's almost too perfect: when Berry Gordy told The Contours that they had been chosen to record his song "Do You Love Me" for Gordy Records, the group was so delighted they leapt on the notoriously steely Motown boss for a hug.

Back in 1962, "Do You Love Me" would have been performed by The Temptations, if only Gordy had been able to find them at the Hitsville USA studio. The Tempts were playing the Detroit gospel-music showcase, but to Gordy's mind, they'd gone AWOL—so when he bumped into The Contours in the hallway, he decided to give the song to them. And, of course, it's now difficult to imagine the song sounding any other way. Can you hear anyone but Billy Gordon screeching the song's impassioned refrain (or any other backing singers instructing dancers to do the twist)?

The song sold over a million copies on its initial release and made No. 3 in the *Billboard* Hot 100 chart. Within a couple of years, it became a standard cover for British Invasion groups (The Hollies, The Dave Clark Five) as well as U.S. proto-punks such as The Sonics; twenty years later, the song was championed by Bruce Springsteen.

"Do You Love Me" would reach its biggest audience in the Eighties, via the movie *Dirty Dancing*. The Contours joined Ronnie Spector on a *Dirty Dancing* tour and, to this day, still play (brilliantly) live. Hugs all round. **SH**

Your Cheating Heart
Ray Charles (1962)

Writer | Hank Williams
Producer | Sid Feller
Label | ABC-Paramount
Album | *Modern Sounds in Country and Western Music Volume Two* (1962)

Although Ray Charles had cut a country song back in 1959, Hank Snow's "I'm Movin' On," the 1962 release of *Modern Sounds in Country and Western Music*—a dozen lily-white country songs translated by Charles and producer Sid Feller into the all-black soul idiom—came as a jolt to a music industry unused to genre-hopping. The album surged to the top of the U.S. charts, catapulting Charles into the mainstream; its success was such that it spawned a sequel, no less impressive, on which is featured "Your Cheating Heart."

Charles cut two Hank Williams songs on the original *Modern Sounds* set—a jaunty "Hey, Good Lookin'" and a strung-out reading of "You Win Again"—but both were topped by *Volume Two*'s take on "Your Cheatin' Heart" (Charles's version restores the missing *g*). Scored by jobbing Hollywood arranger Marty Paich, the weeping-willow strings and cornball backing vocals occasionally threaten to sink the ship; across both *Modern Sounds* records, it is the songs set to brass arrangements by Gerald Wilson that come out on top. But here, Charles's jazz-inflected piano and perfectly pitched vocal delivery save the day.

For that matter, it is Charles's dynamic, committed, and often raw, vocals that elevate all his country-tinged output above the status of mere curios. The key? "I'm not singing it country-western," he put it. "I'm singing it like me." **WF-J**

Cry Baby | Garnet Mimms
& The Enchanters (1963)

Writer | Bert Russell (aka Bert Berns), Norman Meade (aka Jerry Ragovoy)
Producer | Jerry Ragovoy
Label | United Artists
Album | *Cry Baby and 11 Other Hits* (1963)

Raised in a religious household, the teenage Garnet Mimms found his voice as a gospel singer. He formed doo-wop group The Gainors with Howard Tate in 1958, then pushed his talent to the edge with a string of mostly modest hits in the Sixties, before becoming a pastor in the Seventies. Of course, part of what makes "Cry Baby" such a shiver-inducing listen is that it is sung with the kind of fervor that normally rattles church roofs: Mimms's voice moves from a silky, calm baritone to a hands-in-the-air falsetto.

The killer twist is that "Cry Baby" is really a bedroom song, pure yearning distilled into four minutes. Our hero loves a girl who's in love with another guy—and a no-good guy at that. So when he breaks her heart, which he will, guess who'll be around to catch the tears?

"Cry Baby" comes to the boil like rolling coffee; it opens with a gently puttering 6/8 beat and a chorus of sweetly cooing girl singers (the troupe would later include Dionne Warwick and Doris Troy), gathering momentum until Mimms's heart all but explodes. The song simmers back down, and Mimms delivers a head-held-high soliloquy ("I'll always love you, darlin' / And I can see that you got some more tears to shed"), which builds and builds until the next chorus. An exquisite, almost unbearable listen, it was a huge hit (*Billboard* pop No. 4; R&B No. 1) in 1963. **SH**

Ray Charles enters country territory with "Your Cheating Heart" in 1962.

La javanaise
Juliette Gréco (1963)

Writer | Serge Gainsbourg
Producer | Uncredited
Label | Philips
Album | *Juliette Gréco No. 8* (1963)

Outside of his home country, Serge Gainsbourg is known, if at all, for embodying the stereotype of a certain kind of Gallic manhood: truculent, unshaven, permanently smoking, and lecherous. Gainsbourg released a few low-selling solo albums in the late Fifties and early Sixties, but did not find fame until he began to write for others, teaming up with Beat poet and jazz singer Juliette Gréco on an EP of his songs in 1959. An habituée of the bohemian cafés of Saint-Germain-des-Prés in Paris, where she drank with Jean Cocteau and Miles Davis, Gréco was a formidable presence—when they first met, Gainsbourg was too shy to speak.

"La javanaise" proved to be Gainsbourg's first real masterpiece as a songwriter. Based around an exotic jazz theme, it might seem to English speakers to be a simple lament for lost love in the typical French chanson style. Actually, Gainsbourg was attempting something far more ambitious. The song's title is a play on "javanais," a type of French slang popular during the 1950s where the extra syllable "av" is placed into the middle of words to render them almost incomprehensible. Accordingly, the song's lyrics cram as many words containing the "av" sound into them as possible. Non-Francophones need not worry about failing to get Gainsbourg's joke, though—Gréco's winningly sultry delivery and André Popp's lush arrangement make this a gorgeous song regardless. **PL**

Harlem Shuffle
Bob & Earl (1963)

Writer | Bobby Relf, Earl Nelson
Producer | Fred Smith
Label | Marc
Album | N/A

The dance-craze singles of the early Sixties were endlessly entangled in invocations of other hits. Every vocalist worth his salt would name-drop the watusi, the twist, the hully gully; the intention was to guide the listeners' steps, in the manner of the caller at a square dance. "Harlem Shuffle" references Russell Byrd's "Hitch Hike," Major Lance's "The Monkey Time," and The Five Du-Tones' "Shake a Tailfeather," but is rooted mainly in an obscure instrumental by California singer Round Robin. His uptempo go-go affair was named "Slauson Shuffle Time," after a thoroughfare in south Los Angeles. "We wanted to make the Shuffle a national hit," said Bobby Relf. "No one back East knew of Slauson, but they knew Harlem."

The triumphant fanfare that opens the track took on new life as a House of Pain sample in 1992, so much so that modern listeners can be taken aback when it is followed by the original's languid, sloping arrangement. Bob & Earl's gospel-inflected vocals, which beg and plead with us to perform the titular steps, are punctuated by clarion horns that clearly caught the ear of George Harrison—their echoes are distinctly audible on The Beatles' confectionery-based parody "Savoy Truffle" from 1968. The following year, "Harlem Shuffle" slid into the British charts for the first time, reaching No. 7—a testament to Fred Smith's seductive, forward-looking production. **SP**

Juliette Gréco, seen here in 1962, took up singing after a successful movie career in the Fifties.

On Broadway
The Drifters (1963)

Writer | Barry Mann, Cynthia Weil
Producer | Jerry Leiber, Mike Stoller
Label | Atlantic
Album | N/A

As originally written by the husband-and-wife team of Barry Mann and Cynthia Weil, "On Broadway" featured a cheerful lyric about a girl on her way to Broadway and success. The song was in a complex time signature and the melody upbeat. It was originally recorded by The Cookies, although The Crystals' version came out first.

There the song might have foundered had not legendary producers Jerry Leiber and Mike Stoller found themselves a song short for a studio session booked by The Drifters the next day. Mann and Weil sent them "On Broadway," but the two producers felt that it was not quite right. The four of them worked overnight to transform it. The characteristic backing riff was given a more bluesy form and the time signature simplified. Most importantly, the narrative was changed so that its now wannabe *male* star was already on Broadway but down on his luck, with only "one thin dime" left.

Broadway is the home of New York theater and musical. To make it on Broadway is to "make it anywhere," as Liza Minnelli sang of New York itself in 1977. Our wannabe star in The Drifters' version—as sung by Rudy Lewis—has tried and failed. But he will prove his critics wrong and become a star. He will play a mean guitar. As did George Benson, on his transformed cover version. And as did the young session guitarist on the original recording, Phil Spector. **SA**

Louie Louie
The Kingsmen (1963)

Writer | Richard Berry
Producer | Ken Chase
Label | Jerden and Wand
Album | *The Kingsmen in Person* (1963)

Richard Berry—an R&B singer who fronted The Pharaohs—was inspired to create this revered slab of primal rock 'n' roll by "El Loco Cha Cha," recorded by René Touzet & His Orchestra. However, having done so, he initially hid his version away on the B-side of his 1957 single "You Are My Sunshine."

A primeval version in 1961 by Rockin' Robin Roberts & The Wailers spawned several covers, but it was thanks to producer Ken Chase that The Kingsmen recorded the track. The music director at radio station KISN in Portland, Chase ran a teenage dance club (The Chase) and wanted a version of the song that would drive the kids there wild. Recruiting young, clean-cut group The Kingsmen, he took them to Northwest Recorders studio and got them to play as they would on stage.

Chase was a jazz fan and cared about the feel of a recording above all else, so when vocalist Jack Ely came in early after the guitar break, Chase wasn't concerned; the naive ineptitude of the record merely adds to its charm. Driven by Don Galluci's keyboard jabs and Bob Nordby's booming bass, with a frantic guitar solo from Mike Mitchell, Lyn Easton's tumble-down drums, and Ely's delivery so indecipherable that the FBI actually launched an investigation into the track for potentially obscene lyrics, "Louie Louie" was a *Billboard* No. 2 in 1963. It is the definitive garage-punk performance—and one of the most covered songs of all time. **JoH**

The clean-cut Kingsmen unleash *the* frat-rock anthem: "Louie Louie." ➜

One Fine Day | The Chiffons (1963)

Writer | Gerry Goffin, Carole King
Producer | The Tokens
Label | Laurie
Album | *One Fine Day* (1963)

"Some of the demos eventually became records, because [some said] they were so good."

Carole King, 1989

◀ **Influenced by: Will You Love Me Tomorrow**
The Shirelles (1960)

▶ **Influence on: Sweet Blindness** • Laura Nyro (1968)

● **Covered by:** The Mindbenders (1966) • Cliff Richard
(1967) • Rita Coolidge (1979) • Carole King (1980)
Natalie Merchant (1996)

Now chiefly known for prising royalties out of George Harrison after a court ruled the former Beatle's "My Sweet Lord" had unintentionally aped their U.S. No. 1 "He's So Fine," The Chiffons were a pioneering girl group of the early Sixties. They formed in the Bronx, New York, in 1960 and initially comprised school friends Judy Craig, Patricia Bennett, and Barbara Lee Jones, before Sylvia Peterson was drafted in from Little Jimmy & The Tops. Cutting their teeth as backing singers, the group benefited from a rich vein of songs passing through New York's Brill Building and similar hothouses of the time, but "One Fine Day" nearly slipped past altogether.

R&B belter Little Eva, still reaping the rewards of the previous year's "The Loco-motion," was a natural choice to record "One Fine Day," another Gerry Goffin and Carole King composition. She laid down a demo, but production team The Tokens swooped on the track, apparently spotting an opportunity to build on the feats of their protégées' similarly titled "He's So Fine." Sources claim that the original demo remained intact but for the vocal, which The Chiffons re-recorded; it's Carole King's own rolling piano that drives the song.

"One Fine Day" was a U.S. No. 5 hit, but, with the advent of The Supremes and rock's changing landscape, The Chiffons were unable to sustain their early flurry of success. Although they still perform occasionally in an unsettled lineup led by Judy Craig, it is "One Fine Day" that has found the greater longevity, inspiring scores of cover versions, like so many Goffin/King originals. Its message, "One fine day we'll meet once more / And then you'll want the love you threw away before," will always resonate. **MH**

In Dreams | Roy Orbison (1963)

Writer | Roy Orbison
Producer | Fred Foster
Label | Monument
Album | *In Dreams* (1963)

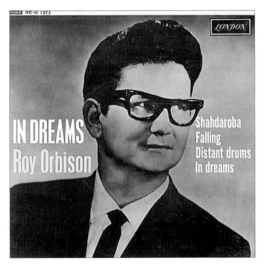

"That was literally a dream song that I dreamt. That sounds like something I would dream up!"

Roy Orbison, 1988

◀ **Influenced by: Surrender** • Elvis Presley (1961)
▶ **Influence on: Wicked Game** • Chris Isaak (1989)
● **Covered by:** Tom Jones (1971) • Chris de Burgh (1995) John Terra (1999) • Jan Keizer (2001) • Big Fat Snake with TCB Band & Sweet Inspirations (2003)

The Big "O"'s signature tune was one of a conspicuous handful that came to him as the Texan rock 'n' roll singer slept. "I woke up the next morning and it was still with me," he revealed. "And I filled in from the front to the back in about twenty minutes." Few artists could piece together such a composition in so little time; "In Dreams" dismisses standard verse-chorus structure in favor of a mini-epic that sails through seven musical movements over a span just shy of three minutes.

One tremulous crescendo of heartache and it is all over. "For a baritone to sing as high as I do is ridiculous," admitted Orbison. "It only comes from the fact that I didn't know what I was doing." But his unparalleled voice is at its most affecting here. The song reached No. 7 in the U.S. charts.

A quarter of a century later, "In Dreams" enjoyed an unlikely revival after extensive use in cult director David Lynch's disturbing movie *Blue Velvet* (1986). (Orbison refused Lynch permission to use the song, but the director went ahead anyway.) Lynch finds a macabre side to the song not immediately obvious in Orbison's sublime, lovelorn delivery, as Dennis Hopper's character, Frank Booth, calls it "Candy-Colored Clown" and dishes out beatings to its orchestral trills. For many, it would never sound the same again.

Lynch's movie brought Orbison back into the limelight, and his second flush of success was capped by a well-loved stint in supergroup The Traveling Wilburys. That distinctive voice never wavered in range or impact, long decades later, even as far as his swan song, *Mystery Girl*, in 1989. There he sealed his legend with the gorgeous "She's a Mystery to Me," a song U2's Bono wrote after a brief obsession—with "In Dreams." **MH**

Sally Go 'Round the Roses
The Jaynetts (1963)

Writer | Zell Sanders, Lona Stevens
Producer | Abner Spector
Label | Tuff
Album | *Sally Go 'Round the Roses* (1963)

The Jaynetts came together in the late Fifties. Initially, membership was fluid. In 1963, the Bronx-based group constituted Mary Sue Wells, Ethel Davis, and Yvonne Bushell. Zell Sanders, who comprised the entire staff of J&S Record Company, was friendly with the girls. Abner Spector, of Chicago's Tuff Records, came to town looking for a girl group, and Sanders proffered The Jaynetts, along with her song "Sally Go 'Round the Roses."

The track was an odd mix of nursery rhyme and beguiling warning. Spector (no relation to Phil) hired pianist Artie Butler to arrange and play most of the instruments on the session. The seemingly nonsensical lyrics—friends warn the heartbroken Sally against going downtown and obliquely advise, "roses they can't hurt you"—provoked many theories, with some even arguing that the song concerned a young woman's struggle with her sexuality. Not that this matters—with its slinky beat, turbulent piano, fairground organ, and muted vocals, "Sally Go 'Round The Roses" stands as a pop original, beautifully eerie and compelling.

Deservedly, the single reached No. 2 in the U.S. charts, though The Jaynetts never had a comparable success. Artie Butler did, however: he went on to arrange The Shangri-Las' hits. Andy Warhol reportedly called "Sally" "the greatest pop record ever made," and played the 45 repeatedly as he painted his own beautifully eerie pop art. **GC**

Be My Baby
The Ronettes (1963)

Writer | P. Spector, E. Greenwich, J. Barry
Producer | Phil Spector
Label | Philles
Album | *Presenting the Fabulous Ronettes featuring Veronica* (1963)

"I was in my car with my girlfriend," Beach Boy Brian Wilson recalled in 1996. "All of a sudden, this disc jockey, Wink Martindale, goes, 'Alright, here we go with "Be My Baby" by The Ronettes.' Whoa, whoa! I pulled over to the kerb and I really did flip out. . . . It wasn't really getting your mind blown, it was more like getting your mind *revamped*." Wilson's epiphany was triggered by 159 seconds of perfection. It opens with Hal Blaine's iconic—and much-imitated—drums, but blossoms into a castanet-clicking, string-swirling sensation. Atop it all soars Brooklyn belle Ronnie Spector, muse of the track's revered producer.

The song was written at Phil Spector's New York penthouse. "I was there," Ronnie told *Rolling Stone*, "but Phil didn't want anybody to know. . . . I put my ear to the wall, and I'm hearing them discuss me: 'She's so innocent, she's from Spanish Harlem . . .' It was so special and great because I knew they were writing for me." Ronnie had already recorded "Why Won't They Let Us Fall in Love" for Spector, but he opted to make "Be My Baby" The Ronettes' debut. The spectacular single—a transatlantic smash—remains Ronnie's signature tune.

Back in 1963, Brian Wilson was so impressed that he wrote a follow-up—which Phil Spector rejected in favor of "Baby I Love You." Wilson's subsequent quest to make equally majestic records just adds to the song's lavish legacy. **BM**

Surfin' Bird

The Trashmen (1963)

Writer | Al Frazier, Carl White, Sonny Harris, Turner Wilson Jr.
Producer | Uncredited
Label | Garrett
Album | *Surfin' Bird* (1963)

Minnesota group The Trashmen inadvertently created "Surfin' Bird" when, live onstage, they combined two popular R&B/doo-wop tracks— "The Bird Is the Word" and "Papa-Oom-Mow-Mow"—by West Coast band The Rivingtons. Bill Diehl, a local radio DJ, was at the performance and persuaded the band to record the track as a single. The two songs, reduced to little more than their respective titles, are repeated in a deranged vocal style that gives "Surfin' Bird" its frenzied, energetic tone. Also influential was the double-time urgency of premier surf band The Ventures' "Pipeline" and The Castaways' surf hit "Liar, Liar."

The recording found them winners of a regional Battle of the Bands contest in Chicago that brought them to the attention of Garrett Records. The label released the track to immediate success, with a No. 4 placing in the *Billboard* Hot 100. Over two decades later, "Surfin' Bird" featured in the soundtrack of Stanley Kubrick's 1987 film *Full Metal Jacket*, where it evoked the adrenaline-rush and violent chaos of combat in the Vietnam War.

To capitalize on the success of "Surfin' Bird," The Trashmen recorded a follow-up in "Bird Dance Beat," following the trend for related dance tracks, but this failed to emulate the impact of their debut. The band, though, have influenced scores of groups, such as The Cramps, Ramones, and The Jesus and Mary Chain. **CR**

Sapore di sale

Gino Paoli (1963)

Writer | Gino Paoli
Producer | Arr. Ennio Morricone
Label | RCA
Album | *Basta chiudere gli occhi* (1964)

With an arrangement by Ennio Morricone that included the saxophone of Gato Barbieri, "Sapore di sale" (Taste of Salt) was one of Italian singer Gino Paoli's greatest hits. In 1963, the song featured at the Cantagiro festival, and on that occasion Paoli made his first real impact on the listening public.

Paoli was inspired to write the song during a difficult moment in his personal life. A married man, he was in the throes of a passionate affair with actress Stefania Sandrelli. Expecting a baby, the lovers had flown to Sicily, and the song expresses Paoli's thoughts as he lay on the beach there, considering both the present and his past.

For once, Paoli's writing is neither melancholy nor overly serious. His song perfectly captures the lightness of summertime: the sun, sea, and days spent in love and lazing on the beach: "Taste of salt / Taste of sea / That you have on your skin / That you have on your lips / When you leave the water / And you come and lie down / Near to me." The song also refers to the salty or slightly bitter taste of lost things, of things left far away, "Where the world is different / Different from here." Nevertheless, the song is a fine evocation of the Italian enjoyment of summer's sensual pleasures.

Paradoxically, the great success of the song added to Paoli's personal distress, and later in 1963 he tried to commit suicide by shooting himself. The bullet is still wedged near his heart. **LSc**

Leader of the Pack
The Shangri-Las (1964)

Writer | Jeff Barry, Ellie Greenwich, George "Shadow" Morton
Producer | "Shadow" Morton
Label | Red Bird
Album | N/A

Les copains d'abord
Georges Brassens (1964)

Writer | Georges Brassens
Producer | Georges Meyerstein-Maigret
Label | Philips
Album | *Les copains d'abord* (1964)

Like the bad boy "from the wrong side of town" who wrecks his bike in the final verse, "Leader of the Pack" is shrouded in the fog of rock lore. In need of a follow-up to his and The Shangri-Las' first hit, "Remember (Walking in the Sand)" of 1964, producer George "Shadow" Morton allegedly found his inspiration when he ran into some leather-bound, gum-snapping chicks at a diner. His tragic tale of a lovelorn bobbysoxer who dumps her sensitive biker dude on her father's orders, hastening his death, was like Shakespeare, except these two meet in a candy store.

Morton wanted a local girl group called The Goodies to sing it. He has said that songwriting titans and label honchos Jerry Leiber and Mike Stoller initially rejected his song on account of its illicit teenage love affair and ultimate catastrophe. So he scooped up the budding Shangri-Las, snuck them into New York's Ultrasonic Studios, and cut the song on the sly. However, various Red Bird associates, including the legendary Ellie Greenwich, who is credited as a songwriter on "Leader," have disputed many or all of these details—not to mention the story that a real motorcycle was driven through a building to capture the song's iconic revving sounds. Whatever the case, "Leader of the Pack" shot to No. 1 on the back of its pulsing bass lines, conversational style, and Mary Weiss's mournful lead vocal. **MO**

Although he is surprisingly little known outside of France, Georges Brassens was an iconic figure at home, where he is still affectionately referred to as *tonton Georges* ("Uncle George") and *notre nounours national* ("our national teddy bear").

One of the greatest masters of classic French chanson, he wrote intimate and infectiously hummable melodies, but it was in his witty, erudite, and poetic words that his greatest appeal lay. Sadly, the fact that his lyrics are so difficult to translate means that only French speakers really "get" Brassens. Even the title of this song does not translate adequately as "Friends First," since it is a sly play on words that sounds like *copains de bord* ("shipmates"). This is the first of several nautical references, which include the Battle of Trafalgar and *The Raft of the Medusa*, Théodore Géricault's unforgettable painting. Then there is the Latin phrase *Fluctuat nec mergitur*, which means "beaten by the waves, but does not founder"—the motto of Paris, the city with which he was always associated, even though he was from the south of France and never lost his accent.

Brassens sang in a gentle, understated baritone and generally accompanied himself on acoustic guitar (though he was also a self-taught pianist), as he does on this, his most famous song. He wrote it for Yves Robert's film *Les copains* (1964), and it was also the title track of an album that year. **JLu**

Samba malato
Nicomedes Santa Cruz (1964)

Writer | Traditional, arr. Nicomedes Santa Cruz
Producer | Uncredited
Label | Philips
Album | *Cumanana* (1964)

Worldwide recognition of the treasures of Afro-Peruvian music didn't really arrive until the release of the compilation *The Soul of Black Peru* on David Byrne's Luaka Bop label in 1995.

Nearly four decades earlier, however, the musician, poet, and writer Nicomedes Santa Cruz had kick-started a revival of Afro-Peruvian music with a series of albums. Inspired by the work of his forebear Don Porforio Vasquez in the Forties, he began collecting, reconstructing, and interpreting this marginalized and nearly extinct musical culture, which he had heard performed by his grandparents and mother. The songs are rich in the languages and rhythms of Africa, brought by slaves to Peru centuries earlier.

His best-known version of "Samba malato" appears on the groundbreaking double LP *Cumanana* and is subtitled "Landó"—the name of the distinctively halting rhythm of the piece, used in a suggestive dance. The arrangement features acoustic guitar, heavy percussion (dominated by *cahón*, the quintessential Peruvian drum), and his earthy lead vocal, answered by the chorus. The minimal lyrics are a mixture of Spanish and creolized words from Kikôngo, a language still spoken in the region of Angola and the Congo. The lyrics of later versions by other Afro-Peruvian artists, such as Lucila Campos, Peru Negro, and Susana Baca, are more elaborate. **JLu**

Walk On By
Dionne Warwick (1964)

Writer | Burt Bacharach, Hal David
Producer | Burt Bacharach, Hal David
Label | Scepter
Album | *Make Way for Dionne Warwick* (1964)

The Sixties were a golden decade for Dionne Warwick and songwriters Burt Bacharach and Hal David. In ten years they had nineteen U.S. Top Forty records, with eight in the Top Ten. One of the most enduring of those hits is "Walk On By."

It almost didn't turn out that way. Originally "Walk On By" was released as the B-side to "Any Old Time of Day," a song that her label, manager, and Warwick herself believed would secure her a hit after a run of misses. But influential New York DJ Murray "the K" Kaufman felt that the B-side was the more likely hit and refused to play "Any Old Time of Day," plugging "Walk On By" instead.

His insistence paid off, with listeners buying "Walk On By" in their droves, making it a huge hit in the United States, while it also made the U.K. Top Ten. Since then, it has been covered by more than forty different artists, from Pucho & His Latin Soul Brothers to Cyndi Lauper.

The song was recorded in a three-hour studio session that also saw "Anyone Who Had a Heart"—which became Warwick's first U.S. Top Ten hit—committed to tape. Bacharach said: "'Walk On By' was the first time I tried putting two grand pianos on a record in the studio. . . . I knew the song had something." And Dionne Warwick's accomplished delivery hit all the right emotional notes; as she said, "I didn't get the guy very often in those days." **DC**

Dionne Warwick in 1964, the year in which, apparently, men were walking on by her. ➡

Don't Gimme No Lip Child
Dave Berry (1964)

Writer | Don Thomas, Jean Thomas, Barry Richards
Producer | Mike Smith
Label | Decca
Album | N/A

For live engagements, Sheffield-born singer (and ex-welder) Dave Berry—real name David Holgate Grundy—would appear clad in black with the collar of his leather jacket upturned, his hair dyed black; occasionally, he favored a cape and leather gloves. He also employed an unsettling stare and beguiling hand movements during appearances.

After a number of moderate successes with covers such as "Memphis, Tennessee" and Bacharach and David's "Baby It's You," his fourth single, "The Crying Game," reached No. 5 in the U.K. in July 1964. While the A-side was a doomy but saccharine ballad, its flip was anything but, an effervescent, swinging Sixties put-down of a song that makes its point in just over two minutes then flaunts out. Written by Don Thomas and his sister, Jean, a demure session vocalist who later appeared as a backing singer on records by Neil Diamond and Barbra Streisand, "Don't Gimme No Lip Child" is a thuggish slab of Brit-blues, distinguished by nasty-minded lyrics, shrill harmonica outbursts, and a stuttering guitar solo by Jimmy Page—then a twenty-year-old session player.

Its surliness struck a chord later with the punk bands, including the nascent Sex Pistols. Covered in early rehearsals alongside a stack of other Sixties garage and freakbeat gems brought in by bass player Glen Matlock, it first emerged on the soundtrack to *The Great Rock 'n' Roll Swindle*. **PL**

E se domani
Mina (1964)

Writer | Giorgio Calabrese, Carlo Alberto Rossi
Producer | Carlo Alberto Rossi
Label | Ri-Fi
Album | *Mina* (1964)

First presented to the public during the Sanremo Music Festival in 1964, sung by Fausto Cigliano and Gene Pitney, "E se domani" (And If Tomorrow) did not even reach the final. One of the song's authors, Carlo Alberto Rossi, then worked hard to convince Mina to sing it and to include it on her forthcoming album. Her first with Ri-Fi, it was entitled *Mina*, and, apart from "E se domani" and "Non illuderti," included only covers of American and Brazilian songs. "E se domani" turned out to be not only one of the best songs on the album but one of the top songs of Mina's career. *Mina* was voted by critics to be best album of 1964, and the singer won the Oscar del disco prize in the same year.

The lyrics of "E se domani" are brief and simple, and are still very well known in Italy today. A lover tries to paint a mental picture of what would happen if she couldn't see her loved one anymore: she would lose not only the man she loves but her whole world—"E se domani / e sottolineo se /all'improvviso / perdessi te / avrei perduto / il mondo intero / non solo te."

Unusually, and because of the great success that "E se domani" was enjoying, the song was recorded as the B-side of two different singles: "Un anno d'amore" in1964 and "Brava" in 1965. The former secured Mina's personal record in the hit parade, remaining at No. 1 in Italy for sixteen consecutive weeks. **LSc**

The Girl from Ipanema
Stan Getz & João Gilberto (1964)

Writer | Antônio Carlos Jobim, Norman Gimbel
Producer | Creed Taylor
Label | Verve
Album | *Getz/Gilberto* (1964)

The Brazilian music known as bossa nova—Portuguese for "new wave" or "new trend"—is rare in that it is largely the invention of one person: Antônio Carlos Jobim. Developed in Rio de Janeiro, bossa nova evolved from samba but was less percussive and harmonically more complex.

U.S. jazz musicians heading south for the sun appreciated its lilting rhythms and cool demeanor. One such, guitarist Charlie Byrd, introduced saxophonist Stan Getz to the music. In 1962, Byrd and Getz recorded an entire album of Brazilian music—*Jazz Samba*—that stayed on the *Billboard* charts for seventy weeks and gave birth to a single hit, Jobim's "Desafinado" (Out of Tune).

A year later, Getz repeated the trick, this time in partnership with the Brazilian guitarist João Gilberto, with Jobim on piano. On two tracks, Getz wanted the original Portuguese lyrics to be translated and sung in English; he asked Gilberto's wife, Astrud, to perform them. She was not a professional singer and had a tendency to sing flat, but she stepped up to the microphone. Her deadpan English, indeed sung slightly flat, was a perfect response to Getz's peerless saxophone.

The song made Astrud's reputation and confirmed Getz as the epitome of cool. Of this classic piece of bossa, the man known as "The Sound" remarked that he soon "got bored with it, but it paid for my kids to go through college." **SA**

A Change Is Gonna Come
Sam Cooke (1964)

Writer | Sam Cooke
Producer | Sam Cooke, Hugo Peretti, Luigi Creatore
Label | RCA
Album | *Ain't That Good News* (1964)

Sam Cooke first found success in the early Fifties, both with gospel group The Soul Stirrers and as a solo singer; "You Send Me" was a U.S. No. 1 in 1957, selling two million copies. He sang, wrote, and co-produced a series of hits including "Wonderful World" (1959), "Chain Gang" (1960), and "Cupid" (1961), and founded his own label, SAR Records.

But arguably Cooke's greatest accomplishment was "A Change Is Gonna Come," a song he claimed came to him in a dream. Cooke's biographer Peter Guralnick traces the inspirations for the song to three events: Cooke talking with student sit-in demonstrators in Durham, North Carolina, after playing a show in May 1963; his hearing Bob Dylan's "Blowin' in the Wind" and feeling that, if a white man was writing something with such a significant message, he should be, too; and the singer's arrest after he attempted to register at a segregated (whites only) Shreveport, Louisiana, Holiday Inn in October 1963. Furthermore, in the same year, Martin Luther King Jr. led the civil rights March on Washington for Jobs and Freedom and gave his famous "I Have a Dream" speech.

On December 21, 1963, at RCA Studios, Los Angeles, Cooke recorded this melancholy civil rights sermon. Singing with a depth of emotion rarely heard outside of the church, he cries: "It's been a long, a long time coming / But I know a change gonna come / Oh yes it will." **JoH**

Dancing in the Street
Martha & The Vandellas (1964)

Writer | William "Mickey" Stevenson, Marvin Gaye, Ivy Jo Hunter
Producer | "Mickey" Stevenson
Label | Gordy
Album | *Dance Party* (1965)

"Can't forget the Motor City," pleads Martha Reeves midway through "Dancing in the Street." As if anyone would. At the time of the record's release, Detroit label Motown was entering its creative and commercial peak. But the city was also in the spotlight during a period when relations between black and white communities across the nation were at their most volatile.

Although Motown's mainstream success helped bridge the cultural gap between white and black America, the gulf was still vast when, in July 1964, Lyndon B. Johnson signed into law the landmark Civil Rights Act, with the aim of eliminating U.S. racial discrimination. Within weeks, as if to show how tough a task this would be, riots broke out in Harlem and the town of Rochester, New York, both triggered by apparent brutality toward local African Americans by white police officers.

Released in the very same month, "Dancing in the Street" sounds like a veiled attempt to address these issues and inspire the black community to action, although Reeves has always held that it was not a call to arms but an invitation to party. Whatever its message, the single still thrills, from that blaring horn fanfare to Reeves's euphoric declaration that "all we need is music." Nearly fifty years after its release, no single better embodies Motown's electrifying aesthetic. "Are you ready for a brand-new beat?" asked Reeves. We were. **WF-J**

I Just Don't Know What to Do with Myself | Dusty Springfield (1964)

Writer | Burt Bacharach, Hal David
Producer | Johnny Franz
Label | Philips
Album | *A Girl Called Dusty* (1964)

Although it had previously been recorded by Tommy Hunt for his album of the same name two years earlier, it was Dusty Springfield who made "I Just Don't Know What to Do with Myself" her own.

The track—very much in the torch-song genre, at which Springfield was to excel—marked the first venture in what was to become a hugely successful relationship with the work of Burt Bacharach, who wrote many more hits for her, including "Wishin' and Hopin'" and "The Look of Love." It also gave listeners a glimpse of the emotional range of her soulful voice, a blend of breathy sensuality and raw passion and feeling that often led listeners to assume she was a black, American vocalist.

Springfield's effortless ability to encompass pop, ballads, country, soul, and more brought comparisons with Elvis, another white performer breaking down barriers, both in performance and society. In the United Kingdom, especially, she led the way for white singers to perform "black" material, opening doors for the likes of Lulu, Sandie Shaw, and Cilla Black, all of whom went on to record soul material. The song has also been recorded by a host of soul artists, including Isaac Hayes and Dionne Warwick. In 2003, The White Stripes famously released a version that recontextualized the song as a punk-rock ballad, with an accompanying video directed by Sofia Coppola and starring model Kate Moss. **CR**

Dusty Springfield on a rooftop in 1963, clearly not knowing what to do with herself. ➡

You've Lost That Lovin' Feeling | The Righteous Brothers (1964)

Writer | Phil Spector, Barry Mann, Cynthia Weil
Producer | Phil Spector
Label | Philles
Album | *You've Lost That Lovin' Feeling* (1965)

> *"This is Spector's greatest production, the last word in Tomorrow's sound Today."*
> **Andrew Loog Oldham, 1965**

◄ **Influenced by: Baby I Need Your Loving** · The Four Tops (1964)
► **Influence on: The Sun Ain't Gonna Shine Anymore** The Walker Brothers (1965)
● **Covered by:** Isaac Hayes (1970) · Tom Jones (1970) Erasure (2003)

The acme of blue-eyed soul, Bill Medley and Bobby Hatfield's finest four minutes was also Phil Spector's last as alpha male in American pop. His next teen symphony, Ike and Tina Turner's "River Deep, Mountain High," flopped in the United States and "the tycoon of teen" retired.

Determined to better anything he or any other producer had ever created, and inspired by the fact that The Beatles and Motown were demonstrating new ways to use the recording studio, Spector licensed The Righteous Brothers from the small Moonglow label after seeing them support The Ronettes. He then instructed the husband-and-wife writing team of Barry Mann and Cynthia Weil to come up with something for them.

Famously, the label stated that the song was five seconds over three minutes, shaving forty-five seconds from the truth, to fool radio stations reluctant to play lengthy songs. However, first-time listeners are more shocked by the opening seconds, when Medley's deep voice seems to slow as it drags its way through "You never close your eyes anymore when I kiss your lips." When Mann heard it, he complained that the song must be playing at 33 rpm.

After that, the song provides hook after hook, introducing a "wall of sound" that arrives, along with Hatfield's harmony, for the first chorus, then disappears for the second verse. From the third verse, when the soaring baritone is on his knees and the tenor is reminding his lover what she used to do, the listener is sucked into the crescendo.

With more than eight million spins, this is the most-played song in the history of American radio. And even if you heard every one, you would never get bored with it. **DH**

You Really Got Me | The Kinks (1964)

Writer | Ray Davies
Producer | Shel Talmy
Label | Pye
Album | *Kinks* (1964)

" 'You Really Got Me' was the ultimate sort of blues riff. I didn't know I was doing it."

Ray Davies, 1984

◄ **Influenced by: Louie Louie** • The Kingsmen (1963)
► **Influence on: I Can't Explain** • The Who (1965)
● **Covered by:** Robert Palmer (1978) • Van Halen (1978)
The 13th Floor Elevators (1978) • Sly and The Family
Stone (1983) • Iggy Pop (1995) • Small Faces (1996)
The Patron Saints (2005)

When R&B beat group The Kinks, from Muswell Hill, north London, entered IBC Studios in Portland Place in July 1964 to record their third single, "You Really Got Me," they were under pressure for a hit after their two previous releases had failed to sell. Both their debut cover of Little Richard's "Long Tall Sally" and singer/rhythm-guitarist Ray Davies's own "You Still Want Me" were competent Merseybeat, but there was little to suggest that here was a band that would revolutionize popular music. Yet that is exactly what happened with "You Really Got Me," after an initial slower version was scrapped at the band's instigation because it lacked grit. The re-recorded song's power-chord, fuzz-guitar riff laid the foundations for heavy rock and the career of The Who, with Pete Townshend openly admitting the song's influence on The Who's inaugural hit, "I Can't Explain," while Ray's lyrical directness and the record's aggressive, driving sound projected a proto-punk attitude.

In the studio, producer Shel Talmy replaced The Kinks' drummer, Mick Avory, with session man Bobby Graham, but, contrary to rumor, it is not Jimmy Page but lead guitarist and Ray's brother, Dave Davies, who plays the riff and primitive "rave up" solo. Dave achieved the sound he wanted from his Epiphone on the track by slicing the speaker cone of his small 4-watt amplifier with a razor blade, patching it with Sellotape, putting pins in it, turning it on full volume, and then feeding the sound through a 30-watt amp on low volume, resulting in the desired distortion.

Released on August 3, "You Really Got Me" turned out to be The Kinks' breakthrough hit, topping the U.K. chart and giving the group a U.S. No. 7 placing. **JoH**

The House of the Rising Sun | The Animals (1964)

Writer | Traditional (credited arranger: Alan Price)
Producer | Mickie Most
Label | Columbia
Album | N/A

> *"On that session we started at 8 a.m. and by 8:15 we had done 'House of the Rising Sun.' … So we made an album."*

Mickie Most, producer, 1981

◄ **Influenced by: Honey Hush** • Big Joe Turner (1953)
► **Influence on: Delta Lady** • Joe Cocker (1969)
● **Covered by:** The Supremes (1964) • Frijid Pink (1969)
Tim Hardin (1969) • Santa Esmeralda (1977)
Tracy Chapman (1990) • Sinéad O'Connor (1994)
The Walkabouts (1996) • Muse (2002)

Pop svengali Mickie Most had the casting vote when it came to selecting the recording that would be the follow-up to The Animals' debut hit, "Baby Let Me Take You Home." The record company was unimpressed with the overlong slow blues of "The House of the Rising Sun," but Most's judgment proved to be sound, as the single would go on to top the charts on both sides of the Atlantic.

Both of the first two singles produced by The Animals had connections to Bob Dylan, who had written and recorded "Baby, Let Me Follow You Down" (aka "Baby Can I Take You Home") and covered the centuries-old traditional American folk song "The House of the Rising Sun" on his debut album. But it was bluesman Josh White's recording of 1937 that sparked Alan Price's keyboard arrangement, and blues-obsessive Eric Burdon's growling vocals that made The Animals' version of the song so striking. This was a reversal of the "taking coals to Newcastle" adage, one might say, as The Animals—from Britain's industrial northeast—were sending back to the United States an ancient American tale about a New Orleans house of ill repute. Yet the song reached the top of the U.S. charts just two months after hitting No. 1 in The Animals' homeland.

Perhaps surprisingly, this landmark release—a key element in the British pop invasion of America—required no painstaking or lengthy recording sessions. "The House of the Rising Sun" was recorded in a London studio early one Sunday morning in just two takes. So quickly did the group nail the track that producer Mickie Most hurriedly squeezed an entire album of recordings out of the remaining session time. He noted: "We completed an album for £24, which was a good deal." **DR**

Eric Burdon (left) and Chas Chandler of The Animals demonstrate that "traditional" needn't mean dull.

Go 'Way from My Window
John Jacob Niles (1964)

Writer | John Jacob Niles
Producer | Moses Asch
Label | Smithsonian Folkways
Album | *John Jacob Niles Sings Folk Songs* (1964)

The city of Louisville has a reputation for producing dark, brooding music. Today, its stars include Will Oldham and Slint, but arguably the spookiest sounds to emerge from Louisville came from the Forties murder balladeer John Jacob Niles.

Niles appears in Martin Scorsese's Bob Dylan documentary, *No Direction Home*, where crackly, vintage television footage shows a white-haired, spindly old man singing in a falsetto voice and gesticulating wildly. Sonically and visually, the term "otherworldly" could have been invented for Niles; his shrill, clear voice is neither masculine nor feminine, and he sings as if thoroughly possessed by the song, his black eyes darting about as he strums at an Appalachian dulcimer.

As Niles later recalled, "In 1908, my father had in his employ a Negro ditch-digger known as Objerall Jacket. As he dug, he sang, 'Go 'way from my window, go 'way from my door.' Just those words, over and over again, on two notes. Working beside Jacket all day, I decided that something had to be done. The results were a four-verse song dedicated to a blue-eyes, blond girl, who didn't think much of my efforts. The song lay fallow from 1908 to 1929, when I arranged it and transposed to a higher key."

With covers including a version by Marlene Dietrich and its title kicking off Bob Dylan's "It Ain't Me Babe," "Go 'Way from My Window" is a landmark twentieth-century folk song. **SH**

Amsterdam
Jacques Brel (1964)

Writer | Jacques Brel
Producer | Uncredited
Label | Barclay
Album | *Enregistrement public à l'Olympia* (1964)

On October 16, 1964, almost three years to the day after recording his first live album at the Olympia in Paris, Jacques Brel returned to the scene for two nights that would also be released as an in-concert LP. "Amsterdam," the opening track, was a new song that would never be recorded in a studio, and it became one of Brel's most significant songs.

For most of its four verses, the singer is an observer in the dockside bars, where sailors drink heavily, eat unpalatable pieces of fish, lust over whores who give their virtue for a piece of gold, and dance to the sound of a rancid accordion. He paints a distasteful picture of human merriment, acknowledging silently that most men wish, deep down, for this paradoxically enticing life. In the last couplet, however, the observer stumbles: "Et ils pissent comme je pleure / Sur les femmes infidèles." Or, as Scott Walker bravely sang in 1967: "And he pisses as I cry / For an unfaithful love."

At forty-five years' remove, with Brel dead more than three decades and a cult figure outside France, it is difficult to grasp how powerful his performance was. Fortunately, a 1966 concert recorded for television offers some insight into the impact of Brel live. The last verse of "Amsterdam" is transformed into a violent, heaving scream, as dynamic as the shower sequence in *Psycho*. At the climax, when Brel turns his back on the spotlight, it is as if he has dropped through a trapdoor. **DH**

Jacques Brel delivers a mesmerizing performance at the Théâtre d'Aubervilliers, Paris, in 1967. ➲

La paloma
Caterina Valente (1965)

Writer | Sebastián de Iradier
Producer | Uncredited
Label | Decca
Album | *Caterina Valente's Greatest Hits* (1965)

"La paloma" (The Dove) is almost certainly the most widely performed and recorded song ever. According to the avant-garde musician Kalle Laar, who produced a six-CD compilation of versions from all over the world for the German label Trikont, there are over 2,000 known recordings.

The version by Italian-born singer Caterina Valente is a lush, easy-listening period piece. Werner Miller's orchestra backs Valente's sultry Spanish vocal with flourishes of harp, a bold brass section, and suitably generic Latin percussion. Elvis recorded an English adaptation retitled as "No More" for his best-selling *Blue Hawaii* album of 1961, but there are hundreds of instrumental takes as well, both by well-known and obscure artists.

Wrongly considered "traditional," "La paloma" was written in the early 1860s by the Basque composer Sebastián de Iradier, after visiting Cuba. He used the distinctively lurching Cuban *habanera* rhythm that would soon become a building block of Argentinean tango. Iradier's other most famous song, "El Areglito," is also a *habanera*; its melody was stolen by Bizet for the song "L'amour est un oiseau rebelle" in his opera *Carmen*.

The earliest known recording of "La paloma" (an instrumental) dates from between 1883 and 1890 and is kept in Havana's Museum of Music. The song has featured in many movies and is the subject of a book and a film devoted entirely to it. **JLu**

Sinnerman
Nina Simone (1965)

Writer | Traditional
Producer | Hal Mooney
Label | Philips
Album | *Pastel Blues* (1965)

In the early Sixties, Nina Simone established the gospel standard "Sinnerman" as a trademark part of her repertoire, using it as a hard-hitting finale to her live shows in New York. It wasn't until after her move from Colpix to Philips in 1964, however, that it was released—the live recording made in Greenwich Village was a glaring omission from the album *Nina at the Village Gate* (1962).

The move to Philips coincided with Simone's increasing involvement with the civil-rights movement. Her first album with the label, *Nina Simone in Concert* of 1964, included "Mississippi Goddam" and "Old Jim Crow," and the civil-rights message continued into the *Pastel Blues* album the following year. The studio recording of "Sinnerman" fit well into this album, alongside covers of the Bessie Smith classic "Nobody Knows You When You're Down and Out" and Billie Holiday's "Strange Fruit," providing an upbeat final track (as it had in her live shows) but maintaining the civil-rights theme with its shouts of "Power!"

Simone probably knew "Sinnerman" from her childhood, hearing it at church meetings led by her mother, a Methodist minister. The song is a traditional spiritual, and appeared in many versions before Simone adopted it, but was made famous by The Weavers in 1959. The recording on *Pastel Blues*, more than ten minutes long, is considered Simone's definitive version. **MW**

The Irish Rover | The Clancy Brothers & Tommy Makem (1965)

Writer | Arr. The Clancy Brothers & Tommy Makem
Producer | Tom Wilson
Label | CBS
Album | N/A

Released as the B-side of "The Rising of the Moon," "The Irish Rover" is one of the best-loved songs by The Clancy Brothers & Tommy Makem. Influenced by American folk revivalists such as The Kingston Trio and The Weavers, the group almost single-handedly sparked the Sixties Irish-ballad revival.

Although the song's roots are disputed, "The Irish Rover" is thought to be a nineteenth-century sea shanty, and is performed as a rollicking barn dance. In keeping with the group's penchant for humor, it is a comical account of a mythical ship that sets sail from the "Cobh [cove] of Cork" with "a cargo of bricks / For the grand City Hall of New York" . . . only to be wrecked. Namesakes of the song include innumerable pubs, restaurants, and boats—even a Catholic student newspaper and a football club. And in 1963, a Canadian band called The Irish Rovers was founded by newly arrived immigrants from Northern Ireland. Incredibly, they're still touring, so have outlived their icons; Liam Clancy passed away in December 2009, the last of this group to do so.

"The Irish Rover" was covered in 1987 by The Pogues and The Dubliners, who were brought together at the suggestion of Dave Robinson (Stiff Records founder) and producer Eamonn Campbell. The single reached No. 8 in the U.K. pop charts, and introduced The Dubliners to a whole new generation of fans. **JLu**

Needle of Death
Bert Jansch (1965)

Writer | Bert Jansch
Producer | Bill Leader
Label | Transatlantic
Album | *Bert Jansch* (1965)

Like many Sixties Brit-folk albums, Bert Jansch's debut is crammed with rewrites of old standards, but nestled among them is this haunting story of addiction and loss. Initially believed by many listeners to be a drug-related self-portrait—Jansch certainly looks bedraggled and bohemian on the LP cover—"Needle of Death" was actually written as an elegy for guitarist David "Buck" Polly, who overdosed on heroin and cocaine in June 1964.

Later anthems, such as The Heartbreakers' "Chinese Rocks" and The Velvet Underground's "Heroin," would paint the life of a junkie as an act of counter-cultural defiance. But Jansch sees Polly's decision to turn to grains of "pure white snow / Dissolved in blood" as a way of escaping a "troubled young life." And, while other opiate-infused songs are often self-focused, detailing the singer's own drug battles, Jansch records the impact of Polly's addiction and death on those closest to him. Over a gentle fingerpicked melody, Jansch sings, "How tears have filled the eyes / Of friends that you once had walked among."

The song hit home with another folk legend, Neil Young, who was inspired to write "Needle and the Damage Done" for 1972's *Harvest* album. During an interview for Jimmy McDonough's 2002 biography, *Shakey*, Young also expressed remorse that he had lifted Jansch's melody almost note for note for his 1974 song "Ambulance Blues." **TB**

Papa's Got a Brand New Bag

James Brown (1965)

Writer | James Brown
Producer | James Brown
Label | King
Album | N/A

By 1965, James Brown was a man ready to make big changes. Having established himself as a supreme writer and performer of doo-wop, soul, and R&B, Brown was striving toward a harder, heavier sound. Due to complicated recording deals with King and Smash Records, "Papa's Got a Brand New Bag" (released as two parts split over both sides of a single) came about as a reworked version of a previous recording, "Out of Sight." This led to King's renegotiating their recording and publishing deals with Brown, whereby he received increased royalties and complete creative control.

The song is regarded as the first example of the sound that made Brown the originator of funk. Whereas "Out of Sight" emphasized the second and fourth beats of a bar, the new version was built around the "downbeat," on the first and third. The trademark horn-rhythm-and-guitar hook provides a rousing backdrop to a tale of an older man unafraid to make new moves on the dance floor. The session featured brothers Maceo and Melvin Parker (saxophone and drums, respectively), who became key contributors to the future James Brown heavy-funk sound.

As critic Dave Marsh wrote, "The only way 'Papa's Got a Brand New Bag' could be more bone-rattling would be if James Brown himself leaped from your speakers, grabbed you tight by the shoulders, and danced you around the room." **CR**

La bohème

Charles Aznavour (1965)

Writer | Charles Aznavour, Jacques Plante
Producer | Uncredited
Label | Barclay
Album | La bohème (1965)

Heralded today as the "Frank Sinatra of France," Charles Aznavour certainly paid his dues. After breaking into showbiz in the Thirties, making his stage debut at nine years old, the Armenian–French *chansonnier* spent the next twenty-five years scuffling, even going so far as to take a job as Edith Piaf's chauffeur. His fortunes changed in the late Fifties, when he landed a recording contract and made the first of many film appearances.

In 1965, he recorded the French tune that would cement his status as one of the century's most brilliant singers: "La bohème." The gorgeous piano ballad was sung from the perspective of a man looking back upon a lost love—with a tear in the eye, a glass of Bordeaux in one hand, and a lit cigarette in the other. Aznavour reminisces about an idyllic bohemian existence: sharing a love nest near Montmartre, painting nude portraits, and not worrying about when the next meal might come. ("My songs have to be listened to," he said in 2001, "everything is in the words.")

His rough singing voice—which Aznavour himself dubbed "strange"—worked to advantage here, making his delivery believable in a way that could never have happened with a classically trained "divo" (see Josh Groban's 2008 version for proof). Aznavour recorded dozens of great tunes, including "She" and "The Old Fashioned Way," but none did more to establish him than this one. **JiH**

Charles Aznavour with the tools of his songwriting trade in 1965. ➜

California Dreamin' | The Mamas & The Papas (1965)

Writer | John Phillips, Michelle Phillips
Producer | Lou Adler
Label | Dunhill
Album | *If You Can Believe Your Eyes and Ears* (1966)

"I couldn't believe anything that good had just walked in off the street."

Lou Adler, 1966

◀ **Influenced by:** Mr. Tambourine Man • The Byrds (1965)
▶ **Influence on:** Sunday Will Never Be the Same • Spanky and Our Gang (1967)
● **Covered by:** The Seekers (1966) • Bobby Womack (1968) The Four Tops (1969) • M.I.A. (1985) The Beach Boys (1986)

John Phillips was more than a decade older than most of his mid-Sixties folk-rock contemporaries, but experience had honed his songwriting and taught him what might grab the public's attention. Phillips formed a hippie folk-pop band around his beautiful young wife, Michelle, the huge-of-voice-and-girth Cass Elliot, and handsome, golden-throated Denny Doherty, and soon had them working New York's Greenwich Village folk scene.

Realizing their contemporaries were finding fame in L.A., the group—named after a Hell's Angels slang term for men and women—headed west. Folk-pop star Barry McGuire introduced them to his producer, Lou Adler, whose initial remark (upon seeing Michelle) was, "Who's the blonde?" Initially, and with reluctance, Adler hired them to sing backing vocals for McGuire, but after hearing the band's original songs he immediately signed them.

John had written "California Dreamin'" in New York after Michelle complained that she hated the cold and missed California (she helped with the lyrics). Recognizing its potential, Adler hired top session players Glen Campbell, Hal Blaine, Joe Osborn, and Larry Knechtel to provide backing. Jazz veteran Bud Shank added wistful flute.

The song celebrated California as a golden paradise, yet its delivery is tense and tinged with unease. "I'd be safe and warm if I was in L.A." the honeyed harmonies chime, but the minor-key melancholy of the piece belies that sentiment. The song immediately established the group internationally, has been covered many times, and regularly appears in films and on TV. Yet less than a decade after the band had formed, Cass Elliot was dead and both John Phillips and Doherty were drug-addled ruins. **GC**

Ticket to Ride | The Beatles (1965)

Writer | John Lennon, Paul McCartney
Producer | George Martin
Label | Parlophone
Album | *Help!* (1965)

"It was George Harrison who influenced me to get a Rickenbacker. 'Ticket to Ride'— what a brilliant song!"

Johnny Marr, 1990

◀ **Influenced by: When You Walk in the Room**
   The Searchers (1964)
▶ **Influence on: Tomorrow Never Knows**
   The Beatles (1966)
● **Covered by:** The 5th Dimension (1967)
   The Carpenters (1969) • The Punkles (1998)

Beatles records were always hits—and big ones—but the commercial success of this most commercial of bands (and their subsequent hagiography) makes it easy to overlook the genuine innovation that underpins their continued appeal.

Exhibit A: "Ticket to Ride." A transatlantic No. 1, naturally, but only for one week Stateside. In truth, the song is not natural A-side material. It's slow paced (and also longer than any previous Beatles track), the drum part is awkwardly start-stop, and the opening hangs grimly on to one key for ten whole bars, including the intro, before shifting. Moreover, the lyrics are resolutely melancholy.

In short, "Ticket to Ride" represents a shift away from pure pop and into less charted, more interesting territory. Key influences here include Tamla Motown (using opening bars as a one-key drone had featured in Motown hits such as Martha & The Vandellas' "Dancing in the Street") and the bright guitar sound of fellow Merseysiders The Searchers. (George Harrison plays his 12-string Rickenbacker here for the last time on a Beatles track.) Sonically, the track is several steps on from previous releases, being clangorous and trebly, and—with the lop-sided drum part—never seems to settle. The booming drums anticipate Ringo Starr's exemplary playing in 1966 on "Tomorrow Never Knows" (both drum parts were suggested by Paul McCartney) and "Rain." This, plus the high bass line and prominent guitars, is perhaps one reason why Lennon later referred to "Ticket to Ride" as "one of the earliest heavy metal records made."

Appropriately enough, it was covered two years later by proto-metallists Vanilla Fudge. By then, though, the seeds planted in "Ticket to Ride" were full-bloom psychedelia. **RD**

(I Can't Get No) Satisfaction | The Rolling Stones (1965)

Writer | Mick Jagger, Keith Richards
Producer | Andrew Loog Oldham
Label | Decca
Album | N/A

SATISFACTION
OFF THE HOOK
LITTLE RED ROOSTER
THE UNDER ASSISTANT
WEST COAST
PROMOTION MAN

"I'm the guy that wrote 'Satisfaction' in my sleep."

Keith Richards, 2003

◄ **Influenced by: Dancing in the Street** • Martha & The Vandellas (1964)
► **Influence on: Sunshine of Your Love** • Cream (1967)
 Covered by: Sandie Shaw (1968) • The Troggs (1975)
● Devo (1977) • Tom Jones (1996) • Cat Power (2000)
 Britney Spears (2000)

Keith Richards has long been known for letting songs come to him rather than sitting down and diligently forcing them out. Yet even by his standards, the success of "(I Can't Get No) Satisfaction" in 1965 was indeed an instance of divine intoxication.

One night in the spring of 1965, while the Stones were on tour in the United States, Richards was passed out in a Florida motel. Suddenly, he awoke and recorded the most famous rock riff ever and the words "I can't get no satisfaction" into the tape recorder he carried around with him. Then he fell back to sleep. The tape was "two minutes of 'Satisfaction' and forty minutes of me snoring," he later mused.

A few weeks later, in May, the Stones were in RCA Studios, in Hollywood, to record a preliminary version of the track (which would later appear on the U.S. LP *Out of Our Heads*, though not the U.K. version). Mick Jagger, splitting the idea of "satisfaction" into distinct spiritual and sexual halves, had written lyrics about the rampant American commercialism that at once fascinated and repelled him—not only was the man on the TV trying to sell him crap he didn't want, but it wasn't helping him get laid either.

Richards envisioned a horn section in place of the three-note guitar riff on which the song was built. To beef up his guitar sound for the time being, he used a Gibson Maestro Fuzzbox, which lent the riff—and the band—its signature dirty, dangerous feel. Richards never got the chance to bring in the horns. "Suddenly," he'd later recall, "I was hearing it on the radio on every station and I thought, 'I'm not going to complain,' although I never considered it to be the finished article." **MO**

Satisfaction proves elusive for The Rolling Stones during a TV rehearsal in 1964. ➲

The Tracks of My Tears
The Miracles (1965)

Writer | Smokey Robinson, Warren Moore, Marvin Tarplin
Producer | Smokey Robinson
Label | Tamla
Album | *Going to a Go-Go* (1965)

Mr. Tambourine Man
The Byrds (1965)

Writer | Bob Dylan
Producer | Terry Melcher
Label | Columbia
Album | *Mr. Tambourine Man* (1965)

With his band The Miracles, the Motown maestro Smokey Robinson had been hitting the U.S. charts since 1960. He inspired Dylan, The Beatles, and the Stones and—like those acts—chose 1965 to unleash one of his greatest albums. *Going to a Go-Go*, laden with treats such as the title track and "A Fork in the Road," opened with this classic.

"The Tracks of My Tears" originated in a melody by guitarist Marvin Tarplin, co-credited with Robinson and their fellow Miracle, Warren Moore. Smokey wrote the eloquent lyrics—whose use of "substitute" inspired Pete Townshend to write The Who's song of that name. But Smokey's dramatic production distinguishes the song from its R&B/doo-wop lineage, with the drums and horns adding an urgency more often associated with the output of Motown's rival label, Stax.

At the outset of their partnership, Motown's chief, Berry Gordy, told Smokey, "Every song should have an idea, tell a story, mean something." It is a measure of Robinson's triumph that even the notoriously hard-to-please Gordy pronounced the track a masterpiece. Though the song rose to only No. 16 in the United States, myriad covers—notably by Aretha Franklin in 1969 and Linda Ronstadt in 1975—testify to the work's enduring appeal. It also enjoyed a silver-screen-sponsored resurgence in the Eighties, thanks to its inclusion in *The Big Chill* and *Platoon*. **BM**

Los Angeles quintet The Byrds' debut hit, "Mr. Tambourine Man," was released in the United States on April 12, 1965; by June 26, it had reached No. 1 in the *Billboard* chart. The song was picked for the band by their manager, Jim Dickson, after he heard its author, Bob Dylan, sing it at the 1964 Monterey Folk Festival, and requested a demo from Dylan's publisher. The meandering tune that arrived, featuring Dylan and Ramblin' Jack Elliott on harmony, failed to impress Dickson's protégés (still known as The Jet Set until November 1964), even after Dickson urged them to radically edit the verses and add a beat-group rhythm. They were finally sold on it when Dylan visited them and, hearing their version, exclaimed: "Wow, man! You can dance to that!"

Only one Byrd played on the single: Jim (later Roger) McGuinn with his Rickenbacker 360 12-string guitar; he also sang, in a style he later described as "halfway between Dylan and Lennon." Backing on the twenty-two takes recorded was provided by session musicians The Wrecking Crew, with drummer Hal Blaine and bassist Larry Knechtel featuring prominently. The ot-her Byrds were not trusted to play, but Gene Clark and David Crosby added exquisite vocal harmonies. The single gave Dylan his first international No. 1 as a composer, encouraging him to go electric, and established The Byrds as folk-rock pioneers. **JoH**

The Byrds walk by Radio City in rainy New York, far from their native California. ➜

Like a Rolling Stone | Bob Dylan (1965)

Writer | Bob Dylan
Producer | Tom Wilson
Label | Columbia
Album | *Highway 61 Revisited* (1965)

" 'Rolling Stone' is the best song I wrote."

Bob Dylan, 1965

◀ **Influenced by: Lost Highway** · Hank Williams (1949)
▶ **Influence on: Hey Jude** · The Beatles (1968)
● **Covered by:** The Turtles (1965) • Cher (1966)
The Jimi Hendrix Experience (1970) • Spirit (1975)
Mick Ronson (1994) • The Rolling Stones (1995)
Nancy Sinatra (1999) • Green Day (2009)

Picking Bob Dylan's best song might be as futile an exercise as selecting Van Gogh's best painting, but most Dylan fans have done it—and "Like a Rolling Stone" is the one they usually choose.

Hypnotic, poetic, acerbic, but with a wicked groove and spit-along chorus, ". . . Rolling Stone" didn't quite come out of nowhere. The 1965 album *Bringing It All Back Home* had signaled Dylan's departure from the leg irons of folk and protest—but that opening snare-drum crack (which Bruce Springsteen later said "sounded like somebody'd kicked open the door to your mind") still got people listening. The title came from Hank Williams and the whirligig gospel organ from Al Kooper, who joined the session almost by default but ended up supplying the cornerstone riff. Dylan, in full sneer, targets a woman, a socialite, who has fallen on hard times. Some believe it's Edie Sedgwick, a prototype 'It Girl' and Warhol muse; others say it is Dylan himself. It doesn't really matter: this is simply powerful writing.

"How does it feel?" Dylan demands, as the lyrics, cut from a short story, become increasingly figurative ("You used to ride on the chrome horse with your diplomat / Who carried on his shoulder a Siamese cat") and the song keeps forgetting to end. It ultimately clocks in at six minutes—unprecedented for a single—yet reached No. 2 in the United States, giving artists the confidence to break radio time limits. It has been covered numerous times, by everybody from Bob Marley to Michael Bolton, but the best alternative version is one of Dylan's own, a vivid, live jive recorded on the fractious U.K. tour of 1966. It appears on *The Bootleg Series: Vol. 4* and is preceded by Dylan's command to "Play it fucking loud." **PW**

Bob Dylan's first Stratocaster outing horrified many fans at the Newport Folk Festival in 1965. ➜

People Get Ready
The Impressions (1965)

Writer | Curtis Mayfield
Producer | Johnny Pate
Label | ABC-Paramount
Album | *People Get Ready* (1965)

Chicago-based vocal group The Impressions, led by Jerry Butler, had their first hit in 1958 with Butler's "For Your Precious Love." When he departed for a solo career, Curtis Mayfield took over the lead, and by 1963 their lineup had settled as a soul trio, Curtis Mayfield's high tenor accompanied by Fred Cash singing tenor and Sam Gooden's bass.

In 1964, Mayfield penned the gospel-infused, civil-rights anthem "Keep on Pushing," which reached the U.S. *Billboard* pop Top Ten. The following year, they hit *Billboard* R&B No. 3 and pop No. 14 with "People Get Ready." A contemplative, uplifting song, it once more combined Mayfield's religious conviction and schooling in gospel music with a subtle message of racial unity and black empowerment. Utilizing a train motif common to gospel spirituals, such as The Fisk Jubilee Singers' "The Gospel Train," Mayfield sings that "faith is the key" and of "hope for all." As Mayfield trades lines with Fred Cash on the gospel call and response, Sam Gooden provides backing harmony over understated strings and brass arranged by Johnny Pate and guitar embellishment from Mayfield. The only person for whom there is no room on the train is "the hopeless sinner who would hurt all mankind just to save his own."

The message wasn't lost on Bob Marley: The Wailers learned much from The Impressions, and Marley's "One Love" references the tune. **JoH**

Who Do You Love
The Preachers (1965)

Writer | Bo Diddley
Producer | Ray Maxwell
Label | Moonglow
Album | N/A

With their matching dog collars and shoulder-length hair, The Preachers from Hermosa Beach must have looked pretty far out, even for 1965. Over the course of their three singles, the quintet channeled snotty pre-punk energy into enduring songs with nose-thumbing titles such as "Stay Out of My World." Their first release, however, was a cover of Bo Diddley's rock 'n' roll classic "Who Do You Love." The single stole from the British Invasion's take on old American blues and R&B and turned up the volume and energy to almost parodic levels. Jettisoning the (very little) subtlety and nuance of Diddley's original, The Preachers produced harmonies that sounded like they were clearing their throats, a surf-guitar break, and an effect as though keyboard player Rudy Garza was bashing his instrument while wearing boxing gloves. A slot on the TV show *Shivaree* saw the band leering at the camera and headbanging like stalwart devotees of Kink Dave Davies.

Singer Richard Fortunato was soon fired by their label, Moonglow, for his over-the-top vocal style, but "Who Do You Love" became a garage-band staple, covered by back-to-basics groups across America—notably, Michigan's Woolies in 1966. The Doors stretched the song into a six-minutes-plus workout on 1970's *Absolutely Live* concert LP, featuring some dizzying slide guitar, but no one did it with as much vim as The Preachers. **PL**

The Carnival Is Over
The Seekers (1965)

Writer | Tom Springfield
Producer | Uncredited
Label | Columbia
Album | N/A

With a Peter, Paul & Mary–esque brand of folk-inflected pop music couched in full, close-blend harmonies, The Seekers scored a string of hits in the early Sixties, including "I'll Never Find Another You," "Morningtown Ride," and the chirpy "Georgy Girl." In the process, they became the first Australian group to enjoy such success abroad. None of those hits, however, had the quiet majesty of "The Carnival Is Over."

The song's melody derives from an old Russian folk song, though composer Tom Springfield probably knew it from Pete Seeger's version of 1953, "River of My People." Judith Durham delivers this lament for a lost love in a characteristically clear, full-hearted vocal, the plaintive melody neatly complementing the pathos of the lyrics. Stately strings rise up during the middle eight, expanding the sound without compromising the power of Durham's controlled lead or the block harmonies behind her. A moving all-round performance, "The Carnival Is Over" sold more than 90,000 copies a day at its peak and gave The Seekers their second and final U.K. No. 1.

In 1986, Nick Cave & The Bad Seeds delivered surely the most unexpected take on "Carnival" for their *Kicking Against the Pricks* covers set. It is an arresting, atmospheric reading, getting to the dark heart of melancholy in the song and awakening new resonance in this Sixties staple. **RD**

Psycho
The Sonics (1965)

Writer | Jerry Roslie
Producer | Buck Ormsby, Kent Morrill
Label | Etiquette
Album | *Here Are The Sonics* (1965)

Long before grunge, the U.S. Pacific Northwest had a reputation for creating blue-collar rock 'n' roll at its most gloriously elemental, away from the glitz of music-business hubs such as Los Angeles and New York. Unlike some of their peers, the bands here were geographically isolated enough to forge their own sound—plus, without ready access to big studios, they had to create a D.I.Y. ethic that was a forerunner of the later punk scene.

Alongside groups such as Seattle's Kingsmen, The Sonics were a group of five teenagers from drizzly Tacoma, Washington, who had a freak local hit when their debut single, "The Witch," was picked up by a local DJ. Swiftly realizing that they weren't earning any royalties from the record's B-side—a frantic cover of Little Richard's "Keep a Knockin'"—the band resolved to write a new composition of their own after one of their regular Saturday-night gigs at local nightclub The Red Carpet. "When we got done playing at about one o'clock in the morning we sat down and wrote and rehearsed 'Psycho.' It took about fifteen minutes," recalled singer and keyboardist Jerry Roslie.

The result was eventually released as a single in its own right and remains a needle-in-the-red, raw-throated shot of rock 'n' roll that's still thrilling decades later: indeed, when The Sonics re-formed at the start of the twenty-first century, they were able to play to packed halls worldwide. **PL**

I've Been Loving You Too Long (to Stop Now) | Otis Redding (1965)

Writer | Otis Redding, Jerry Butler
Producer | Otis Redding, Jerry Butler
Label | Volt
Album | *Otis Blue: Otis Redding Sings Soul* (1965)

Otis Redding began his career in the early Sixties as an R&B bawler in the Little Richard mold. But he defined himself and the burgeoning Stax sound a few years later in the wake of the death of his idol, Sam Cooke, from whom he inherited the mantle of Soul Brother No. 1. For his album *Otis Blue* of 1965, Redding made a play for the mainstream by balancing Richard's sexual bark and Cooke's elegant tenor. The record's centerpiece was the slow-burning plea "I've Been Loving You Too Long."

Only a few months after Cooke was fatally shot by a motel keeper in Los Angeles, Redding brought his composition to the legendary house band (none other than Booker T. & The MG's) at Stax Records. Like Cooke's "A Change Is Gonna Come," Otis's ballad is anchored by an insistent vocal lead that climbs to emotional peaks and settles down into a confessional lament. He begins the song with the title itself—a cry for his departed hero as much as for any unnamed lover.

In part thanks to The Rolling Stones, who included a cover of "I've Been Loving You Too Long" on their first live album, Redding enjoyed breakout success with his ballad. In 1967, he wowed the unwashed masses at the Monterey Pop Festival with it, securing crossover success. But on December 10 of that year, he joined Cooke in the hereafter when his tour plane plunged into an icy Wisconsin lake. **MO**

Stop! In the Name of Love | The Supremes (1965)

Writer | B. & E. Holland, L. Dozier
Producer | B. Holland, L. Dozier
Label | Motown
Album | *More Hits by The Supremes* (1965)

"Stop! In the Name of Love" garnered The Supremes their fourth U.S. pop No. 1 and became the group's in-concert showstopper. By 1965, the trio were Motown's hottest artists, and Berry Gordy was intent on establishing them as superstars. Partly, this was purely commercial—The Supremes possessed a finesse that made them more appealing to the masses than any other black-American outfit of the time. And partly it was emotional—Gordy having become enamored with Diana Ross.

Conceived by Lamont Dozier after he blurted out "Stop! In the name of love" during an argument with his girlfriend, the song took dramatic shape when Brian Holland developed it into a piano-driven, reflective ballad. Gordy recognized the song's quality but, noting that The Supremes' biggest-selling singles had all been propulsive dance numbers, insisted Holland-Dozier-Holland increase its tempo. The song took on a fierce dance groove, with bassist James Jamerson laying down a driving rhythm over James Gittens's electric organ.

The lyric was basic girl-group stuff, with Ross worrying that her boyfriend has become involved with another woman. Yet her vocal is among the singer's most affecting, reminding her beau how good their thing is while demanding he stop playing around. Performed with traffic-cop-style hand gestures, "Stop! In the Name of Love" became one of the group's best-loved songs. **GC**

The Supremes in 1964: from left, Mary Wilson, Diana Ross, and Florence Ballard.

Subterranean Homesick Blues | Bob Dylan (1965)

Writer | Bob Dylan
Producer | Tom Wilson
Label | Columbia
Album | *Bringing It All Back Home* (1965)

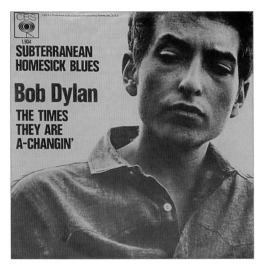

*" 'The pump don't work /
'Cause the vandals stole the
handle.' I'll always love
that line."*

Roger Waters, 1987

◀ **Influenced by: Too Much Monkey Business**
Chuck Berry (1956)
▶ **Influence on: We Didn't Start the Fire**
Billy Joel (1989)
● **Covered by:** Harry Nilsson (1974) • Red Hot Chili
Peppers (1987) • Mountain (2007)

"'Johnny's in the basement / Mixing up the medicine . . . " quoted Thom Yorke in an interview in 1997 for *OK Computer*, an allusion to Radiohead lead guitarist, Jonny Greenwood, and the band's cheekily named "Subterranean Homesick Alien." Although the song bears little trace of Dylan beyond its title, it confirms the original's place in an illustrious rock 'n' roll lineage.

With the release of "It Ain't Me, Babe" in 1964, Dylan bade farewell to folk music. The following year's strident *Bringing It All Back Home* was so iconoclastic that rock 'n' roll would not be so completely turned on its head again until the invention of the Sex Pistols in 1975. "Outlaw Blues" and "On the Road Again" set the pace, but the most live-wire moment on *Bringing It All Back Home* was "Subterranean Homesick Blues"—a nutty retooling of Chuck Berry's "Too Much Monkey Business."

Dylan was hardly shy about stealing stuff from his idol Woody Guthrie. He duly looted lines from Guthrie and Pete Seeger's "Taking It Easy," putting "Mom was in the kitchen preparing to eat / Sis was in the pantry looking for some yeast" through the ol' mental blender. As is mandatory with Dylan lyrics, the song has been scoured for meaning. Key lines emerge from a jumble of jargon, notably the oft-quoted "You don't need a weatherman / To know which way the wind blows."

The end result arguably didn't signify anything more profound than Berry's original lyric, "I don't want your botheration, get away, leave me!" However, thanks to Dylan's gigantic talent and influence, and an iconic film clip of him holding up cue cards of key lyrics from the song, it became his first *Billboard* chart hit—and a fire under the ass of rock 'n' roll. **BM**

The Sounds of Silence | Simon & Garfunkel (1965)

Writer | Paul Simon
Producer | Tom Wilson
Label | Columbia
Album | *Sounds of Silence* (1966)

"It was post-adolescent angst, but it . . . resonated with millions of people."
Paul Simon, 2004

◄ **Influenced by: Masters of War** · Bob Dylan (1963)
▶ **Influence on: Catch the Wind** · Donovan (1965)
● **Covered by:** The Bachelors (1966) · Bud Shank (1966)
The Ventures (1970) · Edward Woodward (1970)
James Last (1974) · Nevermore (2000)
Shaw-Blades (2007)

Written in the aftermath of the assassination of President John F. Kennedy, "The Sounds of Silence" represents a particular moment in American musical history—when the earnest political engagement of the coffeehouse folk scene unexpectedly found mainstream acceptance.

School friends Paul Simon and Art Garfunkel made for an unlikely looking partnership, but the purity of their harmonies was persuasive enough to make up for recent college graduate Simon's slightly naive lyrics here, which apparently took him six months to complete. The first recorded version of the song, which consisted of the pair's vocals accompanied just by Simon's acoustic guitar, was included on their debut album, *Wednesday Morning, 3am*, in 1964. When that record flopped, the duo disbanded, with Simon heading to Europe to attempt to build his career as a solo artist. However, shortly before a show in Denmark, he found out that producer Tom Wilson had overdubbed electric guitar, bass, and drums onto the track and released the new version as a single without consulting its creators.

The duo were reportedly aghast, but their indignation didn't last long—by the end of 1965 "The Sounds of Silence" had reached the top of the charts, becoming the first of a string of No. 1 hits that Simon & Garfunkel would enjoy. Further cementing the song as a totem of Sixties youth alienation, director Mike Nichols included it on the soundtrack to his coming-of-age movie *The Graduate* (1967), starring Dustin Hoffman. Simon & Garfunkel's soundtrack album to the film became one of the biggest-selling albums of 1968, eventually knocking The Beatles' *White Album* from the top of the charts. **PL**

My Generation
The Who (1965)

Writer | Pete Townshend
Producer | Shel Talmy
Label | Brunswick
Album | *My Generation* (1965)

The Who's third single is probably still their best known, a glorious adrenaline-rush anthem for disaffected youth, a caustic expression of rebellion inspired in part by the London mods that followed the band in their early days. "My Generation" was originally envisioned by guitarist and songwriter Pete Townshend as a slow Jimmy Reed–influenced Chicago-blues-style number; indeed, The Who later recorded a blues version on *Live at Leeds* in 1970. However, the uptempo final master take of "My Generation" was explosive, aggressive pop, like nothing else in 1965. Townshend's feedback-drenched, distorted guitar, John Entwistle's thundering bass, and Keith Moon's pounding drums and crashing cymbals underline Roger Daltrey's arrogant sneer of "I hope I die before I get old"—one of the most famous lines in pop. The masterstroke was provided by co-manager Kit Lambert when he told Daltrey to stutter the line "Why don't you all f-fade away," a hint that Daltrey had a considerably stronger phrase in mind.

The song reached the U.K. No. 2 and became the climax of The Who's live set, often ending in howling feedback from Townshend's Rickenbacker guitar, which would be poked into the speaker cabinet and smashed while Moon pushed his drums over and kicked them across the stage. And, like their heyday stage act, "My Generation" remains one of rock's defining statements. **JoH**

Unchained Melody
The Righteous Brothers (1965)

Writer | Alex North, Hy Zaret
Producer | Bill Medley
(credited to Phil Spector)
Label | Philles
Album | *Just Once in My Life* (1965)

The Righteous Brothers (Bobby Hatfield and Bill Medley) recorded on the Philles label owned by Phil Spector; the latter produced their single releases but also took production credit for many of the album tracks and B-sides that were actually produced by Medley. Medley was not concerned by this arrangement, but Spector was privately furious when DJs gave more airtime to the B-side "Unchained Melody" (actually a solo sung by Bobby Hatfield) than his A-side, the Gerry Goffin/Carole King song "Hung on You." "Unchained Melody," originally recorded as an album track, was a solo ballad more suited to Hatfield's tenor voice than Medley's bass, but wound up credited to The Righteous Brothers on the single release.

It was not the first time that "Unchained Melody" had reached the charts. Written as the theme to the prison movie *Unchained* in 1955, the song became a No. 1 hit for Les Baxter, and within weeks was followed by a cover by Al Hibbler that reached No. 3. Later the same year, Roy Hamilton, June Valli, and Harry Belafonte all recorded versions that made the U.S. Top Forty, while a cover by Jimmy Young topped the U.K. charts.

The Righteous Brothers' recording enjoyed a revival after appearing in the movie *Ghost* (1990), when it was re-released. In the United Kingdom this prompted a second re-release of the Brothers' other hit—"You've Lost That Lovin' Feelin'." **MW**

Pete Townshend brings "My Generation" to a destructive climax in 1965.

Et moi et moi et moi

Jacques Dutronc (1966)

Writer | Jacques Lanzmann, Jacques Dutronc
Producer | Jacques Dutronc
Label | Disques Vogue
Album | *Jacques Dutronc* (1966)

Jacques Dutronc began his music career as a session guitarist with acts such as El Toro et les Cyclones and Eddy Mitchell. He subsequently found work as a house writer, with lyricist and scriptwriter Jacques Lanzmann, for the Disques Vogue label. The two Jacques had initially put together this song for French pop singer Benjamin. His success, though, proved short lived, and the label's artistic director, Jacques Wolfsohn, suggested the song as Dutronc's solo debut.

The track proved an immediate success, turning Dutronc into one of the leading players in the French Yé-yé scene of the late Sixties. Taking the fuzzy freakbeat guitar sounds of The Pretty Things and The Kinks as a base, Dutronc added his own biting Gallic attitude, to great effect. The song's tongue-in-cheek lyrical style and sideswipes at the lame elements of the folk-protest movement made it particularly popular with the mod scene in Britain, despite the language barrier, as well as with Les Minets, the mods' French equivalent.

Earlier French garage hits had come from the so-called Yé-yé Girls—the likes of France Gall, Sylvie Vartan, and Françoise Hardy (whom Dutronc went on to marry in the early Eighties). But "Et moi . . ." marked the beginning of an era of insouciant male-fronted French R&B that found an echo in the work of Gallic superstars such as Johnny Hallyday and Serge Gainsbourg. **CR**

Stay with Me

Lorraine Ellison (1966)

Writer | Jerry Ragovoy, George Weiss
Producer | Jerry Ragovoy
Label | Warner Bros.
Album | N/A

The studio was booked, the orchestra was primed, but the singer—Frank Sinatra—was sick. Warner Bros. offered producer Jerry Ragovoy the slot, and he had just enough time to work up an arrangement for a song he had recently written. He had a voice in mind, too. Lorraine (born Marybelle Luraine) Ellison was a respected gospel singer who'd gone secular in 1964 and had an R&B hit, "I Dig You Baby," the following year. She was set to record a song so powerful, so deep, and so spine-chilling that it would effectively define the term "soul music," not to mention her career.

"Stay with Me" (a U.S. R&B No. 11) starts slowly and cautiously. Just under a minute in, at the end of the first verse, the music swells and Ellison erupts, tearing into the word "leave" and holding it in a scream for five seconds. This is the full, sanctified gospel experience, but the object of her love is a cheating ingrate, and as he leaves he is ripping her heart out. Seemingly losing herself in intensity, Ellison remains controlled enough throughout to take the mood right back down again for each verse. In fact, it is her formal, perfect diction between choruses that makes each operatic scream such a shock, no matter how well you know the song. It is difficult to believe she didn't end the session lying sobbing on the floor as her lover wriggled free and disappeared through the door. A real man would have stayed. **DH**

Al-atlal
Umm Kulthum (1966)

Writer | Riyad al-Sunbati, Ibrahim Naji
Producer | Uncredited
Label | Sono Cairo
Album | *El Atlal* (1966)

You're Gonna Miss Me | The
Thirteenth Floor Elevators (1966)

Writer | Roky Erickson
Producer | Lelan Rogers
Label | International Artists
Album | *The Psychedelic Sounds of the 13th Floor Elevators* (1966)

Umm Kulthum (whose name is also transcribed as Oum Kalthoum, Kalthum, or Khalsoum) was the most renowned Arab singer of the twentieth century. On her death, in 1975, nearly four million mourners filled Cairo's streets. Out of her vast legacy of recordings, "Al-atlal" (The Ruins) is widely considered the most iconic, although it was captured quite late in her career, when her voice was arguably past its peak. Even so, she had to stand six feet back from her microphone.

Kulthum had complete mastery of Arab scales (*maqamat*), and her singing was imbued with *shaggan*, or emotional yearning. By 1966, she was moving away from classical Egyptian music toward more modern formats, although "Al-atlal" uses complex traditional Arab scales. After the lengthy, moaning intro, where a large, swooning Egyptian orchestra answers her melismatic phrases, a modern dance rhythm takes over. The words combine two poems by Dr. Ibrahim Naji, and supposedly concern a disintegrating love affair, full of tragic but luminous images ("we outran our own shadows"). However, the song was widely interpreted as an extended metaphor for disillusionment with the Nasser government.

Also in 1966, Kulthum made her only public appearance outside the Middle East. During a marathon six-hour concert in Paris, she sang just three pieces, one of which was "Al-atlal." **JLu**

Most recently used by Dell to advertise their XPS laptop, "You're Gonna Miss Me" is the apogee of early U.S. psychedelic rock, recorded by a band who would routinely hand out free LSD to their audiences, who employed a man playing an electric jug onstage, who reportedly chose their name because the thirteenth letter of the alphabet was "M" (for marijuana), and whose sleevenotes advocated the use of drugs as a gateway to a higher, "non-Aristotelian" state of consciousness.

"You're Gonna Miss Me" is a thrillingly concise blast of red-eyed Sixties punk aggression. Combining singer Roky Erickson's otherworldly yowling, an invigorating surf-guitar break, and Tommy Hall's odd warbling jug noise, the song was initially recorded by Erickson's band The Spades, gaining a release on a small local label before a re-recorded version by the Elevators ("Thirteenth," not the "13th" of the single's label) was picked up by International Artists. "You're Gonna Miss Me" became the Austin, Texas, band's only national U.S. hit, reaching No. 55 on the *Billboard* chart.

Following a handful of increasingly deranged albums and singles, in 1969 Erickson pleaded insanity to escape a drugs charge and wound up being committed to a mental asylum. However, the support of friends and fans such as ZZ Top, R.E.M., and Primal Scream has led to several recent and successful comeback tours for the singer. **PL**

Substitute | The Who (1966)

Writer | Pete Townshend
Producer | Pete Townshend
Label | Reaction
Album | N/A

"Smokey Robinson sang the word 'substitute' so perfectly . . . I decided to celebrate the word itself with a song of its own."
Pete Townshend, 1987

◄ **Influenced by: 19th Nervous Breakdown**
The Rolling Stones (1966)
► **Influence on: Pretty Vacant** · Sex Pistols (1977)
● **Covered by:** Sex Pistols (1979) · The Glitter Band (1986)
Ramones (1993) · Blur (1994) · Richard Thompson
(2006) · Crosbi (2007)

According to its author, Pete Townshend, "Substitute" began life as a spoof on The Rolling Stones' "19th Nervous Breakdown." After the Stones' manager, Andrew Loog Oldham, played him a rough mix of the song, Townshend appropriated it as a blueprint for his own demo, even mimicking Mick Jagger's vocal style.

The title "Substitute" came from Townshend's admiration of Smokey Robinson's use of the word in The Miracles' "The Tracks of My Tears," while the riff was nabbed from "Where Is My Girl" by Robb Storme & The Whispers, a song that Townshend had heard when reviewing singles for the "Blind Date" column in *Melody Maker*.

For the recording, Townshend swapped his then-signature Rickenbacker electric for a 12-string acoustic. But the change of instrumentation lost the song none of the bite of The Who's previous singles, as Daltrey sneers out one of Townshend's most ingenious, self-deprecating lyrics concerning identity, illusion, and reality. The line "I look all white but my dad was black" was deemed too controversial for America and was cut from the U.S. version of the single (and replaced with "I try going forward but my feet walk back"). It was the first track that Townshend produced himself after a split with producer Shel Talmy.

The heavy bass sound on John Entwistle's Motown-inspired riff was the result of his deliberately turning up the volume on his bass for the instrumental break during recording—effectively creating a bass solo. Keith Moon, meanwhile, was reportedly so out of his head on pills that he did not remember the session.

The single reached No. 5 in the United Kingdom and became a staple of their live act. **JoH**

Eight Miles High | The Byrds (1966)

Writer | Gene Clark, Roger McGuinn, David Crosby
Producer | Allen Stanton
Label | Columbia
Album | *Fifth Dimension* (1966)

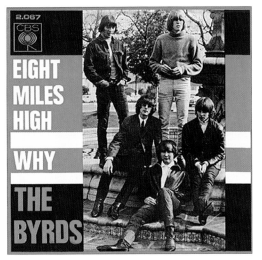

"Of course it was a drug song … we were stoned when we wrote it."
David Crosby, 1980

◀ **Influenced by: India** · John Coltrane (1963)
▶ **Influence on:** Raga rock
● **Covered by:** Golden Earring (1969) · Roxy Music (1980) Hüsker Dü (1984) · Ride (1990) · Robyn Hitchcock and The Egyptians (1996) · Dave Cloud (1999) · Chris Hillman (2005) · The Postmarks (2008)

The Byrds' first tour of the United Kingdom, in 1965, proved something of a flop. Expectations were impossibly high: they had been touted, unwisely, as the "American Beatles"; The Beatles themselves had declared The Byrds their favorite band. Moreover, their particular brand of California cool—taking an age to tune up on stage—plus some indifferent playing didn't help. One very good thing came out of it, though.

The culture shock the band experienced on their visit found its way into "Eight Miles High," one of the most extraordinary singles ever released. (Its original title, "Six Miles High"—the altitude at which commercial airplanes fly—was rejected as sounding less poetic.) Lyrically, the song is a wide-eyed snapshot from the heart of that turbulent tour, taking in Swinging London, and even inter-band rivalry ("Nowhere is there warmth to be found / Among those afraid of losing their ground").

Musically, "Eight Miles High" demonstrates succinctly why the Fabs rated The Byrds so highly. Following an ominous bass intro, Roger McGuinn's trademark Rickenbacker 12-string kicks off the famous four-note riff before unleashing a jagged stop-start flurry of notes. Jazz genius John Coltrane is a clear influence here—particularly his track "India" (1963). Less acclaimed, but equally essential, Michael Clarke provides glorious cymbal work and spine-tingling fills in the verses.

Sadly for The Byrds, it was an an era when radio was waking up to the drug references peppering songs. "Eight Miles High" was banned in the United States, though it made No. 14 on *Billboard*. In the United Kingdom, it stalled at No. 24, ending the band's status as chart contenders. **RD**

Sunny Afternoon | The Kinks (1966)

Writer | Ray Davies
Producer | Shel Talmy
Label | Pye
Album | *Face to Face* (1966)

"I was so sure everything would go right, and I even said to Shel, 'You know it's the one take, Shel. That's it.'"

Ray Davies, 1984

◄ **Influenced by:** Let's All Go down the Strand
Clarence Wainwright Murphy (composed 1904)
► **Influence on:** Everybody Knows (Except You)
The Divine Comedy (1997)
● **Covered by:** Bob Geldof (1992) • Jimmy Buffett (1994)
Stereophonics (1999)

After inventing hard rock (but not heavy metal, as is erroneously supposed) with their early hits "You Really Got Me" and "All Day and All of the Night," The Kinks surprised everyone by diverting their path into semi-comedic music-hall territory. (Their 1965 hit, "A Well Respected Man," had charted similar ground.) "Sunny Afternoon" was a stroke of genius—a combination of honky-tonk piano, guitar squawks, and oompah-band rhythm that seemed to want nothing more than to extol the pleasures of being idle. Or was it more than that?

Like so many songs released between 1966 and 1968, "Sunny Afternoon" seemed to embody the spirit of change that was spreading across the United States and Europe at the time. "Tune in, turn on, and drop out" was a catchphrase for a reason: at the fringes of the counterculture, increasing numbers of people were beginning to understand that they didn't have to be part of the mainstream. Remember, in 1966 The Beatles also advised their fans to relax, turn off their minds, and float downstream. The Kinks, however, got there first.

Musically as well as lyrically, "Sunny Afternoon" was a revelation. The retrograde step that songwriter Ray Davies took with the song—toward the music-hall follies of his youth, rather than in the progressive direction that the band's earlier hits had seemed to indicate—seems now to have been a stroke of genius. The warmth and laconic mellowness of this cut belied the astute minds behind it, an observation that could equally apply to The Beatles (once again), who recorded their own music-hall tribute the following year in the form of "Being for the Benefit of Mr. Kite." Clever chaps, all of them. **JMc**

Paint It Black | The Rolling Stones (1966)

Writer | Mick Jagger, Keith Richards
Producer | Andrew Loog Oldham
Label | Decca
Album | N/A

"It was the lyrics that sent me over to the dark side. There was a path that led to The Doors, the Velvets, and the Banshees."

Marc Almond, 2007

◄ **Inspired by:** *Ulysses* • James Joyce (1922)
► **Influence on:** *Thirteen* • Big Star (1972)
● **Covered by:** Chris Farlowe (1966) • Eric Burdon & The Animals (1967) • After Hours (1987) • Echo & The Bunnymen (1988) • Deep Purple (1988) • Dominion (1998) • Acid Mothers Temple (2003)

The Stones' tenth U.K. single—a transatlantic No. 1—cast a singular shadow over the sunny optimism of 1966 pop. "Paint It Black" is blues, but a more nihilistic blues than anything this band had tried before. (Why the mysterious comma in the title on the cover? A glitch by the record company, according to Keith Richards.) Mick Jagger's lyrics—"I have to turn my head until my darkness goes" references James Joyce's *Ulysses*—make the death of a loved one a catalyst for a blanket worldview of desperation and desolation, with no hint of hope. "It's like the beginnings of miserable psychedelia," Jagger reflected years later. "That's what The Rolling Stones started."

The strongest musical presence here by far is Brian Jones's sitar, an unsettling and slightly menacing presence that makes the song a far more succinct and successful excursion into psychedelia than 1967's patchy *Their Satanic Majesties Request* LP. (The track features on the U.S. *Aftermath* LP, though not the original U.K. version.) In fact, the session had been going nowhere until he picked up the exotic instrument and began plucking out notes. "We'd been doing it with funky rhythms and it hadn't worked," mused Richards later, "and he started playing [the sitar] and everybody got behind it." Compare Jones's playing—skillfully exploiting the instrument's mesmerizing jangling drone—to George Harrison's far flatter use of sitar on "Norwegian Wood." Bill Wyman, who had played comedy organ on an early version, wound up doubling his bass part on the organ's bass pedals.

The snarl of garage punk—rammed home by Charlie Watts's tribal drums, pounding like a migraine—cut with abject misery, "Paint It Black" is pop's most thrilling requiem. **RD**

Summer in the City
The Lovin' Spoonful (1966)

Writer | J. & M. Sebastian, S. Boone
Producer | Erik Jacobsen
Label | Kama Sutra
Album | *Hums of the Lovin' Spoonful* (1966)

Over a two-year period, The Lovin' Spoonful kicked out a string of sunny hits—including the sublime "Do You Believe in Magic" and "Daydream"—that encapsulated all that was great about mid-Sixties pop; top of the heap was "Summer in the City."

It opens with B-movie horror keyboards and the thwack of a snare drum, recorded in a stairwell for über-reverb. Auto horns and jackhammers epitomize the sticky oppression of a sizzling city day. As with The Kinks' wry "Sunny Afternoon," a U.K. hit that same summer, the song's verse is built around downwardly descending shifts through minor chords—"Back of my neck all dirty and gritty. . . . Doesn't seem to be a shadow in the city"—before exploding into major-key relief with the chorus—"But tonight it's a different world!"

The lyrics had been written by Mark Sebastian, sibling of the Spoonful's key songwriter, John, while still a student at Blair Academy. Brother John expanded on that contrast between daytime exhaustion and nighttime euphoria with the keyboard part: "I was going for the scary, minor chord, 'Hit-the-road-Jack' chord sequence that doesn't warn you of what's coming in the chorus."

"We felt the only way we could stick out would be to sound completely different from one single to another," he mused later. A good tactic: chart-wise, the song hit the *Billboard* top spot—their sole U.S. No. 1—and made U.K. No. 8. **RD**

God Only Knows
The Beach Boys (1966)

Writer | Brian Wilson, Tony Asher
Producer | Brian Wilson
Label | Capitol
Album | *Pet Sounds* (1966)

In 1966, Brian Wilson was in Hollywood, tumbling into his own clinical state of Beatlemania. He was the only man on earth who could declare that he was going to make a record as good as *Rubber Soul* and actually pull it off. Brian and The Beach Boys had made nine full-length albums in three years and, against all odds, were showing signs of transforming what seemed like a passing surfer fad into pop's answer to classical music.

Pet Sounds, The Beach Boys' riposte to *Rubber Soul*, was anchored by a stunning ballad, "God Only Knows," about love and the unspeakable despair that can live in its absence. Enlisting more than twenty studio musicians to create a soundscape of accordion, French horn, clarinet, saxophone, and cello, Wilson composed a three-voice hymn that approached spirituality with a tentative faith.

For the first time, someone was writing pop that demanded concentration. The verses stretched at the confines of rock chord progressions, linked by a bridge that didn't reveal its destination until it got there. Carl Wilson's lead vocal, like a shepherd, guided the listener through. Not many love songs open with a downer like "I may not always love you," but when it's followed by "But long as there are stars above you / You'll never need to doubt it," we know, too, that God destroys as much as he creates. Not long after he wrote "God Only Knows," Brian Wilson heard *Sgt. Pepper's* and lost his mind. **MO**

The Beach Boys pose for their public on a couple of customized Mini Mokes in 1966. ➡

(I'm Not Your) Stepping Stone
Paul Revere & The Raiders (1966)

Writer | Tommy Boyce, Bobby Hart
Producer | Terry Melcher
Label | Columbia
Album | *Midnight Ride* (1966)

History has been unkind to one of the great bands of the Sixties. It all comes down to looks, and The Raiders' eighteenth-century Revolutionary War costumes count against them every time. Formed in 1958, the group made the charts in 1965, thanks to the patronage of Dick Clark's television shows. Bizarrely, the men in the tricornered hats were the first great punk band. Tracks such as ". . . Stepping Stone," "Steppin' Out," and the anti-drugs "Kicks" featured fuzzy organ, stinging guitars, and a Jagger-on-steroids snarl, courtesy of Mark Lindsay. Iggy Pop's claim to the title of "Godfather of Punk" is in doubt after hearing Lindsay's delivery of this song, particularly the words "book of Who's Who."

In 1966, Tommy Boyce and Bobby Hart (and their band, The Candy Store Prophets) were part of The Monkees' studio squad. Following The Raiders' release of ". . . Stepping Stone" on *Midnight Ride,* the pair tweaked the title slightly (replacing "Stepping" with "Steppin'") and dragged Mickey Dolenz into Hollywood's Western Recorders Studio to outsnarl Lindsay. He failed, but the track remains the spikiest thing The Monkees ever did, although the irony of singing lyrics about not being walked over would not have been lost on that band. Issued as the B-side of their transatlantic No. 1 "I'm a Believer," The Monkees' version made the *Billboard* Top Twenty in its own right. More important, however, was that snarl's long tail. **DH**

Mas que nada
Sérgio Mendes & Brasil '66 (1966)

Writer | Jorge Ben
Producer | Herb Alpert
Label | A&M
Album | *Herb Alpert Presents . . .* (1966)

Although the original by Jorge Ben had been a big hit in Brazil in 1963, "Mas que nada" (Why, No Way) is best known around the world for the version cut by Sérgio Mendes, aka "The swinger from Rio." Ben had written the song as an homage to another Carioca (resident of Rio), a friend of his called Rosinha, who lived in Copacabana and habitually used the eponymous expression.

A classically trained pianist, Mendes had left Brazil hurriedly in 1964 after the newly installed military dictatorship started breathing down his neck, as they did with many other artists. Initially struggling on the L.A. lounge scene, Mendes hit paydirt when he hooked up with Herb Alpert's A&M label for the *Brasil '66* album. The lead track was his brisk take on "Mas que nada" (titled "Mais que nada"), featuring Mendes on piano; a tight, peppy rhythm section; and airy lead vocals by his newly acquired Chicago-bred singer, Lani Hall. Her phonetically learned pronunciation of the Portuguese lyrics was so convincing that even Brazilians thought she could speak their language—which she couldn't.

The song has enjoyed surprising longevity. In a fortieth-anniversary celebration of his breakthrough, Mendes re-recorded a new hip-hop-meets-samba update of the song with Black Eyed Peas' will.i.am for the album *Timeless*—a title that reflects how he feels about the song. **JLu**

El muerto vivo

Peret (1966)

Writer | Guillermo González Arenas
Producer | N/A
Label | Ariola
Album | N/A

Pere Pubill Calaf, aka Peret, was born in 1935 to Romany Gypsy parents in Barcelona; his recording career began in 1957. Initially playing flamenco, Peret began to add elements from American rock 'n' roll and Cuban dance music. The new sound came to be called "rumba flamenco," or "rumba Catalanya," and was immediately popular. Recorded in 1966, "El muerto vivo" (The Dead Alive) gained wide popularity with music fans of diverse social backgrounds. The buoyant mix of flamenco guitar and rumba rhythms in this and other Sixties recordings by Peret influenced all Catalan Gypsy music and helped to reinvent Spanish pop. Meanwhile, Peret acted in, and provided the music for, the Academy Award–nominated 1963 film *Los Tarantos*—a *Romeo and Juliet*-based story shot in Somorrostro, Barcelona's former Gypsy neighborhood.

When Franco's Spain returned to democracy, Peret found himself out of favor and turned to preaching. Ironically, the Gipsy Kings (Catalan-speaking Romanies from the south of France) then took the sound Peret pioneered to a massive pop audience. The likes of Manu Chao and Ojos de Brujo championed Peret's groovy mix of flamenco and rumba rhythms as Barcelona's rootsy sound, and Peret once again found himself fashionable. He would re-record "El muerto vivo" in 2009 as a duet with Marina of Ojos de Brujo. **GC**

Tomorrow Is a Long Time

Elvis Presley (1966)

Writer | Bob Dylan
Producer | Felton Jarvis
Label | RCA Victor
Album | *Spinout* (1966)

By 1966, only diehard fans expected greatness from Elvis Presley. However, in May and June that year, Presley cut some of his most important recordings since his heyday. Those sessions, best known for the songs on 1967's Grammy-winning gospel album *How Great Thou Art*, which heralded the King's musical comeback, also included a take on Bob Dylan's "Tomorrow Is a Long Time" that was hailed by the composer as his favorite cover.

This was not Presley's only excursion into Dylan's discography. He recorded "Blowin' in the Wind" at home around the same time, and later covered "Don't Think Twice, It's Alright" and "I Shall Be Released." His template for "Tomorrow Is a Long Time," however, was a sparse, bluesy version by Odetta, a folk singer who had influenced Dylan himself. Utterly at odds with Presley's contemporary output, the track was spooky and, at over five minutes, unusually long.

The composer's own version—originally destined for 1963's *The Freewheelin' Bob Dylan*—went unreleased, although a live take adorned his *Greatest Hits Vol. II* in 1971. In the meantime, the song was covered by artists including Rod Stewart (on *Every Picture Tells a Story*) and Nick Drake (on posthumously released demos). But neither they nor subsequent attempts by Sandy Denny and others would even approach the heights of Presley's definitive version. **BM**

Eleanor Rigby | The Beatles (1966)

Writer | John Lennon, Paul McCartney
Producer | George Martin
Label | Parlophone
Album | *Revolver* (1966)

"Prior to that, I thought the music was very good, but [not necessarily important]. For me, 'Eleanor Rigby' was the start."

Paul McCartney, 2009

◀ **Influenced by:** Vivaldi
▶ **Influence on: A Rose for Emily** • The Zombies (1968)
● **Covered by:** The Standells (1966) • Richie Havens (1967) • Vanilla Fudge (1967) • P. P. Arnold (1968) Aretha Franklin (1969) • Four Tops (1969) • John Denver (1970) • The Crusaders (1974)

What a shock this song must have been. Part of it is context: the song debuted on the other side of the deliberately daffy "Yellow Submarine." But even without that jarring clash, "Eleanor Rigby" stands out a mile from the chart-chasing pop that surrounded it. Not in a million years would The Swinging Blue Jeans have tried to record a song about a woman's loneliness and death, accompanied by a string section apparently inspired by Vivaldi and Bernard Herrmann.

Although he got a little help (notably from Ringo, who supplied the vivid image of Father MacKenzie "darning his socks in the night"), "Eleanor Rigby" is a Paul McCartney song, one of his many portraits in which the songwriter stands a distance apart from his subjects. George Martin's string arrangement is played with an impassive steadiness that only lends more weight to the lyric, one of McCartney's most incisive. Lennon and Harrison add backing vocals to McCartney's lead, but "Eleanor Rigby" is one of only a handful of Beatles tracks on which none of the band was required to play an instrument.

Who, though, was Eleanor Rigby? Despite the presence of a gravestone marking the remains of one Eleanor Rigby in Liverpool's Woolton Cemetery, which adjoins the church at which McCartney met Lennon in 1957, the singer maintains that the name is a fiction, inspired jointly by Eleanor Bron, with whom the group had worked on the movie *Help!*, and Rigby & Evens, a wine shop in Bristol that McCartney had noticed while strolling in the city (girlfriend Jane Asher was acting in a play there). "I was looking for a name that sounded natural," said McCartney in 1984. "'Eleanor Rigby' sounded natural." **WF-J**

The Beatles let the train take the strain in 1966. ➔

River Deep—Mountain High | Ike & Tina Turner (1966)

Writer | Phil Spector, Jeff Barry, Ellie Greenwich
Producer | Phil Spector
Label | Philles
Album | *River Deep—Mountain High* (1966)

"I must have sung that 500,000 times. I was drenched with sweat. I had to take my shirt off and stand . . . in my bra to sing."

Tina Turner, 2004

◀ **Influenced by: Be My Baby** • The Ronettes (1963)
▶ **Influence on: Born to Run** • Bruce Springsteen (1975)
● **Covered by:** The Easybeats (1967) • Harry Nilsson (1967) • The Supremes & The Four Tops (1970) • Erasure (1988) • Neil Diamond (1993) • Neil Diamond (1993) • Céline Dion (1996)

The definitive "wall of sound" production from Phil Spector at the peak of his powers, "River Deep—Mountain High" was also a landmark in Tina Turner's career, anticipating her later success as a solo artist without husband Ike.

Spector had been almost a year without a major hit. Working with the songwriting team of Jeff Barry and Ellie Greenwich, who had penned hits such as "Da Doo Ron Ron," "Then He Kissed Me," and "Be My Baby" for him, he put all his efforts into the next single. Tina Turner's voice was just what was needed, maybe the only voice powerful enough for the massive sound he had in mind, but he was obliged to sign Ike & Tina Turner as a duo to his Philles label in order to get her. Bizarrely, the producer effectively paid Ike $20,000 *not* to be involved, and agreed to credit the single to both husband and wife.

Spector spared no expense on the production of the song, with a backing orchestra including such great names as jazz guitarist Barney Kessel and country crooner Glen Campbell, and was effectively staking both his fortune and his reputation on its success. At a final cost of $22,000, the single was released in September 1966; although it did well in Europe, reaching No. 3 in the United Kingdom, it struggled to reach No. 88 in the U.S. charts. This was the final straw for the highly strung Spector, who withdrew from the music business, taking his Philles label with him.

The song had a more appreciative reception on its re-release in the United States, in 1969, and has since been recognized as Spector's masterpiece. And Tina Turner has adopted it as one of her "signature songs," despite having a very impressive list of later hits from which to choose. **MW**

7 and 7 Is | Love (1966)

Writer | Arthur Lee
Producer | Jac Holzman
Label | Elektra
Album | *Da Capo* (1966)

"The Doors idolized Arthur. They took a lot of style from Love. There's no question about that."
Paul Rothchild, producer, 1994

◀ **Influenced by: Get Off of My Cloud** • The Rolling Stones (1965)
▶ **Influence on: Skeleton Key** • The Coral (2002)
● **Covered by:** Alice Cooper (1981) • Billy Bragg (1990) The Ramones (1993) • The Electric Prunes (2001) Amoeba (2004) • Rush (2004)

"7 and 7 Is" was recorded at Sunset Sound Recorders Studio in Hollywood on June 17 and 20, 1966; its breakneck pace and cryptic lyrics provided Love with their only U.S. *Billboard* Top Forty hit. Lead singer Arthur Lee initially composed the song as a Bob Dylan–style folk number in the bathroom at the Colonial Apartments on Sunset Boulevard while the rest of Love slept. "My songs used to come to me just before dawn," he later told writer Phil Gallo. "I hear songs in dreams."

Lee's seemingly surreal words conceal an autobiographical thread in the song that provides a glimpse into Lee's early life. The enigmatic title was inspired by the birth date that Lee shared with his teenage girlfriend, Anita—March 7. The lyric "In my lonely room I'd sit, my mind in an ice-cream cone" refers to Lee's mother making him sit alone in his bedroom when he did badly at school; the "ice-cream cone" was a metaphor for a dunce's cap. Love lead guitarist Johnny Echols once told writer Andrew Sandoval that Lee's mother was a schoolteacher who made Lee feel inadequate, as "he was not really that academically inclined."

When the group got hold of the song, it underwent a metamorphosis from folk into frantic, experimental proto-punk, with alienated, angry vocals, manic guitar, and pounding drums culminating in a slowed-down gunshot—added by producer Jac Holzman to mimic the sound of an exploding atomic bomb.

The song's punishing, speedy tempo required multiple takes, with some sources claiming that Lee replaced drummer Alban "Snoopy" Pfisterer on the finished version. Guitarist Echols, however, insists that the thrilling, "Wipe Out"–style surf-band rumble is all Pfisterer. **JoH**

96 Tears
? & The Mysterians (1966)

Writer | Rudy Martinez
Producer | Rudy Martinez
Label | Pa-Go-Go
Album | *96 Tears* (1966)

Pushin' Too Hard
The Seeds (1966)

Writer | Sky Saxon
Producer | Marcus Tybalt
Label | GNP Crescendo
Album | *The Seeds* (1966)

On their 2009 tour, Bruce Springsteen & The E-Street Band invited audience members to shout out song names to see if they could find something the band couldn't play. In Atlanta, the request was "96 Tears," the organ-driven No. 1 1966 smash from ? & The Mysterians. Springsteen paused before launching into a boisterous version of a song that, like "Louie Louie," has been played by a thousand garage bands around the world.

First released on indie label Pa-Go-Go, "96 Tears" was picked up by Cameo-Parkway and went to No. 1 as America grooved to the yelping vocals and organ riff and ignored the slightly sinister revenge fantasy of the lyrics. The Mysterians, named after a Japanese horror movie, were from Michigan; their singer was "?," who claimed to be 10,000 years old and have been born on Mars, but was probably Rudy Martinez, a Mexican-American never photographed without his sunglasses on.

"96 Tears" inspired a wave of garage acts but didn't feature on the genre-defining *Nuggets* album because, like the rest of Cameo's back catalog, the original version was locked in a vault. (It was finally re-released in 2005.) Even that couldn't stop its becoming a cultural icon, quoted in song by acts as diverse as The B-52's, Tom Russell, and The Cramps, covered by Aretha Franklin and Suicide, and exuberantly belted out by bar bands—including Springsteen's—everywhere. **PW**

Written, according to *Teen Scene* magazine, in ten minutes by The Seeds' lead singer, Sky Saxon (born Richard Marsh), while waiting for his girlfriend in a supermarket parking lot, "Pushin' Too Hard" is a two-chord garage-punk classic and arguably the apotheosis of The Seeds' unique sound.

Saxon later claimed that the song was also partly inspired by the closure of the Pandora's Box club on Sunset Strip. (It had been acquired by Los Angeles City Council following the youth protests against curfew laws outside the club, which led to the so-called Riot on Sunset Strip.) As this happened in November 1966 and The Seeds' second single was first released in March and a hit in August, Saxon's recollection is shaky, but the song did tap into the defiant mood of the youth of southern California, and The Seeds built a large following in L.A. Reaching No. 36 nationally, the single was defined by Saxon's sneering, nasal, whining vocals, the rudimentary but jazzy electric piano from Daryl Hooper, Jan Savage's mix of surf and fuzz guitar, and Rick Andridge's primitive drumming.

Hooper's prominent electric piano surely influenced his City of Angels neighbor, The Doors' Ray Manzarek, and "Pushin' Too Hard" was included on Lenny Kaye's 1972 Elektra Records compilation, *Nuggets: Original Artyfacts of the First Psychedelic Era, 1965–68*, which was an irrefutable influence on the Seventies punk scene. **JoH**

Psychotic Reaction
The Count Five (1966)

Writer | The Count Five
Producer | Hal Winn,
Joseph Hooven
Label | Double Shot
Album | *Psychotic Reaction* (1966)

"I finally came to realize that grossness was the truest criterion for rock 'n' roll," wrote Lester Bangs, whose book *Psychotic Reactions and Carburetor Dung* took its inspiration from this garage-rock anthem. And, of all the noisy, messy records cut by scruffy teens in the mid-Sixties, it is "Psychotic Reaction" that best nails the sweaty thrills of that era's music, from its ghostly harmonica wails to its sudden tempo changes, wacka-wacka guitar strumming, and straight-ahead rock screaming.

The Count Five were really just kids when they formed in San Jose, California, its five members led by nineteen-year-old singer and rhythm guitarist John Byrne. The story goes that Byrne was taking a health-education class at college—on psychosis—when his buddy Rob Lamb opined that "Psychotic Reaction" would make a good name for a song, and Byrne used the title to pin down a melody he'd had going through his head all day.

At their live shows, The Count Five strode onstage in Dracula-style capes before launching into their set, taking every gig as an opportunity to rework "Psychotic Reaction" to achieve maximum craziness. Their efforts paid off. "Psychotic Reaction" hit No. 5 on the *Billboard* chart in 1966, and The Count Five were offered a million dollars' worth of bookings. Instead, they chose to go to college. Asked recently if the band regretted the decision, Byrne replied, "Yes. Wouldn't you?" **SH**

Reach Out (I'll Be There)
The Four Tops (1966)

Writer | Eddie Holland,
Lamont Dozier, Brian Holland
Producer | B. Holland, L. Dozier
Label | Motown
Album | *Reach Out* (1967)

A second U.S. No. 1 for The Four Tops, "Reach Out" marked the peak of their long career. It was a distinct break from their earlier style—darker and more dramatic, with contrasts of major and minor keys—but most noticeable was the newly edgy vocal style of lead singer Levi Stubbs. At the recording session, Motown songwriting-and-production team Holland-Dozier-Holland had encouraged Stubbs to sing at the top of his baritone range. Combined with the call-and-response style of the song, this strain on his voice gave the track a gospel-like fervor and urgency, matched by backing vocals from the quartet and Motown's resident female singers, The Andantes.

After recording the number—allegedly in two takes—the performers presumed it was destined to be an album track. Motown boss Berry Gordy recognized the song as hit material, however, and released it as a single in late 1966; within weeks, it made No. 1 in both the R&B charts and the *Billboard* Hot 100. It did, however, later appear on an album, as the lead track of *Reach Out*.

Another Holland-Dozier-Holland number—"Standing in the Shadows of Love"—returned the Tops to the charts in November 1966, though it was their last big hit. However, the quartet continued as a popular live act, with the same lineup as when they first got together as The Four Aims in the Fifties, until Lawrence Payton's death, in 1997. **MW**

Good Vibrations
The Beach Boys (1966)

Writer | Brian Wilson, Mike Love
Producer | Brian Wilson
Label | Capitol
Album | *Smiley Smile* (1967)

Inspired by The Beatles' ambitious pop, Beach Boy Brian Wilson left the world of simple surf anthems and embarked on creating his own complex opus. The result was 1966's *Pet Sounds*, which cleared the bar set by The Beatles for experimental rock. But Wilson's grandest statement was still to come.

"Good Vibrations" began during the *Pet Sounds* sessions, yet its recording stretched months past that album's release. Driven to capture the sounds he heard in his head, Wilson used eight months and several studios in recording the epic track. This unprecedented attention to detail, although linked to Wilson's mental breakdown of 1967, paid off beyond his wildest expectations.

Wilson's publicist Derek Taylor was credited with calling "Good Vibrations" a "pocket symphony." Equally extravagant and concise, the three-and-a-half-minute single benefited both from staggering ambition and an ear for what works on radio. The baroque music unfolds in chapters, united by romantic imagery, lush harmonies, and unusual instrumentation (including a theremin). It is curiously irresistible, so dense with ideas it demands multiple rotations.

"Good Vibrations" was the band's third U.S. No. 1 hit and its first in the U.K. Thirty-seven years later, the song was re-recorded and united with its intended family on *Smile*, Wilson's intended follow-up solo album to *Pet Sounds*. **JiH**

Dead End Street
The Kinks (1966)

Writer | Ray Davies
Producer | Shel Talmy
Label | Pye
Album | N/A

After The Beatles, The Kinks were always the most sonically adventurous of the great British bands of the Sixties, and in Ray Davies they had perhaps the most distinctive songwriter of their generation. Without watering down his words or themes, Davies was able to find the middle ground between McCartney's sentimentality and Lennon's cynicism, and in "Dead End Street" produced a song about poverty that managed to be sympathetic without being patronizing, and angry without being bitter.

The genius is in the details, as Davies draws out the scene in four short, brilliant opening lines: "There's a crack up in the ceiling / And the kitchen sink is leaking / Out of job and got no money / A Sunday joint of bread and honey." For the narrator, the Sixties is emphatically failing to swing. The sound of the song is also highly individual, with mournful trumpet underpinning a tune that uses tricks from blues and folk, sudden changes of rhythm, and shouted backing vocals to get over the requisite sense of pride and despair. Fellow Kinks Dave Davies and Pete Quaife have both named it as one of the best three songs that Ray ever wrote, and its influence—a jaunty tune backing a desolate tale—can be heard in the work of some of the great British working-class bands that followed, particularly Madness, The Smiths, and Pulp, English essayists all. **PW**

The Kinks inanimatedly encounter Mike Nesmith (seated left) of The Monkees in 1967. ➔

The Sun Ain't Gonna Shine Any More | The Walker Brothers (1966)

Writer | Bob Crewe, Bob Gaudio
Producer | Johnny Franz
Label | Philips
Album | N/A

While the Sixties "British Invasion" spearheaded by The Beatles saw U.K. acts clean up Stateside, it wasn't all one-way traffic. An all-American trio regroomed themselves in Britain as a brooding boy band and became the biggest pop act in 1966—the year of this song, their second U.K. No. 1. They were neither brothers nor were their surnames Walker, but they *looked like* siblings, and damn cute ones, too. Noel Scott Engel (later changed to Scott Walker) was the heartthrob, backed by Gary Leeds and John Maus.

Mariachi-style guitar-strum and trumpets open the mid-tempo number, and then a thunderous Spector-esque wall of sound, with drums and bass emanating from a seemingly huge chasm, envelops the listener into the opening word: "Loneliness." Scott's articulate, mellifluous vocals make perfect plaintive pleas for romance-seeking teen girls. As the song reaches its epic and eponymous chorus, the boys give their all, backed by lush, dramatic, positively cinematic orchestrations arranged by Ivor Raymonde.

Originally recorded in 1965 by Frankie Valli & The Four Seasons, the song topped the U.K. charts for The Walker Brothers in March 1966. (It peaked at No. 13 in the United States.) After their split the following year, only Scott Walker went on to achieve solo fame, becoming the self-styled reclusive "Orson Welles of the record industry." **JJH**

Season of the Witch | Donovan (1966)

Writer | Donovan Leitch
Producer | Mickie Most
Label | Epic
Album | *Sunshine Superman* (1966)

"Season of the Witch" is not as well known as Donovan's "Sunshine Superman" or "Mellow Yellow" (which gave the flower-powered minstrel U.S. No. 1 and No. 2 hits, respectively). However, the song perfectly encapsulated the harder-hitting psychedelic sound he would henceforth embrace, helping him to shake off the "Britain's Bob Dylan" tag he probably wished he'd never courted.

With drummer "Fast" Eddie Hoh, Lenny Matlin on keyboards, and local bassist Bobby Ray, Donovan and producer Mickie Most booked themselves into CBS Studios in L.A. to try out their new approach to pop. Over Ray's heavy backbeat bass, Donovan played a white Fender Telecaster electric guitar, chunking down on the scratchy chords (just two for most of the song) that slowly, creepily increase in volume to a wailing, chilling chorus. The bass, turned up high despite opposition from the CBS engineers, satisfyingly lent weight to what became an iconic riff.

Eschewing the whimsy often associated with him, Donovan crafted sharp-eyed lyrics that snipe at the commercialization and pitfalls of the counterculture ("Beatniks out to make it rich"). An air of menace hangs over the track, the implication that all those acid highs must be paid for one day. As such, it made for the perfect playout music in Gus Van Sant's memorable 1995 study of unbridled, unthinking ambition, *To Die For*. **JJH**

Friday on My Mind | The Easybeats (1966)

Writer | George Young, Harry Vanda
Producer | Shel Talmy
Label | United Artists
Album | N/A

"The Easybeats . . . were like Australia's Beatles. [We] used to hang out there with them thinking, 'This is the way to go!'"
Malcolm Young, AC/DC, 2000

◄ **Influenced by:** The Swingle Singers
► **Influence on:** The Sound of the Suburbs
The Members (1979)
● **Covered by:** The Shadows (1967) • David Bowie (1973)
London (1977) • Peter Frampton (1998) • Richard
Thompson (2003) • Ben Lee (2008)

By the summer of 1966, The Easybeats had been stars in their native Australia for more than a year. However, their name meant nothing to the U.S. and U.K. markets, where their records had not even been released. Irked, the five-piece signed a deal with United Artists, relocated to London, and recorded a new single with Shel Talmy, producer of The Who and The Kinks.

Psychedelia was round the corner, but the breathless "Friday on My Mind" harked back to "it's the weekend!" crackers such as "Rip It Up" and "C'mon Everybody." With opening notes inspired—oddly—by a distinctive easy-listening arrangement from vocal troupe The Swingle Singers, this effusive dose of Sixties power pop concerned the longed-for reward of a night on the town after "the five-day drag." Setting a frantic pace that threatens to send the song toppling, guitars niggle impatiently for that sweet release, as vocalist Stevie Wright counts down the days; the background vocals positively burble with barely suppressed glee.

A deserved U.K. Top Ten hit, "Friday on My Mind" did even better in Australia, where it topped the charts for eight straight weeks. (The Easybeats' success prompted the fledgling Bee Gees to make the trip back to Blighty from Oz, too.) Alas, it proved The Easybeats' swan song. Mired in contractual hell, sidetracked by drugs ("By that time the band was stoned off their nuts most of the time," guitarist George Young admitted), and despite a belated follow-up hit in 1968 with "Good Times" (featuring Small Face Steve Marriott on backing vocals), their momentum foundered. The Young family were to taste chart action again in style come the Seventies, however, via George's siblings Angus and Malcolm in AC/DC. **RD**

I'm a Believer | The Monkees (1966)

Writer | Neil Diamond
Producer | Jeff Barry
Label | Colgems
Album | *More of the Monkees* (1967)

the monkees   stereo
i'm a believer · daydream believer
last train to clarkesville · a little bit me, a little bit you

"I thought, well, what should I do that's just like the most unhip thing you can possibly think of?"

Robert Wyatt, 1996

◄ **Influenced by: Cherry Cherry** · Neil Diamond (1966)
► **Influence on: Sugar Sugar** · The Archies (1969)
● **Covered by:** The Ventures (1967) · The Four Tops (1967)
Wanda Jackson (1968) · Robert Wyatt (1974) · Tin Huey
(1979) · The Frank and Walters (1992) · Sugar Beats
(1997) · The Patron Saints (2008)

The Monkees never got to play their own instruments on this or many of their other classic Sixties pop hits. Were they reviled for it, like Milli Vanilli in the Nineties? No, because there was no pretense in the first place. The Monkees were created specifically to star in a TV show that tapped into Beatlemania. ("Madness!" screamed the press ads. "Running parts for insane boys . . ." referencing Richard Lester's wacky, irreverent, fast-paced Beatles flick, *A Hard Day's Night*.) "To say that The Monkees are a band is like saying Leonard Nimoy is a Vulcan," quipped former *Circus Boy* child actor (and Monkee drummer) Mickey Dolenz. That comment was topical, because *Star Trek,* for which Nimoy sported his trademark pointy ears, and *The Monkees* were both previewed on TV in 1966.

"I'm a Believer" sprang from impeccable Brill Building stock: Neil Diamond penned the tune (originally intended for country star Eddie Arnold) and strummed rhythm guitar; Carole King sang background vocals. Dolenz provided the euphoric lead vocal, supported by Davy Jones—the only Brit in The Monkees. Jones (whose role was to be The Cute One) had previously played the Artful Dodger in *Oliver!* on Broadway and had been on the famous *Ed Sullivan Show* that launched The Beatles live into America's living rooms.

An aggrieved Mike Nesmith (guitarist and, like fourth Monkee Peter Tork, a non-actor with a musical background) told producer Jeff Barry, somewhat sniffily, "I'm a songwriter, and that's no hit." But he probably wasn't complaining when "I'm a Believer" attracted advance sales alone of 1,051,280 and its infectious bubblegum organ and Beatles-tinged guitars and harmonies kept it at No. 1 stateside for seven weeks. **JJH**

Dirty Water
The Standells (1966)

Writer | Ed Cobb
Producer | Ed Cobb
Label | Tower
Album | *Dirty Water* (1966)

As both an archetypal U.S. garage track and the official victory song of the Boston Red Sox, "Dirty Water" lives on today in the affections of aficionados of both Sixties punk and Boston baseball—although this barefaced Rolling Stones tribute was recorded by a band who made a living playing the upmarket supper clubs of Los Angeles and had never actually visited Beantown.

A simple twelve-bar blues written by The Standells' manager and producer, Ed Cobb—the man also responsible for Gloria Jones's Northern Soul classic, "Tainted Love," later covered by Soft Cell—"Dirty Water" was inspired by an inauspicious visit by Cobb to Boston in the early Sixties, when he was mugged on a bridge over the Charles River. Noting also the pollution in Boston Harbor, and throwing in a couple of timely references to the Boston Strangler and the contemporary curfew for female students at Boston University, Cobb gave the song to his charges, The Standells, led by former Mouseketeer Dick Dodd.

"Dirty Water" became a Top Ten hit in June 1966, but the band would never achieve the same kind of commercial success again. Still, the song's adoption by the Red Sox in the Nineties led to the reformed Standells' playing at Fenway Park when the team won the 2004 World Series. Indeed, U2, Steely Dan, The Mars Volta, Aerosmith, and Bruce Springsteen have all covered it live in Boston. **PL**

I Feel Free
Cream (1966)

Writer | Jack Bruce, Pete Brown
Producer | Robert Stigwood
Label | Reaction
Album | N/A

After the curious false start of "Wrapping Paper," their debut single, Cream—Jack Bruce, Eric Clapton, and Ginger Baker (the world's first rock supergroup)—needed to prove that they could live up to the hype surrounding their formation. With "I Feel Free," all fears were assuaged. Serious blues musicians *could* make pop music.

Written by bassist and vocalist Bruce and lyricist Pete Brown, the single, recorded at London's Rye Muse Studios, was a complete palette cleanser. A U.K. No. 11, it was a blast of aggressive joy that arrived just before the point when beat finally gave way to psychedelia. Brown's breezy message of all-consuming love showcases Bruce's remarkable voice. Clapton distills his considerable skills into a guitar solo notable for its brevity. Baker was never happy with his drumming, but it complements the song's frenetic pace perfectly.

Although it was left off the U.K. version of their debut album, *Fresh Cream*, the track opened the U.S. release, establishing the intense love affair that nation was to have with the group. Among the song's admirers was David Bowie, who performed it on his 1972 Ziggy Stardust tour and recorded it on 1993's *Black Tie White Noise* album. The Foo Fighters have also cut a spirited rendition.

"I Feel Free" makes the listener feel elated and then finishes before it outstays its welcome. It remains one of Cream's finest moments. **DE**

You Keep Me Hangin' On
The Supremes (1966)

Writer | B. & E. Holland, L. Dozier
Producer | B. Holland, L. Dozier
Label | Motown
Album | *The Supremes Sing Holland-Dozier-Holland* (1967)

Although steeped in soul and pop, Motown paid close attention to rock music. "You Keep Me Hangin' On" stands as a precursor to Norman Whitfield's harder-edged late-Sixties psychedelic soul productions with The Temptations.

Producers Brian Holland and Lamont Dozier created a dramatic, swooping guitar opening that hooks the listener before The Funk Brothers come crashing in with a tense groove. The Morse code-like riff comes across like an emergency call for emotional rescue. Diana Ross rides the backing with an impassioned, dramatic vocal. (It's a full minute before the other Supremes join in—a sign, perhaps, that Ross was already being groomed for solo stardom.) Backed by thick organ, syncopated tambourine, pulsing bass, crashing drums, and that insidious guitar riff, never had The Supremes sounded quite so desperate. Ross spits like a blues singer when announcing: "And there ain't nothin' I can do about it!" Florence Ballard and Mary Wilson provide stirring, gospel-flavored backing vocals and the conceit of love as something approaching an addiction ramps up the song's drama quota.

"You Keep Me Hangin' On" became a favorite of rock bands. In 2003, songwriter Brian Holland praised Vanilla Fudge's prog-rock workout on the song: "They took it to a totally different place. Most cover records just copied what we did. But Vanilla Fudge made it a whole different ballgame." **GC**

Happenings Ten Years Time Ago
The Yardbirds (1966)

Writer | Yardbirds
Producer | Simon Napier-Bell
Label | Columbia (UK)
Album | N/A

This is the only Yardbirds single to feature both Jimmy Page and Jeff Beck playing guitar together and one of only three songs recorded by the band to feature both men (the others being its B-side, "Psycho Daisies," and "Stroll On," from the soundtrack to Michelangelo Antonioni's *Blow Up*). In a catalog ripe with pioneering experimentation on tracks such as "Still I'm Sad" and "Shapes of Things," it is the group's most progressive release, an early milestone of psychedelic music.

Page had joined the band as a replacement for original bass player Paul Samwell-Smith (who left to become a producer) but soon switched to playing lead guitar. Here, he duals with Beck on an astonishingly dense, multilayered record that utilizes feedback, guitars imitating a police siren and an explosion, reverse tapes, and a thundering riff, topped with a mixed-up, tripped-out lyric sung by Keith Relf that vaguely hints at reincarnation—"Was it real, was it in my dreams? I need to know what it all means." John Paul Jones plays bass, preempting his partnership with Page in Led Zeppelin—a group that initially went under the name of The New Yardbirds.

Released in October 1966, the single broke the band's run of five U.K. Top Ten singles, reaching No. 43; it fared little better in the United States, peaking at No. 30 on the *Billboard* chart and No. 34 on *Cashbox*. Ah, but what do charts know? **JoH**

Tomorrow Never Knows
The Beatles (1966)

Writer | John Lennon,
Paul McCartney
Producer | George Martin
Label | Parlophone
Album | *Revolver* (1966)

In 1963, The Beatles were content to hold a girl's hand. By the time of *Tomorrow Never Knows*, they wanted to make love to the entire universe. Psychedelic drugs, especially LSD, turned the world of pop on its head during the late Sixties and shifted its focus from schoolyard romance to nothing less than spiritual enlightenment.

So it was with "Tomorrow Never Knows," the final track of *Revolver*, released in 1966. One of the first examples of psychedelic rock, it retains its electrifying modernity today. Shortly after John Lennon began experimenting with LSD, he obtained a copy of *The Psychedelic Experience*, written by acid guru Timothy Leary, from which the opening line of the song ("Turn off your mind, relax and float downstream") is borrowed.

The result of this collision between chemistry and philosophy is a revolutionary piece of music. Driven by pounding drums, the track is haunted by drones and strange birdlike cries, as if seagulls were wheeling above some unearthly shoreline. Lennon's vocal outlines the tenets of a new faith against this extraordinary sonic backdrop.

There are many crumbs of historical interest to enjoy in "Tomorrow Never Knows." The reversed, heavily edited guitar solo was lifted from "Taxman," the opening track of *Revolver*, while the song takes its title from a typically enigmatic remark made by Ringo Starr during a BBC television interview. **JD**

The End
The Doors (1967)

Writer | John Densmore, Robert Krieger,
Ray Manzarek, Jim Morrison
Producer | Paul A. Rothchild
Label | Elektra
Album | *The Doors* (1967)

"The End" is one of those songs that you may not like but you have to admire. It's huge, in length and in scope, a monument to taboo-busting and boundary-breaking that was remarkable even in 1967, when popular music really started to explore the parameters of what could be accomplished.

It wasn't meant to be that way. "The End" began life as a standard three-minute pop song, much like The Doors' breakthrough hit "Light My Fire," but got whacked right out of shape during drug-soaked performances in Los Angeles; by the time the track became the closer of their debut album, it weighed in at nearly twelve haunting minutes of sinister organ, Indian-influenced guitar drone, and sparse jazz drumming, set against a raging and controversial spoken-word Oedipal subtext.

This was music unlike anything that went before, inspiring countless bands from Black Sabbath to The Cult to Joy Division. But as Morrison lapsed into sweaty self-parody (as early as 1968, *Rolling Stone* was arguing that organist Manzarek "has what Morrison does not have: subtlety"), The Doors became profoundly uncool. After Francis Ford Coppola borrowed "The End" for the brilliant but overblown *Apocalypse Now*, the song became a benchmark for pomposity, lampooned by hip kids from Zappa to Nirvana. But, despite all that, it is an Ozymandian accomplishment: one of spine-tingling bravura and ambitious splendor. **PW**

Electricity | Captain Beefheart & His Magic Band (1967)

Writer | Don Van Vliet, Herb Bermann
Producer | Richard Perry,
Bob Krasnow
Label | Buddah
Album | *Safe As Milk* (1967)

British DJ John Peel once said, "If there has ever been such a thing as a genius in the history of popular music, it's Beefheart. I heard echoes of his music in some of the records I listened to last week and I'll hear more echoes in records that I listen to this week." For aficionados of Captain Beefheart & His Magic Band, "Electricity" from *Safe As Milk* is one song with echoes of what had come before and signs of what would come next for the group.

Van Vliet (Beefheart, who added the "Van" to his given name in the early Sixties) later claimed that the off-kilter, occasionally dark, material for this album led A&M Records to drop the group. After parting with A&M, they recut the songs with guitarist Ry Cooder (ex-The Rising Sons). Buddah Records picked up where A&M had left off.

The debut album by Van Vliet & Co. is heavily rooted in Delta blues but departs from this template to foreshadow much of the good Captain's future output. "Electricity" is a case in point. Coming on like a psychedelic hoedown, "Electricity" combines bluesy rhythms with full-on creepiness, the latter particularly evident in Van Vliet's stream-of-consciousness lyrics and rasped repetition of the song's title. Drummer John "Drumbo" French's neat high-hat work punctuates the song, while Cooder provides the nagging bottleneck riff. The distinctive theremin warbles come courtesy of Dr. Samuel Hoffman. **CS-J**

Corcovado | Frank Sinatra & Antônio Carlos Jobim (1967)

Writer | Antônio Carlos Jobim, Gene Lees
Producer | Sonny Burke
Label | Reprise
Album | *Francis Albert Sinatra & Antônio Carlos Jobim* (1967)

Bossa nova (Portuguese for "new trend") had been around for some years in Brazil, but took a while to catch on in the English-speaking world. When it did, the songs of Antônio Carlos ("Tom") Jobim appeared in the repertoires of numerous singers. "Corcovado" (the title refers to the Corcovado mountain in Rio de Janeiro, with its famous *Cristo Redentor* statue)—or "Quiet Nights of Quiet Stars" in the English version of the lyrics by Gene Lees—was covered by Tony Bennett, Doris Day, Perry Como, and Johnny Mathis, while jazz greats including Miles Davis established it as a standard.

In 1967, Frank Sinatra embraced bossa nova, too. In a huge departure from his show-stopping style, the fifty-two-year-old embarked on a collaboration with the composer himself, toning down his performance to the understated delivery typical of the genre. Gone too was the big-band backing, replaced with arrangements by Claus Ogerman and his orchestra, who were closely associated with Jobim. The resulting album, *Francis Albert Sinatra & Antônio Carlos Jobim*, was a collection of definitive versions of Jobim songs, especially "Quiet Nights of Quiet Stars," now regarded as a classic. Although it won critical acclaim and a Grammy award, it was not a great commercial success, and a planned second album was reduced to just one side of the 1971 long player *Sinatra & Company*. **MW**

Heroin
The Velvet Underground (1967)

Writer | Lou Reed
Producer | Tom Wilson (Andy Warhol credited)
Label | Verve
Album | *The Velvet Underground and Nico* (1967)

"When I put a spike into my vein / Then I tell you, things aren't quite the same / When I'm rushing on my run / And I feel just like Jesus' son," croons Lou Reed fifteen seconds into the opening verse. It is a watershed moment in rock history. While The Byrds ("Eight Miles High") and Bob Dylan ("Rainy Day Women #12 and 35") had touched on the taboo topic, "Heroin" was the first time a rock band had sung about drug use so unambiguously.

Written back in 1964, while Reed was still honing his skills as a Pickwick Records intern, the nihilistic verse was completely out of sync with the free-love hippie hype of the late Sixties. But "Heroin" was neither a cautionary tale nor a glamorization of junkie pride; it was poetry.

Musically, the song was equally innovative. While its seven minutes and twelve seconds were built around deceptively simple D and G-flat-major chords, the whirlpool of Sterling Morrison's arcing rhythm-guitar arpeggios, John Cale's screeching electric viola, and Maureen Tucker's hypnotic tribal drumming sounded like nothing else in rock, a musical metaphor for a narcotic high. The classically trained Cale's atonal, one-chord drone also mainlined minimalist avant-garde dissonance into pop music for the first time.

Unsurprisingly, the song never got radio airplay, but its legacy lives on in the work of countless musicians, writers, and filmmakers. **MK**

Chelsea Girls
Nico (1967)

Writer | Lou Reed, Sterling Morrison
Producer | Tom Wilson
Label | Verve
Album | *Chelsea Girl* (1967)

German-born model Christa Päffgen—she was given the name Nico by fashion photographer Herbert Tobias—was not a natural singer, but she did have an imposing presence: a tall, blonde, beautiful German, and an inscrutable poseur with a heroin addiction that often turned her crazy.

Right after singing on The Velvet Underground's debut album, she started on her first solo work, *Chelsea Girl*. The title refers to Andy Warhol's 1966 film, *Chelsea Girls,* in which she had starred, the name a reference to the notoriously louche Hotel Chelsea in which it was mostly shot. Her own song about the hotel, all seven minutes, twenty-two seconds of it, consists of a simple electric guitar line played by the Velvets' guitarist Sterling Morrison, with an insistent flute and occasional string accompaniment. Nico flatly intones her tale of the hotel's unstable and drugged inhabitants, the girls of both genders and none, of Bridget "all wrapped up in foil" and Pepper "who thinks she's some man's son." "Here they come now / See them run now ... Chelsea Girls."

Nico herself hated the track, as she did the whole album, because of the flute and string arrangements by Larry Fallon, added without her knowledge by producer Tom Wilson, and the lack of drums. As a snapshot of the hedonistic, nihilistic denizens of Sixties New York, though, "Chelsea Girls" is unbeatable. **SA**

Haunting face, haunting songs: Nico in the Sixties. ➜

For What It's Worth
The Buffalo Springfield (1967)

Writer | Stephen Stills
Producer | Charles Greene, Brian Stone
Label | Atco
Album | *Buffalo Springfield* (1967)

"For What It's Worth" was an antiestablishment anthem for a significant period of youth unrest in the mid- to late Sixties. West Coast group Buffalo Springfield boasted two songwriters who would go on to play lengthy roles in the development of U.S. rock music: Neil Young and Stephen Stills. The latter's timely protest song captured the emerging spirit of teenage independence and briefly catapulted the group to commercial success. The Springfield's only major hit, it peaked at No. 7 and stayed for fifteen weeks on the *Billboard* Hot 100.

A simple, chiming guitar figure undercuts a song describing confrontations between police and teenagers that took place in 1966 on West Hollywood's Sunset Boulevard. Hundreds of hippies would congregate on the sidewalks outside popular clubs Pandora's Box and The Whisky A Go-Go, prompting agitated local businessmen to enlist the help of the L.A. police to clean up the place. The resulting riots, beatings, and arrests were witnessed by Stephen Stills. Disturbed, he quickly set about writing an almost journalistic song about "battle lines being drawn" in an area just a few blocks away from his home.

The line "What a field day for the heat" was a thinly veiled attack on the police—a sensitive subject for a song back in 1967. More recently, the track has soundtracked TV and movies ranging from *The West Wing* to *Forrest Gump*. **DR**

The Look of Love
Dusty Springfield (1967)

Writer | Burt Bacharach, Hal David
Producer | Phil Ramone
Label | Colgems
Album | *Casino Royale* (1967)

The James Bond spoof *Casino Royale* is now best remembered for this classic song. Hired to compose an instrumental soundtrack that would be dominated by Herb Alpert's Tijuana Brass, Burt Bacharach became obsessed with a scene in which Ursula Andress seduces Peter Sellers. He wrote a theme, but it wasn't until Hal David decided to add lyrics to this lightest of bossa novas that "The Look of Love" started to take shape.

As a fan of Dusty Springfield's interpretations of his songs, Bacharach already knew whom he wanted to sing it, but—foreshadowing her Memphis recordings with Jerry Wexler—sessions were tense: both were perfectionists, though from different perspectives, and this turned out to be the only song they ever recorded together. Even once Bacharach was satisfied and the album released, Springfield's doubts remained. She returned to London and her regular producer, Johnny Franz, to record it one more time, a shorter version on which she sounds more confident.

With the film a financial success, there was considerable demand for the song, yet the second version was only released as the B-side to "Give Me Time." Several covers were released, most idiosyncratically by Nina Simone. Then DJs discovered Dusty's version and it finally received a slice of the recognition it deserved, including a nomination for an Academy Award. **DH**

I'd Rather Go Blind

Etta James (1967)

Writer | Billy Foster, Ellington Jordan
Producer | Rick Hall
Label | Cadet
Album | *Tell Mama* (1968)

Etta James was a constant presence on the U.S. singles charts in the early Sixties, thanks to such hits as "Trust in Me" and the song that became her signature, "At Last." Her career derailed mid-decade, however, as she battled heroin addiction and spent time in a psychiatric hospital.

In 1967, James was in need of a comeback. On the recommendation of Leonard Chess, who had originally groomed James into star material, she journeyed to Muscle Shoals, Alabama, to begin recording her seventh album, *Tell Mama*. It would be one of James's finest, featuring a stirring cover of Otis Redding's "Security" and the heartbreaking love song "I'd Rather Go Blind," comprising just two chords, which has only grown more devastatingly beautiful through the years. Indeed, "I'd Rather Go Blind" has aged at least as well as "At Last"—perhaps better, since it is not weighed down by as much nostalgia. The song is the musical equivalent of an open wound. James sounds like a woman tilting toward the abyss, trying, quite unsuccessfully, to accept that her man is leaving. "I'd rather go blind, boy," she pleads, "Than to see you walk away from me."

Originally released as the B-side to "Tell Mama," the song was not a hit. It did, however, factor into the popularity of the parent album (James's first U.S. Top 100 hit in seven years) and greatly aided the vocalist's comeback. **JiH**

(Your Love Keeps Lifting Me) Higher & Higher | Jackie Wilson (1967)

Writer | Raynard Miner, Carl Smith, Gary Jackson, Billy Davis
Producer | Carl Davis
Label | Brunswick
Album | *Higher and Higher* (1967)

If there is one song that expresses the pure, giddy joy of being in love, it is this exuberant classic by Jackie Wilson. In the mid-Sixties, hoping to revive his career after a slump in his fortunes, Wilson had decided to work with Chicago soul producer Carl Davis. Unfortunately, their defining collaboration did not seem set to begin smoothly, because Wilson apparently considered "(Your Love Keeps Lifting Me) Higher and Higher" a ballad.

"We went into the studio, and Jackie started singing it, and it was completely different from what I thought it should sound like," Davis later recalled. "And I told him, 'No, no, no, no. I don't like that!'" Frustrated, Wilson reportedly suggested Davis come out and show him how it should be done. Demonstration over, Wilson "went back in there and in one take he did it," according to Davis.

And the result appears to come from the heart, with Wilson's voice cracking: he can barely believe his old friend disappointment will never be showing his face again, now he's found his "one in a million girls." Alongside him, Motown house band The Funk Brothers provide a pacy and ecstatic turn.

The single would reach No. 1 in the U.S. R&B chart and make the regular Top Ten, but Wilson largely failed to capitalize on the success. However, "(Your Love Keeps Lifting Me) Higher and Higher" was to reveal its lingering power by bringing the Statue of Liberty to life in the 1989 movie *Ghostbusters II*. **MH**

Strawberry Fields Forever | The Beatles (1967)

Writer | John Lennon, Paul McCartney
Producer | George Martin
Label | Parlophone
Album | N/A

The Beatles

"[It] was psychoanalysis set to music."

John Lennon, 1970

◀ **Influenced by: Mr. Tambourine Man**
Bob Dylan (1965)
▶ **Influence on: Rainy Day, Dream Away** • The Jimi
Hendrix Experience (1968)
● **Covered by:** Richie Havens (1969) • Todd Rundgren
(1976) • The Runaways (1980)

While on location in Almería, southern Spain, to act in the Richard Lester film *How I Won the War*, John Lennon had a lot of time between takes to smoke marijuana and think. From this came perhaps the greatest work of the psychedelic era: a dreamy free association of memory and introspection.

The lyric found Lennon invoking a haunt from his childhood, a Salvation Army home called Strawberry Field in Woolton, a suburb of Liverpool; as a child, he had often attended the annual garden party in a neighboring park. But in the song, the physical location only serves as a catalyst for a dissection of his consciousness, a place where "nothing is real, and nothing to get hung about."

Upon returning to London, Lennon shared the song with producer George Martin, who was immediately enchanted by the song's "hazy impressionistic dreamworld." Martin's moody arrangement of brass and strings wonderfully offsets Paul McCartney's mellotron playing and George Harrison's swordmandel (an Indian stringed instrument).

The Beatles spent forty-five hours at Abbey Road Studios recording the song over nearly a month in late 1966. Two possible versions emerged, which Martin—at Lennon's request—seamlessly merged, though the two had originally been recorded in slightly different speeds and keys. Although the *Sgt. Pepper's* album was in the works, manager Brian Epstein was pushing for a single, so the song was paired on a double A-side with "Penny Lane" (written by McCartney about another childhood reverie set in Woolton). Remarkably, it only reached No. 2 in the U.K. charts, the first Beatles single since "Please Please Me" in 1963 to fall short of the top spot. **TS**

White Rabbit | Jefferson Airplane (1967)

Writer | Grace Slick
Producer | Rick Jarrard
Label | RCA Victor
Album | *Surrealistic Pillow* (1967)

"We found that you could either get married and live in a suburb … or you could live like Alice B. Toklas, Picasso, or Diaghilev."
Grace Slick, 2002

◀ **Influenced by:** *Sketches of Spain* · Miles Davis (1960)
▶ **Influence on:** **Where Is My Mind?** · Pixies (1988)
● **Covered by:** George Benson (1971) · The Damned (1980) · Sanctuary (1988) · The Murmurs (1995) Shakespear's Sister (2004) · Lana Lane (2006) Patti Smith (2007)

When asked how she wrote "White Rabbit"—her most famous song—Grace Slick darted back, deadpan: "How? With pencil and paper."

Inspired by Miles Davis's *Sketches of Spain* and Ravel's *Boléro*, Slick's paradoxical bedtime story had grown wings in one of her previous outfits, The Great Society. A wry reflection on the hallucinatory effects of psychedelic drugs, "White Rabbit" drew on the fantastical narrative of Lewis Carroll's 1865 odyssey *Alice's Adventures in Wonderland*, referencing several of its characters, including Alice, the caterpillar, the White Knight, the Red Queen, and the Dormouse, while simultaneously inventing a catchphrase for her generation with the bellowed "Feed your head!"—though Slick insisted "It also means you gotta feed your brains."

By the time of Jefferson Airplane's recording on November 3, 1966, the tempo had been slowed down and the ornamentation stripped to restore Slick's core bolero rhythm. Jack Casady added his funky bass line, Spencer Dryden snake-hipped the Spanish rhythm, Jorma Kaukonen played guitar-aggressor, and Slick commanded with her strident vocals. It was a winning mix, giving the band their second Top Ten hit (despite the lyrics, it was not banned), after "Somebody to Love," also drawn from *Surrealistic Pillow*. "White Rabbit" rapidly became an anthem for a generation, its prediction of the Sixties psychedelic comedown presented with razor-sharp subversion.

The song has maintained its presence in popular culture down the years, featuring in Oliver Stone's movie *Platoon*, Hunter S. Thompson's book *Fear and Loathing in Las Vegas* (in a scene portraying Dr. Gonzo's bad acid trip), and no fewer than three episodes of *The Simpsons*. **KL**

Purple Haze | The Jimi Hendrix Experience (1967)

Writer | Jimi Hendrix
Producer | Chas Chandler
Label | Track
Album | N/A

"Man, in this life, you gotta do what you want, you gotta let your mind and fancy flow, flow, flow free."

Jimi Hendrix, 1968

◄ **Influenced by: The Times They Are A-Changin'**
Bob Dylan (1964)
► **Influence on: Hey Dude** · Kula Shaker (1996)
● **Covered by:** Soft Cell (1983) · Kronos Quartet (1986)
Frank Zappa (1991) · The Cure (1993)
Paul Rodgers and Company (1993)

In the digitally crisp, metal-friendly modern era, it is hard to imagine the outcry caused by the first overdriven electric guitars—but James Marshall Hendrix, the first musician to take effects such as distortion to their maximum limits, was rightly hailed as a pioneer when he emerged from the R&B session scene with songs such as this (a non-album U.K. single, though it was included on the U.S. version of the *Are You Experienced* LP). Opening with a heavily overdriven and dissonant riff based on a tritone (the diminished fifth or *diabolus in musica*, an interval actually regarded as evil in medieval times), "Purple Haze" sounds intimidating to this day. Imagine its impact in the Summer of Love—and all that before the song even finishes its intro....

In "Purple Haze," the then-twenty-five-year-old Hendrix made a deliberately opaque reference to the psychedelic drugs that were transforming the cutting edge of popular culture at the time. Too obscure for The Man to decipher, but manna from heaven to Hendrix's growing army of "heads," his words tell of confusion among a lysergic fog—although, tellingly, he doesn't express a desire to emerge from it. Backing his words up with searing guitar solos, Hendrix paints a picture of total chaos, a heaven or hell in which there are no parameters. "'Scuse me while I kiss the sky!" he asks, sounding like a prophet or demon in doing so.

"Purple Haze" has entered the international vocabulary as a synonym for a state of flux, but the song's intention is anything but unclear: with this track, Hendrix implied that an altered state of consciousness was a prerequisite for those who wished to see the world as he did. Few mission statements are more compelling. **JMc**

Jimi Hendrix performs the uncommon feat of behind-the-head soloing at a 1967 concert in France. ➡

I'm a Man
The Spencer Davis Group (1967)

Writer | Steve Winwood, Jimmy Miller
Producer | Jimmy Miller
Label | Fontana
Album | N/A

The Spencer Davis Group was one of many fine Sixties British blues groups, but what distinguished them from their peers was their precocious lead vocalist, Steve Winwood. Discovered by guitarist Spencer Davis playing piano in his older brother Muff's jazz-and-blues band in Birmingham when he was only fifteen, Winwood (like his brother) joined the guitarist's group in 1963.

Encouraged by their 1966 hit "Keep on Running," Winwood started to write his own material while the band enlisted future Rolling Stones producer Jimmy Miller to upgrade their sound. Their first collaboration, "Gimme Some Lovin'," was quickly followed by "I'm a Man," which reached No. 9 in the U.K. and No. 10 in the U.S. in January 1967. Winwood was still just eighteen. The song—unrelated to Bo Diddley's of the same name—is an urgent slice of R&B. Powered along by Pete York's drums, brother Muff's insistent bass, and Davis's rhythm guitar, with producer Miller on sizzling percussion and Winwood playing both lead guitar and Hammond B-3 organ, the song showcases Winwood's distinctive Ray Charles–influenced high tenor voice.

Singing behind Winwood were vocalists Jim Capaldi, Dave Mason, and Chris Wood. Within three months of the song's success, Winwood announced he was leaving Spencer Davis and joining the three to form his own group, Traffic. **SA**

Venus in Furs
The Velvet Underground (1967)

Writer | Lou Reed
Producer | Tom Wilson (Andy Warhol credited)
Label | Verve
Album | *The Velvet Underground and Nico* (1967)

Despite the credit on the cover, *The Velvet Underground and Nico* was not so much produced by Andy Warhol as facilitated by him. Warhol had taken the band under his wing at the end of 1965 after seeing them play at an East Village bar called Café Bizarre, and went on to fund the recording of the group's debut album after insisting that they use foghorn-voiced German actress Nico as a guest singer. According to Lou Reed, Warhol also served as the group's "protector," his influence frightening studio engineers and label executives away from requesting changes. Given both the sound of the record and the subject matter of its songs, Warhol's help was indispensable.

"Venus in Furs" was inspired by an apparently autobiographical book of the same title by nineteenth-century Austrian author Leopold von Sacher-Masoch, whose name later led to the coining of the word *masochism*. The song is a microcosm of the album's aesthetic: a dark lyric; a simple, memorable melody, almost a minor-key nursery rhyme; and an abrasive, dirgelike backdrop. John Cale's shrieking viola added color to Maureen Tucker's frill-free drumming and Reed's droning guitar (all six strings were tuned to the same note).

The album was greeted by indifference on its original release, but, as Brian Eno quipped, everyone who heard *The Velvet Underground and Nico* went off and formed a band. **WF-J**

An eye to the future: The Velvet Underground, live, in 1966. ➡

Fire | The Jimi Hendrix Experience (1967)

Writer | Jimi Hendrix
Producer | Chas Chandler
Label | Track
Album | *Are You Experienced* (1967)

"Jimi said to Margaret [Redding], 'Let me stand next to your fire' … that's where the idea for the song came from."

Mitch Mitchell, 1990

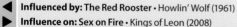

◀ **Influenced by: The Red Rooster** • Howlin' Wolf (1961)
▶ **Influence on: Sex on Fire** • Kings of Leon (2008)
● **Covered by:** Five by Five (1967) • Red Hot Chili Peppers (1988) • Trick Bag (1990) • Kingston Wall (1992) • Nigel Kennedy (1993) • The New Mastersounds (2001) • Joan as Police Woman (2009)

It may seem tasteless to reference the sex tapes leaked onto the Internet in 2008, which revealed the late Jimi Hendrix spending quality time with female friends, but in the context of "Fire," doing so is entirely relevant. Although Jimi had written many lyrics urging his listeners to expand their minds via tuning in, turning on, and dropping out, he wasn't averse to exhorting them to indulge in more carnal pleasures too—and when he sang "I have only one burning desire / Let me stand next to your fire," his intentions were clear.

In a sense, "Fire" owes more of a debt to Jimi's past as an R&B session man than to any of his solo work. The subject matter is funky, hot, and obvious, with many a precedent in the Thirties blues songbook (remember Robert Johnson singing "Squeeze my lemon till the juice run down my leg") and no one is taking themselves too seriously. Jimi isn't in prophet mode here: he's more interested in getting down-and-dirty by the fireside. He asks "Rover" to move over first, a reference to Hendrix attempting to warm himself by the fire with his girlfriend at the house of bassist Noel Redding's mother, where her Great Dane dog was in the way. A generation was in accord.

"Fire" remains one of Hendrix's most popular songs: it's fast (drummer Mitch Mitchell is on brilliant form), funny, and debauched in a way that many of his contemporaries' songs rarely were. As always, his guitar work is exemplary: listen to the solo, and to this day you can hear how much fun he was having. The Experience often opened their live gigs with this song. No wonder that the Red Hot Chili Peppers, one of the most testosterone-laden bands ever formed, covered it so memorably a couple of decades after its writer's death. **JMc**

Waterloo Sunset | The Kinks (1967)

Writer | Ray Davies
Producer | Ray Davies, Shel Talmy
Label | Pye
Album | *Something Else by the Kinks* (1967)

"I've never worked with a song that has been a total pleasure from beginning to end like that one."

Ray Davies, 1984

◀ **Influenced by: Penny Lane** · The Beatles (1967)
▶ **Influence on: For Tomorrow** · Blur (1993)
● **Covered by:** Affairs of the Heart (1983) · Cathy Dennis (1996) · Fastbacks (2001) · David Bowie (2003) · David Essex (2003) · Scrabbel (2005) · Def Leppard (2006) MiG (2007) · The Rushes (2007)

Ray Davies, the lead singer, rhythm guitarist, and principal songwriter of The Kinks, had originally intended to write a song called "Liverpool Sunset" about the death of Merseybeat, but he decided that, as a Londoner, he should write about his home city instead.

The song was very personal to Davies, and the Waterloo area held special significance for him. He had been a patient in St. Thomas's Hospital in Waterloo in his early teens undergoing a tracheotomy, and, while recovering, the nurses had wheeled him on to the hospital's balcony where he could look at the Thames—the "dirty old river" of the song. Davies had also traveled daily through Waterloo as an art student on the way to Croydon Art School and walked along the Embankment with his first wife, Rasa, when they were courting.

In the song, the solitary outsider narrating watches a couple—"Terry and Julie"—meet at Waterloo railway station, cross the river via Waterloo Bridge to north London, happy in their own private bubble. The singer is wistful ("But I don't need no friends"), finding an inner contentment in the ambience of sunset over the London skyline. Terry and Julie are often presumed to be the British actors Terence Stamp and Julie Christie, who starred in *Far from the Madding Crowd* together in 1967, but Davies denies any specifics, stating that the couple are imaginary young innocents wrapped up in each other at the start of a romance—although the name Terry was also that of Ray's nephew in Australia.

Reaching No. 2 in the U.K. charts in the summer of 1967, "Waterloo Sunset" is Davies's finest composition: a beautiful, melancholy yet warm, evocation of twilight London. **JoH**

Ode to Billie Joe
Bobbie Gentry (1967)

Writer | Bobbie Gentry
Producer | Kelly Gordon
Label | Capitol
Album | *Ode to Billie Joe*
(1967)

Having begun her career as a variety singer in the casinos of Las Vegas and the country clubs of Beverly Hills, Bobbie Gentry returned to her humble Chickasaw County, Mississippi, roots for her Capitol Records debut single. Having had "Mississippi Delta" selected for her as the A-side, the singer offered the self-penned "Ode to Billie Joe" for the flip. The latter proved so popular it was decided to go with this as the single. A wise move: it garnered eight Grammy nominations, made No. 1 on *Billboard*, and was an international smash.

The song tells the tale of the eponymous Billie Joe McAllister, the boyfriend of the narrator, who has committed suicide for unknown reasons. The combination of the mysterious nature of the death and the narrator's matter-of-fact reaction as she and her family learn of the event over dinner sets a haunting tone for the song. The odd atmosphere is stressed by the stark arrangement of strings, and Gentry's plain, nylon-string guitar. Writer Herman Raucher was later commissioned to compose both a novel and a film script based on "Ode . . . ."

There's more mystery in the line in which Billie Joe and the narrator are seen throwing something from the Tallahatchie Bridge. In the film version, a ragdoll is thrown into the waters, and Billie Joe kills himself because he fears he may be homosexual. These explanations and all others were rejected by Gentry, who claims the song is entirely fiction. **CR**

The Dark End of the Street
James Carr (1967)

Writer | Chips Moman, Dan Penn
Producer | Q. Claunch, R. Russell
Label | Goldwax
Album | *You Got My Mind Messed Up* (1967)

James Carr received this song in 1966 from a professional and personal couple based in Memphis: twenty-five-year-old producer Dan Penn and former Stax session guitarist Chips Moman, five years Penn's senior. The song was written during a break in a poker game at a music industry convention in Nashville. As Penn told writer Robert Gordon, the duo "were always wanting to come up with the best cheatin' song—ever."

The singer's ambitions were rather less lofty. Born in Coahoma, Mississippi, but raised in Memphis, the illiterate James Carr was eking out a living as a laborer while singing in various gospel groups when he met upstart manager Roosevelt Jamison in 1962. Jamison shepherded him into a deal with the small Memphis label Goldwax; one of the first sides he cut for them (secured in two takes) was this ballad of infidelity, lent grandeur by Carr's proud, passionate baritone.

Now seen as a southern-soul classic, "The Dark End of the Street" was one of several minor hits for Carr. However, hampered by a tragically unstable personality, the singer never made the major breakthrough his talent deserved, and was effectively out of the business before the dawn of the Seventies. His biggest hit, though, has been kept alive by some inferior covers and by Van Morrison, who incorporated a lyrical tribute in his 1979 single "Bright Side of the Road." **WF-J**

Suzanne
Leonard Cohen (1967)

Writer | Leonard Cohen
Producer | John Simon
Label | Columbia
Album | *Songs of Leonard Cohen* (1967)

For Leonard Cohen—poet, future Zen Buddhist monk, and ultimate auteur of fellatio in popular music—this was the song that started it all. The public were first introduced to "Suzanne" on 1967's *Songs of Leonard Cohen* album, but the piece was written at the start of the Sixties when Cohen was living in his native Montreal.

It was here that the singer first met Suzanne Verdal, a beautiful young dancer married to the sculptor Armand Vaillancourt. Cohen would watch the pair dancing together in jazz/beat clubs. He met Verdal briefly, but the pair developed a meaningful spiritual connection several years later when Verdal had separated from her husband and moved to the St. Lawrence River. Says Verdal: "Leonard heard about this place I was living, with crooked floors and a poetic view of the river, and he came to visit me many times. We had tea together many times and mandarin oranges."

The song itself is a perfect evocation of those drowsy, sunny days. Over delicately plucked Spanish guitar, Cohen's description of Suzanne's beauty melts into a wider, flowing contemplation of nature and philosophy—all delivered in his opiated baritone. For Cohen, the song remains a career favorite. For Verdal, the song is a bittersweet pleasure: "He became a big star after the song was launched and he became a songwriter," she says. "Our relationship did change with time." **SH**

Respect
Aretha Franklin (1967)

Writer | Otis Redding
Producer | Jerry Wexler
Label | Atlantic
Album | *I Never Loved a Man the Way I Love You* (1967)

You know a song is special when a new category of the Grammy Awards is created just to give it its dues. Such was the case in 1968, when Aretha Franklin won the inaugural award for Best Female R&B Vocal Performance for her burning rendition of Otis Redding's "Respect."

A lot of people were in dire need of respect in 1967, not least the twenty-five-year-old preacher's daughter herself. The black community was on the verge of burning down her home city of Detroit, rather than suffer another indignity at the hands of a racist bureaucracy. Women were beginning to apply the goals of the civil rights movement in their uphill struggle for social equality. And the spectacularly talented Franklin was struggling to resuscitate her career at Atlantic after several stagnant years with Columbia Records. She had been raised on gospel before wandering into jazz, and new producer Jerry Wexler now wanted her to preach. In two and a half minutes, the soon-to-be-queen of soul would make all of their cases.

Before recording the song, Franklin and her sister, Carolyn, reset its beat and wrote new vocal arrangements, including the iconic spelling out of the title. It wasn't just a rhythmic device. Without plain R-E-S-P-E-C-T, there would be no lovin'. Franklin sang with a devastating mix of clarity and conviction, making "respect" into a universal decree of common sense. **MO**

Montague Terrace (in Blue)
Scott Walker (1967)

Writer | Scott Engel
Producer | John Franz
Label | Philips
Album | *Scott* (1967)

A Day in the Life
The Beatles (1967)

Writer | John Lennon, Paul McCartney
Producer | George Martin
Label | Parlophone
Album | *Sgt. Pepper's Lonely Hearts Club Band* (1967)

Scott Walker had recorded a handful of his own songs with The Walker Brothers, but one look at the track listing for the trio's third album, *Images*, explains why Walker pulled the plug. Among the highlights is "Orpheus," a ballad written by Walker (under his real name, Scott Engel) that offered a foretaste of the singer's later classic "Plastic Palace People." Yet this gem was sandwiched between a soporific cover of Fats Domino's "Blueberry Hill" and a wan reading of Ben E. King's "Stand by Me."

By then in the grip of an obsession with Belgian balladeer Jacques Brel, Walker had little time for such compromises. Leaving behind his bandmates (none of whom was related), he set out on a solo career, taking Walker Brothers producer John Franz with him. The first track on *Scott*, his solo debut, was a rollicking cover of Brel's "Mathilde." The second was this powerful, cinematic piece of storytelling, with Walker's charismatic vocal and imagery-rich lyric ("The window sees trees cry from cold / And claw the moon") wedded to a pungent orchestral score from Wally Stott.

The public initially took Walker's solo career to their hearts, with his first three albums all making the U.K. Top Three. The dark, elusive *Scott 4* and the disjointed *'Til the Band Comes In* failed to chart, though, and it was only with the Walker Brothers' reunion LP, *Nite Flights* (1978), that Walker again triumphed as a unique experimental artist. **WF-J**

The Beatles' *Sgt. Pepper's* was teamwork personified. For the album's dizzying closer, McCartney supplied the middle eight, but Lennon's lyrics dominate. An avid media consumer, his inspiration came partly from newspapers—the "lucky man who made the grade" may have been inspired by a report about ill-fated Guinness heir Tara Browne. The *Daily Mail's* "Far & Near" column famously supplied the line about holes in Blackburn, Lancashire, and Lennon's recent role in Richard Lester's satirical *How I Won the War* emerges, too. In the line "I'd love to turn you on," for the first time the duo deliberately sent their fans a pro-drugs message. (The BBC certainly got it: they banned the song.)

McCartney's burgeoning interest in avant-garde composers such as Stockhausen and Luciano Berio inspired him to suggest the song's famous orchestral "surges"—in which each player took his instrument through every note from lowest to highest, over twenty-four bars. The result, scored by George Martin for a forty-piece orchestra, was described by Lennon as "a sound building up from nothing to the end of the world" and, more pithily, by George Martin as an "orchestral orgasm."

Jaw-droppingly original in conception, with superb ensemble playing throughout (Starr's subtle, jazz-inflected drumming is a dream), and a beautifully judged Lennon vocal, "A Day in the Life" might just be pop's best-ever collaboration. **RD**

John Lennon's handwritten lyrics for "A Day in the Life" have generated much interest at auction. ➜

I READ THE NEWS TODAY OH BOY.
ABOUT A LUCKY MAN WHO MADE THE GRADE
AND THOUGH THE NEWS WAS RATHER SAD
WELL I JUST HAD TO LAUGH
     I SAW THE PHOTOGRAPH.

HE BLEW HIS MIND OUT IN A CAR
HE DIDN'T NOTICE THAT THE LIGHTS HAD CHANGED
A CROWD OF PEOPLE STOOD AND STARED
THEY'D SEEN HIS FACE BEFORE
NOBODY WAS REALLY SURE IF HE WAS FROM THE
     HOUSE OF LORDS

+I SAW A FILM TODAY OH BOY
THE ENGLISH ARMY HAD JUST WON THE WAR
A CROWD OF PEOPLE ~~TURNED AWAY~~
BUT I JUST HAD TO LOOK
{US'T} HAVING READ THE BOOK
   + I LOVE TO TURN YOU ON
+I READ THE NEWS TODAY OH BOY
FOUR THOUSAND HOLES IN BLACKBURN LANCASHIRE
AND THOUGH THE HOLES WERE ~~RATHER~~ SMALL
THEY HAD TO COUNT THEM ALL
NOW THEY KNOW HOW MANY HOLES IT TAKES TO FILL
     THE ALBERT HALL

Alone Again Or | Love (1967)

Writer | Bryan MacLean
Producer | Bruce Botnick, Arthur Lee
Label | Elektra
Album | *Forever Changes* (1967)

"I listened to it once and never again."

Bryan MacLean, 1996

◀ **Influenced by:** Lieutenant Kije Suite · Composed by
Sergei Prokoviev (1933)
▶ **Influence on:** Nantes · Beirut (2007)
● **Covered by:** UFO (1977) · The Damned (1987)
Sarah Brightman (1990) · The Boo Radleys (1992)
The Oblivians (1993) · Calexico (2003)

Few songs define the noir pallor of Sixties psychedelia as intensely as "Alone Again Or." Originally entitled "Alone Again"—the mysterious "Or" was added by the band's wayward leader, Arthur Lee—and intended for Love's debut self-titled 1966 debut album, Bryan MacLean's ode to his faraway girlfriend wasn't completed until the recording of *Forever Changes*, in the summer of 1967. The track's cult status owes much to the wistful mariachi-horn part halfway through that peppers the original string arrangement alongside MacLean's bleak conclusion: "And I will be alone again tonight, my dear." (MacLean later commented: "That was the happiest I ever was with anything we ever did as a band.")

However, the track famously caused rifts between band members when MacLean's own vocals were remixed and replaced with band mate Arthur Lee's harmony vocal, on the grounds that his original lead was "too weak." MacLean eventually admitted that his voice had not been quite strong enough to hold the tune, and he later readdressed the matter by singing a solo version of the track on his album *ifyoubelievein*.

Although the song was deemed "inconsistent" by *Rolling Stone* on its release as a single in 1968—when it reached only No. 99 in the U.S. *Billboard* chart—this beguiling track soon grew in cult status, becoming regarded as a classic expression of its psychedelic times.

"Alone Again Or" has featured in many movies, including the cult classic *Sleepers* (1996). It has been covered by artists as diverse as The Boo Radleys, Calexico, UFO, and Matthew Sweet with Susanna Hoffs. "We *love* love, man!" remarked the latter duo. "And we mean the group, too!" **KL**

Tin Soldier | The Small Faces (1967)

Writer | Steve Marriott, Ronnie Lane
Producer | Steve Marriott, Ronnie Lane
Label | Immediate
Album | N/A

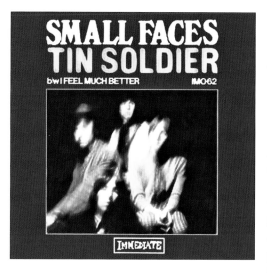

"It refers to a girl [Jenny Rylance] I used to talk to all the time and she really gave me a buzz."
Steve Marriott, 1967

◄ **Influenced by:** Little Girl · John Mayall & The Bluesbreakers (1966)
► **Influence on:** Would You Believe · Billy Nicholls (1968)
● **Covered by:** Quiet Riot (1977) · The Hypstrz (1979) Todd Rundgren (1983)

Written in Ibiza by Steve Marriott in a bid to impress the woman who would a year later become his wife, "Tin Soldier" was never intended to be a song for The Small Faces. The Immediate label fostered a culture of sharing, and so the writer presented the song to Pat (P. P.) Arnold, a former backing singer for the Ike & Tina Turner Revue, who had made her home in London. As Marriott later remembered it, "She freaked, so I thought I'd better hold back." Keeping it for the band, he gave her a song with similar power, "(If You Think You're) Groovy," instead. The band played on her record, she sang on theirs.

Released in December 1967, "Tin Soldier" arrived at a time when the east London quartet could do little wrong. The third of the five Immediate singles released while the band were together, it sits between "Itchycoo Park" and "Lazy Sunday," but would almost certainly win any poll designed to identify their finest work. After the pop psychedelia of the previous year, the song was a return to their mod-soul origins, yet it represented a great leap forward for the band as writers, musicians, and recording artists after the water-treading of their second album.

An early instrumental version reveals all the acoustic guitars that had originally been intended to carry the song, but the finished result was to be a significant influence on the heavy-rock scene that emerged in 1968. The song is a headbanger's delight, with Ronnie Lane playing bass in both rhythm and lead roles while Kenney Jones's percussion—which includes tin-drum effects—pulverizes the backing track. And Marriott's singing? It was time to put away childish things: at 1:35 in, the rock era began in earnest. **DH**

See Emily Play | Pink Floyd (1967)

Writer | Syd Barrett
Producer | Norman Smith
Label | Columbia
Album | N/A

"It changed my life and convinced me there was something very special about music."

Captain Sensible, The Damned, 2000

◄ **Influenced by: Strawberry Fields Forever**
The Beatles (1967)

► **Influence on: Shine On You Crazy Diamond**
Pink Floyd (1975)

● **Covered by:** David Bowie (1973) • The Grapes of Wrath
(1994) • Martha Wainwright (2008)

Pink Floyd briefly allowed themselves to be jolly good at pop singles. Their second offering, "See Emily Play," was 1967's greatest British hit not to bear a Lennon/McCartney imprint.

The song was originally named for an ambitious London show by the Floyd, *Games for May*, but bandleader Syd Barrett rechristened it "See Emily Play" after being inspired by the sight of a "psychedelic schoolgirl," a member of their audience at London's UFO Club. Yet "hardly any [psychedelic] special effects were used," said keyboardist Rick Wright. "Take that 'Hawaiian' bit at the end of each verse: that was just Syd using a bottleneck through echo."

Syd's eventual successor as guitarist, David Gilmour, visited the studio in May 1967 and was disturbed to find his friend "glassy-eyed . . . not terribly friendly." Live, the Floyd would, in bassist Roger Waters's words, "struggle through 'Emily' occasionally." Otherwise, they would play the instrumental "Reaction in G" instead. "We used to tour the country playing our peculiar music, to the absolute fury of the punters . . ." recalled drummer Nick Mason. "Promoters would come backstage feeling totally ripped off because 'See Emily Play' had just been a three-minute spot."

Barrett refused to promote the single on the U.K. TV show *Top of the Pops*. "We finally discovered the reason," said Waters, "was that John Lennon didn't have to do *Top of the Pops*, so he didn't."

David Bowie—who murdered the song on 1973's *Pin Ups*—remarked: "Pink Floyd got a hit, and for a few months they were moderately overground. And Syd just didn't want any part of that, so he opted out. And I understood why . . . they're being accepted. Nobody wants that." **BM**

The rest of Pink Floyd look rather prim beside Syd Barrett's latest sartorial departure in 1967. ➡

A Whiter Shade of Pale
Procol Harum (1967)

Writer | Keith Reid, Gary Brooker, Matthew Fisher
Producer | Denny Cordell
Label | Deram
Album | *Procol Harum* (1967, U.S.)

Indecipherable lyrics and lawsuits make "A Whiter Shade of Pale" one of pop's most enigmatic and enduring creations. During the technicolor, kaftan-wearing summer of 1967, this pop-meets-the-classics single remained top of the British singles chart for six psychedelic weeks.

Procol Harum was created to record the songs of lyricist Keith Reid and vocalist/keyboard player Gary Brooker. "A Whiter Shade of Pale" was the surprise hit of the year for the newly formed group. The complex song combined a somber, Bach-like organ melody with the most surreal lyrics ever to grace a pop song. Tripping "the light fandango" and featuring vestal virgins, a tale-telling miller, and a ceiling that "flew away," no one could quite make sense of it, least of all the record label. Doubts as to whether it should even be released at all were swept aside once a test pressing found its way to pirate radio station Radio London, anchored off Britain's east coast. Rush-released by public demand, the single took just three weeks to make U.K. No. 1. (As was standard practice, the song was omitted from the 1967 U.K. album *Procol Harum*, but made the cut for the U.S. version.)

Inspiration for the song's title came courtesy of a remark overheard by Keith Reid at a party. Reid's friend, disc-jockey-turned-producer Guy Stevens, turned to his wife and observed, "My God, you've just turned a whiter shade of pale." **DR**

The Tears of a Clown | Smokey Robinson & The Miracles (1967)

Writer | Henry Cosby, "Smokey" Robinson, Stevie Wonder
Producer | Cosby, Robinson
Label | Tamla
Album | *Make It Happen* (1967)

When Stevie Wonder set off for the Motown Christmas party of 1966, he took with him some music to which he had been unable to fit any words. Smokey Robinson remarked on its circus feel, and this triggered memories of the lonely clown who has to keep his audiences smiling. (Robinson had written the line "Just like Pagliacci did, I'll try to keep my sadness hid" for the song "My Smile Is Just a Frown.") The Miracles recorded the result, releasing it on their 1967 LP, *Make It Happen*.

Three years later, Smokey himself had become a forlorn figure; tired of life on the road, on a break from recording, he wanted to split from the group and spend more time at home with his young family. Then news came in from Britain: the long-forgotten song had been released as a single (thanks to the enthusiasm of a secretary at EMI, the label that released Motown material there) and hit No. 1. The Detroit office was skeptical but took the cut, slowed it down, and overdubbed a drum track that gave the song more drive. On December 12—three months after hitting No. 1 in Britain—it replaced The Partridge Family in the U.S. No. 1 slot.

So what was it Detroit had missed in 1967? The interplay between bassoon and flute that gives the song its irresistible "circus" feel? One of Smokey's finest lyrics? The peerless backing vocals? Who knows—but EMI's Karen Spreadbury deserved a hefty Christmas bonus that year. **DH**

Sunshine of Your Love
Cream (1967)

Writer | Eric Clapton, Jack Bruce, Pete Brown
Producer | Felix Pappalardi
Label | Reaction
Album | *Disraeli Gears* (1967)

By the standards of 1967, Cream were the ultimate fusion of styles, combining a mastery of the decades-old blues idiom with the most modern jazz departures and a psychedelic rock tinge of their very own. It is fitting that "Sunshine of Your Love" should be so fêted all these years later, therefore, because it too epitomizes this synthesis of new and old. It is both simple and complex; many a guitarist will recall learning Eric Clapton's descending ten-note guitar riff in their very earliest lessons. In the hands of Cream admirers such as a certain Jimi Hendrix, however, the song evolved into a riff-storm of enormous power.

Like all the best compositions, the lyrics (in this case, from the pen of longtime Cream collaborator Pete Brown) do not have to make grammatical sense. Jack Bruce singing "It's getting near dawn" takes the listener back to the first electric blues, the words' voodoo charm diminished not a jot by the fact that the singer—a Royal College–educated jazz master—was culturally about as far from the bayou as could be. The song is strongly emotive, with the narrator—evoking the "tired eyes" of night—taking us to a place where only the object of his desire matters. Smart despite its lovelorn tones, modern despite its ancient roots, "Sunshine of Your Love" was, and remains, a statement encapsulating both the vibe of its era and the talents of its creators. **JMc**

Cold Sweat | James Brown
& The Famous Flames (1967)

Writer | James Brown, Alfred Ellis
Producer | James Brown
Label | King
Album | *Cold Sweat* (1967)

In 1966, James Brown & The Famous Flames played a concert in Abidjan, the capital of Ivory Coast. The effect it had on the West African music scene was electric, sparking the careers of, among others, Fela Kuti, who was soon to claim JB was playing *his* songs. Just how much influence polyrhythmic African music had on Brown can be measured by the direction he took in January 1967, with the recording of "Let Yourself Go," the first tentative step toward the pure groove (and away from melody) that Brown had been searching for.

Recorded four months later, "Cold Sweat," a two-part single and seven-minute LP cut, was a collaboration between Brown and Alfred "Pee Wee" Ellis, his bandleader and alto-sax player. It is little more than a jam session: the lyrics are rudimentary, as if Brown is admitting that the song is entirely about the percussive feel of all the instruments, specifically the interplay between Clyde Stubblefield's much-sampled drums, Maceo Parker's tenor, and Bernard Odum's bass. Typically, Brown's exhortations are now more famous than the solo breaks: "Maceo, come on now, brother. Put it where it's at" and "Give the drummer some."

An R&B No. 1 and a pop No. 7, "Cold Sweat" set Brown on a course that would take him through the next seven years, until his historic concerts in Zaire, in 1974. More importantly, the track revolutionized black music on two continents. **DH**

The First Cut Is the Deepest | P. P. Arnold (1967)

Writer | Cat Stevens
Producer | Mike Hurst
Label | Immediate
Album | *The First Lady of Immediate* (1967)

"[The song] totally related to my life and what had happened to me as a result of my first marriage."

P. P. Arnold, 2004

◀ **Influenced by: Don't Let Me Be Misunderstood**
Nina Simone (1964)
▶ **Influence on: Back to Black** • Amy Winehouse (2006)
● **Covered by:** Rod Stewart (1976) • Martin Simpson
(1983) • Bad Manners (1993) • Bonfire (1998)
Sheryl Crow (2003) • David Essex (2003)

During her first visit to the United Kingdom—touring in support of The Rolling Stones as a member of Ike and Tina Turner's backing band The Ikettes—P. P. Arnold's talent was noted by Mick Jagger. Impressed, the Stones' front man promptly advised his manager, Andrew Loog Oldham, to sign her to his new Immediate label.

Working with musicians such as Keith Emerson of The Nice, and Ronnie Lane and Steve Marriott of The Small Faces, Arnold began developing new material from a number of writers. Following her debut with Oldham's own "Everything's Gonna Be Alright," she went on to score her biggest hit with the Cat Stevens–penned "The First Cut Is the Deepest," a poignant tale of a heartbroken woman trying to give love another chance. Stevens had written the song early in his career while trying to establish himself as a songwriter for hire. On the back of a demo recording he made, the song was sold on to Immediate for P. P. Arnold for £30 and was released in May of 1967. Later that year, Stevens included the track on his own *New Masters* album, though he didn't release it as a single, as he felt Arnold's cover was the definitive recording.

The rousing, up-tempo Arnold version, recorded by Mike Hurst (a former member of The Springfields), featured string and horn sections alongside a harp. Listen closely and you can hear echoes of both the dense layering of Phil Spector's "wall of sound" productions and the idiosyncratic touches that British R&B groups were developing as they moved into more psychedelic territories in the late Sixties.

The song achieved modest chart success (peaking at No. 18 in the U.K.), but it marked the beginning of a recognizable British soul scene. **CR**

I Say a Little Prayer | Aretha Franklin (1968)

Writer | Burt Bacharach, Hal David
Producer | Jerry Wexler
Label | Atlantic
Album | *Aretha Now* (1968)

"Y'know the one that sticks out the most—maybe because she made the song better—was Aretha's record."

Burt Bacharach, 1996

◀ **Influenced by: How I Got Over**
Mahalia Jackson (1961)
▶ **Influence on: Close Your Eyes and Remember**
Minnie Riperton (1970)
● **Covered by:** The Dells (1972) • Susan Cadogan (1975)
Al Green (1978) • Bomb the Bass (1988)

Overshadowing Dionne Warwick is no easy feat, but Aretha Franklin managed it with her treatment of this song. Her version was released nearly a year after Warwick's and didn't chart as highly in the United States, but Franklin's is the name that will forever be associated with the song.

Songwriters Burt Bacharach and Hal David had collaborated with Warwick to produce pop perfection in "Anyone Who Had a Heart" and "Do You Know the Way to San Jose," but Bacharach wasn't totally satisfied with the treatment of "I Say a Little Prayer." "I think I made the tempo a little too fast," he reflected. His initial objections to releasing the song as a single were offset by Warwick's rendition's hitting the Top Five in 1967. However, it wasn't long before another version of the song had him sitting up and taking notice.

After a move of labels from Columbia to Atlantic, Franklin's music had been toughened up to give it the same punch as her voice. The policy justified itself through nine Top Ten hits in the United States during 1967 and 1968, of which "I Say a Little Prayer" was the last. "She changed the melody a bit, some other things, and I thought, 'Hmmmm,'" admitted Bacharach. "But when I got used to it—and she's incredible—I was fine with it." Though not his own work, a classic was born.

The song's timeless quality has ensured an enduring influence. Kevin Rowland, front man of Dexys Midnight Runners, has admitted that his mornings were incomplete without the song, while Rupert Everett led a rousing restaurant rendition sung to Julia Roberts in the 1997 romcom *My Best Friend's Wedding*. More tellingly, it is Bacharach's personal favorite of all the thousands of interpretations of his songs. **CB**

The Snake
Al Wilson (1968)

Writer | Oscar Brown Jr.
Producer | Marc Gordon, Johnny Rivers
Label | Soul City
Album | *Searching for the Dolphins* (1969)

Taking his cue from one of Aesop's fables, the radical jazzman Oscar Brown Jr. composed "The Snake" for his 1962 album *Oscar Brown Jr. Tells It Like It Is*. Its narrative is a parable about trust: a tender woman takes a frozen serpent into the warmth of her care—a scenario that would cause both Sigmund Freud and John Milton to nod in recognition—and, after nursing it back to health, receives a poisonous bite. "'Oh shut up, silly woman!' said that reptile with a grin. / Now you knew darn well I was a snake before you brought me in.'"

Brown's original was a subtle bossa nova, but in the hands of Al Wilson it became a four-to-the-floor stomper. Marty Paich's horn arrangement is quite simply one of the most exciting ever recorded; with each successive verse, the brass stabs become more and more manic, reflecting the drama of the narrative. The impressive extended drum fills, which slither from the right speaker to the left, were played by Hal Blaine on a full-octave kit with twelve drums rather than the usual five.

Wilson revels in the theatricality of it all, hissing his fricatives when playing the snake and adopting a comical squawk when he voices the hapless woman. (The backing singers get in on the act, too, with a kitschy "Ooooh!" at the moment of the bite.) "The Snake" was a guaranteed floor-filler, in particular for the large-trousered fans of Northern-soul in Seventies Britain. **SP**

Oh Happy Day
The Edwin Hawkins Singers (1968)

Writer | Phillip Doddridge, J. A. Freylinghausen; arr. Edwin Hawkins
Producer | Edwin Hawkins
Label | Pavilion
Album | *Let Us Go into the House of the Lord* (1968)

When the forty-six-strong Northern California State Youth Choir needed funds for a trip to Washington, D.C., to attend a youth congress in 1968, they commissioned Century Record Productions to make a live recording of one of their performances. From those basic two-track tapes, eight songs (including the original version of "Oh Happy Day") were chosen for an album, and just five hundred copies were pressed.

Later, copies were circulated in the community. A DJ on San Francisco's underground radio station KSAN-FM began playing "Oh Happy Day," and other stations soon picked up on it. This attracted the attention of Buddah Records' Neil Bogart, who bought the national distribution rights, re-released the album (on Pavilion), issued "Oh Happy Day" as a single, and renamed the group The Edwin Hawkins Singers, after the choir leader.

With a simple backing of piano, drums, bass, and a chorus that included future gospel star Tramaine Hawkins, the soulful lead vocals were by Dorothy Coombs Morrison. She immediately launched a solo career on the back of the success of the single, which eventually sold seven million copies worldwide and earned Hawkins the first of four Grammys. "Oh Happy Day" has been covered by numerous artists, most notably Joan Baez, Glen Campbell, Aretha Franklin (in a duet with Mavis Staples), and Queen Latifah. **JLu**

The Edwin Hawkins Singers, with Hawkins at the piano, perform "Oh Happy Day" in 1970.

Israelites | Desmond Dekker & The Aces (1968)

Writer | Desmond Dekker, Leslie Kong
Producer | Leslie Kong
Label | Pyramid
Album | *Israelites* (1969)

With "Israelites," Desmond Dekker became the first Jamaican artist to achieve truly international popularity. More importantly, the record paved the way for other ska and reggae acts to follow.

Dekker's single "007 (Shanty Town)" had begun to win him a fan base in England, but it seemed ska would remain strictly a Caribbean/English phenomenon until "Israelites" achieved the seemingly impossible. Rising through the charts on both sides of the Atlantic, it reached No. 1 in Britain, the Netherlands, West Germany, Sweden, and Canada, and No. 9 on the *Billboard* Hot 100. The feat was all the more remarkable given that very few listeners understood the lyrics: Dekker's words not only included some obscure cultural references (it was originally titled "Poor Me Israelite"), but were also delivered in an accent impenetrable to most non-Jamaicans.

Unfortunately, having opened up the U.S. and European markets for West Indian music, Dekker never matched the success of "Israelites," even in his adopted home of Britain, though he maintained a steady following in Jamaica through the Seventies. His best-known song has retained its popularity, however, again reaching the U.K. Top Ten on its re-release in 1975. It was covered by Swedish punks Millencolin in 1997 and by beloved London ska institution Madness on the album *The Dangermen Sessions Vol. 1* in 2005. **MW**

Wichita Lineman
Glen Campbell (1968)

Writer | Jimmy Webb
Producer | Al De Lory
Label | Capitol
Album | *Wichita Lineman* (1968)

Jimmy Webb still remembers the phone call. "Glen's looking for a follow-up for 'By the Time I Get to Phoenix,'" relayed the A&R man, "but it's got to be a place." Just twenty-one at the time, Webb wasn't interested at first, but had a crack at it regardless, mapping a song around a memory he held of telephone engineers working on the wires around the town of Liberal, Kansas, and the Oklahoma panhandle. He sent in the sketch with the caveat that it wasn't finished. Producer Al De Lory, whose uncle worked as a lineman in California, disagreed.

At the time, Campbell's solo career had only just taken flight, nearly a decade after his first single. The singer had spent the years making a living as a guitarist for hire, a key part of L.A.'s famous Wrecking Crew of session musicians. De Lory enlisted many members of the Wrecking Crew to work on the song, later adding his own Morse code–mimicking string arrangement and the otherworldly tinkle of Webb's Gulbransen organ.

Since becoming Campbell's biggest hit, "Wichita Lineman" has been covered by artists as varied as The Fatback Band and R.E.M. Webb himself recorded it in the Nineties, despite confessing that his pairing of "time" and "line" in the chorus makes him flinch; he's described it, perhaps harshly, as "the biggest, awfullest, dumbest, most obvious false rhyme in history." **WF-J**

I Heard It through the
Grapevine | Marvin Gaye (1968)

Writer | Norman Whitfield,
Barrett Strong
Producer | Norman Whitfield
Label | Tamla
Album | *In the Groove* (1968)

Motown boss Berry Gordy usually had a pretty good instinct for a hit, but he nearly missed the boat on this one. Several recordings of "I Heard It through the Grapevine" were rejected by Gordy in 1966 and 1967: the original by Smokey Robinson & The Miracles, a much-rumored, never-heard cover by The Isley Brothers, and a slower version by Marvin Gaye. In late 1967, producer Norman Whitfield talked Gordy into releasing a reading by Gladys Knight & The Pips, which climbed to the U.S. No. 2 spot. But it wasn't until August 1968, nearly eighteen months after it was recorded, that Gaye's version emerged, bolted onto his album *In the Groove* by Whitfield against Gordy's wishes.

It would have sat there unnoticed were it not for the reaction of DJs in the United States. Knight's dance-floor stomper was still fresh in listeners' memories, but Gaye's slower recording, both statelier and more impassioned, took flight in a way that Knight's never had, despite its high charting. Eventually released as a single in October 1968, Gaye's version spent a combined ten weeks at the top of the U.S. and U.K. charts, becoming Motown's best-selling single at the time.

The song returned to the U.K. charts in 1986 on the back of a Levi's ad in which Nick Kamen stripped to his underwear in a laundromat while a re-recording played in the background—the budget didn't stretch to Gaye's original. **WF-J**

America
Simon & Garfunkel (1968)

Writer | Paul Simon
Producer | Roy Halee, Simon &
Garfunkel
Label | Columbia
Album | *Bookends* (1968)

"This song explains why I'm leaving home to become a stewardess," says Zooey Deschanel, her eyes gravid with sorrow and anger, as she cues up the needle in Cameron Crowe's movie *Almost Famous* (2000). It is a bravura piece of filmmaking—halting the narrative while we listen to a record—and one that would not work without a soundtrack as nuanced and as effortlessly beautiful as "America." From the gently hummed harmonies at the outset, it builds steadily to take in folk-rock guitar, subdued pipe organ, and triumphant jazz fills from prolific session drummer Hal Blaine.

Thematically, the track resembles the road songs of Chuck Berry seen through the prism of Jack Kerouac. Berry's easy, conversational style is adapted to non-rhyming couplets replete with references to cigarettes and the Greyhound bus, as the narrator travels from Saginaw, Michigan, to New York with his girlfriend, Kathy (presumably Simon's muse Kathy Chitty, seen on the cover of his 1965 solo LP, *The Paul Simon Songbook*). Over just three minutes and 650 miles, youthful optimism congeals into alienation, culminating in the fraught "I'm empty and aching and I don't know why." At this, the song changes gear, the orchestration swelling as the focus pulls back to show countless thousands of travelers on the New Jersey Turnpike, with the peaks of Manhattan like an Emerald City on the horizon. **SP**

Ain't Got No; I Got Life | Nina Simone (1968)

Writer | Galt MacDermot, James Rado, Gerome Ragni
Producer | Joe René
Label | RCA
Album | 'Nuff Said! (1968)

"Now that my people have decided to take over the world ... I'm going to have to do my part."

Nina Simone, 1969

◀ **Influenced by: I Got a Woman** • Ray Charles (1954)
▶ **Influence on: You Remind Me** • Mary J. Blige (1991)
● **Covered by:** Julie Driscoll, Brian Auger & Trinity (1970)
Red Box (1986) • Jim Guthrie (2004) • Le Volume Courbe
(2005) • Mika (2008)

The year 1968 saw the opening of the rock musical *Hair*—a key statement of the 1960s hippie counter-culture, with its message of peace and love, freedom, and drugs—on Broadway and in the West End of London. It was also the year in which Martin Luther King Jr. was assassinated, in April. Three days later, Nina Simone appeared at Westbury Music Fair and dedicated her performance that day to his memory; a recording of the show formed the basis for the album *'Nuff Said!* "I was desperate to be accepted by the civil rights leaders, and when I was, I gave them ten years of singing protest songs," she said in 1991.

Also on the album were three studio tracks recorded a month later, including a medley of two songs from *Hair*, "Ain't Got No" and "I Got Life." In the musical, these appeared as a rock protest anthem and its feel-good response, performed by "the tribe" of hippies in their quest for a drug-induced utopia. Like most numbers from *Hair*, it could easily have been soon forgotten. Its inclusion on the serious-minded *'Nuff Said!* is, on the face of it, surprising, but in Simone's hands the call for freedom takes on a harder-edged civil rights tone in keeping with the other tracks, while still managing to retain the upbeat mood of the original.

"Ain't Got No; I Got Life" was also something of a departure from Simone's usual jazz, gospel, and blues repertoire, appealing more to pop audiences. When released as a single, it became one of her biggest hits and reached a wider, younger audience than she was used to, especially in Europe: it reached No. 1 in the Netherlands, and No. 2 in the British charts. **MW**

Piece of My Heart | Big Brother & The Holding Company (1968)

Writer | Bert Berns, Jerry Ragovoy
Producer | John Simon
Label | Columbia
Album | *Cheap Thrills* (1968)

"When I sing, I feel like when you're first in love."

Janis Joplin, 1968

◀ **Influenced by: Strange Brew** • Cream (1967)
▶ **Influence on: You Had Me** • Joss Stone (2004)
● **Covered by:** Marmalade (1968) • Dusty Springfield (1968) • Bryan Ferry (1973) • Bonnie Tyler (1977) Etta James (1978) • Sammy Hagar (1981) • Faith Hill (1994) • Beverley Knight (2006)

"Onstage I make love to 25,000 people, then I go home alone," said Janis Joplin famously at the height of her late-Sixties fame. And no other song in this blues banshee's repertoire sums up that statement like "Piece of My Heart."

Recorded in 1968 for Big Brother & The Holding Company's *Cheap Thrills* LP, "Piece of My Heart" took the straight-up soul original by Erma Franklin (Aretha's sister) and twisted it into four minutes of guttural pain and screaming guitars.

Janis's vocal owes little to Franklin's smooth take; instead it became the Texan hippy's greatest showcase. From the opening "Oh, come on / come on / come on . . ." through to ". . . deep down in your heart I guess you know that it ain't right / Never never never never never never hear me when I cry at night," Joplin instills the song with her own very real and personal heartache.

"Piece of My Heart," however, is as much about Big Brother & The Holding Company's arrangement as Janis's definitive vocals. Franklin herself said she didn't recognize it when she first heard the cover, generously noting, "Her version is so different from mine that I really don't resent it too much." The snap of the guitars fits perfectly with the 1968 theme, with crunching lead parts taking their cue from Cream and Jimi Hendrix.

Artists from Sammy Hagar to Beverley Knight have covered "Piece of My Heart" since, but Big Brother & The Holding Company's version remains the watermark by which all other efforts are judged. The power of "Piece of My Heart" still endures, helping the *Cheap Thrills* album to No. 338 in *Rolling Stone*'s 500 Greatest Albums of All Time in 2003, thirty-five years after it hit No. 1 in the *Billboard* charts. **JM**

Say It Loud—I'm Black and I'm Proud | James Brown (1968)

Writer | James Brown, Alfred Ellis
Producer | James Brown
Label | King
Album | *Say it Loud—I'm Black and I'm Proud* (1969)

Following the assassination in March 1968 of civil-rights leader Dr. Martin Luther King Jr. in Memphis, Tennessee, and the police shooting of Black Panther Party member Bobby Hutton in Oakland, California, the following month, there was increased pressure on black entertainers to speak for their community. As a self-styled black icon known as "Mr. Dynamite," James Brown was expected to make a stand for black rights, but initially this did not happen. He backed Vice-President Hubert Humphrey against the popular anti–Vietnam War candidate Robert Kennedy in the Democratic primaries; he recorded a single titled "America Is My Home," extolling the virtues of his homeland—"the best country"; and he performed for the U.S. Army in Vietnam, an action condemned by antiwar activists.

In August, though, Brown restored his credibility with young blacks with the hard funk chant "Say It Loud—I'm Black and I'm Proud," a forceful statement of black pride in which Brown cried out "We'd rather die on our feet / Than be livin' on our knees." The politically infused anthem influenced Motown songwriter/producer Norman Whitfield's work with The Temptations and Gil Scott-Heron, among many others. The track's percussive, pounding rhythm and verbal attack provided a blueprint for hip-hop; Eric B and Rakim sampled it on "Move the Crowd" in 1987. **JoH**

Hard to Handle | Otis Redding (1968)

Writer | A. Jones, A. Isbell, O. Redding
Producer | Steve Cropper
Label | Atco
Album | *The Immortal Otis Redding* (1968)

"Hard to Handle" was recorded during sessions in late 1967 that would prove to be Redding's last. From those same sessions came "Sittin' on the Dock of the Bay," the unfinished song that would win the singer a posthumous No. 1.

"Dock of the Bay" is often cited as evidence that the singer was moving in a more reflective, acoustic direction, but "Hard to Handle" refutes such charges. From its swinging opening piano riff, this is rough, tough R&B dance music. Redding was celebrated for the tenderness of his recordings—"These Arms of Mine," "My Girl," "I've Been Loving You Too Long"—yet he was equally at home with up-tempo soul numbers where he could boast of his virility. The opening lyric of "Hard to Handle"—"Hey there, here I am / I'm the man on the scene / I can give you what you want / but you got to come home with me"—sets the scene for two minutes and twenty seconds of stud swagger.

Superbly backed by Steve Cropper (guitar), Duck Dunn (bass), Al Jackson (drums), Booker T. Jones (piano), and The Memphis Horns, Otis's fierce vocal roars through "Hard to Handle." The 1968 single is among Redding's most dynamic recordings, though it reached only No. 51 on *Billboard*'s pop listings (U.K. No. 15). It has since been covered by numerous rock bands, and Jamaican singer Toots Hibbert gave the song a lilting reggae makeover. **GC**

Ⓒ James Brown saying it loud; he believed the track reduced his potential crossover audience.

A minha menina
Os Mutantes (1968)

Writer | Jorge Ben
Producer | Manoel Barenbein
Label | Polydor
Album | *Os Mutantes* (1968)

Fusing a shared love of The Beatles and the psychedelic soul of Sly & The Family Stone with the traditional sounds of samba and bossa nova, brothers Arnaldo and Sérgio Dias Baptista and singer Rita Lee formed Os Mutantes (The Mutants) in 1966. Alongside innovators such as Caetano Veloso and Gilberto Gil, they formed a new movement christened Tropicália, which influenced art, poetry, and theater, as well as music, in the days of the military dictatorship in Brazil.

The group's infectious, upbeat sound had greater energy and, on the surface at least, a lighter disposition than the work of Veloso and Gil. "A minha menina" (literally "This Girl of Mine") typifies the Mutantes' sound from the outset, with nylon-stringed guitar overlaid by fuzz-driven electric guitars, joy-filled vocals, and chaotic hand-clapping. The song became the focal point of the band's self-titled debut album and remains their best-known track, despite limited release as a single. Its influence is evident with the likes of David Byrne (who has consistently championed the band with his Luaka Bop label) and Beck, who named his 1998 album, *Mutations*, for the band.

More recently, "A minha menina" has been used in a McDonald's advertising campaign, and a faithful cover version by The Bees (in English) has been used extensively in television and independent-film soundtracks. **CR**

Sympathy for the Devil
The Rolling Stones (1968)

Writer | Mick Jagger, Keith Richards
Producer | Jimmy Miller
Label | Decca/ABKCO
Album | *Beggars Banquet* (1968)

Following an album entitled *Their Satanic Majesties Request* with a track called "Sympathy for the Devil" was a touch paper to the controversy of rock's original demonic bad boys. Despite the previous album's title, no explicit references to the devil were included therein—in stark contrast to the opening track of the follow-up. The song prompted religious groups and some in the media to label the band as devil-worshippers and a corrupting influence on their youthful fans.

Jagger has claimed the lyrics were influenced by French poet Charles Baudelaire, though the lyrics and themes of the song both bear a strong resemblance to Mikhail Bulgakov's novel *The Master and Margarita*, wherein the devil appears in person in Russia and claims influence over world affairs. During the recording sessions for the track, Senator Robert Kennedy was assassinated, prompting a change in the lyrics to reflect the event. The recording of the song was captured in Jean-Luc Godard's film of the same name.

Jagger initially composed the song as a ballad. At the suggestion of Keith Richards, it evolved into a dark samba rhythm, adding to the sinister, hypnotic nature of the track. The satanic theme of the song, as well as the Stones' overall style and demeanor, became a huge influence, particularly in hard rock and heavy metal, as it proved that dark, gothic music could be catchy, too. **CR**

Pressure Drop
Toots & The Maytals (1968)

Writer | Toots Hibbert
Producer | Leslie Kong
Label | Mango
Album | *Sweet and Dandy* (1968)

In 1967, Frederick "Toots" Hibbert walked out of jail after serving an eighteen-month sentence for alleged marijuana possession and returned to the studio with his musical partners, Nathaniel "Jerry" Mathias and Henry "Raleigh" Gordon. In the years before, the vocal trio had racked up a string of ska and rocksteady hits in Jamaica. With producers Coxsone Dodd and Prince Buster they had recorded tracks like "Bam Bam," twinning bouncing rhythms with Hibbert's powerful voice.

The Maytals' next clutch of songs, though, would propel them into the international mainstream. Helmed by Leslie Kong, the Chinese-Jamaican reggae producer who presided over the debut singles of Bob Marley and Jimmy Cliff, the sessions yielded not only "Pressure Drop," an uplifting number set to an irresistible skank, but also "Do the Reggay"—the song that announced the new phenomenon of reggae to Jamaica.

"Pressure Drop," though, encapsulates Toots & The Maytals' positive, evangelistic energy. Hibbert's lead vocal is every bit as strong as his Stateside inspirations Otis Redding and Curtis Mayfield, and the song's sense of raw euphoria would carry it far beyond Jamaica's shores. "Pressure Drop" was covered by The Clash, released on the B-side of their 1979 single "English Civil War." The Maytals have also recorded versions of the song with both Eric Clapton and Keith Richards. **LP**

Cyprus Avenue
Van Morrison (1968)

Writer | Van Morrison
Producer | Lewis Merenstein
Label | Warner Bros.
Album | *Astral Weeks* (1968)

Named in honor of a Belfast street on the right side of the tracks, "Cyprus Avenue" is commonly misspelled. It is an easy mistake to make. Apparently, the street itself was meant to be Cypress Avenue—every tree lining it is a different species, and presumably there is, or once was, a cypress there—but someone was confused, perhaps wrapped up in the dream state that floors Van Morrison.

For this, the centerpiece of Morrison's turbulent, romantic *Astral Weeks*, our man is transported to a teenage obsession, losing himself in a reverie of beauties in carriages, lonely train drivers, and falling leaves. It zips past like heather on the wind ("A total thing, a flow," according to Morrison himself), the seasoned jazz ensemble tuned to the precocious singer's stream of delirium.

The song became a highlight of Morrison's live set, an elongated show-stopper whistling through jazz and blues styles more rooted in rhythm than the flighty original. On the 1974 live album *It's Too Late to Stop Now*—the title taken from the last hurrah of the live "Cyprus Avenue," in turn nabbed from *Moondance*'s "Into the Mystic"—the song is prodded and squeezed, shifting from swing to boogie to storming rock. Morrison makes mischief, stammering along with the staccato piano as his "tongue gets tied," but his breakdown repetition of "all your revelation" takes the crazy mix of memory and transforms it into a show of reverence. **MH**

Hey Jude | The Beatles (1968)

Writer | John Lennon, Paul McCartney
Producer | George Martin
Label | Apple
Album | N/A

"It's very strange to think that someone has written a song about you. It still touches me."
Julian Lennon, 2002

◄ **Influenced by: Somewhere to Lay My Head**
The Sensational Nightingales (1954)
► **Influence on: Do You Realize??** The Flaming Lips
(2002)
● **Covered by:** Wilson Pickett (1968) · Ella Fitzgerald
(1969) · Grateful Dead (1969)

John Lennon thought it was about him. Judith Simons, a journalist with the *Daily Express*, thought it was about her. It was not until some twenty years after it was released that Julian Lennon was informed that one of the best-selling singles of all time was originally conceived as a song that would comfort him after his parents' split. "I was driving out to see Cynthia Lennon," Paul McCartney revealed at the time. "It was just after John and she had broken up, and I was quite mates with Julian. I was going out in my car just vaguely singing this song, 'Hey Jules, don't make it bad . . .' Then I thought a better name was Jude, a bit more country and western for me."

Finishing touches on the composition were worked through with John (Lennon insisting that McCartney keep in the rather nonsensical lyric "The movement you need is on your shoulder"). The Beatles then began to rehearse the song at Abbey Road Studios in late July 1968, in the midst of the band's work on what became known as *The White Album*. They moved to Trident Studios on July 31 to employ that facility's eight-track capabilities, bringing in a thirty-six-piece orchestra—with McCartney reportedly urging the players to join in on the clapping and singing of the song's extended coda. He had a very specific arrangement in mind as they worked, and his controlling direction in the studio led to friction, particularly with George Harrison, who balked at the criticism of his suggested contributions.

Released less than a month later, the single was the first for the band's new Apple label. It soon climbed the charts on both sides of the Atlantic, staying at No. 1 for nine weeks in the United States and becoming The Beatles' top-selling single. **TS**

Voodoo Child (Slight Return) | The Jimi Hendrix Experience (1968)

Writer | Jimi Hendrix
Producer | Jimi Hendrix
Label | Polydor
Album | *Electric Ladyland* (1968)

I stand up next to a mountain and chop it down with the ledge of my hand...

I'm a Voodoo Chile...

"Eric Clapton thought he discovered the wah-wah pedal. He was really put out when Jimi Hendrix used to use it."
Pete Townshend, 1980

◄ **Influenced by: Mannish Boy** · Muddy Waters (1955)
► **Influence on: Theme from** *Shaft* · Isaac Hayes (1971)
● **Covered by:** Stevie Ray Vaughan & Double Trouble (1984) · The Hamsters (1996) · Kenny Wayne Shepherd (1997) · Angélique Kidjo (1998) · Térez Montcalm (2006) Jacques Stotzem (2009)

Much like the artist who created it, Jimi Hendrix's "Voodoo Child (Slight Return)" enjoys a legacy that is at once crystal clear and swathed in the haze of rock lore. The song was recorded on May 3, 1968, the day after a longer version of the same tune (which also appears on *Electric Ladyland*, as "Voodoo Chile") was laid down with Steve Winwood on organ, Jefferson Airplane's Jack Cassady on bass, and the Experience's Mitch Mitchell on drums. This fifteen-minute version was—though utterly electrifying itself—essentially a standard blues jam played by a distinctly non-standard band and directly inspired by Muddy Waters's haunted, self-mythologizing "Mannish Boy," first recorded in 1955.

The following day, The Jimi Hendrix Experience were back in the studio, with Mitchell again on drums and regular band member Noel Redding on bass. As Hendrix himself put it, "Someone was filming when we started doing ["Voodoo Child"]. . . . They wanted to film us in the studio, to make us—'Make it look like you're recording, boys'—one of them scenes, you know. So, 'OK, let's play this in E, a-one, a-two, a-three,' and then we went into 'Voodoo Child.'"

This time, for the benefit of onlookers unfamiliar with his incandescent style, Hendrix added an introductory guitar riff that managed to capture just about everything that made him rock's undisputed heavyweight champion of guitar—a slithering vamp of wah-wah-pedal splendor that exploded into the devastating punch of his electric genius. "Well I stand up next to a mountain," he began, leaving no one in doubt that he truly was as tremendous as nature itself, poised to chop it all down with his axe. **MO**

The Pusher
Steppenwolf (1968)

Writer | Hoyt Axton
Producer | Gabriel Mekler
Label | ABC Dunhill
Album | *Steppenwolf* (1968)

As Peter Fonda stuffs dollar bills—the profits from a cocaine deal—into a plastic tube, thence into the gas tank of his customized Stars and Stripes chopper, the menacing strains of Steppenwolf's "The Pusher" are heard. A portentous opening for groundbreaking counterculture flick *Easy Rider*.

Written by country singer Hoyt Axton after one of his friends had died of a drug overdose, the song tackles hard drugs head-on ("I've seen a lot of people walkin' 'round / With tombstones in their eyes"), decrying and defying their suppliers with an emphatic and unequivocal refrain: "God damn the pusher." The song did not chart (unlike Steppenwolf's proto-metal "Born to Be Wild," heard over the opening credits of *Easy Rider*, which made U.S. No. 2 for three weeks). But with its cold-eyed lyrics, slack, scratchy rhythm, and whinnying lead guitar, it was a warning to a restless generation. However, Steppenwolf's front man, John Kay—guitar and vocals—was the pro-marijuana author of "Don't Step on the Grass, Sam," and the song is no blanket condemnation of recreational drugs; it draws a fine line between the dealer and his dope and the pusher with his hardcore heroin.

"The Pusher" was covered by artists as diverse as Nina Simone and Blind Melon, and its mesmerizing riff was also sampled by Neneh Cherry for "Trout," a duet with R.E.M.'s Michael Stipe that features in her 1992 set, *Homebrew*. **JJH**

The Weight
The Band (1968)

Writer | Robbie Robertson
Producer | John Simon
Label | Capitol
Album | *Music from Big Pink* (1968)

"The Weight," which formally introduced the world to The Band, is one of those songs that feel instantly familiar the first time you hear them. It is a folktale in the most literal sense, the kind that is handed down from one generation to the next. Perhaps that's why "The Weight" reached only No. 63 in the U.S. pop charts when it was released on the group's debut album. It was such an important song that it already felt old and comfortable.

There was a lot of screaming in the year leading up to the autumn of 1968—Jimi Hendrix's guitar, Keith Moon's drums, The Beatles' acid hymns, and that brought by the bullets that took Martin Luther King and Robert F. Kennedy. The counterculture desperately needed a cool, faithful voice of reason, and here was the band to deliver it. "I pulled into Nazareth, was feeling 'bout half past dead," sang drummer Levon Helm in his comforting tenor. "I just need to find a place where I can lay my head." Above Helm's sturdy country rhythm, Robbie Robertson strummed his rustic acoustic guitar and Richard Manuel filled in the gaps with stately, descending flourishes of piano.

It was, indeed, time to "take a load off," to come home from the psychedelic party. The weight of revolution and drugs and war and self-indulgence was too great to bear. Like the protagonist in the song, The Band delivered its regards to a weary scene. Now it was time to leave Nazareth. **MO**

Steppenwolf's John Kay; no pushin' allowed.

Days
The Kinks (1968)

Writer | Ray Davies
Producer | Ray Davies
Label | Pye
Album | N/A

The Kinks were a famously combustible outfit, punch-ups regularly occurring between front man Ray Davies, guitarist brother Dave, and the other members. This fractiousness, compounded by the disappointing sales of previous single "Wonderboy" and troubled sessions for their next album (which would become *The Kinks Are the Village Green Preservation Society*), prompted Ray Davies, in the summer of 1968, to consider splitting The Kinks and embarking upon a solo career.

Accordingly, then, "Days" plays like a bittersweet farewell, deriving a sophisticated melancholy from its remembrance of both the joy and pain of a perished relationship. Ray sounds as thankful for those titular days as he is thankful that they're over. The mature and wistful lyric marked him as out of step with the psychedelic times; while his contemporaries were taking lucrative trips to the edges of their imagination, he was wringing affecting pop from the down-to-earth.

Even during the session for "Days," The Kinks remained a powder keg, bassist Pete Quaife walking out of the studio after a furious row with Davies. Still, the song's success upon its release in June 1968—charting at No. 10 in the U.K. singles rundown—soothed the mood. Work progressed on the album, which continued in the whimsical, personal vein of "Days." A flop on its release, it has since been recognized as a masterpiece. **SC**

My Way
Frank Sinatra (1969)

Writer | Paul Anka, Claude François, Jacques Revaux, Gilles Thibault
Producer | Don Costa, Sonny Burke
Label | Reprise
Album | *My Way* (1969)

Twenty-seven-year-old former teen idol Paul Anka was on holiday in France when a song playing on the radio caught his attention. Written by singer Claude François after his split from French pop star France Gall, "Comme d'habitude" was a syrupy ballad that Anka disliked but found intriguing. Having quickly snapped up the rights, Anka returned to America and forgot all about the song until an impromptu meal with Frank Sinatra provided his lightbulb moment. Sinatra was complaining about his divorce from Mia Farrow and a recent dip in his career, ending by threatening to retire from the music business altogether. Anka promptly decided to rewrite the lyrics of "Comme d'habitude" to reflect Sinatra's outlook as a man who, looking back over his career, had seen it all and regretted nothing.

Sinatra's final version, which also slightly altered the melody of the original, was recorded in half an hour on December 30, 1968, and rush-released shortly afterward, rapidly becoming an international hit (U.S. No. 27; U.K. No. 5). In Britain, it has spent a record-breaking time in the Top Forty. The song's self-aggrandizing pomp became an anthem for the rest of Sinatra's career until his death, in 1998. Over the years, it has been recorded by more than a thousand different artists, including Elvis Presley and Sid Vicious. It remains the most requested song in karaoke bars. **PL**

The First Time Ever I Saw Your Face | Roberta Flack (1969)

Writer | Ewan MacColl
Producer | Joel Dorn
Label | Atlantic
Album | *First Take* (1969)

British folk icon Ewan MacColl's "The First Time Ever I Saw Your Face" has a most personal backstory. The singer-songwriter, playwright, actor, and activist penned it after being introduced to his third-wife-to-be, Peggy Seeger, having watched her at an audition. But it would take the combination of a stylistic transformation and exposure through a major motion picture to elevate this song to the contemporary-standard status it enjoys today, covered by everyone from Elvis Presley and Johnny Cash to Céline Dion.

Fledgling R&B vocalist Roberta Flack recorded the song for her 1969 debut album, *First Take*. While MacColl's original arrangement, performed by Peggy Seeger, was simple and featured a pleasantly flowing vocal-and-acoustic-guitar treatment, the dreamy tempo of Flack's version is held together by her luminous vocal, effectively minimal high-hat playing, and a sublime double-bass line by jazz legend Ron Carter.

In 1971, actor Clint Eastwood included "The First Time Ever I Saw Your Face" in his feature-film directorial debut, *Play Misty for Me*. On the strength of this, the song became Flack's first U.S. No. 1, in 1972, and earned her a Grammy for Record of the Year in 1973. She would go on to have a successful career in both R&B and adult pop, both as a solo artist and as a duet partner with Donny Hathaway and later Peabo Bryson and Maxi Priest. **YK**

I'm Just a Prisoner (of Your Good Lovin') | Candi Staton (1969)

Writer | George Jackson, Eddie Harris
Producer | Rick Hall
Label | Fame
Album | *I'm Just a Prisoner* (1969)

The title track of Candi Staton's first album, recorded at Fame Studios in Muscle Shoals, Alabama, takes Tammy Wynette's dogged domestic fidelity and marries it to "Chain of Fools" by Aretha Franklin (with whom Staton, as a young girl, had toured in a gospel revue). Like Aretha, she recognizes that she is bound and chained by love, but, like Tammy, she resolves to stand by her man.

The musicians on the track epitomized musical integration—remarkable in a state that had been on the frontline of the civil-rights struggle. The Fame Gang, a multiracial octet of crack session men, were one of the tightest soul ensembles of all time, and they build the track here with sensitivity and precision. The opening few bars are relaxed, based around Freeman Brown's laid-back drums and Junior Lowe's country guitar, but by the time the chorus arrives, it has become a full-blown whirlwind, thanks to Mickey Buckins's surging horn arrangement and Clayton Ivey's funky organ.

Staton, too, starts out calm, even chatty (with a deft conversational touch—"in other words"—lifted from Barbara Lewis's "Baby I'm Yours"), but by the fade, her voice is cracking and hoarse, broken by emotion and the endless takes that producer Rick Hall insisted upon. In later years, disco bunnies would idolize Staton for her 1976 anthem "Young Hearts Run Free," but soul connoisseurs will always prefer her years as a prisoner. **SP**

She Moves through the Fair
Fairport Convention (1969)

Writer | Traditional; Padraic Colum
Producer | Joe Boyd
Label | Island
Album | *What We Did on Our Holidays* (1969)

When folk singer Sandy Denny joined Fairport Convention in 1969, her knowledge of traditional British repertoire encouraged the band to turn away from American folk and folk rock and look closer to home for their material. This new approach bore fruit on the album *What We Did on Our Holidays*, their first for Island.

Included on the album was "She Moves through the Fair," a perfect synthesis of old and new. The song, set to a traditional Irish tune (later to crop up in Simple Minds' "Belfast Child"), was collected around the turn of the twentieth century by musicologist Herbert Hughes and poet Padraic Colum, who slightly altered the lyrics and claimed them as his own. It became well known in the Sixties through a number of recordings, including one by Anne Briggs and Davy Graham.

The Fairport Convention version was, however, something else. Denny's crystal-clear vocals dominate, of course, but the ethereal, psychedelic backing transforms the simple tune into an eerie sound-world, in keeping with the ghostly lyrics. The arrangement, largely by Denny, centers around her own acoustic guitar accompaniment and Ashley Hutchings's eccentric bass line, while the melody floats virtually unaltered above. This ability to breathe new life into traditional material set the tone for Fairport's future, establishing them as Britain's top folk-rock band. **MW**

Many Rivers to Cross
Jimmy Cliff (1969)

Writer | Jimmy Cliff
Producer | Leslie Kong
Label | A&M
Album | *Jimmy Cliff* (1969)

"Many Rivers to Cross," by Jamaican vocalist Jimmy Cliff, was originally released on his eponymous second album (which was repackaged in 1970 for U.S. distribution as *Wonderful World, Beautiful People*). The song was not issued as a single because it was bypassed in favor of two protest songs ("Wonderful World" and "Vietnam") and a cover tune (Cat Stevens's "Wild World"). All of those songs were international hits, but none proved as memorable as "Many Rivers to Cross."

The ballad was both haunting and hope-filled, a tale of a man who is beaten but not broken, on a quest for enlightenment. Cliff—who was going through his own religious awakening and soon converted to Islam—sang each word as though his soul depended on it. Graceful accompaniment from a church organ and gospel-flavored backing vocals underscored the tune's spirituality. Although the song boasted a syncopated reggae rhythm, it belonged to no single genre.

The perfectly realized number would finally get its due on the soundtrack to 1972's *The Harder They Come*, which starred Cliff. The movie and its soundtrack introduced real roots reggae to the world and made Cliff the genre's first true international star. The movie also established "Many Rivers to Cross" as a pop standard, one that has been handled over the years by such diverse talents as Cher, UB40, and Annie Lennox. **JiH**

From left, Fairport's Richard Thompson, Sandy Denny, and Simon Nicol play Copenhagen in 1969.

In the Ghetto | Elvis Presley (1969)

Writer | Mac Davis
Producer | Chips Moman (Felton Jarvis also credited)
Label | RCA
Album | *From Elvis in Memphis* (1969)

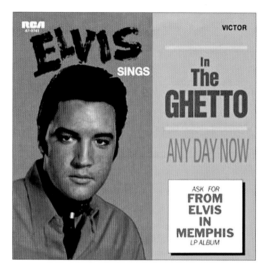

"I think Elvis took a huge chance in doing 'In the Ghetto.' It was a big risk."

Mac Davis, 2006

◀ **Influenced by: The Wind Cries Mary** • The Jimi
Hendrix Experience (1967)
▶ **Influence on: The Sun Refused to Shine**
Richard Hawley (2007)
● **Covered by:** Sammy Davis Jr. (1970) • Nick Cave & The
Bad Seeds (1984) • The Cranberries (2001)

Was this really the same Elvis who only recently could be heard performing unlistenable soundtracks to unwatchable films? The path that returned Elvis to credibility started with his 1968 TV special, which had climaxed with "If I Can Dream," but "In the Ghetto" was another song of considerable substance, musically and lyrically. Guided by the safety-first principle of Colonel Parker, Elvis had never been much for music as social commentary, but a slew of assassinations, including those of Bobby Kennedy and Martin Luther King (the latter in Elvis's Memphis hometown), affected the star profoundly.

Mac Davis—credited as Scott Davis to avoid confusion with another similarly named songwriter—also had an agenda. He wanted to describe the hopeless cycle of life in poverty, what he called "being born into a situation where you have no hope." Davis had in mind a title: "The Vicious Circle." However, as he admitted, "There's nothing that rhymes with 'circle.'"

Elvis harbored doubts about tackling a song that was so outspoken against injustice. But ace producer Chips Moman of Memphis's American Sound Studio knew that musing about giving the number to another artist would be all the convincing Elvis needed. During some of the most productive sessions of his career, Elvis gave everything in twenty-three takes of the song.

"Crying in the Chapel" had been the last time that Elvis breached the U.S. Top Three. That had been 1965. Four years on, he was back where he belonged. The hit was merely the public confirming what the seen-it-all-before session guys had witnessed in the studio: "He just sang great," said trumpet player Wayne Jackson. **CB**

Oh Well, Parts 1 & 2 | Fleetwood Mac (1969)

Writer | Peter Green
Producer | Fleetwood Mac
Label | CBS
Album | N/A

"Part Two was full of Gurdjieffian sonorities and Hispano-Moorish arabesques."

Mick Fleetwood, 1990

◀ **Influenced by: Boom Boom** · John Lee Hooker (1961)
▶ **Influence on: Black Dog** · Led Zeppelin (1971)
● **Covered by:** Big Country (1993) · Jimmy Page & The Black Crowes (2000) · Stephen Pearcy (2006) · Todd Wolfe & Under the Radar (2008) · The Rockets (2009)

While they won early notice for front man Peter Green's faultless blues licks, the original lineup of Fleetwood Mac also excelled both at psychedelic tenderness (their hit instrumental, "Albatross") and ribald, bawdy rock 'n' roll (infamously, drummer Mick Fleetwood regularly affixed a large dildo he named Harold to his drum kit before showtime). "Oh Well, Parts 1 & 2," a non-album single, encompassed these contrasts across its eight or so minutes, shedding light on the troubled genius who led the band—Fleetwood later recalled that "there was an aggressive side to Peter's personality." The track's swaggering first half was all blistering, bluesy attack (Green and sidemen Jeremy Spencer and Danny Kirwan making for a fearsome triple-headed threat) and lyrics that snarled with contempt for their target, some fool who had done Green wrong.

After this came a pastoral second half, a haunting instrumental for cello, acoustic guitar, and flute (the latter performed by Green's girlfriend, Sandra Elsdon). This, according to Fleetwood, expressed the other side of Green's persona, "the reflective, spiritual musician." Preceded by such a spiteful blues, this gentle piece nevertheless possessed a menacing undertow.

Following a lysergic misadventure shortly afterwards, the unhappy Green suffered a nervous breakdown and exited the group. An extended period of upheaval followed, before Fleetwood Mac evolved into the chart-topping AOR behemoth that recorded *Rumours*, with a sound far removed from their Sixties roots. To this day, however, the blues-rock first half of "Oh Well" remains on their setlist—although Harold is no longer seen on Fleetwood's bass drum. **SC**

The Real Thing
Russell Morris (1969)

Writer | Johnny Young
Producer | Ian "Molly" Meldrum
Label | Columbia
Album | *The Real Thing* (1969)

By the time Aussie vocalist Johnny Young wrote "The Real Thing," he had been the star of his own TV show at age sixteen, managed some hits in the mid-Sixties, and then spent a year in the United Kingdom. When he returned Down Under in 1968, he was past his commercial prime and was working as a DJ when he penned his best-known song.

Fortunately, he didn't record it himself. "It wouldn't have been a hit if I'd sung it," Young told the *Sun-Herald*. "My time as a pop star was over." Molly Meldrum, however, heard the song and felt it suited a young singer he was working with, Russell Morris, who had just left Somebody's Image and was looking to start his solo career. To put it mildly, Meldrum was right. The recording married folksy pop with heady psychedelia and ran almost six and a half minutes, but it was so addictive that just one spin felt insufficient. Morris's confident, yet deliciously understated, delivery was complemented by The Chiffons' lovely harmonies, The Groop's soulful backing, and Meldrum's head-spinning production.

"The Real Thing" made Morris a truly big star in Australia, where the song became 1969's biggest-selling single. Many have long considered it one of the greatest rock songs ever recorded Down Under—including, evidently, members of the Australian government, who honored "The Real Thing" with its own postal stamp in 1998. **JiH**

Sister Morphine
Marianne Faithfull (1969)

Writer | Marianne Faithfull, Mick Jagger, Keith Richards
Producer | Mick Jagger
Label | Decca
Album | N/A

"After writing 'Sister Morphine,'" declared Marianne Faithfull in 2002, "I learned that you must be very careful what you write about because it may come true." The song began with Faithfull's partner, Mick Jagger. The Rolling Stones' front man, she recalled, "had the melody for about six months and he would walk around the house strumming it." Faithfull added "the story of a man who has had a terrible car accident. He's dying . . . and the lyrics of the song are addressed to the nurse."

Jagger—with himself on guitar, Jack Nitzsche on piano, Ry Cooder on guitar, and his bandmates Bill Wyman on bass and Charlie Watts on drums—cut the song in 1968. Faithfull added vocals months later, and it was issued on the B-side of 1969's "Something Better"—which was promptly withdrawn when Decca realized what "Sister Morphine" was about. The Stones, again with Cooder and Nitzsche, recut the track later that year—a version that emerged on *Sticky Fingers*.

Keen to keep money from the clutches of her then-manager, Jagger and Richards neglected to credit Faithfull on their album. She did, however, receive a share of the royalties—which, with grim irony, helped fund a career-crippling drug habit. After her renaissance with 1979's *Broken English*, she re-recorded the song for another single. The eerie, bluesy original, however, remains one of rock's most unsettling prophecies. **BM**

Marianne Faithfull in 1969, the year her harrowing hymn to addiction was released. ➔

Okie from Muskogee
Merle Haggard (1969)

Writer | Merle Haggard, Roy Edward Burris
Producer | Fuzzy Owen
Label | Capitol
Album | *Okie from Muskogee* (1969)

Could this be the most controversial song in the country-music canon? Merle Haggard wrote it on a tour bus while passing the Oklahoma town of Muskogee. It began with a throwaway comment that became the song's arresting opening line: "We don't smoke marijuana in Muskogee"; from there, it unfavorably compares the lives of the LSD-taking, draft-card-burning, long-haired hippies from San Francisco with those of the simple, flag-waving, hand-holding folk of Muskogee.

President Nixon was hooked and asked Haggard to play it in the White House; Haggard refused, but didn't recant his reactionary views, delighting conservatives and confusing liberals, who had previously believed that Haggard, an ex-con with a stick-it-to-the-man attitude, was one of them. Folk hippies The Youngbloods recorded a conciliatory response, and the argument began.

Although partly tongue in cheek, "Okie . . ." is undoubtedly a conservative anthem—a rarity in modern music—but Haggard himself is no partisan: he has praised Reagan and JFK equally. His claimed motivations for writing "Okie . . ." have changed over the years, partly as attitudes toward the Vietnam War—which forms the unspoken center of the song—have developed. Whatever the truth, there are few finer artefacts to represent the culture wars that have shaped American politics for three generations. **PW**

Heartbreaker
Led Zeppelin (1969)

Writer | John Bonham, John Paul Jones, Jimmy Page, Robert Plant
Producer | Jimmy Page
Label | Atlantic
Album | *Led Zeppelin II* (1969)

Led Zeppelin's eponymous debut album saw the band dress up English folk in the sharp, pinstripe threads of the blues; on *Led Zeppelin II* they ventured further into the music of cotton fields and crossroads. The opening riff of "Heartbreaker," a menacing, alley-cat swagger, shows how their sound had become more commanding. This was partly due to Jimmy Page's use of a Gibson Les Paul guitar through a Marshall amplifier stack—a muscular combination he favored for the rest of his career and a clear contrast to the nasal, waspish timbre of his earlier guitar work with the group.

Robert Plant's plaintive vocal tells a cautionary tale of torment at the hands of an inconstant woman. Despite this classic blues theme (which Zep had visited in "Dazed and Confused" on their debut LP, married to another memorable riff and a similar slow-fast-slow verse structure), "Heartbreaker" still has a fair amount of English dandification about it, with Plant milking the story for every drop of debauched theater it can yield.

Page's frenetic, improvised solo, which forms the centerpiece of the track, was dubbed in after the main body of the song was recorded. Its dexterity and showmanship inspired a young Edward Van Halen to develop the two-handed tapping technique with which he would carry rock music even further from the bluesman's front porch and into the realm of stadium fantasy. **JD**

Is That All There Is?

Peggy Lee (1969)

Writer | Jerry Leiber,
Mike Stoller
Producer | Phil Wright
Label | Capitol
Album | *Is That All There Is?* (1969)

Peggy Lee's heyday came in the Fifties, yet in 1969, aged forty-nine, she had a surprise Top Forty hit with a most unlikely song: "Is That All There Is?"

The recording almost never came to be. Originally written by Leiber and Stoller with English singer Georgia Brown in mind, the track was offered to Marlene Dietrich and Barbra Streisand before the less popular Lee recorded it, in January 1969. It was only on Lee's insistence that Capitol reluctantly agreed to release it on an album in November of that year, but the single did well, reaching No. 11 in the *Billboard* Hot 100 and winning the 1970 Grammy Award for Best Contemporary Vocal Performance.

As surprising as Lee's comeback was the song itself. In a masterful arrangement by Randy Newman, the world-weary existential lyrics (based on Thomas Mann's short story "Disillusionment") are first spoken as a narrative over a lush orchestral backing but then break into a chorus sung Lotte Lenya–style, with an accompaniment reminiscent of Kurt Weill's settings of Brecht. The song suited the mood of the time. "Is That All There Is?" appealed to a younger audience as much as Lee's older fan base, and was an influence on artists such as Bette Midler and Madonna. It has been covered by singers as diverse as Sandra Bernhard, in 1999, and Chaka Khan, in 2004, though Cristina's jagged 1980 take drew Leiber and Stoller's wrath. **MW**

Sweetness

Yes (1969)

Writer | Jon Anderson,
Chris Squire, Clive Bailey
Producer | Paul Clay, Yes
Label | Atlantic
Album | *Yes* (1969)

Formed from the ashes of the splendidly titled Mabel Greer's Toy Shop, Yes in 1969 were very different from their later prog-rock incarnation. They were, at best, an experimental rock group with a major Beatles hang-up. In fact, Yes had initially wanted Paul McCartney to produce their self-titled debut album, and had auditioned for Apple. It would have made perfect sense, as the record owes a great deal to his *White Album* ballads.

"Sweetness" is gentle, melodic, and brief. It highlights the players' ability, but not once does it slide into the shuddering pomp the band went on to produce for most of the Seventies. Chris Squire's tremoloed bass references McCartney's high-fretboard work, while Tony Kaye's underrated Hammond, Bill Bruford's restrained drumming, and Peter Banks's gently phased guitar all support the serenity of Jon Anderson's vocal and the charmingly open-hearted lyrics. The dramatic buildup in the middle eight is quickly resolved with a gently melodic breakdown, the only hint of the progressive path that Yes were to take.

"Sweetness" was Yes's debut single but did very little and was never performed by them in concert. It was almost as if the band were ashamed of it. However, American fringe actor/director/singer Vincent Gallo admired the song, using it (alongside "Heart of the Sunrise," from 1971's *Fragile*) in his 1998 cult classic, *Buffalo 66*. **DE**

Suspicious Minds | Elvis Presley (1969)

Writer | Mark James
Producer | Chips Moman, Felton Jarvis
Label | RCA
Album | N/A

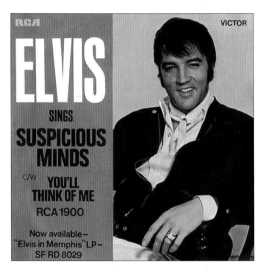

"I give you my word I will never sing a song I don't believe in."

Elvis Presley, 1968

◀ **Influenced by: Crying** · Roy Orbison (1961)
▶ **Influence on: Jealous Guy** · John Lennon (1971)
● **Covered by:** Dee Dee Warwick (1971) · Thelma Houston (1980) · Candi Staton (1981) · Fine Young Cannibals (1985) · Dwight Yoakam (1992) · True West (1998) · Jesper Lundgaard (2002) · Helmut Lotti (2002)

Following a lengthy slide toward commercial oblivion, Elvis Presley reclaimed the title of the King of Rock 'n' Roll during the television show now known as the *'68 Comeback Special*. He would cement his return with a prolific session at Memphis's American Sound Studio, during which he recorded 1969's *From Elvis in Memphis* and the singles "In the Ghetto," "Kentucky Rain," and "Suspicious Minds." The latter would become the singer's eighteenth U.S. No. 1. It was also his last. In retrospect, however, it is hard to imagine a more fitting final chart-topper for the King.

Everything about "Suspicious Minds" worked in unison, from Presley's high-strung vocals to the edgy arrangement and the claustrophobic lyrics detailing a couple "caught in a trap" of jealousy and distrust. Although the lyrics were penned by Memphis tunesmith Mark James, Presley took vocal command of the song in a way that made it feel like an original composition. Indeed, not only did it sound as though he had written the words, he gave the distinct impression that he had lived them. Another telling detail, which caught many a DJ off-guard, was the fake fade-out and surprise fade-in at the end. The result was unlike anything else in the Elvis songbook.

"Suspicious Minds" would be covered by a sizeable number of artists in the years to come, and in a surprising number of ways. Most notably, the Fine Young Cannibals gave it a modern-rock twist in 1985 and Dwight Yoakam took it countryward in 1992, but it has also been handled by jam-rockers Phish, indie stars The Flaming Lips, and *American Idol*'s Clay Aiken. Some of those covers are good in their way, but none compares favorably to the King's royal original. **JiH**

Suite: Judy Blue Eyes | Crosby, Stills & Nash (1969)

Writer | Stephen Stills
Producer | Crosby, Stills & Nash
Label | Atlantic
Album | *Crosby, Stills & Nash* (1969)

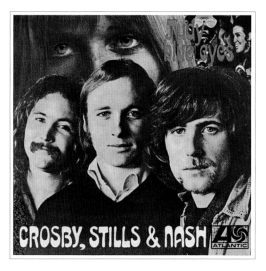

> *"I was left with all these pieces of song and I said, 'Let's sing them together and call it a suite.'"*
>
> **Stephen Stills, 1991**

◄ **Influenced by: All I Have to Do Is Dream** • The Everly Brothers (1958)
► **Influence on: Take It Easy** • Eagles (1972)
● **Covered by:** Liberace (1969)

One of the dangers of being a songwriter by trade is the inevitable compulsion to pour your heart out in song when personal relationships provide your richest creative inspiration. The "Judy Blue Eyes" referred to in Stephen Stills's four-piece suite of songs was Judy Collins; the pair had begun a love affair when Stills guested on the folk singer's 1968 album, *Who Knows Where the Time Goes*. Although "Suite: Judy Blue Eyes" was more than seven minutes long when recorded for Crosby, Stills & Nash's much-heralded debut album, it packed in only a fraction of the notebooks of poetry that Stills had penned during their time together.

Released as the second single on the trio's debut album, following their successful chart debut, "Marrakesh Express," "Suite: Judy Blue Eyes" quickly became an acoustic crowd-pleaser during live performances. Stills's virtuosity climaxes at a memorable vocal high note during the line "It's my heart that's a-suffering, it's a-dying . . ." and audiences always willed him on with generous applause whenever he struggled to make it.

It is hard to believe that the track, recorded back in 1969 at Wally Heider's Los Angeles studios, carries only instrumentation from guitar, bass, guitar-tapping percussion by Stills, and Dallas Taylor's drumming, so rich are the three-part harmonies that fill out the recording. The song was so complicated, convoluted, and varied in styles that Stills's biggest problem was how to end it. In the end, he settled for "the little kicker at the end about Cuba" to wind up the song, which otherwise threatened to continue indefinitely.

The song's highest-profile showcase imaginable came when the movie *Woodstock* captured the group's second live performance. **DR**

Pinball Wizard | The Who (1969)

Writer | Pete Townshend
Producer | Kit Lambert
Label | Track
Album | *Tommy* (1969)

"The whole point of 'Pinball Wizard' was to let [Tommy] have some sort of colorful event and excitement."

Pete Townshend, 1969

◀ **Influenced by: S. F. Sorrow Is Born**
The Pretty Things (1968)
▶ **Influence on: Jesus of Suburbia** · Green Day (2004)
● **Covered by:** Rod Stewart (1972) · Elton John (1975)
Mary McCaslin (1977) · Carl Dixon (2003) · McFly (2005)
The Flaming Lips (2008)

Few would claim that the influential rock opera *Tommy* is The Who's best album. Track for track, it cannot compete with 1971's *Who's Next*, which contains "Baba O'Riley," "Behind Blue Eyes," and "Won't Get Fooled Again." But in the midst of the filler that connects the twisting storyline—of a "deaf, dumb, and blind kid" who becomes a messiah—*Tommy* contained a few true gems, the brightest of which was "Pinball Wizard."

The lyrics were not great, and it took a leap of faith to believe in a hero who ruled the arcade by "sense of smell." Yet The Who sold this song with fury, and the feverish pitch carried equal amounts of virtuosity and ambition. Guitarist Pete Townshend's super-fast strumming was worth the admission price alone. ("I attempted the same mock baroque guitar beginning that's on 'I'm a Boy,'" he revealed later—actually a purposeful nod to Henry Purcell's "Fantasia upon One Note"—"and then a bit of vigorous kind of flamenco guitar.")

Upon its release, *Tommy* was hailed as a masterpiece by some and dismissed as self-indulgent by others, yet almost everyone agreed that "Pinball Wizard" (the last track to be written for the album) was a great song. One dissenting opinion, oddly, came from its author, who later dubbed it "the most clumsy piece of writing [I've] ever done." Townshend was outvoted by fans, who made "Pinball Wizard" a U.S. and U.K. Top Twenty hit and now regard it as a career highlight.

The song's popularity kept *Tommy* on the radio for decades, and paved the way for the story to be retold through Ken Russell's 1975 film, in which Elton John performed "Pinball Wizard." A musical play debuted onstage in 1993, and the song has enjoyed countless revivals. **JiH**

Je t'aime ... moi non plus | Jane Birkin & Serge Gainsbourg (1969)

Writer | Serge Gainsbourg
Producer | Uncredited
Label | Fontana
Album | *Jane Birkin/Serge Gainsbourg* (1969)

"Everyone said, 'Oh, Serge, he's so dangerous.' I said, 'Yes, he is,' but really, he was a pushover."

Jane Birkin, 2009

◄ **Influenced by:** What'd I Say Parts 1 & 2
Ray Charles (1959)
► **Influence on:** Love to Love You Baby
Donna Summer (1975)
● **Covered by:** Donna Summer (1978) • Pet Shop Boys
& Sam Taylor-Wood (1999)

The relationship of one of the best-known couples in the history of French pop didn't get off to the best of starts. Serge Gainsbourg began his first date with Jane Birkin by treading on the young British model's toes during a slow dance, and ended it by passing out drunk on his bed at the Paris Hilton, while a nervous Birkin hid in the bathroom. Yet somehow, despite those inauspicious beginnings and the pronounced generation gap (she was a limpid twenty-one, he a grizzled forty), a relationship flourished.

But if "Je t'aime ... moi non plus" ("I Love You ... Me Neither," in its most popular, though jarring, translation) sounds like the authentic first stirrings of a new-born romantic euphoria, that is a slight deception. Gainsbourg actually wrote the song in 1968 for Brigitte Bardot, with whom he was entangled at the time. The pair recorded it, but Bardot got cold feet about releasing it when she rather belatedly remembered that she was married to someone else. So, when Gainsbourg connected with Birkin later the same year, he pulled the song out of the filing cabinet and they had another go at it, the duo gasping and moaning their way through Arthur Greenslade's slinky arrangement.

Inevitably, the song was banned more or less everywhere it was released. Just as inevitably, it was a massive hit. It became the first foreign-language single to reach No. 1 in the United Kingdom, where it has since spawned an array of archetypally British nudge-wink cover versions. Gainsbourg later recycled the title for a bizarre and fairly grubby film starring Birkin, Warhol collaborator Joe Dallesandro, and, playing an animal lover who loves animals in an appallingly enthusiastic way, Gérard Depardieu. **WF-J**

Is It Because I'm Black?
Syl Johnson (1969)

Writer | Jimmy Jones,
Glenn C. Watts, Syl Johnson
Producer | Willie Mitchell
Label | Twinight
Album | *Is It Because I'm Black?* (1970)

After the assassination of Martin Luther King Jr. in 1968, civil-rights politics and soul music became increasingly radicalized. Sylvester Johnson was early to articulate the new mood. "Is It Because I'm Black?" plays like the sour flip side to Sam Cooke's "A Change Is Gonna Come," with its despondent recognition of the deep-seated inequalities in U.S. society. Referring to King's rhetoric, he sings: "Looking back at my first dreams that I once knew / Wondering why my dreams never came true."

Musically, the song is a taut Chicago blues in the soulful style of B. B. King's contemporaneous hit "The Thrill Is Gone." Johnson was raised in the Windy City, brought up in a house next door to the harmonica player Magic Sam, and had cut his teeth playing with blues legends including Elmore James, Freddie King, and Howlin' Wolf. Guitarist Mabon "Teenie" Hodges lays down a supple groove, backed in a propulsive arrangement by his brothers, bass player Leroy and organist Charles.

Johnson's assessment of race relations is bleak. "Like a child stealing its first piece of candy and got caught / Peeping around life's corner, somewhere I got lost," he sings, simmering with dejection. But on the extended LP version, he finds a way forward. Over the course of seven minutes, "something is holding me back" gradually morphs into the nobler sentiment "keep on keepin' on." Even in the depths of despair, there is hope. **SP**

I Want to Take You Higher
Sly & The Family Stone (1969)

Writer | Sylvester "Sly Stone" Stewart
Producer | Sly Stone
Label | Epic
Album | *Stand!* (1969)

In the wee hours of Sunday, August 17, 1969, the drugged-out, worn-out crowd of around 400,000 who had assembled at Woodstock were literally shaken out of their slumbers by Sly & The Family Stone's electrifying performance of "I Want to Take You Higher." Sly, the razzle-dazzle front man, a black rhinestone cowboy with tassles all a-flailing, shouted out "Higher!" and the crowd responded back in kind. The horns screeched the riffs while Sly's brother Freddie laid down the funky guitar riff over Larry Graham's pioneering slap-bass.

The song had originally been released as the B-side of "Stand!," which made the U.S. No. 22 slot a few months before Woodstock, and then No. 60 as an A-side in its own right. After Sly's da-bomb live version, it was re-released in June 1970, reaching No. 38. Drawing on the track "Higher" from their 1968 LP, *Dance to the Music*, "I Want to Take You Higher" crossed racial and gender divides; it was the epitome of Sly's kaleidoscopic, psychedelic soul. The band were one of the first to openly feature black female singers and instrumentalists (Cynthia Robinson on trumpet and Sly's sister Rose on piano) alongside mixed-race horn players.

In February 2006, the sixty-one-year-old Sly Stone performed "I Want to Take You Higher" at the Grammys. Sporting a peroxide-white Mohawk, he departed after just a few verses. Other recent appearances have been equally unpredictable. **JJH**

Sly Stone takes the 400,000-strong audience higher still at the 1969 Woodstock festival. ➜

The Court of the Crimson King | King Crimson (1969)

Writer | Ian McDonald, Peter Sinfield
Producer | King Crimson
Label | Island
Album | *In the Court of the Crimson King*
(1969)

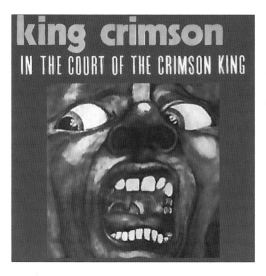

"We've always had … letters. Kids write and say 'I don't understand your lyrics, who IS the Crimson King?'"

Peter Sinfield, 1971

◀ **Influenced by:** The Cheerful Insanity of Giles, Giles, and Fripp · Giles, Giles and Fripp (1968)
▶ **Influence on:** The Devil's Triangle
King Crimson (1970)
● **Covered by:** Doc Severinsen (1970) · Saxon Killing Ground (2001)

"King Crimson appeared on the scene, and we thought they were just magnificent, doing the same kind of things that we wanted to, but so much bigger and better," enthused Genesis front man Peter Gabriel to *ZigZag* magazine in 1971. An epic workout, built around a haunting riff played on the (then novel) Mellotron, "The Court of the Crimson King" is, indeed, a pretty fair encapsulation of all things prog rock. If you want a symphonic theme, changing time signatures, discombobulated drumming, away-with-the-fairies imagery (courtesy of lyricist Peter Sinfield), and undoubted grandeur, look no further.

Band leader and inventive guitarist Robert Fripp was to be the dominant mainstay in Crimson's frequently changing lineups. On this standout track, however—which alternates an all-guns-blazing descending chord sequence with more pastoral, reflective acoustic interludes—he plays support to Ian McDonald's array of keyboard, Mellotron, and vibes, as well as woodwinds and reeds. Ironically, King Crimson's signature song is one of only two tracks that Fripp did not co-write. Recorded at London's Wessex Sound Studios, the roughly ten-minute full version forms a kind of grand finale and summary of its parent album. Although the edited single didn't chart in the United Kingdom, it reached U.S. No. 80 in 1970, split between the two sides of a 45.

Greg Lake gives the song gravitas with his bass and lead vocals, Michael Giles fills in the holes with free-form drumming, but this is essentially Ian McDonald's masterpiece. How strange to think that, a few years on, the same man would be belting out "You're as cold as ice" on keyboards for mainstream rock outfit Foreigner. **JJH**

Whole Lotta Love | Led Zeppelin (1969)

Writer | Jimmy Page, Robert Plant,
John Paul Jones, John Bonham, Willie Dixon
Producer | Jimmy Page
Label | Atlantic
Album | *Led Zeppelin II* (1969)

*"Well, you only get caught
when you're successful.
That's the game."*

Robert Plant, 2000

◄ **Influenced by: You Need Love** · Muddy Waters (1962)
► **Influence on: Whole Lotta Rosie** · AC/DC (1977)
● **Covered by: CCS** (1970) · King Curtis (1971) · Tina
Turner (1975) · Coalesce (1999) · Ben Harper & The
Innocent Criminals (2001) · Prince (2003) · The
Dynamics (2007) · Mary J. Blige (2010)

Having covered two songs penned by bluesman
Willie Dixon on their debut LP ("You Shook Me"
and "I Can't Quit You Baby"), Led Zeppelin decided
on a reworking of his "You Need Love" (written for
Muddy Waters) to open their follow-up album.
Dixon's track had previously been remodeled by
Steve Marriott in the form of "You Need Loving"
for The Small Faces, but Page and Plant went
further by turning the simple blues number into
a symphonic rock opus. The initially uncredited
adaptation led to an out-of-court settlement with
Dixon years after the song's release.

The full-length album version of the song
includes an extended break with a drum solo,
theremin, and a moaning vocal workout from
Plant, which has become known as the "orgasm
section." As Zeppelin did not release singles in the
United Kingdom, the length (5.33 minutes) was
not a problem in that market. However, the length
of the track and the unorthodox bridge section
led to edited shorter versions being released as
singles in other territories.

One of the best-known uses of the song,
or specifically its opening riff, was as the title
theme to BBC Television's *Top of the Pops*. Actually
a faithful 1970 cover played by CCS, the riff
announced the show for more than thirty years.

"Whole Lotta Love" has the distinction of being
the last song performed live by Zeppelin's original
lineup, on July 7, 1980, in Berlin. The song was also
played by the three surviving members at Live Aid
(1985), the Atlantic Records Fortieth Anniversary
(1988), and the Ahmet Ertegun tribute concert
(2007). Jimmy Page also went on to perform a
version of the song with Leona Lewis at the closing
ceremony of the 2008 Beijing Olympic Games. **CR**

I Wanna Be Your Dog
The Stooges (1969)

Writer | Iggy Pop, Dave Alexander, Ron Asheton, Scott Asheton
Producer | John Cale
Label | Elektra
Album | *The Stooges* (1969)

Elvis Presley's "Hound Dog" may have kicked open the kennels, but it was this ode to canine carnality that really let the dogs out into rock 'n' roll. The Stooges shunned late-Sixties hippie-dippy love-song tropes for a rude mating ritual about the agony and the ecstasy of adolescent sex.

Riding guitarist Ron Asheton's distortion-driven three-chord (G, F#, and E) guitar throb and producer John Cale's single-fingered piano drone, vocalist Iggy Stooge (not yet Pop) delivers a snotty-nosed sermon about subservient, screwed-up love that upstages even The Velvet Underground's seminal sagas of sexual deviance.

Rolling Stone reviewer Edmund O. Ward panned the racket as "loud, boring, tasteless, unimaginative, and childish." The song isn't just an adolescent rock shtick about self-abasement, though. It reflects Iggy's obsession with the brutish minimalism of the blues. Muddy Waters's swampy overhaul of Big Joe Williams's classic "Baby Please Don't Go" is transformed into a coarse new cocktail of blues-rock monotony. The single failed to chart, but its nihilistic glee struck a major chord with the late-Seventies blank generation. Covered by everyone from punk pinups Richard Hell and Sid Vicious to post-punk progenitors The Fall, Pere Ubu, and Sonic Youth, the song was performed by R.E.M. and Patti Smith at The Stooges' Rock and Roll Hall of Fame induction, in 2007. **MK**

Kick Out the Jams
The MC5 (1969)

Writer | M. Davis, W. Kramer, F. Smith, D. Thompson, R. Tyner
Producer | J. Holzman, B. Botnick
Label | Elektra
Album | *Kick Out the Jams* (1969)

Recorded as part of their debut live album of the same name over two nights at the Detroit Grande Ballroom, "Kick Out the Jams" is the definitive revolutionary rock call to arms. Though not lyrically political, it became the antiestablishment calling card for a band who performed amid the riots of the 1968 Chicago Democratic Convention and helped form the Marxist White Panther Party.

The controversies surrounding the Motor City Five were myriad, but none was more significant than the incendiary opening epithet of the song —"Kick out the jams, motherfuckers!" This led to stores' refusing to stock the record, an edited version being released, and every live performance of the band putting them at risk of obscenity laws.

The song's title was widely adopted as a slogan by the counterculture movements of the late Sixties and early Seventies. Given the revolutionary leanings of the group, and particularly their manager—White Panther founder John Sinclair—this would be understandable. The band, though, have maintained it was aimed at other groups who indulged in too much "jamming" onstage.

The song is widely viewed as a prototype for punk and garage rock. The MC5 ushered in a Detroit sound that superseded Berry Gordy's Motown, influencing bands from Detroit contemporaries The Stooges to Rage Against the Machine, Monster Magnet, and Primal Scream. **CR**

Fred "Sonic" Smith of MC5, a prime mover in the band's loud, uncompromising sound. ➜

I Want You Back
The Jackson 5 (1969)

Writer | The Corporation
Producer | The Corporation
Label | Motown
Album | *Diana Ross Presents The Jackson 5* (1969)

Sorry, Tito, but it is a Michael Jackson song. The happiest tune ever written about sadness was the debut of The Jackson 5, who would launch the perennial boy-band model with this, the first of four consecutive No. 1 hits, in 1969. And sure, Jackie, Marlon, and Jermaine contribute some lead-vocal cameos along the way. But it can't be a coincidence that the introduction of Michael's vocal cords to the whole world led to arguably the greatest pop song in history.

"I Want You Back" was written by the freshly minted Corporation, a think tank of soul headed up by Motown honcho Berry Gordy, who wanted to plug his Indiana-bred prodigies into Frankie Lymon's faded teen-dream socket. The song's exultant rattle of piano, dancing strings, vibrant funk guitars, and background "oo-oohs" was a perfect fit for the singing Jackson brothers.

From the moment Michael jumped into the Corporation's orgiastic intro, it was clear the kid was on another level. With just an "uh-huh" and a "lemme tell ya, now," his nimble alto revealed a musical and emotional intuition that most of our greatest *adult* singers never reach. "I Want You Back" may be the best his voice ever sounded. Obviously, an eleven-year-old didn't write words like "Tryin' to live without your love is one long sleepless night," but only Michael Jackson could make heartbreak seem so perfectly blissful. **MO**

The Thrill Is Gone
B. B. King (1969)

Writer | Rick Darnell, Roy Hawkins
Producer | Bill Szymczyk
Label | Bluesway/ABC
Album | *Completely Well* (1969)

When B. B. King recorded the biggest U.S. pop hit of his career (a No. 15), in June 1969, the Motown sound, with its lollipop melodies and bouncing bass lines, was pushing King's black audience for the blues to the margins of urban radio broadcasts. It was time to shake up the formula.

King wanted to record a cover of Roy Hawkins's minor 1951 hit, "The Thrill Is Gone," an old favorite from his days as a radio DJ in Memphis. B. B. figured he could lay some trademark guitar licks over the top of the rare minor-key blues lament and come out with something a little moodier and more sophisticated than, say, "Paying the Cost to Be the Boss." He found the ideal collaborator in young producer Bill Szymczyk, who convinced King to cut the track with four session men, rather than his usual band, and to flavor it with sedated rhythm guitar and organ instead of the usual barrage of horns. King sang with dignified remorse about breaking free from a lover's spell, his gruff vibrato almost ghostly over Paul Harris's keys and Gerlad Jemmott's mournful bass.

Then Szymczyk decided to add a twelve-piece string section (arranged by Bert DeCoteaux), believing it would propel the song to mainstream radio. In effect, it propelled string sections— one part classy, two parts pornographic—to mainstream radio for the next decade, rendering "The Thrill Is Gone" a blues-fusion classic. **MO**

B. B. King performs on "Lucille," one of his famous Gibson ES-355 variants, in Denmark in 1969. ➤

- Bob Marley comes to prominence as reggae's most charismatic star

- Abba, formed in 1972, dominate the charts throughout the decade

- David Bowie introduces, then kills off, his Ziggy Stardust persona

- The Sex Pistols form in 1975 and galvanize U.K. punk rock

- *Saturday Night Fever* triggers a global fascination with disco in 1977

1970s

Up Around the Bend | Creedence Clearwater Revival (1970)

Writer | John Fogerty
Producer | John Fogerty
Label | Fantasy
Album | Cosmo's Factory (1970)

"Rock 'n' roll is Southern and that's why I'm Southern. Because what I learned from was Southern."

John Fogerty, 1997

◀ **Influenced by: I've Got a Tiger by the Tail**
Buck Owens (1964)
▶ **Influence on: Out in the Street** • Bruce Springsteen (1980)
● **Covered by:** Hanoi Rocks (1984) • Elton John (1994)
The Bates (2000)

At the end of the 1960s, rock bands that did not count a deified figure among their ranks (Morrison, Hendrix, Clapton, Page, etc.) had to work especially hard just to seem worthy of airplay. If you weren't writing a tripped-out concept album or redefining your instrument, you were liable to be trampled underfoot. Such was the plight of American group Creedence Clearwater Revival and its lead singer, guitarist, and songwriter, John Fogerty, who didn't write sixteen-minute songs about sex and didn't use a wah-wah pedal but still managed to churn out one great hit song after another.

In 1970, writing his fifth album in two years, Fogerty sharpened his genius for "roots rock," as it would be called today, with songs such as "Up Around the Bend" (U.S. No. 4; U.K. No. 3). Using a screaming lead-guitar lick from Hendrix's bag, a driving chord progression courtesy of The Beatles, and Grateful Dead harmonies in the chorus, Fogerty carved out a tune that, in the end, could only have been Creedence Clearwater Revival: tight, melodic, forceful, and done in two and a half minutes. The song was released on a double A-sided single with "Run Through the Jungle" on the flip side.

As with most of Creedence's best work, the beauty of "Up Around the Bend" is in its simplicity. The song invites the listener to a party just up the road, and there's the sense that there won't be any strawberry elevators or rainbow alarm clocks when you get there. It's more wood paneling and beer. "Bring a song and a smile for the banjo / Better get while the gettin's good," Fogerty sings in his trademark raspy howl. "Hitch a ride to the end of the highway." **MO**

Layla | Derek & The Dominos (1970)

Writer | Eric Clapton, Jim Gordon
Producer | Tom Dowd
Label | Polydor
Album | *Layla and Other Assorted Love Songs* (1970)

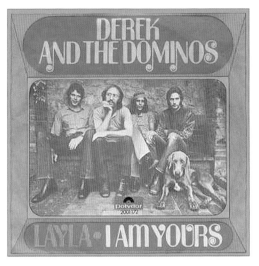

*"I'm very proud of ['Layla'].
I love to hear it. It's almost like
it's not me. It's like I'm listening
to someone that I really like."*
Eric Clapton, 2001

◀ **Influenced by:** As the Years Go Passing By
Albert King (1967)
▶ **Influence on:** Motherless Children • Eric Clapton
(1974)
● **Covered by:** Herbie Mann (1974) • John Fahey (1984)
Henri Salvador (1994) • Bobby Broom (2001)

There is a certain irony that Eric Clapton's most famous song was recorded by a group in which he hid his name and leadership to avoid some of the pressures he had endured in his previous supergroups, Cream and Blind Faith. Sharing the guitar lead with Duane Allman (of The Allman Brothers Band) and writing duties with the rest of the group when they weren't playing covers, Clapton produced just one album with Derek & The Dominos before retreating back into the shadows of addiction and pain.

The song was inspired by *Layla and Majnun*, a twelfth-century poem by Persian poet Nezami Ganjavi, which tells the tale of a man driven to distraction by the woman he cannot have. The real-life Layla was Pattie Boyd, wife of Clapton's best friend, George Harrison, and the woman with whom Clapton had fallen madly in love. Over the course of a double album, he spells out his dilemma of unrequited love, its apex coming with this monumental track, a seven-minute-plus howl of agony and grief, a personal statement almost too raw to comprehend. He wonders whether he will go insane, asking the same question as blues legend Robert Johnson in his darkest hour: is his "love in vain"?

Clapton's original rough version of the song was revved up with an opening lick by Duane Allman taken from an Albert King song, turning its original ballad form into a rocker played out in six overdubbed guitar lines. The four-minute piano finale was a separate song by drummer Jim Gordon and added three weeks later. As for "Layla" herself, Pattie Boyd eventually left Harrison and married Clapton in 1979, although the marriage ended in divorce in 1988. **SA**

War Pigs
Black Sabbath (1970)

Writer | T. Iommi, B. Ward, G. Butler, O. Osbourne
Producer | Rodger Bain
Label | Vertigo
Album | *Paranoid* (1970)

Rain, thunder, and a tolling bell opened Black Sabbath's debut album. If you made it through that nightmare, album two (released just seven months later) offered no respite: the air-raid sirens of its opening song suggested you had awoken to a world that was even worse. The song was "War Pigs," which—despite *Paranoid*'s hit title track—remains the definitive early-Sabbath anthem. Indeed, it was originally envisaged as the album's title song (hence *Paranoid*'s peculiar artwork), an idea that was nixed to avoid putting the band into a political corner regarding the Vietnam War.

The original version (demoed as "Walpurgis") spoke of "bodies burning in red ashes" and "bad sinners . . . eating dead rats' innards." However, alarmed by the public's perception of the band as devil worshipers, Sabbath reworked the lyrics, inadvertently evoking the era's disillusionment and horror. "We knew nothing about Vietnam," observed Ozzy. "It's just an antiwar song." "The world," grumbled bassist and chief lyricist Geezer Butler, "is a right fucking shambles."

The evocative lyrics were complemented by an imaginative structure. After the dead-slow introduction, the song showcased Ozzy's distinctive wail, Tony Iommi's vicious riffing, and Butler and drummer Bill Ward's almost jazzy rhythm section. A blueprint for the next two decades of heavy metal had arrived. **BM**

When the Revolution Comes
The Last Poets (1970)

Writer | Umar Bin Hassan
Producer | East Wind Associates
Label | Douglas
Album | *The Last Poets* (1970)

"Understand that time is running out!" ran the opening words to The Last Poets' eponymous debut album, and that same sense of urgency was maintained throughout the set, conjured from only fiery voices and an endless, restless rumble of percussion. A trio of urban bards from Harlem with links to the Black Panthers, and who formed in May 1968 at a celebration for Malcolm X, The Last Poets were dreaming of an Afrocentric revolution. "When the Revolution Comes" was, by turns, an electrifying call to arms ("Guns and rifles will be taking the place of poems and essays"), and a scabrous attack on those they saw as obstacles.

Often, the Poets took aim at what they perceived as antirevolutionary apathy on the part of a black community lulled by the material comforts of relative upward mobility. Another Harlem poet and a fellow rap primogenitor, Gil Scott-Heron, had gibed at such political lethargy on his epochal "The Revolution Will Not Be Televised" that same year, and Umar Bin Hassan opened his track by warning that the revolution might come while many were glued to their televisions.

Across its two-and-a-half-minute spiel, Hassan dreamed of junkies swapping their drugs for the cause, Jesus walking the streets of Harlem, and "straight-hairs trying to wear Afros," though he knew many of his contemporaries preferred to "party and bullshit." **SC**

Sabbath bassist Geezer Butler in an impressive display of hair guitar.

Band of Gold
Freda Payne (1970)

Writer | Ron Dunbar, Edyth Wayne (Holland-Dozier-Holland)
Producer | Holland-Dozier-Holland
Label | Invictus
Album | *Band of Gold* (1970)

Freda Payne, sister of Seventies-era Supreme Scherrie Payne, spent the Sixties unsuccessfully courting the listening public. Her first two albums were jazz recordings, neither of which did well. The long courtship paid off at the dawn of the new decade, though, as Payne hitched herself to a song that would take her to the top of the charts.

"Band of Gold" came courtesy of Brian Holland, Edward Holland, and Lamont Dozier, who convinced the vocalist to sign with their new Invictus label and try her hand at pop. They handed her a surefire hit, which they co-wrote under the pen name "Edyth Wayne," a move made necessary due to a lawsuit with old employer Motown.

The curious lyrics, still ripe for interpretation, describe a young marriage gone terribly wrong on a honeymoon spent in separate rooms. For some reason, the groom has abandoned his bride in a darkened room "filled with sadness, filled with gloom." The only thing she has left, besides a broken heart, is "a band of gold."

Thanks to Payne's heroic delivery, the song becomes an old-fashioned somebody-done-somebody-wrong anthem. Her voice was complemented, never crowded, by steady accompaniment from The Funk Brothers, Motown's famed house band. The whole package translated to a worldwide hit, which dominated the top spot on the U.K. charts for six weeks. **JiH**

Love the One You're With
Stephen Stills (1970)

Writer | Stephen Stills
Producer | Stephen Stills, Bill Halverson
Label | Atlantic
Album | *Stephen Stills* (1970)

When supergroup Crosby, Stills, Nash, & Young fragmented after recording the terrific but traumatic album *Déjà vu*, the four members set about establishing their solo credentials. "Love the One You're With" was one of a batch of new songs recorded by Stephen Stills at Island Studios in London for what would be his eponymous debut album. A chance remark, overheard by Stills, from musician Billy Preston became the inspiration for both the song and its title, although Doris Troy also claimed to have had that conversation with Stills.

Distancing himself from the CSN&Y West Coast hype, Stills left the United States in 1970, moved to England, and rented (and later bought) Ringo Starr's Surrey country house. A rich vein of form resulted, as Stills poured all his energy into recording enough material for a number of future projects. With its hypnotic percussion and wall of sound built on Stills's searing organ playing, "Love the One You're With" was a transatlantic hit single and included guest harmonies by David Crosby and Graham Nash.

An eclectic musician, Stills embraced blues, Latin, country, and rock on his solo recordings, and "Love the One You're With" had a soul sensibility that later attracted The Isley Brothers and Luther Vandross to record it. Best interpretation of all, perhaps, was Aretha Franklin's gospel soul reading on *Aretha Live at Fillmore West*. **DR**

Fire and Rain
James Taylor (1970)

Writer | James Taylor
Producer | Peter Asher
Label | Warner Bros.
Album | *Sweet Baby James* (1970)

Autobiographical work doesn't get much more potent than James Taylor's "Fire and Rain," penned while in rehab for a debilitating heroin addiction in 1968. It chronicles both his experiences in a U.S. mental institution and the suicide of a friend. According to Taylor himself, the song was written in three parts over three months in 1968: the first in a basement apartment in London, the second in a hospital room in Manhattan, and the third in Austin Riggs hospital in Massachusetts. In his own words: "It's like three samplings of what I went through then."

The lyrics speak for themselves: "Suzanne" was later confirmed as good friend Suzanne Schnerr, who had committed suicide. The poetic line "sweet dreams and flying machines in pieces on the ground" refers to his failed band, The Flying Machine, while his own plea ("Won't you look down upon me, Jesus") begs unashamedly for salvation and sobriety.

Both the album and the single reached No. 3 on the *Billboard* charts. His devastating juxtaposition of sweet-sounding vocals, sparse instrumentation, and apocalyptic lyrics made Taylor an overnight star. "'Fire and Rain' is undoubtedly a great song," mused the record's producer, Peter Asher, twenty-eight years later, "but I'd be hard pressed to say what about it is unusual or which bit of the song is exceptional. The whole thing is." **KL**

Ain't No Mountain High Enough
Diana Ross (1970)

Writer | Nick Ashford,
Valerie Simpson
Producer | Ashford and Simpson
Label | Motown
Album | *Diana Ross* (1970)

Originally a hit for Marvin Gaye and Tammi Terrell in 1967, "Ain't No Mountain High Enough" was dramatically reinvented by producer/composer couple Ashford and Simpson to provide Diana Ross with her solo breakthrough. Ross had been groomed by Motown boss Berry Gordy for solo stardom for at least three years, first taking separate billing on Supremes singles then leaving the band with a farewell concert earlier in 1970, but her first release had been a relative disaster.

"Reach Out and Touch (Somebody's Hand)," another Ashford and Simpson composition, barely scraped the *Billboard* Top Twenty in April 1970, but the follow-up was a surefire smash. Gaye and Terrell's take had been straightforward, finger-clicking soul, an arrangement The Supremes used on a 1968 hookup with The Temptations, and one later borrowed by Amy Winehouse for her single "Tears Dry on Their Own" in 2007. But the new "Ain't No Mountain High Enough" was a sexy anthem, whipping up the tension with two minutes of psychedelic soul before the delayed release of the chorus.

It shot to No. 1 in the United States. Yet it could have all been so different. "Dusty Springfield came by our house and heard it," Valerie Simpson later confided. "But we told her, 'We couldn't give it to you.'" Springfield's loss was Ross's belated gain, confirming the birth of a diva. **MH**

Black Night | Deep Purple (1970)

Writer | Ritchie Blackmore, Ian Gillan, Roger Glover, Jon Lord, Ian Paice
Producer | Deep Purple
Label | Harvest
Album | N/A

"The management were screaming for a single, because there wasn't an obvious single on the album."
Roger Glover, 1988

◀ **Influenced by: On the Road Again** · Canned Heat (1968)
▶ **Influence on: Woman** · Wolfmother (2005)
● **Covered by: Bad Manners** (1997) · Deicide (2006) Pat Travers (2006) · Twilight Guardians (2007)
★ **Other key track:** Smoke on the Water (1972)

"Black Night" has something of the appeal of a vintage motorcycle. Brutish and primal, this gutsy British boogie is propelled along by its central riff as by a large, thumping engine. If it were possible to park this song in a garage, it would leave a puddle of oil on the floor.

Despite being Deep Purple's highest-selling single, the track was not drawn from *In Rock*, the band's fourth album. Instead, "Black Night" was released as a radio-friendly single to promote *In Rock*, ironically outshining that album in posterity. According to vocalist Ian Gillan, the song's title was inspired by the lyrics of an old Arthur Alexander blues song, while the tempo was borrowed from the roadhouse-boogie style characteristic of Canned Heat. The lyrics are fairly perfunctory—Gillan admits they were hastily written in a pub at the end of a fruitless studio session aimed at producing a single.

More important is the way Jon Lord's churning Hammond organ fuses with Ritchie Blackmore's brooding guitar to produce a new element on the periodic table of rock—like lead, only heavier. An interesting footnote to this quintessential metal riff is that, according to guitarist Blackmore, it took unlikely inspiration from the guitar line on Ricky Nelson's cover of the George Gershwin jazz standard "Summertime."

True, the track is not without its precedents. Blackmore's raygun-style, whammy-bar excursions owe no small debt to Hendrix, while Ian Gillan's vocal takes cues from the declamatory style of the traditional bluesman. Be that as it may, "Black Night" signaled that a new breed of heavy rock had awoken—and that its future was not bright, but dark as midnight. **JD**

War | Edwin Starr (1970)

Writer | Norman Whitfield, Barrett Strong
Producer | Norman Whitfield
Label | Gordy
Album | *War & Peace* (1970)

"If you grew up in the Sixties, you grew up with war on TV every night, a war that your friends were involved in."

Bruce Springsteen, 1985

◀ **Influenced by: Ball of Confusion (That's What the World Is Today)** · The Temptations (1970)
▶ **Influence on: What's Going On** · Marvin Gaye (1971)
● **Covered by:** D.O.A. (1982) · Bruce Springsteen & The E Street Band (1986) · Laibach (1994) · Joan Osborne (2002) · Gilbert Montagné (2006)

After Gladys Knight hit No. 1 with "I Heard it Through the Grapevine," Norman Whitfield was Motown's backroom alpha male, the only man with clout enough to take Berry Gordy's baby into the ghetto when the label boss wanted it to have a residency in Vegas.

In March 1970, The Temptations' album *Psychedelic Shack* was released, and Whitfield almost immediately had them back in the studio to work on their apocalyptic next single, "Ball of Confusion," a mid-tempo litany of woe stuffed with guitar effects, blues harmonica, and clavinets. Yet before they had finished, it was obvious that one of the songs on the album had caught the ear of the antiwar lobby as the conflict in Vietnam dragged on. Motown were repeatedly asked for a single release of the song.

The producer had a dilemma: releasing this song, "War," as a single would polarize opinion and kill The Temptations' career. Moreover, after "Ball of Confusion," it felt like a half-strength howl. He trawled the label's B-list for other singers, and when The Undisputed Truth refused to do it, Edwin Starr got the gig. The singer insisted it had to be done his way, and all those grunts, screams, and ad libs ("Listen to me," "Good Gawd, y'all," "Say it, say it, say it, s-a-a-a-y it") were spontaneous. It proved to be the most successful song of his career.

Harnessing the singer's James Brown inflections to a track that owed much to "Ball of Confusion" (which would be released during the sessions) but added a military beat, Whitfield concocted a perennial classic, an American No. 1, and a peacenik chant for ever, its power undimmed through forty years in which it has been frequently banned at sensitive times. **DH**

(To Be) Young, Gifted and Black
Bob and Marcia (1970)

Writer | Nina Simone, Weldon Irvine
Producer | Harry "J" Johnson
Label | Harry J
Album | *Young, Gifted and Black* (1970)

An instant civil-rights anthem penned and initially recorded by Nina Simone, "Young, Gifted and Black" was covered with enthusiasm within weeks of its debut appearance by the likes of soul legend Donny Hathaway and—most conspicuously—reggae duo Bob and Marcia.

Bob Andy had been a member of The Paragons, the Jamaican troupe notable for the original version of "The Tide is High," but had left to pursue a solo career. Struggling away at Studio One—reggae's own Motown—singer Marcia Griffiths was being pushed this way and that by label founder Sir Coxsone Dodd, without finding material or spar strong enough to bring her success. She had performed songs written by sometime-paramour Andy before, but it was not until producer Harry "J" Johnson turned up touting the backing tapes of "Young, Gifted and Black" that they became a recording team. Andy agreed to sing it and suggested Griffiths join him. The results were scintillating.

The snappy mix of the duo's voices embodies optimism and possibility, their harmonies trumpeting their identity, but it's the version that crashed into the U.K. Top Five that has the real spring in its step. With strings arranged by The Johnny Arthey Orchestra—upcoming masters at sprucing up reggae tunes for a learning U.K. market—it's three minutes of pure celebration. **MH**

Ball of Confusion
The Temptations (1970)

Writer | Norman Whitfield, Barrett Strong
Producer | Norman Whitfield
Label | Gordy
Album | N/A

Motown were slow to embrace songs of social awareness, but made up for it with stunning turn-of-the-decade releases by Marvin Gaye (*What's Goin' On*, 1971), Edwin Starr ("War," 1970), and—of course—The Temptations.

Norman Whitfield's tenure as producer had seen The Temptations evolve from soulful pop to psychedelic soul with LPs *Cloud Nine* (1969) and *Psychedelic Shack* (1970), the latter featuring an early version of "War." "Ball of Confusion"—which owed much to Whitfield's affection for Sly & The Family Stone, George Clinton, and Jimi Hendrix—matched a scintillating, slow-burn arrangement to a world vision verging on the paranoid. Underpinned by Funk Brother Bob Babbitt's nagging bassline, four of The Temptations tick off the world's escalating crises, with Dennis Edwards handling the trickier lines. Racism, two-faced politicians, drug abuse, violent civil unrest, mounting bills, war—and, all the while, that incessant bass and beat keep ramping up the tension. Snaggles of psychedelic guitar mirror the singers' head-shaking bewilderment, interspersed by funky brass and a wailing harmonica. When the chorus finally hits, and the harmonies blend, it's sheer relief. The track was recorded in one three-hour stint, prior to the lyrics being written; Babbitt didn't hear the song in its full-on politicized glory until four days later, on his car radio. **RD**

Dancing to the beat of apocalypse—The Temptations in 1970.

Avec le temps
Léo Ferré (1970)

Writer | Léo Ferré
Producer | Gerhardt Lehner
Label | Barclay
Album | *Amour Anarchie* (1970)

There is a phonetic quality to the French language that can infuse even the dullest weather report with a sense of melancholy and sensuality. The expression of sorrow and somber reflection is, of course, intrinsic to Léo Ferré's chosen genre, the chanson. The lyrics of "Avec le temps" speak of the faces and voices you forget as time passes, of a heart that stops beating—and of rays of death on a Saturday night. Translations of such lyrics always seem melodramatic and eccentric.

"Avec le temps" was first released as a single in October 1970, shortly after Ferré recorded it at the age of fifty-four. The singer's age may partly explain the dark subject matter of "Avec le temps," and the song also references tensions in Ferré's life as a popular artist. The Monaco-born singer's upbringing at an oppressive Italian boarding school had left him feeling alienated from society and keen to cultivate the image of an outsider. By expressing himself in lyric-driven songs that followed the rhythm of his mother tongue, he had rebelled against the conformity imposed by Anglo-American pop, and he was adopted as a voice for left-leaning intellectuals and revolutionaries. Yet reconciling this widespread popularity with the fact that he felt at odds with the rest of society must have been difficult. The personal sense of vulnerability he revealed in "Avec le temps" may well have hinted at this conflict. **DaH**

The Man Who Sold the World
David Bowie (1970)

Writer | David Bowie
Producer | Tony Visconti
Label | Mercury
Album | *The Man Who Sold the World* (1971)

One week in 1970, David Bowie's telephone rang every day at the exact same time—but whenever he answered it, there was no one there. Stoked up on thoughts of Tibetan Buddhism and the occult writings of Aleister Crowley and H. P. Lovecraft, Bowie became convinced that it was his late father trying to contact him from the next world.

Such was the mentality that produced the title track of his third LP, a vignette that co-opted the "man who wasn't there" from Hearst Mearns's 1899 nursery rhyme "Antigonish," which had previously been set to music in the swing era. The singer's voice was drenched with phasing to suit the spooky narrative, and double-tracked at emphatic moments (at the word "surprise," the two Bowies sing with comically varied intonation). New recruit Mick Ronson, fresh from gigging with Bowie and bassist Tony Visconti in the short-lived superhero-rock band Hype, provided the record's spiraling, Eastern-flavored guitar motif.

Hidden away on an album full of proto-metal—and with a controversial cover on which the singer reclined like a mermaid in a "man's dress" from Mr. Fish—the song was overlooked by the record-buying public. A post-Ziggy reissue of Bowie's back catalog in 1972 brought it to wider attention, but it achieved its greatest recognition thanks to an unplugged cover by Nirvana, released posthumously in 1995. **SP**

Caught in the spotlight: David Bowie in 1970. ➔

Awaiting on You All
George Harrison (1970)

Writer | George Harrison
Producer | George Harrison, Phil Spector
Label | Apple
Album | *All Things Must Pass* (1970)

Northern Sky
Nick Drake (1970)

Writer | Nick Drake
Producer | Joe Boyd
Label | Island
Album | *Bryter Layter* (1970)

"It was an important album for me," wrote George Harrison in 2000, "and a timely vehicle for all the songs I'd been writing during the last period with The Beatles." Having fought to squeeze his songs onto the Fab Four's records, Harrison splurged on a triple album for his first solo outing.

All Things Must Pass featured guests such as Eric Clapton, Ringo Starr, and the then unknown Phil Collins. Harrison's chief collaborator, though, was producer Phil Spector, who had overseen John Lennon's "Instant Karma" and a controversial mix of The Beatles' *Let It Be*. In a letter to Harrison, Spector judged a demo of a song on Side Three: "The mixes I heard had the voice too buried . . . I'm sure we could do better."

That demo was "Awaiting on You All," Harrison's most rapturously uplifting song since 1967's "It's All Too Much." He would later admit to misgivings about Spector's overwhelming production, but here it only adds to the excitement. And while the lyrics advocate the Krishna philosophy of "chanting the names of the Lord," Harrison throws in a wry reference to the pope's owning "fifty-one per cent of General Motors"—and you suddenly remember that this is the man who wrote "Taxman."

The album became best known for the hit "My Sweet Lord," but "Awaiting on You All" has a timeless exuberance that even Beatles-haters should experience. **BM**

"The greatest English love song of modern times," proclaimed U.K. music magazine *NME* in 2009 about a song nearly forty years old by an artist who never found success during his brief lifetime.

"Northern Sky" was one of two collaborations with John Cale, co-founder of The Velvet Underground, who had worked with producer Joe Boyd on a Nico album and become intrigued with Drake's music. Cale persuaded Boyd to let him work with Drake to develop "Northern Sky", incorporating an ethereal bell-chiming celesta and perfectly blended piano and organ parts behind Drake's favorite acoustic guitar tunings of DADGDG and breathy murmurings. Cale was also responsible for the middle break leading to a soaring vocal refrain from Drake—arguably his most uplifting on record.

Robert Kirby's beguiling chamber-ensemble string arrangements are key to many of Drake's songs and appear elsewhere on *Bryter Later*, but not here. In truth, their presence might have compromised the glowing simplicity of this piece. ("Never felt magic crazy as this"—is there a better, more direct way of describing love?) Kirby told Drake biographer Patrick Humphries that he felt it could have been a single, and recalled that Drake seemed buoyed by the sessions. "I think he felt this was going to be the one," Kirby mused years later, in words that, necessarily, now seem poignant. **JJH**

Maybe I'm Amazed
Paul McCartney (1970)

Writer | Paul McCartney
Producer | Paul McCartney
Label | Apple
Album | *McCartney* (1970)

"Maybe I'm Amazed" was written by Paul McCartney in 1969 for his new wife, Linda. With a George Harrison-esque guitar and Billy Preston-style organ, he single-handedly created something that was every scrap as good as anything in The Beatles' recent catalog—and it was created without all the attendant acrimony that had so dogged his old group's final eighteen months. Just the song, in fact, that McCartney needed to give him confidence in the dark days around the band's demise, as demonstrated in the lines, "Maybe I'm a lonely man in the middle of something that he doesn't really understand."

It is the one track on the largely home-recorded, self-produced *McCartney* album that didn't feel deliberately underdone—except possibly its fade-out, which simply collapses into thin air. Yet that only leaves you wanting more. A later, live version from *Wings Over America* finally placated the fans who had wanted the album track released as a single; it reached the U.S. Top Ten in 1977. That and subsequent live versions are polished and professional, with the added coda McCartney was going to use in the original, but none of these quite hits the spot as did the tentative wonder of the 1970 recording.

"Maybe I'm Amazed" is the only one of Paul McCartney's solo songs to make the *Rolling Stone Top 500 Songs of All Time* list, at No. 338. **DE**

Into the Mystic
Van Morrison (1970)

Writer | Van Morrison
Producer | Van Morrison
Label | Warner Bros.
Album | *Moondance* (1970)

It is all too fitting that the working title of this blue-eyed soul classic was "Into the Misty," as the literal meaning of its lyric is shrouded in a haze. At first listen, the song seems to tell the tale of a lovelorn sailor headed home to his beloved. Van Morrison himself was not completely certain, either. When documenting the lyric for his publishers at Warner Brothers, he couldn't decide if the first line was "We were born before the wind" or "We were borne before the wind." His reported confusion with subsequent lines (were they younger than the sun or the son?) makes it clear the song is more about a feeling than a story.

The pure, rapturous passion of the track belied Morrison's hard road to musical independence. His initial efforts at a solo career after leaving the group Them were marked by a contentious working relationship with producer Bert Berns. Once he was finally making music on his own terms, he realized his singular voice on *Astral Weeks* in 1968. Yet it wasn't until the LP *Moondance* that he assembled a working band to help him get just the sound he wanted. No song on that album stands out as strongly as "Into the Mystic."

While time has proven the song's greatness, earning a place on lists of the best songs of all time, it was never released as a single. Only "Come Running" gained that honor at the time, with "Moondance" getting a delayed release in 1977. **TS**

Get Up (I Feel Like Being a) Sex Machine | James Brown (1970)

Writer | James Brown, Bobby Byrd, Ron Lenhoff
Producer | James Brown
Label | King
Album | N/A

"Get Up (I Feel Like Being a) Sex Machine" marks a change of emphasis, and perhaps the beginning of the end, for the Godfather of Soul. In March 1970, James Brown's funk juggernaut had hit a pothole with the departures of tenor saxophonist Maceo Parker, guitarists Jimmy Nolen and Country Kellum, and most of the rest of the James Brown Orchestra. Drummer Jabo Starks remained, along with organist/singer Bobby Byrd, but a whole new band was required.

Enter The JB's, led by bassist Bootsy Collins and his rhythm-guitarist brother, Catfish. The Collins brothers found the groove that pins "Get Up (I Feel Like Being a) Sex Machine," relegating the usually prominent horn section to the stabbed opening—and anywhere else Brown felt like introducing it, as he snaked through the song, letting the rhythm do its thing, trading plans with Byrd.

Legendary pay disputes, along with the odd fine for duff notes, had strained Brown's relationship with his Orchestra, but The JB's had no such beef with their boss. "Things kinda changed a bit," noted Bootsy in 2002, "because he couldn't really threaten us with fines or taking anything from us as we never had nothing no way." Brown's unaffected young cohorts gave him fresh vigor to face up to the threat from the next generation of funkateers—Sly Stone, Isaac Hayes—and find a new beat. **MH**

Ohio | Crosby, Stills, Nash & Young (1970)

Writer | Neil Young
Producer | David Crosby, Stephen Stills, Graham Nash, Neil Young
Label | Atlantic
Album | N/A

The death of four Kent State University students, shot by the National Guard in Ohio during a protest on May 4, 1970, was the inspiration behind this one-off Crosby, Stills, Nash & Young single—one of rock's most resonant protest songs.

Pressed into action when David Crosby showed him harrowing photos of the shootings published in *Life* magazine, Neil Young wrote the song in a day; the members of Crosby, Stills, Nash, & Young then promptly convened in the Record Plant Studios, Sausalito, California. The recording was more of a team effort than anything on the recent *Déjà vu* album, which, though hugely successful, had mostly showcased four separate performers. "Ohio" was captured live in the studio, ragged harmonies and all, and simmering with audible outrage at the shootings. "Neil wrote 'Ohio' on Monday and recorded it at Record Plant in Hollywood and it was on the airways by Friday; that is just unheard of and I'll never forget it, we got 'Ohio' in one take," explained drummer Johnny Barbata, who was hastily called up for the session.

The dread conveyed in lines such as "tin soldiers and Nixon coming" contrasted sharply with CSN&Y's country-rock single taken from *Déjà vu*, Graham Nash's "Teach Your Children." Nevertheless, the rush-release of the guitar-driven "Ohio" meant that CSN&Y registered two Top Twenty *Billboard* hits in the month of June 1970. **DR**

From left, Nash, Crosby, Young, and Stills harmonize in 1970. ➜

The Only Living Boy in New York
Simon & Garfunkel (1970)

Writer | Paul Simon
Producer | R. Halee, Simon & Garfunkel
Label | Columbia
Album | *Bridge over Troubled Water* (1970)

The beginning of the end for the titans of folk rock came when Art Garfunkel flew down to Mexico to spend five months playing Nately in Mike Nichols's film of Joseph Heller's *Catch-22*. Paul Simon was left alone in NYC, penning tracks for their LP *Bridge over Troubled Water*, an experience commemorated in this wistful, meditative ballad.

Given the subsequent acrimony of their breakup, the lyrics could be read as a passive-aggressive dig at the frizzy-haired absentee, but Garfunkel remembers the song as filled with nothing but affection. By addressing the first line to "Tom" rather than Art, Simon harks right back to the partnership's teenage origins—as Tom & Jerry, the duo had charted in 1957 with the Everly Brothers–styled "Hey, Schoolgirl."

The recording itself builds from the strummed guitar of a lone busker into a lush, layered melancholy, thanks to Larry Knechtel's devotional organ chords, drummer Hal Blaine's Ringo-esque thumps, and Joe Osborn's funky bass flourishes. Just over a minute in, aaahing voices bring to mind the rich choral harmonies on Side Two of The Beatles' *Abbey Road*, released only a few months beforehand. This sixteen-strong choir is comprised entirely of Paul Simon and Art Garfunkel, recorded in an echo chamber and doubled up half a dozen times. It's like hearing those old musical friends jointly heave a last, melodic sigh. **SP**

In a Broken Dream
Python Lee Jackson (1970)

Writer | David Bentley
Producer | Miki Dallon
Label | Young Blood International
Album | *In a Broken Dream* (1972)

Who was the mysterious Python Lee Jackson? The answer is that he was not one man, but four—an Australian beat group who moved to Swinging London with the intention of making it big. Singer David Bentley was armed with a very palpable hit—an angsty breakup ballad called "In a Broken Dream"—but shortly before recording it in 1968, he heard Joe Cocker's histrionic version of "With a Little Help from My Friends" belting from a boutique doorway, and realized that his own voice was not ideal for the material.

The band was signed to John Peel's imprint, Dandelion Records, at the time; the DJ suggested that Rod Stewart, a sandpaper-voiced mod who was at that time between bands, might provide a guide vocal. The result was one of the definitive performances of Stewart's career, a world-weary and nuanced reading that perfectly suited the song's mood of despairing denial, but it remained unreleased until 1970—and did not chart until a reissue cashed in on his post-Faces fame in 1972. By then, the charts were fizzing with bubblegum and glam, and "In a Broken Dream" seemed a vestige of a bygone time. Bentley's laidback Hammond and Jamie Byrne's bass are cut from the Procol Harum template, while Mick Liber's brain-fried guitar work owes much to Bay Area psychedelic bands such as Big Brother & The Holding Company (with Stewart as a male Janis Joplin). **SP**

Oh Lonesome Me
Neil Young (1970)

Writer | Don Gibson
Producer | Neil Young, David Briggs, Kendall Pacios
Label | Reprise
Album | *After the Gold Rush* (1970)

While Neil Young credited a trippy, unproduced screenplay by actor Dean Stockwell and Captain Beefheart collaborator Herb Berman as the inspiration for most of the original songs on his opus *After the Gold Rush*, this standout track was a cover from a more conventional source. Penned by country hitmaker Don Gibson, "Oh Lonesome Me" effectively mines that rich vein of honky-tonk music. Building on a foundation laid by Hank Williams's classic "Lovesick Blues," Gibson takes loneliness to the next level, with the singer essentially declaring himself the most forlorn individual on earth. While Gibson rendered the song in a rollicking, "to hell with it all" manner, Young instead sounds the depths of the lyric, slowing things to a deliciously dolorous crawl.

Backing Young here was the band Crazy Horse, whom he had used on his previous solo album, *Everybody Knows this is Nowhere*. But because of guitarist Danny Whitten's drug addiction, only three tracks with the group made it to *After the Gold Rush*. Whitten was later kicked out of the band and died of an overdose in 1972. Young lamented his demise on 1973's *Tonight's the Night* (released in 1975).

Amazingly, *Rolling Stone* panned *After the Gold Rush* on its release in a scathing review by Langdon Winner. Thankfully, Winner later abandoned rock criticism for a career as a professor of political science. **TS**

54-46 Was My Number
Toots & The Maytals (1970)

Writer | Fred "Toots" Hibbert
Producer | Leslie Kong
Label | Beverley's
Album | N/A

Close-harmony group The Maytals had formed in 1962, initially working with producer Clement "Coxsone" Dodd at his Studio One label. The group went on to record with Prince Buster and Byron Lee, with limited success, before two factors were to dramatically change their fate.

Lead vocalist Fred "Toots" Hibbert was jailed for possession of marijuana. After his release, the band renamed themselves Toots & The Maytals and found a new home at Chinese–Jamaican Leslie Kong's Beverley's label, moves that saw them become the biggest ska crossover group to date.

Hibbert drew upon his time in prison for the lyrical theme of "54-46 That's My Number," the forerunner of this track, though the actual prison number was invented; it featured in the score (though not the soundtrack album) of Jimmy Cliff's *The Harder They Come* (1972). The song is a protest of the singer's innocence, as Hibbert claimed the real reason for his imprisonment was for having bailed out a friend, rather than the stated drugs charge. This more dynamic follow-up version, featuring a rousing vocal intro and subtly retitled "54-46 Was My Number," proved to be a hugely popular song both in Jamaica and overseas, and was to be the first of a string of hits for the group.

The prison and protest themes of the track became an influence for the politicized sections of the punk movement, particularly The Clash. **CR**

Working Class Hero
John Lennon (1970)

Writer | John Lennon
Producer | John Lennon, Yoko Ono, Phil Spector
Label | Apple
Album | *Plastic Ono Band* (1970)

John Lennon's first solo album followed four months of primal-scream therapy with New York psychologist Dr. Arthur Janov, a period that saw him facing his legion of demons. An almost motherless adolescence; the breakup of his band and the support system he resented; the paradox of his iconoclasm; guilt; and contempt for his middle-class upbringing—it was all poured into *Plastic Ono Band*.

As Paul McCartney settled into bucolia and George Harrison spread his wings at last, the other songwriting Beatle had some scores to settle, not least with himself. The conspicuously Dylanesque "Working Class Hero" drips with disdain, typical sarcasm, and bitterness. The song makes its point starkly, in rough-picked folk and a half-spoken, half-sung sneer. There is no respite. As if the song were not already robust enough, Lennon completes his alienation of the more staid elements of his audience with two spits of the word "fucking," the second his memorable dismissal of the "peasants" we will always be. "I put it in because it fit," he told *Rolling Stone*, aware of its effect.

While it's not exclusively personal—education, the daily drudge, corporate fat cats all take a hit—this is Lennon's experience. "I hope it's just a warning to people," he once ventured, but even a flawed hero has his acolytes. **MH**

Box of Rain
The Grateful Dead (1970)

Writer | Phil Lesh, Robert Hunter
Producer | Grateful Dead, Steve Barncard
Label | Warner Bros.
Album | *American Beauty* (1970)

It's a good thing that Phil Lesh knew how to play the bass—since he wasn't ever going to make it as a vocalist. Still, it's ironic that one of the few Grateful Dead tunes that Lesh sang, with his brittle, reedy voice, would become one of the most significant pages in the group's mighty songbook.

The fragile, acoustic-flavored ballad "Box of Rain," so different from the heady psychedelic jams that the band was known for in concert, was composed by Lesh as a tribute to his father, who was dying from cancer. The bassist then handed the music to outside lyricist Robert Hunter, who would pen most of the group's classics. Hunter, obviously moved by the occasion, scribbled down the words that would secure his legend as one of the hippie nation's finest songwriters.

Sharing much in common with another Dead staple, "Ripple," the song was deeply poetic. It was built on one man's experience, yet the message was universal. Lesh's strained voice, choking with emotion, was difficult to listen to once one knew the backstory to the song, but also the perfect vehicle to convey its sentiment. Lesh accompanied himself on acoustic guitar, while David Nelson swung the electric axe and Jerry Garcia sat at piano.

The tune was included on the Dead's country-folk masterpiece *American Beauty*. It was never released as a single, yet that didn't stop it from becoming a fan favorite at concerts. **JiH**

Phil Lesh in his most familiar role, as bass kingpin of The Grateful Dead's interstellar ramblings. ➔

Life on Mars? | David Bowie (1971)

Writer | David Bowie
Producer | Ken Scott, "The actor" (aka David Bowie)
Label | RCA Victor
Album | Hunky Dory (1971)

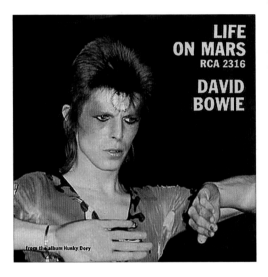

LIFE
ON MARS
RCA 2316

DAVID
BOWIE

from the album Hunky Dory

"There's something Zen-like about that song, even though it's so emotional."

Mick Rock, photographer, 2008

◄ **Influenced by: My Death** · Scott Walker (1967)
► **Influence on: Boy** · Ian Hunter (1975)
● **Covered by:** Barbra Streisand (1974) · The Flaming Lips (1996) · Geoff Keezer (2000) · Seu Jorge (2004) · Tony Christie (2006) · The Dresden Dolls (2006) · The Thing (2008) · Enrico Ruggeri (2009)

"This song was so easy . . ." declared David Bowie in 2008, tongue firmly in cheek. However, "Life on Mars?" had anything but a straightforward genesis.

In 1968, Bowie had written "Even a Fool Learns to Love," its lyrics set to the music of a French song from 1967, "Comme d'habitude," recorded by one of its writers, Claude François. Bowie's song went unreleased, while Paul Anka bought the rights to the original French version, and rewrote it into "My Way." Bowie duly wrote "Life on Mars?" as a parody of Frank Sinatra's recording of Anka's song. "There was a sense of revenge in that," he admitted. The liner notes of Hunky Dory—the album on which the song first appeared—described the song as "inspired by Frankie."

The new lyrics concerned "a sensitive young girl's reaction to the media." "I started working it out on the piano and had the whole lyric and melody finished by late afternoon . . ." Bowie told The Mail on Sunday. "Rick Wakeman came over a couple of weeks later and embellished the piano part and guitarist Mick Ronson created one of his first and best string parts." "The songs were unbelievable," Wakeman marveled. "'Changes,' 'Life on Mars?,' one after another."

Released in 1973 as a single to cash in on the success of Ziggy Stardust, "Life on Mars?" was a U.K. hit. It reached No. 3 and stayed in the charts for thirteen weeks. (The song has since been covered by artists from Barbra Streisand to Arcade Fire.) A striking promotional video, directed by photographer Mick Rock, features Bowie in his orange-haired pomp and wearing a turquoise suit against a brilliant-white backdrop. "I still couldn't tell you what it's about," reflected Rock in 2008, "but that's art." **BM**

Bang a Gong (Get It On) | T. Rex (1971)

Writer | Marc Bolan
Producer | Tony Visconti
Label | Fly
Album | *Electric Warrior* (1971)

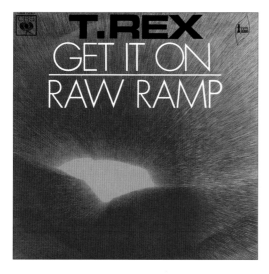

"I'm really Marc Hendrix! I feel I'm a killer guitarist.... Listen to 'Get It On.'"

Marc Bolan, 1972

◄ **Influenced by:** Little Queenie • Chuck Berry (1959)
► **Influence on:** Cigarettes and Alcohol • Oasis (1994)
● **Covered by:** Power Station (1985) • Blondie (1993)
The Glitter Band (1996) • Boy George & Edwyn Collins
(1996) • Neanderthal Spongecake (2002)
Ministry (2008)

After forming as a slightly fey psychedelic-folk group in the late 1960s, Marc Bolan and Tyrannosaurus Rex were riding high in the U.K. charts with their single "Ride a White Swan" when they headed to the United States for a short tour early in 1971. A session in New York provided the first tracks for the *Electric Warrior* album (the group's first as T. Rex), but it was in L.A. that Bolan and producer Tony Visconti really struck gold. Hooking up with Mark Volman and Howard Kaylan—Turtles singers who had recently worked with Frank Zappa—at Kaylan's house in Laurel Canyon after a gig, the band jammed out an idea that Bolan had been working on as a tribute to a Chuck Berry's "Little Queenie" from 1959, the flip side of "Almost Grown." Keeping some of Berry's lyrics (the final recorded version pays tribute to Berry in its fade-out, borrowing a line of his), the result was a handy summation of the glam-rock phenomenon, combining urgent rock 'n' roll with post-hippy posturing. ("When we do it live, it goes on for twenty minutes sometimes and it's just loaded with guitar solos," an ebullient Bolan told an interviewer in 1972.)

The song, titled "Bang a Gong (Get It On)" to avoid its being confused with a hit of the same name by the band Chase, became Bolan's only major hit in the United States. It sold nearly a million copies in the United Kingdom at the peak of "T-Rextasy." By 1972, T. Rex were selling out arenas in their home country and Ringo Starr had signed up to make a documentary (*Born to Boogie*) about them. Only a few years later, however, the band had all but split, and Bolan was killed in an automobile accident in September 1977, just a fortnight before his thirtieth birthday. **PL**

Blackwater Side
Anne Briggs (1971)

Writer | Traditional
Producer | A. L. Lloyd
Label | Topic
Album | *Anne Briggs* (1971)

Scottish folk musician Bert Jansch maintains that, in the context of the British folk scene, Anne Briggs "was more akin to a punk than to anything that had gone before." Young, attractive, and wild, Briggs left her Nottingham home in 1962, aged seventeen, to join a touring folk revue, and soon made her name in London's folk clubs. Her erratic nature and reluctance to record only added to her legend, which continues to grow even today.

Briggs released an EP, *Hazards of Love*, in 1964 and, with singer Frankie Armstrong and folklorist A.L. Lloyd, an album of "traditional erotic songs" two years later. The folk revival was then in full bloom, and Briggs was one of its leading lights. Yet she spent much of the rest of the Sixties rambling drunkenly around England and Ireland, avoiding anything that might have been termed a "career."

Before she disappeared, Briggs's repertoire had included "Blackwater Side," a traditional song learned from Lloyd. Jansch learned it from Briggs in the early 1960s, recording it on his *Jack Orion* album in 1966. Jimmy Page learned it from *Jack Orion*, retitling it "Black Mountain Side" on Led Zeppelin's debut in 1969. Briggs recorded this delicate version for her own belated debut in 1971. A second album followed the same year. Blocking the release of an album entitled *Sing a Song for You* (recorded in 1973, but unreleased until 1996), she's barely sung in public since. **WF-J**

I Don't Want to Talk About It
Crazy Horse (1971)

Writer | Danny Whitten
Producer | Jack Nitzsche, Bruce Botnick
Label | Warner Bros.
Album | *Crazy Horse* (1971)

The musicians who came to be known as Crazy Horse formed around guitarist-singer Danny Whitten in Canton, Ohio, in 1962. Shifting to San Francisco, they became The Rockets, a hot bar band. An L.A. gig led Neil Young to employ them as his backing band on the excellent *Everyone Knows This Is Nowhere* album (1969), on which Whitten and Young traded vocals and guitar interplay. Producer Jack Nitzsche named the band Crazy Horse and began sitting in with them on piano.

After Young fired Crazy Horse from the *After the Gold Rush* recording sessions, because of Whitten's heroin addiction, the group absorbed Nitzsche, guitarist Nils Lofgren, and a recording contract with Warner Bros. This unit recorded one album featuring five remarkable Whitten songs. Sadly, Whitten's continuing drug problems forced the rest of the band into firing him.

"I Don't Want to Talk About It" is a plaintive ballad, and Whitten's mournful voice and pleading lyrics might, in a lesser talent, belong to the navel-gazing singer-songwriter school. Yet the beauty of the melody, the taut interplay between the musicians—Ry Cooder adds exemplary slide guitar—the atmosphere of immense, almost silent, grief, shaped a song of rare beauty. Whitten's spirit exudes a bruised despair. "I Don't Want to Talk About It" could be his hymn to a lover or to heroin, the drug that killed him in 1972. **GC**

A Case of You
Joni Mitchell (1971)

Writer | Joni Mitchell
Producer | Unknown
Label | Reprise
Album | *Blue* (1971)

Although her fourth album is nakedly confessional—"I was at my most defenseless during the making of [it]," she admitted in 1997—Joni Mitchell has shied away from revealing its precise inspirations. Certainly, there's no shortage of suspects. Mitchell's list of lovers in the years leading up to the album included all three of Crosby, Stills, and Nash; at the time of the recording, she was having an affair with James Taylor, who was then in the depths of a crippling heroin habit. It may be this addiction to which Mitchell refers on "A Case of You," when she offers that she's "frightened by the devil" but "drawn to those ones that ain't afraid."

But to dwell on the real-life angst that inspired *Blue* runs the risk of passing over the skill with which it was translated into song. The singer's three previous albums had all been airy, winsome affairs. *Blue*, though, was both emotionally rawer and musically richer.

"A Case of You" is a case in point. Written and performed by Mitchell on an Appalachian dulcimer, it's a perfect blend of unvarnished intimacy and crafted poetry. Taylor added a little empathetic guitar, and there's the merest hint of percussion, but the performance is otherwise all Mitchell, her fluid vocal emphasizing the melody's lovely arc. The song has since been much covered but never matched. **WF-J**

Crayon Angels
Judee Sill (1971)

Writer | Judee Sill
Producer | Henry Lewy
Label | Asylum
Album | *Judee Sill* (1971)

How could such a troubled background produce such a sweet, heavenly sound? A short life punctuated by episodes of reform school, heavy drug-taking, prostitution, and jail somehow managed to produce one of America's most gifted but overlooked songwriters.

"Crayon Angels" was the first track on Judee Sill's debut album and, as a result, the first release on David Geffen's new label, Asylum Records. Although Sill's music was gorgeously easy on the ear, the beauty of the song's melody contrasted greatly with her powerful lyrics. "Phony prophets stole the only light I knew" seemed a dig at music business bigwigs. Even Geffen, initially a big champion of Sill, couldn't devote enough time to nurturing her fragile career after Jackson Browne and the Eagles began their rich run of success for Asylum.

The record deal did give Sill the security to buy a place in California's songwriting haven, Laurel Canyon, but, although a second album followed, commercial success did not. Sill died in 1979, aged thirty-five, but a reappraisal of her work culminated in the release of *Crayon Angel: A Tribute to the Music of Judee Sill* in 2009. An appreciation of her work has surfaced through a new wave of bands typified by Fleet Foxes, who often include "Crayon Angels" in their live performances. **DR**

Famous Blue Raincoat
Leonard Cohen (1971)

Writer | Leonard Cohen
Producer | Bob Johnston
Label | Columbia
Album | *Songs of Love and Hate* (1971)

Although it was released on the Canadian legend's third album in 1971, "Famous Blue Raincoat" had actually been written years earlier and tested extensively live before being taken to the studio. As Leonard Cohen's guitarist and band leader, Ron Cornelius, remembers it, Cohen realized in advance of its release that the song would become one of his best loved: "We played that song a lot before it ever went to tape. We knew it was going to be big. We could see what the crowd did—you play the Royal Albert Hall, the crowd goes crazy, and you're really saying something there."

Cornelius was right. One of the songs Cohen is most readily associated with, "Famous Blue Raincoat" is a lyrically opaque examination of the end of a love affair, written as a letter addressed to a male acquaintance and telling the tale of a love triangle that leads to the end of a relationship. At one concert in 1970, Cohen described the lyric as being an attack on sexual possession, but the reality is something much more cryptic: the power of the epistolary lyrics lies in the fact that they are almost spoken—rather than sung—and matched to an understated waltz underpinned by Elton John arranger Paul Buckmaster's subtle strings.

Cohen has always claimed to be unhappy with the lyrical ambiguity of the song. A host of artists have overcome such reservations to cover it, however, including Lloyd Cole and Joan Baez. **PL**

Chalte Chalte
Lata Mangeshkar (1971)

Writer | Ghulam Mohammed, Kaifi Azmi
Producer | Uncredited
Label | Odeon
Album | *Kamal Amrohi's Pakeezah OST* (1971)

Choosing only one song to represent an artist once listed in *Guinness World Records* as the most recorded singer in history isn't easy. Nor is counting the songs she's voiced as a "playback singer" in around 1,200 Bollywood movies, during a career that began in 1942. One of Lata Mangeshkar's personal favorites, though, and a song that was very popular in India, is "Chalte Chalte," from the 1971 movie *Pakeezah*.

The film's title means "pure of heart," and it concerns a thwarted romance between an aristocrat and a prostitute, played by director Amrohi's then wife, Meena Kumari. Having started work on the film, Amrohi and Kumari subsequently divorced, and the film was abandoned; they later reunited to complete it, but it was more than ten years before it made it to the screen. At first, *Pakeezah* received a lukewarm response from the public, but when Kumari died soon after its release, it became a hit. The film is now remembered as much for its soundtrack as its story.

In the performance of "Chalte Chalte" in the film, Kumari lip-synchs along to Mangeshkar's honeyed, high-pitched voice. There is a folkloric, light classical flavor to the accompaniment, with an initial flourish on santoor (dulcimer) before the percussion, sarangi, and sitar kick in. Near the end, there is a shrieking train whistle motif, which features several times in the movie. **JLu**

Leonard Cohen models a raincoat of indeterminable color in a 1970 publicity photo.

Maggie May | Rod Stewart (1971)

Writer | Rod Stewart, Martin Quittenton
Producer | Rod Stewart
Label | Mercury
Album | *Every Picture Tells a Story* (1971)

"Bob Dylan hit it on the head when he said, 'You don't write songs, you discover them.'"

Rod Stewart, 1976

◄ **Influenced by: Maggie May** · Traditional English folk song (*c*.1800)

► **Influence on: Painkiller** · Turin Brakes (2003)

● **Covered by:** The Pogues (1989) · Blur (1992) · Mathilde Santing (2008) · Massacre (2008) · Matthew Sweet & Susanna Hoffs (2009)

"Maggie May" is always described as Rod Stewart's best-known song, although his versions of "Sailing" and "Handbags and Gladrags" also come close. There is something about "Maggie May" that keeps it from sounding dated, even four decades after its release. The instrumentation sounds ravishing to this day, thanks to the sweetly singing acoustic guitars and mandolin laid down by Stewart's sometime collaborator Ron Wood. Rod's vocal, meanwhile, is a typically rasping performance, with the woodsmoke-and-whiskey edge that he has retained ever since.

Still, there's more to this song than simply its sweet sounds. In "Maggie May," Stewart tells a story (based on personal experience) that always grips the imagination—the tale of a sexually inexperienced male lured into the clutches of an older woman. At the start of the song, he asks her to wake up because he has to break off their relationship in order to attend school—a startling opening line if ever there was one. "All you did was wreck my bed / And in the morning kick me in the head," he laments, leading the listener to ask what sort of relationship this was.

And yet there's true love at the heart of the song: Stewart sings of his promises to adore Maggie forever, despite her age. This was eyebrow-raising stuff back in 1971, which makes the song's adoption as a standard love ballad, played at weddings and funerals alike, all the stranger. Stewart himself has mellowed into a housewife's favorite over the years, too, but look under the covers of this song and there's a biting cultural comment.

The song (and the album from which it came) simultaneously topped the charts in the United Kingdom and the United States. **JMc**

Imagine | John Lennon (1971)

Writer | John Lennon
Producer | John Lennon, Yoko Ono, Phil Spector
Label | Apple
Album | *Imagine* (1971)

"The idea for a song like 'Imagine' came out of Yoko's influence."

John Lennon, 1972

◄ **Influenced by: Let It Be** • The Beatles (1970)
► **Influence on: Don't Look Back in Anger** • Oasis (1995)
● **Covered by:** Andy Williams (1972) • Diana Ross (1973)
Susan Cadogan (1975) • Elton John (1980) • Gerry & The
Pacemakers (1981) • Liza Minnelli (1992) • David Bowie
(1997) • Ray Charles (2001)

Considering its ubiquity, it seems unthinkable that "Imagine" was not a single in the United Kingdom until it was used to promote *Shaved Fish*'s collection of singles and other John Lennon flotsam in 1975, four years after it was first heard. Even then, it reached only No. 6 in the charts—hardly the performance of a future standard.

As the title track of Lennon's second solo album, "Imagine" spearheaded a set of tracks far less stark and confrontational than *Plastic Ono Band* in 1970. With that primal howl of a record, Lennon had worked out a few (very) personal issues—although there would be a notorious dig at former colleague Paul McCartney on *Imagine*'s "How Do You Sleep?"

"Imagine" is a sly dog. Its pillowy sound and simple lyric—a trope inspired by Yoko Ono's potted philosophy in Lennon's treasured copy of her *Grapefruit* book—not to mention the song's rather vague exhortations, disguise subversive ideas. Lennon himself suggested that it was "virtually the Communist manifesto," and it would have that clout if taken literally. However, people being people, exposure has watered its message down to platitude.

"Imagine" was reissued following Lennon's murder in December 1980. This time, it claimed the No. 1 spot that its timeless melody and Lennon's persuasive vocal deserved, joining "(Just Like) Starting Over" and "Woman" in a near-consecutive triumvirate of U.K. chart-toppers as a nation grieved. From there, it began its weary journey via cover versions, awards, and ever-more-frequent polls to unimpeachable classic status. Peer through the baubles, though, and there's still a song in there. **MH**

Laughing
David Crosby (1971)

Writer | David Crosby
Producer | David Crosby
Label | Atlantic
Album | *If I Could Only Remember My Name...* (1971)

Three years before this song's eventual release, ex-Byrd David Crosby was searching for a solo deal in L.A., hawking an acoustic guitar–and-voice demo of "Laughing" as his calling card. He touted it to Paul Rothchild (producer of Love and The Doors, among others) and, encouraged by John Sebastian, cut another version. But then came Crosby, Stills & Nash and a monster first album, plus an era-defining Woodstock set, so the song went on the back burner.

"Laughing" finally surfaced on his all-star solo album and as the B-side to the single "Music is Love." The laid-back Laurel Canyon set (including Graham Nash) teamed up with the Haight-Ashbury hippies (such as Jefferson Airplane's Paul Kantner and Grace Slick) to concoct a West Coast, good-vibe, meandering masterpiece.

Recorded at San Francisco's new hip Wally Heider Recording, the "Laughing" sessions comprised Crosby and a kernel of The Grateful Dead, including Jerry Garcia on pedal steel guitar, Phil Lesh providing a beefy bass sound, and Bill Kreutzmann on drums. Joni Mitchell, one of Crosby's former lovers, also lends her characteristic vocals. The song is laden with echo and overdubs, and Garcia's otherworldly pedal steel guitar is simply stunning. Crosby himself provides sparkling twelve-string guitar as well as his glorious, multi-tracked voice. **JJH**

When the Levee Breaks
Led Zeppelin (1971)

Writer | Memphis Minnie, John Paul Jones, John Bonham, Robert Plant
Producer | Jimmy Page
Label | Atlantic
Album | *Led Zeppelin IV* (1971)

Ensconced at country-retreat-cum-studio Headley Grange, nearing the end of the sessions for their fourth album—which, thanks to the epic "Stairway to Heaven," would prove their most successful—Led Zeppelin took one last swing at their version of a dusty but enduring blues relic.

The original, recorded in 1929 by husband-and-wife duo Kansas Joe McCoy and Memphis Minnie, was inspired by the plight of those caught in the Great Mississippi Flood of 1927. Drenching Zeppelin's earthy take in studio effects—including distinctive reverse-echo on the blistering harmonica and trudging guitars—Jimmy Page built a track that evoked the sheer might of the flood, vocalist Robert Plant wailing beneath the tumult.

The genius stroke, however, was John Bonham's behemoth of a drum track, the secret to the song's colossal heft. To achieve this pulverizing beat, engineer Andy Johns placed the kit at the bottom of a staircase in the old country house and suspended microphones from the ceiling, so Bonham's every kick-drum thud, snare thwack, and cymbal splash was bolstered by the natural reverb of the stairwell. The song was so reliant upon this primal studio trickery that Zeppelin only performed it onstage twice, although Page and Plant revisited the song while touring acoustically in the 1990s. Still, it remains perhaps their most ground-shaking track. **SC**

Robert Plant: in 1971, no one was more the rock god than he. ➡

Surf's Up
The Beach Boys (1971)

Writer | Brian Wilson,
Van Dyke Parks
Producer | The Beach Boys
Label | Brother
Album | *Surf's Up* (1971)

A lesser song might buckle under the weight of its legend, but the wryly titled "Surf's Up" only tantalizes all the more. On its belated release in 1971, it offered a glimpse of the rumored majesty of Brian Wilson's abandoned *Smile* project, surpassing the snippets that had emerged in one form or another since 1967—with the exception, perhaps, of "Good Vibrations." Whatever the relative merits, *Smile*'s mooted centerpiece, "Surf's Up," was a different kettle of fish, a pop symphony out of place and out of time.

Wilson finally got around to finishing *Smile* in 2004, but, apart from the bootlegs and half-conceived songs strewn across *Smiley Smile* (1967) and *20/20* (1969), we're still a frustrating step removed from what The Beach Boys themselves would have made of it.

With Wilson marginalized by his own design and mental state, the remaining Beach Boys obviously realized there was value in "Surf's Up," and Carl Wilson set about rebuilding the track from demo material and new input for the album that would bear its name. It's his characteristically pure vocal hitting the high notes in the first half of the song, with Brian's demo guide taking over for the second movement. "The vocal on that was a little limited," Brian later admitted, "but it did have heart." And it did, wringing beauty and poignancy out of Parks's wild poetry. **MH**

Theme from *Shaft*
Isaac Hayes (1971)

Writer | Isaac Hayes
Producer | Isaac Hayes
Label | Enterprise
Album | *Shaft OST* (1971)

Make no mistake—with the funky wah-wahs, disco drumming (before D-I-S-C-O had been unleashed), and sugary-lush but tight-ass orchestration, Isaac Hayes unleashed a revolutionary sound for the epitome of the blaxploitation movie: *Shaft*.

It starts with Willie Hall's distinctive sixteenth-note high-hat-cymbal rhythm, and then you hear something completely off the wall for its time. An extended "Stax"-atto rhythmic riff from guitarist Charles "Skip" Pitts wafts it way over the drums, followed by Hayes's own heavy keyboard hits. The drums go into a 4/4 disco beat punctuated further by orchestrated brass, woods, and strings while the wah-wah-effects pedals work overtime.

This instrumental opener, performed by a backing band that included several members of The Bar-Kays (bassist James Alexander, guitarist Michael Toles, and Hall), shoots well over the two-minute mark before Hayes intones, "Who's the black private dick / That's a sex machine to all the chicks?" The lyrics then hit a problem over censorship. The famous line, "He's a baaaad motherfucker" had to be blanked, but Hayes got round the problem by getting backup singer Telma Hopkins to drown out his "call" with a "Shut yo' mouth!" response.

In November 1971, "Theme from *Shaft*" reached No. 1 on the *Billboard* Hot 100. The next year, it won the Oscar for Best Original Song. **JJH**

The Revolution Will Not Be Televised | Gil Scott-Heron (1971)

Writer | Gil Scott-Heron
Producer | Bob Thiele
Label | Flying Dutchman
Album | *Pieces of a Man* (1971)

"The Revolution Will Not Be Televised" first surfaced as a vocal-poetry performance accompanied by percussion on Gil Scott-Heron's debut album, *Small Talk at 125th and Lenox* (1970). It was re-recorded as a fully accompanied track a year later for *Pieces of a Man*. The song's popularity was boosted by its inclusion as the B-side of Scott-Heron's debut single "Home Is Where the Hatred Is," both sides of which proved a hit with critics and listeners alike.

In many ways, the track is a distilled essence of the vocal tradition of poetry and folk-rhyme up until that time, but it also captures the spirit of the early 1970s. Alternating between sparkling humor and cold-eyed criticism, the lyrics rail against the dumbing-down of culture and the anesthetic nature of entertainment, which continues to add to the disenfranchisement of voters in the developed nations to this day. The vast array of cultural references name-checked in the machine-gun delivery of the lines takes in contemporary advertising slogans, political and cultural figures, TV culture, and drugs.

The song became a calling card for the counterculture, spreading through student movements, jazz venues, and dance halls. It also acted as the spearhead for jazz- and soul-backed, poetry-oriented artists such as The Last Poets. Decades later, it would also influence the "conscious" hip-hop of Public Enemy and Mos Def. **CR**

It's Too Late | Carole King (1971)

Writer | Toni Stern, Carole King
Producer | Lou Adler
Label | Ode
Album | *Tapestry* (1971)

A small, seismic shift occurred in popular music when this double A-side (with "I Feel the Earth Move") reached *Billboard*'s No. 1 spot on June 19, 1971, and stayed there for five weeks. It was the calling card for an album, *Tapestry*, that went on to shift twenty-two million copies, pick up four Grammys, and set the template for the Seventies singer-songwriter boom.

A pumping piano kicks off over a gently laid-back, percussion-driven jazz samba as King plays a string of figures and a catchy riff. Then, with clear-headed emotional intensity tinged with a homey Jewish Brooklyn twang, King (née Klein) sets out Toni Stern's new-feminist take on a relationship breakup that's too far gone to patch up. It's like a note left on the fridge door—she's leaving him on her terms, but "I'm glad for what we had." "I want songs of hope, songs of love, songs of raw feeling," King told interviewer Barry Miles in 1976. "Not songs about spacey things like 'In the Canyons of My Mind' with butterflies fluttering about."

Recorded at A&M in the old Charlie Chaplin Films Studio on Hollywood's Sunset Boulevard, the let-it-all-hang-out lyrics are carried by a virtually live take, courtesy of consummate L.A. studio musicianship. The verse-chorus segues nicely into some cool jazz-guitar grooves by Danny Kortchmar that blend into a soprano-sax lick from Curtis Amy, while King interplays on electronic keyboards. **JJH**

Dum Maro Dum
Asha Bhosle (1971)

Writer | Anand Bakshi, Rahul Dev Burman
Producer | Rahul Dev Burman
Label | Saregama India Ltd.
Album | N/A

Asha Bhosle was born in Bombay, British India, in 1933, and during her long life she has become arguably the most recorded singer in history. She is especially well known as a Bollywood "playback singer"—these are the singers whose voices come out of the movie stars in the Bollywood movies.

She began working as a playback singer in 1943—her older sister, Lata Mangeshkar, was already doing so—and after a disastrous marriage was left to raise three children alone. She raised the funds to bring them up by singing for Bollywood soundtracks. By her own accounts, she has now recorded more than 12,000 songs.

"Dum Maro Dum" was recorded in 1971 for the film *Hare Krishna Hare Rama* and finds Bhosle working with the great Bollywood composer R. D. Burman. This film takes as its theme the migration of Western hippies to Asia, and as the song is played actress Zeenat Aman mimes along on screen, smoking a spliff. (The title of the track translates as "Puff, take a puff.") Burman cleverly mixes Bollywood effects with rock guitars and psychedelic effects while Asha's high-pitched voice races along with the frantic music, almost crashing into the repeated "ah ah ah"s from Usha Lyer and the chant of "Hare Krishna Hare Rama." "Dum Maro Dum" demonstrates just how crazy, funny, and inventive Bollywood soundtracks can be, at their best. **GC**

Tired of Being Alone
Al Green (1971)

Writer | Al Green
Producer | Willie Mitchell
Label | Hi
Album | *Al Green Gets Next to You* (1971)

It took time and a skilled producer to develop the distinctively sensuous voice of U.S. soul legend Al Green. At the age of ten, Albert Greene, as he then was, had started singing in the Greene Brothers gospel quartet with his siblings. Caught listening to Jackie Wilson by his father, he was ejected from both the group and the family home.

Green wanted to be a soul singer and sing like his heroes Jackie Wilson, Wilson Pickett, and James Brown. Willie Mitchell, of Memphis's Hi Records, recognized Green's talent but also realized his singing skills lay not in forceful soul and R&B but in a more relaxed, personal style. His debut album in 1969, *Green Is Blues*, was a compilation of slow, horn-driven ballads—mostly cover versions of popular songs—but was only a moderate hit. The follow-up, *Al Green Gets Next to You*, consisted almost entirely of Al Green originals and was a huge success.

The song sets Green's sinewy, slightly strained falsetto against a chiming guitar, bass, and insistent drumbeat cushioned by wordless backing vocals, the whole punctuated by abrupt unison interruptions from The Memphis Horn Section. As Green laments his loneliness, the song builds to an anguished climax. It was a peerless piece of music from a collaboration that dominated soul until personal tragedy sent Green back to the church and to ordination as a pastor in Memphis in 1976. **SA**

Al Green on stage in 1973, at the peak of his career as a singer of secular soul. ➡

Won't Get Fooled Again | The Who (1971)

Writer | Pete Townshend
Producer | The Who, Glyn Johns
Label | Track
Album | Who's Next (1971)

"It's interesting that the song has actually been taken as a kind of anthem when really it's such a cautionary piece."
Pete Townshend, 1989

◄ **Influenced by: Street Fighting Man** • The Rolling Stones (1968)
► **Influence on: Jump** • Van Halen (1984)
● **Covered by:** Labelle (1972) • Skrewdriver (1977) Van Halen (1993)
★ **Other key track:** I Can See for Miles (1967)

"The first thing people are going to want to hear after listening to *Tommy*," Pete Townshend told *Rolling Stone*, "is, of course, *Tommy* again." Determined to top that pioneering effort, Townshend conceived *Lifehouse*, a full-blown, sci-fi folly.

Received with utter befuddlement by his bandmates and management, Townshend filleted the piece into the band's bestselling *Who's Next* (1971). This was awash with classics—including "Behind Blue Eyes" and "Baba O'Riley"—and climaxed with the synth-driven masterpiece that originally soundtracked a *Lifehouse* uprising: "Won't Get Fooled Again."

In an early incarnation, the song featured guitar twiddling from Mountain maestro Leslie West. In its final form, it showcased Townshend's slashing guitar, bassist John Entwistle's thunder-fingers, Keith Moon's pyrotechnical drumming, and Roger Daltrey's speaker-rattling scream. (Two decades later, another angst-ridden bass-drum-axe combo arrived in the form of Nirvana. Kurt Cobain duly referred to *Nevermind*'s "Drain You" as their own "Won't Get Fooled Again.")

Trimmed to under half its length for a single, the song gave The Who their first U.K. Top Ten hit since "Pinball Wizard" more than two years earlier. Oddly, for all that the track seems to embody rebellion, it actually climaxes with the bleak "Meet the new boss / Same as the old boss" (a line diplomatically omitted by Daltrey for The Who's show-stopping set at the post-9/11 Concert for New York City).

Nonetheless, it lives on as the theme for *CSI: Miami* (*CSI: New York* uses "Behind Blue Eyes"; the original *CSI* uses "Who Are You") and was played to wall-smashing effect when The Who guested on *The Simpsons*. **BM**

Vincent | Don McLean (1971)

Writer | Don McLean
Producer | Ed Freeman
Label | United Artists
Album | *American Pie* (1971)

"I just wanted to be naked when I would sing songs about delicate subjects and just say the truth."

Don McLean, 2003

◄ **Inspired by:** *The Starry Night* (painting)
Vincent van Gogh (1889)
► **Inspiration for:** "Starry Night" • Tupac Shakur (1999)
● **Covered by:** Chet Atkins (1972) • The King's Singers
(1989) • Justin Hayward (1994) • Josh Groban (2001)
Rick Astley (2005)

Don McLean does a fine line in musical obituaries. His most famous might be "American Pie," wherein he recalls the plane crash that killed Buddy Holly, Ritchie Valens, and The Big Bopper, but arguably his best is "Vincent." Often overshadowed by "American Pie," the wistful "Vincent," which recounted Dutch painter Vincent van Gogh's life and death, still captured a sizeable fan base and was internationally more successful than its predecessor (U.S. No. 12; U.K. No. 1).

Hearing it, it is little wonder that "Vincent"—which was played daily at the Van Gogh Museum in Amsterdam throughout the 1970s—won the hearts of its listeners. The charts may have favored the libertine stylings of the previous decade, but in "Vincent," McLean trod a quieter path. Referencing the artist's schizophrenia, suicide, and relentless drive for perfection, his subtle song has a reverential delicacy. Accompanying this with a simple riff and his unwavering, melodious voice, McLean pays his respect to the misunderstood painter in a way that makes his life and death easier to empathize with.

Somewhat unusually for a chart hit, "Vincent" is extraordinarily intimate. In its gentle climax, McLean is momentarily unaided by music and addresses the artist directly: "But I could have told you / Vincent / This world was never meant for one as beautiful as you."

"I got criticized for the kinds of things I wrote sometimes," McLean reflected in 2003. "'American Pie' was too long and couldn't be a hit; 'Vincent' was too weird." Thankfully, McLean was and is no walkover, and his "weird" song became a long-overdue eulogy for the late artist and set a precedent for singer-songwriters everywhere. **KBo**

City of New Orleans
Steve Goodman (1971)

Writer | Steve Goodman
Producer | Kris Kristofferson, Norbert Putnam
Label | Buddha
Album | *Steve Goodman* (1971)

Outside of folk-music circles, Steve Goodman was never a major star. He did have a taste of commercial success as a recording artist with "Jessie's Jig and Other Favorites," but his real claim to fame was as a "songwriter's songwriter."

Goodman died in 1984, a thirty-six-year-old victim of leukemia, but by then he had already secured his legacy with "City of New Orleans." Released on his self-titled debut album, the song wasn't actually about Crescent City itself, but about a "southbound odyssey" from Chicago, Illinois, to New Orleans on the nightly passenger train known as the City of New Orleans.

Goodman's lyrics, which balanced patriotism and realism in Woody Guthrie–like fashion, transported listeners across every mile of the trip, "past houses, farms, and fields" and by "freight yards full of old black men." His understated delivery—rising up on the chorus, "Good morning, America, how are you?"—and finger-picked guitar made the number feel like some long-lost train song from back in Boxcar Willie's day. In time, it would become a country-folk classic, but it took other voices to get it there.

Artists to cover the song include Arlo Guthrie, Johnny Cash, and John Denver. However, the best-known version is Willie Nelson's chart-topper in 1984, which earned its songwriter a posthumous Grammy for Best Country Song. **JiH**

Peace Train
Cat Stevens (1971)

Writer | Cat Stevens
Producer | Paul Samwell-Smith
Label | Island
Album | *Teaser and the Firecat* (1971)

When he appeared on *The Chris Isaak Hour* in 2009, Cat Stevens said of this much-loved song: "Musically, I was revisiting a very Greek-sounding riff—the kind of thing you'd hear on a Greek island." The song reached No. 7 on the *Billboard* Hot 100 chart, Stevens's first Top Ten hit stateside. Spiritually, though, Stevens's chart-topping hit was about more than channeling his Greek-Cypriot roots: "Peace Train" was a reaction to the horrors of the Vietnam War. Perhaps because of its unashamed optimism, it soon became a hippie anthem. Surprisingly, chart success was not repeated across the Atlantic: Island Records refused to release the single outside of the United States, in a bid to encourage fans to buy the album.

"Peace Train" embodies a snapshot in time for Stevens, capitalizing on the spiritual journey he began when he became sick with tuberculosis at the age of nineteen. The singer later mused: "The words were attached to that time, my peace anthem." Most recently its sentiments were repeated by the renamed Yusuf Islam—Cat Stevens famously converted to Islam at the height of his career, in 1977—in protest about the plight of children in the Iraq War. The song has become a favorite of Yusuf in the years following his Muslim conversion. Fittingly, he performed it at the Nobel Peace Prize ceremony for Bangladeshi economist Muhammad Yunus in 2006. **KL**

Steven Georgiou, aka Cat Stevens, found a large audience for his introspective songs in the 1970s. ➡

Superstar
The Carpenters (1971)

Writer | Leon Russell, Bonnie Bramlett
Producer | Jack Daugherty
Label | A&M
Album | *Carpenters* (1971)

A Nickel and a Nail
O. V. Wright (1971)

Writer | D. Malone, V. Morrison
Producer | Willie Mitchell
Label | Back Beat
Album | *A Nickel and a Nail and Ace of Spades* (1971)

"Superstar" could have been a disaster for The Carpenters. Singer Karen Carpenter thought her brother Richard was "crazy" to suggest the song—a desperate plea from a groupie yearning to sleep with a rock star, which was miles away from their cutesy remit.

Luckily, Richard saw the pop potential in the bittersweet track, which had already been released as a B-side by Delaney & Bonnie under the title "Groupie (Superstar)." It was subsequently covered by Bette Midler, Cher, and Rita Coolidge in Joe Cocker's *Mad Dogs and Englishmen* revue. "I came home from the studio one night and heard a then relatively unknown Bette Midler performing this song on the *Tonight Show*," Richard recalled. "I could barely wait to arrange and record it."

Ditching "I can hardly wait to *sleep* with you again" and replacing it with "*be* with you again" clearly boosted its chances of appealing to Carpenters fans, but it was Richard's souped-up arrangements that really morphed "Superstar" into the triumphant belter it is today.

The opening hoots of an oboe give the song a doleful quality that eclipses its raunchy subject matter. Richard's assured semiorchestral horns and strings in the chorus and deft backing vocals complement Karen's affecting, velvety contralto laments perfectly, making the song both more epic and more emotive than earlier versions. **KBo**

O. V. Wright possessed the most haunted voice in American music. The Memphis-based soul man grew up singing gospel. Aged twenty-four, he cut "That's How Strong My Love Is" for Goldwax. Don Robey, owner of Houston-based Peacock Records, claimed to have Wright under contract as a gospel singer and so began issuing Wright 45s on his Back Beat label.

The songs Wright sang—largely provided by Robey (who bought them off struggling songwriters, then added the pseudonym Deadric Malone to the credits)—all possessed a fierce, brooding quality. Some were slow ballads, others up-tempo dance numbers. Taken together, they constitute deep soul's greatest recordings. Wright's voice was raw, gospel inflected, and blues soaked. ("Soul is church," he once said. "Just changing 'Jesus' to 'baby.' That's all it is.")

"A Nickel and a Nail" finds Mitchell adapting Wright's sound to a sleek funk groove. O. V. rides the rhythm, relaying a tale of misfortune and sorrow. As the song builds, he testifies like a Georgia preacher, the horns kick in, and the track achieves a kind of soul-blues ecstasy. "I get in trouble," Wright laments, "I get in jail." Anyone aware of the singer's all-too-brief life—heroin addiction blighted his career and contributed to his death, aged forty-one—might be forgiven for thinking that the song was autobiographical. **GC**

Logs and straw reinforce the down-home image of sibling duo Karen and Richard Carpenter.

Inner City Blues (Make Me Wanna Holler) | Marvin Gaye (1971)

Writer | Marvin Gaye, James Nyx
Producer | Marvin Gaye
Label | Tamla
Album | *What's Going On* (1971)

The third single from Gaye's *What's Going On* LP lacks the dope-haze sense of optimism of the title track and finds the singer staring into the abyss. With Eddie "Bongo" Brown and bassist Bob Babbitt leading the musicians, the Motown house band conjures up a Latin-flavored voodoo funk from the opening second: if listeners thought all this talk about God and love and ecology meant there was some kind of redemption due to humankind, they were in for a quick, hard lesson in reality.

That Gaye was a master at screwing up his personal life should come as no surprise; here he passes on what he knows to the government: "Rockets, moon shots, spend it on the have-nots," he urges an administration more concerned with glory than lives. (A sentiment echoed seventeen years later in Prince's "Sign o' the Times": "Sister killed her baby 'cause she couldn't afford to feed it / And we're sending people to the moon.") Gaye had firsthand experience of these polarized priorities: his brother Frankie served in Vietnam. "God knows where we're heading," he adds, but this is a cry of confusion, not of religious conviction.

Then the mood changes, those malignant influences overcome by a brief burst of clarity (on the longer, album version). Marvin is left singing with himself and just his piano. Safe in the arms of his mother, he has returned to the comfort of "What's Going On" to see out the LP. **DH**

Papa Was a Rollin' Stone | The Temptations (1972)

Writer | Norman Whitfield, Barrett Strong
Producer | Norman Whitfield
Label | Motown
Album | *All Directions* (1972)

In retrospect, this is the sound of Motown's hottest ensemble tearing itself apart—the vocal quintet would soon sack their producer, thus initiating their own decline. Nevertheless, this seven-minute single (a U.S. No. 1) and its near-twelve-minute album version remain the apex of the psychedelic soul era. That the singers picked up a solitary Grammy while the writer-producer won two shows just how successful and divisive their magnum opus was.

The song comes at you in layers. Bass and high-hat, then strings and a guitar, with a trumpet soloing. Then these disappear and an electric piano fills the space for a bit, creating a foggy, trancelike mood. You would relax, if it weren't for that minatory bass, as ominous as a shark's fin on the horizon. Four minutes in, Dennis Edwards begins singing: "It was the third of September, that day I'll always remember. . . ." Edwards's father had died on that date, and Whitfield used this coincidence to rachet up the tension in the studio. Each of the singers—Edwards, plus Melvin Franklin, Otis Williams, and recent recruits Damon Harris and Richard Street—takes it in turn now to ask questions of their mother while dredging up rumors about their father's reputation. She stonewalls. "Papa was a rollin' stone / Wherever he laid his hat was his home." Wisely, Whitfield lets the Funk Brothers band fill in the gaps in the story. **DH**

I'll Take You There
The Staple Singers (1972)

Writer | Alvertis Isbell (aka Al Bell)
Producer | Al Bell
Label | Stax
Album | *Be Altitude: Respect Yourself* (1972)

With an immediately recognizable bass line lifted from the Harry J Allstars' 1969 classic "The Liquidator" and sun-soaked soul backing from The Muscle Shoals Rhythm Section, The Staple Singers' first U.S. No. 1 single is a long way from Pops Staples's gospel roots. After signing to Stax in 1968, Pops and his daughters found their mojo and—with the aid of producer Al Bell—made the breakthrough with 1971's "Respect Yourself." Bell remained on board for "I'll Take You There," penning its repeated refrain and building on "The Liquidator" to create a mantra for a unified society.

And that's about the size of it—one aspirational lyric, a big borrowed groove, and a mix of testifying and James Brown–style encouragement for the band from singer Mavis Staples. But what might be flimsy in the hands of lesser talents works here because it is honest. When Mavis pleads, "Let me, let me take you," you want to go. Go where, though? Their church turned on The Staple Singers when they began to rack up the R&B hits, leaving Mavis to protest in 1997: "What other place could you take a person but Heaven?"

Taken at the singer's word, it almost seems a pity that the promised land of "I'll Take You There" is somewhere over the rainbow. It is a message of hope ("Ain't no smiling faces / Lying to the races") delivered with joyous bounce, and it deserves to be a template, not a pipe dream. **MH**

Soul Makossa
Manu Dibango (1972)

Writer | Manu Dibango
Producer | Manu Dibango
Label | Fiesta
Album | *Soul Makossa* (1972)

Without "Soul Makossa," disco would be a radically different beast. The Cameroon-born, Paris-based saxophonist's signature recording became a cult hit in Harlem nightclubs in 1972. This, after legendary loft-party DJ David Mancuso stumbled on a rare imported copy in a Brooklyn store and DJ Frankie Crocker of New York's hippest black radio station, WBLS, included the song on his playlist.

As its title suggests, "Makossa" ("twisting dance" in Cameroon's Duala dialect) is a vibrant fusion of traditional African trance ritual rhythms and the brassy soul-jazz funk of King Curtis and James Brown. After Atlantic Records licensed the single from the French Fiesta label, it became Africa's first truly global hit, reaching No. 21 and No. 35 on *Billboard*'s R&B and pop charts respectively in 1973, driven initially by club play. *Rolling Stone*'s Dave Marsh observed later that it was "the only African record by an African" to break into the Top Forty at the time.

The song's influence was epic. At one time there were nine different cover versions in the charts. Kool & The Gang blueprinted their disco smash "Jungle Boogie" on it, while Michael Jackson built its chanted vocal "Mama-se, mama-sa, ma-ma-ko-ssa" into the final bridge of his 1982 *Thriller* opener "Wanna Be Startin' Somethin'." A Tribe Called Quest borrowed its refrain, and Jay-Z, Rihanna, and Wyclef Jean have all sampled it. **MK**

Superstition
Stevie Wonder (1972)

Writer | Stevie Wonder
Producer | Stevie Wonder
Label | Motown
Album | *Talking Book* (1972)

Elected
Alice Cooper (1972)

Writer | A. Cooper, M. Bruce,
G. Buxton, D. Dunaway, N. Smith
Producer | Bob Ezrin
Label | Warner Bros.
Album | *Billion Dollar Babies* (1973)

With its stridently funky groove, "Superstition" was very different from Stevie Wonder's previous Motown hits. And its chart success showed that his mature style was being warmly appreciated.

This was Wonder's second U.S. No. 1: the first, "Fingertips, Part 2," was in 1963, when he had been billed as "Little" Stevie Wonder. In 1971, when Wonder turned twenty-one, he renegotiated a deal with his old label, securing complete creative control over and full rights to his own songs. This was previously unheard of at Motown, but the label eventually capitulated.

The result was what is now known as Wonder's "classic period," which began with *Music of My Mind*, closely followed by *Talking Book*—which included "Superstition" and his next No. 1, "You Are the Sunshine of My Life." For these albums, Wonder often played several different instruments, overdubbing tracks as a sort of virtual one-man band; on "Superstition" (originally written by Wonder for guitarist Jeff Beck), he played drums and multiple keyboards to create the complex cross rhythms, ably supported by a heavy brass riff. But it was his ear-catching use of the Hohner clavinet, combined with synth sounds developed by Tonto's Expanding Head Band (Robert Margouleff and Malcolm Cecil, co-producers with Wonder of *Talking Book*) that gave "Superstition" its inimitable sound. **MW**

The Rolling Stones were settling into tax exile, the Sex Pistols had yet to form, and Marilyn Manson was three years old. In 1972, after the authority-baiting "School's Out," Alice Cooper was rock's No. 1 villain. Los Angeles scenester Kim Fowley—who later masterminded The Runaways—claimed credit for inspiring the follow-up to that smash. He met Alice's producer, Bob Ezrin, who asked him whether he had any ideas. "Yeah," replied Fowley, "what about Alice Cooper for president? Right about election time, you should have this song about Alice being elected, like a kind of [1968 movie] *Wild in the Streets* on record."

The result was "Elected," a Who-style stormer on stage, based on "Reflected," from Alice's 1969 debut, *Pretties for You*. In the studio, Ezrin added orchestral and brass flourishes—much as The Who themselves were to do on 1973's *Quadrophenia*.

The timing could not have been better. "Elected" was released in October 1972, when the Watergate scandal was beginning to envelop Richard Nixon's White House. By the time it was immortalized on *Billion Dollar Babies*, the song sounded like an incisive comment on hypocrisy and the sick side of the Seventies (hence its cameo on the soundtrack of 2005's porno exposé *Inside Deep Throat*). For the record, Alice himself was never interested in a political career. "That," he told bol.com, "would be my hell." **BM**

Motown's boy Wonder in 1973.

Sam Stone
John Prine (1972)

Writer | John Prine
Producer | Arif Mardin
Label | Atlantic
Album | *John Prine* (1972)

In the Seventies, a lot of artists were told they were the "new Bob Dylan," but only one released a debut album that was so convincing, Dylan himself showed up at one gig unannounced and anonymously pitched in on harmonica. Dylan still names John Prine, a drawling folkie from Chicago, as one of his favorite songwriters, and has singled out "Sam Stone" as one of the reasons for that.

The song is one of genuine heft and grace, compassionate but unforgiving, timeless despite being rooted in the politics of its era. While other songs about the Vietnam War were straightforward protests—even the smarter ones, like Creedence Clearwater Revival's "Fortunate Son"—Prine decided to write something different, focusing on a soldier who had served and survived, but found life at home ("the time that he served / Had shattered all his nerves") tougher than Indochina ("But the morphine eased the pain"). The key is in the chorus, chilling in its jauntiness, as Prine croons the line "There's a hole in daddy's arm where all the money goes," as evocative a description of heroin addiction as has ever been set to song.

Stone's fate is set, and he ends up going the same way as that other ruined vet, the Indian Ira Hayes. Perhaps the most moving evocation of Stone's life was from Spiritualized's Jason Pierce, who appropriated key lines on 1997's smack-soaked odyssey "Cop Shoot Cop." **PW**

Willin'
Little Feat (1972)

Writer | Lowell George
Producer | Ted Templeman
Label | Warner Bros.
Album | *Sailin' Shoes* (1972)

It was Jimmy Carl Black, the drummer in Frank Zappa's Mothers of Invention, who first remarked upon them. In Black's words, his bandmate Lowell George had "the ugliest little fuckin' feet." Tickled by the comment, George remembered Black's remark when he was asked by Zappa to leave the Mothers. The name of his new band was born, with "feet" misspelled in honor of The Beatles.

Legend has it that Zappa tossed George from his band after he heard George's song "Willin'," written from the perspective of a road-weary trucker whose peregrinations are fueled by "weed, whites, and wine." Zappa suggested that if he wanted to play this kind of thing, George might want to form his own band. So he did.

Released in 1971, Little Feat's self-titled debut was a ragged thing, and the hurried, clumsy version of "Willin'" on it sounds like little more than a demo. (This despite the presence of Ry Cooder on slide guitar, brought in to help after George hurt his hand.) The recording that appeared on the following year's *Sailin' Shoes* is a vast improvement, slowed down to cruising speed and given a beefier arrangement. As George had hoped it might, the song became something of a truckers' anthem and a highlight of the group's sets. In 1979, Little Feat broke up and George succumbed to a massive heart attack while touring to support his first solo album. He was thirty-four. **WF-J**

It's a Rainy Day, Sunshine Girl
Faust (1972)

Writer | Rudolf Sosna
Producer | Uwe Nettelbeck
Label | Polydor
Album | *Faust So Far* (1972)

Of all the classic first-wave krautrock bands, it is Faust who most strike fear into the casual listener, thanks to their taste for live shows that involve saws, power drills, and all manner of other equipment more suited to the D.I.Y. workshop than the rock show. But, alongside such a predilection for industrial metal in the most literal sense of the words, this veteran experimental act—formed in West Germany in 1971 and signed up by radical journalist Uwe Nettelbeck—also display a Dada-influenced humor and naive tunefulness that belies any such fearsome reputation.

The proof is right here in "It's a Rainy Day, Sunshine Girl". The first track off Faust's second LP, this is krautrock at its most bubblegum—a whimsical sing-along tethered to choppy one-chord guitar and a basic four-to-the-floor backbeat that hammers the tune home over seven increasingly delirious minutes, before a jaunty saxophone brings the song to a slow fade.

The sheer sonic oddity of "It's a Rainy Day, Sunshine Girl" spoke volumes about Faust's freedom to experiment. Holed up in rural Wümme in a schoolhouse converted into a studio, the band pursued a creative curiosity that seemed boundless. "We did everything from jazz to imitating church choirs," recalls Hans Joachim Irmler. "We dissected and examined everything. We were just like children at play." **LP**

Sail Away
Randy Newman (1972)

Writer | Randy Newman
Producer | Lenny Waronker, Russ Titelman
Label | Reprise
Album | *Sail Away* (1972)

Avoid listening closely to the lyrics, and "Sail Away" may come across as a simple paean to the American dream, in which there is always food on the table and "every man is free." But Randy Newman has built his singular aesthetic on such confusions, marrying good-natured, major-key melodies to lyrics sharp enough to cut.

In that sense, "Sail Away" is a Newman archetype. He had written about the South before, most notably in his acidic rewrite of Stephen Foster's sentimental "My Old Kentucky Home," and returned to it later on the likes of "Rednecks," in which neither the apparently racist South nor the putatively liberal northern states escape unharmed. But "Sail Away," an advertising pitch from a slave trader to his potential prey delivered in Newman's inimitable foggy growl, may be his most pungent piece of satire.

Not every subsequent performer of "Sail Away" seems to have quite understood its message. Some have even nervously changed the "climb aboard, little wog" lyric, the line on which the entire song hinges. Still, Newman must be used to it by now, given the treatment that has been dealt out to his repertoire by singers who take his lyrics at face value. Such a misunderstanding even gave Newman his biggest hit as a performer, when his powerfully sarcastic "Short People" became a huge hit in the U.S. at the start of 1978. **WF-J**

Silver Machine | Hawkwind (1972)

Writer | Robert Calvert, Dave Brock
Producer | Dave Brock (aka Dr. Technical)
Label | United Artists
Album | N/A

"Rock is the literature of this generation."
Robert Calvert, 1977

◄ **Influenced by: Astronomy Domine** · Pink Floyd (1967)
► **Influence on: Ladies and Gentlemen We Are Floating In Space** · Spiritualized (1997)
● **Covered by:** James Last (1973) · Doctor & The Medics (1985) · Thin White Rope (1993) · The Church (1999) Sex Pistols (2002)

The story of "Silver Machine" is an ironic one. Hawkwind's best-known song to this day (and a U.K. No. 3 hit), it was sung by their sometime vocalist Ian "Lemmy" Kilmister in a clean tone that was a long way from the shredded style he went on to employ for three decades and more in his next band, Motörhead. Why did he go on to found that other, much more commercially successful act? Because the other members of Hawkwind kicked him out. He left them "Silver Machine" as his primary legacy—and quite possibly their own greatest achievement.

And some achievement it is. When the Sex Pistols reunited again in 2002 and played a series of major concerts, they kicked off their set with "Silver Machine." Whether they did it out of punk-versus-space-rock spite, or just out of recognition that it is an amazing song, they highlighted its importance in Seventies culture. To this day, the song represents many things. It is the biggest space-rock anthem of all, in an acid-fried and long-lasting tradition that stretches from Sixties psychedelia to modern progressive rock. The song is also the definitive biker anthem, alongside Motörhead's own "Iron Horse."

All this is achieved through a simple ascending chord sequence with basic boogie chords, although a smattering of the required trippiness was added courtesy of the analogue synth pulse at the beginning. It just goes to show, one more time, that simple songs always have the most enduring appeal—whether or not you happen to have ingested quantities of psychoactive substances before listening. Hawkwind have never equaled "Silver Machine," but the fact that they wrote it at all deserves your respect. **JMc**

Tumbling Dice | The Rolling Stones (1972)

Writer | Mick Jagger, Keith Richards
Producer | Jimmy Miller
Label | Rolling Stones
Album | *Exile on Main St.* (1972)

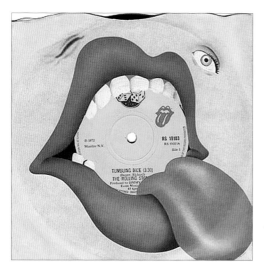

"It's such a great track. So laid back. It really sucks you in with that groove."
Joe Perry, 2002

◀ **Influenced by:** Alimony · Ry Cooder (1970)
▶ **Influence on:** Bad Obsession · Guns N' Roses (1991)
● **Covered by:** Owen Gray (1973) · Linda Ronstadt (1977) Pussy Galore (1986) · Bon Jovi (1995) · Johnny Copeland (1997) · Molly Hatchet (2000) · Barry Goldberg (2002) · Jill Johnson with Kim Carnes (2007)

"I don't really know what people like about it," puzzled Mick Jagger. "I don't think it's our best stuff. I don't think it has good lyrics. But people seem to really like it."

The Rolling Stones' "Tumbling Dice" first saw the light of day in Britain in October 1970, but in a very different incarnation. Then called "Good Time Woman," the song had different lyrics, a faster tempo, Mick Taylor on lead guitar, and Ian Stewart on piano. It had "a very simple structure," recalled Taylor, "that evolved out of us just jamming."

The following summer, the track was reworked in the basement of Keith Richards's French villa. "I remember writing the riff upstairs in the very elegant front room," Keef said, "and we took it downstairs the same evening and we cut it." However, as engineer Andy Johns complained: "That went on for about two weeks. They would just sit and play the intro riff over and over for hours and hours trying to get the groove right. We must have done 150 or 200 takes."

Finally, the key to the song's evolution was Richards taking over guitar (with assistance from Jagger), while Taylor played bass. "Tumbling Dice" was completed in Los Angeles in March 1972. "All of a sudden," Jagger complained during mixing, "the backing track seems so . . . so . . . *ordinaire*."

Actually, the result was anything *but* "ordinaire," despite its largely incomprehensible lyrics. "Part of what makes this special," remarked The Clash's Joe Strummer, "is that the words are a conundrum, like 'Louie, Louie.'" ("It's about gambling and love," confirmed Jagger.) "I really loved 'Tumbling Dice,'" enthused Richards. "Beautifully played by everybody." Ryan Adams agreed: "It's so groovy a track, it's perfect." **BM**

Thirteen
Big Star (1972)

Writer | Alex Chilton, Chris Bell
Producer | Big Star, John Fry
Label | Ardent
Album | *#1 Record* (1972)

Big Eyed Beans from Venus | Captain
Beefheart & The Magic Band (1972)

Writer | Captain Beefheart
Producer | Ted Templeman
Label | Reprise
Album | *Clear Spot* (1972)

A quintessential cult hero, Alex Chilton first found fame with Sixties popsters The Box Tops. They struck gold with hits such as "The Letter," but were essentially a vehicle for their producer and writer, Dan Penn. So, young Alex turned his back on stardom and entered the orbit of obscurity. But before his erratic solo career, he joined fellow singer-songwriter Chris Bell's band, Big Star, whose debut album blended Beatlesque melodies, Stonesy blues, and a soupçon of psychedelia. "Every cut could be a single," marveled *Billboard*.

Amid these delights was something *Rolling Stone* described as "a wistful, funny remembrance of junior high." A lyrical reference to The Rolling Stones' "Paint It, Black" did indeed evoke a sense of nostalgia, but, as the title suggests, "Thirteen" hinted at a slightly seedier relationship. However, its acoustic delicacy made it a quite wondrous two and a half minutes.

"Thirteen" was Chilton's baby. Although he was to dismiss the song as "groping around," and Big Star imploded in 1974 without ever enjoying success, "Thirteen" became a cast-iron classic. Big Star's biggest disciples, Teenage Fanclub, named their 1993 album *Thirteen* after the song, and it has been covered by admirers ranging from Elliott Smith and Wilco to dEUS and Garbage—the latter version even earning the accolade of "really good" from Chilton himself. **BM**

It is hard to believe that Don van Vliet truly expected *Trout Mask Replica*, his third album, to fly off the shelves when it was issued in 1969. But its lack of U.S. success led him to tone down his musical eccentricities. In 1972, he enlisted as his producer Ted Templeman, a former member of Sixties pop act Harpers Bizarre who had, by then, found success working with The Doobie Brothers.

It sounds like a strange collaboration, but it was not strange enough. *Clear Spot* is a world away from the bewildered blues-rock of *Trout Mask Replica*, but the comparatively clean-cut record lacked its predecessor's charisma. The bayou boogie of "Nowadays a Woman's Gotta Hit a Man" and the maladroit balladry of "My Head Is My Only House Unless It Rains" signally failed to catapult Beefheart into the hearts of the nation.

The album's highlight is buried near the end. Driven by the twin-engine guitars of Rockette Morton (real name Mark Boston) and Zoot Horn Rollo (Bill Harkleroad), memorably encouraged here to "Hit that long, lunar note, and let it float," and grounded by the deceptively complex drumming of Ed Marimba (Art Tripp), "Big Eyed Beans from Venus" is the most successful fusion of Beefheart's avant-garde roots with his mainstream leanings. It was also one of the last worthwhile recordings he made; in the early Eighties he abandoned music and became a painter. **WF-J**

Band magic in 1972: from left, Rockette Morton, Zoot Horn Rollo, and Captain Beefheart. ➔

Rocket Man | Elton John (1972)

Writer | Elton John, Bernie Taupin
Producer | Gus Dudgeon
Label | DJM
Album | *Honky Château* (1972)

"We didn't steal that one from Bowie. We stole it from another bloke, called Tom Rapp."

Bernie Taupin, 1988

Influenced by: Rocket Man · Pearls Before Swine (1970)
Influence on: 1st Man in Space · All Seeing I (1999)
Covered by: Kate Bush (1991) · Hank Marvin (1993) The Nixons (1998) · Angie Aparo (2002) · Carl Dixon (2003)

By 1972, the space race was beginning to seem almost mundane, and the awestruck television audiences of the early Apollo missions had dwindled away. This was the atmosphere into which Elton John launched "Rocket Man"—a song that treats space travel not as exotic or enviable but as workaday and isolating.

But Elton wasn't quite going where no man had gone before. The most obvious forerunner is David Bowie's 1969 hit "Space Oddity," which has the same themes and producer (Gus Dudgeon) as "Rocket Man." Lyricist Bernie Taupin, however, prefers to cite a namesake number by Pearls Before Swine, the psychedelic group fronted by lisping folkie Tom Rapp, as his primary influence. Both Taupin and Rapp's compositions draw upon a short story by sci-fi author Ray Bradbury, from his 1951 collection *The Illustrated Man*, about an astronaut whose work enables him to see his family only four times a year.

The bleakness of the song is offset by Elton's emphatic piano and the soaring vocal harmonies from the rest of the band. A futuristic, BBC Radiophonic Workshop element is added by David Hentschel on the ARP Odyssey synthesizer, but otherwise the instrumentation is reassuringly down-to-earth (witness, for instance, the acoustic-guitar flourish from Davey Johnstone that opens each chorus). And that is only appropriate. The lines "I miss the Earth so much, I miss my wife / It's lonely out in space" tap into a long-standing tradition of melancholy in songwriting, but take it to a rarely explored sphere—the world of domesticity. Countless bluesmen had sung of loneliness, but how many of them admitted a yearning for the security of the marital home? **SP**

Mama Weer All Crazee Now | Slade (1972)

Writer | Noddy Holder, Jim Lea
Producer | Chas Chandler
Label | Polydor
Album | *Slayed?* (1972)

"Gene Simmons told us that 'Rock and Roll All Nite' was Kiss's 'Mama Weer All Crazee Now.'"
Noddy Holder, 1987

◄ **Influenced by: L-O-N-D-O-N** · Lord Sutch & Heavy
Friends (1970)
► **Influence on: Rock and Roll All Nite** · Kiss (1975)
● **Covered by:** James Last (1973) · The Runaways (1978)
Mama's Boys (1984) · Quiet Riot (1984) · The Oppressed
(2001) · Reel Big Fish (2009)

In those outrageous stack heels and glitter outfits, glam-rock kings Slade trampled all over the British charts in the first half of the Seventies, gleefully misspelling as they went. "Mama Weer All Crazee Now"—initially titled "My My We're All Crazy Now"—was their third U.K. No. 1 in under a year, and arguably it was the best yet.

The common consensus was that, while Slade on vinyl was a rabble-rousing experience, the group came into their own in the live environment. As Gene Simmons of Kiss mused: "Before Slade, no one really knew shit about how to make an audience riot." And it was witnessing the debris following a Slade show in London that inspired Noddy Holder to provide the perfect images to go with bassist Jim Lea's stomping tune. Explained guitarist Dave Hill: "'Mama Weer All Crazee Now' was written purely on the strength of one night, when we went down really well and the audience was just wild. . . . We saw a lot of kids raving it up and thought 'We're all bloody mad!'"

After the crunching guitar intro, Holder's howl sends the adrenaline into overdrive, even though it was not originally part of the track (it was lifted from one of his vocal warm-ups by producer, and ex-Animal, Chas Chandler). The public lapped up the band's direct approach, as have succeeding generations when confronted by a variety of contrasting bands and artists, including the Ramones, Tom Jones, Oasis, and Nirvana.

"Mama Weer All Crazee Now" comes from a time when Slade seemed to own the charts—and in the Seventies no rock act sold more singles. Slade could not be commended for services to spelling, but they had plenty of lessons to impart about being a great British band. **CB**

Rocky Mountain High
John Denver (1972)

Writer | John Denver, Mike Taylor
Producer | Milton Okun
Label | RCA
Album | *Rocky Mountain High* (1972)

The Night | Frankie Valli
& The Four Seasons (1972)

Writer | Bob Gaudio, Al Ruzicka
Producer | Bob Gaudio
Label | MoWest
Album | *Chameleon* (1972)

Among the male superstars of the Seventies—Neil Diamond, Stevie Wonder, Rod Stewart, Barry Manilow—the late John Denver has the reputation of being the blandest. That is a reflection of the singer-songwriter's easygoing and wholesome style, which appeals to fans of every style of melodic pop from M.O.R. to folk and light country.

The former John Deutschendorf changed his surname to John Denver in part to reflect his love of the American West. "Rocky Mountain High" (a U.S. No. 9) comes across as one of his most personally felt yet universally appealing works. It became the second Colorado state song in 2007 and is also considered Denver's unofficial anthem. The lyrics concern a man's spiritual rebirth and subsequent awareness of the natural power and beauty that surround him as he returns to the Rocky Mountain State that is (as echoed in the chorus) "Co-lo-ra-do-o." Denver's steady voice is placed in the middle of the mix, surrounded by jangly acoustic guitars, soaring pedal steel, and a lone triangle providing minimal percussion.

The song was briefly banned for its use of the word "high," though Denver maintained that this was simply a reference to his euphoria in the presence of the Rockies landscape. But, once word circulated that he reportedly wrote it while using LSD and marijuana, those themes of awakening took on an entirely different subtext. **YK**

As some of the most accomplished practitioners of blue-eyed soul, The Four Seasons were the act that Berry Gordy would play to his Motown songwriters to give them an idea of what they should be aiming for. But if Gordy was expecting good-time pop when he signed the Jersey boys to his West Coast imprint in 1971, he was in for a shock; the resultant album, *Chameleon*, was a dark and mature work that was more in line with the tone of Carole King's recent LP *Tapestry*.

"The Night" opens with Joe Long's aggressively funky bassline and the Seasons' *sotto voce* warning "Beware . . . of his promise," and it is instantly apparent that this is no celebration of nocturnal hedonism. Rather, it is a breakup song—an anguished Valli warns his departing lover to consider carefully or spend many sleepless nights regretting her decision. The message is underscored by the group's unparalleled falsetto harmonies and a menacing arrangement dominated by Billy DeLoach's psychedelic guitar and newcomer Al Ruzicka's moody organ.

Although it was not a hit, "The Night" was championed by the pop archaeologists of England's Northern soul scene, in thrall to Paul Wilson's four-to-the-floor timekeeping and the frantic chorus. Such was the song's appeal among the Northern Soul faithful that it belatedly entered the U.K. Top Ten in 1975. **SP**

Reelin' in the Years
Steely Dan (1972)

Writer | Walter Becker, Donald Fagen
Producer | Gary Katz
Label | ABC
Album | *Can't Buy a Thrill* (1972)

The catchy pop of Steely Dan's second single was so unlike the band's first hit—the cool, seductive Latin-tinged cha-cha "Do It Again"—that they might have been mistaken for two different groups. Donald Fagen sings about a college relationship that went sour, and adds a twist of misogyny, while the band deliver the sneering chorus as a catchy sing-along. Few pop songs kick-start with such searing guitar chords and then opt to veer off and unleash a killer solo with just-in-tune jazzy phrasing—and this from a player, Elliot Randall, who was not even in the band. Together with friend Jeff "Skunk" Baxter and Denny Dias, the three guitarists also display blistering, tightly harmonized guitar segues throughout.

English graduate Donald Fagen and his co-alumnus Walter Becker were the minds behind one of the most lyrically dense but musically savvy rock outfits of the Seventies. Behind the cool shades and anonymous anti-band stance, the duo knew precisely how to pull a melodic punch and carry a syncopated rhythm. Fagen (keyboards and nasal, whining vocals) and Becker (bass) built their eclectic catalog around a meticulous attention to detail, using chord-and-rhythm charts and plenty of studio spit and polish to perfect their pop.

Their nous paid off, chart-wise: released as a single in 1973, "Reelin' in the Years" made No. 11 in the U.S. and became an FM radio staple. **JJH**

Always on My Mind
Elvis Presley (1972)

Writer | Johnny Christopher, Mark James, Wayne Carson Thompson
Producer | Felton Jarvis
Label | RCA Victor
Album | *Separate Ways* (1972)

Although recorded more than five years before his death, Presley's "Always on My Mind" brought down the curtain on the revitalized Elvis, reborn after his famous 1968 television special.

On February 23, 1972, Presley had completed a successful stay at the Las Vegas Hilton and was at the peak of his popularity second time around. And, when he and his regular musicians (including guitarists James Burton and Charlie Hodge, drummer Ronnie Tutt, and pianist Glen Hardin, plus J. D. Sumner & The Stamps on vocals) gathered in RCA's Studio C in Hollywood on March 27, the results were magnificent.

True, many of the songs recorded in those three days suggested he was distracted and spilling his troubled heart out in the studio, but "Separate Ways," "Burning Love," and "Fool" are among the best songs he recorded in the Seventies. It was on the third day of the session that he recorded the song destined to become, in many people's eyes, the full stop at the end of his marriage, and to the end of the Elvis era. A recent flop single by Brenda Lee, "Always on My Mind" had yet to register with the public and was released in November as a double-A-sided single with "Separate Ways," perhaps the ultimate break-up package. Elvis, enthused co-writer Mark James, "recorded a really great and memorable performance." Remember him this way: as a true soul singer. **DH**

Most People I Know . . . | Billy Thorpe & The Aztecs (1972)

Writer | Billy Thorpe
Producer | Billy Thorpe
Label | Havoc
Album | N/A

Regenerating themselves through several lineup changes, Billy Thorpe & The Aztecs are best remembered for their Seventies rock reincarnation that produced "Most People I Know (Think That I'm Crazy)." Billy Thorpe, or "Thorpie," as he was affectionately known, died in 2007. His Mk I version of The Aztecs had been Australia's only group to threaten The Beatles' total chart domination and teen adulation in the mid-Sixties.

As pop evolved into rock in the early Seventies, Thorpe's transformation, both visual and musical, evolved, too. Although not wholly representative of their new, gutsier sound, "Most People I Know" became the band's signature tune at a time when Thorpe continued to lead as vocalist but now strapped on a guitar, sported a pony tail, and fronted one of rock's loudest acts. "Most People I Know" got its first public airing in the summer of 1972, when the band played the Sunbury Music Festival in Victoria. They could not have picked a better time or place to debut their new song. It was an instant favorite with the 40,000 festival-goers at what was dubbed Australia's own Woodstock.

The defiant and personal nature of the song's lyrics also struck a chord with record buyers, who helped the single rocket toward the top of the Australian charts and encouraged the release of *Aztecs Live at Sunbury*, which captured the debut of "Most People I Know" in all its glory. **DR**

Taj Mahal | Jorge Ben (1972)

Writer | Jorge Ben
Producer | Paulinho Tapajos
Label | Philips
Album | *Ben* (1972)

Renowned as the Brazilian singer-songwriter who nearly became a footballer before fusing samba with rock, soul, and, in particular, funk, Jorge Ben had his first hit with "Mas, Que Nada" in 1963. He struck gold again in 1972, when "Taj Mahal" became very popular in Brazil.

It's an upbeat tune, given a "blaxploitation" twist by its brass and expectant rhythm guitar, although the insistent squeaking of a cuica drum (which is rubbed, rather than hit) underlines its samba roots. The Portuguese lyrics refer to the love of India's Mughal Prince Shah Jahan for Princess Mumtaz Mahal, but they don't detail how he built the eponymous mausoleum in her name, instead resorting to a jolly, scatted chorus.

It was this riff that formed the basis of Rod Stewart's "Da Ya Think I'm Sexy?" in 1978, a transatlantic No. 1 smash that Stewart co-wrote with his drummer, Carmine Appice, after being inspired by The Rolling Stones' disco hit "Miss You." Ben successfully sued Stewart for plagiarism. In an amicable settlement, Stewart agreed to pay his royalties to UNICEF.

The African-American bluesman Taj Mahal has recorded a version of "Taj Mahal," substituting the title words with "Jorge Ben." Meanwhile, Jorge Ben himself changed his name to Jorge Benjor in 1989, after finding out some of his royalties had mistakenly gone to George Benson. **JLu**

Jorge Ben leads his band on acoustic guitar in a performance of his feel-good hit in 1972. ➔

Walk on the Wild Side | Lou Reed (1972)

Writer | Lou Reed
Producer | David Bowie, Mick Ronson
Label | RCA
Album | *Transformer* (1972)

"Some people say that I'm a perfectionist. They're right. . . . But I'm also talented and I know when I create something great."
Lou Reed, 1998

◄ **Influenced by:** Sweet Talkin' Guy · The Chiffons (1966)
► **Influence on:** Animal Nitrate · Suede (1993)
● **Covered by:** Vanessa Paradis (1990) · The Skids (1991)
Company B (1996) · Texas Lightning (2005) · Paul
Young (2006) · Editors (2007) · Jesse Malin (2008)
★ **Other key track:** Perfect Day (1972)

After the demise of cult avant-garde rock group The Velvet Underground, Lou Reed was forced to move back in with his parents and take a job in his father's accountancy firm. Fortunately he soon tired of balance sheets and decided to launch a solo career, with the aid of Velvets fan David Bowie. Reed's second album was produced by Bowie—then still in his Ziggy Stardust period—and featured three songs that had originally been commissioned by Reed's former mentor Andy Warhol for a planned musical based on Nelson Algren's 1956 novel *A Walk on the Wild Side*. The show never happened, but Reed kept the title for a song chronicling the lives of some of the Manhattan street hustlers who frequented Warhol's studio, The Factory. Thus the exploits of Holly Woodlawn, Candy Darling, Joe Dallesandro, Jackie Curtis, and Joe "Sugar Plum Fairy" Campbell were immortalized in a portrait that is unflinching but affectionate, featuring backing vocals from female singing trio Thunderthighs and a mellifluous saxophone solo played by Ronnie Ross—Bowie's childhood sax teacher.

Despite containing references to transsexuality, oral sex, and drugs, "Walk on the Wild Side" was a Top Twenty hit in the United States and the United Kingdom—although the BBC famously objected to the line about "colored girls," insisting it be replaced by "all the girls." It was the legendarily truculent Reed's last hit for thirty years, although Herbie Flowers's memorable double-bass part has been repeatedly sampled, most notably by A Tribe Called Quest on 1990's "Can I Kick It?" Flowers was paid no princely sum for his work on *Transformer* but saw that as the nature of session musicianship: "You do the job and get your arse away." **PL**

Virginia Plain | Roxy Music (1972)

Writer | Bryan Ferry
Producer | Peter Sinfield
Label | EG
Album | N/A

"['Virginia Plain'] opened up the whole thing to a lot more people.... I hate to just appeal to a sort of intellectual element."

Phil Manzanera, 1975

◄ **Influenced by: I'm Waiting for the Man** · The Velvet Underground (1967)

► **Influence on: A Glass of Champagne** · Sailor (1975)

● **Covered by:** Spizzenergi (1979) · Slamm (1993) · Griff Steel (2007)

★ **Other key track:** Do the Strand (1973)

Bryan Ferry once claimed that his principal songwriting influence was Smokey Robinson, but the listener would be hard-pressed to spot the connection between that Motown artist and the strangulated croon and sci-fi sound effects of Roxy Music's first single. If there is a precursor, it is in the hypnotically rhythmic style of The Velvet Underground, a group that Roxy's resident boffin, Brian Eno, eulogized as a major influence (on him, and on everyone else who had heard them).

The sonic force of the song is monumental, a wall of sound that collapses into a pile of rubble: Eno coaxing space-age noises out of his suitcase-shaped VCS3 synthesizer, an ad hoc guitar solo by Phil Manzanera, sax parps from Andy Mackay, Ferry's pounding piano (lifted wholesale by glam-rock also-rans Sailor in 1975), and Shangri-Las-style motorbike revs, recorded by a miked-up roadie riding through central London with the cables trailing behind him.

Ferry's oblique, sloganeering lyrics draw on a painting from his art-student days, blending tobacco-ad imagery with a portrait of Warhol acolyte Baby Jane Holzer, whose bouffant hairdo—or "Holzer mane," as he termed it—had caused a fashion sensation in 1964. Indeed, the influence of Warhol himself, as Pop Art guru and erstwhile Velvets producer, is keenly felt throughout the song, every line being steeped in Americana—a world of teenage rebels at the drive-in, hipsters jiving, all-night cha-chas, and the 1933 Fred 'n' Ginger musical *Flying Down to Rio*. The lyric is a collage of pop-culture references that parallel the collision of golden-age cinema and rock 'n' roll in the band's name. And it's all a very long way from "Tears of a Clown." **SP**

You're So Vain

Carly Simon (1972)

Writer | Carly Simon
Producer | Richard Perry
Label | Elektra
Album | *No Secrets* (1972)

It remains one of pop's great mysteries: just who in Carly Simon's No. 1 single "You're So Vain" was the guy who flew his own Learjet and "had me several years ago / When I was still quite naive"?

Simon was initially lukewarm about working on the song with Richard Perry, who had produced Harry Nilsson and Barbra Streisand and was possibly too slick for her liking. It has also been rumored that the golden-voiced Nilsson was originally lined up for backing vocals but bowed out after Mick Jagger showed up at the studios. Perry was a perfectionist, and they recorded the song three different times with three different drummers (using Jim Gordon in the end). But the key figure was neither Simon nor Jagger nor Perry. It was Beatles' *Revolver* artist Klaus Voorman, who provided the signature opening-solo bass licks that set the scene for the anonymous "son of a gun," while Paul Buckmaster (who had beautifully handled the arrangements on Elton John's first two albums) provided the sympathetic orchestration.

The million-selling song spent three weeks at No. 1 in early 1973. Listeners speculated as to whether the refrain, "You're so vain / I'll bet you think this song is about you / Don't you? Don't you?," referred to Jagger, or possibly Warren Beatty, Kris Kristofferson, or Simon's husband James Taylor (not to mention Cat Stevens or Hugh Hefner). Over thirty years later, she's still not telling. **JJH**

Today I Started Loving You Again | Bettye Swann (1972)

Writer | Merle Haggard, Bonnie Owens
Producer | Rick Hall, Mickey Buckins
Label | Atlantic
Album | N/A

Soul blended with country on "Today I Started Loving You Again." It was Bettye Swann's last visit to the *Billboard* Hot 100 before leaving the music business to devote herself to "living life the right way," as she put it, as a devout Jehovah's Witness.

The song, a country standard, was given a soul inflection when Swann signed to Capitol. A chance pairing with new producer Wayne Shuler resulted in *Don't You Ever Get Tired of Hurting Me*, the Louisiana-born singer's 1969 album, which first included her recording of "Today I Started Loving You Again." According to Shuler, he first teamed his new charge with country legend Buck Owens on a groundbreaking version of the song, a rare and controversial white-country-meets-black-soul duet, frowned upon even as recently as the late Sixties. Sadly, the recording remains unreleased and the album used Swann's still terrific solo version. (Intriguingly, Buck Owens was married to the song's co-creator Bonnie Owens who, in turn, later married her writing partner Merle Haggard.)

Bettye Swann had transferred from Capitol to Atlantic by the time the song resurfaced as a hit single in 1973, albeit originally as a B-side to "I'd Rather Go Blind." A million miles from its country origins, her terrific performance was recorded with Jimmie Haskell's string arrangement and some beefy brass at "The Home of The Muscle Shoals Sound," Fame Studios. **DR**

Il mio canto libero
Lucio Battisti (1972)

Writer | Lucio Battisti, Mogol
Producer | Lucio Battisti
Label | Numero Uno
Album | *Il mio canto libero* (1972)

The hit "Il mio canto libero" (Song to Feel Alive) was released at the same time as the album of the same name and became 1973's third-best-selling single in the Italian charts (the album was the year's best seller, remaining at No. 1 for eleven weeks). To this day frequently broadcast on Italian radio, the song is a prominent highlight in the work of Lucio Battisti, and a classic of Italian popular music. It also enjoyed great success abroad, being translated into several languages (there are versions in English, French, German, and Spanish, all sung by Battisti on the album *Images*).

By far the most significant element of the song is the emotional vocal, sung against an accompaniment that, in the original version, begins with a single guitar and builds as the song develops with the introduction of fuller instrumentation and drums, and then brass. The lyric, concerning the love uniting the author and his woman, chimed with the young people of its moment, with their sense of shared alienation, the difficulty of starting to live as adults, and yet hope.

The lyrics have autobiographical references. Mogol wrote it after he had separated from his wife and met his new companion, poet Gabriella Marazzi. He refers to his divorce, his love song "Soaring over all the accusations / Over prejudice and affectations." This was truly a ballad for a generation finding its way to maturity. **LSc**

Superfly
Curtis Mayfield (1972)

Writer | Curtis Mayfield
Producer | Curtis Mayfield
Label | Curtom
Album | *Super Fly* (1972)

There is some debate as to which was the first blaxploitation movie—that is, a film made with black actors for a black audience and concerned with black urban and ghetto themes. Both *Sweet Sweetback's Baadasssss Song* and *Shaft* came out in 1971, swiftly followed by *Super Fly*, for which Curtis Mayfield wrote and performed the soundtrack.

Mayfield, a politically committed soul and R&B singer and composer, was a strong supporter of civil rights, black pride, and black power. His soundtrack to the film is at variance to the film itself. *Super Fly* is about a black cocaine dealer who is trying to quit the business. If the movie's message is ambiguous, Mayfield's soundtrack is anything but: a series of hard-hitting lyrics that criticize the ghetto's glorification of drugs and directly attack some of the movie's characters.

The title track itself—spelled as one word, not two—is a delight, sung in Mayfield's trademark falsetto voice. Its opening bass line and percussion break, now much sampled, lead into a lightly sprung funk line interrupted by brass and percussion chords that support and enhance the vocals. Both the song and soundtrack were huge and immediate commercial successes, the soundtrack being one of the few to easily outgross its film. It is also one of the first soul concept albums, every bit the equal of Marvin Gaye's contemporaneous *What's Going On*. **SA**

Crazy Horses
The Osmonds (1972)

Writer | The Osmonds
Producer | Alan Osmond, Michael Lloyd
Label | MGM
Album | *Crazy Horses* (1972)

The Osmonds are often dismissed as an anemic version of The Jackson 5, but gruff-voiced singer Merrill Osmond cited Led Zeppelin as a major influence, and, as if to prove it, the brothers cut this astonishing, hard-rocking slice of funk metal in 1972. Its churning, guitar-heavy sound revolves around a tribal chant followed by high-pitched *weeeeeooooh* noises, reminiscent of the theremins used in Fifties B-movies (actually teen idol Donny, pounding on his Buchla synth). The band's showbiz tendencies were also given free rein, thanks to brass stabs arranged by Jim Horn.

What's more, there was—as the first line informs us—"a message floating in the air." The song reflects the nascent eco-consciousness of the early Seventies, a warning about the cult of the car "smoking up the sky" with foul pollution. The automotive motif was driven home by Wayne and Alan's guitars, chugging along like diesel engines, and an album cover that showed the five siblings in a breaker's yard under a pall of cartoon fumes.

The heavy riffs of "Crazy Horses" brought the Osmonds admirers in unexpected quarters. After it hit No. 1 in France, they performed there—sporting flared jumpsuits, tailored by Elvis Presley's outfitter, Bill Belew—to an audience of hairy Black Sabbath fans. "We knew what we were faced with," recalled Merrill in 2009. "We vamped 'Crazy Horses' for about a half-hour." **SP**

All the Young Dudes
Mott the Hoople (1972)

Writer | David Bowie
Producer | David Bowie
Label | Columbia
Album | *All the Young Dudes* (1972)

After years of Saturday gigs and little chart success, Dylanesque rockers Mott the Hoople were ready to throw in the towel. Then David Bowie—who carved out a niche as something of a svengali to such icons as Lou Reed, Iggy Pop, and Peter Noone—offered them his as yet unreleased song "Suffragette City." When bass player Pete Overend Watts turned it down, Bowie phoned back within two hours: "I've written a song for you since we spoke, which could be great," he confided.

The tune in question was a football-terrace sing-along of generation-gap angst, replete with Cockney rhyming slang, a reference to British chain store Marks & Spencer, and sly digs at Marc Bolan. "It's no hymn to the youth, as people thought," Bowie said in 1974. "It is completely the opposite." He saw the lyric as part of his *Ziggy Stardust* cycle—the message that the titular dudes were conveying was that the Earth was doomed to imminent destruction within a matter of years. But glitter-faced teens were more interested in Mick Ralphs's epic Gibson Firebird intro, Verden Allen's transcendent church organ, and the contagious hand claps that snake lazily through the chorus. Glamrock stardom was theirs.

The Thin White Duke would return to "All the Young Dudes" intermittently, performing it on 1974's *David Live* and spooling it backwards as the basis for the *Lodger* track "Move On" in 1979. **SP**

Mick Rock's shot of a gleeful young dude almost graced the cover of Mott the Hoople's 1972 album. ➔

Personality Crisis | New York Dolls (1973)

Writer | David Johansen, Johnny Thunders
Producer | Todd Rundgren
Label | Mercury
Album | *New York Dolls* (1973)

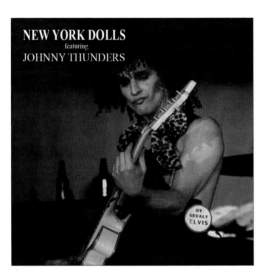

"We were young and screaming our generation's next move. Everybody else took notes and took it to the bank."

David Johansen, 2006

◀ **Influenced by: Brown Sugar** • The Rolling Stones (1971)
▶ **Influence on: Blitzkrieg Bop** • Ramones (1976)
● **Covered by:** Sonic Youth (1993) • Teenage Fanclub (1998)
★ **Other key track:** Looking for a Kiss (1973)

The story of the New York Dolls tends to go as follows: five losers from New York learn a handful of chords on guitar in 1971, raid their girlfriends' wardrobes, play their first gig at a homeless shelter, make two records that don't chart any higher than No. 116 in the United States, do a magnificent amount of drugs, and collapse four years later. Depending on who you ask, that is the story of an above-average bar band with a Marc Bolan fetish—or nothing shy of an account of the birth of punk rock.

"Personality Crisis," the first song on the New York Dolls' first album, will help you decide which way to go. As a convincer, the number takes three minutes and forty-three seconds: "And you're a prima ballerina on a spring afternoon / Change on into the wolfman, howlin' at the moon / Got a personality crisis, you got it while it was hot / It's always hard to know when frustration and heartache is what you got." Singer David Johansen and guitarist Johnny Thunders took three chords from any random girl-group hit or Chuck Berry record, doubled the tempo, and got up on stage in fishnets, acting like they ruled the world. With Sylvain Sylvain's skanky lead guitar on top and Arthur Kane's punishing bass down below, the Dolls were a mesmerizing crisis in heels.

It would never take a genius to make this kind of music, but it was punk rock in 1973, which made it absolutely brilliant. Wrapped up in one album—perhaps even in this song—was the blueprint for what was hot in the rest of the Seventies. In the next few years, the Ramones would take the chords, Kiss would take the makeup, and the Sex Pistols would take the snarl. And all the Dolls ever got was frustration and heartache. **MO**

New York Dolls' David Johansen; not every man can step into a woman's shoes. ➡

The Ballroom Blitz
The Sweet (1973)

Writer | Nicky Chinn, Mike Chapman
Producer | Nicky Chinn,
Mike Chapman
Label | RCA
Album | N/A

On January 27, 1973, The Sweet—glam rock's archetypal hod-carriers with eyeliner—were mincing about on stage at the Grand Hall in Kilmarnock, Scotland, when a hostile crowd bombarded them with bottles. Far from setting them back, this incident became immortalized in song as the follow-up single to the hard-rocking "Hell Raiser." Not that The Sweet penned their own hits, of course—that honor fell to the team of Nicky Chinn and Mike Chapman, the writer-producer masterminds who also oversaw the outputs of Mud and Suzi Quatro.

The Sweet's winning formula was to match bubblegum melodies to Andy Scott's crunching Townshend-style power chords, while ensuring that there were always plenty of hooks to ensnare listeners. "The Ballroom Blitz" is a magnificent conglomeration of gimmicks, from singer Brian Connolly's calls to the rest of the band—"Are you ready, Steve?" ("Uh huh!"); "Andy?" ("Yeah!"); "Mick?" ("OK!")—to the pounding polyrhythms of Mick Tucker's drums and the dubby echo on the word "Blitz-itz-itz" that leads into the middle eight. But bass player Steve Priest provides the most memorable hook of all with his high-pitched, histrionic vocals on the bridge section—his camp intonation of "She thinks *she's* the passionate one!" can also be heard in the midst of The Beastie Boys' come-on song "Hey Ladies" in 1989. **SP**

Jolene
Dolly Parton (1973)

Writer | Dolly Parton
Producer | Bob Ferguson
Label | RCA
Album | *Jolene* (1974)

For a song that is all about low self-esteem and vulnerability, "Jolene" is a robust little number. With a simple chorus of rising chords, Dolly Parton's breakout pop-country hit has been covered by more than thirty artists in an array of genres. There's whimsical folk from Mindy Smith (Parton's favorite), Gothic self-hate from Sisters of Mercy, and plangent despair from The White Stripes. Strawberry Switchblade gave it some Eighties synth, while Olivia Newton-John stripped out all the pathos but really got the disco floor bouncing.

The content of the lyrics isn't open to quite so much reinterpretation. Parton, a successful country singer-songwriter but one without a smash hit, was moved to write it after her husband began receiving admiring glances from a woman who worked in a local bank and, as Parton explained with typically brassy self-deprecation, "had all that stuff that some little short, sawed-off honky like me don't have." The song takes the form of the narrator pleading woman-to-woman with beautiful predator Jolene: "Please don't take my man." "My happiness depends on you, and whatever you decide to do," concludes a desperate but determined Parton. It's hardly a feminist anthem—hence Kirsty MacColl's caustic response, "Caroline," in 1995—but at no point does it ever sound like the husband himself will have any say in what is going to happen. **PW**

Dolly Parton: the most instantly recognizable woman in country music. ➡

Writer | Mort Shuman, Jacques Brel, Eric Blau
Producer | Phil Wainman
Label | Mountain
Album | *Next* (1973)

"[I] had a big poster of the band on my bedroom wall."

Ian Rankin, writer, 2009

◄ **Influenced by:** (Whiskey Bar) Alabama Song
The Doors (1967)

► **Influence on:** Burst • Magazine (1978)

● **Covered by:** Marc Almond (1989) • Gavin Friday
& The Man Seezer (1989)

★ **Other key track:** Delilah (1975)

Released within a year of each other in the first half of the Seventies, versions of two songs by Jacques Brel illustrated diametrically opposed approaches to the Belgian singer-songwriter's often troubling work. Canadian singer Terry Jacks ripped the cynical heart out of "Le moribund" ("The Dying Man") but what was left became the monster summer-sing-along hit "Seasons in the Sun" in 1974. Before that, weird met weirder when The Sensational Alex Harvey Band took the already downbeat "Au suivant" ("Next")—written about the threat of the military to individuality—into some very dark corners, indeed (they totally overshadowed Scott Walker's reading of "Next," released in 1968, in the process).

The reputation of The Sensational Alex Harvey Band's version among music fans of a certain age rests heavily on strong impressions of a performance on U.K. television series *Old Grey Whistle Test*, complete with a string trio in matching masks. The song's sheer strangeness has stuck with people, but it didn't always go down so well live. Playing a Jacques Brel translation while in support of the mundane likes of Blue Öyster Cult and Uriah Heep could be challenging. "That particular point in the set is very much touch and go for people who've never seen us," understated Alex Harvey. "I mean, I think a lot of them get really disturbed by 'Next.' They think it's a piss-take."

However, "Next" gave Harvey the chance to do what he did better than almost anyone else: feed off the energy of the crowd, be it positive or, as often in this case, otherwise. "Nobody's eyes left the stage," he continued. "Ultimately, those people turn out to be some of the best fans we can get, because they'll remember us." **CB**

20th Century Boy | T. Rex (1973)

Writer | Marc Bolan
Producer | Tony Visconti
Label | EMI
Album | N/A

"What kind of kids liked T. Rex? School-hating anarchists."

Morrissey, 2005

◄ **Influenced by: (I Can't Get No) Satisfaction**
The Rolling Stones (1965)
► **Influence on: Teenage Kicks** • The Undertones (1978)
● **Covered by:** Siouxsie & The Banshees (1979)
The Replacements (1984) • The Big Six (1998) • Placebo
(1998) • Naked Raygun (2001)

Two crunching guitar chords smash out like blasts of static, followed by an ecstatic whine midway between Little Richard and Prince. It could almost be the sound of a defibrillator jumpstarting the Electric Warrior's stalled career. For, by 1973, the progenitor of glam rock was looking increasingly irrelevant; podgy and paranoid, he'd watched his star become eclipsed by the upstarts David Bowie and Roxy Music.

"20th Century Boy" was triumphant proof that Marc Bolan still had it in him. Its sound, too, suggests a belated realization that the tried-and-tested T. Rex formula had to change. The squalling saxophone line (played by Howie Casey) is clearly indebted to his rivals' use of the instrument, while the soulful backing vocals betray the influence of his girlfriend, "Tainted Love" singer Gloria Jones—an approach that would be investigated further on the next T. Rex album, *Tanx*. But, while these elements were grafted on by producer Tony Visconti in London, Bolan's own contributions (recorded in Tokyo, while on tour) are just as groundbreaking. The trademark slinky boogie of previous T. Rex hits is gone, ousted by an apocalyptic fuzz-guitar riff that resembles Keith Richards playing Wagner.

The song renewed its fame thanks to a Levi's commercial in 1991—although Bolan himself was more of a satin-flares man—and has enjoyed a panoply of covers, from The Cure to Placebo (for the movie *Velvet Goldmine* in 1998). Almost universally, these cover versions change the line "it's just like rock 'n' roll" to "I'm just like Robin Hood," but that mishearing misses the point. It's not about theft, it's about strutting majesty: a monarch, not an outlaw. **SP**

Rock On
David Essex (1973)

Writer | David Essex
Producer | Jeff Wayne
Label | CBS
Album | *Rock On* (1973)

Search and Destroy
Iggy & The Stooges (1973)

Writer | James Osterberg, James Williamson
Producer | Iggy Pop
Label | Columbia
Album | *Raw Power* (1973)

The cult of retro had emerged in the 1960s—all Twenties pastiche and *Sgt. Pepper's* Victoriana—but soon after it started to focus on the more immediate past, plundering the back catalog of the doo-wop era in search of lost innocence. At the forefront of this Fifties nostalgia was the film *That'll Be the Day* (1973), starring David Essex, for which the young actor penned a potential theme tune loaded with references to "Summertime Blues," "Blue Suede Shoes," and James Dean.

That "Rock On" was not, in the end, used for the film is perhaps unsurprising. Jeff Wayne's incredible, avant-garde production is inspired less by soda-shop pop than by the rhythmic minimalism of Gary Glitter and producer Mike Leander. Essex had demonstrated the song to him by tapping out the beat on a wastepaper basket, and Wayne, admiring this melancholy sparseness, arranged it without any chords. Instead, he structured the track around complex percussive slaps, the echoing heartbeat of Herbie Flowers's double-tracked bass, and an almost atonal violin section pitched somewhere between Bollywood and the sweeping strings of the disco era.

"Rock On" is a record that looks forward as much as back. "Where do we go from here?" wonders Essex, wracked with self-doubt. The answer, it turned out, was musical theater and an orchestral version of *The War of the Worlds*. **SP**

"Search and Destroy" might open with one of the most legendary couplets in all of rock 'n' roll—Iggy's immortal, sneered "I'm a street-walking cheetah with a heart full of napalm / I'm a runaway son of the nuclear A-bomb"—but it was hardly regarded as an instant classic at the time.

The Stooges' U.S. record company, Elektra, had already washed their hands of the band following their free-jazz-inspired *Fun House*, and by the time the band rocked up in London at the request of David Bowie, they were widely regarded as a drug-damaged liability. Twelve days at London's CBS studios, however, spawned the perfect riposte, in the form of the proto-punk classic *Raw Power*.

"Search and Destroy" was that album's opening salvo, sinewy rock 'n' roll propelled forth on new guitarist James Williamson's hard, metallic riffs. Iggy cribbed the song's title from a *Time* magazine article on the Vietnam War, and his apocalyptic delivery, recorded in one, deranged take, suggested he channeled destruction with no little relish. Brothers Ron and Scott Asheton, meanwhile, play the archetypal powerhouse rhythm section, their bass and drums rumbling.

Columbia hated the album and initial sales were poor, but *Raw Power* proved to be a huge influence on the nascent punk movement. Steve Jones of the Sex Pistols claimed he'd learned to play guitar by taking speed and playing along to the album. **LP**

Iggy Pop bends over backward to please his fans. ➡

Desperado
Eagles (1973)

Writer | Don Henley, Glenn Frey
Producer | Glyn Johns
Label | Asylum
Album | *Desperado* (1973)

Following the success of the group's debut album, *Eagles*, in 1972, Don Henley and Glenn Frey took on an increasing share of songwriting duties. "Desperado," which lends its name to the group's second album, is the melancholy fruit of that creative partnership.

Evoking the ghostly honky-tonk pianos of some faded saloon, "Desperado" is a tragic ballad in the narrative style. Ostensibly it tells the story of a hard-bitten outlaw who has one last chance to come in from the cold. A tender allegory about the difficulty of seeking redemption after years of shunning love lies beneath the grizzled frontier rhetoric, however.

Despite rich vocal harmonies arranged by guitarist Bernie Leadon, formerly of seminal country-rock outfit The Flying Burrito Brothers, and an enduring emotional appeal, "Desperado" was never released as single. Such was the song's popularity among fans, though, that it was shrewdly included on the band's first greatest-hits collection, in 1976.

In an intriguing footnote, Linda Ronstadt—who had briefly employed Henley, Frey, and Leadon as part of her backing band in 1971—was asked to leave a Las Vegas venue in 2004, after dedicating her cover version of "Desperado" to controversial filmmaker Michael Moore in front of a staunchly conservative casino crowd. **JD**

Child's Christmas in Wales
John Cale (1973)

Writer | John Cale
Producer | Chris Thomas
Label | Reprise
Album | *Paris 1919* (1973)

For all John Cale's influence over the sound and direction of The Velvet Underground, the group he co-founded with Lou Reed in 1965, he wasn't accustomed to standing front and center. When Cale left the group in 1968, he retreated behind the scenes of the music industry, producing The Stooges' first album and playing on Nick Drake's *Bryter Layter*. When he eventually decided to place himself in the spotlight on a self-produced solo album, *Vintage Violence* (1970), the result was, in Cale's own words, "a very naive record."

By contrast, *Paris 1919* is tangibly the work of someone who's figured out what he wants to do and how to do it. Cale hired Beatles and Pink Floyd collaborator Chris Thomas as his producer, and three-fifths of Little Feat as his backing band. The music that resulted from the collaboration remains some of the most cherished of his career.

The opening track shares a title with a Dylan Thomas memoir, which first appeared in 1950. "Growing up in Wales," Cale admitted, "you can't miss the poetry." But Cale uses Thomas's "A Child's Christmas in Wales" as inspiration rather than source material, threading together a typically elusive narrative ("Ten murdered oranges bled on board ship / Lends comedy to shame") over an arrangement lent color by Lowell George's slide guitar. Cale returned to Thomas later in his career, but never as warmly as here. **WF-J**

Solid Air
John Martyn (1973)

Writer | John Martyn
Producer | John Martyn, John Wood
Label | Island
Album | *Solid Air* (1973)

John Martyn and fellow troubadour Nick Drake met sometime in the late 1960s as labelmates at Island Records. Painfully shy and unable to perform well in public, Drake expected stardom and was deeply upset when it failed to materialize. What confidence he had as the good-looking poster boy of English folk music soon dried up.

It was his friendship with Nick Drake that inspired one of John Martyn's most haunting songs. Written and recorded in 1972, "Solid Air" features Martyn's ethereal, echo-heavy acoustic guitar backed by Danny Thompson's reverberating double bass and a spare accompaniment of keyboards, electric bass, drums, and congas. Luminous vibes and a haunting tenor solo by saxophonist Tony Coe add to the mood. It is Martyn's vocals that stand out, however. Drawled, smeared, yet utterly clear, he is forced to admit that "I don't know what's going on in your mind / But I know you don't like what you find / When you're moving through / Solid air."

"Solid Air" and its parent album confirmed Martyn as an innovative musician straddling the folk-rock border. As for Drake, he died, probably accidentally, from an overdose of antidepressants in 1974, eighteen months after the song and album were released. Largely unrecognized in his lifetime, he is now considered one of the greatest songwriters of the last fifty years. **SA**

I Know What I Like (in Your Wardrobe) | Genesis (1973)

Writer | Banks, Collins, Gabriel, Hackett, Rutherford
Producer | John Burns, Genesis
Label | Charisma
Album | *Selling England by the Pound* (1973)

For all their twenty-minute, multipart symphonies, Genesis knew a good pop tune when they heard it. After guitarist Steve Hackett fell into playing a Beatles-influenced riff over and over at rehearsals for the group's fifth album, *Selling England By the Pound*, keyboard player Tony Banks began improvising around it. Soon the other members jumped on it as a touch of light relief from the more opaque material they had been making. Peter Gabriel came up with a melody line and a lyric inspired by what was to become the album's cover painting, *The Dream*, by Betty Swanwick.

"I Know What I Like (in Your Wardrobe)" is a tale of external pressure on Jacob, a young man (allegedly Genesis roadie Jacob Finster) to conform. The line "There's a future for you in the fire-escape trade" echoes Mr. McGuire's line to Benjamin in *The Graduate*: "There's a great future in plastics." Jacob, however, is simply content to mow lawns for a living and doze in the sun at lunchtime.

With Mike Rutherford playing electric sitar and a to-die-for Mellotron riff from Banks at the close, it all scuttles along with tremendous panache and humor. The song even makes a case for a tiny subgenre: glam-prog. It became a stage favorite in both Gabriel's and Phil Collins's eras of the group, with the former dressed as a yokel meticulously miming mowing and the latter furiously banging away on tambourine. **DE**

Cum on Feel the Noize | Slade (1973)

Writer | Noddy Holder, Jim Lea
Producer | Chas Chandler
Label | Polydor
Album | N/A

> *"Who is this? I love the bloke's voice. He sounds just like me."*
>
> **John Lennon, 1973**

◀ **Influenced by:** Revolution · The Beatles (1968)
▶ **Influence on:** Come on Feel the Illinoise · Sufjan Stevens (2005)
● **Covered by:** Quiet Riot (1983) · One Way System (1983) The Glitter Band (1996) · Oasis (1996) · Bran Van 3000 (1997)

Teachers the length and breadth of the United Kingdom were aghast at the rise of the group originally known as Ambrose Slade, fearing that widespread illiteracy would be the natural result of the band's fondness for phonetic spellings— "the way people write on toilet walls," according to singer Neville "Noddy" Holder. Faced with such establishment opprobrium, the West Midlands four-piece responded with a glorious call to arms, a none-too-quiet riot of chiming power chords and sandpaper vocals. Holder is on the attack throughout: "So you think my singing's out of time, well it *makes me money!*" he gloats exultantly, like his idol John Lennon at his most acerbic.

With Holder's Al Jolson-esque cry of "Baby-baby, baby" (a microphone check left in at the behest of producer Chas Chandler), Don Powell's urgent drum fills, and guitarist Dave Hill's throbbing twelve-bar boogie, "Cum on Feel the Noize" saw Slade's sledgehammer glam reach its peak, spawning future covers by Oasis and Californian cock-rockers Quiet Riot. The original (and best) stormed straight into the U.K. charts at No. 1, and in those days that actually meant something—the feat had not been achieved since The Beatles' "Get Back," four years before.

Slade were unashamed populists—witness the mob-handed backing vocals and hand claps in the chorus—and were in their element playing to the bopping masses on *Top of the Pops*. Hill, in particular, reveled in the dressing-up opportunities provided by the glam era. For this single he excelled himself, turning up at the studio in a bizarre mirrored wimple that led bass player Jim Lea to describe him as a "metal nun." His response? "You write 'em, I'll sell 'em." **SP**

Living for the City | Stevie Wonder (1973)

Writer | Stevie Wonder
Producer | Stevie Wonder
Label | Tamla
Album | *Innervisions* (1973)

"The bass sound on that—I mean, I think it's a Moog, I don't think it's a real bass, but WHEW!"

Lou Reed, 1980

◄ **Influenced by: Inner City Blues (Makes Me Wanna Holler)** • Marvin Gaye (1971)
► **Influence on: The Message** • Grandmaster Flash & The Furious Five (1982)
● **Covered by:** Ike & Tina Turner (1974) • Ray Charles (1975) • Bonnie Tyler (1978)

Innervisions, the third in Wonder's epochal album trilogy released under his new contract with Motown, soundtracked the darkest hours of the American Century, when the optimism of the previous decade was subjugated by Tricky Dick, Watergate, Vietnam, drugs, the oil crisis, rising crime, and urban decline. What the key track did in unambiguous terms was remind the inconvenienced middle classes that African-Americans had been putting up with much worse for far longer.

Wonder's characters come from "hard time" Mississippi, the poorest state in the union, the parents working hard to ensure that their children are eligible for the American dream. The daughter may own old clothes, but she wears them with pride; the son has brains, but what good will they do him when "where he lives they don't use colored people."

And that's where the single, a Top Ten hit, ends. LP buyers, however, had a completely different experience midway through, a spoken interlude beginning with a minute-long playlet as the young man (Wonder, who provides a panoply of voices) boards a bus, arrives in New York, and is hustled into a drug deal, arrested, racially abused, and sentenced to ten years.

When the next verse comes in, Wonder is transformed, singing from the back of his throat with fury for two more verses: "He spends his life walking the streets of New York City." However, the dream is not entirely soured, for the final verse finds the singer hoping his song can make a difference, that we can "make a better tomorrow."

And for this "Yes, we can" message, we should forgive those dated synthesizers. **DH**

I Can't Stand the Rain
Ann Peebles (1973)

Writer | Don Bryant, Ann Peebles, Bernard Miller
Producer | Willie Mitchell
Label | Hi
Album | *I Can't Stand the Rain* (1974)

Ann Peebles is a singer regarded by many as one of the greats—no less a figure than Bonnie Raitt once raved to *Rolling Stone*, "She's my hero!" Peebles was instrumental in defining the Memphis-soul sound, even becoming known as the "female Al Green." Sadly, the Al Green connection didn't help her, and she spent years trying to find a piece of the limelight from behind her Hi Records stablemate, until one serendipitous moment in 1973.

Peebles told *Memphis Flyer*, "One night we were at the house getting ready to go to a concert . . . and it was just pouring down with rain, and thunder was cracking. All of a sudden I popped up and said, 'Man, I can't stand the rain.' And Don [Bryant] looked at me and said, 'Ooh, that's a good song title!'" The concert was forgotten, the song was written that evening, and a hit was made.

Bryant attributed much of the song's success to producer Willie Mitchell. Talking to BBC Radio, he recalled, "Willie always had a certain touch . . . [he] added the electric timbales." Those timbales, part of the equipment newly installed at the studio, were used to create the song's raindrop effects.

The song made No. 6 on the U.S. R&B chart, entered the pop Top Fifty, earned a Grammy nomination, and enabled Peebles to buy her first house. But the highest accolade may have been awarded by John Lennon, who reportedly called it "the greatest song ever." **DC**

Goodbye Yellow Brick Road
Elton John (1973)

Writer | Elton John, Bernie Taupin
Producer | Gus Dudgeon
Label | DJM
Album | *Goodbye Yellow Brick Road* (1973)

In January 1973, the former Reg Dwight was holed up in the Pink Flamingo Hotel in Jamaica with a big pile of pre-written lyrics by his collaborator, Bernie Taupin. Over just three days he composed the greater part of the music for *Goodbye Yellow Brick Road*—a double LP he described as the "White Album" to *Honky Château's* "Revolver."

The title ballad reveals its treasures slowly. It begins with nothing more than Elton and his woozy piano. Gradually, Del Newman's orchestra buoys up the sound until Nigel Olsson comes in with a great crash of soft-rock drums, and we are taken into a wordless refrain that betrays a love of The Beach Boys' psychedelic harmonizing.

And that is not the only love that is betrayed here—Taupin's lyric is a brutal rejection of a former lover, a moneyed figure who took the narrator into a world of penthouses and vodka and tonics, but treated him as just another commodity. He turns his back on the shallow fripperies of big-city life and yearns to be back on the farm, where the focus of life is land husbandry and the predators are avian, not sexual: a "howling old owl in the woods / Hunting the horny-back toad." As Ian Beck's album-sleeve illustration makes overtly clear, this is a response to the escapism of "Over the Rainbow," but one that neatly inverts it, preferring rural authenticity to a world of fantasy. The other man's grass, it seems, is always Technicolor. **SP**

Elton John deals with an oversized sunglasses malfunction during a concert in the early 1970s.

Future Days
Can (1973)

Writer | Karoli, Czukay, Liebezeit, Schmidt, Suzuki
Producer | Can
Label | United Artists
Album | *Future Days* (1973)

The title track of the final album recorded with Can's free-spirited Japanese vocalist Damo Suzuki at the helm, "Future Days" is also one of the Cologne-based group's most enduring and beautiful creations. Recorded after the band returned from a summer holiday, paid for by the surprise chart success of their 1972 single "Spoon," its spun-out nine minutes captures them in an uncommonly laid-back spirit, albeit one not lacking Can's familiar percussive undercurrent.

Unlike "Spoon," "Future Days" is nowhere near a pop song. Commencing in a haze of electronic effects, scrapes, and eddying strings, it's over ninety seconds until the track finally lifts into motion on a bossa-nova-tinged beat courtesy of Jaki Liebezeit, formerly a disciple of European free-jazz trumpeter Manfred Schoof.

Even as the track gently builds, everything is lightly applied. Michael Karoli's guitar wanders idly, as if kicking through surf. Holger Czukay's bass rings like a metronome, barely there. And Damo Suzuki's vocals feel pulled back in the mix, a little submerged—although his melody is serene and optimistic.

Future Days would be Can's last classic album. Following its release, Damo Suzuki dropped out of the band and became a Jehovah's Witness. Without his input, Can would never again capture their element, perfect ebb and flow. **LP**

Essiniya
Nass El Ghiwane (1974)

Writer | Traditional, arranged by Nass El Ghiwane
Producer | Nass El Ghiwane
Label | Disques Ouhmane
Album | *Essiniya (Disque d'or)* (1974)

When Nass El Ghiwane (New Dervishes) arrived on the Moroccan music scene in the late 1960s, they infused traditional music with a radical voice. The band from Casablanca played the Gnaoua music of southern Morocco while adding a contemporary lyricism to songs, making them relevant to North African listeners. With their long hair and hippie clothing, the band were compared to The Rolling Stones, and, although they never attempted to westernize their music (playing dar, bendir, banjo, and darbouka), they possessed a similarly rebellious spirit to the London band.

On its release in 1974, "Essiniya" made a huge impact. The word itself references the round Moroccan tray that tea is served upon and around which people gather. What made the single so radical was the band's refusal to include in the verses any praise for Morocco's king, a custom at the time. By distancing themselves from such sycophancy, Nass El Ghiwane were implicitly criticizing the way Morocco was being run. Listeners embraced them as a radical, independent voice.

Nass El Ghiwane remain very popular across North Africa today. Most of the founder members of this five-piece band have died, yet in their Seventies recordings they established a template for a new North African music, one from which folk-music-influenced genres such as *chabbi* would arise. **GC**

Carpet Crawlers
Genesis (1974)

Writer | Banks, Collins, Gabriel, Hackett, Rutherford
Producer | John Burns, Genesis
Label | Charisma
Album | *The Lamb Lies Down on Broadway* (1974)

"It seemed like prancing around in fairyland was rapidly becoming obsolete." So spoke Peter Gabriel when he unveiled Genesis's double album, *The Lamb Lies Down on Broadway,* the tale of Bronx ghetto-dwelling Puerto Rican protagonist Rael.

One of Gabriel's best-ever melodies, "Carpet Crawlers" is the indisputable highlight of the group's most impenetrable album. Unlike other material on the ninety-minute-long suite, "Carpet Crawlers" was written very quickly, developed by keyboard player Tony Banks and bassist/guitarist Mike Rutherford. The song comes at a point in Gabriel's "punk *Pilgrim's Progress*" when Rael finds a red-carpeted corridor full of people on their knees heading up to a hidden chamber. Beyond the narrative aspects of the song, it has been said that its haunting, repeated refrain, "you've got to get in to get out" represents the need for sperm to fertilize an egg in order to produce a baby—or a "carpet crawler," if you will.

However, you can simply listen to the beauty of this song—the whole band play with passion and, importantly, restraint. Gabriel is at his most soulful, and Phil Collins's chorus vocal is memorable. This is Genesis for people who despise progressive rock, weaving as it does an idiosyncratic yet inclusive soul-folk path. Although unsuccessful as a single release, "Carpet Crawlers" serves as a five-minute distillation of Genesis's glory. **DE**

Águas de março | Antônio Carlos Jobim & Elis Regina (1974)

Writer | Antônio Carlos Jobim
Producer | Aloysio de Oliveira
Label | Verve
Album | *Elis & Tom* (1974)

Already famous in his native Brazil, Antônio Carlos Jobim came to worldwide prominence in the early 1960s, thanks chiefly to an album on which he stayed in the background. American saxophonist Stan Getz and Brazilian guitarist João Gilberto got their names in lights on *Getz/Gilberto* (1964), and the plaintive vocals of João's wife, Astrud Gilberto, ushered "The Girl from Ipanema" into the mainstream. The guiding hand, however, came from Jobim, who co-wrote most of the songs on the album and played piano throughout.

The success of *Getz/Gilberto* allowed Jobim to pursue a healthy career in the United States. In 1974, he joined Brazilian singer Elis Regina in Los Angeles to record an album of Jobim-penned tunes. The duo's version of "Águas de março," a gentle piece of philosophy inspired by the March rains in Rio, wasn't the first to be released; Jobim's original, hurried recording had been given away with a magazine two years earlier. But the after-you interplay between Regina and Jobim on the melodically simple, rhythmically fluid melody, and the empathetic all-star Brazilian band, helped make it the definitive version.

Unusually, Jobim also wrote the song's English-language lyrics, titled as "Waters of March." In a recent survey of Brazilian journalists to find their country's best song of the twentieth century, "Águas de março" came out on top. **WF-J**

Ain't No Love in the Heart of the City | Bobby Bland (1974)

Writer | Michael Price, Dan Walsh
Producer | Steve Barri
Label | ABC Dunmill
Album | *Dreamer* (1974)

Bobby "Blue" Bland's successful career as a blues singer had stalled by the late 1960s. His run of R&B chart successes dried up, financial pressures caused him to break his band up completely, and his musical association with his main composer and arranger, Joe Scott, came to an end.

His career improved when his record company, Duke, was sold to the ABC group. They steered Bland in a more soulful, mainstream direction, complete with rock guitars and string arrangements. Under their guidance, he released two successful albums, written by and featuring the best L.A. session men. The second of these sets, *Dreamer*, produced Bland's biggest hit for years.

"Ain't No Love in the Heart of the City" is a fairly basic song, just a chorus and two verses. Its skill comes in the way in which Bland implicitly links his lost love with a lament for the decline and despondency of his home city. She had "loved me like this old neighborhood," but now that she's gone, "the sun don't shine, from the city heart to the county line." After Marvin Gaye's *What's Going On*, urban deprivation was a constant theme of American black music, and Bland's take on the subject was all the stronger for its subtlety.

Rapper Jay-Z sampled the song's hookline but then laid down a series of hateful lyrics. Heavy metal band Whitesnake also included the song on their first EP and later released it as a single. **SA**

(Looking for) The Heart of Saturday Night | Tom Waits (1974)

Writer | Tom Waits
Producer | Bones Howe
Label | Asylum
Album | *The Heart of Saturday Night* (1974)

If *Closing Time*, Tom Waits's first album, is the sound of a singer looking for his voice, then *The Heart of Saturday Night* is the sound of him finding it. Granted, that voice hadn't yet been shattered by cigarettes, and the louche barfly schtick he'd built for himself was more of a sketch than a portrait. But, even so, Waits's second album is the point at which he started to sound like himself.

For all that, the record's near-title track is unusual for an early Waits song in that he doesn't put his persona at the center of the action. The self-mythologizing first-person narrative found on other mid-Seventies tracks such as "Tom Traubert's Blues" is absent; here, Waits is the observer, watching as the world unfolds before him.

The song's theme is contained within its title: the wide-eyed optimism inspired by the weekend, cash in your pocket, and girl by your side. It's a simple subject, tackled often by songwriters down the years. Savvily, Waits doesn't oversell it, wedding a snapshot lyric to one of his simplest, loveliest melodies.

The Heart of Saturday Night failed to make much of an impression. The singer spent the rest of the decade growing into his Skid Row beatnik role and then growing out of it, before embarking on one of rock's more startling mid-career reinventions with the uncompromisingly clattery *Swordfishtrombones* (1983). **WF-J**

A taxicab-borne Tom Waits eyes the camera on a 1974 visit to London. ➡

Sweet Home Alabama | Lynyrd Skynyrd (1974)

Writer | Ed King, Gary Rossington, Ronnie Van Zant
Producer | Al Kooper
Label | MCA
Album | *Second Helping* (1974)

"I think 'Sweet Home Alabama' is a great song. I've actually performed it live a couple of times myself."

Neil Young, 1995

◀ **Influenced by: Southern Man** · Neil Young (1970)

▶ **Influence on: Ronnie and Neil** · Drive-By Truckers (2001)

● **Covered by:** Charlie Daniels (1981) · Hank Williams Jr. (1987) · Leningrad Cowboys (1993) · Bonfire (1999) · Down By Law (2000) · Jewel (2002)

For the best take on "Sweet Home Alabama," you should probably seek out "Ronnie and Neil," by Alabama rockers Drive-By Truckers, in which singer Patterson Hood relates the full messy story behind this epic and continually misunderstood rallying cry for southern pride. It was recorded by Ronnie Van Zant's Skynyrd in response to Neil Young's "Southern Man" and "Alabama," both of which seemed to blame the entire South for the actions of a racist minority. In the song, Skynyrd—staunch antisegregationists and Neil Young fans, but proud of their roots (all three songwriters were actually from Florida)—admonished Young and praised the state of Alabama, while making equivocal comments about infamous racist governor George Wallace (something later echoed by Randy Newman's scabrous and conflicted "Rednecks").

Young loved it, as did most of Skynyrd's fellow Southerners, who adopted the song as an unofficial anthem (it's the slogan on Alabama's state license plates), but some listeners failed to discern the subtleties of the song's politics and saw it as a simple endorsement of white superiority. Others ignored the lyrics entirely and just grooved to its funky toe-tapping backing rhythm and swinging wah-wah guitar, the two qualities that have made it a staple of film soundtracks and classic-rock compilations. These contradictions are exemplified by the disparate cover versions of the song: one, vicious and stupid, by English Nazi punks Skrewdriver; another, celebratory and tongue-in-cheek, by Dirty South rappers B.A.M.A.; and an anodyne third by MOR folkie Jewel, the latter the theme for a forgettable romantic comedy bearing the song's name. This would be the "the duality of the southern thing," as Drive-By Truckers later put it. **PW**

Piss Factory | Patti Smith Group (1974)

Writer | Patti Smith, Richard Sohl
Producer | Lenny Kaye
Label | MER
Album | N/A

PATTI SMITH   HEY JOE (VERSION)

PISS FACTORY

SPECIAL COLLECTORS EDITION

SRE 1009

"In 'Piss Factory' I wasn't trying to represent any punk rock point of view. I was just representing the fact that we all have a choice."
Patti Smith, 1996

◄ **Influenced by: Desolation Row** · Bob Dylan (1965)
► **Influence on: Marquee Moon** · Television (1977)
● **Covered by:** Swarf Sisters (1997) · The Klone Orchestra (2009)
★ **Other key tracks:** Hey Joe (1974) · Free Money (1975) Because the Night (1978)

Patti Smith had been knocking around the fringes of the music world for a while before she finally got into the studio, so when it was time to record her first single she was locked, loaded, and ready to roll. Smith, a strong personality and powerful performer, saw herself as a poet and writer as much as a singer, but that still didn't prepare anybody for the cathartic might of "Piss Factory," one of the great B-sides in musical history and also one of the most successful fusions of honest-to-god poetry (rather than opaque and self-indulgent lyrics) with rock 'n' roll.

Over Richard Sohl's amazing, insane, jazzy piano, Smith intones a wildly rhythmic, Beat-influenced recollection of her hellish time working in a New Jersey toy factory as a sixteen-year-old in 1964 ("Because you see it's the monotony that's got to me / Every afternoon like the last one / Every afternoon like a rerun") until she makes her closing, bold, climactic promise: "I'm gonna be somebody, I'm gonna get on that train, go to New York City / And I'm gonna be so big, I'm gonna be a big star and I will never return." She was as good as her word.

With an equally unorthodox Patty Hearst–referencing cover of "Hey Joe" on the A-side, the single was paid for by photographer Robert Mapplethorpe (Smith's former lover, whose photos of her later became the LP covers of the Patti Smith Group). Smith had been inspired to record after seeing shows by Television, whose songwriter, Tom Verlaine, played on "Hey Joe (Version)"/ "Piss Factory," so it made perfect sense when the two bands began a residency at CBGB in 1975, and America's Rimbaud-meets–The Rolling Stones version of punk was born. **PW**

Evie
Stevie Wright (1974)

Writer | Harry Vanda, George Young
Producer | G. Young, H. Vanda, Stevie Wright
Label | Albert
Album | *Hard Road* (1974)

Free Man in Paris
Joni Mitchell (1974)

Writer | Joni Mitchell
Producer | Joni Mitchell
Label | Asylum
Album | *Court and Spark* (1974)

In the mid-Sixties, "Little Stevie" Wright enjoyed massive success as lead singer of The Easybeats. That Aussie group was embraced in its homeland with Beatlemania-style passion thanks to a string of No. 1 pop hits, notably "Friday on My Mind."

After The Easybeats disbanded in 1969, Wright wore various hats, at one point appearing in *Jesus Christ Superstar*, before recording his solo debut, *Hard Road*. The effort would reunite him with his old Easybeats mates Harry Vanda and George Young, who were then in the process of becoming Australia's hottest hitmakers.

One of the few truly genuine rock epics, "Evie" was a three-part suite that utilized memorable lyrics and dramatic arrangements to tell the full arch of a relationship in eleven minutes. The first part (subtitled "Let Your Hair Hang Down") was a raucous rocker—clearly an early blueprint for what Vanda and Young would later accomplish with AC/DC—and it told of the courtship of Evie. The second was a tender, believable piano ballad celebrating the good times, while the third (subtitled "I'm Losing You") was an anguished cry of a relationship on its last legs. All three parts could be enjoyed individually, but the synergy found in the complete work was undeniable.

Despite its unfashionable length, "Evie" was a massive hit in Australia and pushed *Hard Road* to No. 2 in the charts. **JiH**

Songs about record labels and their owners are rarely complimentary: witness "E.M.I." by the Sex Pistols. "Free Man in Paris," however, is relatively affectionate. "I wrote that in Paris for David Geffen, taking a lot of it from the things he said," Mitchell told the *Los Angeles Times*. "He begged me to take it off the record. I think he felt uncomfortable being shown in that light."

Mitchell played the song's parent album to Geffen (then president of Asylum) and his latest signing, Bob Dylan. "*Court and Spark*, which was a big breakthrough for me, was being entirely and almost rudely dismissed," she told Cameron Crowe in *Rolling Stone*. "Geffen's excuse was, since I was living in a room in his house at the time, that he had heard it through all of its stages, and it was no longer any surprise to him."

The lyrics depict Geffen, "unfettered and alive," wandering the Champs-Élysées, away from people "calling me up for favors." "If taken at his word (or Joni's translation, per se)," observed Sufjan Stevens, "Geffen comes off as an A&R curmudgeon, wary of the tedium of Hollywood, pining for the romance of Paris. [Ironically] Geffen's indignation is aimed at the very industry he helped create."

The gloriously sunny music featured flute by Tom Scott, backing vocals from David Crosby and Graham Nash, and guitar by José Feliciano. The song became Mitchell's final major hit. **BM**

Joni Mitchell in 1974, the year of her acclaimed set *Court and Spark*. ➜

I Will Always Love You
Dolly Parton (1974)

Writer | Dolly Parton
Producer | Bob Ferguson
Label | RCA
Album | *Jolene* (1974)

"I Will Always Love You" is a story of two cover versions, one that was and one that might have been. The song was originally a modest hit for Dolly Parton in 1974 and 1982. Written to lament the end of Parton's formative (and entirely non-romantic) musical partnership with sharp-dressing country legend Porter Wagoner, "I Will Always Love You" was twice a country No. 1 but never troubled the pop charts. Then Whitney Houston got hold of it in 1992 and turned an understated country love song into a gargantuan, release-the-diva soul ballad. Recorded for the soundtrack of cinematic melodrama *The Bodyguard*, "I Will Always . . ." was No. 1 in the United States for fourteen weeks and sold more than thirteen million singles around the world—a record for a female artist.

Which brings us to the second cover version, the one that never was. While Parton's sprightly tune was still wowing country audiences, it reached the ears of Elvis Presley and his manager, Colonel Tom Parker, who decided it would make ideal chart-fodder for the laboring King. However, when Parton discovered this would mean signing over half the publishing rights, as was the custom when dealing with Parker, she refused. Although it denied us the chance to hear Presley's tonsils wrapped round her perky tune, the decision paid off nearly twenty years later, when Houston's version earned Parton a cool $6 million. **PW**

The Grand Tour
George Jones (1974)

Writer | Norro Wilson, Carmol Taylor, George Richey
Producer | Billy Sherrill
Label | Epic
Album | *The Grand Tour* (1974)

It's revealing that George Jones's autobiography allocates only a handful of its pages to the singer's records. Nashville's Sinatra, a towering talent who's reached the Top Ten of the country singles chart on more than seventy occasions, is reduced by his own pen—or, more likely, that of his ghostwriter—to a collection of anecdotes, many built around the singer's legendary alcohol problem.

The irony in this is that Jones's music often referenced his own life, a classic Nashville tactic for bridging the gap between music-business artifice and country's treasured aspirations toward authenticity. The singer sang of his battles with the bottle—"If Drinkin' Don't Kill Me (Her Memory Will)"—and his romantic travails in countless singles, among them a pair of duets with Tammy Wynette that fictionalized the couple's marriage ("The Ceremony") and divorce ("Golden Ring").

"The Grand Tour" sees Jones guiding the listener around the home he used to share with a wife who's walked out on him, "Taking nothing but our baby and my heart." Jones's longtime producer, Billy Sherrill, occasionally overegged his puddings, but not here: the sympathetic arrangement is undeniably sentimental but never mawkish. Still, "The Grand Tour" isn't Sherrill's record but Jones's, thanks to what might be the finest ever vocal performance by perhaps the greatest interpreter of song in country-music history. **WF-J**

Withered and Died | Richard and Linda Thompson (1974)

Writer | Richard Thompson
Producer | Richard Thompson, John Wood
Label | Island
Album | *I Want to See the Bright Lights Tonight* (1974)

In late 1969, singer-songwriter-guitarist Richard Thompson was in London's Chelsea recording *Liege and Lief* with his band, Fairport Convention. In the next studio was Linda Pettifer (aka Peters), who was taping a jingle for Kellogg's Corn Flakes. The pair connected through Sandy Denny, Fairport Convention's singer and a friend of Pettifer from the London folk-club circuit, and hit it off. They married in 1972, the same year that Linda sang backing vocals on Richard's first solo album after leaving Fairport Convention.

There's a tangible folk and folk-rock influence on *I Want to See the Bright Lights Tonight*, the first record the Thompsons made as a duo. It's audible in the all-together-now chorus of "We Sing Hallelujah"; in the faintly Fairport-esque sound of "The Little Beggar Girl," among others; and in the guest appearances from John Kirkpatrick and Fairport's Simon Nicol. The influence extends to "Withered and Died," a haunting ballad that sounds as if it could be a good deal older than it is.

The pair continued in a similar vein across five subsequent albums until 1982, when Richard left Linda for another woman on the eve of a major tour that Linda got through with the liberal use of "vodka, orange juice, and antidepressants." Twenty years later, the pair had reconciled to such a degree that Richard guested on Linda's long-overdue solo debut, *Fashionably Late*, in 2002. **WF-J**

Louisiana 1927
Randy Newman (1974)

Writer | Randy Newman
Producer | Lenny Waronker, Russ Titelman
Label | Reprise
Album | *Good Old Boys* (1974)

In the autumn of 1926, rain fell relentlessly on the middle south of the United States for months. To avoid the destruction of New Orleans, levees upstream of the city were dynamited, while others ruptured. The city was spared, but the resulting flood the following year killed hundreds and left more than 700,000 homeless across Louisiana and Mississippi.

Half a century later, Randy Newman, a New Orleans native, saw the former governor of Georgia and one-time segregationist Lester Maddox lambasted on Dick Cavett's TV talk show. It was the spark for a song cycle that took a very unorthodox approach to exploring the off-kilter romanticism of the American South. With some shuffling and replacing, the set of songs developed into the album *Good Old Boys*.

"Louisiana 1927" is a brilliant ode to Newman's devastated home state. The lush, full orchestra heard at the song's opening evokes all the pomp of a formal cotillion, only to be undercut by spare piano and Newman's unassuming voice explaining what happened "to this poor crackers' land."

In 2005, disaster struck again when Hurricane Katrina nearly washed New Orleans from the map. The spirit of Newman's song, with its references to shrugging politicians and the bitter plight of the disenfranchised, still rang only too true. Fittingly, Newman re-recorded the track for a benefit album to aid the people of his one-time home. **TS**

You Haven't Done Nothin'
Stevie Wonder (1974)

Writer | Stevie Wonder
Producer | Stevie Wonder
Label | Tamla
Album | *Fulfillingness' First Finale* (1974)

In 1974, Stevie Wonder was at the peak of his abilities. Just twenty-three years old, he had freed himself from the shackles of the Motown hit machine and had recorded three groundbreaking albums that put him at the forefront of the world's music scene. While other soul artists had dabbled with politics and civil rights and then returned to a more conventional pop path, for the debut release from his album *Fulfillingness' First Finale*, Wonder was completely incensed by the turmoil at the heart of U.S. government.

With its opening bark of "We are amazed and not amused by all the things you say and you do," "You Haven't Done Nothin'" rails against U.S. president Richard Nixon, who, at the time of recording, was embroiled in the Watergate scandal. Working with engineers Robert Margouleff and Malcolm Cecil, Wonder played everything on the track, apart from Reggie McBride's bass; Motown stablemates The Jackson 5 added backing vocals.

The single was released in August 1974, the same month Nixon was to resign, and the potency of an acclaimed artist releasing new material that chimed with such a tumultuous event sent the record to the top of the charts. It may not have been one of Wonder's greater melodious statements, but "You Haven't Done Nothin'" remains marvellous and aggressive, dirty funk agit-pop that pioneered the use of the drum machine. **DE**

This Town Ain't Big Enough
for the Both of Us | Sparks (1974)

Writer | Ron Mael
Producer | Muff Winwood
Label | Island
Album | *Kimono My House* (1974)

Formed by Ron Mael (keyboards) and his younger brother Russell (vocals) in Los Angeles at the end of the Sixties, Sparks, as they became known, were always a square peg in a round hole in America. Their music owed more to British beat and Weimar Germany than to the feel-good vibe rolling in from the Pacific. After two albums on Bearsville and a visit to London in late 1972, manager John Hewlett saw the brothers' potential in a U.K. chart dominated increasingly by eccentrics.

The brothers relocated to London, where Simon Napier-Bell protégé and ex–John's Children bassist Hewlett found them a new band—bassist Martin Gordon, guitarist Adrian Fisher, and drummer Norman "Dinky" Diamond—and got a deal with Island Records. The resultant album, *Kimono My House*, is one of the strangest, most discrete works of the 1970s. It was dwarfed by this, its lead single. With sound-effect gunshots added by engineer Richard Digby-Smith, Ron Mael's filmic writing, and Russell Mael's exaggerated staccato delivery, it makes for one of the most breathtaking moments of that decade's pop. That Ron resembled Adolf Hitler and Russell looked like a pretty boy added to their immediate novelty the moment the record crashed onto British weekly chart show *Top of the Pops*. The song reached No. 2 in the U.K. charts. Four decades and nineteen albums later, it is still a cornerstone of their live shows. **DE**

Sparks' siblings Russell (left) and Ron Mael: quite unlike two peas in a pod. ➜

Only Women Bleed | Alice Cooper (1975)

Writer | Alice Cooper, Dick Wagner
Producer | Bob Ezrin
Label | Atlantic
Album | *Welcome to My Nightmare* (1975)

"They kept saying I … didn't write anything. … So Wagner and I wrote those ballads just to show we could write."

Alice Cooper, 1977

◀ **Influenced by: Isn't it a Pity** • George Harrison (1970)
▶ **Influence on: Knockin' on Heaven's Door** • Guns N' Roses (1992)
● **Covered by:** Tina Turner (1976) • Carmen McRae (1976) Julie Covington (1978) • Elkie Brooks (1986) • Lita Ford (1990) • Tina Arena (2008)

Despite its misleading (and controversial) title, "Only Women Bleed" is a ballad rather than part of the shock-rock canon for which Alice Cooper is best known—in fact, Atlantic abbreviated the title to "Only Women" for the shorter version of the single, released ahead of its inclusion on parent album *Welcome to My Nightmare*.

However, it still had some shock value, mainly because of the widespread, but mistaken, idea that the song made reference to menstruation. The lyrics, however, are unambiguous: the song is about women in repressive and abusive relationships. Even this managed to raise some hackles, particularly among feminists, who took issue with the fact that it was written and performed by a man—and, what's more, a man who had adopted a woman's name and was known for his notoriously violent, Grand Guignol–style stage act.

Nevertheless, "Only Women Bleed" was a surprise hit for Cooper (backed with the vicious classic "Cold Ethyl"), which helped to launch the concept album *Welcome to My Nightmare*, the film of its live performance, and a television special, *The Nightmare*, featuring Vincent Price. It was the first time the name Alice Cooper referred solely to the singer; previously it had applied both to him and his band.

"Only Women Bleed" was rumored to be about Cooper's friend Tina Turner, who later recorded the song herself. Many other women also ignored the controversy and embraced the song, including Julie Covington, Etta James, Elkie Brooks, Lita Ford, Tori Amos, and Tina Arena. More disturbingly, Guns N' Roses reinstated it into a macho hard-rock setting, using it to lead into "Knockin' on Heaven's Door" in their live act. **MW**

Jive Talkin' | Bee Gees (1975)

Writer | Barry Gibb, Robin Gibb, Maurice Gibb
Producer | Arif Mardin
Label | RSO
Album | *Main Course* (1975)

"We were over the moon about 'Jive Talkin,'' but when we played it to people at the record company, they didn't want it."
Maurice Gibb, 1998

◄ **Influenced by:** Superstition · Stevie Wonder (1973)
► **Influence on:** I Want Your Sex · George Michael (1987)
● **Covered by:** Ronnie Dyson (1976) · Cedar Walton (1976) · Boogie Box High (1987) The Blenders (1995)
★ **Other key tracks:** Massachusetts (1967) · Nights on Broadway (1975) · You Should Be Dancing (1976)

By 1973, the Bee Gees had hit the commercial buffers, the steady run of smashes now reduced to a trickle, the band notoriously consigned to cabaret turns at low-rent venues. That year's *Life in a Tin Can* album did little to halt the decline, but, on friend Eric Clapton's advice, the follow-up—*Mr. Natural*, in 1974—teamed the Gibbs with legendary R&B producer Arif Mardin, who would coax them in a new direction.

Although *Mr. Natural* failed to spawn hits, band and producer were back in harness for *Main Course* (1975), and this time Mardin had ideas. He encouraged the brothers to listen to Stevie Wonder and other contemporary artists, and suggested Barry Gibb might like to broaden his vocal range. "I asked Barry to take his vocal up one octave," Mardin later revealed. "That's how their falsetto was born."

"Jive Talkin'" showcased the revolutionary vocal sound, but equally inspirational was the early-disco rhythm track pinning the song down. "There's a bridge that we had to cross on the way to the studio," Maurice Gibb recalled, "and every time we crossed it, the car would make a clickety-clack sound." Realizing the funk behind those rickety rhythms, and adding the distinctive ARP 2600 synthesizer bass line from keyboard player Blue Weaver, the Bee Gees found themselves with a dance track that revived their fortunes. Despite coy initial airings under the cloak of a white label, "Jive Talkin'" soared to No. 1 on the U.S. chart and enjoyed No. 5 success in the United Kingdom, setting the pace for a triumphant few years.

In 1977, "Jive Talkin'" popped up again on the *Saturday Night Fever* soundtrack, seamlessly blending with the band's disco zenith, a reminder of where it all began. **MH**

Jesus' Blood Never Failed Me Yet
Gavin Bryars (1975)

Writer | Gavin Bryars
Producer | Brian Eno
Label | Obscure
Album | *The Sinking of the Titanic* (1975)

An avant-garde classical work based on a hymn tune, sung by a London tramp with orchestral accompaniment, and lasting twenty-five minutes in its original version, is unlikely material for a hit recording, but Gavin Bryars's "Jesus' Blood Never Failed Me Yet" has acquired a cult status since its release in 1975.

It originally appeared as the whole of the B-side of *The Sinking of the Titanic*, the first album released by Brian Eno's Obscure Records label, with the title track filling the A-side. Bryars had studied classical music and worked as a jazz double-bass player before turning to composition, inspired by minimalist composers of the New York School, including John Cage and Morton Feldman. The vocal that provides the basis for the piece was recorded during the making of a documentary film about London's homeless, featuring an old tramp singing a favorite hymn. Bryars made a tape loop of the first section of this song and added a slowly evolving orchestral accompaniment that builds to a mighty climax.

The song, and the album, might have gone unnoticed without Brian Eno's backing. He and Bryars had collaborated in the classical performance-art ensemble Portsmouth Sinfonia, and worked together throughout the Seventies on minimalist and "ambient" music that attempted to cross over the classical-pop divide. **MW**

Boulder to Birmingham
Emmylou Harris (1975)

Writer | Emmylou Harris, Bill Danoff
Producer | Brian Ahern
Label | Reprise
Album | *Pieces of the Sky* (1975)

Born into an army family in 1947, Emmylou Harris came to country music in a roundabout way. Her musical passions were first aroused by the Sixties folk revival, obsessing as a teenager over Bob Dylan and Joan Baez. Moving to New York, Harris cut her first album, the folky *Gliding Bird*, in 1970. However, when the album bombed and her marriage collapsed, Harris returned home to live with her parents outside Washington, D.C.

The singer's epiphany came in 1971, when Gram Parsons, just then embarking on a solo career, asked former bandmate Chris Hillman if he knew any female singers with whom he could duet. Hillman had just seen Harris sing in a Washington folk club, and the pair connected over a few songs. Harris thought that would be all she'd ever hear from the famously erratic singer, but Parsons soon flew her out to L.A. to work on his solo debut, effectively serving as Harris's musical mentor for her second-chance musical career.

Harris was heartbroken when, in 1973, Parsons overdosed in a motel in the Californian desert. But the reputation she'd earned as his co-vocalist led to a record contract of her own and to the release of *Pieces of the Sky*. That the record was an immediate success was due in no small part to the presence of "Boulder to Birmingham," Harris's gorgeous tribute to her former friend and the album's undoubted centerpiece. **WF-J**

Emmylou Harris, seen here in concert in 1975, the year her solo career took off. ➡

Fight the Power (Parts 1 & 2)
The Isley Brothers (1975)

Writer | Isley Brothers, Chris Jasper
Producer | Isley Brothers, Chris Jasper
Label | Epic
Album | *The Heat Is On* (1975)

By the mid-Seventies, The Isley Brothers had become true innovators. They expanded on their old funk-rock template and released a series of breathtaking records that wedded Ronald Isley's angelic voice to Ernie Isley's blistering rock guitar.

Although the brother's sheer presence and commercial success had been themselves a political statement, and records such as "It's Your Thing" and "The Blacker the Berry" had indeed been interpreted as radical, "Fight the Power," the lead track from their *The Heat Is On* album, was one that could be seen as incendiary.

The idea came to guitarist Ernie Isley in the shower one morning when he began singing the first two lines straight out. The song talks of rising up against authority and red tape, and, after "rolling with the punches" only to get "knocked to the ground," it is time to make a stand against "all this bullshit going down." Much fuss was made about the use of the word "bullshit" in the chorus, a very radical choice of word in 1975.

This song was a late addition to the ranks of protest numbers, although the Isleys were quick to point out that the power it railed against could indeed be *all* authority rather than a simple issue of black versus white. It certainly captured the post-Watergate mood in the United States—the record scorched to the top of the R&B chart in July and hit the Top Ten of the pop chart as well. **DE**

That's the Way (I Like It)
KC & The Sunshine Band (1975)

Writer | H. W. "KC" Casey, R. Finch
Producer | H. W. "KC" Casey, R. Finch
Label | TK
Album | *KC & The Sunshine Band* (1975)

One of the biggest hits of the disco era, "That's the Way (I Like It)" was the second No. 1 for KC & The Sunshine Band, topping the U.S. charts twice in November and December 1975. Co-writers and -producers Richard Finch and Harry Wayne "KC" Casey got together in the early Seventies, when Finch worked as an engineer at the TK studio in Florida and moonlighted on bass with a band called The Ocean Liners. Casey, a record-store worker, joined the band on keyboards, and the two soon developed a close friendship and songwriting partnership, forming the multiracial and multimember KC & The Sunshine Band in 1973 along with fellow Ocean Liners Jerome Smith (guitar) and Robert Johnson (drums). Their first success, though, was not under their name but for George McCrae with "Rock Your Baby," in 1974, penned and produced by Casey and Finch and backed by The Sunshine Band. The next year, the band released their eponymous album, including the R&B chart-topper "Get Down Tonight" and their first hit, "That's the Way (I Like It)."

Although the lyrics are transparently sexual, emphasized by the "uh-huhs" alternating between Casey and the female backing vocalists, this was a toned-down version of the original recording, which would have jeopardized getting airplay in 1975, though no doubt the suggestiveness added to its appeal on the dance floor. **MW**

Kalimankou denkou
Le Mystère des Voix Bulgares (1975)

Writer | Philip Koutev
Producer | Marcel Cellier
Label | Disques Cellier
Album | *Le mystère des voix bulgares* (1975)

Marcus Garvey
Burning Spear (1975)

Writer | Winston Rodney,
Phillip Fullwood
Producer | Jack Ruby
Label | Island
Album | *Marcus Garvey* (1975)

This is a musical mystery in every sense. When U.K. label 4AD issued the *Le mystère des voix bulgares* album in 1986, they gave no information on the performers. Ivo Watts-Russell, 4AD's co-founder, wrote that he had first heard this music via a cassette given to him by Peter Murphy (vocalist for Bauhaus, another 4AD act), and mentioned that Swiss ethnomusicologist Marcel Cellier had gathered the singers and recorded them singing these ancient songs. This is misleading.

Cellier had traveled in communist Bulgaria, where he heard the Bulgarian State Television Female Vocal Choir (BSTVFVC). This choir, often consisting of up to twenty-one vocalists, were shaped by composer Philip Koutev so as to blend Bulgarian-village polyphony singing with Western classical music's concepts of harmony and form.

"Kalimankou Denkou" is an outstanding example of the choir at work, their piercing voices building a dense, otherworldly music. Cellier took tapes of the BSTVFVC back to Switzerland and issued them locally in 1975. Quickly deleted, the recordings existed only on shared tapes thereafter, which led to 4AD tracking down Cellier and licensing the music.

An underground hit, *Le mystère des voix bulgares* still sounds eerie and beautiful. Ironically, however, in today's post-Communist Bulgaria, there is little interest in polyphonic choirs. **GC**

Winston Rodney began his recording career after a chance encounter with Bob Marley in Jamaica. Marley encouraged Rodney to visit legendary producer Clement "Coxsone" Dodd at his Studio One base in Kingston. Starting out as a duo with co-vocalist Rupert Willington, he debuted with the Dodd-produced "Door Peep" in 1969, adopting the name Burning Spear—the nickname given to Jomo Kenyatta, a political activist imprisoned by the British colonial government in East Africa, who was later to become the first president of Kenya. Vocalist Delroy Hinds subsequently joined, too.

By 1975, Rodney's working relationship with Dodd had broken down, so the trio decamped to work with Jack Ruby on their third album, *Marcus Garvey*. The title track was a tribute to the philosopher and activist who posthumously became the prophet of Rastafarianism; Rodney had become greatly influenced by his message of Pan-African unity and independence. Indeed, such was the success of this track, with its message of oppression and redemption, and funky, polyrhythmic, horn-laden sound, it hooked American and European listeners.

Backed up musically by the Black Disciples—an assortment of some of Jamaica's finest, including bassist Robbie Shakespeare—the track's parent album was an instant success, leading to an international release on Island Records. **CS**

Bohemian Rhapsody | Queen (1975)

Writer | Freddie Mercury
Producer | Roy Thomas Baker, Queen
Label | EMI
Album | *A Night at the Opera* (1975)

"He knew exactly what he was doing. It was Freddie's baby. We just helped him bring it to life."
Brian May, 2002

◀ **Influenced by: This Town Ain't Big Enough for Both of Us** · Sparks (1974)
▶ **Influence on: United States of Eurasia** · Muse (2009)
● **Covered by: Elaine Paige** (1988) · **"Weird Al" Yankovic** (1993) · **Rolf Harris** (1996) · **Lucia Micarelli** (2004) The Royal Philharmonic Orchestra (2005)

Ah, the endless dichotomy of "Bohemian Rhapsody," Queen's insane, seven-minute blancmange of rock, opera, and heavy metal. On the one hand, it is regularly voted the best song ever by the public; on the other, the *Penguin Encyclopedia of Popular Music* pompously states that "the enduring popularity of 'Rhapsody' is a mystery to music lovers; it is to music as a tabloid is to a newspaper."

The song sprang fully formed from the head of Freddie Mercury; when he played it on piano for the band he left gaps where the operatic bits would go. Determination and self-confidence were the watchwords. "Bohemian Rhapsody" tested technology, requiring 180 vocal overdubs, and the band's manager, Pete Brown, thought they were "quite mad" to release it as a single. Yet they did, surreptitiously and with the help of a willing DJ who played a test pressing on British radio, and the joyful lunacy and magpie imagination of "Bohemian Rhapsody" was embraced by the public. Bolstered by a promo video, made so the band didn't have to mime on BBC TV's *Top of the Pops*, it became a U.K. Christmas No. 1 and U.S. Top Ten hit, much to the disappointment of critics who knew better. The lyrics are famously nonsensical—"Scaramouche, Scaramouche, will you do the fandango?"—but there is something of a narrative, of wanton murder and a killer infused with ennui: thematic connections could be made with The Cure's "Killing an Arab" or "Folsom Prison Blues" by Johnny Cash.

"Bohemian Rhapsody" found a new audience after Mercury's death in 1991, when it was again a U.K. No. 1, and it also made No. 2 in the United States in 1992 after it was used in endearing fashion in Mike Myers's metalhead movie *Wayne's World*. It is, if nothing else, one of a kind. **PW**

Gloria | Patti Smith (1975)

Writer | Van Morrison, Patti Smith
Producer | John Cale
Label | Arista
Album | *Horses* (1975)

"I wrote that line when I was twenty years old. A lot of people misinterpreted it as the statement of an atheist."

Patti Smith, 1996

◄ **Influenced by: Sister Ray** · The Velvet Underground (1968)

► **Influence on: C'Mon Billy** · PJ Harvey (1995)

● **Covered by:** Jimi Hendrix (1979) · Eddie & The Hot Rods (1997) · Rickie Lee Jones (2001) · The Standells (2001) · Simple Minds (2001)

Dumb, simple, and brutal, "Gloria," Van Morrison's hymn to lust, became the record every three-chord guitarist wanted to emulate, with The Shadows of Knight taking it into the Top Ten in the United States, and U2, Joe Strummer, and Bruce Springsteen among the legions acknowledging it as a foundation stone of rock 'n' roll.

It is fitting, therefore, that the song became punk's curtain-raiser as the opening track on Patti Smith's debut album, *Horses*. The song is divided in two, with Smith's "Gloria in Excelsis Deo" segueing into "the Van Morrison version." Smith's earlier part has an opening line that few of the punk poets would ever match: "Jesus died for somebody's sins but not mine." You can correctly infer from this that the singer has no plans to return the eponymous heroine to her roots in Catholic doxology.

In Smith's "Gloria," the singer goes to a party where, bored, she looks outside and espies a sweet young thing "Humpin' on the parking meter, leanin' on the parking meter." Smith is transfixed by this sight, but it appears to be Gloria, not her, who is put under a spell: "Here she comes / Crawlin' up my stair." Smith will "take the big plunge," afterward insisting, "and I'm gonna tell the world that I just ah-ah made her mine." Even when, later in the song, Smith is on stage in a stadium with 20,000 girls screaming their names at her, there is only one she wants to remember.

From foreplay to climax, once Gloria got to the singer's room, Van Morrison and Them could make it last twenty minutes; Jim Morrison and The Doors would take half that time but be more explicit. Yet people dismiss the song as pop *reductio ad absurdum*. It just goes to show: the men don't know, but the little girls understand. **DH**

Tangled Up in Blue
Bob Dylan (1975)

Writer | Bob Dylan
Producer | Bob Dylan
Label | Columbia
Album | *Blood on the Tracks* (1975)

If there were an award for heartbreaking albums, then Bob Dylan's *Blood on the Tracks* would have racked up a whole shelf. Though Dylan has said that the songs are inspired by Chekhov's short stories, the timing coincided with the breakdown of his marriage to Sara Lowndes; the couple's son, Jakob, has said that listening to the album, to him, sounds like hearing his parents talking.

"Tangled Up in Blue," the album's opening song, sets the tone. The lyrics track the course of a relationship, but from scattered viewpoints—a songwriting style that grew from Dylan's fascination with Cubism: "There's a code in the lyrics, and there's also no sense of time," he revealed in 1978. "There's no respect for it. You've got yesterday, today, and tomorrow all in the same room, and there's very little you can't imagine not happening."

The song, then, becomes a collage of shards; potent images such as the side of a woman's face in the spotlight at a topless bar, or the book of poetry she later shows him, its lines glowing off the page. Emotionally, it creates a seesaw effect: they're together, they're apart, they're together, and so on. Musically, this same motion is reflected in chords that pull apart and then resolve. Dylan has restructured the lyrics of this nuanced song in his live performances. Once, he even introduced the song by saying that "Tangled Up in Blue" took him ten years to live and two years to write. **SH**

Walk This Way
Aerosmith (1975)

Writer | Steven Tyler, Joe Perry
Producer | Jack Douglas
Label | Columbia
Album | *Toys in the Attic* (1975)

"Let's try to write something funky so we don't have to cover James Brown," suggested guitarist Joe Perry to his bandmates. For their third album, Aerosmith were keen to expand beyond their Stones and Yardbirds foundations. Perry, under the influence of New Orleans funkateers The Meters, devised a riff, and "added it to another one I came up with while watching a *Godzilla* movie."

The lyrics came less easily to singer Steven Tyler. His bandmates eased their frustration with an outing to see Mel Brooks's *Young Frankenstein*. "There's a part in the movie," recalled bassist Tom Hamilton, "where Igor says, 'Walk this way,' and the other guy walks the same way with the same hump and everything. We thought it was the funniest thing we'd ever seen. . . . So we told Steven, the name of this song has got to be 'Walk This Way,' and he took it from there."

A belated U.S. hit in 1976, the song was resurrected a decade later by Run-DMC, who invited Tyler and Perry to guest on the recording. The subsequent hit revived Aerosmith's career and paved the way for rock 'n' rap unions. The song has become a cornerstone of Aerosmith's shows, notably their 2001 Super Bowl performance with Britney Spears. "Tyler wasn't able to persuade Spears to take the 'Ain't seen nothin' till you're down on the muffin' line," lamented *Rolling Stone*. "Sighed Tyler, 'She wasn't having *any* of it.'" **BM**

Steven Tyler in the 1970s; the scarf-bedecked mic stand was apparently his own invention. ➜

Wish You Were Here
Pink Floyd (1975)

Writer | David Gilmour, Roger Waters
Producer | Pink Floyd
Label | Harvest
Album | *Wish You Were Here* (1975)

An album about anxiety brought fame and fortune to Pink Floyd. Fittingly, therefore, they had trouble following *Dark Side of the Moon.* "The only way I could retain interest in the project," remembered leader Roger Waters, "was to try to make the album relate to what was going on there and then, i.e., the fact that no one was really looking each other in the eye, and that it was all very mechanical."

From this frustration emerged the title track. As cynical in its way as the accompanying "Welcome to the Machine" and "Have a Cigar," "Wish You Were Here" was redeemed by Waters's evocative poetry—"Two lost souls swimming in a fish bowl"—and David Gilmour's heartbreaking guitar parts. The requisite Floydian trickiness consisted of a snippet of Tchaikovsky's Fourth Symphony, followed by a segment designed to sound like—in Gilmour's words—"one person sitting in the room playing guitar along with the radio."

The song became a favorite at latter-day Floyd and solo shows; notably when Rick Wright's piano added to its pastoral charms, such as on Gilmour's *Live in Gdańsk,* issued just after the keyboardist's death in 2008. Its most poignant performance came when the estranged Waters and Gilmour reunited with Wright and drummer Nick Mason for Live8 in 2005. Waters dedicated the song to the band's founder, Syd Barrett, displaying the spark of humanity that powers the Floyd machine. **BM**

Time of the Preacher
Willie Nelson (1975)

Writer | Willie Nelson
Producer | Willie Nelson
Label | Columbia
Album | *Red Headed Stranger* (1975)

"Time of the Preacher" is one of those songs that have two wildly different lives. For some, it is the laconic and chilling tune that opens Willie Nelson's unsurpassed country concept album, *Red Headed Stranger,* and then reappears throughout as a narrative theme. For others, it is the song that underscores an unforgettable scene in the classic British TV drama *Edge of Darkness.* Such is the power of a great song—somebody else can take it and give it a second life beyond anything the writer could ever possibly have imagined.

Nelson himself would probably love this juxtaposition. A country songwriter from the genre's rebel liberal fringe, he had written a series of hit songs for Nashville professionals—most notably "Crazy" for Patsy Cline—before striking out his own. In the Seventies, he moved to Austin, Texas, and fomented the Outlaw Country movement. He'd already scored some hits, but nothing to match *Red Headed Stranger,* an album about a preacher who kills his wife and lover. This beautiful, distinctively poetic album somehow managed to sell several million copies, and "Time of the Preacher" epitomizes the album's subtle yet confident qualities. That's largely thanks to Nelson's singular voice, plaintive but determined as he croons the story of the man who "cried like a baby / Screamed like a panther in the middle of the night" after his love left him. **PW**

Rimmel

Francesco De Gregori (1975)

Writer | Francesco De Gregori
Producer | Francesco De Gregori
Label | RCA Italia
Album | *Rimmel* (1975)

"Rimmel" (a word for mascara in Italy) is the song that has probably become most strongly identified with singer-songwriter Francesco De Gregori. It demonstrates the typical characteristics of the popular Roman singer: hermetic lyrics and clear echoes of the American folk-rock music that influenced him, in particular Bob Dylan, James Taylor, and Neil Young.

The song "Rimmel" appears on the album of the same name, which was one of the biggest-selling LPs in Italy in the Seventies. De Gregori's first two—acoustic-guitar-driven—albums had passed relatively unnoticed, but "Rimmel" marked an important change in direction and fortunes for the musician. His lyrics had previously reflected his left-wing political sensibilities, but on "Rimmel," De Gregori—who is commonly known in his native country as "Il principe poeta" (The Poet Prince)—switched his focus to love songs, adding keyboards, drums, bass, and backing vocals to his spare acoustic sound.

With its elegant piano melody and unusual poetic imagery, "Rimmel" is the singer's bittersweet farewell to an ex-lover. It became De Gregori's signature song and, along with at least half of the songs on the album (including "Pezzi di vetro" and "Buonanotte fiorellini"), became part of his greatest hits canon, turning the Poet Prince into a pop superstar. **LSc**

Born to Be with You

Dion (1975)

Writer | Don Robertson
Producer | Phil Spector
Label | Phil Spector Records
Album | *Born to Be with You* (1975)

Recent veneration of "Born to Be with You" and its Phil Spector–produced parent album has perplexed Dion DiMucci. Bobby Gillespie of Primal Scream and Jason Pierce of Spiritualized have been effusive in their praise of this quietly influential record, but its singer always considered it a failure. "It was basically Phil's album," Dion sighed in 1976. "I thought there was a place we could meet musically, and there really wasn't." Admittedly, it was a commercial blot—not even released in Dion's native United States, it made little impact on the U.K. market—but the sonic glory and confessional candor of the project has reached far beyond sales performance.

The song had been a U.S. Top Five and U.K. Top Ten hit in 1956 for The Chordettes. Puzzlingly, it had also been covered in 1973 by British rock 'n' roll revivalist Dave Edmunds, who cloaked his version in a Spector-patented "wall of sound," spurring the producer to triumph at his own game.

Given the pick of any artist on the Elektra label, Spector chose to work with former teen idol and reformed junkie Dion, and their take on "Born to Be with You" is dense, foggy, and powerful. Buffeted by blasts from Wrecking Crew saxophonist Nino Tempo, and underscored by pizzicato strings and listing slide guitar, Dion's vocals (apparently only "sketched") carry the song, bringing careworn grace to Spector's soupy cavalcade. **MH**

Musica ribelle | Eugenio Finardi (1975)

Writer | Eugenio Finardi
Producer | Paolo Tofani
Label | Cramps
Album | *Sugo* (1976)

"Actually, 'Musica ribelle' was not about pure rage; it was a lucid attempt to suggest an originally Italian way to rock."
Eugenio Finardi, 2009

◀ **Influenced by: Mysterious Traveller** · Weather Report (1974)
▶ **Influence on: Extraterrestre** · Eugenio Finardi (1978)
● **Covered by:** Luca Carboni (2009)
★ **Other key tracks:** Amore Diverso (1983) · Le ragazze di Osaka (1983) · La forza dell'amore (1990)

When "Musica ribelle" (Rebel Music) was released by the newly created independent label Cramps in 1975, it was like a stone hitting the stagnant pond of Italian pop music. It was the first true Italian rock song to become a big hit, helped by the B-side, "La radio," a jingle written for Italy's first independent radio station. It became a generational anthem.

Eugenio Finardi, half American on his mother's side, had been singing rock blues in the Milan underground scene for years with friends such as the legendary Demetrio Stratos, but the highly charged social and political atmosphere of the time made him want to contribute to the struggle with his songs. He wanted a sound that had the energy and rebelliousness of British-American rock but was rooted in Italian musical tradition. The result was original and exciting: electric mandolins played through 200-watt Marshall amps, frantic drums louder than the vocal, and wild guitar solos in major keys. The album *Sugo* soon hit the charts, its success largely attributable to its urgency, anger, and political commitment.

The lyrics of "Musica ribelle" capture Finardi's feeling that people were coming together and rising against the system. He sings urgently, "There is something in the air that you just can't ignore / ... / It's a growing wave that follows wherever you go / It's music, rebel music."

"Musica ribelle" was recorded live in one take on the first day of sessions for the album *Sugo*. Finardi sang and played acoustic guitar, Lucio Fabbri piano and violin, and much of the energy of the song came from interplay between Hugh Bullen on bass and Walter Calloni on drums. Together they created an irresistible texture and a truly original sound that has dated very little. **LSc**

Born to Run | Bruce Springsteen (1975)

Writer | Bruce Springsteen
Producer | Bruce Springsteen, Mike Appel
Label | Columbia
Album | *Born to Run* (1975)

"New Jersey became a romantic, mythologized scene of neon light, fast cars, and the shore bars."
Jon Bon Jovi, 1995

◀ **Influenced by:** Da Doo Ron Ron • The Crystals (1963)
▶ **Influence on:** Stuck Between Stations • The Hold Steady (2006)
● **Covered by:** Frankie Goes to Hollywood (1984) • Suzi Quatro (1995) • Joey Tempest (1998) • The Hollies (1999) Melissa Etheridge (2001) • Ray Wilson (2002)

"The words 'born to run' just came to me in bed," claimed Bruce Springsteen. "They suggested a cinematic drama that would work with the music I heard in my head." The Boss's head was full of dreams when the song became the first recorded, in 1974, for his third album. That collection was originally envisaged as a concept affair, with song titles mooted before even a note was written— "Born to Run" itself was previously known as "Wild Angels" or "That Angel."

Springsteen labored at length on the song—"A twenty-four-year-old kid aimin' at the greatest rock 'n' roll record ever," he later drily observed of the process. Fan magazine *Backstreets* reported: "At least four different mixes are known to exist that include strings [and] a female chorus." The lyrics, too, underwent multiple revisions, from an early emphasis on "the American night" and specific New Jersey references, to cameos by James Dean and Elvis Presley.

The song debuted in Springsteen's shows more than a year before its release. A review of one from future manager Jon Landau led to his famous quote: "I saw rock 'n' roll's future and its name is Bruce Springsteen." The song was even recorded—albeit not released—by Hollies singer Allan Clarke before the Boss's version came out.

When "Born to Run" was eventually released, in August 1975, it was as if the famous Spector "wall of sound" had been rebuilt. "He definitely made a concerted effort to write a Phil Spector record," confirmed Springsteen's then-manager and co-producer, Mike Appel. The rousing song finally brought the Boss mainstream popularity and, like Spector's work, helped form the foundations of future rock 'n' roll. **BM**

Leb' Wohl
NEU! (1975)

Writer | Klaus Dinger, Michael Rother
Producer | Conny Plank
Label | Brain
Album | *NEU! '75* (1975)

Formed in 1971 after guitarist Michael Rother and drummer Klaus Dinger absconded from an early incarnation of Kraftwerk, NEU! started their career by inventing one of the most influential drumming styles ever—the driving beat dubbed *motorik*. "Hallogallo," the first track on their first LP (*NEU!*, 1972) not only introduced this superminimal rhythm but laid out NEU!'s formula with crystal clarity: Rother as the serene dreamer, teasing away at a golden E-major chord, and Dinger as the primal, primitive force, thrashing away at his kit until blood flecked the cymbals.

For two albums, NEU! made music out of this fire-and-ice synthesis, but by 1973, the pair's differences had led to a temporary hiatus. In 1975, though, they reconvened at krautrock producer Conny Plank's studio for their climactic, schizophrenic masterpiece: *NEU! '75*. The album peaks with "Leb' Wohl," a nine-minute track nothing like anything they had ever done before. The title meant "Farewell," and this was NEU! at their most wistful, commencing with crashing waves and a distant storm of minimalist piano and building into a tranquil elegy of keys and hushed, echo-soaked vocals.

As the title suggested, that was it for NEU!, and they split again. Hugely influential, they have since been hailed by figures ranging from David Bowie to Noel Gallagher. **LP**

Legalize It
Peter Tosh (1975)

Writer | Peter Tosh
Producer | Peter Tosh, Lee Jaffe
Label | Intel-Diplo HIM
Album | *Legalize It* (1976)

The title track off the ex-Wailer's debut album, "Legalize It" was banned when released in Jamaica in 1975. Attempts to suppress it, however, proved futile, and the track became the hit of the year, catapulting Jamaica's "Bushdoctor" to international fame.

"Herb will become like cigarettes," Peter Tosh predicted in an *NME* interview in 1978. While its pro-ganja lyrics and pot-smoking cover pose—and mythical marijuana-scented sticker—may have promoted sales, this upbeat ballad is more than just a stoner's party anthem. Deep and authoritative, Tosh, backed by an infectious melody courtesy of The Wailers' instrumental quintet, demands: "Legalize it and I will advertise it," while two of the I-Threes (Rita Marley and Judy Mowatt) coo in agreement. His upbeat attack and lyrical provocations about marijuana's medicinal use belie his sincere concern for political issues.

Written in response to his ongoing victimization at the hands of the Jamaican police, "Legalize It" is, at heart, a pro-Rastafarian hymn that celebrates marijuana as a sacrament within the religion. "Herb? Vegetables? We are the victims of Ras clot circumstances. Victimization, colonialism, gonna lead to bloodbath," explained Tosh in *Reggae Bloodlines* (1977). Words that proved tragically prophetic in the light of his violent death, allegedly at the hands of drug dealers, in 1987. **MK**

Don't fear the reefer: Peter Tosh with avian acquaintance. ➜

(Don't Fear) The Reaper
Blue Öyster Cult (1976)

Writer | Donald Roeser
Producer | David Lucas, Murray Krugman, Sandy Pearlman
Label | Columbia
Album | *Agents of Fortune* (1976)

A haunting moment that contrasted with the heavier fare of their catalog, "(Don't Fear) The Reaper" earned Blue Öyster Cult their breakthrough to mainstream success a full nine years after the group formed, and helped parent album *Agents of Fortune* become their first platinum release.

While the group had previously enrolled the likes of rock critic Richard Meltzer and sci-fi author Michael Moorcock to help pen their lyrics, "(Don't Fear) The Reaper" was written by guitarist Donald "Buck Dharma" Roeser and inspired by a bout of heart trouble, during which Roeser feared he might die. There's a certain morbid air to the song's tale of a dead boy coming back to find his girlfriend has waited for him—the lyrics allude to Romeo and Juliet, "Together in eternity"—which was later interpreted by some listeners as a paean to suicide. This interpretation horrified Dharma, who admitted in 1995 that "some people were seeing it as an advertisement for suicide or something, but that was not my intention at all." This dark lyrical undertow is a perfect balance for the song's sweetly sad melody and the haunted Byrdsian harmonies, though. With a prog-rock, mid-song instrumental break excised from the album version, the track became a smash hit—it was voted Best Rock Single of 1976 by *Rolling Stone*—and a much-loved rock classic. **SC**

More Than a Feeling
Boston (1976)

Writer | Tom Scholz
Producer | John Boylan, Tom Scholz
Label | Epic
Album | *Boston* (1976)

Boston were signed to Epic in 1975 on the strength of a demo made by Tom Scholz at his home studio. After six years of trying to break into the music business, the demo, with its lead song, "More Than a Feeling," saw multi-instrumentalist Scholz and singer Brad Delp realize their dream.

"More than a Feeling" is bold, exciting, and brief. It is also remarkable as everything on it, apart from Sib Hashian's drumming, is played by Scholz—the charging rhythm guitar, the searing solos, the acoustic breakdowns. However, it is Delp's impassioned vocals that make Scholz's words so poignant. Taking a routine subject matter—how music can uplift you—they make dreaming of "a girl he used to know" seem rich and meaningful. (The record indirectly referred to in the song has been cited as either "Louie Louie" by The Kingsmen or "Walk Away Renée" by The Left Banke.) In the days before a click of a computer mouse would have brought her back to life, the vision of this long-lost love is forever linked to this tune.

The song is ubiquitous (it is one of the most popular songs ever on the video game *Guitar Hero*) but still, in some ways, underrated. Its message of losing yourself in music has made it something of a slacker anthem, reinforced by Kurt Cobain's referencing its riff on "Smells Like Teen Spirit." Ironic, as Scholz had done something similar for "More than a Feeling." **DE**

Blue Öyster Cult's Eric Bloom enjoys some fretboard-on-fretboard action in a 1970s performance.

Sir Duke
Stevie Wonder (1976)

Writer | Stevie Wonder
Producer | Stevie Wonder
Label | Motown
Album | *Songs in the Key of Life* (1976)

Written as a tribute to bandleader and composer Duke Ellington, who had died in 1974, "Sir Duke" was one of several songs Wonder wrote in homage to his musical heroes: the album *Tribute to Uncle Ray* (1962) was a nod to Ray Charles; "Bye Bye World" (1968) and "We All Remember Wes" were paeans to guitarist Wes Montgomery. As well as Ellington, Wonder name-checks other giants of the swing-band era in "Sir Duke"—bandleaders Count Basie and Glenn Miller, trumpeter and singer Louis "Satchmo" Armstrong, and singer Ella Fitzgerald.

"Sir Duke" kicks off with a distinctive brass intro that gives little preparation for the funky groove that will follow. The horns—two trumpets and alto and tenor sax—return to punctuate the verse, underlining the words "But just because a record has a groove / Don't make it in the groove." It is the mightily swinging instrumental interlude that provides the hook of the song, though, and makes the connection with the "Duke" of the title.

First appearing on his best-selling album *Songs in the Key of Life* in 1976, "Sir Duke" was released as a single in 1977, following the chart-topping success of "I Wish" from the same album. It too reached No. 1 in both pop and R&B charts in the States, getting to No. 2 in the U.K. singles chart. The album, and the two hit singles that it spawned, marked the climax—and the end—of what is considered Wonder's "classic period." **MW**

The Killing of Georgie
(Parts I & II) | Rod Stewart (1976)

Writer | Rod Stewart
Producer | Tom Dowd
Label | Warner Bros.
Album | *A Night on the Town* (1976)

Rod Stewart had enjoyed a pivotal year in 1975, moving to the United States and finally bidding farewell to his cheeky rocker persona—and his band, The Faces. Recording the knowingly titled *Atlantic Crossing* with soul producer Tom Dowd, Stewart moved into the next phase of his career, filing down his edges and courting a mainstream audience. Dividends were swift, with "Sailing," but many felt something had been lost.

Dowd was still in place for *A Night on the Town* and so was the crowd-pleasing soft-soul sheen. Against this backdrop, "The Killing of Georgie (Parts I & II)" stood out all the more. Reputedly a true story about a gay man from Denver who, disowned by his family, took to shadowing The Faces at their New York gigs, the song takes a thorny and progressive subject and treats it to the kind of careworn folk-soul rendering familiar from Bob Dylan's *Blood on the Tracks* (1975). Although Georgie's murder is not specifically related to his homosexuality, the song still demands considerable sensitivity, and Stewart avoids triteness and moralizing with poignancy, aplomb, and a heart-wrenching melody.

The melody in the coda masquerading as Part II appears to draw on The Beatles' "Don't Let Me Down," another welcome sign that Stewart could still exercise an emotional pull even as his muse appeared to be deserting him. **MH**

Rod Stewart performs in Los Angeles in 1975, the year The Faces went their separate ways. ➔

Dancing Queen | Abba (1976)

Writer | Benny Andersson, Björn Ulvaeus, Stig Anderson
Producer | Benny Andersson, Björn Ulvaeus
Label | Polar
Album | *Arrival* (1976)

"I loved it from the very beginning when Benny brought home the backing track.... It was so beautiful I started to cry."

Anni-Frid "Frida" Lyngstad, 1994

◄ **Influenced by: Rock Your Baby** · George McCrae (1974)
► **Influence on: Love to Hate You** · Erasure (1991)
● **Covered by:** Garageland (1995) · Kylie Minogue (1998) S Club 7 (1999) · CoCo Lee (1999) · Sixpence None the Richer (1999) · The Ten Tenors (2006)

From The Rolling Stones' "Satisfaction" to Nirvana's "Smells Like Teen Spirit," there's no lack of identifiable rock anthems. But what about the *pop* epic? Survey random wedding receptions, karaoke bars, and pre-"tweens" slumber parties, and Abba's "Dancing Queen" is likely to land at the top of most shortlists.

By 1976, Abba (couples Björn Ulvaeus and Agnetha Fältskog, and Benny Andersson and Anni-Frid "Frida" Lyngstad) had already established themselves with chart successes such as "Waterloo," "S.O.S.," and "Fernando." However, "Dancing Queen," released late that year, would net them their first and only No. 1 in the United States (it reached the top spot in thirteen other countries worldwide) and across much of Europe. Fältskog has admitted in a television interview that "it's often difficult to know what will be a hit. The exception was 'Dancing Queen.' We all knew it was going to be massive."

The track has all the components necessary for pop immortality: cheerfully defiant upper-range piano chords, sprightly disco strings, and sweetly blended vocals from Lyngstad and Fältskog. Always planned as a dance number, the song was originally going to be titled "Boogaloo," and its backbeat was inspired by the rhythm of George McCrae's disco classic, "Rock Your Baby," from 1974.

"Dancing Queen" lived up to its regal name in two different eras. It was performed in Stockholm as part of a televised concert event on the eve of King Carl XVI Gustav of Sweden's wedding, in June 1976. In the same city almost exactly sixteen years later, modern rock royalty U2 performed "Dancing Queen" in concert, with Andersson guesting on keyboards and Ulvaeus on acoustic guitar. **YK**

Blitzkrieg Bop | Ramones (1976)

Writer | Dee Dee Ramone, Johnny Ramone, Tommy Ramone, Joey Ramone
Producer | Craig Leon
Label | Sire
Album | *Ramones* (1976)

"I like to play punk rock—and that's it."

Joey Ramone, 1985

Influenced by: Saturday Night · Bay City Rollers (1976)
Influence on: St. Jimmy · Green Day (2004)
Covered by: Screeching Weasel (1992) · Yo La Tengo (1996) · Poison Idea (1996) · The Kids (2002) · Rob Zombie (2003) · Joe Strummer & The Mescaleros (2001) The Beautiful South (2004)

Surely any similarities between leather-clad New York punk trailblazers the Ramones and Scottish pop puppets the Bay City Rollers start and end with both being all-male bands formed in the Seventies who have sibling membership (although this was, of course, imaginary in the case of the Ramones)? According to front man Joey Ramone, however, the parallels extended beyond that.

"I hate to blow the mystique," he said, "but, at the time, we really liked bubblegum music and we really liked the Bay City Rollers. Their song 'Saturday Night' [a U.S. No. 1 in early 1976] had a great chant in it, so we wanted a song with a chant in it. . . . 'Blitzkrieg Bop' was our 'Saturday Night.'" Delivering on both its title and the exhortation of the "Hey ho, let's go" intro, it set the Ramones' template: frantic, funny, and thrilling. It wasn't for six long months—until The Damned's "New Rose"—that punks in the United Kingdom began to get what was going on.

As with the rest of the band's debut album, "Blitzkrieg Bop" is credited to the whole group, but the song was really drummer Tommy Ramone's baby, save for a couple of suggestions from bassist Dee Dee Ramone (including a renaming from "Animal Hop" to reference blitzkrieg [lightning war], Hitler's tactic of overcoming opposition by the use of overwhelming force).

Tommy summed up the outfit's musical manifesto in the same year that "Blitzkrieg Bop" was unleashed: "Rock 'n' roll, man, just rock 'n' roll. The way it should be—entertaining, a lot of fun, sexy, dynamic, exciting." The Ramones might not have aimed to change the world, but their overwhelming force on the dance floor made you forget about it for a while. **CB**

Love Hangover
Diana Ross (1976)

Writer | Marilyn McLeod, Pamela Sawyer
Producer | Hal Davis
Label | Motown
Album | *Diana Ross* (1976)

The favored protégée of her label boss (and sometime lover), Berry Gordy, Diana Ross was the brightest star of Motown's firmament in the Sixties. As the Seventies dawned, Ross redefined herself as a solo balladeer expertly blending sentimentality and sophistication, but as the decade wore on, she found herself edged off the dance floor by a coming wave of disco divas, in particular Donna Summer, who'd won fame with her sensual epic, "Love to Love You Baby," in 1975.

"Love Hangover" would be Ross's response to these newcomers, but, distrustful of disco, Motown was initially reluctant to assign the song—which had just been recorded by labelmates The Fifth Dimension—to Ross. The singer echoed her label's reservations, but producer Hal Davis prevailed, assuaging the diva's anxieties by creating a party ambience in the studio, dressing the room with colored lights and a disco strobe.

Ross loosened up with several shots of Rémy Martin, which she shared with the musicians, her breathy postcoital purr announcing a raunchiness absent from her previous recordings. The mid-song tempo shift into a restless but graceful disco groove, meanwhile, assuredly returned Diana to the dance floor, thanks not least to an opulent eleven-minute remix on the twelve-inch, extending the song's ecstatic coda and offering more of Ross's sultry, improvised love coos. **SC**

Cokane in My Brain
Dillinger (1976)

Writer | Lester Bullock
Producer | Jo Jo Hookim
Label | Black Swan/Island
Album | *C.B.200* (1976)

How do you spell New York? Never mind spelling out the letters—in his funky, proto-rap hit, reggae DJ Dillinger spelled it out with the elliptical lyrics "A knife, a fork, a bottle, and a cork." There are many theories as to whether the song's ambiguous lyrics are pro- or anti-drugs, or if they are about the increasing embourgeoisement of American soul music—cheekily pointed up by the replication of the bass line to The People's Choice's disco hit "Do It Any Way You Wanna"—and the prevalence of cocaine on the scene: "No matter where I treat my guest / You see they always like my kitchen best."

The song was initially released as a limited edition in Jamaica on an Island Records imprint, Black Swan, and when sold internationally the following year, it became an underground hit, making it to No. 1 in the Netherlands. Dillinger was also particularly appreciated in the United Kingdom, where punks took him to their hearts, with The Clash name-checking him in their classic "(White Man) in Hammersmith Palais."

The song was a huge hit for Dillinger, and one that he found it hard to move past. In 1977, he released "Marijuana in My Brain," followed by "LSD in My Brain" (1983). Neither reached the heights of their progenitor, which still exerts its pull on popular culture. It was arguably a big influence on the U.S. hip-hop scene and has been remixed in acid-house and drum-and-bass versions. **DC**

Diana Ross, seen here in 1977, took her "Love Hangover" to the dance floor.

Police and Thieves
Junior Murvin (1976)

Writer | Junior Murvin, Lee Perry
Producer | Lee Perry
Label | Island
Album | *Police and Thieves* (1976)

In the mid-Seventies, an escalation of ideologically motivated gang warfare led Jamaican prime minister Michael Manley to place the island "under heavy manners"—in effect, martial law. The country's political and music scenes were closely linked, and many reggae songwriters, from Prince Far I to Leroy Smart, were quick to voice their own take on Jamaica's seeming slide into anarchy.

Helium-voiced singer Murvin Smith Jr. busked his own plea for an end to the violence, "Police and Thieves," while sitting on the porch of the Black Ark, the revolutionary studio in the backyard of Lee Perry's home. In these primitive facilities, the producer had built up a huge backlog of rhythm tracks, using little more than an outmoded four-track console and an Echoplex reverb unit to create his distinctive underwater sound. Swimming with psychedelic phasing, squelching guitar, and a sibilant high-hat, it encapsulated the sheer insanity of the times and seemed tailored to Murvin's plaintive, Curtis Mayfield–inspired falsetto.

In the United Kingdom, "Police and Thieves" became an anthem in 1976 just as the Caribbean carnival in Notting Hill erupted into a full-blown riot. Among the revelers caught up in the fracas were Joe Strummer and Paul Simonon of The Clash, who were inspired to cover the song on their first album—in a style that was, they insisted, "punk reggae," not "white reggae." **SP**

(I'm) Stranded
The Saints (1976)

Writer | Ed Kuepper, Chris Bailey
Producer | The Saints
Label | Fatal
Album | *(I'm) Stranded* (1977)

Formed in Brisbane, Australia, in 1974, The Saints were contemporaries of the Ramones and the Sex Pistols—though blissfully ignorant that these bands were in gestation. The Australian four-piece shared with both those bands a passion for The Stooges, along with a contempt for mainstream rock. Forming their own label, they issued "(I'm) Stranded," a howl of rage against boredom and oppression—Seventies Queensland (the state of which Brisbane is capital) was being run by a corrupt, racist government and brutal police force. The buzz-saw guitar and vocal wail of "(I'm) Stranded" was a rallying cry for Australian punk. Copies of the single were sent to U.K. music papers, one of which, *Sounds*, made it Single of the Week ("and every other week"). This led to EMI—the label that would drop the Sex Pistols in 1977—signing The Saints and bringing them to London.

If The Saints played aggressively, they didn't play "punk"—no ripped jeans and spiky hair for them. This led many in the British media, who had embraced punk as a fashion movement, to reject the band. The Saints expanded their sound further than pretty much any other punk band, bringing in horns and acoustic guitars; their literate, paranoid songs were streets ahead of what British bands were then trying to do. Their music influenced many others, with everyone from Henry Rollins to Nick Cave citing them as an inspiration. **GC**

Hotel California
Eagles (1976)

Writer | Don Felder, Glenn Frey, Don Henley
Producer | Bill Szymczyk
Label | Asylum
Album | *Hotel California* (1976)

Few songs have had their lyrics dissected as much as this brooding classic. "A song about the dark underbelly of the American dream" was how the band's drummer and vocalist, Don Henley, put it. Although the self-destruction and hedonism rife in the Los Angeles music scene appear to be the underlying theme, Henley also had a more personal take on the subject matter of "Hotel California." He dismissed the notion that specific girlfriends featured regularly in the lyrics to many Eagles songs. Having said that, "Some of the more derogatory parts of 'Hotel California,' however, are definitely about Loree Rodkin: 'Her mind is Tiffany-twisted, she got the Mercedes bends / She got a lot of pretty, pretty boys that she calls friends.' That's about her, and I wouldn't be crowing if I were Ms. Rodkin," Henley stated, after his long-term relationship with the Chicago-born socialite had ended.

While Frey and Henley took care of most of the song's lyrics, Don Felder's guitar dueling with the band's relatively new recruit, Joe Walsh, was an equally important part of the single's success. It stretched the release time to six minutes and thirty-one seconds, a length that almost denied it a release by label bosses, who felt it was overlong for radio play. The band stood firm and persuaded Asylum to go with it: a decision fully vindicated by the single's U.S. No.1 and U.K. No. 8 chart peaks. **DR**

Roadrunner
The Modern Lovers (1976)

Writer | Jonathan Richman
Producer | John Cale
Label | Beserkley
Album | *The Modern Lovers* (1976)

From Bobby Troup's much-covered "(Get Your Kicks on) Route 66" to Springsteen's "Born to Run," most driving songs are concerned with the possibility of escape. By contrast, "Roadrunner" concerns itself with a road to nowhere: Route 128, a sixty-mile (96-km) ring road separating Boston from its suburbs. It's not so much a road that only a local could love as one that only a local would notice. Jonathan Richman was born and raised a ten-minute drive away.

Richman left Boston for New York as a teenager in the late Sixties, reputedly in search of The Velvet Underground. He headed home again soon after, but connected with his heroes in 1972, when The Modern Lovers, the band he'd formed on his return, recorded some demos under the watch of former Velvet John Cale. Among them was "Roadrunner," a two-chord, four-minute homage to driving around at night "going faster miles an hour." Richman went on to cut a bewildering number of versions, but it's this pulsating, all-electric, Cale-produced original that's both the best and, today, the best known.

When, in 1977, a different recording of "Roadrunner" was followed into the U.K. charts by a quixotic instrumental called "Egyptian Reggae," Richman briefly joined the mainstream, but this anti-rock, lo-fi artist showed little interest in remaining a part of it. **WF-J**

American Girl | Tom Petty
& The Heartbreakers (1976)

Writer | Tom Petty
Producer | Denny Cordell
Label | Shelter
Album | *Tom Petty & The Hearbreakers* (1976)

Just as its sound has been co-opted by countless bands over the years, the lyrics to "American Girl" have invited endless explanations. The most popular myth spun around the song is that it was written about the real-life suicide of a female student at University of Florida. Petty dismisses the story outright as urban legend. The girl is a composite: "a character who yearned for more than life had dealt her."

The real inspirations behind the song (cut, appropriately, on July 4, American Independence Day) are subtler and rather more poetic. That line about waves crashing on the sea? Petty was living in Encino, California, when he wrote the song: "I was right by the freeway. And the cars would go by. And I remember thinking that that sounded like the ocean to me."

Roger McGuinn of The Byrds quickly picked up on the way that Petty himself had picked up on The Byrds' sound, recording his own version of the song shortly afterward. (On first hearing the song, McGuinn reportedly remarked to his manager that he didn't recall writing it.) Likewise, Petty is unperturbed by the similarity of "American Girl" to The Strokes' "Last Nite." As he recently told *Rolling Stone*, "The Strokes took 'American Girl,' and I saw an interview with them where they actually admitted it. That made me laugh out loud. I was like, 'OK, good for you.'" **SH**

Detroit Rock City
Kiss (1976)

Writer | Paul Stanley, Bob Ezrin
Producer | Bob Ezrin
Label | Casablanca
Album | *Destroyer* (1976)

"It's quintessential Kiss . . ." declared producer Bob Ezrin. "From the sort of cocky attitude, to the storytelling, to the really balls-out playing." The explosive "Detroit Rock City" certainly packs a lot into five minutes. In its original incarnation, on the album *Destroyer*, the song opens with a theatrical montage assembled by Ezrin (who plays the part of a news reporter) and engineer Corky Stasiak. There's even a snippet of Kiss's hit from 1975, "Rock and Roll All Nite." Then a rumbling riff, revived from their vintage live number "Acrobat," introduces singer Paul Stanley's lyrical tale—inspired by a fan's fatal car accident, en route to see Kiss, in North Carolina in April 1975.

The drama is complemented by Gene Simmons's Curtis Mayfield–influenced bass line, Peter Criss's finest drumming, and Ace Frehley's flamenco-inflected guitar solo. The latter was written by Ezrin as "my take on gladiator music." "We thought he was on crack when he suggested it," Simmons admitted. Ezrin also doubled the song's power chords with a piano—an idea that reached fruition when Kiss played it with a symphony orchestra in 2003.

"Detroit Rock City" flopped as a single—its B-side, "Beth," hit the chart instead—but became a perennial live favorite. It even bequeathed its title to a 1999 movie, for which the original lineup re-recorded the song. **BM**

Kiss this: from left, Gene Simmons, Paul Stanley, and Ace Frehley in 1976. ➡

Young Hearts Run Free
Candi Staton (1976)

Writer | Dave Crawford
Producer | Dave Crawford
Label | Tamla Motown
Album | *Young Hearts Run Free* (1976)

By the time Candi Staton came to record "Young Hearts Run Free," she was already a seasoned performer, having garnered Grammy nominations for her highly emotional versions of "Stand by Your Man" and "In the Ghetto."

Written by her producer, Dave Crawford (whose lyrics were inspired by Staton's tales of her marriage to promoter Tyrone Davis), and recorded in Los Angeles, "Young Hearts Run Free" is an almost perfect minidrama. Such a lonely, desperate song has never been dressed up so sweetly. From the ebullient horn introduction onward, its real meaning was frequently missed while being sashayed to on a million dance floors.

"Young Hearts Run Free" is a straightforward plea for women's rights. It is about the desperation of a loveless marriage and a woman trapped by the actions of an artless, philandering man. Although the song is a call for feminism, the protagonist is not strong enough to escape her "duty." But she implores others, most probably her children, not to get themselves into her situation. It is the hope offered by the song that makes it so powerful.

The record (a U.K. No. 2 for Staton) has enjoyed its fair share of covers over the years, but possibly the most poignant is by British folk singer Nancy Wallace. She locates the record's pain, and by stripping it of its disco frippery she makes it clear what a remarkable song it is. **DE**

Chase the Devil
Max Romeo (1976)

Writer | Max Romeo, Lee "Scratch" Perry
Producer | Lee "Scratch" Perry
Label | Island
Album | *War ina Babylon* (1976)

When roots, the spiritual strain of reggae, took off in the mid-Seventies, Max Romeo teamed up with maverick producer Lee "Scratch" Perry to cut some of his finest sincere, gospel-based work, songs brimming with Old Testament blood and fire.

"Chase the Devil," with its first line taken from Isaiah 14:12, casts Romeo as the Archangel Michael, wearing a shirt of iron and driving out Satan. Perry had originally wanted the lyric to be about stringing up the Prince of Darkness, slitting his throat, and setting him on fire, but Romeo, the voice of clemency, persuaded him that it was sufficient to "send him to outer space / To find another race." (This not-in-my-backyard couplet went on to become the basis of The Prodigy's frenetic rave workout "Out of Space" in 1992.)

The recording techniques that Perry used were idiosyncratic—to enhance the sound, he might blow marijuana smoke over the master tapes as they rolled, or bury them in the soil—and the strangeness of the springy backing track reflects his offbeat methods. The Upsetters, Scratch's house band, provide an accomplished rhythm in his favored "one-drop" style—the bass and kick drum hypnotically emphasized on the third beat—distinguished by its ribbiting guiro sound and apocalyptic piano chords. Sparse and unearthly, the sound could almost have been beamed in from another dimension. **SP**

New Rose
The Damned (1976)

Writer | Brian James
Producer | Nick Lowe
Label | Stiff
Album | *Damned Damned Damned* (1977)

Was punk evolution or revolution? The first line of the genre's first single (in the United Kingdom, anyway) seems to provide compelling evidence for the former. Dave Vanian's spoken intro to "New Rose"—"Is she really going out with him?"—immediately establishes a link back to 1964 and "Leader of the Pack" by The Shangri-Las. Throw in Rockpile's Nick Lowe as producer and a cover of The Beatles'"Help!"on the B-side, and punk's position as a musical Year Zero looks less than watertight.

Where many of their contemporaries had one eye on a place in posterity, The Damned lived in the moment. Brian James, who wrote "New Rose" in fifteen minutes flat in his northwest London abode, saw Rat Scabies as "a lunatic in the Keith Moon tradition. [He] drummed like no one else I'd ever played with."The adrenaline surge of Scabies's thunderous opening assault never abates for the track's breathless duration. No surprise, then, that bassist Captain Sensible said that it was recorded "purely on cider and speed,"with Lowe on hand to direct the band to play everything very loud.

Released as a single in October 1976, "New Rose" failed to trouble the U.K. Top Forty, but where the Pistols chose to introduce themselves in relatively obvious terms with "Anarchy in the U.K.," released scant weeks afterwards, it was left to The Damned to remind everyone that there was still room for fun amid the po-faced posturing. **CB**

Anarchy in the U.K.
Sex Pistols (1976)

Writer | Sex Pistols
Producer | Chris Thomas
Label | EMI
Album | *Never Mind the Bollocks Here's the Sex Pistols* (1977)

In the year following their first gig, in November 1975, the Sex Pistols caused constant havoc, starting fights with audience members and getting themselves banned from various venues throughout London. Despite the controversies, or perhaps because of them, EMI signed the Pistols in October 1976, packing them off to the studio to tape their debut single just two days later.

According to *England's Dreaming*, Jon Savage's peerless punk history, the first recording of "Anarchy in the U.K." aimed to capture the chaotic energy of the band's live performances; Glen Matlock suggests it was recorded in two takes. However, when this original version met with a thumbs-down, the group returned to the studio. This time, they took a more measured approach, creating a "wall of sound" that provided a heady backdrop for Lydon's mesmerizing, vicious vocals.

Rushed out in November 1976, "Anarchy in the U.K." may only have had a modest impact were it not for a TV appearance made by the group a few days after its release. When labelmates Queen dropped out of a slot on ITV's *Today* program, EMI drafted the Sex Pistols in to replace them. Goaded to "say something outrageous" by disdainful host Bill Grundy, Steve Jones did just that. Within weeks, Grundy had been suspended and the Pistols had been dropped by EMI, but suddenly punk had caught the limelight. **WF-J**

Poor Poor Pitiful Me
Warren Zevon (1976)

Writer | Warren Zevon
Producer | Jackson Browne
Label | Asylum
Album | *Warren Zevon* (1976)

Rarely had such an illustrious cast been assembled to work on another artist's album as the one that came together for *Warren Zevon*. The singer-songwriter's sophomore release (seven years after his debut) resembled a who's who of Seventies celebs, featuring guest appearances by Phil Everly, Stevie Nicks, Don Henley, and Bonnie Raitt, to name but a few. To top it off, it was produced by Jackson Browne.

This vote of confidence from L.A.'s A-list was a sign these musicians understood something that fans would soon discover: Zevon was a singer-songwriter like no other. He'd illustrate his wicked way with the pen on many of the album's eleven tracks, yet the best summation of Zevon's talent was "Poor Poor Pitiful Me." A musical take on Murphy's Law, "Poor Poor Pitiful Me" told the story of an incredible run of bad luck. With deadpan delivery, Zevon bitched about such unfunny topics as a failed suicide attempt and domestic abuse, and somehow left listeners laughing out loud.

This anthem for the underachiever, while not a hit at the time, proved to be one of Zevon's most lasting and pliable compositions. Linda Ronstadt scored a Top Forty hit in 1978 with a version that tweaked the lyrics to make them fit a female narrator, while Canada's SNFU recorded a punk rendition in 1984 and Terri Clark took the song down a country road in 1996. **JiH**

Underground
The Upsetters (1976)

Writer | Lee "Scratch" Perry
Producer | Lee "Scratch" Perry
Label | Upsetter/Island
Album | *Scratch the Super Ape* (1976)

"I'm an artist, a musician, a magician, a writer, a singer; I'm everything." Lee "Scratch" Perry, reggae producer extraordinaire, in his own words. Or, rather, the man who created rock steady reggae out of ska, helped send Bob Marley's career stratospheric, and was one of the most inventive and prolific pioneers of dub.

At his Black Ark studio in the Seventies, Perry created many classic albums, particularly with songwriters such as Max Romeo and The Congos. Perry told U.K. music journal *New Musical Express* his collaborations were successful because of his approach to producing: "I expect artists to do exactly as I say. I teach them everything; how to play, how to move, everything. I am a dictator!"

Yet one underrated LP was entirely his own unique vision: *Super Ape* by The Upsetters, his house band. There's only a limited amount of vocals on the album, leaving Perry to experiment with creating bewildering dub soundscapes. "Underground" is a highlight of the set, a song that speaks of a certain connection with nature, in this case with "collie weed"—marijuana. The rhythm was originally recorded for a rare dub plate called "From Creation," with guitar pickings turned metallic by being treated with treble and reverb, and hypnotic vocals layered on top.

These sonic visions would live on courtesy of acts like Massive Attack. **DC**

← Warren Zevon in 1978: that same arched eyebrow finds expression in his songs.

God Save the Queen | Sex Pistols (1977)

Writer | S. Jones, G. Matlock, P. Cook, J. Rotten
Producer | Chris Thomas
Label | Virgin
Album | *Never Mind the Bollocks Here's the Sex Pistols* (1977)

"I don't understand it. All we're trying to do is destroy everything."

Johnny Rotten, 1977

◀ **Influenced by:** My Generation • The Who (1965)
▶ **Influence on:** Smells Like Teen Spirit • Nirvana (1991)
● **Covered by:** The Bollock Brothers (1983) • Anthrax (1985) • Quorthon (1997) • Motörhead (2000) • Enrico Ruggeri (2004) • The Enemy (2008) • Nouvelle Vague (2009)

After initially recording "God Save the Queen" for A&M Records earlier in 1977, the Sex Pistols found themselves dropped by the label, having already been dropped from EMI Records following the "Bill Grundy Incident" and the release of their debut single, "Anarchy in the U.K."

Having signed a new deal—at the gates of Buckingham Palace—with Richard Branson's Virgin Records, it was fitting that the release of "God Save the Queen" coincided with the Queen's Jubilee Year. The association of the Queen's reign with fascism, the contention in the lyrics that England had "no future," and Jamie Reid's iconic cover of a defaced portrait of the monarch all ensured that the single caught the public's attention and reinforced the group's notoriety. The song marked the last recording for original Pistols bassist Glen Matlock, who was fired for being "too nice," to be replaced by Sid Vicious.

Banned from the airwaves in the United Kingdom by both the BBC and the Independent Broadcasting Authority, the song was effectively blacklisted. However, the sales of the record pushed it to the No. 1 slot in the *New Musical Express* charts, although the official BBC charts maintained that Rod Stewart held the top spot with "I Don't Want to Talk About It." To launch the single, the band performed on Coronation Day—June 7—aboard a boat on the River Thames, though the party was abandoned when a scuffle broke out and eleven guests were arrested.

There are rumored to be as few as ten copies of the original A&M single, which was given to senior label staff as a "golden handshake." One of the copies that did surface on the open market made more than £12,000 at auction. **CR**

Pistols drawn at a 1977 gig. ➡

Trans-Europe Express | Kraftwerk (1977)

Writer | Ralf Hütter, Emil Schult
Producer | Ralf Hütter, Florian Schneider
Label | Kling Klang
Album | *Trans-Europe Express* (1977)

"Things like 'Trans-Europe Express' came like a train going through the studio. This is the type of music I like best."
Ralf Hütter, 1991

◀ **Influenced by: Bayreuth Return** · Klaus Schulze (1975)
▶ **Influence on: Confusion** · New Order (1983)
● **Covered by:** Señor Coconut y su conjunto (2000)
★ **Other key tracks:** Autobahn (1974) · Radioactivity (1975) · Europe Endless (1977) · Showroom Dummies (1977) · Tour de France (1983)

Kraftwerk's 1974 hit "Autobahn" was conceived to echo the journey of an automobile along one of Germany's famous freeways. Three years on, "Trans-Europe Express" also evoked the wonder of travel—this time, on the TEE, an international train network that stretched from France to Germany, Switzerland, and the Netherlands.

Forming the centerpiece of their album of the same name, "Trans-Europe Express" marked a great technological leap for the band. Recorded using the Synthanorma Sequenzer, a custom-built version of the synthesizer popular with German contemporaries such as Tangerine Dream, "Trans-Europe Express" felt stiff and mechanical but full of motion. A stuttering rhythm beat out the sound of clacking train tracks and a building-then-fading synth wash mimicked the Doppler aural effect, experienced when passing landmarks at speed.

For all its futurism, the parent album is also steeped in more classical references to European modernity: the "parks, hotels, and palaces" of "Europe Endless," or "Franz Schubert." "Trans-Europe Express" itself is a magic blur of past and present, cutting a path from the Champs-Elysées to the late-night cafes of Vienna, with lyrics influenced by pre-recording discussions in Berlin with two fans, Iggy Pop and David Bowie.

Seized upon by New York's hip-hop community, "Trans-Europe Express" formed the hook to Afrika Bambaataa and the Soulsonic Force's 1982 hit "Planet Rock," a landmark in sample culture and the spark for a new wave of futuristic, funky hip-hop dubbed "electro." (Kraftwerk themselves felt far from honored: uncredited on the track, they sued, finally settling out of court with Tommy Boy label head Tom Silverman.) **LP**

Sweet Gene Vincent | Ian Dury (1977)

Writer | Ian Dury, Chas Jankel
Producer | Peter Jenner, Laurie Latham, Rick Walton
Label | Stiff
Album | *New Boots and Panties!!* (1977)

"Gene was at his peak when he was with the guitarist Gallopin' Cliff Gallup, sort of pre-1958. After then, forget it."

Ian Dury, 1998

◄ **Influenced by:** Bluejean Bop • Gene Vincent (1956)
► **Influence on:** Oranges and Lemons Again • Suggs with Jools Holland & His Rhythm & Blues Orchestra (2001)
● **Covered by:** Robbie Williams (2001)
★ **Other key track:** Sex & Drugs & Rock & Roll (1977)

Ian Dury described his influences as "the Stax and Motown labels and Max Miller, with a lot of television thrown in," but often his inspiration was Gene Vincent. It was after Vincent's death in 1971 that Dury formed his first band, Kilburn & The High Roads, and, as well as the music, his stage persona and sartorial style (especially the black leather gloves) paid homage to his hero. Dury, crippled by childhood polio, insisted that it was the singer's style and voice that first impressed him, and that he only later realized Vincent too wore a leg brace.

Dury's tribute song, "Sweet Gene Vincent," appeared on his first solo album, *New Boots and Panties!!*, and was the only track released as a single. The song features Dury's characteristically playful and vivid lyrics, with clever references to Vincent's own songs, including "Blue Jean Bop," "Who Slapped John?" and "Be-Bop-A-Lula"; the song's co-writer, Chas Jankel, commented that after Dury's extensive research on Vincent, the original draft of his lyrics would have taken fifteen minutes to perform. Alas, lyrics brimming with wordplay and references to Essex and east London, all delivered in broad Estuary English, were impenetrable abroad—particularly in the United States—so the album and even "Sweet Gene Vincent" remained very English successes.

Shortly after *New Boots and Panties!!*, Dury and his backing band started to perform as Ian Dury & The Blockheads, and subsequent singles such as "What a Waste" and "Hit Me with Your Rhythm Stick" gained the band more international popularity. "Sweet Gene Vincent" also got a new lease on life, reappearing on several compilation discs and remaining a favorite on their set list right up to Dury's death, in 2000. **MW**

By This River
Brian Eno (1977)

Writer | B. Eno, H. J. Roedelius, D. Moebius
Producer | Brian Eno, Rhett Davies
Label | Polydor
Album | *Before and After Science* (1977)

"By This River," the centerpiece on Side Two of Brian Eno's final solo mainstream "pop" album of the Seventies, is a beautiful, minimalist piece for piano and vocal inspired by collaborative sessions with Cluster's electronic experimentalists Roedelius and Moebius. An aquatic theme runs through much of Eno's work, and "By This River" is a gentle, almost lullaby-like, piece, the pared-down track combining piano and up-close vocal refrain with the minimalism of Eno's ambient recordings. The gently melodic, atmospheric piece nestles exquisitely between the mesmerizing "Julie with . . ." and the haunting "Through Hollow Lands."

The album, divided on vinyl between an "art rock" side and a serene, melancholic, reflective side, was the result of protracted sessions, as Eno, faced with an overabundance of ideas that he wished to pursue, strove to complete the record.

After 1977, and up until 1990's *Wrong Way Up*—his collaboration with John Cale—he would more or less retreat from lead vocals, but "By This River" plays to Eno's strengths as a singer. His gentle voice—reserved, intimate, and with a hint of the forlorn—concludes with a fading multitracked vocal hum of the song's piano refrain.

At the Brighton Festival, which he curated in May 2010, Eno gave an extraordinarily rare live performance of four songs, including "By This River," described as his daughter's favorite. **JL**

Dum Dum Boys
Iggy Pop (1977)

Writer | David Bowie, Iggy Pop
Producer | David Bowie
Label | RCA
Album | *The Idiot* (1977)

Recorded during a fruitful musical partnership with David Bowie some three years after his breakup with The Stooges, Iggy Pop's "Dum Dum Boys" is a poignant reflection on that band's sad demise. The song opens with Iggy chatting to himself—backed only by finger clicks and sparse electric piano—about the fate of various ex-Stooges, the dum dum boys of the title. "What happened to Zeke [Zettner]?" he asks. "He's dead on Jones, man / How about Dave [Alexander]? / OD'd on alcohol / Well, what's Rock [Scott Asheton] doing? / Oh, he's living with his mother."

After this blunt epilogue, the band kicks in. Their sound is far removed from the trademark three-chord chaos of The Stooges, though. The drumbeat is treated with echo, and guitars are layered with effects and distortion—touches that would also feature heavily on another 1977 release, Bowie's *"Heroes."* According to Iggy, Bowie gave him "the concept of the song and he also gave me the title. . . . Then he added that guitar arpeggio that metal groups love today."

Despite his desire to shed old musical skin, Iggy makes it clear that he misses his dum dum boys with the line "Hey, where are you now when I need your noise?" He would find them again in 2003, when the surviving Stooges reunited and hit the road, finally earning the audience and recognition they had deserved three decades before. **TB**

Com'è profondo il mare
Lucio Dalla (1977)

Writer | Lucio Dalla
Producer | A. Colombini, R. Cremonini
Label | RCA Italia
Album | *Com'è profondo il mare* (1977)

Although *Com'è profondo il mare* (Deep Is the Sea) was Lucio Dalla's tenth album, it was the first for which he supplied all the music and lyrics. The eponymous lead-off song of the album carries none of the uncertainty and naivety of his earlier work. Against a restrained background of deceptively relaxed, strummed guitar and spare keyboards, and with a seemingly jaunty whistled introduction, Dalla's voice is flexible and expressive as he shares the profound desperation, pessimism, and negativity that he is feeling.

The song, written while the singer was traveling by boat to the Tremiti islands in the Adriatic, is a meditation on the human condition in Seventies Italy. The opening lines set out his musings: "We are, we are many / We hide at night / For fear of motorists / Of linotypists / We are black cats / We are pessimists / We are bad thoughts / And we have nothing to eat. . . ." Dalla tells the story of a desperate people with no purpose and no future, while all the while the accompaniment resolutely maintains its cheerful-sounding course.

Many of Dalla's fan base thought both the song and the album to be too commercially driven and a betrayal of his earlier work. Roberto Roversi, one of Dalla's earlier songwriters, said, "He simply wanted to be left alone, singing about nothing. These are industrial choices, not cultural ones." The choices were to gain Dalla many new fans. **LSc**

Ghost Rider
Suicide (1977)

Writer | Alan Vega, Martin Rev
Producer | Marty Thau, Craig Leon
Label | Red Star
Album | *Suicide* (1977)

Suicide was the creation of Alan Vega and Martin Rev, sculptor and free-jazz musician, respectively, who met at the Project of Living Artists, a workshop and space in New York's SoHo. Inspired by the raw confrontation of The Stooges and the Pop Art of Warhol and Lichtenstein, the pair envisaged a confrontational performance art that stripped rock'n'roll down to its twitching skeleton.

"Ghost Rider," inspired by the Marvel comic of the same name, is the first track on Suicide's self-titled 1977 debut. Teamed with a pounding drum machine and a one-note rock'n'roll riff punched out by Rev on a Farfisa organ, Vega—in an Elvis-style tremor, his voice slaked in echo and reverb—relates the story of a flame-headed stunt motorcyclist who sold his soul to the devil. The lyrics were not sophisticated: as music journalist Simon Reynolds wrote, they "risked corn and trusted in the timeless power of cliché." But Vega's reliance on pop-cultural themes gave his lyrics a chilling potency: "Bebebebebebebe he's a-screaming the truth / America, America is killing its youth."

As a band, Suicide's influence would far outweigh their sales. Their spirit of anti-musicianship and city-slicker nihilism was to be echoed across New York's early-Eighties no-wave scene, and by the Nineties they were being cited as an influence by artists including Bruce Springsteen, Depeche Mode, and Radiohead. **LP**

Orgasm Addict | Buzzcocks (1977)

Writer | Pete Shelley, Howard Devoto
Producer | Martin Rushent
Label | United Artists
Album | N/A

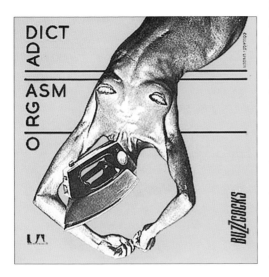

"It was a story everybody could relate to."

Steve Diggle, Buzzcocks, 2001

◀ **Influenced by: I Can't Control Myself** • The Troggs (1966)
▶ **Influence on: Uncontrollable Urge** • Devo (1978)
● **Covered by:** Manic Hispanic (1992) • Momus (1996)
★ **Other key tracks:** Boredom (1977) • What Do I Get (1978) • Everybody's Happy Nowadays (1979)

From "Pictures of Lily" to "I Touch Myself," odes to onanism have provided some of rock's quirkiest moments. But in the pop panoply of self-pleasure, "Orgasm Addict" is hard to beat.

The lyrics—penned mostly by Howard Devoto before he quit to form Magazine—offer a singular and witty portrait of a serial masturbator ("Well you tried it just for once, found it all right for kicks / But now you found out that it's a habit that sticks"). Set against a pell-mell clatter of guitars and drums, a stream of unusual fantasy figures rushes by in a bizarre slideshow, ranging from tramps to bellhops to women who decorate Christmas cakes. (Devoto briefly worked in a bakery.) The whole seedy catalog is delivered in a camp, delightfully hysterical vocal by Pete Shelley—recorded, by chance, on the day Marc Bolan died. The track is one of punk's incontrovertible classics: raucous, subversive, funny, over in less than two minutes.

And banned, of course. The BBC wouldn't touch it. To start with, United Artists' record plant wouldn't even press it—hardly an auspicious beginning for the band, as this was set to be their debut single for the label. Even Shelley himself had reservations, although they were strictly technical ones, rather than a case of literary cold feet. He told *Melody Maker* in 1978 that he already wanted to re-record it: "That song is embarrassing. It's the only one I listen to and . . . shudder."

Thankfully, he didn't. "Orgasm Addict" is a truly wondrous clatter, right up there with The Undertones' "Teenage Kicks" as a superlative vignette of secret adolescent delights. And it seemed entirely appropriate that it should make an appearance in Clark Gregg's 2008 dark comedy about a sex addict: *Choke*. **RD**

Holidays in the Sun | Sex Pistols (1977)

Writer | S. Jones, P. Cook, J. Rotten, S. Vicious
Producer | Chris Thomas
Label | Virgin
Album | *Never Mind the Bollocks Here's the Sex Pistols* (1977)

> *"We had to escape from London at the time. The song pretty well sums up the trip."*
>
> **Steve Jones, 1992**

◄ **Influenced by:** Chatterbox • New York Dolls (1974)
► **Influence on:** Good Times • Towers of London (2006)
● **Covered by:** The Bollock Brothers (1983) • Skid Row (1989) • Green Day (1997) • Hayseed Dixie (2007)
★ **Other key tracks:** Satellite (1977) • Pretty Vacant (1977) • E.M.I. (1977)

Johnny Rotten's opening line—"A cheap holiday in other people's misery"—was a nod toward graffiti that appeared in Paris in 1968 during the campaign for a more egalitarian society by the revolutionary movement Situationist International. Cool credentials, and the Sex Pistols were not above a bit of petty pilfering in the music behind the lyrics, either. The basis of "Holidays in the Sun" was a riff shamelessly stolen from The Jam's "In the City," released earlier in 1977 and itself inspired by the 1966 Who B-side "In the City."

Not that Sid Vicious was hiding the fact. Paul Weller recalled an altercation in a London club. "He just came up to me and he was going on about 'Holidays in the Sun,' where they'd nicked the riff from 'In the City.' Anyway, he just came up and nutted me. So I returned it." Neither party emerged victorious, but honor was partly satisfied.

The lyrics were written as a release from the oppressive atmosphere that surrounded the Pistols at the time. The group first made their way to Jersey, but, as they said, "They threw us out." But their notoriety made an escape essential for their safety. Said Rotten: "Being in London at the time made us feel like we were trapped in a prison-camp environment. . . . The best thing we could do was to go set up in a prison camp somewhere else. Berlin and its decadence was a good idea. The song came about from that."

The riff was not the only thing the Pistols appropriated on this fourth single (and the first not to feature a co-credit for Glen Matlock). The sleeve was a lightly amended version of a Belgian travel brochure. An objection from the company resulted in later copies of the U.K. Top Ten single being issued in a plain white cover. **CB**

Peaches
The Stranglers (1977)

Writer | The Stranglers
Producer | Martin Rushent
Label | United Artists
Album | *Rattus Norvegicus* (1977)

There were various ways to get your song banned from the radio in 1977. While some chose to mock royalty, The Stranglers had the BBC's knickers in a twist for very British, seaside-based reasons.

The band's second single, "Peaches," is driven by one of *the* great bass lines, as simple as it is spectacularly effective. But, until a re-recorded version was released, it was the lyrics that caused the furor, with the B-side, "Go Buddy Go," alone granted airplay. Most of the fuss focused on one word: as front man Hugh Cornwell relates the scene of women parading past him on the beach, he refers to what could be a part of the female genitalia—or the French word for a bathing costume. The latter scenario would be a stretch were it not for the band's Anglo-French bassist, Jean-Jacques Burnel, and later Stranglers songs in the same language (1981's "La Folie," for example).

Burnel had the inspiration for the track after a huge PA he owned with Cornwell was rented by a reggae collective in west London. "I'd never heard bass so dominant," said Burnel. "I thought, 'I'm going to write a song like that,' and the next day I wrote 'Peaches.'" "Rap over loutish thug riff," ran the review in music paper *Sounds*, a fine way of describing the band's first U.K. Top Ten hit. Over two decades later, "Peaches" was still cool enough to carry the opening scene of Jonathan Glazer's sun-basted gangster thriller, *Sexy Beast* (2000). **CB**

Black Betty
Ram Jam (1977)

Writer | Traditional
Producer | Jerry Kasenetz, Jeff Katz
Label | Epic
Album | *Ram Jam* (1977)

Although Ram Jam were a comparatively short-lived band, their version of "Black Betty" has had enduring popularity, and its driving beat and catchy riff have made it a favorite to pump up the excitement at sporting events, particularly those staged at New York's Yankee Stadium.

Ram Jam's unlikely origins lay in the bubblegum pop of the late Sixties, spearheaded by New York producers Jerry Kasenetz and Jeff Katz. One of the pair's hits, "Green Tambourine" by The Lemon Pipers, included Bill Bartlett, who went on to form the group Starstruck, recording a version of "Black Betty" on their own TruckStar label. This had only moderate success, but was picked up by Kasenetz and Katz and re-recorded by Bartlett's new band, Ram Jam.

Originally a work song, one perhaps dating back to the eighteenth century, "Black Betty" was well known in the Thirties and particularly popular on prison farms. The earliest known recording, collected by the musicologists John and Alan Lomax in 1933, was made by convict James "Ironhead" Baker and others in Sugarland Prison, Texas. However, Bartlett's inspiration was a 1939 recording by Huddie "Lead Belly" Ledbetter.

Ram Jam's cover made it to No. 18 in the U.S. charts, and in 1990 a remix of "Black Betty" proved especially popular in the United Kingdom, Europe, and Australia, where, in 2004, the song was resurrected in a cover by Spiderbait. **MW**

Born for a Purpose
Dr. Alimantado & The Rebels (1977)

Writer | Winston "Dr. Alimantado" Thompson
Producer | Winston "Dr. Alimantado" Thompson
Label | Vital Food/Greensleeves
Album | *Born for a Purpose*, aka "Sons of Thunder" (1981)

Reggae singer Dr. Alimantado had built up a strong reputation in Jamaica in the early Seventies with a string of Lee "Scratch" Perry–produced singles. But his only international hit, "Born for a Purpose / Reason for Living," originated in a personal disaster. On Boxing Day, 1976, Dr. Alimantado was struck down and dragged behind a bus while walking home. Thompson believes the incident occurred because he was sporting dreadlocks, something that was frowned upon in Jamaica at that time.

The song came to him while he was recovering; reportedly he had to drag himself on crippled legs across his house to find a pad and pencil to write it down. It was recorded at legendary studio Channel One, with all the musicians playing for free to help Alimantado settle his hospital bills.

With its refrain of "If you feel that you have no reason for living, don't determine my life," the track captured the ideals of the U.K. punk scene, mainly with the help of Johnny Rotten, who played it on his famous one-off radio show with DJ Tommy Vance in 1977. On the show, he described how the song helped him after he was badly beaten up in London: "Just after I got my brains kicked out, I went home and I played it."

An icon for British punks, Dr. Alimantado was name-checked by The Clash on their *London Calling* track "Rudie Can't Fail" with the line "Like the doctor who was born for a purpose." **DC**

Zombie
Fela Kuti & Africa 70 (1977)

Writer | Fela Kuti
Producer | Fela Kuti
Label | M.I.L. Multimedia
Album | *Zombie* (1977)

With its "bitches brew" of biting sociopolitical critique and polyrhythmic funk, "Zombie" is neatly emblematic of Fela Kuti's Afrobeat. The centerpiece and title track of the pioneering Nigerian saxophonist's 1977 album, it features Kuti at his most outspoken, railing against social injustice in a twelve-minute big-band march.

Over Africa 70's frantic staccato jazz horn stabs and nagging riffs, and drummer Tony Allen's lithe-limbed propulsive rhythms, Kuti and his backup singers ridicule the Nigerian military. "Attention! Quick march! Slow march! Salute!" Kuti chants in his trademark broken pidgin English. "Fall in! Fall out! Fall down! Go and kill! Go and die! Go and quench!" Each phrase is followed by the female backing singers' taunting response: "Zombie!"

For the army, such satire was a direct attack, exacerbated by the fact that in the song alpha males are being made to look foolish, in part by women. The backlash was unprecedented. Fela was severely beaten and his elderly mother murdered. His shrine and self-declared liberated zone, the Kalakuta Republic commune, was set on fire, and his studio was destroyed.

But if the military thought they could silence him, they were wrong. "Zombie" quickly became a rallying cry across the continent, playing its part in riots in Ghana and cementing Kuti's belief in individual liberation through music. **MK**

Fela Kuti's articulate defiance gave hope to Africans suffering under oppressive regimes. ➲

Wuthering Heights | Kate Bush (1977)

Writer | Kate Bush
Producer | Andrew Powell
Label | EMI
Album | *The Kick Inside* (1978)

"I was sixteen. . . . By the magic of God, it got on the radio, and I just about died."

k.d. lang, 1997

◀ **Influenced by: A Really Good Time** • Roxy Music (1974)
▶ **Influence on: Silent All These Years** • Tori Amos (1991)
● **Covered by:** Pat Benatar (1980) • White Flag (1992) Angra (1993) • James Reyne (2000) • The Puppini Sisters (2006) • Hayley Westenra (2006)

As startling as punk, "Wuthering Heights" emerged in the same year as the Sex Pistols' "God Save the Queen." And although Kate Bush and Johnny Rotten became friends and mutual admirers, they seemed at odds: he an urchin who scrawled "I hate" on a Pink Floyd shirt; she a hippy nurtured by Floyd's Dave Gilmour. In their iconic songs of 1977, he attacked a British institution; she celebrated a literary classic.

Bush shares a birthday with *Wuthering Heights* author Emily Brontë (July 30), but the book was not a favorite: "I didn't read it until just before I wrote the song. I'd seen the television series years ago. . . . I knew there was Heathcliff and Cathy and that she died and came back. It just fascinated me."

The song's most distinctive feature is its vocal. "I tried to project myself into the role of the book heroine," Bush recalled, "and, because she is a ghost, I gave her a high-pitched wailing voice." In the spare U.K. video, Kate flutters before the camera as she sings the chorus: "Heathcliff, it's me, Cathy, I've come home / I'm so cold, let me in-a-your window." Having fought EMI's conviction that the more traditional "James and the Cold Gun" should be her debut, Bush became—aged nineteen—the first British female to top the chart with a self-composed song.

The singer later admitted, "It was a bit misleading; it seemed to suggest too much fantasy and escapism." Nonetheless, the song remained her best known, and she re-recorded it for a 1986 greatest hits set, *The Whole Story*—"I wanted to put a contemporary mark on it. . . . It sounded like a very little girl singing that to me." Such longevity suits what Bush called "the ultimate love story . . . a love affair that goes beyond death." **BM**

Kate Bush sports red—as she does in the U.S. "Wuthering Heights" video—for a show in Amsterdam. ➡

Uptown Top Ranking
Althea & Donna (1977)

Writer | Althea Forrest, Donna Reid, Errol Thompson
Producer | J. Gibbs, E. Thompson
Label | Lightning
Album | *Uptown Top Ranking* (1978)

Long before the practice of sampling became widespread, Jamaica's sound-system culture had fostered a similar form of musical recycling. The flip sides of most reggae discs were instrumental dub mixes—known as "versions"—that were reused by deejays as backing tracks for otherwise new material. Thus Althea & Donna's signature hit had its origins a decade earlier in Alton Ellis's rocksteady ballad "I'm Still in Love with You," a song that Marcia Aitken covered in 1977 with a beefed-up rhythm track. This, in turn, provided the backing for Trinity's "Three Piece Suit," in which the deejay boasts at length about his dapper tailoring and stylish Argyle socks.

Later the same year, schoolgirls Althea Forrest and Donna Reid gave Trinity's display of dance-hall braggadocio a feminine twist, substituting halter-back tops, heels, and khaki suits for his masculine garb. In "Uptown Top Ranking," a pair of teenagers proclaim their Saturday-night credentials in a streetwise patois designed to alienate their elders. But, for all their moneyed signifiers—the Mercedes-Benz and the visits to Kingston's upmarket Constant Spring shopping center—Althea and Donna insist that they are keeping it real. "Nah pop, no style," they tease. "I strictly roots." In Britain, where it was championed by DJ John Peel, the record thankfully displaced Wings' "Mull of Kintyre" as the U.K. No. 1. **SP**

I Feel Love
Donna Summer (1977)

Writer | Donna Summer, Giorgio Moroder, Pete Belotte
Producer | Giorgio Moroder
Label | Casablanca
Album | *I Remember Yesterday* (1977)

"I Feel Love," the second collaboration between Boston-born disco queen Donna Summer and Italian producer Giorgio Moroder, changed the course of an entire genre. Prior to 1977, disco tracks were typically performed by a live ensemble of session musicians, but Moroder—a synthesizer wizard inspired by Kraftwerk and psychedelic rock epics such as Iron Butterfly's "In-A-Gadda-Da-Vida"—had no need of hired hands.

Instead, "I Feel Love"—conceived as the "future" section of Summer's 1977 LP, *I Remember Yesterday*, a concept album that aimed to meld disco with the music of decades past—was the first noteworthy song to boast an entirely synthesized backing track. With Summer's clear diva vocal over a pulsing beat, wriggling electronic bass line, and smooth, flawless keyboards, "I Feel Love" not only overshadowed the album it was drawn from but took electronic music into the hit parade, topping the U.K. singles chart and reaching No. 6 in the *Billboard* Hot 100.

Divorcing disco from its roots in African-American soul and funk stoked up some controversy at the time. American music critic Nelson George declared that "I Feel Love" was "perfect for folks with no sense of rhythm." But others were seduced wholeheartedly. Brian Eno called it "the sound of the future," and it has subsequently been hailed as a key influence on house and techno. **LP**

Peg
Steely Dan (1977)

Writer | Walter Becker, Donald Fagen
Producer | Gary Katz
Label | ABC
Album | *Aja* (1977)

By 1977's *Aja*, Steely Dan had honed an already smooth sound into an impossibly polished jazz-pop fusion, not a glitch in its sophisticated armory. "There wasn't a single slouch," Walter Becker said of the players on 1976 set *The Royal Scam*, but he and Donald Fagen were even more watchful on the follow-up, bringing in accomplished jazz guitarists Lee Ritenour and Steve Khan, yet still trying out half a dozen more for the guitar solo on "Peg."

Jobbing producer/guitarist Jay Graydon was the man who eventually provided the lick to satisfy Becker and Fagen, his solo oozing organically from the groove, no run-up, no seam. Around him, Steely Dan conjure an enchanting pop song with the catchiest horn section this side of the JB's and a lyric suggesting the sleaze of the casting couch—"This is your big debut. . . . So won't you smile for the camera / I know I'll love you better."

The song manages to get away with its seedy edge through perky refrains, dance-floor suss, and some glorious harmonies. The latter were boosted in no small part by ex-Dan keyboardist and now–Doobie Brother Michael McDonald, presaging his later blue-eyed soul turns.

Of course, "Peg" sounds almost disco, but its funky strut was not left to fester. In 1989, De La Soul exhumed its perfectly preserved form, snatching bass line, brass, and vocal sample to bring the bliss to Daisy Age hit "Eye Know." **MH**

Marquee Moon
Television (1977)

Writer | Tom Verlaine
Producer | Andy Johns, Tom Verlaine
Label | Elektra
Album | *Marquee Moon* (1977)

Television were pioneers of New York punk. And yet their music had little in common with their punk compatriots. While the Ramones and The Heartbreakers spewed out three-chord wonders, Television assembled jazz-inspired epics filled with complex solos and abstract lyrics.

"Marquee Moon," the ten-minute title track from their 1977 debut, was their most ambitious construction. The track's riffs slot together like a jigsaw: a double-stopped guitar opens on the left channel, then a jangling motif joins in on the right, and a simple two-note bass line pulls the song together. That minimalist, entrancing melody provides space for guitarists Tom Verlaine and Richard Lloyd to throw out sublime, extended solos.

However, for front man Verlaine—who took his surname from the French symbolist poet—words were more important than riffs. "I probably spent six times the amount of time on the lyrics than I did on the music back then," he explained. Like the song's sparring guitars, Verlaine's lyrics are dominated by dueling concepts ("The kiss of death, the embrace of life").

The track's sheer un-punkiness made it a target for many U.S. critics. Britain had a more open mind—"Marquee Moon" reached No. 30 in the singles charts, even though the track's length meant it had to be split between two sides of a seven-inch single. **TB**

Like a Hurricane
Neil Young (1977)

Writer | Neil Young
Producer | Neil Young, David Briggs, Tim Mulligan
Label | Reprise
Album | *American Stars 'n Bars* (1977)

The Passenger
Iggy Pop (1977)

Writer | Iggy Pop, Ricky Gardiner
Producer | The Bewlay Bros.
Label | RCA
Album | *Lust for Life* (1977)

In the summer of 1975, with his *Tonight's the Night* album just hitting the shelves and its follow-up, *Zuma*, prepped for release, Neil Young underwent surgery to remove nodes that had developed on his vocal cords. While recuperating afterward, unable to speak and forced to communicate only through sign language, Young went on the lam with a gaggle of roguish road-crew compadres to La Honda, a small town in the Santa Cruz mountains, where a high time was had by all.

Young had separated from his wife Carrie Snodgress a year previously, and one night, at a La Honda hangout called Venturi's, he fell under the spell of a local girl named Gail. Nothing came of it, but the attraction haunted Young and, some nights later, he sat at the organ, writing what would become his next great guitar epic. Still unable to sing, he scrawled a couplet chorus, sketching out the theme of corrosive longing: "You are like a hurricane / There's calm in yer eye."

Young took the song to his band, Crazy Horse, soon afterward. After a couple of false starts, Frank "Poncho" Sampedro put down his rhythm guitar and manned a nearby Stringman synthesizer, leaving more space for Young to solo. (His vocals would have to be recorded later.) The song soon became a highlight of Young's concert set lists, his plaintive, vulnerable vocals giving way to ever-more excursive, emotive guitar soloing. **SC**

When Iggy Pop and David Bowie ask if you have anything for them as potential material for the follow-up to *The Idiot*, it pays to have something impressive in your locker. In a Berlin flat, prog-rocking session player Ricky Gardiner hit them with the memorable chords for "The Passenger."

With all its talk of ripped backsides, "The Passenger" found Iggy letting it all hang out with an observational tale of late-Seventies excesses, inspired by journeys he had taken around the German city. But this dark direction had nothing at all in common with the circumstances in which Gardiner found his inspiration. On what he called "one idyllic spring morning," he was wandering, guitar in hand, "beside the radiant apple blossoms" when he found himself strumming the irresistible chords. It required just one unplugged rendition, recorded on a cassette player, to send Iggy scurrying off to write the lyrics overnight.

Although the song has become what Gardiner admits is "a rock standard," it did not display any contemporary commercial clout at the time, being hidden away as the B-side to "Success," which did not live up to its name. However, its presence in movie soundtracks and advertising (one campaign took it to just outside the U.K. Top Twenty in 1998) has seen it acclaimed after the fact. Cover versions (from Bauhaus to The Banshees) have served only to emphasize the original's brilliance. **CB**

Ragged glory: Neil Young onstage in the Seventies.

Stayin' Alive | Bee Gees (1977)

Writer | Barry Gibb, Robin Gibb, Maurice Gibb
Producer | Bee Gees, K. Richardson, A. Galuten
Label | RSO
Album | *Saturday Night Fever* (1977)

"You never really know if something's a hit or not. Apart from 'Stayin' Alive.'"
Barry Gibb, 2009

◄ **Influenced by:** TSOP (The Sound of Philadelphia)
MFSB (1974)
► **Influence on:** I Was Made for Lovin' You • Kiss (1979)
● **Covered by:** Mina (1978) • Happy Mondays (1991)
Dweezil Zappa (1991) • N-Trance (1995) • Dimension
Zero (2007) • MegaDriver (2007)

In April 1977, the Bee Gees flew to Paris with two tasks in mind—mixing a live album and working on new material for a follow-up to the best-selling *Children of the World*. Residing at the cold and forbidding Château d'Hérouville studios (recently vacated by David Bowie, who'd just recorded *Low* there), the group received a call from their manager, Robert Stigwood. He had bought the rights to an extended essay by writer Nik Cohn entitled "Tribal Rites of the New Saturday Night." Planning to make it into a film, he needed at least four songs from the group for the project.

One of those four, "Stayin' Alive," is fascinating. Worked up by the three brothers on acoustic guitars and written without reading either the article or the screenplay, it captures perfectly the struggle for survival in an inner city ("Life going nowhere, somebody help me") and the escapism provided by a dance floor. The rigid drum beat was achieved by using a loop from the already-recorded "Night Fever."

Saturday Night Fever—as Cohn's essay was renamed for the movie—became one of the highest-grossing movies of all time and made the Bee Gees reluctant (but well-compensated) figureheads of the disco movement. And a lot of that success was down to the strength of this song, captured forever over the opening credits, in which Tony Manero (John Travolta) quickens pulses as he half-walks, half-dances his way to work.

"Stayin' Alive" swiftly topped charts worldwide, though after a first rush of enthusiasm it was soon derided. People mocked the group's falsettos, medallions, satin shirts, and hair—but a lot of the cricicism was simple jealousy. Time has proven just how well written "Stayin' Alive" is. **DE**

Wonderous Stories | Yes (1977)

Writer | Jon Anderson
Producer | Yes
Label | Atlantic
Album | *Going for the One* (1977)

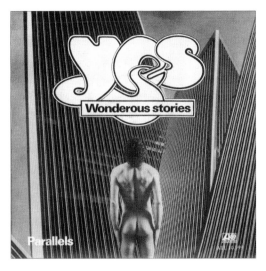

"Originally I wanted Yes to be just The Nice with Vanilla Fudge harmonies."

Jon Anderson, 1975

◄ **Influenced by: I Believe in Father Christmas**
Greg Lake (1975)
► **Influence on: Northern Lights** · Renaissance (1978)
● **Covered by:** Magenta (2009)
★ **Other key tracks:** Close to the Edge (1972) · Awaken
(1977) · Going for the One (1977)

At a time when punk rock was raising its spiky little head, pomp rockers Yes—with prodigal keyboards man Rick Wakeman returned to the fold—defied all the odds and fashioned their best album in years, charting a first U.K. hit single.

Something of a novelty track for an album-orientated prog-rock band, "Wonderous Stories" was Yes's pop moment. No less novel than the music was the bright-blue vinyl 12-inch release put out at the same time as the 7-inch black single that bagged a No. 7 spot on the U.K. chart. Titled "Wondrous Stories" on some releases, the track featured a soaring vocal performance by the song's author, Jon Anderson.

"Wonderous Stories" was an opportunity for Yes to appeal to a wider audience. New album *Going for the One,* from which it was plucked, was less intellectual and far more approachable than the band's previous offerings. It restored Yes to the No. 1 spot in the U.K. album charts and maintained their popularity in the United States, where it peaked at No. 8. The fantasy worlds of early Yes prog-rock epics were stripped away, revealing Anderson's ability to deliver a catchy pop song in under four minutes.

Clearly spiritual, his lyrics had an almost biblical turn of phrase; making a journey "bound for my forgiver," he is directed to "the gate" where his spirit ascends—apparently—heavenward. Anderson, who is often wrongly described as a singer using a falsetto technique, had rarely put his alto-tenor Lancastrian vowels to better use. The song became an FM-radio-friendly staple, although seasoned Yes fans didn't fully warm to the joyous-sounding track, preferring, as did Anderson, *Going for the One*'s alternative "masterwork," "Awaken." **DR**

Go Your Own Way | Fleetwood Mac (1977)

Writer | Lindsey Buckingham
Producer | Fleetwood Mac, R. Dashut, K. Caillat
Label | Warner Bros.
Album | *Rumours* (1977)

" 'Go Your Own Way' was angry and nasty, and— in my opinion—extremely disrespectful."

Stevie Nicks, 2009

◀ **Influenced by: Street Fighting Man** · The Rolling Stones (1968)

▶ **Influence on: The Game of Who Needs Who the Worst** · Cursive (2000)

● **Covered by:** NOFX (1989) · Seaweed (1993)
The Cranberries (1998) · Wilson Phillips (2004)

The lengthy touring that followed Fleetwood Mac's eponymous 1975 album—their first featuring new guitarist/vocalist Lindsey Buckingham and singer Stevie Nicks—took a heavy toll on the relationships within the band, leading to the separation of both Buckingham and Nicks, and bassist John McVie and his keyboardist/singer wife, Christine; drummer Mick Fleetwood's marriage with wife Jenny also hit the rocks. A group whose history had been marked by mental breakdowns and outrageous misfortune, Fleetwood Mac soon devolved into a soap opera, which fueled their massively successful 1977 album, *Rumours*.

The first single from *Rumours*, "Go Your Own Way," was also the most rancorous. Buckingham's song started out as a riff on the Stones' "Street Fighting Man," taut verses bristling into harmony-drenched (but most certainly unharmonious) choruses that flung his broken relationship with Nicks to the winds. Nicks had essayed their relationship herself on the more meditative "Dreams," hoping their friendship could be recovered from the wreckage, but "Go Your Own Way" rang with stung indignation, picking over Buckingham's broken heart with a spiteful honesty and railing against the girl to whom he had offered his world and who had rejected him.

Such autobiography would win Fleetwood Mac the greatest success of their career, but these upheavals—and Nicks's enduring offense at Buckingham's lyrics, cattily claiming that "shacking up is all you want to do"—also ensured this soap opera would continue. Fleetwood Mac's greatest lineup ultimately split when tensions between the duo exploded into a physical fight after sessions for 1987's *Tango in the Night*. **SC**

"Heroes" | David Bowie (1977)

Writer | David Bowie, Brian Eno
Producer | Tony Visconti, David Bowie
Label | RCA
Album | *"Heroes"* (1977)

"It's really that two-chord special. It was that 'Waiting for the Man' thing."

John Cale, 2008

◄ **Influenced by:** Hero • NEU! (1975)
► **Influence on:** Heroes Symphony • Philip Glass (1996)
● **Covered by:** Blondie (1980) • Nico (1981) • Pink Lincolns (1987) • Billy Preston (1993) • TV on the Radio (1996) Oasis (1997) • Philip Glass (1997) • King Crimson (2000) Peter Gabriel (2010)

At twenty-nine, David Bowie was certainly not the first—nor would he be the last—pop star to flee L.A., exhausted by its excesses. "Life in L.A. had left me with an overwhelming sense of foreboding," he said recently. "I had approached the brink of drug-induced calamity one too many times, and it was essential to take some kind of positive action."

After releasing his *Young Americans* album (which Bowie himself described as "plastic soul"), he found Berlin a sanctuary. Bowie had long felt an artistic kinship with Expressionist Berlin (Max Reinhardt and Bertolt Brecht); plus, the city was cheap (he was broke) and it guaranteed anonymity.

In this most divided city, Bowie would devise the Berlin Trilogy (*Low*, *"Heroes,"* and *Lodger*) and his most covered song, "Heroes." While *Low* was recorded at the supposedly haunted Château d'Hérouville, *"Heroes"* was recorded with Tony Visconti and Brian Eno at Hansa Studio 2, which stood right next to the heavily guarded Berlin Wall. For all the surrounding bleakness, however, these were happy sessions, Eno and Bowie frequently "in schoolboy giggling fits" doing impressions of comic heroes Peter Cooke and Dudley Moore.

"Heroes" starts as if already halfway through: piano in full roll, saxes hoisted skyward, Robert Fripp's driving guitars. The song reaches bursting point at Bowie's description of two lovers meeting by the Wall ("The guns shot above our heads / And we kissed / As though nothing could fall"). Though it was a secret at the time, the lovers were in fact Visconti (who was still married) and his new girlfriend. Bowie remembers, "It was very touching because I could see that Tony was very much in love with this girl." To this day, "Heroes" remains a perfect musical expression of romantic defiance. **SH**

Exodus
Bob Marley & The Wailers (1977)

Writer | Bob Marley
Producer | Bob Marley
& The Wailers
Label | Tuff Gong/Island
Album | *Exodus* (1977)

It is one of the neatest jokes in Bob Marley's entire catalog: the piano motif that appears throughout this song comes from the Oscar- and Grammy-winning theme to Otto Preminger's 1960 film *Exodus*, about the founding of Israel. As a single, it had been a global smash in the hands of piano duo Ferrante and Teicher, and clearly the story had resonance in Rasta teachings. This time, however, the subject is the movement of Jah people, but there is also the small matter of the singer and his inner circle having to leave home after an assassination attempt that only just failed. This was more exile than exodus, a two-year period in London during which he was able to craft an album that took his message further than ever.

This was the moment Marley became a global superstar; perhaps as a consequence, his 1977 LP, *Exodus*, is often labeled as his sell-out, soft-centered, pop album. Yet the title cut was one of the most intense musical experiences available in the year punk broke. Much of that comes down to the rhythm track, the way the Barrett brothers played off each other, with Aston's bass high in a busy, psychedelic mix. Over this, Marley takes his place at the head of the long march to the promised land, no longer simply preaching to sufferahs or reggae fans or the Back to Africa movement. Now his army consisted of everybody unhappy with life as it is lived in Babylon. **DH**

River Song
Dennis Wilson (1977)

Writer | Dennis Wilson, Carl Wilson
Producer | Dennis Wilson,
Gregg Jakobson
Label | Caribou
Album | *Pacific Ocean Blue* (1977)

Unexpectedly, Dennis Wilson was the first Beach Boy to release a solo album. Yes, he had contributed a handful of memorable songs to the band's oeuvre, but he was seen as the surfer, the rock 'n' roll heart, the dissolute brother, the friend of Charles Manson, never the grafter.

Released in 1977 (and reissued with *Bambu* in 2008), the frazzled, sun-kissed *Pacific Ocean Blue* met with a cool critical reception. The album was treated as an indulgence, heavy on production values and sonic layers, with no track as guilty as opener "River Song." Still, one man's overegged pudding is another's stirring epic, and this hymn to nature's beauty now rightly stands as a landmark itself, undercutting Dennis's party-boy image.

Exasperated with the city ("So crowded I can hardly breathe"), "River Song" also sells the tranquillity of the country, Wilson's tinkling piano evoking the wash of the river itself. Here the song is delicate, but Wilson soon piles on gospel choirs ("Ninety percent of those voices are mine," he claimed) and rolling drums, expressing the river's widening course. In the end, "River Song" is an exhortation to "run away" and join it, our gravelly singer yearning to ditch the high life and clean up.

The track had been performed live by The Beach Boys in 1973 but was never laid down. By 1977, the band had lapsed into nostalgia and retreads; brother Dennis still had dreams. **MH**

A reggae revolutionary leading the exodus: Bob Marley.

Whole Lotta Rosie | AC/DC (1977)

Writer | Bon Scott, Malcolm Young, Angus Young
Producer | Harry Vanda, George Young
Label | Atlantic
Album | *Let There Be Rock* (1977)

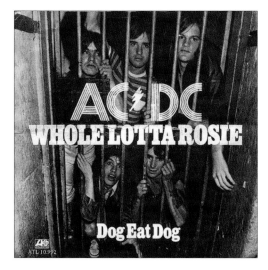

"This chick Rosie lived across the road. She used to check out which bands were in town.... She was too big to say no to."
Bon Scott, 1979

◀ **Influenced by: Lucille** • Little Richard (1957)
▶ **Influence on: Welcome to the Jungle** • Guns N' Roses (1987)
● **Covered by:** Acid Drinkers (1994) • W.A.S.P. (1995) Anthrax (2003) • Guns N' Roses (2009)
★ **Other key track:** Highway to Hell (1979)

If you were looking for a song to sum up AC/DC in all their hard-rocking, sticky-fingered glory, you'd need look no further than "Whole Lotta Rosie." The sweaty climax of the Sydney band's 1977 LP *Let There Be Rock*, it is the testament of a real-life encounter singer Bon Scott had with a plus-size lady—the titular "Rosie," who might be "weighin' in at nineteen stone" but has the enthusiasm and endurance to do it "All through the night time / Right around the clock." As Scott reported, "To get out of bed, I had to climb over her, which was like climbing a mountain."

It is a subject matter that finds its home in the locker room, and true, if you're looking for more cerebral subjects in your rock 'n' roll, AC/DC may not be for you. The rest of us, though, can appreciate "Whole Lotta Rosie" for what it is: a larger-than-life stadium stomp that is silly without being stupid and saucy without being sleazy.

The band snap from a stop-start beginning into a delirious boogie signposted with cymbal-smashing breakdowns and astonishing solos from school-uniform-clad guitarist Angus Young. And while, in these more enlightened times, one might question Bon Scott's descriptions of a larger lady ("Ain't no skin and bones"), one listen to his larynx-challenging delivery suggests his tribute is entirely genuine. (Confirming testimony came from Angus in 2000: "Bon had this fetish about big women. He used to party around with these two girls who were called the Jumbo Jets.")

"Whole Lotta Rosie" has since found a special place in AC/DC's discography. Along with "Nutbush City Limits," new vocalist Brian Johnson performed the song at his audition following the death of Bon Scott in 1980. **LP**

| **The Seventies**

Blank Generation | Richard Hell & The Voidoids (1977)

Writer | Richard Hell
Producer | Richard Gottehrer, Richard Hell
Label | Sire
Album | *Blank Generation* (1977)

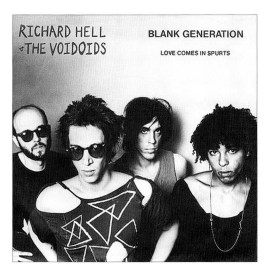

"When anything got into the final analysis, I didn't care. That's what that song 'Blank Generation' was about."

Richard Hell, 1996

◄ **Influenced by:** The Beat Generation · Bob McFadden & Dor (1959)
► **Influence on:** Pretty Vacant · Sex Pistols (1977)
● **Covered by:** Angel Corpus Christi (1989)
   The Heartbreakers (1991)
★ **Other key track:** Love Comes in Spurts (1977)

Although New York punk hardly begged for sloganeering, few of its missives seem as patently anthemic as "Blank Generation," the signature recording by CBGB writer-howler Richard Hell. The song's chorus—"I belong to the blank generation and / I can take it or leave it each time"—lent Hell and his scruffy fellow-travelers a suitably nihilistic maxim to present to interested parties.

Patterned after the 1959 beatnik spoof "The Beat Generation," "Blank Generation" served as the namesake of Richard Hell & The Voidoids' 1977 debut LP. However, the singer had introduced the song years earlier, during his uneasy tenure in Television. As recorded by The Voidoids, "Blank Generation" is wired and neurotic, with Hell's tense vocals giving way to the anarchic guitar spurts of Robert Quine. Yet for all its untamed ferocity, the song retains a jazzlike cadence carried over from the novelty record that inspired it; as with much early punk, "Blank Generation" is more complex than it lets on.

While it never achieved the ubiquity of some of the Ramones' hits, "Blank Generation" resonated beyond CBGB's walls. In 1980, it was used as the title and theme of a low-budget film starring Hell as a struggling downtown musician. The work also found a fan in Malcolm McLaren, who returned from a New York trip and commanded the Sex Pistols to write their "own version" of "Blank Generation," resulting in "Pretty Vacant." Indeed, it is difficult to imagine U.K. punk without Hell's influence. "There was no question that I'd take it back to London," McLaren recounted in the oral history book *Please Kill Me*. "I was going to imitate it and transform it into something more English." **JR**

Bat Out of Hell
Meat Loaf (1977)

Writer | Jim Steinman
Producer | Todd Rundgren
Label | Epic
Album | *Bat Out of Hell* (1977)

In 1977, the best dose of theatrical overkill available to the music-buying punter was either *Bat Out of Hell* or a Queen album—and even Freddie Mercury felt subtle in comparison with Marvin Aday. Everything was exaggerated in Meat Loaf's universe: his operatic singing style, the awe-inspiring album cover, the wall-of-sound production, and the lyrics of this title track, the LP's most memorable cut.

In the grand tradition of two decades of death discs, "Bat Out of Hell" tells the tale of a doomed, lovelorn teenager who rides his motorbike too fast and winds up dead. Aday supplied suitably histrionic vocals over Jim Steinman's marvelous suite of instrumentation, split into discrete movements for maximum drama. Guitar solos wail; a nimble-fingered piano riff gives the song's opening a genuine boost; and the energetic layers of music add up to so much high-octane froth that many writers were moved to describe the song as heavy metal. They were wrong; although the heavy metal of the day did specialize in big, fat, pompous riffage (see Deep Purple), "Bat Out of Hell" was more akin to a symphony.

The album went on to become one of the best-selling of all time, thanks to its fuller-than-full-fat arrangements. But if listening to the whole album daunts, give the title track a spin and marvel at how much subtlety emerges. **JMc**

Lust for Life
Iggy Pop (1977)

Writer | Iggy Pop, David Bowie
Producer | The Bewlay Bros.
Label | RCA
Album | *Lust for Life* (1977)

In West Berlin, Iggy Pop and David Bowie lived a life of Weimar decadence, subsisting on cocaine, red wine, and bratwurst and sitting down once a week to watch broadcasts of *Starsky and Hutch* on the Armed Forces Network. Bowie reworked the station's signature tune—a staccato Morse-code beep—on the ukulele to become the barreling riff of "Lust for Life." The so-called Bewlay Bros. (Pop, Bowie, and co-producer Colin Thurston) laid down the track in 1977 at Hansa Studios, where Bowie would soon cut his album "*Heroes.*"

Iggy prowls through his vocals with a feline growl, name-dropping Johnny Yen, a Venusian gangster from William Burroughs's 1962 novel *The Ticket That Exploded*, from which he also lifted the sentiment that love was "like hypnotizing chickens." Drummer Hunt Sales and his bassist brother Tony (the future Tin Machine rhythm section, no less) provide the song's percussive drive—memorably exploited to score the opening sequence of *Trainspotting* in 1996.

The film connection propelled a reissued "Lust for Life" to the dizzying heights of No. 26 in the U.K. charts, and in the process laid the groundwork for various revisionist takes on its riff, notably The Strokes' "Last Nite" and "Are You Gonna Be My Girl" by antipodean rockers Jet. But Iggy's vivacious swagger is timeless—neither of the past nor of the future. He's just a modern guy. **SP**

Non-Alignment Pact
Pere Ubu (1978)

Writer | Pere Ubu
Producer | Ken Hamann, Pere Ubu
Label | Blank
Album | *The Modern Dance* (1978)

Taking their name from a character in Alfred Jarry's surrealist play *Ubu Roi*, Pere Ubu were formed in 1975 by local music journalists David Thomas (aka Crocus Behemoth) and the late Peter Laughner in Cleveland, Ohio, from the ashes of the Stooges-inspired protopunk band Rocket from the Tombs. At the time, Cleveland was in major decline, but the group's relative isolation allowed them to develop a unique "avant-garage" mixture of abrasive synthesizers, hypnotic bass lines, and Thomas's apocalyptic howling.

After a handful of single releases on their own Hearthan label, including the harrowing "30 Seconds over Tokyo," Pere Ubu unleashed their debut long-player, *The Modern Dance*, after signing to Mercury Records offshoot Blank. "Non-Alignment Pact," the opening track of this uncompromising album of garage-punk pranks and *musique concrète* sound collages, begins with thirty seconds of high-pitched synth squeal and feedback before exploding as a high-energized rockabilly sprawl, with energetic and explosive verses and a shout-along refrain. The whole mess is interspersed with a nihilistic instrument breakdown before rising up with more garage noise and heavyweight riffs. "We were making popular music. That's why we did singles," David Thomas once insisted. "Whether people liked it or not was not our problem." **CS**

Blue Valentines
Tom Waits (1978)

Writer | Tom Waits
Producer | Bones Howe
Label | Asylum
Album | *Blue Valentine* (1978)

Although he emerged in the early Seventies at the same time as a host of other California singer-songwriters, it soon became clear that Tom Waits was channeling a different sort of muse. His beatnik ethos was an admitted homage to heroes such as Jack Kerouac and Ken Nordine, though his spin on it was something wholly original.

While his songs had worn their hearts on their sleeves from the start, Waits's penchant for bent romance reached its apotheosis on his fifth album, *Blue Valentine*. Each successive tale of tragic romance on the disc pulls the listener deeper into beatific heartbreak. From the lush orchestration that supports a growled cover of "Somewhere" from *West Side Story*, on through the finger-snapping lilt of "Romeo Is Bleeding," Waits masterfully conjures the spirit of star-crossed love as experienced on Skid Row.

But it is "Blue Valentines," the album's final track, that seals the deal. The spare jazz guitar of Ray Crawford—well known from his work with organist Jimmy Smith—frames the singer's tale of love gone terribly wrong, lamenting his role as the "burglar that can break the rose's neck." Produced by Bones Howe (who had worked with Elvis Presley before establishing the classic sunshine-pop sound of bands such as The Association), "Blue Valentines" is a masterpiece of both tasteful restraint and unabashed sentimentalism. **TS**

Heart of Glass | Blondie (1978)

Writer | Deborah Harry, Chris Stein
Producer | Mike Chapman
Label | Chrysalis
Album | *Parallel Lines* (1978)

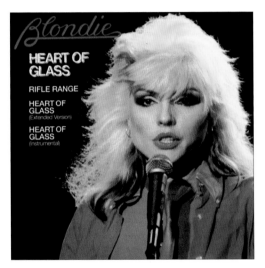

"We didn't expect the song to be that big. We did it as a novelty item to put more diversity into the album."

Chris Stein, 1979

◀ **Influenced by:** I Feel Love • Donna Summer (1977)
▶ **Influence on:** Take Me Out • Franz Ferdinand (2004)
● **Covered by:** The Shadows (1979) • Chet Atkins (1981)
Erasure (1997) • Toshiyuki Yasuda (2002) • Vitamin C
(2003) • Skye Sweetnam (2004) • Faye Wong (2004)
Nouvelle Vague (2006) • The Puppini Sisters (2006)

Toward the tail end of the Seventies, a new-wave band who regularly performed at New York punk mecca CBGB committed heresy. To put the matter bluntly, they released a disco record.

The band was Blondie and the record was "Heart of Glass." Although writers Debbie Harry and Chris Stein were big on the disco scene, not all the band members were happy with the new direction: bassist Nigel Harrison infamously called it a "compromise with commerciality." Stein and Harry originally wrote the song in pre-Blondie days and cut it as a shuffling, disco-tinged demo with the title "Once I Had a Love" in 1975. After featuring it on their tours, they re-recorded the song in 1978, again with the original title. When the band came to record their third album, *Parallel Lines*, with hotshot new producer Mike Chapman, he saw that the track, now more of a rock number, had potential, but he felt it was not radio-friendly.

Then Harry suggested, "Well, maybe it could be like a Donna Summer thing." She, Chapman, and Stein became fired up by the idea, but the rest of the band were incredulous. Matters weren't helped by a frustrating studio session. "It was all done the slow way," Harry was to comment. "We had to practically record each beat by hand."

No one had much confidence in the track—Chapman stuck it in the middle of *Parallel Lines'* B-side—so when it was released as the third single from the album, it surprised them all by becoming No. 1 in the U.K. and U.S. charts. There was an immediate backlash from rock artists—drummer Clem Burke recalls, "Our peers labeled us as disco sellouts"—but "Heart of Glass" sealed Blondie's reputation as pop pioneers and set the template for all rockers wanting to flirt with dance music. **DC**

Ever Fallen in Love … (with Someone You Shouldn't've) | Buzzcocks (1978)

Writer | Pete Shelley
Producer | Martin Rushent
Label | United Artists
Album | *Love Bites* (1978)

"I did have a certain person in mind, but I'll save that for my kiss 'n' tell. The music just seemed to follow, fully formed."

Pete Shelley, 2006

◀ **Influenced by: I Can't Get Next to You** • The Temptations (1969)
▶ **Influence on: I Can't Make You Love Me** • Bonnie Raitt (1991)
● **Covered by:** Fine Young Cannibals (1987) • Pete Yorn (2004) • Thea Gilmore (2004)

"I'd fall in love with somebody and then instantly wonder why they hadn't fallen in love with me. I'd start getting possessive and jealous long before they knew of my existence. It was bad for my mental metabolism." It is easy to forget how music that can elicit such pleasure in the listener can have come from such a painful place for the composer—in this instance, Pete Shelley.

But Shelley's emotional angst found a creative outlet in what became the greatest in a long line of bittersweet Buzzcocks classics. The song took shape in the uninspiring surroundings of an Edinburgh guesthouse, where Shelley's ear was caught by a line from the 1955 Brando and Sinatra musical *Guys and Dolls,* which was playing on the TV. The lacerating, lovelorn lyrics poured out the following day (though the lack of airplay afforded to "Orgasm Addict" the previous year led Shelley to change "piss on" to the more radio-acceptable "spurn" in the song's first line).

During this prolific period, which saw the release of the first two Buzzcocks albums separated by just seven months in 1978, Shelley's unfailing ability to tap into the common romantic consciousness resulted in the single becoming the band's biggest hit in the United Kingdom, reaching No. 12. "The reason some of them have been so popular," he explained, "is that things which have been going on inside my head have been going on inside lots of other people's heads. Therefore, they get the same ideas that I do, the same confusion and the same doubts and fears."

In 2005, a cover of the song starring numerous rock alumni, including Shelley, was released as a charity tribute single to the late DJ John Peel, with the proceeds going to Amnesty International. **CB**

Le Freak | Chic (1978)

Writer | Nile Rodgers, Bernard Edwards
Producer | Nile Rodgers, Bernard Edwards
Label | Atlantic
Album | C'est Chic (1978)

"The Led Zeppelin of dance music."

David Lee Roth, 1997

◀ **Influenced by: Get Down Tonight** · KC & The Sunshine Band (1975)
▶ **Influence on: A Lover's Holiday** · Change (1980)
● **Covered by:** The Corn Dollies (1990) · The Ukulele Orchestra of Great Britain (2006) · Millionaires (2010)
★ **Other key track:** I Want Your Love (1978)

"Le Freak" was the biggest hit of the greatest group that the disco phenomenon ever produced: Chic. Although the band's core members—Bernard Edwards on bass, Nile Rodgers on guitar, and Tony Thompson on drums—had previously played in a variety of New York club outfits, they seemed to appear out of nowhere in 1977, fully equipped with their debut single, "Dance, Dance, Dance (Yowsah, Yowsah, Yowsah)."

Rodgers and Edwards quickly proved to be prodigious writers and producers and, on New Year's Eve, 1977, they were invited to meet Grace Jones at Manhattan's infamous Studio 54 with a view to producing her. Unfortunately, they fell foul of the venue's notorious door policy and were cast out into the snowy night. Retreating to Rodgers's nearby apartment, and fueled by champagne, marijuana, and cocaine, the duo began to jam. After repeatedly singing the phrase "Ah, fuck off!"—inspired by their ill treatment earlier—they gradually metamorphosed the line into "freak out." One of the most popular songs of the disco era was born, a record that conflates America's golden age of dance, in the shape of the Savoy ballroom, with Studio 54 itself, while celebrating an underground dance.

Everything here is in correct, infectious measure. The gnawing guitar and syncopated hand claps, the chorus vocal, and then that breakdown, its six-note bass riff and the drama of the Chic choir (at this point, David Lasley, Luther Vandross, Luci Martin, Diva Gray, and Alfa Anderson) piping up with the simple, repeated refrain: "I say freak."

"Le Freak" sold a million copies in the United States alone. It became one of the best-selling singles in Atlantic's history. **DE**

Milk and Alcohol | Dr. Feelgood (1978)

Writer | John Mayo, Nick Lowe
Producer | Richard Gottehrer
Label | United Artists
Album | *Private Practice* (1978)

"You don't have to be a musician to play rock and roll. You've just got to love it and want to play it."

Lee Brilleaux, 1976

◀ **Influenced by: One Bourbon, One Scotch, One Beer** John Lee Hooker (1974)
▶ **Influence on: Three Times Enough ·** Nine Below Zero (1981)
● **Covered by:** Jimmy Keith & His Shocky Horrors (1995)
★ **Other key track:** She Does It Right (1975)

Dr. Feelgood were key precursors to punk in the United Kingdom. Hailing from Canvey Island, an unloved lump of land in the Thames estuary, they created a fierce R&B sound in the mid-Seventies, a time when others were content to sail around their *Topographic Oceans.*

"Milk and Alcohol" is from the band's second album, *Private Practice,* with guitarist John "Gypie" Mayo. The riff had been written by Mayo and then played to friend and sometime Feelgood producer Nick Lowe, who recalled a night in 1976 when he and the band had witnessed a desultory John Lee Hooker gig at the Starwood Hotel in Los Angeles. Disgruntled at their hero's lackluster performance and fueled by White Russian cocktails (vodka, Kahlua, and milk), the band set off for their accommodation and drove through a red light. Pulled over by the LAPD, manager Chris Fenwick took the rap for the quantity of hash found in the car's glove compartment; in the song, this is altered to "They got me on milk and alcohol."

"Milk and Alcohol" was produced by Richard Gottehrer, who in the Sixties had been in the U.S. garage band The Strangeloves; he had recently produced Richard Hell and Blondie. His all-faders-blazing approach gives the song's military beat a zing, but it is the vocal performance of Lee Brilleaux, a man whose 1994 *New York Times* obituary praised his "sweat-spattered, eye-bulging, finger-wagging performances" that clinches it, the malevolent growl of a weary commentator.

The single—the band's tenth—was released in a choice of brown- or white-colored vinyl and reached the U.K. Top Ten in early 1979. Dr. Feelgood may have cut better songs, but this is the one that remains burned in the memory. **DE**

Don't Stop Me Now | Queen (1978)

Writer | Freddie Mercury
Producer | Queen, Roy Thomas Baker
Label | EMI
Album | *Jazz* (1978)

"It's a work of genius. You will see, in any wedding, party, hen night or celebration, the effect this track has when it comes on."
Brian May, 2009

◄ **Influenced by: The Bitch Is Back** • Elton John (1974)
► **Influence on: I Believe in a Thing Called Love**
The Darkness (2003)
● **Covered by:** The Vandals (2004) • McFly (2006)
Jeroen van der Boom (2006) • Katy Perry (2009)
The Royal Philharmonic Orchestra (2009)

Freddie Mercury, Queen's extravagant front man, was often happiest hiding behind a role in his songs, as on the operatic melodrama of "Bohemian Rhapsody"; his lyrics rarely told us much about the man who wrote them. But both the words and the surging, giddy celebratory spirit of "Don't Stop Me Now" came straight from Mercury's heart, and captured this legendary libertine in all his glory.

The track was recorded in Nice in July 1978, during the earliest sessions for Queen's seventh album, *Jazz* (the group would later decamp to Mountain Studios in Montreux, which they subsequently purchased). For all the song's impressive bombast, the arrangement is relatively sparse by Queen's standards: aside from a gloriously triumphant Brian May solo before the final chorus, it is simply bass, drums, and piano.

But this proves the perfect background for Mercury's vocal tour de force, his ecstatic lead backed by the trademark Queen choir of harmonies egging Freddie along as the legendarily omnivorous singer celebrates his appetite for hedonism with typical camp: he's a "sex machine ready to reload," "a racing car passing by like Lady Godiva." This was, undoubtedly, the ideal soundtrack for the infamously debauched soirée the group held in New Orleans later that year to celebrate the release of *Jazz*.

Reaching No. 9 in the U.K. singles charts, "Don't Stop Me Now" was one of Queen's lesser hits, but it has recently enjoyed a resurgence of popularity: director Edgar Wright used the song brilliantly in his 2004 zombie-comedy *Shaun of the Dead*, while viewers of U.K. TV's *Top Gear* voted it the Greatest Driving Song a year later, recasting the tune as a joyrider's anthem. **SC**

Queen's Freddie Mercury bestrides the stage like a camp Colossus in 1978. ➡

Teenage Kicks
The Undertones (1978)

Writer | John O'Neill
Producer | The Undertones
Label | Good Vibrations
Album | *The Undertones*
(1978)

It is a song that will forever be associated with John Peel, but he wasn't the only Radio 1 DJ who brought The Undertones' debut to the British public's attention. While Peel had songwriter John O'Neill "in shock" when he played it twice in a row on his eclectic evening show, Peter Powell gave it further exposure after Peel left him a note to say, "This is the one."

Not that the band necessarily agreed. The Undertones had more of a punk agenda than has often been credited. O'Neill's cohorts didn't want to record the song (preferring "True Confessions"). "If anything reeked of commercialism or anything obvious, we'd do the reverse of that," he said. The song actually failed to make the cut on the original release of their self-titled album.

Nevertheless, as the title track of the four-song EP on Belfast's Good Vibrations label, it helped them to get a deal with Sire. "We were just the right age at the right time. It's the strength of the voice and the urgency of the drums and guitars. It seemed to capture the moment," O'Neill later commented. But even Peel and Powell's high-profile championing couldn't push a re-release any higher than No. 31 in the U.K. charts.

At Peel's request, the song that so perfectly sums up youthful yearning was played at his funeral, and the line "Teenage dreams so hard to beat" features on his headstone. **CB**

You Make Me Feel (Mighty Real)
Sylvester (1978)

Writer | J. Wirrick, S. James
Producer | Harvey Fuqua, Sylvester James
Label | Fantasy
Album | *Step II* (1978)

Born in Los Angeles, Sylvester James was a successful gospel singer as a child, but fled a repressive home life and as a teenager lived on the streets. In 1967, he moved to the gay ghetto of San Francisco, where he came spectacularly to life. Performing briefly in a musical, he then joined drag group The Cockettes, apparently contributing a repertoire of Bessie Smith blues songs, before launching his solo career as a soul and rock singer.

So far, so average for a new gay boy in town, but in 1977 he signed with Fantasy Records and began to work with renowned Motown producer Harvey Fuqua. The special added ingredient to this combination was provided by synthesizer player Patrick Cowley, who transformed a rough demo of one particular track. Cowley's insistent synthesizer beat pushed Sylvester right onto the dance floor.

That track was the six-and-a-half-minute "You Make Me Feel (Mighty Real)," an inspired tour de force, its fast, bass-heavy beat and insistent synthesizer swooshes supporting Sylvester's exuberant falsetto vocals in a life-affirming anthem for hedonism. More than any Donna Summer or Gloria Gaynor track, this was the soundtrack of gay liberation traced out on the dance floor, sung by an out-and-proud gay man—often appearing in full drag—barely a decade after the Stonewall riots in New York heralded the birth of a new liberation movement. **SA**

Human Fly
The Cramps (1978)

Writer | Poison Ivy Rorschach, Lux Interior
Producer | Alex Chilton
Label | Vengeance
Album | N/A

The Cramps are celebrated as the progenitors of psychobilly—an amalgam of punk and rockabilly with a hefty dose of B-movie schlock—but in truth, their style referenced many genres; they were as likely to draw on *Nuggets*-era garage, Link Wray's power chords, or the demented surf of The Trashmen as they were on inbred rockabilly.

"Human Fly" was The Cramps' second single, cut in Memphis under the supervision of Big Star head honcho Alex Chilton. It was also their first self-penned release, although—as always with The Cramps—to call it an original composition is to miss the point. The opening scale and relentless riff are a reworking of a heroically obscure saxophone instrumental called "The Green Mosquito" from 1958, rendered almost unrecognizable by a wall of fuzz, reverb, and distortion. Front man Lux Interior (who took his stage name from the text of a Chevrolet advert) almost swallows the microphone as he snarls and yowls, making atrocious puns about pushing "the pest aside." Lux's wife and lead guitarist, "Poison" Ivy Rorschach, hammers home the horror-film riff over Nick Knox's caveman drums, while skunk-haired Bryan Gregory, also on guitar, buzzes around them.

The title alludes to the 1958 horror film *The Fly*, but also to The Cramps' modus operandi: as a fly feeds on detritus, so did they, finding rich pickings in pop culture's overlooked morsels. **SP**

Shake Your Body (Down to the Ground) | The Jacksons (1978)

Writer | Michael Jackson, Randy Jackson
Producer | The Jacksons
Label | Epic
Album | *Destiny* (1978)

The Jackson 5's Motown recording contract expired in 1975, leaving the brothers to consider their options. Suspecting under-promotion of recent material, they decamped to Epic, leaving Jermaine—who was wedded to Berry Gordy's daughter, Hazel—to remain with Motown as a solo artist. Changing their name to The Jacksons under legal pressure, the band enjoyed initial success, but after two albums a rethink was on the cards.

For 1978's *Destiny*, the brothers themselves took control, laying down a belated marker in the disco dirt. They took sole production credits, and Michael began to show his songwriting chops, teaming up with Randy to pen this dance-floor stormer that, following on from their cover of Michael's "Blame It on the Boogie," established The Jacksons anew on the club scene. An almost instant blossoming of the now-grown star's talent, "Shake Your Body (Down to the Ground)" would also prove the prototype for Michael's 1979 solo classic "Don't Stop 'til You Get Enough," both driven by skipping bass to futuristic funk thrills.

Arranged by Greg Phillinganes, a version of "Shake Your Body (Down to the Ground)" reached the *Billboard* Top Ten. Its influence spread beyond Michael's solo material to Rockers Revenge's 1982 electro rework of Eddy Grant's "Walking on Sunshine" and, later, to reggae-crossover artist Shaggy's 2000 hit "Dance and Shout." **MH**

(I Don't Want to Go to) Chelsea | Elvis Costello & The Attractions (1978)

Writer | Elvis Costello
Producer | Nick Lowe
Label | Radar
Album | *This Year's Model* (1978)

" 'Ha, bloody ha,' said the first taxi driver that I asked to take me there after the record came out."

Elvis Costello, 1989

◄ **Influenced by: I Can't Explain** · The Who (1965)
▶ **Influence on: Way Too Long** · Audio Bullys (2003)
● **Covered by:** The Nutley Brass (1996)
★ **Other key tracks:** Alison (1977) · Watching the Detectives (1977) · Pump It Up (1978) · Radio Radio (1978) · Accidents Will Happen (1979)

On the cover of his second album, *This Year's Model*, Elvis Costello poses with a Hasselblad like David Hemmings in *Blow-Up*, Michelangelo Antonioni's snapshot of Swinging London. Is it homage or sneering parody? Whatever the case, the image is suitably ambiguous for an LP on which Elvis & The Attractions adopt the tight beat-group stylings (and tighter suits) of their mod forebears, while at the same time deriding those among their peers who insist on living in the past.

The album's leadoff single alludes to the plot of *Blow-Up* in its references to photography and murder, but it is also a rancorous attack on the self-absorbed fashion set of the King's Road. "There's no place here for the miniskirt waddle," jeers Costello, indicating that things had moved on since '66, while taking a sideswipe at the trendy crowd sucked into the area by Malcolm McLaren and Vivienne Westwood's punk boutique, Sex.

"Chelsea" was only the second vinyl outing for Costello with The Attractions (his previous backing group, Clover, would go on to become Huey Lewis's News), and on the song, the new-wave recruits compete to outperform one another. Pete Thomas leads off with a virtuoso drum solo, jousting with the clamorous fuzz-bass of his namesake Bruce, while Steve Nieve chimes in with his circling Vox Continental organ. The band's input radically reshaped the song—while Costello's spidery lead guitar had started off as an approximation of The Who's "I Can't Explain," it was rejigged to emulate rock-steady trio The Pioneers. Ironically, given this influence from the West Indies, the song was dropped from *This Year's Model* in the United States for purportedly sounding "too English." **SP**

One Nation under a Groove | Funkadelic (1978)

Writer | George Clinton, Walter Morrison, Garry Shider
Producer | George Clinton
Label | Warner Bros.
Album | *One Nation under a Groove* (1978)

"Funk is like, who gives a funk? If you feel like dancing, funk it. Funk gives you that attitude that everything's all right."
George Clinton, 1999

◄ **Influenced by: Funky Worm** · The Ohio Players (1973)
► **Influence on: Oops Upside Your Head** · The Gap Band (1979)
● **Covered by:** Chaka Demus & Pliers (1993)
★ **Other key tracks:** Groovallegiance (1978) · Who Says a Funk Band Can't Play Rock?! (1978)

George Clinton's Parliafunkadelicment thang was always a polymorphously perverse project, shifting its identity and style as Clinton's whim and the group's lineup decreed. Funkadelic had long served as the grimy, self-indulgent, and out-there flip side to Parliament's more crafted and pop-orientated sides. However, "One Nation under a Groove" boasted none of Funkadelic's trademark tripped-out touches; the mind-mangling guitar workouts, the fierce polyrhythms, and the wild and freaky noises were gone. Instead, here was a moment of brilliant coherence, perhaps the ensemble's most enduring dance-floor anthem.

Some credit for this sonic volte-face goes to co-writer and new Funkadelic recruit Walter "Junie" Morrison, a former member of fellow funkateers The Ohio Players. He had played the wild synth lines for their 1973 hit "Funky Worm," and coined the addictive hook for Funkadelic's 1979 classic "(Not Just) Knee Deep." Junie layered restlessly funky synth lines throughout, with in-house keyboard genius Bernie Worrell handling the fearsomely slinky synth bass line, throbbing along to an irresistible, hand-clap-emboldened 4/4 beat that played disco at its own game (only funkier).

As ever, there was a concept here, spelled out by call 'n' response vocals shared between Junie, guitarist Garry Shider, and Clinton himself, with Ray Davis (a veteran since the days of Clinton's doo-wop group, The Parliaments) offering deep bass tones. Society's a mess, they suggested, so trust in funk to free you from your hang-ups and make everything better. Thanks to copious sampling from the likes of EPMD, Ice Cube, and X-Clan, the track would form the backbone of the funk of the future. **SC**

Das Model | Kraftwerk (1978)

Writer | Ralf Hütter, Karl Bartos, Emil Schult
Producer | Ralf Hütter, Florian Schneider
Label | Kling Klang
Album | *The Man-Machine* (1978)

"It's about the context of an object, paying money: for beauty we will pay. I think the cynicism is obvious, don't you?"
Ralf Hütter, 2009

◄ **Influenced by: Ricochet, Parts 1 & 2** • Tangerine
Dream (1975)
► **Influence on: Walk Away** • Orchestral Manoeuvres
in the Dark (1981)
● **Covered by: Big Black** (1987) • Rammstein (1997)
Messer Chups (2007)

In 1978, boundary-pushing German electronic pioneers Kraftwerk revealed that, for them, to be light years ahead of anyone else in the music they were making hadn't been enough; they could also break ground in the lyrics department. The words of "The Model"—in which the life of a female fashion model comes under scrutiny ("It only takes a camera to change her mind")—anticipates future developments; in this case, the rise of the obsession with celebrity culture.

Being so far ahead of the field meant having to wait for the rest of the world to catch up, though. Commercially, this song had everything: a throbbing bass chassis (created on a Moog Micromoog synthesizer); a melody that, once heard, is never forgotten; and, for Kraftwerk, a relatively radio-friendly running time (it is by far the shortest track on *The Man-Machine*). However, first issued in 1978 on a 45 pairing it with "Neon Lights," it failed to cause much commotion outside of its native Germany. In 1981, a second attempt, as a double-A-side with "Computer Love" (from the *Computer World* album), just punctured the U.K. Top Forty. It was only right at the close of 1981—and at the third time of asking—that the song was finally recognized as an "instant" classic. Early in 1982, it rose to become the U.K. No. 1.

In some benighted circles, the members of Kraftwerk are seen as emotionless automata. By way of redressing the balance, there is an amusing soundcheck version of "The Model" from a gig in Edinburgh in 1981. In this performance, the closing line, "Now she's a big success, I want to meet her again," was amended to make for a clearly unrobotic action that was rather more intimate than just "meeting." **CB**

Kraftwerk in 1978: from left, Karl Bartos, Ralf Hütter, Florian Schneider, and Wolfgang Flür. ➡

Writer | Howard Devoto, Pete Shelley
Producer | Magazine, Mick Glossop
Label | Virgin
Album | *Real Life* (1978)

"If you take my lack of confidence and you take my pride—well, there you really are shot by both sides."

Howard Devoto, 2000

◀ **Influenced by: Search and Destroy** · Iggy & The Stooges (1973)

▶ **Influence on: Just** · Radiohead (1995)

● **Covered by: No Fun at All** (1997) · Mansun (2004) Radiohead (2007) · Jarvis Cocker (2007)

★ **Other key track:** My Mind Ain't So Open (1978)

If you wonder why there was a parting of the ways between Buzzcocks and Howard Devoto after the release of the *Spiral Scratch* EP, you could do worse than sample the two respective camps' treatment of Pete Shelley's awesome ascending guitar riff. Buzzcocks came up with "Lipstick," which related the end of a relationship—a subject that provided rich and regular material for the band. Devoto's new outfit, Magazine, fashioned a much darker and more sinister affair. "I was shocked to find what was allowed / I didn't lose myself in the crowd," sings Devoto, a line born of disillusion with the lack of individuality on the punk scene. That thought is part of—no question, no quibbles—one of the best debut singles ever.

The memorable phrase that gave the song its title came up during a conversation. "I was totally apolitical," said Devoto. "A socialist friend said to me, 'You'll end up getting shot by both sides.'" The words stuck with Devoto, and he filed them away until the right musical outlet presented itself. With guitar genius John McGeoch creating the chest-tightening tension, Devoto is "Shot by both sides / On the run to the outside of everything."

Critic Paul Morley welcomed the critical outlook of the single in fulsome terms: "Hero, you come at last." Like most of Magazine's output, the song was massively underappreciated at the time, but has been hugely influential since. Radiohead, major Magazine fans, are just one of the bands to have covered it live. As a calling card for Magazine, though, it failed, limping no further than No. 41 in the U.K. singles chart in early 1978. The uncomfortable thought that Devoto was casting pearls before swine comes to mind. What were we all thinking of? **CB**

Public Image | Public Image Ltd (1978)

Writer | Public Image Ltd
Producer | Public Image Ltd
Label | Virgin
Album | *First Issue* (1978)

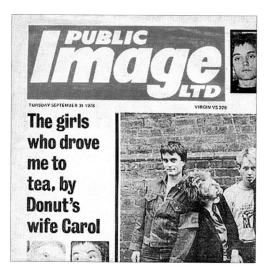

"The PiL album, especially the single, had the immediacy of hardcore and punk, but a more sinister, artful edge."
Mattie Safer, The Rapture, 2007

◀ **Influenced by: Moonshake** · Can (1973)
▶ **Influence on: Higher Than the Sun** · Primal Scream (1991)
● **Covered by:** Alphabeat (2008) · Feeder (2008)
★ **Other key tracks:** Religion (1978) · Death Disco (1979) Poptones (1979) · This Is Not a Love Song (1984)

There was little in 1978 that John Lydon wouldn't do to avoid being pigeonholed as a Sex Pistol. The name Johnny Rotten had already been ditched, but also in his sights was a musical makeover. When asked about his new direction, he said he was setting up an Irish-Cajun-disco-Afro rock band. With Moog synthesizers.

Clearly, it was difficult to know what to expect from Public Image Ltd. But it was obvious what it *wasn't* going to be. "The first thing I wanted was to not sound the same as the Pistols," said Lydon. "After twenty minutes in a rehearsal room, we knew damn well we weren't going to."

"Public Image" had been written during the Pistols period, but the sound was far removed from anything they had achieved. For the ominous intro, it helped enormously having a bassist— Jah Wobble—with a genuine aptitude for the instrument, while Keith Levene's spiky guitars were a relief after the relentless metal of Steve Jones.

Lydon took the title from Muriel Spark's 1968 Booker Prize–nominated *The Public Image*, a slim novel about, as Lydon observed, "what can happen to you if you don't control your public image." In the song, Lydon protested, "I'm not the same as when I began / I will not be treated as property." Wobble admitted, "It set his world to rights. He was full of righteous indignation." And should anyone fail to get the message concerning media manipulation, the point was hammered home by the single's sleeve, produced in the style of a tabloid newspaper.

A Top Ten hit in the United Kingdom showed that there was indeed life after Malcolm McLaren. Said Lydon proudly: "I can look at myself and go: 'My God, you did that? Not bad, boy.'" **CB**

Alternative Ulster | Stiff Little Fingers (1978)

Writer | Stiff Little Fingers, Gordon Ogilvie
Producer | Ed Hollis
Label | Rough Trade / Rigid Digits
Album | *Inflammable Material* (1979)

"I love The Undertones but ... my soundtrack was more 'Alternative Ulster.'"

Bono, 2007

◀ **Influenced by:** Ulster · Sham 69 (1977)
▶ **Influence on:** Church of Noise · Therapy? (1998)
● **Covered by:** London Punkharmonic Orchestra (1998)
Voice of a Generation (1999)
★ **Other key tracks:** Suspect Device (1979) · At the Edge
(1980) · Listen (1982)

Recalling his state of mind while growing up in Northern Ireland during the period known as "The Troubles," Stiff Little Fingers' front man Jake Burns stated in 2002: "There's got to be more to life than waking up scared and going to bed scared." Taking to the streets to participate in peaceful protests against violence would only, he admitted with bitter irony, have resulted in a beating. That left music as one of the few platforms for protest—and Stiff Little Fingers (with journalist Gordon Ogilvie's lyrical input) certainly made use of it.

As the *Guardian* put it in 2003, "Alternative Ulster" found the band relating "the foul brew of brutality and boredom that characterized their experience of their home town." "It was a song written in the classic punk mode about having nothing to do," said Burns. "That was the overriding reality of life in Belfast for a teenager in the mid-Seventies: . . . the sheer tedium of having nowhere to go."

With Eddie & The Hot Rods' Ed Hollis as producer, "Alternative Ulster" was not as rough, but just as ready, as Stiff Little Fingers' debut 45, "Suspect Device." Although "Alternative Ulster" had originally been intended as a free flexi-disc for a local fanzine of the same name, it ended up as a commercial release that gave the Rough Trade label a flying start, selling around 35,000 copies. Recommending the abandonment of any reliance on the R.U.C. and I.R.A., it also reminded the metrocentric punk movement that major events actually did happen outside London. Burns told *Sounds* in 1980: "I get fans asking me just what my alternative Ulster would be. They think I'm advocating a new state or something. But it's a personal alternative." **CB**

(White Man) In Hammersmith Palais | The Clash (1978)

Writer | Joe Strummer, Mick Jones
Producer | The Clash
Label | CBS
Album | N/A

"This was one of the greatest bands of all time coming into their own."

The Edge, 2006

◀ **Influenced by: Police and Thieves** • Junior Murvin (1976)

▶ **Influence on: Jah War** • The Ruts (1979)

● **Covered by: 311** (1999) • Fighting Gravity (1999) Manic Hispanic (2001) • Built to Spill (2003) • Colin Gilmore (2004)

On June 5, 1977, The Clash singer/guitarist Joe Strummer, together with Clash roadie Roadent and DJ Don Letts, attended a reggae all-nighter at the Hammersmith Palais headlined by Jamaican performers Dillinger, Leroy Smart, and Delroy Wilson. This night led to Strummer's writing the song he regarded as his best, "(White Man) In Hammersmith Palais"—not because he was inspired but because he felt that the show was too showbiz and the music "pop reggae," rather than the revolutionary "roots" sounds he had hoped for. Released as a single in June 1978 (and on the U.S. version of debut LP *The Clash*), it saw the band move away from riff-heavy, raw punk and build on the punky reggae hybrid of their cover of Junior Murvin's "Police and Thieves," while lyrically developing Strummer's morality politics.

Over the course of the song, Strummer muses that any armed revolution would fail because it could never beat the British army; calls for unity among black and white youths; and suggests they ask for "some wealth distribution." He then addresses the punk movement, attacking "the new groups" in "Burton suits" out to make it rich, who are "turning rebellion into money"— usually taken to be a dig at The Jam, who wore matching suits and had fallen out with The Clash when supporting on the latter's White Riot tour. Strummer also acidly comments on the rise of the far right National Front in Britain with the supposition that "If Adolf Hitler flew in today / They'd send a limousine anyway."

Lead guitarist Mick Jones, who harmonizes with Joe, conceived the perfect arrangement to back Strummer's lyrics, uniting rock guitar with a reggae beat. **JoH**

Ambition
Subway Sect (1978)

Writer | Vic Godard
Producer | Mickey Foote
Label | Rough Trade
Album | N/A

Subway Sect proved to be one of the most obscure of the original U.K. punk bands. The group was originally formed by Vic Godard and Rob Simmons, residents of Mortlake, west London, at the suggestion of Sex Pistols svengali Malcolm McLaren, who invited them to perform at the 100 Club Punk Special in London in September 1976.

Subway Sect's music and image were in stark contrast to the colorful bluster of the Pistols. Influenced by the New York Dolls and The Velvet Underground, their minimal songs featured a Fender Mustang guitar, chosen for its trebly sound, and Godard's Americanism-free lyrics.

Under the wing of Clash manager Bernie Rhodes, the publicity-shy group were to release just two singles and record one John Peel Session in their first two years of existence. An outtake from an aborted and still unissued album, the second of these singles was "Ambition," which Rhodes eventually released after a plea by Buzzcocks manager Richard Boon, who wanted Subway Sect to open for his group on their upcoming tour. The song was a blistering piece of power pop overlaid with Godard's sarcastic nasal delivery. (Rhodes apparently sped up the recording in an attempt to make it sound more "punk.") The track also features a distinctive trilling synthesizer and—in the background—the sound of ping-pong balls recorded from an arcade game. **CS**

Hong Kong Garden
Siouxsie & The Banshees (1978)

Writer | Siouxsie Sioux, John McKay, Kenny Morris, Steve Severin
Producer | S. Lillywhite, N. Stevenson
Label | Polydor
Album | N/A

The last of the first wave of punk bands to get a record deal—despite connections with punk's inner circle, a fierce live reputation, and an impressive graffiti campaign by an overzealous fan—Siouxsie & The Banshees were finally signed by Polydor on the strength of this song after it was broadcast as a John Peel session on U.K. radio. It had its genesis in a song guitarist John McKay was working on entitled "People Phobia"; McKay also came up with the distinctive oriental-sounding introduction, played on an electronic xylophone.

Taking its title from a Chinese takeaway in Siouxsie's hometown of Chislehurst, "Hong Kong Garden" was written by her as a tribute to the Chinese race after she had witnessed skinheads taunting the owners with racist abuse. As she herself said, "They used to mercilessly torment these people for being foreigners. It made me feel so helpless, hopeless, and ill."

Following months of media intrigue and anticipation, this soaring slice of post-punk euphoria crashed into the U.K. Top Ten yet did not appear on their debut album, *The Scream* (it was later included on the CD reissue). However, its success paved the way for one of the most original and enigmatic bands of the post-punk era. The song later appeared, with an extended orchestral introduction, on the soundtrack of Sofia Coppola's 2006 biopic, *Marie Antoinette*. **CS**

Siouxsie Sioux, aka Susan Ballion, vamps for the camera in the late Seventies. ➔

Being Boiled | The Human League (1978)

Writer | Martyn Ware, Ian Craig Marsh, Philip Oakey
Producer | The Human League
Label | Fast Product
Album | *Travelogue* (1980)

"I have always been cocky. I thought 'Being Boiled,' our first single in 1978, would go Top Ten."
Philip Oakey, 1995

◀ **Influenced by: Showroom Dummies** · Kraftwerk (1977)
▶ **Influence on: Just Fascination** · Cabaret Voltaire (1983)
● **Covered by: Beborn Beton** (1994) · **Heaven 17** (1999) **Simple Minds** (2001)

Those familiar with The Human League only from their 1981 album, *Dare*, might easily be forgiven for failing to recognize their debut single, released three years earlier, as the work of the same band. However, the disparity is less surprising when you consider that front man Phil Oakey was the only factor common to both lineups. Further, "Being Boiled" was recorded for the princely sum of £2.50, a payment made almost invisible down the line by what it took to achieve the immaculate pop gloss of that huge hit album.

For the single, Martyn Ware and Ian Craig Marsh had the music mapped out but needed lyrics. These came courtesy of former Sheffield schoolmate Oakey. It was a bargain-basement budget, but that didn't mean that big ideas were off-limits. Nevertheless, Oakey admitted that his lyrics could have benefited from a little more research. "I'd got some religions mixed up and I thought that, like, Buddhism was the same as Hinduism, and it was sort of a plea for vegetarianism, really, against killing the silkworms to make socks or something. I got really confused about it." "I thought the lyrics were just completely crazy," commented Marsh.

Understandably, the stark and ominous 1978-era Human League sound polarized opinion. Bowie and Vince Clarke were firmly in the pro camp, but John Lydon dismissed it. Outside of celebrity circles, it proved a tough sell. After leaving no chart imprint on its first release, a reworked version (with John Leckie as co-producer) on the *Holiday 80* EP did slightly better. However, it was only when it piggybacked on the post-"Don't You Want Me" demand for Human League product that the track reached No. 6 in the United Kingdom. **CB**

Rock Lobster | The B-52's (1978)

Writer | Fred Schneider, Ricky Wilson
Producer | The B-52's
Label | Boo-Fant
Album | *The B-52's* (1979)

"We just did our own thing, which was a combination of rock 'n' roll, and Fellini, and game-show host, and corn . . . ."
Fred Schneider, 1990

◄ **Influenced by: Beach Party** · Annette Funicello (1963)
► **Influence on: Hey You Girl** · Pitbull (2006)
● **Covered by: Dead Horse** (1991) · Boy Division (2008)
★ **Other key tracks:** 52 Girls (1978) · Planet Claire (1978)
Party Out of Bounds (1980) · Private Idaho (1980)
Summer of Love (1986)

Situated 250 miles (400 km) from the Atlantic Ocean, the college town of Athens, Georgia, is perhaps not the most sensible location to make a beach-party record—but then The B-52's were never the most sensible of bands. That much was clear from their polyester threads and vertiginous beehive wigs, a kitsch aesthetic that carried over into the wacky scat-style backing vocals, twangy riff (reminiscent of the John Barry Seven's 1959 instrumental "Beat Girl"), and marine-biology-obsessed lyrics of their debut single.

Initially released in May 1978 as a limited-edition pressing of 2,000 copies—with lead singer Fred Schneider's workplace, the El Dorado Restaurant, given on the back as a contact address—"Rock Lobster" was re-recorded with producer Chris Blackwell for the band's debut album the following year. This new version, stretched out to almost seven minutes, places Kate Pierson's *Munsters*-theme Farfisa arabesques in the foreground and finds Schneider on vicious form, barking out lines such as "Twisting round the fire, having fun" with unwarranted venom. By the point that he is gleefully enumerating various fish species with far-fetched vocal effects ("In walked a jelly fish / There goes a dogfish"), Ricky Wilson's guitar line has mutated from surf twang into sinister Gang of Four post-punk.

The song is also credited with enticing John Lennon back into the recording studio after a five-year hiatus. Hearing "Rock Lobster" in a Bermuda disco, the former Beatle detected a certain similarity to his wife's vocal style in Cindy Wilson's atonal shriek. "It sounds just like Ono's music," he said in 1980, "so I said to meself, 'It's time to get out the old axe and wake the wife up!'" **SP**

Roxanne | The Police (1978)

Writer | Sting
Producer | Stewart Copeland, Sting, Andy Summers
Label | A&M
Album | *Outlandos d'Amour* (1978)

"It was a total offshoot from what we'd been doing. . . . That was the turning point for The Police, that and Andy joining."

Sting, 1978

◀ **Influenced by:** Soul Rebel · Bob Marley & The Wailers (1970)

▶ **Influence on:** Who Can It Be Now? · Men at Work (1981)

● **Covered by:** Aswad (1997) · George Michael (1999) Fall Out Boy (2005) · Michael Paynter (2008)

At the start of 1978, The Police had no record deal, media support, or money. They had formed in 1977 and tried to ride the U.K. punk-rock explosion. Yet the trio comprised a singer who was, until recently, a school teacher; a drummer who had played with prog-rock ensemble Curved Air; and a guitarist whose CV stretched back to late-Sixties psychedelic bands.

Aware they appeared too old, and were too musically fluent, to genuinely embrace the advent of punk as rock's Year Zero, The Police determined to forge their own path, bringing elements of jazz and reggae into their sound. "Roxanne" was written by Sting after the band played a Parisian punk festival in the winter of 1977. Noting the prostitutes around their hotel, he started thinking of the song's refrain while in the hotel lobby, where there was a poster for *Cyrano de Bergerac*, the famous play in which the protagonist has a beloved named Roxanne. The band shaped the song in the studio in 1978, building a subtle reggae-rock feel around the keen, emotional hook of Sting's unique vocal. Impressed by the track, manager Miles Copeland—older brother of drummer Stewart—won them a record deal.

Released as a single in 1978, "Roxanne" flopped. The band doggedly toured the United States with Miles Copeland, working the media until U.S. radio stations cautiously began playing the song. In 1979, "Roxanne" became a minor U.S. hit, and U.K. radio also began to give the song airtime; soon the media were wondering who this stylish new band were. With "Roxanne," The Police went from being losers in the punk wars to quickly becoming the most successful band to arise out of the entire punk–new wave explosion. **GC**

Another Girl, Another Planet | The Only Ones (1978)

Writer | Peter Perrett
Producer | The Only Ones
Label | CBS
Album | *The Only Ones* (1978)

"After thirty years, you have to be happy you have a song that means so much to so many people."

Peter Perrett, 2009

◀ **Influenced by: Lonely Planet Boy** · New York Dolls (1973)

▶ **Influence on: You Can't Put Your Arms around a Memory** · Johnny Thunders (1978)

● **Covered by:** The Replacements (1989) · London Punkharmonic Orchestra (1998) · Jack Hayter (2002)

The Only Ones are the one-hit wonders who wonder how they never had a hit, and this is their masterpiece. "Another Girl, Another Planet" boasts an unforgettable introduction, wittily drawled lyrics, and an accomplished, fluttering guitar solo. The song has been referenced by famous fans such as Pete Doherty and John Peel. It has even been described as "the greatest rock single ever recorded." It is, in short, the sort of instant classic that screams No. 1—but it never charted higher than No. 57 in the United Kingdom.

The song opens with a quietly stuttering guitar line that is joined by sporadic bass and slowly thumping percussion, rising louder, faster, and higher into a euphoric swirl until vocalist and songwriter Peter Perrett's nasal whine breaks the spell, joining the party with nearly a minute already gone. The first line has to be arresting: "I always flirt with death / I could kill, but I don't care about it." Perrett was a brilliant lyricist, a skill acquired on the streets of south London and in British boarding schools. Many of his songs—this one included, albeit obliquely—reference the drugs that Perrett claims he sold to finance his band's first self-produced album and to which he later became destructively addicted. He went on to work with another talented drug-taker, Johnny Thunders, playing on "You Can't Put Your Arms around a Memory," as The Only Ones staggered through three occasionally brilliant albums before the inevitable split (and just as inevitable reunion in 2007). Their keynote song has appeared in commercials and numerous soundtracks, been covered by Babyshambles, The Replacements, and Blink-182, and even lent its name to an American film. But it has never been a hit. **PW**

Germ Free Adolescents | X-Ray Spex (1978)

Writer | Poly Styrene
Producer | Falcon Stuart
Label | EMI
Album | *Germ Free Adolescents* (1978)

"When you were into reggae you did skanking, slow dancing, and I could do that to it."

Poly Styrene, 2008

◄ **Influenced by:** Heavy Manners · Prince Far-I (1976)
► **Influence on:** Not a Pretty Girl · Ani DiFranco (1995)
● **Covered by:** The Levellers (1997) · Michael Monroe (2003) · Studio 99 (2006)
★ **Other key tracks:** Oh Bondage Up Yours! (1977) · The Day the World Turned Day-Glo (1978) · Identity (1978)

Of all the many distinctive bands to emerge from British punk, few stood out like X-Ray Spex. That was largely due to their extraordinary singer, Marian Elliott (aka Poly Styrene), who was born in Brixton of English and Somali parents, dressed in colorful clothes, had a shock of unruly hair, wore braces on her teeth, possessed an incredible voice (she was a trained opera singer), and had seemingly supernatural confidence for an eighteen-year-old. In appearance, music, and looks, X-Ray Spex were so far ahead of the curve, they were on a different graph. Poly sang sardonically about consumerism and an increasingly disposable lifestyle, but also about femininity, challenging convention with every song. And those songs were brilliant, belligerent, bouncy punk-pop with a branded motif—the out-of-tune sax wielded with malicious intent by Rudi Thomson.

"Germ Free Adolescents" (sometimes "Germ Free Adolescence" on the label, but we'll go with the typical spelling) is unique, and thus typical of the band's string of sensational singles. The Clash's "(White Man) In Hammersmith Palais" is usually said to be the first song to merge punk and reggae, but Poly might have beaten them to it with this track. It is hypnotic, almost psychedelically slow, as it copies the dub reggae records that the band danced to at London punk club The Roxy. The lyrics are about a girl who "cleans her teeth ten times a day," obsessed with cleanliness, terrified of germs. The comment is obvious: it is the ritual purification of daily life that is unnatural, not the dirt. There is also a faint trace of the melancholy that would later develop into full-blown depression; citing pressure, Styrene quit the band and became a Hare Krishna devotee. Unique to the last. **PW**

Runnin' with the Devil | Van Halen (1978)

Writer | Edward Van Halen, Alex Van Halen, Michael Anthony, David Lee Roth
Producer | Ted Templeman
Label | Warner Bros.
Album | *Van Halen* (1978)

"I think Van Halen is the future of rock 'n' roll for the United States, and for the world!"

David Lee Roth, 1978

◀ **Influenced by: Dealer** · Deep Purple (1975)
▶ **Influence on: Lay It Down** · Ratt (1985)
● **Covered by:** Bryan Clark (2003) · Whitney Morgan & The Waycross Georgia Farmboys (2006)
★ **Other key tracks:** Eruption (1978) · Ain't Talkin' 'bout Love (1978) · Jamie's Cryin' (1978)

Deep Purple had petered out, Black Sabbath were sinking, Led Zeppelin were laying low. Meanwhile, success was eating Kiss and Aerosmith alive. Hard rock needed a shot in the arm.

Van Halen were that shot—and how. Their debut album was packed with punches, but the fight was won in the first three and a half minutes: "Runnin' with the Devil," among the most superbly swaggering openers ever etched into vinyl.

Long a feature of their live sets, the song was recorded—albeit in a slightly faster, funkier form—on a 1977 demo financed by Kiss bassist Gene Simmons. "I quickly learned that I didn't like overdubbing," Eddie Van Halen told *Guitar World*. "Gene said, 'Here's what you do in the studio—you play your rhythm parts on one track, and your solo parts on another.' I remember feeling very uncomfortable with separating my lead and fill parts from my rhythm parts. Onstage, I'd gotten used to doing both simultaneously."

Nonetheless, the version on *Van Halen* required one of the album's few guitar overdubs. Further sonic trickery came into play with its introductory car horns (also on the 1977 demo, reputedly at Simmons's suggestion). Those horns, from the band's own vehicles, were linked with an automobile battery, and the result played backward to menacing effect.

The title—inspired by The Ohio Players' 1974 cut "Runnin' from the Devil"—suggested devil worship (hence the song's appearance in Adam Sandler's 2000 movie *Little Nicky*). The lyrics, however, summarized front man David Lee Roth's lone-wolf attitude. "We were not afraid of defying convention," he recalled in 1997. Ten million U.S. sales proved that fortune favored the brave. **BM**

Hammond Song
The Roches (1979)

Writer | Margaret A. Roche
Producer | Robert Fripp
Label | Warner Bros.
Album | *The Roches* (1979)

Shortly after disbanding Simon & Garfunkel, Paul Simon quietly signed on to teach a songwriting course at New York University. Maggie and Terre (pronounced "Terry") Roche didn't study at NYU, but they went there anyway in the hope of pitching some songs to him in the university lobby. His response was to invite them to his class.

For all the ambivalence this suggests, Simon's patronage came in handy. The singer-songwriter paid for the pair to take music lessons, invited them to sing on his 1973 album *There Goes Rhymin' Simon*, and then, two years later, co-produced their debut, *Seductive Reasoning*. The sisters then decided to head south and hang out with an old friend who had moved to Hammond, Louisiana. The visit formed the basis of "Hammond Song."

By the time the song was recorded, The Roches had become a trio, augmented by kid sister Suzzy (rhymes with "fuzzy"). Shows in New York folk clubs were noticed by Warner Brothers and by King Crimson guitarist Robert Fripp, who produced their first record as a three-piece. It seemed an unlikely combination, but Fripp's spacious production (in "audio verité," says the sleeve) gave the trio the room that their bold, cultured harmonies deserved, and Fripp's own out-of-the-ether guitar solos on "Hammond Song" were a perfect fit. As soloists or as a group, they never made a more affecting record. **WF-J**

Heaven
Talking Heads (1979)

Writer | David Byrne, Jerry Harrison
Producer | Brian Eno, Talking Heads
Label | Sire
Album | *Fear of Music* (1979)

Talking Heads' country-and-western-tinged ballad from their third album brought a different slant to their musical style, which is typically pigeonholed as angular, quirky new wave.

Singer David Byrne's lyrics often undermine or expose their subjects in unexpected ways. In "Heaven," though perhaps drawing inspiration from Christian country music, he creates his own notably secular vision of life after death. Portraying an afterlife without pain, sorrow, and challenge, he presents a peculiarly sterile, soulless, and empty utopia: "Heaven is a place . . . where nothing, nothing ever happens." It is a disquieting vision of a cyclical eternity where happiness is stretched to the point of meaningless vacuity. "The band in Heaven . . . play my favorite song, they play it one more time, they play it all night long." Yet there is an element of ambiguity here too: the barest hint that heaven might also offer escape, perfection, and tranquillity.

The track's glacially spacious production—due in part to the manner in which it was recorded at Chris Frantz and Tina Weymouth's New York loft, via an on-street mobile recording unit—enhances the otherworldly tone of the song. An excellent version, arranged for acoustic guitar and bass with backing harmonies, later appeared on the soundtrack of the acclaimed live Talking Heads film *Stop Making Sense*. **JL**

Talking Heads' David Byrne is typically poker-faced during a London performance in 1979. ➔

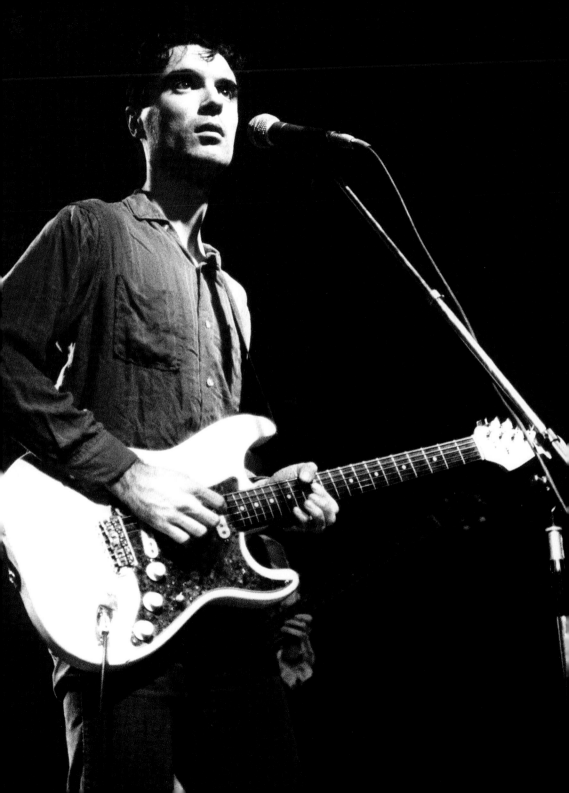

The Eton Rifles | The Jam (1979)

Writer | Paul Weller
Producer | The Jam, Vic Coppersmith-Heaven
Label | Polydor
Album | *Setting Sons* (1979)

"It wasn't a fucking jolly drinking song for the cadet corps."

Paul Weller, 2008

▶ **Influenced by: Substitute** · The Who (1966)
▶ **Influence on: What a Waster** · The Libertines (2002)
● **Covered by:** The Nutley Brass (1996) · Stereophonics (2009)
★ **Other key tracks:** In the City (1977) · English Rose (1978) · The Butterfly Collector (1979)

Will politicians ever learn? David Cameron, the Conservative British prime minister, spoke in 2008 of his love for "The Eton Rifles." Cameron is an alumnus of said fee-paying public school in the English county of Berkshire, but it was wasted money if he is able to miss the point of one of The Jam's finest moments so spectacularly. As Paul Weller said pointedly: "Which part didn't he get?"

The song that Weller wrote in a caravan was inspired by a 1978 clash in Slough between pupils from Eton and left-wing demonstrators, which he used to illustrate his larger point about the inequality of the class struggle in Britain: "Thought you were smart when you took them on / But you didn't take a peep in their artillery room / All that rugby puts hairs on your chest / What chance have you got against a tie and a crest?" The scathing lyrics were matched by musical backing that is ablaze with aggression. But it had been a hard track to get right. Producer Vic Coppersmith-Heaven took to lining the walls and floors of the studio with corrugated iron sheets to create the appropriate acoustics. Without the advantage of the song taking shape in live sets, three separate attempts were needed to capture lightning in a bottle. The end result was "absolutely burning hot," said Coppersmith-Heaven. "We just knew it was going to be a great single."

It was successful as well, becoming The Jam's first U.K. Top Ten entry. If there was a plus side to Cameron's comments, it was helping to get The Modfather to reintroduce "The Eton Rifles" into his live sets, one of the few Jam-era compositions to be granted such exalted status. "It's unfortunate that it's still relevant," Weller reflected. "It's the same bullshit with different faces." **CB**

London Calling | The Clash (1979)

Writer | Mick Jones, Joe Strummer
Producer | Guy Stevens
Label | CBS
Album | *London Calling* (1979)

"By 'London Calling,' we'd become grown men and, having traveled, had become more worldly."

Paul Simonon, 2004

◀ **Influenced by: Dead End Street** • The Kinks (1966)
▶ **Influence on: Don't Break the Red Tape** • The Enemy (2009)
● **Covered by:** The Pogues (1993) • Captain Tractor (1995) One King Down (1999) • The Business (2003) Gelugugu (2003) • Bruce Springsteen (2009)

In the classroom of English first-generation punk, if The Damned were the loons messing around at the back and scaring the girls with frogs, then the Sex Pistols were the snot-nosed tearaways disagreeing with everything they were told because . . . well, just because. That left The Clash as the defiant ones who reminded everyone—repeatedly, and at high volume—how messed up the world had become.

The anger that fueled the band through their first two albums was still present on "London Calling," but it was now allied to a greater maturity. Guitarist Mick Jones reflected, nearly twenty-five years after the single reached No. 11 in the U.K. charts, that "it was Joe [Strummer] that provided the spark that we needed to put down very specific ideas into song." On this occasion, the song made reference to the nuclear scare at Three Mile Island in the United States, police brutality, drugs, meltdown (both financial and climatic), and cultural vacuity. If the manifesto of The Clash could sometimes have benefited from fine-tuning to achieve a sharper focus, presenting such a smorgasbord of society's ills here merely added to the oppressive, apocalyptic atmosphere created by the ominous backing from Jones, bassist Paul Simonon, and drummer Topper Headon.

The song's title was a nod toward the British Broadcasting Corporation's transmissions in World War II, which often began with "This is London calling." By adapting the words to his own ends, Strummer was suggesting that his warnings deserved our attention. Time may have shown him to be right on the mark. As Simonon said, The Clash left the songs about "love, kissing, and having a nice time" to other bands. **CB**

Transmission | Joy Division (1979)

Writer | Ian Curtis
Producer | Martin Hannett
Label | Factory Records
Album | N/A

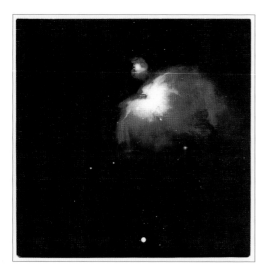

"People had been moving around, and they all stopped and listened.... That's when I realized that was our first great song."

Peter Hook, 1994

◄ **Influenced by: Funtime** · Iggy Pop (1977)
► **Influence on: Obstacle 1** · Interpol (2002)
● **Covered by:** Submarine (1995) · Low (1996)
The Smashing Pumpkins (1998) · New Order (2002)
Bauhaus (2006) · Innerpartysystem (2008) · Hot Chip (2009)

It is typical of Joy Division's stubbornly perverse logic that perhaps their defining song did not appear on either of their studio albums. Instead, "Transmission," the first single proper from the Salford, Greater Manchester, quartet, hit shelves in November 1979, five months after the release of their critically acclaimed debut, *Unknown Pleasures*.

Like their debut album, "Transmission" was recorded by Factory Records' in-house production auteur, Martin Hannett. The band themselves initially disliked Hannett's ghostly, hollowed-out treatment: "We felt that Martin had toned it down, especially with the guitars," complained guitarist Bernard Sumner. But it was Hannett's peculiar studio foibles—like dismantling the drum kit and recording each component one by one to ensure total "sound separation"—that gave the likes of "Transmission" an eerie spaciousness.

Commencing with a loping, minimal Peter Hook bass line, the song speeds forward with machine-like precision, Stephen Morris's robotic drumming presaging the sequenced beats that the band, minus vocalist Ian Curtis, would later explore as New Order. Sumner's slashes of reverb-soaked guitar ramp up the intensity, while Curtis's vocal—an exhortation to "dance to the radio"—starts as a mordant murmur and rises to a climactic shriek.

Following Curtis's suicide in 1980, the song has taken on added significance in its apparent references to his collapsing marriage and his battle with epilepsy. In *24 Hour Party People*, the semi-fictional biopic of Factory Records, Joy Division's performance of the song is interrupted when Ian Curtis suffers a fit. Curtis's widow, Deborah Curtis, also named her 1995 memoir, *Touching from a Distance*, after a lyric in the song. **LP**

Joy Division's Ian Curtis in 1979, the year before he took his own life. ➔

Voulez-Vous | Abba (1979)

Writer | Björn Ulvaeus, Benny Andersson
Producer | Björn Ulvaeus, Benny Andersson
Label | Polar
Album | *Voulez-Vous* (1979)

"It's incredibly inspiring when you get to hear a lot of fresh stuff you like; you get a kick to do something that is just as good."
Benny Andersson, 1979

◀ **Influenced by:** Stayin' Alive · Bee Gees (1977)
▶ **Influence on:** Drama! · Erasure (1989)
● **Covered by:** High Inergy (1979) · HAM (1990) · Erasure (1992) · Culture Club (1999) · Morgana Lefay (2001)
★ **Other key tracks:** Waterloo (1974) · S.O.S. (1975) Knowing Me, Knowing You (1976)

The recording sessions for what was to become Abba's sixth album, *Voulez-Vous*, had proved problematic, inasmuch as the group's busy worldwide touring schedule was getting in the way of their creative processes. Although the quartet had recently completed their Polar Studios in Stockholm, which was to be their base for the rest of their career, their nomadic existence meant that they were often away from home.

They settled in the Bahamas in January 1979 and moved to record backing tracks in Miami. This change of scene energized their songwriting, and one song, entitled "Amerika," propelled by a compelling disco beat, swiftly came to the fore. Björn Ulvaeus and Benny Andersson had been captivated by disco, the craze that was by then sweeping the world, especially the Bee Gees' populist version of it, as well as Chic's faultless ability to marry rhythm and melody.

Recorded at Criteria Studios, Miami, with veteran U.S. R&B producer/engineer Tom Dowd in attendance, the rhythm track that was "Amerika" became "Voulez-Vous." It was one of their most effective grooves: a dense and climactic affair, an early example of what would later be known as eurodisco. Finished at Polar, the track was ostensibly about a pickup at a nightclub; it featured a joint lead vocal from Frida and Agnetha, and the chorus referenced the "ah-has" that had proved such a trademark in their earlier success, "Knowing Me, Knowing You."

Although not one of their biggest hits at the time, the song's relative lack of exposure has made it one of their most enduring numbers. It certainly enlivened Abba. Within a couple of months, they had nearly completed their new album. **DE**

Beat the Clock | Sparks (1979)

Writer | Ron Mael, Russell Mael
Producer | Giorgio Moroder
Label | Virgin
Album | *No. 1 in Heaven* (1979)

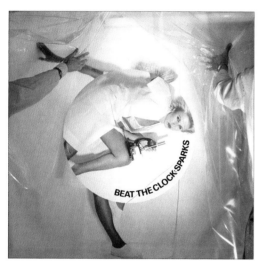

" 'Beat the Clock' was like a Velvet Underground song when I wrote it. . . . But what Giorgio did with it was amazing."

Ron Mael, 2002

◀ **Influenced by: I Feel Love** · Donna Summer (1977)
▶ **Influence on: Planet Earth** · Duran Duran (1981)
● **Covered by:** Bent Boys (1993)
★ **Other key tracks:** Amateur Hour (1979) · Never Turn Your Back on Mother Earth (1974) · The Number One Song in Heaven (1979)

In 1978, Sparks were at a crossroads. L.A.-born brothers Ron and Russell Mael had relocated to England in 1973 and had become overnight sensations. After three successful long-players, they set their sights on success at home. Two fruitless albums later, their operatic pomp rock was out of step with its era.

However, a turning point came after the brothers heard, and fell under the spell of, "I Feel Love" by Donna Summer. Never overenamored of working with rock musicians, they felt that an amalgamation of their songs with dance beats and synthesizers was a logical next step. The last act of their outgoing manager, John Hewlett, was to link the brothers with Giorgio Moroder, then white-hot after his productions with Summer. As the trio began to work together, Ron and Russell dispensed with the idea of a "band" and became one of the first synthesizer duos.

Ron presented Moroder with the songs he had written, and the producer rejected all of them apart from two, one of which was "Beat the Clock." Taken from its piano-based roots, Moroder fashioned it into a snappy piece of disco pop, with live drums played by his cohort Keith Forsey.

Ron's witty lyrics focused on the pace of modern living, with its protagonist entering school at two o'clock, getting his doctorate the same afternoon, and getting divorced by four. His life's ambition is to meet Liz Taylor . . . and suddenly that happens, as well. The record returned Sparks to the U.K. Top Ten, propelled by an effective marketing campaign by Virgin Records, while the serious rock journals sneered about the brothers "going disco." Two years later in Britain, the charts would be full of synth duos. **DE**

Oliver's Army | Elvis Costello & The Attractions (1979)

Writer | Elvis Costello
Producer | Nick Lowe, Elvis Costello
Label | Radar
Album | *Armed Forces* (1979)

"They always get a working-class boy to do the killing. I don't know who said that; maybe it was me."

Elvis Costello, 2002

◄ **Influenced by: Dancing Queen** · Abba (1976)
► **Influence on: Shipbuilding** · Robert Wyatt (1982)
● **Covered by:** Billy Bragg (1988) · Blur (1993)
Raimundos (1997) · Peter Mulvey (2002) · Belle &
Sebastian (2002) · Minibar (2003) · Dirty Pretty Things
(2006) · Bill Janovitz (2008)

The high-water mark of Costello's career (in commercial terms, at least), "Oliver's Army" was doubtless assisted in its ascent of the British charts by its colonization of Benny Andersson's joyous piano motif from "Dancing Queen." But behind the pop shimmer is a broadside against militarism informed by the singer's first visit to Belfast's "Murder Mile" in 1978. The armed force in question is Cromwell's New Model Army—the precursor to the modern British military and the instigators of infamous massacres at Drogheda and Wexford in the seventeenth century.

Costello's words are dense and allusive, taking in a list of then-current global flashpoints including Palestine, the Berlin Wall, Hong Kong, and Johannesburg. At the same time, he subverts the misleading language of army-recruitment posters ("There's no danger / It's a professional career"). But the historical scope is not limited to the late Seventies: from the English Civil War allusion to the name-check of Winston Churchill, "Oliver's Army" inhabits a temporal neverland, one that was also visited by Costello's former Stiff Records labelmate Jona Lewie in his U.K. Christmas hit, "Stop the Cavalry," in 1980.

There is a sense that this is a vicious update of Buffy Saint-Marie's peacenik folk song "Universal Soldier"—a timeless lament for boys sent to fight in men's wars. And amid the devilishly catchy choruses and the rollicking barrelhouse piano was the notorious line "One more widow, one less white nigger," the vocabulary of which was enough to prevent the single charting in the States. Costello refused, point-blank, to change it. "That was the aim," he said in 1982. "A grim heart in the middle of an Abba record." **SP**

Tusk | Fleetwood Mac (1979)

Writer | Lindsey Buckingham
Producer | Fleetwood Mac, R. Dashut, K. Caillat
Label | Warner Bros.
Album | *Tusk* (1979)

"It really worked and it's a glorious noise, something I'm very proud of. I still find it on jukeboxes."

Mick Fleetwood, 1995

◄ **Influenced by: Born in Captivity** · The Alpha Band (1977)
► **Influence on: Brother Sport** · Animal Collective (2009)
● **Covered by:** R.E.M. (1991) · Camper Van Beethoven (2002)
★ **Other key track:** Gold Dust Woman (1977)

Nutty double albums are usually associated with early Seventies prog rock. But the decade's end brought examples ranging from ambitious to bonkers, including The Clash's *London Calling*, Pink Floyd's *The Wall*, and Stevie Wonder's *Journey through the Secret Life of Plants*.

Falling midway on the sanity scale was Fleetwood Mac's *Tusk*. Over the course of twenty songs, the band's melodic might was matched by guitarist Lindsey Buckingham's forays into new wave–flavored experimentation.

The schizophrenia bubbled over on the title track—which, drummer Mick Fleetwood told *Mojo*, "came from a riff we used to jam on in sound checks. When we started the album, we worked on it but everybody lost interest in it. It went in the dustbin for about a year until I pulled it out again. . . . When I said I wanted to record the U.S.C. [University of Southern California] marching band at Dodger Stadium, they were sure I'd gone round the twist, so I paid for it myself."

Singer Stevie Nicks, who twirled a baton in the video, recalled the entity that inspired the song and album title: "In the studio we had two ivory tusks as tall as Mick on either side of the console. The board became 'Tusk.' If something went wrong, it was, 'Tusk is down.' Those thirteen months working in that room were our journey up the sacred mountain to the sacred African percussion place, where all the gods of music lived."

Although the album was deemed a failure, its title track stomped into Top Tens around the world. "Despite having virtually no lyric, it became one of our biggest hits," Fleetwood marveled. "It really worked. . . . Later, we got to play live with the marching band, which was marvelous." **BM**

Gloria
Umberto Tozzi (1979)

Writer | Umberto Tozzi, Giancarlo Bigazzi
Producer | Umberto Tozzi
Label | CBS
Album | *Gloria* (1979)

The late Seventies are now thought of as a time of febrile punk creativity, yet most of Europe was in thrall to a distinct variety of disco. And if Abba's "Dancing Queen" was the cream of that crop, twenty-seven-year-old Tozzi's anthem ran it pretty close. It was the ultimate square's riposte: a huge chorus sung by a man with gorgeous hair and no attitude whatsoever. "Gloria" wasn't the singer's biggest hit—"Ti Amo" had dominated the Italian pop charts in 1977—but it swept the continent (it was also covered by Jonathan King for British consumption and made the U.S. Latin charts).

In 1982, arranger and keyboard player Greg Mathieson brought the song to the New World, where Canadian writer Trevor Veitch turned the lyrics around, from lightweight love song ("Gloria, when I'm with you," sang King, "my life takes on new meaning") to warning ("If everybody wants you, why isn't anybody calling?"). Used on Laura Branigan's debut album, it sold two million copies in the United States, got to No. 2 in the U.S. charts, and swept back across the world once more (it hit No. 1 in Germany, holding Tozzi's own version off the top spot). That colossal riff refused to lie down, also turning up on Olivia Newton-John's "Physical" and Pulp's "Disco 2000"—and the 2004 election campaign by Filipino president Gloria Macapagal-Arroyo. Twenty years later, Tozzi recorded Veitch's version for his own *Best Of* collection. **DH**

Black Eyed Dog
Nick Drake (1979)

Writer | Nick Drake
Producer | Joe Boyd
Label | Island
Album | *Fruit Tree* (1979)

Today, Nick Drake is seen as one of the most important British singer-songwriters of the past half century, but his three albums made minimal impact when released between 1969 and 1972. Drake had expected to be a star, and became angry and depressed when that failed to happen. In early 1974, his producer, Joe Boyd, set up a recording session for a new album. Drake was obviously in no state to record anything, though. Boyd and producer John Wood managed to get four guitar tracks recorded in one evening, doing the vocals and rough mix the next night. All four were bleak and bitter laments, none more so than "Black Eyed Dog." The track lay unreleased for five years, until it was added, along with the other three final tracks, to Drake's third album, *Pink Moon*, as part of 1979's *Fruit Tree* boxed set.

The "black dog" has long been a symbol for the devil and, since the eighteenth century, a euphemism for depression—used most notably by Winston Churchill. Nick Drake once told a journalist that, like bluesman Robert Johnson, he had a hellhound, or black dog, on his trail. With spare, picked guitar lines on just three strings and a tremulous, uncertain voice, Drake lamented, "A black-eyed dog he called at my door / The black-eyed dog he called for more." The lines could have come straight from the Robert Johnson songbook. **SA**

Nick Drake in 1972: a jewel in the crown of English songwriting. ➡

Are "Friends" Electric? | Gary Numan & Tubeway Army (1979)

Writer | Gary Numan
Producer | Gary Numan
Label | Beggars Banquet
Album | *Replicas* (1979)

"We had the first electronic No. 1, and that opened a lot of doors for other bands. I'm proud of that."

Gary Numan, 2009

◀ **Influenced by: The Man-Machine** · Kraftwerk (1978)
▶ **Influence on: Metal** · Nine Inch Nails (2000)
● **Covered by:** Replicants (1995) · An Pierlé (1996)
Moloko (1997) · Information Society (1997) · Republica
(1997) · Rosetta Stone (2000) · Chris Whitley (2006)
Weezer (2008) · The Dead Weather (2009)

Gary Numan's enduring electronic ballad "Are 'Friends' Electric?" saw Tubeway Army's lead singer change tack from the rock/faux-punk direction of the band's previous work. While the song did not entirely dispense with guitars and classic rock instrumentation, it was a bold and stark statement of the electronic sound with which Numan would become synonymous.

A mood piece about isolation in a world overrun by dehumanizing technology (a prescient thought for an age where "friends" now meet on social-networking sites), the song is measured, eerie, and dislocated, with sparse instrumentation driven by a bass line and an off-kilter synth melody. At five-plus minutes, the track is unusually long for a single (the result of Numan melding two disparate song ideas), and it doesn't even feature a chorus.

Replicas, the album that spawned this U.K. No. 1 single, bordered on conceptual in its portrait of a dystopian future; its influences include authors Philip K. Dick and William Burroughs. The "friends," said Numan, "provide services. You can call a 'friend' to play chess with, or indulge your most obscene sexual fantasies, or anything in between."

On the sleeve (and the collectible picture-disc format), Numan sports a proto-goth android look: sinister, removed, distant. He would later attribute his own remoteness to Asperger's syndrome; he subsequently struggled to cope when a sudden surge in his popularity was paralleled by sneering from certain sections of the musical press.

Twenty-three years later, the backing track formed the basis for Sugababes' U.K. No. 1 single "Freak Like Me," produced by Richard X. The hit refurb helped to pave the way toward a critical and commercial upswing in Numan's standing. **JL**

Boys Don't Cry | The Cure (1979)

Writer | R. Smith, L. Tolhurst, M. Dempsey
Producer | Chris Parry
Label | Fiction
Album | N/A

"We were sort of playing pop, just … playing it badly."

Robert Smith, 1987

◄ **Influenced by: Love You More** · Buzzcocks (1978)
► **Influence on: Feed Me with Your Kiss** · My Bloody Valentine (1988)
● **Covered by:** Tuscadero (1995) · Lostprophets (2004) Superbus (2005) · Grant-Lee Phillips (2006) · Reel Big Fish (2006) · Razorlight (2006)

The glumly gothic Cure have a heritage of incongruously poppy songs. Indeed, an early demo won them a contract with a European label who, remembered main man Robert Smith, "thought they could turn us into a teen group."

"Boys Don't Cry"—"a Seventies attempt at a Sixties pop song"—caught the ear of Polydor's Chris Parry. He promptly formed the Fiction subsidiary, signed The Cure, and set them to work on a debut album. The result was *Three Imaginary Boys*, which oddly omitted "Boys Don't Cry," and their debut single, "Killing an Arab." (U.S. label PVC included both songs on a revised version of the album, titled *Boys Don't Cry*, in 1980.)

Issued as a single in 1979, the song flopped. "In a perfect world, 'Boys Don't Cry' would have been a No. 1 hit," maintained Smith, nonetheless relieved that he wouldn't have to "rewrite that song again and again, just to maintain that success." At a festival appearance that summer, he dedicated it to another band on the bill: Motörhead.

A remixed version in 1986 featured a new vocal by Smith, pitched lower this time so that he would not have to replicate the higher lines of the original in TV appearances. The single was used to promote the group's compilation *Standing on a Beach*—which, weirdly, presented listeners with the original version of "Boys Don't Cry."

The song bequeathed a title to the Oscar-winning movie of 1999 starring Hilary Swank. The movie featured neither of the Cure versions, preferring a cover by Nathan Larson, partner of singer Nina Persson of The Cardigans. But The Cure themselves have kept the jangly gem alive: thirty years on, it is a regular and rapturously received highlight of their Olympian live sets. **BM**

Good Times
Chic (1979)

Writer | Nile Rodgers,
Bernard Edwards
Producer | N. Rodgers, B. Edwards
Label | Atlantic
Album | *Risqué* (1979)

"Good Times" was Chic's last pop chart success. It topped the U.S. chart in August 1979, just as the backlash against disco music reached its apogee after the much-publicized "Disco Demolition" at Chicago's Comiskey Park, where DJ Steve Dahl blew up boxes of twelve-inch singles in front of a baying crowd. However, this was disco that didn't suck. Recorded as part of the group's career-best album, *Risqué*, "Good Times" is one very clever record. Set over its simplistic, seductive, and repetitive groove is the ironic suggestion that dancing in the face of the largest economic recession since the Twenties was possibly not the smartest thing. Lyricist Nile Rodgers could sense that change was in the air, and, by adapting the words of old Depression-era standard "Happy Days Are Here Again," he jabbed slyly at the ephemeral opulence of the late Seventies. Not that anyone noticed: they were too busy grooving to it.

Chic suffered badly because of the backlash. Within a year, the group, whose appearance coincided with the popularity of disco, were persona non grata. By 1983, Rodgers and co-leader Bernard Edwards could only achieve major success as producers. However, the influence of "Good Times" has proved outstanding—within two years of its release, Edwards noted at the time, over thirty songs had appeared that owed a debt to its riff, from Queen and Blondie to Eno and Byrne. **DE**

Don't Stop 'til You Get Enough
Michael Jackson (1979)

Writer | Michael Jackson
Producer | Quincy Jones
Label | Epic
Album | *Off the Wall* (1979)

Despite a handful of solo albums on Motown, *Off the Wall* marked the true artistic debut of the star who would rule pop for the next decade. Michael Jackson had recently joined Epic Records, and there was doubt as to whether the twenty-year-old former child star would make a viable adult act. His lead single, "Don't Stop 'til You Get Enough," was the first recording over which he had artistic control, and it got off to a puzzling start. Over a stabbing synth bass that veered sharply from the smooth edges of his old material, Jackson, his boyish tenor bashful and nervous, offered a spoken appeal to the listener. It sounded like a kid rambling about *Star Wars*: "You know, I was wondering, you know . . . if you could keep on, because the force has got a lot of power, and it makes me feel like . . . . "

But just one "oooh!" was all it took. The force was strong with this one, indeed. "Don't Stop" blasts off with a rhythmic symphony of strings and horns that dances around Jackson's mischievous falsetto. Sounding at once sexual and pure, he peppers the verses with the vocal yaps and hiccups that would soon become his signature, expressing the flow of barely contained passion. It isn't black music or white music, not exactly disco or rock—gloriously, it is somehow all of those things at once. Little wonder that it resulted in a U.S. No. 1, Jackson's first in seven years. **MO**

A bejewelled twenty-one-year-old Michael Jackson performs in New Orleans in 1979. ➡

Lost in Music
Sister Sledge (1979)

Writer | Nile Rodgers, Bernard Edwards
Producer | N. Rodgers, B. Edwards
Label | Atlantic
Album | We Are Family (1979)

After Bernard Edwards and Nile Rodgers of Chic had made their production intentions clear, they were offered the pick of Atlantic's roster to work with. The Rolling Stones and Bette Midler were mentioned. However, the duo didn't wish to be responsible for major acts "turning disco." They chose instead to work with Sister Sledge, a four-piece sister act from Philadelphia that so far had enjoyed only minor success.

Rodgers and Edwards set to work getting appropriate material to allow the Sledges—Kim, Joni, and Debbie, led by the wonderfully emotive voice of Kathy—to achieve the recognition they deserved. Recorded alongside Chic's own C'est Chic album and using the same players, the resulting work, We Are Family, bristled with hits, and none is more appealing than "Lost in Music."

The idea for the song derived from the fact that, at Chic's zenith, the hardworking Edwards and Rodgers would use the phrase "lost in music" when they wanted people to leave them alone. "It was the code to stop fucking with me, because I was writing a song!" Rodgers revealed in 2004.

It is a manifesto for freedom, postponing life's stresses for the rapture of the dance floor, set ablaze by the euphoric Sledge vocals. A big hit in the United Kingdom, the widescreen production of "Lost in Music" still sounds like a drive downtown on the busiest night of the year. **DE**

Brass in Pocket
Pretenders (1979)

Writer | Chrissie Hynde, James Honeyman-Scott
Producer | Chris Thomas
Label | Real
Album | Pretenders (1980)

"I hated 'Brass in Pocket' with a vengeance," complained Pretenders front woman Chrissie Hynde. "The guys in the group, the manager, the producer, the record company, are all saying, 'This is a fantastic song, this is a No. 1 record.' And I'm going, 'Well, that's exactly the reasons why I don't like it: it's so obvious.'"

Nonetheless, the band's third single became their first U.K. No. 1 and pushed Pretenders to platinum—not bad for a song that many misunderstood. "They thought the lyrics in 'Brass in Pocket' went—instead of 'gonna use my sidestep'—'gonna use my sausage,'" drummer Martin Chambers told Creem. Other head-scratchers included "Detroit leaning" (driving with one hand on the wheel and an arm on the window) and "brass" (money) itself.

The music was equally intriguing. "I probably pinched the riff off an old Barry White record," guitarist James Honeyman-Scott admitted to NME, "'cos I used to take those riffs and put them back to front again, y'know. Like 'Love's Theme' by Love [Unlimited] Orchestra. . . . [In the middle] there's a little guitar bit that goes der der la la, and that's just something from some Motown record, Steve Cropper or something."

An ambitious handful have covered the song, including Suede in 1992 and Kelis in 2005. Yet "Brass in Pocket" remains forever Hynde's. **BM**

Outdoor Miner
Wire (1979)

Writer | Graham Lewis, Colin Newman
Producer | Mike Thorne
Label | Harvest
Album | N/A

A melodic and delicate indie-style single, "Outdoor Miner" is a relatively rare but welcome demonstration of Wire flirting with mainstream pop. While the band's debut album showcased their punk roots, albeit in an idiosyncratic fashion, Wire's second LP, 1978's *Chairs Missing*—on which an early version of "Outdoor Miner" appeared—tapped into their "art school" background.

Although the song's subject is an insect pest—a fly larva—the lyrics are emotive, in particular the chorus: "He lies on his side, is he trying to hide? / In fact it's the earth, which he's known since birth." The song's "serpentine miner," burrowing through a leaf, is in danger of being crushed under the weight of its own excavation.

The superior seven-inch-single version features a prominent and dexterous piano element, additional vocals, and an extra chorus, and is a good minute longer than the original edit on *Chairs Missing*. This single mix appeared as a bonus track on a reissued CD of the album, but was later removed as the band considered that it detracted from the original LP's integrity.

While Wire were by no means a singles band, "Outdoor Miner" gave them their highest-charting U.K. seven-inch; it made No. 51. But because of allegations of "chart hyping" by their label, EMI, Wire lost both their slot on U.K. music showcase *Top of the Pops* and their chance of pop fame. **JL**

Rapper's Delight
The Sugarhill Gang (1979)

Writer | Edwards, Rodgers, O'Brien, Jackson, Wright, van der Pool Robinson
Producer | Sylvia Inc.
Label | Sugar Hill
Album | *Sugarhill Gang* (1980)

Cooked up by soul-singer-turned-label-owner Sylvia Robinson, who recruited three unknown New Jersey rappers to "sugar up" the street sound blowing up in the Bronx, "Rapper's Delight" combined artist-audience chants and comically throwaway rhymes with a session band's reconstruction of the infectious bass line from Chic's disco smash "Good Times." An infectious party starter, it gave the genre its first calling card: "I said a hip-hop, the hippie, the hippie to the hip, hip-hop, and you don't stop . . . ."

New York radio initially aired the track as a joke, but the punch line had staying power. Label boss Joe Robinson recalls: "All I had to do with it was get one play anywhere and it broke." At one point, "Rapper's Delight" was shifting 75,000 copies a week—hitting the U.S. No. 36 and U.K. No. 3.

Members of New York's early hip-hop fraternity were unimpressed, dismissing the rhymes as plagiarized and accusing the song of reducing the culture's street credo to a commercial "rap" product. As hip-hop historian David Toop later said, The Sugarhill Gang "were to Bronx hip-hop what The Police were to the Sex Pistols." "Rapper's Delight" wasn't the first rapped record—funk band Fatback's "King Tim III (Personality Jock)," released months earlier, owns that title—or the most original, but its success around the world ignited a new urban musical movement. **MK**

California Über Alles | Dead Kennedys (1979)

Writer | Jello Biafra, John Greenway
Producer | Dead Kennedys
Label | Alternative Tentacles
Album | N/A

" 'California Über Alles' was inspired musically more by Japanese Kabuki than anything else."

Jello Biafra, 2005

◀ **Influenced by: Holidays in the Sun** · Sex Pistols (1977)
▶ **Influence on: Giuliani Über Alles** · Hasidic New Wave (1999)
● **Covered by:** Disposable Heroes of Hiphoprisy (1992) Six Feet Under (2000) · Jello Biafra with The Melvins (2005) · The Delgados (2006)

Some bands take time to find their place; others spring fully armored as if from nowhere. So it was with Dead Kennedys, the Californian punks who mixed the tunes and chutzpah of the Sex Pistols with the sloganeering of The Clash and announced their intentions with their very first single, a scabrous, satirical, and unpredictable punk-pop classic. Much of the credit goes to lead singer and songwriter Jello Biafra, a political prankster who ran for mayor of San Francisco in 1979.

With its title cribbed from the German national anthem, "California Über Alles" begins with suitably pounding martial drums and a creeping bass line, before Biafra's sarcastic croon takes over, imagining California as a liberal dictatorship ("Mellow out or you will pay") under the hippie-approved Democrat governor Jerry Brown. The left-baiting and Nazi allusions bring a delicious whiff of iconoclastic tastelessness to the whole enterprise, most notably in the slowed-down middle section of Disney punk—"Now it's 1984 / Knock, knock at your front door / It's the suede-denim secret police / They've come for your uncool niece." A thrash-rock holler closes the song.

Having first released it as a single, the band recorded an almost identical version for their debut album *Fresh Fruit for Rotting Vegetables* (1980) and revisited it in easy-listening style in 1981 as "We've Got a Bigger Problem Now," with Jerry Brown replaced by Ronald Reagan. Then Biafra hooked up with The Melvins to have a (to date) final go in 2005, this time in honor of the election of Arnold Schwarzenegger as California governor. It has also been recorded and retooled by artists as diverse as Disposable Heroes of Hiphoprisy and The Delgados. **PW**

Typical Girls | The Slits (1979)

Writer | Ari Up, Palmolive, Viv Albertine, Tessa Pollitt
Producer | Dennis Bovell
Label | Island
Album | *Cut* (1979)

"They made really cool music. They were so inspiring in the way they combined dub and funk and punk."

Jill Cunniff, Luscious Jackson, 1999

◄ **Influenced by:** Identity · X Ray Spex (1978)
► **Influence on:** She Walks on Me · Hole (1994)
★ **Other key tracks:** Adventures Close to Home (1979)
Instant Hit (1979) · Love und Romance (1979)
Shoplifting (1979) · Spend, Spend, Spend (1979)

Punk was underpinned by the D.I.Y. ethos, the unshakeable belief that a self-chosen path was infinitely preferable to tagging along with the herd. "Typical Girls," one of The Slits' finest three minutes, exhorted women to take the same route as themselves and look beyond a magazine-defined agenda of anxiety that consisted of fretting about "spots, fat, and natural smells." The alternative, they suggested, was to ask yourself "who's bringing out the new, improved model?"

Given this independent stance, it was ironic when an influential figure in the punk vanguard—Mick Jones, no less—encouraged Ari Up and company to alter their distinctive style and bring it more into line with what had become the accepted punk template. "Like a Clash song, smack-boom-boom-boom, one-two-three-four," recalled Ari to *Harp* magazine in 2005. Malcolm McLaren, Slits manager for the briefest time, had already advised them to turn down the bass and turn up the lead guitars.

Despite such counsel, "Typical Girls" is conclusive evidence that the group did right in sticking by their sound and refusing to iron out the kinks that gave the song its unique character. With its elements of spiky blues, speeded-up reggae (dub producer Dennis Bovell was at the controls), and classic girl-group pop, it seemed like three great records rolled into one. The song did not become a huge hit (it reached No. 60 in the United Kingdom after Island fruitlessly lobbied for the cover of "I Heard It through the Grapevine" to be the A-side). Rather, its importance lies in its influence on what was to come. It proved that, in what was (and still is) a male-dominated industry, women were now making music on their own terms. **CB**

Atomic | Blondie (1979)

Writer | Debbie Harry, Jimmy Destri
Producer | Mike Chapman
Label | Chrysalis
Album | *Eat to the Beat* (1979)

" 'Atomic' was pieced together from every spaghetti western I ever saw and a bunch of other things."

Jimmy Destri, 2003

◀ **Influenced by: I Feel Love** · Donna Summer (1977)
▶ **Influence on: Into the Groove** · Madonna (1985)
● **Covered by:** The Mission (1992) · Sleeper (1996)
★ **Other key tracks:** Rip Her to Shreds (1976) · Denis (1978) · Hanging on the Telephone (1978) · Picture This (1978) · Dreaming (1979) · Union City Blue (1979)

In 1981, Ennio Morricone had a hit with "Chi Mai," but the Italian legend's presence had been felt in the U.K. charts not long before. Co-writer Jimmy Destri admitted that Blondie's 1980 No. 1 single "Atomic"—itself a remixed version of the eponymous song on Side Two of the previous year's *Eat to the Beat*)—was shot through with heavy influences from Morricone's soundtracks for Sergio Leone's Sixties spaghetti westerns, starring Clint Eastwood.

When describing his experience of the writing process, the Blondie guitarist admitted that the music for "Atomic" did not exactly leap into his head fully formed. Destri elaborated: "Sometimes, a song will spill out in fifteen minutes, like 'Maria.' Sometimes, it will take a year. Like 'Atomic.'" Fortunately, coming up with the words was a rather quicker affair for Debbie Harry, whose writing style was rooted in on-the-spot improvisation. "I would write while the band were just playing the song and trying to figure it out," she said. "I would just be scatting along with them and I would just start going, 'Ooooooh, your hair is beautiful.'"

Chrysalis did not drag its heels in exploiting the band's potential as a hit-making machine. In just under three years, beginning in early 1978, Blondie crafted ten U.K. Top Ten hits, including five chart-toppers (with "Atomic" being the third of those, although it stalled at No. 39 in the United States). At one point, Harry had a word with the record label about pulling so many songs off the parent albums. "I thought it was a little bit upsetting, a little bit much." However, like "Heart of Glass" before it (pulled from 1978's *Parallel Lines*), "Atomic" was a canny mix of pristine pop and disco danceability that no one could resist. **CB**

Blondie's Debbie Harry, captured by glam-rock chronicler Mick Rock in 1978. ➡

Gangsters | The Specials (1979)

Writer | Jerry Dammers
Producer | The Specials
Label | 2-Tone
Album | N/A

"It's not that we're just trying to revive ska. It's using those old elements to try forming something new."

Jerry Dammers, 1979

◀ **Influenced by:** Al Capone • Prince Buster (1964)
▶ **Influence on:** The Prince • Madness (1979)
● **Covered by:** Fun Boy Three (1994) • Citizen King (1999)
   The Louisville Sluggers (2001) • Dub Pistols (2007)
★ **Other key tracks:** A Message to You, Rudy (1979)
   Nite Klub (1979) • Too Much Too Young (1980)

The Coventry Automatics, a multiracial seven-piece from England's West Midlands, had been attempting unsuccessfully to fuse punk with roots reggae before they found a suitable sound in the crude and uptempo genre of ska, introduced to them by rhythm guitarist Lynval Golding via his father's collection of aged 45s. The band's de facto leader, Jerry Dammers, rechristened them The Specials—intended to sound like a drunken approximation of "the Sex Pistols"—and set up his own label, 2-Tone, with a monochrome livery that became synonymous with the ska revival.

The 2-Tone label's first release was a single split between The Specials and The Selecter. The Specials only had enough cash to record one track, which was based on Prince Buster's 1965 ska number "Al Capone." Its opening squeal of brakes was a direct sample, while toaster Neville Staple altered the first line to "Bernie Rhodes knows, don't argue," in reference to the band's manager. Over a lilting rhythm significantly more uptempo than anything from Sixties Kingston, Terry Hall wails like a muezzin about the antics of unscrupulous concert promoters—the line "Don't interrupt while I'm talking / Or they'll confiscate all your guitars" refers to an incident in Paris when Golding's prized Telecaster was held to ransom before a gig.

The 2-Tone scene produced a legion of imitators decked out in the rude-boy apparel of the label's mascot, Walt Jabsco (a cartoon man based on The Wailers' Peter Tosh), but at times the darker undercurrents of the music passed unnoticed. "The Specials there," said presenter Peter Powell when they performed the single on British TV institution *Top of the Pops*. "Good-time music from Coventry." **SP**

Cars | Gary Numan (1979)

Writer | Gary Numan
Producer | Gary Numan
Label | Beggars Banquet
Album | *The Pleasure Principle* (1979)

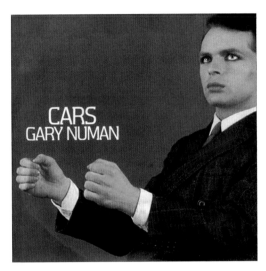

"Gary Numan had more influence on me than Kraftwerk ever did—he's the dark side of electronica."

Dave Clarke, DJ, 1997

◄ **Influenced by: Always Crashing in the Same Car**
David Bowie (1977)
► **Influence on: Koochy** · Armand Van Helden (2000)
● **Covered by:** Frank Zappa (1980) · Hole (1995)
Shampoo (1995) · Fear Factory (1998) · The Leisure
Society (2009) · Nine Inch Nails (2009)

"Cars," Gary Numan's first solo single, is arguably the song with which he is most readily identified. The track showcased the electronic sound that would become his trademark.

Built around a simple but memorable synth hook, the melodic "Cars" nevertheless masks a darker perspective, as is true of many of Numan's songs. The singer revealed that the track is "about the way I think of the modern motor car as a personal tank. I can always drive away at the first sign of trouble." As the lyrics testify: "Here in my car / I feel safest of all / I can lock all my doors."

A significant proportion of the song is instrumental, taking for inspiration the likes of Kraftwerk's "Autobahn" and David Bowie's "Always Crashing in the Same Car." The work of author J.G. Ballard also influenced Numan's songwriting—for example, the science-fiction author's "auto"-erotic novel *Crash* would later provide the title of a Numan composition.

On its original release, "Cars" topped the U.K. charts and became a U.S. Top Ten hit. The song's enduring appeal is such that it has been remixed and reissued as a single in the United Kingdom on three further occasions, reaching the Top Twenty twice, as a promotional "vehicle" for Numan compilations (and, in one instance, as part of an advertising campaign for a lager brand). In 2002, a fascinating pared-down choral version, produced by Flood, also appeared on Numan's *Hybrid* album.

In 2009, the Scottish government chose Numan to front a "Go Green" driving campaign, discouraging drivers from making short trips. With "Cars" as its soundtrack, some commented that Numan's petrolhead status made him a somewhat unsuitable candidate for the role. **JL**

Babylon's Burning | The Ruts (1979)

Writer | The Ruts
Producer | Mick Glossop
Label | Virgin
Album | *The Crack* (1979)

"It's a short, simple statement and it all leads to one word: anxiety. Everyone's anxious. Everyone's worried."

Malcolm Owen, 1979

◀ **Influenced by:** War in a Babylon · Max Romeo (1976)
▶ **Influence on:** Babylon's Burning the Ghetto · Lethal Bizzle (2007)
● **Covered by:** Zion Train (1996) · London Punkharmonic Orchestra (1998) · Die Toten Hosen (2000) · Don Letts (2005) · Kid Loco (2005)

Reggae and punk had been bedfellows from the start—the DJ at punk club The Roxy, Don Letts, had spun dub sides before the scene produced any records of its own for him to play, while Bob Marley name-checked everyone from The Clash to pub-rockers Dr. Feelgood on his 1977 cut "Punky Reggae Party." And more than most, second-wave punks The Ruts wore their reggae influences on their tattered sleeve; tracks such as "Staring at the Rude Boys" and "Jah War" were infused throughout with Jamaican patois.

"Babylon's Burning" takes a rasta millenarian concept visited by the likes of Marley and Max Romeo and sets it to a blistering guitar onslaught, accompanied by apocalyptic sirens and alarms that evoke the violence in London's Southall in spring 1979. The spirit of cultural cross-pollination was taken further by British rapper Lethal Bizzle in his twenty-first-century grime version, built around a seemingly subaquatic Ruts sample.

The Ruts' technical abilities set them apart from their punk contemporaries. Singer Malcolm Owen, guitarist Paul Fox, and drummer Dave Ruffy were all veterans of a jazz-funk covers band called Hit & Run, and their sophisticated arrangements derived as much from a love of Captain Beefheart's 1972 LP, *Clear Spot*, as from the Ramones' two-minute thrashes. Meanwhile, John "Segs" Jennings's thunderous bass lines were learned by studying Tony Henry from Rastafari collective Misty in Roots. But for all the promise implicit in "Babylon's Burning" and its mother album, *The Crack*, The Ruts' moment in the sun was brief. In early 1980, Owen's addiction to heroin forced the cancellation of numerous tour dates; in July he was found dead from an overdose. **SP**

Message in a Bottle | The Police (1979)

Writer | Sting
Producer | Nigel Gray, The Police
Label | A&M
Album | *Reggatta de Blanc* (1979)

"We played it at Sting's wedding, a decade after the group disbanded, and it was still burning."

Stewart Copeland, 1993

◄ **Influenced by: Watching the Detectives** • Elvis Costello (1977)
► **Influence on: Daylight Goes** • Grand National (2004)
● **Covered by:** Excel (1989) • Leatherface (1991) Maxi Priest (1996) • Machine Head (1999) • Wolfgang (2001) • John Mayer (2003)

The the band's first release to achieve a No. 1 chart placing (staying there for three weeks in the United Kingdom), Sting's "Message in a Bottle" is a strong contender for The Police's greatest song: quite an achievement, given their impressive run of hits as a "singles" band.

Sting already had the riff playing in his mind for some time before inspiration took hold and the complete song was formed. The resulting track brings out the talents of all three band members, with a pivotal performance from guitarist Andy Summers complemented by the light, yet aggressive, percussive brilliance of drummer Stewart Copeland.

Sting's lyrics address the misery of isolation, using the central metaphor of an island castaway. ("Loneliness hits me, but I use it," the singer once admitted. "I *glorify* in it.") It was not the first or last time that Sting would confront the subject: in "Can't Stand Losing You" the narrator is contemplating suicide, while The Police had previously scored a hit with the (surprisingly upbeat) "So Lonely." The lyrics, however, reveal a neat twist in the final verse, and a startling discovery: "Walked out this morning, don't believe what I saw / Hundred billion bottles washed up on the shore / Seems I'm not alone in being alone / Hundred billion castaways, looking for a home."

Despite the bleak subject matter, the track's energy and arena-anthemic qualities lend it a dynamism that raises it above indulgent self-pity. For Andy Summers, "It was always my favorite song to play live, the best track we recorded, and probably the fans' favorite before 'Every Breath You Take.' It had all the trademarks. There was something joyous about it." **JL**

- In 1980 John Lennon is shot dead by a deluded gunman in New York

- MTV is launched in 1981 in New York, encouraging music video production

- Michael Jackson's 1982 album, *Thriller*, yields seven best-selling singles

- Bob Geldof organizes global Live Aid concerts for famine relief in 1985

- The golden age of hip-hop begins with Run-DMC's *Raising Hell* in 1986

1980s

The Winner Takes It All | Abba (1980)

Writer | Benny Andersson, Björn Ulvaeus
Producer | Benny Andersson, Björn Ulvaeus
Label | Polar
Album | *Super Trouper* (1980)

ABBA
THE WINNER TAKES IT ALL · ELAINE
A Special Collectors Item

" 'The Winner Takes It All' is so sad … it seems such a genuine account of them crackin' up."
Ian McCulloch, Echo & The Bunnymen, 1998

◄ **Influenced by:** Go Your Own Way · Fleetwood Mac (1977)
► **Influence on:** Total Eclipse of the Heart · Bonnie Tyler (1983)
● **Covered by:** The Corrs (1999) · Martine McCutcheon (2002) · Anne Sofie von Otter (2006)

By 1980, the disco backlash could be felt well beyond half-filled dance clubs in New York City. Not surprisingly, Sweden's Abba—always one of the more trend-conscious acts—decided to veer away from the dance-oriented music of *Voulez-Vous* (1979) and pursue a more adult-contemporary pop sound with *Super Trouper*.

The band was living out its own soap opera as it went into Sweden's Polar Studios to begin recording. Björn Ulvaeus and Agnetha Fältskog had gone through a divorce the previous year, and fans wondered how that might play out in the studio. What was widely perceived as the answer to that question came with "The Winner Takes It All"—an anguished lament, which was released months prior to the parent album.

Ulvaeus claimed that the song was not autobiographical, stating that "there wasn't a winner or a loser in our [divorce]." Fältskog's lead vocals, full of heartbreak and remorse, tell a different story. Listening to her mourn through the pained lines—especially "But tell me does she kiss / like I used to kiss you? / Does it feel the same / when she calls your name?"—it's hard to believe she's doing anything other than drawing inspiration from personal experience. Andersson, who wrote his part when he was drunk, later admitted, "I remember presenting it to the girls, and there were tears."

Super Trouper produced five other singles, including the title track and "Happy New Year," but none matched the worldwide success, nor boasted the staying power, of "The Winner Takes It All." Now regarded as one of Abba's best, the song features prominently in the musical *Mamma Mia!* and its film version. **JiH**

Rapture | Blondie (1980)

Writer | Debbie Harry, Chris Stein
Producer | Mike Chapman
Label | Chrysalis
Album | *Autoamerican* (1980)

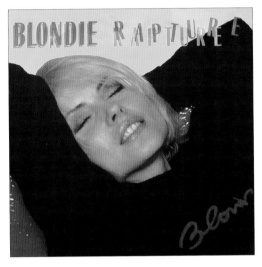

"Debbie and Chris were always so ahead of everyone else; Blondie had just the best videos."

Andy Warhol, 1986

◀ **Influenced by:** Rapper's Delight · The Sugarhill Gang (1979)

▶ **Influence on:** The Adventures of Grandmaster Flash on the Wheels of Steel · Grandmaster Flash & The Furious Five (1981)

● **Covered by:** Erasure (1997) · Alicia Keys (2010)

Did The Sugarhill Gang shake their fists in frustration when their new wave pals Blondie hit the hip-hop jackpot and "Rapture" became the genre's first No. 1? With their first stab at rap, the New York hipsters thrust into the mainstream a scene that was skirting the fringes with Kurtis Blow and The Sugarhill Gang.

"Rapture," the second single to be released from *Autoamerican* (after "The Tide Is High"), started as a parody, with a self-conscious pun in the title; but the song's relevance and brilliance—with ethereal come-ons from Debbie Harry, coquettish chimes, grinding guitar—made it a standout in the genre. Another string to its bow? It was a rap chart-topper with original music, not a looped sample. "We did two versions," recalled guitarist Chris Stein. "One slow: a Christmas rap with Fast Freddie, the rapper, duetting with Debbie ... After we cut that track, we felt it should be faster, peppier." Saxophonist Tom Scott "added the final funk punch."

Students of hip-hop history will find treasures in the rap. Debbie retooled the "Rapper's Delight" lyric "Hip-hop you don't stop" into "You don't stop ... punk rock," and namechecked DJs Fab 5 Freddy and Grandmaster Flash (the accompanying video went one better by featuring New York artist Jean-Michel Basquiat). The invading Martian theme marked the song as a sequel to "The Attack of the Giant Ants" on 1976's *Blondie*.

"Rapture" signaled the the last hurrah of Blondie's hitmaking in the Eighties (bar their sunken "Islands of Lost Souls," released in April 1982). But the breadth of its influence—from rock to rap—ensured that the group remained very much the beating heart of pop. **KBo**

While You See a Chance
Steve Winwood (1980)

Writer | Steve Winwood, Will Jennings
Producer | Steve Winwood
Label | Island
Album | *Arc of a Diver* (1980)

Almost churchy in its synthesized organ intro, "While You See a Chance" represents a Damascene conversion of sorts; a beacon too, and not just for Steve Winwood. The ultra-polished AOR that would dominate the early CD age, and spur a new market of affluent middle-aged males, is in its DNA.

After his former band Traffic stalled, Winwood experimented with performing solo on his 1977 album *Steve Winwood*. *Arc of a Diver* found him playing every instrument and producing the whole album alone. "The only problem now is writing, which is coming slower for me," he admitted. "I want to write with as many people as possible—form new writing relationships."

Chief co-writer on *Arc of a Diver* was Will Jennings. He assisted with the positive vibes and seize-the-day romance of "While You See a Chance," its lead single. "Will just came up with the lyric," Winwood told *Mojo*, "and it was right for me, right for him, and right for the song."

A perfectionist sheen dominates the song. It is a mature take on the electronic pop that was swallowing the mainstream at the start of the 1980s—resolutely modern yet rooted by Winwood's undiminished blues vocal. The squirty keyboards would date eventually, but not before the single broke the U.S. Top Ten—and, in its wake, other veterans like Eric Clapton and Phil Collins found new leases of life. **MH**

Heartattack and Vine
Tom Waits (1980)

Writer | Tom Waits
Producer | Bones Howe
Label | Asylum
Album | *Heartattack and Vine* (1980)

Tom Waits doesn't write music that is simple, or facile, or easily understood. Thirty years old when he recorded the *Heartattack and Vine* LP, he'd seen enough of the filth and dross of life to put it into song, but not so much that he retreated from it.

The album's title track is a sparse, uneasy composition with pauses between stabs of warm, overdriven guitar and Waits's hoarse, semi-shouted vocal. "There ain't no devil," he repeatedly warns us, "just God when he's drunk." Referring to the dregs of life in Los Angeles, Waits portrays a seething mass of humanity, flawed but not without redemption. "If you want a taste of madness, you'll have to wait in line," he sneers; adding, "You'll probably see someone you know on Heartattack and Vine."

It's a drug song (he refers to "lines" and "china white") but it's also a people song—a bleak but somehow celebratory picture of life lived in gleeful desperation when there is no alternative. Though he sued to stop Levi's using Screamin' Jay Hawkins's version of the song in a commercial, the grimly comic irony can't have escaped him.

Over the decades, Waits has worn many faces, but he's never quite shed his reputation as a Mad Hatter of the late-night piano stool. The *Heartattack* album and its title track form a perfect way in for anyone wishing to acquaint themselves with his work for the first time. **JMc**

Like a fine wine, Sixties veteran Steve Winwood improved with age.

Kings of the Wild Frontier | Adam & The Ants (1980)

Writer | Stuart "Adam Ant" Goddard, Marco Pirroni
Producer | Chris Hughes
Label | CBS
Album | *Kings of the Wild Frontier* (1980)

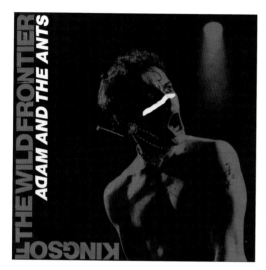

"Adam was just the coolest person on the planet. He epitomized the brilliantly elegant side of punk."
Justine Frischmann, Elastica, 1995

◄ **Influenced by: The Good, the Bad and the Ugly**
Ennio Morricone (1966)
► **Influence on: The Beautiful People** · Marilyn Manson (1996)
★ **Other key tracks:** Dog Eat Dog (1980) · Antmusic (1980) · Physical (You're So) (1980)

"Through imitation," proclaimed Adam Ant in 1981, "you eventually arrive at something that is distinctly yours." By his own admission, there was nothing original about the essential ingredients of Adam & The Ants. The band plundered African tribal drums, Duane Eddy-style twangy guitar, elaborate pirate costuming and Native American war paint. Rolling them into one potent package, however, was their own genius.

"Marco [Pirroni, guitarist] and I decided to be very flamboyant—very escapist, very razzmatazz, very heroic, very noble—and go into certain areas that were corny but we actually sincerely like," Ant told the *Daytona Beach Morning Journal.* (Drummers Terry Lee Miall and Merrick, and bassist Gary Tibbs, completed the lineup.)

The single, a rousing commentary on the oppression of Native American tribes, became the band's first British Top Fifty hit in August 1980, blasting their freshly distilled sound and look into the national consciousness with a brash swagger. "The extent of its success surprised us . . ." Pirroni admitted to *Mojo.* "I was trying to get everything I liked into that record. And it worked."

The chartbusting "Dog Eat Dog" and "Antmusic" followed, pushing the parent album to platinum in the United Kingdom and gold across the Atlantic. "With the 'Kings of the Wild Frontier' single," Ant marveled to *The Face,* "'Antmusic for Sexpeople'— which had been an ideal—became a reality."

After disbanding the group to go solo in 1982, Ant retained the sound defined by "Kings of the Wild Frontier," ultimately influencing acts from Elastica to Nine Inch Nails. "You have to have the artistry to back the gimmickry," he said, "because that's what show business is all about." **EP**

Redemption Song | Bob Marley & The Wailers (1980)

Writer | Bob Marley
Producer | Bob Marley & The Wailers, Chris Blackwell
Label | Island
Album | *Uprising* (1980)

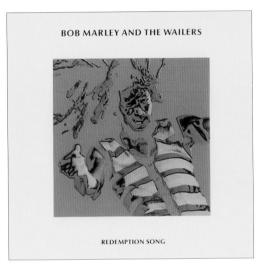

BOB MARLEY AND THE WAILERS

REDEMPTION SONG

"Way I see . . . it looks simple but it's true. Rasta for the people! Capitalism and communism are finished. It Rasta now!"

Bob Marley, 1979

◄ **Influenced by: There's a Reward** • Joe Higgs (1975)
► **Influence on: Black Uhuru Anthem** • Black Uhuru (1983)
● **Covered by:** Flying Pickets (1996) • Stevie Wonder (1996) • Johnny Cash & Joe Strummer (2003) • Don Campbell (2003)

A prolific writer, Bob Marley released fourteen studio albums (and a further posthumous one) in his fifteen-year musical career, so there are many classic songs that represent his work with The Wailers. Nevertheless, "Redemption Song" holds a special place in the hearts of reggae fans.

The last track on *Uprising,* the final studio album of his lifetime, "Redemption Song" is unique for being a solo recording—just Marley and his acoustic guitar. The familiar groove and backing from The Wailers are absent for this one song (although a version with the whole band was released posthumously, and an earlier version of "Redemption Song" appeared on a 1977 single).

By the time of *Uprising*, Marley was suffering from the cancer that claimed his life, though he never spoke about it. With hindsight, there's a detectable sadness in the song—as well as a call to arms for those who would come after him. A fierce defender of Rastafari beliefs and a protestor against the oppression that he saw visited upon his people, Marley wove the words of Jamaican orator Marcus Garvey into the lyric.

"Redemption Song" is a quiet reinforcement of the joyous uprising that Marley felt was needed, and believed, optimistically, that he would see. A live version of the song—recorded at his last concert, in Pittsburgh on September 23, 1980—appears on the box set *Songs for Freedom*, which was released in 1992.

A testament to the musical legacy left behind by Marley is that "Redemption Song" is one of his most widely covered songs. Its themes are kept alive in interpretations from artists as varied as Stevie Wonder, The Chieftains, Sinéad O'Connor, and Nina Simone. **SO**

Dead Souls
Joy Division (1980)

Writer | Ian Curtis, Peter Hook, Bernard Sumner, Stephen Morris
Producer | Martin Hannett
Label | Factory
Album | *Still* (1981)

"Joy Division were a heavy metal band," opined The Smashing Pumpkins' Billy Corgan in 2005 (and he should know, since his output is indebted to the Manchester quartet, and he joined the band's surviving members in New Order for a 2001 tour).

The best evidence for Corgan's claim is the coruscating "Dead Souls." It was written in 1979, amid a creative surge that also created the classic "These Days" and "Atmosphere." While it may not have entered the public consciousness in the same way as the band's swan song, "Love Will Tear Us Apart," it is no less emotive or haunting.

The song was first issued in March 1980, with the sepulchral "Atmosphere," on *Licht und Blindheit*—a (very) limited edition single on the French independent label Sordide Sentimental. It reappeared on the Factory label's compilation *Still*, which gave Joy Division their highest chart placing (No. 5) in their native Britain. "Dead Souls" was one of only two previously released studio tracks on the album.

After a two-minute instrumental introduction, "Dead Souls" got underway with "Someone take these dreams away / that point me to another day." Curtis's fierce demands reflected his alienation and desperation to escape the band's bleak environment. Or, as writer Jon Savage put it, "'Dead Souls' is an unsettling evocation of psychic possession and the presence of past lives." **GK**

Master Blaster (Jammin')
Stevie Wonder (1980)

Writer | Stevie Wonder
Producer | Stevie Wonder
Label | Tamla
Album | *Hotter than July* (1980)

Since 1975, when they shared the bill at a gig in Kingston, Jamaica, Stevie Wonder and Bob Marley had developed similar careers. In 1973, each had success, with the albums *Innervisions* and *Catch a Fire*, respectively. Wonder followed up in 1976 with *Songs in the Key of Life*. After Marley released the equally acclaimed *Exodus*, the two again shared a stage, in Philadelphia in 1979.

In 1980, Wonder had another hit with *Hotter than July*. The title came from a track that Wonder had written in tribute to Marley and his music. With an irresistible reggae feel, it referenced Marley's *Exodus* cut "Jamming," and also mentioned the Jamaican superstar in the lyrics.

"Master Blaster (Jammin')" became one of Wonder's biggest hits, reaching No. 2 in the United Kingdom, and spending seven weeks at the top of *Billboard*'s R&B chart. On an album that Wonder used to campaign for a public holiday to celebrate Martin Luther King's birthday, "Master Blaster" also carried political themes.

Bob Marley and Stevie Wonder were set to play together again during Wonder's tour for *Hotter than July*, planned for 1981. Unfortunately, Marley's cancer overwhelmed him and he died in May that year. Fittingly, however, Marley's son Stephen covered "Master Blaster" for the 2003 tribute album *Conception: An Interpretation of Stevie Wonder's Songs*. **SO**

Everybody's Got to Learn Sometime | The Korgis (1980)

Writer | James Warren
Producer | The Korgis
Label | Rialto
Album | *Dumb Waiters* (1980)

Oddball prog rock had not made stars of British folkies Stackridge. They split amid the onslaught of punk, but bassist James Warren and drummer Andy Davis reinvented themselves as smart poppers The Korgis. After a hit in 1979 with "If I Had You," Davis quit, leaving Warren with multi-instrumentalists Stuart Gordon and Phil Harrison.

With a synthesizer borrowed from Peter Gabriel, The Korgis added lush layers to their polished pop. Nowhere was this sophistication more evident than on the halting, haunting "Everybody's Got to Learn Sometime." Warren maintained that the lyrics were "the ones that first came into my head," yet the song's four simple lines proved remarkably moving. Unfortunately, its air of forgiveness was not mirrored within the group. Global success, rued Warren to *Bristol Rocks*, "only served to exacerbate and intensify the tensions that existed in the band." With no further hits, The Korgis splintered within two years.

Nonetheless, the song has been covered by a host of admirers, from synth-poppers Erasure to Italian crooner Zucchero and alternative rockers Glasvegas. In 1995, dance act Baby D took "(Everybody's Got to Learn Sometime) I Need Your Loving" into the U.K. Top Three—a year after producer Jon Brion contributed his version, fronted by Beck, to the soundtrack of Michel Gondry's *Eternal Sunshine of the Spotless Mind*. **BM**

I'm Coming Out
Diana Ross (1980)

Writer | Bernard Edwards, Nile Rodgers
Producer | B. Edwards, N. Rodgers
Label | Motown
Album | *Diana* (1980)

Having worked with Motown Midas-touchers Nickolas Ashford and Valerie Simpson on *The Boss* (1979), Diana Ross turned to another hit-making team—Chic's Bernard Edwards and Nile Rodgers—for the follow-up, *Diana*. She was looking to update her sound, and few were turning out groovier singles than Chic.

Yet the road to boogie wonderland was full of potholes. The producers and the star clashed in the studio, and Ross worried that the songs sounded too *Saturday Night Fever* at a time when listeners were buying "Disco Sucks" stickers. Thus, the final mix toned down the Chic-style funk.

Fortunately, *Diana* still delivered, notably on the smash singles "Upside Down" and "I'm Coming Out." The latter provided Ross with one of her greatest anthems, a self-affirming song often used to kick off her concerts. It was built on a beat faster than most could play, since the tempos were accelerated in the mix to highlight Ross's voice. That tactic paid handsome dividends, and her high-arching soprano sounded stronger than it had since her Supremes classics. The biggest gamble was Meco Monardo's trombone solo, but that just further distinguished the song from the field.

"I'm Coming Out"—along with "Upside Down"—made *Diana* Ross's biggest-selling solo disc and was brilliantly used on The Notorious B.I.G.'s "Mo Money Mo Problems." **JiH**

Back in Black
AC/DC (1980)

Writer | Brian Johnson, Angus Young, Malcolm Young
Producer | Robert John "Mutt" Lange
Label | Atlantic
Album | *Back in Black* (1980)

Back in Black wasn't just another album for AC/DC: it marked their return after the death of singer Bon Scott the previous year. As a tribute and a statement, it was a multiplatinum triumph, thanks to songs such as the monstrous title track.

"Back in Black" was based on a typically unforgettable guitar figure from Malcolm Young, buffed to a glossy sheen by "Mutt" Lange, and leavened by the leather-larynxed Brian Johnson, Bon Scott's successor. If fans had been expecting mellow introspection, they were immediately relieved: "Back in Black" was that rare thing—a song that was both catchy and crunching.

Almost three decades on, the influence of the song is incalculable. "Most bands," observed Charlie Benante of Anthrax, "learned how to play by listening to this record." The Beastie Boys, meanwhile, sampled it on "Rock Hard" in 1985. Beasties engineer George Drakoulias remembered: "Rick [Rubin, producer] played it on a Walkman for Angus and Malcolm Young, and they weren't upset about it, just intrigued. It was like, 'Ah, interesting! I see what you've done there! But aren't the drums very loud?'"

In 2009, an all-star panel in *Classic Rock* magazine voted "Back in Black" the best AC/DC song. One accolade even came from John Oates, of Hall & Oates, who declared it "perfectly simple and elegant in a heavy sort of way." **JMc**

Let My Love Open the Door
Pete Townshend (1980)

Writer | Pete Townshend
Producer | Chris Thomas
Label | ATCO
Album | *Empty Glass* (1980)

"It's got three chords in it, hasn't it?" Pete Townshend remarked to the BBC in 1983. "When I was getting the songs together for a gig I did recently, I realized that all the songs I wanted to play had the same three chords in them. . . . I did it on a computerized organ machine, and then decided to put a vocal on it—just singing the first thing that came into my head—and that's what came out."

Simplicity was key to "Let My Love Open the Door." Townshend's writing for The Who in the preceding decade had been sandbagged by self-importance and self-doubt; but, freed from the supergroup's conceptual and sonic shackles, he sounded gloriously cheerful. The song duly matched the No. 9 position of The Who's biggest U.S. hit, "I Can See for Miles," released in 1967.

Though the lyric sounds romantic, the song was interpreted as a lesson learned from Indian spiritual teacher Meher Baba, of whom Townshend was a follower. "When you go to the tavern—which is to God—and you ask for his love . . . you have to give him [an] empty glass," he explained. "There's no point giving him your heart if it's full already."

The song had an earthly effect too. "I released *Empty Glass*," Townshend told *Playboy*, "and then went on to do the Who tour, and I could see the difference immediately. There were all these girls coming backstage asking, 'Which one of you wrote "Let My Love Open Your Door"?'" **BM**

Geno | Dexys Midnight Runners (1980)

Writer | Kevin Rowland, Kevin Archer
Producer | Pete Wingfield
Label | EMI
Album | *Searching for the Young Soul Rebels* (1980)

"He was the greatest soul singer that ever lived, apart from James Brown."

Kevin Rowland, 1980

◀ **Influenced by: Michael (The Lover)** • Geno
Washington & The Ram Jam Band (1966)
▶ **Influence on: Ghost Town** • The Specials (1981)
★ **Other key tracks:** Dance Stance (1979) • There, There,
My Dear (1980) • I Love You (Listen to This) (1985)
This Is What She's Like (1985)

Back in '68 in a sweaty club, Kevin Rowland saw soul journeyman Geno Washington, heard the crowd chanting the singer's name, and decided he could do this job. It took him a dozen years to get around to it, but he and songwriting partner Kevin "Al" Archer finally quit punk also-rans The Killjoys to—according to Rowland—"wear great clothes and make soulful music." The clothes were *Mean Streets*-inspired dockers' threads; the music brass-led R&B from the rough side of the tracks.

"Geno," their second single, stomped to No. 1 in the United Kingdom. ("I went up to him," marveled Duran Duran's Nick Rhodes. "'That's great, Kevin. You're No. 1.' 'Urrggghhh,' and he storms off. . . . Unbelievable!") Its raw power evoked Northern soul, while the brass was pure ska. In the 2-Tone era of The Specials, Rowland's wildhearted outsiders fitted perfectly.

A tribute in implication only, "Geno" ends up sneering at its subject. Rowland tips his woolly hat to Washington's way with a crowd, but Geno's washed-up, his song is "so tame". Now it's Rowland's time, but don't worry, he'll "remember your name." Nonetheless, Rowland told *Sounds*, "I know he blew it, played the cabaret circuit and pissed everyone off but he's criminally underrated, especially the band he had about '65. The fire and emotion he performed with, total conviction . . . it's that strength and passion we try to put in."

But perhaps Washington had the last laugh. The song's success brought Dexys Midnight Runners a whole new audience, tuned to one song only. ("It might have detracted from our live set," ventured Archer, "and alienated the original fans.") But what a song! **MH**

Guilty | Barbra Streisand and Barry Gibb (1980)

Writer | Barry Gibb, Robin Gibb, Maurice Gibb
Producer | B. Gibb, A. Galuten, K. Richardson
Label | Columbia
Album | *Guilty* (1980)

"Barbra sings something once and it's magic . . . each time she sings, it's good."

Barry Gibb, 1980

◀ **Influenced by:** How Deep Is Your Love • Bee Gees (1977)
▶ **Influence on:** Above the Law • Barbra Streisand with Barry Gibb (2005)
● **Covered by:** Tom Jones & Gladys Knight (1997) • Bee Gees (1998)

"When you write for yourself," explained Barry Gibb, "you're the only instrument, so you have certain limitations in your mind and in your heart. If you're writing for someone else, and that person has the range that Barbra has, it stretches you out."

In 1978, Gibb broke the record for most No. 1 compositions in a calendar year. Hits by his band the Bee Gees joined smashes by Yvonne Elliman, Frankie Valli, and Andy Gibb. This platinum touch made him a natural choice for Streisand, who had stormed into the pop arena in 1979, with Donna Summer on "No More Tears (Enough is Enough)."

"I was a little nervous," Gibb confessed to *Billboard*'s Craig Rosen. "She intimidated me to some extent." Reassurance came from Neil Diamond, with whom Streisand had duetted on "You Don't Bring Me Flowers"—"He said that she is an absolute pleasure."

Absolute pleasure is a good way to describe the Gibb-penned *Guilty* album and its title track. With one performer at the peak of his powers, and another whose talent has rarely been surpassed, it could hardly fail. "Certain things he does on the demos that are so wonderful rhythmically, I can't do sometimes," Streisand confessed. "But then he encourages me to make the song my own." (Gibb's demos for the album were released on iTunes in 2006.) Shimmering and seductive, "Guilty" still sounds effortlessly elegant.

The collaboration was originally played down, Streisand fretting that the public might be tired of superstar pairings. A chart-topping album and three hits—including the No. 1 "Woman in Love"—proved her wrong. "It was," she reflected, "such a lovely experience." **BM**

Love Will Tear Us Apart | Joy Division (1980)

Writer | Ian Curtis, Peter Hook, Stephen Morris, Bernard Sumner
Producer | Martin Hannett
Label | Factory
Album | N/A

"It was not your common rock 'n' roll session . . . but it did sound great."

The Edge, U2, 2006

◀ **Influenced by:** Be My Wife · David Bowie (1977)
▶ **Influence on:** As It Is When It Was · New Order (1986)
● **Covered by:** Paul Young (1983) · Swans (1988) · Opium Den (1995) · Simple Minds (2001) · New Order (2002) Fall Out Boy (2004) · Nouvelle Vague (2004)
★ **Other key track:** Shadowplay (1979)

"There was an atmosphere in the building, like something amazing was happening . . ." reported U2 guitarist The Edge of the session that produced the post-punk era's greatest song. "It was a very intense vibe. I think they may have been listening to Wagner."

The fledgling U2—in London to meet Joy Division's producer Martin Hannett—weren't the only ones to be impressed. The strident yet aching "Love Will Tear Us Apart" has been continually covered, quoted, tapped for soundtracks, and cited as an inspiration for three decades.

Its inspiration was singer and lyricist Ian Curtis's decaying relationship with his wife, Deborah. Its title was an ironic twist on The Captain & Tennille's 1975 smash, "Love Will Keep Us Together."

As a single, it took hold slowly. Factory label boss Tony Wilson denied that its eventual success was due to the publicity attending Curtis's suicide one month after its release: "The week before he died there was a massive demand from shops for 'Love Will Tear Us Apart.' It was going to happen."

Nonetheless, the singer's death hardly harmed the song's mythological status. Its title even adorns his tombstone in Macclesfield (Cheshire, England) Cemetery—an eerie echo of the single's artwork. It duly clung to indie charts for years, haunting the surviving members of Joy Division—who evolved into New Order—and being dubbed the "Stairway to Heaven" of the Eighties.

One key figure remained unmoved. "'Love Will Tear Us Apart' isn't particularly upsetting," Deborah Curtis told *Q*, "because I feel so angry about it. There's no point in writing a song that I'm not going to hear until he's dead. He should have told me at the time." **BM**

Wardance | Killing Joke (1980)

Writer | Jaz Coleman, Paul Ferguson, Kevin "Geordie" Walker, Youth
Producer | Killing Joke
Label | Malicious Damage
Album | *Killing Joke* (1980)

"Killing Joke were a band with such a good energy."

Kate Bush, 1985

◀ **Influenced by: Electric Funeral** · Black Sabbath (1970)
▶ **Influence on: On the Beach** · The Comsat Angels (1980)
● **Covered by:** The Mad Capsule Markets (2001)
★ **Other key tracks:** The Wait (1980) · Requiem (1980)

Staring hard into his crystal ball told Jaz Coleman, Killing Joke's main mischief-maker, that it was a question of *when,* not *if,* we were all to be engulfed in a nuclear fireball before the Eighties were very old.

"Wardance" was the band's inimitable way of embracing the inevitable. As jester Jaz said: "Enjoy it, have a laugh about it, revel in it. Don't look away from it." Opening a live set with this aural battering ram in 1981, he told the crowd: "Let's be realistic—we've only got a few years left. So let's make the most of it."

That meant losing yourself in music that could loosen the fillings in your teeth. "Wardance" is simple, savage, and skull-crushing: harsh, robotic vocals and skin-peeling guitar grinding like metal being pulled apart after a car crash. Some copies of the single came with fake military call-up papers, emphasizing the band's belief in what was coming over the horizon.

Such sentiments didn't seem to be appreciated when the British band—featuring future session star and super producer Martin "Youth" Glover—played it at a Campaign for Nuclear Disarmament benefit concert in London. Coleman, however, found it "hilariously funny." If certain elements in the United Kingdom didn't get the joke, overseas audiences were more attuned, especially in Germany. "They loved it," said Coleman. "They were like wild pigs rushing all over the place."

In the end, the world kept spinning and Coleman's dash to Iceland in 1982 in a bid to avoid the apocalypse proved unnecessary. But, as he warned in 1979, "Our music's destructive—it's not supposed to make people happy. It's supposed to shake them up." **CB**

Ace of Spades
Motörhead (1980)

Writer | Ian "Lemmy" Kilmister, "Fast" Eddie Clarke, "Philthy" Phil Taylor
Producer | Vic Maile
Label | Bronze
Album | *Ace of Spades* (1980)

Lemmy is, let's face it, familiar with the occasional amphetamine rush. Generously, the Motörhead main man shared its aural equivalent with us on "Ace of Spades." A life lived defiantly against a stacked deck was conjured up from dice, cards, and other gambling imagery. However, the references could have been less persuasive had Lemmy used his personal preferences: "I'm more into the one-armed bandits actually," he wrote in his autobiography.

Aside from its crunching catchiness, the track's success lay in its simplicity. But milestones, even ones this memorable, can also be millstones. It was the song that introduced many to the band, reaching No. 15 in the United Kingdom in 1980. Yet for many people, the relationship never progressed beyond that stage. Lemmy has said that it has been used to open sets "just to get it out of the way."

Other times, however, he has been more benevolent. "I like dressing in the same socks for three weeks running," he told *Q*, "pedaling out there and raising the trammeled face to the rafters and croaking out 'Ace of Spades' again."

The song's ubiquity might have lessened its impact, especially after its use in commercials for everything from potato chips to Swedish furniture; but "Ace of Spades" was a pile-driving way of narrowing the gap between punk and metal, and remains an all-time anthem. **CB**

Start!
The Jam (1980)

Writer | Paul Weller
Producer | Vic Coppersmith-Heaven, The Jam
Label | Polydor
Album | *Sound Affects* (1980)

Some said Paul Weller's admiration for Pete Townshend led to readily identifiable similarities in his songs. With "Start!" the press switched to wondering if he was borrowing from another music legend. "It was obvious, wasn't it?" quipped Weller to *Uncut*. "I think we copied James Brown."

In less lighthearted moments, Weller robustly defended the similarities between the band's second U.K. chart-topper and The Beatles' *Revolver* opener "Taxman." "I use anything," he declared, "and I don't really care whether people think it's credible or not, or if I'm credible to do it."

For the *Sound Affects* album (their fifth in less than four years, Weller wanted what he called a "stripped down" ambience compared to what had gone before: "I thought 'Going Underground' was a peak and we were getting a little safe with that sound. That's why we've done 'Start!'" A decision was taken to introduce the public to a new side to the band—one where Weller's brittle guitar provided a nervous urgency, befitting the song's original title, "Two Minutes."

In a touché moment, when asked if "Taxman" composer George Harrison had been in contact, Weller said: "Nah. He's in no position to talk, is he?" Harrison, of course, had run into legal troubles nine years earlier, as a result of similarities between his "My Sweet Lord" and "He's So Fine" by The Chiffons. **CB**

Motörhead's Lemmy shows he's not above a little flutter on the slot machines.

Once in a Lifetime | Talking Heads (1980)

Writer | David Byrne, Chris Frantz, Jerry Harrison, Tina Weymouth, Brian Eno
Producer | Brian Eno, Talking Heads
Label | Sire
Album | *Remain in Light* (1980)

"It was the perfect example of … where they combine quirkiness with a real melodic ear."

Rick Wright, Pink Floyd, 1996

◀ **Influenced by:** Oh Lord Give Us More Money
Holger Czukay (1979)
▶ **Influence on:** Don't Scandalize Mine · Sugar Bear (1988)
● **Covered by:** Big Daddy (1991) · Phoebe One (1998)
Phish (2002) · The Exies (2007)

After three albums of tightly wound new wave, Talking Heads summoned the spirit of Africa to create a fascinating, funky classic.

Band leader David Byrne recalled: "Both Brian [Eno, producer] and I had been reading a lot about African music and sensibilities and the effect it has—people going into trances through playing multiple rhythms—and I thought that sounded pretty good. A lot of the investigations that began with the record I did with Brian [*My Life in the Bush of Ghosts*, released belatedly in 1981] came to fruition on the Talking Heads record."

At Compass Point Studios in the Bahamas, the Heads labored on what drummer Chris Frantz called "just extended grooves." One was "Weird Guitar Riff Song," a prototype for "Once in a Lifetime." Back in the States, Byrne found inspiration in "evangelists I recorded off the radio." One particular sermon, he recalled, "had an incantation, a groove. It was about hell and damnation and had the line about living in a shotgun shack. I thought, I can use that."

Byrne's head-smacking performance as a possessed preacher in the song's video entranced those new to the Heads (the video is now exhibited in the New York Museum of Modern Art). "Once in a Lifetime" has been sampled by Jay-Z ("It's Alright"), covered live by The Smashing Pumpkins and referenced by Marilyn Manson in his autobiography, *The Long Hard Road Out of Hell* (1998). The song became a fan favorite too, hence its thunderous performance in the band's 1984 concert movie *Stop Making Sense*. "We used to have so much fun playing this song live," remembered Frantz in 1992. "It was a soaring feeling, and the audience was right there with us." **BM**

Vienna | Ultravox (1980)

Writer | Billy Currie, Midge Ure, Chris Cross, Warren Cann
Producer | Ultravox, Konrad "Conny" Plank
Label | Chrysalis
Album | *Vienna* (1980)

Ultravox
'VIENNA'

"It's fun to debate whether Ultravox were better with John Foxx or Midge Ure."

Moby, 2000

◀ **Influenced by:** ISI • NEU! (1975)
▶ **Influence on:** Guiding Light • Muse (2009)
● **Covered by:** Celestial Season (1995) • Clawfinger (2001) Russell Watson (2000)
★ **Other key tracks:** Sleepwalk (1980) • All Stood Still (1980)• Passing Strangers (1980)

Partly pretentious, mostly melancholy, "Vienna" was ahead of its time. Despite winning a Brit award for best British single, it never reached No. 1 in Ultravox's native land. Gallingly, it was held at No. 2, for three weeks, by one-hit wonder Joe Dolce's "Shaddap You Face." (It reached No. 13 after being reissued in 1993.)

While their contemporaries were thrashing out punk, Ultravox were pioneers of early Eighties electro-pop. However, their breakthrough came only after they had been dropped by the Island label, replaced singer and founder John Foxx with Midge Ure—of The Rich Kids and, briefly, Thin Lizzy—and evolved from their glam-rock origins. "Vienna," the ambitious culmination of these upheavals, became their signature song.

A simple but eerie battlefield beat introduced the track, before it segued into lushly romantic orchestral synthesizers and moody lyrics. As bassist Chris Cross told *Mojo,* "Trying to make something 'over-pompous,' so that it's obvious to the listener, is pretty difficult to do." Slick production and Ure's plaintive vocals did the trick.

The Chrysalis label, judging the song too depressing and slow, refused to fund the innovative video (which includes a classic shot of a tarantula walking across the director's face). Filmed in Vienna and London, it was inspired by the 1949 movie *The Third Man.*

According to Ure, the stirring song is about a holiday romance, although he initially indulged the misconception that it referred to the early-twentieth-century Vienna Secession art movement. It also provided a handy punch line. Asked his least favorite city to play, The Clash's Joe Strummer replied, "Vienna. It means nothing to me!" **GK**

Caballo viejo
Simón Díaz (1980)

Writer | Simón Díaz
Producer | Nucho Bellomo
Label | Palacio
Album | *Caballo Viejo* (1980)

Regarded as a national treasure in Venezuela, Simón Díaz has perpetuated and popularized his country's rich roots music, both as a TV presenter and a musician with more than seventy albums under his belt. One of his specialities is *musica llanera*—cowboy music from the *llanos* (plains) of the Orinoco river—and his most famous song is "Caballo viejo," composed one day while filming a folk group on location in Apure state. The trigger for this was the group's young singer Emilia, with whom Díaz became suddenly, giddily infatuated; he felt compelled to tell her about it in a song.

Celebrating the singer's unconsummated desire in dignified, poetic language, "Caballo viejo" recounts how when such an "old horse" meets a "chestnut filly," he goes a little bit *loco*. The flowing mid-tempo backing, subtly suggesting a horse's gait, is typically Venezuelan, driven by a country harp, *cuatro* (four-stringed guitar), bass, and deftly twirled maracas—thought to be a local Amerindian invention.

In 1987, the French group Gipsy Kings adapted the lyrics and tune of "Caballo viejo" as a turbo-charged *rumba flamenca* and retitled it "Bamboleo." As the lead track of their international debut, it was a global megahit, and launched their career in style. The likes of Celia Cruz, Plácido Domingo, and Julio Iglesias have also had some success with their own versions. **JLu**

I Got You
Split Enz (1980)

Writer | Neil Finn
Producer | David Tickle
Label | Mushroom
Album | *True Colours* (1980)

Split Enz's breakthrough hit arrived eight years into the career of the flamboyant and arty New Zealand group whose albums had ricocheted between oddball experimentation, leftfield whimsy, and charming pop.

The Enz had relocated to London for a dispiriting few years, just as punk was beginning. When founder members and co-writers Phil Judd and Mike Chunn exited the group, front man Tim Finn's younger brother Neil took over lead guitar. His inexperience led to material that was simpler and more immediate. This proved fortuitous, as Neil's songs betrayed a knack for melodic pop. "I Got You" perfectly fused the wonderful oddness of Split Enz's early records with a bright, radio-friendly clarity. Nervy, anxious verses, singing of a paranoid romance, led to a nagging, addictively upbeat chorus, propelled by brashly joyous synth and Finn's Beatlesque harmonies. "The Beatles were our main influence . . ." observed Tim Finn, "so, in a way, we were getting back to our roots."

The single won the group international attention; topping the charts at home, reaching No. 12 in the United Kingdom, and No. 53 in the United States. It didn't secure long-term success for Split Enz, but it was Neil Finn's first introduction to charts he would regularly grace with Crowded House (whom his brother briefly joined), bringing his gift for perfect pop to the fore. **SC**

It Must Be Love
Madness (1981)

Writer | Labi Siffre
Producer | Clive Langer, Alan Winstanley
Label | Stiff
Album | N/A

After nine hit singles and three successful albums, Madness were flying high at the turn of the 1980s. With their Nutty Boys personas proving popular with the public, they were reluctant to record someone else's sweet-natured love song. However, keyboardist Mike Barson had heard Labi Siffre's single (a U.K. hit in 1971) and thought it would fit well with singer Suggs's voice. He introduced it to his bandmates during rehearsals and they began playing it as an encore at gigs.

At one concert, Stiff label boss Dave Robinson heard "It Must Be Love" and set about persuading the band that the song was a potential hit. Robinson was so convinced, he bet that if it didn't make the Top Five in the United Kingdom, he would give the band his record company.

The first version of the song was recorded in a home studio in Newcastle upon Tyne, England. As the result sounded merely like a good demo, it was rerecorded and finessed in London. This second take helped it reach No. 4 in the U.K. chart. (A reissue in 1992 also climbed into the U.K. Top Ten.)

Labi Siffre liked the distinctive reworking so much that he appeared in the single's video. Producer Trevor Horn, taken by its pizzicato strings, emulated them on ABC's 1982 album *The Lexicon of Love*. Most fittingly, when Norman Cook—aka Fatboy Slim—and Zoë Ball married in 1999, they had Suggs sing it at the wedding. **DC**

Tom Sawyer
Rush (1981)

Writer | Geddy Lee, Alex Lifeson, Neil Peart, Pye Dubois
Producer | Rush, Terry Brown
Label | Anthem
Album | *Moving Pictures* (1981)

Groovy isn't a word often associated with polished prog rockers Rush. But as the Eighties dawned, they streamlined LP-length conceits into song-sized classics such "The Spirit of Radio."

A contemporary take on Mark Twain's *The Adventures of Tom Sawyer* busted them out of the prog ghetto. Ominous synths, bassist Geddy Lee's distinctive vocals, Alex Lifeson's blistering guitar, and Neil Peart's spectacular drumming were par for the course. But the song had a weirdly funky feel, hence its sampling by hip-hop acts including Mellow Man Ace and Young Black Teenagers.

The Canadian trio shared the credits with poet Pye Dubois. "His original lyrics," said Peart, "were kind of a portrait of a modern day rebel—a free-spirited individualist. . . . I added the themes of reconciling the boy and man in myself, and the difference between what people are, and what others perceive them to be—namely me, I guess."

"Right up until the end it was a struggle," Lee told *Classic Rock*. "Alex went through a hundred different sounds for the guitar solo. There's always one song that haunts you and drives you crazy."

"Tom Sawyer" has been used in movies such as Rob Zombie's *Halloween* remake, TV shows including *Family Guy*, *Chuck*, and *The Sopranos*, and even a 2000 car commercial. "We really don't have a problem with it," the band declared, "as it was tastefully done." **BM**

Girls on Film | Duran Duran (1981)

Writer | Simon Le Bon, Nick Rhodes, Andy Taylor,
John Taylor, Roger Taylor
Producer | Colin Thurston
Label | EMI
Album | *Duran Duran* (1981)

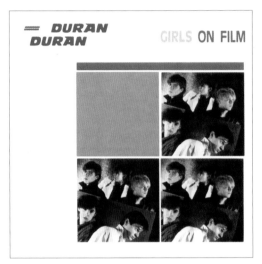

"We knew exactly what we were doing with the 'Girls on Film' video."

John Taylor, 2001

◀ **Influenced by:** Love Is the Drug • Roxy Music (1975)
▶ **Influence on:** Girls and Boys • Blur (1994)
● **Covered by:** The Living End (1999) • Billy Preston (2002)
Girls Aloud (2003)
★ **Other key tracks:** Careless Memories (1981) • Planet
Earth (1981) • Night Boat (1981)

Duran Duran were the first band to realize everything the 1980s had to offer. For the quintet from Birmingham, England, image was paramount—but it was crucial to back up the looks with accessible, well-crafted songs. "Girls on Film," their first U.K. Top Five hit, covered all the bases. It addressed the glamorous life into which they were soon to be pitched, boasted what would later be revealed as a typically robust chorus, and was accompanied by a video that everyone was talking about.

Ex-10cc members and pop polymaths Kevin Godley and Lol Creme were drafted in to create the mini-film: a riot of naked females, mud wrestling, and somewhat bemused miming from Duran Duran themselves. "Having a girl with an ice cube on her nipple was actually a talking point," keyboardist Nick Rhodes recalled to *Q* in 2007. "It seems quaint and quite tasteful now."

Predictably, the raunchy video met with distaste from the BBC, while the newborn MTV had to edit it heavily, but an impact had been made. Quickly grasping the power of the promo, Duran Duran became synonymous with lavish visuals—a perfect fit with a garish decade. "Video to us is like stereo was to Pink Floyd," Rhodes told *Rolling Stone*.

The song itself—featured on their first demo—had a blurry birth, with compositional input from former singer Andy Wickett. Immediately prior to its release, Wickett was reportedly persuaded to sign a waiver, selling the rights to songs in which he may have played a part. The clicking shutter that opens "Girls on Film" proved prescient: as Wickett slipped from view, Duran Duran became a familiar sight in the media glare. **MH**

Duran Duran's John Taylor (left) and Simon Le Bon enjoy the limelight in 1981. ➡

I Love Rock 'n Roll | Joan Jett & The Blackhearts (1981)

Writer | Jake Hooker, Alan Merrill
Producer | Ritchie Cordell, Kenny Laguna
Label | Boardwalk
Album | *I Love Rock 'n Roll* (1981)

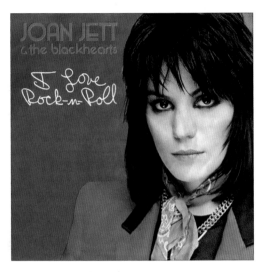

*"I had a crush on Joan Jett.
I usually finish my DJ set with
'I Love Rock 'n Roll'."*

Alison Goldfrapp, 2006

◄ **Influenced by: Old Time Rock & Roll** · Bob Seger
& The Silver Bullet Band (1978)
► **Influence on: Everybody Get Up** · Five (1998)
● **Covered by:** Ghoti Hook (1998) · Britney Spears (2002)
Queen of Japan (2002) · Hayseed Dixie (2002)
Showaddywaddy (2006)

Tracing an inspirational arc from Suzi Quatro, through L7 to Britney Spears, Joan Jett's "I Love Rock 'n Roll" topped the *Billboard* chart in the United States for seven weeks in 1982. Its raw chords, raunchy lyrics, and anthemic chorus stood out in a year where hits wore their glossy production on their sleeves. At the same time, the song's gritty black-and-white video was one of the most played in early MTV history.

Quitting all-girl teen group The Runaways in 1979, Jett sought to break free from the limitations of glam rock. After spotting the original version of "I Love Rock 'n Roll," by The Arrows, on British television in 1976, she recorded the track with Sex Pistols Steve Jones and Paul Cook (the punk degenerates had taken The Runaways under their wing during their tour of the United Kingdom).

However, this incarnation appeared only as a B-side in Holland. "We buried the first version . . ." Jett declared, "because the record company weren't pushing it." With its "So put another dime in the jukebox, baby" refrain, the song—re-recorded in 1981—harks back to rock's golden age. Britney Spears's version, released two decades later, however, prompted Jett to remark, "I doubt she loves rock 'n' roll."

The film *Wayne's World* used the track to hilarious effect in 1992 and it appears in music video game *Guitar Hero*. Undoubtedly great news for Jett, who kept all her rejection letters from record companies, one having the temerity to suggest to her that "You have no songs . . . and you can't be hard if you're a girl." In 2003, *Rolling Stone* magazine confirmed Jett's credibility, naming her—alongside Joni Mitchell—as one of just two women in their "100 Greatest Guitarists" list. **SS**

Mickey | Toni Basil (1981)

Writer | Mike Chapman, Nicky Chinn
Producer | Greg Mathieson, Trevor Veitch
Label | Radialchoice
Album | *Word of Mouth* (1981)

"I was always a cheerleader, and I remember the echoing in the basketball courts of … us stomping, chanting."
Toni Basil, 2006

◄ **Influenced by: Kitty** · Racey (1979)
► **Influence on: Girlfriend** · Avril Lavigne (2007)
● **Covered by:** "Weird Al" Yankovic (1983) · B*Witched (2000) · Zebrahead (2009)
★ **Other key track:** You Gotta Problem (1982)

Toni Basil's major label career began, and nearly ended, in 1966 with "Breakaway." She had better luck as a choreographer, working on videos (including Talking Heads' "Once in a Lifetime"), tours (including David Bowie's *Diamond Dogs* extravaganza) and movies (including *Easy Rider*). One of the latter—The Monkees' 1968 cult classic *Head*—factored into her second coming.

Fifteen years after "Breakaway" flopped, Basil got another shot at pop stardom. Record executives thought she could score a hit with a remake of Racey's "Kitty." Basil agreed, on one condition: changing the title to "Mickey," to reflect her crush on Monkee Mickey Dolenz.

The result turned out to be one of pop's best sugar highs. The song was unabashedly silly, with a shout-along hook that children of the era can recite in their sleep. "The record company asked me not to put the chant on," she revealed, "because they were very concerned it would 'ruin the tune'."

But the thunderclap drumbeat, cheesy organ, cheer-squad chorus, and Basil's screeching lead demanded attention. It was a simplistic yet confounding morsel of bubblegum: a novelty love song for the MTV age that evoked both 1960s girl groups and 1970s glam. It even spawned a conspiracy theory: that the lyrics described an unrequited crush on a gay friend.

With help from its video—who can forget those cheerleader outfits?—"Mickey" took the top spot in the United States and climbed to the upper reaches elsewhere. Despite her starry associations (new wave nutjobs Devo are among the names on the *Word of Mouth* album), Basil is now remembered as a one-hit wonder, but what a wonderful one hit. **JiH**

Computer Love | Kraftwerk (1981)

Writer | Ralf Hütter, Emil Schult, Karl Bartos
Producer | Ralf Hütter, Florian Schneider
Label | EMI
Album | *Computer World* (1981)

"One group I saw around that time who blew me away was Kraftwerk. They were amazing."

Madonna, 1994

◀ **Influenced by: Telemusik** · Karlheinz Stockhausen (1966)
▶ **Influence on: Computer Love (Sweet Dreams)** The Egyptian Lover (1984)
● **Covered by: Balanescu Quartet** (1992) · **Camouflage** (1992) · **The Album Leaf** (2001)

After *The Man-Machine*, released in 1978, it took electro pioneers Kraftwerk three years to produce *Computer World*. Though a relatively short gestation by the standards the band set later, it was nonetheless remarkable—because, during it, they fully dismantled, then rebuilt and rewired their Kling Klang studio in Düsseldorf. However, admitted leader Ralf Hütter to *Mojo*, "When the album was finished we didn't even have computers. When we went on tour we got our first computer, an Atari."

Succeeding years have not dimmed *Computer World*'s relevance. Its themes—the rise of computers in society, the electronic retention of personal data by corporations, and the way that humans relate to the world through technology—remain very much twenty-first-century concerns.

"Computer Love" was the plaintive cry of a lonely man surrounded by technology, looking for romance via that same technology—predating, by years, the advent of online dating. It was released as a single, backed with an English version of *The Man-Machine*'s "Das Model"—a dream coupling that, thanks to a successful reissue, made Kraftwerk the first German act to top the U.K. chart.

Their colossal influence—on electronic music, hip-hop, and pop—ensnared even Coldplay. For "Talk," on *X&Y* (2005), Chris Martin wanted to use the chiming melody from "Computer Love." "This is what would pass for modern music nowadays," he enthused, "yet they were doing it twenty-five years ago." For permission, Martin wrote to the band in schoolboy German and nervously awaited their reply. Eventually he received a one-word answer: "Yes." **DC**

O Superman | Laurie Anderson (1981)

Writer | Laurie Anderson
Producer | Laurie Anderson
Label | Warner Bros.
Album | *Big Science* (1982)

"I love 'O Superman.'"

Kate Bush, 1985

◄ **Influenced by: Piece in the Shape of a Square**
Philip Glass (1968)
► **Influence on: Obsession** • Army of Lovers (1991)
● **Covered by:** David Bowie (1997) • MANDY vs Booka
Shade (2008)
★ **Other key track:** Sharkey's Day (1984)

Laurie Anderson has spent her career operating outside the mainstream. In the 1970s, she worked New York City's avant-garde performance art scene, palling around with fellow eccentrics like writer William S. Burroughs and comedian Andy Kaufman. One piece, *Duets on Ice*, featured Anderson playing violin while wearing skates, which were frozen in a block of ice. The performance ended when the ice melted.

Anderson was thus an unlikely candidate to score a hit. That she didn't soften her heady approach to do so makes the accomplishment all the more amazing.

"O Superman" was conceived as a cover of the aria "O Souverain, o juge, o père," from Jules Massenet's 1885 opera *Le Cid*. It turned out to be a minimalist manifesto—featuring two chords, "ha" repeated countless times, and Anderson's spoken words through a vocoder.

The song commented, with oblique humor, on the United States's involvement in Iran: "When justice is gone, there's always force. And when force is gone, there's always Mom. Hi Mom!" Her aim was to make humane, warm imagery as compelling as horror. "It's certainly the case in 'O Superman.'" enthused David Bowie in 1983. "That's a very delicate balance; a marvelous piece of work."

Seemingly too long for radio—over eight minutes—it still soared to No. 2 in the United Kingdom but nonetheless remains Anderson's sole hit. Its influence, however, can be felt in the dance and electronic genres. In particular, "O Superman" has proved ripe for mashups, which have pitted it against artists including Dolly Parton and Tears for Fears. And, in 1997, David Bowie covered the song live. **JiH**

In the Air Tonight
Phil Collins (1981)

Writer | Phil Collins
Producer | Phil Collins, Hugh Padgham
Label | Virgin
Album | *Face Value* (1981)

"It's wonderful that an urban myth has grown up around it . . ." Phil Collins told *Uncut*, concerning rumors that "In the Air Tonight" is about a murder. "Because I can say with hand on heart that I have *no idea* what it's about."

The song took shape in 1979. Collins played it to his colleagues in Genesis—but, as he told *Melody Maker*, "it was kind of too simple for the band." Manager Tony Smith and Collins's U.S. label boss Ahmet Ertegun duly persuaded him to develop his demos for a solo outing.

A key development was his cameo on the third album by former Genesis singer Peter Gabriel. "Phil was playing drums," remembered engineer Hugh Padgham, "and I opened the reverse talkback mic. We heard the most unbelievable, distorted, crunching sound." Impressed by this and other percussive innovations, Collins hired Padgham to work on his own album, *Face Value*.

Despite Collins's reputation for mainstream balladeering, the eerie song remains one of his best loved. In 1985, he played it on both sides of the Atlantic for Live Aid. It also achieved an odd ubiquity in rap: adapted by Lil' Kim for the tribute album *Urban Renewal*, cited by Eminem in "Stan," and sampled by Doug E Fresh and DMX. As Daryl Steurmer, who played guitar on the original, said: "I remember thinking, 'Wow, good song, Phil—you've got a nice little career ahead of you there.'" **BM**

Edge of Seventeen
Stevie Nicks (1981)

Writer | Stevie Nicks
Producer | Jimmy Iovine
Label | Modern
Album | *Bella Donna* (1981)

"Nobody wanted me to do it and possibly risk the future of Fleetwood Mac," Stevie Nicks told *Billboard*'s Craig Rosen of her solo debut. However, *Bella Donna* found a home for the prolific Nicks's output. Its biggest hit was "Stop Draggin' My Heart Around," yet its greatest cut was one of her most personal creations.

The song was inspired by Jane Petty, first wife of Nicks's friend Tom (who duetted on "Stop Draggin' My Heart Around"). Jane's thick Southern accent caused Stevie to mishear her saying "age of seventeen" as "edge of seventeen." Originally a paean to the Pettys' love for each other, the song received a new theme after a week in December 1980 that saw both the assassination of John Lennon, and the death of Nicks's uncle Jonathan from cancer. "The white-winged dove in the song is a spirit that is leaving a body," she said, "and I felt a great loss at how both Johns were taken."

The track proved a powerful meditation on mortality. Musically, however, it eschewed the ethereal, acoustic tangles of Nicks's Mac classics like "Sara." Its restrained heavy rock established a bleak tension that she and her band would draw into a ten-minute epic in concert.

Still her greatest solo achievement, "Edge of Seventeen" has since graced the soundtrack of *Grand Theft Auto IV* and had its riff sampled on the Destiny's Child smash "Bootylicious." **SC**

Stevie Nicks takes the stage in Los Angeles as a soloist with her backing singers in 1981. ➔

Via con me
Paolo Conte (1981)

Writer | Paolo Conte
Producer | Italo "Lilli" Greco
Label | RCA
Album | *Paris Milonga* (1981)

A former marimba player who cut his teeth in several Italian jazz bands during the early 1960s, Paolo Conte worked for much of his early career as a lawyer in his hometown of Asti, near Genoa. He eventually started writing songs with his brother, creating hits for other artists. It was only in 1974, prompted by the renowned producer Italo "Lilli" Greco, that Conte released his debut solo album.

"Via con me" is his best-known song and comes from his fourth album, which found him at the height of his powers. It established Conte as the leading exponent of *canzone d'autore* (Italy's esoteric cousin of the singer-songwriter genre) and later featured in the movie *French Kiss* (1995).

Conte's love of prewar American jazz is obvious in the suavely swinging accompaniment, but he gives this a European twist, with echoes of French chansonniers and a dash of Django Reinhardt.

"Via con me" is a track typical of Conte's playful relationship with language, mixing both his own tongue and a trademark half-scatted English. Most of the lyrics are in Italian, with Conte casually proposing in a gravelly speak-singing tone that an unnamed lover come away with him.

The phrase that jumps out at most English speakers is "It's wonderful, it's wonderful," which Conte slurs into something like "swunerful, swunerful." And yes, he really is saying "chips, chips, dat to doo di do, chi boom, chi boom." **JLu**

Under Pressure
Queen & David Bowie (1981)

Writer | Queen, David Bowie
Producer | Queen, David Bowie
Label | EMI
Album | *Hot Space* (1982)

Six years after their first U.K. No. 1—the iconic "Bohemian Rhapsody" in 1975—Queen topped the charts again. This time they were assisted by the Thin White Duke himself.

Although "Under Pressure" proved a match made in heaven, it was the product of providence. Queen owned Mountain Studios in Switzerland, where Bowie was a neighbor and visitor. "Someone suggested that we should all go into the studio and play around one night," recalled Queen's Brian May. This jam spawned the genesis of "Under Pressure," which was finished during what May described as "an extremely long night."

Neither May nor Bowie was happy with the result. Nonetheless, with front man Freddie Mercury's affecting "Why can't we give love that one more chance?" the song presented an emotional plea for tolerance and compassion in a pressure-cooker world. It was the highlight of Queen's uncharacteristically funky *Hot Space*.

Queen wasted no time wowing audiences with the track. Bowie, however, didn't perform it until a year after Mercury's untimely death; duetting with Annie Lennox at a 1992 concert in honor of the Queen vocalist. "Under Pressure" has since been heard in the most unexpected places—even serving as an official wake-up call for the crew of Space Shuttle flight STS-116 on December 14, 2006. **BC**

Our Lips Are Sealed
_Go-Go's_ (1981)

Writer | Jane Wiedlin, Terry Hall
Producer | Richard Gottehrer, Rob Freeman
Label | I.R.S.
Album | _Beauty and the Beat_ (1981)

Girl band the Go-Go's burst onto the Los Angeles punk scene in the late 1970s, but, within a few years, they'd put their rebellious beginnings behind them, thanks in part to the success of their debut album, _Beauty and the Beat_. Packed with quirky, exuberant tunes, it topped the _Billboard_ chart and transformed the group into superstars.

The newly crowned pop princesses were shot to the top by "We Got the Beat," but more enduring was "Our Lips are Sealed." With chugging guitar and pulsing bass, the buoyant ditty fitted seamlessly into the band's goodtime frivolity. But this sonic sugar-coating masked a tale of infidelity concerning the song's co-writer, guitarist Joe Wiedlin.

"I met Terry Hall, the singer of The Specials," she told _Songfacts_, "and ended up having kind of a romance. He sent me the lyrics to 'Our Lips Are Sealed' later in the mail, and it was kind of about our relationship, because he had a girlfriend at home and all this other stuff." Wiedlin polished the lyrics before it was recorded. "I was really afraid to show it to the band in case they didn't like it . . ." she confessed. "But luckily they did like it."

Terry Hall was equally impressed, and released the song with his new outfit, Fun Boy Three, in 1983. "They did a really great version of it . . ." enthused Wiedlin. "It was a lot gloomier than the Go-Go's version." **SF**

Genius of Love
Tom Tom Club (1981)

Writer | A. Belew, C. Frantz, S. Stanley, T. Weymouth
Producer | S. Stanley, T. Weymouth, C. Frantz
Label | Sire
Album | _Tom Tom Club_ (1981)

The boingy bass, synth chirrups, and lazy beats of "Genius of Love" crop up on cuts by acts from Grandmaster Flash ("It's Nasty") and De La Soul ("Shoomp") to Mariah Carey, whose 1995 single "Fantasy" was little more than a straight copy.

Tom Tom Club was formed in 1980 by Talking Heads rhythm section (and married couple) Tina Weymouth and Chris Frantz, when relations in the day-job band were at their lowest ebb. Complaining about early pressings of the Heads' 1980 album _Remain in Light_ crediting singer David Byrne rather too heavily, Frantz asserted: "It wasn't an administrative error. It was an error by a member of the band who is used to taking credit for everything that happens."

For the new band, the pair recruited Talking Heads' touring guitarist Adrian Belew, Jamaican producer Steven Stanley, and session players including Weymouth's singer sisters Laura, Loric, and Lani. After the proto-hip-hop track "Wordy Rappinghood," "Genius of Love" established Tom Tom Club's sunshine sound.

A woozily sung tribute to a mighty fine boyfriend, it praises this "maven of funk mutation" and namechecks Funkadelic bassman Bootsy Collins, disco pioneer Hamilton Bohannon, and, most stridently, James Brown. With its lolloping gait and squeaky hook, "Genius of Love" fuels grooves and bank balances to this day. **MH**

Ghosts | Japan (1981)

Writer | David Sylvian
Producer | Steve Nye, Japan
Label | Virgin
Album | *Tin Drum* (1981)

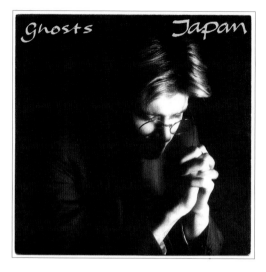

"If I listen to that track now, I'm still amazed it did as well as it did."

David Sylvian, 1993

◀ **Influenced by: Art Decade** • David Bowie (1977)
▶ **Influence on: Mad World** • Tears for Fears (1983)
● **Covered by:** Mathilde Santing (2008)
★ **Other key tracks: Adolescent Sex** (1977) • Life in Tokyo (1979) • Gentlemen Take Polaroids (1980) Cantonese Boy (1981)

"It's a little oblique, to say the least," remarked Japan's singer David Sylvian. Indeed, "Ghosts" was certainly unconventional, yet it was also the British quartet's biggest hit.

Earlier recordings made apparent the group's influences, from the New York Dolls and Roxy Music to David Bowie and Erik Satie. "Ghosts," however, saw Japan create a striking sound of their own: a sparse, electronic backing, featuring an Oriental motif, behind a haunting—and haunted—vocal. "The best thing that Dave's written," enthused the group's keyboard player Richard Barbieri.

The eerie atmosphere perfectly fit Sylvian's words, in which ghosts act as a metaphor for unspecified anxieties. "At the time I wrote the lyrics," he confessed to *NME*, "I wasn't happy with them. I wasn't one hundred percent sure." "There's a lot of me in there," he added. "But I'm not a depressive . . . I actually find 'Ghosts' optimistic, not pessimistic."

Japan were riding high at this time, but Sylvian felt the band had reached a zenith. The media pressure he felt, as "the most beautiful man in pop," as well as internal fractures, meant that by the end of 1982, they had performed live for the last time. Splitting at their height fulfilled the song's prophecy: "Just when I thought I could not be stopped / when my chance came to be king / the ghosts of my life blew wilder than the wind."

In his solo career, Sylvian distanced himself from his former band's work. But he continued to perform "Ghosts" live—and the track, in partially re-recorded form, was one of only two Japan songs to feature on his 2000 retrospective *Everything and Nothing*. **JL**

Tainted Love | Soft Cell (1981)

Writer | Ed Cobb
Producer | Mike Thorne
Label | Some Bizzare
Album | *Non-Stop Erotic Cabaret* (1981)

"We're grateful for the song. But eventually it became a bit of a millstone. It ended up being more famous than we did."

David Ball, 2008

◀ **Influenced by: Tainted Love** · Gloria Jones (1964)
▶ **Influence on: SOS** · Rihanna (2006)
● **Covered by:** David Benoit (1994) · Wild Strawberries (2000) · Marilyn Manson (2002) · Paul Young (2006)
★ **Other key tracks:** Say Hello, Wave Goodbye (1981) Torch (1982)

"A mixture of cold electronics with an overpassionate, overexuberant, slightly out-of-key vocal," is how Marc Almond describes the song for which his band Soft Cell are best known: a cover of a 1964 classic by U.S. singer-songwriter Gloria Jones (later Marc Bolan's girlfriend). It was Almond's partner-in-crime David Ball's idea to fuse "Northern soul [cult soul records beloved of British youths] with German electronics." "Tainted Love" was Soft Cell's second single, and their record label was reportedly going to make it their last, if it didn't sell. They need not have worried—the tune went to No. 1 in seventeen countries and broke the record for the longest stay on the U.S. *Billboard* chart.

Perhaps the secret of the song was what Almond told *The Times*: "I feel I can put my baggage into other people's songs better." The lyrics were taken as a commentary on the advent of AIDS—"It wasn't an intentional tie-in," Almond observed, "but it took on this other meaning."

Whatever its meaning, the song went on to be used commercially to sell everything from jeans to soft drinks; it turned up in movies and TV shows (including a Danny DeVito striptease on *Friends*), and it was covered by everyone from P. J. Proby to Marilyn Manson, as well as in other languages. (The Spanish version, by La Unión, is called "Falso amor.")

Ball came to regard the song as "a bit of a millstone," but Almond looked on it fondly: "It's been a good friend, because when I play a concert and it's going down like a lead balloon, all I have to do is bring out 'Tainted Love' and suddenly I have everybody." And, as Gloria Jones remarked, "Their version is far better than mine." **DC**

Walking on Thin Ice | Yoko Ono (1981)

Writer | Yoko Ono
Producer | John Lennon, Yoko Ono, Jack Douglas
Label | Geffen
Album | N/A

" 'Walking on Thin Ice' is a very difficult song for me to sing . . . there are so many memories. "

Yoko Ono, 2009

◀ **Influenced by: Ashes to Ashes** · David Bowie (1980)
▶ **Influence on: Hunter** · Björk (1997)
● **Covered by:** Elvis Costello & The Attractions (1984)
We've Got a Fuzzbox and We're Gonna Use It (1989)
★ **Other key tracks:** Why (1970) · Kiss Kiss Kiss (1980)
Hard Times Are Over (1981) · No, No, No (1981)

"Walking on Thin Ice" was among Yoko Ono's greatest achievements. Yet if she could erase the day of its recording, no doubt she would. It was cut on December 8, 1980—just hours before Ono's husband, John Lennon, was shot to death by psychotic fan Mark Chapman. "John wasn't supposed to be there," revealed producer Jack Douglas. "I'd worked with him that night, and he'd stayed around to help her out." Lennon reportedly died clutching a mix of the song.

In the aftermath, Ono told *Uncut*, "I was in a funk . . . I would be in bed and then I would go out to the studio to finish 'Walking on Thin Ice.' . . . After John's passing, people told me, 'Walking on Thin Ice,' they're playing it in the clubs all the time."

Striking enough on its own merit, the track became more meaningful in the context of Lennon's murder. The very title evokes a precarious situation, strengthened by the lyrics: "I'm paying the price / for throwing the dice in the air / Why must we learn it the hard way / and play the game of life with your heart?" Ono's delivery—softly sung rather than screeched in the fashion that had annoyed Beatles fans—was eerily resigned, as if she saw something coming that she couldn't stop.

The song's danceable groove, highlighted by a mesmerizing bass line and Lennon's avant-garde guitar, gave Ono her first chart success. (It was added to a 1997 reissue of her 1981 album, *Season of Glass*.) The song has been remixed by Spiritualized's Jason Pierce and the Pet Shop Boys, and covered by Elvis Costello and The Attractions on the tribute album *Every Man Has a Woman* (1984), while a 2003 re-release topped the U.S. dance chart. **JiH**

Please Don't Touch | Motörhead/Girlschool (1981)

Writer | Johnny Kidd, Guy Robinson
Producer | Vic Maile
Label | Bronze
Album | N/A

"Motörhead are a real laugh. We had a fantastic time doing it."

Kelly Johnson, Girlschool, 1982

◄ **Influenced by: Summertime Blues** • Eddie Cochran (1958)
► **Influence on: Plastic Girl** • The Busy Signals (2007)
● **Covered by:** The Meteors (1989) • Stray Cats (1994)
★ **Other key tracks:** Emergency (1981) • Bomber (1981)

Everything was going swell in Motörhead's world in 1980, with the hit "Ace of Spades" under their bullet belts. Then drummer Phil "Philthy Animal" Taylor lived up to his nickname during a friendly test of strength, and broke his neck.

Taylor's bandmates—bassist and front man Lemmy, and guitarist "Fast" Eddie Clarke—filled their downtime by recording with labelmates Girlschool. The result was the *St. Valentine's Day Massacre* EP, commonly credited to Headgirl, on which Motörhead (with Girlschool's Denise Dufort on drums) covered Girlschool's "Emergency," while the girls tackled Lemmy and Co.'s "Bomber." The bands united on "Please Don't Touch"—a career highlight for both.

The song, a 1959 single by Johnny Kidd & The Pirates, best known for "Shakin' All Over," appeared an unlikely choice. But Lemmy had long been a fan of 1950s rock; hence *Fools Paradise*, his 2006 covers album, as The Head Cat (featuring the Stray Cats' Slim Jim Phantom).

Headgirl's version wasn't punk, metal, or any of the other labels that Lemmy so despised being used on his music. It was rock 'n' roll—and, according to Lemmy's sleevenotes on the 1984 compilation *No Remorse*, an improvement on the original. The ferocious vocals and roaring tune made it a track that punks, metal-heads, and even pop fans could agree on.

"'Please Don't Touch' was such a crossover record," Girlschool's Kelly Johnson enthused to *Creem*. "So many different people bought it." The EP duly crashed the U.K. Top Five—landing Headgirl on *Top of the Pops* and further cementing Motörhead's status as one of the most influential bands in rock. **JiH**

Super Freak

Rick James (1981)

Writer | Rick James, Alonzo Miller
Producer | Rick James
Label | Motown
Album | *Street Songs* (1981)

Rick James signed to Motown in 1966, having gone AWOL from the Navy to front R&B group The Mynah Birds. He finally achieved superstardom fifteen years later with an anthem perfectly tailored for the synth-funk bad boy.

"Super Freak" was a fierce slab of digital sleaze, featuring James lustfully crooning about "a very kinky girl, the kind you don't take home to mother." The Temptations (featuring James's uncle, Melvin Franklin) provided backing vocals, but it was a 180-degree turn from the wholesome fare of Sixties-era Motown. "I just put 'Super Freak' together really quickly," James told *Musician* in 1983. "I wanted a silly song that had a bit of new wave texture to it. So I just came up with this silly little lick and expounded on it."

"Super Freak" sent *Street Songs* triple platinum, and James enjoyed his newfound fame to the hilt, even guesting on TV's *The A-Team*, singing his hit at a prison concert. Only a few years later, however, James found himself incarcerated in Folsom Prison for real, for kidnapping and assault.

His career would not recover. But "Super Freak" lived on, thanks to MC Hammer heavily sampling it for his 1990 smash, "U Can't Touch This," and Jay-Z looping it for his 2006 track "Kingdom Come." The original, meanwhile, brilliantly soundtracked a scandalous dance routine by a seven-year-old girl in the 2006 comedy *Little Miss Sunshine*. **SC**

Don't Stop Believin'

Journey (1981)

Writer | Steve Perry, Neal Schon, Jonathan Cain
Producer | Mike Stone, Kevin Elson
Label | Columbia
Album | *Escape* (1981)

Critically despised though it was, Adult-Oriented Rock gave the world mighty tunes: Nirvana looted Boston's "More Than a Feeling"; only hard hearts don't melt at REO Speedwagon's "Keep on Loving You"; and the most downloaded pre-2000 song of the twenty-first century? "Don't Stop Believin'."

The all-time anthem began with keyboardist Jonathan Cain, who joined Journey for *Escape*. "He brought 'Don't Stop Believin','" guitarist Neal Schon told *Billboard*'s Craig Rosen. "I came up with a coupla chords and jammed them out and then he and Steve [Perry, vocalist] finished it."

With Schon riffing "like a locomotive," Cain and Perry developed a lyrical tale of young lovers. (Thanks to this and two hit ballads—"Who's Crying Now" and "Open Arms"—*Escape* became *the* make-out album for American teens.)

The anthemic "Don't Stop Believin'" has featured in TV's *Scrubs*, *Family Guy*, *Laguna Beach*, and—most stupendously—the very end of *The Sopranos*. "I didn't want the song to be part of a bloodbath, if that was going to be the closing moment," Perry told *People*. "In order for me to feel good about approving the song use, they had to tell me what happened. And they made me swear that I would not tell anybody." However, he told *Blender*, "When I saw the show, I thought it was perfect. I was shouting in my house, throwing my arms up: '*Woooooh!*'" **BM**

Rick James combines leather and an off-the-shoulder number in a 1982 performance.

The Eighties | 493

Pretty in Pink | The Psychedelic Furs (1981)

Writer | The Psychedelic Furs
Producer | Steve Lillywhite
Label | CBS
Album | *Talk Talk Talk* (1981)

"We helped the sale of pink clothes worldwide."

Tim Butler, 2004

- ◄ **Influenced by:** Sweet Jane · The Velvet Underground (1970)
- ► **Influence on:** Mr. Brightside · The Killers (2004)
- ● **Covered by:** Pink Lincolns (1987) · Automatic Seven (1997) · The Dresden Dolls (2005)
- ★ **Other key track:** Mack the Knife (1981)

Despite coining a phrase, The Psychedelic Furs' fifth single was only a minor hit on its initial release (peaking at No. 43 in the U.K. singles chart)—although Vince Clarke, then of Depeche Mode, declared it his favorite track in the world. This depiction of transient love affairs would not become the band's signature tune until its revival for a teen movie of the same name.

Inspired by David Bowie and The Velvet Underground, The Psychedelic Furs' guitar-driven sound—punctuated by saxophone and aggressive drums—was the perfect vehicle for Richard Butler's nicotine-stained vocals. "Pretty in Pink" duly struck a balance between new wave rock and accessible pop.

Female names recur in Butler's lyrics. Here, Caroline returns from the debut album's "India," apparently nude—"pretty in pink." Prey to uncaring lovers, she is used, then cast aside: "The one who insists he was first in the line," rasps Butler, "is the last to remember her name."

Cryptic mumbling concludes the song. Butler told *Creem* about a fan, who "had written out what he thought I was saying at the end of 'Pretty in Pink.' The lyrics had purposely been buried in the mix so people could make up their own interpretations. And he had all this great stuff written out—things about Oedipus and Greek mythological characters and the rain and spitting at turntables."

The song inspired director John Hughes's movie *Pretty in Pink*, released in 1986, the soundtrack of which featured a glossy, new, "saxed–up" version. Bassist Tim Butler marveled that the band were asked to re-record the track because "the guitar on the original was slightly out of tune." **JL**

Ghost Town | The Specials (1981)

Writer | Jerry Dammers
Producer | John Collins
Label | 2 Tone
Album | N/A

Ghost Town
Why?
Friday Night Saturday Morning

"It's that classic, no future, nihilistic punk thing. 'Ghost Town' might well have been the only punk No. 1."

Billy Bragg, 2002

◄ **Influenced by:** What a Feeling · Gregory Isaacs (1980)
► **Influence on:** Hell Is Around the Corner · Tricky (1995)
● **Covered by:** Terry Hall (1995) · The Prodigy (2002)
Get Cape. Wear Cape. Fly (2006) · The Aggrolites (2009)
Kode9 & The Spaceape (2009)
★ **Other key track:** Do Nothing (1980)

Eerie sirens, ominous organs, haunting Japanese fake clarinets, and anguished cries—this was the baleful sound of a country in crisis. Jerry Dammers's prescient masterpiece duly hit No. 1 in the United Kingdom the day after riots erupted across the land. The song's lyrics mark a despair with rising unemployment and the most unpopular government of the postwar era—as well as the band's more personal frustration at the violence they encountered at gigs.

It was also the sound of a band in crisis. Rifts between its members grew ever wider, as Dammers pushed forward his vision of a new sound: a mix of the group's ska roots and electronic "easy listening" grooves. Things came to a head in the recording session, where Dammers defied the group's practice of playing together live, by working out each part separately beforehand. "Neville [Staples, vocalist] would not try the ideas . . . " he told *The Guardian* in 2002. "I remember Lynval [Golding, guitarist] rushing into the control room while they were doing [the brass section], going, 'No, no, no, it sounds wrong! Wrong! Wrong!' In the meantime, Roddy [Radiation, guitarist] is trying to kick a hole through the wall . . . ."

Just before The Specials were to perform their hit on British television, Staples, Golding, and front man Terry Hall announced they were leaving the group. "'Ghost Town,'" said Hall, "was the perfect way for us to say 'bye.'" The trio reappeared as Fun Boy Three.

Despite being so of its time, "Ghost Town" has been used and sampled many times—most memorably in British sitcom *Father Ted*, in one episode of which it is the only record, played over and over, at a village disco. **DC**

I'm in Love with a German Film Star | The Passions (1981)

Writer | David Agar, Barbara Gogan,
Clive Timperley, Richard Williams
Producer | Peter Wilson
Label | Polydor
Album | *Thirty Thousand Feet over China* (1981)

*"It was a song that almost
seemed to write itself."*
David Agar, 2009

◄ **Influenced by: Fade Away and Radiate** · Blondie
(1978)
► **Influence on: The Metro** · Berlin (1981)
● **Covered by:** The Names (2002) · Foo Fighters (2005)
Chris Whitley (2005)

Having released three singles and one album
in 1980, The Passions were in search of a
breakthrough when they entered Clink Street
Studios in London to begin their sophomore
effort. Guitarist Clive Timperley (formerly of The
101-ers, with The Clash's Joe Strummer) and
bassist David Agar were simply jamming a three-
chord progression, when vocalist Barbara Gogan
blurted out the line, "I'm in love with a German
film star." At that, drummer Richard Williams
snuffed out his cigarette and commented, "That's
a hit single"—and he was right.

The object of Gogan's desires wasn't Klaus
Kinski, Marlene Dietrich, or, for that matter, even
German or a star. The mysterious, forlorn lyrics
were in tribute to former Sex Pistols roadie Steve
Connelly—who had a few parts in minor German
films and TV shows, before entering the stage
lighting industry. Yet Gogan's wispy delivery
was the musical equivalent of a wide-eyed teen
daydreaming over a Hollywood pin-up.

She was accompanied, to perfection, by a
moody arrangement of echoing, decaying guitar,
icy keyboards, and the otherworldly beats of a
drum channeled through a vocoder. The whole
package was as strange as it was enticing and
hypnotic—an odd post-punk offering from an
entity originally known as a guitar band.

The song peaked at No. 25 in the U.K. charts,
a height that the band wouldn't come close to
for the brief remainder of its career. The Passions,
who broke up in the mid-Eighties, are now
remembered as a "one-hit wonder." But that hit
was highly influential, and has since been covered
by both the Foo Fighters and the Pet Shop Boys
(producing artist Sam Taylor-Wood). **JiH**

Radio Free Europe | R.E.M. (1981)

Writer | Bill Berry, Peter Buck, Mike Mills, Michael Stipe
Producer | Mitch Easter, R.E.M.
Label | Hib-Tone
Album | N/A

"I don't like listening to a song and being able to pick out every single word."
Michael Stipe, 1983

◀ **Influenced by: When My Baby's Beside Me** · Big Star (1972)
▶ **Influence on: Agoraphobia** · Deerhunter (2008)
● **Covered by: The Replacements** (1985) · **Just Say No** (1992) · **Alan Pinches** (1997)
★ **Other key track: Sitting Still** (1981)

Melodic and mysterious, "Radio Free Europe" was a perfect calling card for R.E.M.'s mesmerizing debut *Murmur*. Front man Michael Stipe's Southern drawl and vague vocals ("Keep me out of country in the word / Deal the porch is leading us absurd"—perhaps) and Peter Buck's ringing, Byrdsy guitar swiftly became the band's hallmarks.

The title namechecked a U.S. radio station that broadcast Western propaganda to the Eastern Bloc. "Whatever Michael was getting at there didn't even matter because it was a good phrase, something we all knew," said Buck. "I thought, isn't that strange—America is spreading cultural imperialism through pop music. So the song was kinda about that." (Buck and Stipe recalled an oddball ad for RFE featuring The Drifters' "On Broadway" and wondered what the song could have meant east of the Iron Curtain.)

"Radio Free Europe" gave the Georgia foursome a lowly *Billboard* No. 78 placing. That, however, was the re-recorded *Murmur* version. This landmark song was first released, in an initial pressing of one thousand, on the independent label Hib-Tone. "I purposely did not want any lyrics understood . . ." Stipe revealed. "I hadn't written any of the words yet, so I just kind of blabbered." Nonetheless, the Hib-Tone release registered with the underground press—"One of the few great American punk singles," enthused *Village Voice*.

R.E.M. were unhappy with the mix and the mastering, but this version zipped along with an urgency that many prefer over the more famous recording. And the band eventually learned to live with it: the Hib-Tone version appeared on their 1988 retrospective *Eponymous* and 2006's hits set, *And I Feel Fine*. **RD**

The Message | Grandmaster Flash & The Furious Five (1982)

Writer | Clifton "Jiggs" Chase, Ed "Duke Bootee" Fletcher, Melvin "Melle Mel" Glover, Sylvia Robinson
Producer | C. Chase, E. Fletcher, S. Robinson
Label | Sugar Hill
Album | *The Message* (1982)

It was the moment when the pioneers of hip-hop, stars of the 1970s South Bronx party scene, whose DJ invented quick mixing, hit the big time. Yet Grandmaster Flash & The Furious Five don't really appear on "The Message"—except on the label.

The track, from an idea by session musician Duke Bootee, was engineered by Sugar Hill label boss Sylvia Robinson into a politicized hip-hop track for her stars, Flash and his MCs. But only one, Melle Mel, appears on the record, thanks to a verse of social commentary he had used on their 1980 release, "Super Rappin'."

"The Message" is the only hip-hop song in the American Library of Congress's National Recording Registry. As Public Enemy's Chuck D noted, it "gave a platform for every single rap group that came afterwards"—and Melle Mel's "ha ha ha ha ha" even inspired the laughter on Genesis's hit "Mama." "When 'The Message' became the hottest song that summer," recalled Red Hot Chili Peppers front man Anthony Kiedis, "it started dawning on me that you don't have to be Al Green or have an incredible Freddie Mercury voice to have a place in the world of music."

However, the division of the group for their biggest hit led to a fatal rift. Flash split the band, suing Sugar Hill over royalties and the use of his name. But "The Message" lives on—it even turned up in the 2006 kids' movie *Happy Feet*. **DC**

365 Is My Number | King Sunny Adé & His African Beats (1982)

Writer | King Sunny Adé
Producer | Martin Meissonnier
Label | Island/Mango
Album | *Juju Music* (1982)

African audiences had been under the spell of King Sunny Adé for well over a decade, but it wasn't until Island Records boss Chris Blackwell signed him to his fledgling world music imprint, Mango, in 1982, that his music went global.

Recorded in Togo and mixed in London, "365 Is My Number/The Message" is a polymorphic mix of traditional Nigerian Yoruba praise song, calypso reggae riffs, instrumental surf-guitar strums, and African electric funk. While the litany of "talking" drums, congas, bongos, and weirdly tuned electric guitars give "365 Is My Number" its magnetism, it is producer Martin Meissonnier's deft, dub-wise integration of "synchro" synthesizers that makes the instrumental "The Message" so inviting for Western ears. Not that Adé actually panders to any Western pop clichés. Instead, he caricatures them with burlesque Hawaiian slide guitar licks and Spanish-tinged chords, undercut by a deep-rooted authenticity.

The Yoruba lyrics and polyrhythmic complexity was not a formula for mainstream chart success, however. Ultimately, Adé proved too experimental to live up to Island Records' desire to bill him as "the African Bob Marley."

However, "365 Is My Number/The Message" did manage to achieve a Hollywood footnote on the soundtrack to Jim McBride's 1983 remake of *Breathless*, starring Richard Gere. **MK**

Grandmaster Flash on the wheels of steel in the early 1980s.

Do You Really Want to Hurt Me | Culture Club (1982)

Writer | Culture Club
Producer | Steve Levine
Label | Virgin
Album | *Kissing to Be Clever* (1982)

"I don't write songs for heterosexuals and I don't write songs for homosexuals. I just write songs for everyone."

Boy George, 1983

◀ **Influenced by: The Tracks of My Tears** • The Miracles (1965)

▶ **Influence on: Hold Me Now** • Thompson Twins (1983)

● **Covered by:** Violent Femmes (1991) • Diana King (1997) Mike Post (1998) • Mark Eitzel (1998) • Blue Lagoon (2005)

Style has always mattered as much as substance in pop music. The scales tilted toward the former with the dawn of MTV, which began broadcasting in 1981 and made stars out of colorful, though limited, talents such as Men Without Hats and Bow Wow Wow. With Culture Club's hit-packed debut album, *Kissing to Be Clever*, the public would meet an act that was equal parts style and substance.

The London band—led by androgynous fashion icon Boy George, a former member of Bow Wow Wow, singing under the stage name Lieutenant Lush—played a blend of new wave, reggae, and blue-eyed soul. But was the mix marketable? EMI didn't think so, and passed on the group after paying for demos. Virgin, however, took a chance and signed the act, but the gamble didn't look like it would pay off when the group's first two singles—"White Boy" and "I'm Afraid of Me"—floundered.

The third time proved the charm: "Do You Really Want to Hurt Me," with its easy Island groove and George's softly soulful vocals, became a worldwide smash. "People have said to me," marveled George to *NME*, "what about 'Do You Really'? Was it about S&M? And it makes me scream. They said that in America. I couldn't believe it. It made me laugh because I write about basic emotions, in my own way."

Culture Club never strayed far from the template created by "Do You Really Want to Hurt Me." The modern torch song remains one of the group's most popular offerings—and one that has been handed down to new generations, thanks to its inclusion in the movies *The Wedding Singer* (1998) and *Shrek* (2001). **JiH**

Electric Avenue | Eddy Grant (1982)

Writer | Eddy Grant
Producer | Eddy Grant
Label | ICE
Album | *Killer on the Rampage* (1982)

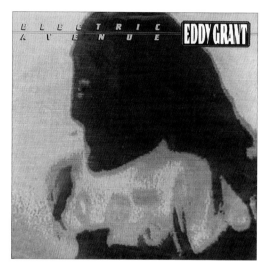

"Back then, the concept of a black entrepreneur hadn't yet been assimilated into British society."

Eddy Grant, 2008

◄ **Influenced by: Downpressor Man** · Peter Tosh (1977)
► **Influence on: Avenues** · Refugee Camp All-Stars (1997)
● **Covered by:** Raggadeath (1997) · Tait (2003) · Skindred (2009)
★ **Other key tracks:** I Don't Wanna Dance (1982) · War Party (1982)

Jaunty hits can hide darker truths. Bruce Springsteen's sceptical "Born in the U.S.A." became a flag-waving anthem, and the Red Hot Chili Peppers' ode to drug use—"Under the Bridge"—sounded like a love song.

With a stomping beat, chirpy synth, and memorable chorus, "Electric Avenue" was a guaranteed party hit. But one look at the video, with an angry Eddy Grant barking direct to camera, revealed the real story.

Originally from Guyana, Grant graduated from working-class beginnings to lead The Equals (who scored in 1968 with "Baby Come Back"), open Britain's first black-owned recording studio, and launch his own label, ICE. The U.K.—Grant's home for over twenty years—provided a springboard for his success, including pioneering the hybrid sound of soca. But, by 1981, Grant was disillusioned with Britain's class and racial struggles, and relocated to Barbados.

Killer on the Rampage is full of political fire and rebellion. It included "I Don't Wanna Dance," Grant's swan song to Britain, and "War Party," which was banned during the Falklands conflict. While the sound of "Electric Avenue" suggested a funky, vibrant place, its lyrics evoked unrest in a predominantly black area of south London (Electric Avenue is a real street in Brixton, the scene of a 1981 riot). "That's how I try to write," said Grant. "You take it how you want, but I am basically a writer of protest."

A 2001 remix brought Grant back into the U.K. Top Five after his career was blighted by litigation. "It just shows that it's really all about just making the best music you can," he told *Blues & Soul*, "and then just waiting for the end result." **SO**

Sweet Dreams (Are Made of This)
Eurythmics (1982)

Writer | Dave Stewart, Annie Lennox
Producer | Dave Stewart
Label | RCA
Album | *Sweet Dreams (Are Made of This)* (1983)

"Eurythmics weren't selling any records to speak of," Dave Stewart told *NME*. "The Tourists were long split up; and then me and Annie [Lennox] split. Yet we were still going around with the same hopes."

"We had been so stitched up when we started out as The Tourists in '78," Lennox told *Smash Hits*, "and even as Eurythmics at the beginning, we just had to take things into our own hands. That line in 'Sweet Dreams' about being 'used and abused' refers directly to my own experiences. Not just in love, but in this business too."

Their first smash fitted the vogue for soulful vocals atop electronic backings. The Eurythmics, however, added twists. "Things that you think are sequencers are real," Stewart told *Performing Songwriter*. "Like Annie and I playing milk bottles on 'Sweet Dreams.'" A memorable video was, Stewart assured *Q,* "inspired by the Luis Buñuel movie *L'Âge d'or*." "It was all about absurdity and how the world is absurd," he elaborated to *Artists House Music*, "and yet we're singing 'Sweet dreams are made of this.' It's an ironic statement."

The song has been sampled by acts from Britney Spears to 50 Cent, and covered by multitudes from Bebel Gilberto to Marilyn Manson. "In a single lyric," Manson wrote, "it summed up . . . the mentality of nearly everyone I had met since forming the band: 'Some of them want to abuse you / Some of them want to be abused.'" **BM**

Atomic Dog
George Clinton (1982)

Writer | George Clinton, Garry Shider, David Spradley
Producer | G. Clinton, T. Currier
Label | Capitol
Album | *Computer Games* (1982)

Wigged out Parliament/Funkadelic front man George Clinton dissolved the two groups at the dawn of the 1980s and signed as a solo artist to Capitol. But his debut recordings featured P-Funk alumni in sprawling jams.

At one session, a druggily paranoid Clinton believed the engineers were cutting tracks without him. They were only experimenting but, having burst into the studio, Clinton was determined to lay a vocal over their weird backward drum track. Ad libbing a canine theme, to find the right key, Clinton laid down lyrics that influenced a generation of rappers. Then a forward-running drum track was mixed on top of the backward one, keyboardist Bernie Worrell added a funky melody, and a whomping track that was to be sampled over eighty times was born. Ice Cube alone has used it seven times, while Clinton himself is said to have been in Dr. Dre's studio when Snoop Doggy Dogg's homage "Who Am I (What's My Name)?" was created.

"Atomic Dog" has been used in a bewildering range of movies and TV shows, from *The Wire* and *Menace II Society* to *Rugrats Go Wild*. As Clinton told National Public Radio in 2006: "I like being silly because the kids are the only ones who relate to it for a minute. And then you go to another age bracket, and they relate to it for a minute, then it's too old for anybody." **DC**

Eurythmics in 1983, the year that "Sweet Dreams" broke into the charts.

The Eighties | 503

State of Independence | Donna Summer (1982)

Writer | Vangelis, Jon Anderson
Producer | Quincy Jones
Label | Geffen
Album | *Donna Summer* (1982)

"It is Brian Eno's favorite song. He played it all the time."

Chris Martin, Coldplay, 2008

◀ **Influenced by: State of Independence** • Jon & Vangelis (1981)

▶ **Influence on: The Places You Find Love** • Quincy Jones (1989)

● **Covered by:** Moodswings featuring Chrissie Hynde (1991)

Michael Jackson? Seventies prog rockers? Brian Eno? Only one song ticks all three boxes.

It originated on *The Friends of Mr. Cairo*, a 1981 collaboration between Yes singer Jon Anderson and keyboard maestro Vangelis (who had been mooted to join Yes in 1974). Yet it was cherry-picked by super-producer Quincy Jones for Donna Summer's follow-up to her first post-disco success *The Wanderer*. (The intended follow-up—a gospel set called *I'm a Rainbow*—was rejected by Geffen, who paired her with Jones.) "It's a song that really expresses what I've been feeling lately," Summer declared. "It's got an optimism and sense of purpose that is based in reality."

Jones stuck closely to the original song's arrangement, but he gave it a lush, stirring production. His premier client, Michael Jackson, was among guests in an "all star choir" that also featured Dionne Warwick, Michael McDonald, Lionel Richie, and Brenda Russell (the woman responsible for 1988's "Piano in the Dark" and Summer's 1987 single "Dinner with Gershwin"). "When Quincy calls," Summer observed, "people drop what they're doing."

Another noted guest, Stevie Wonder, even contributed sleeve notes for the song: "Just as all creation is one with the universe, may we too be one with each other." Jones later credited this gathering as an inspiration for "We Are the World."

At the time of release, "State of Independence" met a more muted reception than the album's first single, the effervescent "Love Is in Control (Finger on the Trigger)." Today, however, it is widely celebrated—not least by producer and musician Brian Eno, who describes it as "one of the high points of twentieth century art." **BM**

Save a Prayer | Duran Duran (1982)

Writer | Duran Duran
Producer | Colin Thurston
Label | EMI
Album | *Rio* (1982)

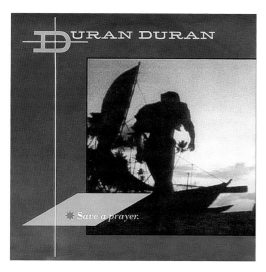

"A bit of pretension never hurt anybody. Except for Spandau Ballet."
John Taylor, 1982

◀ **Influenced by: If You Could Read My Mind**
Gordon Lightfoot (1970)
▶ **Influence on: Teddy Picker** · Arctic Monkeys (2007)
● **Covered by:** Tony Hadley (1997)
★ **Other key tracks:** Planet Earth (1981) · Hungry Like the Wolf (1982) · Rio (1982)

One of the first songs whose visuals meant as much as its music, "Save a Prayer" is one of pop's all-time great ballads. Duran Duran addressed the unexpectedly deep issue of doomed love with the third single from their second album, *Rio*—front man Simon Le Bon singing about a one-night stand over a moving blend of synth-pop and English chanson.

It has become a cliché to mention the videos for the *Rio* singles, but there is good reason to do so. The "Save a Prayer" clip depicted the band wearing skimpy beachwear while lounging around bars and temples in Sri Lanka, implying that they inhabited a parallel world of total glamour. "'Save The Prayer' is a bit epic . . ." gushed bass guitarist John Taylor to *Sounds*. "It's all got religious overtones: Buddhist temples, processions. Great. In one scene we had about 125 extras, and we just paid them a ballpoint pen each and they think it's great!"

It was hard to take "Save a Prayer" seriously: no one really believed that the band lived the life depicted in the video (directed by Australian film director Russell Mulcahy, of *Highlander* fame). But, in their home country, the United Kingdom, this dreamlike vision stood in stark contrast to the gray lives of many fans—little wonder, then, that the song was an instant and enduring hit. (A live version was a U.S. hit in 1985.)

The exotic myth remains a glorious dream for fans, who continue to flock to Duran gigs. Although the band grew up, wised up, and began making more mature music, "Save a Prayer" is as appealing as ever, with numerous covers, including ones by Spandau Ballet's Tony Hadley, Shut Up and Dance, and Eve's Plum. **JMc**

Candy Girl | New Edition (1982)

Writer | Maurice Starr, Michael Jonzun
Producer | M. Starr, M. Jonzun, Arthur Baker
Label | Streetwise
Album | *Candy Girl* (1983)

"We thought it would be played in Boston, and that would be it."

Ricky Bell, 1984

◄ **Influenced by:** ABC · The Jackson 5 (1970)
► **Influence on:** Candy · LL Cool J featuring Ralph Tresvant & Ricky Bell (1997)
● **Covered by:** Baby DC featuring Imajin (1999)
★ **Other key tracks:** Is This the End? (1983) · Popcorn Love (1983)

Unlikely as it sounds, "Candy Girl" was the first U.K. No. 1 to feature rapping. There was the traditional tough guy bragging, but also birthday-card poetry like "She walks so fast / She looks so sweet."

The nice kids responsible—in their teens when they came to prominence—were spotted at a Boston talent show by pop svengali Maurice Starr (real name Larry Johnson), of the Jonzun Crew. He enlisted his brother and Jonzun Crew colleague Michael to co-write their breakthrough hit, "Candy Girl." It was deliberately indebted to The Jackson 5—Starr was no novice—but also suffused with the squeaks, beats, and quirks of the electro scene that the Jonzun Crew helped create.

"Candy Girl" was the first of New Edition's U.S. R&B chart-toppers, but little afterward would match the joy and propulsive energy of this initial smash. Maturity proved a thorny issue: the group forced Starr out of the equation, then lost Bobby Brown to the allure of a solo deal in 1986 (although Ralph Tresvant had taken the lead on "Candy Girl"). "Not knowing what questions to ask," Ricky Bell rued, "we were five boys from the projects that had everything ripped off."

All turned out well for Maurice Starr—who later masterminded New Kids on the Block. This time, an all-white band made hay while the sun shone, sticking together for a succession of hits and laying the foundations for the cult of the boyband in the 1990s.

New Edition enjoyed solo success before periodically reforming. And, along the way, Ricky Bell, Michael Bivins, and Ronnie DeVoe produced a Nineties classic as sensational as their Eighties debut—Bell Biv DeVoe's "Poison," which peaked at No. 3 in the *Billboard* Hot 100. **MH**

Mad World | Tears for Fears (1982)

Writer | Roland Orzabal
Producer | Chris Hughes, Ross Cullum
Label | RCA
Album | *The Hurting* (1983)

"It's very much a voyeur's song. It's looking out at a mad world from the eyes of a teenager."

Curt Smith, 2004

◀ **Influenced by: Matthew and Son** • Cat Stevens (1966)
▶ **Influence on: American Princess** • Prozak (2008)
● **Covered by:** Michael Andrews featuring Gary Jules (2003) • Brai nclaw (2004) • The Red Paintings (2005) Sara Hickman (2006) • Tara MacLean (2007) • Zonaria (2008) • Elisa (2009)

Emerging from Bath, England, Roland Orzabal and Curt Smith were cut off from burgeoning scenes in cities such as London and Sheffield. This dislocation shows on their debut *The Hurting*: its songs are precocious and intriguingly in hock to psychologist Arthur Janov's work on primal therapy. But they are also solidly commercial, and "Mad World" provided their U.K. breakthrough.

"I remember it being written in an hour or two in Roland's little flat above a pizza place," Smith told the *Boston Globe*. They had no expectations of a hit, yet it slotted into a new pop vogue. Inventive percussive effects and discordant guitars recall the work of the then nearly defunct Japan, while disguised synth-pop hooks rub along easily with post–Vince Clarke Depeche Mode.

Like "Suffer Little Children," their flop first single, "Mad World" shed light on Orzabal's interest in Janovian theory, hinting at a troubled childhood. "Dreams in which you're skipping," he told *Smash Hits*, "won't do much for you at all." "And," added Smith, "it wouldn't have rhymed either." There's no comfort in his mad world; where every child is "made to feel the way" they should, where there's "no tomorrow."

In 2003, a vastly rearranged version became an unlikely U.K. Christmas No. 1. American composer Michael Andrews added a cover—featuring singer Gary Jules—to his soundtrack for the cult 2001 movie *Donnie Darko*. (Andrews's original choice for its closing scene was U2's "MLK"—canned for budgetary reasons.) Two years later, a groundswell of popular opinion saw it released as a single. Sparse and ghostly, Andrews's arrangement found new poignancy in the song, opening it up to an entirely new audience. **MH**

Black Metal
Venom (1982)

Writer | Anthony Bray, Jeffrey Dunn, Conrad Lant
Producer | Keith Nichol, Venom
Label | Neat
Album | *Black Metal* (1982)

"Home taping is killing music," observed a sleevenote on the *Black Metal* album, ". . . so are Venom." What the British trio lacked in technical prowess, they compensated for with brutal ferocity. And their revving din and shout-outs to Beelzebub inspired a legion of followers.

Venom's debut *Welcome to Hell* introduced their galloping, bastardized Motörhead riffage. The 1982 sequel pumped up the volume, its title track opening with the earsplitting sound of a chainsaw cutting metal. "On the actual album version we cut it in such a way that as soon as the needle touched the actual vinyl—*CRZZZZK!*—it went straight into that racket," Sulfur-throated bassist Conrad "Cronos" Lant told *The Quietus*. "So straight away, for the uninitiated, you get that sense of panic: 'Oh fuck, my stereo's broken!'"

The lyrics conjured images of witchcraft and armageddon, implied that their producer was the devil, and implored listeners to "Lay down your soul to the gods rock 'n' roll."

The band never secured crossover success, but proved an indelible influence on the likes of Metallica and Slayer, who embraced the trio as blessed relief from metal's eyeliner 'n' spandex-clad pretty boys. As Cronos cackled in 2008: "Yes, we sing about Satanism, and witchcraft, and paganism, and sex and drugs and rock 'n' roll. This *is* the devil's music, apparently." **SC**

Shipbuilding
Robert Wyatt (1982)

Writer | Clive Langer, Elvis Costello
Producer | E. Costello, C. Langer, A. Winstanley
Label | Rough Trade
Album | N/A

In April 1982, Prime Minister Margaret Thatcher told the press to "rejoice" in news that British forces had taken control of the Atlantic island of South Georgia. But not everyone regarded the Falklands conflict as something to celebrate.

Many artists used their music to channel anger at what they saw as a war manufactured to distract attention from domestic hardship, but it took one of the generation's best wordsmiths to drive home the high price of the campaign—with lines that were alternately searing and sublime. Clive Langer wrote the jazz-flecked track—but his lyrics, he admitted, were "crap." He played it to Elvis Costello, who seized on "this ironic notion that we might be building ships to send the children of the ship workers to be killed senselessly."

On his demo, Langer had attempted an impersonation of Soft Machine drummer turned solo artist Robert Wyatt. The real thing was duly persuaded to cut the song—bestowing lines like "Diving for dear life / When we could be diving for pearls" with a perfect, plaintive hopelessness.

Both Langer and Costello came to regard their contributions as highlights of their careers. In May 1983, a re-release took the song to No. 35 in the United Kingdom. Less than a month later, however, a wave of nationalistic fervor took the Conservative Party to the biggest election victory for almost forty years. **CB**

Cattle and Cane | The Go-Betweens (1982)

Writer | Grant McLennan, Robert Forster
Producer | John Brand
Label | Stunn
Album | *Before Hollywood* (1982)

THE GO-BETWEENS

CATTLE AND CANE

"I don't like the word nostalgic; to me, it's a sloppy yearning for the past."

Grant McLennan, 1983

◄ **Influenced by: Who Loves the Sun** · The Velvet Underground (1970)

► **Influence on: Lazy Line Painter Jane** · Belle & Sebastian (1997)

● **Covered by:** The Wedding Present (1992) · Jimmy Little (1999)

The case for why The Go-Betweens—a group of tunefully bookish Australians, led by sensitive singer-songwriters Grant McLennan and Robert Forster—"should have been huge" usually begins with "Cattle and Cane." It's a good start: the tune is the best known from a solid songbook.

The band relocated to London in the early 1980s, yet McLennan's heart remained Down Under. The song—written to please his mother, by whom he was raised after his father died—originated at a squat occupied by Nick Cave's band The Birthday Party. "Nick had brought this acoustic guitar," McLennan recalled, "and at that stage he couldn't play guitar very well. Well, neither could I, but I could play a little bit better. Weird chords came to me. The phrase 'the railroad takes him home' came straight away. I knew that I wanted three verses and I wanted a different point of view to come in at the end of the song. So I asked Robert to contribute an overview. I think we nailed that song. I still get such a rush when I hear it because it's such a different sounding song and you don't write many songs like that."

The wistful lyrics relay three vignettes of a young man growing up in Queensland. The words—spoken rather than sung—are beautifully framed by folksy art-rock that seems equal parts Joy Division and Leonard Cohen.

The result was embraced by fans but generally ignored by the public. It has, however, aged well: in 2001, "Cattle and Cane" was named one of the Top Thirty Australian songs of all time. Grant McLennan's death in 2006 brought to an end what *Village Voice* critic Robert Christgau described as "the greatest songwriting partnership working today." **JiH**

Uncertain Smile | The The (1982)

Writer | Matt Johnson
Producer | Mike Thorne
Label | Some Bizzare
Album | *Soul Mining* (1983)

"I see myself changing a lot, becoming a lot more cynical."

Matt Johnson, 1982

◀ **Influenced by: Hot on the Heels of Love**
Throbbing Gristle (1979)
▶ **Influence on: Divine** · Sébastien Tellier (2008)
● **Covered by:** Pierce Turner (1986) · Poésie Noire (1990)
★ **Other key tracks:** Perfect (1983) · Infected (1986)
The Beat(en) Generation (1989)

Deceptively jaunty, the swinging "Uncertain Smile" was a typically misleading record from arch-manipulator Matt Johnson, aka The The. The protagonist was a man obsessed: a "broken soul" watching the ignorant object of his affections "from a pair of watering eyes." This lyrical lust was soundtracked by bouncing guitar and almost comedic saxophone. The song (a reworking of the 1981 single "Cold Spell Ahead") seemed free of effort—but our hero needed to go to sleep just to clear his head of his unrequited love.

Johnson released his 1981 debut album *Burning Blue Soul* under his own name, reverting thereafter to The The, a name of an earlier band, to put a wall between artist and audience. That debut had been raw and unapproachable, and the mooted follow-up *The Pornography of Despair* was never even released, although one can assume "Uncertain Smile" was earmarked for it.

The single was recorded in New York with Soft Cell's producer Mike Thorne, Uptown Horns session player Crispin Cioe, and the integral assistance of a xylimba—a cousin of the marimba, giving the song its distinctive, percussive shimmy. Cioe's alto sax and flute provided solos between the verses and generally allowed "Uncertain Smile" to float lighter than air—lighter than its lyrical mood at the very least.

When a The The album eventually appeared, 1983's stunning *Soul Mining* featured a reboot of "Uncertain Smile," now produced by Paul Hardiman in tandem with Johnson. Gone were Cioe's contributions; in their place, a sleeker sound and a preposterous—but brilliant—piano solo from Jools Holland of Squeeze. There is endless value in either version. **MH**

Valley Girl | Frank Zappa (1982)

Writer | Frank Zappa, Moon Unit Zappa
Producer | Frank Zappa
Label | Barking Pumpkin
Album | *Ship Arriving Too Late to Save a Drowning Witch* (1982)

Frank & Moon Zappa
Valley Girl

Ship Arriving Too Late To Save A Drowning Witch

"Anybody who knows the whole story behind that song could not possibly be offended by it."

Moon Unit Zappa, 1982

◀ **Influenced by: Supernaut** · Black Sabbath (1972)
▶ **Influence on: Ya Hozna** · Frank Zappa (1984)
● **Covered by:** The Lewinskys (2003)
★ **Other key tracks:** You Are What You Is (1981) · No Not Now (1982) · Teen-Age Prostitute (1982)

In a bid to see more of her father, Moon Unit Zappa slipped a note under the door of Frank's home studio, offering to record her take on the local San Fernando Valley patois. He accepted her offer and, early one morning, led her to his vocal booth. "I managed to improvise several tracks . . ." she recalled, "reciting things I'd heard people really talk about and elaborating on subjects that amused my father. He edited the tracks together, and my life has never been quite the same again." The song is a satirical comment on the "Valspeak" that was popular among teenage girls in California's San Fernando Valley region.

Frank married Moon's vocal to a piece he had begun the previous year, at the end of a session with drummer Chad Wackerman, then added a few lyrics and—with Ike Willis and others—a chorale background. The final piece of the jigsaw was Scott Thunes's bass.

The record became a radio hit even before it was released. The only Zappa single to enter the U.S. charts, "Valley Girl" remained there for twenty-two weeks, reaching No. 32 in the *Billboard* Hot 100. According to Zappa, however, "They didn't buy that record because it had my name on it. They bought it because they liked Moon's voice. It's got nothing to do with the song or the performance. It has everything to do with the American public wanting to have some new syndrome to identify with."

"Valley Girl" was nominated for a Grammy in the category "Best Rock Performance by a Duo or Group with Vocal," but lost to Survivor's "Eye of the Tiger." Meanwhile, Frank failed to prevent the cash-in *Valley Girl* movie (1983), starring a teenage Nicolas Cage. **AG**

A smoking performance by the man with the most famous mustache in rock. ➡

Thriller
Michael Jackson (1982)

Writer | Rod Temperton
Producer | Quincy Jones
Label | Epic
Album | *Thriller* (1982)

From an album of superlatives and firsts, the mock horror of *Thriller*'s title track was an odd fit alongside the innovation of "Billie Jean" and "Beat It." Yet "Thriller" became one of Michael Jackson's signature songs, thanks to its groundbreaking video—a fourteen-minute zombie parody directed by John Landis (*An American Werewolf in London*).

The song's marriage of a catchy hook with kitschy effects was sealed with a rap from horror movie veteran Vincent Price. "I've known Vincent ever since I was eleven years old . . ." Jackson told *Smash Hits*. "Béla Lugosi and Peter Lorre are dead now and the only giant who goes back to those days is Vincent Price. So I thought he was the perfect voice."

Landis's mini-epic, with its much-emulated zombie dance, claimed the Guinness World Record for being the most successful music video ever. "Thriller" was the first such clip to have a narrative, a Hollywood director, a budget of over half a million dollars, *and* a theatrical release.

To meet demand, MTV played it twice an hour, making Jackson one of the first black artists on the channel. Sales of the album tripled thanks to the video, and it was then released as a home video, with an accompanying documentary, to cover costs. In more ways than one, "Thriller" changed the music industry forever. **GK**

Shock the Monkey
Peter Gabriel (1982)

Writer | Peter Gabriel
Producer | Peter Gabriel, David Lord
Label | Charisma
Album | *Peter Gabriel* (1982)

"Most people saw that as a sort of animal rights song," conceded Peter Gabriel, "but it wasn't." Gabriel's oblique lyrics had long been open to interpretation. His last album with Genesis, *The Lamb Lies Down on Broadway,* released in 1974, barely made sense even with its story on the sleeve. His first solo hit, "Solsbury Hill," was a metaphor for being inspired to leave Genesis, while "Games Without Frontiers" (1980) owed its popularity more to a whistle-along hook than its anti-nationalistic lyrics.

"Shock the Monkey" was also interpreted as a reference to experiments by psychologist Stanley Milgram, obliging Gabriel to explain to Stinkzone: "[It] was more about jealousy than Milgram's experiments. . . . 'Shock the Monkey' was only connected to Milgram through the title reference."

But the message was arguably less important than the music. On his fourth self-titled solo album (known as *Security* in the U.S.), Gabriel gave full reign to the claustrophobic rhythms that fueled the highlights of 1980's *Peter Gabriel*. "Shock the Monkey" added a dollop of funk to the formula (plus backing vocals by Van der Graaf Generator's Peter Hammill). It earned Gabriel his biggest U.S. hit to that point, and set the scene for another cocktail of rhythm and sex—the globe-conquering "Sledgehammer," released in 1986. **BM**

Save It for Later
The Beat (1982)

Writer | R. Charlery, A. Cox, E. Morton, D. Steele, D. Wakeling
Producer | Bob Sargeant
Label | Go-Feet
Album | *Special Beat Service* (1982)

British group The Beat were never satisfied with being just another ska band. They scored hits with songs that infused their 2-Tone sound with paranoia ("Mirror in the Bathroom"), politics ("Stand Down Margaret"), and pop standards (Smokey Robinson's "The Tears of a Clown," Andy Williams's "Can't Get Used to Losing You").

There was little that was recognizably 2-Tone about the first single from the group's final album, *Special Beat Service*. A lilting slice of urbane pop, given extra shine by deft strings and brass, "Save it for Later" swapped their usual buoyant bonhomie for affecting melancholy. While a mature wisdom colors Dave Wakeling's lyrics, he had penned the song as a teenager, before the group formed. He sensed life was about to get complicated, and that the adults offering him advice didn't necessarily know any better than he did. "It was like, keep your advice to yourself," he explained to Songfacts. "Save it, for later." Wakeling admitted the title was also a teenager's dirty joke: a pun on "fellator." "I didn't know," he admitted, "it was going to be a joke that lasted for thirty years."

The song's aching sense of adolescent confusion struck a chord with The Who's Pete Townshend. His performance of it was the highlight of his 1986 live album, *Deep End Live!*—after he phoned Wakeling to learn the song's idiosyncratic tuning. **SC**

Great Southern Land
Icehouse (1982)

Writer | Iva Davies
Producer | Keith Forsey, Iva Davies
Label | Regular
Album | *Primitive Man* (1982)

While AC/DC and INXS hit the headlines, another Australian act enjoyed more low-key success—and produced one of the nation's best-loved anthems.

Icehouse were the brainchild of Iva Davies, an Iggy Pop fan with a Bryan Ferry-esque voice and pre-Duran Duran good looks. After the multi-platinum success of 1980's *Icehouse,* Davies began the follow-up in a home studio full of technology and artwork that became the *Primitive Man* cover.

"This piece of art, for me, has had a strangely simplistic, naive, and yet sophisticated quality . . ." he declared. "It could have been the work of artists thousands—indeed hundreds of thousands—of years apart in history, and this led me to question whether anything had really changed at all during that time. The first song I wrote in this room was 'Great Southern Land' and it was from this song that I drew the title *Primitive Man*."

Davies's then-manager had urged him to "write me an epic" and "Great Southern Land" duly evoked Australia's historical and mythical heritage—a tale told by "the motion of the wind in the mountains." The song soared into the country's Top Five, and has remained a favorite.

Davies continued to experiment with epic songs, notably on *Code Blue* (1990), apparently finding it easier to express himself in song than in conversation. As he observed, "There's no point in talking about a song. You've gotta listen to it." **BM**

Party Fears II | The Associates (1982)

Writer | Billy Mackenzie, Alan Rankine
Producer | The Associates, Mike Hedges
Label | Associates/Beggars Banquet
Album | *Sulk* (1982)

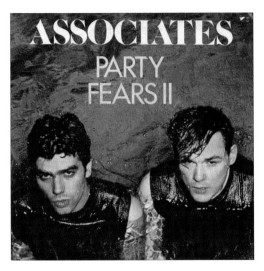

"I don't think of our songs as being unusual but I suppose they are."
Billy Mackenzie, 1982

◀ **Influenced by: Ashes to Ashes** · David Bowie (1980)
▶ **Influence on: Nobody's Diary** · Yazoo (1983)
● **Covered by:** The Divine Comedy (2006)
★ **Other key tracks:** Gloomy Sunday (1982) · It's Better This Way (1982) · Arrogance Gave Him Up (1982)

Less was never more for Billy Mackenzie and Alan Rankine in anything they did during their all-too-brief flirtation with fame. The Scottish duo found astonishingly inventive ways to get rid of a £60,000 record company advance, including Mackenzie's beloved dogs guzzling smoked salmon and Rankine buying chocolate guitars for appearances on TV. "If anything," remarked Rankine to *The Guardian* in 2007, "I think people have been holding back a bit in their recollections. It was madness."

As you might expect from a group influenced by Nat King Cole, Bryan Ferry, David Bowie, Dusty Springfield, Billie Holiday, Can, and Kraftwerk, that approach applied equally to the music they made. "Every day was like nineteen hours of work," said Rankine. "We only stopped when we'd run out of ideas. 'Here's the verse: full on. Here's the intro: full on. Here's the chorus: no difference.'"

All this came together gloriously on "Party Fears II." The piano-led paean seemed to be perpetually on the brink of collapse, but held it together long enough to make No. 9 in the U.K. singles chart in 1982.

The framework of the song had come together five years earlier, amid hangover hazes. "The alcohol loves you, while turning you blue," sang Mackenzie in his remarkable voice, which could stand without shame next to those of his heroes. "It was so poppy," Rankine told *Q*, "it sounded like an advert for soap powder, but we knew we had a hit."

As for the lyrics, Mackenzie was giving little away, teasing that they could apply to marital discord or a clash of political ideologies. Decadent decay had seldom sounded so seductive. **CB**

Situation | Yazoo (1982)

Writer | Vince Clark, Alison Moyet
Producer | Vince Clarke, Eric Radcliffe, Daniel Miller
Label | Mute
Album | N/A

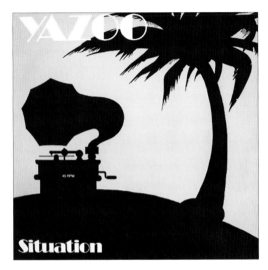

"I love Yazoo . . . the only record that's stirred any emotion in me for the last ten years."
Boy George, 1982

◀ **Influenced by:** The Robots • Kraftwerk (1978)
▶ **Influence on:** Theme from S'Express • S'Express (1988)
● **Covered by:** Tom Jones (1994)
★ **Other key tracks:** Only You (1982) • Don't Go (1982) Nobody's Diary (1983)

"Her voice, combined with those modern techniques. . . . It's a masterpiece of modern technology with a voice that's *singing*," marveled Robert Plant. Yazoo (known in the United States as Yaz) were an ungainly combination: ex–Depeche Mode geek Vince Clarke and soul belter Alison Moyet. But the meeting of machine and passion set a template for Eighties synth pop, and revivals beyond.

There was no design to it when Clarke answered Moyet's advert for a "blues band" to accompany her, but it worked nevertheless. The irony was, Clarke fled the trappings of Depeche Mode's success only to find further triumph. Yazoo's debut "Only You" was an instant hit, outstripping Mode's singles at this point. The track was an electronic torch song, soon to find classic status itself, but its B-side "Situation" was a different matter entirely. This was dance music.

The track was promptly remixed and issued in its own right in the United States. "They took the master over there and Americanized it by adding bongos and an awful jazz synth break," sniped Depeche's Andy Fletcher. (The song was added to the U.S. version—and U.K. CD—of Yazoo's 1982 album *Upstairs at Eric's*.)

"Situation" was later sampled on a diverse range of hits, from Los del Rio's holiday favorite "Macarena" to girl band The Saturdays' "If this is Love." But its real legacy was helping to shape Eighties techno and the commercial end of acid house: its pulse and sharp synth riff could be traced in cuts coming out of Detroit a half-decade later. Years after Clarke and Moyet split to exploit their separate skills, their quirky blend was still making its presence felt. **MH**

Rock the Casbah | The Clash (1982)

Writer | Topper Headon, Mick Jones,
Joe Strummer
Producer | Mick Jones
Label | CBS
Album | *Combat Rock* (1982)

*"It's such a groove. Long live
groove. Screw the rest of it."*
Joe Strummer, 1988

◀ **Influenced by: Shah Shah a Go Go** · The Stranglers
(1979)
▶ **Influence on: 51st State** · The Enemy (2009)
● **Covered by:** Solar Twins (1999) Rachid Taha (2004)
Something for Kate (2007)
★ **Other key track:** Should I Stay or Should I Go (1982)

The Clash's figureheads, Joe Strummer and Mick
Jones, were punk's Lennon and McCartney, but
drummer Topper Headon—the driving force
behind "Rock the Casbah"—was definitely more
George than Ringo.

"He ran out in the studio and banged down
the drum track . . . " Strummer told the *Los Angeles
Times*. "Then he ran over to the piano and he
banged down the piano track to it, and then ran
over to the bass and he banged down the bass
part. This is, like, I suppose, within twenty-five
minutes and 'Rock the Casbah' is there, boom."

That was much of the boogie-woogie backing
track sorted. But Headon's original, lascivious
lyrics were replaced by Strummer's account
of popular defiance against a ban on rock
music in a middle-eastern state—inspired by
a story he had heard in which "you get lashed
for owning a disco album in Iran." (Headon's
drug habit meant that his days in the band
were numbered—he was replaced by original
Clash skin-basher Terry Chimes in the video for
the "Casbah" single.)

The track didn't fare better than No. 30 on its
U.K. release in 1982 (a 1991 reissue performed
much better). However, it went Top Ten on
Billboard. A sign of how far the danceable track
penetrated the United States is its presence on
everything from Will Smith's single "Will 2K,"
released in 1999, to the über-cool Wes Anderson
movie *The Royal Tenenbaums* in 2001.

However, while the song did much to raise The
Clash's profile in America, the same country did as
much to dismay Strummer—during the first Gulf
War, "Rock the Casbah" was misappropriated in
1991 by U.S. troops in Iraq. **CB**

Buffalo Gals | Malcolm McLaren (1982)

Writer | Malcolm McLaren, Anne Dudley, Trevor Horn
Producer | Trevor Horn
Label | Charisma
Album | *Duck Rock* (1983)

"The interesting thing about that record is that it's an adventure story."
Malcolm McLaren, 1982

◀ **Influenced by: Zulu Nation Throw Down** · Afrika Bambaataa & The Soulsonic Force (1980)
▶ **Influence on: Close (To the Edit)** · Art of Noise (1984)
● **Covered by:** Malcolm McLaren & The World's Famous Supreme Team versus Roger Sanchez & Rakim (2005)
★ **Other key track:** Double Dutch (1983)

Rarely short of a grand folly or two, Malcolm McLaren was the svengali behind the Sex Pistols and Bow Wow Wow, and conceived an ambitious project for his solo debut. *Folk Dances of the World*—eventually titled *Duck Rock*—was a grab-bag of styles from across the globe: a melting pot of hip-hop, South African pop, and tribal rhythms.

Producer Trevor Horn—formerly of Yes and the Buggles, and mastermind of ABC's glossy *Lexicon of Love* album—seemed an unlikely collaborator, but he saw method in McLaren's madness. His *Lexicon of Love* arranger, Anne Dudley, came along to paper over the cracks.

"Buffalo Gals" was the first fruit of the union: a meld of traditional country dance song—copyrighted by Cool White in the mid-nineteenth century—and hip-hop scratch techniques. As McLaren dictated square dance instructions, hip-hop crew the World's Famous Supreme Team wove a tapestry of scratches, beats, and samples. The result was an ungainly yet addictive beast that cracked the U.K. Top Ten. "I put it out first because I thought it was the most radical," McLaren told *Smash Hits* reporter and future Pet Shop Boy Neil Tennant. "It would make people think about the way they listen to music and use music."

"Buffalo Gals" was crucial in breaking hip-hop into the mainstream—not least via its video, which inspired outbreaks of breakdancing. Not for the first or last time, McLaren had exploited a form for his commercial and artistic gain, yet simultaneously benefited the genre itself. He later invented new hybrids to recapture the moment—the popera of *Fans*, the Strauss-house of *Waltz Darling*—but hillbilly-hop was his most triumphant success. **MH**

A New England
Billy Bragg (1983)

Writer | Billy Bragg
Producer | Oliver Hitch
Label | Utility
Album | *Life's a Riot with Spy vs Spy* (1983)

He may have lifted the first lines from Simon and Garfunkel and the melody from Thin Lizzy, but Billy Bragg set out his stall in convincing style with this early gem.

A plaintive love song, it also has a political context. "When I say I don't want to change the world, I mean it," he explained. "But just because you don't want to change the entire system doesn't mean you should close your eyes to everything." The lyrics feature his trademark observations of British life ("All the girls I loved at school are already pushing prams"), wry wit, and an ability to find the poetic in the prosaic ("I saw two shooting stars last night / I wished on them, but they were only satellites").

Musically, it has the classic Bragg formula of man and guitar. At two minutes fourteen, it is short and snappy, testament to his formative days in the (rightly) forgotten punk band Riff Raff. A stint in the army had focused his mind and *Life's a Riot with Spy vs Spy* was the result.

The mini-album reached No. 1 in the U.K. indie chart and featured in influential DJ John Peel's Christmas countdown of listeners' favorites from the past year. Kirsty MacColl had a U.K hit with her 1985 version, for which Bragg penned an extra verse. "'A New England' was like having access to an unreleased Beatles song or something," she enthused. "A real pressie!" **EB**

Blister in the Sun
Violent Femmes (1983)

Writer | Gordon Gano
Producer | Mark Van Hecke
Label | Slash
Album | *Violent Femmes* (1983)

Violent Femmes' debut peaked at No. 171, produced no hits, and featured songs written while founding member Gordon Gano was still in high school. All of that, combined with ten smoking tracks, made *Violent Femmes* the stuff of legends.

It started with "Blister in the Sun," which showcased everything that made this band and album so wonderful. The song twitched with teen angst, beginning with Brian Ritchie's addictive acoustic bass and Victor DeLorenzo's slamming brushwork on his single-tom kit. Then Gano joined in, adding nervy electric guitar and a conflicted coming-of-age story that was more *Revenge of the Nerds* than *Catcher in the Rye*. The lyrics, whispered near the song's end, tell of sexual frustration, a crappy relationship, and masturbation—no wonder so many were able to identify.

Milwaukee's finest pursued similar topics on the album's other nine tracks—and the results were nearly as good. As a whole, *Violent Femmes* was a pivotal moment in indie rock history and ranks as one of the all-time great debuts.

"Blister in the Sun" has never gone out of rotation on college campuses, handed down from one disenfranchised student to another. Add in its use in movies such as *Grosse Point Blank* and the track became as well known as many 1980s hits. Its popularity pushed *Violent Femmes* to platinum status, nearly eight years after its release. **JiH**

Violent Femmes' Gordon Gano (left) and Victor DeLorenzo (right) perform in California in 1985. ➡

Let's Dance | David Bowie (1983)

Writer | David Bowie
Producer | David Bowie, Nile Rodgers
Label | EMI America
Album | *Let's Dance* (1983)

*"He told me that he wanted
me to do what I did best—
make hits."*

Nile Rodgers, 2000

◀ **Influenced by: Good Times** · Chic (1979)
▶ **Influence on: Last Dance** · George Clinton (1983)
● **Covered by:** Falco (1984) · Atrocity (1997) · Second Skin
(2000) · M. Ward (2003) · The Futureheads (2006)
Nona Reeves (2007) · Sophie Ellis-Bextor (2007)

The lead single from Bowie's second album of the Eighties made his intentions clear. He was—for the moment—casting aside the image of "that weird guy with mismatched pupils," and setting his sights on the mainstream. With a clutch of hits from the *Let's Dance* album, and the globe-straddling *Serious Moonlight* tour, Bowie became—for the first time—a global pop brand.

The title song's distinctive introduction—later redeployed on Puff Daddy's "Been Around the World"—featured vocals and drums escalating to a funky feast typical of co-producer, and Chic main man, Nile Rodgers.

The single version, shorn of an extended horn and percussion workout—but not Bowie's tremulous "If you should fall into my arms and tremble like a flower"—became an international smash, topping the U.S. and U.K. charts. "The truth is," Bowie admitted in 2002, "I told Nile, 'Why on earth you think that's a single, I have no idea. . . . I wanted 'China Girl' to be the first single."

The song featured a memorable guitar solo from Stevie Ray Vaughan, prompting Jimmy Page to nominate "Let's Dance" as his favorite Bowie song. Yet despite the stylish radio-friendliness, there is foreboding when the singer whispers, "Let's dance, for fear tonight is all."

This darker undercurrent is given credence by the video, made on location in Australia with director David Mallet. Jettisoning his penchant for artier promos, Bowie is relegated to a bystander as the video's narrative follows the fortunes of an Aboriginal teenager. The song's red shoes, symbolic of corrupting consumerism, are finally crushed underfoot and discarded as Western society succumbs to nuclear fallout. **JL**

This Charming Man | The Smiths (1983)

Writer | Morrissey, Johnny Marr
Producer | John Porter
Label | Rough Trade
Album | N/A

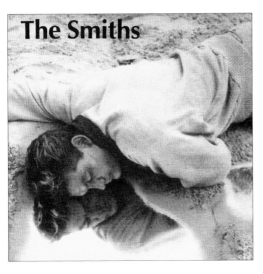

"I'd heard 'Walk Out to Winter' (by Aztec Camera) on Radio 1, and I felt a little jealous. My competitive urges kicked in."
Johnny Marr, 2008

◀ **Influenced by: Walk Out to Winter** · Aztec Camera (1983)
▶ **Influence on: Animal Nitrate** · Suede (1993)
● **Covered by:** Death Cab for Cutie (1996) · Braid (2000) Darling (2000) Stars (2001)
★ **Other key track: How Soon Is Now?** (1984)

The Smiths' first single, "Hand in Glove," earned the lauded Manchester four-piece a session with John Peel on BBC Radio 1. Guitarist Johnny Marr—keen to outdo Eighties indie rivals Aztec Camera—penned "This Charming Man" especially for the slot with the legendary DJ.

The result was a track that acted as the ultimate showcase for Marr's Byrds-esque jangling arpeggios and Morrissey's oblique, controversial lyrics. The tale of a young boy getting a bicycle puncture—to whom ". . . in this charming car / This charming man" stops to offer solace and more—was hailed as a cute allusion to Morrissey's supposed homosexuality.

Lyrically, however, "This Charming Man" is light years beyond brazen tales of late-night encounters. Speaking at the time, Morrissey said he was tired of hearing about the song's alleged theme: "I hate it when people talk to me about sex in a trivial way." In fact, his inspiration went further than simply chronicling a tryst. "A jumped-up pantry boy" refers to the 1972 movie *Sleuth*, starring Laurence Olivier and Michael Caine as lovers of the same woman.

The single version (added to the U.S. version of their debut, *The Smiths*) differs markedly from the John Peel session cut (released in 1984 on *Hatful of Hollow*). The spruced-up track features a feistier effort from Marr on his 1954 Fender Telecaster, while Andy Rourke's lolloping bassline is testament to his talent for meshing, to stunning effect, with his band's lead guitarist.

"This Charming Man," which has since been covered by various artists, remains a classic and has topped *Mojo* magazine's list of the greatest U.K. indie records of all time. **JM**

Relax | Frankie Goes to Hollywood (1983)

Writer | Peter Gill, Holly Johnson, Mark O'Toole
Producer | Trevor Horn
Label | ZTT
Album | *Welcome to the Pleasuredome* (1984)

"We used to pretend it was about motivation, and really it was about shagging."
Mark O'Toole, 1984

◀ **Influenced by: Don't Make Me Wait** · Peech Boys (1982)
▶ **Influence on: Animal** · Def Leppard (1987)
● **Covered by:** Brooklyn Bounce (1997) · Powerman 5000 & Danny Boy (2001) · The Dandy Warhols (2004)
★ **Other key track:** Rage Hard (1986)

One of the most controversial songs of the 1980s, "Relax" was a subversive slow burner. Frankie's debut took three months to top the U.K. charts in January 1984 (and even longer to reach the U.S. Top Ten later that year).

Sales rocketed when British DJ Mike Read objected to its lyrics and whipped it off the air. "Many people . . ." protested Read, "said they were really pleased I had done so." The BBC promptly banned the song, which rocketed to No. 1. Each week at the top (five in total) was an embarrassment for the broadcaster.

"Relax" remained in the U.K. charts for forty-two consecutive weeks. To add insult to injury, it climbed back up to No. 2 in the summer when its follow-up, "Two Tribes," took the top spot, helped by record label ZTT's marketing ("Frankie Says Relax" T-shirts were, by this time, ubiquitous). At the end of the year, during which "Relax" was the biggest-selling single of the year (apart from Band Aid), the BBC lifted the ban and it was played on the Christmas edition of *Top of the Pops*.

Singer Holly Johnson is the only band member who performs on the single. According to ZTT's co-founder and producer Trevor Horn, the boys were back home in Liverpool by the time he had reworked the song for the fourth and final time. Among musicians used along the way were Norman Watt-Roy and Charley Charles, of Ian Dury & The Blockheads.

"Relax" has featured in advertisements, movies, and games, and been fruitfully remixed—notably in 1993, when it reached No. 5 in the United Kingdom. "It also," boasted Johnson, "heralded a new era of technological advancement in pop, influencing the dance music boom." **GK**

Frankie Goes to Hollywood and female friends, with Holly Johnson biting down on the whip. ➜

Song to the Siren | This Mortal Coil (1983)

Writer | Tim Buckley, Larry Beckett
Producer | Ivo Watts-Russell, John Fryer
Label | 4AD
Album | *It'll End in Tears* (1984)

"You can feel the nervousness … yet it's so hauntingly pretty."
Robert Plant, 1985

◀ **Influenced by:** 1/1 • Brian Eno (1978)
▶ **Influence on:** If I Had Glass Hands and Glass Feet
School of Seven Bells (2008)
● **Covered by:** Sally Oldfield (1996) • The Czars (2000)
Susheela Raman (2001) • Robert Plant (2002) • David
Gray (2007) • John Frusciante (2009)

Some cover versions become better known than the originals. This Mortal Coil's version of Tim Buckley's heartbreaking lament—from *Starsailor* (1970)—is one of them. And, despite a queue of people aiming to add something to the song, it really should have been the last word.

This Mortal Coil was a studio-only affair with a fluid line-up, largely drawn from the influential 4AD label. This track featured two-thirds of the Cocteau Twins—guitarist Robin Guthrie and vocalist Liz Fraser. "Song to the Siren" was intended as a B-side, but its perfect evocation of lovelorn imagery, with Fraser extracting even more melancholy melody than Buckley, saw it promoted to the A-side of the first Mortal Coil single.

The number's otherworldly qualities appealed to director David Lynch, who included it in his 1997 movie *Lost Highway* (although it didn't feature on the soundtrack album). Initially, however, it was a song that people knew about rather than bought, albeit one that maintained a prolonged presence on the independent chart.

The artists themselves came to regard it as a nuisance. "I was really sick when I saw that getting played on the radio all the time," grumbled Guthrie, "and the Cocteaus had never been played. So the only way we could get played on the radio was to do somebody else's song under a different name." He, however, was in the minority. "I like the Tim Buckley original . . ." enthused Led Zeppelin's Robert Plant, "but I'll go with this version. It's so rewarding to hear it on U.S. college radio."

Despite this definitive reading, the song has since been tackled by artists including Robert Plant, John Frusciante, and Sinéad O'Connor. **CB**

Everything Counts | Depeche Mode (1983)

Writer | Martin L. Gore
Producer | Daniel Miller, Depeche Mode
Label | Mute
Album | *Construction Time Again* (1983)

"Everybody knows that bands make lots of money— sometimes far too much for what they do."

Dave Gahan, 1989

◀ **Influenced by: Metall Auf Metall** · Kraftwerk (1977)
▶ **Influence on: Pug** · The Smashing Pumpkins (1998)
● **Covered by:** In Flames (1997) · Meat Beat Manifesto (1998) · Yendri (2000)
★ **Other key tracks:** Love in Itself (1983) · Told You So (1983)

In the early 1980s, the notion that fresh-faced synth-poppers—from the sterile British suburb of Basildon, Essex—would become world-conquering rock giants was unimaginable. But that's what happened to Depeche Mode.

Despite European chart success with the jaunty singles "Just Can't Get Enough" and "See You," the band were eager to be more than just another pop act. This desire to move forward sonically eventually saw them morph into hard-edged, techno-rockers.

The aural turning point came with their eighth U.K. single, "Everything Counts." Using Synclavier and Emulator samplers to capture the clanging noise of everyday objects, they produced a more industrial sound. Dave Gahan's vocals had a new, vitriolic edge, while Martin Gore's lyrics took a cynical swipe at corporate greed and corruption. He drily named his own publishing company Grabbing Hands Music after the emotionally searing chorus, "The grabbing hands / Grab all they can / All for themselves." (Fittingly, the band didn't have a formal contract with Mute Records.)

Rather than alienate listeners used to Depeche Mode's softer approach, "Everything Counts" proved equally popular: both the single and its parent album, *Construction Time Again*, attained Top Ten status in the U.K. The song even enjoyed a triumphant 1989 re-release, in singalong live form, from their candid *101* concert movie. "Merchandise finances tours," Gahan explained to *Q* magazine. "People talk about million-dollar deals with merchandisers. Before you know it, you may as well be running a chain of T-shirt shops." With the U.S. caving to the group's more aggressive sound, the world was theirs. **BC**

Dear Prudence
Siouxsie & The Banshees (1983)

Writer | John Lennon, Paul McCartney
Producer | Mike Hedges, Siouxsie &
The Banshees
Label | Wonderland
Album | N/A

In their punk days, Siouxsie & The Banshees unleashed a full-throttle version of "Helter Skelter" on their debut *The Scream*. But a second Beatles cover gave them their biggest hit.

Written by John Lennon (though credited to Lennon and McCartney), "Dear Prudence" appeared on *The Beatles*, commonly known as *The White Album*. After touring Scandinavia, listening incessantly to Liverpool's finest, The Banshees reimagined "Dear Prudence" for a one-off single. "There weren't any new Banshees songs written . . ." admitted bassist Steve Severin, "and we wanted Robert [Smith, moonlighting from The Cure] to be playing on a new single." Drummer Budgie added that their other choice, "Glass Onion," lost to "Dear Prudence" because "it was the only song that Robert was familiar with."

Although The Banshees' take remains faithful to the original, Smith's psychedelic guitar and Siouxsie's upbeat vocal elevate its mood from melancholy to celebratory. On the Christmas edition of British music show *Top of the Pops*, Smith appeared with both "Dear Prudence" and The Cure's "The Love Cats."

"People seem to think that all we had to do was cover 'Dear Prudence' and we'd have a hit," protested Severin. "Nothing's ever that simple. It's because of the way we did it, the way we recorded it, that it was successful." **BC**

It's Like That
Run-DMC (1983)

Writer | Darryl McDaniels, Joseph Simmons,
Larry Smith
Producer | Russell Simmons, Larry Smith
Label | Profile
Album | *Run-DMC* (1984)

Leather jumpsuits, rhinestones, and furs were the look and funky disco the sound in the early days of rap. Then Run-DMC dropped their debut single and changed the face of hip-hop forever.

"It's Like That" set the tone for all that was to come. Against hard drums, Joseph "Run" Simmons and Darryl "DMC" McDaniels despaired of the ills of the world. Run—DJ and sideman for rap pioneer Kurtis Blow—had been paid $100 to write a rhyme for Blow by superproducer Larry Smith. But when Smith created a sparse beat, Run persuaded his older brother Russell—Kurtis Blow's promoter, and co-founder of rap's über-label Def Jam—to let him cut a demo. Russell insisted that his younger brother finish high school first, but that $100 rhyme formed half of "It's Like That." "I wanted some help . . ." Run told *The Face*. "I went to D and . . . he came up with some important hooks and plugged up gaps in a few verses."

Throughout the song, Run and DMC alternate lines and finish each other's sentences, creating an energy and unity that lasted almost two decades.

In 1997, a remix by house music producer Jason Nevins introduced "It's Like That" to a new generation, as the track catapulted to No. 1 in the United Kingdom, Australia, and across Europe. "We don't do house at all . . ." DMC told *Stealth Magazine*. "But, when we heard it, we thought it was a good record." **DC**

Run-DMC—Joseph "Run" Simmons (left) and Darryl "DMC" McDaniels—make hip-hop history. ➜

Rock of Ages | Def Leppard (1983)

Writer | Steve Clark, Robert John "Mutt" Lange, Joe Elliott, Rick Savage, Pete Willis, Rick Allen
Producer | Robert John "Mutt" Lange
Label | Vertigo
Album | *Pyromania* (1983)

"We'd always gone for the big hooks. We got some down pretty much on the Pyromania album."
Joe Elliott, 1989

◄ **Influenced by: My My, Hey Hey (Out of the Blue)**
Neil Young (1979)
► **Influence on: Pretty Fly (for a White Guy)**
The Offspring (1998)
● **Covered by:** Kelly Hansen (2000)
★ **Other key track:** Animal (1987)

All but ignored in their homeland until 1986, Brit bashers Def Leppard conquered the United States in 1983 with *Pyromania*—thanks in no small part to the extraordinary, lush production of "Mutt" Lange. The album was duly kept off the top of the chart only by *Thriller*.

"We ended up," singer Joe Elliott told *Mojo*, "doing the backing vocals before we put the guitars down—to a bass! And we layered them so much, they were like a football crowd. . . . One hundred and seventy-six voices singing 'Rock of Ages.' We'd come out of there not being able to talk, never mind sing."

Although "Photograph" was the biggest hit off *Pyromania*, "Rock of Ages" was indicative of Leppard's knack for huge choruses, monster riffs, and endearingly dopey lyrics. The song's title was inspired by the hymn "Rock of Ages," but the seriousness ended there. Indeed, its Teutonic introduction is just gibberish improvised by Lange, who had tired of counting the band in with "one, two, three, four."

"'Rock of Ages' is a parody actually . . ." Elliott admitted. "It's making fun out of every anthem that's ever been written. We even rechristened it 'Another One Bites the Stroke by Joan Jett's Rainbow.' . . . We wanted a bit of light relief on the album. It's kind of kindergarten stuff, but it fits the song, and it's good fun."

Two keyboard players enhanced the sound: Thomas Dolby ("I didn't really want to get tarred with the heavy metal brush," he told *The Quietus*, hence his pseudonym Booker T. Boffin) and Tony Kaye of Yes. "I was doubling the guitar parts . . ." Kaye told yesfans.com, "so you ended up with this great wall of sound." **BM**

Gimme All Your Lovin' | ZZ Top (1983)

Writer | Frank Beard, Billy Gibbons, Dusty Hill
Producer | Bill Ham
Label | Warner Bros.
Album | *Eliminator* (1983)

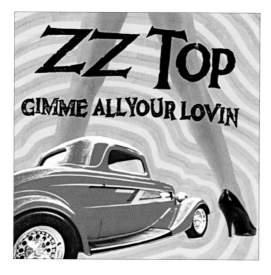

"I kind of enjoy the oddball attitude that is thrust on us. It keeps 'em guessing."

Billy Gibbons, 1984

◄ **Influenced by: Life in the Fast Lane** • The Eagles (1976)
► **Influence on: Growing on Me** • The Darkness (2003)
● **Covered by:** Lonestar (2002)
★ **Other key tracks:** Beer Drinkers & Hell Raisers (1973) Jesus Just Left Chicago (1973) • Cheap Sunglasses (1979) • Sharp Dressed Man (1983)

After fourteen years of performing Southern rock in the grand old Lynyrd Skynyrd and Allman Brothers tradition, Texan trio ZZ Top discovered sequencers and embarked on a new, enormously successful direction.

The rise of MTV, with its focus on a marketable image, coincided with a brush-up in the group's appearance—enormous beards, comedy guitars, and hot-rod cars became the centerpoint of their new look. The album that tied these strands together was *Eliminator*, led by the still-essential "Gimme All Your Lovin'"— good ol' boy spelling and all.

This song works because it's so utterly simple. After an iconic drum intro and lead guitar motif, the song stays on the same note through the first verse until the chorus, when the chord progression performs an unusual trick: dropping downward without the benefit of a bridge. This gives it almost a stoner-metal feel—like 1970s Status Quo with a Deep South twang. (The song, observed Barney Hoskyns in *NME*, "achieved in three minutes and fifty-nine seconds what dear old Status Quo have been striving to do for twenty whole years.")

And, of course, it is about good, old-fashioned sex—a subject handled with even less subtlety on the follow-up single "Legs" (in many ways a continuation of its predecessor).

Americans loved the new ZZ Top because they combined riffs with a pop chorus and vocal hook that anyone could sing. Brits liked them because of their irresistible depiction of Americana. Everyone else liked them because the cars and guitars looked great on TV—and because "Gimme All Your Lovin'" was a great song. **JMc**

Every Breath You Take
The Police (1983)

Writer | Sting
Producer | Hugh Padgham, The Police
Label | A&M
Album | *Synchronicity* (1983)

"It's a nasty little song," Police chief Sting admitted to *NME*. "Really rather evil. It's about jealousy and surveillance and ownership."

Sting wrote the track on a piano, at James Bond author Ian Fleming's estate in Jamaica. "I knew it was the biggest hit we'd ever have . . ." he told the BBC, "despite the cries from the other members of the band that it was simplistic." Indeed, the song became a sticking point in the *Synchronicity* sessions. "We knew we had a killer song," guitarist Andy Summers remarked to *Billboard*'s Craig Rosen, "and we didn't want to fuck it up."

"Stewart [Copeland, drummer] would say, 'I want to fucking put my drum part on it!'" producer Hugh Padgham told *Sound on Sound,* "and Sting would say, 'I don't want you to put your fucking drum part on it! I want you to put what *I* want you to put on it!' and it would go on like that."

Summers added a guitar figure inspired by classical composer Béla Bartók. "My guitar completely made it classic and put the modern edge on it," he bragged to *Record Collector.*

Misinterpreted as romantic, "Every Breath You Take" became one of the most played songs on U.S. radio. "The twist is there's no escape," Sting told *Q* in 1999. "It's circular: this guy is trapped and enjoying it. . . . If I wrote it now, I think I would make it move on—break the guy out of the cycle he's in." **BM**

99 Luftballons
Nena (1983)

Writer | Joern-Uwe Fahrenkrog-Petersen, Carlo Karges
Producer | R. Heil, M. Praeker
Label | CBS Schallplatten
Album | *Nena* (1983)

Nuclear paranoia was rife in the early 1980s and Germany was particularly sensitive to the mood, with the dissected city of Berlin on the frontline for World War III.

Into this unhappy stew came Nena's era-defining "99 Luftballons," a deceptively chirpy synth-pop take on nuclear annihilation. The premise is simple: ninety-nine balloons are released into the German sky and mistaken for UFOs by nervy generals, who push the button that calls down apocalypse.

Nena were named after their singer, Gabriele "Nena" Kerner, whose husky vocals pushed the song to No. 1 in Germany in 1983. Sniffing success, the band's manager suggested an English-language version, and British musician Kevin McAlea—an associate of Kate Bush—was approached to translate the lyrics.

The English version, renamed "99 Red Balloons," and released in 1984, reached No. 1 in the U.K. Both versions were played by U.S. radio—and, unpredictably, it was the German one that the American public took to, driving it to No. 2.

In content and style the song is emblematic of the 1980s and has featured on decade-aping movie soundtracks such as *Grosse Point Blank.* It has been sung (impressively, in the original German) by Homer Simpson, and referred to in *Scrubs* and the *Grand Theft Auto* game. **PW**

Zungguzungguguzungguzeng
Yellowman (1983)

Writer | Winston "Yellowman" Foster
Producer | Henry "Junjo" Lawes
Label | Greensleeves
Album | *Zungguzungguguzung-guzeng* (1983)

Funk overlords James Brown and George Clinton are often cited as the most-sampled artists. It's likely that early Eighties reggae records could compete, if the baffling array of releases on different labels didn't make keeping track so hard.

"Zungguzungguguzungguzeng" is a prime example. The albino Yellowman was among the MCs who rose to represent Jamaica after Bob Marley's passing—a new breed for whom commercial potential had the edge over Rasta philosophy. He batted aside prejudice against his complexion and sleazy lyrics to become one of the biggest MCs in dancehall.

"Zungguzungguguzungguzeng" (a reference to Jamaica's emergency number) first appeared in 1982, as "Zungguzuzeng," on the Volcano label. Volcano's mastermind was the song's producer Henry "Junjo" Lawes, often credited with popularizing dancehall. The track itself hit the mainstream when Greensleeves issued it in 1983, and reggae and hip-hop acts began to loot both the melody and the bass and drums "riddim."

Few, however, rivaled the smiling sensation that was "Zungguzungguguzungguzeng" itself, with its injunction to "Jump fe happiness and jump fe joy," and cheeky references to the "First Lady of dancehall," Lady Ann. Indeed, Yellowman remained positive even after cancer ravaged his jaw—a setback that he ultimately conquered. **BM**

Blue Monday
New Order (1983)

Writer | G. Gilbert, P. Hook, S. Morris, B. Sumner
Producer | New Order
Label | Factory
Album | N/A

"The idea," claimed singer and guitarist Bernard Sumner, "was that I'd come back onstage, press the play button, let all the sequencers and computers play 'Blue Monday' as an encore, and fuck off." New Order had spent their first three years running from the gloom of their previous incarnation, Joy Division. Now they were setting their sights on New York dance floors rather than Manchester wastelands.

Their passport to paradise came from a messy synth-jam, "Prime 5-8-6" (a more polished version of which is on 1983's *Power, Corruption and Lies*), nods to Sylvester's "You Make Me Feel (Mighty Real)" and obscure Italo-disco artists Klein+MBO, an eerie choir sample from Kraftwerk's "Uranium," and an outright steal from Donna Summer's "Our Love." Typically, accident played a part. Painstakingly programmed drums were wiped when drummer Stephen Morris tripped over a power cable, while the offbeat melody is reportedly due to keyboard player Gillian Gilbert starting the sequencer at the wrong time.

Peter Saville's iconic, floppy disc sleeve was so costly that, once sales went stratospheric, the Factory label actually lost money. A disastrous live appearance on the BBC's *Top of the Pops* stalled the single's climb, but the hypnotic classic's influence was cemented: "Blue Monday" presaged the worldwide explosion of dance music. **MB**

The Trooper | Iron Maiden (1983)

Writer | Steve Harris
Producer | Martin Birch
Label | EMI
Album | *Piece of Mind* (1983)

"Iron Maiden is like an old warhorse. 'The Trooper,' the charging . . ."

Bruce Dickinson, 1993

◀ **Influenced by:** Lights Out · UFO (1977)
▶ **Influence on:** Paschendale · Iron Maiden (2003)
● **Covered by:** Sentenced (1993) · Jughead's Revenge (1996) · Vital Remains (1996) · Supernova (1999) · Zen Guerrilla (2001) · Rage (2002) · Highland Glory (2005) Hellsongs (2008)

Resisting the onslaught of punk, the formative Iron Maiden fought valiantly for metal. Championing legends like Deep Purple, they had little in common with their spiky-haired foes—other than a ferocious attack.

"The Trooper" is the most explosive weapon in their formidable arsenal. Its lightning-flash introduction never fails to ignite audiences, whose roaring sing-alongs can be heard on Maiden's live albums. (A version from 2005's *Death on the Road* smashed into the U.K. Top Five.)

The lyrics concerned—as composer Steve Harris confirmed—"the Crimean War with the British against the Russians. The opening is meant to try and recreate the rhythm of the galloping horses in [Alfred, Lord Tennyson's 1854 poem] *The Charge of the Light Brigade*."

Harris's galloping bass fueled the song, fleshed out by Nicko McBrain's thunderous drums, Dave Murray and Adrian Smith's lacerating guitars, and Bruce Dickinson's "air raid siren" vocals. Even the band's original singer, Paul Di'anno, conceded to *Classic Rock*: "Bruce sounds incredible on many later Maiden tracks such as 'The Trooper.'"

Machine Head and Coheed and Cambria are among fans to have covered the song. In a more permanent tribute, Harris had Derek Riggs's single sleeve artwork tattooed on his arm.

"Most of the songs that we've written about war aren't glorifying war . . ." the bassist told *Brave Words & Bloody Knuckles*. "I was always taught to be proud of the flag and the whole British thing, doing your duty. . . . Some of our songs are trying to put you in that position, asking how you'd feel in that situation. It's important to think about these things, isn't it?" **BM**

Two Tribes | Frankie Goes to Hollywood (1984)

Writer | Peter Gill, Holly Johnson, Mark O'Toole
Producer | Trevor Horn
Label | ZTT
Album | *Welcome to the Pleasuredome* (1984)

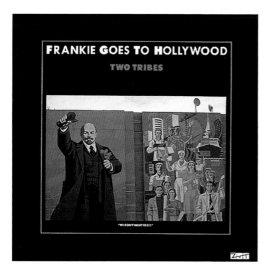

"An American funk line and a Russian line. It's the most obvious demonstration of two tribes that we have today."
Holly Johnson, 1984

◀ **Influenced by: I Feel Love** • Donna Summer (1977)
▶ **Influence on: Paranoimia** • The Art of Noise (1986)
● **Covered by:** Rosetta Stone (2000) • Doctor & The Medics (2008)
★ **Other key track:** One February Friday (1984) • War (1984) • The Power of Love (1984)

If the Cold War hadn't been so terrifying when Frankie Goes to Hollywood recorded their second single, we would have laughed at them. But any young fan who encountered the song on its release heard a devastating account of an age in which humanity could be consumed in a nuclear holocaust at any moment. Frankie and their associates knew this perfectly well—and got great mileage out of it.

The band, guided by their record label ZTT and producer Trevor Horn, had scored a smash with "Relax," and needed a song of serious weight to avoid one-hit-wonder status. "Two Tribes" proved to be the right contender—but only just. "The demo wasn't any good," recalled engineer Steve Lipson—who, with Horn, keyboardist Andy Richards, and synthesizer programmer JJ Jeczalik, essentially created the sound (just as they'd done with "Relax"). However, Lipson told *Sound on Sound*, "It was the only track that he [Horn] could envision being the follow-up single."

The result was storming, and Godley and Creme's accompanying video—depicting then-U.S. president Ronald Reagan tussling with Russian leader Konstantin Chernenko—was promptly banned. The song spent nine weeks atop the U.K. chart, its sales boosted by a series of entertainingly ludicrous remixes.

Taken out of context, "Two Tribes" boils down to a synthesized bass line, Anne Dudley's orchestral stabs, and singer Holly Johnson's apocalyptic delivery. In context, it was scary as hell. No wonder we all bought into it: owning "Two Tribes," its parent album *Welcome To The Pleasuredome*, and (go on, admit it) a Frankie T-shirt seemed a potent protest. **JMc**

Runaway | Bon Jovi (1984)

Writer | Jon Bon Jovi, George Karakoglou
Producer | Lance Quinn, Tony Bongiovi
Label | Mercury
Album | *Bon Jovi* (1984)

"If you see this song down at the beach, buy it a drink —it's finally old enough."

Jon Bon Jovi, 2003

◀ **Influenced by: All for Leyna** · Billy Joel (1980)
▶ **Influence on: Ryders** · Saigon featuring Memphis Bleek (2008)
● **Covered by: Alex Mitchell** (2006)
★ **Other key tracks:** She Don't Know Me (1984) · Burning for Love (1984) · You Give Love a Bad Name (1986)

"R2D2 We Wish You a Merry Christmas" was Jon Bon Jovi's first commercial release, but "Runaway" proved a more enduring early classic.

It was first demoed at New York's Power Station studio—where Jon was a gofer—in 1981. His cousin, Power Station founder Tony Bongiovi, was sufficiently impressed to assemble The All Star Review—drummer Frankie La Rocka (later to join the Spin Doctors), guitarist Tim Pierce (not, as has been suggested, Skid Row's Dave Sabo), bassist Huey McDonald (later to join Bon Jovi) and Bruce Springsteen's keyboard player Roy Bittan—for a 1982 recording.

The result blueprinted the Bon Jovi sound: muscular rock, sparkly keys, and Jon's fierce puppy vocals. "Nobody thought it was going to do anything . . ." he told *Spin*. "I was so tired of record companies shutting the door in my face, finally I said, 'Fuck it, I'm going to a radio station that has nothing to lose by saying I like it or I hate it.' I played it for a DJ named Chip Hobart, who put me and Twisted Sister on this same [radio only] album. . . . If it wasn't for him, 'Runaway' would have ended up in the garbage."

The song's success in New York led to Bon Jovi scoring a major label deal in 1983. The following year it was released as a single from the album *Bon Jovi*, reaching No. 39 on the *Billboard* Hot 100.

"The first time you heard 'Runaway,' it had 'hit' written all over it . . ." observed Richie Sambora, the guitarist recruited for Jon's new band. "It was instantly one of those songs you knew would sound good on the radio. If it hadn't been released by an unknown band—if Journey or one of those bands had released it—it would have been No. 1, no problem." **BM**

Born in the U.S.A. | Bruce Springsteen (1984)

Writer | Bruce Springsteen
Producer | Bruce Springsteen, Jon Landau,
Chuck Plotkin, Steve Van Zandt
Label | Columbia
Album | *Born in the U.S.A.* (1984)

*"It had implications
that I didn't tune into
at the time."*
Bruce Springsteen, 1996

◀ **Influenced by: Love, Reign O'er Me** • The Who (1973)
▶ **Influence on: Banned in the U.S.A.** • Luke (1990)
● **Covered by:** Stanley Clarke (1985) • Eric Rigler (2003)
Richard Shindell (2007) • Casiotone for the Painfully
Alone (2009)
★ **Other key track:** Born to Run (1975)

"Any work out there is open to different types of interpretation," said Bruce Springsteen of his most misunderstood song. "That is part of the roll of the dice. I probably could have made a record that would have been more easily understood, but . . . that was the right record."

The "right record" was born in January 1982, amid acoustic recordings that became 1982's *Nebraska*. It was revived when Springsteen reunited with his E Street Band a few months later. A rockabilly arrangement, featuring bassist Garry Tallent and drummer Max Weinberg, was one of several to be cast aside.

The final version came when the band were, in Weinberg's words, "just hacking around." Explosive drums and keyboard fanfares formed a backdrop to lyrics about the struggles of Vietnam veterans. (A film script sent to Springsteen by director Paul Schrader inspired the title; the Boss repaid the favor by providing the eventual title track, "Light of Day," for the movie, released in 1987, starring Michael J. Fox, Gena Rowlands, and Joan Jett.)

Millions heard the song, but not all listened—then-president Ronald Reagan cited the song's "message of hope." Over a decade later, however, Springsteen conceded to *NME* that *Born in the U.S.A.*'s red, white, and blue styling "was certainly oversimplified, if you just saw the image and didn't go to the show and get a sense of where it was coming from and what it was about."

But the song's raging spirit—best captured in an earth-shaking version on *Live/1975–85*—spoke volumes about the American character. As Talking Head David Byrne observed, "'Born in the U.S.A.' was a patriotic anthem—despite all intentions to the contrary." **BM**

World Destruction
Time Zone (1984)

Writer | Afrika Bambaataa, Bill Laswell
Producer | Bill Laswell/Material, Afrika Bambaataa
Label | Celluloid
Album | N/A

Joe Elliott or John Lydon? Amazingly, Def Leppard's front man was Afrika Bambaataa's first choice as guest vocalist for the second single by his and producer Bill Laswell's Time Zone project.

Bambaataa's lyrics ranged from Islam toppling the world's superpowers to a nuclear nightmare: territory more suited, surely, to someone who made "Anarchy in the U.K." rather than "Rock! Rock! (Till You Drop)." Laswell duly suggested Public Image Ltd's Lydon, who fitted Bambaataa's request for "somebody that's really wild."

Lydon spent only a few hours working on the song, but that was enough to leave his inimitable stamp; his vocals contrasted perfectly with Bambaataa and gave the track a deranged edge that suited the subject matter. He also recorded a version whose frank judgments on Her Majesty The Queen meant it has never been released.

The single made more of a mark in clubs than on charts. An influential blend of rock and hip-hop, "World Destruction" was also crucial in bringing Lydon and Laswell together—a union that spurred a renaissance for Public Image Ltd.

The song also found its way into *The Sopranos*. "That episode . . . was written the week of September 11," *Sopranos* creator David Chase told NJ.com in 2006. "Very presciently . . . there's this line: 'The Democratic-Communist relationship won't stand in the way of the Islamic force.'" **CB**

Immigrés/Bitim Rew
Youssou N'Dour (1984)

Writer | Youssou N'Dour
Producer | Youssou N'Dour
Label | Celluloid
Album | *Immigrés* (1984)

"Immigrés/Bitim Rew" launched Senegalese star Youssou N'Dour's international career, leading to later successes such as "7 Seconds," his 1994 hit duet with Neneh Cherry.

Invited to perform for the Association of Senegalese Taxi Drivers in Paris in 1983, N'Dour was struck by their plight and wrote "Immigrés" to remind them that, even if they were forced to work abroad, they could always return to the land that knew them best. (The alternative title, "Bitim Rew," means "outside the country.") The song first appeared on the eighth volume of the cassettes that N'Dour produced for the local market. It was remixed for its 1984 release on the Celluloid label, and again in 1988 for Virgin.

N'Dour's imploring vocal was a high, muezzin-like wail on this astonishing example of the polyrhythmic *mbalax* style. The song featured an exhilarating percussion break, with the late Alla Seck hammering over a guitar, hand claps, cymbals, the cracking of the *sabar* drum, and the strange, pitch-shifting *tama* (talking) drum. Abruptly, the plunging bass, brass, keyboards, and N'Dour returned, before several false endings.

The song eased N'Dour's transition into the international market, and a 1983 show in Paris introduced him to his biggest champion, Peter Gabriel. "Astounding . . ." Gabriel recalled to *NME*, "like liquid gold from the sky." **JLu**

It's My Life
Talk Talk (1984)

Writer | Mark Hollis, Tim Friese-Greene
Producer | Tim Friese-Greene
Label | EMI
Album | It's My Life (1984)

After dropping out of studying child psychology, Mark Hollis played with new wave band The Reaction. Following their demise, his brother introduced Hollis to Simon Brenner, Lee Harris, and Paul Webb—and, in 1981, Talk Talk were born.

By 1984, Brenner had been replaced by long-term collaborator Tim Friese-Greene. "It's My Life," the first fruit of this new partnership, was a hook-laden slice of synth-pop, underlined by Webb's funky bass and Hollis's doleful voice. The song did well across Europe, and entered the U.S. Top Forty.

The accompanying video mocked the concept of lip-syncing. Shots of Hollis at London Zoo with his mouth obscured were interspersed with footage from nature documentaries. Appalled, EMI demanded that it be reshot. The group were duly filmed with cheesy grins and comic miming. This reluctance to toe the industry line later manifested itself in increasingly uncommercial albums, culminating in 1991's Laughing Stock.

In the meantime, "It's My Life" became a staple in clubs and finally made a splash in Talk Talk's home country on its third re-release in 1990 (after a second attempt in 1985) to promote Natural History: the Very Best of Talk Talk. Then, in 2003, a version by No Doubt, fronted by Gwen Stefani, became an international hit. Thanks to the cover, the reclusive Hollis earned a Broadcast Music Incorporated songwriting award. **CS**

Smooth Operator
Sade (1984)

Writer | Sade, Ray Saint John
Producer | Robin Millar
Label | Epic
Album | Diamond Life (1984)

With a voice like melted chocolate, Sade Adu sashayed onto the Eighties music scene to no little acclaim, being duly rewarded with a Grammy for Best New Artist and a Brit award for Best Album. "We were picked up on because we were different from anything else that was going on at that time," she told Q.

The band, which took the name of their front woman, featured Stuart Matthewman (sax and guitar), Andrew Hale (keyboards), and Paul Denman (bass). The missing member was guitarist Ray Saint John, who had co-written "Smooth Operator" with Adu two years earlier.

A blend of cool vocals—delivered in a breathy, Monroe-esque style—with jazzy saxophones and poppy bongo beats, "Smooth Operator" was Diamond Life's fourth and final single. It spent ten weeks in the U.K. chart and broke the band in the United States.

Despite the media's pigeon-holing, Adu fought to adhere to the style she envisaged for the band, and disliked the labels frequently applied to their sound. "Our music is clearly pop, because it's easy to understand," she grumbled to Melody Maker. "All the songs I've ever loved—even jazz stuff—are things that tell a story."

"Smooth Operator," meanwhile, has become shorthand for love 'em and leave 'em guys who are too cool to call. **SO**

I Feel for You | Chaka Khan (1984)

Writer | Prince
Producer | Arif Mardin
Label | Warner Bros.
Album | *I Feel for You*
(1984)

*"I resent the stupid
electronics and I hate
stupid love songs."*
Chaka Khan, 1985

◀ **Influenced by: I Feel for You** • Pointer Sisters (1982)
▶ **Influence on: Who's Zoomin' Who** • Aretha Franklin
(1985)
● **Covered by:** The Flying Pickets (1991) • El Caco (2008)
★ **Other key tracks:** I'm Every Woman (1979) • Ain't
Nobody (1983)

Chaka Khan was under pressure. Her self-titled
1982 album had gone gold, and "Ain't Nobody,"
released in 1983, had become a classic. Could she
cut a fitting follow-up? Most definitely: "I Feel for
You"—a cover of Prince's 1979 original—heralded
the fusion of R&B with rap, and won Khan her
second solo Grammy.

Producer Arif Mardin—the man behind
the Bee Gees' equally pioneering "Jive Talkin',"
and Khan's "I'm Every Woman"—inadvertently
created the stuttering rap by Melle Mel (a
colleague of arranger Reggie Griffin, from hip-
hop label Sugar Hill). Mardin's hand slipped on
the sampler, hence the distinctive repetition of
"Chaka Khan." He had intended to fit her name to
the percussion, so the error paid off.

However, when she heard lines like "Let me
rock you, Chaka Khan / Let me rock you, that's all
I wanna do," the star was mortified. "I thought
'Oh God . . . how am I going to live this down?'"
she told *Rolling Stone*. "Every time a guy walks up
to me on the street, I think he's going to break
into that rap. And most of them do."

Nonetheless, the cocktail of Khan's expressive
voice, Mel's ear-catching rap, samples from Stevie
Wonder's "Fingertips Part 2," and Wonder himself
playing harmonica proved a gold-selling U.S. and
U.K. hit, reaching No. 1 in the U.K. singles chart and
No. 3 on the *Billboard* Hot 100. Prince repaid the
compliment by contributing songs to Khan's 1988
CK album and, later, performing her arrangement
of "I Feel for You" live. (Khan also covered Prince's
"Sign o' the Times" in 2007.)

"I look at that," Mardin later told *Performing
Songwriter*, "as one of the songs I'd like to take with
me to a desert island." **GK**

The Killing Moon | (1984)

Writer | Will Sergeant, Ian McCulloch,
Les Pattinson, Pete de Freitas
Producer | The Bunnymen
Label | Korova
Album | *Ocean Rain* (1984)

"It's up there with 'Suzanne' by Leonard Cohen, 'Blowin' in the Wind,' 'In My Life.'"

Ian McCulloch, 2009

◀ **Influenced by:** The Seventh Seal · Scott Walker (1969)
▶ **Influence on:** Crown of Love · Arcade Fire (2004)
● **Covered by:** Pavement (1997) · Wendy Rule (1997) · Eva
O (1998) · The Quakes (2003) · Grant-Lee Phillips (2006)
Nouvelle Vague (2006) · Something for Kate (2006)
★ **Other key track:** Back of Love (1982)

Great songwriters can dash off hits in their sleep. Paul McCartney opened his eyes humming "Yesterday"; Keith Richards came up with the riff for "Satisfaction" in the middle of a snooze; and Bunnymen singer Ian McCulloch awoke from slumber with a soaring hook and the words "Fate up against your will" echoing in his mind.

He sketched out the "meat of the song" on an acoustic guitar, then handed it over to the band. Bassist Les Pattinson added the ominous opening bars, and Will Sergeant applied layers of chiming, vibrato-heavy guitar. "Will took it to another level," McCulloch enthused. "He turned it into this amazing thing, a real classic." The result, declared the singer—never one for modesty—was "The most beautiful and best thing we had ever done."

He was right. In less than six minutes, Echo & The Bunnymen evolve from abrasive post-punks into masters of anthemic, doom-laden psychedelia. McCulloch's Leonard Cohen-esque lyrics ("In starlit nights I saw you / So cruelly you kissed me / Your lips a magic world") swirl over a slow-building orchestral backdrop that swells with passion and danger.

A Top Ten hit in the United Kingdom, the track has since won a new generation of fans, thanks to its use in Eighties nostalgia flicks such as *Grosse Point Blank* (1997) and *Donnie Darko* (2001). "We didn't know much about *Donnie Darko*," admitted Sergeant to *Record Collector*. "It was presented to us as some little underground cult film, and it went on to make millions." The track was originally used during the film's opening sequence; in the director's cut, however, it plays during a Halloween party near the end of the film, as originally intended. **TB**

You Spin Me Round (Like a Record) | Dead or Alive (1984)

Writer | Pete Burns, Mike Percy, Tim Lever,
Steve Coy
Producer | Mike Stock, Matt Aitken, Pete Waterman
Label | Epic
Album | *Youthquake* (1985)

*" 'You Spin Me Round' is a
hallmark in British music
and it will never ever date."*

Morrissey, 1985

◄ **Influenced by: Fashion** · David Bowie (1980)
► **Influence on: Rock Me Amadeus** · Falco (1986)
● **Covered by:** Templebeat (1997) · Second Skin (1998)
Dope (2000) · Hate Dept. (2000) · Thalía (2002) · Jessica
Simpson (2006) · Danzel (2007) · Thea Gilmore (2008)
Indochine (2009)

With Pete Burns, the "look" came first: the Englander's androgynous appearance was so striking that promoters encouraged him to start a band. It wasn't until he actually started performing—first with The Mystery Girls, then Nightmares in Wax, before he founded Liverpool's Dead or Alive in 1980—that it became clear that Burns's voice was as impressive as his look.

Dead or Alive's debut, *Sophisticated Boom Boom*, was a minor success, thanks to a cover of KC & The Sunshine Band's "That's the Way (I Like It)," a U.K. Top Forty hit. That set the stage for the synth-pop extravaganza *Youthquake*, produced by the then-fledgling production team Stock, Aitken, and Waterman, who went on to mastermind the likes of Kylie Minogue. (Meanwhile, Dead or Alive's guitarist Wayne Hussey joined goth lords The Sisters of Mercy.)

"You Spin Me Round (Like a Record)"—with its whirlwind groove, new wave vocals, and string arrangements modeled on Wagner's "Ride of the Valkyries"—was a slam-dunk choice for the first single. Yet it took a surprising amount of time for the general public to catch on. The song spent fourteen weeks in the U.K.'s Top 75 before finally reaching No. 1, setting a record for the slowest climb to the top of the chart. In the United States, it reached No. 11 in September 1985.

Once "You Spin Me Round" made it to the top, however, it never really left. The song's popularity has never slipped, and artists ranging from rapper Flo-Rida to pop moppet Jessica Simpson have covered or sampled it. Dead Or Alive themselves have re-released the song three times; on each occasion it has been a hit—most recently in 2006, when it reached No. 5 in the U.K. chart. **JiH**

The Boys of Summer | Don Henley (1984)

Writer | Don Henley, Mike Campbell
Producer | Don Henley, Danny Kortchmar,
Greg Ladanyi, Mike Campbell
Label | Geffen
Album | *Building the Perfect Beast* (1984)

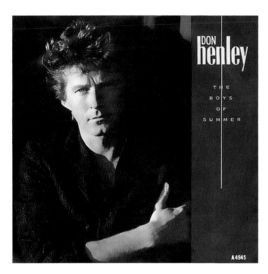

"I knew I had something there. I said, 'This is good and I know it's good.' It's great."

Don Henley, 1986

◄ **Influenced by: Caney Creek** • The Dillards (1973)
► **Influence on: Runaway Trains** • Tom Petty & The
Heartbreakers (1987)
● **Covered by:** Roger Daltrey (1998) • DJ Sammy (2002)
Bree Sharp (2002) • The Ataris (2003) • Paul Young
(2006)

Four years after the split of the Eagles, singer Don Henley was driving near San Diego when he was passed by a top-end Cadillac—at the time, the definitive establishment status symbol. To his horror, he saw a Deadhead sticker (denoting the driver's love of the ultimate anti-establishment band, The Grateful Dead) on the rear of the car, and was immediately inspired to write. (Dead fanzine *The Golden Road* was unamused, complaining: "The Eagle has blasphemed!")

Henley received a helping hand from his guitarist, on loan from Tom Petty's band The Heartbreakers: "I got so inspired by the track that Mike Campbell had given me [originally written for Petty's *Southern Accents*] that it just sort of wrote itself. It came just screamin' out of me. And I was jumping up and down in the car 'cause I knew I had something there."

The song became a lament for both a summer relationship and the 1960s counterculture. Sung in Henley's bruised tenor, the song hit home thanks to its wistful tone, sparse production, and the "I can see you . . . I can tell you" hook. The song was as smooth as silk, perfect for FM radio and baby-boomer nostalgia. The video, a striking black-and-white montage directed by Jean-Baptiste Mondino, won several accolades.

"The Boys of Summer" transcends everything that Henley recorded before or since—the mighty Eagles even played it live when they re-formed in 1994. One of the Eighties most distinctive songs, it has come to epitomize that decade, with its images of Wayfarer sunglasses and, indeed, that infamous Deadhead sticker—a cultural reference as relevant to the youth of today as platform heels. **JMc**

Rock You Like a Hurricane
Scorpions (1984)

Writer | H. Rarebell, K. Meine, R. Schenker
Producer | Dieter Dierks
Label | Harvest
Album | *Love at First Sting* (1984)

The Scorpions existed far beyond parody. As if titles like "Rock You Like a Hurricane" weren't enough of a clue, drummer and co-writer Herman Rarebell's 1986 solo album was titled *Herman ze German and Friends.*

Helmed by singer Klaus Meine and guitarist Rudy Schenker (brother of Michael, a sometime Scorpion), the band won footholds in Europe and Japan in the 1970s. By early 1984—with Rarebell, bassist Francis Buchholz, and guitarist Matthias Jabs—they had struck gold (and platinum) in the United States with *Blackout.*

This enviable evolution, coupled with a formidable live reputation, made *Love at First Sting* a dead cert. Its fortunes were hardly hampered by one of *the* Eighties metal anthems—"Rock You Like a Hurricane." The hit was helped by an entertainingly ludicrous video that aroused the ire of music censors the Parents Music Resource Center.

"We don't go looking for hit singles . . ." Meine told *Circus.* "We want good songs and it's got to stay rough. . . . It's important that it rocks, that it's wild and that fans can see it in concert. We're not looking for something American radio will play." Nonetheless, they wound up with an anthem that was as suited for the airwaves as it was for arena shows and sports events—and which has lost none of its power in the past quarter-century. **BM**

Plateau
Meat Puppets (1984)

Writer | Curt Kirkwood
Producer | Uncredited
Label | SST
Album | *Meat Puppets II* (1984)

They toured with Black Flag and recorded for the pioneering punk label SST, but the Meat Puppets were never *really* a hardcore band. Arizona kids raised on drugs and classic rock, their early shows were riotous, with the trio covering The Grateful Dead and Neil Young between their own haywire thrash. Their second album replaced full-pelt hurtle with sun-damaged psychedelic country, steeped in classic songwriting but still brilliantly unique. "Plateau" crystallized this new sound: Curt Kirkwood's woozy drawl murmuring mystical riddles over a tangle of acoustic guitars and muted drums.

The hardcore kids didn't "get" *Meat Puppets II,* but *Rolling Stone* raved about it. And while the band never broke through to the mainstream, Kurt Cobain invited Curt and his brother Cris to Nirvana's *Unplugged* session, from which covers of three of their songs (including "Plateau") introduced the band to a new generation.

"I guess they liked our stuff 'cos we took a step away from formulaic hardcore in the early Eighties but still had the attitude," Kirkwood told *Mojo.* "Also, both Kurt and I have that high and lonesome country thing in our voices. . . . It was clear that we were on the same trip—Kurt wanted to extend the end part of 'Plateau' for half an hour, and I'd written that song to be cyclical, so you could just space out." **SC**

Tenderness | General Public (1984)

Writer | Micky Billingham, Roger Charlery, Colin Fairley, Gavin MacKillop, Dave Wakeling
Producer | General Public, G. MacKillop, C. Fairley
Label | Virgin
Album | ... All the Rage (1984)

"There was a darker side to the song, because it came out in that period of AIDS."
Dave Wakeling, 2008

◀ **Influenced by:** Wings of a Dove • Madness (1983)
▶ **Influence on:** Cherish • Madonna (1989)
● **Covered by:** Galactic (2003)
★ **Other key tracks:** Never You Done That (1984) • Hot You're Cool (1984) • As a Matter of Fact (1984) • Burning Bright (1984)

After ska revivalists The Beat (known as the English Beat in North America) broke up in 1983, guitarist Andy Cox and bassist David Steele launched Fine Young Cannibals. Meanwhile, vocalist Dave Wakeling and toastmaster Ranking Roger started General Public. The former experienced greater success, but the latter, too, had their moment in the sun.

Inexplicably, the band scored only minor success in their native Britain. In the United States and Canada, however, they scored a well-deserved hit with "Tenderness." This bouncy pop gem was built on a keyboard riff that rang like bells, slap-happy drums, and Wakeling's poignant vocals (plus a recurring female "sigh" that escalated in orgasmic fashion).

"I write my own songs from a point of view of feeling really strongly about something . . ." Wakeling told Songfacts. "I have to be moved to the point where sometimes I'm shaking a bit . . . 'Tenderness' was very much like that."

"The notion was that you were driving around in there, in America, searching for the tenderness—whereas, of course, it's in your heart all the time. So it's like you're looking in the outside world for something that can only be discovered in yourself—because love is a verb, not a noun."

The track glistened with a radio-friendly sheen, yet boasted the down-and-dirty guitar of The Clash's Mick Jones, who guested with General Public just long enough to toughen it up. "He was my favorite guitarist of all time," enthused Wakeling.

General Public petered out, but "Tenderness" lived on—thanks to its inclusion in movies such as *Weird Science* (1985) and *Clueless* (1995), and to its timeless, uplifting power. **JiH**

Wood Beez (Pray Like Aretha Franklin) | Scritti Politti (1984)

Writer | Green Gartside
Producer | Arif Mardin
Label | Virgin
Album | *Cupid & Psyche 85* (1985)

"I don't really have Aretha as an iconographic symbol or cipher . . . just an apt device."
Green Gartside, 1985

◀ **Influenced by: Don't Stop 'til You Get Enough**
Michael Jackson (1979)
▶ **Influence on: I Feel for You** · Chaka Khan (1984)
● **Covered by:** Audio Thieves (2006)
★ **Other key tracks:** The Sweetest Girl (1981) • Hypnotize (1985) • Perfect Way (1985)

From the dubby romanticism of Scritti Politti's early work, "Wood Beez" was a headlong dive into blue-eyed funk. Front man Green Gartside had jettisoned the original line-up, switched labels, and honed in on pure pop. The result? A fluid groove that pressed hip buttons while maintaining a commercial veneer. As he foretold in 1982: "There's absolutely no point in making music, no point in having a bash at pop, and theorizing about it, without actually having popular records."

Gartside had rarely written a song without a philosophical tract to go with it, but "Wood Beez" spoke plainly. It ticked the classic soul box with its title, had a customary dabble with words ("There's nothing I wouldn't take / Oh, even intravenous") and generally expressed unconditional love.

"Aretha was singing what are arguably inane pop songs and had left her gospel roots," Gartside explained to *NME*. "But she sang them with a fervor, a passion. . . . Hearing her was as near to a hymn or a prayer as I could get."

The song's power lay in Gartside's honeyed vocal and the assured playing of his new cohorts, New Yorkers Fred Maher and David Gamson. Arif Mardin's impeccable production was the icing upon the sweetest of cakes.

"Wood Beez" more than held its own with the smart R&B coming out of America at the time—even its cutesy title matched Prince's language larks—and introduced Gartside to circles he thought beyond him. Within three years, he would work with Chaka Khan and Al Jarreau, feature on Madonna's *Who's That Girl* soundtrack, and entice Miles Davis to guest on "Oh Patti (Don't Feel Sorry for Loverboy)," released in 1988. **MH**

I Will Dare
The Replacements (1984)

Writer | Paul Westerberg
Producer | Paul Westerberg, Peter Jesperson, Steve Fjelstad
Label | Twin Tone
Album | *Let It Be* (1984)

Unlike their peers, The Replacements never had high-art pretensions. Instead, they crafted wry pop rock that addressed their audience's key concern: how to survive adolescence.

"I Will Dare," which opened their third album, was a tender take on a perennial teen concern—the first days of a new romance. Westerberg imagined the fumbling questions asked by the couple, capturing the worry of a lover waiting for a call. Underneath that anxiety, though, lay hope, with Westerberg pledging, "If you will dare, I will dare."

The promise of new love was accompanied by a new sound. The group stopped ripping off the New York Dolls, and looked to their heroes Big Star for inspiration. Westerberg played that most un-punk of instruments, the mandolin, while R.E.M.'s Peter Buck played a Byrdsy guitar solo.

The jangling masterpiece spoke to the college rock crowd, and inspired Westerberg wannabes like the Goo Goo Dolls. "I remember the first time I heard it," recalled Replacements manager Peter Jesperson, "thinking, 'Oh my God, we're gonna be rich.'" But while their heirs made big bucks, the band dissolved in a mess of pills and booze, earning little from their pioneering efforts.

Westerberg would later note that the title of their breakthrough song could have served as The Replacements' slogan: "We'll dare to flop," he said. "We'll dare to do anything." **TB**

How Soon Is Now?
The Smiths (1984)

Writer | Johnny Marr, Morrissey
Producer | John Porter
Label | Rough Trade
Album | N/A

"I wanted an intro that was almost as potent as 'Layla'," Johnny Marr told *Guitar Player* in 1990. "When it plays in a club or a pub, everyone knows what it is." Boy, did he deliver! "How Soon Is Now?" is a triumph, thanks to Marr's genius layering of sliding and oscillating vibrato guitar, Mike Joyce and Andy Rourke's tight rhythm section, and Morrissey's defiantly anti-pop lyrics.

It all started, said Marr, by trying to create "a stomping groove" like the Seventies hits "Disco Stomp" by Hamilton Bohannon and "New York Groove" by Hello. "I suddenly got the riff," he told the *Guardian*. "It all came together . . . When Morrissey first sang, 'I am the son / And the heir,' John Porter went, 'Ah great, the elements!' Morrissey continued, 'Of a shyness that is criminally vulgar.' I knew he'd hit the bull's-eye there and then."

"How Soon is Now?" appeared on the B-side of "William, It Was Really Nothing," then on the 1984 compilation *Hatful of Hollow*. Fans loved the seven-minute masterpiece, but its belated 3.53 minute single release in 1985 peaked at an unimpressive No. 24 in the United Kingdom. It was hoped the song would "break" America, but it didn't even chart there.

Happily, cover versions by the likes of Love Spit Love (whose version became the theme tune for TV series *Charmed*) ensure its enduring success. **LS**

The Smiths' Johnny Marr (left) and a none-too-shy Morrissey perform in London in 1984. ➔

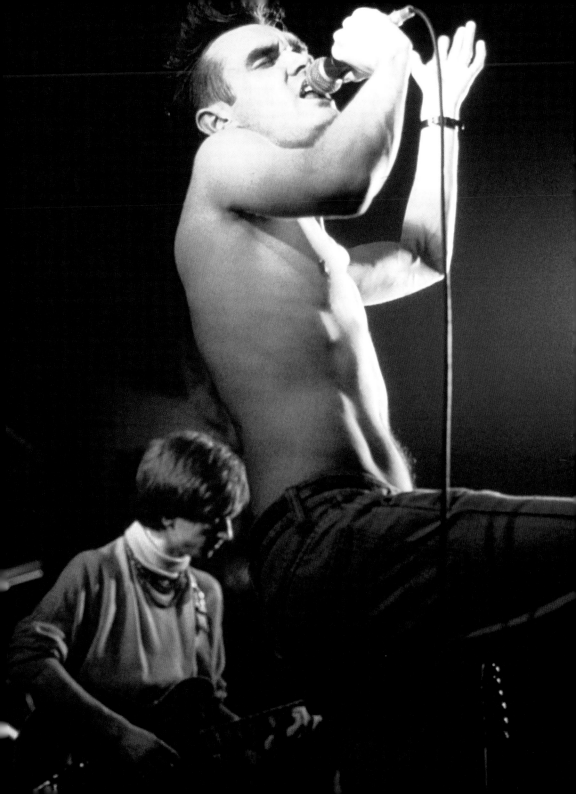

Rattlesnakes | Lloyd Cole & The Commotions (1984)

Writer | Neil Clark, Lloyd Cole
Producer | Paul Hardiman
Label | Polydor
Album | *Rattlesnakes* (1984)

"In fact, I had never even read Simone de Beauvoir."

Lloyd Cole, 1990

◀ **Influenced by:** Walk on the Wild Side · Lou Reed (1972)
▶ **Influence on:** Lloyd, I'm Ready to be Heartbroken Camera Obscura (2006)
● **Covered by:** Tori Amos (2001)
★ **Other key track:** Perfect Skin (1984)

"Rattlesnakes" is a lovely vignette, a perfect distillation of the album whose title it shares. Lloyd Cole's lyrical hallmarks are here—studiedly offhand mentions of literary characters, a sense of movie-cool America, couplets bursting with imagery ("Her heart's like crazy paving / Upside down and back to front")—in a pithy story. "Jodie" is armed with a gun and a bruised heart, haunted by a "never-born child" but reckless with her own wellbeing. However, she also "looks like Eva Marie Saint in *On the Waterfront*," so it's not all bad news.

Littered with cultural allusions and evocative names, such as that of French writer Simone de Beauvoir, The Commotions' debut album divided opinion, but Cole stood by his method. "I'd just come out of studying literature, so in a way it was natural to write like that," he protested to *The Observer* in 1990. "To hear it referred to as name-dropping is a bit odd; it's not as though I'd met Mailer or anything."

Cole's cracked delivery came straight from Lou Reed and Bob Dylan, but the music owed a debt to The Byrds' country-soul, with co-writer Neil Clark's jangly guitar to the fore.

The strength of the songs was undeniable— the album also boasted the classics "Perfect Skin," "Forest Fire," and "Are You Ready to be Heartbroken?"—and nowhere was the early Commotions sound more fully realized than on "Rattlesnakes." With strings arranged by Anne Dudley—then pushing boundaries with Art of Noise—it barreled along, urgent but compassionate. Remarked Tori Amos, who covered the song on her *Strange Little Girls*: "I loved the way that he was so aware of the pain that she was in." **MH**

Im Nin' Alu | Ofra Haza (1984)

Writer | Rabbi Shalom Shabazi
Producer | Bezalel Aloni
Label | Hed-Arzi
Album | *Yemenite Songs* (1984)

"I hope a lot more people buy Ofra Haza. Which they should have done in the first place."

Jonathan More, Coldcut, 1987

◀ **Influenced by: Hayyaati Albi** • Om Kalsoum (1950)
▶ **Influence on: Temple of Love** (1992) • The Sisters of Mercy (1992)
● **Covered by: Anjali** (2006)
★ **Other key tracks: Yachilvi Veyachali** (1984) • Lefelach Harimon (1984)

From the Eurovision Song Contest to goth gods, via pioneering dance records? Ofra Haza had an extraordinary career—and this was the song that was most responsible.

Haza was born in 1957 to impoverished parents from Israel's Yemeni Jewish community. This ancient group had a strong musical tradition, and Haza grew up singing both secular material and Diwan songs—devotional pieces that cover religious and secular subjects, and are performed on festive occasions.

She began singing in public aged thirteen, was voted "Best Israeli Female Singer" in 1981, and represented her country in the 1983 Eurovision Song Contest. In 1984, reportedly as a tribute to her parents, she reached back to her roots for *Yemenite Songs,* bringing the Diwan to a modern audience. Contemporary Israeli musicians brought a pop flavor to the songs.

Yemenite Songs duly won Haza international recognition. In late 1987, the distinctive wails of its opening track, "Im Nin' Alu," were sampled on a version of M|A|R|R|S' dance classic "Pump Up the Volume" and Coldcut's remix of "Paid in Full" by hip-hop legends Eric B & Rakim—without Haza's consent. "We put it on because we thought it's a nice piece of music," Coldcut's Jonathan More protested to *NME*. "And I think it'll gain, potentially, a range of listeners which might never otherwise have heard of it."

This accidental publicity made Haza in demand around the world. Before her death in 2000, she notched up collaborations with admirers ranging from punk godfather Iggy Pop, through goth rock legends The Sisters of Mercy, to house heroes The Black Dog. **GC**

Purple Rain | Prince & The Revolution (1984)

Writer | Prince
Producer | Prince & The Revolution
Label | Warner Bros.
Album | *Purple Rain* (1984)

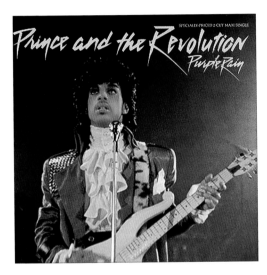

"It was so different. It was almost country. It was almost rock. It was almost gospel."

Bobby Z, The Revolution, 1999

◀ **Influenced by: We've Got Tonite** • Bob Seger (1978)
▶ **Influence on: Like You'll Never See Me Again**
Alicia Keys (2007)
● **Covered by:** The Flying Pickets (1991) • Randy
Crawford (1995) • Teddybears (1995) • LeAnn Rimes
(1998) • Etta James (2006)

Channeling the soul of Sly Stone and the spirit of Jimi Hendrix, Prince alchemized purple into platinum. "Purple Rain" is the title song from his most successful album, with over thirteen million sold in the United States alone, and winning Prince an Oscar for Best Original Song Score in 1984.

Its origins lie in The Purple One's tour for his breakthrough album, *1999*—which, like the rest of his pre-*Purple Rain* work, was funk-based. According to the Revolution's keyboardist Matt Fink, Prince was baffled by the appeal of hard rocker Bob Seger, who was playing in the same cities. Fink duly suggested Prince write a crossover ballad in the Seger vein.

"The song was basically Prince's," Revolution guitarist Wendy Melvoin told *Vogue*, "but we [she and keyboardist Lisa Coleman] did embellish it considerably. He encouraged us to work together and began asking for parts and arrangements, so we carried four-track recorders around in our hotel rooms and worked on things when we had spare time." Thus Prince crafted one of his signature songs, later ranked 143rd in *Rolling Stone*'s 500 Greatest Songs of All Time. It followed "When Doves Cry" and "Let's Go Crazy" into the upper reaches of transatlantic charts, going gold in the United States.

The song was recorded live at a benefit gig in Minneapolis in 1983, but for the album it was edited down from eleven minutes to just eight by ditching one verse and a solo. But the unmistakable, undulating opening guitar hints at the epic to come. Bluesy guitar—echoed by live drums, and soulful lyrics—creates an emotional crescendo before tapering into a finale of tinkling piano and sad strings. A true anthem. **GK**

State of Shock | The Jacksons featuring Mick Jagger (1984)

Writer | Michael Jackson, Randy Lee Hansen
Producer | Michael Jackson
Label | Epic
Album | *Victory* (1984)

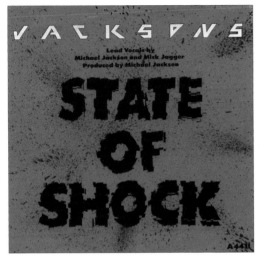

"I think it could have been much better produced but, you know, I enjoyed doing it."

Mick Jagger, 1984

◀ **Influenced by: State of Shock** · Ted Nugent (1979)
▶ **Influence on: Hooked on Polkas** · "Weird Al" Yankovic (1985)
● **Covered by:** DJ Flash & King MC (1984)
★ **Other key tracks:** Torture (1984) · Body (1984) · One More Chance (1984)

By 1983, Michael needed the Jacksons like Tina Turner needed Ike. *Thriller* was on its way to becoming the best-selling album of all time, elevating Michael to the throne of "The King of Pop." So he was throwing his brothers a bone by rejoining them for a follow-up to *Triumph in* 1980.

The resulting batch of songs, recorded amid heavy sibling squabbling, hardly bore comparison with The Jacksons' Seventies offerings—with one exception: a funky collaboration with Rolling Stones front man Mick Jagger. "State of Shock," The Jacksons' last Top Ten hit, was one of the era's best disco-rock hybrids, and arguably the finest duet that either MJ recorded.

The song (whose co-writer was not the much-admired guitarist Randy Hansen) was one of three that Jackson demoed with Queen singer Freddie Mercury in 1982. "I was initially going to be on *Thriller*," marveled Mercury. "Can you imagine that?" For reasons that can only be speculated upon, Mercury was replaced by Jagger—who, on entering a New York studio in May 1984, was told by Jackson to run through scales to warm up his vocal cords. "If Michael Jackson says 'warm up,'" remarked engineer Bruce Swedien, "you warm up—even if you are Mick Jagger."

Their voices worked surprisingly well together, both on harmony parts and volleyed leads. Every word is sung with urgency, underscored by nasty guitar and drums that sounded as if they were being beaten with hand grenades.

Although, as Jagger observed, "a lot of people didn't like it," "State of Shock" peaked at No. 3 in the United States and was the only real triumph—either artistically or commercially—to emerge from *Victory*. **JiH**

Private Dancer
Tina Turner (1984)

Writer | Mark Knopfler
Producer | John Carter
Label | Capitol
Album | *Private Dancer*
(1984)

Freedom
Wham! (1984)

Writer | George Michael
Producer | George Michael
Label | Epic
Album | *Make It Big*
(1984)

Tina Turner scored classic hits, such as "River Deep—Mountain High," with her husband Ike in the Sixties and early Seventies. But it wasn't until *Private Dancer* went multiplatinum that she was propelled to superstardom at the age of forty-five.

The album's title track had been destined for Dire Straits' *Love over Gold*. Composer Mark Knopfler recorded the song but felt the lyrics weren't appropriate for a male singer and shelved it. However, his manager knew Turner's manager, and suggested the song might work for her.

Turner hoped to put her vocals over the Dire Straits recording, but contractual obstacles obliged her to redo it, with band members John Illsley, Guy Fletcher, Alan Clark, and Hal Lindes. With Knopfler unable to join them, lead guitar duties were taken by Jeff Beck. "I asked her to sign my guitar . . ." Beck recalled. "She suddenly pulls out this flick knife and starts carving her name—'T-I-N-A'—across my beautiful guitar!"

The song is a beautifully atmospheric tale of a woman in a gentlemen's club. "Someone said, Why did you select 'Private Dancer'? Is it because you've been a hooker?" Turner recalled. "And I was shocked, because . . . I had done private parties for the rich people in Dallas, and I called that a private performance. And private dancing was very close to that type of thing, so I didn't see her as a hooker . . . I can be naive about some of these things." **SO**

Fantastic made Wham! one of the biggest bands in their native United Kingdom. The follow-up to that 1983 debut, however, transformed George Michael and Andrew Ridgeley into international superstars. *Make It Big*'s joyous lead single was "Wake Me Up Before You Go-Go," a worldwide No. 1. "Careless Whisper" achieved similar results, as did a third, "Freedom."

Of that trio, "Freedom" best illustrates why Wham! were a big deal. It sounds like a Motown classic, but feels contemporary. It's giddy and up-tempo; yet the lyrics, which place Michael in the role of heartsick lover, are uncommonly touching. "'Freedom' was the least likely to get to No. 1 . . ." he noted. "I always considered it a bit of a risk but I really wanted us to put it out."

Michael wrote the song en route to recording in France: "On the way to the airport, in the taxi, I got the chorus line for 'Freedom' and when I got there it kept going round in my head, so we worked on it and did 'Freedom' on the third day. I loved 'Freedom' so much, I thought the ideas I'd had earlier on in the year just weren't up to it."

After the band split in 1986, Michael had few nice things to say about his time in Wham! Tellingly, however, he recorded a follow-up of sorts, "Freedom '90," and used a small bit of the old song—performed on organ—at the start of the smash "Faith." **JiH**

Tina Turner combines big hair and a small dress on stage in 1985.

I Want You Back
Hoodoo Gurus (1984)

Writer | Dave Faulkner
Producer | Alan Thorne
Label | Big Time
Album | *Stoneage Romeos* (1984)

Long before The Hives and White Stripes resurrected garage rock, Australian bands tipped a hat to the late Sixties and created a colossally influential scene of their own. Radio Birdman set the pace, with bands like The Scientists carrying the gospel overseas. At the same time, The Saints spearheaded Australia's punk revolution, with others such as The Victims taking up the challenge.

The Hoodoo Gurus, formed in 1980, took the best of both. Guitarist Dave Faulkner and drummer James Baker had been in The Victims, responsible for the classic "Television Addict." Guitarist Brad Shepherd, who joined in 1981, had also played alongside Baker, in The Scientists. They originally intended to simply play covers, but chose to make the most of Faulkner's writing talents.

Stoneage Romeos was their stunning debut. Lyrically, it acknowledged everyone from Sky Saxon to the Ramones; yet amid the rambunctious recipe that blueprinted their career was what sounded like a tender lament.

"I Want You Back" was a jangly slice of pretty power pop. But its tale of a failed relationship was an analogy, inspired by Shepherd's predecessor, who co-founded the band. "When Rod Radalj left the Gurus, he was very dismissive of us . . ." Faulkner told *Harp*. "It was me saying, 'You'll regret it.' . . . It's not a song about 'I wish you'd come back,' but 'You'll wish you *were* back!'" **BM**

Sally Maclennane
The Pogues (1985)

Writer | Shane MacGowan
Producer | Elvis Costello
Label | Stiff Records
Album | *Rum, Sodomy & the Lash* (1985)

A perfect song, Shane MacGowan told *The Daily Telegraph*, "should hit you . . . in the feet, in the groin, in the heart, and the soul." MacGowan's sentiment sums up this high-spirited ballad.

The second single by the Irish-blooded folk-punks to hit the U.K. Top 100, this classic drinking anthem views working-class life through the bottom of a beer glass. It's boisterous, yet tinged with tragedy: MacGowan's rough-diamond vocals recount a cautionary tale of death through joyous overindulgence, centered around harmonica-playing Jimmy and the colorful characters in his local bar. The lyrics raise a toast "to the greatest little boozer and to Sally Maclennane"—although, according to the *Independent*, the latter was "not a lady but a brand of stout."

"Sally Maclennane" was taken from The Pogues' second album, *Rum, Sodomy & the Lash*, which was produced by Elvis Costello. A fan of the group, Costello had taken them on their first major tour as his support act, and he would later marry their bass player, Cait O'Riordan. With its acoustic guitar, banjo, accordion, tin-whistle, and stand-up drumming splendor, the song is typical of the band's "it rocks but it's not really rock music" oeuvre.

Never a huge hit, the rabble-rousing "Sally Maclennane" will nonetheless forever be a favorite among craic-revelers the world over. **BC**

The Pogues' Shane MacGowan, whose song "Sally Maclennane" celebrates the glass that refreshes. ➡

Voices Carry | 'Til Tuesday (1985)

Writer | M. Hausman, R. Holmes, A. Mann, J. Pesce
Producer | Mike Thorne
Label | Epic
Album | *Voices Carry* (1985)

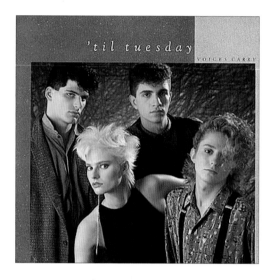

"Being content with my work is the most important thing."

Aimee Mann, 1985

◄ **Influenced by: Only the Lonely** · The Motels (1982)
► **Influence on: I Touch Myself** · Divinyls (1991)
● **Covered by:** Gang Green (1986) · Morella's Forest (1995) · Vitamin C (2005) · Toxic Audio (2005) · Tiffany (2007) · MGMT (2009)

Aimee Mann gave up the music conservatory for punk rock, then gave up punk rock to start a new wave band. The vocalist must have known what she was doing: within months of forming, 'Til Tuesday were Boston's hottest independent act.

Epic signed the quartet and sent them to New York to record their debut. As tapes rolled, executives smelled a hit in "Voices Carry"—Mann's bitter, paranoid relationship tale with an all-female cast. The thought of one woman singing about an affair with another, however, made the suits nervous and they convinced Mann to change the sex of the song's controlling antagonist from female to male.

That compromise didn't hurt Mann's delivery, which was perfectly in tune with the lyrical arc. She sounded hollow and beaten as her character identified the losing situation; then, bristling at the lover's manipulative ways, full of defiance. Ultimately, she zoomed into a frenzy that left it unclear how this relationship would end. The music followed the same path—distant and icy at first, then steadily drawing closer to the fire.

Two decades later, Mann cut a solo, acoustic version of "Voices Carry" for iTunes. "The song represents the beginning of my career," she told *Tastes Like Chicken*, "and I felt that maybe it was time to be able to share a different version of it."

The original "Voices Carry" became a hit in the United States, Canada, and Australia. Mann went on to fashion a fine solo career after the group disbanded in 1988, guested with Rush, and was nominated for an Oscar for her *Magnolia* soundtrack. Yet her voice would never carry in quite the same way as it did on 'Til Tuesday's first single. **JiH**

The Sun Always Shines on T.V. | A-ha (1985)

Writer | Pål Waaktaar
Producer | Alan Tarney
Label | Warner Bros.
Album | *Hunting High and Low* (1985)

"To a Scandinavian, melancholia is not negative. It's more like an itch you must scratch."

Magne Furuholmen, 2009

◄ **Influenced by:** It's My Life · Talk Talk (1984)
► **Influence on:** Beautiful Day · U2 (2000)
● **Covered by:** Hubi Meisel (2002) · Delays (2006)
Atrocity (2008) · And One (2009) · Nadja (2009)
★ **Other key tracks:** Hunting High and Low (1985) · Take on Me (1985) · Train of Thought (1985)

After the hard-worked triumph—and numerous re-releases—of the global hit "Take on Me," A-ha reaped immediate rewards with "The Sun Always Shines on T.V." Going one better than their breakthrough, it climbed to the summit of the U.K. chart and into international Top Twenties on its first release. With Wham! splitting and Duran Duran struggling to keep their Taylors, the Norwegian trio became the teen band of choice, and were not going to put a foot wrong.

Producer Alan Tarney—who had been at the helm for the vocal operatics and the tinny synths and beats of "Take on Me"—helped the band evolve. Morten Harket's remarkable voice was still to the fore, but this time he was backed by a wall of sound. Muscular where "Take on Me" was lithe, "The Sun Always Shines on T.V." reveled in its own drama; a churchy intro built into a crescendo of clatter, guided by Magne Furuholmen's chiming synths.

Cathedrals of noise apart, it's a dour affair. Harket gave flesh to guitarist and writer Pål Waaktaar's existential angst: "I fear the crazed and lonely looks the mirror's sending me / These days." In this light, the title is a cry of despair: if life is so terrible, how come it always looks so bright on television? The band shared Abba's Scandinavian gift for couching misery in glorious melody (a lesson also learned by avowed A-ha fan Chris Martin of Coldplay).

The song bore an unusual legacy: many fans gleefully spotted the similarities in U2's No. 1 "Beautiful Day," which was released in 2000; and Morrissey recast its message—"the sun *never* shines on T.V."—in a brief rendition before a Norwegian audience in 2004. **MH**

Into the Groove | Madonna (1985)

Writer | Madonna, Stephen Bray
Producer | Madonna, Stephen Bray
Label | Sire
Album | N/A

"Madonna has been incredibly important to the 1980s, musically … a little disco queen who … became an icon."

Jon Bon Jovi, 1990

◀ **Influenced by: Ain't No Big Deal** · Barracuda (1983)
▶ **Influence on: Don't Wanna Lose This Groove**
Dannii Minogue (2003)
● **Covered by:** Ciccone Youth (1986) · Mina (1988) · Dale
Bozzio (2000) · Superbus (2002) · Missing Persons
(2005) · The Medic Droid (2008)

"With the music and *Desperately Seeking Susan*," Madonna told *Time*, "I think I'm affecting people in the same way either way. My personality is getting across." The movie certainly scored a double whammy: Madonna stole Rosanna Arquette's thunder (Arquette won a BAFTA for best supporting actress, despite playing the lead), and gave the world "Into the Groove."

The singer presented a demo for a scene set in the Danceteria club. The movie's producers were delighted—Madonna's label less so, as they were still promoting the previous year's *Like a Virgin*. The song duly failed to feature on the soundtrack album. However, when DJs began bootlegging it, a polished "Into the Groove" was added to a European reissue of *Like a Virgin* and made the B-side of "Angel" in the United States.

Written and produced with ex-boyfriend Stephen Bray—whom Madonna met when they were both members of The Breakfast Club—"Into the Groove" is simultaneously fluffy and forceful. Singing about a subject close to her heart—she trained as a dancer—Madge flounced to the top of the U.K. chart for the first time. "Holiday" climbed back to No. 2, while "Crazy for You" began its ascent. Madonna mania had hit. The song has been remixed many times; notably in 2003, when Madonna united with Missy Elliot to create "Into the Hollywood Groove" for a Gap advert. It has also been covered by a number of artists, including Dannii Minogue, who combined the song with her single "Don't Wanna Lose This Feeling."

"Into the Groove" survives to Madonna's setlists today. "There are still those people," she complained in 1987, "who, no matter what I do, will always think of me as a little disco tart." **GK**

Madonna in the 1980s, with a great many reinventions of her pop persona still to come. ➡

Running Up That Hill (A Deal with God) | Kate Bush (1985)

Writer | Kate Bush
Producer | Kate Bush
Label | EMI
Album | *Hounds of Love* (1985)

"That song is going to puzzle a lot of people. . . . It's actually not that religious."

Kate Bush, 1985

◀ **Influenced by:** No Self Control · Peter Gabriel (1980)
▶ **Influence on:** Speed of Sound · Coldplay (2005)
● **Covered by:** Blue Pearl (1990) · Elastic Band (1994)
Distance (1998) · Faith & The Muse (2001) · Placebo
(2003) · Within Temptation (2003) · Chromatics (2007)
Little Boots (2009)

Two days before Kate Bush unveiled "Running Up That Hill" in 1985—on BBC chat show *Wogan*, of all places—*NME* included her in a "Where are they now?" feature. (She had vanished after the commercially disappointing *The Dreaming* in 1982.) Within months, *NME* was eating its hat, trumpeting "Running Up That Hill" as the best single ever recorded by a British, non-black artist. The song became her first U.K. Top Ten hit in five years—entering at No. 9 and reaching No. 3—and got her noticed in the United States for the first time, reaching No. 30 on the *Billboard* chart. (EMI had wanted "Cloudbusting" to be the first single, but Bush prevailed.)

The song was one of the first written for her album *Hounds of Love*. "If these two people could swap places," Bush declared, "if the man could become the woman and the woman the man . . . perhaps they could understand the feelings of that other person in a truer way."

The galloping drums—which inspired Talk Talk's "Life's What You Make It"—were programmed by Bush's then-partner, Del Palmer. "He wrote this great pattern . . ." she recalled. "So I just put the Fairlight [synthesizer] on top of it and that was the basis of the song, with the drone."

The final piece of the puzzle was the title. "The song was originally called 'Deal with God'—to me that is the title and I still believe it should be, [but] I was told that if I insisted on it, radio in ten countries would refuse to play it." Bush compromised, so as not to sabotage the album, and the results were conclusive: now she was pioneering *and* commercially successful. "It's so rewarding," Bush said, "after working for a long time, to see that your work is being received with open arms." **GK**

West End Girls | Pet Shop Boys (1985)

Writer | Neil Tennant, Chris Lowe
Producer | Stephen Hague
Label | Parlophone
Album | *Please* (1986)

"They'll be remembered for 'West End Girls' . . . I don't know anybody who doesn't know that song."

Brandon Flowers, The Killers, 2006

◄ **Influenced by:** The Message · Grandmaster Flash & The Furious Five (1982)

► **Influence on:** Jump · Madonna (2005)

● **Covered by:** My Morning Jacket (2005) · The Hotrats (2009)

★ **Other key track:** Rent (1987)

Described by *NME* as "Marc Almond overdosing on mean streets and clublands," the Pet Shop Boys' first hit—and still their best-known track— did extremely well on its second release.

First issued in 1984, and produced by New York dance legend Bobby Orlando, "West End Girls" was initially a minor underground hit. After the Boys signed to EMI, producer Stephen Hague was brought in to slow the original tempo and help Chris Lowe realize his potential as a synthesizer maestro. (Hague proceeded to assist New Order— whose "Blue Monday" was exactly the sound that Neil Tennant had envisaged for the Pet Shop Boys.)

The song's genesis came two years earlier, in 1983. Tennant, assistant editor of British pop magazine *Smash Hits*, had gone to bed after watching a Jimmy Cagney gangster film. The killer opening lines—"Sometimes you're better off dead / There's a gun in your hand and it's pointing at your head"—came to him as he was falling asleep. Subsequent lyrics were inspired by T. S. Eliot's poem *The Waste Land*, using different narrative voices to portray a class-ridden London where Cockney East End boys have little in common with well-to-do West End girls. The video follows Tennant and Lowe around various landmarks of London's West End.

Although influenced by hip-hop, Tennant forced himself to use his distinctive English accent—he didn't want to mimic a New York rapper. The blend of hypnotic rhythm and cinematic synthpop with intelligent lyrics propelled the track to No. 1 on both sides of the Atlantic. Twenty years after its release, "West End Girls" won an Ivor Novello award for Song of the Decade, 1985–1994. **GK**

She Sells Sanctuary | The Cult (1985)

Writer | Ian Astbury, Billy Duffy
Producer | Steve Brown
Label | Beggars Banquet
Album | *Love* (1985)

She Sells Sanctuary

"I took a perverse pride from writing as many Top Twenty singles as I did using the same three chords."

Billy Duffy, 2001

◀ **Influenced by: Dazed and Confused** · Led Zeppelin (1969)
▶ **Influence on: Available** · The National (2003)
● **Covered by: Britt Black** (2005) · Keane (2007) · The Dandy Warhols (2007)
★ **Other key track:** Love Removal Machine (1987)

Despite Ian Astbury snarling like Jim Morrison on crystal meth and his "world turns around" refrain, the power of "She Sells Sanctuary" lies in Billy Duffy's unmistakable, hypnotic hook. The guitarist's trademark three-chords-and-the-truth—delivered via his beloved 1970s white Gretsch—turned the song into a two-fingered salute to the post-punk era.

The song's parent album *Love* edged the band from their goth-punk past as Southern Death Cult to a future dominated by AC/DC rhythms and Led Zeppelinesque arrangements. Recording in a studio that Zeppelin had used, Duffy channeled Jimmy Page for the song's intro: "I found a violin bow and started to play the guitar with it [to] amuse Ian."

Of the mixes released on singles, the best loved featured Steve Brown at the helm. The plan was to get Steve Lillywhite, but The Cult's management sent a demo to his office marked simply "To Steve." That office also managed Mr. Brown—so, remarked Duffy, "We got the wrong Steve." Nonetheless, on the strength of this song, Brown secured work with the Manic Street Preachers.

The song proved irresistible and influential. "In Seattle," Astbury recalled, "Andrew Wood from Mother Love Bone [later to spawn Pearl Jam] told me . . . that it gave them a touchstone." The connections didn't end there: "She Sells Sanctuary" was remixed by *Nevermind* producer Butch Vig, and is echoed in "Times Like These," released in 2003 by the Foo Fighters.

"I don't think there could be a Cult show without 'She Sells Sanctuary,'" Ian Astbury observed in 2007. "It just wouldn't be the same, either for us or the audience." **SS**

Close to Me | The Cure (1985)

Writer | Robert Smith
Producer | Robert Smith, David Allen
Label | Fiction
Album | *The Head on the Door* (1985)

"It reminds me of 'Jimmy Mack'—that's the sound I thought it should have."

Robert Smith, 1985

◄ **Influenced by: Jimmy Mack** · Martha & The Vandellas (1966)

► **Influence on: So Human** · Lady Sovereign (2009)

● **Covered by:** Dismemberment Plan (1995) · The Get Up Kids (1999) · -M- (1999) · Kaki King (2008) · I Was a Cub Scout (2008)

"Of all the songs we've written," Cure main-man Robert Smith told *Q*, "'Close to Me' doesn't spring to mind as one of our best. . . . It was a slightly surreal moment on the record and it wasn't even a definite album track during the recording. It was only when I did the vocal and got really extreme on the production, making it really claustrophobic sounding, that it came to life. Up till that point it was average."

Don't be misled by the ever-contrary Smith—after all, he has claimed for two decades that each Cure album and tour will be the last. "Close to Me" is one of their best and most bewitching songs.

Still, contrariness sticks close to "Close to Me." Smith had deliberately attempted a three-minute pop song in the Beatles-meets-Buzzcocks vein of "Boys Don't Cry," yet it was the band's lowest-charting U.K. single in four years. However, the video—written and directed by Tim Pope—became one of their most popular. It featured all five members of the band packed into a wardrobe teetering on a the edge of a cliff. The wardrobe eventually topples over into the sea, filling with water as the band continues to play.

"It was awful . . ." complained Smith to *Record Mirror*. "The most uncomfortable video we've ever done. We spent ten hours in the water." (The story continued in the 1990 clip for a Paul Oakenfold remix, from the *Mixed Up* album: the remix itself reached No. 13 in the U.K. singles chart.)

The song's charm lies in its delicate simplicity and Motown-esque hand claps. "It's the only one on the album that's got no effects or anything on it," Smith chirped. "We recorded it straight off, like you'd do it in a room with just a cassette recorder—the way they used to record things." **BM**

Under Mi Sleng Teng
Wayne Smith (1985)

Writer | Noel Davey, Lloyd James, Ian Smith
Producer | Lloyd James
Label | Jammy's
Album | *Sleng Teng* (1986)

On February 23, 1985, reggae music was changed forever. At a sound system clash in Kingston, Jamaica, DJ/producer Lloyd "Prince Jammy" James blew away the competition when he played what is widely considered to be the first wholly digital reggae "riddim." The moment the bass pounded out of the speakers, there was pandemonium. Digital dancehall, or ragga, was born.

The song came into being when Noel Davey was practicing singing to preset rhythms on his electronic "music box" keyboard. One day he and Wayne Smith slowed down a rock 'n' roll preset—reportedly based on Eddie Cochran's "Somethin' Else"—to a reggae rhythm's pace, and stumbled on the distinctive bassline that formed the basis of the "Sleng Teng" rhythm.

Smith took the track to Prince Jammy, who recorded a number of artists toasting over it, including Smith's own paean to marijuana, "Under Mi Sleng Teng." The track became a massive hit, spawning innumerable imitators.

The digital revolution hit Jamaica's session musicians hard, as producers moved to emulate the "Sleng Teng" sound, casting aside bassists and drummers who had previously played on everything recorded on the island. Jammy himself shelved over fifty "analog" rhythms that he had waiting to be released. As his DJing assistant Tupps said, "the 'Sleng Teng' dominate bad, bad." **DC**

Cruiser's Creek
The Fall (1985)

Writer | Mark E. Smith, Brix Smith
Producer | John Leckie
Label | Beggars Banquet
Album | N/A

One of the few times that The Fall's maverick ship sailed close to commercial waters was in the mid-1980s. Crucial to that development was Mark E. Smith's partnership with American guitarist Laura Elisse Salenger, aka Brix, whom he married in 1983.

The sound remained typically robust—driving drums, thumping bass—but melodies started to creep in. "I don't want to sell forty thousand records, I want to sell a million," Brix told *NME*. "It doesn't really mean anything unless you get a gold disc." (She was to remain unfulfilled.)

"Cruiser's Creek" was formed around a nagging guitar riff, reminiscent of a West Coast garage band. However, if the song was part earworm, it was still part earache on the vocals, with Smith sounding off in his trademark barks and yelps. Mixed in were derisive references to the likes of Red Wedge, the left-wing musical collective that included Billy Bragg and Paul Weller.

In November 1985, "Cruiser's Creek"—which initially found its way onto vinyl versions of *This Nation's Saving Grace* only outside the United Kingdom—was played on the band's second appearance on TV's alternative music showcase *The Tube* (the first had been at the request of DJ John Peel). It was a nationally broadcast reminder that Morrissey, Marr, Rourke, and Joyce weren't the only Smiths from the northwest of England making gloriously addictive sounds in the mid-1980s. **CB**

The Fall's Mark E. Smith, photographed in 1989, signals that he is his own man. ➔

Life in a Northern Town | The Dream Academy (1985)

Writer | Nick Laird-Clowes, Gilbert Gabriel
Producer | D. Gilmour, N. Laird-Clowes, G. Nicholson
Label | Blanco y Negro
Album | *The Dream Academy* (1985)

THE
DREAM
ACADEMY

LIFE IN
A NORTHERN
TOWN

"Romanticism is coming back. You can . . . make beautiful music and not get sneered at."

Kate St. John, 1985

◄ **Influenced by: The Thoughts of Mary Jane**
Nick Drake (1969)
► **Influence on: Sunchyme** · Dario G (1997)
● **Covered by:** Voice Male (2003) · Neema (2006)
★ **Other key tracks:** Test Tape No. 3 (1985) · Poised on the Edge of Forever (1985)

The Dream Academy shone briefly but brightly in the mid-Eighties. Singer/guitarist Nick Laird-Clowes, keyboard player Gilbert Gabriel, and multi-instrumentalist Kate St. John wowed the States in particular, snaring a *Billboard* Top Ten hit with this epic single. A grab bag of pop culture nostalgia and earthy imagery, "Life in a Northern Town" was also sumptuous "big music," powered by strings, chants, thunderous drums, and soaring cor anglais.

Laird-Clowes had earlier surfaced in The Act with Mark Gilmour, brother of Pink Floyd's David. The Floyd guitarist was duly persuaded to produce Laird-Clowes's new project. "We had the benefit of his experience of the Sixties and early Seventies, as well as modern technology," remarked Gabriel in 1985, nailing the peculiar sonics of "Life in a Northern Town." This new opportunity to re-create orchestras at the touch of a button fired The Dream Academy's music.

Alongside an unlikely nod to minimalist composer Steve Reich, the single sleeve featured a dedication to Nick Drake, whom Laird-Clowes acknowledged as an influence, suggesting he had tapped into a "leyline" with the late singer-songwriter when penning the lyrics. The song's eerie whimsy almost bears him out.

Far from Drake's rural idylls, the distinctive chorus chant found a new lease of life in 1997 when British dance producers Dario G built their "Sunchyme" around it, scoring a U.K. hit. Its euphoria was a world away from the original's plaintive, rainswept Northernisms. Laird-Clowes, however, stuck closer to home with writing credits on Pink Floyd's 1994 album *The Division Bell*, and—with Gilmour's assistance—scoring Griffin Dunne's movie *Fierce People* (2005). **MH**

The Whole of the Moon | The Waterboys (1985)

Writer | Mike Scott
Producer | Mike Scott
Label | Ensign
Album | *This Is the Sea* (1985)

"Mike Scott was the best songwriter in the world at that time."

Bono, 2006

◀ **Influenced by: 1999** · Prince (1982)
▶ **Influence on: N17** · The Saw Doctors (1989)
● **Covered by:** Terry Reid (1991) · Jennifer Warnes (1992) Human Drama (1998) · Mandy Moore (2003)
★ **Other key tracks:** Don't Bang the Drum (1985) · This Is the Sea (1985) · Fisherman's Blues (1988)

In the first half of the 1980s, chief Waterboy Mike Scott became known for making "the big music"—a tag derived from a track of the same name on their album *A Pagan Place*, released in 1984. None came bigger than "The Whole of the Moon"; but the song refused to be rushed, either in composition or in popular acclaim.

When recording commenced on *This Is the Sea* in early 1985, "The Whole of the Moon" was, as Scott put it, "markedly unfinished." It had started life on the back of an envelope during a New York winter, but it took until late spring in London to reach a state of completion. (According to Scott, he "couldn't have written" the song without having read Mark Helprin's novel *Winter's Tale*, but denies that the song is about Helprin.)

Such a sweeping song, with lyrics praising the artistic vision of those who had inspired Scott, required an equally epic production. Thanks to keyboards by multi-instrumentalist (and future World Party front man) Karl Wallinger—"a one-man orchestra," according to Scott—and soaring trumpets from Roddy Lorimer, it got one.

But big music didn't guarantee big sales. The track was only a moderate hit (reaching the U.K. Top Thirty) in October 1985. It wasn't until a re-release six years later, promoting a greatest hits album, that an appreciative audience took it into the Top Three. (Scott grumbled good-naturedly that Cher's "The Shoop Shoop Song" had denied him the No. 1 spot.) Recognition also came in the form of an Ivor Novello award in 1991, but Scott was most impressed by the endorsement of Bob Dylan: "He told me he liked 'The Whole of the Moon.' Bob Dylan telling me that he likes a song of mine means a lot." **CB**

Marlene on the Wall | Suzanne Vega (1985)

Writer | Suzanne Vega
Producer | Lenny Kaye, Steve Addabbo
Label | A&M
Album | *Suzanne Vega* (1985)

"I loved Marlene Dietrich for her image. And that cruel streak, which I find attractive. Then I read biographies and feel sad."

Suzanne Vega, 1999

◄ **Influenced by:** Help Me • Joni Mitchell (1974)
► **Influence on:** Marlene Dietrich's Favorite Poem
Peter Murphy (1989)
● **Covered by:** Underwater City People (2005)
★ **Other key tracks:** Neighborhood Girls (1985) • Luka
(1987) • Tom's Diner (1987)

A cult song about a poster doesn't come along often. But, in the mid-Eighties (post-Joni, pre-Jewel), successful female singer-songwriters such as Suzanne Vega were rare too.

A struggling New York musician, Vega was rejected twice by A&M—who thought subtle folk-pop wouldn't sell—before they signed her. Patti Smith's guitarist Lenny Kaye produced her album and "Marlene on the Wall" broke her in the U.K. The success of Vega's cool delivery, Leonard Cohen-inspired lyrics, and acoustic-based music was particularly remarkable in an era when everyone else was trying to be Madonna.

Inspired by a poster of Hollywood legend Marlene Dietrich, Vega wrote about a girl on a voyage of self-discovery. "I went through a fairly promiscuous period . . ." she confessed to *Q*. "It was too hectic. You discover that having sex with virtual strangers is very empty too." Hence "Marlene watches from the wall / Her mocking smile says it all / As she records the rise and fall / Of every soldier passing."

"The idea of using a poster as a reference point is a very pop idea . . ." Vega told *SongTalk*. "As opposed to 'Today I am a small blue thing' [the chorus of another song from her debut album], in which some people think I'm speaking in code. . . . That was a truthful song. The lines came out of my life."

Vega later dismissed "Marlene on the Wall" as "full of detail from my life that might not mean anything to anybody else" and "a little wide of the mark." But this beautiful, breezy song paved the way for her smashes "Luka" (1986) and "Tom's Diner" (1987), and welcomed listeners into two decades of wonderful music. **GK**

How Will I Know | Whitney Houston (1985)

Writer | G. Merrill, S. Rubicam, N. M. Walden
Producer | N. M. Walden
Label | Arista
Album | *Whitney Houston* (1985)

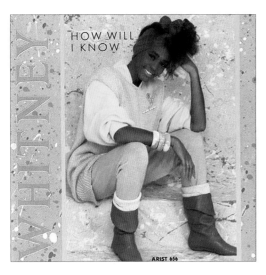

"Hearing the first take of 'How Will I Know' on the phone, we knew we were on to something special."

George Merrill, 1985

◄ **Influenced by: Who's Zoomin' Who?** · Aretha Franklin (1985)
► **Influence on: Waiting for a Star to Fall** · Boy Meets Girl (1988)
● **Covered by:** Dionne Warwick (1985)
The Lemonheads (1996) · Hit the Lights (2008)

Before Bobby Brown, before the substance problems, and before the erratic television appearances, Whitney Houston was a clean-cut superstar, who scored an international smash with this ridiculously catchy, feel-good, pop classic.

"How Will I Know" seemed a perfect song for the young singer with the powerful, gospel-honed voice. But writers George Merrill and Shannon Rubicam originally wrote it with a different woman in mind. "They asked us to write for Janet Jackson's next record . . ." Merrill told *Songfacts*. "They passed on it because it wasn't right for her at the time—she was in the midst of doing her *Control* album."

Jackson's loss was Houston's gain. The cutesy pie lyrics—"I try to phone, but I'm too shy (can't speak)"—dealt with the age-old conundrum, "Do they like me as much as I like them?" The simple R&B beat was given extra oomph by Premik Russell Tubbs's saxophone solo, with an added cherry on top—Houston's extraordinary voice.

Narada Michael Walden produced it, although there was initial reluctance from the songwriters when he wanted to make a few changes. "Narada added his very punchy track and he did some rearranging on it . . ." recalled Rubicam. "So it really was far more powerful than the demo we did."

At one point during the video, Houston sings, "I'm asking you, 'cause you know about these things," while looking up at a screen featuring her godmother, Aretha Franklin. It was a fitting homage, as the melody of "How Will I Know" echoed Franklin's song, and another Walden production, "Who's Zoomin' Who?" Merrill and Rubicam also capitalized on their associations, entering the limelight as Boy Meets Girl. **OM**

Manic Monday
Bangles (1985)

Writer | Christopher (aka Prince)
Producer | David Kahne
Label | Columbia
Album | *Different Light*
(1985)

"Prince sent a message through saying, 'If you want to just use the tracks, you can, and just re-record the vocals,'" said Bangles guitarist Vicki Peterson. "We gratefully declined." Audibly influenced by his own "1999," the Minneapolis maestro composed "Manic Monday" for his *Purple Rain*–era protégées Apollonia 6. However, he pulled it from their album, possibly because Apollonia did not have a good enough voice.

Meanwhile, as Bangles singer Susanna Hoffs told popdose.com, "He heard and saw the video for a song that we did on our first record called 'Hero Takes a Fall.' . . . He started to come to our shows, and he would come up and play a long and amazing guitar solo on that song . . . 'When Doves Cry' was becoming a huge hit on the radio, so it all happened at the same time . . . we hung out a little bit, and we got to know him a little bit."

The quartet decorated "Manic Monday" with their West Coast jangle, bringing Mamas and Papas sunshine to Minneapolis soul. *All Over the Place* (1984) had failed to produce hits, but the new song's appealing cadences and easy chorus took the Bangles to No. 2 in both the United States and the United Kingdom.

Peterson recalled Prince visiting while they cut the track. When they apologized for the lack of keyboards, he whispered, "You don't need the keyboards. It's gonna go." Good spot. **MH**

Sun City | Artists United
Against Apartheid (1985)

Writer | Steven Van Zandt
Producer | Steven Van Zandt,
Arthur Baker
Label | Manhattan
Album | *Sun City* (1985)

Bruce Springsteen and Miles Davis probably didn't have much in common. There was, however, one unifying principle: they weren't going to play Sun City, the luxury resort in South Africa. Dozens of others were also willing to bypass a paycheck to protest the country's apartheid rule. Midway through U.S. President Ronald Reagan's administration, criticized for a policy on apartheid that many believed wasn't tough enough, these "rockers and rappers, united and strong" helped create the decade's greatest protest song.

"Sun City" was the brainchild of guitarist Steven Van Zandt. Having quit Springsteen's band in 1984, he recruited the players, then helped assemble the song. The result justified the effort, as "Sun City" spurred many to think about South Africa for the first time. Naysayers included Joni Mitchell, who objected to the original lyric singling out her friend Linda Ronstadt for playing in South Africa. U.S. radio also largely ignored the song, concerned about its political sentiments.

However, "Sun City" stood out for more than just its significance. Among the first rap-rock hybrids, the song was packed with stirring performances and an irresistible chorus. And, while it may not have influenced the end of apartheid (a decade after the song's release), "Sun City" did achieve the seemingly impossible: persuading Lou Reed to dance on video. **JiH**

Kerosene
Big Black (1986)

Writer | Big Black
Producer | Iain Burgess, Big Black
Label | Homestead
Album | *Atomizer* (1986)

As a kid, Steve Albini spent time in Missoula, a small city in Montana. A recent report found that the northwestern area of the state—which includes Missoula—had the highest rate of illicit drug use in the United States. That has always been one way to make the time pass. On "Kerosene," Albini and his cohorts wrote about other options, as they created Big Black's most fully formed and disturbing track. Courtney Love ambivalently cited the song as one that changed her life.

Intended to make what Albini called "big-ass vicious noise that makes my head spin," the band's debut album moved up several gears from the EPs that preceded it. *Atomizer* was still an all-out attack, but there was art at work, too. Albini's guitar sounded like he was coaxing clashing chimes from broken glass. The unsettling mood it created was the perfect welcome for what followed. Big Black's tackling of taboo topics often brought fierce criticism, and "Kerosene" was no different, being interpreted as concerning the gang rape and murder (using kerosene) of a woman.

Bassist Dave Riley disagreed: "The song is about American small towns where life is so boring, there's only two things to do: go blow up a whole load of stuff for fun, or have a lot of sex with the one girl in town who'll have sex with anyone. 'Kerosene' is about a guy who tries to combine the two pleasures." Uneasy but essential listening. **CB**

Ay te dejo en San Antonio
Flaco Jiménez (1986)

Writer | Santiago Jiménez
Producer | Chris Strachwitz
Label | Arhoolie
Album | *Ay te dejo en San Antonio y mas!* (1986)

Flaco Jiménez is the master-blaster of Tex-Mex Conjunto music. Born Leonardo (the nickname "Flaco" means "skinny") and raised in the southern Texas city of San Antonio, Jiménez is the best-known Mexican accordionist. His ability to cook up a spicy musical chilli has led the likes of Ry Cooder, The Rolling Stones, Dwight Yoakam, The Chieftains, and many others to call upon him. But it is as a solo artist and as a member of two Texan ensembles, The Texas Tornadoes and Los Super Seven, that he has enjoyed his greatest successes.

Flaco was schooled by his father, master accordionist Santiago Jiménez. Playing Mexican-American events, Flaco learned not only how to play accordion and sing but also how to work a crowd. He was befriended by rising San Antonio rocker Doug Sahm and began to cross over into rock and country music. Sahm and Jiménez would regularly play together, later forming The Texas Tornadoes (with Freddy Fender and Augie Meyers). Working with Arhoolie Records, he brought his particular brand of Mexican conjunto music to a much wider audience than any artist before.

"Ay te dejo en San Antonio" (I'm Going to Leave You in San Antonio) is a song Flaco learned from his father, and it won him the first of his (so far) five Grammy awards. With its traditional roots and Flaco's dynamic delivery, the song powerfully demonstrated the strength of Tex-Mex music. **GC**

Time of No Reply
Nick Drake (1986)

Writer | Nick Drake
Producer | Frank Kornelussen, Joe Boyd
Label | Hannibal
Album | *Time of No Reply* (1986)

"Time of No Reply"—one of Nick Drake's earliest studio recordings, from late 1968—features the singer-songwriter in stripped-down form. A solo performance on acoustic guitar, it is a blues-inspired, autumnal number that hints at the darkness to come in Drake's all-too-brief life.

The lyrics muse on a sense of youthful alienation: "The sun went down and the crowd went home / I was left by the roadside all alone / I turned to speak as they went by / But this was the time of no reply." The sparse arrangement lends it a pensive quality, yet the melodic folk guitar endows the song with a glimmer of optimism.

The track was mooted for inclusion on Drake's debut LP *Five Leaves Left*, but was relegated to the vaults when other compositions took precedence. In 1986, for the CD release of 1979's posthumous *Fruit Tree* box set, Drake's friend and producer Joe Boyd supplemented his three original albums with a set of unreleased recordings. This album, *Time of No Reply*, opened with the title track, first revealed some eighteen years after it was recorded.

In 2004 came further rare recordings. *Made to Love Magic* included a version of "Time of No Reply," augmented with an arrangement by Robert Kirby, who had provided orchestration for *Five Leaves Left*. Based on Kirby's original score from 1968, this "new" version proved a fascinating and worthy footnote to the song's history. **JL**

Wide Open Road
The Triffids (1986)

Writer | David McComb
Producer | Gil Norton, The Triffids
Label | White Hot
Album | *Born Sandy Devotional* (1986)

For a band that had no significant hits, Perth-based indie rockers The Triffids cast a long shadow across Australian music. They were fronted by the booming, dread-filled voice of charismatic singer David McComb, who also wrote the bulk of their most distinctive material, conjuring a quintessentially Australian sense of place.

This cinematic song did that best. Over a brooding bass line, punctuated by a startling gunshot snare motif, McComb raged at a lover's desertion: "I drove out over the flatlands / Hunting down you and him." A minimal but hugely effective arrangement was embellished with chiming guitar and "Evil" Graham Lee's subtle pedal-steel licks, over a metronomic, Suicide-influenced beat. McComb recalled: "It seemed to naturally evoke . . . the stretch of highway in between Caiguna and Norseman, where The Triffids' Hiace [van] monotonously came to grief with kangaroos."

"Wide Open Road" limped to No. 64 in the Australian singles chart, though it fared better in Britain. But it was not until 2008 that they were inducted into the Australian Recording Industry Association's Hall of Fame—too late for McComb, whose transplanted heart gave out on February 2, 1999, three days after a minor car accident.

Fellow Aussies, including Weddings Parties Anything and The Church, have covered the song, but no one has matched the original. **JLu**

There Is a Light That Never Goes Out | The Smiths (1986)

Writer | Morrissey, Johnny Marr
Producer | Morrissey, Johnny Marr
Label | Rough Trade
Album | *The Queen Is Dead* (1986)

THE SMITHS

"When we first played it, I thought it was the best song I'd ever heard."

Johnny Marr, 1993

◀ **Influenced by: There She Goes Again** • The Velvet Underground (1967)
▶ **Influence on: Losing My Religion** • R.E.M. (1991)
● **Covered by:** The Divine Comedy (1996) • Neil Finn (2001) • The Ocean Blue (2002) • The Magic Numbers (2006) • Noel Gallagher (2009)

"There Is a Light That Never Goes Out" has become The Smiths' defining song, not because it is their most beautiful, moving, witty, or poignant—although it is all of these things—but because it is the one that best captures what the band appeared to represent. "There Is a Light . . ." could have been the hit the band craved (they never rose higher than No. 10), but guitarist Johnny Marr preferred to release the rockier "The Boy with the Thorn in His Side," and the moment was lost.

The Smiths have always been typecast as purveyors of music for the most miserable souls among us, a finding that misses the humor of singer Morrissey's lyrics and the vibrancy of Marr's rhythms—"I wanted," said Marr, "to be Phil Spector with a guitar." "There Is a Light . . ." is undeniably melancholic, with stirring strings and maudlin vocals, but the gloom is offset by the beautiful music and unique lyrics. Morrissey seemed, at this point in his career, incapable of writing a dull line, and "There Is a Light . . ." is sharply immediate. He imagines lovers driving in a town in which the narrator no longer feels welcome: "Driving in your car / I never, never want to go home / Because I haven't got one / Any more."

There is the trademarked sexual reticence—"And in the darkened underpass / I thought: Oh God, my chance has come at last / But then a strange fear gripped me and I just couldn't ask"—but also affecting melodrama: "And if a ten-ton truck / Kills the both of us / To die by your side / Well, the pleasure, the privilege, is mine." Stirring stuff, which some believe was directed at Marr himself, and which has delighted bedroom brooders ever since. A live version by Morrissey, issued in 2005, confirmed its timeless appeal. **PW**

Some Candy Talking | The Jesus and Mary Chain (1986)

Writer | Jim Reid, William Reid
Producer | The Jesus and Mary Chain
Label | Blanco y Negro
Album | N/A

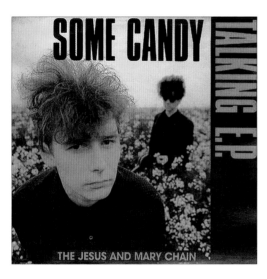

" 'Candy' is just a nice word."

Jim Reid, 1986

◀ **Influenced by: I'm Waiting for the Man** • The Velvet Underground (1967)
▶ **Influence on: Teen Age Riot** • Sonic Youth (1988)
● **Covered by:** Richard Hawley (2006) • The Caulfield Sisters (2006)
★ **Other key track:** Never Understand (1985)

Scottish duo The Jesus and Mary Chain were punk rock in all but their sound. They had a bratty, defiant snarl, fought with their label over the use of profanity in song titles, and were infamous for twenty-minute live sets that provoked crowds to violence. Yet the group's brand of post-punk, so melodic at its core, had more in common with The Shangri-Las than the Sex Pistols.

Brothers Jim and William Reid had honed their blend of searing, Velvet Underground-style guitar and pretty, Beach Boys-esque melodies by the time they recorded *Psychocandy* in 1985. However, "Some Candy Talking"—often considered to be their finest song—didn't make the cut for that noise-pop masterpiece.

The tune appeared a few months later on an EP bearing the same title. The sneering, leering song—juxtaposing Jim Reid's brittle vocal delivery with a mountain of electric feedback—was unlike anything most listeners had heard before. The lyrics seemed sweet and simple, relaying the story of a man going to meet the girl he adores— although some believed "Candy" to be a reference to heroin. Reid sings: "To see if I can get a taste tonight / A taste of something warm and sweet / That shivers your bones and rises to your heat." But, the singer protested to *NME* at the time, "It isn't, and I don't think anybody would think so."

The BBC *did* think so, and banned it, but "Some Candy Talking" crashed the U.K. Top Twenty anyway. More significantly, it secured the Mary Chain's rank as founding fathers of noise-pop, shoegazing, and alt-rock. And, two years later, William came clean to the *Observer:* "It's obvious to us now that it *was* a drug song and all the people who criticized us at the time were right." **JiH**

No Sleep Till Brooklyn
Beastie Boys (1986)

Writer | Michael "Mike D" Diamond, Adam "King Ad-Rock" Horovitz, Adam "MCA" Yauch, Rick Rubin
Producer | Rick Rubin, Beastie Boys
Label | Def Jam
Album | *Licensed to Ill* (1986)

"If you're not gonna have as much equipment as AC/DC," observed Mike D, "you really shouldn't play instruments." The Beastie Boys duly ditched pluckily played punk for hip-hop—and created rap's first U.S. chart-topping album with *Licensed to Ill*. It was essentially a white take on Run-DMC, whose pioneering blend of rock and rap the Beasties took to a new level. Most notably, "No Sleep Till Brooklyn"—the title adapted from Motörhead's *No Sleep 'til Hammersmith*—was based on a riff from the 1975 classic "T.N.T." by AC/DC (whose "Back in Black" they had sampled on 1984's "Rock Hard").

The metal link was secured with the recruitment of guitarist Kerry King from Slayer, who were recording the Rick Rubin-produced thrash landmark *Reign in Blood*. "We were in the same studio," King told writer Alan Light, "and [Rubin] came down and said, 'Hey, what do you think about doing the lead down the hallway?' . . . It took five minutes. It might have taken two takes, because it wasn't supposed to be anything intricate. They were spoofing metal, so to speak."

The song remains a favorite, thanks in part to its inclusion in 2008's *Guitar Hero World Tour*. However, the Beasties have been heard to amend its lyrics in concert. "MCA's in the back 'cos he's skeezin' with a ho," for example, has become "MCA's in the back at the mahjong hall." **GK**

Raining Blood
Slayer (1986)

Writer | Jeff Hanneman, Kerry King
Producer | Rick Rubin, Slayer
Label | Def Jam
Album | *Reign in Blood* (1986)

Consistently voted thrash metal's finest album, Slayer's *Reign in Blood* is bookended by horrific songs, executed at insane speeds. The opener, "Angel of Death," is infamous for its controversial lyrics. The numbingly fast finale, "Raining Blood," pulls off the near-impossible task of being thematically interesting as well as making grown men want to run down the street uprooting trees. Make no mistake: it's *that* good.

Privately regarding devil worship as laughable hokum, guitarists and songwriters Kerry King and Jeff Hanneman were nonetheless in fully satanic mode at this point in Slayer's career, writing songs that merrily invoked Old Nick. ("To a Journey fan, we suck," King conceded to *Kerrang!*.) Still, it was *fun* hokum and annoyed the establishment. In "Raining Blood" (a pun on the album title), Satan sits in a hellish cavern, while blood rains on him from sinners impaled on stalactites. Or is he a serial killer? No one knows, including the band.

"Raining Blood" is distinguished by its recurring lead guitar riff, abrupt changes in tempo, and singer Tom Araya's gleefully morbid vocals. "Now I shall reign in blood!" he bellows, before the song's apocalyptic climax leaves the listener trembling as it devolves into sounds of a thunderstorm— actually the bloody precipitation of the title. It is the perfect ending to the perfect metal album, and is unlikely to be bettered. **JMc**

Beastie Boys in the mid-Eighties: from left, Mike D, MCA, and King Ad-Rock.

First We Take Manhattan | Jennifer Warnes (1986)

Writer | Leonard Cohen
Producer | C. Roscoe Beck, Jennifer Warnes
Label | Cypress
Album | *Famous Blue Raincoat* (1986)

"I did know what it meant at the time I wrote it."

Leonard Cohen, 1988

◀ **Influenced by: Masters of War** · Bob Dylan (1963)
▶ **Influence on: Democracy** · Leonard Cohen (1992)
● **Covered by:** R.E.M. (1991) · Warren Zevon (1991) · Joe Cocker (2000) · Tyskarna från Lund (2003) · Sirenia (2004) · Maxx Klaxon (2005) · Boris Grebenshchikov (2005)

Jennifer Warnes had greater commercial moments than *Famous Blue Raincoat*. The shortlist includes "Up Where We Belong" and "(I've Had) the Time of My Life"—both soundtrack hits that won Academy Awards. Artistically, however, nothing suited her better than that collection of Leonard Cohen songs. The legendary Canadian poet had befriended Warnes in the early Seventies, hiring the Seattle songbird as a backing vocalist. Once the latter's star had commercially eclipsed that of her mentor, she used her position to spread the word about him. *Famous Blue Raincoat* included several Cohen staples but opened with a song that fans had yet to hear. "While she was preparing to record," Cohen told *Q* magazine, "she heard 'First We Take Manhattan' and wanted to do it."

With lyrics that were hypnotically poetic, dense, and deceiving, the song bristled with drama. In biting and tongue-in-cheek ways it addressed narcissism and fascism, but other avenues for thought were revealed with each spin. "'First We Take Manhattan' is Leonard Cohen being prophetic," Warnes told the *Austin-American Statesman*. "He won't admit it. But I think he sensed what was going to happen. He called it—back in those days, before 9/11—a terrorist's song."

Cohen released his own version on *I'm Your Man* in 1988, and R.E.M. and Joe Cocker were among those who took shots at it later—on *I'm Your Fan* and *No Ordinary World* respectively. What sells Warnes's rendition is her warm, graceful voice and all-star band, which included guitarist Stevie Ray Vaughan burning through one of his best leads. "First We Take Manhattan" was further confirmation of what this singer could accomplish with the right song. **JiH**

True Colors | Cyndi Lauper (1986)

Writer | Tom Kelly, Billy Steinberg
Producer | Cyndi Lauper, Lennie Petze
Label | Portrait
Album | *True Colors* (1986)

"It was like I'd peeled off everything on the surface and that was the real me there—real feelings."

Cyndi Lauper, 1987

◀ **Influenced by: Bridge Over Troubled Water**
Simon & Garfunkel (1970)
▶ **Influence on: Shining Through** · Fredro Starr
featuring Jill Scott (2001)
● **Covered by:** Leatherface (2000) · Sarina Paris (2001)
Erlend Bratland (2008)

The world had seen various facets of Cyndi Lauper's musical character: the explosive-haired rabble-rouser on "Girls Just Want to Have Fun," the credible balladeer on "Time After Time," even the onanist's friend on "She Bop." But "True Colors," the first single from her second album, brought everything back to basics, artifice stripped away. It was a risk—handsomely repaid by a U.S. No. 1.

"True Colors" was the work of Tom Kelly and Billy Steinberg, writers of Madonna's "Like a Virgin." Steinberg had intended it to be a song about his mother, but Kelly persuaded him to broaden its subject to universal sympathy ("Show me a smile then / Don't be unhappy . . ."), and provided the you've-got-a-friend appeal of the first verse. Together the writers fashioned a cheering gospel song akin to The Beatles' "Let It Be" or a more ornate version of Bill Withers's "Lean on Me." Lauper, however, had other ideas.

To the delight of Steinberg (Songfacts reported him saying, "It was so much more adventurous than our demo"), the singer's co-production with Lennie Petze let the words speak for themselves. The arrangement was stark yet pretty, and Lauper's childlike speech guided the melody. "I did everything I could to get across the pure emotion . . ." she told *Creem*. "I wanted it to be really internal, to go right inside." Her close, unadorned delivery hit the mark.

Many have covered "True Colors," from Elaine Paige and Eva Cassidy to Phil Collins and Aztec Camera. But few could hope to equal the heart and soul of Lauper's original. "She produced it and did a beautiful job," Steinberg enthused. "That song, more than any other song I've written . . . seems to have the most universal appeal." **MH**

Move Your Body
Marshall Jefferson (1986)

Writer | Marshall Jefferson
Producer | Virgo (Marshall Jefferson, Adonis Smith, Vince Lawrence)
Label | Trax
Album | N/A

"You can't make one song and say you deserve to be a millionaire," Marshall Jefferson told *The Face* in 1994. He should know: having had a hand in Sterling Void's "It's Alright," Ten City's "Devotion," Liquid's "Sweet Harmony," and his own "Move Your Body—the House Music Anthem," he influenced dance records for the best part of a decade.

In the early Eighties, when U.S. disco had gone underground, Jefferson was introduced to its offspring at Chicago's Music Box club. "My only perspective on disco had been very negative," he told *NME*, "so I knew what I didn't like about it: the commercial sound. When I first went to the Music Box and heard this really black dance music, 'deep house,' the heaviness hit me, and I knew I liked it."

He began making his own demos, and scored a few club hits, but it was "Move Your Body" that set him on the road to becoming a godfather of house. Originally released as a four-track demo—*Move, Dub, Drum and House Your Body*—it was refined by Jefferson after his label declined to pay $1,600 for the twenty-four-track epic that he was planning. Its distinctive use of a piano was so innovative that many refused to call it house.

Anyone who has ever raved into the small hours will know the spine-shiver elicited by the opening piano riff before the addictively bouncy beat and rhythmic strings kick in. "Lost in house music is where I want to be"—millions were. **GK**

Rise
Public Image Ltd (1986)

Writer | John Lydon, Bill Laswell
Producer | John Lydon, Bill Laswell
Label | Virgin
Album | *Album* (1986)

Public Image Ltd's album of 1984, *This Is What You Want . . . This Is What You Get*, was an unworthy successor to the likes to *Flowers of Romance* and *Metal Box*. But any suspicion that ex-Sex Pistol John Lydon was a spent force whose anger had become diluted was set straight by "Rise"—its lyrics inspired by torture techniques in apartheid-era South Africa. "'Rise' is quotes from some of the victims," Lydon told *Smash Hits*. "I put them together because I thought it fitted in aptly with my own feelings about daily existence."

The logical choice would have been to set such incendiary words to abrasive music. Lydon wrongfooted everyone by framing them in something much more seductive—with, appropriately enough, an almost world music feel. The lineup included jazz drummer Tony Williams and keyboard wizard Ryuichi Sakamoto.

Complementing the unusual music, Lydon countered the oft-quoted lyric "Anger is an energy" ("It sure beats apathy," he told KROQ) with the Irish blessing, "May the road rise with you." Another talking point was the single's packaging. Called precisely that—"Single"—on the sleeve, it was a pastiche of consumerism that extended to the parent album, cassette, and CD releases. "You can't keep pumping out happy-go-lucky records and completely avoid reality," declared Lydon. No chance of that here. **CB**

Public Image Limited's John Lydon rises onstage, 1986. ➡

Love Can't Turn Around | Farley "Jackmaster" Funk (1986)

Writer | V. Lawrence, J. Saunders, I. Hayes, D. Pandy
Producer | Keith Farley, Jesse Saunders
Label | House
Album | N/A

"House is a 4/4 beat with some sounds around it. How can you lose?"

Farley "Jackmaster" Funk, 2006

◀ **Influenced by: I Can't Turn Around** · Isaac Hayes (1975)
▶ **Influence on: Flowerz** · Armand Van Helden (1999)
● **Covered by:** BustaFunk (2000)
★ **Other key tracks: All Acid Out** (1986) · **The Funk Is On** (1986) · **It's You** (1987)

"Now this is how it started, my dream's all broken-hearted." The first line of "Love Can't Turn Around" could well sum up the feelings of Chicago DJ Steve "Silk" Hurley about his roommate's platinum-selling smash.

Hurley had been putting on house music nights and sharing an apartment with fellow DJ Farley "Funkin'" Keith Williams—before the latter changed his name to Farley "Jackmaster" Funk. But their friendship faltered over "Love Can't Turn Around." Hurley had been playing an instrumental reedit of an old Isaac Hayes song, "I Can't Turn Around," which he had rechristened "Love Can't Turn Around." He alleged that his former friend appropriated it. "Farley's a sharp guy," he told *i-D* magazine. "He's the hottest radio DJ in town, but he's not an artist." (Hurley soon scored a hit of his own with "Jack Your Body.")

By whatever means he achieved the track, Farley had his instrumental backing, but still needed a vocal. Vince Lawrence provided the verses, based on unrequited love for a girl who was "just a friend." But, by the early hours of their final day in the studio, Farley and producer Jesse Saunders still had no singer to deliver them.

Enter the larger-than-life Darryl Pandy, who had been pestering the DJs for two years to put him on a record. They were sceptical—"I sing a little better than Luther [Vandross]," Pandy announced—but desperate times call for desperate measures. As Vince Lawrence recalled, "We brought this guy in, and he sang the fuck out of that tune." Two decades' worth of reissues and remixes confirm that, whatever its origins, this house classic—the first to chart in the United Kingdom—will never fail to fill dance floors. **DC**

Dear God | XTC (1986)

Writer | Andy Partridge
Producer | Todd Rundgren
Label | Virgin
Album | *Skylarking* (1986)

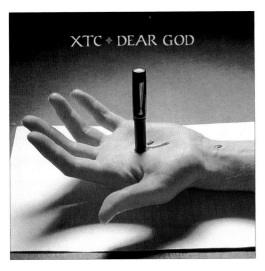

"A lot of people felt threatened by that song. It was sort of a kick below the Bible belt, if you will."

Andy Partridge, 2000

◀ **Influenced by:** God · John Lennon (1970)
▶ **Influence on:** One of Us · Joan Osborne (1995)
● **Covered by:** Sarah McLachlan (1996) · Tricky (2003)
★ **Other key tracks:** Making Plans for Nigel (1979)
Generals and Majors (1980) · Ball and Chain (1982)
Senses Working Overtime (1982)

Having claimed, in 1966, to be "more popular than Jesus," John Lennon discovered that making controversial, religious comments in the United States was not a great idea. But for XTC—a band often labeled as Beatlesesque—something similar two decades later proved to be a career-saver. According to bassist Colin Moulding, their record label was "only days away from letting us go." Then "Dear God," front man Andy Partridge's angry letter to the Almighty, started picking up airplay—enough for it to be promoted from a B-side.

The song was Partridge's way of divesting himself of what he perceived as the shackles of organized religion. "I was killing off the last shreds of doubt in my mind about the existence of God," he said. "All that stuff they punched into me as a kid." Although *Skylarking* was initially released without the track, it was quickly slotted into subsequent pressings (displacing "Mermaid Smiled"), and the song undoubtedly became a key factor in the album's success.

At producer Todd Rundgren's inspired suggestion, the opening verse was sung by a child—a young girl named Jasmine Veillette (although a boy lip-synced to her voice in the video). Partridge himself doubted that the lyric was convincing: "How do you fit into a three-and-a-half-minute nursery rhyme/political idea such a massive subject?" But it was convincing enough for him to receive hate mail, while a radio station in Florida was threatened with a firebombing. "I found that," he marveled, "so medieval."

It was certainly an unusual formula for career rehabilitation. "It really pissed off some people," Partridge told *Mojo*, "but I'm glad it did. As a song, though, I still think it's a petulant failure." **CB**

Don't Want to Know If You Are Lonely | Hüsker Dü (1986)

Writer | Grant Hart
Producer | Bob Mould, Grant Hart
Label | Warner Bros.
Album | *Candy Apple Grey* (1986)

Hüsker Dü's guitarist Bob Mould and drummer Grant Hart blueprinted two generations of music. Their evolution—from the frantic thrash of 1981's *Land Speed Record* to the chiming, mature pop of their later work—was no hasty, cynical shift. The double set *Zen Arcade* of 1984 scattered melodic gems between chainsaw punk, while 1985's *New Day Rising* and *Flip Your Wig* fused jagged attacks with conventional songcraft.

The trio (completed by bassist Greg Norton) left hardcore imprint SST for Warner Bros. in 1986. Their major-label debut, *Candy Apple Grey*, pitted punk blasts like "Crystal" against acoustic laments and tortured piano balladry. However, the strongest track returned to their established formula—but with newfound focus and skill.

"Don't Want to Know If You Are Lonely" is one of the great breakup songs. Hart's lyrics smarted with the vulnerability and paranoia of a post-relationship aftermath, torn between fears that his ex was still pining for him and that the ex was with someone else. Set to a nagging melody and one of Mould's patented, searing hooks, it became the lead single from *Candy Apple Grey*.

It never charted, and Hüsker Dü split following 1987's *Warehouse: Songs and Stories*. However, groups like the Pixies and Nirvana rode Hart and Mould's formula—nuanced lyrics, punk dynamics, pop melodies—to the mainstream. **SC**

Kiss | Prince & The Revolution (1986)

Writer | Prince
Producer | Prince & The Revolution
Label | Paisley Park
Album | *Parade* (1986)

Less than a fortnight after completing the *Purple Rain* tour—and just before the release of *Around the World in a Day*—Prince began to record his next album. As he sped through songs for *Parade*, his protégés Mazarati were in an adjoining studio with producer David Rivkin, aka David Z.

When Mazarati asked for a song, Prince popped into another room and conjured a demo for "Kiss." "It was just an acoustic guitar version," recalled Rivkin in Per Nilsen's book *DanceMusicSexRomance—Prince: the First Decade*. "So I had the license to go nuts and do whatever I wanted with it. We stayed up all night and we made that track the song we're familiar with."

The next day, Prince was astonished to hear a full-blooded version, with bass (which he subsequently omitted), drums, piano, and Mazarati on vocals—and promptly took the song back. He did, however, grant an "arranged by" credit to Rivkin, and "background voice" to Mazarati. "We were flattered," the band's Tony Christian allowed, "that Prince would even put something that we had done on his record." Rivkin said: "As far as I'm concerned, he has paid me back over and over."

Prince's distributors, Warner Bros., were not impressed. "They said, 'We can't put this out,'" recalled Rivkin. "'There's no bass and it sounds like a demo.'" However, aided by a mischievous video, "Kiss" became the maestro's third U.S. No. 1. **BM**

Prince returns to the mic in a London club following a show at Wembley Arena in 1986. ➡

Attencion Na SIDA
Franco (1987)

Writer | Franco
Producer | Uncredited
Label | African Sun Music
Album | *Attention Na SIDA* (1987)

François Luambo Makiadi—aka "Franco"—was a Congolese composer, singer, and guitarist, whose influence on African popular music is unrivaled. "Attention na SIDA" (Beware of AIDS), about the looming HIV/AIDS pandemic, was both his masterpiece and his swan song. Within eighteen months of its release, he had succumbed to a mysterious wasting disease, believed to be the one against which he had campaigned so urgently.

Franco's songs often voiced social commentary but, under the iron rule of President Mobutu, artists usually had to cloak their words in metaphor. There's nothing cryptic here, though. Over an infectiously stuttering, folkloric rhythm, backed by spiraling guitars, Franco called on the world's finest minds to "conquer this plague."

Franco delivered much of his message in crystal-clear French to reach the widest possible audience. He alternated between his trademark speak-singing, and doomy, spoken-word entreaties, punctuating verses with the infectious chorus "Look after your body, and I'll look after mine."

Franco wrote the song when he was in Paris. Keen to capture it when it was fresh, he recruited Victoria Eleison, a Zairean group visiting Europe at the time. Franco's introductory guitar riff recycled part of the pornographic "Jacky," a song that once landed him in jail for a month. The irony was probably intentional. **JLu**

Under the Milky Way
The Church (1987)

Writer | Karin Jansson, Steve Kilbey
Producer | The Church, Greg Ladanyi, Waddy Wachtel
Label | Mushroom
Album | *Starfish* (1987)

Although a sensation in their homeland from the get-go, this Australian quartet took the long road to international success. The trek included charting nine singles and releasing four albums Down Under, as well as getting the boot from two major international labels. The path eventually led to Los Angeles—where they recorded the song that would change their fortunes.

Written by bassist/vocalist Steve Kilbey and his then-girlfriend Karin Jansson, "Under the Milky Way" was a moody, hypnotic masterpiece that beguiled everyone. The moony-eyed lyrics conveyed untold despair, undefined (and unrequited) longing, and deeply poetic imagery.

With eye-popping instrumentation—built on twelve-string acoustic guitar, yet possessing a near-symphonic wallop—the package came across like an anthem for, well, something. "There are songs that operate as a premise for you to have your own adventure," Kilbey said. "'Under the Milky Way' is definitely one of those songs."

It was also the band's first international hit, charting in the Top Forty in the United States and elsewhere. The Church couldn't capitalize on this success, however, and their star soon faded—except in Australia, where they still boast a loyal following. A startling range of cover artists—from Kill Hannah to Echo & The Bunnymen and Zero 7 singer Sia—testifies to their legacy. **JiH**

Bamboleo
Gipsy Kings (1987)

Writer | Tonino Baliardo, Jahloul Bouchikhi, Simon Diaz, Nicolas Reyes
Producer | Dominique Perrier
Label | P.E.M.
Album | *Gipsy Kings* (1987)

When "Bamboleo" became a hit, many thought it just another Euro-pop confection, to be sung all summer, then forgotten. Instead, the Gipsy Kings became the world's most famous Gypsy musicians.

This family band emerged in France from the Provençal Gitan community who journey every May to Les Saintes-Maries-de-la-Mer to celebrate Sara-la-Kali, their patron saint. In the 1960s, flamenco singer Jose Reyes and his sons met their cousins at these festivals and formed Los Reyes.

Inspired by Catalan Gypsy singer Peret's mixing of flamenco with Latin rumba rhythms, they developed their dynamic dance music. After Jose Reyes's death in the 1970s, his son Nicolas became the band's lead vocalist. Jose's son-in-law, Jahloul "Chico" Bouchikhi, completed the lineup.

"Bamboleo" (sung in a Gitan blend of Spanish, Catalan, and Romany) was based on "Caballo Viejo" (Old Horse) by Venezuelan singer Simon Diaz. The Gipsy Kings reinvented the song until they had created a roaring, rumba-flamenco anthem.

Its pumping rhythm and catchy chorus helped their album sell over seven million copies, and the band became international stars. "The reason for the incredible success of the Gipsy Kings is that you can feel the fingers flying over the neck . . ." David Bowie enthused to *Q*. "There's nothing there—just these guys playing guitars. And that in itself is theater, because it's so stunningly real." **GC**

This Corrosion
The Sisters of Mercy (1987)

Writer | Andrew Eldritch
Producer | Jim Steinman
Label | Merciful Release
Album | *Floodland* (1987)

It took the epic visions of front man Andrew Eldritch and producer Jim Steinman to create The Sisters of Mercy's biggest hit. Eldritch was an introvert whose dislike of the "goth rock" tag made him desperate to escape the niche in which his band had been placed. Steinman, meanwhile, had spent a decade in demand after composing the most over-the-top album ever made, Meat Loaf's *Bat Out of Hell*.

"This Corrosion," Eldritch told *Q*, "just demanded Steinman's touch, if 'touch' is discreet enough a word for what he does. Whenever I said, 'Isn't that slightly over the top?' he'd say, 'No.'" Together they conjured the fiendishly effective idea of recording the New York Choral Society and multi-tracking the tapes to make dozens of singers sound like hundreds. The Wagnerian results were bolted onto an electronic pop song—nearly nine minutes even in demo form—that was equal parts New Order and The Addams Family.

The elliptical lyrics were inspired by the exit of guitarist Wayne Hussey (founder of The Mission). "It is, of course, directed at somebody," Eldritch told *Melody Maker*. "I find it embarrassing watching people humiliate themselves for their absurd idea of rock 'n' roll." The chorus—"Hey now, hey now now, sing this corrosion to me"—still elicits sing-alongs at Sisters shows. As Eldritch proudly declared, "It's my war cry." **JMc**

Camarón
Pata Negra (1987)

Writer | C. Lancero, R. Amador, R. Pachón
Producer | Ricardo Pachón
Label | Nuevos Medios
Album | *Blues de la Frontera* (1987)

The most celebrated movers and shakers of Spain's 1980s flamenco revival, Pata Negra ("black leg") took their name from the tastiest type of Iberian ham that money can buy. The core of the group was Raimundo Amador Fernández and his brother Rafael, and they pushed flamenco into exciting new territory, fusing it with blues in a style they dubbed *bluslería*. *Blues de la Frontera*, their last album together, was voted the top album of the decade in the Spanish music press.

"Camarón" is an homage to their friend and colleague, the celebrated flamenco singer Camarón de la Isla. The music is an unlikely but perfectly judged fusion of bluesy electric guitar licks and a flamenco rhythm based on the 12/8 meter of *tanguillos de Cádiz*. This is one of the many *palos* (styles) of flamenco that have originated in Cádiz, the city with which Camarón is most strongly associated.

It was actually in their hometown of Seville that Raimundo first met Camarón, along with his guitarist Paco de Lucía. Later, Raimundo would collaborate with them on the album *La Leyenda del Tiempo* (1979), playing Spanish guitar alongside the great Tomatito. After a stint in the band Veneno (named after its founder Kiko Veneno), the brothers formed Pata Negra. They eventually split over "musical differences" but have re-formed several times. **JLu**

Amandari
Ali Farka Touré (1987)

Writer | Ali Farka Touré
Producer | Nick Gold
Label | World Circuit
Album | *Ali Farka Touré* (1987)

Ali Farka Touré was one of the most revered artists from Mali—a poor, landlocked country often perceived as the original source of the blues. He was dubbed "the bluesman of Africa" and "the African John Lee Hooker"—and, of all his songs, "Amandrai" most closely bears this out.

Touré first recorded "Amandrai" at Radio Mali in the 1970s. The song is about serenading a secret lover—termed "my little sister"—by means of music. Its rhythm and melody are typical of songs in Tamascheq, the language of the Touareg—just one of several in which Touré sang. (When he first heard John Lee Hooker and Albert King, he declared, "This music has been taken from here," noting that it was close to Tamascheq music.)

"Amandrai" received its first international release on Touré's striking, self-titled 1987 album. The CD version included a studio recording with just his guitar and voice, as well as one recorded live in London, with the click and boom of percussion.

Touré revisited it in a fuller arrangement on the Grammy-winning *Talking Timbuktu* (1994), recorded in Los Angeles. His group, Asco, contributed percussion, joined by John Patitucci on acoustic bass, Jim Keltner on subtle drums, and Ry Cooder. "We did that record in three days," Cooder told the BBC in 2006 (the year of Touré's death). "We could have done [it] in one day except that I had to go to bed and he didn't." **JLu**

Ali Farka Touré's music found ready appreciation among Westerners attuned to the blues.

Push It | Salt-N-Pepa (1987)

Writer | Hurby "Luv Bug" Azor, Ray Davies
Producer | Hurby "Luv Bug" Azor
Label | Next Plateau
Album | N/A

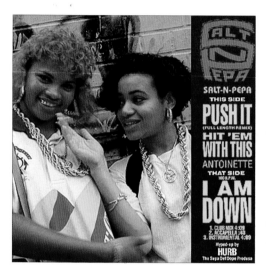

"They were like real women, you know what I mean?"

Amy Winehouse, 2004

◄ **Influenced by: The Bird** • The Time (1984)
▶ **Influence on: Money Honey** • Lady Gaga (2008)
● **Covered by:** Numb (1996) • Ten Masked Men (2000) Harry (2003) • Girls Aloud (2008)
★ **Other key tracks:** Tramp (1987) • My Mic Sounds Nice (1987)

"This dance ain't for everybody / Only the sexy people." With this paraphrasing of Prince protégés The Time, Salt-N-Pepa set the tone for their breakthrough hit: a slice of pop-rap heaven, boasting raunchy riffs and sassy lyrics—"Can't you hear the music's pumpin' hard, like I wish you would?" "We was," admitted Cheryl "Salt" James, "a little raw back in the day."

The addictive hook and spunky rapping—including a quote from The Kinks' "You Really Got Me," released in 1964—made it a dance floor perennial. "The music," enthused *People*, "more melodic and complex than most rap, gives the record an incredible twist."

"Push It" was originally the flipside to "Tramp." "We recorded it in [rapper] Fresh Gordon's bathroom," Salt told *Essence*. "We needed something quick for the B-side because we wanted to put out the single the next day." Californian DJ Cameron Paul remixed it and sent his version to Next Plateau Records. That was released as a single and retrospectively added to Salt-N-Pepa's debut, *Hot, Cool & Vicious* (1987). It reappeared on *A Salt with a Deadly Pepa* (1988).

Voted into *Rolling Stone*'s 500 Greatest Songs of All-Time, it has been sampled by various artists. 2 Many DJ's memorably mixed it with "No Fun" by The Stooges on their mashup masterpiece *As Heard on Radio Soulwax pt 2* (2002).

At a Detroit show in 2008, Salt-N-Pepa claimed that the song wasn't about sex, but about dancing. Always passionate about feminist and social issues, they dedicated it to single mothers, lower taxes, and the Obamas. "We are," declared Salt, "pushing it for change in America with Barack and Michelle Obama." **OM**

Bring the Noise | Public Enemy (1987)

Writer | C. Ridenhour (Chuck D), H. Shocklee, E. Sadler
Producer | Bill Stephney, Hank Shocklee, Carlton Ridenhour (Chuck D), Eric Sadler
Label | Def Jam
Album | *Less than Zero* (1987)

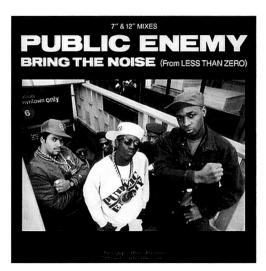

"I thought, 'What the hell is that?' It was unlike anything else that had come before."

Roots Manuva, 2008

◀ **Influenced by:** Niggers Are Scared of Revolution
The Last Poets (1970)
▶ **Influence on:** AmeriKKKa's Most Wanted · Ice Cube
(1990)
● **Covered by:** Anthrax featuring Public Enemy (1991)
Staind and Fred Durst (2000)

How do you get from the sweet soul of The Isley Brothers to the dense dissonance of Public Enemy? The answer, in the case of "Bring the Noise," is by sampling the horns from Marva Whitney's "It's My Thing"—a response to the Isleys' "It's Your Thing."

But that doesn't do justice to the revolutionary sample collage assembled by its producers (later known as The Bomb Squad). As George Clinton remarked, "Public Enemy would take a little piece of those songs and actually make arrangements out of them." (Inevitably, Clinton's much-sampled group Funkadelic feature on "Bring the Noise.")

Oddly, this potent brew of noise and Black Nationalism first appeared on the soundtrack to *Less than Zero* (1987), a tale of dissolute, rich Californians. It was released as a single as a double A-side with the smooth R&B of The Black Flames. (Equally incongruously, the album also featured Roy Orbison singing a song by Glenn Danzig.)

Eventually, "Bring the Noise" was issued in its own right, and became the opening track on Public Enemy's ground-breaking *It Takes A Nation of Millions to Hold Us Back* (1988)—although front man Chuck D told *Hip Hop Connection* that "[Def Jam producer] Rick Rubin actually wanted us to keep 'Noise' and 'Rebel' off the album, but me and Hank [Shocklee] argued and said, 'Fuck that!'"

Chuck's vocals have been sampled countless times ("Bass! How low can you go?" became the title of a U.K. hit by Simon Harris in 1988) and the track was remixed by house producer Benny Benassi in 2007. It has had a wide influence in hip-hop, although sample clearance costs mean that nothing is ever likely to sound the same again. As Shocklee remarked, "It wouldn't be impossible. It would just be very, very costly." **DC**

True Faith | New Order (1987)

Writer | New Order, Stephen Hague
Producer | New Order, Stephen Hague
Label | Factory
Album | *Substance* (1987)

"New Order had become really stagnant and really repetitive, but now I think they're brilliant."

Robert Smith, The Cure, 1988

◀ **Influenced by: Planet Rock** · Afrika Bambataa
& The Soul Sonic Force (1982)
▶ **Influence on: The Real Thing** · Gwen Stefani (2004)
● **Covered by:** The Boo Radleys (1993) · Dreadful
Shadows (1995) · Aghast View (1997) · Flunk (2005)
Code 64 (2005) · Anberlin (2009)

Having risen from the ashes of Joy Division, by 1987 New Order had been firmly established for six years in the United Kingdom, with hits such as "Blue Monday." It was "True Faith," though, that finally broke them into the American mainstream, when it reached No. 32. Not bad for a song written and recorded—along with its outstanding B-side, "1963"—in just ten days.

As with many of the Mancunian quartet's songs, the title doesn't feature in the lyrics, which vocalist Bernard Sumner penned when he was accidentally locked in the group's apartment for a day. "We got a bill for thousands ... off the taxman, I think," he told *News of the World*. "We thought, 'Hell, we'd better try to write a Top Forty hit here.' So we got our heads together, and 'True Faith' was the result." Sumner's line "Now that we've grown up together / They're all taking drugs with me" was changed to ". . . They're afraid of what they see" for added radio friendliness. The group, however, performed the original lyric onstage.

Peter Hook's melodic bass almost didn't make the cut. "Let's just say it was a bit of a battle for me to get on there," he told *Q*. "Musically, we were moving towards straight dance and I was keen on keeping the New Order I'd known and loved."

Nonetheless, the blend of Gillian Gilbert's danceable synths, Stephen Morris's dramatic drums, and the edgy lyrics made "True Faith" irresistible, while French choreographer Philippe Decouflé's surreal video—in which outlandishly costumed dancers slap each other in time to the music—won the BPI (British Phonographic Industry) award for best promotional video in 1988. "It was," producer Stephen Hague told *Sound on Sound*, "just 'mission accomplished.' " **GK**

It's a Sin | Pet Shop Boys (1987)

Writer | Neil Tennant, Chris Lowe
Producer | Stephen Hague, Julian Mendelsohn
Label | Parlophone
Album | *Actually* (1987)

"Your career gets hijacked by a big hit. In our case it's 'Go West' and 'It's a Sin.'"

Neil Tennant, 2009

◄ **Influenced by: Passion** · The Flirts (1982)
► **Influence on: Like a Prayer** · Madonna (1989)
● **Covered by:** Gamma Ray (1999) · JJ72 (2001) · Paul Anka (2005) · And One (2009)
★ **Other key tracks:** What Have I Done to Deserve This? (1987) · Always On My Mind (1987)

One afternoon in 1982—four years before the Pet Shop Boys' debut, *Please*, hit shelves—Neil Tennant and Chris Lowe were working in a studio in London's Camden Town. Lowe began playing music that to Tennant—a recovering Catholic schoolboy—sounded religious. At that point, words flooded forth and, some five minutes later, the lyrics to "It's a Sin" were complete.

The public wouldn't get to hear the song until 1987, when "It's a Sin" served as a cornerstone of the duo's third record, *Actually*, which followed their remix effort *Disco* in 1986. The wait was worth it: in the interim, the song had morphed into a grandiose dance-pop epic told through whirling synthesizers and orchestral blasts.

Tennant bared his soul for judgment, crying out sharply, "So I look back upon my life / Forever with a sense of shame / I've always been the one to blame." Yet the music—rich with drama and boogie—turned this confession into a party. Toss in extravagant extras—like Tennant reciting from the Latin Confiteor and the countdown to a rocket launch—and you had the Pet Shop Boys at their most deliciously theatrical. The video, directed by Derek Jarman, expanded on the song's lyric, with Tennant being arrested by an Inquisitor.

Coming on the heels of the chartbusting "West End Girls," "It's a Sin" confirmed the duo as one of the world's best dance-pop acts. The song was a smash in the United States, the United Kingdom, and throughout Europe. It remains a staple of the band's shows—notably when Killers front man Brandon Flowers joined them at the 2009 Brit Awards—and has inspired covers by acts as diverse as Paul Anka and power metallers Graveworm. **JiH**

Pump Up the Volume
M|A|R|R|S (1987)

Writer | Martyn Young, Steve Young
Producer | Martyn Young, John Fryer
Label | 4AD
Album | N/A

Ivo Watts-Russell, boss of independent London label 4AD, created M|A|R|R|S by challenging his acts AR Kane and Colourbox to collaborate. The aim was a fusion of the underground dance scene with recordings of other songs, manipulated using sampling technology. The collaboration was not an obvious success, with the atmosphere between the groups so frosty that they opted to create separate tracks before adding finishing touches to each other's work. The result was a double A-side single, on which "Anitina," largely created by AR Kane, was hopelessly eclipsed by Colourbox's brilliant "Pump Up the Volume."

The song took a mind-boggling array of vocal and instrumental samples—most notably Eric B & Rakim's "Paid in Full," and Israeli singer Ofra Haza's "Im Nin' Alu"—and somehow made them work. Crucial to the success of the remix was the involvement of DJs Dave Dorrell and CJ Mackintosh, whose hip-hop scratches in particular gave the song a distinctively gritty urban edge.

The track sold 200,000 in the United Kingdom and 500,000 in the United States, where it was nominated for a Best Instrumental Performance Grammy. M|A|R|R|S broke up shortly afterward but, in their short lifespan, they introduced the public to a radically new sound and to the revolutionary concept of producers and DJs as artists in their own right. **CE-S**

Birthday
The Sugarcubes (1987)

Writer | The Sugarcubes
Producer | Ray Shulman, Derek Birkett
Label | One Little Indian
Album | *Life's Too Good* (1988)

As a solo artist, Björk has drawn headlines for attacking paparazzi and for her racy videos and outlandish outfits. She has also delivered a succession of daring albums.

The Icelandic pop princess was equally creative and controversial upon her arrival, making a big splash with "Birthday," The Sugarcubes' international debut single. Its lyrics were vaguely mysterious, and the storyline made harder to follow by Björk's unorthodox whisper-to-wail delivery. "I can't understand what 'Birthday' is about," she claimed in *Exposure*. "I always write the melodies, then the words come later. I'm not a poet . . . I just translate feeling into words."

Careful attention, however, revealed that Björk had entered taboo territory, describing an affair between a five-year-old girl and a much older male. "The song's called 'Birthday' because it's his fiftieth birthday," she told *Raw*, "but not many people can figure it out from the lyrics."

Yet the woozy, Cocteau Twins-esque ballad was oddly endearing, sounding a siren-like call to those weary of slick 1980s pop. Championed by U.K. DJ John Peel, "Birthday" paved the way for the success of The Sugarcubes' full-length debut, *Life's Too Good* (1988). It introduced Icelandic music to listeners across the globe and made the public hungry to see what Björk would do next—a pursuit that has proved endlessly fascinating. **JiH**

Björk and The Sugarcubes in 1987: an oblique pleasure. ➡

Beds Are Burning | Midnight Oil (1987)

Writer | Rob Hirst, James Moginie, Peter Garrett
Producer | Wayne Livesey, Midnight Oil
Label | CBS
Album | *Diesel and Dust* (1987)

"It felt like screaming into a fog of indifference."

Jim Moginie, 2008

◄ **Influenced by: Clampdown** · The Clash (1979)
► **Influence on: Zombie** · The Cranberries (1994)
● **Covered by: Split Lip** (1996) · Augie March (2001)
Novaspace (2003) · Misery Inc. (2007)
★ **Other key tracks:** Dream World (1987) · Gunbarrel
Highway (1987) · The Dead Heart (1987)

Well before vocalist Peter Garrett ran as a Nuclear Disarmament Party candidate in the 1984 Australian Senate race, fans Down Under had figured out that Midnight Oil was one of Oz's most political—and best—bands. The rest of the world got the picture with *Diesel and Dust.*

Inspired by a tour through Australia's aboriginal settlements, the concept album addressed indigenous suffering as well as environmental concerns. Punk at heart, but not in sound, the tuneful opus was their international breakthrough. *Diesel and Dust* featured many fine tracks, including "The Dead Heart" and "Dreamworld," but just one all-time modern rock anthem.

"Beds Are Burning" was a no-nonsense cry for social justice; but the band sugared the pill with a shout-along chorus, shimmering guitar leads, and throbbing R&B-influenced rhythms. Most fans didn't get the politics—which demanded that the Australian government give back land to the native Pintupi—only that "Beds Are Burning" was perhaps the most addictive offering on radio that year. Garrett was such a convincing salesman at the microphone that listeners probably would have bought whatever he was pedaling.

"There was a sense of hopelessness about the issue at the time . . ." guitarist Jim Moginie told Identity Theory. "When the album was ready to be released, we were prepared to be shouted down by every closet racist in the country."

"Beds Are Burning" became a big hit, helping to make Midnight Oil, briefly, one of the world's biggest bands. It is still regarded as hugely influential—indeed, the Rock and Roll Hall of Fame has named "Beds Are Burning" as one of the five hundred songs that shaped the genre. **JiH**

Yé Ké Yé Ké | Mory Kanté (1987)

Writer | Mory Kanté
Producer | Nick Patrick
Label | Barclay
Album | *Akwaba Beach* (1987)

"It's their way of communicating their interest."

Mory Kanté, 1998

◀ **Influenced by: Lan Naya** · Bembeya Jazz National (1985)
▶ **Influence on: Tekere** · Salif Keita (1995)
● **Covered by:** Picco (2008)
★ **Other key tracks:** Akwaba Beach (1987) · Nanfoulen (1987)

Mory Kanté was the first African musician to score a million-selling single with the Afro-pop classic "Yé Ké Yé Ké," a dance-floor smash across Europe. It appeared on his 1987 album *Akwaba Beach*, although he had recorded a more traditional version for *A Paris*, which was released in 1984. Blowing up just after the marketing term "world music" was coined, the song encouraged a surge of international interest in African artists.

Kanté comes from a long line of *griots*—a hereditary caste of musicians found in West African countries. Though a multi-instrumentalist and singer, he is best known for playing the *kora*—West Africa's twenty-one-stringed harp, which tinkles away throughout "Yé Ké Yé Ké." Of the epithets the song has earned him, "doyen of techno kora music" is among the more accurate.

The production has a modern sheen, with crashing drums and stabbing brass, belying the fact that Kanté based it on a traditional Guinean love song called "Yékéké." "It's the sound that young women make when they dance," Kanté told *Folk Roots*. "You can do *yéké* with the bottom, then *yéké* with the top."

Kante sings in classic call-and-response mode with female vocalist Djanka Diabate, who performs the catchy chorus: "Yékéké n'nimo, Yéké yéké." *N'nimo* means "my sister-in-law"—a phrase used by men in Guinea as a non-threatening way of flirting with women.

"Yé Ké Yé Ké" has since been covered in more than a dozen languages, including Chinese, Arabic, Hebrew, and Hindi. It has also been remixed many times, notably in 1994 by German techno duo Hardfloor, whose version featured on the soundtrack for the 2000 movie *The Beach*. **JLu**

Just Like Heaven | The Cure (1987)

Writer | Robert Smith, Simon Gallup, Porl Thompson, Boris Williams, Laurence Tolhurst
Producer | David Allen, Robert Smith
Label | Fiction
Album | *Kiss Me Kiss Me Kiss Me* (1987)

"The best pop song The Cure have ever done. . . . It was one take and it was perfect."

Robert Smith, 2003

◀ **Influenced by: Another Girl, Another Planet**
The Only Ones (1978)
▶ **Influence on: Taking Off** · The Cure (2004)
● **Covered by:** Dinosaur Jr. (1989) · Goldfinger (1999)
30footFALL (1999) · In Mitra Medusa Inri (2001)
Gatsby's American Dream (2005) · Katie Melua (2005)

"I knew as soon as I'd written it that it was a good pop song . . ." The Cure's Robert Smith declared to *Blender*. The song was conjured in "a small two-bedroom flat in north London," before Smith took it to sessions in the south of France. Drummer Boris Williams inspired him to speed up the song, and introduce the instruments one by one.

Smith gave an instrumental version to French TV show *Les Enfants du Rock*, aiming to make this "obvious single . . . familiar to millions of Europeans." The scheme backfired: "Just Like Heaven" failed even to make France's Top Thirty. Nonetheless, the song became their most popular: even fans who balk at "Friday I'm in Love" have no problem jigging to this jangly gem.

Covers abound, from Dinosaur Jr.'s Smith-endorsed, "passionate . . . fantastic" overhaul, to Katie Melua's tentative tiptoe. The latter adorned the 2005 movie *Just Like Heaven*—the second blockbuster to bear a Cure-inspired title, after *Boys Don't Cry*, released in 1999.

Closer to Smith's heart, however, was the original video. The song, he revealed, is "about a seduction trick. . . . It was something that happened on Beachy Head, on the south coast of England. The song is about hyperventilating—kissing and fainting to the floor. Mary [his wife] dances with me in the video because she was the girl, so it had to be her. The idea is that one night like that is worth one thousand hours of drudgery."

"My favorite Cure song of all-time," enthused the video's director, Tim Pope. "Who else could write music as uplifting and celebratory as this?" He added that Mary Poole "can honestly lay claim to being the only featured female in any Cure video, ever." **BM**

The One I Love | R.E.M. (1987)

Writer | Bill Berry, Peter Buck, Mike Mills, Michael Stipe
Producer | R.E.M., Scott Litt
Label | I.R.S.
Album | *Document* (1987)

"It's probably better that they just think it's a love song at this point."

Michael Stipe, 1987

◄ **Influenced by: Break It Up** • Patti Smith (1975)
▶ **Influence on: Morning Glory** • Oasis (1995)
● **Covered by:** Butthole Surfers (1989) • Moog Cookbook (1996) • Sufjan Stevens (2006)
★ **Other key tracks:** It's the End of the World as We Know It (and I Feel Fine) (1987) • Everybody Hurts (1992)

After plugging away in the alternative rock scene during the early Eighties, college radio favorites R.E.M. finally made a colossal breakthrough. The key to their success was what singer and lyricist Michael Stipe told *Rolling Stone* was "a made-up song, not from any real story."

Their first Top Ten hit on *Billboard*'s Hot 100 registered them as a force to be reckoned with. "I wanted to write a song with the word 'love' in it," Stipe remarked in 1992, "because I hadn't done that before." But what many construed as a romantic message was actually much darker. As Stipe explained: "The song sounds like a love song until that line ["A simple prop to occupy my time"], and then it gets ugly. I thought it was too brutal to actually record."

Brutal or not, the soaring song helped *Document* go platinum, and ushered R.E.M. into the mainstream. "We used to play it," guitarist Peter Buck recalled, "and I'd look into the audience, and there would be couples kissing. Yet the verse is . . . savagely anti-love. . . . People told me that was 'their song.' *That* was your song? Why not 'Paint it Black' or 'Stupid Girl' or 'Under My Thumb'?" (The song, which reached No. 16 in the U.K. chart following its re-release in 1991, contains just three verses—identical but for minor variations.)

"The One I Love" marked the start of a fruitful relationship with Scott Litt. He went on to produce a further five R.E.M. albums, and mixed singles for R.E.M. fans Nirvana.

After *Document*'s success, R.E.M. signed a multi-million dollar deal with Warner Bros., beginning their rise to stadium status. And at those stadiums, this song's baffling but rousing chorus of "Fire!" echoes to the skies. **SF**

Fairytale of New York
The Pogues (1987)

Writer | S. MacGowan, J. Finer
Producer | Steve Lillywhite
Label | Stiff
Album | *If I Should Fall from Grace with God* (1988)

"The opening line of 'Fairytale of New York' is 'Christmas Eve, babe, in the drunk tank,'" observed The Pogues' former manager, Frank Murray. "You know you're not getting an ordinary Christmas song when it starts like that."

"Fairytale of New York"—its title inspired by J. P. Donleavy's novel *A Fairy Tale of New York* (1973)—took two years to write, and a month to record. Often voted Britain's favorite Christmas song, its original release was pipped to the No. 1 spot by "Always On My Mind," by the Pet Shop Boys.

In a bid for international success, Murray took The Pogues on tour in America. During a bout of pneumonia, Shane MacGowan perfected the lyrics to a duet that he'd planned to sing with bassist Cait O'Riordan. After she quit the band, producer Steve Lillywhite took the song to his wife, singer Kirsty MacColl. "Kirsty really made that record," opined MacGowan. "She had the character down properly. There was a lot of chemistry between us. She was a great laugh." The result "just sounded perfect," according to Murray, and—according to pianist Jools Holland—"like a little symphony."

Avoiding the slush usually associated with festive singles, MacGowan charted the spiraling fortunes of a "bum" and a "slut on junk" who have failed to ignite Broadway. "You don't normally get Christmas songs that are so utterly hopeless," said Nick Cave. "There should be more of 'em." **SO**

Paradise City
Guns N' Roses (1987)

Writer | Guns N' Roses
Producer | Mike Clink
Label | Geffen
Album | *Appetite for Destruction* (1987)

Given their advanced intoxication, it's unsurprising that Guns N' Roses have varying accounts of their signature song's origins. Bassist Duff McKagan declared: "I wrote the chords to that song when I first moved to LA, when I didn't know anybody and was feeling a little down." Guitarist Slash dated it to a post-show jam in San Francisco: "I came up with the jangly intro . . . Duff and Izzy [Stradlin, guitarist] picked it up . . . while I came up with the chord changes." At its live premiere, in Los Angeles in October 1985, McKagan announced, "We just wrote this one today."

Slash's suggested "Where the girls are fat and they've got big titties" was promptly vetoed. Wrote biographer Marc Canter, "The verse before 'tell me who ya gonna believe' had different lyrics from those that appeared on the album. Duff sang a lot of the leads toward the end, while Axl [Rose, vocalist] filled in the back-up vocals."

Rose explained the lyrics in a press release: "The verses are more about being in the jungle. The chorus is like being back in the Midwest or somewhere. It reminds me of when I was a little kid." On *Appetite for Destruction*, he insisted on "a screaming synth," to Slash's displeasure.

Regardless, it joined "Sweet Child o' Mine" and "Welcome to the Jungle" as *Appetite*'s hit highlights and became one of *the* rock stormers of the past quarter-decade. **BM**

Defying the rules of rock, Axl Rose performs in a Guns N' Roses shirt in 1987. ➜

Never Let Me Down Again
Depeche Mode (1987)

Writer | Martin L. Gore
Producer | Depeche Mode, Dave Bascombe, Daniel Miller
Label | Mute
Album | *Music for the Masses* (1987)

Depeche Mode were quick to muddy their synth sound after a 1981 split with Vince Clarke. Their music began to embrace a darker hue that shifted the band away from the mainstream, but secured a loyal fan-base. By *Black Celebration* (1986), they were leather-clad goths in search of a hit.

The answer came with "Never Let Me Down Again," which brimmed with punishing beats, heavily treated guitar, and a killer chorus. There was a black humor to "Promises me I'm as safe as houses / As long as I remember who's wearing the trousers," but as Dave Gahan blared "Never let me down" over Gore's delicate counterpoint and massed Wagnerian choirs during the extended fade, the effect was almost sick with horror.

"Never Let Me Down Again" became one of Depeche Mode's lowest-charting hits in their homeland in half a decade. Unruffled, Gore assured *Record Mirror,* "It's nice to be more of a cult band than a hugely successful group."

However, the song and its parent album confirmed their stealthy triumph in the United States, with fans flocking to see the newly muscular Mode. A performance in the tour movie *101* even debuted an arm-waving routine for the song that persists at shows to this day. Oddly, this breakthrough reestablished Depeche Mode as contenders at home, reinforced in 1990 by the masterful *Violator.* **MH**

Faith
George Michael (1987)

Writer | George Michael
Producer | George Michael
Label | Epic
Album | *Faith* (1987)

Well before Wham! called it quits in 1986, people thought George Michael had what it took to become a successful solo artist. But few could have predicted how quickly he ascended from teeny-bop idol to pop icon. All it took was one album—but *what* an album. *Faith* boasted seven singles, sold millions, and scored a Grammy. "Just before the break-up of Wham! I was very introspective and depressed..." he recalled. "Now I've come through that period...and it's given me optimism and faith."

The title cut was striking in its simplicity. After a softly played organ, quoting Wham!'s "Freedom," the song bounced into gear with a rapidly strummed acoustic guitar. Punk legends The Damned had left "a horrible aluminum body guitar" at Denmark's Puk Studio, engineer Chris Porter told *Billboard*'s Craig Rosen. "That's what you hear, and it became the signature sound of the record. He said he wanted a Bo Diddley kind of rhythm...everything stark and dry."

"Faith" became one of Michael's greatest hits—especially in the United States, where it was the top single of 1988. An iconic video helped—although, he admitted, "I can't play the guitar in the video. I can play guitar but not that well. If you look in the video, some of the time I've got a glove on and other times I haven't. That's because I'd grazed my fingers on the strings." **JiH**

Need You Tonight

INXS (1987)

Writer | Andrew Farriss,
Michael Hutchence
Producer | Chris Thomas
Label | WEA
Album | *Kick* (1987)

Hit-makers in the United States and their native Australia since the early Eighties, INXS had to wait until 1987 for worldwide success. Key was this slinky little number, whose video helpfully showcased Michael Hutchence's good looks.

Guitarist Andrew Farriss wrote the music before jetting to Hong Kong to rendezvous with the singer. "The cab came to pick me up to take me to the airport . . ." he recalled. "I told the cab driver to wait: 'Please don't go, because I have to go to the airport, but I have to finish writing a song first.' He looked at me like, 'What a weirdo. Yeah, writing a song—sure, mate.'"

Coincidentally, Hutchence had written a set of lyrics the night before Farriss arrived: "Andrew was playing these tapes of stuff he'd done, and I . . . got a microphone and pulled out these 'Need You Tonight' lyrics. I started singing on the track straight off, and the song finished—it stopped at the end—and it was exactly how you hear it on the record." The only change from this demo, Farriss recalled, "was we put a stop in the middle of it."

The song's abrupt ending segued straight into the next album track, "Mediate"—a trick they replicated for an accompanying video. Never intending to release it as a single, the band were swayed by the reactions of friends to the recording. "It was ridiculously casual . . ." admitted Farriss. "It must be the secret to it all, I'm sure." **BM**

With or Without You

U2 (1987)

Writer | U2
Producer | Daniel Lanois,
Brian Eno
Label | Island
Album | *The Joshua Tree* (1987)

When U2 began work on the follow-up to *The Unforgettable Fire* (1985), there was—according to guitarist The Edge—"little to be excited about . . . 'With or Without You' was really just a chord pattern; it didn't have melodies or guitar parts." Even after further work, "'With or Without You' still sounded awful." Bassist Adam Clayton agreed: "The chords just went round and round and round. It was hard to find a . . . new way into it."

Happily, fate intervened. While The Edge road-tested a prototype guitar that "gave me infinite sustain, like a violin," Virgin Prunes front man Gavin Friday persuaded them to persevere with the song. With the addition of a keyboard arpeggio from producer Brian Eno, the music was complete.

As usual, singer Bono wrote the words. "That song is about torment," he recalled in the band's 2006 autobiography, "sexual but also psychological—about how repressing desires makes them stronger."

The result was their first U.S. No. 1. "We really agonized over which single was going to lead . . ." The Edge told *NME*. "'With or Without You' became the obvious choice . . . it's the one that seems to smooth the transition from the last thing to this record the easiest." *Friends* fans will remember "With or Without You" soundtracking key moments of drama amid the comedy. The song remains a spinetingling highlight of U2's concerts. **BM**

Freak Scene | Dinosaur Jr. (1988)

Writer | J Mascis
Producer | J Mascis
Label | SST
Album | *Bug* (1988)

"Rock 'n' roll was about a bunch of ambivalent people getting together, hating each other, and playing loud music."
Lou Barlow, 2005

◀ **Influenced by: Schizophrenia** • Sonic Youth (1987)
▶ **Influence on: Smells Like Teen Spirit** • Nirvana (1991)
● **Covered by:** Godeater (2001) • Belle & Sebastian (2008)
★ **Other key tracks:** Don't (1988) • Keep the Glove (1988)
No Bones (1988) • Pond Song (1988) • They Always
Come (1988) • The Wagon (1991)

The original lineup of Dinosaur Jr. barely survived the sessions for their third album, *Bug*. But this friction fueled their greatest anthem: a tale of relationship dysfunction set to an electrifying, quiet/LOUD! dynamic, reflecting the passive-aggressive tensions within the group. "The lyrics spelled out that [singer-guitarist J Mascis] was unhappy," bassist Lou Barlow told *Mojo* in 2005. "There was a 'Bug' in the ointment, and it was me."

Barlow and drummer Murph recorded their parts within three days, leaving Mascis alone to complete the album, multi-tracking layer upon layer of guitar. And "Freak Scene" was very much Mascis's "guitar hero" moment. The jangling, acoustic verses flared into deafening, distorted riffage and squalling but melodic solos.

The lyrics drew upon the frustrations between Mascis and Barlow, describing a situation "so fucked, I can't believe it"—although the song closed on a note of hopeful reconciliation, with Mascis drawling, "When I need a friend, it's still you." The song's success—it hit No. 7 on the U.K. indie chart—saw the group lured to major label Sire Records, albeit without Barlow, who was sacked in May 1989 after a miserable tour in support of *Bug*. (Barlow went on to form Sebadoh.)

With the song's crunch recognized as a key influence on the likes of the Pixies and Nirvana, Dinosaur Jr. coasted through the grunge era, but never again would they capture the slacker generation's ennui as succinctly as on "Freak Scene." Perhaps sensing that their flammable chemistry was key to the group's sound, Mascis buried his arsenal of hatchets with Barlow in 2005, and the reunited group continue to tour and record. **SC**

Follow the Leader | Eric B. & Rakim (1988)

Writer | Eric B., Rakim
Producer | Eric B., Rakim
Label | UNI
Album | *Follow the Leader* (1988)

"The message is that you have the capability to do anything you want."
Rakim, 1988

◄ **Influenced by: Listen to Me** • Baby Huey (1971)
► **Influence on: Root Down** • Beastie Boys (1994)
● **Covered by:** Parliament Funkadelic & P-Funk Allstars featuring Rakim (1995)
★ **Other key tracks: Just a Beat** (1988) • **Microphone Fiend** (1988) • **Lyrics of Fury** (1988)

Cut-up-and-keep mixmasters Coldcut made Eric B. & Rakim's name across the world with a 1987 slice and dice of "Paid in Full." Not that Eric B. appreciated it: "They were trying to make us sound like a bunch of clowns," he protested to *NME*.

In 1988 they needed no help: "Follow the Leader" showed the pair at their best. Eric B. created a woozy, sinister patchwork of belly-shaking bass and dynamic, *Mission Impossible*-style samples, while Rakim spat catchphrases that would linger for years. "Every time you hear it," Eric bragged, "you'll hear something different."

Heavy on the James Brown samples, the duo's debut *Paid in Full* had set a template for late Eighties hip-hop. But then Public Enemy demonstrated another way: layering beats and samples to emulate an orchestra of the apocalypse. "Follow the Leader" was in this mold, evoking danger with every stab of brass, every rat-a-tat of machine-gun bass, every word of Rakim's relentless onslaught.

It sounded almost incongruous for Rakim to be preaching hope: "I have to raise ya / from the cradle to the grave, but remember / You're not a slave." "If people put their mind to it," he declared, "they can reach out and grab themselves a life, 'cause it's out there waiting. But you can't sleep on yourself, 'cause there's competition out there in the real world."

Against the title track's full-steam assault, the rest of the *Follow the Leader* album sounded almost tame (though Chris Rock listed the album at No. 12 on his *Vibe* magazine Top 25 Hip-Hop Albums of All Time). The single provided a high-water mark for the duo's career, and they split in 1992, having failed to touch it again. **MH**

Where Is My Mind?
Pixies (1988)

Writer | Charles Thompson
Producer | Steve Albini
Label | 4AD
Album | *Surfer Rosa* (1988)

The Pixies' full-length debut was filled with taboo topics, including voyeurism, mutilation, and sexual fetishes. Ironically, its defining moment—and songbook highlight—was inspired by vocalist Charles "Black Francis/Frank Black" Thompson's happy memories of a scuba diving trip.

The deceptively simple lyrics waltz between surrealism and children's poetry, and the tempo changes so frequently, and so convincingly, that it's hard to categorize the song. The tune is full of remarkable performances, from Black's flexible vocals to Joey Santiago's biting guitar, yet there's an undeniable sense of band chemistry.

"Where is My Mind?" wasn't released as a single, but its popularity among fans helped *Surfer Rosa* spend over a year on the U.K. indie chart—though it took seventeen years for the album to be certified gold in the United States.

But the true measure of this song isn't properly told in sales figures alone. Like The Velvet Underground, the Pixies influenced innumerable aspiring musicians, especially Thom Yorke and Kurt Cobain. "Where is My Mind?" has been sampled by M.I.A., and covered by acts as diverse as Placebo, Nada Surf, and James Blunt. Its legacy was secured by the final scene of David Fincher's movie *Fight Club* (1999), in which—against a backdrop of collapsing buildings—it suddenly sounded like the loveliest song in the world. **JiH**

Waiting Room
Fugazi (1988)

Writer | I. MacKaye, G. Picciotto, J. Lally, B. Canty
Producer | Ted Niceley, Fugazi
Label | Dischord
Album | *13 Songs* (1989)

By the mid-1980s, punk had lost its way. Instead of embracing diversity, the movement rejected innovation. If you wanted to be classified as true punk, you had to play by strict, stifling rules: three chords and nothing longer than three minutes.

In 1988, Fugazi shattered those strictures. Founded by Ian MacKaye, a veteran of hardcore act Minor Threat, the group channeled everything from The Stooges, to dub and free jazz. "Waiting Room"—their debut EP's opening track—served as Fugazi's revolutionary declaration. Vocalists MacKaye and Guy Picciotto barked demands, urging listeners to think for themselves and find their own way in the world: "But I don't sit idly by / I'm planning a big surprise / I'm gonna fight for what I want to be . . . "

The music was similarly radical: an almost funky bass line kicked off the track, and tightly wound, stop-start guitars backed the shouted call to action. Other punks, MacKaye recalled in 2002, didn't know what to make of this brave new sound: "When 'Waiting Room' came out, everyone thought that was totally bizarre reggae music."

That confusion wouldn't last long—alternative types everywhere adopted the song as their anthem. Even jocks latched onto its inspirational message: American footballers the Washington Redskins have used the track to pump up fans during home games since 2001. **TB**

Pixies' Black Francis takes on the burden of the world in a 1991 portrait.

The Eighties | 609

Touch Me I'm Sick | Mudhoney (1988)

Writer | M. Lukin, M. Arm, D. Peters, S. Turner
Producer | Jack Endino
Label | Sub Pop
Album | N/A

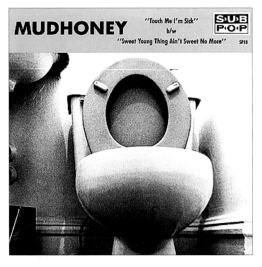

"I couldn't believe something like that came from Seattle."

Courtney Love, 1994

◄ **Influenced by: Scene of the Crime** • Iggy & The Stooges (1981)
► **Influence on: Teenage Whore** • Hole (1991)
● **Covered by:** Sonic Youth (1988) • Naked Lunch (2001) My Ruin (2005)
★ **Other key track:** Here Comes Sickness (1989)

Often overlooked in retrospectives, Mudhoney (formed in Seattle in 1988) have nonetheless been called "the band that made grunge rock possible." Green River (featuring Mudhoney's Mark Arm and Steve Turner) and Soundgarden had produced earlier single releases, but when Sub Pop became a full-time working label in 1988, "Touch Me I'm Sick" was their calling card.

"It was just a limited edition, maybe 800 pieces," recalled Sub Pop founder Bruce Pavitt to *Dazed & Confused*. "But people all over America started raving about it. People that we really respected. That fall, Mudhoney released *Superfuzz Bigmuff*, which amazingly did very well in England. . . . We sent Mudhoney over there with Sonic Youth and we released a split single where they covered each other's songs." (The original version reappeared in 1990 on *Superfuzz Bigmuff Plus Early Singles*.)

Featuring Mark Arm's sleazy shrieks and a simplistic guitar riff distorted out of all proportion, the song is an aural representation of what "grunge" might look like if you met it after midnight in a spit-and-sawdust bar. Not for nothing has "Touch Me I'm Sick" earned the accolades "classic" and "anthem."

Mudhoney have continued to make albums, but this remains their signature song. Its legacy includes director Cameron Crowe's movie *Singles* (1992)—a paean to grunge-era Seattle. This featured a reworking, performed by Citizen Dick—a fictitious band featuring Matt Dillon and three members of Pearl Jam. Its title? "Touch Me I'm Dick." As a bizarre coda, Mudhoney visited the White House with Pearl Jam the day after Kurt Cobain's body was discovered in 1994. "It was," Arm reflected, "an odd afternoon." **SO**

Feed Me with Your Kiss | My Bloody Valentine (1988)

Writer | Kevin Shields
Producer | My Bloody Valentine
Label | Creation
Album | *Isn't Anything* (1988)

"I get too much enjoyment out of blasting my head off and it's taken its toll."

Kevin Shields, 1992

◀ **Influenced by: The Living End** · The Jesus and Mary Chain (1986)
▶ **Influence on: Revolution** · Spacemen 3 (1989)
★ **Other key tracks:** Nothing Much to Lose (1988) You Made Me Realise (1988) · Blown a Wish (1991) Only Shallow (1991) · To Here Knows When (1991)

Those were the days—when My Bloody Valentine actually made records. People now know Kevin Shields only as the guy behind the creation of two classic albums, a very long time ago—who then, as he admitted to *The Guardian*, "lost it."

Yet the November 1988 EP on which "Feed Me with Your Kiss" was the lead track was the band's eighth release in four years. By Shields's standards, these thirty-plus tracks represented a fearsome level of productivity. It was worth it, too: "Feed Me with Your Kiss" proved that the Valentines (formed in Dublin, Ireland, in 1983) had evolved from the insubstantial sappiness of their earlier efforts to a sound that *NME* aptly labeled "skin-flaying."

Innovators such as Sonic Youth, Dinosaur Jr., and Hüsker Dü were obvious influences—artists who, as Shields said, "don't have any respect for the 'correct' way of playing the guitar but are more interested in getting new sounds out whichever way they can." On *Loveless* (1991), Shields laid layer upon layer upon layer of six-string shimmer to the songs, but "Feed Me with Your Kiss" was more direct, and equally thrilling.

Don't pay much attention to the song's lyrical content (which was never the point of the Valentines anyway): immerse yourself instead in the slabs of sound that, played live, could—as Shields told *Melody Maker*—make you "literally lose your balance and feel sick."

"People have been making a loud racket with guitars for years, so it's not a revolutionary thing," Shields said in 1988. But few were taking music to as interesting and pulverizing places as My Bloody Valentine, as the subsequent work of admirers, from The Smashing Pumpkins and U2 to Deerhunter, testifies. **CB**

Buffalo Stance | Neneh Cherry (1988)

Writer | N. Cherry, C. McVey, P. Ramacon, J. Morgan
Producer | Bomb the Bass (T. Simenon, M. Saunders)
Label | Circa
Album | *Raw Like Sushi* (1989)

"I loved Neneh Cherry when I first saw her. I thought 'Buffalo Stance' was wicked."

Mel B, the Spice Girls, 1996

◀ **Influenced by: Buffalo Gals** · Malcolm McLaren (1982)
▶ **Influence on: Wannabe** · Spice Girls (1996)
● **Covered by:** The Rifles (2009)
★ **Other key tracks:** Kisses on the Wind (1989)
Manchild (1989) · The Next Generation (1989)

A heady blast of R&B, rap, pop, hip-hop, and dance, "Buffalo Stance" celebrated strong women, lambasting gold-diggers and pimps. It was the perfect soundtrack for its feisty Swedish singer, Neneh Cherry. "Most of the music I hear today is completely dishonest and devoid of energy," she complained. "'Buffalo Stance' is meant to be hard, fast, sexy . . . and raw."

The song began as the B-side to "Looking Good Diving," a 1986 single by Cameron McVey's duo Morgan McVey. That B-side was a remix by the Wild Bunch, comprised of future super-producer Nellee Hooper and members of Massive Attack. The single flopped, and McVey began to focus on production and songwriting. Keen to keep the spotlight on Cherry, he is credited on her *Raw Like Sushi* as "Booga Bear."

Bomb the Bass—who helped kick-start acid house—produced the song, hence Cherry's namechecking "Timmy" (Tim Simenon) and demanding "Bomb the Bass: rock this place!"

"It's about sexual survival," Cherry told *Rolling Stone*. "It's about being a woman of the Eighties and having something to say. . . . You have to know yourself pretty well, and then just stick your fingers up to the rest of the world and do it."

Cherry's mixed background yielded a beguiling blend of American rapping and British asides. With a funky quote from Miami's "Chicken Yellow (Let Me Do It to You)," this headspinning mix entranced a generation, including Amy Winehouse, the Spice Girls, and Swedish popstress Robyn. "As a young girl," remarked the latter, "I was quite empowered by that song. She was saying the things you wanted to say and she looked the way you wanted to look." **OM**

Fast Car | Tracy Chapman (1988)

Writer | Tracy Chapman
Producer | David Kershenbaum
Label | Elektra
Album | *Tracy Chapman* (1988)

"Tracy Chapman wrote a coupla good songs . . ."

Joni Mitchell, 1990

◄ **Influenced by: Down to Zero** · Joan Armatrading (1976)

► **Influence on: Sometimes I Rhyme Slow** · Nice & Smooth (1992)

● **Covered by:** Amazing Transparent Man (2003) Hundred Reasons (2004) · Mutya Buena (2007)

Scan the list of top-selling songs in 1988 and it couldn't be fluffier. Kylies, Tiffanys, and Whitneys were dominating the airwaves as the Reagan era came to a close, and the record-buying public were desperate for anything jolly to go with their poodle hair and acid-wash denim.

So a young black woman singing socially aware folk tunes about poverty, alcoholism, and domestic violence was the polar opposite of what was then topping the charts. Nonetheless, *Tracy Chapman*—the debut album by a fresh-out-of-college singer-songwriter—hit No. 1 on both sides of the Atlantic.

The likes of 10,000 Maniacs and Suzanne Vega had ushered in a folk revival, particularly in the United States. Musically, this paved the way for Chapman, but the political issues she broached in her songs were more uncomfortable and, initially, she struggled for airplay.

At Nelson Mandela's seventieth birthday concert in June 1988, a nervous Chapman stood alone onstage at London's Wembley Stadium. She played acoustic guitar and sang "Fast Car"—a song she had had to sing live for producer David Kershenbaum, since it was written after the shows and demos that won her a record deal. The Mandela appearance promptly shot the song into transatlantic Top Tens.

Chapman was taken aback by the song's success, which set her career in motion: "I never thought I would get a contract with a major label. All the time since I was a kid listening to records and the radio, I didn't think there was any indication that record people would find the kind of music that I did marketable. I didn't see a place for me there." Fortunately, there was. **SO**

Straight Outta Compton
N.W.A. (1988)

Writer | Ice Cube, MC Ren, Eazy-E, Dr. Dre
Producer | Dr. Dre, Yella
Label | Ruthless
Album | *Straight Outta Compton* (1988)

N.W.A weren't the first gangsta rappers. By 1988, their West Coast predecessor Ice-T had built a career on pimping and gangbanging rhymes. But N.W.A were the first to go multi-platinum thanks to the unholy trinity of bitches, bullets, and bad language. *Straight Outta Compton*—produced in six weeks for only $8,000—sold over three million copies, an estimated eighty percent of which were bought by suburban teens.

Listen to the thrilling opening title track, and you will quickly grasp why N.W.A infiltrated the mainstream. While Ice-T spat cautionary tales of street life, N.W.A produced the hip-hop equivalent of action movies. MTV banning the track's video only served to boost its sales.

In the song, each member of the band played a cold-hearted super-villain—perfect adolescent antiheroes. The air of menace is amped up by Dr. Dre's chaotically churning production. Samples of Funkadelic, Ronnie Hudson & the Street People, The Winstons, and Wilson Pickett are smashed against sirens, scratches, and shouts.

Those elements may now sound like rap clichés, but in 1988 they were revolutionary. Previously, only feel-good hip-hop acts had enjoyed chart success. Now, labels realized that they could hawk tales from the frontline to shock-craving adolescents. By the end of 1988, gangsta rap was unstoppable. **TB**

Opel
Syd Barrett (1988)

Writer | Syd Barrett
Producer | Malcolm Jones
Label | Harvest
Album | *Opel* (1988)

Christmas 1988 offered two stocking fillers for Pink Floyd fans. One was the band's live *Delicate Sound of Thunder*; the other was a collection of unreleased material by Syd Barrett. Though the former trounced its rival in sales, in terms of songs, Barrett was the clear winner—with the opening, six-minute title track proving his finest solo effort.

Barrett had mentioned the song to Malcolm Jones, the Harvest label's A&R man, in spring 1969. Thrilled at the thought of Barrett returning to action, Jones set about producing his first solo album; but the sessions proved longwinded, with backing band the Soft Machine often baffled by Barrett's oblique instructions. Alarmed at the cost of the work, Harvest's parent label, EMI, urged Jones to relinquish his duties to Floyd's Roger Waters and David Gilmour. The duo completed *The Madcap Laughs*, but omitted "Opel."

"Syd obviously intended to include it on the album . . ." rued the producer. "It is one of his best tracks and it's tragic that it wasn't included." Indeed, it is hard to comprehend how Waters and Gilmour could have overlooked—or been unmoved by—the stark, beautiful piece.

"What was so stunning about Syd's songs," Waters told *Rolling Stone,* "was, through the whimsy and the crazy juxtaposition of ideas and words, there was a very powerful grasp of humanity. They were quintessentially human songs." **BM**

Everyday Is Like Sunday | Morrissey (1988)

Writer | Morrissey, Stephen Street
Producer | Stephen Street
Label | His Master's Voice
Album | *Viva Hate* (1988)

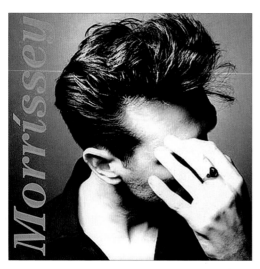

"There are very few aspects of Englishness I actually hate."
Morrissey, 1988

◀ **Influenced by: Sketch for Dawn** · The Durutti Column (1985)
▶ **Influence on: Everybody's Changing** · Keane (2003)
● **Covered by:** 10,000 Maniacs (1992) · The Pretenders (1995) · Colin Meloy (2003) · KT Tunstall (2008)
★ **Other key track:** Suedehead (1988)

When The Smiths' singer and lyricist Stephen Morrissey embarked on a solo career, few of his fans could predict the direction he would take. His debut album, *Viva Hate*, surprised many with its unashamedly poppy songs. But while "Suedehead" was catchy and "Angel, Angel Down We Go Together" was dramatic, the standout for Morrissey-watchers was "Everyday Is Like Sunday"—a strident yet wistful evocation of winter life in a deserted seaside town.

The song began with a melody by producer Stephen Street. He had submitted demos to Morrissey, intending them for B-sides to singles from The Smiths' final album, *Strangeways, Here We Come*, released in 1987. Instead, Street told *NME*, "I got a letter back from him saying, 'I don't see any point in continuing The Smiths, would you like to make a record with me?'" With The Durutti Column's Vini Reilly replacing Johnny Marr as Morrissey's guitar foil, they forged ahead.

"Every day is silent and gray," sang Morrissey in a more forceful voice than the pleading croon he had employed on many of The Smiths' best-known songs. His depiction of the silent streets and tedium of the song's unnamed location was perfect; a lyrical slew of very English images.

As was often the case with The Smiths, the music—almost jubilant at times—contrasted with the lyrics, which his detractors regarded as simple miserablism. Yet, in his own way, Morrissey seemed to be celebrating the hushed, depressed nature of this aspect of England. What's wrong with Sundays anyway? As with so many of this misunderstood maverick's songs, there's more than one meaning. "Everyday Is Like Sunday" remains one of Morrissey's best-known songs. **JMc**

Orinoco Flow | Enya (1988)

Writer | Enya, Roma Ryan, Nicky Ryan
Producer | Nicky Ryan
Label | WEA
Album | *Watermark* (1988)

"I was hoping someone would enjoy it, but I didn't realize how many listeners there would be."

Enya, 2008

◀ **Influenced by:** Night Scented Stock · Kate Bush (1980)
▶ **Influence on:** Now We Are Free · Lisa Kelly (2003)
● **Covered by:** The Section Quartet (2001) · Celtic Woman (2005) · Bit by Bats (2008) · Libera (2008)
★ **Other key tracks:** Storms in Africa (1988) · Watermark (1988) · Book of Days (1991) · Caribbean Blue (1991)

Many label Irish singer and composer Enya as unhip. Others worship her as a mystical Celtic priestess—one who knows magic, converses with forest creatures, and keeps the Emerald Isle safe from evil wizards. (The latter group may well be right—she does, after all, live in a castle.)

That people would still be talking about Enya today seemed highly unlikely at the start of her solo career. After appearing with her family band Clannad—best known for "Theme from Harry's Game"—in the early Eighties, the singer drew little attention with her eponymous 1987 debut; but things changed once Enya delivered her sophomore set, thanks to "Orinoco Flow."

If the title doesn't ring a bell, you're not alone—most know the tune as "Sail Away." ("Sail away" is the chorus, and the song's only two easily decipherable words.) It was actually named after London's Orinoco Studios, where longtime Enya collaborator Nicky Ryan, a devoted follower of The Beach Boys and Phil Spector, fashioned a new "Wall of Sound" for his protégée.

The mix included synthesized folk melodies and heavily layered vocals, the latter forming a simple travelogue through such exotic ports of call as Fiji, Bali, and Babylon. "I like to curate different ideas and put them all in one song," Enya explained to the *Daily Telegraph,* "and see the journey of what it will become."

The result was the catchiest new age song ever heard—one that turned out to be bigger than its genre. "Orinoco Flow" pushed *Watermark* past the eight million sales mark and reached No. 1 in several countries. It became the singer's signature tune, and set the stage for Enya to metamorphose into one of the world's most popular artists. **JiH**

One | Metallica (1988)

Writer | James Hetfield, Lars Ulrich
Producer | Flemming Rasmussen, Metallica
Label | Elektra
Album | . . . And Justice for All (1988)

"Physical pain is nothing compared to mental scarring— that shit sticks with you forever."

James Hetfield, 1991

◀ **Influenced by: Buried Alive** · Venom (1982)
▶▶ **Influence on: Soldier of Misfortune** · Filter (2008)
● **Covered by:** Die Krupps (1993) · Apocalyptica (1998)
Total Chaos (2001) · Crematory (2003) · Korn (2003)
Rodrigo y Gabriela (2004) · Beat Crusaders (2008)

"So which song is the obligatory ballad?" asked journalists when Metallica's fourth album, . . . *And Justice for All*, was announced in 1988—with good reason. The San Francisco-based thrashers had included a mellow, downbeat song on their previous two albums: "Fade to Black" on *Ride the Lightning* (1984) and "Welcome Home (Sanitarium)" on *Master of Puppets* (1986). However, "One" is rather different from its predecessors.

After a cheesy but thrilling barrage of warfare sound effects, the song moves into a melodic lament, based on singer and guitarist James Hetfield's tale of a suicidal soldier left blind, deaf, and limbless by a landmine explosion. "Tied to machines that make me be . . . cut this life off from me!" barks Hetfield earnestly, while the guitars switch from clean arpeggios in the verses to distorted riffage in the chorus.

All Metallica ballads end with a climax of enormous riffs and, when the expected huge guitars arrive, the results are spectacular. Lead guitarist Kirk Hammett delivers a fusillade of notes over a riff pattern anchored to drummer Lars Ulrich's unforgettable double bass-drum riff. (And check out the orchestra-enhanced version on their live album *S&M*, recorded in Berkeley in 1999.)

"One" remains a staple of Metallica's live set, two decades after its release, and the song's video—the band's first—enjoys regular airings. Although it comes across as a little naive these days, the footage underlines Metallica's clear artistic vision. Intercut with scenes from the 1971 war movie *Johnny Got His Gun*—whose Dalton Trumbo–penned story had inspired the song—the video evokes the horrors of war, with the music as an appropriately grim soundtrack. **JMc**

The Mercy Seat | Nick Cave & The Bad Seeds (1988)

Writer | Nick Cave, Mick Harvey
Producer | Nick Cave & The Bad Seeds
Label | Mute
Album | *Tender Prey* (1988)

"The brutality of the Old Testament inspired me, the stories and grand gestures."

Nick Cave, 2008

◀ **Influenced by:** 25 Minutes to Go • Johnny Cash (1965)
▶ **Influence on:** Prison Shoe Romp • 16 Horsepower (2003)
● **Covered by:** Johnny Cash (2000) • Kazik Staszewski (2001) • Unter Null (2010)
★ **Other key track:** Deanna (1988)

Prison songs are designed to shock. Johnny Cash, for instance, wove casual, attention-grabbing violence ("I shot a man in Reno, just to watch him die") into "Folsom Prison Blues."

The Bad Seeds took the inmate anthem to a new, harrowing high with "The Mercy Seat." Nick Cave takes on the persona of a death row prisoner awaiting execution. As that fateful appointment gets closer, the inmate moves from denying his crime to admitting his guilt. His grip on reality also loosens as death approaches. The prisoner sees the face of Jesus in inanimate objects; criticizes his good hand ("That filthy five") for not stopping its murderous brother, and compares the electric chair to God's throne in heaven (from which "all history does unfold"), which he will see all too soon.

That journey is made more traumatic by a discordant cacophony summoned up by the Bad Seeds. The metallic chug of a bass guitar smacked with drumsticks serves as the track's foundation. Military drumming, off-key harpsichord notes, and unrelenting, pounding guitars are thrown on top—a bare yet chaotic melody on which Cave hangs his lyrics. Perfecting that wall of dissonance, said engineer Tony Cohen, "knocked ten years off my lifespan. . . . There was so much on there to try and make any sense [of]."

It was worth it. "The Mercy Seat" made a fan of Cave's childhood hero Cash, who recorded a stripped-back cover for his *American III: Solitary Man* (2000). "[That] version is so good," said Cave in 2003. "He just claims that song as he does with so many." Various other artists have covered the song, including Stromkern (1997), Anders Manga (2006), and The Red Paintings (2007). **TB**

Ederlezi
Goran Bregović (1988)

Writer | Goran Bregović
Producer | Goran Bregović
Label | Diskoton
Album | *Dom Za Vešanje* (1988)

Goran Bregović is the most celebrated and controversial musician to emerge from the former Yugoslavia. Despite criticism for not crediting the Gypsy musicians from whom he borrows, he is recognized for helping to popularize Balkan music.

After leading prog-rock band White Button in the 1970s, Bregović decamped to Paris, and began work with fellow Bosnian, filmmaker Emir Kusturica. Their success owed much to the combination of Kusturica's colorful stories and Bregović's evocative soundtracks. "I'm not great at composing music for films," he told Cafe Babel. "I've just been lucky to work with directors who do not need real composers."

Nonetheless, "Ederlezi," the theme for the 1988 film *Dom Za Vešanje* (*Time of the Gypsies*), is a composition of great beauty. It features when the Gypsies take to the river to celebrate the arrival of spring, and a magnificent, orchestral version of Bregović's music is heard.

For "Ederlezi," Bregović adapted an ancient Roma hymn, gave it a lush arrangement, and employed a young Gypsy singer, Vaska Jankovska, whose haunting voice wails across the song.

The eerie "Ederlezi" was quickly recognized as a classic of both soundtrack music and contemporary Balkan music. It is played today by brass bands across the Balkans and featured on the soundtrack of the 2006 comedy, *Borat*. **GC**

Ale Brider
Klezmatics (1988)

Writer | Traditional, arranged by The Klezmatics
Producer | The Klezmatics
Label | Piranha
Album | *Shvaygn = Toyt* (1988)

The traditional music of Eastern Europe's Jewish communities, klezmer was the soundtrack to weddings and festivities across the centuries until the Nazis murdered the Ashkenazi Jews who produced these lovely, clarinet-led sounds.

The style disappeared from Europe, and was largely ignored in Israel; but it survived in New York, albeit in an underground manner. The city's large Jewish diaspora meant many klezmer musicians migrated there and influenced all kinds of American music: Gershwin's "Rhapsody in Blue," for example, opens with a wistful klezmer melody.

In the 1980s, young Jewish New York musicians began researching their roots, resulting in a klezmer revival that spread into jazz, folk, and rock 'n' roll. The Klezmatics are the most celebrated of all klezmer revivalists and their brilliant, irreverent approach has won them a wide, diverse audience. The Klezmatics remind listeners of Jewish history and persecution, and link this to the struggles of gays and other minority groups. Their album title, *Shvaygn = Toyt,* translates as Silence = Death, a phrase associated with the failure of the Reagan administration to deal with AIDS.

"Ale Brider" (We're All Brothers) is a rousing labor anthem that found the Klezmatics joined by Les Miserables Brass Band. No matter what your religion, sexuality, or musical tastes are, it's guaranteed to get you on the dance floor. **GC**

Love Shack
The B-52's (1988)

Writer | K. Pierson, F. Schneider, K. Strickland, C. Wilson
Producer | Don Was
Label | Reprise
Album | *Cosmic Thing* (1989)

Ten years after from the immortal "Rock Lobster" (1979), The B-52's risked becoming "that other band from Athens, Georgia." While old pals R.E.M. were blooming, The B-52's hadn't managed a memorable hit since "Private Idaho" in 1980. *Bouncing Off the Satellites*, in 1986, was a low point, both on the charts and on a personal level.

Three years later, they made an amazing comeback with *Cosmic Thing*, a multimillion-selling, Top Ten smash. That success can be credited almost entirely to "Love Shack." The song came from a demo recorded by guitarist/keyboardist Keith Strickland. An attempt at adding vocals proved so disappointing that "Love Shack" was nearly scrapped. However, reported *Rolling Stone*, "They gave it one last shot the next day and nailed it on the first take."

"When we handed it in," recalled Was, "I don't think there was a single person who said, 'Hah! That's the hit The B-52's have been needing for the past twelve years!'" They were, therefore, vindicated when it went gold and was nominated for a Grammy. "Now maybe people won't be saying we're a novelty band," said Strickland.

A joyous blend of surf rock and new wave, "Love Shack" opens with Fred Schneider's robotic directions, before Kate Pierson soars in from on high. With that, the party is on—climaxing with Cindy Wilson's "Tin roof … rusted!" **JiH**

A Little Respect
Erasure (1988)

Writer | Vince Clarke, Andy Bell
Producer | Stephen Hague
Label | Mute
Album | *The Innocents* (1988)

With tattered hearts on sleeves, dance pop duo Erasure released their soul-shattering love letter to an unrequited crush—and, in doing so, injected the charts with a heavy hit of realism.

This wasn't just any love letter. Andy Bell is credited as being one of the first openly gay singers and his candor paid off, with legions of fans both straight and gay. "If I hear a lyric from another song, and it moves me emotionally, I think 'That guy knows exactly what I'm going through,'" he told the BBC. "And when you can do the same with one of your own lyrics, that's the best kind of writing you can do."

Bell's openness—something you might expect from a man so comfortable in his own skin that he dresses in rubber catsuits onstage—isn't the only reason "A Little Respect" is so brilliant. Synth handyman Vince Clarke wrote Depeche Mode's first three smashes then played in Yazoo and The Assembly. Here, his craftsmanship gives "A Little Respect" a bedrock Abba beat, ratcheting the band's pop kudos up a notch or two and making their slightly abstract style (see "Sometimes" and "Who Needs Love Like That") more accessible.

Surrounded at the time in droll electro doom and glossy pop from the Stock, Aitken, and Waterman hit factory, it would have been easy for "A Little Respect" to sound contrite. Instead it stood tall and sounded refreshingly human. **KBo**

Wicked Game | Chris Isaak (1989)

Writer | Chris Isaak
Producer | Erik Jacobsen
Label | Reprise
Album | *Heart Shaped World* (1989)

"I banged into it pretty quick. I wish they could all be that quick."

Chris Isaak, 1991

◄ **Influenced by: Blue Moon** · Elvis Presley (1956)
▶ **Influence on: Dark Therapy** · Echobelly (1995)
● **Covered by:** R.E.M. (1995) · HIM (1996) · Crossbreed
(1998) · JJ72 (2003) · Heather Nova (2005) · Girls Aloud
(2005) · Giant Drag (2006) · Ima Robot (2006) · Stone
Sour (2007) · Turin Brakes (2007)

Perhaps a mutual love of pompadours and rock 'n' roll crooners such as Roy Orbison inspired director David Lynch to use songs from Chris Isaak's critically acclaimed but little-known debut album *Silvertone* (1985) in his movie *Blue Velvet* (1986). "Three years later," Isaak told *Q* magazine, "he said—and he's a real straight guy—'I have hardly any budget for music but I know somebody who's cheap and punctual.'" The singer's music duly featured on the soundtrack of Lynch's dark romantic thriller *Wild at Heart*, released in 1990. This time, it came from Isaak's third album, *Heart Shaped World*.

In the movie, Lynch used an instrumental version of "Wicked Game," but the music director of an Atlanta radio station, who was also an avid Lynch fan, picked up the soundtrack album, featuring the song with Isaak's vocals. Within months of his airing this version of the track, it had spread to stations nationwide. "This," Isaak told *Country Music International*, "was really neat: after the record had been out and gone down the line, to have it come back and be a hit. I remember sitting on my couch in my house watching *Hawaii Five-O* and somebody calling me and going, 'You're in the Top Ten and still going up!'" (Herb Ritts's sultry new video for the song—replacing one by Lynch, and featuring supermodel Helena Christensen topless on a beach—didn't hurt.)

Of his lyrical inspiration, Isaak told *Rolling Stone*: "There was a girl on the way over. It was one of those things where they call—they say, 'I'm comin' over.' You know you shouldn't, but you let 'em. . . . By the time she got there, I had the song pretty much finished. We didn't do much guitar playin' after she got there!" **SO**

Personal Jesus | Depeche Mode (1989)

Writer | Martin Gore
Producer | Depeche Mode, Flood
Label | Mute
Album | *Violator* (1989)

"I was listening to it ... because I wanted to really take a step away from the world."
Marilyn Manson, 2004

◀ **Influenced by: Rock and Roll (Part 2)** · Gary Glitter (1972)
▶ **Influence on: Reach Out** · Hilary Duff (2008)
● **Covered by:** Lollipop Lust Kill (2002) · David Gogo (2002) · Gravity Kills (2002) · Pat MacDonald (2003) Marilyn Manson (2004) · Tamtrum (2009)

On the whole, Depeche Mode's seventh studio album was more restrained than its stadium-sized predecessor, *Music for the Masses* (1987). However, *Violator*'s opener—the booming "Personal Jesus"— was Depeche at their anthemic best.

Inspired by Priscilla Presley's book *Elvis and Me*, Martin Gore's lyrics were taken at face value and dubbed blasphemous by some. "It's a song about being a Jesus for somebody else, someone to give you hope and care," Gore told *Spin* magazine. "[The book is] about how Elvis was her man and her mentor and how often that happens in love relationships; how everybody's heart is like a god in some way." Discerning listeners understood the irony in this tale of a supposed savior—one who would answer a call and "make you a believer"— and read it as cautionary advice against putting anyone on a pedestal. "No one is perfect," observed Gore, "and that's not a very balanced view of someone, is it?"

The song rings with appropriately messianic significance, thanks to an industrial sound, crafted by producer Flood and keyboard player Alan Wilder, that marries synth-pop and radio-friendly rock. Dave Gahan's vocals are little short of gigantic, complemented by the first prominent use of guitar on a Depeche hit. "They wanted," confirmed Flood, "to push into new territory."

"Personal Jesus" was unleashed when Depeche Mode were approaching worldwide domination. The song was a smash that—combined with the follow-up "Enjoy the Silence"—helped make *Violator* the biggest album of their career. Marilyn Manson and Johnny Cash covered the number, and—decades later—fans still worship their "Personal Jesus." **JiH**

Soy gitano
Camarón de la Isla (1989)

Writer | Camarón de la Isla, V. Amigo, J. F. Torres
Producer | Ricardo Pachon
Label | Philips
Album | Soy gitano (1989)

I Am the Resurrection
The Stone Roses (1989)

Writer | Ian Brown, John Squire
Producer | John Leckie
Label | Silvertone
Album | The Stone Roses (1989)

José Monge Cruz—aka Camarón de la Isla—was the greatest male flamenco singer of the last century. His phenomenal talent, turbulent life, and early death have seen him dubbed the Spanish Jimi Hendrix.

Camarón was born into a poor Gypsy family in Andalusia, Spain, in 1950. He began singing in local taverns aged eight, and his rare talent was soon recognized. Aged sixteen, he was sent to Madrid, where he met gifted young flamenco guitarist Paco de Lucia. Together, the duo pushed flamenco forward with Camarón's beautifully raw, expressive voice matched by Paco's mercurial playing. Initially, only flamenco aficionados appreciated them—but, as word got out, they became stars across Spain. Quincy Jones and Mick Jagger, among others, announced that they wanted to work with Camarón (to which the singer replied, "Who's Mick Jagger?").

Camarón was a simple man, with little understanding of how to deal with fame. "The only thing that I do," he declared, "and that I have done in my life, is to sing, because it is all I know how to do." Ultimately, he resorted to alcohol and drugs, and his performances became erratic. But Camarón's behavior never affected his artistry in the recording studio. "Soy gitano" (I Am Gypsy) is a defiant statement of pride in his people. Recorded with the London Philharmonic Orchestra, it demonstrates just how far Camarón pushed flamenco, and it remains an anthem. **GC**

Part swinging jab at religion, part "murderous attack" of a band associate, part instrumental wig-out, "I Am the Resurrection" sealed The Stone Roses' classic debut album and confirmed their swaggering self-confidence.

It was the final track recorded during the Mancunians' last session with producer John Leckie at Rockfield Studios, Wales. Ian Brown's voice is full of the bite that Oasis front man Liam Gallagher later tried desperately to best. The lyrics—which Brown claimed were inspired by a painted notice outside a church, and are a dig at the Catholic church in particular—also capture the Madchester scene of which the Roses were godfathers. "Don't waste your words, I don't need anything from you / I don't care where you've been or what you plan to do," is Brown at his arrogant best, aware that his band was creating something nigh-on unsurpassable.

However, "I Am the Resurrection" is perhaps best remembered for its final four minutes: a showcase for Hendrix-inspired guitarist John Squire, thunderous bassist Mani, and funky drummer Reni. Mani informed NME in 2009 that he, Squire, and Reni nailed the instrumental coda in one perfect take. Leckie, however, remembers it differently: "We spent a good few days arranging and rehearsing that end," he told the BBC, "so it sounded like something special." **JM**

Ian Brown of The Stone Roses in 1989, looming large over British pop. ➲

Me Myself and I | De La Soul (1989)

Writer | P. Huston, D. Jolicoeur, V. Mason, K. Mercer, E. Birdsong, G. Clinton, P. Wynne
Producer | Prince Paul, De La Soul
Label | Tommy Boy
Album | *3 Feet High and Rising* (1989)

"We were surprised how big it got. Sometimes the simplest thing is what people can relate to."
Posdnous, 2009

◀ **Influenced by: (Not Just) Knee Deep** · Funkadelic (1979)
▶ **Influence on: Hot Potato** · Freestyle Fellowship (1993)
★ **Other key tracks:** Eye Know (1989) · Ghetto Thang (1989) · The Magic Number (1989) · Say No Go (1989) Ring Ring Ring (Ha Ha Hey) (1990)

The offbeat humor, Afrocentric interests, and jazzy hooks of the Native Tongues posse—a loose collective of friends and contemporaries, including De La Soul, A Tribe Called Quest, Queen Latifah, and The Jungle Brothers—heralded hip-hop's "D.A.I.S.Y. Age" (da inner sound, y'all). A bewildered media pigeonholed them as hippies, simply because their clothes, music, and lyrics didn't fit rap stereotypes back in the day.

De La Soul spelled out their frustrations on "Ain't Hip to be Labeled a Hippie," the flip side to one of several singles issued from their epochal debut album, *3 Feet High and Rising*. The A-side took a more positive stance, parlaying a proud statement of their oddball selves into the Long Island troupe's first R&B chart-topper.

Producer Prince Paul lifted liberally from the golden age of funk, cramming in everything from the rubbery synth intro of Funkadelic's "(Not Just) Knee Deep," to the grouchy granny from The Ohio Players' "The Worm" and the groove of Edwin Birdsong's "Rapper Dapper Snapper." Over this glorious party, the trio celebrated their individualism with winning wit and smarts. Trugoy (Jolicoeur) declared "De La Soul is from the soul"; Posdnuos (Mercer) chided the press for calling him a hippy because he wore glasses. "We were just being ourselves," Trugoy told *Rolling Stone* in 2009.

A vibrant video furthered the point. In a school detention, De La Soul's medallion and baseball cap-sporting classmates mock them for their African necklaces and asymmetrical haircuts. Still the hippy tag lingered—in response, the group illustrated the harder *De La Soul Is Dead* (1991) with a broken flowerpot, formally announcing the demise of the D.A.I.S.Y. Age. **SC**

Epic | Faith No More (1989)

Writer | Mike Bordin, Roddy Bottum, Billy Gould, Jim Martin, Mike Patton
Producer | Matt Wallace, Faith No More
Label | Slash
Album | *The Real Thing* (1989)

"I love Faith No More. Their song 'Epic' was my burlesque number at the bar I used to work at."

Lady Gaga, 2009

◄ **Influenced by:** Fight like a Brave · Red Hot Chili Peppers (1987)
► **Influence on:** My Name Is Mud · Primus (1993)
● **Covered by:** The Automatic (2007) · Atreyu (2008) Love Is All (2008)
★ **Other key track:** Midlife Crisis (1992)

"Acid-head dirtbags" was how drummer Mike Bordin referred to himself and his Faith No More colleagues. It was probably one of the only labels this wonderfully perverse band allowed in close proximity. The funk-metal tag didn't sit well with them, and—never lost for words—Bordin remarked, "We're not a heavy metal band because we don't have jack-off guitar solos every song and we don't have some dick singing fake opera." Nonetheless, Jim Martin's six-string sound was central to the genesis of "Epic." "I was just noodling around on the demo," the oddball axeman told *Guitar* magazine, "and there was one little part at the beginning of the solo that grabbed me. Sometimes, that's all it takes."

The replacement of Chuck Mosley with Mike Patton as front man gave the group extra dimensions, including lyrics whose opaque nature had fans struggling to decipher their meaning. Interpretations of the song duly range from "success" to "masturbation." Just as oblique was the "Epic" video—featuring a flopping fish and an exploding piano—which was played on what keyboard player Roddy Bottum called "stress rotation" on MTV. ("That's heavier than heavy rotation," he quipped to *Select*.) However, it all added up to a Top Ten U.S. chart placing.

Most groups would have used such success as a jugular vein into the mainstream, but acclaim didn't sit well with Faith No More. "That this band is now getting support from the straight populace—that's kind of erotic, kind of weird," said Patton. "We sold a lot of records and we had the radio hit . . ." bassist Billy Gould told *Terrorizer*. "Maybe we second-guessed ourselves a little bit, to try and keep our intentions pure." **CB**

Like a Prayer | Madonna (1989)

Writer | Madonna, Patrick Leonard
Producer | Madonna, Patrick Leonard
Label | Sire
Album | *Like a Prayer* (1989)

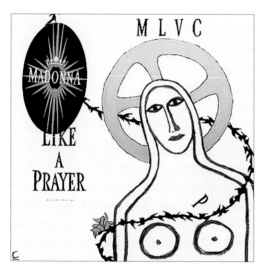

"I really love 'Like a Prayer' because it was the first one I learned every word to."

Britney Spears, 2008

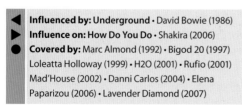

◀ **Influenced by: Underground** · David Bowie (1986)
▶ **Influence on: How Do You Do** · Shakira (2006)
● **Covered by:** Marc Almond (1992) · Bigod 20 (1997)
Loleatta Holloway (1999) · H2O (2001) · Rufio (2001)
Mad'House (2002) · Danni Carlos (2004) · Elena
Paparizou (2006) · Lavender Diamond (2007)

"That song means a lot more to me than 'Like a Virgin,'" Madonna told *Billboard*'s Craig Rosen. "I wrote it and it's from my heart."

One of the star's most enduring and biggest-selling singles—more than five million copies sold worldwide—"Like a Prayer" was co-written with producer Patrick Leonard. "Pat had the chord changes for the verse and the chorus . . ." she told *SongTalk*. "I really wanted to do something really gospel oriented and a cappella . . . just my voice and an organ. So we started fooling around with the song, and we'd take away all the instrumentation so that my voice was naked. Then we came up with the bridge together, and we had the idea to have a choir. In almost everything I do with Pat, if it's up-tempo, there's a Latin rhythm or feeling to it. . . . We both think that we were Latin in another life."

The accompanying video—featuring burning crosses, masturbation, and an interracial plot—prompted an inevitable outcry. (The Andrae Crouch gospel choir, who sang on the song, refused to appear in it.) The controversial content of the video also resulted in the canning of a tie-in commercial for Pepsi-Cola in which the song appeared. At the MTV Video Music Awards in 1989, Madonna gleefully thanked Pepsi "for causing so much controversy!"

The artwork on the single cover features an illustration of the icon by the star's brother Christopher and the letters "M.L.V.C." (Madonna Louise Veronica Ciccone). A displaced letter "P," near her heart, distances Madonna from her ex-husband Sean Penn—reflecting music that deals with the anguish of love and presents a more human persona than before. **SS**

W.F.L. (Think about the Future) | Happy Mondays (1989)

Writer | P. Davis, M. Day, P. Ryder, S. Ryder, G. Whelan
Producer | Paul Oakenfold, Terry Farley
Label | Factory
Album | N/A

"Our music is not even about having a future— but, right now, we're it."

Shaun Ryder, 1989

◀ **Influenced by: Burning Down the House** · Talking Heads (1983)
▶ **Influence on: Weekender** · Flowered Up (1992)
● **Covered by:** Manic Street Preachers (1993)
★ **Other key tracks:** Step On (1990) · Kinky Afro (1990) Grandbag's Funeral (1990)

After the demise of The Smiths, the Manchester scene had a Technicolor overhaul, and the result was Madchester. While The Stone Roses jingle-jangled, the Happy Mondays staggered from studio to stage, creating the funkiest white rock of its time.

"Wrote for Luck" had been released in 1988 as the lead single from the fantastic *Bummed*, but two remixes—renamed "W.F.L."—shot the group into the spotlight. The producers were all-important because, as singer Shaun Ryder quipped, the group's unfamiliarity with music production meant that a mixing desk might as well have been a machine for cutting sheet metal. The Martin Hannett–produced original was handed to Erasure's Vince Clarke, who transformed it into "W.F.L." However, the version that secured the Mondays' fortunes was the "Think about the Future" mix, blessed with what Ryder described as Paul Oakenfold's "smooth mellowness." "There was a vibe," said Oakenfold, "and the vibe was a good vibe." Ryder's voice was raised, giving his words—part poetry, part thuggery—deserved prominence. Oakenfold, he observed, "brought that sort of trance to it.... All the right ingredients."

Following this triumph, hailed by *NME* as the year's best dance record, Oakenfold inspired the Mondays to even greater heights as co-producer of *Pills 'n' Thrills and Bellyaches* (1990). And while the group ultimately crashed and burned, Oakenfold became the world's most celebrated DJ. "It was Happy Mondays," he told *Soundgenerator*. "I was doing all my own music. I never had any desire to remix or produce anyone.... The record company asked me and I said, 'Yeah, I'll have a go.' And that's how it happened. And then that blew up and then everyone was asking me." **CB**

Getting Away with It | Electronic (1989)

Writer | Bernard Sumner, Johnny Marr, Neil Tennant
Producer | B. Sumner, J. Marr, N. Tennant
Label | Factory
Album | N/A

"Getting away with it...
Electronic!"

"I looked under 'G' for 'guitarist' in the Yellow Pages *and Johnny's was the first name in there."*

Bernard Sumner, 1999

◄ **Influenced by: Heaven Knows I'm Miserable Now**
The Smiths (1984)

► **Influence on: Miserablism** · Pet Shop Boys (1991)

● **Covered by:** Skin (2003)

★ **Other key tracks:** Lucky Bag (1989) · Get the Message (1991) · Feel Every Beat (1991) · Soviet (1991)

"It didn't sound like The Smiths and it didn't sound like New Order," observed Johnny Marr. "We'd done something really unique." The Smiths guitarist first worked with Bernard Sumner on Quando Quango's 1984 single "Atom Rock," co-produced by the New Order front man. "We just knew each other in passing," Marr recalled, "like a lot of musicians in Manchester." The pair reunited in Electronic, whose debut single also boasted Pet Shop Boy Neil Tennant. The latter, Sumner told Neil Chase, "said that he'd heard that I was making a record with Johnny and he'd like to be involved with it. I've always been a big fan of Pet Shop Boys' music and so I was very pleased."

The lavish song combines—to sublime effect—acoustic guitar, piano (inspired by Marr and Sumner's love of Italian house music), sweeping strings, and a captivating chorus. The lyrics—opening with "I've been walking in the rain just to get wet on purpose / I've been forcing myself not to forget just to feel worse"—were inspired by Smiths front man Morrissey. "'Getting Away with It,'" recalled Tennant, "is looking at Morrissey's persona of being miserable . . . and saying that he's been getting away with it for years. It's meant to be humorous."

Electronic's "supergroup" credentials were given further credence on "Getting Away with It" with drumming by ABC's David Palmer and orchestration from Anne Dudley of Art of Noise. The song did not appear on initial U.K. pressings of the band's debut album in 1991, but bolstered reissues. "I didn't know what the hell to do after The Smiths," Marr reflected in 2006, "so Electronic taught me to trust my instincts and make the bullshit part of being in a band secondary." **JL**

Monkey Gone to Heaven | Pixies (1989)

Writer | Charles Thompson
Producer | Gil Norton
Label | Elektra
Album | *Doolittle* (1989)

"I just wanted to capture the song's innocence and angelic beauty."

Gil Norton, 2005

◀ **Influenced by: Green Eyes** · Hüsker Dü (1985)
▶ **Influence on: Today** · The Smashing Pumpkins (1993)
● **Covered by: Far** (1999) · Hamell on Trial (2004) · The String Quartet (2004) · Feeder (2008)
★ **Other key tracks:** Debaser (1989) · Here Comes Your Man (1989) · Wave of Mutilation (1989) · Tame (1989)

Kim Deal came to the Pixies via a classified advertisement for a bassist who enjoyed the music of both Peter, Paul & Mary and Hüsker Dü. With "Monkey Gone to Heaven," the Pixies combine those unlikely influences, but that isn't all that the group tossed into the blend.

In under three minutes, and fewer than one hundred words, singer-songwriter Charles "Frank Black" Thompson applies his surrealist imagery to such environmental concerns as the greenhouse effect, ozone depletion, and water pollution. There are also references to what he told *The Alternative Press* was "what I understand to be Hebrew numerology. . . . I didn't go to the library and figure it out."

The group sugar the pill with one of their most memorable melodies, a folky chorus, their patented loud-soft structure, and another gripping lead from guitarist Joey Santiago. The Pixies also introduce guest musicians in the form of a string section (two cellists and two violinists): a surprise that somehow comes off like the most natural addition in the world. "Kim was playing a grand piano in the studio, picking the strings with a plectrum . . ." producer Gil Norton told *Sound on Sound*. "We ended up putting that on the chorus. Then I thought, 'Let's add strings to that, they'll sound fantastic.'"

"Monkey Gone to Heaven" gave the group their first hit in their homeland, reaching No. 5 on the U.S. Modern Rock chart. The song—combined with the follow-up single "Here Comes Your Man"—made *Doolittle* the band's biggest-selling album. Still, the record's sales were dwarfed by its influence: *Doolittle* provided a roadmap for the alt-rock explosion of the Nineties. **JiH**

Can't Be Sure
The Sundays (1989)

Writer | D. Gavurin, H. Wheeler
Producer | Ray Shulman
Label | Rough Trade
Album | *Reading, Writing and Arithmetic* (1990)

For an understated, measured song, The Sundays' debut single caused a stir. Excited critics thought that their quest for a new Smiths had finally come to an end. "Can't Be Sure" has none of Morrissey's bite and little of Johnny Marr's swagger, save a certain jangle to David Gavurin's guitar. However, closer listening reveals Harriet Wheeler's blank sarcasm—first in the song's wry signature line ("England my country, the home of the free / Such miserable weather"—quoted onstage in 2006 by none other than Morrissey), and then "Did you know desire's a terrible thing? / The worst that I can find."

The Sundays' nearer neighbors were the Cocteau Twins, with Wheeler's little girl tone emulating Liz Fraser's swoops, and Gavurin building spirals of guitar on two-note refrains—gorgeous atmospherics created with simple tools. Lyrically, however, The Sundays were more open.

Peculiarly English as it is, the song made an impact across the Atlantic. "There is a 'people power' thing about the American music scene that's quite encouraging," Gavurin told *Vox*. "If people ring in and say, 'I like that!' they'll play it." However, The Sundays were devils for losing impetus, and a reluctance to come up with new material wasted their rich promise. Despite a hit reworking of "Here's Where the Story Ends" by Tin Tin Out, and a brief renaissance with 1997's "Summertime," The Sundays became a curio. **MH**

Lullaby
The Cure (1989)

Writer | R. Smith, S. Gallup, B. Williams, P. Thompson, R. O'Donnell, L. Tolhurst
Producer | R. Smith, D. Allen
Label | Fiction
Album | *Disintegration* (1989)

"We didn't want to release 'Lullaby,'" grumbled Robert Smith, in a *Times* interview to promote the single and its parent album. "I actually want to get rid of some of the people who bought the last album . . . 'Lullaby' is my least favorite track, but I suppose it's a sensible choice because it sounds very Cure-like."

Disintegration was a monochrome contrast to the colorful *Kiss Me Kiss Me Kiss Me* (1987), with only the singles "Lullaby," "Love Song," and "Fascination Street" providing relief—although, Smith conceded, "Even on 'Lullaby' there was a somber side to it."

Interpretations of the eerie song vary. Fans have suggested child abuse, whereas the band's video director Tim Pope divined an allegory of Smith's druggy past. The composer, however, suggested a more mundane inspiration for its creepy theme: "Spiders are one of the phobias I've not been able to overcome." The lyrics duly reference Mary Howitt's poem *The Spider and the Fly* (1829).

A favorite with fans, the song was covered by Led Zeppelin's Jimmy Page and Robert Plant on a tour in 1995. The band included ex-Cure guitarist Porl Thompson—"Jimmy Page was his idol," allowed Smith, "so I could understand it." Plant described The Cure as "one of the most underrated rock bands to come out of England," and enthused to *Q* about "Lullaby" in 1990: "I love Robert Smith's beckoning you into his vulnerability. It's an interesting little world, like H. G. Wells' [novel] *History of Mr. Polly*." **BM**

Free Fallin'
Tom Petty (1989)

Writer | Tom Petty, Jeff Lynne
Producer | Jeff Lynne, Tom Petty,
Mike Campbell
Label | MCA
Album | *Full Moon Fever* (1989)

After seven Heartbreakers albums, Tom Petty sounded in need of a change on *Let Me Up (I've Had Enough)* in 1987. He took a break and joined Bob Dylan, George Harrison, Jeff Lynne, and Roy Orbison in the Traveling Wilburys, then his first solo album followed. However, *Full Moon Fever* was "solo" in name only: Heartbreakers guitarist Mike Campbell and Lynne co-produced, and Harrison, Orbison, and Heartbreakers Howie Epstein and Benmont Tench contributed. The result was Petty's best album since *Damn the Torpedoes* in 1979: its greatness revealed with this plaintive opener.

"Free Fallin'" is a gorgeous slice of pop heaven. Warm, acoustic strumming introduces a melancholic ride through San Fernando Valley. Petty's stunning delivery brings to life one of his most memorable characters: the "good girl" who "loves her mama . . . Jesus and America," and is "crazy 'bout Elvis." The production is just as awe-inspiring, as layered vocals complement the jangly backing. "We had a multitude of acoustic guitars," Petty told *Rolling Stone*, "so it made this incredibly dreamy sound."

"Free Fallin'" helped make *Full Moon Fever* the biggest-selling album of Petty's career. It featured in Cameron Crowe's movie *Jerry Maguire* (1996), while John Mayer, Stevie Nicks, and Beck covered the song in concert. Petty came to regard it as something of an albatross; however, as he told *Esquire*, "I'm grateful that people like it." **JiH**

Nothing Compares 2 U
Sinéad O'Connor (1989)

Writer | Prince
Producer | S. O'Connor, N. Hooper
Label | Ensign
Album | *I Do Not Want What I
Haven't Got* (1989)

Amid his success with *Purple Rain*, Prince penned "Nothing Compares 2 U" for his protégés, The Family. Credits for their album were distributed among the group, but Prince laid claim to this ballad: "Kind of an indication," said saxophonist Eric Leeds, "of how personal he felt about that song."

Five years later, a feisty, shaven-headed girl from Dublin followed up her cult favorite *The Lion and the Cobra* with the blockbusting *I Do Not Want What I Haven't Got*. The album was propelled into the stratosphere by a bare, beautiful rendition of Prince's composition. "I think we just took that song as far as we could," he told *Rolling Stone*, "then someone else was supposed to come along and pick it up."

While Soul II Soul's strings entranced listeners, TV viewers were captured by the emotional video: a close-up of its star, singing direct to camera. At the climax, O'Connor let tears roll down her cheeks. She has described these tears variously as acted and as spontaneous—but, as she told *Q*, "Acting isn't pretending, it's using your past experiences, summoning them up to tell a story that's not a lie but the truth." The striking video helped the song to No. 1 around the world, and at the MTV Awards in 1990, it won Video of the Year—a first for a woman. This success prompted Prince to play it himself at gigs. However, O'Connor claimed she fell out with him after he objected to her swearing. "I told him to go fuck himself," she said. **SO**

The Humpty Dance | Digital Underground (1989)

Writer | Gregory "Shock-G" Jacobs, George Clinton, Bootsy Collins, Walter "Junie" Morrison
Producer | Gregory "Shock-G" Jacobs
Label | Tommy Boy Music
Album | *Sex Packets* (1989)

"Digital Underground is unlike any group."
Tupac Shakur, 1991

◀ **Influenced by: Let's Play House** · Parliament (1980)
▶ **Influence on: If U Can't Dance** · Spice Girls (1997)
● **Covered by:** F.O. the Smack Magnet (2000)
★ **Other key tracks:** Doowutchyalike (1989) · The Way We Swing (1989) · Gutfest '89 (1989) · Rhymin' on the Funk (1989) · The Danger Zone (1989)

Rap in the late 1980s was polarized between N.W.A. and Public Enemy's sonic assaults, and MC Hammer and the Fresh Prince's radio-friendly jams. Digital Underground—busting through a door left ajar by De La Soul—offered a new way: the way of the funky.

The group wore their influences proudly on their sleeves: the groundbreaking grooves and wigged-out worldview of George Clinton's Parliament-Funkadelic empire. Inspired by Clinton's maxim, "All the grown adult actors have come and went, but Bugs Bunny is still runnin' strong," producer Gregory "Shock-G" Jacobs created his alter ego: Humpty Hump. The character "started from the Warner Bros. cartoons," he said, "and it evolved from there."

Digital Underground's debut "Underwater Rimes/Your Life's a Cartoon" announced their intentions, but "The Humpty Dance" brought them to prominence. Tommy Boy label president Monica Lynch had suggested that Humpty Hump be given his own track. So, one night while the rest of the group went clubbing, Shock-G stayed in the studio—and, blending a Parliament groove with a beat from Sly & The Family Stone's "Sing a Simple Song," created "The Humpty Dance." Wittily scandalous lyrics completed the classic.

A massive club hit, it soared into the U.S. pop chart. Producers seized upon its superbly squelchy sonics, which turned up in tracks by giants such as Jay-Z, Ice Cube, and Will Smith. Digital Underground even recorded "The Humpty Dance Awards," in which they thanked everyone who had sampled it. The song had another legacy, too: in appearances to promote "The Humpty Dance," the Underground were joined by a young dancer edging his way to stardom: Tupac Shakur. **DC**

Back to Life (However Do You Want Me) | Soul II Soul (1989)

Writer | Nellee Hooper, Jazzie B, Simon Law, Caron Wheeler
Producer | Jazzie B, Nellee Hooper
Label | 10
Album | *Club Classics Vol One* (1989)

"A happy face, a thumpin' bass, for a lovin' race."
Jazzie B, 1989

◀ **Influenced by: The Jam** · Graham Central Station (1976)
▶ **Influence on: Unfinished Sympathy** · Massive Attack (1991)
● **Covered by:** Dodgy (1994) · The Reelists featuring Ms. Dynamite (2002)

In the late 1980s, the reggae-tinged Soul II Soul were a welcome antidote to the chemical euphoria of acid house. London DJs Jazzie B and Daddae Harvey teamed up with producer Nellee Hooper and created the aptly named album *Club Classics Vol One*. "Back to Life" closed that album, with an a capella version of the song, sung by Caron Wheeler—who had previously worked as a backing singer for Erasure, Howard Jones, and Elvis Costello. After the succcess of "Keep on Movin'," the album's first single, "Back to Life" was re-recorded with the addition of similar instrumentation: funky drums, thumping bass, and lush strings. Two versions were cut: one with the original vocal track and another with the addition of new lyrics and the refrain "However do you want me / However do you need me." The second version was chosen for release, and another club classic was born.

The single became a worldwide hit, turning a London sound system into a global brand with its own range of clothing. The no-nonsense Jazzie B even walked out on British TV show *Top of the Pops*: "They had us down as just another black dance act, so they wouldn't let us do it live. I said, 'Fuck this, let's go!' . . . But the record stayed at No. 1 for another five weeks."

The influential rhythm track has been sampled many times, and the song has been used on TV in *The Fresh Prince of Bel-Air* and *The L Word*. Jazzie B has been given the key to several U.S. cities and, in 2008, he was awarded the Order of the British Empire. After twenty years of the project, he commented, "Soul II Soul was always as much of a lifestyle statement as it was a musical movement or a sound system." **DC**

Nothing Has Been Proved | Dusty Springfield (1989)

Writer | Neil Tennant, Chris Lowe
Producer | N. Tennant, C. Lowe, J. Mendelsohn
Label | Parlophone
Album | *Reputation* (1990)

NOTHING HAS BEEN PROVED.
Dusty Springfield

"It didn't really register with me at the time. I didn't understand call-girls and naughties."

Dusty Springfield, 1989

◄ **Influenced by: Private Dancer** • Tina Turner (1984)
► **Influence on: Jesus to a Child** • George Michael (1996)
● **Covered by:** Pet Shop Boys (2006)
★ **Other key tracks:** I Just Don't Know What to Do with Myself (1964) • Some of Your Lovin' (1965) • Goin' Back (1966) • You Don't Have to Say You Love Me (1966)

The Pet Shops Boys breathed new life into Dusty Springfield's career by requesting her presence on their smash hit of 1987, "What Have I Done to Deserve This?" They then set about organizing a full-scale return for the British soul star, which included collaborating on "Nothing Has Been Proved" for *Scandal*—the 1989 movie about Christine Keeler and the Profumo Affair. *Scandal* and Springfield were a bittersweet combination: when the scandal had come to a head in 1963, Springfield had been embarking on her solo career.

"We suggested Dusty," Neil Tennant said, "because she's a voice from the Sixties." Twenty-six years later, a careworn Springfield was looking back to a time when she was on top. Of course, "Nothing Has Been Proved" is not about her—the Pet Shop Boys had even made a demo themselves. The uncluttered lyric is a concise and fluid telling of the affair, delivered as if Springfield were a diarist or newsreader—even down to "'Please Please Me's number one." The detail anchors the whole story to its mundane setting. "It's a scandal," fluttered Tennant in the background, "such a scandal"—ironic to the core.

Springfield invests the tawdry unraveling of the outrage with convincing emotion, her smoky voice—accompanied by Angelo Badalamenti's subtle orchestration—compelling us to listen to the lyric as we would watch a film. The tension is ramped up with, "In the news, a suicide . . ." and a key change in the third verse/bridge. Deftly handled, the dry exposition turns into drama.

"We've all got things to do," sighed Springfield at the fade, bringing us down to earth again. Courtney Pine's saxophone eases the song away, back to the daily drudge, the melodrama over. **MH**

Headlights on the Parade | The Blue Nile (1989)

Writer | Paul Buchanan
Producer | The Blue Nile
Label | Linn
Album | *Hats* (1989)

"It's less about places than about a dialogue between the people on the record."

Paul Buchanan, 1995

◄ **Influenced by:** Time it's Time • Talk Talk (1986)
► **Influence on:** Barefoot in the Head • A Man Called Adam (1990)
★ **Other key tracks:** Stay (1984) • Tinseltown in the Rain (1984) • The Downtown Lights (1989) • From a Late Night Train (1989) • Let's Go Out Tonight (1989)

Four albums in a quarter of a century may seem slothful, but Scottish trio The Blue Nile's music is so exquisitely crafted that it is a wonder it makes it out of the studio at all. "Headlights on the Parade" is the centerpiece of *Hats*—the night-and-lights classic that followed five years after their acclaimed debut *A Walk across the Rooftops*. Like its parent album, "Headlights on the Parade" shimmers in the rain, bristles with romance, and mocks its refined setting with real passion from singer Paul Buchanan.

Buchanan's soul-soaked croon lifts The Blue Nile from their roots as a showcase band for hi-fi manufacturer Linn. Their meticulously programmed synthesizers sound fantastic, but—as with Alison Moyet in Yazoo—the human element raises the art. In "Headlights on the Parade," our protagonist asks for trust but admits that words are not enough. It "would be easy to say I love you," sighs Buchanan, searching for a way to express himself. The headlights "light up the way."

The Blue Nile breathe autumn, drizzly dusks, and trysts under streetlamps. "We wanted to make music that was believable to people who had real lives," explained Buchanan in 2006. "Headlights on the Parade"—at six minutes, hardly radio-friendly—bolstered their list of non-hit singles, including the equally heartrending "Tinseltown in the Rain" in 1983 and "The Downtown Lights" in 1989.

Hats is a grown-up record, creased by experience. But songs like "Headlights on the Parade"—with its motorik pulse and chiming, fluttering synths—sound almost Balearic. Unlikely as it seems, the deft playing and mood setting of Buchanan, Robert Bell, and Paul Joseph Moore can turn neon lights into Ibizan sunsets. **MH**

Chloe Dancer/Crown of Thorns
Mother Love Bone (1989)

Writer | Jeff Ament, Bruce Fairweather, Greg Gilmore, Stone Gossard, Andrew Wood
Producer | Mark Dearnley
Label | Stardog
Album | N/A

Seattle's Mother Love Bone were rooted in the sound that made their hometown famous: bassist Jeff Ament and guitarist Stone Gossard had been in grunge pioneers Green River. However, their influences and ambitions were far from the sludgy punk and metal of their contemporaries. Thanks to flamboyant front man Andrew Wood, Mother Love Bone were a grander affair: wedding glam metal flourishes to classic rock greatness.

Wood wore an unabashed love for Freddie Mercury and Elton John on his lamé sleeve, and their gift for impassioned balladry seeped into "Chloe Dancer/Crown of Thorns"—the standout track from the group's debut EP, *Shine* (1989).

Over melancholic piano, Wood sings of thwarted but undying love, nobly denying that his cause is truly lost. As the intro gives way to "Crown of Thorns," the band stir up a nuanced groove that builds to heroic crescendos, with breathtaking grace and tender power.

An edited version of the song appeared on their debut album, *Apple* (1990), but Wood—aged twenty-four—was dead of a heroin overdose before it hit the shelves. Mother Love Bone's legacy lived on, however, in Ament and Gossard's next band, Pearl Jam. Meanwhile, "Chloe Dancer/Crown of Thorns" featured on the soundtrack of Cameron Crowe's movie *Singles* (1992), alongside "Would?"—Alice in Chains' tribute to the late singer. **SC**

Rhythm Nation
Janet Jackson (1989)

Writer | Janet Jackson, James "Jimmy Jam" Harris, Terry Lewis
Producer | J. Harris, T. Lewis, J. Jackson
Label | A&M
Album | *Janet Jackson's Rhythm Nation 1814* (1989)

"Children are the future," intoned Janet Jackson at a press conference in 1989. "Yeah," replied a cynical voice, "future record buyers." Critics may have been unconvinced, but the public had no problem with the socially conscious Janet: *Rhythm Nation* topped the U.S. chart, sold six million copies in that country alone, and became the first album to spawn seven Top Five hits.

"The thing we set out to do was not make *Control Part Two* . . ." producer Jimmy Jam told *Billboard*'s Craig Rosen, referring to Jackson's hit album of 1986. "The actual *Rhythm Nation* idea wasn't formed until about six or seven songs into the project. . . . We were watching a lot of CNN and there were a lot of world events that were happening that were screwed up. That was on Janet's mind while we were making the album." "There was a major drug issue back then," Jackson recalled to *The Times* in 2009. "Crack cocaine was being introduced in the inner cities, and it was cheap. I remember seeing something on CNN about a little kid who was homeless, sleeping in the back of a car. And that was what it all sparked from."

Jimmy Jam and Terry Lewis's pounding, grinding music—based on a sample from Sly & The Family Stone's bittersweet "Thank You (Falettinme Be Mice Elf Agin)"—matched the stark lyrics. Jackson's brother Michael suggested the military look of the song's video, and an iconic image was born. **BM**

Janet Jackson performs in her militaristic "Rhythm Nation" outfit in 1990.

- Nirvana and other Pacific Northwest bands introduce grunge in 1991

- Death Row Records, founded in 1991, releases West Coast rap music

- The Spice Girls form in 1994 and become the best-selling girl group

- Oasis and Blur battle to dominate the Britpop music scene in 1995

- The 1997 *Buena Vista Social Club* album reinvigorates world music

1990s

Painkiller | Judas Priest (1990)

Writer | K. K. Downing, Rob Halford, Glenn Tipton
Producer | Chris Tsangarides, Judas Priest
Label | CBS
Album | *Painkiller* (1990)

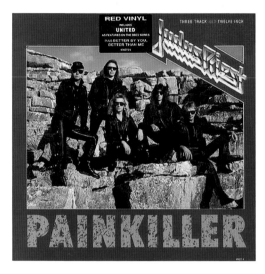

"Obviously, the intro to 'Painkiller' is a pretty memorable point in my career."
Scott Travis, 2007

◀ **Influenced by: Wake up Dead** · Megadeth (1986)
▶ **Influence on: Angel in Black** · Primal Fear (2001)
● **Covered by:** Angra (1996) · Death (1998)
  Biomechanical (2005)
★ **Other key tracks:** Battle Hymn (1990) · A Touch of Evil (1991) · Night Crawler (1992)

The dawning of the Nineties should have spelled the end for Judas Priest. Every one of their albums had gone gold in the Eighties, and they had emerged victorious from a difficult court case that accused them of inciting a suicide attempt. But they had been metal gods since 1974, so surely it was time to let Megadeth take over? "We're at the point, really, where I think what our fans want is more of a failure than a success," rued guitarist K. K. Downing to metal magazine *Kerrang!* "They want a record that's gonna fail, but they're gonna love it to death!"

Downing was ultimately vindicated. After the sonic detour *Turbo* in 1986, and the inconsistent *Ram it Down* of 1988, *Painkiller* was acclaimed as Judas Priest's best album ever. Warning is served by the first fifteen seconds of the opening title track: new recruit Scott Travis (formerly of Racer X) smashing seven shades of hell out of his drums. Then comes the razor-sharp guitars of Downing and Glenn Tipton, and the unmistakable shriek of singer Rob Halford. *Village Voice* summed it up: "[Halford] has been howling about the same law-breaking nightcrawling beasts . . . while K. K. Downing and Glenn Tipton flutter and twiddle . . . for the last sixteen years. They've just never done it this urgently."

Painkiller, and its title track in particular, proved that Judas Priest were far from finished, although some old-school fans were bewildered by the material. "We started touring with five tracks off that album," Downing told *Classic Rock Revisited,* "and, by the time we finished, we were playing two. It was a bit of a hard sell." Two decades on, however, fans new and old rank "Painkiller" as a pivotal moment in metal. **BM**

Loaded | Primal Scream (1990)

Writer | Bobby Gillespie, Andrew Innes, Robert Young
Producer | Andrew Weatherall
Label | Creation
Album | *Screamadelica* (1991)

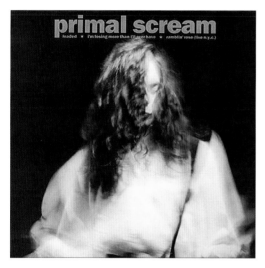

"We're a rock 'n' roll band, but we like going to clubs and getting pretty wasted."
Bobby Gillespie, 1991

◀ **Influenced by:** Sympathy for the Devil • The Rolling Stones (1968)
▶ **Influence on:** Butcher Blues • Kasabian (2004)
★ **Other key tracks:** Higher Than the Sun (1991) • Inner Flight (1991) • Movin' on Up (1991) • Rocks (1994) Burning Wheel (1997) • Kowalski (1997) • Star (1997)

With a new perspective on an old song, Primal Scream and Andy Weatherall instantly opened up all sorts of possibilities for the merging of rock with dance. On a whim, the Scream gave "I'm Losing More Than I'll Ever Have"—from their self-titled, second album—to DJ and producer Weatherall, hoping he could exploit its full potential.

His overhaul was front-ended with Peter Fonda's defiant drop-out speech from the Roger Corman movie of 1966, *The Wild Angels* (previously used by Mudhoney on the *Superfuzz Bigmuff* EP in 1988). However, Weatherall's real genius was to transform a mournful lament into an influential indie-dance classic—and Primal Scream's first Top Twenty U.K. hit to boot. (In its wake, Weatherall's remix of My Bloody Valentine's "You Made Me Realise" passed largely unnoticed. Years later, however, the Valentines' main man Kevin Shields himself remixed—and briefly joined—the Scream.)

The producer has been modest about the part he played in the song's success: "It was just random elements coming together. I was just one of them that came in, sort of bumping into doors." However, singer Bobby Gillespie saw how powerful the combination had been, acknowledging that "Loaded" was a turning point in the group's career: "We've always written great songs, but we've never known how to turn them into hit singles. He [Weatherall] can take that quintessential element from one of our songs and make it really focused. He's got vision and inspiration." To top it off, the Scream made a memorable showing on BBC TV's *Top of the Pops*—their demeanor suggesting that the band had gotten fully into the spirit of the song. **CB**

Iceblink Luck | Cocteau Twins (1990)

Writer | Elizabeth Fraser, Robin Guthrie, Simon Raymonde
Producer | Cocteau Twins
Label | 4AD
Album | *Heaven or Las Vegas* (1990)

"Heaven or Las Vegas is quite uplifting, isn't it? I wonder how that happened."

Liz Fraser, 2000

◀ **Influenced by: Down** • A. R. Kane (1989)
▶ **Influence on: Fallen** • One Dove (1991)
● **Covered by:** Mephisto Walz (2000)
★ **Other key tracks:** Pearly Dew Drops Drops (1984)
Blue Bell Knoll (1988) • Pitch the Baby (1990)
Fifty-Fifty Clown (1990)

Vaunted as much for singer Liz Fraser's gobbledygook as for their dense dream-pop, the Cocteau Twins found a third way in 1990. Suddenly, on their sixth album, *Heaven or Las Vegas*, they displayed the will to make their music accessible to a wider audience, and—crucially—Fraser's lyrics became comprehensible.

That's not to say the band began dealing in straightforward love songs. However, "Iceblink Luck"—with its "You, yourself, and your father. . . . You're really both bonesetters / Thank you for mending me babies"—offered emotional insight, particularly in light of the birth of Fraser and guitarist Robin Guthrie's daughter a year earlier. "As soon as I got pregnant," Fraser told *Select*, "I don't know what happened, but I suddenly started to realize what things mattered. . . . Suddenly I had confidence which I'd never ever had in my life."

That the Cocteaus were dealing in the personal was unexpected. Fans were not alienated, however. There was no let-up in Fraser's soaring voice, which swoops on the verse. Then, double-tracked, it turns an earworm of a chorus into an anthem, ever more ecstatic with each iteration. In Guthrie and Simon Raymonde's chiming music there is a fresh clarity to the production: crisper beats and sparkling guitar enhance a melody that suggests a hit. "In a way, we just made the same record over and over again," Guthrie conceded in 2000. "We just did it with a different level of confidence." Enhanced by experience, "Iceblink Luck" represented the Cocteau Twins' finest hour—its tenderness and relative transparency proving that they could now speak to people without compromising their essential, bewitching mystery. **MH**

Cocteau Twins' Liz Fraser in 1990, the year of the group's greatest commercial success. ➔

Birdhouse in Your Soul
They Might Be Giants (1990)

Writer | John Flansburgh,
John Linnell
Producer | Clive Langer, Alan Winstanley
Label | Elektra
Album | *Flood* (1990)

"Birdhouse in Your Soul" probably remains the only song written from the point of view of a blue, canary-shaped nightlight. Nonetheless, insisted John Linnell—one half of "the two Johns"—"We don't want it to sound weird. That isn't the idea."

Linnell and John Flansburgh were friends who began making music together in New York after college. Eventually signed to Elektra, the duo snared the mainstream with their third album, *Flood*. With its chirpy charms and engaging video, "Birdhouse in Your Soul" flew up the U.K. chart. At home, Flansburgh told popculturecorn.com, "People are familiar with the song, but it never charted. I think probably the main reason people know it is because it got MTV play."

"The melody and chords were cooked up years earlier," Linnell told *Rolling Stone*, "and the lyrics had to be shoehorned in to match the melody, which explains why the words are so oblique—I mean beautiful." The song's trumpet solo, reported *Rolling Stone*, "is sampled from a studio session by Frank London, who played the memorable trumpet-plunger hook in LL Cool J's 'Going Back to Cali.'"

The group's lyrics were often subject to multiple interpretations. "Some of our songs are very hard to explain . . ." admitted Flansburgh, "[But] I feel like we could write a song with the title 'I Wanna Fuck You' and people would still say, 'I don't understand . . . explain to me what that song means.'" **SO**

Energy Flash
Joey Beltram (1990)

Writer | Joey Beltram
Producer | Joey Beltram
Label | Transmat
Album | *Beltram Vol. 1* (1990)

Electronic dance music is a fast-mutating creature with enough subgenres to defeat the most determined discographer. However, back in 1990, the trailblazing "Energy Flash" united the scene. Its deceptively simple, hardcore beat and distorted high hat pulsated alongside one of the first on-the-record odes to Ecstasy, via a menacing vocal loop. Voted *Muzik* magazine's track of the Nineties, the relentlessly invigorating single has since appeared on innumerable dance compilations, having laid a foundation for many subgenres that followed—from deep house to darkcore.

An early proponent of Chicago house, Beltram began spinning records at the age of twelve. After cutting his first dance record for New York's Nu Groove label in 1988, he hopped the Atlantic to play in Europe, traveling through Belgium in 1989. The journey served him well, introducing him to the R&S label (who licensed the track to techno pioneer Derrick May's Transmat label). By the time he was nineteen, Beltram had fine-tuned his pioneering blend of Chicago house, Detroit techno, and Belgian hardcore for "Energy Flash."

"Melodically, it's one of the simplest records you ever heard," explained progressive house DJ Richard Ford of the single's enduring appeal. "But it shows that house is about sound. This is dirty, sleazy, seedy—but most of all fantastic. It marked the R&S label in its heyday. It still works big time today." **EP**

Bonita Applebum
A Tribe Called Quest (1990)

Writer | W. Allen, R. Ayers, E. Birdsong, W. Booker, Q-Tip, A. Shaheed Muhammad, C. Stepney
Producer | A Tribe Called Quest
Album | *People's Instinctive Travels and the Paths of Rhythm* (Jive, 1990)

"Bonita Applebum" was by no means rap's first love song, but few offered seduction with the sophistication of New York's A Tribe Called Quest. With the vocals drenched in backward echo, their rhymes sound like intimate whispers, setting up rapper Q-Tip as a lover man for the 1990s—a considerate partner promising to kiss his girl "where some brothers won't" and a willing practitioner of safe sex—"If you need 'em, I got crazy prophylactics."

Q-Tip could hardly fail in his quest for Bonita, reputedly a girl he knew from high school. His lustful poetry is wrapped in a dulcet bedroom groove sampled from "Daylight," by Roy Ayers's protégés RAMP, while an erotic sitar lick, lifted from Rotary Connection's "Memory Band," caresses the foreground. Cannonball Adderley's "Soul Virgo" is among the other sources.

A poppier remix, laying Tip's vocals over the beat to "Why"—Carly Simon's 1982 collaboration with Chic's Bernard Edwards and Niles Rodgers—entranced many listeners. However, it is the original "Bonita Applebum" that is the keeper, stirring up a subtle, downbeat mood that A Tribe Called Quest mined further on the acclaimed, jazz-soaked *The Low End Theory* (1991). Indeed, "Bonita Applebum" is the track that blueprinted Tribe's unique, jazzy sound—making them standard-bearers for rap and the song a hip-hop standard. **SC**

Little Fluffy Clouds
The Orb (1990)

Writer | Youth, Alex Paterson, Steve Reich
Producer | Youth
Label | Big Life
Album | *The Orb's Adventures Beyond the Ultraworld* (1991)

At the beginning of the 1990s, along came chill-out music. Two former punks—Alex Paterson and Jimmy Cauty, mutual acquaintances of Killing Joke bassist-turned-producer Youth—led the pack. Their baby, The Orb, married samples from a huge library of sources to pulsating, ambient sound.

The gorgeous "Little Fluffy Clouds" was Paterson and Youth's first venture after Cauty split to focus on the more dance-oriented KLF, and the first chill-out track to infiltrate the mainstream. It opens, as Paterson informed *Melody Maker*, with "a [BBC] Radio Four interview I did about ambient music." However, the title and recurring speech comes from singer Rickie Lee Jones, from an interview on a promo edition of her album *Flying Cowboys* (1989). During the interview, Jones recalled cloud formations from the desert skies of her youth, all "purple and red and on fire." Jones's publishers promptly demanded compensation; while the singer was obliged to point out that her apparently stoned tone was actually because she had a cold.

Among the song's other samples is an extract from a piece by modern classical composer Steve Reich. "There in the middle of it," Reich recalls, "is my composition 'Electric Counterpoint.' Since The Orb were not very well known at the time, I suggested to [Reich's label] Nonesuch that they not go after them for money, which probably upped my stock in the remix world." **JMc**

Three Days | Jane's Addiction (1990)

Writer | Perry Farrell, Eric Avery, Dave Navarro, Stephen Perkins
Producer | Dave Jerden, Perry Farrell
Label | Warner Bros.
Album | *Ritual de lo Habitual* (1990)

"I get so caught up in these songs, I can actually feel the band pushing themselves to their limits."
Alice Cooper, 1994

◀ **Influenced by: The Song Remains the Same**
Led Zeppelin (1973)
▶ **Influence on: Boatman** • DJ Frane (1999)
★ **Other key tracks:** Been Caught Stealing (1990)
Classic Girl (1990) • Stop! (1990)

"What could beat two days of sex and drugs and violent movies?" singer Perry Farrell asked an audience in 1987. "*Three* days of sex, drugs, and violent movies." This set the scene for his band's most astounding song: a near eleven-minute epic that twisted and turned from poetry to Zeppelinesque classic rock. It originated with a bass line conceived by Eric Avery in 1985, before he founded Jane's Addiction with Farrell the following year. After modifications in 1986, "Three Days" was played live in 1987, mothballed for a year, then extended and slowed down in preparation for *Ritual de lo Habitual*.

Its lyrics concerned Xiola Bleu, an ex-lover of Farrell's, who stayed with the singer and his partner, Casey Niccoli, when she attended her father's funeral in early 1986. Farrell never saw Xiola again: she died alone, aged nineteen, of an overdose in June 1987—hence "I miss you, my dear Xiola" in his spoken introduction. "She was very young, very intelligent, and very beautiful . . ." Niccoli told *Details*. "So we kind of put her on a pedestal."

By 1990, Jane's Addiction were falling apart. Their headlining sets at Farrell's Lollapalooza festival degenerated into fistfights, and the band split in 1991. Guitarist Dave Navarro later joined the Red Hot Chili Peppers, with whom he occasionally played excerpts of "Three Days" after their song "Warped."

Recording "Three Days" provided a welcome shining moment amid the group's disintegration. "The whole band came in and played 'Three Days' from beginning to end," recalled co-producer Dave Jerden. "That was the last time they played together in the studio, and the only time on that record. It was a magic moment." **BM**

Dub Be Good to Me | Beats International (1990)

Writer | Norman Cook, James "Jimmy Jam" Harris, Terry Lewis
Producer | Norman Cook
Label | Go!
Album | *Let Them Eat Bingo* (1990)

"It's got scratching noises on it and a bass line that doesn't follow the rest of the song."

Norman Cook, 1990

◀ **Influenced by: Just Be Good to Me** · The S.O.S. Band (1983)
▶ **Influence on: Just Be Good to Me** · Groove Diggerz featuring Lindy Layton (2009)
● **Covered by:** Faithless & Dido (2002) · Jack Peñate (2007) · The Ting Tings (2009)

"Tank fly boss walk, jam nitty gritty / You're listening to the boy from the big bad city / This is jam hot, this is jam hot." Schoolyards and clubs across Europe and the United States reverberated to the introductory rap of "Dub Be Good to Me" for many months in 1990.

The brainchild of Norman Cook, the song was an intoxicating cocktail. It was originally written as an instrumental track titled "The Invasion of the Estate Agents." The opening rap was from Johnny Dynell's cut "Jam Hot" of 1983. The song itself was The S.O.S. Band's extraordinary "Just Be Good to Me," embellished with a bass line from The Clash's classic of 1979, "The Guns of Brixton." (That, Cook enthused, "was me tipping my hat off to The Clash, as I was such a big fan.") The finishing touch was an eerie excerpt of "Man with a Harmonica," from Ennio Morricone's *Once Upon a Time in the West* movie soundtrack, released in 1968.

The plaintive, lovelorn lyrics suited singer Lindy Layton perfectly. "It was Lindy's idea to do a cover," Cook declared. "I knew it would go well with other beats because I'd tried it as a DJ." Cook formed Beats International after leaving The Housemartins (whose Paul Heaton formed The Beautiful South). Despite that band's success, Cook was surprised when "Dub Be Good to Me" topped the U.K. chart. "To have a No. 1," he told *The Face*, "you have to sell to grannies and ten-year-olds. I didn't think grannies would get into a record like that. It took six hours to make. I'm still shocked."

Beats International never matched the success of their signature song "Dub Be Good to Me," and disbanded after their second album. Cook, however, eventually became a household name— as Fatboy Slim. **OM**

Kool Thing | Sonic Youth (1990)

Writer | Kim Gordon, Thurston Moore,
Lee Ranaldo, Steve Shelley
Producer | Sonic Youth, N. Sansano, R. Saint Germain
Label | DGC
Album | Goo (1990)

"Chuck D seemed totally cool. He's just a homeboy. He lives in Long Island—down to earth."

Thurston Moore, 1990

◀ **Influenced by: Femme Fatale** · The Velvet
  Undergound & Nico (1969)
▶ **Influence on: Swimsuit Issue** · Sonic Youth (1992)
● **Covered by:** Steve Wynn (1991) · Tub Ring (2004)
★ **Other key tracks:** Expressway to Yr. Skull (1986) · Teen
  Age Riot (1988) · The Sprawl (1988) · Dirty Boots (1990)

Sonic Youth had become a byword for the harsh, dissonant, no-wave sound after a decade's worth of underground, alt-rock releases. However, in June 1990, they surprised long-time fans with the release of "Kool Thing"—their first single for a major label. The track was demoed as "DV2," produced by Dinosaur Jr.'s J. Mascis and Gumball's Don Fleming. But the four-minute edit of "Kool Thing" became one of the New York band's most radio-friendly tracks. Foregoing the band's art-noise roots in favor of a melodic guitar riff, the single's conventional verse-chorus-verse structure features a series of rasping exchanges between Sonic Youth's Kim Gordon and Public Enemy's Chuck D, on the subject of sexual equality.

The Chuck D collaboration came about purely by accident, when Sonic Youth found themselves working in the same New York City studio as Public Enemy, who were recording their third album *Fear of a Black Planet*. "I think they were kind of curious about us," Thurston Moore told *City Limits*. "Their scene is aware ours exists, but it all melts together. So, you know, we might as well be Blondie. . . . Chuck was around, Kim asked him if he'd come in, do the song, say those lines—and he elaborated on it a bit, and grooved along. . . . We were honored, really."

The accessibility of "Kool Thing" threatened to catapult Sonic Youth into the mainstream. However, despite the song's subsequent inclusion in the computer games *Rock Band* and *Guitar Hero*, the Youth retained their low-key integrity. "Maybe in some sort of small indie circle we're rock personalities or whatever," reflected guitarist Lee Renaldo. "But I don't think any of us see ourselves as rock stars." **EP**

Sonic Youth: clockwise from bottom left, Lee Ranaldo, Steve Shelley, Kim Gordon, and Thurston Moore. ➡

Only Love Can Break Your Heart | Saint Etienne (1990)

Writer | Neil Young
Producer | Saint Etienne
Label | Heavenly
Album | *Foxbase Alpha* (1991)

"We were thinking of doing 'Ambulance Blues' ... but it was too long. And too difficult."

Bob Stanley, 1991

s

Many have dipped into Neil Young's back catalog; few have matched the emotional resonance of his recordings, let alone given them a fresh, intoxicating spin. However, with their audacious interpretation of "Only Love Can Break Your Heart," originally from *After the Gold Rush*, Saint Etienne turned a plaintive ballad into haunting yet danceable pop.

"Psychic TV had just done 'Only Love ... '" the band's Bob Stanley admitted to *Melody Maker*, "and we thought it was a really good idea. ... We saved up two hundred quid and went into the studio to do two songs, but we hadn't written any, so we decided on 'Only Love Can Break Your Heart' and '[Let's] Kiss and Make Up' by The Field Mice."

Saint Etienne's collected elements—house music piano, Soul II Soul–style drums, a peppering of Led Zeppelin's bombastic "When the Levee Breaks" in the refrain—should never have suited the song. However, the simple yet effective composition—reportedly made in two hours—transcends these early Nineties clichés, giving the song the power to outlast most of its indie dance contemporaries.

Named after a French soccer team but obsessed with swinging Sixties London, Saint Etienne are often associated with photogenic chanteuse Sarah Cracknell. However, this—their debut single—was a pre-Cracknell release, sung by Moira Lambert from fellow indie outfit Faith Over Reason. Production-wise, "Only Love Can Break Your Heart" sounds pleasingly coordinated with the rest of *Foxbase Alpha*—although this means that Lambert doesn't always get the credit she deserves, because many listeners assume that Cracknell is singing. The single became the band's only appearance on *Billboard*'s Hot 100, peaking at No. 97 but topping the dance chart. **GR**

Crazy | Seal (1990)

Writer | Seal
Producer | Trevor Horn
Label | ZTT
Album | *Seal* (1991)

"Seal and I exchanged sweet emails when I was about to cover his song."
Alanis Morissette, 2005

◀ **Influenced by: The Wind Cries Mary** · The Jimi Hendrix Experience (1967)
▶ **Influence on: Space Cowboy** · Jamiroquai (1994)
● **Covered by:** Talisman (1996) · Iron Savior (2002) Mushroomhead (2003) · Alanis Morissette (2005) Helena Paparizou (2006)

One of the weirdest yet strongest songs to emerge from the late Eighties influx of acid house music was "Killer" by Adamski. As proved by Adamski's subsequent career trajectory, Seal's rich vocals were, for many, the most captivating element of the song. Not slow to recognize this fact, legendary Eighties production supremo Trevor Horn signed up to produce the singer-songwriter's first album. Seal's solo career was launched in style with "Crazy," a fusion of soul, pop, rock, and R&B, which—despite later smashes like "Kiss from a Rose"—remains arguably his most enduring moment.

Full of drug and dance scene references, "Crazy" blends soulful lyrics and husky vocals with Horn's trademark sweeping orchestration and a voguish electronic backing—a combination that, in the wake of this and Massive Attack, became the template for a whole strand of dance music.

"I had no doubts about 'Crazy,'" Seal told *Q*. "I always thought it was a potential No. 1—even though it never was! It's the first song I wrote on the guitar, and the first song where I said everything I wanted to say in a concise way. Before that my songs had been too long. But as soon as I wrote the hook, I knew it was a potential hit." The song reached No. 2 in the U.K. charts and was a Top Ten hit in the United States.

"When I did the Gap campaign," Alanis Morissette told *Songwriter Universe*, "the lovely folks there asked me to submit a list of my favorite songs. 'Crazy' was one of the first . . . because it brings back so many memories of my teenage years. . . . 'You're never going to survive / Unless you get a little crazy' is to me one of the simplest yet most profound statements." **SO**

Mustt Mustt (Lost in his Work)
Nusrat Fateh Ali Khan (1990)

Writer | Nusrat Fateh Ali Khan
Producer | Michael Brook
Label | Real World
Album | *Musst Musst* (1990)

Diaraby Nene
Oumou Sangare (1990)

Writer | Oumou Sangare
Producer | Ahmadou ba Guindo
Label | Samassa
Album | *Moussolou* (1990)

An extraordinary singer with the humility of a saint, Nusrat Fateh Ali Khan became Pakistan's premier cultural envoy after giving its modal qawwali music worldwide exposure. This was largely because of his association with the WOMAD organization and Real World label—both the brainchild of Peter Gabriel. Gabriel teamed him with Canadian producer Michael Brook for a four-day session, and the result was the fusion masterpiece *Musst Musst*.

Qawwali is a blend of Islamic (Sufi) poetry and Hindustani music. Khan supported such fusion because, in the Qur'an, Allah is said to favor diversity —and Khan considered music the best way to celebrate this. He had already updated qawwali, speeding up and shortening traditional pieces that could last up to an hour and were performed with just harmonium, drums, and chorus vocals. "Musst Musst" ("intoxicated" or "high") features a West African *djembe* drum, funky bass, and electric guitars. Over this, Khan recites Urdu poetry and improvises in his trademark wordless style, similar to scat.

Musst Musst "was a seminal album for me and completely changed the face of British music," enthused Nitin Sawhney, who noted it "also features one of the best remixes of all time from Massive Attack." The latter gave "Mustt Mustt" their patented trip-hop vibe for a version that achieved international success and helped kick-start Britain's "Asian Underground" movement. **JLu**

In Mali, as in many West African countries, music as a profession has, for centuries, been the almost exclusive preserve of a hereditary caste called griots or jelis, who mostly sang for wealthy patrons. In recent decades, though, non-griot artists from the Wassulu region—most of them women—have had huge success with their own funky music. Their undisputed queen is Oumou Sangare, who made her name with "Diaraby Nene" (the title translates as "thrill of love" or, more evocatively, "shivers of passion").

Sangare's lyrics (which she considers more important than the music) have long focused on women's issues, attacking traditional practices such as polygamy, female circumcision, and forced marriage. A woman singing about her passion for a man may not sound radical at all; however, in this tradition-bound society, "Diaraby Nene" provoked outrage from some (and admiration from many). Not even bothering to veil its message in metaphors, the song speaks quite frankly and graphically about unfettered female desire: "I put my hand low on his stomach / My skin shivers . . ." The frisky, plunking sound of the six-stringed *kamalengoni* harp drives the lurching, hypnotic rhythm. However, what grabs most attention is Sangare's fabulous soaring vocal, its moans of pleasure needing no translation. **JLu**

Nusrat Fateh Ali Khan in 2001: his devotional music also attracted nonbelievers in droves.

1952 Vincent Black Lightning
Richard Thompson (1991)

Writer | Richard Thompson
Producer | Mitchell Froom
Label | Capitol
Album | *Rumor and Sigh* (1991)

"The Vincent is a rather wonderful, rare, and beautiful beast," Richard Thompson told writer Anil Prasad of his ode to a vintage motorcycle and its rider. "It is an object of myth. There's not many I can think of in Britain." Thompson could have been talking about himself. Having helped launch English folk rock with Fairport Convention, and duetted with then-wife Linda on two seminal albums, he influenced singers, songwriters, and guitarists (a tribute album in 1994 featured admirers ranging from Dinosaur Jr. to The Blind Boys of Alabama). Arguably, however, he didn't have a definitive solo song until he found it for *Rumor and Sigh*.

This dramatic tragedy kicks off with an acoustic guitar picked with remarkable speed and dexterity. The lyrical arc begins as biker James Adie woos Red Molly with compliments ("Red hair and black leather, my favorite color scheme") and a warning ("But I'll tell you in earnest, I'm a dangerous man"). Following a trail blazed by The Shangri-Las' classic "Leader of the Pack," James revs past the point of no return. The song climaxes on his deathbed: "I see angels on Ariels in leather and chrome / Swooping down from heaven to carry me home."

"It's a story that relates back to older British and Scottish ballad forms where we have an antihero central character," Thompson observed. "And even though he may die in the end, he sort of triumphs and gets one over on society first." **JiH**

Balada conducatorolui
Taraf de Haïdouks (1991)

Writer | Stephane Vande Wyer
Producer | V. Kenis, S. Karo, M. Winter
Label | CramWorld
Album | *Musique des tziganes de Roumanie* (1991)

When communism ruled Eastern Europe, Western music was banned, and ancient folk-music styles were preserved. Thus, when the Berlin Wall fell, there were numerous musical treasures waiting to be discovered. First off the block were a Romanian Gypsy group, discovered by Belgian promoter Stephane Karo. He named them Taraf de Haïdouks, meaning "band of outlaws."

"Balada conducatorolui" (Ballad of the Dictator) got the outlaws' discography off to a striking start. The group's seventy-year-old leader, Nicolae Neacşu, draws raw sounds from his violin while fourteen-year-old Marinel Sandu sets up a sparkling rhythm pattern on a small *cymbalum* (hammered dulcimer). The toothless Neacşu narrates the events that led to the overthrow of the tyrant, at one point tugging horse's hair across the violin's strings to create the most extraordinary effect—as if the earth were opening up.

Taraf de Haïdouks performed the song in Tony Gatlif's superb French movie of 1993 *Latcho drom* (Romany for "safe journey"). This won them great acclaim, with violin maestro Yehudi Menuhin and contemporary classical group The Kronos Quartet lining up to praise Neacşu's musical genius. Such fame saw them appearing on the world's most prestigious stages and in several films. Neacşu died in 2002, but the Taraf continue to share their unique, ancient sound. **GC**

Calling All Angels
Jane Siberry with k.d. lang (1991)

Writer | Jane Siberry
Producer | Jane Siberry
Label | Warner Bros.
Album | *Until the End of the World* (1991)

Upstaging R.E.M., Depeche Mode, and U2 is a daunting task. However, Jane Siberry accomplished it in style when "Calling All Angels" became the best-loved song from the soundtrack to Wim Wenders's *Until the End of the World*. (It reappeared in 1993 on her album *When I Was a Boy*.)

Siberry was the missing link between fellow Canadians Joni Mitchell and Sarah McLachlan, yet her maverick approach to music and business was more akin to Ani DiFranco or Madonna. She started her own label, gave away her possessions, and, predating Radiohead, allowed fans to determine prices for downloads.

"Calling All Angels," however, reins in the weirdness in favor of heartbreaking beauty. Wintry, electronic sounds form a backdrop to acoustic guitar and world-weary lyrics. Joining the chorus is another Canadian maverick, k.d. lang. Siberry duly credited lang with making her "a much better singer." "Something went into my system when I sang 'Calling All Angels' with her," she told *Impact*. "Just being around someone who understands singing the way she does, you pick up all sorts of things." The wispy image endured, however. "Many people don't get me," Siberry told *Perfect Sound Forever*. "Like when I go to comedy clubs . . . I start to heckle! This vile, venomous language comes out of me! 'This isn't the girl who sang 'Calling All Angels' is it?' [Pause] 'Oh, yes, it is.'" **BM**

I Can't Make You Love Me
Bonnie Raitt (1991)

Writer | Mike Reid, Allen Shamblin
Producer | Don Was, Bonnie Raitt
Label | Capitol
Album | *Luck of the Draw* (1991)

After eighteen years in the business, Bonnie Raitt topped the U.S. charts with her Grammy-winning tenth album, *Nick of Time* (1989). With success came pressure, and the singer-guitarist was under the gun to show that *Nick of Time* was not a fluke. She accomplished that in style with *Luck of the Draw*.

Raitt spent six months recording the album's twelve songs, half of which were released as singles. The most striking was "I Can't Make You Love Me," Raitt's crowning moment. "It was," she told phillymag.com, "an incredible gift to be given that song." The heart-wrenching ballad is a one-sided love story, painfully depicting a relationship on its deathbed. The lyrics were inspired by a news story about a man who shot at his girlfriend's car in an attempt to make her stay with him. When a judge asked the perpetrator what he had learned from the situation, he reportedly answered, "You can't make a woman love you if she don't."

Raitt did the vocals in one take, explaining to producer Don Was that she simply couldn't summon up the requisite emotions a second time. In retrospect, she didn't need a second take—she had nailed the lovesick feel perfectly. Her tear-jerking delivery was wonderfully complemented by equally forlorn piano from Bruce Hornsby. The song was a Top Ten U.S. hit that helped *Luck of the Draw* garner a boatload of Grammys and become the best-selling album of Raitt's career. **JiH**

Jesus Built My Hotrod | Ministry (1991)

Writer | A. Jourgensen, P. Barker, G. Haynes, B. Rieflin
Producer | Al Jourgensen, Paul Barker
Label | Sire
Album | *ΚΕΦΑΛΗΞΘ* aka *Psalm 69: The Way to Succeed and the Way to Suck Eggs* (1992)

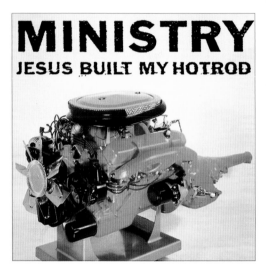

"I don't wanna see these guys wearing cowboy hats and long hair and Easy Rider *shades, playing hardcore beats."*
Thurston Moore, Sonic Youth, 1992

◀ **Influenced by: Surfin' Bird** · The Trashmen (1963)
▶ **Influence on: Some Dispute Over T-Shirt Sales**
Butthole Surfers (1993)
● **Covered by:** Shining (1999) · The BossHoss (2006)
★ **Other key tracks:** TV Song (1991) · N.W.O. (1991)
Just One Fix (1991)

"Warner Bros. gave us $700,000," gloated Ministry main man Al Jourgensen, "and we turned in this stupid little hillbilly song with Gibby Haynes singing on it. Basically we spent all of that cash on drugs."

Jourgensen formed Ministry at the dawn of the 1980s, as a vehicle for skewed synth-pop. As the decade wore on, they evolved into a shuddering, mercilessly heavy, industrial metal beast. Jourgensen also pursued side projects with alternative figureheads: Lard (with Dead Kennedys front man Jello Biafra), Pailhead (which allied the drug-guzzling, libertarian Jourgensen with Ian MacKaye, abstemious leader of Fugazi), and 1,000 Homo DJs (with Trent Reznor of Nine Inch Nails).

"Jesus Built My Hotrod," the first salvo from the long and debauched sessions for *ΚΕΦΑΛΗΞΘ,* boasts blitzing guitar riffs and truly gonzoid vocals from Gibby Haynes, scrambled front man of Texan freaks Butthole Surfers. The music's precision-tooled attack is married to Haynes's batshit babble, as he snarls "Jerry Lee Lewis was the devil!" before barking a high speed, sinister spiel of lusty talk and rock 'n' roll gibberish ("Ding dang a dong bong bing bong / Ticky ticky thought of a gun"). The result sounds like "Surfin' Bird" performed by murderous robots on cheap, nasty drugs.

A bombastic video cut together footage of Haynes spazzing wildly, Jourgensen rocking out in leathers and dreadlocks, and tire-squealing footage of drag racing and NASCAR pile-ups. Its unhinged mania easily captured the imaginations of Beavis and Butthead–types the world over. Thereafter, Jourgensen toured Ministry's pulverizing circus across the globe, while Haynes recycled the lyrics for the Buttholes' "Some Dispute over T-Shirt Sales," on *Independent Worm Saloon.* **SC**

No More Tears | Ozzy Osbourne (1991)

Writer | Ozzy Osbourne, Zakk Wylde, Randy Castillo, Mike Inez, John Purdell
Producer | Duane Baron, John Purdell
Label | Epic
Album | *No More Tears* (1991)

"All that stuff about heavy metal and hard rock, I don't subscribe to any of that. It's all just music."

Ozzy Osbourne, 2000

◄ **Influenced by: I Am the Walrus** · The Beatles (1967)
► **Influence on: No More Tears** · Darrell Deese (2008)
● **Covered by:** Black Label Society (1999)
   Shaaman (2006)
★ **Other key tracks:** Crazy Train (1980) · I Don't Know
   (1980) · Diary of a Madman (1981)

"Smells Like Teen Spirit" is the rock anthem most associated with 1991. However, while Nirvana took over magazine covers and swept "hair metal" aside, a few veterans escaped the purge. Ozzy Osbourne had long defied logic, not least by becoming more successful as a solo artist than he had been in metal pioneers Black Sabbath. (Indeed, by 1991, Sabbath were re-recruiting Ozzy's successor Ronnie James Dio, in a bid to bolster their flagging fortunes.) Yet surely even Ozzy was due to decline, after twenty years of self-abuse and being arrested for attempting to kill his wife and manager Sharon.

Instead, he forged into the new decade with his biggest-selling album. It boasted the hit "Mama, I'm Coming Home" and future Grammy winner "I Don't Want to Change the World"—yet most remarkable was its epic title track. The seven-minute masterpiece opens with a rumbling bass line devised by Mike Inez (latterly of Alice in Chains). Thereafter, it showcases Ozzy's evil tale of a serial killer menacing strippers, and Zakk Wylde's pyrotechnical guitar—ingredients that might have made it no more than an excellent heavy metal song. The key elements in its greatness are John Sinclair's orchestral keyboards and Beatlesque breakdown—entirely appropriate for Ozzy, who once said, "When I heard The Beatles, I wanted to *be* a Beatle." (Sinclair's own rock associations included a stint with Spinal Tap.)

With a memorable video of a woman nearly drowning in her own tears, "No More Tears" became a rightful classic. Yet, while Ozzy continued to prosper, there was a sad coda: two of the song's co-writers—drummer Randy Castillo and producer John Purdell—died of cancer, in 2002 and 2003, respectively. **BM**

Smells Like Teen Spirit | Nirvana (1991)

Writer | Kurt Cobain, Krist Novoselic, Dave Grohl
Producer | Butch Vig, Nirvana
Label | DGC
Album | *Nevermind* (1991)

> *"I don't exactly know what 'Teen Spirit' means, but you know it means something and it's intense as hell."*
> **Butch Vig, 1992**

◀ **Influenced by: More Than a Feeling** · Boston (1976)
▶ **Influence on: I'll Do Anything** · Courtney Love (2004)
● **Covered by:** Tori Amos (1992) · Xorcist (1993)
The Flying Pickets (1994) · J.B.O. (1995) · Beki Bondage
(2000) · Blanks 77 (2000) · Melvins (2000) · Willie
Nelson (2001) · Paul Anka (2005)

Sometimes inspiration comes from the most unlikely of places. In 1991, Bikini Kill riot grrrl Kathleen Hanna scrawled "Kurt" next to the words "smells like teen spirit" on his wall—teasingly linking Nirvana front man Kurt Cobain to a brand of deodorant for girls. This set his creative cogs into overdrive, dreaming up a song that bassist Krist Novoselic described as capturing the singer's hatred of "the mass mentality of conformity."

Cobain's bandmates were similarly particular in their tastes and did not warm to the grunge grumbler's original version of "Smells Like Teen Spirit," even after an hour and a half of playing the same four-chord riff (whose similarity to one by Boston they eventually acknowledged). However, when Novoselic suggested slowing the song down—and Dave Grohl raised a ruckus on drums—the Seattle trio created a listless (albeit paradoxically thrilling) anthem to moan about for years. And moan they did. The success of the song—an apathetic murmur alternating with a distorted riot—wasn't theirs to celebrate. "I was trying to write the ultimate pop song," said Cobain, dismissively. "I was basically trying to rip off the Pixies. . . . We used their sense of dynamics, being soft and quiet and then loud and hard."

"What the kids are attracted to in the music," opined *Nevermind*'s producer Butch Vig, "is that . . . he doesn't necessarily know what he wants but he's pissed." Or, as satirist Weird Al Yankovic put it in his song "Smells Like Nirvana" (much more fun than reverential covers by Tori Amos and Patti Smith): "Now I'm mumblin' and I'm screamin' / And I don't know what I'm singin'. . . . We're so loud and incoherent / Boy, this oughta bug your parents." **KBo**

Kurt Cobain and Nirvana, promulgators of Seattle grunge, perform in Cork, Ireland, in 1991. ➔

VANDALISM:
BEAUTIFUL AS A ROCK
IN A COP'S FACE

Summertime | DJ Jazzy Jeff & The Fresh Prince (1991)

Writer | Robert Bell, Ronald Bell, G. Brown,
L. Mahone, R. Mickens, C. Simpkins, C. Smith,
W. Smith, A. Taylor, D. Thomas, R. Westfield
Producer | L. "Hula" Mahone, C. "K. Fingers" Simpkins
Label | Jive
Album | *Homebase* (1991)

> *"I would listen to that by the pool and talk about boys."*
>
> **Eva Mendes, 2007**

◀ **Influenced by: Summer Madness** • Kool & The Gang
(1975)
▶ **Influence on: Summertime** • Kenny Chesney (2005)
● **Covered by:** The Wipeouts (2007)
★ **Other key tracks:** Parents Just Don't Understand
(1988) • You Saw My Blinker (1991)

N.W.A. prompted much hand wringing in 1991 with their album *Efil4zaggin*. However, at the same time, Jeff Townes (DJ Jazzy Jeff) and Will Smith (the Fresh Prince) provided a powerful antidote to gangsta rap with "Summertime." "Hip-hop has many different styles," observed Ice-T at the time. "You got the Jazzy Jeff & The Fresh Prince style, which is very pop and fun."

Now a compilation staple, the slow-grooving "Summertime" samples Kool & The Gang's B-side "Summer Madness" from 1975 and Jack Bruce's "Born to Be Blue" (from *Things We Like,* released in 1970). Among contributors to the song was rapper Juice, an associate of producer K. Fingers. However, as he told BallerStatus.com, "We got sued by Kool & The Gang for the sample and nobody made money." (Legendary rapper Rakim denied rumors that he helped ghostwrite the rhymes, although Smith's delivery is certainly reminiscent of his.)

Fusing a laid-back rap with a soulful vocal from LaVette Goodman, "Summertime" is a welcome, mellow respite from Smith and Townes's usual busy sound. "They have one foot in house and rap, and the other in mainstream R&B," noted record executive Barry Weiss. Jive's then senior vice president scored a marketing coup by premiering the "Summertime" video immediately after an episode of Smith's smash TV sitcom, *The Fresh Prince of Bel-Air.*

The Grammy-winning cut remains Smith and Townes's biggest joint hit. Although Hollywood success all but eclipsed the former's on-off recording career, he told *Jet* in 2004: "There's no experience I've ever had that beats standing in the middle of a stage with 70,000 people and those first couple of seconds of 'Summertime' come on." **EP**

Give It Away | Red Hot Chili Peppers (1991)

Writer | Flea, John Frusciante, Anthony Kiedis, Chad Smith
Producer | Rick Rubin
Label | Warner Bros.
Album | *BloodSugarSexMagik* (1991)

" 'Give It Away' was never about melody. It was a party song."

Anthony Kiedis, 2004

◄ **Influenced by:** Loopzilla · George Clinton (1982)
► **Influence on:** What I Got · M.I.A. (2008)
● **Covered by:** Bjørn Berge (2002)
★ **Other key tracks:** Under the Bridge (1991) · Soul to Squeeze (1991) · Suck My Kiss (1991) · Californication (1999) · By the Way (2002) · Snow (Hey Oh) (2006)

Having raised a funk-rock ruckus for years, Red Hot Chili Peppers hit the mainstream with their album *BloodSugarSexMagik*. With producer Rick Rubin and a change of label (not to mention the hit "Under the Bridge"), the sound that the Peppers had made their own hit the world.

BloodSugar's first single sprang from a jam session. "This idea of 'give it away' was tornadoing in my head for a while," recalled singer Anthony Kiedis. "When Flea started hitting that bass line, that tornado just came out of my mouth." A memorable video directed by French filmmaker Stéphane Sednaoui—the group dancing in a desert, wearing silver bodypaint and shiny pants—and Kiedis's chanting "Giveidaway, giveidaway, giveidaway now" helped "Give It Away" become an international Top Ten hit. Ironically, "the number one radio station that Warner's wanted to break the song on—a station out of Texas—told [us] to 'come back when you have a melody in your song,'" said Kiedis.

At first listen, the lyrics seem to be simply about sex. "Where you say, 'What I got you gotta get and put it in ya,'" observed Krusty the Clown when the Peppers guested on *The Simpsons*, "how about just, 'What I'd like is I'd like to hug and kiss ya'?"

However, the chorus to the song is about altruistic behavior. Kiedis said that the lyrics were inspired by a discussion about selflessness and generosity that he had with an ex-girlfriend, German singer Nina Hagen: "I was going through her closet one day . . . when I came upon a valuable exotic jacket. . . . 'Take it, you can have it,' she said. . . . 'It's always important to give things away: it creates good energy.'" **SO**

One | U2 (1991)

Writer | U2
Producer | Daniel Lanois, Brian Eno
Label | Island
Album | *Achtung Baby* (1991)

"Achtung Baby *was bigger than life. It was unique. A song like 'One' was beyond ridiculous.*"

Jon Bon Jovi, 2000

◀ **Influenced by:** The Cross • Prince (1987)
▶ **Influence on:** Yellow • Coldplay (2000)
● **Covered by:** Information Society (1999) • Johnny Cash (2000) • Warren Haynes (2004) • Joe Cocker (2004) • Cowboy Junkies (2005) • Professional Murder Music (2005) • Keziah Jones (2008)

"I thought this might be the end," recalled drummer Larry Mullen in the autobiography *U2 by U2,* published in 2006. The band had decamped to Berlin, on the eve of reunification, in a desperate search for inspiration, only to find themselves riven by dissent. "We weren't getting anywhere," said bassist Adam Clayton, "until 'One' fell into our laps and suddenly we hit a groove."

Just as the band had begun to think that their disagreements might remain unresolved, producer Daniel Lanois—who also played on the track—suggested guitarist The Edge combine two chord progressions with which he had been toying. Suddenly the band found their stride and improvised the rest of "One" in less than an hour. Singer Bono conjured the words, inspired by a festival called Oneness, spearheaded by the Dalai Lama. "I love and respect the Dalai Lama," said Bono, "but this event didn't strike a chord. I sent him back a note saying, 'One—but not the same.'"

Although the song galvanized the recording of *Achtung Baby,* the drama continued. "I walked in literally as the boys had completed the last mix and said, 'I've got a great guitar part for the end of 'One,'" remembered The Edge. "It was like telling them someone had died . . . I ran in, put the amp up, plugged it in, played the guitar part once, they mixed it ten minutes after, and it was done."

"One" yielded a controversial video featuring U2 in drag and so entranced Guns N' Roses singer Axl Rose that he took to showing up on the band's subsequent tour. In 2005, U2 re-recorded the slow burner with soul star Mary J. Blige. However, as Bono admitted, "The song is a bit twisted . . . I could never figure out why people want it at their weddings." **BM**

Losing My Religion | R.E.M. (1991)

Writer | B. Berry, P. Buck, M. Mills, M. Stipe
Producer | Scott Litt, R.E.M.
Label | Warner Bros.
Album | *Out of Time* (1991)

"I found myself incredibly moved to hear the vocals in conjunction with the music."
Peter Buck, 2003

◄ **Influenced by: Every Breath You Take** • The Police (1983)

► **Influence on: We Both Go Down Together**
The Decemberists (2005)

● **Covered by:** Tori Amos (1995) • Rozalla (1995)
Swan Dive (1997) • Scary Kids Scaring Kids (2006)

"Our career can be divided into the two parts," observed R.E.M. guitarist Peter Buck. "Pre-'Losing My Religion' and post-'Losing My Religion.' . . . Afterward, we had hit singles, platinum albums . . ." Many groups have to compromise to reach such heights. R.E.M. achieved it with their integrity intact, as the defiantly non-mainstream "Losing My Religion"—with its mandolin-driven melody and enchanting simplicity—clearly illustrates.

"I was drinking wine," Buck recalled, "and watching The Nature Channel with the sound off and learning how to play the mandolin. . . . I played 'Losing My Religion' all the way through, and then played really bad stuff for a while. I woke up in the morning not knowing what I'd written. I had to relearn it by playing the tape. That's where songs come from for me: someplace where you're not really thinking about it." "I described R.E.M. once as a bunch of minor chords with some nonsense thrown on top," said singer Michael Stipe. "'Losing My Religion' has that quality. You always want to sing along, and you always want to keep singing when it's over."

Catchiness camouflages ambiguity: as with R.E.M.'s 1987 hit, "The One I Love," the lyrics are not what they seem. Rather than a personal declaration of lost faith, Stipe said the phrase "losing my religion" refers to Southern slang for losing your temper or being "at the end of your rope." A melodramatic video featuring religious imagery such as Saint Sebastian and Stipe wearing angel wings fueled further misconceptions. Nonetheless, "Losing My Religion" swept the board at the MTV Video Music awards in 1991, confirming Stipe's belief that "once a song . . . goes out to people, it's as much theirs as it is mine." **BC**

Life Is a Highway
Tom Cochrane (1991)

Writer | Tom Cochrane
Producer | Joe Hardy
Label | Capitol
Album | *Mad Mad World* (1991)

Red Rider enjoyed massive success in Canada during the Eighties, yet were considered something of a one-hit wonder (for the Pink Floyd rip "Lunatic Fringe") everywhere else. A nearly identical scenario played out in the Nineties for vocalist Tom Cochrane, once he left the band.

"Life Is a Highway," Cochrane's debut solo single, is a country-rocker that demands listeners' attention. The radio-friendly track is so contagious that, whether or not you like it, you find yourself singing along—and the chorus gets stuck in your head for days. On the surface, "Life Is a Highway" is a classic road song, in the lineage of "Route 66." Cochrane, however, claims that it has a deeper, Zen-like meaning: "It's a celebration of life and doing what you can when you can. And really don't sweat the rest because you can't control everything."

The song was a No. 1 hit in Canada, where it helped Cochrane earn four Juno awards and signaled the start of a prosperous solo career. It also did big business in the United States, reaching No. 6. In 2006, Rascal Flatts found success with a version featured in the Disney movie *Cars*. However, there was a dark side to the joyful song. "I've had people send me letters telling me their kid died in a car crash and they found the 'Life Is a Highway' tape in the tape deck," Cochrane told melodicrock.com. "Sometimes you don't want to hear that stuff." **JiH**

Always on the Run
Lenny Kravitz (1991)

Writer | Lenny Kravitz, Slash
Producer | Lenny Kravitz
Label | Virgin America
Album | *Mama Said* (1991)

"As far as I'm concerned," Lenny Kravitz admitted in 1989, "state of the art was in 1967." The writer-producer-performer was talking about his debut album *Let Love Rule*, which was indeed late Beatlesque. Between albums, Kravitz had written and produced Madonna's unimpeachably modern "Justify My Love," but his second set, *Mama Said*, drew more clearly on Sly & The Family Stone, Led Zeppelin, and righteous Seventies soul.

Although its brass was rooted in James Brown, the lead single "Always on the Run" strayed to the Jimmy Page side of the tracks. And who better to be a six-string foil than the era's premier top-hatted guitar hero? Guns N' Roses guitarist Slash and Kravitz first played together on *Mama Said* opener "Fields of Joy." "We enjoyed that experience," Kravitz reflected in 2000, "and thought that it would be nice to write a song together." "As I was warming up," Slash recalled, "I played a funky guitar riff that I'd come up with recently but hadn't found a place for in any of the songs I was working on at the time with Guns." The multitalented Kravitz played drums, adding bass and vocals later, and the result is a classic rock strutter, paving the way for future funky triumphs such as "Are You Gonna Go My Way" and "Fly Away." "We recorded 'Always on the Run' in under an hour," marveled Slash. "The raw, spontaneous energy of that track is right there in the final product." **MH**

Lenny Kravitz performs in 1990: his art and tailoring nodded toward Jimi Hendrix. ➡

Treaty | Yothu Yindi (1991)

Writer | S. Kellaway, P. Kelly, W. Marika, C. Williams, M. Munuŋgur, G. Yunupingu, M. Yunupingu
Producer | Mark Moffatt
Label | Mushroom
Album | *Tribal Voice* (1992)

> *"Yothu Yindi became successful through their really good stage show, which mixed aspects of their own culture with rock."*
>
> **Neil Finn, Crowded House, 2000**

◀ **Influenced by: Black Boy** · Coloured Stone (1984)
▶ **Influence on: Celebrate** · Christine Anu (2000)
★ **Other key tracks:** Djäpana (Sunset Dreaming) (1991) Yolngu Boy (1991) · My Kind of Life (1991) · It's Okay (One Blood) (2006)

In 1988—the bicentennial of British settlement in Australia—Prime Minister Bob Hawke was presented with a statement calling for recognition of the rights of Aboriginal landowners. Hawke promised to provide this, but by 1990 no such action had occurred. Yothu Yindi's "Treaty" is a spirited reminder.

The song—based on a historic recording by one of the band's relatives—fuses rock with an indigenous *djatpangarri* song style, and uses *bilma* (clapsticks) and *yirdaki* (didgeridoo), alongside more conventional instruments. The lyrics, in English and the Gumatj language, include the pointed "Promises can disappear / Just like writing in the sand." Initially, "Treaty" flopped as a single, but when remixers Filthy Lucre gave it a dance-floor-friendly house vibe, it climbed to No. 11 on the Australian chart. It was the first song by a predominantly Aboriginal group to chart in their homeland, and the first song in any Aboriginal Australian language to win major international recognition. It even showed up on *Billboard*'s dance chart. Commercial success aside, "Treaty" has developed an iconic cultural status. The group recorded an update ("Treaty 98") and performed the song at the Sydney Olympics in 2000. The following year, the Australian Performing Rights Association declared it one of the Top Thirty Australian songs of all time.

Progress has been made towards the goals that the song set out to achieve. In 1992, the *terra nullius* doctrine—which classified Australia as "unowned land" before British settlement—was overturned. And, in February 2009, Kevin Rudd's government issued its apology to Australia's "stolen generation." However, as of 2010, there is still no treaty. **JLu**

Unfinished Sympathy | Massive Attack (1991)

Writer | Robert Del Naja, Grant Marshall,
Shara Nelson, Jonathan Sharp, Andrew Vowles
Producer | Massive Attack, Jonny Dollar
Label | Wild Bunch
Album | *Blue Lines* (1991)

"The title came up as a joke at first, but it fitted the song and the arrangements so perfectly . . . "

Robert "3D" Del Naja, 2009

◄ **Influenced by: Back to Life (However Do You Want Me)** • Soul II Soul (1989)
► **Influence on: Play Dead** • Björk (1993)
● **Covered by:** Tina Turner (1996)
★ **Other key tracks:** Daydreaming (1991) • Safe from Harm (1991) • One Love (1991) • Protection (1995)

A cinematic blend of sweeping strings and emotionally layered hip-hop beats, electric soul, and samples, "Unfinished Sympathy" is like nothing that had gone before. Shara Nelson's searching vocals seal the song as a groundbreaking, beautiful, soul classic.

The masterpiece began as one of Nelson's melodies. Input from associates such as Andrew "Mushroom" Vowles, with his subtle sampling and scratching skills, and co-producer Jonny Dollar, who arranged for a forty-piece string section to record at Abbey Road, proved crucial. "We removed the chorus and we decided to fill the dead space with strings," recalled Robert "3D" Del Naja. "That's how it changed from a conventional pop song into something sort of symphonic." (The title is a play on Schubert's *Unfinished Symphony*.)

Massive Attack are known for their creative sampling. Here, the bells in the beat are from Bob James's 1975 song "Take Me to the Mardi Gras," and the "Hey, hey, hey, hey" lyric is based on the Mahavishnu Orchestra's opening vocal in "Planetary Citizen." Ironically, Mushroom objected to Nellee Hooper's remix of "Unfinished Sympathy," grumbling "You don't hear of people remixing Led Zeppelin or the Mahavishnu Orchestra."

The video was innovative, too. Filmed in one continuous shot as Nelson walked through Los Angeles, it has been much emulated, notably in The Verve's "Bitter Sweet Symphony." The song also inspired British dance giant Fatboy Slim. Of his "Right Here, Right Now," he declared: "The blueprint for it was 'Unfinished Sympathy.' I just thought about the strings and about how evocative it was. . . . I thought, 'I'd really like to make a record that's remembered in ten years' time.'" **GK**

Justified & Ancient | The KLF
featuring Tammy Wynette (1991)

Writer | Jimmy Cauty, Bill Drummond, Ricky Lyte
Producer | The KLF
Label | KLF Communications
Album | N/A

This hip-hop house track by two musical guerrillas features Tammy Wynette—"the first lady of country"—and a recurring quote from Jimi Hendrix's "Voodoo Chile"? Unsurprisingly, this delightfully bonkers song has a deranged history.

It first appeared as "Hey Hey We Are Not the Monkees" on *1987 (What the Fuck is Going On?)* by Jimmy Cauty, future co-founder of The Orb, and former Echo & The Bunnymen/Teardrop Explodes manager Bill Drummond. They called themselves The JAMs, or Justified Ancients of Mu Mu, after a sect in *The Illuminatus! Trilogy*—a series of cult books published in the 1970s—who infiltrated and subverted a secret world order, The Illuminati. Cauty and Drummond intended to do the same to the music industry through sampling.

By 1991, the duo—renamed The KLF—had enjoyed three Top Five U.K. hits. Their best-selling album *The White Room* closed with the lullaby "Justified and Ancient," which—in late 1991—was drastically revamped as the transatlantic smash "Justified & Ancient (Stand By the JAMs)." "Jimmy and I were about to drop the track," Drummond wrote in his book, *45*. "But things turned round after Cauty had the idea of enlisting Tammy. Twenty minutes after he suggested it, [I] was chatting to the heroine of heartache backstage at a Tennessee concert hall." The track became her biggest hit on *Billboard*'s pop chart. **PW**

Enter Sandman
Metallica (1991)

Writer | Kirk Hammett, James Hetfield, Lars Ulrich
Producer | B. Rock, J. Hetfield, L. Ulrich
Label | Elektra
Album | *Metallica* (1991)

Metallica fans divide into two camps. Thrashers prefer the band's older, more aggressive music and were let down when they changed direction at the start of the Nineties. More relaxed folks like Metallica songs from both sides of the divide. But no matter where you stand, "Enter Sandman" is a masterful composition, and, with a full-fat production from Bob Rock, it was perfect for MTV and radio.

After the sinister introduction, the verse sits atop a chunky riff devised by lead guitarist Kirk Hammett. "Soundgarden had just put out *Louder Than Love*," he told *Rolling Stone*. "I was trying to capture their attitude toward big, heavy riffs." "That was the most straightforward, simplest song we had ever written," recalled drummer Lars Ulrich, who modified the guitarist's work. "We did that in two days." The "sandman" theme was one that singer and lyricist James Hetfield had mooted for six years. "Me being brought up in Denmark and not knowing about a lot of this shit, I didn't get it," admitted Ulrich in *Kerrang!* "Then James clued me in. Apparently the sandman is like this children's villain."

Every successful band has its "Stairway to Heaven"—a song that takes them to a new level of recognition and without which they would not have come so far. "Enter Sandman"—a hit that remains a near-permanent inclusion in the band's setlists—is Metallica's. **JMc**

Metallica's Kirk Hammett gives a riffological masterclass in 1991. ➜

Weather with You | Crowded House (1991)

Writer | Neil Finn, Tim Finn
Producer | Mitchell Froom,
Neil Finn
Label | Capitol
Album | *Woodface* (1991)

*"It's a pleasure to write a song.
… It's a wonderful feeling."*

Neil Finn, 1998

◄ **Influenced by: I'm Only Sleeping** · The Beatles (1966)
► **Influence on: Girl Inform Me** · The Shins (2001)
● **Covered by:** Voice Male (1999) · Clouseau (2000)
Aswad (2002) · Andrea Zonn (2003) · Ian McCulloch
(2003) · Jimmy Buffett (2006)

With all due respect to the Everlys, no brotherly reunion can claim to be as important in pop as that of Neil and Tim Finn in 1991. The New Zealanders, who had spent years falling in and out of each other's bands, reunited when younger brother Neil was in creative dire straits. "We had two glorious weeks locked in a room with a couple of acoustic guitars," recalled Tim Finn. "Came out with fourteen songs." Among the results was the wonderfully thoughtful and joyous "Weather with You," which took the band from success to superduper stardom—Princess Diana even referred to them as her favorite band.

Crowded House had enjoyed critical acclaim but commercial nonchalance with their second album, *Temple of Low Men* (released in 1988)—which the group quipped was nearly called *Mediocre Follow-Up*—and relative success with the song "Don't Dream It's Over." However, "Weather with You"—originally snubbed, then penciled in, for a Finn brothers album—won them an army of fans worldwide.

Maybe it is the change in production that makes the song so appealing, replacing the heaviness of previous efforts with something easier on the ear. Maybe it is the irresistible acoustic riffs in place of the earlier use of organs. Maybe it is the harmonies, harking back to the Beach Boys brothers' sweetly infectious tones. Or maybe it is Neil Finn's dog, Lester, featured in the upbeat video. Who knows? However—like the song's story of someone's moods having such a strong influence on their surroundings that they alter the weather for everyone around them— "Weather with You" seems to bring in the sunshine with every listen. **KBo**

You Got the Love | The Source featuring Candi Staton (1991)

Writer | Anthony Stephens, Arnecia Michelle Harris, John Bellamy, Jamie Principle
Producer | J. Truelove, E. Abdullah, C. James
Label | Truelove Electronic Communications
Album | N/A

the source featuring candi staton
YOU GOT THE LOVE

"When the song didn't happen in America, I thought, 'Oh well, another one bites the dust.'"

Candi Staton, 2006

◄ **Influenced by: Move On Up a Little Higher**
Mahalia Jackson (1948)
► **Influence on: I Know** • New Atlantic (1991)
● **Covered by:** Florence & The Machine (2008)
★ **Other key tracks:** He Called Me Baby (1970) • Young Hearts Run Free (1976) • Suspicious Minds (1982)

"They were calling my house saying I had a No. 1 record in England," recalled American soul singer Candi Staton in an interview with the *Guardian* in 2006. "And I said, 'What song? I haven't released any song.'" This is almost the final paragraph in the convoluted history of a song that has sold two million copies worldwide and been a Top Ten hit on three separate occasions in the United Kingdom.

The origins of the track lie in a documentary about a morbidly obese man trying to lose weight. The producers asked Staton to provide a song to soundtrack the film, and she gave them the spiritually beseeching "You Got the Love." The song has a spiritual message: God has "got the love I need to see me through." The film was eventually shelved, and Staton forgot about her anthem. Then, in 1989, European DJ Eren Abdullah mixed the a cappella version of the song with a renowned house music track by Frankie Knuckles and Jamie Principle, "Your Love." The result was released on a bootleg EP.

Two years later, the heartbreaking track was officially released in the United Kingdom by DJ John Truelove, this time credited to The Source featuring Candi Staton. It was as it flew up the charts that Staton received her perplexing congratulatory telephone call. Truelove released two remixed versions, in 1997 and 2006.

In 2004, the song was used to play out the final minutes of *Sex and the City's* last episode. Meanwhile, Staton started performing the song with The Source—although, as she admitted to The Quietus in 2009: "At first I didn't even know how to sing it! I didn't even know when to come in on time!" **DC**

Blind Willie McTell
Bob Dylan (1991)

Writer | Bob Dylan
Producer | Bob Dylan, Mark Knopfler, Jeff Rosen
Label | Columbia
Album | *The Bootleg Series Volumes 1–3 (Rare & Unreleased) 1961–1991* (1991)

Bob Dylan tipped his hat to Blind Willie McTell—the early twentieth-century vocalist-guitarist best known for "Statesboro Blues"—on several occasions. He covered the Georgia-born bluesman's "Broke Down Engine" and "Delia," and referenced him in the words of "Highway 61 Revisited" and "Po' Boy." His greatest tribute came in 1983, with the recording of "Blind Willie McTell." Fans, however, wouldn't get to hear the song until much later.

Dylan intended the track for *Infidels*, which marked his welcome return to secular music. That "Blind Willie McTell"—now considered a career highlight—didn't make the final cut is hard to fathom, given that *Infidels* is hardly bursting with Bob's best. Dylan later explained the omission to *Rolling Stone*: "It was never developed fully. I never got around to completing it. There wouldn't have been any other reason for leaving it off the record."

Whispered about by fans for years, "Blind Willie McTell" eventually showed up in 1991 on *The Bootleg Series Volumes 1–3*. The work is one of uncommon beauty, built on a familiar piano melody from "St. James Infirmary Blues" and filled with exquisite language. There's visceral conviction to the vocal delivery, as Dylan delivers five short vignettes, each closing with a reverential line about McTell. The song's greatest accomplishment, however, is to prompt listeners to take the next step and search out McTell's own recordings. **JiH**

Move Any Mountain–Progen 91
The Shamen (1991)

Writer | Colin Angus, The Shamen
Producer | The Shamen
Label | One Little Indian
Album | *En-Tact* (1990)

Much of the dance music of 1991 seemed to exist in the shadow of The Shamen. If you had not been exposed to the Beatmasters version assailing the airwaves, there were numerous remixes of "Move Any Mountain–Progen 91"—so many, in fact, that they were released as an album (*Progeny*) in their own right. The song had started life as "Pro>Gen," which took hold in the clubs during 1990. Espousing then-newcomer Mr. C's belief that "No one can do a Shamen song better than The Shamen," it was re-recorded and became one of three hits (with "Hyperreal" and "Make It Mine") from *En-Tact* that established the group as techno figureheads.

The words of the song encapsulate the optimism of the moment. "This was it," said founder Colin Angus. "We could take control; we had the power. That's what the 'Move Any Mountain' lyric is all about. Large numbers of people all with the same vibe." Large enough, indeed, to take the song into the U.K. Top Three and even to make inroads into the U.S. market. However, this "anything is possible" ethos was tested to its extreme when—during the trip to Tenerife where the "Move Any Mountain" video was filmed—bassist Will Sinnott (aka Will Sin) drowned. "I realized that what The Shamen's about was positivity," said Angus. "That positivity is like the spirit of the music, and positivity acknowledges the need for change. So for those reasons I elected to carry on." **CB**

How I Could Just Kill a Man
Cypress Hill (1991)

Writer | L. "B-Real" Freese, L. "DJ Muggs" Muggerud, S. "Sen Dog" Reyes, L. Fulson, J. McCracklin
Producer | DJ Muggs
Label | Ruffhouse
Album | *Cypress Hill* (1991)

Cypress Hill's debut single was almost a "how to" guide for Nineties hip-hop. Unleashed before Dr. Dre's cannabis-championing *The Chronic*, "How I Could Just Kill a Man" (known in demo form as "Trigga Happy Nigga") kicked off with B-Real praising the power of the herb: "Hey don't miss out on what you're passin' / You're missin' the hoota of the funky Buddha." The music enhances the toking experience: the beats, from Manzel's "Midnight Theme," are lazy and dirty; the bass line, from Lowell Fulsom's "Tramp," is rumbling; and a squealing guitar from the solo of Jimi Hendrix's "Are You Experienced?" dominates the chorus. These hazy sonics helped Cypress Hill to unite gangbangers and headbangers. (The line "All I wanted was a Pepsi" at the song's close is from Suicidal Tendencies' thrash epic "Institutionalized").

"How I Could Just Kill a Man" soundtracked a climactic scene in the Tupac Shakur film *Juice* (1992). It also pushed gangsta rap closer to the mainstream, when the band played the Lollapalooza festival and had white rock crowds chanting along with the menacing chorus: "Here is something you can't understand / How I could just kill a man." B-Real claimed that he hadn't intended to glorify violence and only advocated gunplay in self-defense. Whatever his intention, this funky firecracker helped create an audience for the coming generation of socially unconscious, trigga-happy rappers. **TB**

Cop Killer
Body Count (1992)

Writer | Ice-T, Ernie C
Producer | Ice-T, Ernie C
Label | Sire
Album | *Body Count* (1992)

Rap pioneer Ice-T was not the first musician to openly discuss murdering a police officer (see "I Shot the Sheriff"), but he was the first to turn the concept into an international controversy. Gangsta rappers N.W.A. had attracted attention for "Fuck tha Police," and unrest about the behavior of urban law enforcers had been noted in many U.S. cities, but no one expected the elements to explode in 1992, culminating in the Los Angeles riots.

"Cop Killer" initially passed unnoticed, buried at the end of the debut by Ice's heavy metal side project Body Count. "The white kids are very open for a black rock band, if it's done right," he told *Q*. "They just want to make sure you're not posing, y'know? . . . We like Anthrax, Slayer, Motörhead, and real thrash bands like Minor Threat." However, after the riots—and with censorship still a political hot potato—lyrics like "I know your family's grieving—fuck 'em!" sparked boycotts and protests. The storm spiraled out of proportion; ultimately, Ice requested that his label's parent company, Warner Bros., reissue the album without the offending track.

In throwing himself to the lions, Ice laid his career on the line for rap, rock, and freedom of speech. "Cop Killer," as he said himself, "was a protest record, man. It was a record of anger and some people didn't understand it, but a lot of people really heard that fuckin' record and they knew what I was singing about." **JMc**

Pretend We're Dead | L7 (1992)

Writer | Donita Sparks
Producer | Butch Vig, L7
Label | Slash
Album | *Bricks are Heavy* (1992)

" 'Pretend We're Dead,' a song we love, is as pop as we went."

Donita Sparks, 1998

◀ **Influenced by: Wooly Bully** · Sam the Sham & The Pharoahs (1965)
▶ **Influence on: I Wanna Be Your Lush** · Fluffy (1996)
● **Covered by:** CSS (2007)
★ **Other key tracks:** Shove (1990) · Everglade (1992) Mr. Integrity (1992) · Andres (1994)

Nirvana drove a stake through the charts, creating a hole through which many like-minded bands followed. L7—a female four-piece from Los Angeles, named after 1950s slang for "square"—were one. They had two albums (and a tour with Nirvana) under their belts by the time that grunge hit the mainstream, and they trailed their third with this thundering anthem about the perils of apathy. The lyrics, explained drummer Dee Plakas, referred to "people not paying attention to what's going on, politically, socially—shutting your ears and eyes."

Co-produced by *Nevermind*'s Butch Vig, "Pretend We're Dead" was picked up by MTV. The video shoot hadn't been without incident: a camera crane fell on guitarist Suzi Gardner. "I've been a dim bulb ever since," she mourned. Gardner was, however, responsible for one of the song's distinctive elements: "I wanted to do a backwards solo, but it just wasn't working out so hot. So I wrote a solo frontwards, played the tape backwards, learned it backwards, then played it like that."

The song secured L7 enviable exposure—literally when it came to Britain's live TV show *The Word*, on which singer-guitarist Donita Sparks dropped her pants to cap a riotous, drum-kit-trashing performance. That spectacle was matched in 1992 at the sodden Reading festival in the United Kingdom, when Sparks hurled a used tampon into a mud-slinging crowd. (Fifteen years later, she joined Brazilian band CSS onstage in LA for their customary cover of the song.)

"Pretend We're Dead" became a karaoke favorite thanks to *Rock Band 2* and, when it turned up on the soundtrack to *Grand Theft Auto III: San Andreas*, its classic status was confirmed. **PW**

My Drug Buddy | Lemonheads (1992)

Writer | Evan Dando
Producer | The Robb Brothers
Label | Atlantic
Album | *It's a Shame about Ray* (1992)

"When we heard it, we were like, 'That's a pretty cool subject to write a song about.'"

Nathan Followill, Kings of Leon, 2003

◄ **Influenced by: Sin City** · The Flying Burrito Brothers (1969)
► **Influence on: Sorted For E's & Wizz** · Pulp (1995)
● **Covered by:** Juliana Hatfield and Evan Dando (1994) Anthony Green (2005)

Evan Dando made it all sound so easy. "She's coming over," sang the Lemonheads' puppyish singer, against a loping, countrified backdrop. "We'll go out walking / Make a call on the way / She's in the phone booth now / I'm looking in / There comes a smile on her face . . ." And if you couldn't guess what "she" was smiling about, the song's title made it clear.

Pink Floyd's guitarist David Gilmour cited it as a song he wished he had written. "I probably shouldn't say that," he admitted to *Q*. "I really liked Evan Dando and the Lemonheads. *It's a Shame about Ray* is a great album."

The album was indeed full of mini masterpieces, but "My Drug Buddy"—with backing vocals by Juliana Hatfield—had the most resonance. Few singers were as up-front about their drug use as the disarmingly naive Dando, who cheerfully admitted his fondness for getting high in interviews and on songs like "Alison's Starting to Happen" (allegedly about an acid trip).

It's a Shame About Ray—the band's fifth album—was a surprise hit in the wake of their smash cover of Simon & Garfunkel's "Mrs. Robinson" (added to a hasty reissue of the album, on which "My Drug Buddy" was abbreviated to "Buddy"). But Dando was still being honest, telling one interviewer he couldn't talk because he had just been on a crack and smack binge.

As the decade progressed, Dando disappeared from view and many feared that he would go the same way as his idol Gram Parsons, who died of a drug overdose at the age of twenty-six. But Dando hung on, cleaned up, and went back on the road, performing "My Drug Buddy" without a hint of regret. **PW**

Shake Your Head | Was (Not Was) (1992)

Writer | David Was, Don Was, Jarvis Stroud
Producer | David Was, Don Was, Steve "Silk" Hurley
Label | Fontana
Album | Hello Dad . . . I'm in Jail (1992)

*"Ozzy . . . it was so absurd,
we had to try. He was perfect!
I couldn't believe it."*
Don Was, 1984

◀ **Influenced by: Kissing with Confidence** · Will Powers (1983)

▶ **Influence on: Everybody's Free (to Wear Sunscreen)** Baz Luhrmann (1999)

● **Covered by:** C. C. Catch (2003)

Heavy metal legend Ozzy Osbourne rapping over an electro backing? That's what awaited listeners on the second album from Detroit duo Was (Not Was), *Born to Laugh at Tornadoes,* in 1983. "The lovable loon proves quite the capable soul man," marveled *Creem.* Alongside the Ozzy showcase "Shake Your Head (Let's Go to Bed)," the album featured unusual guests, such as Mitch Ryder and Mel Tormé. Former U.S. President Richard Nixon was apparently also asked to contribute piano to one track.

The then unknown Madonna had recorded vocals for "Shake Your Head," but her record label, Sire, put a stop to their use. "I've always imagined the vocalist as extensions of ourselves," Don Was later conceded, "and I couldn't relate to female vocals being our voice."

In 1988, Was (Not Was) finally cracked the mainstream with their third album, *What Up, Dog?* thanks to the hits "Walk the Dinosaur" and "Spy in the House of Love." A compilation album was assembled to cash in on this belated exposure, and house music producer Steve "Silk" Hurley was commissioned to remix "Shake Your Head."

This time, the now highest-earning female singer on earth vetoed the use of her voice. "Madonna refused to be on the track with me," cackled the Prince of Darkness. "That's what they must teach in Kabbalah: stay the fuck away from Ozzy." Instead, actress Kim Basinger was brought in to make the song an unlikely duet, and a Top Five hit in the United Kingdom.

Meanwhile, for an alternative remix in the United States, producer "Silk" Hurley was given the wrong vocal tracks, and a twelve-inch single, featuring the Queen of Pop, was "mistakenly" pressed. It was hastily withdrawn. **AG**

Motorcycle Emptiness | Manic Street Preachers (1992)

Writer | J. D. Bradfield, R. Edwards, S. Moore, N. Wire
Producer | Steve Brown
Label | Columbia
Album | *Generation Terrorists* (1992)

"The ultimate early Manics . . . longing for something you're never going to get."
Nicky Wire, 2002

◄ **Influenced by: Sweet Child o' Mine** · Guns N' Roses (1987)

► **Influence on: Some Kind of Bliss** · Kylie Minogue (1997)

● **Covered by:** Stealth Sonic Orchestra (1996) Millennium (2001)

Where most bands struggle with the "difficult second album," Manic Street Preachers pioneered the "difficult debut album." Though it lacked the ferocity of their singles on the Heavenly label, the Welsh quartet promised *Generation Terrorists* would be "the most important benchmark for rock in this decade"—and that they would split up after it. To no one's surprise, it wasn't, and they didn't.

Still, amid all the hype, the Manics had the good sense to release the altogether lovely "Motorcycle Emptiness." It was based on an early demo entitled "Go! Buzz Baby, Go!" in which weedy vocals rouse themselves for a yelled "Motorcycle emptiness!" In its revised form, the song benefited from elegiac guitar by James Dean Bradfield—a raised middle finger to anyone who mocked their fondness for Guns N' Roses.

"It was the first song that Nick [Wire, bassist] and Richey [Edwards, lyricist] wrote as a fifty-fifty partnership," recalled Bradfield, "and I remember thinking, 'God, this is really going to work.' When it came to recording our first album, our producer Steve Brown said that I needed to put a 'dime store riff' on it—a riff that would become the signature of the song. The song metamorphosed into something that we never realized that it would."

Blending sloganeering lyrics with a classic rock backing, "Motorcycle Emptiness"—the fifth single to be lifted from *Generation Terrorists*—bridged the gap between their truculent early work and later albums that have kept them in feather boas and Nietzsche. Although Wire rued that it never became "our worldwide smash," he proudly declared that "Even today it sounds like no other band." Its fleeting stay in the British chart indeed belies its classic uniqueness. **KBo**

Creep | Radiohead (1992)

Writer | C. Greenwood, J. Greenwood, E. O'Brien, P. Selway, T. Yorke, A. Hammond, M. Hazlewood
Producer | Sean Slade, Paul Q. Kolderie
Label | Parlophone
Album | *Pablo Honey* (1993)

"Jonny played the piano at the end and it was gorgeous. Everyone who heard 'Creep' just started going insane."

Paul Q. Kolderie, 1997

◄ **Influenced by: The Air That I Breathe** · The Hollies (1974)
► **Influence on: Jeannie's Diary** · Eels (2000)
● **Covered by:** The Pretenders (1995) · Sentenced (1998) Scarling (2003) · Sophie Koh (2006) · Korn (2007) Anberlin (2007) · Amanda Palmer (2009)

It's ironic that Radiohead felt alienated for so long from a song that explored that very subject. The band has created an acclaimed body of work—but there was once real doubt that they would release anything that could stop people referring to them as the group with the "outsider's song," as front man Thom Yorke called it.

"Creep" tells of a man's pursuit of a female, whose unattainability reinforces his own sense of inadequacy. It was written "in a drunken haze" by Yorke, who thought it was "crap." "I didn't like it," agreed guitarist Jonny Greenwood. "It stayed quiet. So I hit the guitar hard—really hard." That gave the song a primal pre-chorus blast that became central to its success. "Thom mumbled something like, 'That's our Scott Walker song' . . ." producer Paul Q. Kolderie told *Mojo*, "except I thought he said, 'That's *a* Scott Walker song.' . . . Sean [Slade, co-producer] said, 'Too bad their best song's a cover.'"

The song stiffed in the United Kingdom as a single in 1992 but went Top Forty in the United States. Pressure was duly applied for a domestic re-release. Radiohead had already changed its radio-unfriendly lyrics, after reminding themselves that many bands they admired had done the same. Issuing it again in the United Kingdom, however, was a step too far. "Over our dead bodies," declared guitarist Ed O'Brien. Nonetheless, "Creep" hit the Top Ten in 1993, becoming a worldwide hit. "I suppose," admitted Yorke, "the song won in the end." It has duly been covered by a number of artists.

But the band has had their revenge. Tired of its ubiquity, they have only intermittently wheeled "Creep" out in concert since the late 1990s. **CB**

Radiohead's Thom Yorke: one of rock's great vocalists. ➤

Killing in the Name | Rage Against the Machine (1992)

Writer | Rage Against the Machine
Producer | Garth Richardson, Rage Against the Machine
Label | Epic
Album | *Rage Against the Machine* (1992)

"There's plenty of professors at junior colleges who maybe share the same opinions as us. But they don't rock."
Tom Morello, 2007

◀ **Influenced by:** Kick Out the Jams · MC5 (1969)
▶ **Influence on:** Cochise · Audioslave (2002)
● **Covered by:** Biffy Clyro (2008) · FourPlay String Quartet (2009)
★ **Other key tracks:** Bullet in the Head (1992) · Tire Me (1996) · Guerrilla Radio (1999)

A fuming four-piece from Los Angeles, Rage Against the Machine were armed with politically piercing manifestos. If they couldn't change the world, they would at least do a good job of shaking it up with a blend of alternative rock, punk, hip-hop, heavy metal, and funk.

Typically for the confrontational band, their first single, "Killing in the Name," refused to play nicely, and frothed with radio-unfriendly, parent-perturbing, blue language that reached a potty-mouthed crescendo with word-slayer Zach de la Rocha's rousing war cry, "Fuck you, I won't do what you tell me." (The band weren't angry *all* the time. As drummer Brad Wilk assured *Kerrang!* "We don't wake up in the morning and rage against the milk carton because we can't get it open.")

If the song's words—decrying the likes of the Ku Klux Klan—weren't enough of a wake-up call, Tom Morello's spiky guitar and Tim Commerford's throbbing bass certainly did the trick. "We wrote that song before we even had a gig," recalled Morello. "So when we started clobbering people with those riffs and the 'fuck you,' it was exciting from the very beginning." His distinctive squeaks were influenced by "noises that I heard on Dr. Dre and Public Enemy records," Morello told *Rolling Stone*. "We were melding hard rock, punk, and hip-hop, and I was the DJ."

"When we play that song live, I've really seen nothing like it," Morello said in 2007. "When that last chorus comes in—I think if you look under the dictionary for the definition of the word 'apeshit' there'd have to be a picture of people losing their mind to the song." The track received radio play despite the profanity, including one accidentally uncensored airing on BBC Radio One. **KBo**

Connected | Stereo MC's (1992)

Writer | Harry Wayne "KC" Casey, Richard Finch, Nick Hallam, Rob Birch
Producer | Stereo MC's
Label | 4th & B'way
Album | *Connected* (1992)

"Everyone connected, basically."

Rob Birch, 2001

◀ **Influenced by: Let Me Be Your Lover** · Jimmy "Bo" Horne (1978)
▶ **Influence on: Here We Go** · Stakka Bo (1993)
● **Covered by:** Tiger Hifi (2009)
★ **Other key tracks:** Elevate My Mind (1990) · Step It Up (1992) · Deep Down & Dirty (2001)

A sophisticated cocktail of soul, pop, dub, and hip-hop, "Connected" was the title track of the third Stereo MC's album, and their biggest worldwide hit. With a supremely stylish bassline sampled from the disco gem "Let Me Be Your Lover," by Jimmy "Bo" Horne (written by two of KC & The Sunshine Band), the song helped make the Stereo MC's one of the first credible—and commercially successful—British hip-hop acts.

The band emerged in London in 1985, when rapper Rob Birch and DJ/producer Nick "The Head" Hallam helped found the Gee Street label as a means to promote their music. They evolved with the recruitment of singer Cath Coffey and drummer Ian "Owen If" Rossiter, plus backing vocalists Verona Davis and Andrea Bedassie.

For *Connected*, Birch told *Chaos Control*, "We ended up taking the music several stages further than we had gone before and playing things ourselves on bass and keyboards, and getting other people in to play things like the horns."

Stereo MC's slotted into Britain's early Nineties indie dance scene (and were still going strong in the twenty-first century, despite a nine-year hiatus between their third and fourth albums). "Connected"—with its addictive "ah ah ah ah" chorus—duly ticked both the "infectious party anthem" and "super cool" boxes. The album won Best British Album at the 1994 Brit Awards.

"I remember performing the track in late 1992," Birch told *Q*. "The *Connected* album had only been out for a while, and we thought people were just starting to get into it. When we came on to the intro of the track, the whole audience was singing along to the tune and there was just an amazing vibe and energy." **OM**

Inkanyezi Nezazi
Ladysmith Black Mambazo (1992)

Writer | Joseph Shabalala
Producer | Joseph Shabalala
Label | Gallo
Album | *Inkanyezi Nezazi* (1992)

Ever since it was featured in a series of ads for Heinz products in 1997, Ladysmith Black Mambazo's song "Inkanyezi Nezazi" has been widely known as "the baked beans song." But the song was inspired by the biblical story of the three wise men going to Bethlehem to see the baby Jesus.

Founded in 1964, Ladysmith Black Mambazo are South Africa's leading musical ambassadors. Their a cappella style is called *isicathamiya* or *mbube*, and gained a much wider audience in 1986 after they contributed to Paul Simon's *Graceland* album. Then the Heinz campaign brought them back into the spotlight a decade later. Shabalala's stirring lead vocal is in Zulu and soars above the other singers, whose rich harmonies respond to him in rhythmic waves of sound, punctuated by percussive effects they create entirely with their voices.

The song first appeared as the title track of a 1992 album; the ad version is an abridged re-recording made for the 1997 album *Heavenly*. In 1998, in response to the attention generated by the commercial, the original 1992 version was re-released on a CD single, which included "Supafunkee" dub and club remixes by Roger Sanchez and Kings of Tomorrow. The cover didn't show the group, but a look-alike of Heinz's distinctive blue-green baked beans logo. The message was clear: Beanz meanz Mambazo. **JLu**

Sodade
Cesária Evora (1992)

Writer | Luis Morais, Amandio Cabral
Producer | Paulino Vieira
Label | Lusafrica
Album | *Miss Perfumado* (1992)

Cesária Evora is the "barefoot diva"—a singer with an impossibly beautiful voice, whose rise to fame is a literal rags to riches story. She hails from the impoverished Cape Verde off the coast of Senegal, grew up in an orphanage, and sang in bars from her teens. Most of the bars vanished in 1975, when the colony was granted independence.

Jose da Silva, a Cape Verdean émigré, witnessed the singer perform in Portugal and set up the Lusafrica label to record her. He recognized a great vocal stylist and believed that if others heard her, they too would respond. And they did when she released *Miss Perfumado*, showcasing Cape Verdean *mornas*. *Morna* is a melancholic ballad form played on string instruments and, in Evora's hands, it sparkles with bewitching beauty.

"Music is just the universal language," she told the *Sonoma County Independent*. "Even if you don't understand the language . . . you listen because you like the rhythm of the song."

"Sodade" is Evora's most famous—and most personal—song. She sings of the quality that gives *morna* its gorgeous blue soul: *sodade*, the exile into which so many Cape Verdeans are forced, and the melancholy of those left behind. Evora sings this gorgeous song seemingly effortlessly, her velvet voice caressing the melody and riding the supple rhythm. Here is *morna* at its most beautiful and intimate. **GC**

Cesária Evora, who cut her first album at age forty-seven, now enjoys international stardom. ➜

Remedy | The Black Crowes (1992)

Writer | Chris Robinson, Rich Robinson
Producer | The Black Crowes, George Drakoulias
Label | Def American
Album | *The Southern Harmony and Musical Companion* (1992)

"I think they put their records together very nicely. They work out their guitar parts very well."
Rod Stewart, 1993

◀ **Influenced by: Night of the Thumpasorus Peoples**
Parliament (1975)
▶ **Influence on: Fly Away** · Lenny Kravitz (1998)
● **Covered by:** Matchbox Twenty (2007)
★ **Other key tracks:** Hard to Handle (1990) · Darling of the Underground Press (1992)

"Rock with a funky-tinged country gospel influence" is how Chris Robinson described The Black Crowes to *Rock's Backpages*. In 1992, they were hopelessly out of step with prevailing trends. Grunge was fully bedded-in, but the snakeskin troupe remained in hock to The Faces, The Allman Brothers, The Band, and *Exile On Main Street*–era Stones. In Chris's brother Rich, they had a guitarist with the louche swagger of Keith Richards or Ronnie Wood, and they were going to use him.

A rollicking cover of Otis Redding's "Hard to Handle" overshadowed The Black Crowes' 1990 debut *Shake Your Money Maker*. But *The Southern Harmony and Musical Companion* in 1992 was fully rounded and filler-free. "Remedy," the lead single, proved that the Crowes were equally skilled at funky soul and grimy rock 'n' roll.

The album was cut with the minimum of takes, in just eight days, evolving right until recording began. "Chris and Rich were counting down the intro to 'Remedy,'" guitarist Marc Ford told *Guitar*, "when they stopped and said, 'Okay, we're changing this part right now.' And the rest of the band is going, 'Are you serious?!'"

The lyrics, Chris Robinson told VH1's *Storytellers*, were inspired by a dead bird on a Philadelphia hotel windowsill—"Nice omen!"— and attitudes to sexuality in the AIDS era. The song found a fluid groove for the singer, dancing barefoot on his Afghan rug. Driving guitars cranked up the innuendo-rich verses ("If you let me come on inside / Will you let it glide?"), while gospel backing plumped up the choruses' bump-and-grind analogy. The icing on the cake was Ed Hawrysch's Wurlitzer, bringing Sly Stone–style sparseness to the funky finale. **MH**

No Rain | Blind Melon (1992)

Writer | Glen Graham, Shannon Hoon, Brad Smith, Rogers Stevens, Christopher Torn
Producer | Rick Parashar, Blind Melon
Label | Capitol
Album | *Blind Melon* (1992)

"I always thought it was Sesame Street. I never thought it was Grateful Dead."

Rogers Stevens, 2007

◀ **Influenced by: Jane Says** · Jane's Addiction (1988)
▶ **Influence on: Interstate Love Song** · Stone Temple Pilots (1994)
● **Covered by:** Dave Matthews Band (2006) · Emmerson Nogueira (2008)

"We were thinking like, 'Oh, this sounds like the theme song from *Sesame Street*," guitarist Rogers Stevens told ultimate-guitar.com. "'It's a great kids' song or something." The jangly, uplifting guitars and finger-clicking melody that open "No Rain" certainly belie its theme: the crippling effects of depression and drug dependency.

The principal writer was bassist Brad Smith, who told *Details* that it was about a former girlfriend: "She had a hard time with depression. I was telling myself that I was writing it about her . . . and I realized I was writing it about myself at the same time." The title, he added, came from her sleeping "even when it was sunny outside . . . she'd complain that there wouldn't be any rain, because that would give her an excuse to stay in."

Blind Melon's debut album cover, featuring a photograph of drummer Glen Graham's younger sister Georgia, inspired the song's much-loved video (directed by Samuel Bayer), which received heavy airplay on MTV. The band became so sick of the clip's ubiquity that they refused to discuss its bee-costumed heroine, but Pearl Jam wrote "Bee Girl" (on their 2003 album *Lost Dogs*) about her.

Singer Shannon Hoon—a fan of The Grateful Dead, whose "Ripple" is a distant ancestor of "No Rain"—was reportedly high on LSD during the video shoot. Sadly, his weakness for illicit substances cost him his life. He died of a drug overdose in 1995, aged just twenty-eight.

"It was crazy," recalled guitarist Christopher Thorn. "We had booked a club tour before we knew 'No Rain' was going to be a hit. So we were sort of halfway through a club tour and then suddenly the song goes up the charts. . . . Those were really fun days." **OM**

Walk | Pantera (1992)

Writer | Darrell "Dimebag" Abbott, Vinnie Paul,
Phil Anselmo, Rex Brown
Producer | Terry Date
Label | ATCO
Album | *Vulgar Display of Power* (1992)

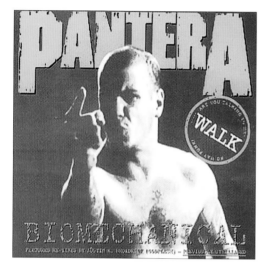

"You done talk behind my back. Here's my face now —talk to me like that now."
Phil Anselmo, 1992

◀ **Influenced by: Desecrator** · Exhorder (1990)
▶ **Influence on: Redneck** · Lamb of God (2006)
● **Covered by:** Kilgore (1998) · Godsmack (2001) · Linkin Park & Disturbed (2001) · Avenged Sevenfold (2007) Peppermint Creeps (2008)

Darrell "Dimebag" Abbott was coming into his prime as a songwriter and guitarist when he recorded Pantera's second major-label album (their sixth release, if you count the band's regrettable glam metal years). A standout on an album full of standouts, "Walk" was based on a staccato riff that was as easy to play as to mosh to.

The song arose during the warm-up for a show. "It came after I picked up a guitar after a day or two …" recalled Dimebag. "Like when you haven't had a piece of ass for a long time!"

"Respect!" bellowed singer Phil Anselmo, while drummer Vinnie Paul and bassist Rex Brown tagged along with Dimebag—who delivers a mind-boggling solo. The song upholds integrity ("You can't be something you're not / Be yourself, by yourself") and warns detractors, "Run your mouth when I'm not around …"

"You get back into town," Anselmo complained, "and all your friends—who you thought were your friends—are all snickering behind your back and talking about this and that. . . . That's what 'Walk' is about. It's like, 'Show some respect, and just walk on, man.'"

With its distinctive "walking" time signature and one of Dimebag's best solos (which *Guitar World* voted the fifty-seventh greatest of all time), the song was a high point in any Pantera show. By the time the band imploded, it had become a new generation's "Whole Lotta Rosie." Covers by Fall Out Boy and Avenged Sevenfold have kept "Walk" in the public eye, and its chorus is often chanted at concerts and sporting events. Its status was only enhanced by Dimebag's death in 2004 at the hands of a psychopath. Had he lived, he might even have bettered it. **JMc**

Real Love | Mary J. Blige (1992)

Writer | Mark C. Rooney, Mark Morales, Kirk "Milk Dee" Robinson, Nathaniel "Gizmo" Robinson
Producer | Mark Morales, Mark C. Rooney
Label | Uptown
Album | *What's the 411?* (1992)

"I worked for my success, you know? I deserve this and I'm not giving up."

Mary J. Blige, 1995

◀ **Influenced by: Top Billin'** · Audio Two (1987)
▶ **Influence on: It's All Gravy** · Romeo featuring Christina Milian (2002)
● **Covered by:** Mike Doughty (2000) · The Twilight Singers (2004) · Toby Lightman (2004)
★ **Other key track:** Sweet Thing (1992)

All trips to the mall should be as fruitful as the one seventeen-year-old Mary Jane Blige made in the late Eighties, when she recorded a version of Anita Baker's "Caught Up in the Rapture" on a karaoke machine. The tape found its way to Andre Harrell, who signed Blige to his Uptown label.

Working with the producer then known as Puff Daddy, Blige drew from both the old-school soul played by her parents and hip-hop blasted on the streets of New York. "It wasn't until Puffy came along," the singer told *Scotland on Sunday,* "that anybody knew what to do with me." The first single from Blige's debut album was the R&B chart-topper "You Remind Me," but the second provided her with a crossover smash.

"Real Love" was Blige at her best. Her platinum pipes rang with gospel-infused soul, earning comparisons with Chaka Khan and Aretha Franklin. Yet the joyful love song was built on beats from Audio Two's hip-hop classic "Top Billin'." Ironically, although Audio Two secured writing credits on Blige's song, the "Top Billin'" drums were themselves sampled from The Honey Drippers' "Impeach the President"—a 1973 funk classic that, like "Top Billin'," has been sampled countless times.

Also key to the success of "Real Love" was a remix by Puff Daddy and Stetsasonic's Daddy-O. This sampled Betty Wright's irresistible "Clean Up Woman"—but, more importantly, it introduced Puffy's protégé, The Notorious B.I.G.

"Real Love" helped *What's the 411?* sell three million copies in the United States alone, while the single reached No. 7 on the *Billboard* Hot 100 and No. 1 on their R&B singles chart. Moreover, it crowned Blige with the title she still holds: "the Queen of Hip-Hop Soul." **JiH**

Deep Cover | Dr. Dre introducing Snoop Doggy Dogg (1992)

Writer | Dr. Dre, Snoop Dogg, Colin Wolfe
Producer | Dr. Dre
Label | Solar
Album | *Deep Cover* (1992)

Leaving N.W.A. in 1991, when the gangsta rappers were peaking in popularity, seemed an odd career move. How could Dr. Dre go solo without Eazy-E and Ice Cube by his side? The answer came in the form of Calvin Broadus, aka Snoop Doggy Dogg. Dre, a gifted talent-spotter, promptly invited Snoop to grace his debut solo single.

Built on Grand Canyon–deep bass, the track mined similar ground to N.W.A.'s "Fuck tha Police." "It's saying, 'Fuck these undercover police that'll set up your ass,'" Snoop told *Playboy*. "This motherfucker and I were doing business. I was trusting him, and all the while he had a wire on. And my girl coming in, happens to tap him on the back and that wire falls out. . . . It's not, 'Hey, he's undercover. Kill him.' It's what you feel like because you trusted him."

The two rappers boasted intriguingly different styles but meshed beautifully. With drums from Sly & The Family Stone's much-sampled "Sing a Simple Song," and a recurring "I can feel it" from The Undisputed Truth's "(I Know) I'm Losing You," the song's hypnotic groove and violent imagery formed the blueprint for "G-Funk."

The *Deep Cover* soundtrack only hit No. 166 in the United States, yet it's likely that everyone who bought it did so for the title track. "Deep Cover" set the stage for the duo's 1992 album, *The Chronic*, and the world was theirs. **JiH**

Out of Space | The Prodigy (1992)

Writer | Howlett, Miller, Perry, Mau. Smith, Max. Smith, Thornton, Randolph
Producer | Liam Howlett
Label | XL
Album | *Experience* (1992)

A slice of techno pop madness called "Charly"—sampling a cartoon cat from a public information film—catapulted The Prodigy into the U.K. charts. But it also saw them derided as a novelty act and the inventors of "kiddie rave."

Despite that mixed reception, they issued four more singles in just eighteen months, all of which reached the U.K. Top Twenty. Of these, the third, "Out of Space," best captures the delirium of the British rave scene in the early 1990s.

A fan of both Public Enemy and Pink Floyd, main man Liam Howlett threw together clattering breakbeats, bubbling synths, and a skanking reggae breakdown, proclaiming "I'm gone sent into outer space / To find another race." The insistent, high-pitched refrain, "I'll take your brain to another dimension / Pay close attention," is a warped sample of Ultramagnetic MC Kool Keith.

By 1993, Howlett had become disillusioned with the rave scene. "I remember a specific gig in Scotland," he told self-titledmag.com, "where I was onstage and felt like, 'Fuck it, I want to go home right now and do something else.'" But "Out of Space" endures—it's the only track from their early days that The Prodigy still play live. Howlett couldn't resist meddling with the mix when Audio Bullys reworked the song for a 2005 re-release—but, as he said, "You can't beat the original. The original is a classic now." **DC**

Didi
Khaled (1992)

Writer | Khaled Hadj Brahim
Producer | Don Was
Label | Barclay
Album | *Khaled* (1992)

"In music," Khaled Hadj Brahim observed to Afro Pop, "there are artists who sing about politics—engaged artists—and also artists who sing about love . . . and artists who make you laugh. Me, I'm coming from those artists who make people laugh and talk about love."

Khaled began scoring hits in his early teens in Algeria and developed into the nation's most gifted (and popular) rai singer. Rai grew from Bedouin traditional songs, about politics, society, and relationships, to a sound that absorbed all kinds of influences. By the time Khaled was hailed "king of rai," the music incorporated Western pop, funk, and rock, yet retained strong Arabic roots.

War between Algeria's military government and fundamentalists in the 1980s forced Khaled and other rai singers to flee to France. There, the Barclay label signed him and hired super-producer Don Was to helm his major-label debut.

"Didi," the opening song and first hit from that album, became a hit in France, and his popularity spread internationally. In the Arabic world, "Didi" became an anthem and *Khaled* the largest-selling Arabic album ever (over seven million copies sold). "Didi" featured Khaled's magnificent voice up front, over a propulsive dance floor groove that kept the song swinging. As an Arabic-Western pop hybrid, it was a masterpiece, and announced, in no uncertain terms, rai's international arrival. **GC**

Animal Nitrate
Suede (1993)

Writer | Brett Anderson, Bernard Butler
Producer | Ed Buller
Label | Nude
Album | *Suede* (1993)

You could plot their musical influences on a small map: David Bowie, The Smiths, David Bowie, The Only Ones, David Bowie. But alternative British music had never seen anything quite like the Suede phenomenon. Acclaimed as the best band in the country before they had even released a record, Suede justified the hype with a trio of scintillatingly sordid singles.

These culminated in "Animal Nitrate," a seedy but energetic smash that artfully combined Bernard Butler's glam guitars with Brett Anderson's cocky celebration of amyl nitrite and underage gay sex. "The songs that specifically revolve around the gay world, like 'Animal Nitrate,' are written because I'm involved in it through my friends . . ." Anderson told *Mojo*. "When people say that I'm just using gay imagery, it depresses me, because my friends go through emotional turmoil. I've felt that on their behalf, and written songs for them."

Few expected the song to go mainstream, but Suede got their big break when they gate-crashed the Brit Awards—the British music industry's annual knees-up. Their act offered a refreshing contrast to the grunge ushered in by Nirvana. Britpop was born, but Suede were overtaken when Blur and Oasis rewrote the rules of what an *NME*-approved indie band could accomplish. They did, however, leave the best legacy that any band can wish for—genuinely great hits. **PW**

La solitudine

La solitudine
Laura Pausini (1993)

Writer | A. Valsiglio, P. Cremonesi, F. Cavalli
Producer | L. Pausini, A. Valsiglio, M. Marati
Label | Atlantic
Album | *Laura Pausini* (1993)

With "La solitudine," Italian singer Laura Pausini won best newcomer at the Sanremo Music Festival in February 1993 and was immediately catapulted onto the international stage while still only eighteen years old. The following summer, the single was broadcast on radio networks all over Europe.

Melodic, cute, and catchy, the song tells of a teenage girl who suffers following the departure of her boyfriend. The lyrics are simple and straightforward, capturing the girl's feelings in exactly the words that a teenager would use. "Marco has left and won't be coming back," she laments, going on to describe the loneliness of the city without him: "The 7:30 train is a soulless heart of metal"; "At school the desk is empty, Marco is inside me." She wonders if he, too, is thinking of her and suffering as much as she is ("I wonder if you think of me / If you ever speak with your friends / So as not to suffer for me anymore").

Though shy, Pausini won over a young audience with her soulful voice and soon had admirers around the world, with a particularly strong following in Latin America. She has even recorded several albums in Spanish and has won a number of Latin Grammys. Cover versions of "La solitudine" have been released in a number of different languages, and the English version, "Loneliness," was translated by Tim Rice. **LSc**

Rumba Argelina

Rumba Argelina
Radio Tarifa (1993)

Writer | Fain S. Dueñas (lyrics: traditional)
Producer | Juan A. Arteche
Label | Sin Fin
Album | *Rumba Argelina* (1993)

Radio Tarifa was the brainchild of multi-instrumentalist Fain Sanchez Dueñas. Feeling stultified by the Madrid rock scene, he discovered flamenco through the music of guitarist Paco de Lucía, and began experimenting with medieval European music in 1984. Then he became interested in Arabic and Persian music, bringing these and other influences together in Radio Tarifa. The core group was essentially a trio, with charismatic front man Benjamin Escoriza on vocals and Vincent Molina playing various wind instruments. Dueñas took care of all the percussion instruments.

"Rumba Argelina" is the title track of the group's critically acclaimed debut album and combines influences of *chaabi* pop music (from Morocco and Algeria) with the traditional lyrics of a flamenco rumba: "Gypsy if you love me / I'd buy you the best cave / You can find in Granada." That may not sound like a very flattering proposal, but it's a reference to the city's cave-dwelling gypsy *barrio* (neighborhood) of Sacromonte—not to some Neanderthal fantasy.

Initially released by Sin Fin in Spain, where it attracted critical acclaim and an unusually broad fan base, the album was licensed by World Circuit in 1996, gaining it much wider recognition. In 2006, however, after three more albums, Radio Tarifa announced an indefinite hiatus. **JLu**

Loser | Beck (1993)

Writer | Beck Hansen, Carl Stephenson
Producer | Carl Stephenson, Tom Rothrock
Label | Bong Load
Album | *Mellow Gold* (1994)

"They said it was a slacker anthem, but it was a completely silly song, just a takeoff on rap."
Beck, 1996

◀ **Influenced by: I Walk on Guilded Splinters**
Johnny Jenkins (1972)
▶ **Influence on: Fresh Feeling** · Eels (2001)
● **Covered by:** The BossHoss (2005)
★ **Other key tracks:** Beercan (1994) · Soul Suckin Jerk
(1994) · Jack-Ass (1996) · Where It's At (1996)

"At first I thought it was a joke . . ." Beck told *Option*, of the reaction to "Loser." "But when the commercial stations started playing it, and the thing started getting on the charts, I figured it must be for real. It was so freaky."

The Los Angeles musical magpie, originally a fan of alternative figureheads Sonic Youth, was turned on to folk via a Mississippi John Hurt album. His subsequent work reflected these influences, with a hip-hop topping. Bong Load label founder Tom Rothrock duly introduced him to "this guy who does hip-hop beats and stuff"—producer Carl Stephenson. In January 1992, the pair assembled "Loser," based on Johnny Jenkins's version of Dr. John's "I Walk on Guilded [sic] Splinters"—a track, featuring guitar by Duane Allman, that has also been sampled by Oasis and Soul II Soul.

"I started writing these lyrics to the verse part," Beck recalled. "When he played it back, I thought, 'Man, I'm the worst rapper in the world' . . . I started singing, 'I'm a loser baby, so why don't you kill me.'"

The track sat unused for a year before Rothrock put it out as a single in 1993. When LA radio leapt on it, DGC—home of Sonic Youth—won a major label bidding war. Their 1994 re-release made "Loser" a smash and Beck an unwitting "slacker" icon. (The song reached No. 10 on the *Billboard Hot 100*.) An experimental video for "Loser" was directed by Steve Hanft, a friend of Beck's.

"If I'd known the impact it was going to make," Beck rued, "I would have put something a little more substantial in it." However, the legacy of "Loser" lives on, from the brainiac Eels to the beer-soaked Kid Rock. **BM**

French Disko | Stereolab (1993)

Writer | Tim Gane, Lætitia Sadier
Producer | Phil Wright
Label | Duophonic
Album | N/A

"If I can open one person's eyes, then that's enough."

Lætitia Sadier, 1994

◄ **Influenced by: Neuschnee** · NEU! (1973)
► **Influence on: Wrapped Up in Books**
   Belle & Sebastian (2003)
● **Covered by:** Editors (2006) · The Raveonettes (2008)
★ **Other key tracks:** Jenny Ondioline (1993) · Wow and
   Flutter (1994) · Miss Modular (1997)

The left-leaning pop peddled by McCarthy—the band co-founded by Tim Gane in the mid-Eighties—was terrific. But Stereolab, his next "groop" (as they became colloquially known), were even better—and there are few greater examples of that brilliance than "French Disko."

Over a hypnotic, NEU!-style rhythm, French singer Lætitia Sadier (sometimes known as Seaya Sadier) combined English and her native tongue in a plea not to accept the grotesque absurdities of life with resigned sighs and shrugs. "I say there are still things worth fighting for," she proclaimed. "*La résistance.*"

It was an early entry in a body of work that constantly sought to poke, prod, and probe the economic and social framework of society. It could all have been turgid, hectoring material, were it not for the music's delicious lightness of touch.

The propulsive track—formerly named "French Disco"—had featured on the *Jenny Ondioline* EP, released in 1993; but this new version gave the band its one and only entry on the U.K. singles chart: a sole week at No. 75 (although it topped the indie rundown). "We've never had a big hit," Gane admitted, "but we make a good living out of something we love doing, which is our definition of success. It's quite nice not having the pressure of having hits."

"I do not like to think that we are known to your average MTV viewer," Gane told an interviewer in America in 1994. With the hedonism of Britpop just around the corner, there were fewer bands than ever willing or able to question the status quo (although Blur recruited Sadier for *Parklife's* gorgeous ballad "To the End"). Stereolab were, therefore, invaluable. *La résistance* indeed. **CB**

Into Dust
Mazzy Star (1993)

Writer | Hope Sandoval, David Roback
Producer | David Roback
Label | Capitol
Album | *So Tonight That I Might See* (1993)

Red Hot Chili Peppers front man Anthony Kiedis had fallen off the wagon after years of sobriety. In "Aeroplane" he sang: "I'm turning into dust again / My melancholy baby, the star of Mazzy, must push her voice inside of me." The lines referenced Hope Sandoval, and the saddest song she ever sang.

Mazzy Star began after Sandoval joined guitarist David Roback's band Opal (her predecessor, Kendra Smith, quit during a tour with The Jesus and Mary Chain, of whom more later). "We were friends, Hope and I," Roback told *Rolling Stone*. "But I don't think we were really part of the music scene. . . . We were both sort of alienated— that's what we had in common."

Acclaim for the duo's new band translated into sales when their second album, *So Tonight That I Might See,* yielded the hit "Fade into You." But listeners discovered an even better song near the end of the set—a sparse account of a decaying relationship. "David's guitar part was just so moving," Sandoval recalled, "we didn't even stop and write. He just played the guitar part, I sang, we recorded it, and that was it. "

Sandoval was customarily reticent about her inspiration for the lyrics. Around that time, however, she was living with William Reid of The Jesus and Mary Chain. Tellingly, Reid recalled the relationship as "an act of self-destruction—two messed up people clinging to each other." **BM**

Rid of Me
PJ Harvey (1993)

Writer | Polly Jean Harvey
Producer | Steve Albini
Label | Island
Album | *Rid of Me* (1993)

Hell hath no fury like a woman scorned— especially if that woman is Polly Harvey. Over the past two decades, she has penned a clutch of songs featuring unbalanced females exacting revenge on straying lovers. And of all Harvey's retribution fantasies, the title track of her second album is perhaps the most disturbing.

"Rid of Me" opens with a muted, percussive guitar, and threats muttered at a cheating beau: "I'll tie your legs / Keep you against my chest / Oh, you're not rid of me." Suddenly, the band flares into a maelstrom of bluesy punk, enhancing Harvey's screams that the torture will continue until her victim admits he wishes he "never, never met her."

Few artists would dare open their first major label album with such a demented display. (Harvey had signed to Island the previous year.) In 2004, she admitted to *Filter* that she had been desperate to "demonstrate that I was not going to be the kind of usually expected major artist material. . . . I just wanted the people involved to know that I can only do things that follow my heart."

This brutal honesty made the song all the more powerful. Harvey declared that she had shocked herself, while a *Melody Maker* writer was so startled that she crashed her car while listening to it. "Rid of Me" even found a place in the 1995 movie *Strange Days*, featuring a frenzied performance of the song by Juliette Lewis. **TB**

PJ Harvey scoffs at commentators who suggest that her lyrics imply a twisted soul.

Streets of Philadelphia | Bruce Springsteen (1993)

Writer | Bruce Springsteen
Producer | Bruce Springsteen, Chuck Plotkin
Label | Epic Soundtrax
Album | *Philadelphia (Music from the Motion Picture)* (1993)

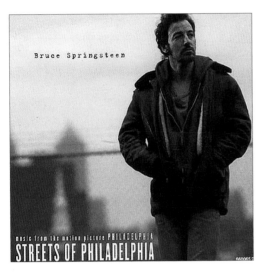

Bruce Springsteen

music from the motion picture PHILADELPHIA
STREETS OF PHILADELPHIA

"This is the first song I ever wrote for a motion picture. So I guess it's all downhill from here."

Bruce Springsteen, 1994

◄ **Influenced by: Justify My Love·** Madonna (1990)
► **Influence on: The Shining ·** Badly Drawn Boy (2000)
● **Covered by:** Richie Havens (1997) · Ray Conniff (1997)
Reilly & Maloney (2003) · Garland Jeffreys (2003)
Molly Johnson (2006) · Liv Kristine (2006) · Bettye
Lavette (2007) · David Gray (2007)

By 1992, Bruce Springsteen had ditched the E Street Band and released two albums that failed to ignite critics or customers. So his career was at a low point when director Jonathan Demme asked him to contribute to *Philadelphia*, his movie about AIDS and injustice. "I thought," Demme recalled, "what we need is the most up-to-the-minute, guitar-dominated, American rock anthem about injustice to start the movie off."

The director originally chose Neil Young, but decided to use his "Philadelphia" to close the movie. From Springsteen, he got a gentle lament with a hip-hop backing. Springsteen recorded all the music himself in August 1993, adding only backing vocals by Tommy Simms. A later version, featuring jazz stars Ornette Coleman and Little Jimmy Scott, appears halfway through the movie.

"Bruce's gift is to locate the heart in some character's dilemma," the song's co-producer, Chuck Plotkin, told *Billboard*'s Craig Rosen. "I don't think he has ever set out to write something about a character that didn't come from his own experience or imagination, but he certainly managed to do it this time."

"Streets of Philadelphia" shot Springsteen back into international charts and hearts. Aided by a Demme-directed video featuring the star singing live while walking through neighborhoods in Philly, the ballad won four Grammys, an MTV award, and an Oscar. Accepting the latter, Springsteen said: "You do your best work and you hope that it pulls out the best in your audience and some piece of it spills over into the real world and into people's everyday lives. And it takes the edge off the fear and allows us to recognize each other through our veil of differences." **SO**

Laid | James (1993)

Writer | Tim Booth, Jim Glennie, Larry Gott
Producer | Brian Eno
Label | Fontana
Album | *Laid* (1993)

"I'm interested in … what it means to be a man, at the mercy of your sexual desires."
Tim Booth, 2005

◀ **Influenced by:** Orange Crush • R.E.M. (1988)
▶ **Influence on:** Glass of Water • Coldplay (2008)
● **Covered by:** Matt Nathanson (2003) • Better Than Ezra (2005)
★ **Other key tracks:** Sit Down (1989) • Come Home (1990) • She's a Star (1997)

Morrissey's favorite band when they were mid-Eighties folk-pop oddballs, James matured into reluctant frontrunners with *Gold Mother,* released in 1990, followed two years later by *Seven.* By this point, they were in the unlikely position of shifting hundreds of thousands of units but chose to pull back from the brink, enlisting Brian Eno to bring out their moody, mystical side. In 1993, *Laid* announced a stripped-back James, still vast and echoing, but creating that space with little fuss.

Rolling tattoos of drums drove its title track, whipping up a sexual fever as singer Tim Booth "messed around with gender roles" (on the album cover, the band members stand resplendent in frocks, munching on bananas). Later affectionately dismissed by Booth as "slightly wacky," "Laid" is a gloriously implausible anthem. (Movie director Kevin Smith, who walked down the aisle to it, said simply: "This song always gives me a boner.")

The lyrics tell a raucous tale of bedroom fireworks: "The neighbors complain about the noises above / But she only comes when she's on top." Then it crashes headlong into fireworks of a different kind, as the couple fight "with kitchen knives and skewers." Ain't love grand?

James's star was waning in the United Kingdom, where "Laid" sauntered to the lower reaches of the Top Thirty. But the United States suddenly welcomed them: the single climbed into *Billboard*'s Hot 100 while becoming a radio hit—and later turned up, performed by singer-songwriter Matt Nathanson, on the soundtrack to *American Pie*'s sequel *American Wedding* (2003). As for the dueling protagonists of the song, the struggle continues: "You're driving me crazy / When are you coming home?" **MH**

Open Up | Leftfield-Lydon (1993)

Writer | Paul Daley, Neil Barnes, John Lydon
Producer | Leftfield
Label | Hard Hands
Album | *Leftism* (1995)

"They didn't ask me in because they wanted a pop star floating around."

John Lydon, 1993

◀ **Influenced by: Burn Hollywood Burn**
Public Enemy (1990)
▶ **Influence on: Firestarter** · Prodigy (1996)
★ **Other key tracks:** Release the Pressure (1992)
Song of Life (1993) · Afro-Left (1995) · Original (1995)
21st Century Poem (1995)

By the early Nineties, Public Image Ltd had lost the cutting edge that once made the band a vital force—but that didn't mean front man John Lydon had stopped springing surprises. His work with Afrika Bambaataa, on Time Zone's "World Destruction," was an early indicator that rock and hip-hop were not mutually exclusive. With "Open Up," he was at it again, collaborating with Leftfield to advance the rock/dance explorations of Andrew Weatherall and Primal Scream.

"Musical McDonald's" was Lydon's stance on dance, but Paul Daley changed his mind with choice cuts from his collection. Leftfield's other half, Neil Barnes, envisaged how Lydon's snarling delivery would mesh perfectly with the duo's skull-crushing electronica. "I knew he would come out with something special," Barnes reflected, "because he was really nervous. Put John on the spot—that's the best way. We treated him like we treat anybody else. We weren't star-struck. We made him work and he liked that."

Ever the punk, Lydon initially claimed that his lyrics were spur of the moment, but he later admitted that he hit the studio word perfect. "I'm one of those horrible perfectionists with a gross sense of insecurity," he confessed to *NME*.

But those words plunged the track into controversy after "Open Up" was issued in late 1993. The phrase "Burn, Hollywood, Burn" was interpreted as glee regarding forest fires raging across California at the time—despite the lyrics having been written long beforehand (the track's release was delayed for months by legal wrangling). The actual inspiration, Lydon explained, was a revenge fantasy: "Not getting a movie part and burning down the studio in sheer frustration." **CB**

Possession | Sarah McLachlan (1993)

Writer | Sarah McLachlan
Producer | Pierre Marchand
Label | Nettwerk
Album | *Fumbling Towards Ecstasy* (1993)

"It was just sort of a sicko fantasy in my brain that wouldn't go any further."

Sarah McLachlan, 1996

◄ **Influenced by: Desire** · Talk Talk (1988)
► **Influence on: You Oughta Know** · Alanis Morissette (1995)
● **Covered by:** Transfer (2001) · Evans Blue (2006) · Smile Empty Soul (2007)

"Scary" isn't an adjective often ascribed to Canadian singer-songwriter Sarah McLachlan, or to her beguiling blend of folk and Fleetwood Mac. And the chorus of "Possession"—"And I would be the one to hold you down / Kiss you so hard"—seems at first simply about passion.

However, the rocky cut was inspired by an obsessed fan—who, the year after its release, took his own life. "I had a few . . ." she explained, "who were writing me a lot of letters based on this romantic, sexual fantasy world that I wasn't in, but they believed me to be there with them."

"I am the person who is the subject of the song 'Possession,'" wrote one such fan, Uwe Vandrei, in a lengthy Internet post. "Ms. McLachlan has breached the confidentiality of my letters . . . I have suffered profound emotional hardships because of the song 'Possession' and the subsequent controversy associated with it." He committed suicide just weeks later.

The song had already courted controversy, thanks to a provocative video that re-created female archetypes from historical paintings. McLachlan ignored her label's advice—"Don't second-guess MTV"—and was rewarded with a ban in the United States. Nonetheless, the star—whose soothing music belies a steely determination—enjoyed ever-escalating sales. She continued to perform "Possession," hence a barnstorming version on her live album *Mirrorball*, released in 1999.

"Almost every letter I get these days," she told *Rolling Stone*, "the writer says, 'I'm not one of those psycho fans.' But ever since then I haven't gotten any letters that were freaky like that, which is great, because I used to get them all the time." **BM**

Cannonball
The Breeders (1993)

Writer | Kim Deal
Producer | Kim Deal, Mark Freegard
Label | Elektra
Album | *Last Splash* (1993)

The Breeders began as a side-project for Pixies bassist Kim Deal and Tanya Donnelly of Throwing Muses. By their second album, *Last Splash*, Donnelly was long gone and Deal (accompanied by her twin sister Kelley) was mining a seam of brilliantly left-handed subterranean sounds.

Kim writes pop to her own recipe. On "Cannonball," that means off-kilter hooks discovered while goofing around in the studio, shrieks of feedback, choruses yelled through harmonicas, false endings, and eerily hummed harmonies—threaded together by a slithering bass line and a stop-start beat. The lyrics seem similarly lackadaisical, although Kim has since claimed that the song was an elaborate mockery of the writings of the Marquis de Sade.

Radio embraced this addictive, off-center track, while Kim Gordon (of Sonic Youth) and Spike Jonze's video made indie rock sirens of the Deal sisters. Its success helped parent album *Last Splash* go platinum, and The Breeders spent a year on the road with Nirvana and, later, the Lollapalooza festival (before remaining on hiatus until 2002 when they released *Title TK*).

The ramshackle charms of "Cannonball" have endured. It appeared in *NME*'s list of the 50 Greatest Indie Anthems Ever, was sampled on French disco producer Mirwais's filthy hit "Disco Science," and still fills indie club dance floors. **SC**

C.R.E.A.M.
Wu-Tang Clan (1993)

Writer | Coles, Diggs, Grice, Hawkins, Hunter, Jones, Smith, Woods, Hayes, Porter
Producer | The RZA
Label | Loud
Album | *Enter the Wu-Tang (36 Chambers)* (1993)

New York was losing the rap race. Although hip-hop had been born and raised on the city's streets, the genre's biggest artists—Dr. Dre and Snoop Dogg—now hailed from California. But, in 1993, Staten Island's Wu-Tang Clan brought hip-hop back east. *Enter the Wu-Tang (36 Chambers)* was a lethal cocktail of street tales and sizzling samples, far removed from the G-Funk of Dre and crew.

"C.R.E.A.M." defined the differences between East and West Coast rap. The chorus—"Cash rules everything around me / C.R.E.A.M. get the money / Dollar, dollar bill y'all"—sounded like the brainless capitalism of Californian gangstas, but the track was more complex. The Clan portrayed hustling and drug dealing as a means of survival, not as a route to riches and bitches.

Not that Wu-Tang were averse to making money. "Taking care of business is part of the fight [in hip-hop]," U2's Bono observed to *NME*. "There was a piece in the *New York Times* on our friend The RZA." The RZA's raw production—born in a cheap, crowded studio—upped the gritty air. A scratchy, spiraling piano riff from The Charmels' Isaac Hayes/David Porter–penned "As Long as I've Got You" repeated over and over, supplemented only by a minimal, dirty beat. These sparse sounds and bleak lyrics helped inspire the next great generation of New York rappers and threw the Empire State back in the game. **TB**

The Breeders' Kim Deal contributes to *MTV Live and Loud: Nirvana Performs Live* in 1993.

Because the Night
10,000 Maniacs (1993)

Writer | Bruce Springsteen, Patti Smith
Producer | Paul Fox
Label | Elektra
Album | *MTV Unplugged* (1993)

"When we did 'Because the Night'," singer Natalie Merchant told *The Arizona Republic*, "we weren't putting a lot of emphasis on it. I just always liked the song and thought it would be interesting to do it acoustically because it's such a powerful song electric." Despite these modest origins, the cover became 10,000 Maniacs' biggest hit—and Merchant's sensational swan song.

It was penned by Bruce Springsteen, who gave it to Patti Smith. Having tinkered with the lyrics, she too enjoyed her biggest hit with the song. Merchant heard it in a restaurant while devising a set list for MTV's *Unplugged*. "Patti Smith and Bruce Springsteen are such different artists," she told the *Los Angeles Times*. "Patti the punk poetess and Bruce the guitar-playing, working-class hero. The two of them collaborating on the song seemed to me to be symbolic of what 10,000 Maniacs had managed to do. We had somehow retained our alternative label—our subversive vision, if you will—yet we were accepted in the mainstream."

Ironically, as "Because the Night" took over U.S. radio, Merchant announced her departure from the group. "She wanted to be a solo act by the time she was thirty," keyboardist Dennis Drew told the *Jamestown Post-Journal*, "and she turned thirty in October [1993]." Under the guidance of Springsteen's manager, Jon Landau (a coincidence, she said), Merchant became a solo star. **BM**

Ching söörtükchülerining yryzy
Huun-Huur-Tu (1993)

Writer | Kaigal-ool Khovalyg
Producer | Alexander Bapa
Label | Shanachie
Album | *60 Horses in My Herd* (1993)

Tuva—the landlocked republic at the heart of Asia—is the home of the four-piece Huun-Huur-Tu. Their "throat singing" has made them popular on the Western world music circuit. Ancient nomadic hunter-herders who roamed the Tuvan steppes developed throat singing, creating a deep, rhythmic growling effect that brings forth eerie harmonics and otherworldly noises. A singer can produce two or three notes at once: a low drone and a higher melody is produced from the overtones of the drone note. The quartet combines this with traditional Tuvan instruments.

The group's philosophy is one of updating Tuvan folklore. Their origins in a nomadic culture that values superb horse riding skills explain why many of their songs concern horses. "Ching söörtükchülerining yryzy" (Song of the Caravan Drivers) employs a rhythm derived from singing on horseback—as Huun-Huur-Tu's ancestors did. Bandleader Kaigal-ool Khovalyg sings in a warm manner while the group backs him with vocals, stringed instruments, and shamanic drums.

Tuva was ruled by the Soviet Union, and the decline of communism allowed Tuvan throat singing to reach the west. Ry Cooder was among the musicians so impressed that they collaborated with Huun-Huur-Tu; they also played with Frank Zappa before his death, and "Song of the Caravan Drivers" is dedicated to him. **GC**

It Ain't Hard to Tell
Nas (1994)

Writer | Jones, Large Professor, Kool & The Gang, Porcaro, Bettis, Handy, C. Redd, G. Redd, Smith, Horne
Producer | Large Professor
Label | Columbia
Album | *Illmatic* (1994)

Bloodlust and bling came to characterize rap as the Nineties wore on. But in 1994, the spotlight shone on two New York rappers whose fame rested on jaw-dropping lyrical skills and astonishing production. One was The Notorious B.I.G.; the other was Nasir bin Olu Dara Jones, aka "Nasty" Nas.

Like B.I.G., Nas worked his way up with cameos, notably on "Live at the Barbeque" in 1991 by Main Source (featuring his producer, Large Professor). He was hailed as a successor to legendary rapper Rakim, but *Illmatic* exceeded all expectations. Its maker just twenty years old, this mature masterpiece became a hip-hop landmark.

For all its excellence, *Illmatic* might have remained a cult favorite had its closing track, and first hit, not nudged Nas into the mainstream. "It Ain't Hard to Tell" took its distinctive brass squeak from the 1971 single "N. T." by Kool & The Gang (a second-long sample that nonetheless meant the entire Gang featured on the track's credits). The recurring "Yeah!" came from Mountain's much-sampled live version of "Long Red" from 1972, and its beat is thought to be from Stanley Clarke's 1978 album cut "Slow Dance."

But the most obvious sample, and the one that guaranteed airplay, was from Michael Jackson's *Thriller* hit "Human Nature." The blend of this sumptuous music and Nas's evocative flow made "It Ain't Hard to Tell" a natural hit. **BM**

Inner City Life
Goldie presents Metalheads (1994)

Writer | Clifford "Goldie" Price, Diane Charlemagne, Rob Playford
Producer | Clifford "Goldie" Price
Label | FFRR
Album | *Timeless* (1995)

Drum 'n' bass was a British music movement that grew out of the hard-core house and break-beat sub-genres. Typified by time-stretched break beats and ominous bass lines, the scene became characterized as overly dark, thanks to its often violent, criminal imagery.

But one man was determined to change that: Goldie. Admittedly, he too seemed dangerously belligerent: "I was hearing all these other dark tunes," he told British TV's Channel 4, "and I'd be going home and thinking, I'm going to need to cut these people down." But Goldie also had a wide range of influences—"I'm a really big Pat Metheny fan," he told djvibe.com—and grand plans.

At the end of 1994, the first sound of that plan was heard: the epic "Inner City Life." It boasted swirling strings, a clattering break beat that evolved throughout the track, and Diane Charlemagne's sweet, soulful vocals on top.

On the *Timeless* album, Goldie took his musical ideas further, incorporating "Inner City Life" into a three-movement, twenty-one-minute symphonic piece. *Timeless* reached No. 7 in the United Kingdom, reaped a slew of awards, and led Goldie to work with David Bowie and Oasis's Noel Gallagher on his follow-up, *Saturnz Return*. In 2008, his symphonic ambitions were realized when an orchestra and chorus piece he composed was played at London's Royal Albert Hall. **DC**

End of a Century | Blur (1994)

Writer | D. Albarn, G. Coxon, A. James, D. Rowntree
Producer | Stephen Street
Label | Food
Album | *Parklife* (1994)

"This is about a late twenties couple, watching videos and eating pizza . . . they're in love."
Damon Albarn, 1995

◀ **Influenced by: End of the Season** · The Kinks (1967)
▶ **Influence on: Modern Way** · Kaiser Chiefs (2005)
● **Covered by:** Squeeze (1995)
★ **Other key tracks:** Popscene (1992) · For Tomorrow (1993) · Girls & Boys (1994) · This Is a Low (1994) · To the End (1994) · The Universal (1995)

A heartfelt lament, "End of a Century" was the last of four U.K. hits—after "Girls & Boys," "To the End," and the title track—from Blur's third studio album, Britpop masterpiece *Parklife*.

The album's most ear-catching opening line ("She says, 'There's ants in the carpet'") was inspired by the house that singer Damon Albarn shared with his partner of the period, Justine Frischmann of fellow Britpop group Elastica.

The melancholy lyrics evoke a mundane relationship at the dying end of the twentieth century: "We all say, 'Don't want to be alone' / We wear the same clothes cause we feel the same / Kiss with dry lips, when we say good night / End of a century, oh it's nothing special."

Unlike many of their contemporaries, Blur did not shy away from experimenting with different sounds and instruments. A flügelhorn forms the bridge before Albarn sweetly—and saucily—harmonizes with guitarist Graham Coxon: "Can you eat her? / Yes you can."

Issued as a single in November 1994—in a *Star Trek*–inspired sleeve, with the Starship *Enterprise* numbered "UN-1" (meaning "you 'n' I")—"End of a Century" rose to only No. 19 in the U.K. singles chart at the time. But it became one of the ten most popular Blur songs on last.fm and has always been a live favorite, partly owing to the video being filmed at a triumphant Alexandra Palace performance in London.

At Blur's 2009 reunion gigs, Albarn changed a line from the original lyrics, "And the mind gets dirty, as you get closer to thirty," to "And the mind gets filthy, as you get closer to fifty"—a wry acknowledgement of the years that had passed since the song's release. **OM**

Connection | Elastica (1994)

Writer | Justine Frischmann
Producer | Marc Waterman
Label | Deceptive
Album | *Elastica* (1995)

"I would agree that 'Connection' was naughty. That's the naughtiest thing we've done."

Justine Frischmann, 1995

◄ **Influenced by: Three Girl Rhumba** • Wire (1977)
► **Influence on: Sing Back Connection** • Moloko vs. Elastica (2007)
● **Covered by:** Talbot Tagora (2008)
★ **Other key tracks:** Stutter (1993) • Line Up (1994) Waking Up (1994) • Car Song (1995)

An artfully sexy song that is impossible not to move to, "Connection" opens with a grinding guitar riff. "That was actually done on a keyboard," leader Justine Frischmann told *Melody Maker*. "But the sound is called 'distorted guitar.'"

The distinctive introduction was, however, highly reminiscent of Wire's "Three Girl Rhumba." Wire's publishers duly sued, but accepted an out-of-court settlement on the eve of the release of the upstarts' debut album. "Personally," Wire's Bruce Gilbert told *NME*, "I have absolutely no problems with Justine or the Elastica project and I like the music. It's fascinating to some degree—it has to be flattering—really, it's quite curious. But if Wire did have an influence I'd rather it be from an attitude point of view rather than from a musical point of view."

His colleague Colin Newman disagreed, telling *Atlanta Weekly*: "I really didn't like Britpop. I didn't want to be anywhere associated with what [Elastica] were doing."

The supremely cool Frischmann, who rated the post-punk pioneers among her favorites, remained unruffled. "I was delighted," she told cdnow.com in 2000, "to see the first two Wire albums re-released after our first album started doing quite well."

Elastica were influenced by new wave and punk but gave their brittle songs a pop twist. They also achieved something that many Britpop contemporaries only dreamed of: Stateside sales.

Elastica endured whispers about their alleged plagiarism and speculation about Frischmann's involvement with Blur's Damon Albarn. But this ignores the strength of songs like "Connection," which takes a blueprint and makes it their own with hooks, hand claps, and spiky singing. **OM**

Confide in Me | Kylie Minogue (1994)

Writer | S. Anderson, D. Seaman, O. Barton
Producer | Brothers in Rhythm
Label | Deconstruction
Album | *Kylie Minogue* (1994)

KYLIE MINOGUE

"Deconstruction don't like to be so safe, so it was a welcome change."

Kylie Minogue, 1994

◀ **Influenced by: Justify My Love** • Madonna (1990)
▶ **Influence on: Stronger** • Sugababes (2002)
● **Covered by:** The Sisters of Mercy (1997) • Nerina Pallot (2006) • Angtoria (2006) • Noël Akchoté (2007)
★ **Other key tracks:** If You Don't Love Me (1994) Nothing Can Stop Us (1994)

"Stick or twist, the choice is yours." Kylie Minogue chose to twist at the end of her contract with PWL—the label with whom she scored smashes like "I Should Be So Lucky," but by whom she was regarded as a puppet of her producers.

She promptly decamped to hipper-than-thou dance label Deconstruction. The first fruits were a collaboration with remix crew Brothers in Rhythm (Steve Anderson and Dave Seaman), and the signs were good: "Confide in Me" was a huge hit in her adopted homeland Britain and native Australia.

Exploiting the then-voguish trip-hop sound, with brooding strings reminiscent of Massive Attack's "Unfinished Sympathy," Minogue and her team showed a feel for the times. The murky setting suited her high-pitched vocal, creating a haunting lullaby that is worlds away from her shrill hits of earlier days.

Controversy loomed when songwriter Owain Barton claimed the strings mirrored the melody of his "It's a Fine Day" (originally by indie group Jane, and transformed into a hit for dance act Opus III). Later pressings added Barton's name to the credits. The shamanic guitar signature was a lift from The Doors' epic of 1967, "The End," while clattering beats rooted the track to the dance floor.

The B-sides to "Confide in Me" were knowingly picked covers of songs by Saint Etienne and Prefab Sprout, both perennially popular with critics, if not the public. This illustrated the dichotomy at the heart of Minogue's new direction: at last she had found respect, but at the expense of her pop princess crown. And indeed the big hits dried up before 2000's triumphant "Spinning Around" comeback—but Minogue had made her first truly artistic statement. **MH**

Your Ghost | Kristin Hersh featuring Michael Stipe (1994)

Writer | Kristin Hersh
Producer | Lenny Kaye, Kristin Hersh
Label | Sire
Album | *Hips and Makers* (1994)

"At around 4 a.m., which is when I write all my songs, I started hearing 'Your Ghost.'"

Kristin Hersh, 2009

◀ **Influenced by: Hymn** · Patti Smith Group (1979)
▶ **Influence on: E-Bow the Letter** · R.E.M. featuring Patti Smith (1996)
● **Covered by:** Paul Durham (2003) · The McCarricks (2007) · Greg Laswell (2009)

Throwing Muses' leader was not thinking about releasing her first solo album when she started laying down tracks that eventually formed *Hips and Makers*. Kristin Hersh simply had tunes running around in her head and wanted them out. Reasoning that these folksy, acoustic-based songs did not make sense for the spiky Muses (contemporaries of the Pixies), she decided to record them on her own.

A demo made its way to Hersh's most famous friend, R.E.M.'s Michael Stipe, who assumed the unofficial role of musical advisor. "Michael would call me now and then," Hersh recalled, "essentially just saying, 'don't fuck this up.'" One conversation occurred while a rough recording of "Your Ghost" played in the background, and Hersh realized that Stipe's voice was the track's missing ingredient.

The resulting collaboration was as bewitching as anything that either icon had sung. Hersh's lyrics screamed with quiet desperation, illuminating by soft candlelight the creepiness in the commonplace. The combination of strummed guitar and Jane Scarpantoni's low, rumbling cello sounded pretty at first, but it didn't take long for the menace to sink in. The whole arrangement was unsettling, the musical equivalent of a puzzle where the pieces do not fit—and, indeed, that was the case. "None of the notes I'm singing go with the notes I'm playing," Hersh admitted.

The single, released amid R.E.M. mania, helped *Hips and Makers* become the biggest record of Hersh's career, despite resistance from radio. "There are stations in America that wouldn't play 'Your Ghost,'" she fumed, "because they were playing 'too many women's songs.'" **JiH**

Doll Parts
Hole (1994)

Writer | Courtney Love
Producer | Paul Q. Kolderie,
Sean Slade
Label | DGC
Album | *Live Through This* (1994)

"There's being really low," observed Joni Mitchell to *Guitar World*, "and then there's pretending to be low because it's trendy to be miserable. There's so much falseness in that stuff. There's a line in a Courtney song that stopped me: 'I fake it so real, I am beyond fake.' That, at least, has an element of truth and revelation in it."

One of Courtney Love's early inspirations, British singer Julian Cope, had told her to live her life as if being followed by a movie camera. And, even before she began a relationship with Nirvana's front man Kurt Cobain, Love had plenty of exposure to show business and its fakery—from stripping, through singing with Faith No More, to verbal catfights with Madonna.

The plaintive "Doll Parts" is often interpreted as having a Cobain connection. Yet she wrote this wry comment on fame before either of them were household names: it was first recorded for a John Peel BBC radio session in November 1991 (this mellower version was released on 1995's *Ask for It* mini-album). Its title has been variously attributed to Jacqueline Susann's 1966 novel *Valley of the Dolls* and the name of one of drummer Patty Schemel's former groups (although Schemel didn't join Hole until 1992).

Whatever its inspiration, "Doll Parts"—like the rest of *Live Through This*—confirmed Love as a magnificent, maturing writer. **BM**

7 Seconds | Youssou N'Dour
featuring Neneh Cherry (1994)

Writer | Y. N'Dour, N. Cherry,
C. McVey, J. Sharp
Producer | Booga Bear, J. Dollar
Label | Columbia
Album | *The Guide (Wommat)* (1994)

"Peter Gabriel presented me to the world," Senegalese singer Youssou N'Dour told *The Times*. "He helped me a lot." But while his singing on Gabriel's album *So* (1986) earned N'Dour recognition, it was the single "7 Seconds" in 1994 that turned him into an international superstar.

"We did it as an experiment," admitted Neneh Cherry, who had gained success with her own hip-hop-inspired work and had met N'Dour years earlier at her parents' home in Sweden. Shocked by the single's enormous commercial success, she told the *Independent*, "That tune grew on its own, completely out of proportion. It was out there doing its own thing. But that is a dream when you write a song."

"7 Seconds"—which reappeared on Cherry's album *Man* in 1996—sold millions and spent an unprecedented sixteen weeks atop the French charts. The song's drifting synthesizer chords and gentle boom-box-beat were enhanced by a moody black-and-white video.

The soul of "7 Seconds" is N'Dour's heartfelt vocals, sung in Wolof and French, enhanced by Cherry's haunting English-language chorus. Written about the innocence of the first seven seconds of life after birth, the collaborators refused to bow to pressure to translate the entire song into English. "Why does it always have to be the dominant language?" Cherry reasoned. **EP**

Hole's Courtney Love, by common consent the First Lady of grunge, performs in 1994.

Live Forever | Oasis (1994)

Writer | Noel Gallagher
Producer | Oasis, Mark Coyle, Owen Morris
Label | Creation
Album | *Definitely Maybe* (1994)

"People said to me after 'Live Forever,' where are you gonna go after that. . . . It's a good song, but I think I can do better."
Noel Gallagher, 2006

◄ **Influenced by: Shine a Light** • The Rolling Stones (1972)
► **Influence on: Club Foot** • Kasabian (2004)
● **Covered by:** The Royal Philharmonic Orchestra (1997) Joe Dolan (1999) • Counting Crows (2000) • MGMT (2009)

"It was written in the middle of grunge and all that," said Oasis's chief songsmith Noel Gallagher. "And I remember Nirvana had a tune called 'I Hate Myself and I Want to Die,' and I was like . . . 'Well, I'm not fucking having that.' . . . Kids don't need to be hearing that nonsense." Three years after penning the track while he was supposed to be working on a Manchester building site—and just four months after Kurt Cobain's death—"Live Forever" became his group's first U.K. Top Ten hit.

Despite Oasis's predilection for aping The Beatles, "Live Forever" is lovingly culled from The Rolling Stones. Noel had been listening to *Exile on Main St.*'s "Shine a Light" and based his melody upon it. (Paul McCartney gave the song a thumbs-up nonetheless.)

The result—arguably his finest achievement—smoothed Noel's takeover of his brother Liam's group. Noel told *Q*, "I remember playing it to them on an acoustic guitar one night . . . and it's one of the greatest moments I've ever had as a songwriter. They were just completely and utterly fuckin' speechless." On vocals, Liam's usual sneer is replaced by eloquent yearning, befitting lyrics that turn their mom Peggy's gardening obsession into something altogether more affecting.

Voted the greatest song of all time by readers of *Q* in 2006, the final cut features a soaring guitar solo that Noel would struggle to live up to. Further fret-twiddling was excised by Owen Morris, one of the song's co-producers.

After trailing their breakthrough album, *Definitely Maybe*, "Live Forever" became a live favorite—and a Britpop documentary made in 2003, starring Noel and Liam themselves, borrowed its title. **JM**

Cut Your Hair | Pavement (1994)

Writer | Stephen Malkmus
Producer | Pavement
Label | Matador
Album | *Crooked Rain, Crooked Rain* (1994)

"I don't want to be remembered for lyrics. I want to be remembered for having a big nose that's a little crooked."
Stephen Malkmus, 2008

◀ **Influenced by:** So You Want to be a Rock 'n' Roll Star
The Byrds (1967)
▶ **Influence on:** Could You Wait? · Silkworm (1997)
● **Covered by:** Airport Girl (2003)
★ **Other key tracks:** Gold Soundz (1994) · Grounded
(1995) · Shady Lane (1997) · Stereo (1997)

In the heady post-*Nevermind* afterglow, it seemed that even lo-fi worshippers of British cult heroes The Fall could infiltrate the mainstream. Championed by influential indie rockers like Sonic Youth, and briefly proclaimed by the British music press as the "next Nirvana," Pavement knew something strange was up when U.S. teen magazine *Sassy* sounded a "Cute Band Alert" in their honor.

The lead single from *Crooked Rain, Crooked Rain* was Pavement's sly, wry response to the music industry merry-go-round onto which they had inadvertently stumbled. Front man Stephen Malkmus described "Cut Your Hair" as "a metaphor song," in which hopeful new groups engaged in undignified popularity contests to secure the media's affections, ending up like girls getting haircuts to win the attention of aloof boys.

Over a melodic, chiming chug, Malkmus dropped dry references to the group's own soap opera, including the recent exit of wildcard original drummer Gary Young. He noted sharply that "Songs mean a lot when songs are bought," and closed the piece with repeated, manic screams of "Career!"

Reminiscing in 2008, Malkmus was tinged with regret: "It's too bad it wasn't quite the song that could've really pushed the band," he told *Spin*. "For all the mistakes that were made marketing Pavement, it comes down to the song; and the song was pretty good, but it just wasn't the song of the time. The Offspring song ["Come Out and Play"], "Cannonball" by The Breeders—those were bigger songs people could get behind."

Regardless, the group located an audience that appreciated their scruffy, and wonderful, pop. "Cut Your Hair" remains an endearing indie anthem. **SC**

All Apologies
Nirvana (1994)

Writer | Kurt Cobain
Producer | Nirvana, Scott Litt
Label | DGC
Album | *MTV Unplugged in New York* (1994)

Kurt Cobain's suicide casts a retrospective shadow over his lyrics. On Internet message boards, fans morbidly posit that the lyrics to "All Apologies"—the closing song on Nirvana's final studio album, *In Utero*—are a veiled farewell and apology for taking his life. But while the lyrics' sense of displacement and alienation offers a window on the depression and confusion that dogged Cobain throughout his years, the song dates to 1990.

Nirvana demoed a version in 1991 and played it at the U.K.'s Reading Festival in August 1992. Cobain dedicated the song to Courtney Love, who had given birth to their daughter Frances Bean a week before, and led the audience in cheers of support for his troubled partner. Their adversarial relationship with the world bleeds through the lyric, Cobain dreaming sweetly of "choking on the ashes of her enemy." But the chorus's troubling hook—"Married / Buried"—suggested there were no easy resolutions in Cobain's worldview.

The song's graceful, Beatlesque arrangement veered from the mangled grunge that preceded it on *In Utero*. Cobain made it one of only two hits to feature in the group's *MTV Unplugged* appearance in 1993. The cello-embellished, shredded vocal "All Apologies" was a highlight of that set. Like the rest of their *Unplugged* performances, it was a first take, and suggested where Cobain's muse might have taken him next. **SC**

Hurt
Nine Inch Nails (1994)

Writer | Trent Reznor
Producer | Trent Reznor
Label | Interscope
Album | *The Downward Spiral* (1994)

The vitriolic 1989 debut album *Pretty Hate Machine* proved Nine Inch Nails mastermind Trent Reznor a maestro of industrial noise and rancorous lyrics. Its full-length follow-up added startling depth.

The Downward Spiral focuses on a character (often identified as Reznor) trying to expunge everything—sex, religion, society—that holds him back, until he is left facing death. The coda, "Hurt," is a tortured evocation of addiction.

With lyrics that begin "I hurt myself today / To see if I still feel," Reznor cracks open his angst-ridden shell to expose the vulnerability within. The music is stripped of NIN's customary assault, bar climactic drums by Chris Vrenna (the only musician other than Reznor to play on it).

Eight years later, Johnny Cash covered "Hurt." "There's more heart and soul and pain in that song," he told *Rolling Stone*, "than any that's come along in a long time." In his hands, the track became a heartrending meditation on mortality—made more poignant by Cash's death in 2003.

"I was flattered," Reznor told *The Daily Telegraph*, "but it also felt like someone was kissing your girlfriend." He was swayed by Mark Romanek's video, featuring Cash and his wife June Carter. "It had such an emotional impact," Reznor admitted. "Hearing someone, who's actually one of the best in the world at what they do, say, 'I choose to cover your song.'" **SF**

Trent Reznor of Nine Inch Nails bares his soul in 1994. ➜

Black Hole Sun | Soundgarden (1994)

Writer | Chris Cornell
Producer | Michael Beinhorn, Soundgarden
Label | A&M
Album | *Superunknown* (1994)

SOUNDGARDEN BLACK HOLE SUN

"We're growing up and realizing the importance of melody. Maybe we've been listening to Bryan Ferry or something."

Chris Cornell, 1994

◀ **Influenced by: Tomorrow Never Knows** · The Beatles (1966)
▶ **Influence on: Blown Wide Open** · Big Wreck (1997)
● **Covered by:** The Moog Cookbook (1996) · Judith Owen (2003) · Rachel Z (2004) · Copeland (2006) Tre Lux (2006) · Peter Frampton (2006)

Long before Kurt Cobain and company got together, Chris Cornell was drumming and singing for a group that helped pioneer the Seattle sound. Soundgarden was one of the earliest groups to sign to the Sub Pop label and the first of the grunge groups to receive mainstream recognition. "We," recalled Cornell, "were the ones to beat."

By June 1994, Cobain was dead but grunge had become the new aristocracy. Riding the crest of that wave, Soundgarden topped the *Billboard* chart with *Superunknown*, and the "Black Hole Sun" video's collection of eerie suburbanites with fixed grins smearing their faces became an award-winning classic.

Superunknown displayed a refreshing sense of melody, enhanced by Cornell's evolution from Robert Plant–style screecher to brooding crooner, and the group's experimentation. The keyboard-type sounds on "Black Hole Sun" were achieved via a Leslie speaker, previously favored by The Beatles, Pink Floyd, Led Zeppelin, and Jimi Hendrix. "It's very Beatlesque," guitarist Kim Thayil told *Guitar World*, "and has a distinctive sound. It ended up changing the song completely."

The lyrics are hard to fathom, although *Rolling Stone*'s singling out "Times are gone / For honest men" offers a clue. "It's really difficult for a person to create their own life and their own freedom," observed Cornell. "It's going to become more and more difficult, and it's going to create more and more disillusioned people who become dishonest and angry."

Despite this unhappy theme, the song had a stirringly sing-along feel—making it an unlikely summer anthem. "Maybe," Cornell quipped, "I could rename it 'Endless Black Hole Summer.'" **SO**

Interstate Love Song | Stone Temple Pilots (1994)

Writer | R. DeLeo, S. Weiland, D. DeLeo, E. Kretz
Producer | Brendan O'Brien
Label | Atlantic
Album | *Purple* (1994)

"It has a few different themes. Honesty, lack of honesty, my new relationship with heroin."

Scott Weiland, 2006

◀ **Influenced by: I Got a Name** · Jim Croce (1973)
▶ **Influence on: My Own Prison** · Creed (1997)
● **Covered by:** Hootie & the Blowfish (1998)
  Velvet Revolver (2007) · Brad Mehldau (2009)
★ **Other key tracks:** Plush (1992) · Lounge Fly (1994)
  Vasoline (1994) · Sour Girl (1999)

Stone Temple Pilots' 1992 debut album, *Core,* boasted enough metallic muscle and radio-friendly hooks to ride on the coattails of the grunge phenomenon. Its breakthrough single, "Plush," struck some as eerily reminiscent of Pearl Jam, and front man Scott Weiland's vocals could easily have been mistaken for the wounded burr of that group's Eddie Vedder in a blindfold test.

Core ultimately secured the San Diego quartet eight platinum discs and a Grammy for "Plush." But it also won them a blitz of critical brickbats and accusations of shameless bandwagon jumping.

The follow-up, 1994's *Purple,* answered their critics with much stronger, more diverse and more ambitious songwriting. Its flagship track, "Interstate Love Song," swapped the grunge for grand classic rock. Originally penned by bassist Robert DeLeo while touring *Core,* the song began as a bossa nova pastiche. "The entire chord structure," DeLeo explained in 2006, "is an Antônio Carlos Jobim [Brazilian bossa nova pioneer] thing."

The gem took shape while the group was recording *Purple* in Atlanta, Georgia. Blending acoustic guitar, colossal drums, Weiland's road-worn harmonies and a swaggering guitar hook, "Interstate Love Song" was timeless enough to win Stone Temple Pilots an audience wider than impatient Pearl Jam fans. It held pole position in *Billboard's* Modern Rock charts for fifteen weeks. Weiland's struggles with addiction—which inspired the song's regretful lyrics, and scuppered a high-profile tour when he was arrested for possession of heroin and cocaine—sent the group into a tailspin. Remarkably, they managed two more platinum albums, but "Interstate Love Song" remains their shining moment. **SC**

Waterfalls | TLC (1994)

Writer | Organized Noize, M. Etheridge, L. Lopes
Producer | Organized Noize
Label | LaFace
Album | *CrazySexyCool* (1994)

"This is not just a song with a nice tune by three popular girls. This is a song that means something."

Lisa "Left Eye" Lopes, 1995

◄ **Influenced by: Waterfalls** · Paul McCartney (1980)
► **Influence on: Stole** · Kelly Rowland (2002)
● **Covered by:** New Mind (2000) · Steve Poltz (2003)
★ **Other key tracks:** Ain't 2 Proud 2 Beg (1992) · Creep (1994) · Diggin' on You (1994) · No Scrubs (1999) Unpretty (1999)

With their 1992 album, *Ooooooohhh . . . On the TLC Tip!* TLC had scored multiplatinum success with sassy songs that were positive and empowered. The first singles off *CrazySexyCool*—"Creep" and "Red Light Special"—suggested they were getting sultry second time around. However, the third single—a wise, melancholic song that painted the R&B trio in a more mature light—became their signature track.

The chorus echoed Paul McCartney's "Waterfalls" and featured guest vocals from future Gnarls Barkley star Cee-Lo Green. Its "don't go chasing waterfalls" refrain warned of a world where kids get mixed up in crime and end up "another body laying cold in the gutter." The second verse warned against sleeping around in the era of AIDS—safe sex was a pet cause for TLC, who once wore condoms attached to their costumes. "When you become a 'star,'" observed Rozonda "Chilli" Thomas, "you are a role model."

A mini-epic video accompanied "Waterfalls." Directed by F. Gary Gray, and featuring the Wu-Tang Clan's young protégé Shyheim, it depicted the verses' doomed drug dealer and AIDS victim. "It's the video that brings the whole song to light," said Lisa "Left Eye" Lopes.

Lopes's rap—a remorseful but hopeful spiel colored by her own chaotic life—sealed the message. She was struggling with her own waterfalls, not least tabloid infamy after accidentally incinerating her partner's home. A car crash claimed Lopes's life in 2002.

In this context, lines like "Only my faith can undo / The many chances I blew" grounded the song with an emotional punch that has not diminished since it topped the charts. **SC**

Cornflake Girl | Tori Amos (1994)

Writer | Tori Amos
Producer | Eric Rosse, Tori Amos
Label | Atlantic
Album | *Under the Pink* (1994)

"It's about this idea that women are the good guys and men the bad guys, which just isn't true all the time."

Tori Amos, 1994

◀ **Influenced by: Hounds of Love** · Kate Bush (1985)
▶ **Influence on: Fidelity** · Regina Spektor (2006)
● **Covered by:** Jawbox (1996) · Tripod (2007)
　 Imogen Heap (2010)
★ **Other key tracks:** Sister Janet (1994) · Daisy Dead Petals (1994) · All the Girls Hate Her (1994)

Tori Amos is proof of the power of advertising. The musical maverick was once a rosy-cheeked unknown cooing about Kellogg's cereal in a commercial. Nine years later, she released "Cornflake Girl"—her breakthrough rhapsody.

Amos likes to mix her inspiration. The principal influence that the confessional singer-songwriter cited for this song was Alice Walker's novel *Possessing the Secret of Joy*, which delves into the world of ritual female genital mutilation in Africa. Amos explained, "The fact is that women have betrayed one another. I agree with Alice Walker when she talks about the cellular memory that is passed down, which all women have to come to terms with. Whether it is the women taking the daughters to the butchers to have their genitalia removed, or the mothers that bound the feet of the daughters, it is often women who betray their own kind, not just men."

"Cornflake Girl" could sound depressing in the wrong hands, but Amos's charm conjures up a song that is as otherworldly as its subject. The piano cascades, soft percussion, and ghostly chorus set it apart from the plod of Britpop and post-grunge dominating transatlantic charts at the time.

Like Kate Bush before her, Amos creates an epic sound while keeping it lean. The occasionally inscrutable lyrics ("Rabbit, where'd you put the keys, girl?") are delivered with the modest confidence of a woman at the top of her game; unafraid of showing vulnerability and passion.

Amos called herself a "cornflake girl," but there is nothing "cornflake-y" about a woman at ease writing about female mutilation, breast-feeding a piglet on an album sleeve, lending her vocals to a Nineties dance smash, and covering Slayer. **KBo**

Hallelujah
Jeff Buckley (1994)

Writer | Leonard Cohen
Producer | Andy Wallace
Label | Columbia
Album | *Grace* (1994)

"Hallelujah" is a soaring, sensual paean to love and loss. Before releasing the song in 1984, writer Leonard Cohen spent years wrestling with the biblical and sexual lyrics—producing eighty draft verses and making it ripe for interpretation (there are more than two hundred covers, from Bob Dylan to Bon Jovi).

Jeff Buckley's cover in 1994 proved definitive and continues to connect with people worldwide. "The hallelujah is not a homage to a worshipped person, idol, or god," Buckley explained, "but the hallelujah of the orgasm."

A cult classic in the Nineties, it became omnipresent in the Noughties. The emotional power of Buckley's octave-spanning voice made it perfect soundtrack fodder for TV shows such as *The West Wing*. His outstanding talent, good looks, and untimely death at the age of thirty—mirroring the early demise of his singer-songwriter father Tim—created a marketable package. Yet it was not until 2008, eleven years after his death, that Buckley had his first chart-topper. On the back of a rendition on U.S. talent show *American Idol*, "Hallelujah" reached No. 1 on download charts.

"I don't want to do any more covers," Buckley told *Rolling Stone* in 1994. "It's good to learn to make things your own, but the education's over." Little did he know that "Hallelujah" was to become his greatest legacy. **GK**

Red Right Hand
Nick Cave & The Bad Seeds (1994)

Writer | N. Cave, M. Harvey, T. Wydler
Producer | Tony Cohen
Label | Mute
Album | *Let Love In* (1994)

The Nick Cave songbook is populated by malevolent, menacing figures. But the lead character of "Red Right Hand"—a charismatic cultist on the edge of town—is his most successful and disturbing creation.

The lyrics were largely ad-libbed. "I had the title," Cave told *Rolling Stone*, "and basically I knew what I wanted to sing about, and it was a matter of just going in and putting it down." He portrays God as a U.S. televangelist, a huckster who rewards his followers with money, cars, and self-respect. But this deity "ain't what he seems": beneath that benevolent exterior lurks the vengeful God of the Old Testament. He hides his "red right hand"—a term used by poet John Milton in *Paradise Lost* to describe the Lord's wrath—in his "dusty black coat." Follow him, Cave warns, and you'll be reduced to "one microscopic cog / In his catastrophic plan."

A spaghetti western backing from The Bad Seeds adds to the apocalyptic feel. The track opens with a church bell, organ, and echo-laden guitar from Blixa Bargeld. Underpinning everything is an almost funky bass line. (According to Cave biographer Ian Johnstone, the recording was inspired by soul acts like Isaac Hayes.)

The song's gothic grooves have become a favorite with directors craving soundtrack spookiness, and "Red Right Hand" features in all three *Scream* movies. **TB**

Nick Cave performs in 1994 in London's much-lamented Tower Records store. ➜

Sabotage | Beastie Boys (1994)

Writer | Beastie Boys
Producer | Beastie Boys, Mario Caldato Jr.
Label | Grand Royal
Album | *Ill Communication* (1994)

"Hip-hop was always the single most important influence— hip-hop and punk rock."

Mike D, 1994

◄ **Influenced by: Waiting Room** · Fugazi (1988)
► **Influence on: Break Stuff** · Limp Bizkit (2000)
● **Covered by:** Phish (1999) · The Bosshoss (2005)
Beatsteaks (2007) · Cancer Bats (2010) · The Penelopes
(2009) · Switchfoot (2010)

With ear-splitting vocals and a jagged riff, "Sabotage" revealed to the wider world what fans had known since 1992's *Check Your Head*. The Beastie Boys were now just as likely to rock your world with punk-funk guitar noise as with two turntables and a microphone.

Beginning life as a jazzy hippie jam during early sessions for *Ill Communication*, "Sabotage" took shape when Adam Yauch dreamed up its dramatic, stop-start dynamic. The final track was completed only two weeks before the album was submitted to their parent label.

The song's holler-along qualities swiftly made it a frat-rock anthem, even though the Beasties themselves had long ditched the frat-boy persona of their "(You Gotta) Fight for Your Right (To Party!)" days. But it was an ingenious video that made the song a crossover hit. Filmed by the then-unknown Spike Jonze, the clip affectionately lampooned the cheesy detective thrillers that swamped Seventies TV schedules. The Beasties donned costumes, wigs, and sideburns to play cops and robbers, vaulting over vintage cars and executing laughable stunts.

The video played the Beasties' gift for arcane pop-cultural humor to the fore, enjoying heavy rotation on MTV. However, while nominated in five categories at 1994's MTV Video Music Awards, it scooped not one gong, provoking Yauch to storm the stage (as his alter-ego, video director Nathanial Hörnblowér) while R.E.M.'s Michael Stipe was accepting an award—fifteen years before Kanye West's similar misbehavior at 2009's awards. The latter event did, however, belatedly honor the "Sabotage" video.

The song made another reappearance in 2009, in J. J. Abrams's *Star Trek* movie. **SC**

The Most Beautiful Girl in the World | Prince (1994)

Writer | Prince
Producer | Prince, Ricky Peterson
Label | NPG
Album | N/A

"Eligible bachelor seeks the most beautiful girl in the world to spend the holidays with."

Prince, 1994

◀ **Influenced by: Takin' Me to Paradise** • J. Raynard (1983)
▶ **Influence on: Take It from Here** • Justin Timberlake (2002)
● **Covered by:** Raheem (2008)
★ **Other key track:** Alphabet Street (1988)

Feeling enslaved by his deal with Warner Bros., Prince renamed himself as an unpronounceable symbol and released "The Most Beautiful Girl in the World" independently. Warner executives, he complained, "are the same people who would tell Mozart he writes too many notes or say that *Citizen Kane* is a long movie."

"Do you know what a sense of freedom it gave me to release 'The Most Beautiful Girl in the World' on an independent label?" he asked *The Age*. Cannily, the Artist (as he was colloquially known) organized a publicity campaign to promote his single and unveiled the gorgeous, twinkling ballad on CBS TV's Miss America pageant.

His muse for the lyrics was twenty-year-old Mayte Garcia. "She looked at me for what I was," Prince said of the dancer whom he married on Valentine's Day in 1996. "When he looks at you," reflected Garcia, "he makes you feel like you're the center of his universe. That's very beguiling."

The single earned Prince his first U.K. No. 1 as a performer and reached No. 3 on *Billboard*'s Hot 100, selling more than half a million copies Stateside. (Remixes appeared on *The Beautiful Experience* EP in 1994 and the album *The Gold Experience* in 1995.)

But it was the statement—not the sales—that mattered to him. "It was truly a beautiful experience . . ." he told an award ceremony audience. "Perhaps one day all the powers that are will realize that it's better to let a man be all that he can be than to try to limit his output to just what they can handle. 'Our sources tell us that there's just too much music.' Well, my sources—all of you—tell me to be all I can be. For this I am eternally grateful." **EP**

Sour Times | Portishead (1994)

Writer | G. Barrow, B. Gibbons, A. Utley, L. Schifrin, H. Brooks, O. Turner
Producer | Portishead, Adrian Utley
Label | Go!
Album | *Dummy* (1994)

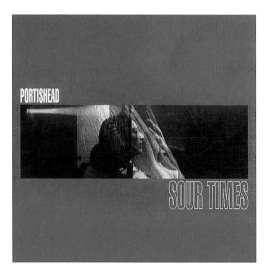

"When it comes to taking ourselves seriously, Beth really doesn't take herself seriously at all."

Geoff Barrow, 2008

◀ **Influenced by: Danube Incident** · Lalo Schifrin (1968)
▶ **Influence on: Teardrops** · The 411 (2004)
● **Covered by:** The Blank Theory (2002) · Bryn Christopher (2008)
★ **Other key tracks:** Glory Box (1994) · Numb (1994) All Mine (1997) · The Rip (2008) · We Carry On (2008)

In 1994, the echoes of grunge were still reverberating around the globe. But, in the United Kingdom, new local heroes were stepping up—and, in Bristol, Portishead were helping to pioneer the ephemeral but fondly remembered genre known as trip-hop. Nonetheless, protested main man Geoff Barrow to suicidegirls.com, "'We write music for people to chill out to'—that's the biggest misconception you could ever have."

"Sour Times," Portishead's second single, was certainly more chilling than chilled. Fusing hip-hop beats with Beth Gibbons's lovelorn lyrics and doleful vocals, it resembled a funked-up 1960s noir soundtrack. "I don't actually think the songs are that desperate," Gibbons protested to *Hot Press*. "I do have an emptiness—but, then again, everyone has, to a lesser or greater degree. I tend to dwell on mine more than other people do, which I'm sure manifests itself in my lyrics."

Amid the song's wonderfully claustrophobic mix of influences, from John Barry to Billie Holiday, the eerie dulcimer sample and bass riff came from "Danube Incident" by U.S. composer Lalo Schifrin—the man responsible for the original *Mission: Impossible* theme, as well as music for *Dirty Harry* and *Bullitt*.

The track didn't make much impact on its first release, but aided by a video drawn from Portishead's short film *To Kill a Dead Man* (and a reissue in 1995), it joined the hit "Glory Box" as springboards from which *Dummy* rocketed to classic status. Some believed Portishead could never match that album. But a version of "Sour Times" from *Roseland NYC Live* in 1998—on which Gibbons's vocal builds into a fierce crescendo—makes the original seem almost tame. **GR**

Army of Me | Björk (1995)

Writer | Björk, Graham Massey
Producer | Björk, Nellee Hooper, Graham Massey
Label | One Little Indian
Album | *Post* (1995)

Army Of Me

"The track is about telling someone who is full of self-pity, and doesn't have anything together, to get a life."

Björk, 1995

◀ **Influenced by: Dig It** · Skinny Puppy (1986)
▶ **Influence on: Love Again** · Baxter (1998)
● **Covered by:** Helmet (1996) · Beanbag (2001)
Powerman 5000 (2004) · Abandoned Pools (2005)
Caliban (2006) · Drama (2010)

"Army of Me" was among the first songs that Björk recorded after the Sugarcubes disbanded in 1992. Yet the Icelandic pop queen did not feel this brash, storming number made sense for her post-'cube *Debut*—and she was right. Its aggressive call to arms would have ruined the pretty electronic pop picture painted on her first major label solo outing. It did, however, work perfectly as the opener on her second solo album, *Post*.

Having delivered the "polite, shy" *Debut*, Björk wanted to go in the other direction, and showcase her other side: the side that is not to be messed with. She might be the only performer on the planet that is equally effective cooing like a baby or hissing like a snake, and it's all the latter on "Army of Me," a song Björk wrote for her brother.

The vocalist sounded dangerous as she sang with fangs fully bared, warning her sibling to stop feeling sorry for himself. "And if you complain once more," she snarled, "you'll meet an army of me!" An equally wrenching mix of old school industrial rock and electronic music, built on explosive samples (and samples of explosions), underscored the words.

The introductory single from *Post*, "Army of Me" stomped into international charts. It was the first of six hits from the album—surpassing the tally of *Debut*, which managed a mere five.

The original release was accompanied by multiple remixes, including a rock revamp with Skunk Anansie. A decade later, twenty versions were assembled as *Army of Me: Remixes and Covers*, the proceeds of which were donated to the United Nations Children's Fund—a heartwarming end to an angry song. **JiH**

Champagne Supernova
Oasis (1995)

Writer | Noel Gallagher
Producer | Owen Morris
Label | Creation
Album | *(What's the Story) Morning Glory?* (1995)

"The number of people who've started clubs called Champagne Supernova is unbelievable," said Noel Gallagher, ahead of the release of *(What's the Story) Morning Glory?* the album that the song brought to a climax. Gallagher went on to name his London home "Supernova Heights," after the track helped propel *Morning Glory* to multiplatinum status.

"Champagne Supernova" catches Oasis in their mid–Britpop pomp. Epic guitar parts, enigmatic lyrics, and a vocal that Noel's brother Liam would struggle to better made it a fan favorite. Lead guitar and backing vocals were supplied by Paul Weller—the "super-sub," according to the album's liner notes. His lush licks make "Champagne Supernova" sing in a way no other *Morning Glory* track can match.

Musically, it soars. Lyrically, it has taken a critical battering. "Some of the lyrics were written when I was out of it," Noel admitted to *NME* in 1995. He is said to have conceived its name after mishearing the title of the Pixies album *Bossanova* while watching a documentary about champagne. "It's about when you're young and you see people in groups and you think about what they did for you—and they did nothing." However, as he told *The Sunday Times* in 2009, "Are you telling me, when you've got 60,000 people singing it, they don't know what it means? It means something different to every one of them." **JM**

The Fever
Garth Brooks (1995)

Writer | Steven Tyler, Joe Perry, Bryan Kennedy, Dan Roberts
Producer | Allen Reynolds
Label | Capitol
Album | *Fresh Horses* (1995)

"I'd rather stay with country radio," said Garth Brooks in 1992, "so people know where they can find me." But by 1995, he had joined the all-time best sellers—and could do whatever he wished.

Fresh Horses was intended to showcase Nashville's best country writers. However, Brooks was unmoved by the songs submitted: "It was like people were guessing where we were going." Eventually, he co-wrote eight of the ten tracks.

The album featured "Fever," from Aerosmith's *Get a Grip*. But the song contained lyrics that even front man Steven Tyler's bandmates had objected to: "The buzz that you be gettin' from the crack don't last / I'd rather be O.D.in' on the crack of her ass." A rewrite was called for.

"I had a couple of buddies . . . that had a song called 'Roll Out the Barrel and Send in the Clowns,'" Brooks told the *Boston Globe*. "It was a rodeo tune and that lyric kept going in my head. Then when I heard Aerosmith's 'Fever,' I thought, 'Wow, if you put the two together . . .'"

Tyler, reported Brooks, "was very sweet and emphasized how much they love their music, 'so take care of it when you're cutting it.' I thought that was a cool thing to hear from a guy who's known for being so freewheeling." But "The Fever"—with revisions by Dan Roberts and Bryan Kennedy—still proved to be too much for U.S. country radio, which blacklisted it. **BM**

Where were we when they were getting high? Oasis siblings Liam (left) and Noel.

The Nineties | 727

Kung Fu | Ash (1995)

Writer | Tim Wheeler
Producer | Owen Morris
Label | Infectious
Album | *1977* (1996)

"I'm always a lover of three minutes of magic."

Tim Wheeler, 2009

◀ **Influenced by: Teenage Lobotomy** · Ramones (1977)
▶ **Influence on: Buck Rogers** · Feeder (2001)
★ **Other key tracks:** Day of the Triffids (1995) · Luther Ingo's Star Cruiser (1995) · Angel Interceptor (1995) Girl from Mars (1996) · Goldfinger (1996)

When Ash recorded this slice of power pop, they were exactly what British and Irish rock needed. The group—two of whom were just seventeen years old when the track was penned—specialized in short, sharp blasts of joy; a welcome change from the grunge and Britpop that dominated the charts. "Smarter than your average bear," noted U2's Bono approvingly.

"Kung Fu" captured the group at their pithiest and punkiest. Lasting just two minutes and seventeen seconds, the song sped through a list of chop-socky and teen culture references, with the first eight seconds taken up by a sample from the 1980 martial-arts movie *Gui da gui* (*Encounters of the Spooky Kind*). *The Karate Kid*'s Mr. Miyagi, Jackie Chan, Fu Manchu, Bruce Lee, and the X-Men had their hosannas sung by front man Tim Wheeler, who wrote the song in five minutes on the day after Christmas in 1994, while waiting for a plane at Belfast International Airport.

The group laid down "Kung Fu" the next day, in one take, with Oasis producer Owen Morris. "We wanted to write a really crap Ramones song," Wheeler confessed, "and it was meant to be the B-side, but it turned out too good."

So good, in fact, that in 1996 Hollywood picked up the track and played it over the closing credits of the U.S. release of Chan's 1995 Hong Kong action film, *Rumble in the Bronx*.

Not everyone, however, was so impressed. The single's sleeve features a photograph of Manchester United soccer player Eric Cantona launching a kung-fu style flying kick against a spectator at a match in January 1995. Cantona promptly sent a disgruntled fax to the group's label. It read: "I spit on your record." **TB**

Writer | Billy Corgan
Producer | Flood, Alan Moulder, Billy Corgan
Label | Virgin
Album | *Mellon Collie and the Infinite Sadness* (1995)

"It's kind of a restless period with a lot of sexual energy and you're stuck in fucking nowhere."

Billy Corgan, 1996

◄ **Influenced by: Everything's Gone Green**
New Order (1981)
► **Influence on: Turn My Way** · New Order (2001)
● **Covered by:** Vaux (2006) · Jacksoul (2006) · Lismore (2006) · Kuusimäki (2007) · Young Love (2007)

"Psychedelic music by a heavy-metal band from the 1920s" was how Pumpkins figurehead Billy Corgan described *Mellon Collie and the Infinite Sadness*. The ambitious album was dominated by hammering rock and progressive symphonies, yet its most enduring track sounded like New Order playing "Rhiannon" by Fleetwood Mac.

The song had, Corgan said, "been kicking around for a while," but co-producer Flood had lost patience. "He just said, 'Not good enough,' and was ready to drop it . . ." Corgan told the *Chicago Tribune*. "I thought, 'No fucking way, this is not another toss-off song.' It really inspired me to finish it and prove him wrong. So that night I wrote the entire song in about four hours. The next day Flood heard it one time and said, 'It's on the album.'"

Aided by a distinctive video, the track became a gold-selling U.S. single, reaching No. 12 on the *Billboard* Hot 100. It was nominated for the Record of the Year and Best Rock Performance at the Grammy Awards and spawned a sequel of sorts with "Perfect" on 1998's *Adore*.

"I can't really say why I picked the year 1979," Corgan told VH1's *Storytellers*. "It's as good as any other year, I suppose. Plus it sounds good in a rhyme scheme."

Corgan also told *Storytellers* about the song's inspiration: "I was about eighteen years old and I was driving down the road near my home, and it was really heavily raining, as only it can seem to rain in a gloomy way in Illinois. I remember just sitting at a traffic light. . . . It doesn't sound very glamorous, but it emotionally connotates, for me, a feeling of waiting for something to happen. And not being quite there yet, but it's just around the corner. And little did I know that I was right." **BM**

Common People | Pulp (1995)

Writer | Nick Banks, Jarvis Cocker, Candida Doyle, Steve Mackey, Russell Senior
Producer | Chris Thomas
Label | Island
Album | *Different Class* (1995)

> *" 'Common People' should've been a No. 1 any week. The lyrics are hilarious."*
>
> **Noel Gallagher, Oasis, 1995**

◀ **Influenced by:** Fanfare For the Common Man
Emerson, Lake & Palmer (1977)
▶ **Influence on:** Sliding Through Life on Charm
Marianne Faithfull (2002)
● **Covered by:** William Shatner & Joe Jackson (2004)
Tori Amos (2005)

"She came from Greece / She had a thirst for knowledge / She studied sculpture at St. Martin's College"—so opens a call to arms against class tourism that catapulted Pulp from cult group to the mainstream. Front man Jarvis Cocker's creation of the two-fingered organ intro on a cheap Casio set the tone for a time when Britpop had its own class war in the shape of Blur vs. Oasis.

Producer Chris Thomas, whose credentials included the Sex Pistols and Roxy Music, was hired, said Cocker, because "he had a neck brace on—our kind of person." In his hands, the song built to its sing-along crescendo with sociopolitical sentiments to rival "God Save the Queen."

The lyrics depict a working-class man's encounter with a wealthy art student whose idea of glamor involves hanging out in London's East End. "It seemed to be in the air, that kind of patronising social voyeurism, slumming it, the idea that there's a glamor about low-rent, low-life," Cocker told *Q* in 1996. "I felt that of [Blur's] *Parklife*, for example, or *Natural Born Killers*—there is that 'noble savage' notion."

Cocker claimed to have forgotten the girl's real identity but admitted to half-truths in his autobiographical lyrics. She may not have studied sculpture, but the line scanned better. And, although it implies that she wanted to bed him, he resorted to poetic license to enhance the narrative. Cocker had the last laugh as the song propelled him from left-field eccentric to pop star and British national treasure.

Nearly a decade after it became a British Top-Ten hit, the song enjoyed a peculiar renaissance when *Star Trek* veteran William Shatner released his version in 2004. **SS**

Where the Wild Roses Grow | Nick Cave & Kylie Minogue (1995)

Writer | Nick Cave
Producer | Nick Cave & The Bad Seeds,
Tony Cohen, Victor Van Vugt
Label | Mute
Album | *Murder Ballads* (1996)

NICK CAVE AND THE BAD SEEDS ♦ KYLIE MINOGUE Where The Wild Roses Grow

"'Where the Wild Roses Grow'
was written very much with
Kylie in mind. I'd wanted to write
a song for Kylie for many years."
Nick Cave, 2007

◄ **Influenced by: Down in the Willow Garden** • Hobart
Smith & Texas Gladden (c. 1940)
► **Influence on: Burst Lethargic** • The Silence Kits (2006)
● **Covered by:** Chicks on Speed & Kriedler (2001)
Chiasm (2006)
★ **Other key track:** Stagger Lee (1996)

Death and violence have always haunted the music of Nick Cave & The Bad Seeds. So it came as no surprise when *Murder Ballads* consisted of nothing but these morbid subjects. What was unexpected was one of Cave's guest singers.

"Where the Wild Roses Grow" saw alt-rock's dark emperor unite with pop princess Kylie Minogue. Although the artists had nothing in common bar their Australian roots, Cave had long wished to work with her. His bandmate Mick Harvey duly called Minogue's then-boyfriend, Michael Hutchence of INXS. "So," Cave told *Great Australian Albums*, "Michael's going, 'Hey, do you wanna do a song with Nick Cave?' and she's going, 'Oh yeah, I'll do that!'"

"We actually left messages with each other's mothers," recalled Minogue. "Can you imagine—Nick Cave calling: 'Hi, is that Mrs. Minogue? Is Kylie there?' . . . The first day I met Nick was the day that I did my vocals, and that was so lovely."

The traditional folk ballad "Down in the Willow Garden," on which the song is based, is the confession of a man awaiting execution for stabbing his lover to death. Cave twisted this into a dialogue between the killer and his slain sweetheart. The result was disturbing yet sensual, with sumptuous strings backing Cave and Minogue's heart-wrenching vocals.

Aided by a dreamlike video, the song soared up the British and Australian charts, and became the group's most successful single worldwide. "I was on *Top of the Pops* two weeks running . . ." Cave told writer Debbie Kruger. "This little kid [came] up to me in a Power Rangers outfit, and he goes, 'Are you that old guy that was on with Kylie Minogue the other night?'" **BC**

Insomnia
Faithless (1995)

Writer | Rollo, Maxi Jazz, Sister Bliss
Producer | Rollo, Sister Bliss
Label | Cheeky
Album | *Reverence* (1996)

Unleashed in an era of uplifting "handbag house," "Insomnia" crept with nocturnal stealth through rave culture into suburban bedrooms. As its title suggested, this climactic, hands-in-the-air dance anthem was not one to put on before bedtime. When rapper Maxi Jazz darkly muttered, "I toss and I turn without cease / Like a curse / Open my eyes and rise like yeast," it evoked the unbearable comedown after an all-nighter.

Perhaps it is the universality of the lyrics—married with ominous beats and an addictive refrain—that has kept the song fresh. It has been remixed more than fifty times and charted three times in the United Kingdom, peaking at No. 3.

While Jazz delivered the lyrics, producers Rollo and Sister Bliss provided the thumping techno bass and ticking-clock-esque synthesizer. The former almost got them into hot water when they were accused of plagiarism by Norwegian act Biosphere. Conversely, Faithless were not amused by alleged similarities when German DJs Sash! released "Encore une fois" (Once Again).

Future superstar Dido—Rollo's sister—fondly recalled singing it "every day onstage for a year and a half." Like Faithless's audiences, she was swept away by the keyboard melody that explodes after the rap. "One of Rollo's sayings is music is all about tension and release," observed Bliss, "and it's one of the principles we adhere to." **GK**

Scream
Michael & Janet Jackson (1995)

Writer & Producer | M. Jackson, J. Jackson, J. Jam, T. Lewis
Label | Epic
Album | *HIStory: Past, Present and Future, Book I* (1995)

"He was very upset and very angry," Janet Jackson told MTV of Michael Jackson's first release since 1993's abuse allegations, "and he had so much pent up in him that he wanted to get out and say."

Michael hadn't collaborated with Janet since she sang backing vocals on *Thriller*'s "P.Y.T. (Pretty Young Thing)." Now he enlisted Jimmy Jam and Terry Lewis—the producers who transformed his sister into an R&B vixen—for his cathartic return.

"We had the title but we really didn't know what the song was going to be about," Jam told *Q*. The producers recorded potential tracks for the star's approval: "An L.A. studio put in a new sound system which was supposed to be specially for Michael—and he blew it up the first day!"

Lewis recalled an "unassuming" Michael recording in December 1994. "He sang 'Scream' for thirty minutes, and that was it," he told the *Omaha World-Herald*. "After it was over, he had to take a nap. You can feel the energy on the tape."

A spectacular song demanded a spectacular video. "They gave me about three weeks to prepare for something they wanted to be enormous," director Mark Romanek told the *Chicago Tribune*. His seven-million-dollar production was music's costliest clip, but it was money well spent. This compelling mix of raw emotion, punchy production, and otherworldly visuals restored the King of Pop's crown. **EP**

Hell Is Round the Corner
Tricky (1995)

Writer | Isaac Hayes, Tricky
Producer | Tricky, Mark Saunders
Label | Fourth & Broadway
Album | *Maxinquaye* (1995)

There is a lot of anger on Tricky's extraordinary debut, *Maxinquaye*, but the artist otherwise known as Adrian Thaws did not dispense with all of it. Some he reserved for Portishead and their use of the same Isaac Hayes sample ("Ike's Rap II," from the 1971 album *Black Moses*) on "Glory Box" that formed the basis of "Hell is Round the Corner."

"I'm paranoid, but when they heard my track in the studio, they brought out Portishead's so fast: boom, boom, boom," he told *Select*. His first instinct was to take the track off his album: "But I listened to my song and thought I was willing to put it next to anything. Let people throw stones." The sample wasn't the only overlap that "Hell is Round the Corner" had with his contemporaries. Tricky's lyrics also featured on Massive Attack's "Eurochild," from their album *Protection*.

Ultimately, there was room for all these innovative releases. But the dense, oppressive "Hell is Round the Corner" is the darkest of the moody pieces. "When I had a psychic reading," he explained to *Melody Maker*, "this woman was really positive. She was, 'No, the world isn't in trouble, we're all going to be alright.' Sorry, I just don't feel that ... I think we've all got a touch of psychosis."

Two versions were issued in August 1995 on *The Hell EP*—also featuring the Gravediggaz. The original remains a magnificent moment from one of the era's essential albums. **CB**

Born Slippy Nuxx
Underworld (1995)

Writer & Producer | Rick Smith, Karl Hyde, Darren Emerson
Label | Junior Boy's Own
Album | *Trainspotting* (1996)

Drunken ramble? Thumping techno? Nineties zeitgeist? "Born Slippy Nuxx"—named after a greyhound on whom Underworld won a tidy sum at the races—is all of these things and more.

First released as the B-side to the original "Born Slippy," the track fell by the wayside. Thankfully, director Danny Boyle loved it and persuaded the trio to loan "Born Slippy Nuxx" to his big-screen adaptation of the novel *Trainspotting* in 1996.

"We were reluctant to be involved in the film," vocalist Karl Hyde confessed to About, "Because, not having read Irvine Welsh's book, but having heard people's rather one-sided description ... we were like, 'We don't sit comfortably with our music being associated with drugs, violence, or anything like that, we don't see dance music that way at all ...' [But] it was pretty clear that we'd been misled." The song promptly became one of the most iconic tracks of the Nineties.

Kicking off with innocuous synth chimes, "Born Slippy Nuxx" swirls into a whirlwind of relentless techno throbbing, topped with Hyde's barbed stream of consciousness. While this rambling was interpreted as an anthem about getting drunk, Hyde intended the opposite. "When I lost my place, I'd repeat the same line," he told the *Guardian*. "That's why it goes, 'Lager, lager, lager, lager.' The first time we played it live, people raised their lager cans and I was horrified." **KBo**

You Oughta Know
Alanis Morissette (1995)

Writer | Alanis Morissette, Glen Ballard
Producer | Glen Ballard
Label | Maverick
Album | *Jagged Little Pill* (1995)

Alanis Morissette put the "grr" in Grammy with this award-winning, fist-in-the-air angst anthem. Smarting from a messy break up, she channeled her rage into a storming song that shifted her from the ditzy pop of her youth to worldwide stadiums. "You Oughta Know" was a slap in the face and a step in the right direction.

Signed by Madonna's Maverick label, Morissette paved the way for a new generation of take-no-prisoners female singer-songwriters. "She reminds me of me when I started out," Madonna told *Rolling Stone*, "Slightly awkward but extremely self-possessed and straightforward."

There is certainly something of the determined and candid Ciccone in lyrics like, "Are you thinking of me while you fuck her?" These verbal volleys were a jolt to the charts and the undisclosed identity of her ex-boyfriend became as intriguing as the subject of Carly Simon's "You're So Vain."

But "You Oughta Know" is not just an angry by numbers kiss-off. "That song wasn't written for the sake of revenge," Morissette announced, "It was written for the sake of release."

It is also an arresting hunk of rock with a walloping hook courtesy of then Red Hot Chili Peppers bandmates Flea and Dave Navarro (and keyboards by Benmont Tench of Tom Petty & The Heartbreakers). In 2009, Britney Spears sang a tellingly faithful cover on her *Circus* tour. **KBo**

Back for Good
Take That (1995)

Writer | Gary Barlow
Producer | Chris Porter, Gary Barlow
Label | RCA
Album | *Nobody Else* (1995)

After four years of reheated disco and lightweight love songs, Take That scored their biggest and most enduring hit with "Back for Good," a ballad that took leader Gary Barlow only ten minutes to write. The group's farewell came a year later with a cover of the Bee Gees' "How Deep Is Your Love"—but this song will be forever linked with the splintering of the U.K.'s biggest boy band, triggered by the exit of Robbie Williams. After the group imploded, Williams spiced up early solo gigs with a sarcastic, punked-up version of the song.

"Back for Good" has since become a wedding staple, despite its maudlin evocation of unrequited love. Its use as a love theme between two characters in the original U.K. version of *The Office* gave it a new lease of life in the 2000s.

"It's a very easy song," Barlow admitted in 2008. Inspired by a friend's suggestion that the best pop songs were the least complex, he thought, "Let me see if I can write a song using just three or four chords." On top of an ascending four-chord progression, Barlow laid down a plaintive lament with which anyone who has loved and lost can identify. In the final section, the backing vocals and lead vocal trade places, to touching effect.

Long admired by Oasis's Noel Gallagher, the song received another champion in the next decade. Coldplay's Chris Martin eulogized it and even performed it live. **JMc**

Stupid Girl | Garbage (1995)

Writer | D. Erickson, S. Manson, S. Marker, B. Vig, T. Headon, M. Jones, P. Simonon, J. Strummer
Producer | Garbage
Label | Almo Sounds
Album | *Garbage* (1995)

"It's our version of Madonna's 'Express Yourself,' about people who squander their potential."

Shirley Manson, 1996

◀ **Influenced by: Train in Vain** • The Clash (1979)
▶ **Influence on: Hot n Cold** • Katy Perry (2008)
● **Covered by:** Zosja (2003) • Alexz Johnson (2005)
★ **Other key tracks:** Driving Lesson (1995) • Alien Sex Fiend (1995) • Only Happy When It Rains (1995) Queer (1995) • Push It (1998) • Special (1998)

The label "perfect pop" was often bandied about in the 1990s, applied to acts ranging from Take That to Saint Etienne. But it made perfect sense when applied to Garbage, formed by über-producer Butch Vig. Having helmed Nirvana's *Nevermind*, Vig turned his part-time playing into a full-time group. The most notable of his recruits was Scottish singer and keyboard player Shirley Manson. Despite being the band's only non-American, Manson was an instant fit, her emotional vocals offsetting the boys' semi-electronic rock.

"A lot of the songs come from jamming," Vig told *The Band*. "'Stupid Girl' happened that way." Among the song's masterstrokes was a loop from The Clash brought to the studio by guitarist Steve Marker—while its distinctive grinding sound was, bassist Duke Erikson told *Addicted to Noise*, "initially a mistake [which], when we slowed it down, actually fit the timbre and pace of the song and became the hook."

The song was topped by Manson's lyrics about a manipulative female doomed to a life of shallowness and deceit, although she said it was "about a million girls and boys that we all know." "It could just as easily be called 'Stupid Boy,'" she told *Raw* in 1996. "It's just a song of reproach."

The song's success was aided by a remix by Danny Saber—whose arrangement Garbage took to playing live—and a distinctive video by Samuel Bayer, who had directed Nirvana's "Smells Like Teen Spirit" promo.

"There was a lot of talk about the dress I wore in the 'Stupid Girl' video," Manson told *Spin* in 1997. "Everybody was, like, 'Which designer?' or 'What style is that? It's so gorgeous.' I got it for fifteen dollars at a teen store in Madison." **JMc**

Miss Sarajevo | Passengers (1995)

Writer | Passengers
Producer | Brian Eno, Bono, Adam Clayton, The Edge, Larry Mullen Jr.
Label | Island
Album | *Original Soundtracks 1* (1995)

"I was impersonating my father singing in the bath impersonating Pavarotti."
Bono, 2006

◀ **Influenced by: The Great Gig in the Sky** · Pink Floyd (1973)
▶ **Influence on: Live Like Horses** · Elton John & Luciano Pavarotti (1996)
● **Covered by:** George Michael (1999)

"There has always been a bit of tension between U2 and Brian Eno," reported the group's manager Paul McGuinness, "because Brian regards himself as a creative force. I think he finds it frustrating that, within the parameters we've set, he is not a writer, he is one of the producers."

Ten years after their association with Eno began—on *The Unforgettable Fire*—U2 reached a solution to this impasse: collaborating with their producer on a soundtrack for Peter Greenaway's movie *The Pillow Book*. When this fell through, they formed a new collective—Passengers—and wrote songs for imaginary films.

Meanwhile, opera superstar Luciano Pavarotti was pestering U2's front man Bono: "He had been crank-calling the house. He told me that if I didn't write him a song, God would be very cross." Eventually, the maestro turned up at U2's studio, film crew in tow, and persuaded Bono (and guitarist The Edge) to grace his annual charity concert in Modena, Italy—at which "Miss Sarajevo" was premiered in September 1995.

Bono's lyrical inspiration was a beauty contest in the war-torn capital of Bosnia and Herzegovina. The album's sleeve notes duly hail "the dark humor of the besieged Sarajevans, their stubborn refusal to be demoralized," suggesting that "surrealism and Dadaism are the appropriate responses to fanaticism." With Pavarotti on tenor vocals and a string arrangement by orchestrator-to-the-stars (Massive Attack and Madonna among others) Craig Armstrong, the majestic song emerged triumphant. Bono came to regard "Miss Sarajevo" as his favorite U2 song, and his performances of it on their *Vertigo* tour in 2005 and 2006 raised many a goosebump. **BM**

River of Deceit
Mad Season (1995)

Writer | L. Staley, M. McCready, B. Martin, J. B. Saunders
Producer | Mad Season, B. Eliason
Label | Columbia
Album | *Above* (1995)

Hardly joyful at the best of times, the Seattle grunge scene had, by late 1994, become very gloomy indeed. In the extended wake of Kurt Cobain's suicide, Pearl Jam nearly imploded while making the bitter *Vitalogy*, Screaming Trees began to splinter, and Alice in Chains slowly sank.

The latter's inactivity was spurred by singer Layne Staley, whose heroin addiction—long a lyrical inspiration—had begun to govern his entire life. However, he was tempted out to play by Pearl Jam guitarist Mike McCready and The Walkabouts bassist John Baker Saunders, who met in rehab. With Screaming Trees drummer Barrett Martin, they became Mad Season, and recorded a bleak and bluesy album. "River of Deceit" was its shimmering highlight, equaling the best of its makers' primary groups. "I told him," McCready recalled to *Rolling Stone,* "'You do what you want. . . . You're the singer.' He'd come in, and he'd do these beautiful songs."

Staley despaired of fans following his narcotic example, and regretted his involvement with heroin. His message in "River of Deceit" was simple: "My pain is self chosen." "I was under the mistaken theory I could help him out," reflected the then-sober McCready. "I wanted to lead by example." Sadly, Saunders overdosed in 1999, followed by Staley three years later. "River of Deceit" remains their eerie epitaph. **BM**

Dear Mama
2Pac (1995)

Writer | Shakur, Jefferson, Sample, Pizarro, Hawes, Simmons, Thomas
Producer | Pizarro, Thomas, Moses
Label | Interscope
Album | *Me Against the World* (1995)

"When I was pregnant in jail, I thought I was gonna have a baby and the baby would never be with me. But I was acquitted a month and three days before Tupac was born. I was real happy—because I had a son." So runs Afeni Shakur's introduction to the video of her son's best-loved hit.

Afeni had been imprisoned for her involvement with African-American revolutionaries the Black Panthers. In a grim twist, Tupac's tribute to her was released while he was incarcerated on a sexual-assault charge (compounding the irony, Tupac was one of the few gangsta rappers to empathize with women, with songs such as "Brenda's Got a Baby").

His gorgeous song heavily featured a sample of "In All My Wildest Dreams," from The Crusaders keyboardist Joe Sample's album, *Rainbow Seeker*. But its chorus and theme were based on "Sadie," from *New and Improved* by soul veterans The Spinners (aka The Detroit Spinners). Tupac's candid interpretation, however, did not shy away from detailing his mother's personal flaws, notably her drug addiction.

"The wonderful thing about that song," Afeni reflected on the first anniversary of her son's 1996 death, "is that [it] is something that I share with millions, probably, of women across this country, and probably across the world. . . . It's a gift from Tupac to women who've maybe not been perfect, who've made mistakes." **BM**

Tupac Shakur performs in 1994; to him, Thug Life meant succeeding despite deprivation. ➜

The Bomb! (These Sounds Fall into My Mind) | The Bucketheads (1995)

Writer | Kenny "Dope" Gonzalez, Daniel Seraphine, David "Hawk" Wolinski
Producer | Kenny "Dope" Gonzalez
Label | Henry Street Music
Album | *All in the Mind* (1995)

The early to mid-Nineties produced a wealth of chart-friendly house songs, although many have not stood the test of time. "The Bomb! (These Sounds Fall into My Mind)," however, still sounds as fantastically fresh as it did in 1995. With its simple refrain—"these sounds fall into my mind"—laid over a storming disco beat, the song heavily samples "Street Player," from *Chicago 13* by Chicago.

Bucketheads main man Kenny "Dope" Gonzalez twisted the original lyric—"street sounds swirling through my mind"—and kept the brass. With extra disco sparkle and driving drums, a fourteen-minute club anthem was born in 1994, edited to manageable length by Armand Van Helden and commercially released the following year. The project was a way for Gonzalez to indulge his populist leanings—away from his acclaimed work as part of Masters at Work and Nuyorican Soul—while still fusing disco, house, hip-hop, and Latin styles. The track's success left a legacy of producers cleverly using samples in a more commercial way, as well as a whole host of disco gems being updated.

The Bucketheads are just one of several acts who have sampled "Street Player" (the original version of which was recorded by Rufus and Chaka Khan. Chicago then covered it and added the much-sampled horns). However, it is unlikely that any of them will enjoy the same longevity as the magnificent "The Bomb!" **OM**

Guilty by Association | Joe Henry and Madonna (1996)

Writer | Vic Chesnutt, Rob Veal
Producer | Joe Henry, Pat McCarthy
Label | Columbia
Album | *Sweet Relief II: Gravity of the Situation (The Songs of Vic Chesnutt)* (1996)

"The weird thing is how my sister-in-law became a cultural icon," said Joe Henry. "I thought you had to shoot a president to do that." The country rocker's association with pop's greatest star was once limited to being married to her sister Melanie. However, in 1996, they united in aid of Vic Chesnutt, a singer-songwriter paralyzed in a car crash at the age of eighteen. Although championed by R.E.M.'s Michael Stipe, Chesnutt failed to sell enough albums to pay his medical expenses—hence a tribute collection, featuring admirers from R.E.M. to Nanci Griffith.

"The song I covered," Henry told *Q*, "is 'Guilty by Association,' which Vic wrote about the albatross of Michael Stipe's celebrity. Somehow Vic got Michael to sing backing vocals on the song without him knowing that the song was about him. So when I asked if I could do that song—because I didn't know what it was about either—somebody said, 'Why don't you get Madonna to sing Michael's part?' Seeing as how the irony is so rich and it was going to benefit Vic, I was willing to make the phone call. She was a good sport."

The result was a career highlight for both stars, whose voices blended over a beautiful, Pink Floydian backing. The association continued, and Henry co-penned songs on Madonna's *Music*, *Confessions on a Dance Floor*, and *Hard Candy*. Sadly, Chesnutt died on Christmas Day, 2009. **BM**

A irmandade das estrelas
Carlos Núñez (1996)

Writer | Carlos Núñez, Kepa Junkera
Producer | Ry Cooder, Paddy Maloney
Label | RCA Victor
Album | *A irmandade das estrelas* (1996)

Carlos Núñez has gained wide recognition playing one of the world's most derided instruments—the bagpipes. His brilliance on the *gaida* (the Spanish bagpipes) allowed for a reconsideration of the instrument and made Núñez heavily in demand, both as a solo artist and as a sideman with the likes of The Chieftains, Ry Cooder, Sharon Shannon, and Sinéad O'Connor. Núñez hails from Galicia, a region in northwestern Spain with a strong folk music tradition. Galicians are extremely proud of their roots music, in which the *gaida* features predominantly, and their music has many affinities with the Celtic music of Ireland and Brittany.

Born in 1971, Núñez began learning the *gaida* aged eight. A musical prodigy, he was befriended by Irish traditional music supergroup The Chieftains as a young man and has played with them so often that they refer to Núñez as "the seventh Chieftain." His debut solo album, 1996's *A irmandade das estrelas* (The Brotherhood of Stars), was a big hit in Spain, selling more than 100,000 copies—the first time Celtic music sold enough to go platinum in Spain—and winning a wide international audience for Galician music.

Núñez's beautiful playing on "A irmandade das estrelas" is haunting yet peaceful. He has further broadened the audience of Galician music by working with musicians from other traditions, including flamenco and Basque music. **GC**

Brooklyn's Finest | Jay-Z featuring
The Notorious B.I.G. (1996)

Writer | Carter, Wallace, Satchell, Bonner, Morrison, Webster, Jones, Pierce, Middlebrooks, Napier, Franklin
Producer | R. "Clark Kent" Franklin, Damon Dash
Label | Roc-A-Fella
Album | *Reasonable Doubt* (1996)

"Me an' Biggie an' Busta [Rhymes], we all went to school together," Jay-Z told VladTV.com. "I remember B.I.G. would never talk about rappin'… Busta was *always* talkin' 'bout rappin'. We went at it one time in the lunchroom. I got 'em good!"

By 1996, B.I.G. (aka Biggie) was a star, and Jay-Z was working on his debut. At the behest of Jay's right-hand man Damon Dash, Biggie agreed to cut a track with his old rival. "I was adamantly against it…" producer and friend Irv Gotti told *XXL*. "I said, 'What I'm scared of is you doin' it with Biggie and you comin' off like his little man.'… Go 'head and listen to that record—'It's time to separate the pros from the cons / The platinum from the bronze …'—he's goin' at him real tough." (Producer Clark Kent, who originally made the backing for Dash's act Future Sound, added the "Jay-Z and Biggie Smalls, nigga shit ya drawers" hook.)

As predicted, B.I.G. came off best, not least in his laconic response to rival rapper 2Pac's claims to have bedded Biggie's wife, Faith Evans: "If Fay had twins, she'd probably have two Pac's / Get it? Tu–pac's." Jay, who also came under fire from 2Pac, got off shots of his own in the song's trigger-happy introduction, based on the movie *Carlito's Way*. Jay and B.I.G. became friends, but the latter's murder in 1997 put paid to hopes of an album-length collaboration. The storming "Brooklyn's Finest" proves what could have been. **BM**

Novocaine for the Soul | Eels (1996)

Writer | Mark "E" Everett, Mark Goldenberg
Producer | Mark "E" Everett, Mark Goldenberg, Mike Simpson
Label | DreamWorks
Album | *Beautiful Freak* (1996)

"The song is about not feeling, or being afraid to feel."

E, Eels, 1996

◀ **Influenced by: The Tears of a Clown** • Smokey Robinson & The Miracles (1967)
▶ **Influence on: Your Woman** • White Town (1997)
● **Covered by:** The Moog Cookbook (2005)
★ **Other key tracks:** Fucker (1996) • My Beloved Monster (1996) • Cancer for the Cure (1998)

This brooding breakthrough for Eels was an unlikely hit in the era of "Macarena" and the Spice Girls. Indeed, there is plenty in "Novocaine for the Soul" that just should not work in the pop charts.

The title name-checks what front man E described as "a chemical that Steven Spielberg invented . . . dentists in America put it in your mouth to make it feel numb before they drill your teeth." A warped sample from Fats Domino's song "Let the Four Winds Blow," released in 1961, is layered with a twisted tinkle on a toy instrument, sinister strings, and grunge guitars that would not sound out of place in film noir. "A big lightbulb went on above my head," E told *Drop-D Magazine*, "when I realized that I could use sampling in the context of my songs and that it would add another dimension to the music." The result was a skulking pop odyssey.

"'Novocaine for the Soul' is not really an optimistic song," he told French radio in 1996, "because it's about everything that the rest of the [*Beautiful Freak*] record is the opposite of. 'Novocaine for the Soul' is about not feeling your feelings—but the whole record is about getting down to the bottom of what's underneath everything on the surface. It's actually, I think, a very optimistic album."

Nonetheless, the song is strangely uplifting. "It's like the Motown formula," he said. "They would take a really sad lyric and put happy music to it." The accompanying video features the band suspended on wires, as if in flight. (Director Mark Romanek was inspired by the movie *Mary Poppins*.) E's reassuring calm and plain-speaking honesty perfectly offset the mish-mash of melancholy, and "Novocaine for the Soul" rewards repeat listens. **KBo**

Ready or Not | Fugees (1996)

Writer | W. Hart, T. Bell, Enya, N. Ryan, R. Ryan
Producer | Wyclef Jean, Lauryn Hill, Pras Michel, Jerry Duplessis
Label | Ruffhouse
Album | *The Score* (1996)

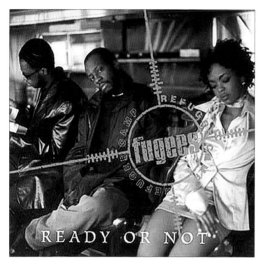

"I would have been flattered had they asked me."

Enya, 1997

◀ **Influenced by: Ready or Not Here I Come (Can't Hide from Love)** • The Delfonics (1968)
▶ **Influence on: I Don't Wanna Know** • Mario Winans featuring Enya & P. Diddy (2004)
● **Covered by:** The Course (1997)

The last thing hip-hop needed in 1994 was more gangstas—especially the Fugees, who proved unconvincing thugs on their debut *Blunted on Reality*. The genre needed a breath of fresh air, which the trio delivered with their sophomore outing. *The Score* is packed with positive messages and killer songs, including covers of old favorites, such as Roberta Flack's "Killing Me Softly with His Song" and Bob Marley's "No Woman, No Cry." However, most striking is "Ready or Not," which is now considered the group's finest moment.

The song sparkles with originality, despite its hefty samples of The Delfonics and "Boadicea" by Enya. "I was completely hurt," the latter told *The New York Times*, "because on the back of their album, the other people who are sampled are credited and I'm not. . . . When their manager heard about it, he got in touch with me and Nicky and Roma [Ryan, Enya's collaborators] and apologized. I was concerned about my fans because a lot of rap albums have obscene language and I didn't want people to think I would be involved. But their manager explained the band's message and that it's different because it's hip-hop, not rap. . . . I know what it's like to work so hard in the studio, so we decided to let them leave the song on." She was eventually paid royalties.

All three Fugees (Wyclef Jean, Lauryn Hill, and Pras Michel) perform on the track, but the best lines belong to Hill: "So while you imitatin' Al Capone / I be Nina Simone and defecating on your microphone." "Ready or Not" spent two weeks in the No. 1 spot in the U.K. charts; the song helped the Grammy Award-winning *The Score* sell more than eighteen million copies and become a hip-hop landmark. **JiH**

Firestarter
Prodigy (1996)

Writer | Howlett, Flint, Deal, Horn, Dudley, Jeczalik, Langan, Morley
Producer | Liam Howlett
Label | XL
Album | *The Fat of the Land* (1997)

Following *Music for the Jilted Generation* in 1994, The Prodigy spent two years on the road, aiming to bury their rave origins and achieve international success. Yet it was only after the band took a break from touring—and unleashed "Firestarter"—that they accomplished that mission.

With a revised name—Prodigy—they amped up the rock and hip-hop that had made *Jilted*'s "Their Law" and "Poison" so popular. "Firestarter" boasts brutal beats and guitars, with memorable samples: a bit of The Breeders ("Cannonball"); a dash of Art of Noise. "Not really a song," noted Pet Shop Boy Neil Tennant. Prodigy supremo Liam Howlett concurred, "It's more like . . . an energy!"

Vocalist Keith Flint used the song as a coming-out party for his punk-style, front-man persona. "He expresses himself onstage dancing," Howlett told writer Ben Thompson, "but I guess he felt like he'd done as much as he could do in that area, and he just needed something else to let himself go with. . . . We both just sat down and wrote the lyrics. Basically, they're just a description of Keith: what happens with him onstage, the way he is—his headstrong personality. That record sums him up."

The startling video and violent lyrics caused controversy, albeit nothing compared to the later "Smack My Bitch Up." Nonetheless, "Firestarter"—released a year before its parent album—became Prodigy's first worldwide smash. **JiH**

Professional Widow (Armand's Star Trunk Funkin' Mix) | Tori Amos (1996)

Writer | Tori Amos
Producer | Tori Amos, Armand Van Helden
Label | Atlantic
Album | N/A

"Courtney Love gives good copy," Tori Amos remarked to Australia's *Herald Sun*. The original, harpsichord-driven version of "Professional Widow" is thought to be about Love, whom Nine Inch Nails main man Trent Reznor blamed for "meddling" in his relationship with Amos. The latter refused to refute this: "We have mutual friends. I don't want to put them in a bad position." But the song was also about herself: "'Widow' is my hunger for the energy I felt some of the men in my life possessed: the ability to be king."

When an Atlantic executive suggested that DJ Armand Van Helden produce a dance remix of the song, Amos made just one suggestion: that it be different. "I was free to experiment," said Van Helden, "and, having just returned from Ibiza, I was feeling extra creative." His bass-heavy, eight-minute-plus remix retains just two lines of the original—repeated over and over—and an inscrutable interlude referring to boxing legend Muhammad Ali. But not "Starfucker, just like my daddy"—one of the lyrics that Amos herself censored on her *Welcome to Sunny Florida* concert DVD. The aim was a hit, after all.

And they got one: "Professional Widow" topped the U.S. Dance Play and U.K. singles charts, boosted Van Helden's reputation, and enhanced a reissue of Amos's *Boys for Pele* (from which the original song came). **AG**

Nancy Boy | Placebo (1996)

Writer | Brian Molko, Stefan Olsdal, Robert Schultzberg
Producer | Phil Vinall
Label | Elevator Music
Album | *Placebo* (1996)

PLACEBO. NANCY BOY
PART 1 OF 2
7243 8 94031 21

"It's obscene. A song this rude should not be No. 4 in the charts."

Brian Molko, 1997

◀ **Influenced by: Disappearer** · Sonic Youth (1990)
▶ **Influence on: Underdog** · Kasabian (2009)
● **Covered by:** Norwegian Celery Farmers (2001)
★ **Other key tracks:** Slackerbitch (1996) · Eyesight to the Blind (1996) · Miss Moneypenny (1996) · Teenage Angst (1996) · 36 Degrees (1996)

With a sprinkle of glam, a spike of punk, and a heap of attitude, Placebo shook up the mainstream with the gender-defying "Nancy Boy." It appeared to flaunt the trio's debauchery—a lifestyle that singer/guitarist Brian Molko reveled in.

With lyrics such as "Different partner every night / So narcotic outta sight," the song seemed a naive celebration of sex, drugs, and cross-dressing. However, Molko told *Melody Maker*, "It criticizes people who think it's fashionable to be gay—guys who think that they are going to try it out because they're in a milieu where it's cool, but they haven't actually felt the desire themselves."

While the risqué lyrics guaranteed exposure, the track's sheer exuberance hooked listeners. Staccato guitars and explosive drums provided an intoxicating backdrop for Molko's acerbic, high-pitched vocals. The payoff was a Top Five U.K. hit.

However, the band had spawned a Frankenstein's monster. "Some people say that this is the best song that we ever wrote," Molko grumbled onstage, "and we say bull-s-h-i-t!" Concerned that the song was pigeonholing them and having lost emotional connection with it, they excluded "Nancy Boy" from their set list for four years. "I've always felt that it was the most moronic of all the songs that we've ever written," Molko informed *Kerrang!* "In fact, during rehearsals, I'd apologize to the rest of the band for the lyrical content of that song."

Fortunately, a change of heart accompanied the release of their album *Once More with Feeling: Singles 1996–2004.* "We realized that we'd have to exhume the corpse eventually," explained Molko, "and, because of the break, it actually became fun to play again." **BC**

Devil's Haircut | Beck (1996)

Writer | Beck Hansen, John King, Michael Simpson, James Brown, Phil Coulter, Thomas Kilpatrick
Producer | Beck Hansen, Dust Brothers
Label | Geffen
Album | *Odelay* (1996)

"What was that song about?"

Beck, 2001

◄ **Influenced by: I Can Only Give You Everything**
Them (1966)
► **Influence on: Legend of a Cowgirl** · Imani Coppola
(1997)
● **Covered by:** Doug Munro's Big Boss Bossa Nova
(2007)

Beck Hansen followed his breakthrough of 1994, *Mellow Gold*, with underground albums that shored up his credibility—but the loping hip-hop blues of his smash "Loser" increasingly seemed like a fluke collision with the mainstream. This ambiguous success played out in the dense, cut-up lyrics of "Devil's Haircut," from *Mellow Gold's* "proper" sequel, *Odelay*. "Everywhere I look there's a dead end waiting," murmured Beck, afraid of donning the "Devil's Haircut" and becoming a corporate sellout.

For *Odelay*, Beck hooked up with the Dust Brothers, who had produced the Beastie Boys' acclaimed *Paul's Boutique*. Arriving late in sessions for the album, following a stint on Lollapalooza in 1995, the track was recorded—with later single "The New Pollution"—in a two-day burst. They worked quickly, and a little of that chaos remains in the cut-and-paste anthem. For the propulsive break beat, the Brothers lifted from funk drummer Bernard "Pretty" Purdie (1968's "Soul Drums") for the chorus and Van Morrison's Sixties band Them (a cover of James Brown's "Out of Sight") for the verses. Beck played the riff to Them's garage rock anthem "I Can Only Give You Everything" on a heavily distorted guitar for the head-caving hook, which stomped thuggishly over the groove.

"Devil's Haircut" proved Beck was no one-hit wonder. This brilliantly addictive pop smash—with anarchic blasts of feedback guitar (amped up on a remix by Noel Gallagher of Oasis) and brain-scrambling boho lyrics—never compromised Hansen's iconoclastic cool. Indeed, *Odelay's* success enabled Beck to pursue his wayward course with the cocky, genre-juggling confidence he has displayed ever since. **SC**

I'll Be There for You . . . | Method Man featuring Mary J. Blige (1996)

Writer | N. Ashford, V. Simpson
Producer | Prince Rakeem aka The RZA
Label | Def Jam
Album | N/A

The Beautiful People
Marilyn Manson (1996)

Writer | M. Manson, T. Ramirez
Producer | Trent Reznor, Dave "Rave" Ogilvie, Marilyn Manson
Label | Nothing
Album | *Antichrist Superstar* (1996)

Romance rarely figured on the Wu-Tang Clan's early agenda. New York's rap crew revolutionized the genre, but through raging rhymes and innovative production, not love songs. However, on tour, Method Man—the Clan's laconic front man—missed Shortie, his girlfriend. He promptly flew her to Los Angeles and wrote a rap for her. The result was the grinding "I'll Be There for You"—based on Marvin Gaye and Tammi Terrell's "You're All I Need to Get By"—on his solo album, *Tical* (1994).

"I didn't know the original song," Def Jam chief executive Lyor Cohen told the *New York Times.* "Everybody told me that it was this old Marvin Gaye record, and I said, 'Wow, if we could only get Mary J. and Meth together on it.' I was just thinking of making Meth bigger and more mainstream and using her as a vehicle." Blige obliged, and Cohen bribed the reluctant Meth with money for a Lexus. The oddly spooky yet romantic revamp appeared as "I'll Be There for You/You're All I Need to Get By." Aided by Def Jam's costly video, the song—featuring mixes by RZA and Puff Daddy—went platinum.

"The song is real . . ." Meth declared. "Everybody wants to be the toughest—calling women ho's, whatever. . . . If that's the kind of women you be with, it's your own damn fault. Everybody's saying, 'Guns, guns, kill, kiiiillll, murdermurdermurder.' But there has to be someone in your life that you show your real love to." **BM**

Nietzschean philosophy combined with an attack on vacant celebrity and the fascism of conventional beauty made "The Beautiful People" an implausible candidate for classic heavy metal. But the song—and its turbulent parent album *Antichrist Superstar*—helped propel the goth-metalers into the face of mainstream America. More significantly, it transformed outspoken titular front man Manson into a provocative poster boy for disaffected youth, and Satan incarnate in the minds of God-fearing conservatives.

Written by Manson and his partner-in-crime, bassist Twiggy Ramirez, "The Beautiful People" was composed of complex ideology far removed from its primitive beginnings in a hotel room on tour. Reflecting the conceptual themes of *Antichrist Superstar*, it juxtaposed Social Darwinism with German philosopher Friedrich Nietzsche's view of master/slave morality: "It's not your fault that you're always wrong / The weak ones are there to justify the strong." The term "the beautiful people," Manson told *Kerrang!* was inspired by Marylin Bender's 1960s book on President Kennedy.

A tribal beat echoed the passion for Adam & The Ants held by its co-producer, Trent Reznor of Nine Inch Nails. Scythe-riff guitars complemented Manson's manic vocals, resulting in what Allmusic hailed as a "song that even the group's detractors couldn't get out of their heads." **SF**

Marilyn Manson: parents were wary of the effect he might have on their children. ➜

Criminal | Fiona Apple (1996)

Writer | Fiona Apple
Producer | Andrew Slater
Label | Work
Album | *Tidal* (1996)

"After I saw myself at the MTV Awards, I realized 'Wow, I do kind of come off a bit intense.'"

Fiona Apple, 1997

◀ **Influenced by: Stoned Soul Picnic** · Laura Nyro (1968)
▶ **Influence on: Miniature Disasters** · KT Tunstall (2005)
● **Covered by:** Amazing Transparent Man (2003)
Natalie Cole (2006)
★ **Other key tracks:** Sleep to Dream (1996) · Slow Like Honey (1996) · Shadowboxer (1996)

Intense and traumatized, Fiona Apple had been writing songs since she was a young girl. "Everyone assumed I'm crazy," she told *Mojo*, "because I'm not running around chewing bubblegum and singing Debbie Gibson songs." Released when she was just eighteen, Apple's debut album, *Tidal*, was extraordinarily accomplished. Her deep, rich voice, and producer Andrew Slater's imaginative arrangements, evoked comparisons ranging from Billie Holiday to Laura Nyro. While much of the album drifted in a beguiling, jazzy haze, "Criminal" was a rollicking, bluesy belter, whose self-lacerating lyrics Apple mitigated with a tongue-in-cheek delivery.

The song was distinguished for the public by a striking Mark Romanek video that saw Apple mostly in underwear among unclad, faceless bodies. "I called Mark and we talked about his idea that the song is about guilty pleasures and sexual deviance . . ." she told *Interview* magazine. "Feeling a little bad about it, but enjoying it all the same. It corresponded with my meaning of the song." Pushed by MTV, "Criminal" became her breakthrough song, gathering awards and propelling *Tidal* to multiplatinum. "I'm a huge fan of her music," wrote Marilyn Manson in 1997.

Ill-suited to success, Apple gave a bitter speech at an MTV awards show that began: "This world is bullshit." Many of her reservations sprang from the "Criminal" video—whose bevy of "female extras who are paid to be pretty" exacerbated Apple's poor self-image—and the awards confirmed a conviction that she had "sold out." "I'd saved myself from misfit status," she wrote on her website, "but I'd betrayed my own kind by becoming a paper doll in order to be accepted." **SO**

Crash into Me | Dave Matthews Band (1996)

Writer | Dave Matthews
Producer | Steve Lillywhite
Label | RCA
Album | *Crash* (1996)

"This song is about the worship of women."

Dave Matthews, 1987

◀ **Influenced by:** Willow · Joan Armatrading (1977)
▶ **Influence on:** Why Georgia · John Mayer (2001)
● **Covered by:** Stevie Nicks (2005)
★ **Other key tracks:** Ants Marching (1994) · So Much to Say (1996) · Christmas Song (1996) · Proudest Monkey (1996) · Say Goodbye (1996)

The Dave Matthews Band's major-label debut, 1994's *Under the Table and Dreaming*, produced five singles and went platinum within months. Yet the Virginia quintet had plenty to prove, such as whether their irregular rock mix—featuring violin and saxophone, but lacking electric guitar—could sustain the public's interest.

They accomplished all of that, and more, on *Crash*—and, really, with one song. Matthews had never released anything like "Crash into Me," and its sophistication clearly distanced his group from their jam band peers. With sweetly strummed acoustic guitar, "Crash into Me" sounded like a straightforward ballad—but its lyrics suggested that the narrator's obsession tended toward the maniacal. There was definitely some degree of stalking going on, complete with a description of spying on the subject. "I wrote this song rather than peering in the window, for fear of being arrested," Matthews deadpanned on *VH1 Storytellers*.

Voyeurism had rarely sounded sexier than on the song's most quoted lyric. However, Matthews told *Blender* magazine, "That's probably the worst line that I've ever written. I've had to answer for that line more than anything. We were recording 'Crash into Me,' and then it got to the end. I'm always rambling on so, to amuse myself and [producer] Steve Lillywhite, I sang, 'Hike up your skirt a little more and show the world to me.' I guess it stuck in people's minds."

The song was a hit that helped *Crash* sell more than seven million copies in the United States alone. It also provided the Dave Matthews Band with new fans, who helped to make them one of America's biggest acts for the ensuing ten years. **JiH**

On & On | Erykah Badu (1996)

Writer | Erykah Badu, JaBorn Jamal
Producer | Bob Powers,
JaBorn Jamal
Label | Motown
Album | *Baduizm* (1997)

*"There are no gimmicks:
just me, a microphone,
three backing singers.…
It's beautiful. It's tribal."*
Erykah Badu, 1999

◀ **Influenced by: Fine and Mellow** · Billie Holiday (1939)
▶ **Influence on: A Long Walk** · Jill Scott (2002)
★ **Other key tracks:** Otherside of the Game (1996)
Next Lifetime (1996) · 4 Leaf Clover (1996) · Appletree
(1996) · No Love (1996) · Sometimes … (1996) · Bag
Lady (2000) · Soldier (2008) · Honey (2008)

In the late 1990s, it looked as if neo-soul—a U.S. movement kick-started by Erykah Badu and her friends The Roots—might conquer the world. It didn't: hip-hop and R&B were more persuasive, and neo-soul was too smooth to compete. However, the scene's early hits remain essential listening, and among the best is Badu's first single, "On & On."

Badu was raised in Dallas. She played bars and clubs as a hip-hop MC and singer and evolved a sultry, laid-back style that was the polar opposite of the octave-scaling likes of Whitney Houston and Mariah Carey. Billie Holiday was a much more obvious reference, but there was more to Erykah than jazz: "On & On" features a rock-solid beat and slick bass that sounds totally modern. "I think I need a cup of tea," croons the singer, delivering a message of universal hippiedom without ever becoming too self-indulgent. The chorus echoes every love and peace anthem that you have ever heard—in the simplest terms—keeping excitement at coffee-table level. An extraordinary, award-winning video showed its star to be genuinely beautiful rather than a typical R&B vixen.

Although her music evolved in rewarding ways, "On & On" remains a definite highlight of Badu's back catalog. "When my first album, *Baduizm*, came out in 1997," she told *Interview*, "one thing rolled after the other. I got about fifteen awards that year, including Grammys, a BET, and American Music awards. I met the love of my life, [OutKast's] André Benjamin, and had a baby when my second album, *Live*, was released. It was my magnum opus year—the kind of year everyone dreams about." **JMc**

Woo-Hah!! Got You All in Check | Busta Rhymes (1996)

Writer | Trevor "Busta Rhymes" Smith, Galt MacDermot
Producer | Rashad Smith, Trevor Smith
Label | Elektra
Album | *The Coming* (1996)

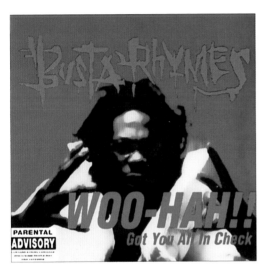

"Being Busta Rhymes isn't just about hyper energy and wilin' out all the time. That's just the most marketable side."

Busta Rhymes, 2003

◀ **Influenced by: Space** · Galt MacDermot (1973)
▶ **Influence on: Tribute** · Nonpoint (2000)
● **Covered by:** DJ Sega (2008)
★ **Other key tracks:** The Finish Line (1996) · Flipmode Squad Meets Def Squad (1996) · Everything Remains Raw (1996) · Hot Fudge (1996) · Dangerous (1997)

Wonderful rap songs come along with reassuring regularity; weird and wonderful rap songs are more rare. In the early Nineties, only Cypress Hill and the Wu-Tang Clan made genuinely surprising contributions to the mainstream. However, another maverick was making waves.

Busta Rhymes began with Leaders of the New School, protégés of Public Enemy (whose Chuck D gave Trevor Smith his stage name). Ragga-tinged roaring, a six-foot frame, and kinetic charisma made Busta a natural scene stealer. He cemented his reputation on two remixes: A Tribe Called Quest's "Scenario" (1992) and Craig Mack's "Flava in Ya Ear" (1994). However, these remarkable cameos barely prepared listeners for his nutty solo debut. Its title was a quote from a rap in The Sugarhill Gang's 1980 single "8th Wonder." The off-kilter music was based on a piece from the soundtrack to the movie *Woman Is Sweeter* (1973), by *Hair* co-writer Galt MacDermot.

An arresting video showcased director Hype Williams's trademark "fish-eye" visuals. It promptly enjoyed heavy MTV rotation without, unusually, featuring on their rap show first. (A second video, for the "World Wide Remix," put Busta in a padded cell with the remix's guest—the Wu-Tang's unhinged Ol' Dirty Bastard.) Busta became the Yosemite Sam of hip-hop: a seemingly furious but curiously lovable cartoon character.

"The lyrics is the first one that has to be in order," he told *The Source*. "Then you take the concept, attitude, then ya gotta get the music that's gonna fit the shit you writing about. . . . When I came onstage it was a whole 'nother level of intensity and energy, and ranting and raving, because everything else was in order." **BM**

No Diggity
Blackstreet featuring Dr. Dre (1996)

Writer | C. Hannibal, T. Riley, W. "Skylz" Stewart, R. Vick, Queen Pen, B. Withers
Producer | T. Riley, W. "Skylz" Stewart
Label | Interscope
Album | *Another Level* (1996)

Singer and producer Teddy Riley was the go-to R&B hitmaker for much of the late 1980s and early 1990s. He created New Jack Swing, topped the charts with the ultra-smooth trio Guy, and co-produced Michael Jackson's *Dangerous*. But as gangsta rap replaced New Jack as the sound of urban America, his magic touch faded. To get back on top, Riley had to reinvent himself—and R&B.

That reinvention came in 1996, when Riley heard the gospel moan and acoustic riff that opens Bill Withers's 1971 track, "Grandma's Hands": "I said, 'That's a groove people are gonna go crazy over.'" Riley sped up the sample, slapped on a stomping piano riff, and scribbled lyrics about a "playette"—a snake-hipped temptress interested only in the spending power of her suitors. Initially, the other members of Blackstreet dismissed the track as corny. However, Riley pushed ahead, hiring rapper and producer Dr. Dre to spit an opening verse, and Queen Pen to rhyme from the femme fatale's perspective.

The mix of gangsta rap, classic soul, and a mesmerizing gospel groove won over hip-hop fans and R&B lovers, and—in November 1996—topped *Billboard*'s Hot 100, ending the three-and-a-half-month reign of Los Del Rio's "Macarena." It stayed at No. 1 for four weeks, going platinum—and attracting the approval of Michael Jackson, who recalled Riley to work on 2001's *Invincible*. **TB**

Woke Up This Morning
Alabama 3 (1997)

Writer | Jake Black, Rob Spragg, Piers Marsh, Simon Edwards, Chester Burnett
Producer | M. Vaughan, The Ministers at Work
Label | Elemental
Album | *Exile on Coldharbour Lane* (1997)

For London trio Alabama 3's best-known song, Rob Spragg explained, "We started with a Howlin' Wolf loop, but a lot of blues lyrics are quite misogynist. So I turned it round to be about a woman who's had enough and gets a gun." The lyric is based on the story of a British woman who shot her abusive husband. Samples from Mississippi Fred McDowell's "Standing at the Burial Ground" and Muddy Waters's "Mannish Boy" complete the song.

David Chase, creator of HBO drama *The Sopranos*, heard it on U.S. radio and promptly abandoned plans to open each episode with a different track. "It's totally ironic," co-founder Jake Black remarked to *The Times*, "that we, who disapprove of anything villains do, should be picked for the theme song of a show that shows the human side of villains." "We've met some nice men in Armani suits with fat hands and fat rings and eaten some nice Italian food," Spragg told *Q*. "But we're very happy to be associated with a program of that caliber. While in no way endorsing the use of guns in any fetishistic manner, obviously."

Weekly exposure, however, didn't bring the band fame and fortune. "Geffen dropped us," Spragg told the *Observer*, "then, a month later, *The Sopranos* picked up 'Woke Up.' Then, two years later, Sony signed us up over there, but they didn't know what the fuck to do with us. A Welshman and a Scotsman singing country techno—they couldn't figure it out. So they dropped us." **BM**

Alabama 3's Rob Spragg (aka Larry Love)—country, but not as we knew it. ➜

Block Rockin' Beats | The Chemical Brothers (1997)

Writer | Tom Rowlands, Ed Simons,
Jesse B. Weaver Jr. (aka Schooly D)
Producer | The Chemical Brothers
Label | Freestyle Dust
Album | *Dig Your Own Hole* (1997)

"We wanted machines to sound like they were sweaty and deranged and wild."
Tom Rowlands, 2008

◀ **Influenced by: Coup** · 23 Skidoo (1983)
▶ **Influence on: Gangster Trippin'** · Fatboy Slim (1998)
● **Covered by:** DJ Sundance (2007)
★ **Other key tracks:** Leave Home (1995) · Song to
the Siren (1995) · Life Is Sweet (1995) · The Private
Psychedelic Reel (1997) · Hey Boy Hey Girl (1999)

Were one to accuse The Chemical Brothers of
basing their musical career on The Beatles'
"Tomorrow Never Knows," they would most
probably agree. However, their magpie methods
produced some of the greatest sonic thrillers
to hit the mainstream since Public Enemy. "We
don't see the whole of music as one long, linear
progression through time," Ed Simons told *Mojo*,
"but pockets of innovation and greatness that we
can go back and access."

This approach paid off and plagued them, in
equal measure, with "Block Rockin' Beats." The
track's sole credited sample is the title phrase,
lifted from gangsta rap godfather Schooly D's
"Gucci Again." However, fans—all twelve of
them—of British band 23 Skidoo gleefully pointed
out its similarity to their buried treasure of 1983,
"Coup" (not to mention The Crusaders' track, "The
Well's Gone Dry," released in 1974). "It's not
actually a straight sample; they replayed it," said
the band's Alex Turnbull. "But, yes, it's been quite
good for us." (23 Skidoo were belatedly adopted
by the Chemicals' parent label, Virgin.)

These unseemly accusations could not detract
from the explosive appeal of "Block Rockin' Beats"
itself. "We had a residency at a club, and we
wanted stuff to play . . ." Simons told *Artist Direct*.
"'Block Rockin' Beats' was something that was
played at like four in the morning, but then it
became something that can be played on
[influential U.S. radio station] KROQ." British radio
listeners also warmed to the song. Following a
trail blazed by "Setting Sun" in 1996, their
collaboration with Noel Gallagher of Oasis, "Block
Rockin' Beats" became the Chemicals' second
single to enter the U.K. chart at No. 1. **BM**

Breakdown | Mariah Carey (1997)

Writer | Mariah Carey, Anthony Henderson, Charles Scruggs, Steven Jordan
Producer | M. Carey, S. Jordan, S. Combs
Label | Columbia
Album | *Butterfly* (1997)

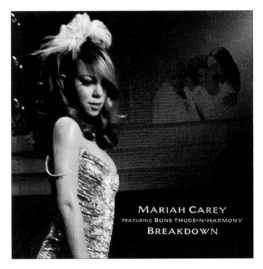

MARIAH CAREY
FEATURING BONE THUGS-N-HARMONY
BREAKDOWN

"This is the direction I've always wanted to head. But I don't want people to think I've gone completely bonkers."
Mariah Carey, 1997

◄ **Influenced by:** Tha Crossroads · Bone Thugs-n-Harmony (1996)
► **Influence on:** Lil Love · Bone Thugs-n-Harmony featuring Mariah Carey and Bow Wow (2007)
★ **Other key tracks:** Emotions (1991) · Fantasy (1995) Honey (1997)

"You know how you work constantly and then you don't realize when you're about to fall down, because you're so wrapped up in what you're doing? That's where this song is coming from." "Breakdown" seemed simply a heartfelt comment on Mariah Carey's collapsed marriage to Tommy Mottola—the theme of her best yet most serious album, *Butterfly*. However, it was also a snapshot of psychological exhaustion that proved eerily prophetic.

The song marks the increasing influence of hip-hop in Carey's work by featuring Krayzie Bone and Wish Bone, from Eazy-E's platinum-selling protégés, Bone Thugs-n-Harmony. "I was very inspired by them when I came up with the song . . ." she told *Blues & Soul*. "I wrote the song to fit in with that type of style they do and I realized it's really hard to sing those types of rhythm. They make it sound so easy. Now, having experienced the difficulty at first hand, I respect them even more."

Despite the singer declaring *"No way* is that about me," the song is clearly autobiographical. In 2001, Carey's very public physical and emotional breakdown began in earnest with messages on her website—largely complaining about overwork—including: "What I'd like to do is just take a little break or at least get one night of sleep without someone popping up about a video or a thing where all I really want to do is just be me." Fortunately, she recovered and returned to the business of being a megastar. And, as she told MTV in 2006, "I definitely still love *Butterfly* . . . not to be like, 'Whoa! I'm so ahead of my time,' but perhaps it *was* a little ahead of its time because [of] songs like 'Breakdown.'" **BM**

Chan Chan | Buena Vista Social Club feat. Compay Segundo (1997)

Writer | Muñoz Máximo, F. Repilado
Producer | Ry Cooder
Label | World Circuit
Album | *Buena Vista Social Club* (1997)

In 1996, guitar legend Ry Cooder visited Cuba and gathered a group of veteran musicians to recapture the sounds of Havana's pre-revolutionary club scene. He ended up with the album *Buena Vista Social Club*. In the process, however, he broke the United States's Trading with the Enemy Act and was fined $25,000 (reduced from half a million by the outgoing President Clinton). However, Cooder told *Uncut*, "If you really wanna get good and you really wanna be involved in great music, you must be with masters."

Of the musicians, Compay Segundo was the elder statesman. "When Compay wasn't there," Cooder observed, "it wasn't the same." Nearing ninety when the sessions took place, he had been influenced by nineteenth-century Cuban troubadours, such as Sindo Garay, whom he remembered singing at his house when he was a child. Also known as Francisco Repilado, Compay was given his stage name—which translates as "second compadre"—after he started out singing second vocals in musical partnerships.

"Chan Chan" is a Spanish-tinged, minor-key ballad that displayed Segundo's absolute mastery of the Cuban song. He was also an innovator: frustrated by the limitations of the Cuban guitar, the *tres*, he added more strings to make his own instrument, the *armónico*. In 1997 the song became a calling card for the Buena Vista Social Club. **DC**

Between the Bars | Elliott Smith (1997)

Writer | Elliott Smith
Producer | Rob Schnapf, Tom Rothrock
Label | Kill Rock Stars
Album | *Either/Or* (1997)

It was an odd moment in Oscar history. Celine Dion's *Titanic* theme "My Heart Will Go On" was up against *Good Will Hunting*'s "Miss Misery" by the almost unknown singer-songwriter Elliott Smith. To the surprise of no one—least of all Smith himself and presenter Madonna, who sneered "What a shocker" on opening the envelope—the *Titanic* theme triumphed. However, the nomination led listeners to Smith's *Either/Or*, where they found the original version of another of his five songs from the movie. The lilting, barely there "Between the Bars" lasts less than two and a half minutes, yet makes an enduring impression. The title evokes jail cells or musical notation, yet the song is a wry, Tom Waits–style ode to alcohol-sodden romance.

Smith created an orchestral version of "Between the Bars" with soundtrack maestro Danny Elfman. "I was able to work with Elliott . . ." Elfman told *Premiere*. "I could make a piece of score end to the same key, and flow into the introduction of Elliott's songs, so you really couldn't tell the difference." "I didn't have any idea [the songs] would be as prominent as they were," Smith told writer Barney Hoskyns. "If I hadn't written them, I would have thought they'd been written for the movie." But "Between the Bars" has outlived its Hollywood association. Numerous admirers have covered it, and in 2006 Madonna named it as the song of the past twenty years that she wished she had written. **BM**

Elliott Smith performs in 1999: in an age of posturing, his songs conveyed genuine feeling.

Everybody (Backstreet's Back)
Backstreet Boys (1997)

Writer | Max Martin, Denniz PoP
Producer | Martin "Max Martin" Sandberg, Dag "Denniz PoP" Volle
Label | Jive
Album | *Backstreet's Back* (1997)

The Backstreet Boys were already huge in several countries by the time they got around to recording their sophomore effort, *Backstreet's Back*. A notable exception was the Boys' native United States, where their self-titled debut hadn't been released.

The group had a gem of a track in "Everybody (Backstreet's Back)"—a thumping dance anthem with strong individual vocal performances and an instantly memorable chorus—yet record executives thought it might be confusing for U.S. audiences. The reasoning was understandable— how could Backstreet be back when this was its introduction to the United States?—yet misguided, in that semantics should never get in the way of a good beat. However, reaction to the tune was so overwhelmingly positive that the U.S. debut was reissued with "Everybody" included.

All the effort would turn out to be worth it: fans around the globe embraced the slamming song (much as they would with another Max Martin composition: Britney Spears's "Baby One More Time"). It was that rarest of things: a boy band cut that dudes could admit to liking, yet sweet enough to woo young ladies, who would quickly pin pictures of these boys to their walls. "Everybody (Backstreet's Back)" went platinum, while the U.S. album on which it appeared sold a staggering fourteen million copies in the band's homeland alone. **JiH**

4,3,2,1 | LL Cool J feat. Method Man, Redman, Canibus & DMX (1997)

Writer | LL Cool J, E. Sermon, R. Rubin, A. Yauch, A. Horovitz, Redman, Method Man, Canibus, DMX
Producer | Erick Sermon
Label | Def Jam
Album | *Phenomenon* (1997)

LL Cool J has spent two decades defying attempts to write him off. In the late Eighties, the wimpy "I Need Love" and his support of Nancy Reagan's "Just Say No" campaign torpedoed his credibility. His response was the storming *Mama Said Knock You Out*.

Having commercially outlasted all his rivals bar the Beastie Boys, LL could afford to take it easy. Yet amid smooth-talking, sample-heavy hits were flashes of his original hardness. *Mr. Smith* had yielded a stunning remix of "I Shot Ya" that matched LL with young bucks like Mobb Deep and Foxy Brown. Upping the stakes, *Phenomenon* featured a stone-cold classic that teamed the master with four of the Nineties' hottest MCs. Method Man, Redman, DMX, and newcomer Canibus took a verse each. However, the latter's appeared to challenge LL—who used his closing verse to castigate the "little shorty with the big mouth." Canibus responded with the vitriolic "Second Round K.O.," the first in a series of "diss" records from both sides. Wyclef Jean, Canibus's mentor, was dragged into the battle, and the upstart's debut album featured a photograph of himself with an adaptation of LL's signature microphone tattoo (embellished with "4321").

Amid this ludicrous battle, the original song was virtually ignored. Yet its jerky, reggae-tinged music (keyboard, bass line, and drums by EPMD's Erick Sermon), and extraordinary lineup mark it as one of the greatest posse cuts in hip-hop history. **BM**

Şimarik
Tarkan (1997)

Writer | Sezen Aksu
Producer | Mehmet Sogutoglu
Label | Istanbul Plak
Album | *Ölürüm Sana* (1997)

Dubbed "The Prince of Pop" by the Turkish media, Tarkan is a German-born singer of Turkish descent, who became a musician after his family moved back to Istanbul. His full name is Tarkan Tevetoglu, but, as with Madonna and Kylie, one word is enough for the fans.

"Şimarik" (meaning "spoiled" in English) broke Tarkan outside Turkey after it was released during 1999 in Europe, becoming a Top Ten hit in several countries and a No. 1 in Belgium. Before that, it had been a huge hit in Turkey, where the slick, big-budget video raised the game in the burgeoning local pop scene.

The dance-floor-friendly rhythm is remarkably close to the classic "Dem bow" beat of reggaeton, but the song's most memorable asset—and the one that made it such a smash—is the lip-smacking "kiss kiss" motif at the end of every verse.

"Şimarik" was penned by the Turkish diva Sezen Aksu, with whom Tarkan had previously collaborated, but they fell out due to a copyright dispute over this song. As a result, Aksu sold the rights, and new versions soon became hits elsewhere. American singer Stella Soleil covered "Şimarik" in English as "Kiss Kiss" in 2001 and had moderate success in the United States. A year later, Holly Valance took a version reconditioned by Juliette Jaimes and Steve Welton-Jaimes to the top of the U.K. and Australian charts. **JLu**

Spice Up Your Life
Spice Girls (1997)

Writer | V. Beckham, M. Brown, E. Bunton, M. Chisholm, G. Halliwell, R. Stannard, M. Rowe
Producer | Richard Stannard, Matt Rowe
Label | Virgin
Album | *Spiceworld* (1997)

Pop was dying in 1996. Grunge and Britpop had hammered all the joy out of music. A key demographic—kids—spent their allowances on video games instead. Enter the Spice Girls: saviors of the form (and the industry, not that they got credit for that). Co-writer and producer Richard Stannard told dontstopthepop.com about his first encounter with the group: "I had just had a meeting with Jason Donovan. As I left the room, Mel B came running down the corridor, told me I had a nice arse and jumped on my back.... I spent the rest of the day in a daze telling Matt Rowe about this insane but brilliant band."

The Spice Girls had brought the universe to heel with smashes such as "Wannabe." They began their second campaign with this rumbling rumba blockbuster. "The girls had been so successful all over the world," Stannard recalled, "I wanted to create something with a tribal feel. It started with the drums and went from there. . . . Not only was the track written and recorded on the same day, it was also the only track where I recorded all five girls singing at the same time, with five mics. It somehow added to the hugeness of the sound and I think you can hear the girls playing off each other." The Spices were good for another year. By the time the dust had settled, Madonna was back, Britney was on the way, and pop lived to fight another day. **BM**

Given to Fly | Pearl Jam (1997)

Writer | Mike McCready, Eddie Vedder
Producer | Brendan O'Brien, Pearl Jam
Label | Epic
Album | *Yield* (1997)

"I was going through this crazy Led Zeppelin phase, so maybe some of that came out."

Mike McCready, 1998

◀ **Influenced by: Going to California** · Led Zeppelin (1971)
▶ **Influence on: Given to Fly** · Ola (2006)
● **Covered by:** String Quartet Tribute (2006)
★ **Other key tracks:** Alive (1991) · Jeremy (1991) · Pilate (1997) · Leatherman (1997) · Wishlist (1997)

Being glum has proved profitable for many musicians. In 1997, however, Pearl Jam turned their frowns upside down; the previous year's miserable *No Code* having left front man Eddie Vedder burned out. "I remember him saying it would be great if other people could come in with ideas," recalled bassist Jeff Ament. "So we all went home and wrote a bunch of songs."

Guitarist Mike McCready conceived the one that saved them—although not before everyone pointed out its resemblance to Led Zeppelin's "Going to California." "It's just one of those amazing coincidences," quipped Zeppelin singer Robert Plant. "Do you think that somebody sang it to them in the cradle . . . ?" "It's probably some sort of rip-off of it, I'm sure," McCready conceded to *Massive!* "Whether it's conscious or unconscious—but that was definitely one of the songs I was listening to, for sure. Zeppelin was definitely an influence on that."

Vedder used it as a vehicle for a lyric whose principal character has been variously interpreted as Jesus Christ or Greek mythology's doomed Icarus. "It's a fable, that's all," the singer told the *Philadelphia Inquirer.* "The music almost gives you this feeling of flight—and I really love singing the part at the end, which is about rising above anybody's comments about what you do and still giving your love away. You know—not becoming bitter and reclusive, not condemning the whole world because of the actions of a few."

The stirring song signaled a rebirth. Pearl Jam abandoned the megastardom of their grunge heyday, but issued ever brighter and more enjoyable albums, culminating in their positively chirpy *Backspacer,* released in 2009. **BM**

Paranoid Android | Radiohead (1997)

Writer | Radiohead
Producer | Nigel Godrich, Radiohead
Label | Parlophone
Album | *OK Computer* (1997)

"Never be in a room with strangers who've taken cocaine."

Thom Yorke, 1999

◀ **Influenced by: Happiness Is a Warm Gun**
The Beatles (1968)
▶ **Influence on: Rodeohead** · Hard 'N Phirm (2005)
● **Covered by:** Brad Mehldau (2002) · Christopher O'Riley (2005) · Easy Star All Stars (2006) · Sia (2006) Lachi (2009)

If you had written your most bloodcurdling songs, would you premiere them at an Alanis Morissette show? Ever happy to provoke misery, Radiohead—the superstar's support act—did just that. "'Paranoid Android,'" bassist Colin Greenwood told *Select*, "used to have this appalling, ten-minute, Brian Auger Hammond solo at the end of it, which went on and on, with Jonny [Greenwood, guitarist] just jamming. We'd beg him not to do it. That was quite full on. There'd be little children crying at the end, begging their parents to take them home."

The finished epic (an homage to DJ Shadow and The Beatles) does, however, boast two of Greenwood's finest moments: unhinged playing that links the first section to the second, and the "rain down" verse. (Unimpressed with his own handiwork, the guitarist said, "If I was working in a shop or a factory, I'd go out for a cigarette break.") Singer Thom Yorke's lyrics are based on an encounter in a Los Angeles bar where "everyone was out of their minds on coke." "The 'kicking squealing Gucci little piggy' in 'Paranoid Android' was inhuman . . ." he told *Q*. "Someone spilled a drink over her and she turned into this fiend."

These ingredients hardly made "Paranoid Android"—its title looted from sci-fi spoof *The Hitchhiker's Guide to the Galaxy*—a likely candidate for chart success. Inspired by a conversation with R.E.M.'s Michael Stipe about the United States's domestic turmoil, Yorke unhelpfully claimed that the song was "about the fall of the Roman Empire." Six years and many rapturous performances later, however, he told *GQ*: "Everybody was talking about it—'Hmm,' like, 'serious song'—and I was, 'C'mon, it's a fucking joke!'" **BM**

Come to Daddy (Pappy Mix)
Aphex Twin (1997)

Writer | Richard D. James
Producer | Richard D. James
Label | Warp
Album | N/A

Prodigy's "Firestarter" video, starring Keith Flint as a pyromaniac sewer rat, caused moral outrage. Fortunately, few of the offended souls were exposed to this infinitely more unsettling release the following year. Flint seemed positively quaint compared to the creation that Richard D. James—aka Aphex Twin—had envisaged as a death metal jingle.

The ever-contrary James regarded "Come to Daddy" as too tame. "You do notice that you'll start to clench your fists and that's always a good sign," he told *Loaded*. "But the clench factor wasn't tight enough for me." For everyone else, its 200 beats per minute industrial intensity was a slice of sonic horror, completed by ghoulish lyrics. "I did the track in its original form about two and a half years ago," James told *Zebra*, "the same day I received this mad letter from this fan that ended with 'I want your soul, I will eat your soul.' I couldn't make head or tail of it at all, but I thought it sounded pretty good."

Director Chris Cunningham matched the music with an urban nightmare video. Childlike creatures (all, spookily, bearing James's face) pursue an elderly lady, who then confronts a demon. To complete the unsettling experience, James released two other versions of the song, which bore no resemblance to this one. Indeed, the "Little Lord Faulteroy Mix" (on the same *Come to Daddy* EP) was rather lovely. "There was," he declared, "never anything serious intended." **CB**

Never Ever
All Saints (1997)

Writer | Robert Jazayeri, Shaznay Lewis, Sean Mather
Producer | C. McVey, M. Fiennes
Label | London
Album | *All Saints* (1997)

A heartbroken soliloquy from Nicole Appleton, in the style of girl group pioneers The Shangri-Las, opens All Saints' first U.K. No. 1—a prime slab of doo-wop soul. Its slow-burning melody mirrored its chart life: the track took over two months to reach the top, falling as low as No. 9 over the festive period before peaking in January 1998.

Founding members Melanie Blatt and Shaznay Lewis met at studios on West London's All Saints Road in 1995, before co-opting Blatt's theater school chums Nicole and Natalie Appleton. In 2004, after the band split, Lewis claimed that Blatt and the Appletons had presented London Records' boss with recordings made without her. Ironically, "Never Ever" was the song that piqued his interest: "He asked who had written it, so then they were forced to come back and get me."

In vests and combat trousers, All Saints offered a street-smart counterpoint to the glitz of the Spice Girls. They also brought a fresh sound to the table. "Never Ever" combined old soul with new beats and the "Amazing Grace" chord sequence to produce a modern pop classic. Lyrically, the song detailed Lewis's dismay at a broken relationship, but her sweetly crooned vocals with Blatt, and the swelling chorus, hinted at upbeat redemption. In the end, there was rich compensation: a No. 1 smash and Brit awards for the single and video. The girl group bar had been raised. **MH**

Aphex Twin's Richard D. James looks through a picture frame darkly.

Song 2 | Blur (1997)

Writer | D. Albarn, G. Coxon, A. James, D. Rowntree
Producer | Stephen Street
Label | EMI
Album | *Blur* (1997)

"It wasn't so much reinvention as needing a new form of stimulus."

Damon Albarn, 1997

◄ **Influenced by: Smells Like Teen Spirit** • Nirvana (1991)
► **Influence on: The Fight Song** • Marilyn Manson (2000)
● **Covered by:** Avril Lavigne & David Desrosiers (2004)
Plain White T's (2006) • My Chemical Romance (2006)
★ **Other key tracks:** Beetlebum (1997) • Coffee & TV (1999) • No Distance Left to Run (1999)

"Song 2"—the track's working title—is famous for its rallying cry, "Woo hoo." Inspired by the Pixies' quiet–loud–quiet dynamics (co-opted by Nirvana), the song is a "blink and you'll miss it" adrenaline rush. Depending on who you choose to believe, the band came up with the song in somewhere between ten and thirty minutes. "Damon [Albarn, singer] went 'Woo hoo' because he had nothing else prepared," claimed producer Stephen Street, "but it's something everyone understands." Albarn was more dismissive: "It's just headbanging."

"Song 2" and its parent album are ripostes to Britpop, for which Blur had been banner carriers. Newfound U.S. influences particularly energized guitarist Graham Coxon. Previously, he had—as he admitted to *Pulse!*—"made my guitar the background and not very expressive at all in the overall song. This is just the opposite, really." Appropriately a U.K. No. 2 hit, the song made Blur's first significant impact in the United States. "Our choice of singles has been spectacularly inept for the American market, really," confessed Albarn. "With 'Song 2,' we've released something that is at least tangible. . . . It feels right in America."

Dedicated to deceased *Music Week* journalist Leo Finlay, an early champion of the band, the track (and its video) harked back to "Popscene," released in 1992. Its success was a vindication after that song's commercial failure. However, although it became popular as a song and a sports theme, not everyone grasped Blur's peculiar irony. "The American army wanted to use it as the theme for video packages when they unveiled the brand new Stealth bomber," marveled Coxon. "We couldn't agree to it, of course." **JL**

Time of Your Life (Good Riddance) | Green Day (1997)

Writer | Billie Joe Armstrong, Mike Dirnt, Tré Cool
Producer | Rob Cavallo, Green Day
Label | Reprise
Album | *Nimrod* (1997)

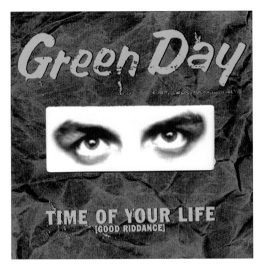

"When we put that out, we knew we had kick-ass ballads."

Tré Cool, 2001

◀ **Influenced by: She's Leaving Home** • The Beatles (1967)
▶ **Influence on: I Miss You** • Blink-182 (2003)
● **Covered by:** Raymond och Maria (2004) • Glen Campbell (2008) • Dwight Yoakam (2009)

"We knew that there were going to be some people that weren't going to like it," observed Green Day front man Billie Joe Armstrong of his band's best-loved song, "because it's not a 'one-two-three-four-let's-go' punk rock tune." (Along with The Offspring, Green Day had eclipsed all their fellow punk revivalists.)

The group struggled with credibility when they accidentally sold ten million copies of their 1994 album *Dookie*. Battered by a backlash, and wounded by sales of "only" two million for 1995's *Insomniac*, the trio (completed by bassist Mike Dirnt and drummer Tré Cool) prevented further fractures by taking a break.

Regrouping added depth and variety to their sing-along stew. Most refreshing was "Good Riddance (Time of Your Life)," a song Armstrong had composed even before *Dookie*, and which first emerged, in demo form, on the B-side of the *Insomniac* single "Brain Stew." "That song took less than ten minutes to write," Armstrong recalled. "It was an acoustic song from the get go. If I'd put drums on it, it would have turned into a power ballad and God forbid that ever happens! I had wanted to work with strings for a while, being such a big Beatles fan.... I think it came out right."

The song ended up being rechristened "Time of Your Life (Good Riddance)" for its single release and the result was an international hit, used to memorable effect in TV behemoth *Seinfeld*. A bittersweet kiss-off to an ex-girlfriend had been reincarnated as an ode to joy. And, according to Dirnt, it was no sell out: "This is a real beautiful song. Who cares what people think? ... Punk is not just the sound, the music. Punk is a lifestyle. We're just as much punk as we used to be." **SO**

Broken Heart | Spiritualized (1997)

Writer | Jason "Spaceman" Pierce
Producer | Jason "Spaceman" Pierce
Label | Dedicated
Album | *Ladies and Gentlemen We Are Floating in Space* (1997)

"Writing 'I have a broken heart' after having a broken heart would be a pretty trite thing to do."

Jason Pierce, 2009

◀ **Influenced by: I Fall to Pieces** • Patsy Cline (1961)
▶ **Influence on: Lost Souls** • Doves (2000)
● **Covered by:** Islands (2008)
★ **Other key tracks:** No God Only Religion (1997)
The Individual (1997) • Electricity (1997)

Keyboardist Kate Radley left Jason Pierce—and, later, his band Spiritualized—and married The Verve's front man, Richard Ashcroft. Pierce's next album, the critically acclaimed *Ladies and Gentlemen We Are Floating in Space* included "Broken Heart," a track described by *Mojo* as "almost bent double with sorrow." Never letting facts get in the way of a good story, journalists drew the inevitable conclusion: break-up was followed by broken heart.

However, Pierce has remained steadfast in his denials—the song was written more than two years before the split with Radley. "The last album was given a weight, that it was about my lost love," he told *Uncut.* "I denied that, but that story was better than the reality so that's what they ran with. . . . It's a bit like people want to read in between the lines before they've read the lines." Whatever the details of its development, "Broken Heart" found the composer at his most vulnerable. If the inspiration was not the break-up with Radley, then someone got to him beforehand to do damage in deep places. The sense of loss—and of losing yourself in your recreation of choice—was overwhelming, and so intimate that it was easy to feel the song (which reappeared on *The Abbey Road EP,* released in 1998) was almost too personal to be eavesdropping on.

Pierce prepared himself by listening to heartbreak classics of previous generations, from the likes of Patsy Cline and Jimmy Scott, and it shows. "If you write a song like that," he told *Mojo,* "you have to make it feel like what it's like to have a broken heart. That's what making albums is all about. Otherwise it's just field recordings." However, such soul-baring honesty clearly comes from a very painful place. **CB**

Into My Arms | Nick Cave & The Bad Seeds (1997)

Writer | Nick Cave
Producer | Nick Cave & The Bad Seeds, Flood
Label | Mute
Album | *The Boatman's Call* (1997)

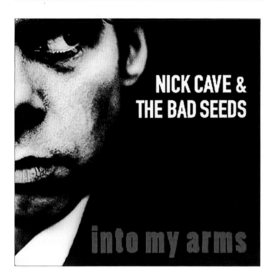

"The actualizing of God through the medium of the love song remains my prime motivation as an artist."

Nick Cave, 1999

◄ **Influenced by:** Hallelujah · Leonard Cohen (1984)
► **Influence on:** I See a Darkness · Bonnie "Prince" Billy (1999)
● **Covered by:** Yots.K (2009)
★ **Other key tracks:** Tupelo (1985) · Nature Boy (2004) The Lyre of Orpheus (2004) · Dig, Lazarus, Dig!!! (2008)

Nick Cave's career is a tale of two texts. In his twenties and thirties, he was preoccupied with the "mean-spirited, jealous, cruel God" of the Old Testament, a deity who runs amok in the Bad Seeds' early work. However, as Cave approached forty, his righteous anger eased, and the New Testament called to him. "It became quite difficult to despise things all the time," he told the *L.A. Weekly*. "Within the New Testament there is a message of forgiveness, and I found that that began to inform the way I lived."

This benevolent spirituality (Cave refuses to regard himself as a Christian) emerged on "Into My Arms." The song first appeared in 1995, when Cave performed a live soundtrack to the 1928 silent movie *La passion de Jeanne d'Arc* in London. The song then began featuring in the set lists of The Bad Seeds more than a year before its eventual release.

As Cave begins to play a gentle, mournful piano melody, with accompaniment from bassist Martyn P. Casey, he admits that he can't believe in the angels and "an interventionist God" prescribed by his loved one. However, despite that lack of faith, he hungers for divine protection, and hopes that love alone will shield and sustain them. Cave recognizes that love isn't a gift from God, but that God emerges out of love.

This vision of love as the ultimate higher power has made "Into My Arms" a hymn for both the secular and religious. Newlyweds frequently pick the track for their first dance (in 2006, *InStyle* magazine featured it in their list of top wedding reception songs) and, in 1997, Cave performed the song at the funeral of his friend, INXS singer Michael Hutchence. **TB**

Doo Wop (That Thing) | Lauryn Hill (1998)

Writer | Lauryn Hill, Johari Newton,
Tejumold Newton, Vada Nobles
Producer | Lauryn Hill
Label | Ruffhouse
Album | *The Miseducation of Lauryn Hill* (1998)

"It's pretty, but it's raw—and that's the way I like it."

Lauryn Hill, 1999

◄ **Influenced by: Together Let's Find Love**
The 5th Dimension (1971)
► **Influence on: Video** · India.Arie (2001)
● **Covered by:** Devendra Banhart (2006) · Amy
Winehouse (2007) · Rihanna (2008)

The Fugees' *The Score* was a coming-out party for Lauryn Hill. Although Wyclef and Praz were impressive on the trio's 1996 set, Hill stole the show with her sensual and street-savvy vocals. But while she had shown she could hit the mark with cover songs, could she do it with an original— and without Wyclef's guidance? "Doo Wop (That Thing)" erased all doubts.

The music evoked a raucous block party, with uplifting horns and sweet backing vocals. "The song itself is based on doo-wop . . ." Hill told MTV. "Supreme-y, Marvelette-type style, with this hip-hop thing." She volleyed between crooning like a classic beehive-haired diva and rapping like a b-girl—and was equally convincing as both.

The socially conscious lyrics were loaded with both sensitivity and sarcasm. Hill preached against the man "more concerned with his rims and his Tims than his women," and cried, "It's silly when girls sell their soul because it's in." Looking after the interests of her sisters is important to Hill. "There are a lot of young black girls who I meet in my travels who don't have a lot of self-esteem . . ." she explained to *Teen People*. "I communicate to them that they are beautiful."

"Doo Wop (That Thing)" debuted at No. 1 in the United States and hit No. 3 in the United Kingdom. Hill's desire for control even extended to the song's video: "I was six months' pregnant, and trying to hide it in a zebra print dress," she told *The Times*, "but it was a lot of fun." Meanwhile, *The Miseducation of Lauryn Hill* was on its way to becoming one of hip-hop's all-time biggest sellers, shifting eight million in the United States alone. And Hill's future? "I love my people, black people, and I will continue to make music for them." **JiH**

Miseducated? Lauryn Hill in 1999. ➔

Kelly Watch the Stars | Air (1998)

Writer | Jean-Benoît Dunckel, Nicolas Godin
Producer | Jean-Benoît Dunckel, Nicolas Godin
Label | Source
Album | *Moon Safari* (1998)

"Moon Safari *was like travels through our childhood."*

Jean-Benoît Dunckel, 2001

◄ **Influenced by: Zoolook** · Jean-Michel Jarre (1984)
► **Influence on: Give it Away** · Zero 7 (2001)
★ **Other key tracks**: Modular Mix (1995) · Sexy Boy (1998) · All I Need (1998) · Jeanne (1998) · Le Voyage de Pénélope (1998) · You Make It Easy (1998) · Talisman (1998) · Playground Love (2000)

"When we started out," Air's Nicolas Godin told *Prefix*, "we produced ourselves and we were so happy to do it." Nowhere is this do-it-yourself philosophy more evident than on "Kelly Watch the Stars." Godin, with Jean-Benoît Dunckel, created a homemade vibe that was uniquely theirs. "We've done music since we were children," he declared, "and we know how to play pretty well, so we don't need computers." Putting Godin's voice through a vocoder and adding swirling, strutting synths, "Kelly Watch the Stars" helped rocket Air to giddy levels of success. Indie movie darling Sofia Coppola and chanteuse Charlotte Gainsbourg promptly demanded the duo's services.

The pair also extended the hand of friendship to fellow French bands. *Uncut* writer David Stubbs remembered "visiting Air at a studio in Versailles and seeing them hook up with members of the very young but frighteningly versatile Phoenix in the studio, jamming through a variety of versions of 'Kelly Watch the Stars' on [traditional] and analogue instruments." Phoenix duly provided an "American Girls Remix" of the song. Three other versions appear on the tenth-anniversary edition of *Moon Safari*.

The lyrical repetition of "Kelly, watch the stars" seemingly signified nothing beyond an access point into the dreamscapes created by the electronic backing. Unsurprisingly, Godin and Dunckel have never explained the song's meaning. Only its surreal video—in which a ping-pong player named Kelly is knocked out, then revived by watching the stars—gives a clue as to what "Kelly Watch the Stars" is truly about. And, as Godin said to the *Face*, "What would I say to an alien? 'Air are your brothers, man.'" **JM**

You Get What You Give | New Radicals (1998)

Writer | Gregg Alexander, Rick Nowels
Producer | Gregg Alexander
Label | MCA
Album | *Maybe You've Been Brainwashed Too* (1998)

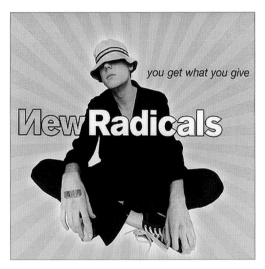

"I think I'll crack his skull open if I see him."

Marilyn Manson, 1998

◀ **Influenced by: Way Down Now** · World Party (1990)
▶ **Influence on: The Game of Love** · Santana featuring Michelle Branch (2008)
● **Covered by:** LMC featuring Rachel McFarlane (2006) Timo Raisanen (2008)

Prime power-pop that ate the world, "You Get What You Give" notched one million plays on U.S. radio—not bad, considering that it peaked at a modest No. 36 on *Billboard*'s Hot 100.

Following two solo albums ("A beacon leading me towards more personal emotionalism," enthused Weezer's Rivers Cuomo), Michigan-born singer-songwriter Gregg Alexander formed New Radicals with multi-instrumentalist Danielle Brisebois in 1997. The act was essentially a showcase for Alexander, who—after the success of the single and its parent album—disbanded his hodgepodge of session musicians to concentrate on writing and production.

But while they passed in a flash, New Radicals burned themselves into pop's fabric with this life-affirming anthem. "We have a whole society that's completely lost touch with the idea of doing something that makes them feel alive . . ." Alexander told MTV. "Celebrity culture and all the information that gets thrown at us—those are the other things that I think people that should use a more discerning, questioning eye towards."

The song was blessed with a startling kiss-off: "Fashion shoots with Beck and Hanson / Courtney Love and Marilyn Manson / You're all fakes, run to your mansions / Come around, we'll kick your ass in!" On MTV, Alexander deadpanned: "I wanted to make sure they got as much exposure as possible." ("I'm not mad that he said he'd kick my ass," Manson protested. "I just don't want to be used in the same sentence with Courtney Love.")

In 2005, Beck recalled encountering an apologetic Alexander, who denied the attack was personal. "I was kind of pleased," admitted Beck. "He's a big guy." **MH**

Music Sounds Better with You
Stardust (1998)

Writer | T. Bangalter, B. Cohen, D. King, F. Musker, A. Quême
Producer | Thomas Bangalter
Label | Roulé
Album | N/A

"When we recorded the song," recalled Alan "Braxe" Quême, "we had no idea that it would become a hit." As 1997 closed, Braxe—a dance producer signed to Thomas Bangalter of Daft Punk's Roulé imprint—had just released his first single and been invited to play a slot at the Rex Club, Paris. He encouraged Bangalter and singer Benjamin "Diamond" Cohen to guest with him and, at their rehearsal, the short-lived Stardust was born.

Sifting through record boxes, the trio alighted on Chaka Khan's 1981 track "Fate," and looped its bass line and funky guitar lick. With Diamond's vocal—"inspired by Michael Jackson"—over the top, the embryonic "Music Sounds Better with You" went down well at the Rex and prompted the trio to knock it into shape at Bangalter's studio. Most of the vocals were excised, leaving lean couplets that were as memorably perfect as the musical hooks.

Released during a hiatus between Daft Punk albums, the streamlined track demonstrated a commercial edge previously missing from that act's work. It peaked at No. 2 in the U.K., topped *Billboard*'s club chart, and was promptly mashed, to thrilling effect, with Madonna's "Holiday" for a promo release. But Stardust opted not to continue and went their separate ways—Braxe to endless collaborations, Diamond to remixes and his own label. The song was later incorporated into live sets by both Madonna and Daft Punk themselves. **MH**

Erase/Rewind
The Cardigans (1998)

Writer | Nina Persson, Peter Svensson
Producer | Tore Johansson
Label | Stockholm
Album | *Gran Turismo* (1998)

After The Cardigans' saccharine "Lovefool" became a worldwide hit in 1996, the Swedish pop darlings seemed hell-bent on an edgier follow-up. The quintet duly adopted black leather and rousing guitars for *Gran Turismo*. The infectious "Erase/Rewind" perfectly showcased Nina Persson's icy vocals and a melodic combination of synthesizer and classical guitar. "It's Ingmar Bergman dressing Garbage in steel," said journalist Caitlin Moran.

Though the band seemed to wear their sex appeal with ease, Persson was uncomfortable with the focus on her—discomfort that was reflected in her vocals. "I was very fucked up throughout the entire recording," she told *The Independent*. "I remember finding a dead bat in the woods near the studio one day. I took it back, nailed it to the wall, and sang every word to the bat, and to nobody else." Nonetheless, the broad appeal of "Erase/Rewind" earned the song a place on very different 1999 movie soundtracks: the romantic comedy *Never Been Kissed* and futuristic thriller *The Thirteenth Floor*. It was remixed by Kleerup in 2008.

A constant in The Cardigans' music was a preoccupation with tortured, imperfect love. Relationships, the singer observed, are "a source of agony to all people. Obviously, I'm not the first person to write songs about love, and I won't be the last. All you can hope as a songwriter is that your lyrics will move people." **EP**

The Cardigans: from left, Nina Persson, Lars Olof Johansson, Peter Svensson, and Bengt Lagerberg. ➔

Teardrop | Massive Attack (1998)

Writer | Robert Del Naja, Grant Marshall, Andrew Vowles, Elizabeth Fraser
Producer | Massive Attack, Neil Davidge
Label | Wild Bunch
Album | Mezzanine (1998)

"We get on really well together, as long as we don't talk about music."
Robert "3D" Del Naja, 1998

◀ **Influenced by: Sometimes I Cry** • Les McCann (1974)
▶ **Influence on: Kneight Riduz Wuz Here** • Krayzie Bone featuring Kneight Riduz (2001)
● **Covered by:** Elbow (2004) • Newton Faulkner (2006) José González (2007) • Simple Minds (2009) • Anneke van Giersbergen & Danny Cavanagh (2009)

Massive Attack's *Mezzanine* marked a change in direction, from hip-hop inspired music to a darker, guitar-driven sound—which Andrew "Mushroom" Vowles disliked so strongly that finally he left the band. The hauntingly beautiful "Teardrop" is the album's most accessible track, and the most ubiquitous; it is the theme for U.S. TV drama *House*.

The song began as a harpsichord melody by co-producer Neil Davidge. He and Mushroom developed it into a melancholic piece with piano and beats, and titled it "No Don't." However, tensions developed, as detailed in a *Q* magazine feature on the band. Mushroom envisaged a soul vocalist for the song. But his bandmates Grant "Daddy G" Marshall and Robert "3D" Del Naja wanted the Cocteau Twins' Elizabeth Fraser, whom they had encountered in a local supermarket.

Enraged, Mushroom is thought to have offered the piece to Madonna, with whom Massive Attack had collaborated on a tribute to Marvin Gaye. "It seemed like an act of treachery," complained Marshall, who was obliged to explain to Madonna that they were keeping the song. In the event, with Mushroom retaining "No Don't," Marshall, Del Naja, and Davidge re-created the demo's sounds.

Mushroom was to concede "It sounds good now," and the song became the band's biggest hit. "It very much sounded like it had a heartbeat running through it," noted director Walter Stern, whose video featured a foetus singing the track.

A few days before recording "Teardrop," Fraser reread letters from a former flame, singer-songwriter Jeff Buckley. Not long after, she received a call informing her that Buckley was missing, presumed drowned—infusing the already eerie "Teardrop" with added poignancy. **GK**

Iris | Goo Goo Dolls (1998)

Writer | John Rzeznik
Producer | Rob Cavallo, The Goo Goo Dolls
Label | Reprise
Album | *City of Angels—
Music from the Motion Picture* (1998)

"I was like, 'Well, gentlemen, I think we've turned a corner. There's no way back to the garage now.'"
John Rzeznik, 1999

◀ **Influenced by: Piano Man** · Billy Joel (1973)
▶ **Influence on: You and Me** · Lifehouse (2005)
● **Covered by:** Ronan Keating (2006) · New Found Glory (2007) · Finley (2008) · Boyz II Men (2009) · Jai (2009)
★ **Other key tracks:** Name (1995) · Black Balloon (1998) Dizzy (1998) · Slide (1998) · Stay with You (1998)

"If you give a monkey a guitar, a paper, and a pen," opined Goo Goo Dolls main man John Rzeznik, "he'll eventually write a hit song." For their part, the Goo Goo Dolls toiled for a decade—enduring critical barbs about their debt to Paul Westerberg's band The Replacements—before at last striking gold with the gorgeous "Name," from the band's fifth album, *A Boy Named Goo* (1995).

Subsequently struck with writer's block, Rzeznik's problems eased when he was invited to contribute to the soundtrack of the movie *City of Angels*. "I was kind of trying to write it from the perspective of [lead actor] Nicolas Cage," Rzeznik told MTV, "where he's about to give up his immortality—and he's sort of pondering that thought because he's so in love and he wants to feel something real for once."

The "really pretty name" of country singer Iris DeMent inspired the title. "I was trying to be pretentious and arty by calling it that," said Rzeznik. "I figured if [Smashing Pumpkins'] Billy Corgan can get away with it, so can I. So I figured, what the hell, I'll tap into the pretentious market."

Originally planning to record it alone, Rzeznik instead "did a demo with drum machines for the band. They pounded out a different version." The result—topped by the composer's coruscating vocal—was a richly heartrending ballad that became one of the era's biggest songs; it was still being covered, imitated, and reissued more than a decade later. Its inclusion on both the *City of Angels* soundtrack and the Goo Goo Dolls' own 1998 album *Dizzy Up the Girl* boosted both records to multiplatinum sales. "'Iris' was like a blessing . . ." Rzeznik reflected. "It just came out of nowhere." **BM**

Bok Espok
Kepa Junkera (1998)

Writer | Kepa Junkera
Producer | Kepa Junkera
Label | Alula
Album | *Bilbao 00:00h* (1998)

Many music aficionados are unaware that Spain's Basque region—often in the news due to actions of ETA, a Basque separatist organization—is home to a strong music scene. Anything sung in the Basque language is considered "Basque music," which can range from Basque singer-songwriters to Basque heavy metal. Of particular note is the traditional yet very contemporary folk scene.

Kepa Junkera is among today's finest young Basque musicians. He plays the *trikitixa* (a diatonic accordion) and leads a band that includes *txalaparta* (horizontal planks bashed with vertical sticks like a giant zylophone), *pandero* (tambourine), and *alboka* (the duophonic double reed pipe). The *trikitixa* has been popular since the late nineteenth century, but *trikitixa* playing changed little until Junkera began to revolutionize its sound and repertoire in the 1980s.

On *Bilbao 00:00h* Junkera was joined by traditional musicians from around the world, showing how the *trikitixa* could fit alongside African, Irish, and other acoustic music traditions. For "Bok Espok," Junkera enlisted the help of Swedish folkies Hedningarna for a typically inventive jam session that combines high-energy tempos with rich melodic passages. The song is ample proof that Junkera's visionary approach to Basque music makes for great party tunes as well as more contemplative listening. **GC**

Save Me
Aimee Mann (1999)

Writer | Aimee Mann
Producer | Aimee Mann
Label | Reprise
Album | *Magnolia* (1999)

Few are the songwriters whose work has soundtracked a whole film. Onetime 'Til Tuesday singer Aimee Mann didn't quite shoulder that responsibility for Paul Thomas Anderson's *Magnolia*—there were also contributions from Supertramp, Gabrielle, and The Devlins. But Mann's music inspired Anderson's script, and it is for her work that the soundtrack is remembered. (Additionally, in the movie, the cast sing Mann's "Wake Up," cocaine is snorted off her *I'm With Stupid* CD, and a character references her song "Deathly.") To quote the song, the imagery from filmmaker and musician proved "a perfect fit."

The most famous phrase from "Save Me"—"the freaks / Who suspect they could never love anyone"—was inspired by a conversation between Mann and a friend. "He just had this fear about himself that he was unable to sustain love. . . . I felt that was very sad and I think I understand it."

Half a million soundtrack sales for *Magnolia* meant that Mann was able to break free from the depressingly familiar cycle dictating that, the better she became, the further she was from popular acclaim. She failed to win an Academy Award (it went to "You'll Be in My Heart" from the Disney movie *Tarzan*), but, ever the amused outsider, Mann has introduced live versions of "Save Me" as the track that "lost an Oscar to Phil Collins and his cartoon monkey love song." **CB**

No One Will Ever Love You
The Magnetic Fields (1999)

Writer | Stephin Merritt
Producer | Stephin Merritt
Label | Merge
Album | *69 Love Songs* (1999)

As its drily descriptive title suggests, all of the songs collected on The Magnetic Fields' magnum opus, the triple-volume *69 Love Songs,* share a single theme: love. Across the 173 minutes, composer, bandleader, and singer Stephin Merritt essays all kinds of love via all kinds of song. This impressively ambitious project marked Merritt out as a superior pop stylist, ably switching from genre to genre without breaking a creative sweat. The sixty-nine songs are only occasionally pastiche: more often, Merritt's genre exercises pack subtle emotional punches and are deftly moving.

"No One Will Ever Love You" is just such a song. By Merritt's own admission, it was conceived as an attempt to capture, in a single song, all the twisted heartache of *Tusk,* Fleetwood Mac's troubled but brilliant double album of 1979. He would later jokingly introduce singer Shirley Simms in concerts as "Shirley Nicks," but her vocal—restrained, pristinely wracked—and the song's aching, dulcet melancholy actually recall Christine McVie in the Mac's *Rumours* era.

With Merritt's words, Simms sings of broken dreams and emotionally distant lovers. Indifference, the song suggests, rather than hate, is the antithesis of love. With a dignity that only makes its message more haunting, the opening couplet—"If you don't mind / Why don't you mind?"—captures the desolation of a love grown cold. **SC**

Surfacing
Slipknot (1999)

Writer | S. Crahan, C. Fehn, P. Gray, C. Jones, J. Jordison, C. Taylor, M. Thomson, S. Wilson
Producer | Ross Robinson, Slipknot
Label | Roadrunner
Album | *Slipknot* (1999)

"Slipknot preach individualism," chief visionary Shawn "Clown" Crahan told the *Guardian,* "and we help our maggots to get rid of conformity."

If the brutal sounds and horror movie visuals didn't clue you in, the Iowa nine-piece's "new national anthem" left no doubt about their worldview. Its chorus was splattered across their album artwork, elevating angst to a manifesto: "Fuck it all / Fuck this world / Fuck everything that you stand for / Don't belong / Don't exist / Don't give a shit / Don't ever judge me."

Inevitably, this was interpreted more as nihilism than protest, particularly by younger fans. "If their parents aren't raising them, then someone has to," drummer and bandleader Joey Jordison told *The Face.* "Someone's gotta tell them how it is."

Musically, the song was distinguished by guitarist Mick Thomson's pitch-shifted squeal. And while he compared "Surfacing" to prog gods Rush, the tumultuous track better evoked the head-splitting thrills of standing in a collapsing building.

However, the band united on their rallying cry. "Surfacing," percussionist Chris Fehn told *Songfacts,* "encompasses the attitude of the band and the attitude of how we feel about life: don't judge me. Everything that you think that you know about the world, and about Slipknot, and about your own life, might not be the case. . . . So I think it's just openmindedness, and just be cool." **BM**

Scar Tissue
Red Hot Chili Peppers (1999)

Writer | Anthony Kiedis, Chad Smith, Flea, John Frusciante
Producer | Rick Rubin
Label | Warner Bros.
Album | *Californication* (1999)

The success of *BloodSugarSexMagik* in 1991 led the Red Hot Chili Peppers' youthful guitarist John Frusciante to quit mid-tour in 1992, unable to handle the pressure. So it is ironic that his return to the band in 1998—following one album, 1995's *One Hot Minute,* featuring Jane's Addiction guitarist Dave Navarro—led to the Peppers' most successful album to date.

Mimicking the introspection of their ballad "Under the Bridge," and reteaming with Stephane Sednaoui, who had directed the "Give It Away" video, was a winning combination for "Scar Tissue," *Californication*'s first single. What the song lacks in customary Chilis-style funk, it makes up for in laidback beauty. Of the song's lyrics, singer Anthony Kiedis recalled: "Rick Rubin and I had been talking about sarcasm a lot . . . I guess I was also thinking of Dave Navarro, who was the King of Sarcasm, faster and sharper than the average bear." He later wrote: "All those ideas were in the air when John started playing this guitar riff, and I immediately knew what the song was about. It was a playful, happy-to-be-alive, phoenix-rising-from-the-ashes vibe. . . . I'll never forget looking up at the sky above that garage [at bassist Flea's house] out toward Griffith Park with the birds flying overhead, and getting a dose of Jonathan Livingston Seagull. I really did have the point of view of those birds, feeling like an eternal outsider." **SO**

Ms. Fat Booty
Mos Def (1999)

Writer | Mos Def, L. "Ayatollah" Dorrell, C. Singleton, E. Snyder
Producer | L. "Ayotollah" Dorrell
Label | Rawkus
Album | *Black on Both Sides* (1999)

For hip-hop fans bored with the bling and bravado of the Nineties rap scene, Mos Def's debut album was a delight. Here, a socially conscious rapper was exploring complicated issues, from the appropriation of black music by white performers on "Rock N Roll" to the planet's H_2O woes on "New World Water." On "Ms. Fat Booty" he gave old-school, sexist party jams an ultramodern twist.

"Ms. Fat Booty" starts off like thousands of hip-hop tracks, with the rapper describing a beautiful woman he met in a club ("Ass so phat that you could see it from the front"). Backed by soulful beats and a sample of Aretha Franklin's 1965 single "One Step Ahead," he boasts to friends how, after weeks of dating, he became her "champion lover."

It is here that the traditional hip-hop tale ends, and the player becomes the played. Def falls in love with Ms. Fat Booty and starts to suffer "flu-like symptoms when shorty not around." These feelings aren't mutual. She skips dates, and their relations end after nine months, the would-be Mrs. Def claiming she can't handle the commitment.

Critics predicted mainstream success could not be far away, but Mos Def had other ideas. He focused on acting, in movies such as *Monster's Ball* and *The Italian Job*. Having set such high standards with *Black on Both Sides* and his 1998 collaboration with Talib Kweli as Black Star, it would be another five years before he released an album. **TB**

Caught Out There | Kelis (1999)

Writer | Pharrell Williams, Chad Hugo
Producer | The Neptunes
Label | Virgin
Album | *Kaleidoscope* (1999)

"Men come up to me and go, 'Hey, my girlfriend left that on my answering machine.'"
Kelis, 2000

◀ **Influenced by: Tyrone** · Erykah Badu (1997)
▶ **Influence on: Black Beatles** (Beatles vs. Black-Eyed Peas vs. Ludacris vs. Kelis) · Loo & Placido (2005)
● **Covered by: Tune Robbers** (2006)
★ **Other key tracks:** Suspended (1999) · Good Stuff (1999) · Get Along with You (1999) · Milkshake (2003)

Dedicated to "all the women out there that have been lied to by their men" (thus acquiring an instant fan base of millions), this rage-filled vocal eruption from Kelis Rogers made every estrogen-fueled revenge song that came before it—including Alanis Morissette's hit "You Oughta Know"—sound vaguely apologetic. The performance, with its memorable chorus of "I hate you so much right now," followed by a visceral scream, was spurred by personal experience. "I'm a mess when I've broken up, but after that I'm mad," Kelis explained to Scotland's *Daily Record*. "And that madness is so intense."

Kelis's elastic vocals, shifting artfully between bluesy ballad and riot grrrl roar, are complemented by whirring space-age hip-hop, courtesy of production super-duo Pharrell Williams and Chad Hugo (aka The Neptunes, with whom Kelis worked as guest vocalist on Ol' Dirty Bastard's "Got Your Money," also from 1999). "They had this futuristic sound that I related to," she told *Billboard*. "We all feel we're from a different planet."

This otherworldliness extended to her style, a pink-and-orange afro lending her the look of a psychedelic soul sistah in the accompanying Hype Williams–directed video. Fully realizing her revenge fantasy, she trashes her cheating lover's apartment before leading a march of angry women, yelling the song's indelible hook.

"The *aaaaaaah!!* just lets it all go," Kelis told *USA Today*. "It's the finishing touch on the whole phrase. I think people connect with the song because it's a real situation. You hear a million and one songs that focus on the love and beauty and pain and sadness. But nobody sings about the anger that comes after the crying and loneliness." **EP**

Why Does My Heart Feel So Bad? | Moby (1999)

Writer | Moby
Producer | Moby
Label | V2
Album | *Play* (1999)

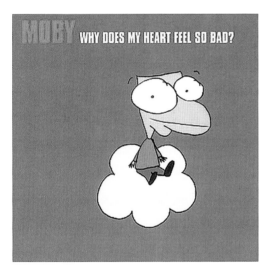

"What's wrong with me? I've got this strange and bizarre love for old soul ballads."

Moby, 2001

◄ **Influenced by: Pacific** · 808 State (1989)
► **Influence on: One Perfect Sunrise** · Orbital (2004)
● **Covered by:** Da Capo Players (2002) · The String Quartet (2002)
★ **Other key tracks:** Porcelain (1999) · Honey (1999) Natural Blues (1999)

Moby's fifth studio album, *Play* was a showcase for his ingenious sampling. Turning his back on standard techno sources, he instead sampled old gospel and folk tunes. The deeply soulful "Why Does My Heart Feel So Bad?" was the most impressive of the lot: a powerful ballad that was both classic and contemporary in the way it combined heart-wrenching vocals—courtesy of The Shining Light Gospel Choir—and Moby's beats to create a unique chill-out track.

"The song I took the woman's vocal from actually goes 'glad,' not 'bad'," Moby told *The New York Times*. "It's an upbeat, happy song. But me being me, I guess, I put these minor chords under it and manipulated the vocal, and it became something else." Elton John recorded his own version in 2000, retaining Moby's backing. "It's particularly interesting for me," Moby enthused to *Interview*, "because the first song I ever learned to play on the guitar was 'Crocodile Rock,' when I was nine years old."

The track was written years earlier—"a really bad techno song," Moby confessed to *Rolling Stone*. "Just mediocre, generic techno." The decision to let it simmer, allowing the mournful blues to bubble to the top, paid off handsomely.

"Why Does My Heart Feel So Bad?" was one of nine singles from *Play*. But before the album sold multimillions, it became a cultural touchstone after becoming the first record ever to have each of its songs licensed for use in movies, television, and commercials. Notably, "Why Does My Heart Feel So Bad?" was featured in the trailer for the 2001 movie *Black Hawk Down*. Quizzed as to why he licensed his songs so freely, Moby replied that it had seemed the only way to get them heard. **JiH**

I Try | Macy Gray (1999)

Writer | Macy Gray, Jeremy Ruzumna, Jinsoo Lim, David Wilder
Producer | Andrew Slater
Label | Epic
Album | *On How Life Is* (1999)

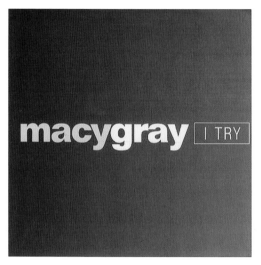

"Everybody seems to love that song. It's definitely what got these deals started."

Macy Gray, 1999

◀ **Influenced by:** Baby, I Love You · Aretha Franklin (1967)
▶ **Influence on:** Trouble Sleeping · Corinne Bailey Rae (2006)
● **Covered by:** The Girlfriends (2000) · Andrew Tinker (2007) · Ben Taylor (2008)

Macy Gray's debut single "Do Something" signaled the arrival of an intriguing new voice, described as "Chaka Khan meets Betty Boop" and "Tina Turner on helium." The subsequent release of "I Try"—which first appeared in the 1997 Jennifer Aniston movie *Picture Perfect*—was Gray's exquisitely arranged trump card.

"I was immediately impressed with her talent," producer Andrew Slater told *Entertainment Weekly*. He mixed "I Try" more than one hundred times before settling on an edit that he found so engaging, he promptly became her manager. "She had a voice like a muted trumpet," he enthused, "and she was a great songwriter."

The star's neo-soul contemporaries, such as Lauryn Hill and Erykah Badu, offered a more beat-driven sound. In contrast, "I Try" opened with soaring retro strings, with Gray's unique vocals luxuriating among a band of real musicians.

The soulful, mid-tempo, break-up ballad turned the idiosyncratic Gray—who grew up in the same neighborhood as Marilyn Manson, in Canton, Ohio—into a worldwide star. She earned a Grammy for Best Female Vocal Performance in 2000 and her first album, *On How Life Is*, hurtled up charts worldwide. It sold three million in her home country alone, while "I Try" went gold in Britain.

The debut album was described as "riddled with scat-sung quotes (from The Beatles to *The Godfather* to Prince), and loving glances to a pre-rock age," by the *Philadelphia Inquirer*, with whom Gray shared her influences: "I grew up on my parents' record collection. I loved James Brown, but also listened to Elvis. I took classical piano for seven years. . . . In college I did the jazz thing. . . . It all comes out of you, if you let it." **EP**

Macy Gray, trying hard in 1999. ➲

U Don't Know Me | Armand Van Helden (1999)

Writer | Kossi Gardner, Duane Harden,
Armand Van Helden
Producer | Armand Van Helden
Label | Armed
Album | *2Future4U* (1999)

*"Fantastic lyrics, melody,
great beats . . . "*

Ian Brown, 2000

◄ **Influenced by: The Captain** · Johnny "D" & Nicky P.
aka Johnick (1996)
► **Influence on: Runnin'** · Doman & Gooding featuring
Dru & Lincoln (2009)
★ **Other key tracks:** Aliene (1999) · Rock da Spot (1999)
Flowerz (1999) · My My My (2004) · NYC Beat (2007)

"The weird thing about dance music," observed Armand Van Helden in 2008, "and this is a strange one, is that you can basically make one hit and DJ for the rest of your life." If this is true, he broke the mold with a string of classic dance songs and remixes. The best of these, "U Don't Know Me," would set up many DJs for life.

The song sliced sounds from R&B singer Carrie Lucas's 1979 song "Dance with You" with beats from house producer Jaydee's 1992 smash "Plastic Dreams." This canny cocktail was enough to attract both underground musos and mainstream record-buyers in their droves.

"I first met up with Armand when he was running clubs in Boston . . ." singer Duane Harden told *Ministry*. "He asked me to sing over one of his tracks. I stayed there all night and just threw down some lyrics. I'm usually inspired by whatever bullshit I'm going through at the time. . . . I wanted to change some parts, but Armand told me to leave it as it was. Now I can see why."

To the full-length version of the track, Van Helden added a spoken introduction from *Dial M for Monkey*, an offshoot of kids' cartoon *Dexter's Laboratory*. "Neither Armand or I had any idea that so many people would like and understand the song," Harden recalled.

Despite its idiosyncratic construction, the result was a celebratory triumph. In the wake of his remix of Tori Amos's "Professional Widow," Van Helden scored a second chart-topper in the United Kingdom and a worldwide hit.

"Duane, the singer of the song, has perfect delivery," enthused Stone Roses front man turned solo star Ian Brown. "All in all, a song everybody can relate to. Best No. 1 of all time." **KBo**

Race for the Prize | The Flaming Lips (1999)

Writer | Wayne Coyne, Michael Ivins, Steven Drozd
Producer | The Flaming Lips, Dave Fridmann, Scott Booker
Label | Warner Bros.
Album | *The Soft Bulletin* (1999)

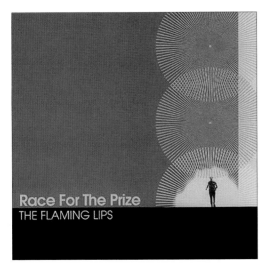

"We wanted to experiment with unexpected sounds but not sacrifice a song's emotional impact."

Wayne Coyne, 1999

◀ **Influenced by: The Whole of the Moon**
The Waterboys (1985)
▶ **Influence on: Kids** · MGMT (2005)
● **Covered by:** Palm School Choir (2008)
★ **Other key tracks:** Waitin' for a Superman (1999) · Do You Realize?? (2002) · The Yeah Yeah Yeah Song (2007)

Preposterous by conventional standards, "Race for the Prize" was a chart-aimed pop dart compared to The Flaming Lips' other work of the time. On its release, the band were still sliding off the back of their psychedelic folly *Zaireeka* of 1997—a set of four discs designed to be played simultaneously, provided that your friends were willing to haul their CD players to your home. The shift to the commercial, human, single-disc stance of *The Soft Bulletin* was therefore quite a leap.

"We wanted to do something more emotional and expressive," singer Wayne Coyne told *Uncut*. "Steven [Drozd, guitarist] had 'Race for the Prize' [originally attempted for *Zaireeka*] and the lyrics I put to it made it feel like we'd turned a corner." Those lyrics told the sweet, proud tale of a pair of scientists risking—"for the good of all mankind"—their lives and reputation to find "the cure that is their prize" (the song is subtitled "Sacrifice of the New Scientists").

The arrangement swings from fragile to awesome. Coyne's voice wavers to emphasize the scientists' physical size, then a thunderous keyboard line spirals heavenward in place of a chorus. Any potential for corniness is crushed by the sheer conviction of these crazed messiahs.

In 1998, Dave Fridmann—Mercury Rev's bassist and producer for both bands—had overseen the Rev's Disneyfied epic *Deserter's Songs*, etching a path from the psychedelic underground to the neon-lit mainstream. The Lips found the door ajar, and Fridmann helped them through. The ensuing success of "Race for the Prize" paved the way for the universal adulation that met both the Lips (for 2002's *Yoshimi Battles the Pink Robots*) and their spiritual descendants, such as MGMT. **MH**

Title	Time	Artist	
Mich Beim Wich...	2:50	Funny van Dannen	
ng (Trample Rid...	3:37	Ghetto Flex	
ood	5:55	Gorillaz	Clin
nc	3:42	Gorillaz	Den
Touch You	2:52	Hot Hot Heat	Kno
nc – Mini, mini,...	1:57	Jaques Dutronc	
It_Like_It's_H...	0:32	Jay-Z	
	3:40	John Frusciante	Live
	2:58	John Frusciante	Shac
(Nirvana Cove...	3:28	John Frusciante	
oom	2:44	Mary Timony	The
e Thousand Per...	3:43	Mary Timony	
	3:42	Mazzy Star	Maz.
– The Weeping S.	4:20	Nick Cave	
ong	4:43	Nick Cave & The...	Mur
	4:09	Oasis	D'Yo
y (w/Johnny Depp)	4:11	Oasis	Help
m – Wish You Were ...	4:29	pearl jam	
Dogg ft Pharrell- Dr...	4:30	SNOOP DOGG	
w wow yippi yo yipp...	4:06	Snoop Doggy Dog	
Patrol – Crazy In Love...	4:13	Snow Patrol	
trol – Never Gonna ...	2:09	snow patrol	
dy Wants to Rule th...	4:11	Tears for Fears	
ing in a Submarine	2:48	The Arcade	
Go	6:02	Th	
In Heaven			
rops In My Wine			

ardrops In My Wine

ver

ann Tiersen & Francoiz

Redemption Song

Jesus Almost Got Me

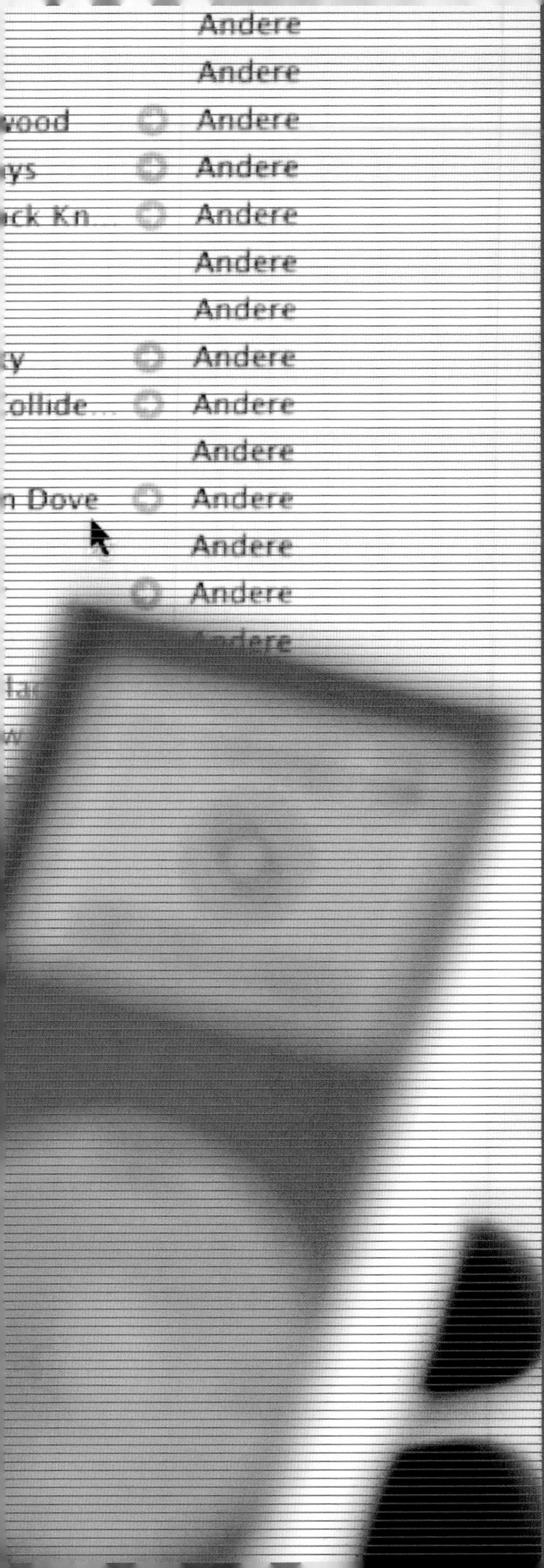

Andere
Andere
wood   Andere
ys   Andere
ck Kn   Andere
Andere
Andere
ky   Andere
ollide…   Andere
Andere
n Dove   Andere
Andere
Andere
Andere

- Britney Spears energizes pop with *Oops!…I Did It Again* in 2000

- The iPod, launched in 2001, puts "1,000 songs in your pocket"

- MySpace, founded in 2003, is used by unknown artists to gain exposure

- Michael Jackson's death in 2009 is met by unprecedented mourning

- Eminem becomes the best-selling rapper of all time with 2009's *Relapse*

2000s

One Armed Scissor | At the Drive-In (2000)

Writer | Omar Rodriguez-Lopez, Cedric Bixler-Zavala, Tony Hajjar, Jim Ward, Paul Hinojos
Producer | Ross Robinson
Label | Grand Royal
Album | *Relationship of Command* (2000)

"Omar and I would get ridiculed for playing Tom Waits and dub music in the tour bus."

Cedric Bixler-Zavala, 2004

◄ **Influenced by: Smallpox Champion** · Fugazi (1993)
► **Influence on: Bleed American** · Jimmy Eat World (2001)
● **Covered by:** Paramore (2007)
★ **Other key tracks:** Proxima Centauri (1999) Arcarsenal (2000) · Pattern Against User (2000)

Creative differences can often fuel bands' best work—and so it was with insurgent Texas punks At the Drive-In. With their breakthrough album *Relationship of Command,* a rift developed between the free-form, experimental instincts of singer Cedric Bixler-Zavala and guitarist Omar Rodriguez-Lopez, and the tight riffs and more traditional punk rock immediacy favored by guitarist Jim Ward.

Producer Ross Robinson harnessed this combustible energy and committed it to tape. On "One Armed Scissor," Bixler-Zavala delivered the tale of a space station in terminal free fall "hurtling back to Earth" that was a metaphor for the pressures the band had experienced on tour. Rodriguez-Lopez and Ward ricocheted breathlessly between the chorus's brilliantly blunt, high impact riff, and more atmospheric, ethereal, rhythmically complex verses.

Despite Robinson's involvement, At the Drive-In were no "nu-metal" Neanderthals: rather, they updated the righteous dynamics of Fugazi for the twenty-first century, while Bixler-Zavala and Rodriguez-Lopez's wild Afros won comparisons with the MC5.

A live performance of the song in 2000 for BBC TV's *Later . . . with Jools Holland* foreshadowed At the Drive-In's demise. With their equipment malfunctioning as the cameras rolled, Bixler-Zavala and Rodriguez-Lopez hurled themselves about the stage, embracing the chaos and creating an unforgettable TV moment, while Ward visibly fumed with frustration. A few months later, it was over. The Afro-sporting duo explored their experimental impulses with the polymorphous The Mars Volta. Ward, meanwhile, recorded three albums of polished emo-punk as Sparta. **SC**

At the Drive-In's Cedric Bixler-Zavala in one of the band's famously high-energy performances. ➡

Hate to Say I Told You So | The Hives (2000)

Writer | Randy Fitzsimmons, aka Niklas Almqvist,
aka Nicholaus Arson
Producer | Pelle Gunnerfeldt
Label | Burning Heart
Album | *Veni Vidi Vicious* (2000)

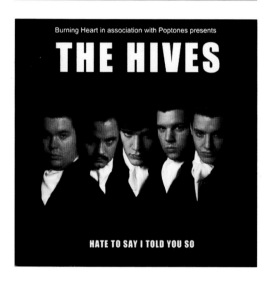

Burning Heart in association with Poptones presents

THE HIVES

HATE TO SAY I TOLD YOU SO

" 'Hate To Say I Told You So'
popular. Yes. Didn't think
people had such good taste."
Nicholaus Arson, 2004

◀ **Influenced by: All Day and All of the Night** · The
Kinks (1964)
▶ **Influence on: Cherry Cola** · Eagles of Death Metal
(2006)
● **Covered by:** Richard Cheese and Lounge Against the
Machine (2002)

There was nothing new about The Hives. But the
Swedish quintet's ballsy brio more than made
up for their originality deficit. Out front, Howlin'
Pelle Almqvist was a junior Jagger, yelping over
irresistible garage punk—influenced by The
Misfits, Elvis, Little Richard, The Saints, the Sex
Pistols, and AC/DC. (Almqvist and his brother
Niklas formed the band in 1993.) The band
members' immaculate black-and-white suits and
spats just added to the energizing effect.

Leading the charge was "Hate to Say I Told You
So"—its title borrowed from Sixties girl group The
Shangri-Las—but even that took time to become
an overnight sensation. Both it and the equally
magnificently manic "Main Offender" had been
ignored in major markets on their first fly-by, on
the band's second album, *Veni Vidi Vicious*.

Only later—in 2001, when the track kicked
off *Your New Favourite Band*, a compilation of the
many highlights from previous releases—did
"Hate to Say I Told You So" strike a scuzzy chord
on both sides of the Atlantic. It even wound up
on the 2002 *Spider-Man* soundtrack album, and
was parodied by "Weird Al" Yankovic (on "Angry
White Boy Polka") in 2003.

Stage shows were a blur of activity, but there
was craft with the chaos. When asked how tracks
such as "Hate to Say I Told You So" evolved,
guitarist Nicholaus Arson (whose alter ego was
Hives songwriter Randy Fitzsimmons) summed
it up as: "Rehearse / time / songs / pretty good /
better / very good / fucking excellent / amazing."

It was all carried off with utter conviction and a
knowing wink. "Sarcastic fun" was the description
preferred by Howlin' Pelle, who behaved like a rock
star and so became one. **CB**

Frontier Psychiatrist | The Avalanches (2000)

Writer | R. Chater, T. DiBlasi, D. Fabay, B. Kaempfert, G. McQuilten, H. Rehbein, D. Seltmann, C. Sigman
Producer | Robbie Chater, Darren Seltmann
Label | Modula
Album | *Since I Left You* (2001)

"Our record is . . . probably the most amazing thing to ever come out of Melbourne."
Darren Seltmann, 2001

◀ **Influenced by: Napalm Brain/Scatter Brain·** DJ Shadow (1996)
▶ **Influence on: Non-Stop Party Now** · Girl Talk (2003)
★ **Other key tracks:** Rock City (1997) · Since I Left You (2000) · A Different Feeling (2000) · Pablo's Cruise (2000) · Electricity (2000) · Avalanche Rock (2000)

With a handful of low-key releases behind them, The Avalanches broke out of Australia with the dizzying collage of *Since I Left You*—an eighteen-song, breakneck party patchwork of more than nine hundred samples.

What could have been a nauseous mess turned out to be a seamless mélange of obscure movie snippets, cheesy pop clips, and the first Madonna sample cleared for release. "Frontier Psychiatrist" was the album in microcosm—busy, daft, composed of countless unconnected parts, yet somehow entirely natural as a whole.

Those parts were typically eclectic. In *Since I Left You*'s dense list of credits, The Avalanches admitted to borrowing portions of Bert Kaempfert's 1968 song "(You Are) My Way of Life" (performed by The Enoch Light Singers).

While these orchestral fanfares fuel the track, the narrative drive comes from its snatches of comedy dialogue—some from the 1969 Disney movie *The Computer Wore Tennis Shoes*; others, written by John Robert Dobson, from Canadian duo Johnny Wayne and Frank Shuster's album *Frontier Psychiatrist*. "Dexter is criminally insane!" must have been a glorious find for a band boasting a member called Dexter Fabay.

The Avalanches attempted to take their concoctions on the road, leading to haphazard gigs where Robbie Chater managed to break both legs—mercifully on separate occasions. Chaos disguised the fact that "Frontier Psychiatrist" and its cousins only thrived on record, where Chater and his chums could painstakingly piece together their inspired sonic mish-mash. That a follow-up album has been little more than a rumor for the best part of a decade tells its own story. **MH**

One More Time | Daft Punk (2000)

Writer | Daft Punk, Anthony Moore
Producer | Daft Punk
Label | Virgin
Album | *Discovery* (2001)

"People are often afraid of things that sound new."

Thomas Bangalter, 2001

◄ **Influenced by: One More Time** • Third World (1985)
► **Influence on: One Mo' Gin** • Play-N-Skillz featuring Lil Jon, Bun B & Krayzie Bone (2008)
● **Covered by:** The Gossip (2008) • Starburkes & The Tea Leaf (2009) • Richard Grey (2009) • Marc Mysterio & Téo Moss (2009)

It's hard to imagine anyone hearing disco house stormer "One More Time" and not automatically tearing up the dance floor. Except, perhaps, hard-core Daft Punk fans who felt that the French duo had betrayed their roots by going for a more commercial sound—a perceived legacy of Thomas Bangalter's involvement with Stardust's "Music Sounds Better with You." Not that it bothered Bangalter: "We care less now than we used to about what critics say about our music . . ." he told *DJ Times*. "The healthy thing is that people either loved it or hated it."

Bangalter and his partner Guy-Manuel de Homem-Christo sampled horns and laid them over thumping bass and a compressed kick drum. With singer Romanthony's vocoder-laden vocals and joyous lyrics—"Music's got me feeling so free / We're gonna celebrate"—a classic was born.

Today you can barely move for R&B stars' auto-tuned vocals. At the turn of the century, it seemed more of a novelty—and not a universally popular one. "It reminds me of the late Seventies when musicians in France tried to ban the synthesizer . . ." Bangalter observed to *Remix*. "[Romanthony] loved it. He has done a lot of different things and he always tries to innovate, which is what we like to do on our records. He never had his voice treated like an instrument like that." (Romanthony's "unplugged" version appeared on *Daft Club*, which was released in 2003.)

Bangalter denied that the song featured any samples, and none are credited on the album sleeve, although it is believed to quote M Diggo's cover of "I Put a Spell on You" (1978), featuring Eddie Johns. But whatever its ingredients, the result was delicious. **OM**

Stan | Eminem featuring Dido (2000)

Writer | Eminem, Dido, Paul Herman
Producer | Mark "The 45 King" James, Eminem
Label | Aftermath
Album | *The Marshall Mathers LP* (2000)

"It says so much in this mad little story."

Dido, 2003

◄ **Influenced by:** Thank You · Dido (1999)
► **Influence on:** U Didn't Care · Canibus (2001)
● **Covered by:** Eminem featuring Elton John (2005)
★ **Other key tracks:** My Name Is (1999) · The Way I Am (2000) · The Real Slim Shady (2000) · Kim (2000) Marshall Mathers (2000) · Under the Influence (2000)

"I got sent the tape, and I just thought it was brilliant," gushed Dido upon the release of the controversial Eminem song that sent her low-key career stratospheric. She owed her gratitude to producer Mark "The 45 King" James, who picked her two-year-old ballad—the appropriately titled "Thank You"—for "Stan," Eminem's cautionary tale of an obsessed fan who kills himself after writing to his idol and not hearing back. "It reminded me of a country song," she told *Word*, "'cos his lyrics tell a story from beginning to end."

The British singer-songwriter played Stan's doomed, pregnant wife in the accompanying video and performed with Eminem in concert and on *Saturday Night Live*. Her previously dormant 1999 album, *No Angel*, promptly ascended to multiplatinum status.

Hip-hop's golden boy Eminem was already basking in the international success of his own 1999 debut, *The Slim Shady LP*, which won a Grammy Award for Best Rap Album. His clever, venomous raps had earned him a cartoonish reputation—but, for fans and critics alike, "Stan" raised the bar. Showcasing masterful storytelling and technical brilliance rather than shock value, it became the jewel in the crown of his Grammy-winning *The Marshall Mathers LP*. "It kinda shows the real side of me," he told *Rolling Stone*.

"Thank You" was revived again in 2006, on Snoop Dogg's "Round Here." Then, in 2008, producer Swizz Beatz claimed he was working on a "totally genius" sequel to "Stan." Eminem was quick to shut that down: "There isn't a 'Stan Two' and there won't be," he told *Billboard*. "Stan drove his car off a bridge and I'm not writing a song as Stan's ghost. That would just be really corny." **EP**

Oh My Sweet Carolina | Ryan Adams feat. Emmylou Harris (2000)

Writer | Ryan Adams
Producer | Ethan Johns
Label | Bloodshot
Album | *Heartbreaker* (2000)

The standout track on Ryan Adams's solo debut was written in a moment of genuine desperation. The singer had split from his long-term girlfriend; Whiskeytown, the punk-country band he fronted for five years, had broken up; and he could barely afford the rent on his New York City apartment. And so, sitting in a Manhattan dive bar, Adams started to write this homesick song.

Like other great traveling numbers, it opens with the singer leaving his Southern home in an attempt to "find me something / But I wasn't sure just what." He skips from city to city, never filling the void in his soul. Only when he loses everything does he realize that the key to his happiness may lie back with friends and family in North Carolina. The track ends with the longing "Oh my sweet disposition / May you one day carry me home."

Silky, somber backing vocals by Emmylou Harris heighten the melancholy. "Emmy was an icon to me . . ." he told writer Barney Hoskyns. "I had put a lotta time into listening to her. . . . I'd almost *studied* those records."

Producer Ethan Johns kept things simple on *Heartbreaker*. Minimal guitar, a few piano chords, and gentle drums perfectly captured the yearning at the song's core. Adams likes to play up his punk credentials, but his finest five minutes ended up winning over a more mature fan—Elton John, who has covered the song in concert. **TB**

Fuck the Pain Away Peaches (2000)

Writer | Merrill Nisker
Producer | Merrill Nisker
Label | Kitty-Yo
Album | *The Teaches of Peaches* (2000)

Since Peaches's turn-of-the-millennium debut, the Canadian-born, Berlin-dwelling Merrill Nisker has shocked and delighted audiences in equal measure with her Groovebox beats, throbbing bass lines, raunchy shows, and penchant for profanity. "I make hip-hop, rock, kind of electro music, so my music is centered around good-time stuff," said the one-woman band. "But if you sing along, after a while you'll realize it, like 'Wait a minute, what am I singing along with?'"

Her breakthrough single is the perfect example of the former drama teacher's ability to sugarcoat her subversive message. "The music must first be good," she told *Billboard*. "Then I can offend, make people think and make them dance." She defends her expletive-laden directness: "Artists like Busta Rhymes and 50 Cent get away with so much more lyrically, without being questioned. But, because I'm a woman, there's that double standard."

The song has made odd inroads into the mainstream. It featured in the movies *Lost in Translation, My Little Eye*, and *Jackass Number Two*, and has been covered in concert by Of Montreal.

Challenging the glossy sexuality pedaled by the likes of Britney and Christina, Nisker sported full body hair with her skimpy stagewear. "It's so dull, this idea that sexy is blonde hair and big tits," she reasoned in the *Observer*. "Everyone is sexual. . . . I'm just saying, 'Find your own, it's okay.'" **EP**

Merrill Nisker, aka Peaches; sex and gender issues are thoroughly aired. ➔

Feel Good Hit of the Summer | Queens of the Stone Age (2000)

Writer | Josh Homme, Nick Oliveri
Producer | Queens of the Stone Age
Label | Interscope
Album | *[Rated] R* (2000)

"I guess we take more drugs than Hanson!"

Josh Homme, 2002

◄ **Influenced by: Apathy** · Subhumans (1985)
► **Influence on: Feel Good Hit of the Summer Part 2**
Atmosphere (2009)
● **Covered by:** Yourcodenameis: Milo (2007)
★ **Other key track:** Regular John (1998) · Avon (1998)
Monsters in the Parasol (2000)

Rarely does a rock song with only eight words make the charts—much less one that sounds like a shopping list for Seventies-era Aerosmith.

"Feel Good Hit of the Summer"—with its oft repeated "Nicotine, Valium, Vicodin, marijuana, ecstasy, and alcohol . . . c-c-c-c-c-cocaine!"—was almost banned from *[Rated] R* by U.S. record executives (only the absence of references to anyone actually taking these substances changed their minds). Indeed, the album's age restriction-aping title had been inspired by it. "We knew we'd get grief from the censors for that lyric," singer/guitarist Josh Homme told the *Guardian*, "so we just thought that we'd beat them to it."

[Rated] R was the successful follow-up to Queens of the Stone Age's 1998 self-titled debut. It launched their brand of "Palm Desert" rock into the mainstream, particularly in Europe where they enjoyed a heartier welcome than at home in America. "Feel Good Hit" seemed to echo Homme and his partner-in-crime Nick Oliveri's roots in the stoner rock group Kyuss—but QotSA were endeavoring to chisel their own niche. "It has taken me years," Homme remarked, "to really develop something that does sound different."

With backing vocals from Judas Priest metal god Rob Halford, the track announced itself with grinding bass reminiscent of dirty old Motörhead. Indeed, QotSA were garnering a good time reputation reminiscent of Motörhead main man Lemmy. "I'm an equal opportunity everything person," Homme said of his inspiration. "That whole list is the drug of my choice." However, he remarked, "People might perceive us as a bunch of drug-pumped loonies, but making music is like poetry or art to us." **SO**

Ms. Jackson | OutKast (2000)

Writer | OutKast, David "Mr. DJ" Sheats
Producer | Earthtone III
Label | LaFace
Album | *Stankonia* (2000)

"My mom just laughs about 'Ms. Jackson.' She and Dré are really pretty cool—they talk."

Erykah Badu, 2001

◀ **Influenced by: Strawberry Letter #23** • The Brothers Johnson (1977)
▶ **Influence on: Ms. Jackson** • Styles P featuring Jadakiss (2007)
● **Covered by:** The Vines (2002)

OutKast were a multiplatinum force to be reckoned with when rappers Antwan "Big Boi" Patton and "André 3000" Benjamin entered the studio in 1999 to record their fourth album. There was, however, room for growth—the Atlantans hadn't scored a huge single or broken big abroad.

Those items were dramatically crossed off the list with *Stankonia*. The album's blend of funk, jazz, and hard rock was simultaneously experimental and radio friendly. Its first single—the blistering "B.O.B."—performed disappointingly; but the second—"an acoustic song that started on guitar and then became what it is now," Benjamin told *Remix*—took OutKast to superstardom.

Aside from a wry interlude by Big Boi, "Ms. Jackson" was curiously remorseful—addressing, from a father's perspective, raising a child in a broken home. The R&B-infused track was heartfelt—the child in question was the son Benjamin had with neo-soul superstar Erykah Badu. "He wanted to give the world something to think about," remarked Badu, whose own verdict on the relationship was the epic "Green Eyes" on the *Mama's Gun* album (2000).

But "Ms. Jackson" wasn't directed at Badu. Opening with "This one right here goes out to all the babies' mamas' mamas," Benjamin used the lyrics as an open letter of apology to Badu's mother. In a metaphor that extended to the cinematic video, he sang, "You can plan a pretty picnic / But you can't predict the weather."

"Ms. Jackson" was a No. 1 smash in the United States and popularized the band abroad, hitting No. 2 in the United Kingdom and Australia. "We are very proud of him, my whole family . . ." Badu told *Jet*. "He is a really good person." **JiH**

Romeo | Basement Jaxx (2001)

Writer | Felix Buxton, Simon Ratcliffe
Producer | Felix Buxton, Simon Ratcliffe
Label | XL
Album | *Rooty (2001)*

"We found out Yoko was a fan of Basement Jaxx. She liked 'Romeo'... that was quite exciting."

Simon Ratcliffe, 2009

◀ **Influenced by: Runaway** · Nuyorican Soul (1996)
▶ **Influence on: Needy Girl** · Chromeo (2004)
● **Covered by:** Basement Jaxx (2001)
★ **Other key tracks:** Red Alert (1999) · Where's Your Head At? (2001) · Do Your Thing (2001) · Jus 1 Kiss (2001) · Good Luck (2003) · Oh My Gosh (2005)

"Cuz you see, my dear, I have had enough / Of keeping quiet about all this stuff / You're neurotic like a yo-yo / You used to be my Romeo . . ." A lament by a neglected lover who is finally standing up for herself evokes memories of disco classics like Gloria Gaynor's "I Will Survive" and the Barbra Streisand–Donna Summer diva-fest "No More Tears (Enough Is Enough)." But Basement Jaxx put a fresh spin on the theme, conjuring one of their most delightful hits in the process.

The U.K. house duo's "Romeo" is a luscious, bhangra-tinged party song. The vocals of guest Kele Le Roc—attitude-laden one minute, sweetly plaintive the next—match the song's spiky lyrics, while Corryne Dwyer's chanted backing vocals add to its infectious joyfulness.

DJs Simon Ratcliffe and Felix Buxton started Basement Jaxx after the success of their south London club night, Rooty, in the early Nineties. Their second, highly successful album—released in 2001 and from which "Romeo" was the first of four hits—was named after that club.

The song's superb video paid homage to Bollywood, with mass dancing, handsome men fighting over a beautiful heroine, a riot of colors, and, of course, tears too. It suited the party vibe, as—like many Basement Jaxx songs—"Romeo" has an unashamed pop element.

The strength of the song was proved when it reappeared on the B-side of another *Rooty* single, "Where's Your Head At." A gorgeous, bossa-nova-style version of "Romeo" let its true beauty out. This can be found on the bonus CD with the hits set *The Singles* (released in 2005), which also boasts a 2 Many DJs mash-up of "Romeo" with The Clash's classic "The Magnificent Seven." **OM**

Can't Get You Out of My Head | Kylie Minogue (2001)

Writer | Cathy Dennis, Rob Davis
Producer | Cathy Dennis, Rob Davis
Label | Parlophone
Album | *Fever* (2001)

"It's like, on the arcade game, I've gone up to the next level. I'm clinging on, trying to stay sane."

Kylie Minogue, 2002

◀ **Influenced by: Can't Get It Out of My Head** · Electric Light Orchestra (1974)
▶ **Influence on: Can't Get Blue Monday Out of My Head** · Kylie Minogue vs. New Order (2002)
● **Covered by:** The Flaming Lips (2002) · Jack L (2003) Carmen Consoli (2003)

Called simply the "la la la" song by Kylie Minogue herself, "Can't Get You Out of My Head" was the hypnotic anthem that turned the Australian pop princess into a bona fide music icon. Selling over four million copies and topping the charts in every European country bar Finland, it was, Minogue's manager Terry Blamey told *Music Week*, "one of those songs where just everything came together—the video, the imagery, and the song."

"The moment Kylie and I heard the demo, we knew how strong it was," Blamey recalled—a reaction not shared by British singers Jimmy Somerville and Sophie Ellis-Bextor, both of whom turned it down. Penned by solo artist turned songwriter Cathy Dennis and former Mud guitarist Rob Davis, the song's infectious hooks were the ideal match for Minogue's sex-kitten delivery.

"You've got the Kraftwerk beat, you've got echoes of Motown," noted former EMI boss Tony Wadsworth. "It's just a classic-sounding record that probably could have been made ten years before or could be listened to in ten years' time and still sound fresh."

The futuristic video was as captivating as the song, Minogue's white jumpsuit gaping precariously as she performed a beguiling, robotic dance. The clip scooped an MTV award—and, in the United States, which had spent a decade resisting Minogue's charms, pushed the single into the Top Ten and its parent album to platinum.

After winning three Ivor Novello awards in 2002 and cementing Kylie Minogue's transition from kitsch to cool, co-writer Cathy Dennis was inundated with telephone calls. "It's mainly, 'Can you write me a hit like that one?'" she told the *Guardian*. "The answer is usually 'No.'" **EP**

Vuelvo al sur
Gotan Project (2001)

Writer | A. Piazzolla, F. E. Solanas
Producer | P. C. Solal, C. H. Müller, E. Makaroff
Label | ¡Ya Basta!
Album | *La revancha del tango* (2001)

"Vuelvo al sur" was one side of the debut single by the innovative, Paris-based Gotan Project, who propelled Argentinean tango into the twenty-first century. Their debut album, *La revancha del tango*, shifted over a million copies, drawing a new, youthful audience to the music.

The simple guitar arpeggio by Eduardo Makaroff emphasizes that "Vuelvo al sur" is a *milonga*—a precursor to the tango. Another key element is Nini Flores's melancholic *bandoneón*—a giant concertina. The acoustic percussion shows the influence of Argentinean folklorist Domingo Cura, but programmed beats lend a contemporary feel. Halfway through, sultry Catalonian singer Cristina Villalonga materializes.

The title translates as "I return to the South." It is unclear whether lyricist Fernando E. Solanas was talking about Argentina in general, or "Sur"—the south side of Buenos Aires, and its spiritual and cultural epicenter. Or he might also have been referring to co-writer Astor Piazzolla's fractious relationship with the country.

Either way, there's a strong "bringing it all back home" theme to Gotan Project's work. As Makaroff observed before a 2005 concert in Buenos Aires: "The lyrics of many of the famous tango songwriters would always talk about going back to this city, and so we're returning to the South and to the place that's in our hearts." **JLu**

Clandestino
Manu Chao (2001)

Writer | Manu Chao
Producer | Manu Chao, Renaud Letang
Label | Virgin France
Album | *Clandestino* (1998)

Paris born, Barcelona based, and a true citizen of the world, José Manuel Thomas Arthur (Manu) Chao is a superstar across much of Europe and Latin America. For many followers, this imp is an iconic figure, railing against the ills of globalization and governmental abuse.

Chao's rise to stardom began with the pioneering Mano Negra. Often described as "the French Clash," they blended punk energy with Latin flavors. When an anarchic tour of Colombia finished them off in the mid-Nineties, prolonged travel saw Chao in Brazil, Peru, Chile, North Africa, Senegal, and Mali. Recordings made on a portable eight track—released as *Clandestino*—proved that working outside the confines of a group had been liberating. The songs demonstrated his maturing writing, as he blended reggae, rumba, and African flavors into brilliant, Latin rock 'n' roll.

Chao's songs concern love, sun, marijuana, and—on his anthem—the suffering of "*clandestinos*" (illegal immigrants). "I wrote it about the border between Europe and those coming from poorer nations," he told the *Guardian* in 2007. "It's a decade since I wrote it, and things have gotten worse."

Initially an underground hit, *Clandestino* went on to sell over five million copies. Chao escaped celebrity by returning to travel. "I have what the Spanish call 'a worried ass,'" he explained. "I literally cannot stay in one place too long." **GC**

Manu Chao's internationalism extends to singing in many languages, often in the same song. ➡

Iag bari
Fanfare Ciocărlia (2001)

Writer | Henry Ernst
Producer | Henry Ernst, Helmut Neumann
Label | Piranha
Album | *Iag bari* (2001)

Romanian Gypsy band Fanfare Ciocărlia seemingly arose from nowhere in 1996 to storm the world with their gonzo sound: Balkan brass. Brass bands have existed in the Balkans since Ottoman times and the Gypsies have reshaped them into outfits that play ferocious party music with Asian flavors.

Fanfare Ciocărlia create whiplash fast, rock hard Balkan funk. Surprisingly, none were professional musicians. All farmers and local factory workers, they played at weddings and parties but were unknown beyond the local region. Then German sound engineer Henry Ernst arrived. He loved Romania's Gypsy music and was looking for something special. In Fanfare Ciocărlia he found it.

Ernst took the group to Germany, where they wrecked audiences. Playing up to two hundred beats per minute on battered brass instruments, Fanfare Ciocărlia created a wild, roaring sound. Their furious groove got dance floors heaving and helped festivals lift off. Fanfare Ciocărlia became stars, and many of their songs have been remixed by DJs trying to reinvent the raw Balkan groove.

"Iag bari" (which translates as "the big longing"), the title track of their third album, recorded in Bucharest, showcases Dan Armeanca, a celebrated Gypsy musician from Bucharest. He joined the band because he loved their forceful sound. The band's pumping groove makes this one of their most popular tunes. **GC**

Oiça lá ó Senhor Vinho
Mariza (2001)

Writer | Alberto Janes
Producer | Jorge Fernando
Label | World Connection
Album | *Fado em mim* (2001)

Showing that binge drinking isn't solely a British phenomenon, "Oiça lá ó Senhor Vinho" ("Hey listen, Mr. Wine") is a cautionary tale from Europe on the demon drink. "I heard it once because I was working in a fado house called Senhor Vinho," Mariza recalled. "It was a nice combination: working [there] and singing a song about wine."

Ever since the Portuguese singer recorded it for her debut album, the song's upbeat, festive tone has made it a favorite at her concerts. But, unlike most of her material, it isn't part of the urban folk tradition of fado. "Oiça lá ó Senhor Vinho" is actually a *malhão*, a dance from the far north of Portugal. The song opens with the thumping sound of the *adufe* drum, typical of the traditional music of Beira Baixa, east of Lisbon.

This—and other songs in Mariza's early repertoire—got her typecast as heir to the crown of the late, great Amália Rodrigues, who popularized it as the title track of a 1971 album. Tiring of the straightjacket of fado, Rodrigues had recorded her first album of Portuguese folk music.

Rodrigues's version has no percussion, is more rhythmically square, and seems to have a whiff of the *saudade* ("longing") that is typical of fado—and maybe even a hint of a hangover. Mariza's has a distinctly African swing that hints at her mixed Mozambican/Portuguese heritage. Both are highly recommended. **JLu**

You and Whose Army?
Radiohead (2001)

Writer | Radiohead
Producer | Nigel Godrich, Radiohead
Label | Parlophone
Album | *Amnesiac* (2001)

This troubling track started off as a way for Radiohead front man Thom Yorke to deal with voices in his head that were, he told *Mojo,* "driving me round the bend." But the singer soon found a different focus. In his crosshairs was Britain's then prime minister, Tony Blair. "Once I came up with that 'You and Whose Army' phrase," Yorke recalled, "I was able to stick other ideas on there and Blair emerged as the song's real subject matter. The song's ultimately about someone who is elected [by the people] . . . then blatantly betrays them."

Yorke explained that both the song's parent album, *Amnesiac,* and its predecessor from 2000, *Kid A,* were influenced by a book he was reading on the studio innovations of The Beatles and their producer George Martin. Yorke and Jonny Greenwood duly envisaged something "kind of Ink Spots-esque" for the "You and Whose Army" vocals.

With admirable throwback innovation, Yorke's voice was fed through—of all things—an eggbox positioned near his microphone. When his narcoleptic vocal was further treated with a device called a Palm Speaker, it created a low-key but unnervingly threatening projection of finger-pointing lines about "you and your cronies." It all seemed like less of an angry plea to the powers-that-be to stop, and more of a resigned warning that their actions would have consequences. But it was all an admirably long way from "Creep." **CB**

Romando y tomando
Lupillo Rivera (2001)

Writer | Martin Ruvalcaba
Producer | Pedro Rivera
Label | Sony
Album | *Despreciado* (2001)

The biggest contemporary star yet to arise from the Mexican-American populace of the United States, Lupillo Rivera was born in La Barca, Mexico, and grew up in Los Angeles. His father, Pedro, was a well-known *corrido* singer who founded the label Cintas Acuario to promote himself and fellow *corrido* singers. The label scored its greatest success with Chalino's narco-corrido anthems—until that singer's murder. Pedro then encouraged his son Lupillo and daughter Jenni to record narco-corridos. They mixed an urban LA flavor into their sound while singing about dealing kilos, living fast, and dying young.

Lupillo has gone on to enjoy huge success across the American Southwest and into Mexico. His fierce image plays up the image of a Mexican drug baron, while his good looks and ability to sing a *ranchera* ballad wins over female fans. On the cover of his best album, *Despreciado*, Lupillo stands dressed in black, Stetson in hand, in front of an expensive late-model car. He is backed by a banda brass band, who blow a weird Mexican funk descended from Austrian military marching bands and village brass bands—music reinvented by *campesinos* (Mexican peasants) as party music. Lupillo's fame has made him a controversial figure and in 2007 his SUV was peppered with machine gun fire as he left a Guadalajara restaurant. Fortunately, he survived to sing about it. **GC**

New York City Cops
The Strokes (2001)

Writer | Julian Casablancas
Producer | Gordon Raphael
Label | Rough Trade
Album | *Is This It?*
(2001)

"What I heard in The Strokes," declared Rough Trade boss Geoff Travis, "was . . . the songwriting skills of a first-rate writer and music that is a distillation of primal rock 'n' roll, mixed with the sophistication of today's society." The band's debut album duly laid waste to a scene dominated by cheesy pop and the post-grunge fallout.

"New York City Cops" was a prime example of their Stooges influence (though the only band that all five Strokes agreed on was The Velvet Underground). But the song was deemed insensitive in the wake of 9/11 and dropped from the U.S. release in favor of "When It Began."

Producer Gordon Raphael recalled "the emotional decision" of taking it off, "in solidarity to the cops and firemen. I will never forget that meeting—in a shell-shocked New York no one had ever experienced—though musically the album is not as holistically powerful as the U.K. version." It remains on international releases, with cheeky cover art depicting a pert bottom and gloved hand, redolent of Spinal Tap's *Smell the Glove*.

The song, reported Raphael, "was recorded live except for the vocals"—immediacy that made it a live staple. An incendiary performance at New York's Radio City Music Hall in 2002 featured the White Stripes' Jack White on guitar. It culminated in the boys receiving hugs from Stripes drummer Meg White—a sweet act of solidarity. **SS**

Fell in Love with a Girl
The White Stripes (2001)

Writer | Jack White
Producer | Jack White
Label | Sympathy for the Record Industry
Album | *White Blood Cells* (2001)

Lego must be kicking themselves. The Danish company declined a request from yet-to-be-famous musician Jack White to package mini sets of their toys with his band's single, "Fell in Love with a Girl." Nonetheless, the video featured Lego versions of Jack and his partner Meg thrashing their instruments. "When someone brings a Lego sculpture of your head to dinner and says, 'This is what the video's going to be,'" Jack observed, "you pretty much say, 'That's it, go ahead.'" The result was brilliantly distinctive, earning three awards from MTV and plaudits from TV show *Family Guy*.

But while the visuals were gimmicky, the band's punky homage to matters of the heart was the real deal. From its opening punches, this garage powerhouse doesn't stick around a moment longer than necessary. "We completely avoided the blues on *White Blood Cells* on purpose," Jack recalled. "The thinking was, 'What can we do if we completely ignore what we love the most?'" The mysterious Meg's hyperactive drumming and Jack's rasping guitar, accompanied by his swaggering howls, were rambunctious and purposeful. The band even got within touching distance of pop, with irresistible "ah ahs" in the frenzied chorus.

With this lean hunk of rock, the duo proved that their charmingly simplistic formula was a force to be reckoned with. **KBo**

Get Ur Freak On | Missy Elliott (2001)

Writer | Missy "Misdemeanor" Elliott, Timothy "Timbaland" Mosley
Producer | Timbaland, Missy Elliott
Label | Elektra
Album | *Miss E... So Addictive* (2001)

MISSY "MISDEMEANOR" ELLIOTT
GET UR FREAK ON

"It could be about dancing, the bedroom—whatever. ... Get your freak on!"

Missy Elliott, 2007

Influenced by: Naag Wang • Jazzy B (1994)
Influence on: Love Will Freak Us • Dsico (2002)
Covered by: KT Tunstall (2005) • Eels (2008)
Other key tracks: The Rain (Supa Dupa Fly) (1997)
Beep Me 911 (1997) • One Minute Man (2001) • Work It
(2002) • Teary Eyed (2005)

"When me and Tim get together, we go to Saturn," Missy Elliott told *Slate* of her innovative, long-time production partnership with Timothy "Timbaland" Mosley. Their sound was never more otherworldly than on the groundbreaking "Get Ur Freak On." Elliott's jolting, boastful rap over Timbaland's aggressive bhangra beat shook the hip-hop scene into a new era of experimentation.

"Tim was playing some new stuff one day," Elliott told *Blender*. "He'd picked up all kinds of music while traveling—and overseas they have the hot, different flavor." "That beat took me ten minutes," Timbaland added. "And Missy did her part just as fast."

This space-age hybrid won Elliott a 2002 Grammy for Best Rap Solo Performance. A remix with vocals from Nelly Furtado appeared on the *Lara Croft: Tomb Raider* (2001) movie soundtrack and became a dance floor staple that year.

The *Lara Croft: Tomb Raider* association is complemented by Elliott's video's dark jungle setting and camouflage-clad, CGI-enhanced dance sequences. There is no shortage of star turns from the hip-hop community—look out for enthusiastic cameos from Nate Dogg, Eve, LL Cool J, Ludacris, Master P, Busta Rhymes, Ja Rule, Timbaland, and Nicole Wray.

"I don't really try to figure out the difference between what y'all call bhangra or ragas or whatever," Timbaland told the *New York Times*. But his genre-defying exoticism triggered a landslide of reinterpretation, from Jay-Z's "Beware of the Boys" to Truth Hurts' "Addictive." "I didn't want to make an album that was just in a category of hip-hop or R&B or mainstream," Elliott declared. "I wanted to make an album for everybody." **EP**

21 Seconds | So Solid Crew (2001)

Writer | Aminu, Dawkins, Harvey, Maffia, Moore, Neil, Phillips, Vincent, Walters, Weir, Williams
Producer | Mahtari "Synth" Aminu
Label | Relentless
Album | *They Don't Know* (2001)

"Creativity like that only happens once in a blue moon."
Megaman, 2010

◀ **Influenced by: Da Mystery of Chessboxin** • Wu-Tang Clan (1993)
▶ **Influence on: Pow! (Forward)** • Lethal Bizzle (2004)
● **Covered by:** Ambulance (2002)
★ **Other key tracks:** Haters (2001) • Way Back When (2001) • Solid Soul (2001) • Broken Silence (2003)

Five minutes, divided by ten vocalists, equals twenty-one seconds, give or take an intro and outro. That was the concept behind So Solid Crew's ticking time bomb breakthrough single: each MC or singer had twenty-one seconds to showcase their talents. "It's not about seeing how many times any one individual can get their face on TV," MC Harvey told the *Daily Telegraph*. "It's about everyone getting their chance."

Previously, party raps or soulful vocals typified Britain's garage scene. But then So Solid Crew hit. Boasting around thirty members from rough London housing estates, the collective made songs more inspired by gangsta rap, dealing with issues in their neighborhoods. "A lot of artists," complained bandleader Megaman, "have lost the plot in the gap between how the music sounds in the underground and how it gets released to the mainstream. And that's what we want to cut out: we want to cut out *changing* it."

Helped by a glossy video that belied the crew's independent status—but won Best British Video at the 2002 Brit Awards—"21 Seconds" smashed into the U.K. singles chart at No. 1. "We didn't get lucky," Asher D explained to the *Guardian*. "We had a talent and we put ourselves in the position where we [could] excel—fast."

Despite this explosive success, So Solid Crew's fame descended into notoriety. In the same year as they topped the charts and won awards for "21 Seconds," Scat D was arrested for breaking a girl's jaw, two people were shot at one of their shows, and Asher D was arrested for firearms possession. "We took everything in one go," Megaman declared, "and, when we was finished with the industry, it felt abused." **DC**

Stay Together for the Kids | Blink-182 (2001)

Writer | Tom DeLonge, Mark Hoppus, Travis Barker
Producer | Jerry Finn
Label | MCA
Album | *Take Off Your Pants and Jacket* (2001)

Stay Together For The Kids

"Is this a damaged generation? Yeah, I'd say so."

Tom DeLonge, 2002

Influenced by: Who's Gonna Ride Your Wild Horses • U2 (1991)
Influence on: Emergency • Paramore (2005)
Covered by: Madelyn (2007)
Other key tracks: First Date (2001) • The Rock Show (2001) • Give Me One Good Reason (2001)

"We get e-mails about 'Stay Together,'" Blink-182 guitarist and singer Tom DeLonge told *Blender*. "Kid after kid after kid saying, 'I know exactly what you're talking about! That song is about my life!' And you know what? That sucks."

Originally dismissed as Green Day wannabes, Blink-182 had, by 2001, become multiplatinum contenders. But much of their success was built on a goofy image and bouncy hits. A bleakly powerful song on their 2001 album, therefore, surprised all but the most attentive fans.

DeLonge conceived "Stay Together for the Kids" as a teenager, when scrape marks across the family driveway provided an inescapable clue to his parents' disintegrating marriage: "I knew my dad had dragged out his furniture single-handedly. That's the first image that went through my head. It was a horrible thing."

Previously best known for running naked down Los Angeles streets for a video, Blink-182 provided grittier visuals for this song: a wrecking ball swinging through a ruined home. A first version was made on September 10, 2001—but the events of the following day obliged them to reshoot the destruction, to make it less reminiscent of that witnessed by millions on television.

Blink's next, self-titled album in 2003 ramped up the seriousness, creating a masterpiece comparable to Green Day's *American Idiot*. Yet sales declined and inter-band relationships deteriorated to divorce-like levels. "When we wanted to go out and do something more serious," rued DeLonge, "there were problems. I wish we had thought about it a little bit earlier—we really played that 'we don't fucking care' card for so long that it became a trap." **BM**

Schism | Tool (2001)

Writer | Danny Carey, Justin Chancellor, Maynard James Keenan, Adam Jones
Producer | David Bottrill, Tool
Label | Volcano
Album | *Lateralus* (2001)

"I definitely feel like we're still underground."

Justin Chancellor, 2001

◀ **Influenced by: Larks' Tongues in Aspic** · King Crimson (1973)
▶ **Influence on: Question!** · System of a Down (2005)
● **Covered by:** The String Tribute to Tool (2001)
★ **Other key tracks:** Sober (1993) · Intolerance (1993) Ænema (1996) · Parabola (2001) · Lateralus (2001)

Despite their unwieldy, prog-inspired sound and aggressively anti-star mentality, Tool rose to the top of the alt-rock/metal heap with *Ænima* in 1996—at which point vocalist Maynard James Keenan opted not to undertake a follow-up but to focus on his side project, A Perfect Circle.

Waiting for Keenan (and for legal issues to be sorted), the band laid the groundwork for their greatest achievement, *Lateralus*. The album was hypnotic from start to finish, fusing the best of prog with the heartiest of metal—yet one track stood out. Dark, menacing, and resoundingly epic, "Schism" encapsulated much that fans loved about the band—jarring lyrics, brooding vocals, and complex rhythm work. Long known for roller-coaster arrangements, Tool made "Schism" a showcase for complicated meter changes. (Forty-seven, calculated one fan.)

The characteristically oblique words refer to the band's disquiet at Keenan's involvement with A Perfect Circle. "It came out a month before September 11," the singer told *Revolver*, "and the second verse says, 'I know the pieces fit / 'cause I watched them tumble down / No fault, no one to blame / It doesn't mean I don't desire to / Point the finger, blame the other, watch the temple topple over / To bring the pieces back together, rediscover communication.' When Tool was on the brink of breaking up, it was our ability to communicate with each other that saved us."

Lateralus debuted atop *Billboard*'s album chart, on its way to double platinum sales in the United States. "Schism," meanwhile, extended the Tool Army's ranks, eventually swallowing enough Grammy voters to secure the song the Best Metal Performance trophy in 2002. **JiH**

Rock Star
N*E*R*D (2001)

Writer | Pharrell Williams, Chad Hugo
Producer | The Neptunes
Label | Virgin
Album | *In Search of . . .* (2002)

After the Neptunes gained major buzz for their funky, idiosyncratic sound—producing hits for acts as diverse as Ol' Dirty Bastard and Britney Spears—it was no surprise that Pharrell Williams and Chad Hugo wanted to get out of the kitchen and serve themselves a slice of the spotlight.

Teaming up with childhood pal Shay Haley, they formed N*E*R*D. "We wanted to put an identity—actual perspectives—out, versus just coloring other people's perspectives," Williams told the *Dallas Observer*. This high-minded mission led them to scrap the 2001 version of *In Search of . . .*.

The re-recording, released in March 2002, featured live instruments, courtesy of Minneapolis rockers Spymob. The standout single, "Rock Star," was a potent pastiche of puffed-up rap-rock, with Williams's ferocious falsetto signaling a genre-bending statement of intent. The aggressive arrangement appealed to beat junkies who wouldn't be caught dead listening to Limp Bizkit.

"'Rock Star' is about power," Williams remarked to *Rolling Stone*. "In rap music, there's a lot of songs about fakes and wannabes, but there's not a lot of those songs in rock."

"We're all about bringing the rock and rap worlds together," Shay Haley told the *Minneapolis Star Tribune*. "And the jazz and the R&B worlds, and the soul and the country worlds. Whatever it is, you know, N*E*R*D plays it." **EP**

Fallin'
Alicia Keys (2001)

Writer | Alicia Keys
Producer | Alicia Keys
Label | J
Album | *Songs in A Minor* (2001)

Alicia Keys's early demos provoked a bidding war between record labels. The victors, Columbia, saw her as the latest in a lineage of pretty R&B singers, happy to sing others' songs while pouting seductively in music videos. But this graduate of New York's School for the Performing Arts—a brilliant pianist with a voice to match—wanted to sing her own songs.

Keys wrote "Fallin'" during her Columbia doldrums, and it was the source of much of her unhappiness there: label bosses refused to allow her to release the ballad, trying instead to give it to another artist, a move Keys successfully fought. Industry legend Clive Davis presciently saw Keys's true potential, signed her to his J Records in 2000, and encouraged her to spread her wings.

A slow-burning ballad with the passion of a gospel hymn, "Fallin'" described a turbulent relationship. "I was going through it bad," Keys recalled, "but [the song] helped me work things out." It wasn't an obvious hit, but Keys had an unlikely champion waiting in the wings.

At Clive Davis's behest, TV legend Oprah Winfrey invited Keys to perform on her chat show. The host's vast audience swiftly sent "Fallin'" to the top of the *Billboard* chart, where it stayed for six weeks—kick-starting the career of an artist too smart to shake her booty on camera, and too talented not to succeed on her own terms. **SC**

Alicia Keys captivates a hometown crowd at the Beacon Theatre in New York in 2001. ➜

More Than a Woman
Aaliyah (2001)

Writer | Timothy "Timbaland" Mosley,
Steve "Static" Garrett
Producer | Timbaland
Label | Blackground
Album | *Aaliyah* (2001)

No relation to the Bee Gees' 1977 classic of the same name, "More Than a Woman" was a captivating statement of intent that defined a promising career cut tragically short. At just twenty-two, singer and budding actress Aaliyah was killed in a plane crash in the Bahamas on August 25, 2001, two weeks after completing work on the "More Than a Woman" video.

Released after her death, "More Than a Woman" became Aaliyah's only U.K. No. 1 and remained in the *Billboard* Hot 100 for twenty-four weeks. The exotic instrumentation—a hypnotic bass line and swirling digital strings—borrows heavily from the track "Alouli Ansa," as recorded by Syrian diva Mayada El Henawy.

"I'm an adult now and I wanted that to show through on the album," she declared. "So, my writers and I, we talk. They ask me how I'm feeling, just as a person, at this point in my life." Singing Steve "Static" Garrett's hot and heavy lyrics, Aaliyah's beguiling restraint demonstrated a left-field approach that set her apart from R&B contemporaries such as Brandy and Monica.

Describing her working relationship with producer and mentor Timbaland on BET's *106 & Park*, she talked up their creative match: "It really is magic. . . . When we go in the studio, he's playing the track, I'm telling him what I'm feeling and it just evolves from there." **EP**

911
Gorillaz (2001)

Writer | D. Albarn, V. Carlisle, D. Porter, J. Hewlett,
D. Holton, R. Johnson, O. Moore
Producer | D. Albarn, J. Hewlett, T. Girling, J. Cox
Label | Parlophone
Album | *Bad Company* (2002)

After the attacks on New York's World Trade Center on September 11, 2001, Detroit rappers D-12 were stranded in London when all international flights were canceled. The five band members—minus their most famous component, Eminem—took refuge at the studio of animated hip-hop band Gorillaz, alongside The Specials' front man, Terry Hall. (The sessions are detailed in the Gorillaz "autobiography," *Rise of the Ogre*.)

Just days later, this unlikely collective emerged from the studio with "911," a commentary on the attacks that captured the frustration, anger, and despair experienced by so many in the immediate aftermath of the tragedy. The track fused politically charged lyrics from D-12 with Middle-Eastern flavors and an ominous lilting beat, and its mournful hook echoed The Specials' 1981 hit "Ghost Town."

The single marked a departure from D-12's customary brand of schoolboy humor and remains a largely unrecognized gem from the genre-mashing Gorillaz, the brainchild of Blur front man Damon Albarn and *Tank Girl* creator Jamie Hewlett. Keen to stay true to their virtual vision, Gorillaz dropped the single online in November 2001. In June of the following year, "911" reemerged on the soundtrack to the action movie *Bad Company*, starring Anthony Hopkins and Chris Rock as CIA agents out to foil a terror plot. **EP**

Tiempo de soleá
Ojos de Brujo (2002)

Writer | Marina Abad, Juan Luis Levrepost, Ramón Giménez, Eldys Isaac Vega
Producer | Carlos Jaramillo
Label | La Fábrica de Colores
Album | *Bari* (2002)

Ojos de Brujo ("Eyes of the sorcerer") are second only to Manu Chao in having put Barcelona on the map of twenty-first-century music. The group is the most significant flowering of a multimedia collective of artists known as La Fábrica de Colores ("The Color Factory"). They set up an eponymous record label to escape the corporate interference that they experienced while making their first album, *Vengue*, in order to release *Bari*, the album on which this song first appeared.

"Tiempo de soleá" ("Lamenting Times") is fairly typical of the mix-and-match fusion of styles that has become a trademark of this group, whose music takes in influences as diverse as flamenco, Catalan rumba, hip-hop, funk, and reggae. Here, the flamenco guitar flourishes and *palmas* (hand claps) of Ramón Giménez combine with the Latin American–style percussion of Xavi Turrull, who plays both congas and a *cajón*, the Peruvian box-drum. DJ Panko's scratching gives it a hip-hop spin, and singer Marina "Las Canillas" Abad contributes a slow-burning vocal.

The lyrics of this song express the group's solidarity with the young glue-sniffing kids—many of North African descent—that they see around their neighborhood in the old town of Barcelona. True to the somber theme, the song is based on a *soleá*—one of the forms of flamenco that most commonly expresses sorrow. **JLu**

Freak Like Me
Sugababes (2002)

Writer | G. Clinton, B. Collins, G. Cooper, E. Hanes, L. Wilson Hill, M. Valentine, G. Numan
Producer | Richard "X" Phillips
Label | Universal Island
Album | *Angels with Dirty Faces* (2002)

When British trio Sugababes debuted in 2000 with "Overload," they projected a fairly wholesome image. In 2002, following the departure of Siobhan Donaghy and the arrival of Heidi Range, their style was more funky vamps than girls next door. Key to this transformation was their cover of Adina Howard's horny 1994 R&B hit "Freak Like Me." For that, Range, Mutya Buena, and Keisha Buchanan had to thank a reluctant star producer. Richard X had made a name for himself by mashing up synthesizer classics with soul and funk vocals. One of his anthems—Gary Numan and Tubeway Army's "Are 'Friends' Electric?" versus the a cappella version of "Freak Like Me"—was first issued on X's own label Black Melody, as "We Don't Give a Damn about Our Friends," under the name Girls on Top.

As his fame spread, X was offered a deal with Virgin, and the chance to make his bootlegs legitimate. He got a thumbs-up from Numan but was declined permission to use Howard's vocals. However, the Universal Island label was looking for a song for their new signings, the Sugababes. "Somebody had the bootleg . . ." Heidi Range told about.com, "and we loved it and tried it out."

The 'babes pop sensibilities blended brilliantly with Howard's funk and Numan's cold electro. The spectacular result topped the U.K. chart—a first for a mash-up—and Numan presented the Sugababes with a Q Award for Best Single. **DC**

Mundian to bach ke | Panjabi MC (2002)

Writer | Rajinder Rai, Glen Larson, Stuart Phillips
Producer | Rajinder Rai
Label | Instant Karma
Album | *The Album* (2003)

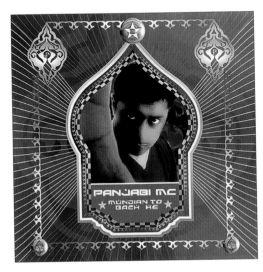

"I was like, 'What the hell is that?' The whole club went off!"

Jay-Z, 2008

▶ **Influenced by: Knight Rider** · Stu Phillips & Glen Larson (1982)
▶ **Influence on: Beware of the Boys** · Panjabi MC featuring Jay-Z (2003)
● **Covered by:** Countdown Singers (2004)

The number has filled dance floors around the world. But most people who have shaken their stuff to "Mundian to bach ke" ("Beware of the Boys") probably have no clue as to what the hypnotic Punjabi lyrics were saying. "He's talking to a girl that's just coming of age," explained composer Rajinder Rai—aka British bhangra guru Panjabi MC—to the *Washington Post*. "He's saying, 'You look good, but beware of the boys.'"

Finger-wagging message aside, Labh Janjua's haunting vocals meld perfectly with Raj's infectious *dhol* drums and single-stringed *tumbi*. Adding to the energy is an unexpected bass line from the theme of cult 1980s television series *Knight Rider*. "It felt right to do a bhangra mix of it," Rai explained of his unusual choice. "It just seemed more like a bhangra key." And, he told the *New York Daily News*, "It mixes the Eastern spiritual side with the power of the bass of the West."

In fact, Rai's refreshing blend of East and West had been kicking around the United Kingdom's underground bhangra scene since 1998. It became dance-floor dynamite in 2002 and finally enjoyed a major commercial release in early 2003. Raj attributed the single's gradual success to heavy play by non-Asian DJs in every major European city, and its gradual adoption by MTV.

The evolution of the song climaxed with a hit version featuring hip-hop titan Jay-Z. "I discovered the Panjabi MC record in a London club..." he told *Time Out*. "I called the guy the next day, to say I'm gonna do a remix, and he's like, 'Who is this?'" But Jay-Z's interest in the song was hugely influential. "It right knocked people out," recalled Raj. "I thought: this is taking bhangra to a level where bhangra's never been." **EP**

A Little Less Conversation | Elvis Presley vs JXL (2002)

Writer | Mac Davis, Billy Strange
Producer | JXL, Ad Bradley, Billy Strange
Label | RCA
Album | *ELV1S: 30 #1 Hits* (2002)

"I loved the remix. . . . I thought, well, this is the damnedest thing I'd ever seen!"

Mac Davis, 2006

◀ **Influenced by: Save Me** • Aretha Franklin (1967)
▶ **Influence on: Rubberneckin' (Paul Oakenfold Remix)**
Elvis Presley (2003)
● **Covered by:** The Bosshoss (2005) • Nicholis Louw
(2008) • Elvis Lounge featuring Andrea Canta (2009)

Elvis Presley's output was variable in the mid-Sixties—and, even when he released a gem, the public seemingly didn't want to know. "A Little Less Conversation" performed poorly in 1968, reaching No. 69 in the United States, while the movie from which it came, *Live a Little, Love a Little*, was no smash. It was mooted for inclusion in his 1968 "comeback special" television spectacular, to which end the star recorded a new vocal for the track. But when it was passed over, this funk-fest—written with Aretha Franklin in mind—lay in undeserved obscurity for over three decades.

The song's recovery was kick-started by its inclusion in 2001's ultra-cool heist movie *Ocean's Eleven*. The rehabilitation was completed by a Nike commercial featuring a remix—the first ever allowed by the Presley estate—created by Dutch DJ Tom Holkenborg (aka Junkie XL or, in the interests of taste, JXL). "It was already a funky and uplifting track," said Holkenborg, "and had elements I really liked, but wanted to beef up."

The energetic makeover opened up the song to a new generation. Its No. 1 position in the United Kingdom edged Presley ahead of The Beatles for the most British chart-toppers: eighteen to seventeen. The song was promptly added to the multi-platinum *ELV1S: 30 #1 Hits* and reappeared on the U.S. version of JXL's *Radio JXL: A Broadcast from the Computer Hell Cabin*.

Co-writer Mac Davis, also responsible for Presley's classic "In the Ghetto," found it gave him newfound credibility with his kids. "The treatment of the song," observed co-composer Billy Strange, "was new enough that younger people got into it." Twenty-five years after his death, Presley was still the King of Rock 'n' Roll. **CB**

Gimme the Light
Sean Paul (2002)

Writer | Sean Paul Henriques, Troy "Troyton" Rami
Producer | Troy "Troyton" Rami
Label | VP
Album | *Dutty Rock* (2002)

"There's a lot of speech we use that Americans don't get right off," Jamaican-born singer Sean Paul Henriques told *Newsweek,* after his intoxicating dancehall anthem broke the U.S. market. Mixing Americanized hip-hop references with Jamaican patois was his only concession to new listeners—who sat up and took notice of the raw, edgy sound. "I just turned the tables," he reasoned. "Instead of puttin' a little dancehall into a rap album, I put a little rap into my dancehall." (Fittingly, the track's "Pass the Dro-voisier" remix featured the ragga-influenced Busta Rhymes.)

Sean Paul's brand of hard dancehall was an underground sound until "Gimme the Light" became a huge club hit. The song's success was due to his distinctive, rapid-fire rasp, and to little-known Miami-based producer, Troyton Rami. Rami had originally used the backing track as the basis for an entire dancehall album in 2001, *Buzz Riddim*. This included an early version of "Gimme the Light" that sneaked out as a single in 2001 on the Black Shadow label.

Sean Paul certainly didn't have MTV viewers in mind when he wrote the lyrics for his ode to sparking up a spliff. Commenting on the hip-hop lingo for marijuana in the song's hook, "Gimme the light, pass the dro," he told the *Miami Times:* "It's a party song. I'm glad people take that in that context. I'm not telling kids to go do this." **EP**

I Believe in a Thing Called Love
The Darkness (2002)

Writer | J. Hawkins, D. Hawkins, E. Graham, F. Poullain
Producer | Pedro Ferreira
Label | Must Destroy Music
Album | *Permission to Land* (2003)

The arch-revivalists of rock ridiculousness instantly rankled with pompous critics when they first surfaced. The Darkness's high-octane shows regularly closed with front man Justin Hawkins throwing his shirt to the audience and being escorted from the stage, his feather-chapped legs straddling a lackey's shoulders. But their debut E.P., released on a tiny London label, proved they had songwriting chops to justify their swagger.

"I Believe in a Thing Called Love" opens with AC/DC-flavored cockiness and is a brilliant pop song. The music is an unashamedly Def Leppard-esque blend of radio-friendly choruses and fist-pumping riffing, while Hawkins's joyous vocals suit the dopily optimistic lyrics. The front man's every gesture drips with winning audaciousness. His "Touching you / Touching me" hook evokes Neil Diamond's "Sweet Caroline," and there is a comical yelp of "Guitar!" before his brother Dan's impeccably flashy fretwork. Meanwhile, the foolhardy swoops into falsetto on the chorus are a flourish that has since inspired many an unwise karaoke moment.

A wildly multiplying fan base saw past the pastiche and took to their hearts a group who, like Queen, fused heavy-rock flash with irresistible pop. Perhaps inevitably, The Darkness soon slipped into irredeemable self-parody, but for these three and a half minutes they were sublime. **SC**

Justin Hawkins assumes he has permission to land during a London concert in 2003.

Ashes of American Flags
Wilco (2002)

Writer | Jeff Tweedy, Jay Bennett
Producer | Wilco
Label | Nonesuch
Album | *Yankee Hotel Foxtrot* (2002)

Wilco's *Yankee Hotel Foxtrot* endured a famously difficult birth. First, leader Jeff Tweedy lost his writing foil Jay Bennett in a conflict over the album's experimental direction. Then their label, Reprise, refused the finished article. Wilco took the songs to the Internet, where nearly three hundred thousand downloads had Reprise changing their minds, but it was too late—the official, belated release went to Nonesuch.

In the midst of this chaos, there was a classic album: a numbed, beautiful meditation on the American (and Tweedy's) psyche. Its fulcrum is "Ashes of American Flags," a rock ballad—disguised by heartrending crescendos and queasy horns—that plods, wheezes, pauses, and battles on in the face of insecurity and consumer sickness. Tweedy's open wounds ("All my lies are always wishes / I know I would die if I could come back new") keep it personal, but the title—also used for a later tour DVD—proved provocative.

That it appeared so soon after September 11 —on an album sporting two towers on its cover, rubbing shoulders with a song called "War on War" and another where "tall buildings shake"—touched a nerve. There's a skewed patriotism to "I would like to salute / The ashes of American flags"—and even though the track, like the rest of the album, was written before the attacks, it is tempting to hear this as an anthem for a scarred America. **MH**

Like I Love You
Justin Timberlake (2002)

Writer | J. Timberlake, C. Hugo, P. Williams,
G. Thornton, T. Thornton
Producer | P. Williams, C. Hugo
Label | Jive
Album | *Justified* (2002)

Justin Timberlake faced an uphill struggle to transcend his saccharine pop pedigree as a Disney Mouseketeer and one-fifth of *NSYNC, the second biggest-selling boy band of all time. Indeed, his biggest claim to fame was having dated and dumped Britney Spears. "The bubblegum sound is old," he declared to *Entertainment Weekly,* while admitting elsewhere that he felt "a little exposed" by his solo debut.

He need not have worried. The Neptunes' Pharrell Williams and Chad Hugo certainly gave Timberlake a head start, but "Like I Love You" didn't rely on their digital funk, flamenco guitar, or rap protégés Clipse. Instead, it was Timberlake's surprising vocal range—flexing effortlessly between his familiar boy-band tenor, a limber falsetto, and a seductive whisper—that captured the attention of long-time fans and naysayers alike.

Inevitable comparisons with Michael Jackson followed, bolstered by the "Billie Jean"–inspired video, showcasing Timberlake's Jackson-esque moves and a look that copied the King of Pop right down to his fedora and fingerless gloves. "I wanted the emphasis to be on the dancing," he said, "and the interaction between me and the girl." "To me the song sounds kinda vintage, very bare," he told *Blender.* "I compare it to Prince's band, or [Prince's protégés] The Time in the year 3000. That's what it sounds like to me." **EP**

You Know You're Right
Nirvana (2002)

Writer | Kurt Cobain
Producer | Adam Kasper
Label | DGC
Album | *Nirvana* (2002)

With its pouting chorus and gothic glory, Nirvana's final single—released eight years after Kurt Cobain's suicide—seems steeped in the angst that prefaced their front man's death.

Nirvana debuted the song onstage in late 1993. Early the following year, with the lyrics still in embryonic form, Cobain recorded an acoustic demo that surfaced on 2004's *With the Lights Out*.

The studio version was recorded during the group's final session, in January 1994. Of the tracks attempted, "You Know You're Right" was the most complete. "Kurt came in Sunday [January 30] in the afternoon and did some vocals," recalled studio owner Robert Lang. "Then they did some guitar tracks and then we went and had dinner. . . . The whole vibe was really good."

Cobain's widow, Courtney Love, performed the song with her band Hole on MTV's *Unplugged* in 1995. "This is a song that Kurt wrote . . ." she said. "If it works, it's dedicated to my mother-in-law."

Nirvana's version was delayed by a dispute between Love and Nirvana's surviving members. Dave Grohl and Krist Novoselic wanted it issued on a box-set of unreleased material. Courtney successfully argued for it to open a single "best of" disc, inspired by The Beatles' compilation *1*. "I remember the first time I heard it on the radio," Novoselic enthused, "because I turned it up and said, 'This sounds real good!'" **SC**

All the Things She Said
T.A.T.U. (2002)

Writer | S. Galoyan, T. Horn, M. Kierszenbaum, E. Kiper, V. Polienko, I. Shapovalov
Producer | Trevor Horn
Label | Interscope
Album | *200 km/h in the Wrong Lane* (2002)

Britney Spears's "Baby One More Time" proved that a doe-eyed schoolgirl wielding a catchy hook could create an empire. Three years later, Russian psychologist turned pop svengali Ivan Shapovalov enhanced that formula when he masterminded Lena Katina and Yulia Volkova's international debut.

Candidly declaring T.A.T.U. an "underage sex project," Shapovalov dressed his waiflike protégées in rain-soaked school uniforms for the Sapphic kiss that dominated the controversial "All the Things She Said" video. "Lena has a voice. And Yulia has a sexual energy," he boasted to the *New Yorker*, as the inevitable tabloid frenzy erupted around their titillating tale of lesbian schoolgirl lust.

Aside from the publicity storm, Shapovalov's masterstroke was enlisting producer Trevor Horn to helm the English-language version of T.A.T.U.'s original Russian track, "Ya soshla s uma." The blend of pleading, angst-ridden vocals and Horn's intoxicating, thumping electronica became the first U.K. No. 1 single by a Russian act.

The lesbian shtick was over by 2003 when Volkova confirmed she was pregnant by a long-term boyfriend. The girls also ditched Shapovalov, complaining in their official bio: "We just had to do whatever he was telling us to." But having inspired multiple covers, mash-ups, and remixes in genres from metal to acoustic balladry, their anthemic tour de force has long outlived the hype. **EP**

Untitled
Interpol (2002)

Writer | Paul Banks, Carlos Dengler, Daniel Kessler
Producer | Peter Katis
Label | Matador
Album | *Turn on the Bright Lights* (2002)

Interpol had been building a reputation since front man Paul Banks and guitarist Daniel Kessler, having met in Paris, recruited bassist Carlos Dengler and drummer Sam Fogarino and issued two independent EPs. But while the press fawned over fellow New York scenesters The Strokes, Interpol were dismissed as mere Joy Division imitators.

Their debut album began to turn things around. Much of *Turn on the Bright Lights* does indeed sound like Joy Division's rockier moments, yet there are plenty of gems. (The ballad "NYC" became a favorite of R.E.M.'s Michael Stipe.)

For many, however, the standout is the bewitching opening track, "Untitled." There is barely anything to it: a childlike guitar riff, a rumbling rhythm section, a two-line lyric, and a dive-bombing guitar effect. But the whole is much greater than the sum of its parts. "It's not a total blow-you-away, rock 'n' roll adrenalin rush . . ." Dengler told *Uncut*. "What we offer involves other emotions, which are difficult to communicate other than on that deep, deep level."

Fogarino described the experience of playing in Interpol: "You know when you feel somebody staring at you from across a room and you don't know why? No matter what they're trying to project—positive or negative, whether they want to beat you up or kiss you—you feel it. So, magnify that by, like, three thousand. Intense, yeah?" **BM**

Slob
Weezer (2002)

Writer | Rivers Cuomo
Producer | Weezer, Rod Cervera, Chad Bamford
Label | Geffen
Album | *Maladroit* (2002)

Goofy sing-alongs like "Buddy Holly," "Pork and Beans," and "Beverly Hills" are the hits for which Weezer are best known. Yet their fans' favorites seem to be the ones in which bandleader Rivers Cuomo takes himself to task: "Slob," for example.

After 1996's proto-emo *Pinkerton*, Cuomo lost interest in the band that had made him a star. A sold-out summer tour in 2000, however, reminded him of the affection with which Weezer were regarded. Continuing in the spirit of band-fan interaction, Weezer prepared for their fourth album by posting demos on their website. Of the resulting *Maladroit*, Cuomo informed Rocknews.com: "It should say, 'Produced by the message board fans.' . . . For example, 'Slob' . . . that was actually a song from the summer of 2000 and it was really cool, but we just forgot about it. Then the fans on the message board kept saying, 'Hey, you guys gotta play 'Slob.''"

The powerful song painted a desolate picture of Cuomo's post-*Pinkerton* malaise. ("I drank some of Grandaddy's beer" nods to Californian indie rockers Grandaddy, often compared to Weezer.) It was, he told *Guitar World*, "written in a very emotionally extreme moment. It's not often that I feel that way. Maybe once a week or something I'll get overwhelmed by a situation in my life and write a song about it. . . . Most of the time I'm a pretty cool character." **BM**

Strange and Beautiful (I'll Put a Spell on You) | Aqualung (2002)

Quelqu'un m'a dit
Carla Bruni (2002)

Writer | Matt Hales, Kim Oliver
Producer | Matt Hales, Jim Copperthwaite
Label | B-Unique
Album | *Aqualung* (2002)

Writer | Carla Bruni, Alex Dupont
Producer | Louis Bertignac
Label | Naive
Album | *Quelqu'un m'a dit* (2002)

When Matt Hales—singer for British band The 45s—received a call from an advertising agency looking for music, all he had was a track he had recorded in his hall, on an out-of-tune piano.

The commercial was for Volkswagen's new Beetle. The track was the haunting "Strange and Beautiful (I'll Put a Spell on You)." Together, they became a British phenomenon. Hales soon had BBC radio calling up, wanting to play his track and asking who they should say it was by. Put on the spot, he came up with the name Aqualung (coincidentally the title of a classic 1971 album by Jethro Tull, about whom he would have to field endless questions when the song was a hit).

In 2002, "Strange and Beautiful" was released as a U.K. single, hitting the Top Ten. American interest followed, and the song was used on the soundtrack of *The O.C.* In 2005, Hales signed a deal to release his songs worldwide, hence the 2005 album *Strange and Beautiful,* comprising songs from his British releases, *Aqualung* and *Strange and Beautiful.* It sold over 300,000 copies in the United States and Hales was feted by stars such as R.E.M.'s Michael Stipe and actor Leonardo DiCaprio. Back in Britain, Hales remained known almost solely for the commercial. "People probably think I died," he told the *Guardian* in 2007. "Or [I'm] struggling away pitching songs to ads going, 'Remember me? I can help you sell cars!'" **DC**

Carla Bruni is annoyingly blessed. As heiress to a tire manufacturing empire, she had no need to work, but took up modeling—leading to associations with Mick Jagger and Eric Clapton. At thirty-five, she became a million-selling musician, too. The song that sealed Bruni's musical fortunes is the title track of her debut album. Translating as "Someone Told Me," it features guitar and piano by producer Louis Bertignac, formerly of French superstars Téléphone. But most notable is Bruni's impeccably wispy voice, and a confident French delivery that belies her Italian origins.

"The French 'chanson' label makes sense to me because I do spontaneously write in French . . ." she told *RFI Music.* "I've spent as much of my life listening to [Georges] Brassens as The Beatles—if not more, in fact. In my teens, I was absolutely hypnotized [by] Bob Dylan and Leonard Cohen. . . . My influences are really mixed between French, English, and Italian. The only place where I would definitely say I'm coming from is folk. I do a sort of 'white' blues, a style I can sing really simply."

The song itself is desperately melancholic. "I love," singer Jane Birkin enthused to Bruni in *Interview,* "that part where you say that 'our lives aren't worth much,' and they are 'passing in an instant, like wilting roses.'" It was a sentiment that fitted perfectly on the soundtrack of 2009's "unromantic comedy" *(500) Days of Summer.* **BM**

Carla Bruni, latterly the First Lady of France, performs in 2003.

Heartbeats | The Knife (2002)

Writer | Karin Dreijer Andersson, Olof Dreijer
Producer | Karin Dreijer Andersson, Olof Dreijer
Label | Rabid
Album | *Deep Cuts* (2003)

"I'm not good at making very happy tracks about nonsense."
Karin Dreijer Andersson, 2009

◀ **Influenced by: Falling** • Julee Cruise (1989)
▶ **Influence on: When I Grow Up** • Fever Ray (2009)
● **Covered by:** José González (2003) • Scala & Kolacny Brothers (2006) • Emmerson Nogueira (2008)
★ **Other key tracks:** You Take My Breath Away (2003) Pass This On (2003)

"Haunting" and "electro" are not words often used together. Unless, perhaps, you are talking about the beautiful "Heartbeats" by The Knife.

The Stockholm siblings' love of synth pop, minimal beats, and electronica came together to create a moving masterpiece. Singer Karin Dreijer Andersson's hypnotic vocals recall both Björk and Siouxsie Sioux, with her icy delivery of magical lines like "And you, you knew the hand of a devil / And you kept us awake with wolves' teeth / Sharing different heartbeats in one night."

"Heartbeats" achieved worldwide recognition when a cover by José González was used in a Sony commercial in 2006. The group's fellow Swede had covered "Heartbeats" on his album *Veneer* in 2003. That interpretation was acoustic and completely different from the original, but equally stunning. "It's the first time we've said yes to a thing like that," Karin was to comment. "The only reason we thought it was okay was it wasn't us performing. It's not fun to sell music for commercials but it gives you money—to help our label."

This independent outlook was enforced by The Knife's selective interview policy and refusal to perform live until 2005, as well as a propensity to wear masks in promotional material. "If we could choose not to do any photos at all, we would . . ." grumbled Karin, "because I don't think it has anything to do with the music." (Although, she later claimed, "Our goal was never to be secret.")

The Knife have described their music as "emotional electronic power pop" (equally applicable to their latter-day protégée Robyn). Ultimately, you may discern one hundred different influences in "Heartbeats," but the song remains resolutely original nonetheless. **OM**

Fuck Me Pumps | Amy Winehouse (2003)

Writer | Amy Winehouse, Salaam Remi
Producer | Salaam Remi
Label | Island
Album | *Frank* (2003)

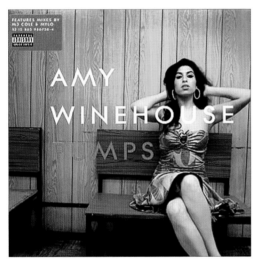

"I'm a musician. I'm not someone who's trying to be diplomatic, you know, trying to get my fifteen minutes."

Amy Winehouse, 2004

◀ **Influenced by:** Afro • Erykah Badu (1997)
▶ **Influence on:** Mercy • Duffy (2008)
★ **Other key tracks:** Help Yourself (2003) • (There Is) No Greater Love (2003) • Take the Box (2003) • Round Midnight (2003) • Stronger Than Me (2003) • What It Is (2003) • Know You Now (2003)

The Amy Winehouse who released her 2003 debut album was much more restrained than the tattooed, substance-abusing tabloid star she became. But if the younger Winehouse seemed demure, *Frank*'s body of lyrics revealed the sharp edge of her jazzy, seductive soul.

Nowhere was this clearer than on "Fuck Me Pumps"—a wittily acerbic take on the party girls who yearn for "a rich man / Six foot two or taller," and aspire only to appearing in the gossip pages on the arm of a footballer. Winehouse's delicious vocals sweeten the song's lyrical bite—as does deft production from co-writer Salaam Remi, who also worked with the Fugees, Nas, and Ms. Dynamite, and who grounded the song's lilting, spare jazzy guitar with subtle hip-hop beats.

Winehouse paints her target as something of a sorry figure, taking too much ecstasy and waking up every morning to find her conquest of the night before has bolted. But there's affection in the portrait, too, and sympathy: "He could be your whole life / If you got past one night / But that part never goes right." There is compassion, too: Amy tells her hapless heroine not to mind being called a "skank," and sings "Without girls like you, there'd be no fun."

The video for the track closes with Winehouse kicking off a pair of the titular de Havillands. "In the video," she complained to popjustice.com, "I mouth the words 'Fuck me,' but they took the audio out in the edit! The first time I saw it I was, like, 'Fuck! Where's my 'fuck'?! I say 'fuck' there!'"

Winehouse later found herself plastered across the very gossip pages for which her party girl had ached. But songs like this proved that she had the talent to back up the feeding frenzy. **SC**

Strict Machine | Goldfrapp (2003)

Writer | Alison Goldfrapp, Will Gregory, Nick Batt
Producer | Goldfrapp
Label | Mute
Album | *Black Cherry* (2003)

" 'Strict Machine' is quite a humorous song."

Alison Goldfrapp, 2003

Influenced by: Knock on Wood • Amii Stewart (1978)
Influence on: Some Girls • Rachel Stevens (2004)
Other key tracks: White Soft Rope (2003) • Hairy Trees (2003) • Train (2003) • Lovely Head (2003) • Deer Stop (2003) • Sartorious (2003)

Goldfrapp's fans were sitting comfortably. They had heard the striking *Felt Mountain* in 2000, thoroughly enjoyed the mix of electro-cabaret and trip-hop, and suspected that was the kind of music they would continue to get. Then Goldfrapp threw them a curveball with *Black Cherry*.

Recording in a darkened English studio, vocalist Alison Goldfrapp and synth wiz Will Gregory brought old school sounds back to the future with their sophomore album. The cinematic soundscapes of *Felt Mountain* were gone, replaced by a harder, club-friendly vibe that drew from Seventies disco and glam rock—a tub-thumping mix that gelled best on "Strict Machine."

"I'm drawn to [glam] in the same way as I'm drawn to disco . . ." Alison told *Artist Interviews*. "It's sort of opulence and dressing up and a kind of fantasy, decadence. . . . I think glam and disco have a very similar thing there." (That was not the song's only link to vintage pop—bassist Charlie Jones is Robert Plant's son-in-law, and co-writer Nick Batt helmed DNA's remix of Suzanne Vega's "Tom's Diner.")

"Strict Machine" was decidedly cold, distant, and foreign—yet Goldfrapp turned those traits into strengths. The lyrics, inspired by a scientific experiment on rats, had the narrator in a cage, receiving satisfaction only when plugged into the "strict machine." But she wasn't complaining—she liked the arrangement. "I'd just broken up with someone and as a result I immediately started having more fun," Alison explained to *Q*. "I became more experimental—and so did the music."

The story was wrapped in futuristic grooves, the kind that would make HAL 9000 boogie, tied with a sexy ribbon. A perfect love song for the digital download era. **JiH**

Alison Goldfrapp performs at the now-demolished Astoria Theatre, London, in 2003. ➡

Step into My Office, Baby | Belle & Sebastian (2003)

Writer | C. Geddes, M. Cooke, R. Colburn, S. Martin, S. Jackson, B. Kildea, S. Murdoch
Producer | Trevor Horn
Label | Rough Trade
Album | *Dear Catastrophe Waitress* (2003)

"Office romances? Don't do it!"

Stevie Jackson, 2005

◀ **Influenced by: Conventioneers** · Barenaked Ladies (2000)
▶ **Influence on: Lovers in the Backseat** · Scissor Sisters (2004)
★ **Other key tracks:** Love on the March (2003) Desperation Made a Fool of Me (2003)

It wasn't only fans who were skeptical about Trevor Horn producing quirky Scottish group Belle & Sebastian's sixth album, from which "Step into My Office, Baby" was the lead single. Band members were also among those questioning the suitability of the man behind Frankie Goes to Hollywood and other over-the-top productions. But Horn won them over. Chief songwriter Stuart Murdoch recalled him saying: "Think of it like this. We had an outside toilet when I was a boy. I used to like going outside to use the toilet. You get very used to it. But I wouldn't have an outside toilet now."

Doubts effectively flushed away, Horn's sure-footedness paid off. "He made everything sound good and he kept the whole thing moving in a disciplined, fun way," said guitarist Stevie Jackson about the sessions. "The only one which he took in a different direction was 'Step into My Office,' which he had a big hand in arranging."

Murdoch was free to fine-tune Belle & Sebastian's bittersweet vignettes. The saucy "Step into My Office, Baby" related to what the *Daily Telegraph* politely described as a "whirlwind corporate romance," in this case between a young worker and his lady boss: "She gave me some dictation / But my strength is in administration."

Introductory, almost Adam & The Ants-esque drums lead into delicious tempo changes and a jaunty backing juxtaposed with jaundiced lyrics (plus a bit of French horn). Trevor Horn, recalled violinist and singer Sarah Martin, "wanted to work his 'hit single' magic with that song in particular, always aiming for it to sound good on the radio." The first of the group's singles to feature on an album, it reached the U.K. Top Forty and earned an Ivor Novello songwriting award nomination. **CB**

Run | Snow Patrol (2003)

Writer | Gary Lightbody, Iain Archer, Jonny Quinn, Mark McClelland, Nathan Connolly
Producer | Garrett "Jacknife" Lee
Label | Fiction
Album | *Final Straw* (2003)

"Songs aren't monolithic— at least the good ones aren't. What Leona Lewis has done has touched hearts."

Gary Lightbody, 2008

◄ **Influenced by: Promenade** • U2 (1985)
► **Influence on: SRXT** • Bloc Party (2007)
● **Covered by:** Tre Lux (2006) • Three Graces (2008) Leona Lewis (2008) • Voice Male (2009) • Jennylyn Mercado (2010)

"It was written in my bedsit bedroom [in] 2000," Snow Patrol leader Gary Lightbody recalled. "I was living, still, like a student, even though I graduated in '98. . . . I was trying to light up my own life really, and it just got a life of its own. God bless it."

After toiling in obscurity for the best part of a decade, the Northern Irish and Scottish band's fortunes were turned around by "Run." Lightbody composed the song after recovering from splitting his head open, the result of a drunken fall in Glasgow. "The words 'light up, light up' gave this sense of a beacon," he told *Q* magazine. "There had to be a light at the end of a tunnel."

The track benefited from an epic style of production that Garrett Lee later brought to Bloc Party and Editors. "It was an experiment for us," Lightbody told the *Daily Mirror*. "When we recorded it, we made it gigantic—we'd never really attempted a song like it before." Embellishments included viola, violin, and cello—the latter played by James Banbury, formerly of The Auteurs.

"Run" became Snow Patrol's first international hit. Lightbody told 4Music that, before its success, "We never had a track that was played on daytime radio. We never had a track that, if you played a festival, people would sing every word back to you. It was just one of those songs that just seemed to become public property."

"Run" was the second single released from *Final Straw*—2003's "Spitting Games" was the first—and reached No. 5 in the U.K. charts. A lung-busting rendition by Leona Lewis, 2006 winner of *The X Factor*, returned the song to the charts in 2008. "The success of 'Run' is obviously brilliant," its composer remarked to musicradar.com. "I won't have to worry about bills for a long time." **BM**

Maps | Yeah Yeah Yeahs (2003)

Writer | Karen Orzoleck, Nick Zinner, Brian Chase
Producer | David Andrew Sitek, Yeah Yeah Yeahs
Label | Interscope
Album | *Fever to Tell* (2003)

"There's a lot of loooove in that song. But there's a lot of fear, too."

Karen O, 2006

◄ **Influenced by:** U.F.O. • E.S.G. (1981)
► **Influence on:** The Other Side of Mt. Heart Attack
Liars (2006)
● **Covered by:** The White Stripes (2004) • Arcade Fire
(2005) • Dept. of Good and Evil featuring Rachel Z
(2007) • Rogue Wave (2009)

Like exposed flesh surrounded by barbed wire, "Maps" stood out on the first full-length album by this trio of New York noiseniks. Most of *Fever to Tell* showcased Karen O's yelping vocals, Nick Zinner's combustible riffs, and Brian Chase's thunderous drums, but this ballad featured vulnerable vocals and an explosively emotional sound.

"We had just started touring a lot," O told *Prefix*. "There was a lot of emotional unrest going on. The dirt was being kicked up and the water was getting really murky.... I just had fallen in love and settled down with someone, but I was constantly going away and coming back. All that caused the bleeding heart song."

The lyrics touched on O's relationship with Liars singer Angus Andrew, who also prompted the genuine tears she shed at the "Maps" video shoot. "He was three hours late and I was just about to leave for tour," she explained to *NME*. "I didn't think he was even going to come and this was the song that was written for him. He eventually showed up and I got myself in a real emotional state." (It has been suggested that the song's title is an acronym for "My Angus Please Stay.")

The heartache of the repeated refrain, "Wait! They don't love you like I love you" clearly touched a nerve with the record-buying public. "Maps" broke Yeah Yeah Yeahs into *Billboard*'s Hot 100 and apparently inspired the guitar break in Kelly Clarkson's "Since U Been Gone" ("Like getting bitten by a poisonous varmint," O told *Rolling Stone*). "Maps" topped an *NME* poll of alternative love songs and has been covered live by The White Stripes (it was also sampled by Radiohead).

"I exposed myself so much with that song," O concluded, "I kind of shocked myself." **JH**

The Yeah Yeah Yeahs' Karen O gives it some tongue in a London performance in 2004. ➡

Toxic
Britney Spears (2003)

Writer | C. Dennis, C. Karlsson, P. Winnberg, H. Jonback
Producer | Bloodshy & Avant
Label | Jive
Album | *In the Zone* (2003)

In 2001, Britney Spears told fans, "I'm Not a Girl, Not Yet a Woman." Two years later, the transition was over—at twenty-one, ready to support her most mature album to date, Spears was all woman.

The lead single—"Me against the Music," a duet with Spears's most obvious role model, Madonna—only hinted at the greatness soon to follow. The brashly mature "Toxic" was a true game-changer, firmly sealing the casket on the bubblegum pop the singer had peddled on her first two albums.

Spears purrs like a kitten (one more apt to claw than cuddle) at the start of the song. She is convincingly hot and bothered as she tells of a relationship that is equally poisonous and addictive. Love isn't the drug she is singing about, and the "hit" Spears so desires seems much more carnal. The sentiment is deepened by a sweaty electro-pop arrangement, with a string effect borrowed from "Tere mere beech mein," by Indian singer Lata Mangeshkar.

The whole package feels ominous and a little bit dangerous, yet—like the fix Spears is singing about—damn irresistible. "It's basically about a girl addicted to a guy," she told MTV.

An international smash, "Toxic" earned Spears her first Grammy and has been covered by acts from Mark Ronson to Marillion. Spears applied the blueprint to later offerings with successful results, but nothing beats the original. **JiH**

Destroy Rock & Roll
Mylo (2003)

Writer | Myles "Mylo" MacInnes
Producer | Myles MacInnes
Label | Breastfed
Album | *Destroy Rock & Roll* (2004)

With a roll call starrier than "We are the World," Myles MacInnes's first single name-checks stars from Michael Jackson and Bruce Springsteen to David "Boo-wie" and Cyndi "Looper."

"Destroy Rock & Roll" was produced by the former BBC journalist in his bedroom on the Isle of Skye, off the coast of Scotland. With its magpie samples and deadly disco hook, the song cost only £350: the cost of a secondhand iMac and free Pro Tools software. The enterprising Mylo released it on his own label, Breastfed.

The title track was initially released as 250 singles, their sleeves hand-sprayed by Mylo himself. A 2005 reissue reached No. 15 in the U.K. chart. Its major component was an extract from "Invocation for Judgement Against and Destruction of Rock Music," by the religious group Church Universal and Triumphant, Inc. (as released on the Faithways International label's *The Sounds of American Doomsday Cults*). Recorded on December 15, 1984, this denounces major music stars (and, in the original sermon, contemporary movies like *Ghostbusters* and *Beat Street*)—hence one of pop's oddest hooks: "Missing Persons, Duran Duran, Missing Persons, Duran Duran ..."

The shoestring production, blending religious rhetoric with thumping bass, proved that great bedroom music needs just a little imagination and a lot of chutzpah. **GK**

Mr. Brightside
The Killers (2003)

Writer | Brandon Flowers, David Keuning
Producer | Jeff Saltzman, The Killers
Label | Lizard King
Album | *Hot Fuss* (2004)

"I was asleep and I knew something was wrong," Killers front man Brandon Flowers told *Q* magazine. "I have these instincts. I went to the Crown and Anchor [a Las Vegas pub] and my girlfriend was there with another guy." Guitarist Dave Keuning married Flowers's story to his music, and The Killers' first classic was minted.

Keuning and Flowers met in Las Vegas, bonding over a love of acts like Oasis, U2, and Beck. With an early incarnation of The Killers, they secured a residency at a local dive bar, where they recruited bassist Mark Stoermer and drummer Ronnie Vannucci. The quartet debuted on record in September 2003, with the release of "Mr. Brightside" on the Lizard King label. Relentless touring and promotion set the scene for the following year's *Hot Fuss*.

Critics fell over themselves to pinpoint the band's Eighties influences, most of which they readily admitted. But, as Flowers pointed out, "I like David Bowie just as much, you know, from the early Seventies." The song duly tips a hat to "Queen Bitch" from *Hunky Dory*, albeit with a beefed-up production—"'Mr. Brightside' had like thirty guitar tracks," admitted Keuning.

"Mr. Brightside" describes madness borne of despair—"I can make myself miserable in minutes with what my mind can conjure up," said Flowers. But it never fails to raise smiles at Killers shows. **BM**

Televators
The Mars Volta (2003)

Writer | Bixler-Savala, Rodriguez-Lopez
Producer | Rubin, Rodriguez-Lopez
Label | Universal
Album | *De-Loused in the Comatorium* (2003)

There was little on The Mars Volta's contorted, ambitious debut suited for release as a single. *De-Loused in the Comatorium* was a concept album retelling the last days of the group's suicidal artist friend Julio Venegas. Its violent yet erudite prog rock was slaked in Latin rhythms, charged with punk energy, and given to passages of turbulent drones mixed into twelve-minute riff-fests.

The mournful "Televators," however, was a relatively palatable slice of the Volta's mad, impassioned magic. Its ballad tempo, and the aching caress of Omar Rodriguez-Lopez's guitar, masked powerfully grief-stricken lyrics, tenderly delivered by front man Cedric Bixler-Zavala (like his partner, formerly of Texas punks At the Drive-In). Bixler-Zavala broke into a heartbroken lament for his friend, describing Venegas lying dead after he leapt several stories from a window.

The brutal, poetic beauty of Bixler-Zavala's words captures the group's ambivalence over Venegas's death, expressing their relief at his release from the agony his life had become, and their pain at his loss. But there is also a note of bruised optimism: a sense that, through his art—and their own—he would live on. "Televators," with its haunting imagery, its melancholic melody, and its nuanced sentiments of grief, regret, and hope, proved that even The Mars Volta's ballads could be complex, passionate, and long-lived. **SC**

Through the Wire | Kanye West (2003)

Writer | K. West, C. Weil, D. Foster, T. Keane
Producer | Kanye West
Label | Roc-A-Fella
Album | *The College Dropout* (2004)

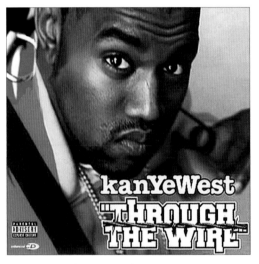

"I didn't expect him to speed it up and make me sound like a chipmunk."

Chaka Khan, 2008

◀ **Influenced by: Through the Fire** • Chaka Khan (1984)
▶ **Influence on: Through the Wire (L.L.T. Remix)**
Lo Life Thugs (2003)
● **Covered by:** Soul Providers (2006)
★ **Other key tracks:** All Fall Down (2004) • Slow Jamz
(2004) • Jesus Walks (2004)

Displaying the commercial nous that characterized his production work for Alicia Keys and Jay-Z, Kanye West's debut single made hay of his near-fatal 2002 car crash. As the song remarks, he turned "tragedy to triumph" with smart rhymes and a sped-up Chaka Khan hook. West even informed Khan of the therapeutic powers of her original song. "He told me a story about how my song helped him recover in the hospital after his accident," Khan told concertlivewire.com, "and that really moved me."

West announced his arrival as a recording artist mere weeks after the collision, insisting, "they can't stop me from rapping. . . . I'll just spit it through the wire." He had undergone extensive facial surgery, but was not prepared to allow his wired-up jaw and resulting fuzzy diction to block his trajectory. Unsurprisingly for a man blessed with a name meaning "the only one" in Swahili, West had the faith, or perhaps the ego, to believe that God had saved him for this purpose. "He still had a job for me . . ." he told the *Guardian*. "In certain situations he just talks through me."

The song is elevated by witty lines—"I look like Tom Cruise on *Vanilla Sky*"—and references to hip-hop stars The Notorious B.I.G., Ma$e, and Jay-Z. Plus, of course, West's trademark use of a high-speed soul sample. "I didn't expect him to do my voice at five thousand rpms," Khan said drily, "but otherwise it's great and I'm honored."

West made this gimmick his calling card, although his debut album, *The College Dropout*, showed more versatility and helped to inspire a generation of R&B artists. "I love him and I love that track," Khan told *Metro*. "The way he's used my sample is so clever." **MH**

Writer | Jack White
Producer | Jack White
Label | XL
Album | *Elephant* (2003)

"It's about me, Meg, and the people we're dating. The world constantly tries to dissect people."

Jack White, 2004

◄ **Influenced by: Symphony No. 5 in B flat** · Anton Bruckner (1878)

► **Influence on: It Takes a Seven Nation Army to Hold Us Back** · Apathy featuring Emilio Lopez (2004)

● **Covered by:** Vyvienne Long (2004) · The Flaming Lips (2005) · Hard-Fi (2005) · C. W. Stoneking (2008)

Detroit duo Jack and Meg White (they were once married, although for a time they claimed they were brother and sister) make much of their simplicity and integrity. Some may scoff at their sticking to certain chords; dressing only in red, black, and white; and shunning drugs and groupies, but few can deny that their take on the world of pop has opened up unique personal territory for them. "Seven Nation Army" takes their reductionist approach to its logical conclusion and scores maximum points as a result.

"7 Nation Army" sounds as if it has been recorded with a full band, including bass, the instrument they always eschewed. In fact, Jack created the central hook by dropping his guitar's range using an octave pedal. "I wrote that riff in a soundcheck in Australia . . ." he recalled to MTV. "I used to call the Salvation Army 'Seven Nation Army' because I thought that's what the name was. So I was working around that and it just became a song about gossip. When I wrote that, I thought if I ever got asked to write the next James Bond theme, that would be the riff for it."

This insistent, bluesy riff fuels the song: with few flourishes or elaborations on that simple figure, "7" is a statement of intent that has rarely been matched this decade—although Hard-Fi, Audioslave, and Alice Russell are among the artists to have covered the song.

The song opened *Elephant*, with Jack overruling the duo's management and label's contention that "There's No Home for You Here" should be the album's first single. Initially, however, as he confessed to the *Observer*, "It wasn't like we all thought, 'This riff is really catchy' or anything. . . . It felt like no big deal at all." **JMc**

Fix Up, Look Sharp
Dizzee Rascal (2003)

Writer | Billy Squier, Dylan Mills, Nick Denton
Producer | Dizzee Rascal
Label | XL
Album | *Boy in da Corner* (2003)

Despite drumming for Alice Cooper, Cher, Ted Nugent, and Gary Moore, it is doubtful that the late Bobby Chouinard will go down in rock 'n' roll history. But he should: his instantly recognizable drums from Billy Squier's "The Big Beat" (on 1980's *The Tale of the Tape*) have driven over forty hip-hop gems, from UTFO's "Roxanne Roxanne" to Jay-Z's "99 Problems." And few did so little—yet so much—with the blistering break as seventeen-year old Dylan Mills, aka Dizzee Rascal. He simply looped it, and rhymed over the top. The result was astonishing, not least because Dizzee did not try to imitate the U.S. rappers who dominate hip-hop.

In a distinctive London accent, he dropped resolutely British references: Dizzee was "flushin' MCs down the loo [toilet]," and "old school like [bargain store] Happy Shopper." You might have been a "Topman" (the name of a clothes store), but he was not trying to be your "mate." There was, however, the approving aside, "Sweet as a nut."

Originally linked to the U.K. garage scene (and its fierce offshoot, "grime"), Dizzee claimed an affinity to rock that was borne out by the headbanging power of "Fix Up, Look Sharp." "I sense such a free spirit from someone like [Nirvana's] Kurt Cobain," he told *X-Ray*. "But then I looked at my own stuff and I can see some similarities. . . . Everyone should be able to make any kind of music." **BM**

Crazy in Love
Beyoncé (2003)

Writer | Beyoncé, Rich Harrison, Shawn Carter, Eugene Record
Producer | Rich Harrison, Beyoncé
Label | Columbia
Album | *Dangerously in Love* (2003)

"The song talks about how, when you're in falling in love, you do things that are out of character and you don't really care . . ." Beyoncé told writer Dennis Hensley. "The song comes from me actually looking crazy one day in the studio. I said, 'I'm looking crazy right now,' and Rich Harrison, the producer, was like, 'That's the song!'"

And thus "Crazy in Love"—Beyoncé's second solo smash, after 2002's "Work It Out"—was born. However, when Harrison first played the former Destiny's Child singer the sample on which the tune is based, she dismissed the distinctive horn riffs, sampled from a 1970 Chi-Lites single, as too retro. "I wasn't sure," she admitted to MTV, "if people were going to get it."

Nevertheless, she gave Harrison a tight deadline and, two hours later, he had written the verses and the hook. Beyoncé came up with the bridge while her boyfriend Jay-Z provided the rap. "When I first heard Jay's version," Harrison remembered, "I was in my car screaming, 'Whoaaaa!'"

The song has been reinvented as an elegiac lament by Antony & The Johnsons, a country jig by Tracy Bonham, and a swing pastiche by The Puppini Sisters. Its most obvious descendant—Amerie's "1 Thing"—was helmed by the same producer, Harrison. "Crazy in Love" also featured in *Bridget Jones: The Edge of Reason*—apt for one of fiction's most famous singletons. **OM**

Beyoncé has proved unquestionably that she's not just another pretty face in pop. ➡

Rebellion (Lies) | Arcade Fire (2004)

Writer | Win Butler, Régine Chassagne, Richard Reed Parry, Tim Kingsbury, Howard Bilerman
Producer | Arcade Fire
Label | Merge
Album | *Funeral* (2004)

arcade fire

rebellion (lies)

"It gave me incredible hope... and made me extremely jealous."
Larry Mullen, U2, 2009

Influenced by: Transmission · Joy Division (1979)
Influence on: You're All I Have · Snow Patrol (2006)
Covered by: The Penelopes (2008)
Other key tracks: Brazil (2004) · Wake Up (2004)
Neighborhood #1 (Tunnels) (2004) · Crown of Love
(2004) · Neighborhood #2 (Laïka) (2004)

In Arcade Fire's baroque power-pop world, everything sounds apocalyptic. Owen Pallett's string arrangements tear through the melody. Massed voices bicker and bitch like a Greek chorus. And, above it all, singer Win Butler testifies his damaged heart out. It would be fearsome—if "Rebellion (Lies)" wasn't so funny.

It is not a laugh a minute, but as a protest song it seethes with sarcasm. We are in mid-Noughties North America—stuffy with paranoia—but Montreal's Arcade Fire believe that it is all "just a lie, scare your son and scare your daughter." "Sleeping is giving in," they sneer. "People say that you'll die faster than without water," they spit. "But we know it's just a lie." "It wasn't written out of a political sentiment," Butler remarked, "but it is kind of about a pied piper image." The song builds from a lone bass signature—gradually layering piano, strings, insistent drums, and warring shrieks—to become a rabble-rouser. It slides from New Wave to Waterboys-esque "big music" via Celtic soul: an ornate mix that shaped mainstream indie rock for the second half of the Noughties.

Although Arcade Fire's debut album *Funeral* commemorates—in title at least—a turbulent year for much of the group, the music is bright, grandiose, even triumphant. It made fans of David Bowie and U2, and permeates later work by the stadium-quelling likes of Coldplay.

Rather than waste time and energy hiding "the night underneath the covers" themselves, Arcade Fire licensed "Rebellion (Lies)" to the Red Campaign, working to combat the spread of AIDS in Africa. Here was one band whose rage proved not to be empty rhetoric, and gave mobilized youth everywhere a new anthem. **MH**

Take Me Out | Franz Ferdinand (2004)

Writer | Alex Kapranos, Nick McCarthy, Bob Hardy, Paul Thomson
Producer | Tore Johansson
Label | Domino
Album | *Franz Ferdinand* (2004)

"We were clever right from the beginning."

Alex Kapranos, 2009

◀ **Influenced by: Damaged Goods** · Gang of Four (1978)
▶ **Influence on: I Can't Give You What I Haven't Got**
The Living End (2004)
● **Covered by:** Scissor Sisters (2004) · Biffy Clyro (2005)
The Magic Numbers (2006) · Guillemots (2006)

"Someone said, 'God, that song works even though it does everything a song shouldn't do —it changes all the time and slows down as well.' But," Franz Ferdinand main man Alex Kapranos explained to *NME*, "that's exactly what we wanted: to create that lurching feeling you get when you go on a roller coaster and your stomach falls away." Crank up the abrupt—and loud—introduction to this bombshell, and you will be treated to some of the best post-punk marching music ever recorded. It is easy to see why the Scottish art rockers' second single was such a huge floor-filler.

The band named themselves after the man whose assassination sparked World War I, and the "Take Me Out" single sleeve is a pastiche of propaganda art from the time. The music's influences, however, are entrenched in the 1980s, mixing the angular, staccato noise of the Fire Engines and Gang of Four with the clever pop of Orange Juice. "This song is about the tensions between two people, in a sexual sense," said Kapranos. "That situation where two people are in love with each other but neither will admit it, as if they'd take rejection over acceptance just to end the tension in the situation. But we were also using the phrase 'take me out' to refer to the tensions between two snipers pointing guns at each other and how you'd rather be shot than continue the tension that's there."

Kapranos famously said that the band wanted to make music that would make girls get up and dance, and "Take Me Out" emphatically achieves this aim. The iconic guitar riff—several stupidly catchy notes—has both boys and girls marching on the spot. **GR**

Perfekte Welle
Juli (2004)

Writer | Simon Triebel, Andreas Herde
Producer | O.L.A.F. Opal
Label | Island
Album | *Es ist Juli* (2004)

From John Lennon's "(Just Like) Starting Over" to Nirvana's infamous "I swear that I don't have a gun," reality can render hit songs ironic. And so it proved for German pop-rockers Juli and their smash "Perfekte Welle." The band was formed by bassist Andreas "Dedi" Herde, guitarists Simon Triebel and Jonas Pfetzing, and drummer Marcel Römer. Singing in English had won them attention but not improved their commercial prospects. With photogenic singer Eva Briegel, they switched to German and evolved into a hit-making force.

A resurgence of support for German bands singing in their own language was spearheaded by Juli's debut single, "Perfekte Welle." Its lyrical theme of a surfer catching a wave proved a fitting metaphor for their hard-fought success: the melodic yet hard-hitting gem peaked at No. 2 during months on German and Austrian charts. Rarely off the radio, its reign eventually coincided with the tsunami that hit Indonesia and neighboring regions in December 2004. The song was promptly removed from playlists for fear of giving offence.

Happily, this controversy did not hinder Juli's fortunes. Their second album, *Ein neuer Tag* (2006), spawned two further radio-friendly smashes, "Dieses Lieben," and "Wir Beide." "Perfekte Welle," meanwhile, has been extensively covered and latterly awarded that most modern of accolades: a place on the computer game *Rock Band*. **BM**

I Predict a Riot
Kaiser Chiefs (2004)

Writer | A. White, N. Baines, N. Hodgson, R. Wilson, S. Rix
Producer | Stephen Street
Label | B-Unique
Album | *Employment* (2005)

"You can beat around the bush," front man Ricky Wilson said, "but it is British, indie pop-rock." There is no mistaking the Kaiser Chiefs' origins, especially with the recruitment of quintessentially English producer Stephen Street, helmsman for the Kaisers' most obvious antecedents, Blur. With Radiohead going bleepy and Oasis on the wane, the mid-Noughties saw a new breed storm European charts and U.S. campuses. Franz Ferdinand, Bloc Party, and honorary Brits The Killers had angular guitars and arched eyebrows. However, the Kaisers were unashamed rabble-rousers—most thrillingly demonstrated on their first single, "I Predict a Riot."

The lyrics pay backward tribute to the band's hometown Leeds. "I used to DJ with my friend Nick," drummer Nick Hodgson told the *Guardian*. "We'd drive home past a big nightclub and there were always lots of police and people fighting. I went home and wrote the riff on the piano and started singing some words. It says: 'A friend of a friend / He got beaten.' That was a friend of Nick, the DJ. At our club night, Pigs, we had a band on, Black Wire. They were going mad and so were the crowd. You could see the bouncers moving in and I said to the club's boss, 'I predict a riot.'" What could have been a depressing dissection of British nightlife became an air-punching anthem, thanks to the band's explosive energy. At gigs, Hodgson confirmed, "Everyone goes the most berserk for it." **BM**

Can't Stand Me Now | The Libertines (2004)

Writer | Carl Barât, Pete Doherty, Richard Hammerton
Producer | Mick Jones
Label | Rough Trade
Album | *The Libertines* (2004)

"The hardest thing in the world is to tell someone you love you don't want to be around them."
Carl Barât, 2004

◀ **Influenced by:** Janie Jones • The Clash (1977)
▶ **Influence on:** Skag Trendy • The View (2007)
● **Covered by:** Apache Raid (2009)
★ **Other key tracks:** Cyclops (2004) • Dilly Boys (2004)
Never Never (2004) • What Became of the Likely Lads
(2004) • Music When the Lights Go Out (2004)

It is a classic rock 'n' roll tale: boy meets boy; boys form band (The Libertines). Boy number one (Pete Doherty) descends into drug addiction, while boy number two (Carl Barât) watches in despair. Boy one burgles boy two's apartment and ends up in jail. Boy two gives his childhood friend one last chance. . . . Of course, this story does not have a happy ending. As The Libertines headed into the studio to record the follow-up album to *Up the Bracket*—released in 2003—it became clear that Doherty wasn't willing to kick his band, or his body-wrecking habits.

You can hear the last gasps of Barât and Doherty's love-hate relationship on the album opener, "Can't Stand Me Now." After a slow-building, jagged intro, singer and guitarist Barât throws out, "An ending fitting for the start / You twist and tore our love apart." Doherty replies, "No, you've got it the wrong way round / You shut me up and blamed it on the brown [i.e. heroin]." In the chorus, the pair take turns singing, "You can't stand me now"; toward the end, Doherty is heard playing the harmonica—a Christmas gift from Barât. The track's tension and antagonism were brutally real: during recording, security guards were hired to stop Barât and Doherty fighting.

Ironically, this document of disintegration became The Libertines' biggest hit, reaching No. 2 in the U.K. chart. It also played a poignant role in the group's final breakup. In February 2004, at the last of a three-night stand at London's Brixton Academy, Doherty thought Barât gave him an evil look as they played "Can't Stand Me Now." He smashed his guitar, kicked over Barât's amplifier, and stormed off the stage. Soon after, Doherty quit the band for good. **TB**

Float On | Modest Mouse (2004)

Writer | Isaac Brock, Dann Gallucci, Eric Judy
Producer | Dennis Herring
Label | Epic
Album | *Good News for People Who Love Bad News* (2004)

"No one is really more surprised about this success than me."

Isaac Brock, 2004

◀ **Influenced by: Monkey Gone to Heaven**
Pixies (1989)
▶ **Influence on: Shine a Light** · Wolf Parade (2005)
● **Covered by:** Ben Lee (2004) · Goldspot (2006)
★ **Other key tracks:** I've Got It All (Most) (2004)
The World at Large (2004)

Modest Mouse ranted and raved their way to the top of the indie rock mountain, then signed with Epic for their major label debut, the bitingly pessimistic *The Moon & Antarctica*, released in 2000. Many listeners expected a similar dose of cynicism from the follow-up album—especially given that singer-songwriter Isaac Brock had been hit with a bogus date-rape allegation and had spent time in jail for driving under the influence of alcohol. However, Brock went the other direction with the first single from *Good News for People Who Love Bad News:* the downright peppy and optimistic "Float On." "It was a completely conscious thing," he told *The A.V. Club*. "I was just kind of fed up with how bad shit had been going, and how dark everything was, with bad news coming from everywhere. . . . I just want to feel good for a day."

"Float On" is a classic Mouse track, full of slashing guitar, semi-howled vocals, and curiously bookish rhymes picked out in the lyrics. Yet the song also boasts a hook big enough to land Moby Dick. A rhythmic march of a song, it is a "first of its kind" anthem that is as suited to stadiums as it is to dorm rooms.

Heavy modern-rock radio rotation for this breakthrough hit pushed *Good News for People Who Love Bad News* to platinum status and a Grammy nomination. It also paved the way for the group's next album—*We Were Dead Before the Ship Even Sank*, released in 2007 and featuring Smiths guitarist Johnny Marr—to hit No. 1 in the United States. "Every once in a while this sort of thing happens in music," Brock told *Rolling Stone*. "Whoever tries to figure it out fails, because even the people in the bands can't figure it out." **JiH**

Jesus of Suburbia | Green Day (2004)

Writer | Billie Joe Armstrong, Mike Dirnt, Tré Cool
Producer | Rob Cavallo, Green Day
Label | Reprise
Album | American Idiot (2004)

"You can't look at it and say, 'This is a catchy number—God, I love the dance to this song.'"

Billie Joe Armstrong, 2005

◄ **Influenced by: Summer of '69** · Bryan Adams (1984)
► **Influence on: American Eulogy: Mass Hysteria/ Modern World** · Green Day (2009)
● **Covered by:** CMH Band (2007)
★ **Other key tracks:** Boulevard of Broken Dreams (2004) American Idiot (2004) · Holiday (2004)

Demons of the past met demons of the present on Green Day's *American Idiot*. Singer and guitarist Billie Joe Armstrong's powerful lyrics blend autobiography with rage against the nation, filtered through the tales of three characters: Jesus of Suburbia, St. Jimmy, and Whatshername. "It's not," Armstrong admitted, "the most linear story in the world."

"Jesus of Suburbia" is a nine-minute epic rock opera. "We had great individual sections," bassist Mike Dirnt told *Kerrang!* "but we needed to get them to fit together, and sometimes it was a case of writing almost anything . . . to get from one part to the other. It was quite grueling."

The song is divided into five chapters: "Jesus of Suburbia," "City of the Damned," "I Don't Care," "Dearly Beloved," and "Tales of Another Broken Home." Fans delighted in identifying the various inspirations: David Bowie's "Moonage Daydream" ("Jesus of Surburbia"); Black Sabbath's "Children of the Grave" ("I Don't Care"); Mott the Hoople's "All the Young Dudes," Mötley Crüe's "On with the Show," *and* Bryan Adams's "Summer of '69" ("City of the Damned").

For Armstrong, the opening lines—"I'm the son of rage and love / The Jesus of Suburbia"— crystallized the album's theme. "When people are singing it back to you," he declared, "they're not just reflecting the things about the song that *you're* wrapped up in, but it's also the way that *their* lives are wrapped up in it . . . all the emotional baggage that you come with. You finally have an outlet for it—that's what 'Jesus of Suburbia' is to me." Fans agreed wholeheartedly. In a *Rolling Stone* readers' poll carried out in 2009, it topped a list of favorite Green Day songs. **BM**

Mein Teil | Rammstein (2004)

Writer | C. Schneider, C. Lorenz, T. Lindemann, P. Landers, R. Kruspe-Bernstein, O. Riedel
Producer | Jacob Hellner, Rammstein
Label | Universal
Album | *Reise, Reise* (2004)

"The Pet Shop Boys seemed to have liked the song."

Till Landemann, 2007

◄ **Influenced by:** Just One Fix • Ministry (1992)
▶ **Influence on:** Blood • Emigrate (2007)
● **Covered by:** Hayseed Dixie (2007) • Panzerballett (2009)
★ **Other key tracks:** Keine Lust (2004) • Amerika (2004) Ohne dich (2004)

From little red roosters to love guns, songwriters have been crafting odes to the male appendage for decades. Yet there has never been a song quite like "Mein Teil." German industrial metal loonies Rammstein had long mined taboo topics, including incest and sadomasochism. However, they saved the real shocker for the most notorious track from their fourth album. "Mein Teil"—"My Part"—is inspired by a case of cannibalism, where one man cooked and ate another man's penis. "This was not our imagination," singer Till Lindemann protested to *Playboy*. "It really has happened."

The song generated inevitable protests. "The controversy is fun, like stealing forbidden fruit," keyboardist Doktor Christian Lorenz told *The Times*. "But it serves a purpose. We like audiences to grapple with our music, and people have become more receptive." Fans can overlook the subject matter—especially if they do not understand German—because, musically, the song is a supreme example of melodic *Neue Deutsche Härte* ("new German hardness"). It hits with the force of a sledgehammer, repeatedly striking blows with a deep, clean mix of crashing industrial sounds and heavy metal. Lindemann rages through the lyrics like a madman stalking his prey, and only if you understand what he is saying does the biting sarcasm come through: "Because you are what you eat and you know what it is—it is my part."

Despite, or perhaps because of, its lyrics, the song proved very popular. It earned Rammstein a Grammy nomination, and—in one of the weirder twists of the band's unconventional career—was remixed for a single by the Pet Shop Boys. According to drummer Christoph Doom Schneider, their version was "dancey." **JiH**

Portland, Oregon | Loretta Lynn featuring Jack White (2004)

Writer | Loretta Lynn
Producer | Jack White
Label | Interscope
Album | *Van Lear Rose* (2004)

The highlight of *Van Lear Rose*—country legend Loretta Lynn's collaboration with White Stripes front man Jack White—"Portland, Oregon" proved the perfect blend of her heartfelt storytelling and White's sympathetic production. The White Stripes met Lynn after dedicating their album *White Blood Cells* to her in 2001. "She has written so many songs saying it like it is," Meg White told *Mojo*, "and saying things that people didn't dare to say at the time." Lynn wrote to thank them, and planned a duet with White on a song she was calling "Portland Oregon and a Sloe Gin Fizz." "It's a little up-tempo thing," she explained, "and I think he'll like that one!"

The lyric is a diary entry, dramatizing an event from her relationship with husband Oliver "Doolittle" Lynn. She had long mined this seam of bruised wisdom, and "Portland, Oregon" is further evidence to support White's claim that Lynn is "the greatest female singer-songwriter of the twentieth century." White's woozy production—with glorious slide guitar evoking *Exile on Main St*–era Rolling Stones—captures a vibe of boozy wrongdoing, as Lynn sings of flirting with a friend to win the attention of her husband. In the lyric, too, much "gin fizz" results in a regretted one-night stand. Years before, Lynn had pretended she was having an affair. Doolittle waited behind a shower curtain, intending to kill his wife if he caught her with a man. The traumatic experience made for a fantastic song. **SC**

Points of Authority . . . Jay-Z with Linkin Park (2004)

Writer | C. Bennington, M. Shinoda, J. Hahn, L. West, B. Delson, R. Bourdon, T. Marrow, A. Henderson, B. Squier, F. Pappalardi, N. Landsberg, J. Ventura
Producer | Mike Shinoda, David May
Album | *Collision Course* (2004)

Two decades after Run-DMC's "King of Rock," cocktails of hard rock and hip-hop were hardly novel. Linkin Park and Jay-Z, however, united to conjure a six-track smash that climaxed with a career highlight for both acts.

Linkin Park had become stars in 2000, courtesy of their hip-hop-spiced debut *Hybrid Theory* and hits such as "One Step Closer." They amped up the hip-hop elements in 2002 for *Reanimation*, with a remixed "Points of Authority" emerging as "Pts. Of.Athrty." An interesting effort, *Reanimation* was put into perspective in 2003 by a Jay-Z single that *rocked*. From *The Black Album*, "99 Problems" was a skull-crushing mix of an Ice-T phrase, Billy Squier's "The Big Beat," lines from UGK's "Touched," and a snippet of Mountain's "Long Red."

A mash-up of this freshly minted classic with two of Linkin Park's heaviest hits could hardly fail, and so it proved at a secret show initiated by MTV. "Our fans," said the Park's Mike Shinoda, "we basically just told 'em, 'It's a show, it's small. . . . By the way, what else do you listen to?' If somebody's gonna put down, 'My other favorite artist is Jay-Z,' then they gotta come!" ("And," added Jay, "if they put, 'I don't wanna hear none o' that rap shit,' you're not coming!")

Alhough "Numb / Encore" was the project's hit, the brutal "Points of Authority / 99 Problems / One Step Closer" delivered the biggest thrills. A new standard for rock 'n' rap had been set. **BM**

Jack White (in red) and Loretta Lynn at the Hammerstein Ballroom, New York, in 2003.

The Art Teacher
Rufus Wainwright (2004)

Writer | Rufus Wainwright
Producer | Marius De Vries
Label | Geffen
Album | *Want Two* (2004)

Rufus Wainwright won fame with operatic takes on his battles with drugs, family, and lovers. His most accomplished song, though, abandoned that template entirely. "The Art Teacher" was recorded onstage in Montreal. "He's such a charismatic and remarkable live performer," said producer Marius De Vries, "it felt right that something on there should be live." On it, Wainwright replaces lush orchestration with sparse, Philip Glass–like, repetitive piano and a mournful French horn solo.

The song is sung from the perspective of a rich housewife. But while the song displays Wainwright's trademark wit—his leading lady wears a "uniform-ish, pantsuit sort of thing"—it does not distract from the heartbreaking tale of unrequited love. The bored housewife dreams of an art teacher who took her school class to New York's Metropolitan Museum. "I was just a girl then," Wainwright croons. "He asked us what our favorite work of art was / But never could I tell him: it was him." The teacher told the girl that he liked the Turners, and the now-adult protagonist claims that from that point she never "turned to any other man." Well, not quite. She confesses to marrying "an executive company head," and says she now owns a Turner. But it only reminds her of that childhood crush. Sung by a gay man, these lines are poignant—any gay person who has once hidden their sexuality can relate to a narrator trapped in a loveless lie. **TB**

Dry Your Eyes
The Streets (2004)

Writer | Mike Skinner
Producer | Mike Skinner
Label | 679
Album | *A Grand Don't Come for Free* (2004)

Original Pirate Material, Mike Skinner's debut album as hip-hop act The Streets, was packed with observations of British life, ranging from the deeply touching to the downright hilarious. His follow-up was, unexpectedly, a concept album. Chronicling a period in which the protagonist loses and finds one thousand pounds, while finding and losing a girl, it is full of life's lessons. However, it was not until the strikingly candid "Dry Your Eyes" became a hit that The Streets became a name on everyone's lips.

The song originally featured Coldplay's Chris Martin on the chorus. "I thought that he would sound really good on it," Skinner told *NME*. "I asked him to do it and he did. After that I don't really know. I don't think his record company liked it. But maybe he didn't like it."

"Dry Your Eyes" details every heartbreaking moment as a relationship ends: Skinner describes being crushed as he begs his girl to reconsider. In a mid-song break, strings swell and he intones, "And I'm just standing there / I can't say a word 'cause everything's just gone / I've got nothing / Absolutely nothing." And, for that breath-holding moment, you're right there with him. "'Dry Your Eyes' is the moment of complete panic when your girlfriend finishes with you . . ." he explained. "I always like to tell how it is. I think that is my strong point." **SO**

Chicago
Sufjan Stevens (2005)

Writer | Sufjan Stevens
Producer | Sufjan Stevens
Label | Asthmatic Kitty
Album | *Illinois* (2005)

"Patriotic songs with strong melodies," said Sufjan Stevens, of his ambitious "Fifty States Project." "It's the basis of what I'm doing, just focusing on traditional songwriting." His aim—to compose an album about each U.S. state—gave rise to the critically lauded *Illinois* (also known as *Sufjan Stevens Invites You to: Come on Feel the Illinoise*). The album's "Chicago" is arguably this indie troubadour's greatest single achievement.

A stunning standout song amid an excellent (albeit oblique) concept album, "Chicago" sees Stevens eschew his pared-back, acoustic approach for a multi-instrumental sound. Beginning with stirring strings, before sliding back to Sufjan's delicate vocal, "Chicago" was hailed for both its emotional lyrics and musical majesty. Fans battled over the song's meaning, with some claiming "You came to take us / All things go, all things go" refers to a personal relationship with Christ. Others believe his cry for "Freedom / From myself and from the land" is a simple reference to escaping the landlocked fields of Illinois and the Midwest.

A city vibe is evident throughout the song. A raft of horns, strings, and percussion adds a sense of occasion and celebration to the song, contributing to the universal acclaim for its parent album. Three further versions were issued in 2006 on its successor, *The Avalanche*, a collection of outtakes from the *Illinois* sessions. **JM**

Todo cambia
Mercedes Sosa (2005)

Writer | Julio Numhauser
Producer | "Chango" Farías Gómez
Label | Universal Classics
Album | *Corazón Libre* (2005)

Having co-founded the left-wing *nueva canción* (new song) group Quilapayún in 1965, Chilean singer-songwriter Julio Numhauser found himself in the firing line when General Augusto Pinochet ousted the socialist government in 1973. Numhauser had to leave Chile for exile in Sweden, where he wrote "Todo cambia" ("Everything changes"). It has since become a Latin American anthem.

The song first appeared on his debut solo album of the same name in 1982, with Numhauser's earnest vocal backed by acoustic guitar and *zampoña* (panpipes). The lyrics feature a series of beautifully poetic images, underlining the need to accept change as something that happens naturally. Everything changes, declares the singer, except his love. Mexican singers Nicho Hinojosa and Guadalupe Pineda are among the artists who have covered "Todo Cambia." However, what brought the song an international audience was when it became part of the repertoire of the late singer Mercedes Sosa, initially featuring on her album *Live in Europe* in 1990. Having been exiled to Europe in 1979 after her own country, Argentina, was engulfed by a "dirty war," Sosa knew exactly what Numhauser meant. Her peerless interpretive skills give his words all the gravity they deserve. She recorded the song several times, arguably the finest of which was this stark, stripped-down arrangement for the *Corazón Libre* album. **JLu**

I Bet You Look Good on the Dancefloor | Arctic Monkeys (2005)

Writer | Alex Turner
Producer | Jim Abbiss
Label | Domino
Album | *Whatever People Say I Am, That's What I'm Not* (2006)

"With the Arctic Monkeys, a lot of it is about the wordplay. 'Cos they are quite stunning lyrics."

Noel Gallagher, Oasis, 2006

◀ **Influenced by:** Disco 2000 • Pulp (1995)
▶ **Influence on:** The Age of the Understatement
The Last Shadow Puppets (2008)
● **Covered by:** Sugababes (2006) • Tom Jones
& Joe Perry (2007)
★ **Other key track:** Fake Tales of San Francisco (2005)

He wrote one of the fastest-selling debut albums in British chart history, yet Arctic Monkeys front man Alex Turner considers himself an accidental hero. "I only started singing because nobody else would do it, really," the nineteen-year-old told the *Daily Record*. Nonetheless, his debut single, "I Bet You Look Good on the Dancefloor," stayed at the top of the U.K. charts for five weeks, and *NME* dubbed Turner the "coolest man on the planet."

Propelling the Sheffield teenager's dizzying success were his band's driving guitars and clattering drums. Meanwhile, Turner's wry, observational lyrics mixed highbrow references with low-rent scenarios, delivered in an inimitable Northern English brogue. Like Pulp's Jarvis Cocker, also from Sheffield, Turner wrote about the world he knew, winning fans with lines such as, "Oh there is no love / Montagues or Capulets / Just bangin' tunes and DJ sets and / Dirty dance floors and dreams of naughtiness."

Catchy, funny, and effortlessly relatable, the band's demos won them an army of loyal, web-savvy followers. They spread the word via online message boards, catapulting the boys into a record deal, and ultimately into music history.

"The Arctic Monkeys have worked right outside the record company structure and that is really radical," commented *NME*'s associate editor, Alex Needham. Turner, he added, "is almost like a new breed of rock star—almost like year zero. He has come straight from the audience on to the stage."

Turner, however, claimed to be unmoved by his first hit. "It's a bit shit," he complained to the *Guardian*. "The words are rubbish. I scraped the bottom of the barrel. . . . I'd hate to be just known for that song because it's a bit crap." **EP**

Hard to Beat | Hard-Fi (2005)

Writer | Richard Archer
Producer | Richard Archer,
Wolsey Wright
Label | Necessary
Album | *Stars of CCTV* (2006)

"We'd been listening to a lot of French house—people like Daft Punk and Stardust."

Richard Archer, 2006

◄ **Influenced by: Music Sounds Better with You**
Stardust (1998)
► **Influence on: Vogue vs. Hard to Beat** · Madonna vs.
Hard-Fi (2006)
● **Covered by:** Studio Group (2006)

"The driving force to actually make something happen," Hard-Fi chief Richard Archer explained to musicOMH.com, "is that the town we come from, there's nothing to do there. We come from a town called Staines in west London, near Heathrow. It's an insular little satellite town. It's close enough to the city that no bands will ever come and play there—they'll always play London. So nothing ever happens there. We were bored of being [broke], bored of being bored."

Having returned from London to Staines after the death of his father and the dissolution of his group Cooltempo, Archer penned new songs while licking his wounds. However, instead of offering to finance demos, his publishing company chose to drop him. Undefeated, Archer assembled Hard-Fi with local musicians and recorded new songs in a disused office, rented for a princely three hundred pounds. These new songs were strong, brash, guitar pop, with fire and focus. One, however, stood head and shoulders above the rest.

A hymn to the empowering rush of love, albeit one written in down-to-earth terms, "Hard to Beat" possesses an irresistible backbeat—all house-y hand claps and rasping high hats—with swooping strings and desperate horns. This heroic punk-funk quickly evolved from indie dance-floor-filler into a crossover smash.

Vindication was sweet for Archer. "Hard to Beat" scored him a U.K. Top Ten entry, a freak American hit, and—doubtless—lots of licensing money from the rousing tune's regular use on televised sports events. Although he is yet to pen another song quite as compelling or successful, one has to concede that Hard-Fi's breakthrough set a tough standard to match. **SC**

Fix You
Coldplay (2005)

Writer | G. Berryman, J. Buckland, W. Champion, C. Martin
Producer | Ken Nelson, Coldplay
Label | Parlophone
Album | *X&Y* (2005)

Coldplay's album *A Rush of Blood to the Head* marked a dramatic sea change in 2002. Their debut *Parachutes* had sold impressively, but the follow-up shifted eleven million copies worldwide. The pressure to deliver again was immense, and reports emerged that EMI's share value depended on Coldplay's third album. Three years later, a still shell-shocked Chris Martin declared: "Shareholders, stocks—all that stuff—It Has Nothing To Do With Me."

Fortunately, *X&Y* did the job. Coldplay delivered what was expected of an arena-filling band—anthems, universal themes, bellow-along choruses—but "Fix You" went above and beyond the call of duty. The track's charming rhymes and gradual scene setting lodge it firmly in the brain, while sustained organ chords lend it a spiritual might (echoing, as bassist Guy Berryman observed, Jimmy Cliff's 1969 classic "Many Rivers to Cross").

The organ was given to Martin's wife Gwyneth Paltrow by her late father Bruce. "I plugged it in, and there was this incredible sound I'd never heard before," the singer marveled to *USA Today*. "All these songs poured out from this one sound." The semireligious bent of "Fix You" is cemented in its final third, as the band join voices for a spine-tingling choral burst. It established "Fix You" as a live favorite and a go-to soundtrack for emotional TV moments, and earned Coldplay an Ivor Novello nomination for Best Song, musically and lyrically. **MH**

Let's Make Love and Listen to Death from Above | CSS (2005)

Writer | Adriano Cintra, Luísa Hanae "Lovefoxxx" Matsushita
Producer | Adriano Cintra
Label | Trama
Album | *Cansei De Ser Sexy* (2005)

Take five cool women—including flamboyant, catsuit-wearing lead singer, Lovefoxxx—and one multitalented man and what do you have? Brazilian sextet CSS, an abbreviation of "Cansei de ser sexy"—the Portuguese translation of a phrase attributed to Beyoncé, "tired of being sexy." The tongue-in-cheek name suits these fun, São Paulo–based popstrels right down to the ground.

Their best-known song, "Let's Make Love and Listen to Death from Above," is a tantalizing electro-pop teaser that name-checks fellow dance-punks Death from Above 1979. CSS took their ode to the now-defunct Canadian band to another level with the video for "Let's Make Love . . ." featuring band members wearing elephant masks—both of Death from Above 1979's album sleeves feature the duo with trunks. The song itself has, as pitchfork.com observed, "a great ripply disco bass line and glassy keyboard tweets and a rock guitar breakdown that actually sounds something like Death from Above."

The song was plucked as a single from their debut album. Voguish producers—including Diplo, Spank Rock, Simian Mobile Disco, Calvin Harris, and Hot Chip—lined up to remix it, contributing to the song's overwhelming cool factor. As well as being on trend, it was also tons of fun with Lovefoxxx's energetic delivery of playfully seductive lyrics like: "Wine then bed / Then more / Then again." **OM**

CSS's front woman Lovefoxxx, latter-day champion of the Lycra catsuit, performs in 2007. ➔

Best of You | Foo Fighters (2005)

Writer | Dave Grohl, Taylor Hawkins, Nate Mendel, Chris Shiflett
Producer | Nick Raskulinecz, Foo Fighters
Label | Roswell
Album | *In Your Honor* (2005)

"I didn't really think of an interesting melody. I just wanted to scream the whole way through."

Dave Grohl, 2005

◄ **Influenced by: Something I Learned Today** · Hüsker Dü (1984)
► **Influence on: Armor and Sword** · Rush (2007)
● **Covered by:** Pieter Embrechts, Thomas De Prins & The New Radio Kings (2009)
★ **Other key track:** Friend of a Friend (2005)

"'Best of You' is a song of resistance," Dave Grohl told MTV. "It's about the refusal to be taken advantage of by something that's bigger than you, or someone you're in love with." A decade into his band's career—and after no shortage of hits and classics—Grohl had finally written his anthem.

Mark Pellington directed the unsettling yet moving video, featuring the band playing on the roof of a disused hospital and provocative images of anger and pain. "His wife had just died . . ." recalled drummer Taylor Hawkins, "and he had a real emotional attachment to the song. At first he said that he couldn't even do it, because it hit him so hard." The sound and vision combined to give the Foo Fighters their first U.S. platinum single. However, it was onstage that the song had the most impact. "I thought, 'There's no way I'll be able to play this live. There's blood in my throat,'" Grohl recalled. "But now it's great. It's a release. When you go out and sing words from the heart, you scream twice as hard."

Two stadium performances in 2007 were of particular significance. The first was Prince's cover version, performed in Miami at the Super Bowl. "When I saw it, tears came to my eyes because I grew up listening to Prince," said Grohl. "When someone like that covers one of your songs, you gotta pinch yourself because it doesn't feel real." Then, at the Live Earth show in Britain, a rendition was beamed around the world, confirming the Foo Fighters as a band worthy of the biggest arenas.

The most remarkable rendition, however, graces *Skin and Bones*. On this live Foo Fighters album released in 2006, the song holds all its original fire and more—played on acoustic guitar by Grohl alone. **BM**

Hoppípolla | Sigur Rós (2005)

Writer | Jónsi Birgisson, Kjartan Sveinsson, Orri Páll Dýrason, Georg Hólm
Producer | Sigur Rós, Ken Thomas
Label | EMI
Album | *Takk...* (2005)

"This is as liberating as an orgasm."

Gary Lightbody, Snow Patrol, 2006

Takk . . . (Icelandic for "thanks") was quite the swerve for Sigur Rós. It immediately showed a greater desire to connect than their preceding album by actually containing song titles. The mainstream duly harvested its rich crop of accessible tracks for commercials, trailers, and incidental television music. And none was more enthusiastically juiced than "Hoppípolla."

It is easy to see the appeal: humble beginnings quickly give way to a bursting, spiraling piano signature with strings and horns woven through it, a handsome evocation of pride and elation. It is a rapturous, big sound, but a small story. "The lyrics are wrapped in the almost impenetrable cocoon of singer Jónsi Birgisson's made-up language, Hopelandi," Snow Patrol's Gary Lightbody told *Q*. "It's like holding a glass to the wall to hear next door." "Hoppípolla" translates as "jump in puddles," and is a memory of childhood, the song's anthemic swoops signifying the abandon of youth. As Birgisson puts it (approximately), "I get a nosebleed / But I'll always stand up again."

Uptake for the song was extraordinary, with the BBC using it to soundtrack teasers for its *Planet Earth* series in 2006. "Hoppípolla," the perfect fit for a show of such global reach, consequently reached the U.K. Top Thirty six months after its release. However, this was the tip of the Icelandic iceberg. "Hoppípolla" has become a byword for emotional splendor: driving drama in the trailer for the movie *Slumdog Millionaire*, soundtracking televised sports tournaments, and underscoring reality TV tearjerkers. Observed Birgisson: "Every dramatic ending—cue it up!" So did the impact of "Hoppípolla" come as a surprise to Sigur Rós? Not quite. Its working title was "The Money Song." **MH**

Hope There's Someone | Antony & The Johnsons (2005)

Writer | Antony Hegarty
Producer | Antony Hegarty
Label | Secretly Canadian
Album | *I Am a Bird Now* (2005)

"Quite frankly, I think he is the greatest singer in history."

Rufus Wainwright, 2004

◄ **Influenced by: In This Hole** · Cat Power (2000)
► **Influence on: We're All Going to Die** · Malcolm Middleton (2007)
★ **Other key tracks:** You Are My Sister (2005) · Fistful of Love (2005) · Free at Last (2005) · For Today I Am a Boy (2005) · Spiralling (2005)

Death will come to each and every one of us, but few have expressed the universal fear of dying—and, specifically, dying alone—so singularly as the English-born Antony Hegarty. "I'm scared of the middle place between light and nowhere / I don't want to be the one left in there," he sings in that remarkable voice, holding nothing back. It can make for an uncomfortable and otherworldly—but unforgettable—experience. As one of Hegarty's heroes and admirers, Boy George, said in 2005: "Antony's vulnerability is so honest and powerful." Indeed, the song's swelling climax sounds as if Hegarty has actually experienced passing from life to death rather than just writing a song about it.

The total lack of compromise in his work obliged the mainstream to move toward him—rather than the other way around—in order to find out more. ("I think he's brave," Kate Bush observed to *Q*, "and I like that.") This culminated in the Antony & The Johnsons album *I Am a Bird Now*, which opens with "Hope There's Someone," winning the U.K.'s Mercury Music Prize.

The song also provides succor in situations that Hegarty had not envisaged. He was dismayed to hear of its regular airings at funerals: "Oh God," he told the *Guardian*, "That sounds like a nightmare. It's a song for the living, not a tribute to the dead." He was less put out by the news that the sister of his band's bassist was employing "Hope There's Someone" to help people find their misplaced faith. "We're talking about a group of two thousand, Christian fundamentalist women," Antony told *Magnet*. "Who would have ever fathomed that song could have an application like that?" **CB**

Welcome to Jamrock | Damian Marley (2005)

Writer | Damian Marley, Stephen Marley, Ini Kamoze
Producer | Stephen Marley
Label | Ghetto Youths United
Album | *Welcome to Jamrock* (2005)

"America is in one of its worst recessions right now, and even still, it's a lot better off than Jamaica."

Damian Marley, 2009

◀ **Influenced by: World-A-Music** • Ini Kamoze (1984)
▶ **Influence on: Stand Up Jamrock** • Bob Marley (2005)
● **Covered by:** DJ Shepdog (2009)
★ **Other key tracks:** The Master Has Come Back (2005)
Road to Zion (2005) • Confrontation (2005) • Pimpa's
Paradise (2005) • Hey Girl (2005)

Damian Marley, youngest son of reggae master Bob Marley, was conceived in the media spotlight: his mother is Cindy Breakspeare, holder of the Miss Jamaica and Miss World titles when she was Bob's lover. He grew up making music and toasting (the Jamaican style of rhyming, over a reggae bass line, that predated and influenced rap). His skills endeared him to collaborators such as Cypress Hill and Nas, and helped win him an audience on his own terms, rather than as "the son of Bob Marley."

"Welcome to Jamrock"—produced by his older brother Stephen—launched Damian internationally. "Jamrock" refers to Jamaica, and the song observes how the nation is marketed to tourists—often employing Bob Marley as a sunny icon. "I look up to my father," Damian told suite101. com, "and I look up to him as a musician, and then, his topics are the greatest topics. And they're the kind of topics that I would like to write about— that can teach people and have something conscious, something to say."

Damian's fiery toasts talk about violent crime, rampant poverty, and corrupt politicians as three of the Caribbean island's more pressing concerns. Sirens, guns, and a chilling chorus— "Out in the street, they call it murder!"—add to the ominous feel. A pumping groove by master Jamaican rhythm section Sly Dunbar and Robbie Shakespeare fuels the seismic song. This first appeared in 1984 on their production of Ini Kamoze's reggae classic "World-A-Music," from which the "Out in the street . . ." sample also originates. Initially an urban anthem, "Welcome to Jamrock" crossed from the streets to radio, gave Damian a huge reggae-rap crossover hit, and won him two Grammys. **GC**

Little Bear
Guillemots (2006)

Writer | Fyfe Dangerfield
Producer | Fyfe Dangerfield, Nick Ingman
Label | Polydor
Album | *Through the Windowpane* (2006)

Romantic pop quartet Guillemots emerged in 2005 and made a name for themselves supporting Rufus Wainwright. They stepped into the spotlight with *Through the Windowpane*, which veered from stark balladry to samba, all steeped in poetry and Fyfe Dangerfield's openhearted croon. "The question we get asked a lot," Dangerfield complained to popjustice.com, "is, 'Was it a conscious decision to make all the songs different on the record?' I don't understand that. It seems to be frowned upon if your songs don't all sound the same."

"Little Bear" opens the set, jarring in its simplicity. Strings circle, telling their own story with the mute eloquence of a silent movie score—there are similarities to the 1982 soundtrack for *The Snowman*—before Dangerfield enters with faintly discordant piano. The arresting opener spurred Paul McCartney to comment: "I think it's a very brave way to open an album. It's beautiful orchestration—really not what you'd expect."

Oddly for a first track, "Little Bear" signals a retreat, the singer shrinking from a relationship beyond control. Dangerfield resists making explicit the meaning of his songs—"They are what they mean to everybody," he insists—but the lyrics are shot through with regret and fear ("I wouldn't want to cause you anything / That might break your lovely face"), and Dangerfield's emotive voice leaves little doubt. **MH**

Consolation Prizes
Phoenix (2006)

Writer | T. Mars, F. Moulin, C. Mazzalai, L. Brancowitz
Producer | Phoenix
Label | Virgin
Album | *It's Never Been Like That* (2006)

Phoenix boasted impeccable ties with French pop: guitarist Laurent Brancowitz had been in the haphazard Darlin' with Daft Punk's Thomas Bangalter and Guy-Manuel de Homem-Christo, and front man Thomas Mars had sung Air's *Virgin Suicides* theme "Playground Love" under the nom de plume Gordon Tracks. While all things Parisian appeared to revolve around house and disco, Phoenix turned up with a fresh dab of 1970s pop, evoking the polished, perfumed likes of Steely Dan and Fleetwood Mac.

Their 2000 debut, *United*, showed promise, and 2004's *Alphabetical* had a perfectionist air. Critical acclaim, however, was not enough to motivate record buyers, so *It's Never Been Like That* saw Phoenix stripping back and learning to appreciate the rough edges. Its second single, "Consolation Prizes," has a joie de vivre you don't get by thinking too hard, reveling in its skiffle shuffle and stop-start, finger-snapping gait.

It's not all a bed of roses. Cut through the second-language phrasing ("If one is easy then hard is two"), and you'll find Mars coming clean. He doesn't want second best; he doesn't want to be anyone else's second best. "Cut off your hair, yeah, that's it! / If you look like that, I swear I'm gonna love you more," he scoffs. It was bittersweet pop—hard lessons learned, plus a sprightly tune that won't budge from the head. **MH**

Not Ready to Make Nice | Dixie Chicks (2006)

Writer | Natalie Maines, Martie Maguire,
Emily Erwin, Daniel Wilson
Producer | Rick Rubin
Label | Columbia
Album | *Taking the Long Way* (2006)

*"I couldn't sing it for the first
hundred times without crying."*

Martie Maguire, 2006

◀ **Influenced by: Courtesy of the Red, White, and Blue
(The Angry American)** • Toby Keith (2002)
▶ **Influence on: Dear Mr. President** • Pink (2006)
● **Covered by:** Wanessa (2007)
★ **Other key tracks:** Everybody Knows (2006) • I Hope
(2006) • The Long Way Around (2006)

"Traitors," "Dixie Sluts," and "Saddam's Angels" are
just three of the insults hurled at the Dixie Chicks
in 2003 after singer Natalie Maines was reported
as telling an audience in London, England, that
she was ashamed President George W. Bush was
from her home state of Texas.

The reports enraged Republican country and
western fans. The band endured death threats,
radio blacklisting, and events where former fans
gathered to destroy CDs. As band member Martie
Maguire told *Der Speigel,* "We don't feel a part of
the country scene anymore."

The Dixie Chicks enjoyed support from artists
including Bruce Springsteen and Madonna, while
country legend Merle Haggard told the Associated
Press: "Almost the majority of America jumped
down their throats for voicing an opinion. It was
like a verbal witch hunt and lynching."

The band released nothing new until 2006,
when "Not Ready to Make Nice" addressed the
controversy: "It's a sad, sad story when a mother
will teach her daughter that she ought to hate a
perfect stranger / And how in the world can the
words that I said send somebody so over the edge
/ That they'd write me a letter sayin' that I better /
Shut up and sing or my life will be over?" Bloody
but unbeaten, it marked a departure from their
traditional country sound, and—despite little
airplay—reached No. 4 in the United States.

There were still dissenting voices. Veteran
entertainer Pat Boone told Fox News: "I think it's
outrageous for any of these performers to be
bashing our president." But vindication came in
2007 when the band performed the song at the
Grammys, before winning Record of the Year, Song
of the Year, and Best Country Performance. **DC**

Crazy | Gnarls Barkley (2006)

Writer | Brian Burton, Thomas Callaway,
Gian Franco Reverberi, Gian Piero Reverberi
Producer | Brian "Danger Mouse" Burton
Label | Downtown
Album | *St. Elsewhere* (2006)

*"The first time Cee-Lo did that,
he went out of body."*

Brian "Danger Mouse" Burton, 2006

Influenced by: Nel Cimitero di Tucson · Gianfranco &
Gian Piero Reverberi (1966)
Influence on: American Boy · Estelle featuring Kanye
West (2008)
Covered by: The Kooks (2006) · Alice Russell (2008)
Violent Femmes (2008)

The economy was in the can, war was raging in cities that most Westerners couldn't pinpoint on the world map, and there wasn't much worth listening to on pop radio. To the rescue—at least in regard to the latter—came unlikely saviors Gnarls Barkley.

The duo—rapper-singer Cee-Lo, from Atlanta's Goodie Mob, and producer Danger Mouse, who came to fame with 2004's *The Grey Album*—definitely delivered a remedy for our ailing ears. *St. Elsewhere* was a refreshing cocktail of what Cee-Lo dubbed "electric industrial Euro soul." Yet it would forever live in the shadow of its lead single.

"Crazy" was a force of nature that made the album and the band seem like afterthoughts. Listeners were swept away by its blend of modern beats and old-school soul. The vocals sounded appealingly androgynous, which only heightened their evocativeness. With subtle production touches, such as warm string arrangements, and the best sing-along chorus in memory, the result was one of the decade's most unforgettable songs.

"'Crazy' was one take . . ." Danger Mouse told Pitchfork. "It's like [Cee-Lo] sang it on the mic, and that's why it sounds the way it does. . . . He was like, 'What do you think of that—how was that?' and I was like, 'Ohhh, that was all right' [laughs]."

The tune was so good that it became a hit months before its actual release, after being leaked to radio. Once people could actually buy the track, fans really went bananas: in the United Kingdom, it became the first single to top the charts on download sales alone. It also became a Top Ten hit in Europe, North America, and Australia and has since been covered by acts ranging from Prince and Nelly Furtado to Ray Lamontagne. **JiH**

Love Is a Losing Game | Amy Winehouse (2006)

Writer | Amy Winehouse
Producer | Mark Ronson
Label | Island
Album | *Back to Black* (2006)

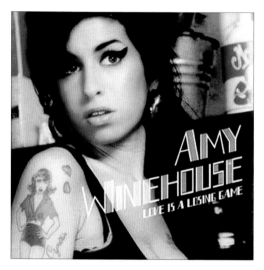

"This is the best female vocalist I've heard in my entire career and one of the best writers."

George Michael, 2007

> ◄ **Influenced by: Remember (Walkin' in the Sand)**
> The Shangri-Las (1964)
> ► **Influence on: If He Should Ever Leave You**
> Tom Jones (2008)
> ● **Covered by:** The City Champs (2009)

Amy Winehouse's debut album in 2003, *Frank*, drew comparisons to the jazz greats, and made the singer a star in her native United Kingdom. The rest of the world didn't get nearly as excited, although that soon changed with the release of *Back to Black*.

One of the most influential albums of the decade, *Back to Black* tapped into the girl-group vibe of the early Sixties and inspired a revival of old-school soul/R&B music. It paved the route to stardom for fellow revivalists Duffy and Adele but also influenced new music from established stars such as Raphael Saadiq and Tom Jones.

"Love Is a Losing Game" didn't boast the novelty factor of "Rehab" or sassy fun of "You Know I'm No Good," but featured Winehouse's most achingly beautiful vocal work. "All the songs," she explained, "are about the state of my relationship at the time with [her partner] Blake [Fielder-Civil]."

This mature, timeless song features forlorn wisdom delivered via deceptively catchy lyrics. A sparse yet velvety arrangement complements the message and the result is far beyond convincing retro-soul. "Love Is a Losing Game," more than anything else on the critically acclaimed *Back to Black*, sounds like a long-lost gem from the Sixties that has been rediscovered.

Although "Rehab" became the most popular Winehouse song to cover, "Love Is a Losing Game" has the best chance of becoming a true standard. That process has already started, with Prince including it in his shows, George Michael choosing it as his favorite among his choices on the BBC radio program *Desert Island Discs*, and students analyzing the lyrics, alongside those of Bob Dylan and Billie Holiday, at Cambridge University. **JiH**

Amy Winehouse performs in 2007; her fashion sense has been as influential as her music. ➔

Ain't No Other Man | Christina Aguilera (2006)

Writer | Christina Aguilera, Chris E. Martin, Charles Roane, Kara DioGuardi, Harold Beatty, Robert Marin
Producer | DJ Premier, C. Roane, C. Aguilera, R. Lewis
Label | RCA
Album | *Back to Basics* (2006)

"She's doin' it. But good music is not out there right now. We gotta save the planet!"
DJ Premier, 2006

◄ **Influenced by: Car Wash** • Christina Aguilera featuring Missy Elliott (2004)
► **Influence on: Until I Stay** • Jully Black (2007)
● **Covered by:** Frida Sanden (2007) • David Davis (2008) • Jordin Sparks (2008)

"The whole 'big band' kind of element, the feel of all these horns and things going on . . ." enthused Christina Aguilera, "It's feel-good music!" *Christina Aguilera* had been her poppy debut, *Stripped* her creative emergence, and *My Kind of Christmas* her . . . well, you can guess. *Back to Basics,* however, was her fabulous folly: "a throwback album to the 1920s, Thirties, Forties, using elements of old blues, jazz, and soul."

The double set's second half was helmed by Linda Perry, who produced the *Stripped* classic "Beautiful" (and followed it up here with the fantastic "Hurt"). The first half, however, was steered by "the more beat-driven producers that give me those throwback elements of old horn blares, horn sounds, different scratches, and sampling these obscure bits and pieces—to create a modern-day sound, with underlying, hard-hitting beats."

The standout was "Ain't No Other Man," whose swaggering, brassy stomp was based on gems dug from the crates by DJ Premier of Gang Starr. One was "The Cissy's Thing," by early Seventies Texan funkateers The Soul Seven. The other was the delightful "Hippy, Skippy, Moon Strut (Opus #1)" by New York Latino outfit The Moon People; first released as "(I'll Be a) Happy Man" in 1968 and then, with organ overdubs by Dave Cortez, as "Happy Soul (with a Hook)."

"Ain't No Other Man" became Aguilera's first U.S. platinum single since her 1999 debut "Genie in a Bottle." "That was an amazing experience," Premier later reflected. "I didn't know what to expect because I had my way and she had her way but I definitely learned things from her that I never did in production before." **BM**

Supermassive Black Hole | Muse (2006)

Writer | Matt Bellamy
Producer | Rich Costey, Muse
Label | Helium 3
Album | *Black Holes & Revelations* (2006)

"I was going out dancing in clubs around New York. That helped create tracks like 'Supermassive Black Hole.'"

Matt Bellamy, 2006

◄ **Influenced by: Do Somethin'** · Britney Spears (2005)
► **Influence on: Where Did All the Love Go?**
Kasabian (2009)
● **Covered by:** Threshold (2007) · Billy Lunn (2009)
Tiffany Page (2010) · Theshold (2010)
★ **Other key track:** Knights of Cydonia (2006)

With their first three albums, Muse accomplished the impossible: they made it okay to like prog rock again. Unexpectedly, the fourth—*Black Holes & Revelations*—seemed as appropriate for rock club dance floors as it was for Dungeons & Dragons tournaments. The album featured acoustic balladry and new wave influences, but the most drastic departure was what drummer Dominic Howard described as "Prince-influenced, groove-based, rock weirdness." For a band long saddled with the "next Radiohead" tag, "Supermassive Black Hole" was a shocking turn of events.

The song mixes swaggering rock—highlighted by Matt Bellamy's cobra-like strikes of twisting guitar and Howard's steady stomps—with a funky groove. "It's the most different to anything we've ever done," Bellamy told *Rockmag*. "We've had some Belgian influences: Millionaire, dEUS, Evil Superstars, Soulwax. . . . We've added a bit of Prince and Kanye West . . . with Rage Against The Machine riffs underneath. We've mixed a lot of things in this track, with a bit of electronica. It's different—quite funny."

Above this glorious racket was Bellamy's pristine falsetto, singing lyrics that were variously interpreted as a twisted love song or his reaction to fame. The latter was boosted by the song's inclusion in the first *Twilight* movie. "[Director] Catherine Hardwicke wanted to use 'Supermassive Black Hole' in a very long scene, with not a lot of dialogue in the foreground," Muse's manager Cliff Burnstein told *Billboard*. "We thought, 'This is fun—this is a nice woman who writes these books, she's a fan of ours, let's get involved in this.' No one was really thinking at the time, 'This is a huge opportunity.'" **JiH**

We Are Your Friends
Justice vs. Simian (2006)

Writer | Gaspard Augé, Xavier de Rosnay, James Ford, Simon Lord, Alex MacNaughton, James Shaw
Producer | Justice
Label | Ten

Many songs are awarded "club anthem" status, but not many truly deserve it. The massive "We Are Your Friends" is a notable exception. Gaspard Augé and Xavier de Rosnay—the DJs/producers behind Justice—created the classic in 2003, using a resung excerpt of "Never Be Alone," from the album *We Are Your Friends* by British electro-rock band Simian. "We ran a remix competition in France around the time we released that song," said Simian's James Ford. "We just gave the parts out. We had ten remixes come back from unknown Frenchies, and Justice was one of them. I believe it's only the first or second thing they ever did!"

"We tried to make it a pop song," de Rosnay told MTV. "We love techno for the energy when we are DJing but ninety-nine percent of the music we listen to is pop." With a rabble-rousing chorus—"We! Are! Your! Friends! You'll never be alone again!"—the song led to a deal with the Ed Banger label for Justice, while Simian splintered (two of them forming the more dancey Simian Mobile Disco). The record that bore both their names was released in 2006. (A version on Justice's live *A Cross the Universe* incorporates elements of Ministry's "Just One Fix" and Klaxons' "Atlantis 2 Interzone"—the latter produced by Simian's James Ford.) Its fantastic video—all party animals and collapsing objects—promptly triumphed at the 2006 MTV Europe Music Awards. **OM**

Pop the Glock
Uffie (2006)

Writer | Anna Catherine "Uffie" Hartley, Fabien "Feadz" Pianta, Johann "Johan52" Mattar
Producer | Fabien "Feadz" Pianta
Label | Arcade Mode

Born in Miami in 1987, electro MC Uffie grew up in Hong Kong before finding a base and a breakthrough in Paris in her teens. Her boyfriend Feadz was a modest name on the French disco scene—thriving in the wake of smashes from Daft Punk and Mr. Oizo—and he encouraged the budding rapper to guest on his tracks. Together, they created the sexy, futuristic—yet perceptibly old school—"Pop the Glock," a one-woman calling card and passport to a record deal. The single snuck out as a limited edition of 200 on Arcade Mode, but a swift reissue on Ed Banger found its hipster audience. Uffie's name was dropped in the right circles, albeit without "Pop the Glock" racking up the chart positions that its deadpan sassiness and icy catchiness deserved.

The track's shape and delivery owed much to the groundbreaking audacity of 1980s female MCs such as Roxanne Shanté and the She Rockers, aping their refreshing directness and beating the boys at their own game. Uffie's rhymes were inspired by the 1987 track "Top Billin'," by U.S. hip-hop duo Audio Two (brothers of another pioneering female rapper, MC Lyte).

Solo singles came and went meekly, forcing Uffie to rely on a late 2009 re-release of "Pop the Glock" to kick-start the campaign for her debut album. As she remarked in 2006, "People need something this fresh!" **MH**

Uffie in 2007: sympathetic to boys who are feeling freaky hot. ➡

Ovunque proteggi

Vinicio Capossela (2006)

Writer | Vinicio Capossela
Producer | Vinicio Capossela
Label | Warner Music (Italy)
Album | *Ovunque proteggi*
(2006)

First, he was "the young Paolo Conte"; then he was "the Italian Tom Waits"; then he decided to be himself. Vinicio Capossela arrived on the music scene at the start of the Nineties, and was garlanded for his albums *All'una e trentacinque circa* (*Around 1:35 AM*) and *Modi* (inspired by the suicide of Jeanne Hébuterne, lover of artist Amedeo Modigliani). Yet, after three albums, he was dissatisfied and unsure how to move forward. His next albums, *Il ballo di San Vito* and *Canzoni a manovella*, found him immersing himself in regional traditional music.

Six years of silence followed, however, until 2006, when *Ovunque proteggi* (*Wherever You Protect*) took the Italian charts by storm. He described it as his "hairy and horned" album, but few could have understood exactly how hairy and horned it was going to be. The title track, a gorgeous piano ballad, made sense of Italian culture and history: this is what makes us unique, he warned, be aware. Our country is small, but its history runs deep—protect everything. "That too much is for a short while / And is still not enough / And is only once."

Capossela set up studios in caves and sang about burning Troy (slang for prostitutes), Medusa, the Colosseum, and ancient Sicilian religious festivals. When he toured, he insisted that he only play in stone auditoriums. At last, Capossela was his own man, and all the stronger for it. **DH**

Please Read the Letter

Robert Plant & Alison Krauss (2007)

Writer | Charlie Jones, Jimmy Page,
Michael Lee, Robert Plant
Producer | T. Bone Burnett
Label | Rounder
Album | *Raising Sand* (2007)

After Led Zeppelin split in 1980, singer Robert Plant long resisted playing their songs in his solo shows but sporadically worked with the band's founder, producer, and guitarist, Jimmy Page. In the mid-Nineties, Plant was asked by MTV to play an *Unplugged* show, and asked Page to join him. A successful souvenir, *No Quarter*, and tour ensued.

Page and Plant's later album of new material (*Walking into Clarksdale*, released in 1998) contained "Please Read the Letter," a song later considerably reworked for Plant's album with American bluegrass singer and fiddle player Alison Krauss. "In its first incarnation," Plant remarked in 2007, "it really needed to be like it is now." The track was co-written by the duo with Plant's former rhythm section: his son-in-law Charlie Jones, and former Cult drummer Michael Lee. "It's a song of yearning," Plant told *Entertainment Weekly*. "There's nothing rock 'n' roll about it. There's an air of fragility within the song. It's about unfinished business."

Plant and Krauss first performed together at a concert celebrating the music of Lead Belly, then approached T. Bone Burnett about recording together. Burnett, acting as musical director, suggested songs that the pair might cover. Plant told *Mojo*, "What we achieved on 'Please Read the Letter' gave the signature for our entire group." The song went on to win the Grammy award for Record of the Year in 2009. **AG**

Crank That (Soulja Boy)
Soulja Boy (2007)

Writer | DeAndre Way
Producer | DeAndre Way
Label | Collipark
Album | *Souljaboytellem.com*
(2007)

At sixteen years old, DeAndre Way became the youngest person to write, produce, and perform a No. 1 single on the *Billboard* Hot 100. "I was just making songs in my house and putting them online," Way—now better known as Soulja Boy—told *Billboard* in 2007, the year his debut single went global. "Crank That," with its bouncy West Indian steel drum beat and dance-friendly hip-hop vocals, quickly gained momentum on MySpace, attracting the attention of producer Mr. Collipark, who signed the young rapper. "He's a genius, man," gushed Collipark to New Zealand's *The Press*. "It's like catching Michael Jackson before he actually hit wax."

Not unlike Jackson, Way's performance was an integral part of his success. He released a YouTube video of his infectious song's accompanying dance, which promptly became one of the site's all-time most-watched clips, with more than 700 million views and innumerable parodies. A triple platinum single and full-blown international phenomenon, "Crank That" was nominated for Best Rap Song at the 2008 Grammy Awards. But it also drew criticism for the line "Superman that ho." "Superman is just a dance," Way protested to the Associated Press. "People don't want to go to a club and hear [about] people getting shot or hear about your life story. People want to . . . have fun and dance and party." **EP**

My People
The Presets (2007)

Writer | Julian Hamilton, Kim Moyes
Producer | Julian Hamilton, Kim Moyes
Label | Modular
Album | *Apocalypso* (2008)

"My People" is electro punk brilliance in a pumping package. Little wonder that it holds the record for the most weeks spent in the Australian Top 100 by a native-released single.

"The initial thing was the kick drum and the bass line," drummer and programmer Kim Moyes told *Disco Workout*. "That was the real start of the track: 'Do do do do do, doo doo doo'—it sounded real 'early 2000 electroclash,' fucking stupid. But what was cool about it was the thing that became the verse. And from there it was a bit of a labor. It took six months and many versions, but we kept hacking into it to make it sound like 'us.'"

The lyrics tackled immigration in Australia. "It's about the way we view outsiders," said singer and keyboardist Julian Hamilton. "Overseas, you become a lot more aware of how people view you as an Australian and it's inspired by everything we saw on the news about back home—[Prime Minister] John Howard, the boat people [asylum seekers], the detention centers, the Cronulla riots [racially motivated violence in New South Wales]."

Initially, there was concern that a contentious song with monster bass would win little airplay. Moyes told *Rolling Stone*: "There were even doubts about how much Triple J [Australia's biggest independent station] would get behind it, let alone any commercial stations." Happily, these fears proved unfounded. **OM**

Flux | Bloc Party (2007)

Writer | Kele Okereke, Gordon Moakes, Matt Tong, Russell Lissack
Producer | Garrett "Jacknife" Lee
Label | Wichita
Album | *A Weekend in the City* (2007)

"Our management really hate it. They told us not to release it."

Kele Okereke, 2007

◀ **Influenced by:** Swastika Eyes · Primal Scream (1999)
▶ **Influence on:** Mindestens in 1000 Jahren
Frittenbude (2008)
● **Covered by:** Brand New Rockers (2009)
★ **Other key tracks:** Banquet (Phones Disco Edit) (2004)
Hunting for Witches (2007) · Waiting for the 7:18 (2007)

"I don't know what people are going to make of it," Bloc Party front man Kele Okereke admitted to *NME*. His concern was a new single (stuck to the cover of that week's *NME*), which dispensed with much of what had made the band stars in the United Kingdom and cult heroes worldwide.

Gone were the angular rhythms and spiky vocals that had dominated their debut, *Silent Alarm*. In their place were a muted but screaming guitar, impassioned singing, and, most strikingly, a trancelike techno pulse. "I used to go to this trance club . . ." Okereke remembered. "It's where I met Russell [Lissack, guitarist] and I fell head over heels for it. I started to think about space and rhythm, and realized that those things could be equally as emotive as melody. Remembering those experiences was definitely in my mind when we were making 'Flux.'"

His bandmates were unconvinced. "I felt awkward in the early stages of putting the song together," remembered drummer Matt Tong, "because I don't think the band really knew what we were supposed to be doing."

However, "Flux" became Bloc Party's fourth Top Ten hit in the United Kingdom, and was added to a reissue of *A Weekend in the City,* which had arrived earlier in 2007. It became a highlight of their brilliant live show, and pointed to the barricade-storming thrills of 2008's *Intimacy*— vindicating Okereke's view that the song was "extremely important in the canon of our band."

"I love the playful[ness] of pop music," he said. "That's what 'Flux' is to me. Sometimes I don't want to be in a rock band. I hate the perception that something is more authentic because somebody is playing a guitar." **BM**

My Moon My Man | Feist (2007)

Writer | Leslie Feist, Jason "Gonzales" Beck
Producer | Leslie Feist, Jason "Gonzales" Beck, Renaud Letang
Label | Art & Craft International
Album | *The Reminder* (2007)

"Most of the people I've ended up playing with, it's kind of love first, a friendship first."

Leslie Feist, 2007

◄ **Influenced by:** Lover's Spit • Broken Social Scene (2004)
► **Influence on:** Drumming Song • Florence & The Machine (2009)
★ **Other key tracks:** 1234 (2007) • I Feel It All (2007) Sea Lion Woman (2007) • Honey Honey (2007)

"My body was lunging desperately for new melodies," Canadian singer-songwriter Feist told *Time Out* of her third album. "It's like when you sit at a computer for too long, you just have to go 'whaaaaghgh' and shake it out."

One of these "new melodies" was "My Moon My Man." A lolloping love song, it marked a major move for Leslie Feist and the pared-back indie sound for which fans adored her. It was written with collaborator, fellow Canadian, and electro darling Jason "Gonzales" Beck, who also worked with Feist's touring partner Peaches.

"My Moon My Man" fits snugly with *The Reminder's* themes of love and longing. "Take it slow / Take it easy on me / Shed some light / Shed some light on things" catches Feist at a vulnerable moment. Speculation about the song's subject centered on her relationship with Kevin Drew—co-founder of indie collective Broken Social Scene, with whom Feist often sang.

Lyrical content aside, the song retains much of Broken Social Scene's skittering sound. The fascinating mix of xylophones, pianos, percussion, and guitars owes much to her previous work, yet is imbued with a sense of solo vigor.

The track helped usher Feist into the mainstream. While the delightful "1234" was used to advertise Apple iPods, "My Moon My Man" was picked up by Verizon Wireless in the United States and featured in the television drama *Grey's Anatomy*. Both were accompanied by seemingly one-shot videos, although Feist confessed that "My Moon My Man" was an assemblage. "We went into it play-date style, making two videos in three days," she told *Variety*. "I thought 'My Moon My Man' was the winner." **JM**

D.A.N.C.E.
Justice (2007)

Writer | X. de Rosnay, G. Augé, J. Chaton
Producer | Justice
Label | Ed Banger
Album | † (2007)

Bassy 1980s funk? Flashy synth stabs? A chorus of children? It could only be a tribute to Michael Jackson. They swore their tongues were nowhere near their cheeks, but French house duo Justice's song is too deadpan to be serious. The hero of "D.A.N.C.E." is "neither black nor white," yet, as the children regretfully trill, was once "such a P.Y.T." It could be grotesque, were it not delivered with such joie de vivre. "We wanted it," Xavier de Rosnay assured MTV, "to be an emotional pop song."

Justice swaggered out of the shadows in 2006 with their Simian remix, "We Are Your Friends." Thereafter, they developed their prog rock-infused, orchestral disco. For "D.A.N.C.E.," de Rosnay and his partner Gaspard Augé set off for England to gather a choir, recruiting eight children for their "style and attitude" rather than technical prowess. The candy-colored result sits happily alongside the filter disco pioneered by compatriots Daft Punk—and followed by the likes of Bob Sinclar and Digitalism—but also echoes their rockier contemporaries Phoenix.

Alongside the references to "Black or White" and "P.Y.T. (Pretty Young Thing)," "D.A.N.C.E." notches up nods to Jackson's "Whatever Happens," "Workin' Day and Night" . . . and it's all "just easy as ABC." In the end, the tone is awestruck—"The way you move is a mystery"—but a delicious suspicion of mischief lingers. **MH**

re: Stacks
Bon Iver (2007)

Writer | Justin Vernon
Producer | Justin Vernon
Label | Self-released
Album | *For Emma, Forever Ago* (2007)

"This my excavation and today is Kumran" was the oblique opening line on the climax to an extraordinary album. "It's referring to the excavations where they found the Dead Sea Scrolls," Bon Iver's Justin Vernon told *Drowned in Sound*. "When they found them, it changed the whole course of Christianity, whether people wanted to know it or not. A lot of people chose to ignore it, a lot of people decided to run with it and, for many people, it destroyed their faith. So I think I was just looking at it as a metaphor for 'whatever happens after that is new shit.'"

"re: Stacks" was the soothing conclusion to a beautiful but harrowing collection. Frustrated after his band fell apart, Vernon headed to a remote cabin in Wisconsin. There he crafted an album dwelling on "an ancient, long-lost love." Despite this well-worn theme, *For Emma, Forever Ago* was a triumph.

"re: Stacks," Vernon told *Treble*, refers to gambling chips and "how things stack up." But its closing lines—"This is not the sound of a new man or crispy realization / It's the sound of the unlocking and the lift away / Your love will be / Safe with me"—reflected his liberation after months in the wilderness. "The biggest thing that happened out there," he said, "was I managed to make peace with a lot of dark circles that had started to pool in different areas of my life." **BM**

With Every Heartbeat | Robyn with Kleerup (2007)

Writer | Robyn, Andreas Kleerup
Producer | Andreas Kleerup
Label | Konichiwa
Album | N/A

"That song was trying to be mini and rural pop art, pinstriped—you know, Stravinsky."

Andreas Kleerup, 2009

◀ **Influenced by:** La Ritournelle · Sébastien Tellier (2004)

▶ **Influence on:** The Girl and the Robot · Röyskopp featuring Robyn (2009)

● **Covered by:** Athlete (2007) · Girls Aloud (2008) The Hoosiers (2008)

A teen star with "Show Me Love" in 1997, Robin Carlsson spent the ensuing years consolidating her place in her native Sweden. However, she suppressed her style in favor of radio-friendly pop, and it took collaboration with local synth duo The Knife to break the stranglehold. Jive Records were unmoved by the resulting "Who's That Girl?" and Robyn left to set up her own label, Konichiwa Records, where she could let "the most killingest pop star on the planet" off the leash.

This electro-pop reinvention was an immediate success at home, where the *Robyn* album topped the chart in 2005. Yet it took a repackaged version to break her worldwide, two years later—and the revamped album's trump card was "With Every Heartbeat," with another fellow Swede, producer Andreas Kleerup.

A No. 1 in the United Kingdom, "With Every Heartbeat" had a trance feel. But, embellished with strings and Robyn's emotion-drenched vocal, it became a heartbreaking epic in the style of Massive Attack's "Unfinished Sympathy." "'With Every Heartbeat' is not a typical No. 1 song," Robyn observed. "It doesn't really have a chorus and it has a weird string break in the middle. . . . The song deserved to be a No. 1, so I'm not surprised, but it wasn't expected either."

"I wrote the lyrics about Kleerup breaking up with his girlfriend," revealed the hard-nosed singer. "I borrowed his life and wrote a really sad song." Kleerup gave her the green light and they produced a peerless pop nugget in the grand Scandinavian tradition. "It's like Ingmar Bergman," Kleerup offered, to explain this peculiar national trait. "Life is kind of crappy and then you make it, you know, comprehensible." **MH**

Someone Great | LCD Soundsystem (2007)

Writer | James Murphy
Producer | The DFA
Label | DFA
Album | *Sound of Silver* (2007)

someone great lcdsoundsystem

"It sounds like a long-lost Human League record and it's absolutely beautiful."

Mark Ronson, 2007

◄ **Influenced by:** Me and Giuliani Down by the Schoolyard (A True Story) • !!! (2003)
► **Influence on:** Can I Be • Kid Cudi (2009)
● **Covered by:** Winter Gloves (2008) • Lissy Trullie & The Fibs (2008) • Banjo or Freakout (2009)
★ **Other key track:** All My Friends (2007)

Songs about death aren't often danceable. With "Someone Great," James Murphy—singer and founder of LCD Soundsystem and co-founder of dance-punk label DFA—created an extraordinary electro elegy.

It's unclear whether the song concerns the death of a person or a relationship. However, *Sound of Silver*, on which it appears, is dedicated to the singer's therapist, Dr. George Kamen. Lines such as "I miss the way we used to argue / Locked, in your basement" do point to his doctor, or perhaps a friend or lover. Some have even speculated that it's about the death of an unborn child. Unusually, the customarily candid Murphy declined to elucidate.

The origins of "Someone Great" lay in LCD Soundsystem's instrumental mix *45:33*, created as part of a promotion for Nike in 2006. "It was actually the first thing I started with . . ." Murphy told *The Village Voice*. "It was going to be just that and then grow out. . . . While I was working on it, I kept singing things on the subway home while I was listening to my iPod to check the mixes. And it started turning into a song. And I thought, 'Maybe I should do the vocals for the Nike thing,' but it didn't seem appropriate in that context. . . . So we asked [Nike], and they were okay with it. I'm really glad because I really like it as a song." A pulsing synth, flickering beats, rhythmic scratching, and a glockenspiel melody complement his poignant lament.

The bittersweet lyrics—"The worst is all the lovely weather / I'm sad, it's not raining"—proved Murphy had more depth than earlier, droll songs like "Losing My Edge" and "Daft Punk Is Playing at My House" implied. A mournful masterpiece. **GK**

Paper Planes | M.I.A. (2007)

Writer | Maya Arulpragasam, Wesley Pentz, Mick Jones, Joe Strummer, Paul Simonon, Topper Headon
Producer | Wesley "Diplo" Pentz, Dave "Switch" Taylor
Label | XL
Album | *Kala* (2007)

"I couldn't say no to Kanye West and Jay-Z and T.I. and Lil Wayne."

M.I.A., 2009

◀ **Influenced by: Rump Shaker** • Wreckx-N-Effect (1992)
▶ **Influence on: Swagga Like Us** • Jay-Z & T.I. featuring Kanye West & Lil Wayne (2008)
● **Covered by:** Ryu Maginn & Veze Skante (2007) Rihanna (2008) • Built to Spill (2008) • Street Sweeper Social Club (2009)

"I just woke up and just sang the whole song in one go. It was in the morning and I wasn't thinking too much. I hadn't brushed my teeth." Her dental hygiene might have left something to be desired, but M.I.A.'s 2007 recording of "Paper Planes" proved serendipitous.

At producer Diplo's suggestion, the track was based on The Clash's spooky "Straight to Hell," from 1982's *Combat Rock*. M.I.A. added lyrics and sound effects of a gun and cash register—references to the negative perception of immigrants and refugees. "America is so obsessed with money," she said, "I'm sure they'll get it."

America didn't. On MTV and a notorious appearance on David Letterman's chat show, the song was censored. But then "Paper Planes" was used in a trailer for the movie *Pineapple Express,* and in *Slumdog Millionaire.* Suddenly, it was inescapable. "America was going through an economic crisis, and I made a song that actually has to do with how immigrants are portrayed . . ." M.I.A. told the *Los Angeles Times.* "That was more what 'Paper Planes' was representing—not a war protest song like some people thought."

The track's profile rose even further when it was sampled for Jay-Z and T.I.'s posse smash "Swagga Like Us." M.I.A. performed the song with her high-profile admirers at the 2009 Grammy awards, despite being due to give birth. In April that year, over eighteen months since its first release, "Paper Planes" was awarded double platinum status in the United States.

"I'm glad 'Paper Planes' happened when it did . . ." she told *Spin.* "It was much more relevant than when people were like, 'Yeah, I got my Hummer and things are good.'" **BM**

Mercy | Duffy (2008)

Writer | Aimee Ann Duffy, Steve Booker
Producer | Steve Booker
Label | A&M
Album | *Rockferry* (2008)

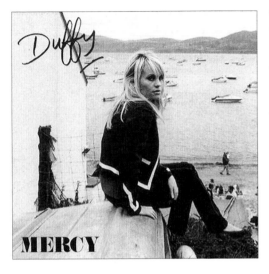

"I don't call myself a soul singer. I've no idea what I am."

Duffy, 2008

◀ **Influenced by: Stand By Me** · Ben E. King (1961)
▶ **Influence on: Choo Choo** · Diane Birch (2009)
● **Covered by:** OneRepublic (2008) · The Fratellis (2008)
John Mayer (2008)
★ **Other key tracks:** Rain on Your Parade (2008)
Rockferry (2008) · Warwick Avenue (2008)

In 2004, Aimee Ann Duffy finished second on the Welsh television talent show *Wawffactor* and released a chart-topping EP of songs sung in her native tongue. That was enough to make her a star at home, but something else was needed for Duffy to gain fame and fortune outside Wales. The missing ingredient arrived via an iPod playlist—stocked by former Suede guitarist Bernard Butler—featuring soul stars such as Al Green and Bettye Swan.

Duffy proved a star pupil, internalizing those classic voices while finding her own on *Rockferry*. The proof came with "Mercy"—a retro-soul blast that would have fit snugly next to any nostalgic gem on Butler's playlist.

The song was the last to be recorded for the album. "It was like this melodic poem in my mind," she told *Mojo*, "which I just had to get out, and I knew exactly what I wanted it to sound like. Steve [Booker, co-writer] was very patient. He sat at the piano and put chords underneath it and we built the song from the bottom up."

The empowering cry for liberation from a lover's suffocating grasp evoked a foregone era when artists like Aretha, Dusty, and The Supremes ruled the world. Thanks to Duffy's mesmerizing vocals and an addictive beat, "Mercy" stopped listeners in their tracks.

It cracked the Top Ten throughout Europe, went platinum in the United States and Australia, and made Duffy the first Welsh female to hit No. 1 on the U.K. singles chart since Bonnie Tyler in 1983 ("Total Eclipse of the Heart"). The tune combined with the album's other triumph, "Warwick Avenue," to push *Rockferry* to worldwide sales of more than six million. **JiH**

Sabali
Amadou & Mariam (2008)

Writer | Mariam Doumbia, Marc Antoine Moreau, Damon Albarn
Producer | Damon Albarn
Label | Because
Album | *Welcome to Mali* (2008)

Mariam Doumbia and Amadou Bagayoko met in the Seventies at the Institute for the Young Blind in Bamako, the capital of Mali. Bonding over a love of music, they became friends, then a couple. They also began to make music together and became global stars of the Malian music scene—the official theme for the 2006 soccer World Cup was theirs.

In 2000, Blur singer and Gorillaz mastermind Damon Albarn was approached by the charity Oxfam to be a representative in Mali. Albarn agreed, but tailored the role to his strengths by working with local musicians. It wasn't until 2005, though, that Amadou & Mariam's path crossed with Albarn's. For his Africa Express project, he took British musicians to Mali to play with the local stars. Impressed by his passion, the duo called on Albarn to collaborate on their 2008 album, *Welcome to Mali*. He co-wrote and produced the opening track "Sabali," giving the duo's trademark sound an electronic sheen. Explaining his focus on Mariam's voice at the expense of her partner's guitar, Albarn told nonesuch.com, "I wanted to hear her voice separated from Amadou for a moment."

Issued as the lead single from the album, "Sabali" won worldwide acclaim, with Pitchfork placing it at No. 15 in their top two hundred tracks of the Noughties. In 2009, the superstars of African music rounded off an excellent decade by playing at the inauguration of President Obama. **DC**

Divine
Sébastien Tellier (2008)

Writer | Sébastien Tellier, Amandine de La Richardière
Producer | G. de Homem-Christo, E. Chedeville
Label | Record Makers
Album | *Sexuality* (2008)

Hearing a great song during the Eurovision Song Contest is a phenomenon that you might witness once in a lifetime. In 2008, one of those moments arrived when Sébastien Tellier performed "Divine" at the talent show's Belgrade final.

Why France's Eurovision committee asked the critically acclaimed composer and singer to represent the country is something of a mystery. Tellier is a bearded, straggly-haired oddball who dresses like a *Miami Vice* villain. And his chosen track, "Divine"—originally written for his fourth album, an erotic concept affair with the self-explanatory title *Sexuality*—was too smart for the show. It grooved along like classic Beach Boys, but with sampled voice fragments, reminiscent of producer Trevor Horn's early Eighties work with Yes and Art of Noise—a blend that made sense given that it was co-produced by Daft Punk's Guy-Manuel de Homem-Christo.

Before the contest, French parliamentarians declared it an "outrage against French culture" that their national entry was sung in English, so the singer reluctantly added a couple of lines *en Français* for the finale. Unsurprisingly, "Divine" didn't win over Eurovision's one hundred million viewers: out of twenty-five countries, France came joint eighteenth with Sweden. However, a week after the Belgrade showdown, the track entered Sweden's chart, eventually hitting No. 4. **TB**

Mariam sings over Amadou's Afro-pop guitar stylings at the Glastonbury festival in 2009.

Mykonos | Fleet Foxes (2008)

Writer | Robin Pecknold
Producer | Phil Ek
Label | Sub Pop
Album | N/A

"The songs are about close friends and family, but I don't want to give everything away."
Robin Pecknold, 2008

◀ **Influenced by: Suite: Judy Blue Eyes** • Crosby, Stills & Nash (1969)

▶ **Influence on: Wild Honey Never Stolen** • J. Tillman (2010)

● **Covered by:** Rock Paper Scissors (2008)

★ **Other key track:** White Winter Hymnal (2009)

The rapid rise to fame in 2008 of Fleet Foxes, a five-piece "baroque harmonic pop" band from Seattle, owed much to "Mykonos." The song is the centerpiece of the band's second EP, *Sun Giant,* which was hastily put together in early January 2008 after they finished recording their self-titled debut album (*Sun Giant* was repackaged with a reissue of *Fleet Foxes* within months of its release).

The genesis of the afterthought EP was plain commercial necessity. Sue Busch of the Sub Pop label told *HitQuarters* that the quintet had nothing to sell on tour: "So we just pressed those up super quickly. . . . People really, really wanted it, so we eventually put it out as a proper release."

The song's primarily acoustic sound owes much to the vocal harmonies of Simon & Garfunkel, The Beach Boys, and Crosby, Stills & Nash—all influences readily acknowledged by composer Robin Pecknold. Lyrically, however, the song is a little more enigmatic. For the debut album, Pecknold had clearly penned two songs about his older brother, Sean. It seems likely that this tune, too, is about Sean—perhaps a plea for him to face up to some personal demons. But why this is associated with Mykonos, one of the group of islands known as the Cyclades and a popular tourist destination, remains unclear.

Sean himself subsequently directed the much-heralded, stop-motion animated video for "Mykonos," which clouded things further. The video depicts the eerie journey of a pair of small paper triangles over land and sea, watched by rows of eyes. The song itself appears to be in two pieces, beautifully stitched together by the band. *Billboard* duly described the second part as "salvation for the ears." **AG**

Time to Pretend | MGMT (2008)

Writer | Ben Goldwasser, Andrew VanWyngarden
Producer | Dave Fridmann
Label | Columbia
Album | *Oracular Spectacular* (2008)

"Unless you hear the whole song, you probably don't realize we're joking."

Ben Goldwasser, 2008

◀ **Influenced by:** Overpowered by Funk · The Clash (1982)
▶ **Influence on:** One More Time to Pretend (MGMT vs. Daft Punk) · Immuzikation (2008)
● **Covered by:** Kaiser Chiefs (2008) · Digital Leather (2009) · Paolo Nutini (2009)

When "Time to Pretend" blew up as iTunes' coveted "pick of the week" in 2008, the exposure spurred both sales and outrage. Curiously, the song's most incendiary verse—an expletive-infused narrative about a rock star's life of debauchery—was chosen for the thirty-second teaser. "It seemed as if one of those conservative Christian coalitions mobilized armies of parents to write in and start attacking us," singer Andrew VanWyngarden told the *Guardian*. "People were accusing us of being 'wild druggies.'"

VanWyngarden and MGMT co-founder Ben Goldwasser wrote the song—originally called "The Mantis Sailing Home"—in college, as an ode to their pet praying mantis (whose favorite song, they giggled, was The Clash's "Overpowered by Funk"). It was first released on an EP in 2005, and later re-recorded with Flaming Lips/Mercury Rev producer Dave Fridmann. (The nagging synth motif appears in both, but Fridmann's version is slightly faster and more of a head-rush.)

Although the 2005 version helped them score a deal with Columbia, the eccentric college boys couldn't even get a date, let alone live out their rock star fantasies—rendering the offending verse entirely ironic. "That's the funniest thirty seconds of the song they could have chosen," Goldwasser told Australia's *Herald Sun*.

The shimmering guitars, retro synths, and T. Rex–style vocals (and psychedelic video) yielded an intoxicating breakthrough hit, an achievement as bemusing to the boys as their accidental rock 'n' roll reputation. "We were never ambitious about starting a band, promoting ourselves, trying to play all the shows, and the things most bands do to get attention," explained Goldwasser. "The song is all about how we're not that kind of band." **EP**

Sweet Disposition
The Temper Trap (2008)

Writer | Dougy Mandagi, Lorenzo Sillitto
Producer | Jim Abbiss
Label | Liberation
Album | *Conditions* (2009)

The transfixing, delay-soaked guitar draws you in. The falsetto vocals tingle your spine. The blissfully simple lyrics perfectly encapsulate a passionate and all-encompassing love. Unadulterated, hands-in-the-air joy ensues when the chorus kicks in. This is the stunning "Sweet Disposition," a late summer anthem by Melbourne quartet The Temper Trap.

The song came together remarkably easily. Drummer Toby Mundas told undertheradar.com: "Lorenzo [Sillitto], our guitarist, came into the rehearsal room one day with the main riff and we jumped on it quite quickly and jammed it out. Dougy [Mandagi, singer/guitarist] came back with the lyrics by the next practice and it was pretty much finished in two or three rehearsals." The words, Mandagi said, are "about the passing of the essence of youth, and how, when you're older, you tend to overanalyze things."

The singer's falsetto vocals, while audibly influenced by Jeff Buckley and Thom Yorke, were also shaped by his early experiences as a choirboy in Indonesia. The urgency and potency of the lines "A moment / A love / A dream aloud / A kiss / A cry" made "Sweet Disposition" the perfect accompaniment to the 2009 movie *(500) Days of Summer,* about the aching despair of a lost first love. The song also has been used in commercials worldwide—upping its ubiquity, but never detracting from its beauty and brilliance. **OM**

L.E.S. Artistes
Santogold (2008)

Writer | Santi White, John Hill
Producer | Jonnie "Most" Davis, John Hill, Santi White
Label | Lizard King
Album | *Santogold* (2008)

Erupting in a starburst of hype at the end of 2007, Santogold defied categorization with a two-track single that set tongues wagging. "Creator" was a Switch production, echoing his associate—and Santogold's most obvious precursor—M.I.A. "Creator" was one for the head, not the feet—but "L.E.S. Artistes" was the tune, a trumping of The Strokes' revivalist template.

The arrival was hard-won. Already past thirty when "L.E.S. Artistes" broke, Philadelphia-born Santi White had cut her teeth fronting punk pretenders Stiffed, then dipped her toe into mainstream waters, singing a ragga-tipped redraft of The Jam's "Pretty Green" for Mark Ronson's *Version.* Lured by Lizard King to make a solo record, White took Stiffed cohort John Hill with her and—with a handful of hip collaborators—sculpted a searing grab-bag of indie, reggae, funk, and post-punk winners. "I hope," she announced, "that I help break down boundaries and genre classifications." "L.E.S. Artistes" drove home the nonconformist point. Melodic but spiky, it thumbed its nose at New York hipsters (the Lower East Side artistes of the confusing title) and sneered, "Stop trying to catch my eye / I see you good, you forced faker."

Ever the chameleon, in 2009 she changed her name to Santigold, following legal threats from singer, filmmaker, jeweler, and all-around renaissance man Santo Gold. **MH**

Santogold (Santi White): fakers shouldn't expect to slink past her unremarked. ➔

Sex on Fire | Kings of Leon (2008)

Writer | Caleb Followill, Nathan Followill, Jared Followill, Matthew Followill
Producer | Angelo Petraglia, Jacquire King
Label | RCA
Album | *Only by the Night* (2008)

"It's about a great sexual relationship with hot, hot sex that you remember forever."

Caleb Followill, 2008

◀ **Influenced by: I'm on Fire** · Bruce Springsteen (1984)
▶ **Influence on: Sometime Around Midnight** · The Airborne Toxic Event (2009)
● **Covered by:** James Morrison (2008) · Sam Winters (2009) · Alesha Dixon (2009) · Tina Cousins (2009) Sugarland (2009)

A band that hardly needs any introduction. The three brothers and one cousin, from a religious background in Tennessee, gained a cult following in Europe for the rousing garage rock of their first and second albums. By the third, they had moved toward the mainstream, with a sound that was slightly more clean-cut. But it was "Sex on Fire," the first single from their fourth album, that sealed the Kings' ability to fill arenas.

The worldwide smash nearly never found its audience. Singer Caleb Followill was playing around with a melody in the studio when he starting singing, "This sex is on fire." He thought: "It was terrible, but the rest of the band were like, 'It's good, it's got a hook.'" Caleb wrote the lyrics while on painkillers (after a fight with his brother Nathan), so was conveniently hazy about their inspiration. "I think my girlfriend hopes it's based on her," he told the *Sun*. "Maybe it is my girlfriend because we've had some good times together . . . but I'm not really sure."

"Sex on Fire" is ambitiously epic, with soaring guitars and Caleb's passionate vocals belting out "Yeaaaah," before the brilliantly unsubtle chorus ("You, your sex is on fire") kicks in. But the song's crossover appeal left some old-school Kings of Leon fans feeling disgruntled. A contestant on *The X Factor*—Britain's *American Idol*—wowing the judges with his rendition could only have added to their woes. And the final nail in the coffin? Simon Cowell was actually singing along.

But to focus on the hit's popularity, rather than its excellence, misses the point. The song's brilliance lies in its simplicity and the visceral beauty of the vocals and guitars. Quite simply, Kings of Leon are on fire. **OM**

One Day Like This | Elbow (2008)

Writer | Guy Garvey, Craig Potter, Mark Potter, Pete Turner, Richard Jupp
Producer | Craig Potter
Label | Fiction
Album | *The Seldom Seen Kid* (2008)

"Mostly I write about life and love and death and friendship and desire and frustration."

Guy Garvey, 2008

◀ **Influenced by: Hey Jude** · The Beatles (1968)
▶ **Influence on: Lifelines** · Doves (2009)
● **Covered by:** Snow Patrol (2008)
★ **Other key tracks:** Lullaby (2008) · Every Bit the Little Girl (2008) · Li'l Pissed Charmin' Tune (2008) · Grounds for Divorce (2008)

Elbow's music is often beautifully understated and intimate, but with "One Day Like This" the band made a successful bid for a stadium sing-along.

The song was borne of the euphoria at finally finding a home (with the Polydor imprint Fiction) for their fourth album, *The Seldom Seen Kid*. "We were buzzing. We'd just got our new deal and it was like a breath of fresh air," singer and multi-instrumentalist Guy Garvey told the *Manchester Evening News*. "It was dead simple. We wanted to do something very uplifting and very positive. That's where the line 'One day a year like this would see me right' comes from." The song, the last to be written for the album, came together at speed—although Garvey has spoken of how the momentum was temporarily slowed by the difficulty of accommodating the word "chamois" (soft suede leather) in his lyric.

As the singer had anticipated, "One Day Like This" became a festival favorite, with Garvey repeatedly looking out at fields of people singing the song "with a big grin on their faces." After years of being underappreciated, Elbow began to collect awards with gratifying regularity. *The Seldom Seen Kid* won the Mercury Prize, Elbow beat Coldplay to the Brit award for Best British Band, and "One Day Like This" picked up an Ivor Novello award for Best Song Musically and Lyrically (meanwhile, the album's first single, "Grounds for Divorce," won Best Contemporary Song.)

With the wonderful warmth that characterizes everything he does, Garvey told radio station Xfm: "This song is about love in a very simple way—but, ultimately, it's about the fact that the five of us are old friends who really enjoy doing what we're doing." **CB**

Viva la Vida
Coldplay (2008)

Writer | Guy Berryman, Chris Martin, Jonny Buckland, Will Champion
Producer | Coldplay, B. Eno, M. Dravs, R. Simpson
Label | Parlophone
Album | *Viva la Vida or Death and All His Friends* (2008)

After three multiplatinum albums, and becoming one of the world's biggest bands, Coldplay had passed most of the usual milestones. Yet the group still hadn't scored a U.S. or U.K. No. 1 single. With "Viva la Vida," from their fourth album, they finally passed that one, too.

The transatlantic smash, which also reached the Top Ten in Australia and throughout Europe, is appropriately grand. Strings introduce the instantly addictive riff, before singer Chris Martin begins the seemingly sad tale of a man who "used to rule the world." The music is glorious—as anthemic as anything in U2's songbook—and the language fittingly exquisite for the title, which translates as "Long Live Life." Martin chose it, reported *Rolling Stone*, after seeing the phrase on a painting by Frida Kahlo. "She went through a lot of shit . . ." he explained, "and then she started a big painting in her house that said 'Viva la vida.' I just loved the boldness of it. Everyone thinks it comes from Ricky Martin, which is fine."

"Viva la Vida" helped to make its parent album a best-seller in 2008, but the song was met with at least three accusations of plagiarism, from Creaky Boards, Joe Satriani, and Yusuf Islam (Cat Stevens). "It is," drummer Will Champion remarked to hamptonroads.com, "only—for some reason, God only knows why—the successful songs that seem to be the ones that are accused of being stolen." **JiH**

Dog Days Are Over
Florence & The Machine (2009)

Writer | Florence Welch, Isabella Summers
Producer | James Ford, Isabella Summers
Label | Moshi Moshi
Album | *Lungs* (2009)

The spiraling range of Kate Bush, gritty passion of PJ Harvey, and spiritual soul of Aretha Franklin can all be traced in Florence Welch. On hearing her for the first time, her manager recalled, "I had literally never heard someone with such a powerful voice!" This delightfully eccentric singer created a modern masterpiece with "Dog Days Are Over"— which, thanks to downloads, was still on the U.K. chart two years after its first release, alongside its original B-side, a cover of "You Got the Love" by The Source featuring Candi Staton.

Beginning with a simple acoustic riff, "Dog Days Are Over" slowly builds with hand claps and mandolin, while Florence's knockout voice swells and soars. There is a teasing moment of silence and a gentle refrain before the onslaught begins, carrying the song to its stunning climax.

Incredibly, most of the music came from a small Yamaha keyboard. Welch claimed that the "really accidental beat" was "hands on the wall while hitting a drum underneath it at the same time." Additional percussion was found in the studio's kitchen: "We were in there banging away on everything: the sink, the pans, the microwave."

Welch was inspired to write "Dog Days Are Over" by a giant art installation of the same name that she cycled past every morning. Seemingly a glorious ode to the passing of bad times, the song—as Welch confessed—meant nothing. **OM**

Florence Welch with The Machine in 2009: a voice to blow away cobwebs. ➡

The Fear | Lily Allen (2009)

Writer | Lily Allen, Greg Kurstin
Producer | Greg Kurstin
Label | Regal
Album | *It's Not Me, It's You* (2009)

"I'm aware that I am a part of that culture, but it's not something that I feel particularly comfortable with."
Lily Allen, 2009

◀ **Influenced by: I Hate Camera** · The Bird and the Bee (2007)
▶ **Influence on: Starry Eyed** · Ellie Goulding (2010)
● **Covered by:** Elviin (2008) · Ehda (2009) · JLS (2009) Tinchy Stryder (2009)
★ **Other key tracks:** Fag Hag (2009) · Kabul Shit (2009)

A curtain raiser for Lily Allen's second album, "The Fear" adopted the electro-pop sound that dominated 2009: a significant step from the scrubbed-up ska of her debut. The switch was not born of necessity—*Alright, Still* was a mammoth hit—but demonstrated Allen's adroitness.

"The Fear" gives a grid reference to Allen's position after half a decade in the spotlight—and to her typical second-album concerns about loss of privacy and the difficulties of following immediate success. The lyric, as ironic as it is judgmental, decries celebrity culture, spearing the obsessions with fame at all costs ("I don't care about clever / I don't care about funny"), weight, and stars' behavior that exercise gossip magazines. But this was no sermon—Lily knew she was up to her neck in the whole pantomime.

The track first emerged in 2008 as a demo on Allen's traditional launch pad, her MySpace page. Then called "I Don't Know," its catchy chorus still shone, but Greg Kurstin's fluid production of the single showed the song in its best light. Kurstin has a superior pop pedigree—as part of The Bird and the Bee with Inara George, daughter of Little Feat's Lowell, he produced work characterized by strong hooks perking up jazz chords; Allen's "The Fear" clearly bears his fingerprints.

"We listened to things like Keane and Coldplay," Allen told dose.ca. "I wanted to make something that was going to sell a lot of records. . . . I'm being facetious when I say that. It's more that I love those guys." Regardless, the gossip magazine-reading, fame-hungry masses bought "The Fear" in their droves, sending it into international charts as they rehearsed its lyrics in their bedrooms for the next year's TV talent show auditions. **MH**

Summertime Clothes | Animal Collective (2009)

Writer | Noah Lennox, David Portner, Brian Weitz
Producer | Ben H. Allen
Label | Domino
Album | *Merriweather Post Pavilion* (2009)

"It must be weird to be in a band with good musicians."

Noah "Panda Bear" Lennox, 2009

◄ **Influenced by: Comfy in Nautica** · Panda Bear (2007)

► **Influence on: Glazin** · Black Dice (2009)

★ **Other key tracks:** My Girls (2009) · Brother Sport (2009) · Bleeding (2009) · Taste (2009) · Lion in a Coma (2009) · Also Frightened (2009) · In the Flowers (2009)

They may sound like characters from a wacky kids TV show, but Avey Tare, Deaken, Geologist, and Panda Bear (aka David Portner, Josh Dibb, Brian Weitz, and Noah Lennox respectively) are the four creative minds behind the idiosyncratic quartet that goes by the name of Animal Collective.

After seven years of highly productive tinkering, largely outside the realms of mainstream play, the Baltimore band released their most radio-friendly edit with the 2009 single, "Summertime Clothes." The result is a rich, kaleidoscopic electro-pop soundscape of soaring harmonies and distorted synthesizers, reminiscent of The Beach Boys at their psychedelic, blissed-out peak (with echoes of The Beatles' "Getting Better"). The sound is similarly euphoric, elevating the simple vocal refrain "I want to walk around with you" into an uplifting declaration of loved-up delight.

"In general, I write the most complex Animal Collective songs . . ." Portner admitted to *VoxPop*. "But I wanted to keep the almost naive simplicity of this song." Explaining the tapestry of influences behind the Collective's sound, Lennox told the *Sun*: "The first thing that swept me away was Top Forty radio, then classic rock radio when I was in high school. Then I started getting into dance music: fully electronic stuff, like The Orb and Aphex Twin. From there, I went backwards to Detroit and Chicago house music. I also like Daft Punk a whole lot."

The band fine-tuned the material live before recording it. "It's kind of like you're going up a mountain," Portner told the *New Zealand Herald,* "and you collect all this stuff, and then you reach the peak . . . and everything feels really strong and the energy of the shows is really intense." **EP**

Rain Dance
The Very Best feat. M.I.A. (2009)

Writer | Esau Mwamwaya, Johan Karlberg, Etienne Tron, Maya Arulpragasam
Producer | Radioclit (J. Karlberg, E. Tron)
Label | Moshi Moshi
Album | *Warm Heart of Africa* (2009)

It should have been a mess. Malawian singer Esau Mwamwaya met Swede Johan Karlberg and Frenchman Etienne Tron, aka producers Radioclit, in London. Having established that Mwamwaya sang, the trio began work, as The Very Best, on their debut album. Among its tracks was "Rain Dance," featuring a much-fêted guest. "We knew M.I.A. for many years from London," Karlberg told Afro Pop. They recruited her for the Santogold collaboration "Get It Up," but also played her "Rain Dance"—"She really liked it so she jumped on that as well. And then we lost the multitrack files . . . so what's actually on the album is a demo."

After an advance listen to M.I.A.'s soon-to-be classic "Paper Planes," Karlberg posted a version with Mwamwaya on MySpace, on the day that the song's parent album, *Kala,* was released. This cheeky hype paid off, and the trio capitalized on media interest with a fantastic mixtape, featuring Mwamwaya singing over a number of tracks.

When "Rain Dance" and *Warm Heart of Africa* proved to be equally joyous fusions of East and West, it seemed there were no surprises left. But then M.I.A., on a U.S. tour and driving through arid landscapes, listened to the song. Confused to still hear water falling after the track's sound effects ended, she realized it was raining in the desert. Recalled Karlberg: "She was like, 'That's what happens when I listen to 'Rain Dance!'" **BM**

Empire State of Mind
Jay-Z & Alicia Keys (2009)

Writer | A. Keys, Jay-Z, A. Hunte, J. Sewell-Ulepic, B. Keyes, S. Robinson, A. Shuckburgh
Producer | Hunte, Sewell-Ulepic, Shuckburgh
Label | RocNation
Album | *The Blueprint 3* (2009)

"I'm the new Sinatra," boasts Shawn Carter, aka Jay-Z, on "Empire State of Mind"—the epic love letter to New York City that won him four weeks at the top of *Billboard*'s Hot 100. Not since Frank Sinatra's 1980 release of "Theme from New York, New York" has one track been so enthusiastically adopted as the theme song of the Big Apple.

Jay's hip-hop swagger and Alicia Keys's passionate hook soar over a soulful piano riff, based on The Moments' 1970 track, "Love on a Two-Way Street." The result is a moving tribute to the five boroughs where both Jay and Keys were born and raised. For Angela Hunte, who penned the hook, the song was an antidote to homesickness while she was in London with her writing partner, Janet Sewell-Ulepic. She told *Billboard*: "Before we left the hotel that night, we knew we would write a song about our city."

Eight months later, Jay-Z was handed the track. He penned his own verses and, Hunte recalled, "recorded it that night." When Alicia Keys was added to the mix, Hunte said, "she just nailed it."

Just as hip-hop has overtaken Sinatra's big band sound as the musical force of New York City, so "Empire State of Mind" has confirmed Jay-Z as his city's contemporary Chairman of the Board. "'Empire State of Mind' is about inspiration," he declared. "It's about hope. I think that's what connects with people." **EP**

Jay-Z and Alicia Keys celebrate their "Empire State of Mind" at the American Music Awards in 2009.

Tenalle chegret
Tinariwen (2009)

Writer | Ibrahim Ag Alhabib
Producer | Jean-Paul Romann
Label | Independiente
Album | *Imidiwan: Companions* (2009)

Although only recently given an international release, "Tenalle chegret" ("The Long Thread") was written shortly after the Touareg rebellion of the early Nineties and deals with its aftermath. The song is a typically atmospheric example of Tinariwen's slow-burning style. Over a loping groove, twangy electric guitars curl around Ibrahim Ag Alhabib's careworn, murmured vocal, answered by a chorus of singers.

The words are about the difficult discussions among the Touareg after the rebellion. A cease-fire was signed with the government in Mali, but this caused a previously unified rebel movement to splinter into factions. That spelled much confusion, frustration and discord—hence the line, "Those who desired to lead have failed the mission."

Acoustic Touareg folklore played on flutes, fiddles, and drums is the main root of Tinariwen's music, but they transpose it onto mostly modern, electric instruments. *Assouf* is what they call their distinctive guitar style, which draws on that of fellow Malian Ali Farka Touré, Moroccan *chaabi*, Algerian Berber and *rai* music, and plenty of western pop (their "Oualahila ar tesninam" sounds oddly like Fleetwood Mac's "Oh Well"). Stars such as Santana, Robert Plant, and The Rolling Stones have sung Tinariwen's praises, and they even inspired Coldplay, whose song "Strawberry Swing" was deliberately designed to sound like them. **JLu**

Harry Patch (In Memory Of)
Radiohead (2009)

Writer | Radiohead, Harry Patch
Producer | Radiohead
Label | Self-released
Album | N/A

Even for a band whose innovation and talent put them light-years beyond their peers, basing a song on an interview with the last British survivor of World War I's trenches sounds ambitious. But "Harry Patch (In Memory Of)" makes the listener stand stock still, struck by its utter beauty.

"The way he talked about war had a profound effect on me," Radiohead front man Thom Yorke said of a 2005 interview with Patch (who died at the age of one hundred and eleven on July 25, 2009, shortly after the song was recorded). "It would be very easy for our generation to forget the true horror of war, without the likes of Harry to remind us."

Recorded in an abbey, the stunning orchestral arrangement was by guitarist Jonny Greenwood (whose previous experience included composing the soundtrack to Paul Thomas Anderson's 2008 movie *There Will Be Blood*). There is no standard verse-chorus-verse, and slow-burning strings are the song's only music. Yorke's otherworldly falsetto adds potency to Patch's lines: "Give your leaders each a gun and let them fight it out themselves," and "Next will be chemical, but they will never learn." The majestic tribute was released through Radiohead's waste.uk.com for a modest download fee, with the proceeds going to the armed forces charity, the British Royal Legion. "I very much hope," wrote Yorke, "the song does justice to his memory as the last survivor." It does, and more. **OM**

Saïd Ag Ayad adds Touareg rhythms to Tinariwen's blueslike West African music in 2005.

The Noughties | 895

Go Do | Jónsi (2010)

Writer | Jón Thór Birgisson
Producer | J. T. Birgisson, Peter Katis, Alex Somers
Label | Parlophone
Album | Go (2010)

"I think you should only follow your instinct. Just write a song."

Jón Thór "Jónsi" Birgisson, 2010

◀ **Influenced by: Wedding Dress** • Samamidon (2008)
★ **Other key tracks:** Animal Arithmetic (2010) Boy Lilikoi (2010) • Grow Till Tall (2010) • Sinking Friendships (2010)

Sigur Rós front man Jón Thór "Jónsi" Birgisson has a simple explanation for why he decided to start solo projects away from the rest of the band. He told the English press, "All of them had babies—three babies in one year. It felt like the perfect time for me to do something on my own."

In 2009, he released the mostly instrumental album *Riceboy Sleeps* with the musician and graphic designer who had produced most of Sigur Rós's album covers: Alex Somers. The same year, Jónsi made the first tentative steps toward a collaboration with acclaimed composer Nico Muhly, who had previously worked with Jónsi's fellow Icelandic star Björk. That collaboration led to Jónsi's English-language album, *Go*.

Jónsi and Muhly began work from afar: initially, Jónsi would send acoustic tracks to Muhly via email, with Muhly then going "apeshit on this bitch," as he told the music magazine *Reykjavík Grapevine*. When they eventually got into the studio, not much had actually been arranged, so Muhly was working on the fly, throwing out ideas, discarding half of them. "Not to mention the piano parts," he confided to the *Grapevine*, "which were all hysteria. Complete hysteria." Luckily, Jónsi liked what he was hearing. Muhly told *Paste* magazine: "I was at the studio with fifteen tracks of piccolo. No one ever lets you get away with all that shit."

"Go Do" is the album's first single, featuring layers of flute and a skipping rhythm courtesy of Finnish percussionist Samuli Kosminen, who created the sounds by slapping and beating on a blue plastic suitcase. As *Paste* heard it from producer Peter Katis, "Samuli's playing made it so much busier and we just went crazy. We didn't show a lot of restraint as far as production." **DC**

Ragged applause from Jónsi at the Coachella Valley Music and Arts Festival. ➔

Me and the Devil | Gil Scott-Heron (2010)

Writer | Robert Johnson
Producer | Richard Russell
Label | XL
Album | *I'm New Here* (2010)

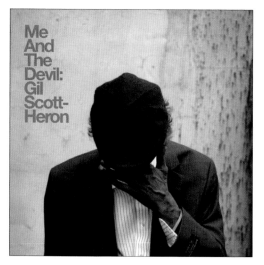

"There are times that I could have been a better person. That's why you keep working on it."

Gil Scott-Heron, 2010

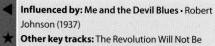

Influenced by: Me and the Devil Blues · Robert Johnson (1937)

Other key tracks: The Revolution Will Not Be Televised (1971) · The Bottle (1974) · "B" Movie (1980) New York Is Killing Me (2010)

Gil Scott-Heron has been hailed as the godfather of rap for the searing, spoken-word sociopolitical commentaries he produced in the Seventies. But by the time hip-hop got seriously political, in the late Eighties, Scott-Heron was in trouble, having developed a cocaine habit.

He produced no new work between 1982 and 1994, and the man who had rapped about the revolution not being televised was reduced to doing the voice-over on a U.K. commercial for an orange soda. It was to be another sixteen years before his voice was heard again.

In 2006, Scott-Heron was languishing in a jail cell in New York's notorious Riker's Island for violating the terms of his parole on a drugs possession charge. How he came to be recording again involves the strange tale of a Scottish publisher and the boss of an English indie record label.

Jamie Byng, director of Canongate Books, was a teenage fan of Scott-Heron who became a close friend after his company reprinted two novels that the poet had produced in the Seventies. Richard Russell, maverick boss of XL Recordings, used to be a hip-hop DJ, and, when he had the idea of making new music with Gil Scott-Heron, he contacted Byng for an introduction.

Russell visited Scott-Heron in prison and struck up a firm, creative relationship. By the time Scott-Heron was a free man, they had enough material for a new album, *I'm New Here*. The songs expressed the poet in reflective mood. The first single was a reworking of bluesman Robert Johnson's "Me and the Devil Blues," with a dense and fractured soundscape sculpted by Damon Albarn—perfectly matching Scott-Heron's dark musings on the state of his soul. **DC**

Stylo | Gorillaz (2010)

Writer | Gorillaz, Mos Def
Producer | Gorillaz
Label | Parlophone
Album | *Plastic Beach* (2010)

"Last thing I remember is thinking, Lord, don't let this happen to me."
Bobby Womack, 2010

◀ **Influenced by: Planet Rock** · Afrika Bambaataa & The Soulsonic Force (1982)
★ **Other key tracks:** Clint Eastwood (2001) · Tomorrow Comes Today (2001) · Dare (2005) · Feel Good Inc. (2005) · Superfast Jellyfish (2010)

The 2005 Gorillaz album *Demon Days* appeared to signal the close of Damon Albarn and Jamie Hewlett's comic book. Albarn, restless creator, had meatier fish to fry: exemplary supergroup enterprise The Good, The Bad & The Queen; a tearful encore with Blur; a more sensible simian in the opera *Monkey: Journey to the West*. But there was life in the old ape yet. The loose environmental concept album *Plastic Beach* emerged in 2010 in a fizz of publicity that hardly screamed "side-project," and "Stylo" was its brooding trailblazer.

Where the band's previous phases had been cloaked in the fun gloss of cartoon characters, here the emphasis was on collectivism. *Plastic Beach* brims with VIPs, all subsumed by the name but each an integral part. "Stylo" showcases two chief contributors, bright-eyed rapper Mos Def and big soul name Bobby Womack, who lend their gritty luster to the dirty beats and teeth-rattling bass.

Mos Def drawls "electric" rhymes through a megaphone for dusty authenticity, but it's the veteran Womack who stamps his authority, reputedly risking more than vocal cords as he bellows over Albarn's spectral coos and Kraftwerk-meets-Knight-Rider groove. A diabetic, Womack improvised to the very edge of his health, finishing flat-out on the studio floor. It was worth the effort; he bursts through with righteous force, beating down young(ish) pretender Albarn, just as Steven Tyler had gatecrashed Run-DMC's "Walk This Way."

Pop reggae legend Eddy Grant soon spoiled the festivities, claiming similarities with his own 1983 electro-dubber "Time Warp." But originality is not the point of "Stylo"; it mines known seams, pasting together the best of funk, hip-hop, and techno to create a greatest hits of cool. **MH**

10,001 Songs You Must Hear...

If those 1001 songs have left you begging for more, here is the ultimate playlist: 10,001 songs to download and listen to before you die. Artists and songs that are reviewed in the book are highlighted in bold type and indexed.

!!!
Heart of Hearts
Me and Giuliani Down by the Schoolyard (a True Story)
? & The Mysterians
96 Tears, 184
***N Sync**
Bye Bye Bye
2 Play featuring Raghav & Naila Boss
It Can't Be Right
2Pac
Brenda's Got a Baby
Dear Mama, 738
Hail Mary
I Get Around
3rd Bass
Pop Goes the Weasel
5.6.7.8's
Woo Hoo
5th Dimension
Together Let's Find Love
10cc
Dreadlock Holiday
The Things We Do for Love
16 Horsepower
Haw
Prison Shoe Romp
23 Skidoo
Coup
30 Seconds to Mars
Kings and Queens
50 Cent
I Get Money
In da Club
Just a Little Bit
100 Proof Aged in Soul
Everything Good Is Bad
411
On My Knees
Teardrops
808 State
Pacific
1000 Clowns
[Not] The Greatest Rapper
1910 Fruitgum Company
1,2,3 Red Light
Indian Giver
Simon Says
10,000 Maniacs
Because the Night, 704
Candy Everybody Wants
Hey Jack Kerouac
Trouble Me

A

A Falta de Pan
Mirabrás
A Filetta
N'en tarra n'en celu
A. R. Kane
Down
Aaliyah
Are You That Somebody?
Back and Forth
More Than a Woman, 814
Try Again
Aaron Neville
Tell It Like It Is
Abba
Dancing Queen, 366
Does Your Mother Know?
Fernando
Gimme! Gimme! Gimme! (A Man After Midnight)
Knowing Me, Knowing You
Mamma Mia
Money, Money, Money
S.O.S.
Take a Chance on Me
Thank You for the Music
The Winner Takes It All, 458
Voulez-Vous, 436
Waterloo
ABC
Tears Are Not Enough
The Look of Love
Abdalhalim Hafez
Karia Al-Fingan (The Fortune Teller)
Abdel Aziz el Mubarak
Ya izzana
Abdel Gadir Salim
Mal wa ihtagab
Abdou
Kima bekkani n'bekkih
Abe Lyman & His Californians
Amen
Abida Parveen
Aandhi chali
Abyssinia Infinite featuring "Gigi" Shibabaw
Gela
AC/DC
Back in Black, 467
Dirty Deeds Done Cheap
For Those About to Rock (We Salute You)
Guns for Hire
Highway to Hell
Playing with Girls
Safe in New York City
Shot Down in Flames
T.N.T.
This Means War
Thunderstruck
War Machine
Who Made Who
Whole Lotta Rosie, 402
You Shook Me All Night Long
Accept
Fast as a Shark
Ace
How Long
Ace of Base
All That She Wants
Acidman
Under the Rain
Ad Libs
The Boy from New York City
Adam & The Ants
Antmusic
Dog Eat Dog
Kings of the Wild Frontier, 462
Physical (You're So)
Stand and Deliver
Zerox
Adam Ant
Goody Two Shoes
Adam Wade
The Writing On the Wall
Adamski
Killer
Add N to (X)
Plug Me In
Addis Black Widow
Innocent
Addisi Brothers
Slow Dancin' Don't Turn Me On
Adele
Chasing Pavements
Adem
These Are Your Friends
Adeva
Warning
Adnan Sami Khan
Lift kara de
Adriana Varela
Cada vez que me recuerdas
Adverts
Gary Gilmore's Eyes
Aerosmith
Amazing
Baby, Please Don't Go
Draw the Line
Dude (Looks Like a Lady)
Helter Skelter
Jaded
Janie's Got a Gun
Jig Is Up
My Fist Your Face
Pink
Sweet Emotion
Walk This Way, 354
Afghan Whigs
My Curse
Africa Unite
Mentre fuori piove
African Business
In Zaire Business
Africando
Doley mbolo
Afrika Bambaataa
Renegades of Funk
Afrika Bambaataa & Soul Sonic Force
Looking for the Perfect Beat
Planet Rock
Afroz Bano
Thumri in misra tilak kamod
Afterhours
Quello che non c'è
Aftershock
Slave to the Vibe
Age of Chance
Who's Afraid of the Big Bad Noise
Agustin Lara
Veracruz
A-ha
Cosy Prisons
Cry Wolf
Hunting High and Low
Stay on These Roads
Take on Me
The Living Daylights
The Sun Always Shines on T.V., 559
Train of Thought
Ahlam
Matheer
Ai Jing
My 1997
Aimee Mann
4th of July
Save Me, 778
The Moth
Air
All I Need
Cherry Blossom Girl
Jeanne
Kelly Watch the Stars, 772
Le voyage de Pénélope
Modular Mix
Playground Love
Sexy Boy
Talisman
You Make It Easy
Air featuring Beck
The Vagabond
Air featuring Françoise Hardy
Au fond du rêve doré
Air featuring Jarvis Cocker
One Hell of a Party
Airborne Toxic Event
Sometime around Midnight
Airto Moreira
Samba de flora
Aisha Kandisha's Jarring Effects
Aisha
Aking
Against All Odds
Al Dexter & His Troopers
Too Late to Worry

Al Donohue
Jeepers Creepers
Al Green
Full of Fire
Here I Am (Come and Take Me)
I'm Still In Love with You
Let's Get Married
Look What You Done for Me
L-O-V-E (Love)
Sha-La-La (Makes Me Happy)
***Tired of Being Alone*, 290**
You Ought to Be with Me
Al Hibbler
He
Al Hirt
Java
Sugar Lips
Al Jarreau
Moonlighting
Al Jolson
Anniversary Song
Avalon
I'm Sitting on Top of the World
Swanee
Al Martino
I Love You Because
I Love You More and More Every
  Day
Just Yesterday
My Heart Would Know
Think I'll Go Somewhere and
  Cry Myself to Sleep
Al Morgan
Jealous Heart
Al Stewart
Year of the Cat
Al Wilson
I've Got a Feeling (We'll Be
  Seeing Each Other Again)
***The Snake*, 220**
Alaap with Anuradha
Pawdwal
Na dil mang ve
Alabama 3
***Woke Up This Morning*, 754**
Alain Peters
Mangé pour le coeur
Alan Dale
Cherry Pink and Apple
  Blossom White
Alan O'Day
Undercover Angel
Alanis Morissette
Pollyanna Flower
Wunderkind
***You Oughta Know*, 735**
Albert Hammond
It Never Rains in Southern
  California
Albert King
As the Years Go Passing By
Alberto Naranjo y Su
Trabuco
Calipso de el callao
Alberto Rojo
Chacarera del fuego
Aldebert
Carpe diem

Aleksandar Sarievski
Zajdi, zajdi, jasno sonce
Alena Busilyova & Siberian
Gypsies
Probil vanyka lion y propil
Alex Chilton
Downtown
Alexander O'Neal
Criticize
If You Were Here Tonight
Alfredo Gutiérrez
Dos mujeres
Alfredo Marceneiro
Louco
Alfredo Zitarrosa
Doña soledad
Ali Akbar Khan with Asha Bhosle
Guru bandana
Ali Farka Touré
Amandari, 590
Hawa dolo
Savane
Alias
More Than Words Can Say
Alice Cooper
Clones (We're All)
Dirty Diamonds
***Elected*, 301**
Gimme
It's Me
Might As Well Be on Mars
***Only Women Bleed*, 346**
School's Out
Alice Cooper featuring Guns
N' Roses
Under My Wheels
Alice Cooper Group
Billion Dollar Babies
I'm Eighteen
No More Mr Nice Guy
Alice Donut
My Boyfriend's Back
Alice in Chains
Check My Brain
Get Born Again
Head Creeps
No Excuses
Rooster
Alicia Keys
***Fallin'*, 812**
Like You'll Never See Me
  Again
You Don't Know My Name
Alick Nkhata
Shalapo
Alien Ant Farm
Smooth Criminal
Alim Qasimov
Mugham shour
Alison Limerick
Where Love Lives
Alison Moyet
Love Resurrection
Alive and Kicking
Tighter, Tighter
Alizée
Moi . . . Lolita
All Saints

Never Ever, 765
Pure Shores
All Seeing I
1st Man in Space
Beat Goes On
Allan Sherman
Hello Muddah, Hello Fadduh!
  (a Letter from Camp)
Alle Möller Band
Bail
Allman Brothers
Jessica
Ramblin' Man
Allman Brothers Band
Hot 'Lanta
One Way Out
Whipping Post
Alpha Band
Born in Captivity
Alpha Blondy
Apartheid Is Nazism
Alpha Blondy & The
Wailers
Travailler c'est trop dur
Alphabeat
Fascination
Alphaville
Forever Young
Alsou
Before You Love Me
Altered Images
Happy Birthday
I Could Be Happy
Altern-8
***Infiltrate*, 202**
Alternative TV
Love Lies Limp
The Force Is Blind
Althea & Donna
***Uptown Top Ranking*, 392**
Alvin Robinson
Something You Got
Alvin Stardust
Jealous Mind
Alvino Rey & His Orchestra
Cement Mixer (Put-Ti Put-Ti)
Deep in the Heart of Texas
Alyson Williams
Sleep Talk
Amadou & Mariam
Koulibaly
Sabali, 881
Sénégal Fast Food
Amal Murkus
Hkaye
Amália Rodrigues
Barco Negro
Foi Deus, 55
Aman Aman
Sien drahmas al dia
Amazing Rhythm Aces
Third-Rate Romance
Amédée Breaux
Jolie Blonde
Amélie-les-Crayons
Ta p'tite flame
America
A Horse with No Name

I Need You
Lonely People
Sister Golden Hair
Tin Man
American Breed
Bend Me, Shape Me
Step Out of Your Mind
American Music Club
Western Sky
Amerie
1 Thing
Ames Brothers
Can Anyone Explain? (No, No, No!)
Melodie d'Amour
Sentimental Me
The Naughty Lady of Shady Lane
Amii Stewart
Knock on Wood
Amon Duul II
Luzifer's Ghilom
Amon Duul II
Restless Skylight-Transistor-Child
Amorf Ordogok
Parti Lany
Amr Diab
Wala Ala Balo
Amy Grant
Baby Baby
Amy Winehouse
Back to Black
***Fuck Me Pumps*, 827**
Help Yourself
Know You Now
***Love Is a Losing Game*, 864**
Rehab
Round Midnight
Stronger Than Me
Take the Box
(There Is) No Greater Love
What It Is
An Hyangnyon
The Song of Sim'chong
Ana Hato (with Deane Waretini)
Pokarekare, 23
Ancka Lazar
Od enga vrta bom zapeu
Ando Drom
Zsa Mo
Andrea Bocelli
Con te partirò
Andreas Johnson
Glorious
Andrew W. K.
Party Hard
Andrews Sisters
Ac-Cent-Tchu-Ate the Positive
Along the Navajo Trail
Civilization (Bongo, Bongo, Bongo)
Cuanto La Gusta
Don't Fence Me In
Down in the Valley
Get Your Kicks on Route 66!
I Hate to Lose You
I Wanna Be Loved
Is You Is or Is You Ain't (Ma' Baby)
Mister Five by Five
Andy Gibb
I Just Want to Be Your Everything

902

Does Your Mama Know About Me

Bobby Vee
Come Back When You Grow Up
How Many Tears
I'll Make You Mine
Look at Me Girl
Run to Him
Take Good Care of My Baby
The Night Has a Thousand Eyes

Bobby Vinton
Blue on Blue
Blue Velvet
Coming Home Soldier
Just as Much as Ever
Mr. Lonely
My Melody of Love
Roses Are Red (My Love)
The Days of Sand and Shovels

Bobby Womack
So Many Sides of You

Bobo Rondelli
Mia dolce anima

Bodines
Therese

Body Count
Cop Killer, 675

Bola de Nieve
Vete de mi

Bomb the Bass
Beat Dis
Bug Powder Dust

Bombay S. Jayashri
Shambho mahadeva

Bon Iver
re: Stacks, 875

Bon Jovi
Blood on Blood
Burning for Love
Have a Nice Day
In These Arms
Lie to Me
Livin' on a Prayer
Runaway, 536
She Don't Know Me
Someday I'll Be Saturday Night
You Give Love a Bad Name

Bone Thugs-n-Harmony
1st of the Month
Tha Crossroads

Bone Thugs-n-Harmony featuring Mariah Carey and Bow Wow
Lil Love

Bonnie "Prince" Billy
I See a Darkness
New Partner

Bonnie Lou
Daddy-O

Bonnie Raitt
I Ain't Gonna Let You Break My Heart Again
I Can't Make You Love Me, 657
Runaway
You
You Got It

Bonnie Tyler
Total Eclipse of the Heart

Bono

Can't Help Falling in Love

Bonobo
Black Sands

Bonzo Goes to Washington
5 Minutes (C-C-C-Club Mix)

Boo Radleys
Lazarus
Wake Up, Boo!

Boogie Down Productions
Love's Gonna Get 'Cha (Material Love)
South Bronx
The Bridge Is Over

Booker Newbury III
Love Town

Booker T. & The MG's
Green Onions
Groovin'
Hang 'Em High
Melting Pot
Soul-Limbo

Boom
Shima Uta

Boomer Castleman
Judy Mae

Boozoo Chavis
Lula Lula Don't You Go to Bingo

Boredoms
Anarchy in the UKK

Boston
Amanda
More Than a Feeling, 363

Boston Pops Orchestra
I Want to Hold Your Hand

Boswell Sisters
Alexander's Ragtime Band
The Object of My Affection

Bottle Rockets
Radar Gun

Boubacar Traoré
Benidiagnamogo

Boukman Eksperyans
Vodou adjae

Bow Wow Wow
C30 C60 C90 Go!
I Want Candy

Box Tops
Cry Like a Baby
Neon Rainbow
Soul Deep
Sweet Cream Ladies, Forward March
The Letter

Boy George
The Crying Game

Boy Meets Girl
Waiting for a Star to Fall

Boyd Bennett
Seventeen

Boyz II Men
The End of the Road

Boz Scaggs
Hard Times
Lido Shuffle
Lowdown

Brad
20th Century

Bran Van 3000
Astounded
Drinking in L.A.

Brand Nubian
Feels So Good

Brandy & Monica
The Boy Is Mine

Brass Construction
Movin'

Brave Old World
Chernobyl

Bravery
An Honest Mistake

Bread
Aubrey
Hooked on You
If
It Don't Matter to Me
Make It with You
Sweet Surrender

Breeders
Cannonball, 703
Fortunately Gone

Brenda Fassie
Vuli ndlela

Brenda Holloway
Every Little Bit Hurts

Brenda Lee
Ain't Gonna Cry No More
All Alone Am I
Break It to Me Gently
Dum Dum
Fool #1
He's So Heavenly
I'm Sorry
Sweet Nothin's
Truly, Truly, True

Brenda Russell
Piano in the Dark

Brenton Wood
Baby You Got It
Gimme Little Sign
The Oogum Boogum Song

Brewer & Shipley
One Toke Over the Line

Brian Eno
1slash1
By This River, 382

Brian Eno & David Byrne
America Is Waiting

Brian Holland
Don't Leave Me Starvin' for Your Love

Brian Hyland
Gypsy Woman
Itsy Bitsy Teenie Weenie Yellow Polka-Dot Bikini
Sealed with a Kiss

Brian Setzer Orchestra
Sleep Walk

Brian Wilson
Love and Mercy

Brick
Dazz
Dusic

Brides of Destruction
Natural Born Killers

Bright Eyes

First Day of My life
Four Winds
Lover I Don't Have to Love

Brighter Side Of Darkness
Love Jones

British Sea Power
Waving Flags

Britney Spears
. . . Baby One More Time
Do Somethin'
I'm a Slave 4 U
Oops! . . . I Did It Again
Toxic, 834
Womanizer

Broken Bells
October
The High Road

Broken Social Scene
Lover's Spit
Stars and Sons

Bronski Beat
Smalltown Boy

Brook Benton
Hotel Happiness
It's Just a Matter of Time
Lumberjack
Mother Nature, Father Time
Rainy Night in Georgia
The Boll Weevil Song
The Same One
Think Twice

Brooklyn Bridge
Worst That Could Happen

Bros
I Owe You Nothing

Brotherhood of Man
Save Your Kisses for Me
United We Stand

Brothers Four
Greenfields

Brothers Johnson
Stomp!
Strawberry Letter #23
Get the Funk Out Ma Face
I'll Be Good to You

Browns
The Three Bells

Brownstone
5 Miles to Empty

Brownsville Station
Martian Boogie
Smokin' in the Boys Room

Bruce Channel
Hey! Baby

Bruce Dickinson
Tattooed Millionaire

Bruce Foxton
Freak

Bruce Hornsby & The Range
The Way It Is

Bruce Springsteen
Badlands
Born in the U.S.A., 537
Born to Run, 359
Devils & Dust
I'm on Fire
Land of Hope and Dreams
One Step Up

One Fine Day, 132
Sweet Talkin' Guy
Chi-Lites
Have You Seen Her
Oh Girl
There Will Never Be Any
Peace
Chills
Pink Frost
Rain
China Crisis
African and White
Choc Stars
Celio
Chordettes
Born to Be with You
Lollipop
Mr. Sandman
Chords
Sh-Boom
Chris Barber's Jazz Band
Petite fleur
Chris Bartley
The Sweetest Thing This Side
of Heaven
Chris Chameleon
Saved
Chris Cornell
Billie Jean
You Know My Name
Chris Crosby
Young and in Love
Chris de Burgh
The Lady in Red
Chris Hodge
We're on Our Way
Chris Isaak
Wicked Game, 622
Chris Kenner
I Like It Like That
Chris Montez
Let's Dance
Some Kinda Fun
Christie
Yellow River
Christie Anu
Island Home
Christina Aguilera
Ain't No Other Man, 866
Beautiful
Genie in a Bottle
Christina Aguilera featuring
Missy Elliott
Car Wash
Christine Anu
Celebrate
Christine Lauterberg
Erika's Alptraum
Christophe
Succès fou
Christopher Cross
Arthur's Theme (Best That You
Can Do)
Chromeo
Bonafied Lovin' (Tough Guys)
Fancy Footwork
Needy Girl
Chubby Checker

Limbo Rock
Pony Time
Popeye (the Hitchhiker)
Slow Twistin'
The Twist
Chuck Berry
Johnny B. Goode, 89
Little Marie
Little Queenie
Maybellene
My Ding-a-Ling
No Particular Place to Go
Promised Land
School Day
Too Much Monkey Business
Chuck Berry with Eric Clapton
Wee Wee Hours
Chuck Brown & The Soul
Searchers
We Need Money
Chuck D
No
Chumbawamba
Tubthumping
Church
Under the Milky Way, 588
Ciara featuring Justin Timberlake
Love Sex Magic
Cibelle
Deixa
Cibo Matto
Birthday Cake
Cilla Black
You're My World
Cinderella
Gypsy Road
Nobody's Fool
Cinkusi
Pet je kumi
Circle Jerks
Wasted
CJ Bolland
Sugar Is Sweeter
Clancy Brothers & Tommy
Makem
The Irish Rover, 151
Clan/Destine
Crazy Horse
Clannad
Robin (the Hooded Man)
Clap Your Hands Say Yeah
Over and Over Again (Lost & Found)
Clarence Carter
Slip Away
Snatching It Back
Too Weak to Fight
Clarence "Frogman" Henry
(I Don't Know Why) But I Do
On Bended Knees
Clarence Wainwright Murphy
Let's All Go Down the Strand
Clark Sisters
You Brought the Sunshine
Clash
(White Man) In Hammersmith
Palais, 421
Clampdown
Janie Jones

London Calling, 433
Overpowered by Funk
Rock the Casbah, 518
Should I Stay or Should I Go
The Magnificent Seven
This Is England
This Is Radio Clash
Train in Vain
Classics IV
Everyday with You Girl
Spooky
Stormy
Traces
What Am I Crying for?
Claude King
Wolverton Mountain
Claude Vamur
Tre D'Yion
Claudine Clark
Party Lights
Clawfinger
Biggest & the Best
Clefs of Lavender Hill
Stop! Get a Ticket
Cliff Nobles & Co.
The Horse
Cliff Richard
Devil Woman
Don't Turn the Light Out
We Don't Talk Anymore
Cliff Richard & The Drifters
Move It!, 89
Cliffie Stone
Popcorn Song
Clifton Chenier
Calinda
Climax
Precious and Few
Climax Blues Band
Couldn't Get It Right
Clinic
Come Into Our Room
Clint Black
Nobody's Home
Clint Holmes
Playground in My Mind
Clipse
Grindin'
Clipse with Slim Thug
Wamp Wamp (What It Do)
Clique
Sugar on Sunday
Clor
Love and Pain
Clotaire K
Beyrouth ecoeuree
Club Dogo
Boing
Clueso
Chicago
Clyde McPhatter
Lover, Please
Coasters
Charlie Brown
Searching
Yakety Yak, 90
Coati Mundi
Me No Pop I

Cocteau Twins
Aikea-Guinea
Blind Dumb Deaf
Blue Bell Knoll
Bluebeard
Cocteau Twins
Carolyn's Fingers
Fifty-Fifty Clown
Iceblink Luck, 644
Pearly Dew Drops Drops
Pitch the Baby
Rilkean Heart
Sugar Hiccup
Treasure Hiding
Cocteau Twins & Harold Budd
Sea, Swallow Me
Colbie Caillat
Have Yourself a Merry Little
Christmas
Cold War Kids
Hang Me Up to Dry
We Used to Vacation
Coldcut and Lisa Stansfield
People Hold On
Colder
Shiny Star
Coldplay
Clocks
Fix You, 854
Glass of Water
Speed of Sound
Viva la Vida, 888
Yellow
Collapsed Lung
Eat My Goal
Color Me Badd
I Wanna Sex You Up
Colourbox
Baby I Love You So
Coloured Stone
Black Boy
Coma
Spadam
Commander Cody
Hot Rod Lincoln
Commodores
Easy
Lady (You Bring Me Up)
Nightshift
Sail On
Still
Sweet Love
Common
Love Is . . .
The Sixth Sense
Common featuring Prince and
Bilal
Star 69 (PS with love)
Common featuring Lily Allen
Drivin' Me Wild
Communards with Sarah Jane
Morris
Don't Leave Me This Way
Company Flow
8 Steps to Perfection
Company of Strangers
Motor City (I Get Lost)
Compay Segundo

912

Wake Up Everybody
Harper's Bizarre
Anything Goes
Chattanooga Choo Choo
The 59th Street Bridge Song
(Feelin' Groovy)
Harry Belafonte
Banana Boat Song (Day-O)
Harry Chapin
Cat's in the Cradle
Harry Connick Jr.
Promise Me You'll Remember
Harry James
11:60 P.M.
All or Nothing at All
Back Beat Boogie
On a Little Street in Singapore
One Dozen Roses
Sleepy Lagoon
Velvet Moon
Harvey Danger
Flagpole Sitta
Hasidic New Wave
Giuliani Über Alles
Hasil Adkins
Chicken Walk
No More Hot Dogs
Hassan Hakmoun
Lala Aisha
Hatebreed
Live for This
Hawkwind
Silver Machine, 304
Health
Die Slow
Heart
Barracuda
The Battle of Evermore
These Dreams
Wait for an Answer
Heatwave
Boogie Nights
Heaven 17
(We Don't Need This) Fascist
Groove Thang
Temptation
Hedningarna
Gorrlaus
Hege Rimestad
Skinfakse
Helen Forrest
Time Waits for No One
Helen Reddy
Angie Baby
Bluebird
Delta Dawn
I Am Woman
I Can't Hear You No More
I Don't Know How to Love
Him
Keep on Singing
Peaceful
The Happy Girls
Helen Schneider
Rock 'n' Roll Gypsy
Helloween
Mr. Torture
Helmet

In the Meantime
Hemant Kumar
Sun ja dil ki dastaan
Henri Rene
Tap the Barrel Dry
Henri Salvador
Dans mon île, 93
Henry Busse
With Plenty of Money and You
Henry Gross
Shannon (Henry Gross)
Henry Mancini & His
Orchestra
Moon River
Henson Cargill
Skip a Rope
Herb Alpert
A Banda (Ah Bahn-Da)
A Taste of Honey
Flamingo
My Favorite Things
Rise
Spanish Flea
The Lonely Bull (El solo torro)
This Guy's in Love with You
Herbert Grönemeyer
Mensch
Was soll das?
Herbert Grönemeyer with
Antony Hegarty
Will I Ever Learn
Herbie Hancock with Norah
Jones
Court and Spark
Herbie Mann
Hijack
Hercules and Love Affair
Blind
Herman Dune
Bristol
Herman's Hermits
A Must to Avoid
Can't You Hear My Heartbeat
Dandy
East West
Just a Little Bit Better
Leaning on the Lamp Post
Listen People
Mrs. Brown You've Got a
Lovely Daughter
No Milk Today
Silhouettes
There's a Kind of Hush
Wonderful World
Hey
One of Them
Hibari Misora
Ringo Oiwake
High Llamas
Checking In, Checking Out
Highwaymen
Cotton Fields
Michael (Row the Boat Ashore)
Hijas del Sol
Kotto
Hilary Duff
Reach Out
Hildegarde

Leave Us Face It (We're in Love)
Hilltoppers
P.S. I Love You
Hinder
Lips of an Angel
Hiru Truku
Neska Soldadua
Hives
Hate to Say I Told You So, 792
Walk Idiot Walk
Hoagy Carmichael
Hong Kong Blues
Huggin' and Chalkin'
Ole Buttermilk Sky
Hobart Smith, Texas Gladden
Down in the Willow Garden
Hold Steady
Chips Ahoy!
Constructive Summer
Positive Jam
Stuck Between Stations
The Smidge
Your Little Hoodrat Friend
Hole
Celebrity Skin
Doll Parts, 711
Miss World
She Walks on Me
Teenage Whore
Holger Czukay
Good Morning Story
Oh Lord Give Us More Money
Hollies
Bus Stop
Carrie-Anne
He Ain't Heavy, He's My Brother
Just One Look
Long Cool Woman (in a Black
Dress)
On a Carousel
Stop Stop Stop
The Air That I Breathe
Hollywood Argyles
Alley-Oop
Hombres
Let It Out (Let It All Hang Out)
Hondells
Little Honda
Younger Girl
Honey Cone
One Monkey Don't Stop No Show
Stick-Up
Want Ads
Honeycombs
Have I the Right?
Honeydrippers
Rockin' at Midnight
Hoodoo Gurus
(Let's All) Turn On
I Want You Back, 556
What's My Scene?
Hoosier Hot Shots
She Broke My Heart in Three Places
Hooters
And We Danced
Satellite
Hootie & The Blowfish
Hey Hey What Can I Do

Only Wanna Be with You
Hope Blister
The Outer Skin
Horace Heidt
Ti-Pi-Tin
Horace Heidt & His Musical
Knights
Friendly Tavern Polka
Hot
Angel in Your Arms
Hot Butter
Popcorn
Hot Chip
Over and Over
Playboy
Hot Chocolate
Disco Queen
You Sexy Thing
Hot Hot Heat
Bandages
Hotlegs
Neanderthal Man
House
Endless Art
House of Love
Christine
I Don't Know Why I Love You
Shine On
House of Pain
Jump Around
Howard Jones
Life in One Day
New Song
Howlin' Wolf
Back Door Man, 119
The Red Rooster, 119
Hudson & Landry
Ajax Liquor Store
Hudson Brothers
Rendezvous
Hues Corporation
Rock the Boat
Huey Lewis & The News
Stuck with You
The Heart of Rock and Roll
Huggy Bear
Her Jazz
Hugh Masekela
Don't Go Lose It Baby
Grazing in the Grass
Stimela
Hugo Winterhalter & His
Orchestra
Canadian Sunset
Hukwe Zawose
Sisitizo la amani duniami
Human Beinz
Nobody But Me
Human League
Being Boiled, 424
Human
(Keep Feeling) Fascination
Love Action (I Believe in Love)
Human Resource
Dominator
Hunters & Collectors
Throw Your Arms around Me
Huong Thanh

H

You're Only Lonely
J. Geils
Must of Got Lost
J. Geils Band
Flamethrower
Love Stinks
J. J. Barnes
Real Humdinger
J. J. Cale
Lies
J. J. Cale & Eric Clapton
Hard to Thrill
J. Raynard
Takin' Me to Paradise
J. Tillman
Wild Honey Never Stolen
Jack Blanchard & Misty Morgan
Tennessee Birdwalk
Jack Johnson
Sitting, Waiting, Wishing
Jack Jones
Call Me Irresponsible
Dear Heart
The Impossible Dream (The Quest)
Jack McVea & His All Stars
Open the Door Richard!
Jack Owens
How Soon (Will I Be Seeing You)
Jack Scott
Burning Bridges
My True Love
What in the World's Come Over You
Jack Smith
You Call Everybody Darling
Jack White & Alicia Keys
Another Way to Die
Jackie Brenston & His Delta Cats
Rocket 88, 51
Jackie DeShannon
Put a Little Love in Your Heart
What the World Needs Now Is Love
Jackie Moore
Sweet Charlie Baby
Jackie Wilson
Baby Workout
My Heart Belongs to Only You
Night
Since You Showed Me How to Be Happy
Whispers (Gettin' Louder)
(Your Love Keeps Lifting Me) Higher & Higher, 199
Jackson 5
ABC
Corner of the Sky
Dancing Machine
I Am Love
I'll Be There
I Want You Back, 254
Little Bitty Pretty One
Lookin' Through the Windows
Mama's Pearl
Sugar Daddy
Jackson Browne
Doctor My Eyes
Lawyers in Love
Somebody's Baby

The Pretender
Jacksons
Body
Enjoy Yourself
Heartbreak Hotel
One More Chance
Shake Your Body (Down to the Ground), 413
Torture
Jacksons featuring Mick Jagger
State of Shock, 553
Jacques Brel
Amsterdam, 148
Ne me quitte pas, 102
Orly
Jacques Dutronc
Et moi et moi et moi, 170
Jacques Renard & His Orchestra
As Time Goes By
Jade
Don't Walk Away
Jaggerz
The Rapper
Jah Wobble featuring Dolores O'Riordan
The Sun Does Rise
Jah Wobble's Invaders of the Heart featuring Sinéad O'Connor
Visions of You
Jaime Roos
Brindis por Pierrot
Jak de Priester
Stellenbosch Lovesong
Jali Musa Diawara
Haidara
Jam
A Town Called Malice
English Rose
In the City
Start!, 473
That's Entertainment
The Eton Rifles, **432**
Jam & Spoon
Stella
James
Come Home
Laid, 699
She's a Star
Sit Down
Tomorrow
James & Bobby Purify
I Take What I Want
I'm Your Puppet
Let Love Come Between Us
Shake a Tail Feather
James Blunt
Wisemen
James Brown
Ain't It Funky Now
Bring It On
Get On the Good Foot
Get Up (I Feel Like Being a) Sex Machine), 272
Give It Up or Turn It a Loose
Hot Pants (She Got to Use What She Got to Get What She Wants)
I Don't Want Nobody to Give Me Nothing (Open the Door)

I Got a Bag of My Own
I Got the Feelin'
I Got You (I Feel Good)
It's a Man's Man's Man's World
King Heroin
Let a Man Come In and Do the Popcorn (Part I)
Licking Stick – Licking Stick
Living in America
Money Won't Change You
Papa Don't Take No Mess
Papa's Got a Brand New Bag, 152
Rapp Payback
Say It Loud – I'm Black and I'm Proud, 227
Super Bad
There It Is
James Brown & The Famous Flames
Cold Sweat, 217
James Carr
The Dark End of the Street, 208
James Darren
All
Goodbye Cruel World
James Darren
Her Royal Majesty
James Dean Bradfield
An English Gentleman
James Ingram & Linda Ronstadt
Somewhere Out There
James Ingram & Michael McDonald
Yah Mo Be There
James Ray
Itty Bitty Pieces
James Taylor
Don't Let Me Be Lonely Tonight
Fire and Rain, 263
Your Smiling Face
You've Got a Friend
Jamie Lidell
When I Come Back Around
Jamie T
Sheila
Jamiroquai
Blow Your Mind
Deeper Underground
Space Cowboy
Jan & Dean
Dead Man's Curve
Drag City
Surf City
The Little Old Lady (from Pasadena)
Jan Blohm
Groen trui
Jan Delay
Klar
Jan Garber
A Beautiful Lady in Blue
A Melody from the Sky
Jan Pavlovic
Fujara Song
Jane Birkin & Mickey 3d
Je m'appelle Jane
Jane Birkin & Serge Gainsbourg
Je t'aime . . . moi non plus, 247
Jane Child

Don't Wanna Fall in Love
Jane Siberry with k.d. lang
Calling All Angels, 657
Jane's Addiction
Been Caught Stealing
Classic Girl
Jane Says
Just Because
Kettle Whistle
Ripple
Stop!
Ted, Just Admit It . . .
Three Days, 648
Janet Jackson
All for You
Got 'til It's Gone
If
Rhythm Nation, 638
When I Think of You
Janis Ian
At Seventeen
Society's Child
Janis Joplin
Me and Bobby McGee
Jaojoby
Pecto
Japan
Adolescent Sex
Cantonese Boy
Gentlemen Take Polaroids
Ghosts, 488
Life in Tokyo
Quiet Life
Japandroids
Young Hearts Spark Fire
Jarmels
A Little Bit of Soap
Jarvis Cocker
Running the World
Jason DeRulo
Whatcha Say
Javier Ruibal
Perla de la medina
Jay & The Americans
Cara Mia
Come a Little Bit Closer
Livin' above Your Head
She Cried
Walkin' in the Rain
Jay & The Techniques
Apples, Peaches, Pumpkin Pie
Keep the Ball Rollin'
Jaye P. Morgan
Danger, Heartbreak Ahead
If You Don't Want My Love
Pepperhot Baby
That's All I Want from You
Jayhawks
Blue
Trouble
Waiting for the Sun
Jaynetts
Sally Go 'Round the Roses, 134
Jay-Z
December 4th
Hard Knock Life (Ghetto Anthem)
Izzo (H.O.V.A.)

931

934

Mother Love Bone
Chloe Dancer/Crown of Thorns,
638
Motherlode
When I Die
Motion City Soundtrack
Truth Hits Everybody
Mötley Crüe
Dr. Feelgood
Girls, Girls, Girls
Saints of Los Angeles
Shout at the Devil
Motörhead
Ace of Spades, 473
Dancing on Your Grave
Doctor Rock
Eat the Rich
Hellraiser
Iron Fist
Listen to Your Heart
Locomotive
R.A.M.O.N.E.S.
Rock Out
Whorehouse Blues
**Motörhead featuring Ice-T
and Whitfield Crane**
Born to Raise Hell
Motörhead/Girlschool
Bomber
Emergency
Please Don't Touch, 491
Motorleague
Hymn for the Newly Departed
Mott the Hoople
All the Young Dudes, 18
Mountain
Mississippi Queen
Moussa Poussy
Toro
Mousse T. vs Hot 'n' Juicy
Horny
Moussu T e lei Jovents
Mademoiselle Marseille
Mouth & MacNeal
How Do You Do?
Movies
Autograph
Mr. Acker Bilk
Stranger on the Shore
Mr. Mister
Broken Wings
Mr. Scruff
Get a Move On!
Ms. Dynamite
It Takes More
Mtume
Juicy Fruit
Muddy Waters
Mannish Boy
You Need Love
Mudhoney
Here Comes Sickness
Touch Me I'm Sick, 610
Mudvayne
Determined
Muhammid Jasimuddin Hiru
Asharh maishya
Mulatu Astatke & The

Heliocentrics
Esketa Dance
Múm
A Little Bit, Sometimes
Green Grass of Tunnel
Mumford & Sons
Little Lion Man
**Munadjat Yulchieva & Ensemble
Shavkat Nirzaev**
Kelmady
Mungo Jerry
In the Summertime
Munir Nurettin Selcuk
Aheste cek kürekleri
Murmaids
Popsicles and Icicles
Murray Head
One Night in Bangkok
Musafir
Hanji mara lalou sa
Muse
Guiding Light
Knights of Cydonia
Muscle Museum
Plug-In Baby
Supermassive Black Hole, 867
Time Is Running Out
United States of Eurasia
Music
Take the Long Road and Walk It
Music Explosion
Little Bit o' Soul
Music Machine
Come On In
Talk Talk
Musical Youth
Pass the Dutchie
Müslum Gürses
Bakma bana oyle
My Bloody Valentine
Blown a Wish
Feed Me with Your Kiss, 611
Nothing Much to Lose
Only Shallow
Soon
To Here Knows When
You Made Me Realise
My Chemical Romance
Helena
Vampires Will Never Hurt You
Welcome to the Black Parade
My Morning Jacket
One Big Holiday
What a Wonderful Man
Mylène Farmer
Désenchantée
Mylo
Destroy Rock & Roll, 834
Drop the Pressure
Myrtille
Les pages
Mystikal
Shake Ya Ass

N

Nada Surf
Popular

Nails
88 Lines about 44 Women
Najat Atabou
Baghi narjah
Najma
Nikala
Najma Akhtar
Dil laga ya thar
Nana Tsiboe
Kai onyame
Nanci Ajram
Akhasmak ah
Nanci Griffith
From a Distance
Love at the Five and Dime
Nancy Sinatra
How Does That Grab You, Darlin'?
Jackson
Lightning's Girl
Love Eyes
Some Velvet Morning
Sugar Town
*These Boots Were Made for
Walking*
You Only Live Twice
Nancy Wilson
Face It Girl, It's Over
Tell Me the Truth
Napoleon XIV
*They're Coming to Take Me Away,
Ha-Haaaa!*
Nas
If I Ruled the World
It Ain't Hard to Tell, 705
Made You Look
Nas el Ghiwane
Mahmouna
Naseebo Lal
Mera sacha si pyar
Nashville Pussy
Fried Chicken and Coffee
Nass El Ghiwane
Essiniya, 334
Nat King Cole
*(I Love You) for Sentimental
Reasons*
All for You
Blossom Fell
Calypso Blues
Gee, Baby, Ain't I Good to You
Looking Back
Orange Colored Sky
Pretend
Ramblin' Rose
Someone You Love
*The Christmas Song (Merry
Christmas to You)*
*Those Lazy-Hazy-Crazy Days of
Summer*
Too Young
When I Fall in Love, 85
Nat King Cole Trio
(Get Your Kicks on) Route 66, 39
Nature Boy, 43
Natacha Atlas
Amulet
Ana Hina
Yalla Chant

Natalie Cole
Inseparable
I've Got Love on My Mind
Jump Start
Natalie Cole & Nat King Cole
Unforgettable
Natalie Imbruglia
Goodbye
Torn
Natalie Merchant
My Skin
Natasha Bedingfield
I Wanna Have Your Babies
National
Available
Brainy
Natural Four
Can This Be Real
Naughty by Nature
Hip Hop Hooray
O.P.P.
Nava
Hey You
Né Ladeiras
Carandilheira
Ne Te
Princess
Neal Hefti & His Orchestra
Batman Theme
Ned Miller
Do What You Do Do Well
From a Jack to a King
Ned's Atomic Dustbin
Happy
Kill Your Television
Neil Diamond
America
Cherry Cherry
Cracklin' Rosie
Desiree
Girl, You'll Be a Woman Soon
Holly Holy
I Am . . . I Said
*I Thank the Lord for the Night
Time*
If You Know What I Mean
I've Been This Way Before
Kentucky Woman
Longfellow Serenade
Play Me
Solitary Man
Song Sung Blue
Stones
*Sweet Caroline (Good Times Never
Seemed So Good)*
The Story of My Life
Walk on Water
What's It Gonna Be?
Yesterday's Songs
You Are the Best Part of Me
**Neil Diamond featuring Beth
Nielsen Chapman**
Deep Inside of You
**Neil Diamond featuring Natalie
Maines**
Another Day (That Time Forgot)
Neil Finn
Sinner

938

P

PQR

Raspberries
Go All the Way
I Wanna Be with You
Ratt
Lay It Down
Round and Round
Ray Anthony & His Orchestra
At Last
Count Every Star
Dragnet
Ray Charles
At the Club
Born to Lose
Busted
Crying Time
Georgia on My Mind
Here We Go Again
Hit the Road Jack
I Can't Stop Loving You
I Chose to Sing the Blues
I Got a Woman
In the Heat of the Night
Let's Go Get Stoned
My Baby Don't Dig Me
No One to Cry To
Smack Dab in the Middle
Take These Chains from My Heart
What'd I Say, 101
You Are My Sunshine
You Don't Know Me
Your Cheatin' Heart, 127
Ray Charles Singers
Love Me with All Your Heart (Cuando calienta el sol)
Ray Conniff
Somewhere My Love
Ray McKinley & His Orchestra
Big Boy
You Came a Long Way (from St. Louis)
Ray Noble
Isle of Capri
Let's Swing It
Paris in the Spring
Ray Noble & His Orchestra
By the Light of the Silv'ry Moon
Linda
Ray Parker Jr.
Ghostbusters
Ray Parker Jr. & Raydio
A Woman Needs Love (Just Like You Do)
Ray Price
For the Good Times
I Won't Mention It Again
Ray Stevens
Ahab, the Arab
Everything Is Beautiful
Gitarzan
Misty
Mr. Businessman
Santa Claus Is Watching You
The Streak
Raydio
You Can't Change That
Raze
Break 4 Love

Razorlight
America
Golden Touch
Somewhere Else
Razor's Edge
Let's Call It a Day Girl
Re Nillu
La città del sol
Ready for the World
Love You Down
Oh Sheila
Real Roxanne
Bang Zoom! Let's Go Go!
Real Sounds of Africa
Soccer Fan
Rebecca Malope
Inombolo yocingo
Rebels
Wild Weekend
Red Foley
Chattanoogie Shoe Shine Boy
Red Hot Chili Peppers
Aeroplane
Behind the Sun
By the Way
Californication
Fight Like a Brave
Give It Away, 663
Havana Affair
Scar Tissue, 781
Snow (Hey Oh)
Soul to Squeeze
Suck My Kiss
Under the Bridge
Venice Queen
Red House Painters
Evil
Summer Dress
Red Ingle & The Natural Seven
Cigarettes, Whiskey, and Wild, Wild Women
Serutan Yob (A Song for Backward Boys and Girls under 40)
Temptation (Tim-Tayshun)
Red Norvo
Please Be Kind
Red Snapper featuring Karime Kendra
The Rough and the Quick
Redbone
Come and Get Your Love
Maggie
Redgum
I Was Only 19 (A Walk in the Light Green)
Redskins
Bring It Down
Keep On Keeping On
Reels
Quasimodo's Dream
Reem Khelani
Sprinting Gazelle
Reflections
(Just Like) Romeo & Juliet
Poor Man's Son
Refugee Camp All-Stars
Avenues

Reggie Rockstone
Mobile Phone
Regina Spektor
On the Radio
Fidelity
R.E.M.
At My Most Beautiful
Everybody Hurts
Fall on Me
I Wanted to Be Wrong
Imitation of Life
It's the End of the World as We Know It (and I Feel Fine)
Losing My Religion, 665
Nightswimming
Radio Free Europe, 497
Sitting Still
The One I Love, 601
You Are the Everything
Orange Crush
R.E.M. featuring Patti Smith
E-Bow the Letter
R.E.O. Speedwagon
Can't Fight This Feeling
Keep on Loving You
Renaissance
Northern Lights
Rene & Rene
Lo mucho que te quiero (The More I Love You)
Renegade Soundwave
Probably a Robbery
The Kray Twins
Rentals
Friends of P
Replacements
Alex Chilton
Bastards of Young
I Will Dare, 548
I'll Be You
Republika
Mamona
Rex Smith
You Take My Breath Away
Reyna Lucero
Carrao carrao
Rheingold
Dreiklangdimensionen
Rialto
Untouchable
Rich Boy featuring Polow Da Don
Throw Some D's
Richard and Linda Thompson
Wall of Death
Withered and Died, 343
Richard Ashcroft
A Song for the Lovers
Check the Meaning
Richard Dejardins
Et j'ai couché dans mon char
Richard Harris
MacArthur Park
My Boy
Richard Hawley
(Wading Through) The Waters of My Time
The Sun Refused to Shine

Richard Hayes
The Old Master Painter
Richard Hayman & His Orchestra
Ruby
Richard Hell & The Voidoids
Blank Generation, 403
Love Comes in Spurts
Richard Thompson
1952 Vincent Black Lightning, 656
Richie Valens
Donna
Rick Astley
Never Gonna Give You Up
Rick Cunha
I'm A Yo Yo Man
Rick Dees
Disco Duck
Dis-Gorilla
Rick James
Mary Jane
Super Freak, 493
Rick Ross
Hustlin'
Rick Springfield
Jessie's Girl
Speak to the Sky
Rickie Lee Jones
Chuck E.'s in Love
The Horses
Ricky Martin
Livin' La Vida Loca
Ricky Nelson
A Wonder Like You
Be-Bop Baby
Believe What You Say
For You
Lonesome Town, 94
Poor Little Fool
She Belongs to Me
Stood Up
Teen Age Idol
Teenager's Romance
The Very Thought of You
Travelin' Man
Young World
Ride
Dreams Burn Down
Leave Them All Behind
Right Said Fred
Don't Talk Just Kiss
I'm Too Sexy
Righteous Brothers
Dream On
Go Ahead and Cry
Just Once in My Life
Melancholy Music Man
My Babe
Rock and Roll Heaven
(You're My) Soul and Inspiration
Unchained Melody, 169
You've Lost That Lovin' Feeling, 144
Rihanna
SOS
Rihanna featuring Jay-Z
Umbrella

Rilo Kiley
Give a Little Love
Portions for Foxes
Ringo Starr
Back Off Boogaloo
It Don't Come Easy
It's All Down to Goodnight Vienna
Oh My My
The No No Song
You're Sixteen
Rinocerose
Le mobilier
Rip Chords
Hey Little Cobra
Three Window Coupe
Rita Pavone
Remember Me
Rita Ribeiro
Isso
Ritchie Valens
La Bamba, 90
Riverside
Conceiving You
Rivieras
California Sun
Roachford
Cuddly Toy
The Way I Feel
Road Apples
Let's Live Together
Rob Base & DJ E-Z Rock
It Takes Two
Rob Dougan
One and the Same
Rob Thomas
Lonely No More
Rob Zombie
Never Gonna Stop
   (the Red Red Kroovy)
Superbeast
The Lords of Salem
Rob Zombie & Alice Cooper
Hands of Death
   (Burn Baby Burn)
Robbie Fulks
Let's Kill Saturday Night
Robbie Nevil
C'est la vie
Robbie Robertson
Night Parade
*Somewhere Down the Crazy
   River*
Robbie Williams
Angels
Feel
Millennium
She's the One
Robert Cray Band
I Guess I Showed Her
Robert Forster
From Ghost Town
Robert John
Sad Eyes
Robert Johnson
Cross Road Blues, 29
Hellhound on My Trail, 30
Robert Knight
Everlasting Love

Robert Miles featuring Maria
   Nayler
One & One
Robert Palmer
Addicted to Love
*Bad Case of Loving You (Doctor,
   Doctor)*
Looking for Clues
Robert Parker
Barefootin'
Robert Plant
Big Log
Burning Down One Side
If It's Really Got to Be This Way
Little by Little
Nirvana
One More Cup of Coffee
Tall Cool One
Robert Plant & Alison Krauss
Please Read the Letter, 870
Robert Plant & The Strange
   Sensation
Freedom Fries
Robert Wyatt
Shipbuilding, 509
The Duchess
Roberta Flack
Feel Like Makin' Love
Killing Me Softly with His Song
*The First Time Ever I Saw Your
   Face*, 235
Where Is the Love
Roberto Angelini
Il Sig. Domani
Roberto Goyeneche
Bandoneón arrabalero
Roberto Rivas
Arroz con concolon
Robin Luke
Susie Darlin'
Robin McNamara
Lay a Little Lovin' on Me
Robin S.
Show Me Love
Robins
Riot in Cell Block No. 9, 59
Robyn
Be Mine
Dancing on My Own
Robyn with Kleerup
With Every Heartbeat, 876
Roches
Hammond Song, 430
Rocker's Revenge featuring
   Donnie Calvin
Walking on Sunshine
Rocket from the Crypt
On a Rope
Rockingbirds
Gradually Learning
Rockwell
Somebody's Watching Me
Rod Stewart
Baby Jane
Every Beat of My Heart
Forever Young
Handbags and Gladrags
I Can't Deny It

If Not for You
Leave Virginia Alone
Maggie May, 284
Oh God, I Wish I Was Home Tonight
Secret Heart
Some Guys Have All the Luck
*The Killing of Georgie (Parts I &
   II)*, 364
The Motown Song
These Foolish Things
You Wear It Well
Young Turks
*Tonight's the Night (Gonna Be
   Alright)*
Roger Daltrey
Under a Raging Moon
Roger Miller
Chug-a-Lug
Dang Me
Engine Engine #9
England Swings
Husbands and Wives
King of the Road
Roger Sanchez
Another Chance
Roger Waters
4:41AM (Sexual Revolution)
Home
Three Wishes
Towers of Faith
Roger Williams
Born Free
Rogey Quigley
A Kind of Loving
Róisín Murphy
Overpowered
Rokia Traoré
Bowmboï
Rolf Harris
Sun Arise
Tie Me Kangaroo Down, Sport
Rolling Stones
19th Nervous Breakdown
Angie
As Tears Go By
Brown Sugar
Dandelion
Don't Stop
*Doo Doo Doo Doo Doo
   (Heartbreaker)*
Emotional Rescue
Get Off of My Cloud
*Have You Seen Your Mother, Baby,
   Standing in the Shadow?*
Honky Tonk Women
(I Can't Get No) Satisfaction, 156
It's All Over Now
Jumpin' Jack Flash
Mother's Little Helper
One Hit (to the Body)
Out of Tears
Paint It Black, 175
Ruby Tuesday
She's a Rainbow
Shine a Light
Street Fighting Man
Streets of Love
Sympathy for the Devil, 228

Terrifying
Tumbling Dice, 305
The Last Time
Time Is on My Side
Undercover of the Night
Waiting on a Friend
*You Can't Always Get What You
   Want*
Rollins Band
Liar
Romantics
Talking in Your Sleep
What I Like About You
Romeo featuring
   Christina Milian
It's All Gravy
Romeo Void
Never Say Never
Romica Puceanu
Vantule, bataia ta
Ron Sexsmith
God Loves Everyone
Lebanon, Tennessee
Strawberry Blonde
Ronettes
Be My Baby, 134
Born to Be Together
Roni Size featuring Onallee
Brown Paper Bag
Ronnie Dove
Happy Summer Days
Hello, Pretty Girl
One More Mountain to Climb
Ronnie Dyson
*(If You Let Me Make Love to You
   Then) Why Can't I Touch You?*
Ronnie Milsap
It Was Almost Like a Song
Ronny & The Daytonas
Bucket "T"
G.T.O.
Rooftop Singers
Walk Right In
Roots
Don't Say Nuthin'
The Seed (2.0)
Roots featuring Erykah Badu
You Got Me
Roots Manuva
Clockwork
Witness (One Hope)
Rosanne Cash
Runaway Train
Seven Year Ache
Rose Murphy
I Can't Give You Anything But Love
Rose Royce
I Wanna Get Next to You
Roseanne Cash featuring
   Bruce Springsteen
Sea of Heartbreak
Rosemary Clooney
*Botch-A-Me (Ba-Ba-Baciami
   Piccina)*
Come On-a My House
Half as Much
Hey There
This Ole House

Rosie & The Originals
Angel Baby
Rosie Vela
Magic Smile
Roudoudou
Peace and Tranquility to Earth
Roxanne Shanté
Go On Girl
Roxette
It Must Have Been Love
Roxy Music
A Really Good Time
Do the Strand
Jealous Guy
Love Is the Drug
More Than This
Oh Yeah (on the Radio)
Virginia Plain, 315
Roy Brown
Good Rockin' Tonight, 43
Roy Clark
Yesterday, When I Was Young
Roy Davis Jr.
Gabriel
Roy Hamilton
You Can Have Her
Roy Head & The Traits
Treat Her Right
Roy Orbison
Breakin' Up Is Breakin' My Heart
Crying
Dream Baby (How Long Must I Dream)
In Dreams, 133
It's Over
Life Fades Away
Mean Woman Blues
(Oh) Pretty Woman
Running Scared
She's a Mystery to Me
Roy Orbison, Johnny Cash, Jerry Lee Lewis, & Carl Perkins
Big Train (from Memphis)
Roy Rogers
Hoppy, Gene, and Me
Royal House
Can You Party
Royal Teens
Short Shorts
Royalettes
It's Gonna Take a Miracle
Röyksopp
Poor Leno
Röyksopp featuring Robyn
The Girl and the Robot
Rubén Blades
Desapariciones
Hopes on Hold
The Man Who Sailed around His Soul
The Song of the End of the World
Ruben Rada
Botija de mi pais
Ruby
Paraffin
Ruby & The Romantics
Our Day Will Come

Ruby Hunter
Down City Streets
Rudy Vallee
The Stein Song (University of Maine)
Vieni vieni
Rufus & Chaka Khan
Ain't Nobody
Rufus Thomas
(Do the) Push and Pull
Do the Funky Penguin
Walking the Dog
Rufus Wainwright
Do I Disappoint You
Oh What a World
The Art Teacher, 850
Rugbys
You, I
Rumble Strips
Motorcycle
Rumillajta
Atahualpa
Run-DMC
Down with the King
It's Like That, 528
It's Tricky
King of Rock
Rock Box
Run's House
Sucker MC's
Rupert Holmes
Escape (The Pina Colada Song)
Rush
Armor and Sword
Distant Early Warning
Dreamline
New World Man
Nobody's Hero
One Little Victory
Show Don't Tell
Test for Echo
The Big Money
The Spirit of Radio
Tom Sawyer, 477
Rush featuring Aimee Mann
Time Stands Still
Russ Hamilton
Rainbow
Russ Morgan
I've Got a Pocket Full of Dreams
The Merry-Go-Round Broke Down
Russ Morgan & His Orchestra
Cruising Down the River
Dance with a Dolly (with a Hole in Her Stockin')
Louise
So Tired
Sunflower
There Goes That Song Again
Russell Morris
The Real Thing, 240
Rusty Draper
Are You Satisfied?
Shifting, Whispering Sands
Ruthless Rap Assassins
And It Wasn't a Dream
Ruts
Babylon's Burning, 454
Jah War

Ry Cooder
Alimony
Ryan Adams
Goodnight Rose
New York, New York
Wonderwall
Ryan Adams featuring Emmylou Harris
Oh My Sweet Carolina, 796
Rye Rye featuring M.I.A.
Bang

S

Sa Ding Ding
Ha ha li li
Sabah
Fistani
Sabahat Akkiraz
Agit
Saban Bajramovic
Opa Cupa
Sabri Brothers & Party
Dyn ek sytam
Sabrina
Boys (Summertime Love)
Sade
No Ordinary Love
Paradise
Smooth Operator, 539
The Sweetest Taboo
Safet Isovic
Kraj Vrbasa
Sai Htee Saing
Than lwin chong char
Saigon featuring Memphis Bleek
Ryders
Sailcat
Motorcycle Mama
Sailor
A Glass of Champagne
Sain Zahoor
Auquhian Rahwan
Sainkho Namtchylak
Order to Survive
Saint Etienne
Avenue
How We Used to Live
Only Love Can Break Your Heart, 652
Saints
(I'm) Stranded, 370
Salaam & His Cultural Imami Group
Moko baba
Salad
Drink the Elixir
Sali Sidibe
Djen Magni
Salif Keita
Soro (Afriki)
Tekere
Yambo
Salih Jacob
Azizah
Saliva
Your Disease

Sally Nyolo
Bikoutsi
Salsoul Orchestra
Nice & Nasty
Salt-N-Pepa
My Mic Sounds Nice
Push It, 592
Tramp
Salt-N-Pepa with En Vogue
Whatta Man
Saltwater Band
Saltwater Music
Sam & Dave
I Thank You
Soul Man
Soul Sister, Brown Sugar
When Something Is Wrong with My Baby
You Got Me Hummin'
Sam Brown
Stop
Sam Cooke
A Change Is Gonna Come, 141
Another Saturday Night
Chain Gang
It's Got the Whole World Shakin'
Lost and Lookin'
Shake
Twistin' the Night Away
When a Boy Falls in Love
You Send Me, 87
Sam Donahue & His Orchestra
I Never Knew
My Melancholy Baby
Sam Mangwana
Maria Tebbo
Sam Neely
Rosalie
Sam Roberts
Brother Down
Sam The Sham & The Pharaohs
How Do You Catch a Girl
Lil' Red Riding Hood
Wooly Bully
Samba Mapangala & Orchestra Virunga
Malako
Sambasunda
Ecek (Move)
Samite
Embalasasa
Sammi Smith
Help Me Make It Through the Night
Sammy Davis Jr.
I've Gotta Be Me
The Candy Man
Sammy Hagar
I Can't Drive 55
Sammy Johns
Chevy Van
Sammy Kaye
Taking a Chance on Love
That's My Desire
The Four Winds and the Seven Seas
The Old Lamp-Lighter
There Will Never Be Another You

951

What Is This Thing Called Love?

Tommy Dorsey featuring Edythe Wright
Stardust

Tommy Edwards
I Really Don't Want to Know
It's All in the Game

Tommy Hunt
I Am a Witness

Tommy James & The Shondells
Ball of Fire
Mirage
Mony Mony
Nothing to Hide
Out of the Blue
She
Sweet Cherry Wine

Tommy Roe
Dizzy
Everybody
Hooray for Hazel
Jam Up and Jelly Tight
Sheila
Sweet Pea

Tommy Sands
Teenage Crush

Tommy Tucker Time
Johnny Doughboy Found a Rose in Ireland

Tommy Tutone
867-5309/Jenny

Tomte
Ich sang die ganze Zeit von Dir

Tone Loc
Funky Cold Medina

Tones on Tail
Go!

Toni Basil
Mickey, 481
You Gotta Problem

Toni Braxton
You're Makin' Me High

Toni Childs
Don't Walk Away

Toni Fisher
The Big Hurt

Tony Allen
Asiko

Tony Bennett
Because of You
Cold, Cold Heart
Rags to Riches
Stranger in Paradise

Tony Joe White
Polk Salad Annie

Tony Martin
Here
I Get Ideas
I Said My Pajamas (and Put On My Pray'rs)
There's No Tomorrow

Tony Orlando & Dawn
Bless You
Candida
Knock Three Times
Look in My Eyes, Pretty Woman
Mornin' Beautiful
Say, Has Anyone Seen My Sweet

Gypsy Rose?
Tie a Yellow Ribbon Round the Old Oak Tree

Tony Orlando and Dawn

Tony Pastor & His Orchestra
Bell Bottom Trousers
Robin Hood

Tony Reidy
The Coldest Day in Winter

Tony! Toni! Toné!
If I Had No Loot

Tool
Ænema
Intolerance
Lateralus
No Quarter
Parabola
Schism, 811
Sober
Stinkfist
Vicarious

Toots & The Maytals
54-46 Was My Number, 275
Toots & The Maytals
Pressure Drop, 229

Tore Bruvoll & Jon Anders Halvorsen
Ungjentdraum

Tori Amos
1000 Oceans
A Sorta Fairytale
All the Girls Hate Her
Cornflake Girl, 719
Daisy Dead Petals
Playboy Mommy
Professional Widow (Armand's Star Trunk Funkin' Mix), 745
Silent All These Years
Sister Janet
Sleeps with Butterflies
Tear in Your Hand
Teenage Hustling
Time

Tornadoes
Telstar

Tose Proeski
Magija

Toto
Africa
Rosanna

Totó la Momposina
La candela viva

Towers of London
Good Times

Toys
A Lover's Concerto
Baby Toys

T'Pau
China in Your Hand

Tracey Dey
Gonna Get Along without You Now
Teenage Cleopatra

Tracy Chapman
Fast Car, 613
Give Me One Reason

Trade Winds
Mind Excursion

Tragically Hip

Ahead by a Century

Train
Drops of Jupiter

Tramaine
Fall Down

Trammps
That's Where the Happy People Go

Tran Duy Tinh
Cannon Fire Lulls the Night

Transatlantic
The Whirlwind

Transglobal Underground
I, Voyager

Transvision Vamp
Baby I Don't Care

Trashmen
Bird Dance Beat
Surfin' Bird, 135

Traveling Wilburys
Handle with Care

Travis
Driftwood
Sing

Treacherous Three
The Body Rock

Treble Charger
American Psycho

Tremeloes
Here Comes My Baby
Silence Is Golden
Suddenly You Love Me

T.Rex
20th Century Boy, 325
Bang a Gong (Get It On), 279

Tribalistas
Velha infância

Tribe Called Quest
Bonita Applebum, 647
Scenario

Tricarico
Vita tranquilla

Tricky
Goodbye Emmanuelle
Hell Is Round the Corner, 733
Makes Me Wanna Die

Tricky & PJ Harvey
Broken Homes

Tricky Woo
Fly the Orient

Triffids
Field of Glass
Hometown Farewell Kiss
Wide Open Road, 575

Trilok Gurtu & The Frikyiwa Family
Agne Yano

Trini Lopez
Sinner Man

Trio
Da Da Da (I Don't Love You You Don't Love Me Aha Aha Aha)

Trio Matamoros
Lágrimas Negras, 22

Trio Reynoso
Teresita

Troggs

I Can't Control Myself
Love Is All Around
Wild Thing
With a Girl Like You

Trouble Funk
Still Smokin'

Trust
Antisocial

Truth Hurts
Addictive

Tryo
Serre-moi

Tsehatu Beraki
Selam

Tshala Mwana
Kalume

Tsinandali Choir
Chakrulo

TTC
Dans le club

Tune Weavers
Happy, Happy Birthday Baby

Turbonegro
Prince of the Rodeo
Vaya con Satan

Turin Brakes
Painkiller
The Boss
Underdog (Save Me)

Turtles
Elenore
Happy Together
It Ain't Me Babe
She'd Rather Be with Me
She's My Girl
You Know What I Mean
You Showed Me

TV on the Radio
Ambulance
Halfway Home
Lover's day
Wolf Like Me

Tweet
Oops

Twinkle Brothers
Pierso godzina (Don't Betray My Love)

Twisted Sister
I Wanna Rock

Two Door Cinema Club
Something Good Can Work

Tymes
So Much In Love
Wonderful! Wonderful!
You Little Trustmaker

Tyrone Davis
Can I Change My Mind
Is It Something You've Got
Turn Back the Hands of Time

U2
All I Want Is You
Bad
Beautiful Day
Gloria
Hold Me, Thrill Me, Kiss Me, Kill Me

Contributors

Andrew Greenaway (AG) sold his soul for rock 'n' roll, then bought it back for half the price: barg'in! Editor of the website www.idiotbastard.com, his book on Frank Zappa's Broadway the Hard Way tour was published in 2010.

Billy Chainsaw (BC) leads a diverse life. The film editor of alternative culture magazine *Bizarre*, he also curates art shows, writes for *Empire* and *Kerrang!*, and has appeared in music videos including Nick Cave & The Bad Seeds' "Fifteen Feet of Pure White Snow."

Bruno MacDonald (BM) contributed to, and was assistant editor on, *1001 Albums You Must Hear Before You Die*. He edited 2010's *Rock Connections* and 1996's still-in-print *Pink Floyd: Through the Eyes of . . .*, and co-wrote 2007's *Rock & Roll Heaven*. He has contributed to magazines including *Radio Times* and *Record Collector* and lives in London with his saintly wife and several ailing houseplants.

Chris Bryans (CB) has contributed to *Time Out*, the *Observer* and *1001 Albums You Must Hear Before You Die*. In the unlikely event that a film is made of his life, he'd like Jaz Coleman in the lead.

Chris Shade (CS) has finally given up on having a hit single and after traveling around South America, Kazakhstan, and Cambodia lives with his young family in a small cathedral city where he drinks red wine and listens to Krautrock and dub.

Craig Reece (CR) has written for *NME*, the *Independent* and *Scotland on Sunday*. He has DJed around the world and runs the independent label Starla Records of Scotland.

Daryl Easlea (DE) has written for a variety of publications, including *Record Collector*, *Mojo*, and the *Guardian*. He compiles and annotates CDs and was born to dance. He wrote *Talent Is an Asset: The Story of Sparks*.

David Crawford (DC) has worked for publications such as *Screen International* and *Radio Times*, writing on subjects ranging from Mozart and Smokey Robinson through to music in Communist Berlin.

David Hutcheon (DH) is a contributor to the *Sunday Times*, *Mojo*, *The Times*, *FRoots*, *Songlines*, *Today in English*, and *Southeast Asia Globe*.

David Hutter (DaH) was born in Germany and briefly lived in both England and France during his teens. He now lives in London and works as a freelance writer and editor.

David Roberts (DR) is a freelance writer, author, and former Managing Editor of the *Guinness Books of British Hit Singles & Albums*. He was chief copywriter and film interviewer to the British Music Experience visitor attraction at the 02 arena.

Eleanor Babb (EB) is a freelance photographer, community artist, and recovering subeditor. She has been a Billy Bragg fan since taping a Town and Country Club gig off the radio at the age of thirteen.

Eloise Parker (EP) is features editor at the U.S. edition of *OK!* magazine. Based in New York, she appears regularly on *Entertainment Tonight* and is a former entertainment correspondent for the Press Association.

Garth Cartwright (GC) is New Zealand born and South London based. He is an award-winning freelance journalist and author of *Princes Amongst Men: Journeys with Gypsy Musicians*.

Gary Rose (GR) is a writer, music fanatic, and occasional DJ who lives in Brighton. He works for the BBC, where he reviews radio and TV programs for the *Radio Times*.

Gerry Kiernan (GK) was continuously turned away at a young age from the Haçienda-club epicenter of "Madchester" but made up for it by writing music features and interviewing bands for independent arts and culture magazines.

James Harrison's (JJH) first song purchase was "Hippy Hippy Shake" by The Swinging Blue Jeans. He is recovering from being Richard Hawleyfied and dips into Jonquil, Wap Wap Wow, and, for Eighties metal, Bronz.

Jamie Dickson (JD) wrote rock features and reviews for the *Daily Telegraph* after studying popular music at Leeds University. He contributed to *1001 Albums You Must Hear Before You Die* and is currently features editor with *Cabinet Maker*.

Jamie Healy (JH) is a writer and subeditor for *Radio Times*. He was once turned down for a job in a record shop on the grounds of his music taste being "suspiciously too varied."

Jay Ruttenberg (JR) is editor of the *Lowbrow Reader* and a staff writer at *Time Out New York*. His work has appeared in the *New York Times*, *Spin*, *Vibe*, and *Details*.

Jim Harrington (JiH) is the longtime music critic for the *Oakland Tribune*. He spends his days following the Chicago Blackhawks and Oakland A's, listening to Throwing Muses and Roxy Music, and goofing around with his daughter.

Joe Minihane (JM) is a freelance writer based in London with a worrying obsession with all things Americana.

Joel McIver (JMc) is the author of sixteen books on rock music and contributes to several magazines, including *Classic Rock*, *Metal Hammer*, and *Rolling Stone*. He also presents a series on Scuzz TV.

Johnny Law (JL) works at Channel 4, loves Josef K A-sides, Blur B-sides, and Men without Hats albums. He is a member of garage—and occasionally dining room—band the Erotic Utensils.

Jon Harrington (JoH) is a regular contributor to *Mojo*. He has also written for *Record Collector* and *1001 Albums You Must Hear Before You Die*.

Jon Lusk (JLu) is a New Zealand–born writer living in London. He specializes in popular and unpopular music from around the world. He recently co-edited the third edition of *The Rough Guide to World Music*.

Kat Lister (KL) is a London-based music journalist whose work has appeared in *NME*, *Clash*, and *Time Out*. In her spare time, she enjoys obsessing over Bob Dylan and promoting her music night, Dig a Pony.

Keeley Bolger (KBo) has contributed to *1001 Albums You Must Hear Before You Die*; written for the *Sun*, the BBC, and Channel 4; and is the author of *How to Win the X Factor*.

Louis Pattison (LP) is a writer and editor who has been published in *NME*, *Uncut*, the *Guardian*, the *Observer*, and *Plan B* magazine.

Louise Sugrue (LS) has written for *1001 Albums You Must Hear Before You Die*, *Record Collector*, *InStyle*, *RSA Journal*, and the *Daily Telegraph*.

Lynda Scott (LSc) was born in Milan, where she still lives. She studied art history and works in a gallery in addition to writing and translating.

Marcus Weeks (MW) works as a freelance musician and author. He is an award-winning composer of avant-garde music and plays trombone in various jazz and rock ensembles.

Matthew Horton (MH) is a freelance music journalist and editor of new music site shabbyculture.com. He also reviews albums for the BBC and writes for Virgin Media.

Matthew Oshinsky (MO) is a news editor at the *Wall Street Journal* in New York City. He has written about music and culture for the Daily Beast and Harvard University Press, among others.

Olivia McLearon (OM) is a freelance writer from London. After discovering Madonna at age eight, there followed a teenage obsession with Britpop—skipping over her SAW phase between 9 and 10—and her passion for music has burned brightly ever since.

Pat Long (PL) lives in London with his collection of Penguin crime paperbacks.

Peter Watts (PW) is a freelance journalist who has written for *The Times*, *Independent on Sunday*, *Sunday Times*, and *Uncut*.

Robert Dimery (RD) is a writer and editor who has worked on Tony Wilson's *24 Hour Party People* and *Breaking Into Heaven: The Rise and Fall of the Stone Roses*, plus countless other popular music publications. He was also general editor of the immensely popular *1001 Albums You Must Hear Before You Die* and has worked for a variety of magazines, including *Time Out London* and *Vogue*.

Shanthi Sivanesan (SS) saw Lene Lovich on *Top of the Pops* and her life took a turn toward the new wave. But beyond Madonna-stalking and an unwavering glam metal obsession, she eked out a career in music journalism at Virgin's *Hotline* and other magazines.

Simon Adams (SA) is a long-standing contributor to *Jazz Journal* and other music magazines. When not listening to music, he ekes out a living as a writer of reference books and children's nonfiction.

Siobhan O'Neill (SO) has rocked for a long, long time. Now it's time for her to write instead. She's seen glam, punk, hair, grunge, and stoner. Now she's putting pen to paper. No more rocking for her. (With apologies to Tenacious D.)

Sloan Freer (SF) is a multimedia arts journalist and film critic. Former digital TV editor of the *Observer*, her credits also include *Q*, *Metal Hammer*, *Bizarre*, *Total Film*, *Radio Times*, and *Kerrang!*

Sophie Harris (SH) is a writer and broadcaster living in New York. She writes about music for *Time Out New York*, *Mojo*, and *The Times* and is a regular BBC commentator.

Stephen Patience (SP) spends most of his working life editing words by other people, on topics ranging from music to design, but from time to time he gets around to writing something himself.

Stevie Chick (SC) has contributed to titles including the *Guardian*, *Mojo*, *NME*, *The Times*, and *Kerrang!* and edits occasional 'zine *Loose Lips Sink Ships*.

Theunis Bates (TB) is a London-based journalist with *Time*, AOL News, and *Fast Company* magazine.

Tim Sheridan (TS) has contributed to *Mojo*, *Downbeat*, *Paste*, *All Music Guide*, *Raygun*, and *Launch*, among others. He also served as head writer for Steven Tyler of Aerosmith. He's not kidding.

Will Fulford-Jones (WF-J) is the editor of *Time Out*'s essay collection *1,000 Songs to Change Your Life*. He lives in London.

Yoshi Kato (YK) has written for Vibe, Pulse, and DownBeat, among others.

Picture Credits

Every effort has been made to credit the copyright holders of the images used in this book. We apologize for any unintentional omissions or errors and will insert the appropriate acknowledgment to any companies or individuals in subsequent editions of the work.

2 Trinity Mirror/Mirrorpix/Alamy **18** Time & Life Pictures/Getty Images **21** Redferns **25** Getty Images **27** Getty Images **31** Retna **32** Time & Life Pictures/Getty Images **38** Getty Images **41** Time & Life Pictures/Getty Images **45** Michael Ochs Archives/Getty Images **46** Hulton-Deutsch Collection/Corbis **49** Ted Williams/Corbis **52** Michael Ochs Archives/Getty Images **56** Photofest/ Retna **61** Redferns **63** Getty Images **65** Getty Images **66** Michael Ochs Archives/Getty Images **73** Time & Life Pictures/Getty Images **74** LA Media/Sunshine/Retna Pictures Picture Shows **77** Michael Ochs Archives/Getty Images **80** Redferns **83** Premium Archive **86** Michael Ochs Archives/Getty Images **88** Redferns **92** Retna **97** Roger Viollet/Getty Images **98** Time & Life Pictures/ Getty Images **104** Time & Life Pictures/Getty Images **106** Hulton-Deutsch Collection/Corbis **108** Redferns **113** Redferns **115** Redferns **118** Getty Images **123** Dezo Hoffmann/Rex Features **126** LA Media/Sunshine/Retna Picture Shows **128** Getty Images **131** Michael Ochs Archives/Getty Images **136** Photofest/Retna UK **139** Retna **143** Popperfoto/Getty Images **147** Monitor Picture Library/Retna UK **149** Roger-Viollet/Rex Features **153** Getty Images **157** Monitor Picture Library/Retna UK **159** Retna **161** Getty Images **165** Redferns **168** Retna **177** Monitor Picture Library/Retna UK **181** Getty Images **187** Monitor Picture Library **188** Dezo Hoffmann/Rex Features **197** Michael Ochs Archives/Getty Images **203** Christian Rose/Dalle/Retna Pictures **205** Getty Images **211** AFP/Getty Images **215** Alain Dister/Dalle/Retna Pictures **221** Michael Ochs Archives/Getty Images **226** Michael Ochs Archives/Getty Images **232** Redferns **236** Redferns **241** LA Media/Sunshine/Retna Pictures Picture Shows **249** Tunick/Retna **253** Leni Sinclair/Dalle/Retna Pictures **255** Redferns **256** Getty Images **260** Michael Ochs Archives/ Getty Images **267** Michael Ochs Archives/Getty Images **269** Michael Ochs Archives/Getty Images **273** Michael Ochs Archives/ Getty Images **277** Getty Images **282** Sunshine/Retna Pictures **287** Chris Walter/Photofeatures/Retna Pictures **291** Retna **295** Michael Putland/Retna **296** Sunshine/Retna Pictures **300** Redferns **307** Redferns **313** Redferns **319** Mick Rock/Retna Pictures **321** Peter Mazel/Sunshine Photo/Retna Pictures **323** Sunshine/Retna Pictures **327** Mick Rock/Retna Pictures **333** Retna **337** Michael Putland/Retna UK **341** Redferns **345** Peter Mazel/Sunshine Photo/Retna Pictures **349** Retna **355** Sunshine/Retna Pictures **361** Fikisha Cumbo/Retna Pictures **362** Getty Images **365** Barry Schultz/Sunshine/Retna **368** Retna **373** Michael Putland/RetnaCelebs **376** Barry Schultz/Sunshine **379** Paul Slattery/Retna Pictures **386** Drian Boot/Retna **389** Leni Sinclair/Dalle/Retna Pictures **391** Barry Schultz/Sunshine **394** Peter Mazel/Sunshine/Retna Pictures **400** Retna **411** Neal Preston/Retna UK **417** Bettmann/Corbis **423** Redferns **431** Steven Richards/Retna UK **435** Steven Richards/ Retna UK **441** Redferns **445** Redferns **451** Mick Rock/Retna Pictures **456** Nik Wheeler/Corbis **498** Getty Images **502** Redferns **508** Redferns **513** Ferrandis/Dalle/Retna **521** Wirelmage **525** Richard Mann/Retna **529** Chase Roe/Retna **544** Michael Ochs Archives/Getty Images **549** Paul Slattery/Retna Pictures **554** Chase Roe/Retna **557** Andy Catlin/Retna UK **561** Retna **567** Steve Double/Retna UK **572** Retna **578** Paul Rider/Retna UK **583** Vincent/Dalle **587** Michael Putland/Retna Pictures **591** Jak Kilby/ Retna **597** Tim Jarvis/Retna UK **603** Andre Csillag/Rex Features **608** Steve Double/Retna Pictures **614** Getty Images **625** Steve Double/Retna UK **639** Bernhard Kuhmstedt/Retna UK **640** PYMCA/Alamy **645** Alastair Indge/Retna Pictures **651** Steve Double/ Retna UK **654** Redferns **661** Ed Sirrs/Retna Pictures **667** Martyn Goodacre/Retna Pictures **671** Redferns **681** Ian Patrick/Retna Pictures **685** Joanne Savio/Retna/Corbis **692** Getty Images **697** Retna **702** FilmMagic **710** Michael Ochs Archives/Getty Images **715** Bernhard Kuhmstedt/Retna UK **721** Steven Richards/Retna UK **726** Paul Slattery/Retna Pictures **734** ÊJay Blakesberg/Retna **739** Getty Images **744** Retna **749** Muinomede/Dalle/Retna Pictures **755** Retna **759** Elliott Smith/Retna USA **764** Steve Double/ Retna UK **771** Michael Schreiber/Retna Limited **775** Redferns **780** Vernhet/Dalle/Retna Pictures **785** Redferns **788** Martin Ruetschi/Keystone/Corbis **791** Retna **797** Redferns **803** Robin Francois/Retna Pictures **806** Cody Smyth/Retna **813** Retna **819** James Quinton/Retna Credit **822** Amanda Rose/Retna UK **825** Eric Fougere/Corbis **829** Rob Cable/Retna UK **833** Debbie Brady/Retna UK **839** Kobus van Rensburg/Elite Photo Agency/Retna **842** Getty Images **848** Robert Spencer/Retna **855** Timothy Cochrane **860** Mattia Zoppellaro/Retna Pictures **865** Mattia Zoppellaro/Retna Pictures **869** Gregory Warran/Retna **874** Timothy Cochrane/Retna Pictures **880** George Chin/Retna Pictures **885** Jay Brooks/Retna Pictures **889** George Chin/Retna Pictures **893** Getty Images **894** Micky Simawi/RetnaUK **897** Getty Images

Quintessence would like to thank the following individuals and organizations for their assistance in the creation of this book:

Helena Baser, Becky Gee, Carol King, Nicole Kuderer, Jon Lusk, Joel McIver, Anthony McAndrew at Retna, Hayley Newman at Getty.

Rob Dimery would like to thank Bruno MacDonald and A Torre, Portuguese Restaurant, Crystal Palace, London, UK.

Bruno MacDonald would like to thank Herita MacDonald for her patience.